THE
WRITER'S
HANDBOOK
2004

Barry Turner has worked on both sides of publishing, as an editor and marketing director and as an author. He started his career as a journalist with *The Observer* before moving on to television and radio. He has written over twenty books including *A Place in the Country*, which inspired a television series, and a best selling biography of the actor, Richard Burton.

His recent work includes a radio play, travel articles, serializing books for *The Times*, editing the magazine *Country* and writing a one-man show based on the life of the legendary theatre critic, James Agate. Barry is currently working on a book about the last months of World War II. This is his seventeenth year as editor of *The Writer's Handbook* and his sixth as editor of *The Statesman's Yearbook* and *SYBWorld*, a politics and economics website.

THE
WRITER'S
HANDBOOK
2004

EDITOR
BARRY TURNER

MACMILLAN

First published 1988
This edition published 2003 by
Macmillan
an imprint of Pan Macmillan Ltd
Pan Macmillan, 20 New Wharf Road,
London N1 9RR
Basingstoke and Oxford
Associated companies throughout the world
www.panmacmillan.com

ISBN 0 333 908120

Credits
Editor *Barry Turner*
Editorial Assistants *Jill Fenner, Jeni Giffen, Mick & Shirley Card, Jean Mighall*
Poetry Editor *Peter Finch*
Contributors *Jude Garvey*
　　　　　　David Hooper
　　　　　　Brian MacArthur
　　　　　　Kate Pool
　　　　　　Bob G. Ritchie
Tax and Finance Adviser *Ian Spring*

Typeset by Heronwood Press, Medstead, Hants
Printed and bound in Great Britain by Mackays of Chatham plc, Kent

Contents

The Rise and Fall of English

Barry Turner argues that English deserves
better of its home country

That English will one day, not far ahead, become *the* world language is regarded as self-evident. Chinese, ranked first by the number of native speakers, has long since given up on ambitions for linguistic ascendancy. And while Spanish is gathering strength, particularly in the Americas, no-one thinks of it as a serious rival.

Nearly a quarter of the world's population, up to 1.5 billion people, are already fluent or competent in English. The official language in seventy-five countries, English is the language of international business and entertainment. Eighty per cent of the world's electronically stored information is in English. In the European Union, which frequently judges Britain to be the least enthusiastic member, English is the dominant language. Up to a few years ago who would have thought that the European Central Bank would conduct all its business in English even though it is the native tongue of only one member of the eighteen-strong governing council?

The imminence of an Anglophone world inspires national pride. We may have lost an empire but, by God, we rule the linguistic waves. Well, up to a point we do. The English we speak is recognizably the English learned as a first or second language in other countries but, as any traveller knows, they often speak and write it better than we do.

For the sad story of how this has been allowed to happen, start with the founding precept of one of the great lexicographers. Language, said Sir Ernest Gowers, 'is an instrument for conveying ideas from one mind to another'. The challenge is in finding how to handle words in a way that makes our meaning clear. That in Britain we no longer achieve this, or anything approaching this, is made obvious at almost every point of daily communication from the interview on a breakfast programme to the written instructions for constructing an item of flat pack furniture.

The culprits are many and varied. The rot set in early in the 1960s when schools adopted a libertarian approach to education which involved giving up on difficult subjects including grammar. Led on by politicians dedicated to mediocrity, (or 'equality' to use the accepted term) teachers were encouraged to set standards by the lowest common denominator. The impact on English was catastrophic as the best educationalists soon came to recognise. But it is easier to destroy than to build and the return to formal and effective learning still has a long way to go. One has only to listen to the delegates to an NUT conference to know that for many teachers clarity of thought let alone clarity of language is way beyond their capacity. Dimly aware of their failings, the incompetents look to technology to compensate for poor linguistic skills. We are now committed to making our children computer literate; no matter that most are illiterate in every other sense.

The decline of English language teaching in schools had its knock-on effect on academia. A recent survey found that nine out of ten graduates submit applications that are full of spelling and grammatical errors. Are we surprised? Pupils who are unable to express themselves clearly become students who are unable to express themselves clearly. Worse still, some then become university and college lecturers. To judge their standard of communication refer to any book list for higher learning. Much blame for the decline of written English is loaded on the purveyors of tabloid newspapers and pulp fiction. But junk books have always been with us. What is new is the half baked academic book with its impenetrable waffle laced with fashionable jargon. The problem is compounded by publishers who no longer see it as a part of their remit to pay for decent editors and by critics (invariably fellow academics) who are the last to shout out loud that Professor Gubbins – who must be a clever fellow otherwise how did he become a professor? – is a sloppy thinker who can't string six words together without descending into cliché or platitude.

Some disciplines are worse than others. The prime villains are sociologists, promoters of the art of stating the obvious in ever more abstruse language. In what Ferdinand Mount has called 'the worst Cambridge clotted manner', a recently published author speaks of 'face to face interaction' in which 'the participants are immediately present to one another and share a common spatial-temporal reference system'. And that was one of the clearer passages in the book.

The weasel words of sociology have carried over to management studies, a discipline that has grown more rapidly than any of the industries it is supposed to benefit. The essence of good management, it seems, is to avoid saying what you really mean. So it is that meetings have become 'brain storming sessions' and desks are 'work units'. Employees are no longer sacked, they are 'outplaced'. Job losses translate into 'efficiency savings'. Nobody has aims anymore; they have 'mission statements'. An opinion is a 'corporate vision'. And those who do well in life – the rich – are 'high net worth individuals'. The language of mystification has only one motive. It is to persuade the uninitiated that simple ideas are actually highly complex, a let out for those who are none too sure of their academic credentials.

And so to politics. It is axiomatic that politicians must be able to argue their case. What is not so obvious is the need for them to talk all the time on every conceivable subject in a language that deliberately misleads. The media must take their share of responsibility. Radio and television with their ever expanding multiplicity of channels, feed off politics. It is rare for the standard interview with the great and the good to illuminate a topical issue but there is air and screen time to be filled – so – get in old Tufton Bufton who is always good for a few words, if not necessarily in the right order. On he comes with his mind set, a master practitioner of unrestrained verbosity.

'Well, John, at the end of the day we need to go forward, grasping our opportunities, rabbit, rabbit, mumbo jumbo ...'

'Thank you, Sir Tufton, that's all we have time for.'

And where politicians go, there too goes the tyranny of politically correct language; clumsy and inelegant.

'We ask brother to be silent while the chair is speaking.'

What is to be done? The argument against the equivalent of the Academie Française was best put by Dr Johnson who asserted that such an institution, setting out inflexible rules on grammar and word usage, would be contrary 'to the spirit of English liberty'. But this is quite different from advocating sensible guidelines for the effective use of English. Clarity of expression is a noble objective. As that master of language, Fritz Spiegl points out, 'Words are precious tools. You *can* use a screwdriver as a chisel but it will never be the same again'.

To restore our pride in lucid and succinct communication, a drive for English language competence in schools, even if it upsets the egalitarian lobby, should take priority over all the other educational objectives. This is not special pleading. A campaign for literacy, if successful, will raise standards in every other area of learning. And not just for the young. We need to extend the opportunity to acquire linguistic skills to all age levels.

At this point, defenders of the prevailing order will claim that writing courses are de rigueur throughout higher education. But so many of these programmes are less to do with the craft of writing than with the exercise of free expression; let-it-all-hang-out therapy by another name. The results may have some psychological value for students but do little to raise levels of competence.

To confess an interest, my own pet project is The National Academy of Writing, a new teaching institution based in Birmingham. Founded by professional writers to support emerging talent, the Academy will promote standards of excellence in all writing disciplines. Starting with short summer courses and master classes, many of them held in schools and colleges, the aim is to offer one-year programmes covering all the creative industries from books and journalism to film and television. If it is to be successful the impact of the Academy will be felt throughout education. To restore English to first place in the national curriculum, a lead has to come from somewhere. In the absence of political will, the Academy may be best placed to front the campaign.

For further information on the National Academy of Writing contact: Martin Eggleston, Development Manager, The National Academy of Writing, Calthorpe House, 30 Hagley Road, Edgbaston, Birmingham B16 8QY. Email: info@writingacademy.org
(see Writers' Courses, page 576)

UK Publishers

AA Publishing

The Automobile Association, Fanum House, Basingstoke, Hampshire RG21 4EA
☎01256 491573 Fax 01256 491974
Email michael.buttler@theAA.com
Website www.theAA.com
Managing Director *Stephen Mesquita*
Editorial Director *Michael Buttler*

Publishes maps, atlases and guidebooks, motoring, travel and leisure. About 100 titles a year.

Abacus

See **Time Warner Books UK**

ABC–Clio

26 Beaumont Street, Oxford OX1 2NP
☎01865 517222 Fax 01865 517228
Email salesuk@abc-clio.com
Website www.abc-clio.com
Acquisitions Editor *Simon Mason*

Formerly Clio Press Ltd. *Publishes* academic and general reference works, social sciences and humanities. Markets, outside North America, the Web, CD-ROM publications and reference books of the American parent company.
Royalties paid twice-yearly.

Abington Publishing

See **Woodhead Publishing Ltd**

Absolute Classics

See **Oberon Books**

Absolute Press

Scarborough House, 29 James Street West, Bath BA1 2BT
☎01225 316013 Fax 01225 445836
Email sales@absolutepress.demon.co.uk
Website www.absolutepress.demon.co.uk
Managing/Editorial Director *Jon Croft*

FOUNDED 1979. *Publishes* food and wine-related subjects as well as travel guides. About 10 titles a year. SERIES *Outlines* Monographs on gay and lesbian creative artists; *Gay Times Travel Guides* Launched in 2001, co-published with *Gay Times*. No unsolicited mss. Synopses and ideas for books welcome.
Royalties paid twice-yearly.

Abson Books London

5 Sidney Square, London E1 2EY
☎020 7790 4737 Fax 020 7790 7346
Email absonbooks@aol.com
Publisher *M.J. Ellison*

FOUNDED 1971 in Bristol. *Publishes* language glossaries and curiosities. No unsolicited mss; synopses and ideas for books welcome.
Royalties paid twice-yearly.

Academic Press

See **Elsevier Ltd**

Academy Group Ltd

John Wiley & Sons, 4th Floor, International House, 7 High Street, Ealing Broadway, London W5 5DB
☎020 8326 3800 Fax 020 8326 3801
Chairman *John Jarvis*
Commissioning Editor *Maggie Toy*
Approx. Annual Turnover £2 million

FOUNDED 1969. Became part of the **John Wiley & Sons, Inc.** group in 1997. *Publishes* architecture and design. Welcomes unsolicited mss, synopses and ideas.
Royalties paid annually.

Acair Ltd

Unit 7, 7 James Street, Stornoway, Isle of Lewis HS1 2QN
☎01851 703020 Fax 01851 703294
Email acair@sol.co.uk

Specialising in matters pertaining to the Gaidhealtachd, Acair publishes books in Gaelic and English on Scottish history, culture and the Gaelic language. 75% of their children's books are targeted at primary school usage and are published exclusively in Gaelic.
Royalties paid twice-yearly.

Actinic Press

See **Cressrelles Publishing Co. Ltd**

Acumen Publishing Limited

15A Lewins Yard, East Street, Chesham, Buckinghamshire HP5 1HQ
☎01494 794398 Fax 01494 784850
Email steven.gerrard@acumenpublishing.co.uk
Website www.acumenpublishing.co.uk

Managing Director *Steven Gerrard*
FOUNDED in 1998 as an independent publisher for the higher education market. *Publishes* academic books on philosophy, history and politics. 15 titles in 2002. No unsolicited mss. Synopses and ideas for books welcome; send written proposal as per Acumen guidelines.
Royalties paid annually.

Addison Wesley Longman
See **Pearson Education**

Adlard Coles Nautical
See **A.&C. Black (Publishers) Ltd**

Advance Publishing
The Garage, Beeches Road, West Row, Bury St Edmunds, Suffolk IP28 8NP
☎01353 7494904
Email editors@advance-publishing.co.uk
Website www.advance-publishing.co.uk
Senior Editor *Julie Underwood*
Editor *Margaret Burrows*
FOUNDED 2002. *Publishes* fiction, biography, autobiography, history, humour, science fiction, travel, war and crime. Unsolicited mss and synopses considered if accompanied by return postage.
Royalties paid twice-yearly.

African Books Collective
The Jam Factory, 27 Park End Street, Oxford OX1 1HU
☎01865 726686 Fax 01865 793298
Email abc@africanbookscollective.com
Website www.africanbookscollective.com
FOUNDED 1990. Collectively owned by its 17 founder publishers. Exclusive distribution in N. America, UK, Europe and Commonwealth countries outside Africa for 76 African participating publishers. Concentration is on scholarly/academic, literature and children's books. Mainly concerned with the promotion and dissemination of African-published material outside Africa. Supplies African-published books to African libraries and organisations and *publishes* resource books on African publishing. TITLES *The African Writers' Handbook*; *African Publishers Networking Directory*; *Women in Publishing and the Book Trade in Africa*; *The Electronic African Bookworm: A Web Navigator*; *Courage and Consequence: Women Publishing in Africa*.

Age Concern Books
1268 London Road, London SW16 4ER
☎020 8765 7200 Fax 020 8765 7211
Email books@ace.org.uk
Website www.ageconcern.org.uk
Approx. Annual Turnover £400,000
Publishing arm of Age Concern England. *Publishes* related non-fiction only. No fiction. About 18 titles a year. Synopses and ideas welcome for new practical handbooks.

Airlife Publishing Ltd
101 Longden Road, Shrewsbury, Shropshire SY3 9EB
☎01743 235651 Fax 01743 232944
Email editor@airlifebooks.com
Website www.airlifebooks.com
Editorial Head *Peter Coles*
Approx. Annual Turnover £3 million
Specialist aviation titles for pilots, historians and enthusiasts. Also twentieth century naval and military history. About 70 titles a year. TITLES *Quest for All-Weather Flight*; *Russian Air Power*; *Rapid Reaction Forces*; *Boeing F-15E Strike Eagle*. Unsolicited mss, synopses and ideas for books welcome.
Royalties paid annually; twice-yearly by arrangement.

Ian Allan Publishing Ltd
Riverdene Business Park, Molesey Road, Hersham, Surrey KT12 4RG
☎01932 266600 Fax 01932 266601
Email info@ianallanpub.co.uk
Website www.ianallanpub.co.uk
Chairman *David Allan*
Managing Director *Tony Saunders*
Specialist transport publisher – atlases, maps, railway, aviation, road transport, military, maritime, reference. About 80 titles a year. Send sample chapter and synopsis with s.a.e. Manages distribution and sales for third party publishers.
IMPRINTS **Midland Publishing** (see entry); **OPC** Railway titles.

J.A. Allen & Co.
An imprint of Robert Hale Ltd, Clerkenwell House, 45–47 Clerkenwell Green, London EC1R 0HT
☎020 7251 2661 Fax 020 7490 4958
Email allen@halebooks.com
Publisher *Caroline Burt*
Approx. Annual Turnover £750,000
FOUNDED 1926 as part of J.A. Allen & Co. (The Horseman's Bookshop) Ltd. Bought by **Robert Hale Ltd** in 1999. *Publishes* equine and equestrian non-fiction. About 20 titles a

year. Mostly commissioned but willing to consider unsolicited mss of technical/instructional material related to all aspects of horses and horsemanship.

Royalties paid twice-yearly.

Allen Lane
See **Penguin Group (UK)**

Allison & Busby
Suite 111, Bon Marche Centre, 241 Ferndale Road, London SW9 8BJ
☎020 7738 7888 Fax 020 7733 4344
Email all@allisonbusby.co.uk
Website www.allisonandbusby.co.uk

Publishing Director *David Shelley*

FOUNDED 1967. *Publishes* literary fiction, crime fiction, biography and writers' guides. About 40 titles a year. TITLES *Little Green Men* Christopher Buckley; *The Encyclopaedia of Cult Children's TV* Richard Lewis; *Homage* Julian Rathbone. Send synopses with two sample chapters, not full mss. No replies without s.a.e.

Alpha Press
See **Sussex Academic Press**

Alton Douglas Books
See **Brewin Books Ltd**

Amber Lane Press Ltd
Cheorl House, Church Street, Charlbury, Oxfordshire OX7 3PR
☎01608 810024 Fax 01608 810024
Email jamberlane@aol.com

Chairman *Brian Clark*
Managing Director/Editorial Head *Judith Scott*

FOUNDED 1979 to publish modern play texts. *Publishes* plays and books on the theatre. About 4 titles a year. TITLES *Strange Fruit* Caryl Phillips; *A Madhouse in Goa* Martin Sherman; *Kiss of the Spider Woman* Manuel Puig (play texts); *Strindberg and Love* Eivor Martinus. 'Expressly *not* interested in poetry.' No unsolicited mss. Synopses and ideas welcome.

Royalties paid twice-yearly.

AMCD (Publishers) Ltd
PO Box 182, Altrincham, Cheshire WA15 9UA
Email web@amcd.co.uk
Website www.amcd.co.uk

Managing Director *John Adams*

FOUNDED 1988. *Publishes* financial directories, books on China, local history, business books and foreign language dictionaries. Took over the Jensen Business Books imprint in 1993 and is well placed in electronic reference after developing its own software. In conjunction with JHC (Technology) Ltd, AMCD offers publishers access to the electronic book market with their reference, dictionary and directory Pop-Up software packages which can handle most languages. About 5 titles a year. Welcomes ideas (by e-mail only) for business books, children's books and books on European history, China or the Far East. No poetry, fiction or historical romance.

Royalties paid twice-yearly.

Amsco
See **Omnibus Press**

Andersen Press Ltd
20 Vauxhall Bridge Road, London SW1V 2SA
☎020 7840 8703/8700 Fax 020 7233 6263
Email andersenpress@randomhouse.co.uk
Website www.andersenpress.co.uk

Managing Director/Publisher *Klaus Flugge*
Editorial Director *Janice Thomson*
Editor, Fiction *Audrey Adams*

FOUNDED 1976 by Klaus Flugge and named after Hans Christian Andersen. *Publishes* children's high-quality picture books and fiction sold in association with Random House Children's Books. Seventy per cent of the books are sold as co-productions abroad. TITLES *Elmer* David McKee; *I Want My Potty* Tony Ross; *Badger's Parting Gifts* Susan Varley; *little.com* Ralph Steadman; *Cat in the Manger* Michael Foreman; *Preston Pig Books* Colin McNaughton; *Junk* Melvin Burgess; *You* Sandra Glover; *I Love You, Blue Kangaroo* Emma Chichester Clark. Unsolicited mss welcome for picture books; synopsis in the first instance for books for young readers up to age 12. No poetry or short stories.

Royalties paid twice-yearly.

Authors' Rating The secret of Andersen's success is publishing children's books that are loved by adults. That and a wicked sense of fun that has been known to upset the education establishment – and hooray for that.

Chris Andrews Publications
15 Curtis Yard, North Hinksey Lane, Oxford OX2 0NA
☎01865 723404 Fax 01865 725294
Email chris.andrews1@btclick.com
Website www.cap-ox.co.uk

Managing Director *Chris Andrews*

Approx. Annual Turnover £350,000

FOUNDED 1982. *Publishes* coffee table scenic travel guides. Also calendars, diaries, cards and posters. TITLES *Romance of Oxford*; *Romance of the Cotswolds*; *Romance of the Thames & Chilterns*. Unsolicited synopses and ideas for travel/guide books will be considered; phone in the first instance. Also owns the **Oxford Picture Library** (see entry under **Picture Libraries**).

The Angels' Share
See **Neil Wilson Publishing Ltd**

Anness Publishing Ltd
Hermes House, 88–89 Blackfriars Road, London SE1 8HA
☎020 7401 2077 Fax 020 7633 9499
Email info@anness.com
Website www.aquamarinebooks.com *or*
  www.lorenzbooks.com *or*
  www.southwaterbooks.com

Chairman/Managing Director *Paul Anness*
Publisher/Partner *Joanna Lorenz*

FOUNDED 1989. *Publishes* highly illustrated co-edition titles: general non-fiction – cookery, crafts, interior design, gardening, photography, decorating, lifestyle and children's. About 700 titles a year. IMPRINTS **Lorenz Books**; **Aquamarine**; **Hermes House**; **Peony Press**; **Southwater**.

Anthem Press
See **Wimbledon Publishing Company**

Antique Collectors' Club
Sandy Lane, Old Martlesham, Woodbridge, Suffolk IP12 4SD
☎01394 389950 Fax 01394 389999
Email sales@antique-acc.com
Website www.antique-acc.com

Managing Director *Diana Steel*
Sales Director *Mark Eastment*

FOUNDED 1966. Has a five-figure membership spread over the UK and the world. The Club's magazine *Antique Collecting* is sold on a subscription basis (currently £25 *p.a.*) and is published 10 times a year. It is sent free to members who may also buy the Club's books at special pre-publication prices. *Publishes* specialist books on antiques and collecting, the decorative arts, architecture and gardening. The price guide series was introduced in 1968 with the first edition of *The Price Guide to Antique Furniture*. Subject areas include furniture, silver/jewellery, metalwork, glass, textiles, art reference, ceramics, horology. Recent TITLES *Tiaras* Geoffrey Munn; *Frederick Sandys*

Betty Elzea; *20th Century Ceramic Designers* Andrew Casey; *Scottish Wild Flowers* Mary McMurtrie. Unsolicited synopses and ideas for books welcome; no mss.
  Royalties paid twice-yearly as a rule, but can vary.

Anvil Press Poetry Ltd
Neptune House, 70 Royal Hill, London SE10 8RF
☎020 8469 3033 Fax 020 8469 3363
Email anvil@anvilpresspoetry.com
Website www.anvilpresspoetry.com

Editorial Director *Peter Jay*

FOUNDED 1968 to promote English-language and foreign poetry, both classic and contemporary, in translation. English list includes Peter Levi, Dick Davis, Dennis O'Driscoll and Carol Ann Duffy. Translated books include Bei Dao, Celan, Dante, Lalic, Baudelaire, Lorca and Neruda. Preliminary enquiry required for translations. Unsolicited book-length collections of poems are welcome from writers whose work has appeared in poetry magazines. Please enclose adequate return postage.

Authors' Rating With a little help from the Arts Council, Anvil has become one of the foremost publishers of living poets.

Apollos
See **Inter-Varsity Press**

Apple
See **Quarto Publishing** under **UK Packagers**

Appletree Press Ltd
The Old Potato Station, 14 Howard Street South, Belfast BT7 1AP
☎028 9024 3074 Fax 028 9024 6756
Email reception@appletree.ie
Website www.appletree.ie

Managing Director *John Murphy*
Publishing Manager *Paul Harron*

FOUNDED 1974. *Publishes* cookery and other small-format gift books, plus general non-fiction of Irish and Scottish interest. TITLES *Little Cookbook* series (about 40 titles); *Ireland: The Complete Guide*. No unsolicited mss; send initial letter or synopsis.
  Royalties paid twice-yearly in the first year, annually thereafter. For the *Little Cookbook* series, a standard fee is paid.

Aquamarine
See **Anness Publishing Ltd**

Arc Publications

Nanholme Mill, Shaw Wood Road,
Todmorden, Lancashire OL14 6DA
☎01706 812338 Fax 01706 818948
Email arc.publications@btconnect.com
Website www.arcpublications.co.uk

Publishers *Rosemary Jones, Angela Jarman*
General Editor *Tony Ward*
Associate Editors *John Kinsella*
    (International), *Jo Shapcott* (UK), *Jean Boase-
    Beier* (Translations), *Angela Jarman* (Music)

FOUNDED in 1969 to specialise in the publication of contemporary poetry from new and
established writers both in the UK and abroad.
AUTHORS John Kinsella and Alison Croggan
(Australia), Donald Atkinson, Mika Haugova
(Slovakia), Yannis Kondos (Greece), Tony
Curtis (Ireland), Alamgir Hashmi (Pakistan),
C.K. Stead (New Zealand), Jackie Wills, Julia
Darling and Herbert Lomas (UK). About 20
titles a year. Authors submitting material
should ensure that it is compatible with the
current list, include a history of published
works and enclose an s.a.e. if they wish mss to
be returned. Electronic submissions are not
accepted. IMPRINT **Arc Music** specialises in
profiles of contemporary composers (particularly where none have existed hitherto) and
symposia which take a 'new approach' to well-
visited territory. Commissioned work only.
    Royalties as per contracts

Arcadia Books

15–16 Nassau Street, London W1W 7AB
☎020 7436 9898 Fax 020 7436 9898
Email info@arcadiabooks.co.uk
Website www.arcadiabooks.co.uk

Managing Director *Gary Pulsifer*

Small, independent publishing house, FOUNDED
in 1996, specialising in translated fiction from
around the world. Winner of the **Sunday
Times Small Publisher of the Year Award**
2002-03. *Publishes* literary fiction, gay fiction,
biography, autobiography, gender studies, travel
writing. TITLE *The Deposition of Father McGreevy*
Brian O'Doherty. Does not welcome unsolicited material.
    Royalties paid twice-yearly.

Authors' Rating A quality publisher that has
great success with translated fiction.

Architectural Press

See **Elsevier Ltd**

Argentum

See **Aurum Press Ltd**

Aris & Phillips Ltd

Oxbow Books, Park End Place, Oxford
OX1 1HN
☎01865 2241249 Fax 01865 794449
Email arisand phillips@oxbowbooks.com
Website www.arisandphillips.com

Editorial Director *David Brown*

FOUNDED 1972. *Publishes* academic archaeology and Egyptology, and Greek, Latin and
Hispanic texts and translations. In 2003 the lists
were sold to Oxbow Books who maintain the
imprint and the series. About 20 titles a year.

Arnold

See **Hodder Headline Ltd**

Arrow

See **Random House Group Ltd**

Artech House

46 Gillingham Street, London SW1V 1AH
☎020 7596 8750 Fax 020 7630 0166
Email jlancashire@artechhouse.co.uk
Website www.artech-uk@artechhouse.com

Managing Director (USA) *William M. Bazzy*
Senior Commissioning Editor *Dr Julie*
    Lancashire

FOUNDED 1969. European office of Artech
House Inc., Boston. *Publishes* electronic engineering, especially telecommunications, computer
communications, computing, optoelectronics,
signal processing, digital audio and video, intelligent transportation systems and technology
management (books, software and videos).
60–70 titles a year. Unsolicited mss and synopses
in the specialised areas listed are considered.
    Royalties paid twice-yearly.

Ashgate Publishing Ltd

Gower House, Croft Road, Aldershot,
Hampshire GU11 3HR
☎01252 331551 Fax 01252 317446 (Ashgate)/
344405 (Gower)/3685954 (Lund Humphries)
Email info@ashgatepub.co.uk
Website www.ashgate.com *and*
www.gowerpub.com

Chairman *Nigel Farrow*

FOUNDED 1967. *Publishes* business and professional titles under the **Gower** imprint and
humanities, social sciences, law and legal studies
under the **Ashgate** imprint. In December 1999
acquired **Lund Humphries**, publisher of art
books and exhibition catalogues.

    DIVISIONS **Ashgate** *Sarah Davies* Social sci-
ences; *John Smedley* History/Variorum collected

studies; *Rachel Lynch* Music and history; *Erika Gaffney* Literary studies; *Sarah Lloyd* Philosophy and religion; *Pamela Edwardes* Art history; *John Hindley* Aviation studies. **Gower** *Jo Burges, Jonathan Norman* Business, management and training; *John Irwin* Law and legal studies. **Lund Humphries** *Lucy Myers*. Access the websites for information on submission of material.

Ashgrove Publishing

55 Richmond Avenue, London N1 0LX
☎020 7713 7540 Fax 020 7713 7541
Email gmo73@dial.pipex.com
Website www.ashgrovepublishing.com
Chairman/Managing Director *Brad Thompson*
Approx. Annual Turnover £75,000

Acquired by Hollydata Publishers in 1999, Ashgrove has been publishing for over 20 years. *Publishes* mind, body, spirit, health, cookery, sports. 4 titles in 2002. No unsolicited mss; approach with letter and outline in the first instance.
Royalties paid twice-yearly.

Ashmolean Museum Publications

Ashmolean Museum, Beaumont Street, Oxford OX1 2PH
☎01865 278010 Fax 01865 278018
Email publications@ashmus.ox.ac.uk
Website www.ashmol.ox.ac.uk
Contact *Declan McCarthy*

The Ashmolean Museum, which is wholly owned by Oxford University, was FOUNDED in 1683. The first publication appeared in 1890 but publishing did not really start in earnest until the 1960s. *Publishes* European and Oriental fine and applied arts, European archaeology and ancient history, Egyptology and numismatics, for both adult and children's markets. About 8 titles a year. No fiction, American/African art, ethnography, modern art or post-medieval history. Most publications are based on and illustrated from the Museum's collections. No unsolicited mss.
Royalties paid annually.

Associated University Presses (AUP)

See **Golden Cockerel Press Ltd**

Atlantic Europe Publishing Co. Ltd

Greys Court Farm, Greys Court, Nr Henley on Thames, Oxfordshire RG9 4PG
☎01491 628188 Fax 01491 628189
Email info@AtlanticEurope.com

Website www.AtlanticEurope.com *and* www.curriculumVisions.com
Directors *Dr B.J. Knapp, D.L.R. McCrae*

Closely associated, since 1990, with Earthscape Editions packaging operation. *Publishes* full-colour, highly illustrated children's non-fiction in hardback for international co-editions and text books. Not interested in any other material. Main focus is on National Curriculum titles, especially in the fields of mathematics, science, technology, social history and geography. About 50 titles a year. Unsolicited synopses and ideas for non-fiction curriculum-based books welcome by e-mail only – does not accept material sent by post. *Fees* paid.

Atom

See **Time Warner Books UK**

AUP (Associated University Presses)

See **Golden Cockerel Press Ltd**

Aurum Press Ltd

25 Bedford Avenue, London WC1B 3AT
☎020 7637 3225 Fax 020 7580 2469
Email editorial@aurumpress.co.uk
Managing Director *Bill McCreadie*
Editorial Director *Piers Burnett*
Approx. Annual Turnover £3 million

FOUNDED 1977. Committed to producing high-quality, illustrated/non-illustrated adult non-fiction in the areas of general human interest, art and craft, lifestyle, sport and travel. About 60 titles a year. IMPRINTS **Argentum** Practical photography books; **Jacqui Small** High-quality lifestyle books.
Royalties paid twice-yearly.

Authentic Lifestyle

See **Paternoster Publishing**

AuthorsOnline

15–17 Maidenhead Street, Hertford, Hertfordshire SG14 1DW
☎01992 586788 Fax 01992 586787
Email theeditor@authorsonline.co.uk
Website www.authorsonline.co.uk
Owner *AuthorsOnLine Ltd.*
Managing Director *Gary Lee*
Editor *Richard Fitt*
Approx. Annual Turnover £1 million

FOUNDED 1997. *Publishes* new and reverted rights work in both electronic format via their website and traditional hard-copy. All genre welcome. Also offers a service to help authors self-publish in both formats. Submit mss by post or e-mail. Further information available via the website.

Autumn Publishing Ltd
Appledram Barns, Birdham Road, Chichester, West Sussex PO20 7EQ
☎01243 531660 Fax 01243 774433
Email autumn@autumnpublishing.co.uk
Website www.autumnpublishing.co.uk
Managing Director *Michael Herridge*
Editorial Director *Ingrid Goldsmid*
FOUNDED 1976, part of the Bonnier Group. *Publishes* baby and toddler books, children's activity, sticker and early learning books. About 200 titles a year. No responsibilty accepted for the return of unsolicited mss.

Award Publications Limited
1st Floor, 27 Longford Street, London NW1 3DZ
☎020 7388 7800 Fax 020 7388 7887
Email info@awardpublications.co.uk
FOUNDED 1958. *Publishes* children's books, both fiction and reference. IMPRINT **Horus Editions**. No unsolicited mss, synopses or ideas.

Azure
See **Society for Promoting Christian Knowledge**

Baillière Tindall
See **Elsevier Ltd**

Duncan Baird Publishers
Castle House, 75–76 Wells Street, London W1T 3QH
☎020 7323 2229 Fax 020 7580 5692
Email james@dbairdpub.co.uk
Managing Director *Duncan Baird*
Editorial Director *Bob Saxton*
Approx. Annual Turnover £5 million
FOUNDED in 1992 to publish and package co-editions overseas and went on to launch its own publishing operation in 1998. *Publishes* illustrated cultural reference, world religions, health, mind, body and spirit, lifestyle, graphic design. 45 titles in 2002. No unsolicited mss. Synopses and ideas welcome; approach in writing in the first instance with s.a.e. No fiction or UK-only subjects.
Royalties paid twice-yearly.

Bantam/Bantam Press
See **Transworld Publishers**

Barefoot Books Ltd
124 Walcot Street, Bath BA1 5BG
☎01225 322400 Fax 01225 322499
Email sales@barefootbooks.com
Website www.barefootbooks.com
Publisher *Tessa Strickland*
UK Editor *Natasha Carr*
FOUNDED in 1993. *Publishes* high-quality children's picture books, particularly new and traditional stories from a wide range of cultures. 30 titles in 2002. TITLES *The Genius of Leonardo*; *The Gigantic Turnip*; *Tales From Old Ireland*. No unsolicited mss.
Royalties paid twice-yearly.

Authors' Rating Writers of children's books would do well to keep track of Barefoot which, from small beginnings, is building a quality list that must be the envy of bigger publishers.

Baring & Rogerson
See **Eland Publishing Ltd**

Barny Books
The Cottage, Hough on the Hill, Near Grantham, Lincolnshire NG32 2BB
☎01400 250246/01522 790009 Fax 01400 251737
Managing Director/Editorial Head *Molly Burkett*
Business Manager *Tom Cann*
Approx. Annual Turnover £10,000
FOUNDED with the aim of encouraging new writers and illustrators. *Publishes* mainly children's books but also adult fiction and non-fiction. Offers schools' projects where students help to produce books. TITLES *Iron Jim* Andy Howarth; *Once Upon a Wartime* (series); *Hell, Fire and Damnation* Mario Martinez; *Trusty the Traitor* Ben Bartlett; *The Boy From Donington – Matthew Flinders* Molly Burkett and the students of Donington School; *Sutton Hoo, Bloody Mary & The Martyrs* Jenny Webb and students at Suffolk Schools. Too small a concern to have the staff/resources to deal with unsolicited mss. Writers with strong ideas should approach Molly Burkett by letter in the first instance. Also runs a readership and advisory service for new writers (£10 fee for short stories or illustrations; £25 fee for full-length stories).
Royalties Division of profits 50/50.

Authors' Rating A gutsy small publisher with a sense of fun which appeals to youngsters.

Barrington Stoke
10 Belford Terrace, Edinburgh EH4 3DQ
☎0131 315 4933 Fax 0131 315 4934
Email info@barringtonstoke .co.uk
Website www.barringtonstoke.co.uk
Chairman *Patience Thomson*
Managing Director *Lucy Juckes*
Editorial Head *Anna Gibbons*
Approx. Annual Turnover £400,000
FOUNDED in 1998 to publish books for 'reluctant, disenchanted and under-confident' young readers. Produces a series of audio books and issues teachers' notes to acccompany teenage fiction titles. Approx 30 titles a year. DIVISIONS **4u2read.OK** for children aged 8–13 with a reading age below 8; **Fiction** for 8–13-year olds TITLES *Living With Vampires; Tod in Biker City*. **Teenage Fiction** TITLES *Runaway Teacher; No Stone Unturned*. Books commissioned via literary agents only. *No* unsolicited material.
Royalties paid twice-yearly.

B.T. Batsford
See **Chrysalis Books Group**

BBC Books
BBC Worldwide Ltd , 80 Wood Lane, London W12 0TT
☎020 8433 2000 Fax 020 8433 3707
Website www.bbcworldwide.com
Acting Director of Books *Robin Wood*
Approx. Annual Turnover £30 million
Publishes TV tie-in and some stand-alone titles, including books which, though linked with BBC television or radio, may not simply be the 'book of the series'. Also TV tie-in titles for children. 100 titles a year. TITLES *Delia's Vegetarian Collection; Rick Stein's Food Heroes*; tie-in script book to *The Office; How to Be a Gardener* Alan Titchmarsh; *A History of Britain* Simon Schama; and autobiographies – Terry Wogan, Steve Redgrave, Esther Rantzen. Unsolicited mss (which come in at the rate of about 40 weekly) are rarely accepted. However, strong ideas well expressed will always be considered, and promising letters stand a chance of further scrutiny.
Royalties paid twice-yearly.

Authors' Rating BBC Worldwide is now Britain's ninth biggest book publisher with a growth rate that rivals would die for. The biggest expansion is in children's books and talking books. The BBC archive is a treasure trove still waiting to be fully exploited. But BBC Audiobooks is already well on the way to dominating the market.

Bedford Square Press
See **NCVO Publications**

Beeline
See **Blackstaff Press Ltd**

Belair
See **Folens Limited**

Belitha Press
See **Chrysalis Children's Books**

Ben Gunn
See **SB Publications**

David Bennett Books
See **Chrysalis Children's Books**

Berg Publishers
1st Floor, Angel Court, 81 St Clements Street, Oxford OX4 1AW
☎01865 245104 Fax 01865 791165
Email enquiry@bergpublishers.com
Website www.bergpublishers.com
Editorial & Managing Director *Kathryn Earle*
Production Director *Sara Everett*
Publishes scholarly books in the fields of history, fashion, cultural studies, social sciences and humanities. About 52 titles a year plus two journals, *Fashion Theory* and *Textile: The Journal of Cloth and Culture*. TITLES *The Sari* Mukulika Banerjee and Daniel Miller; *Nazi Chic: Fashioning Women in the Third Reich* Irene Guenther; *The Material Culture Reader* ed. Victor Buchli; *Shorn Women: Gender and Punishment in Liberation France* Fabrice Virgili. IMPRINT **Oswald Wolff Books**. No unsolicited mss. Synopses and ideas for books welcome.
Royalties paid annually.

Berghahn Books
3 Newtec Place, Magdalen Road, Oxford OX4 1RE
☎01865 250011 Fax 01865 250056
Email editorialUK@berghahnbooks.com
Website www.berghahnbooks.com
Chairman/Managing Director *Marion Berghahn*
Approx. Annual Turnover £700,000
FOUNDED 1994. Academic publisher of books and journals. 65 titles in 2002. TITLES *The History of the Armenian Genocide; Western*

Historical Thinking; Conservation and Mobile Indigenous Peoples. No unsolicited mss; will consider synopses and ideas for books. Approach by e-mail in the first instance. No fiction or trade books.

Royalties paid annually. *Overseas associate* Berghahn Books Inc., New York.

Berkswell Publishing Co. Ltd
PO Box 420, Warminster, Wiltshire BA12 9XB
☎01985 840189 Fax 01985 840243
Managing Director *John Stidolph*

FOUNDED 1974. *Publishes* books for churchwardens including *The Churchwarden's Yearbook.* No fiction. About 4 titles a year. Unsolicited mss, synopses and ideas for books welcome.

Royalties paid according to contract.

Berlitz Publishing Co. Ltd
See **Inset Guide**

BeWrite Books
See entry under **Electronic Publishing and Other Services**

BFI Publishing
British Film Institute, 21 Stephen Street, London W1T 1LN
☎020 7255 1444 Fax 020 7636 2516
Website www.bfi.org.uk
Head of Publishing *Andrew Lockett*
Approx. Annual Turnover £600,000

FOUNDED 1980. Part of the **British Film Institute**. *Publishes* academic, schools and general film/television-related books and resources. About 34 titles a year. TITLES *Film Classics* (series); *Modern Classics* (series); *World Directors* (seires); *The Cinema Book*, revised edition, eds. Pam Cook and Mieke Bernink; *BFI Film & Television Handbook* (annual) Eddie Dyja. E-mail submissions preferred.

Royalties paid annually.

BFP Books
Focus House, 497 Green Lanes, London N13 4BP
☎020 8882 3315 Fax 020 8886 5174
Chief Executive *John Tracy*
Commissioning Editor *Stewart Gibson*

FOUNDED 1982. The publishing arm of the Bureau of Freelance Photographers. *Publishes* illustrated books on photography, mainly aspects of freelancing and marketing pictures. No unsolicited mss but ideas welcome.

Big Fish
See **Chrysalis Children's Books**

Clive Bingley Books
See **Facet Publishing**

Birlinn Ltd
West Newington House, 10 Newington Road, Edinburgh EH9 1QS
☎0131 668 4371 Fax 0131 668 4466
Email info@birlinn.co.uk
Website www.birlinn.co.uk
Managing Editor *Hugh Andrew*

FOUNDED 1992. Acquired **John Donald Publishers** in 1999 (see entry). *Publishes* local and military history, Gaelic, humour, Highland history, adventure, Scottish reference, guidebooks and folklore. 70 titles in 2002. Acquired **Polygon/Polygon@Edinburgh** in 2002. No unsolicited mss; synopses and ideas welcome.

Royalties paid.

Bite
See **Hodder Headline Ltd**

Black & White Publishing Ltd
99 Giles Street, Edinburgh EH6 6BZ
☎0131 625 4500 Fax 0131 625 4501
Email mail@blackandwhitepublishing.com
Website www.blackandwhitepublishing.com
Director *Campbell Brown*

FOUNDED 1990. *Publishes* general fiction and non-fiction, including memoirs, sport, cookery, humour and guidebooks. Text only submissions via website or synopsis and sample chapter by post with s.a.e. or return postage. IMPRINT **Itchy Coo** Scots language resources for use in schools.

Royalties paid twice-yearly.

A.&C. Black (Publishers) Ltd
Alderman House, 37 Soho Square, London W1D 3QZ
☎020 7758 0200 Fax 020 7758 0222
Email enquiries@acblack.com
Website www.acblack.com
Chairman *Nigel Newton*
Managing Director *Jill Coleman*
Publishing Director, Reference *Jonathan Glasspool*
Approx. Annual Turnover £10 million

Publishes children's and educational books, including music, for 3–15-year-olds, arts and crafts, ceramics, fishing, ornithology, nautical, reference, sport, theatre and travel. About 125 titles a year. Acquisitions brought the Herbert Press' art, design and general books, Adlard Coles' and Thomas Reed's sailing lists, Christopher Helm, Pica Press and T&AD Poyser's natural history and ornithology lists into A.&C. Black's stable. Bought by **Bloomsbury Publishing** in May 2000. Owns *Whitaker's Almanack* and children's publisher **Andrew Brodie Publications**.

IMPRINTS **Adlard Coles Nautical**; **Christopher Helm**; **The Herbert Press**; **Pica Press**. TITLES *New Mermaid* drama series; *Who's Who; Writers' & Artists' Yearbook; Know the Game* sports series; *Blue Guides* travel series; *Rockets* and *Graffix* children's series. Initial enquiry appreciated before submission of mss.

Royalties Payment varies according to contract.

Black Ace Books

PO Box 6557, Forfar DD8 2YS
☎01307 465096 Fax 01307 465494
Website www.blackacebooks.com

Managing Directors *Hunter Steele, Boo Wood*

FOUNDED 1991. *Publishes* new fiction, Scottish and general; some non-fiction including biography, history, philosophy and psychology. 36 titles in print. IMPRINTS **Black Ace Books**, **Black Ace Paperbacks** TITLES *Succeeding at Sex and Scotland, Or the Case of Louis Morel* Hunter Steele; *La Tendresse* Ken Strauss MD; *Count Dracula (The Authorized Version)* Hagen Slawkberg; *Caryddwen's Cauldron* Paul Hilton; *The Sinister Cabaret* John Herdman. No children's, poetry, cookery, DIY, religion. 'No submissions at all, please, without first checking our website for details of current requirements and submission guidelines.'

Royalties paid twice-yearly.

Black Dagger

See entry under **BBC Audiobooks**

Black Lace

See **Virgin Books Ltd**

Black Spring Press Ltd

Burbage House, 83–85 Curtain Road, London EC2A 3BS
☎020 7613 3066 Fax 020 7613 0028
Email general@dexterhaven.demon.co.uk

Directors *Robert Hastings, Alexander Hastings*

FOUNDED 1986. *Publishes* fiction and non-fiction, literary criticism, biography. About 5 titles a year. TITLES *The Lost Weekend* Charles Jackson; *The Big Brass Ring* Orson Welles; *The Tenant* Roland Topor; *The Terrible News* collection of Russian short stories by Zamyatin, Babel, Kharms, *et al.* No unsolicited mss.

Royalties paid annually.

Black Swan

See **Transworld Publishers**

Blackstaff Press Ltd

4C Heron Wharf, Sydenham Business Park, Belfast BT3 9LE
☎028 9045 5006 Fax 028 9046 6237
Email info@blackstaffpress.com
Website www.blackstaffpress.com

Managing Editor *Patsy Horton*

FOUNDED 1971. *Publishes* mainly, but not exclusively, Irish interest books, fiction, poetry, history, politics, illustrated editions, natural history and humour. About 25 titles a year. Unsolicited mss considered, but preliminary submission of synopsis plus short sample of writing preferred. Return postage *must* be enclosed.

IMPRINT **Beeline** Lively popular fiction in small paperback format.

Royalties paid twice-yearly.

Authors' Rating Regional and proud of it, this Belfast publisher is noted for bringing on young talent and for 'wonderfully well-presented catalogues and promotional material'.

Blackwell Publishing

9600 Garsington Road, Oxford OX4 2DQ
☎01865 776868 Fax 01865 714591
Website www.blackwellpublishing.com

Also at: 108 Cowley Road, Oxford OX4 1JF
☎01865 791100 Fax 01865 791347

Chief Executive *René Olivieri*
President *Robert Campbell*
Chairman *Nigel Blackwell*

Blackwell Publishing was formed by merging Blackwell Science (FOUNDED 1939) and Blackwell Publishers (FOUNDED 1926). It publishes around 700 books a year and 674 journals in medicine, veterinary medicine, dentistry (IMPRINT **Blackwell Munksgaard**), nursing and allied health, science (particularly biology, chemistry and geology), social sciences, business and humanities. Journals are delivered online through **Blackwell Synergy**.

Royalties paid annually.

Authors' Rating Blackwell Science's main business is in scientific journals, mostly produced in partnership with learned societies, and medical publishing.

John Blake Publishing Ltd

3 Bramber Court, 2 Bramber Road, London
W14 9PB
☎020 7381 0666 Fax 020 7381 6868
Email words@blake.co.uk
Managing Director *John Blake*
Deputy Managing Director *Rosie Ries*

FOUNDED 1991 and expanding rapidly. Bought
the assets of Smith Gryphon Ltd in 1997 and
acquired Metro Publishing in 2001. *Publishes*
mass-market non-fiction. No fiction, children's, specialist or non-commercial. About
100 titles a year. No unsolicited mss; synopses
and ideas welcome. Please enclose s.a.e.
  Royalties paid twice-yearly.

Authors' Rating The formula for success
– sensational titles linked to the famous and
infamous – needs a former tabloid journalist to
make it work as other less savvy publishers
have found to their cost

Blandford Press

See **Octopus Publishing Group**

Bloodaxe Books Ltd

Highgreen, Tarset, Northumberland
NE48 1RP
☎01434 240500 Fax 01434 240505
Email editor@bloodaxebooks.co.uk
Website www.bloodaxebooks.com
Managing/Editorial Director *Neil Astley*

Publishes poetry, literature and criticism, and
related titles by British, Irish, European,
Commonwealth and American writers. 95 per
cent of the list is poetry. About 30 titles a year.
TITLES include three major anthologies, *Staying
Alive; real poems for unreal times* Neil Astley
(ed.); *The Bloodaxe Book of 20th Century Poetry*
Edna Longley (ed.); *The New Poetry* Hulse,
Kennedy and Morley (eds.); *Sixty Women Poets*
Linda France (ed.); *Poems* J.H. Prynne; *Poems
1960–2000* Fleur Adcock; recent collections
by Selima Hill, Helen Dunmore and Peter
Reading. Unsolicited poetry mss welcome;
send a sample of no more than 10 poems with
s.a.e., 'but if you don't read contemporary
poetry, don't bother'. No e-mail attachments.
Authors of other material should write in the
first instance.
  Royalties paid annually.

Authors' Rating Assisted by regional Arts
Council funding, Bloodaxe is one of the liveliest and most innovative of poetry publishers
with a list that takes in some of the best of the
younger poets.

Bloodlines

See **The Do-Not Press**

Bloomsbury Publishing Plc

38 Soho Square, London W1D 3HB
☎020 7494 2111 Fax 020 7434 0151
Website www.bloomsburymagazine.com
Chairman/Chief Executive *Nigel Newton*
Publishing Directors *Alexandra Pringle,*
  Liz Calder, Kathy Rooney, Sarah Odedina,
  Arzu Tahsin
Approx. Annual Turnover £61 million+

FOUNDED in 1986 by Nigel Newton, David
Reynolds, Alan Wherry and Liz Calder. Over
the following years Bloomsbury titles were to
appear regularly on *The Sunday Times* bestseller
list and many of its authors have gone on to win
prestigious literary prizes. In 1991 Nadine
Gordimer won the **Nobel Prize for
Literature**; Michael Ondaatje's *The English
Patient* won the 1992 **Booker Prize**; in 1997
Anne Michaels' *Fugitive Pieces* won both the
Orange Prize for Fiction and the Guardian
Fiction Prize. J.K. Rowling's *Harry Potter and the
Philosopher's Stone, Harry Potter and the Chamber of
Secrets* and *Harry Potter and the Prisoner of Azkaban*
won the **Nestlé Smarties Book Prize** in 1997,
1998 and 1999 respectively. Margaret Atwood's
The Blind Assassin won the **Booker Prize** in
2000. Published *The Encarta World English
Dictionary* in 1999. Acquired **A.&C. Black
(Publishers) Ltd** in May 2000 and **Peter
Collin Publishing Ltd** in September 2002.
Started **Bloomsbury USA** in 1998.
  Publishes literary fiction and non-fiction,
including general reference; also audiobooks.
AUTHORS include Margaret Atwood, T.C.
Boyle, Sophie Dahl, Jeffrey Eugenides, Neil
Gaiman, Daniel Goleman, David Guterson,
Ethan Hawke, John Irving, Jay McInerney,
Tim Pears, Celia Rees, J.K. Rowling, Will
Self, Donna Tartt, Rupert Thomson, Barbara
Trapido, Joanna Trollope and Benjamin
Zephaniah. Unsolicited mss and synopses wel-
come; no poetry.
  Royalties paid twice-yearly.

Authors' Rating With Harry Potter accounting for some 40 per cent of Bloomsbury's
turnover, the hunt is on for other strong sellers as
investment in overseas marketing and electronic
publishing takes off. Reference has strengthened
with the buy-in of A.&C. Black and there is an
expectation of increased sales in the US with the
launch of a new children's list. The latest acquisition is Berlin-Verlag, the German publisher of
many authors sold by Bloomsbury in English

language markets. With the German booktrade in the doldrums it is likely that Bloomsbury has made a shrewd purchase which will pay handsome dividends as trade recovers. Bloomsbury is flavour of the month for new writers. The problem, of course, is finding a way through the crowd of other hopefuls. Have a go by all means but don't expect a quick response.

BMJ Books

BMA House, Tavistock Square, London WC1H 9JR
☎020 7387 4499 Fax 020 7383 6662
Email jhudson@bmjbooks.com
Website www.bmjbooks.com
Chief Executive *Richard Smith*
Managing Director (Books) *John Hudson*
Approx. Annual Turnover £2.5 million
FOUNDED 1988. Part of the British Medical Journal Publishing Group. Book publishing developed initially from collections of BMJ articles but majority of titles now commissioned independently of the Journal. *Publishes* books on clinical medicine aimed at medical professionals. About 40 titles a year. All books available for sale electronically. No unsolicited mss; will consider e-mailed synopses and ideas for books.
Royalties paid twice-yearly.

BMM
See **SportsBooks Limited**

Boatswain Press
See **Kenneth Mason Publications Ltd**

Bobcat
See **Omnibus Press**

The Bodley Head
See **Random House Group Ltd**

The Book Guild Ltd

Temple House, 25 High Street, Lewes, East Sussex BN7 2LU
☎01273 472534 Fax 01273 476472
Email info@bookguild.co.uk
Website www.bookguild.co.uk
Chairman *George M. Nissen, CBE*
Managing Director *Carol Biss*
FOUNDED 1982. *Publishes* fiction, children's fiction, human interest, media, academic, natural history, naval and military, biography, art. About 80 titles a year. Expanding mainstream list plus developing the human interest/media genre.
DIVISIONS
Human Interest *A Challenge Too Far?* Rona

Cant; *Echoes from a War* Graham Watson; *Nearly on Top* David Strutt. **Biography** *Forced Out* Simon Bywater. **Mind, Body, Spirit** *How to be a Successful Therapist* Celia Johnson; *Love and Old Age* Professor Cedric Mims. **Fiction** *Penalty Chick* Bryony Hill; *69 North* Robert Jackson. **Literature** *Byron's Diary* Julian Fane; *Dear Saucy Pat; The Life of Patrick Brontë* Coreen Turner. **Children's Fiction** *The Zoo* Massimo Gava. Unsolicited mss, ideas and synopses welcome.
Royalties paid twice-yearly.

Authors' Rating Regularly advertises for authors who may be asked to cover their own production costs. But in promoting its services, The Book Guild is more up-front with its clients than the typical vanity publisher who promises the earth and delivers next to nothing.

Book House
See **Salariya Book Company Ltd** under **UK Packagers**

Border Lines Biographies
See **Seren**

Boulevard Books & The Babel Guides
71 Lytton Road, Oxford OX4 3NY
☎01865 712931 Fax 01865 712931
Email raybabel@dircon.co.uk
Website www.babelguides.com
Managing Director *Ray Keenoy*
Specialises in contemporary world fiction by young writers in English translation. Existing or forthcoming series of fiction from Brazil, Italy, Latin America, Low Countries, Greece, and elsewhere. The Babel Guides series of popular guides to fiction in translation started in 1995.
DIVISIONS
Latin American *Ray Keenoy* TITLE *Hotel Atlantico* J.G. Noll. **Italian** *Fiorenza Conte* TITLE *The Toy Catalogue* Sandra Petrignani. **Brazil** *Dr David Treece* TITLE *The Jaguar.* **Low Countries** *Prof. Theo Hermans.* **Greece** *Marina Coriolano-Likourezos.* **Babel Guides to Fiction in Translation** Series Editor *Ray Keenoy* TITLES *Babel Guide to Italian Fiction in Translation; Babel Guide to the Fiction of Portugal, Brazil & Africa in Translation; Babel Guide to French Fiction in English Translation; Babel Guide to Jewish Fiction; Babel Guide to Scandinavian Fiction.* Suggestions and proposals for translations of contemporary fiction welcome. Also seeking contributors to forthcoming Babel Guides (all literatures).
Royalties paid annually.

Bounty
See **Octopus Publishing Group**

Bowker (UK) Ltd
3rd Floor, Farringdon House, Wood Street,
East Grinstead, West Sussex RH19 1UZ
☎01342 310450 Fax 01342 310463
Email sales@bowker.co.uk
Website www.bowker.co.uk
Commercial Director *Doug McMillan*
Publisher *Geraldine Turpie*

Part of the Cambridge Information Group
(CIG), based in Maryland in the USA. *Publishes*
library reference, library science, bibliography,
biography, business and professional directories. TITLES *Books In Print; Ulrich's Periodicals
Directory.* Unsolicited material will not be read.
Royalties paid annually.

Boxtree
See **Macmillan Publishers Ltd**

Marion Boyars Publishers Ltd
24 Lacy Road, London SW15 1NL
☎020 8788 9522 Fax 020 8789 8122
Email marion.boyars@talk21.com
Website www.marionboyars.co.uk
Editor *Julia Silk*
Editor, Non-fiction *Ken Hollings*

FOUNDED 1975, formerly Calder and Boyars.
Publishes biography and autobiography, fiction,
literature and criticism, music, philosophy, psy-
chology, sociology and anthropology, theatre
and drama, film and cinema, women's studies.
About 30 titles a year. AUTHORS include
Georges Bataille, Ingmar Bergman, Heinrich
Böll, Hortense Calisher, Jean Cocteau, Carlo
Gébler, Julian Green, Ivan Illich, Pauline Kael,
Ken Kesey, Toby Litt, Kenzaburo Oe, Hubert
Selby, Igor Stravinsky, Frederic Tuten, Eudora
Welty, Judith Williamson, Tom Wiseman,
Hong Ying. Unsolicited mss not welcome for
fiction or poetry; submissions from agents only.
Unsolicited synopses and ideas welcome for
non-fiction.
Royalties paid annually. *Overseas associates*
Marion Boyars Publishers Inc.

Boydell & Brewer Ltd
PO Box 9, Woodbridge, Suffolk IP12 3DF
☎01394 411320

Publishes non-fiction only, principally medieval
studies. All books commissioned. No unsolicited material.

Bradt Travel Guides
19 High Street, Chalfont St Peter,
Buckinghamshire SL9 9QE
☎01753 893444 Fax 01753 892333
Email info@bradt-travelguides.com
Website www.bradt-travelguides.com
Managing Director *Hilary Bradt*
Editorial Head *Tricia Hayne*
Approx. Annual Turnover £450,000

FOUNDED in 1974 by Hilary Bradt. *Specialises*
in travel guides to off-beat places. 13 titles in
2002. SERIES country guides and island guides
(Azores, Falklands, St Helena); wildlife guides
(Galapagos, Arctic, Antarctica); and the
'Eccentric' series (Britain, London, America).
No unsolicited mss; synopses and ideas for
travel guidebooks (not travelogues) welcome.
Royalties paid twice-yearly.

Brassey's
See **Chrysalis Books Group**

Nicholas Brealey Publishing
3–5 Spafield Street, London EC1R 4QB
☎020 7239 0360 Fax 020 7239 0370
Email rights@nbrealey-books.com
Website www.nbrealey-books.com
Managing Director *Nicholas Brealey*

FOUNDED 1992. Innovative books for business
that address the most critical and interesting
issues of the new century – from business to
consumer behaviour, from self-help to leadership, from global change to cross-cultural
understanding. Recently acquired the US publisher Intercultural Press, a specialist publisher
in the field of crossing cultures. 20 titles a year.
TITLES *Shackleton's Way; Power Up Your Mind;
The Rich and How They Got That Way; The
Soul of the New Consumer; The Power Laws; The
80/20 Principle; Riding the Waves of Culture; The
Dance of Change.* No fiction, poetry or leisure
titles. No unsolicited mss; synopses and ideas
welcome.
Royalties paid twice-yearly.

Authors' Rating Looks to be succeeding in
breaking away from the usual computer-speak
business manuals to publish information and
literate texts. Lead titles have a distinct trans-
Atlantic feel.

The Breedon Books Publishing Co. Ltd
Breedon House, 3 Parker Centre, Derby
DE21 4SZ
☎01332 384235 Fax 01332 364063

Email anton@breedonpublishing.co.uk
Editorial Director *A.C. Rippon*
Approx. Annual Turnover £1 million
FOUNDED 1983. *Publishes* local history, old photographs, heritage and sport. 56 titles in 2002. Unsolicited mss, synopses and ideas welcome if accompanied by s.a.e. No poetry or fiction.
Royalties paid annually.

Breese Books Ltd
10 Hanover Crescent, Brighton, East Sussex BN2 9SB
☎01273 687 555
Email MBreese999@aol.com
Website www.sherlockholmes.co.uk *and* www.abracadabra.co.uk
Chairman/Managing Director *Martin Ranicar-Breese*

FOUNDED in 1975 to produce specialist conjuring books and then went on to become a leading publisher of Sherlock Holmes pastiches. No unsolicited submissions; Breese Books works with a regular team of authors.

Brepols Publishers
Christchurch Lodge, Christchurch Passage, Hampstead, London NW3 1JG
☎020 7794 8947 Fax 020 7794 9905
Email johan.van.der.beke@brepols.net
Website www.brepols.net/publishers/
Editorial Director *Johan Van Der Beke*
UK office of the Belgian academic publisher. FOUNDED 1796. *Publishes* scholarly monographs and collections in any field of pre-modern humanities. 150 titles a year. IMPRINT **Harvey Miller Publishers** Editorial Director *Johan Van Der Beke* FOUNDED 1974. *Publishes* academic studies in medieval and Renaissance art history only. 10–12 titles a year. No unsolicited mss; synopses and ideas welcome. Email contact preferred.
Royalties paid twice-yearly.

Brewin Books Ltd
Doric House, 56 Alcester Road, Studley, Warwickshire B80 7LG
☎01527 854228 Fax 01527 852746
Email admin@brewinbooks.com
Website www.brewinbooks.com
Chairman/Managing Director *Alan Brewin*
FOUNDED 1976. *Publishes* books on all aspects of Midland life and history including social, hospital, police, military and family histories as well as biographies. New range of contemporary fiction

being introduced. 25 titles in 2002. TITLES *Sutton Coldfield in the Forties* John Bassett; *Remembering the Great War in Gloucestershire & Herefordshire* Ray Westlake. Not interested in children's, poetry or novels. Approach by letter, but do not send full mss. Unsolicited synopses and ideas welcome.
IMPRINTS **Alton Douglas Books; History Into Print**.
Royalties paid twice-yearly

Brimax
See **Octopus Publishing Group**

Bristol Classical Press
See **Gerald Duckworth & Co. Ltd**

British Academic Press
See **I.B. Tauris & Co. Ltd**

The British Academy
10 Carlton House Terrace, London SW1Y 5AH
☎020 7969 5200 Fax 020 7969 5300
Email secretary@britac.ac.uk
Website www.britac.ac.uk
Publications Officer *James Rivington*
Assistant Publications Officer *Janet English*
Publications Assistant *Vicky Baldwin*
FOUNDED 1902. The primary body for promoting scholarship in the humanities, the Academy publishes many series stemming from its own long-standing research projects, or series of lectures and conference proceedings. Main subjects include history, philosophy and archaeology. About 20 titles a year. SERIES *Auctores Britannici Medii Aevi; Early English Church Music; Fontes Historiae Africanae; Records of Social and Economic History.* Proposals for these series are welcome and are forwarded to the relevant project committees. The British Academy is a registered charity and does not publish for profit.
Royalties paid only when titles have covered their costs.

The British Library
96 Euston Road, London NW1 2DB
☎020 7412 7704 Fax 020 7412 7768
Email blpublications@bl.uk
Publishing Manager *David Way*
Approx. Annual Turnover £950,000
FOUNDED 1979 as the publishing arm of The British Library to publish works based on the historic collections and related subjects. *Publishes* bibliographical reference, manuscript studies, illustrated books based on the Library's

collections, and book arts. TITLES *The British Library Guide to Calligraphy, Illumination and Heraldry; The British Library Writers' Lives Series; Encyclopedia of Ephemera; Medieval Herbals.* About 50 titles a year. Unsolicited mss, synopses and ideas welcome if related to the history of the book, book arts or bibliography. No fiction or general non-fiction.

Royalties paid annually.

The British Museum Press
46 Bloomsbury Street, London WC1B 3QQ
☎020 7323 1234 Fax 020 7436 7315
Website www.britishmuseum.co.uk
Managing Director *Andrew Thatcher*
Director of Publishing *Alasdair Macleod*

The book publishing division of The British Museum Company Ltd. FOUNDED 1973 as British Museum Publications Ltd; relaunched 1991 as British Museum Press. *Publishes* ancient history, archaeology, ethnography, art history, exhibition catalogues, guides, children's books, and all official publications of the British Museum. About 50 titles a year. TITLES *Dangerous Tastes: The Story of Spices; The British Museum Book of Haiku; The British Museum Dictionary of Ancient Egypt (2nd edn); Antony Gormley Drawing.* Synopses and ideas for books welcome.

Royalties paid twice-yearly.

Brockhampton Press Ltd
See **Caxton Publishing Group**

Andrew Brodie Publications
See **A.&C. Black (Publishers) Ltd**

John Brown Citrus Publishing Ltd
The New Boathouse, 136–142 Bramley Road, London W10 6SR
☎020 7565 3000 Fax 020 7565 3050
Chairman *John Brown*
Managing Director *Dean Fitzpatrick*

FOUNDED 1987. Contract magazine publisher. TITLES include *theAAMagazine, Waitrose Food Illustrated* and *The Oldie.*

Brown, Son & Ferguson, Ltd
4–10 Darnley Street, Glasgow G41 2SD
☎0141 429 1234 Fax 0141 420 1694
Email info@skipper.co.uk
Website www.skipper.co.uk
Chairman/Joint Managing Director
  T. Nigel Brown

FOUNDED 1850. *Specialises* in nautical textbooks, both technical and non-technical. Also Scottish one-act/three-act plays. Unsolicited mss, synopses and ideas for books welcome.

Royalties paid annually.

Bryntirion Press
Bryntirion, Bridgend, Mid-Glamorgan CF31 4DX
☎01656 655886 Fax 01656 665919
Email office@emw.org.uk
Press Manager *Huw Kinsey*

Owned by the Evangelical Movement of Wales. *Publishes* Christian books in English and Welsh. TITLES *A Light in the Land; On the Wings of the Dove.* No unsolicited mss; synopses and ideas welcome.

Royalties paid annually.

Bucknell University Press
See **Golden Cockerel Press Ltd**

Business Books
See **Random House Group Ltd**

Business Education Publishers Ltd
The Teleport, Doxford International, Sunderland, Tyne & Wear SR3 3XD
☎0191 525 2410
Email info@bepl.com
Website www.bepl.com
Managing Director *Mrs A. Murphy*
Approx. Annual Turnover £400,000

FOUNDED 1981. *Publishes* business education, economics and law for BTEC and GNVQ reading. Currently expanding into further and higher education, computing, IT, business, travel and tourism, occasional papers for institutions and local government administration. Unsolicited mss and synopses welcome.

Royalties paid annually.

Buster Books
See **Michael O'Mara Books Ltd**

Butterworth-Heinemann
See **Elsevier Ltd**

C&B (Collins & Brown)
See **Chrysallis Books Group**

Cadogan Guides
Highlands House, 165 The Broadway, Wimbledon, London SW19 1NE
☎020 8544 8051 Fax 020 8544 8081
Email info.cadogan@virgin.net
Website www.cadoganguides.com
Managing Editor *Christine Stroyan*

FOUNDED 1982. *Publishes* three series of travel guides: to countries and regions, cities and for parents (*Take the Kids*). Most titles are commissioned. No unsolicited material.

Calder Publications Ltd
51 The Cut, London SE1 8LF
☎020 7633 0599 Fax 020 7928 5930
Email info@calderpublications.com
Website www.calderpublications.com
Chairman/Managing Director/Editorial Head *John Calder*

Formerly John Calder (Publishers) Ltd. A publishing company which has grown around the tastes and contacts of John Calder, the iconoclast of the literary establishment. The list has a reputation for controversial and opinion-forming publications; Samuel Beckett is perhaps the most prestigious name. The list includes all of Beckett's prose and poetry. *Publishes* autobiography, biography, drama, literary fiction, literary criticism, music, opera, poetry, politics, sociology, ENO opera guides. SERIES *Thought Bites* Short polemical texts on current political and social issues. AUTHORS Antonin Artaud, Marguerite Duras, Martin Esslin, Erich Fried, P.J. Kavanagh, Robert Menasse, Robert Pinget, Luigi Pirandello, Alain Robbe-Grillet, Nathalie Sarraute, L.F. Celine, Eva Figes, Claude Simon, Howard Barker (plays). *No new material accepted.*
Royalties paid annually.

Authors' Rating Known for his patronage of eccentric talents, John Calder is one of the few publishers to carry the flag for the English language '... which is in great danger of disappearing under the American vernacular'.

California University Press
See **University Presses of California, Columbia & Princeton Ltd**

Cambridge University Press
The Edinburgh Building, Shaftesbury Road, Cambridge CB2 2RU
☎01223 312393 Fax 01223 315052
Website www.cambridge.org
Chief Executive *Stephen R.R. Bourne*

The oldest printer and publisher in the world with long-established branches in the USA and Australia and more recently established branches in Spain, Africa, South America and East Asia. Winner of The Queen's Award for Export Achievement in 1998. Over the last ten years, Cambridge has opened many new offices around the world. Its books are sold in more than 200 countries. Publications include the Cambridge Histories and Companions, encyclopedias and dictionaries; the **Canto** series; popular science and scientific and medical reference; major ELT courses; coursebooks for the National Curriculum; Cambridge Reading; and Cambridge Low Price Editions for the developing world. *Publishes* academic/educational and reference books for English-language markets worldwide, at all levels from primary school to postgraduate, together with a list of Spanish titles. Also ELT, Bibles and some 170 academic journals. Over 23,000 authors in 106 different countries and about 1800 new titles a year.

PUBLISHING GROUPS
Bibles *C.J. Wright* **ELT** *A.C. Gilfillan* **Humanities and Social Sciences** *R. Fisher* **Education** *J.G.Tuttle* **Journals** *C. Guettler.* Synopses and ideas for educational, ELT and academic books are welcome (and preferable to the submission of unsolicited mss). No fiction or poetry.
Royalties paid twice-yearly.

Authors' Rating CUP retains its traditional strength in the academic market with an increasing number of titles which reach out to the general reader.

Camden Large Print
See entry under **BBC Audiobooks**

Camden Press Ltd
43 Camden Passage, London N1 8EA
☎020 7226 4673
Chairman *Bob Borzello*

FOUNDED 1985. *Publishes* social issues; all books are launched in connection with major national conferences. DIVISION **Publishing for Change** *Bob Borzello* TITLE *Living with the Legacy of Abuse.* IMPRINT **Mindfield** TITLES *Hate Thy Neighbour: The Race Issue; Therapy on the Couch.* No unsolicited material. Approach by telephone in the first instance.
Royalties paid annually.

Campbell Books
See **Macmillan Publishers Ltd**

Candle Books
See **Angus Hudson Ltd** under **UK Packagers**

Canongate Books Ltd
14 High Street, Edinburgh EH1 1TE
☎0131 557 5111 Fax 0131 557 5211
Email info@canongate.co.uk

Website www.canongate.net
Publisher *Jamie Byng*
Managing Director *David Graham*
Submissions Editor *Francis Bickmore*
Approx. Annual Turnover £4.5 million

FOUNDED 1973. *Publishes* a wide range of literary fiction and non-fiction. Historically there is a strong Scottish slant to the list but its output is increasingly international and Canongate has a growing reputation for originating unusual projects (typified by the Pocket Canons Bible series). Key AUTHORS include Michel Faber, Robert Sabbag, Laura Hird, Charles Bukowski, Anthony Bourdain, John Fante, Richard Brautigan, Dorit Rabinyan, Martin Strong, Will Ferguson, Jennifer Clement, Knut Hamsun, Chester Himes, Iceberg Slim, Yann Martel, Dan Rhodes, Alasdair Gray and Toni Davidson. No unsolicited mss. Please contact before sending new material. Also works closely with **Grove/Atlantic** in New York, developing a reciprocal relationship whereby Canongate US is publishing 20 books a year in America and Atlantic UK is distributed alongside Canongate in the UK and Commonwealth.

IMPRINTS **Canongate Classics** Adult paperback series dedicated solely to important works of Scottish literature; **Canongate Crime** Paperback series featuring writers from all around the world, includes **Canongate Crime Classics** dedicated to reprinting lost classics of the genre; **Canongate International** Fiction in translation; **Mojo Books** An imprint in collaboration with Emap's *Mojo* magazine that combines informed, incisive music writing with Canongate's extensive list of existing music titles.
Royalties paid twice-yearly.

Authors' Rating The living proof that there is good in the world of publishing, Canongate attracts original work that finds new markets. Fewer titles are on offer in the latest list but each is given the attention that few big publishers can rival.

Canto
See **Cambridge University Press**

Capall Bann Publishing
Auton Farm, Milverton, Somerset TA4 1NE
☎01823 401528 Fax 01823 401529
Email enquiries@capallbann.co.uk
Website www.capallbann.co.uk
Chairman *Julia Day*
Editorial Head *Jon Day*
FOUNDED 1993 with three titles and now have

well over 200 in print. Family-owned and -run company which *publishes* British traditions, folklore, computing, boating, animals, alternative healing, environmental, Celtic lore, mind, body and spirit. About 40 titles a year. TITLES *Tarot Therapy; How to Talk with Fairies; Spiritual Journey; Crystals Folklore & Healing; Return of Yesterday's People.* Unsolicited proposals for books welcome. No e-mailed submissions – correspondence only, please. No fiction or poetry.
Royalties paid twice-yearly.

Jonathan Cape Ltd
See **Random House Group Ltd**

Capstone Publishing Ltd
8 Newtec Place, Magdalen Road, Oxford OX4 1RE
☎01865 798623 Fax 01865 240941
Email info@wiley-capstone.co.uk
Website www.capstoneideas.com
Joint Managing Directors *Mark Allin, Richard Burton*
FOUNDED 1997. Part of **John Wiley & Sons, Inc.** *Publishes* business books. 45 titles in 2002. Unsolicited synopses and ideas for books welcome; write or e-mail in the first instance with synopsis, c.v. and one or two sample chapters.
Royalties paid twice-yearly.

Carcanet Press Ltd
4th Floor, Alliance House, 30 Cross Street, Manchester M2 7AQ
☎0161 834 8730 Fax 0161 832 0084
Email pnr@carcanet.u-net.com
Website www.carcanet.co.uk
Chairman *Kate Gavron*
Managing Director/Editorial Director *Michael Schmidt*
In the last 30 years Carcanet has grown from an undergraduate hobby into a substantial venture. Robert Gavron bought the company in 1983 and it has established strong European, Commonwealth and American links. Winner of the **Sunday Times Small Publisher of the Year** award in 2000, it took over the Oxford Poets list from **Oxford University Press** in 1999 which it now publishes as a distinct imprint. Primarily a poetry publisher but also *publishes* academic, literary biography, fiction in translation and translations. About 60 titles a year, including the *PN Review* (six issues yearly). AUTHORS Homero Aridjis, John Ashbery, Eavan Boland, Joseph Brodsky, Donald Davie, Natalia Ginzburg, Robert

Graves, Elizabeth Jennings, Edwin Morgan, Les Murray, Frederic Raphael, Leonardo Sciascia, Iain Crichton Smith, Pedro Tamen, Charles Tomlinson. Poetry submissions (hard copy only): 6–10 poems with covering letter and return postage if the material is to be sent back. Prospective writers should familiarise themselves with the Carcanet list.

Royalties paid annually.

Authors' Rating Ever in the forefront of imaginative publishing, Carcanet has taken a step closer to the source of its literary creativity by setting up a postgraduate Writing School at Manchester Metropolitan University. (See entry under **Writers' Courses, Circles and Workshops**.)

Cardiff Academic Press
St Fagans Road, Fairwater, Cardiff CF5 3AE
☎029 2056 0333 Fax 029 2055 4909

Managing Director *R.G. Drake*

Academic publishers.

Carfax Publishing
See **Taylor & Francis Group plc**

Carlton Publishing Group
20 Mortimer Street, London W1T 3JW
☎020 7612 0400 Fax 020 7612 0401
Email enquiries@carltonbooks.co.uk
Website www.carlton.com

Managing Director *Jonathan Goodman*
Editorial Director *Piers Murray Hill*
Approx. Annual Turnover £17 million

FOUNDED 1992. Owned by Carlton Communications. Has two main divisions: **Carlton Books** *publishes* illustrated leisure and entertainment books aimed at the mass market. Subjects include TV tie-ins, lifestyle (fashion, beauty, health and well-being), popular science, design, history, music, sport and puzzles. **André Deutsch** *publishes* autobiography, biography, history, current affairs and the arts. Acquired **Prion Books Ltd** in 2003.

DIVISIONS **Carlton Books**; **André Deutsch**; **Granada Media**; **Manchester United Books**. No unsolicited mss; synopses and ideas welcome. No novels, science fiction, poetry or children's fiction.

Authors' Rating Linked to the largest programme producer in the ITV network, Carlton Books has built a reputation on co-editions for the international market and television tie-ins. Noted for speed of taking a book from first idea to publication.

Carroll & Brown Publishers Limited
20 Lonsdale Road, London NW6 6RD
☎020 7372 0900 Fax 020 7372 0460
Email mail@carrollandbrown.co.uk

Managing Director *Amy Carroll*
Approx. Annual Turnover £4 million

FOUNDED in 1989 as a packaging operation and commenced publishing in 2000. *Publishes* practical cookery, health, fitness, lifestyle, mind, body and spirit. TITLES *Are You Smarter Than You Think?; Tarot for Today; Great Healthy Food for the Menopause; Power Yoga for Beginners*. Synopses and ideas for illustrated books welcome; approach in writing in the first instance. No fiction.

Payment Fees or royalties paid.

Frank Cass & Co Ltd
Crown House, 47 Chase Side, Southgate, London N14 5BP
☎020 8920 2100 Fax 020 8447 8548
Email info@frankcass.com
Website www.frankcass.com

Chairman *Frank Cass*
Managing Director *Stewart Cass*
Managing Editor (Books) *Andrew Humphrys*
Managing Editor (Journals) *Anthony Bastock*

Publishes books and journals in the fields of politics, international relations, military and security studies, history, Middle East and sports studies, economics, development studies.

DIVISIONS **Woburn Press** Educational list: history of education, education policy and practice TITLES *Her Majesty's Inspectorate of Schools Since 1944* John E. Dunford; *Going Comprehensive in England and Wales* Alan C. Kercknoff. IMPRINTS **Vallentine Mitchell/ Jewish Chronicle Publications** (see entry). Unsolicited mss considered but synopsis with covering letter preferred.

Royalties paid annually.

Cassell Illustrated
See **Octopus Publishing Group**

Cassell Military/Cassell Reference
See **The Orion Publishing Group Limited**

Castle Publications
See **Nottingham University Press**

Kyle Cathie Ltd
122 Arlington Road, London NW1 7HP
☎020 7692 7215 Fax 020 7692 7260
Email general.enquiries@kyle-cathie.com

FOUNDED 1990 to publish and promote 'books we have personal enthusiasm for'. *Publishes* non-fiction: cookery, food and drink, health and beauty, mind, body & spirit, gardening, homes and interiors, reference and occasional books of classic poetry. TITLES *Exercise Bible* Joanna Hall; *Teenage Survival Guide* Marina Baker; *100 Great Pasta Dishes* Ann Franco Taruschio; *21st Century Beauty Bible* Sarah Stacey & Josephine Fainley. About 25 titles a year. No unsolicited mss. 'Synopses and ideas are considered in the fields in which we publish.'

Royalties paid twice-yearly.

Catholic Truth Society (CTS)

40–46 Harleyford Road, London SE11 5AY
☎020 7640 0042 Fax 020 7640 0046
Email f.martin@cts-online.org.uk
Website www.cts-online.org.uk

Chairman *Most Rev. Peter Smith*
General Secretary *Fergal Martin*
Approx. Annual Turnover £750,000

FOUNDED originally in 1868 and re-founded in 1884. *Publishes* religious books – Roman Catholic; a variety of doctrinal, moral, biographical, devotional and liturgical publications, including a large body of Vatican documents and sources. Unsolicited mss, synopses and ideas welcome if appropriate to their list.

Royalties paid annually.

Causeway Press Ltd

PO Box 13, 129 New Court Way, Ormskirk, Lancashire L39 5HP
☎01695 576048 Fax 01695 570714

Chairman/Managing Director
M. Haralambos
Approx. Annual Turnover £2 million

FOUNDED in 1982. *Publishes* educational textbooks only. 17 titles in 2003. TITLES *Mathematics for AQA; Mathematics for Edexcel; Psychology in Focus; Business Accounting; Business Studies; Economics; Business Studies for GCSE; Sociology in Focus; Politics in Focus.* Unsolicited mss, synopses and ideas welcome.

Royalties paid annually.

Cavendish Publishing Limited

The Glass House, Wharton Street, London WC1X 9PX
☎020 7278 8000 Fax 020 7278 8080
Email info@cavendishpublishing.com
Website www.cavendishpublishing.com

Executive Chairman *Sonny Leong*

FOUNDED 1990. *Publishes* academic law books. 160 titles in 2002. No unsolicited mss; send synopsis accompanied by a letter in the first instance.

Royalties paid twice-yearly. *Overseas associate* Cavendish Publishing (Australia) Pty Ltd.

Caxton Publishing Group

20 Bloomsbury Street, London WC1B 3JH
☎020 7636 7171 Fax 020 7636 1922
Email office@caxtonpublishing.com
Website www.caxtonpublishing.com

Chairman *Stephen Hill*
Managing Director *John Maxwell*
Approx. Annual Turnover £4 million

FOUNDED 1999. *Specialises* in reprinting out-of-print works for the 'value' market worldwide and commissioning new general non-fiction publications in reference, cookery, gardening and children's. 200 titles a year.

DIVISIONS/IMPRINTS **Brockhampton Press Ltd** Children's fiction and non-fiction. **Caxton Editions Ltd** General non-fiction, reference and military. **Knight Paperbacks Ltd** Fiction. No unsolicited mss; synopses and ideas welcome; send letter in the first instance.

Royalties paid twice-yearly.

CBA Publishing

Bowes Morrell House, 111 Walmgate, York YO1 9WA
☎01904 671417 Fax 01904 671384
Website www.britarch.ac.uk

Publications Officer *Jane Thorniley-Walker*
British Archaeology Editor *Simon Denison*
Young Archaeologists' Club
  Co-ordinator *Alison Bodley*
Approx. Annual Turnover £80,000

Publishing arm of the **Council for British Archaeology**. *Publishes* academic archaeology reports, practical handbooks, yearbook, *British Archaeology* (bi-monthly magazine), *Young Archaeologist* (Young Archaeologists' Club magazine), monographs, archaeology and education. TITLES *Cataractonium: Roman Catterick and its Hinterland (Vol I, II); Pottery in Medieval Southampton; Early Post-medieval Vessel Glass in England; Stirling Castle: The Restoration of the Great Hall.* Please contact by telephone before submitting mss and proposals.

Royalties paid for hardback and commercial publications.

CBD Research Ltd

Chancery House, 15 Wickham Road, Beckenham, Kent BR3 5JS
☎020 8650 7745 Fax 020 8650 0768
Email cbd@cbdresearch.com

Website www.cbdresearch.com
Chairman *G.P. Henderson*
Managing Director *S.P.A. Henderson*
Approx. Annual Turnover £500,000
FOUNDED 1961. *Publishes* directories and other reference guides to sources of information. About 6 titles a year. No fiction.
    IMPRINT **Chancery House Press** Non-fiction of an esoteric/specialist nature for 'serious researchers and the dedicated hobbyist'. Unsolicited mss, synopses and ideas welcome.
    Royalties paid quarterly.

Centaur Press
See **Open Gate Press**

Century
See **Random House Group Ltd**

Chadwyck-Healey
See **ProQuest Information and Learning Ltd**

Chambers Harrap Publishers Ltd
7 Hopetoun Crescent, Edinburgh EH7 4AY
☎0131 556 5929 Fax 0131 556 5313
Email admin@chambersharrap.com
Website www.chambersharrap.com
Managing Director *Maurice Shepherd*
Administrator *Stephanie Divens*

Publishes dictionaries and reference. The imprint was founded in the early 1800s to publish self-education books, but soon diversified into dictionaries and other reference works. The acquisition of Harrap Publishing Group's core business strengthened its position in the dictionary market, adding bilingual titles, covering almost all the major European languages, to its English-language dictionaries. About 25 titles a year. Send synopsis with accompanying letter rather than completed mss.

Chancery House Press
See **CBD Research Ltd**

Channel 4 Books
See **Macmillan Publishers Ltd**

Paul Chapman Publishing Ltd
See **Sage Publications**

Chapman Publishing
4 Broughton Place, Edinburgh EH1 3RX
☎0131 557 2207 Fax 0131 556 9565
Email editor@chapman-pub.co.uk
Website www.chapman-pub.co.uk

Managing Editor *Joy Hendry*
A venture devoted to publishing works by the best of Scottish writers, both up-and-coming and established, published in *Chapman*, Scotland's leading literary magazine. Has expanded publishing activities considerably over the last three years and is now publishing a wider range of works though the broad policy stands. *Publishes* poetry, drama, short stories, books of contemporary importance in 20th-century Scotland. About 4 titles a year. TITLES *Ye Cannae Win* Janet Paisley; *Clan MacHine* Ian McDonough; *Wild Women Series – Wild Women of a Certain Age* Magi Gibson. No unsolicited mss; synopses and ideas for books welcome.
    Royalties paid annually.

Chapmans Publishers
See **The Orion Publishing Group Ltd**

Charnwood
See **F.A. Thorpe (Publishing)**

Chartered Institute of Personnel and Development
CIPD House, Camp Road, London SW19 4UX
☎020 8971 9000 Fax 020 8263 3333
Email publish@cipd.co.uk
Website www.cipd.co.uk

Part of CIPD Enterprises Limited. *Publishes* people management and training titles. A list of 200 titles. TITLES *The Motivation Handbook; HR Forecasting and Planning; Essentials of Employment Law.* Unsolicited mss, synopses and ideas welcome.
    Royalties paid annually.

Chatham Publishing
See **Gerald Duckworth & Co Ltd**

Chatto & Windus Ltd
See **Random House Group Ltd**

Cherrytree Books
See **Evans Brothers Ltd**

Chicken House Publishing
2 Palmer Street, Frome, Somerset BA11 1DS
☎01373 454488 Fax 01373 454499
Email doublecluck.com
Chairman/Managing Director *Barry Cunningham*

Children's publishing house FOUNDED in 2000. *Publishes* books 'that are aimed at real children' – fiction, original picture books, gift books and fun non-fiction. Aiming to publish about 25 titles a year. 'We are always on the lookout for new talent.' Unsolicited material welcome; send letter with synopsis and sample chapters.

Royalties paid twice-yearly.

Authors' Rating A new kid on the street, Chicken House, according to its founder, Barry Cunningham, is a 'small, creative company which has made strategic alliances around the world'. These alliances certainly give new authors a strong international profile – just the thing in an ever more competitive market.

Child's Play (International) Ltd

Ashworth Road, Bridgemead, Swindon, Wiltshire SN5 7YD
☎01793 616286 Fax 01793 512795
Email allday@childs-play.com
Website www.childs-play.com

Chief Executive *Neil Burden*

FOUNDED in 1972, Child's Play is an independent publisher specialising in learning through play, whole child development, life-skills and values. *Publishes* books, games and A-V materials. TITLES Books: *Big Hungry Bear; There Was an Old Lady; Our Cat Cuddles; Royston Knapper; Children of the Sun; Ten Beads Tall; Pocket Pals; Sliders; Roly Poly Books; Book Buddies; Mrs Honey's Tree; Big Books and Storysacks*; Games: *Dizzy Bizzy; Safe Places; Arithmetic Lotto.* Unsolicited mss welcome. Send s.a.e. for return or response. Expect to wait two months for a reply.

Royalties Outright or royalty payments are subject to negotiation.

Chimera

See **Pegasus Elliot Mackenzie Publishers Ltd**

Chivers

See entry under **BBC Audiobooks**

Christian Focus Publications

Geanies House, Fearn, Tain, Ross-shire IV20 1TW
☎01862 871011 Fax 01862 871699
Email info@christianfocus.com
Website www.christianfocus.com

Chairman *R.W.M. Mackenzie*
Managing Director *William Mackenzie*
Editorial Manager *Willie Mackenzie*
Children's Editor *Catherine Mackenzie*
Approx. Annual Turnover £1.2 million

FOUNDED 1979 to produce children's books for the co-edition market. Now a major producer of Christian books. *Publishes* adult and children's books, including some fiction for children but not adults. No poetry. About 80 titles a year. Unsolicited mss, synopses and ideas welcome from Christian writers. See website for submission criteria. Publishes for all English-speaking markets, as well as the UK.

IMPRINTS **Christian Focus** General books; **Mentor** Study books; **Christian Heritage** Classic reprints.

Royalties paid annually.

Christian Heritage

See **Christian Focus Publications**

Christian Publishing

See **First Century Ltd**

Chrome Dreams

See entry under **Audio Books**

Chrysalis Books Group

The Chrysalis Building, Bramley Road, London W10 6SP
☎020 7314 1400
Email <firstinitialsurname>@chrysalisbooks.co.uk
Website www.chrysalisbooks.co.uk

Chairman *Marcus Leaver*
Approx. Annual Turnover £33.9 million

Chrysalis Books, owned by Chrysalis Group Plc, specialises in illustrated non-fiction, publishing under the IMPRINTS **B.T. Batsford**; **Brassey's**; **C&B (Collins & Brown)**; **Conway Maritime Press**; **Paper Tiger**; **Pavilion**; **Putnam Aeronautical Books**; **Robson Books**; **Salamander**; **Vega**.

IMPRINTS
B.T. Batsford Publisher *Roger Huggins*. FOUNDED in 1843 as a bookseller, and began publishing in 1874. Acquired by Chrysalis in 1999. A world leader in books on chess, arts and craft. *Publishes* non-fiction, architecture, heritage, bridge and chess, film and entertainment, fashion, crafts and hobbies. About 100 titles a year. *Royalties* paid twice in the first year, annually thereafter.
Brassey's Publisher *John Lee*. Acquired by Chrysalis in 1999. *Publishes* military history and technology. *Royalties* paid annually.
C&B (Collins & Brown) Publisher *Will Steeds*. *Publishes* a range of lifestyle categories especially in the areas of practical art, photography and needlecrafts.
Conway Maritime Press Publisher *John Lee*. *Publishes* naval history, maritime culture

and ship modelling. *Royalties* paid annually.

Paper Tiger Publisher *Will Steeds*. Acquired by Chrysalis in 2001 (part of C&B). *Publishes* science fiction and fantasy art.

Pavilion Books Editorial Director *Kate Oldfield*. Acquired by Chrysalis in 2001. *Publishes* illustrated books in biography, cookery, gardening, humour, art, interiors, music, sport and travel. Unsolicited mss not welcome. Ideas and synopses for non-fiction titles considered. *Royalties* paid twice-yearly.

Putnam Aeronautical Books Publisher *John Lee*. *Publishes* classic aeronautical histories, technical and reference.

Robson Books Publisher *Jeremy Robson*. FOUNDED 1973. Acquired by Chrysalis in 1998. *Publishes* general non-fiction including biography, cookery, gardening, sport and travel. About 90 titles a year. Unsolicited synopses and ideas for books welcome (s.a.e. essential for reply). *Royalties* paid twice-yearly.

Salamander Publisher *Jo Messham*. FOUNDED 1973. *Publishes* colour illustrated books on collecting, cookery, interiors, gardening, music, crafts, military, aviation, sport and transport. Also a wide range of books on American interest subjects. No unsolicited mss but synopses and ideas for the above subjects welcome. Outright fee paid instead of royalties.

Vega Publisher *Will Steeds* ESTABLISHED 2001. *Publishes* mind, body, spirit.

Authors' Rating Having grown rapidly by acquisitions, Chrysalis publishes up to 700 titles a year covering just about every area of general non-fiction. But recent staff cutbacks suggest a greater concentration on core markets with a corresponding contraction of the publishing programme. US co-editions account for half the company's sales.

Chrysalis Children's Books

64 Brewery Road, London N7 9NT
☎020 7697 3000 Fax 020 7697 3001
Email <firstinitialsurname>@chrysalisbooks.co.uk
Website www.chrysalisbooks.com
Head of Children's Books *Steve Evans*
Publisher *Chester Fisher*

Part of the **Chrysalis Books Group**. *Publishes* all kinds of children's books from fun books to illustrated classics and educational books under the following

IMPRINTS:
Belitha Press Editorial Manager *Joyce Bentley*. FOUNDED 1980, acquired by Chrysalis in 2002. *Publishes* children's non-fiction in all curriculum areas. TITLES *Start Writing; Art for All; History Mysteries; Monster Machines*. No unsolicited mss. Synopses and ideas for books welcome from experienced children's writers.

Big Fish Editorial Head *Honor Head*. Acquired by Chrysalis in 2002. *Publishes* innovative interactive children's books including pop-ups, unique formats, licensed characters and books-plus. Synopses and ideas welcome from experienced children's writers.

David Bennett Books Editorial Head *Liz Flanagan*. FOUNDED 1989, acquired by Chrysalis in 2002. *Publishes* children's picture and novelty books, interactive and board books, baby gifts and non-fiction for babies and toddlers. No unsolicited mss.

Learning World Editorial Head *Joyce Bentley*. *Publishes* books to help parents guide their children's educational development and to support schoolwork at home.

Pavilion Children's Books Editorial Head *Liz Flanagan*. Acquired by Chrysalis in 2002. *Publishes* fiction and non-fiction children's books with visual flair for ages 5+ including picture and gift books. No unsolicited mss.

Zigzag Editorial Head *Honor Head*. Acquired by Chrysalis in 2000. *Publishes* interactive non-fiction for ages 5–14 on popular subjects. Most books contain CD-ROMs and Internet links. No unsolicited mss.

Churchill Livingstone
See **Elsevier Ltd**

Cicerone Press
2 Police Square, Milnthorpe, Cumbria LA7 7PY
☎01539 562069 Fax 01539 563417
Email info@cicerone.co.uk
Website www.cicerone.co.uk
Managing/Editorial Director *Jonathan Williams*

FOUNDED 1969. Guidebook publisher for outdoor enthusiasts. About 20 titles a year. No fiction or poetry. TITLES *Walks and Climbs in the Pyrenees; Tour of Mont Blanc; Walking in Hampshire* and *Long Distance Walking* series of guides. No unsolicited mss; synopses and ideas considered.
Royalties paid twice-yearly.

Cico Books
1st Floor, 32 Great Sutton Street, London EC1V 0NB
☎020 7253 7960 Fax 020 7253 7967
Email mail@cicobooks.co.uk

Managing Director *Mark Collins*
Publisher *Cindy Richards*

FOUNDED in 1999 by Mark Collins and Cindy Richards (both formerly with **Collins & Brown**) 'to offer flexibility by being small, selling co-edition rights to overseas publishers'. *Publishes* lifestyle and interiors, mind, body and spirit. About 12 titles a year. No unsolicited mss, synopses or ideas.
Royalties paid twice-yearly.

Clarion
See **Elliot Right Way Books**

T.&T. Clark
35 Dick Place, Edinburgh EH9 2JA
☎0131 466 0082 Fax 0131 466 0082
Email ggreen.tandtclark@blueyonder.co.uk
Website www.tandtclark.co.uk

Managing Director/Editorial Head
Geoffrey Green

FOUNDED 1821. Part of the **Continuum International Publishing Group Ltd**. *Publishes* religion, theology and philosophy for academic and professional markets. About 35 titles a year, including journals. TITLES *Church Dogmatics* Karl Barth; *The Romans Debate* Karl Donfried; *In the Beginning* Joseph Ratzinger. Unsolicited mss, synopses and ideas for books welcome.
Royalties paid twice-yearly.

James Clarke & Co.
PO Box 60, Cambridge CB1 2NT
☎01223 350865 Fax 01223 366951
Email publishing@jamesclarke.co.uk
Website www.jamesclarke.co.uk

Managing Director *Adrian Brink*

Parent company of **The Lutterworth Press** (see entry). *Publishes* scholarly and academic works, mainly theological, directory and reference titles. TITLES *Libraries Directory* (book and CD-ROM versions); *Encyclopedia of the Middle Ages; Deep Economy: Caring for Ecology, Humanity and Religion; Literature and Sacrament: the Sacred and the Secular in John Donne.* Approach in writing with ideas in the first instance.

Peter Collin Publishing Ltd
See **Bloomsbury Publishing Plc**

Collins
See **HarperCollins Publishers Ltd**

Collins & Brown
See **Chrysalis Books Group**

Colonsay Books
See **House of Lochar**

Colourpoint Books
Unit D5, Ards Business Centre, Jubilee Road, Newtownards, Co. Down BT23 4YH
☎028 9182 0505 Fax 028 9182 1900
Email info@colourpoint.co.uk
Website www.colourpoint.co.uk

Partners *Sheila M. Johnston, Norman Johnston, Malcolm Johnston, Wesley Johnston*

FOUNDED 1993. *Publishes* school textbooks and transport (covering the whole of the British Isles), plus books of Irish and general interest. No fiction. 25 titles in 2002. Unsolicited material accepted but approach in writing in the first instance; include return postage, please.
Royalties paid twice-yearly.

Columbia University Press
See **University Presses of California, Columbia & Princeton Ltd**

Compendium Publishing Ltd
1st Floor, 43 Frith Street, London W1D 4SA
☎020 7287 4570 Fax 020 7494 0583
Email compendiumpub@aol.com

Managing Director *Alan Greene*
Editorial Director *Simon Forty*

FOUNDED 1996. *Publishes* and packages for international publishing companies – general non-fiction: history, reference, hobbies, children's and educational transport and militaria. No unsolicited mss; synopses and ideas preferred.
Royalties paid twice-yearly.

Condor
See **Souvenir Press Ltd**

Conran Octopus
See **Octopus Publishing Group**

Constable & Robinson Ltd
3 The Lanchesters, 162 Fulham Palace Road, London W6 9ER
☎020 8741 3663 Fax 020 8748 7562
Email enquiries@constablerobinson.com
Website www.constablerobinson.com

Non-Executive Chairman *Benjamin Glazebrook*
Managing Director *Nick Robinson*
Directors *Jan Chamier, Nova Jayne Heath, Adrian Andrews*
Approx. Annual Turnover £5 million

Constable & Co FOUNDED in 1890 by Archibald

Constable, a grandson of Walter Scott's publisher. Robinson Publishing Ltd FOUNDED in 1983 by Nick Robinson. In December 1999 Constable and Robinson combined their individual shareholdings into a single company, Constable & Robinson Ltd.

IMPRINTS **Constable** (Hardbacks) Editorial Director *Carol O'Brien Publishes* biography and autobiography, crime fiction, general and military history, psychology, travel, climbing, landscape photography and outdoor pursuits guidebooks. **Robinson** (Paperbacks) Senior Commissioning Editor *Krystyna Green Publishes* crime, science fiction, *Daily Telegraph* health books, the Mammoth series, psychology, true crime, military history and *Smarties* children's books. Unsolicited sample chapters, synopses and ideas for books welcome. No mss; no e-mail submissions. Enclose return postage.

Authors' Rating The merging of two small but highly regarded independent publishers promises well for authors who enjoy close attention from their editors. Emerged with an excellent result from a recent Society of Authors survey of author/publisher relations.

Consultants Bureau
See **Kluwer Academic/Plenum Publishers**

Consumers' Association
See **Which? Books/Consumers' Association**

The Continuum International Publishing Group Limited
The Tower Building, 11 York Road, London SE1 7NX
☎020 7922 0880 Fax 020 7922 0881
Website www.continuumbooks.com
Chairman & Managing Director *Philip Sturrock*
Approx. Annual Turnover £16 million

FOUNDED in 1999 by a buy-out of the academic and religious publishing of Cassell and the acquisition of Continuum New York. *Publishes* academic, religious and general books. 300 titles in 2002.

DIVISIONS
Humanities and Journals Publishing Director *Janet Joyce Publishes* literature; history; linguistics; film; theatre and media; religious and theological journals. TITLES *Companion to Twentieth Century Theatre* (ed. Chambers); *Text and Discourse; New History of Jazz* (Shipton); *Journals for the Study of Old/New Testament.* **Professional and Philosophy** Editorial Director *Anthony Haynes*

Publishes education, business, politics and international relations, philosophy. TITLES *Guerilla Guide to Teaching* (Cowley); *Free Radical* (Benn). **Academic Religious Books** Publisher *Philip Law Publishes* theology, biblical studies, religious studies.

IMPRINTS **Continuum; T.&T. Clark** (see entry); **Sheffield Academic Press; Handsel Press**. TITLES *Acts of the Apostles* (Barrett); *Scientific Theology* (McGrath); *Sense and Sensitivity* (Hunter & Davies). Unsolicited synopses and ideas within the subject areas listed above welcome; approach in writing in the first instance.

Overseas subsidiaries The Continuum International Publishing Group Inc., New York; Morehouse Publishing Group Inc., Harrisburg, PA.

Royalties paid twice-yearly.

Authors' Rating The rapidly expanding religious and academic list owes much to the skilful acquisition of small but interesting companies including a US-based publisher of religious books which will strengthen trans-Atlantic sales.

Conway Maritime Press
See **Chrysalis Books Group**

Thomas Cook Publishing
PO Box 227, Peterborough PE3 8XX
☎01733 402009 Fax 01733 416688
Head of Publishing *Donald Greig*
Approx. Annual Turnover £3.4 million

Part of the Thomas Cook Group Ltd, publishing commenced in 1873 with the first issue of Cook's Continental Timetable. *Publishes* guidebooks, maps and timetables. About 20 titles a year. No unsolicited mss; synopses and ideas welcome as long as they are travel-related.
Royalties paid annually.

Leo Cooper
See **Pen & Sword Books Ltd**

Corgi
See **Transworld Publishers**

Coronet
See **Hodder Headline Ltd**

Countryside Books
2 Highfield Avenue, Newbury, Berkshire RG14 5DS
☎01635 43816 Fax 01635 551004
Email info@countrysidebooks.co.uk

Website www.countrysidebooks.co.uk
Publisher *Nicholas Battle*
FOUNDED 1976. *Publishes* local interest paperbacks on regional subjects, generally by English county. Local history, dialects, genealogy, walking and photographic, aviation and military, some transport. Over 400 titles available. Unsolicited mss and synopses welcome but no fiction, poetry, natural history or personal memories.
Royalties paid twice-yearly.

Cressrelles Publishing Co. Ltd
10 Station Road Industrial Estate, Colwall, Malvern, Worcestershire WR13 6RN
☎01684 540154 Fax 01684 540154
Email simonsmith@cressrelles4drama.fsbusiness.co.uk
Managing Director *Leslie Smith*

Publishes a range of local interest books, drama and chiropody titles. IMPRINTS **Actinic Press** Specialises in chiropody; **J. Garnet Miller** Plays and theatre texts; **Kenyon-Deane** Plays and drama textbooks. Submissions welcome.

Cromwell
See **First Century Ltd**

Croom Helm
See **Routledge**

Crossway
See **Inter-Varsity Press**

The Crowood Press Ltd
The Stable Block, Crowood Lane, Ramsbury, Marlborough, Wiltshire SN8 2HR
☎01672 520320 Fax 01672 520280
Email enquiries@crowood.com
Website www.crowood.com
Chairman *John Dennis*
Managing Director *Ken Hathaway*

Publishes sport and leisure titles, including animal and land husbandry, climbing and walking, maritime, country sports, equestrian, fishing and shooting; also chess and bridge, crafts, dogs, gardening, natural history, aviation, military history and motoring. About 70 titles a year. Preliminary letter preferred in all cases.
Royalties paid annually.

James Currey Publishers
73 Botley Road, Oxford OX2 0BS
☎01865 244111 Fax 01865 246454
Email editorial@jamescurrey.co.uk
Website www.jamescurrey.co.uk

Chairman *James Currey*
Managing Director/Editorial Director *Douglas H. Johnson*
FOUNDED 1985. A specialist publisher. *Publishes* academic paperback books on Africa, the Caribbean and Third World: history, anthropology, economics, sociology, politics and literary criticism. Approach in writing by post with synopsis if material is 'relevant to our needs'.
Royalties paid annually.

Curzon Press
See **Routledge**

Custom Publishing
See **The Orion Publishing Group Limited**

Cygnus Arts
See **Golden Cockerel Press Ltd**

Dalesman Publishing Co. Ltd
Stable Courtyard, Broughton Hall, Skipton, North Yorkshire BD23 3AZ
☎01756 701381 Fax 01756 701326
Email editorial@dalesman.co.uk
Website www.dalesman.co.uk
Editor *Terry Fletcher*

Publishers of *Dalesman*, *Cumbria and Lake District* and *Peak District* magazines, and regional books covering Yorkshire, the Lake District and the Peak District. Subjects include crafts and hobbies, geography and geology, guidebooks, history and antiquarian, humour, travel and topography. Will consider mss on subjects listed above. About 20 titles a year.
Royalties paid annually.

Terence Dalton Ltd
Water Street, Lavenham, Sudbury, Suffolk CO10 9RN
☎01787 249291 Fax 01787 248267
Website www.lavenhamgroup.co.uk
Director/Editorial Head *Elisabeth Whitehair*
FOUNDED 1967. Part of the Lavenham Group Plc, a family company. No unsolicited mss; send synopsis with two or three sample chapters. Ideas welcome.
Royalties paid annually.

The C.W. Daniel Co. Ltd
1 Church Path, Saffron Walden, Essex CB10 1JP
☎01799 521909 Fax 01799 513462
Email cwdaniel@dial.pipex.com
Website www.cwdaniel.com

Managing Director *Ian Miller*
Approx. Annual Turnover £1 million

FOUNDED in 1902 by a man who knew and was a follower of Tolstoy, the company was taken over by its present directors in 1973. Output increased following the acquisition in 1980 of health and healing titles from the Health Science Press, the purchase of Neville Spearman Publishers' metaphysical list in 1985 and the list of L.N. Fowler in 1998. *Publishes* New Age: alternative healing and metaphysical. About 15 titles a year. No fiction, diet or cookery. Unsolicited synopses and ideas welcome; no unsolicited mss.

Royalties paid annually.

Darton, Longman & Todd Ltd

1 Spencer Court, 140–142 Wandsworth High Street, London SW18 4JJ
☎020 8875 0155   Fax 020 8875 0133
Email mail@darton-longman-todd.co.uk
Website www.darton-longman-todd.co.uk

Editorial Director *Brendan Walsh*
Editor/Rights Officer *Rachel Davis*
Approx. Annual Turnover £1 million

FOUNDED 1959. In July 1990 DLT became a common ownership company, owned and run by staff members. A leading ecumenical, predominantly Christian, publisher, with a strong emphasis on spirituality, theology and the ministry and mission of the Church. About 50 titles a year. TITLES *Jerusalem Bible; New Jerusalem Bible; God of Surprises; Landmarks.* Sample material for books on theological or spiritual subjects considered.

Royalties paid twice-yearly.

David & Charles Children's Books

See **Gullane Children's Books**

David & Charles Publishers

Brunel House, Forde Close, Newton Abbot, Devon TQ12 4PU
☎01626 323200   Fax 01626 323317
Email mail@davidandcharles.co.uk
Website www.davidandcharles.co.uk

Managing Director *Budge Wallis*

FOUNDED 1960, owned by F.&W. Publications. *Publishes* illustrated non-fiction for international markets, specialising in needlecraft, crafts, art techniques, practical photography, interiors and equestrian. No fiction, poetry or memoirs. About 50 titles a year. TITLES *The Cross Stitcher's Bible; Yesterday's Countryside; Watercolour in a Weekend; Photos That Sell; The A–Z of Creative Photography; The Complete Equine Veterinary Manual.* Unsolicited mss will be considered if return postage is included; synopses and ideas welcome for the subjects listed above.

Royalties paid twice-yearly or flat fees.

Christopher Davies Publishers Ltd

PO Box 403, Swansea, West Glamorgan SA1 4YF
☎01792 648825   Fax 01792 648825
Email editor@cdaviesbookswales.com

Managing Director/Editorial Head
   Christopher T. Davies
Approx. Annual Turnover £50,000

FOUNDED 1949 to promote and expand Welsh-language publications. By the 1970s the company was publishing over 50 titles a year but a subsequent drop in Welsh sales led to the establishment of a small English list which has continued. *Publishes* biography, cookery, history, sport and literature of Welsh interest. About 3 titles a year. TITLES *An A–Z of Wales and the Welsh; Welsh Birthplaces; Carwyn: A Personal Memoir; Who's Who in Welsh History.* No unsolicited mss. Synopses and ideas for books welcome.

Royalties paid twice-yearly.

Authors' Rating A favourite for Celtic readers and writers.

Giles de la Mare Publishers Ltd

PO Box 25351, London NW5 1ZT
☎020 7485 2533   Fax 020 7485 2534
Email gilesdelamare@dial.pipex.com

Chairman/Managing Director *Giles de la Mare*
Approx. Annual Turnover £35,000

FOUNDED 1995 and commenced publishing in April 1996. *Publishes* mainly non-fiction, especially art and architecture, biography, history, music. TITLES *Married to the Amadeus* Muriel Nissel; *Venice: An Anthology Guide* Milton Grundy; *History at War* Noble Frankland; *Flint Architecture of East Anglia* Stephen Hart; *19th Century British Painting* Luke Herrmann; *Handsworth Revolution* David Winkley; *The Life of Henry Moore* Roger Berthoud. Unsolicited mss, synopses and ideas welcome after initial telephone call.

Royalties paid twice-yearly.

Debrett's Peerage Ltd

Brunel House, 55–57 North Wharf Road, London W2 1LA
☎020 7915 9633   Fax 020 7753 4212
Email people@debretts.co.uk

Website www.debretts.co.uk
Chairman *Christopher Haines*
FOUNDED 1769. The company's main activity (in conjunction with **Macmillan**) is the three-yearly *Debrett's Peerage and Baronetage* (published 2003) and annual *Debrett's People of Today* (published in 2003 and also available on CD-ROM and online). Debrett's general books are published under licence through **Headline**.
Royalties paid twice-yearly.

Dedalus Ltd
Langford Lodge, St Judith's Lane, Sawtry, Cambridgeshire PE28 5XE
☎01487 832382 Fax 01487 832382
Email DedalusLimited@compuserve.com
Website www.dedalusbooks.com
Chairman *Juri Gabriel*
Managing Director *Eric Lane*
Approx. Annual Turnover £200,000
FOUNDED 1983. *Publishes* contemporary European fiction and classics and original literary fiction. 12 titles in 2002. TITLES *The Dedalus Book of Absinthe; The Arabian Nightmare* Robert Irwin; *Memoirs of a Gnostic Dwarf* David Madsen; *Dragon's Eye* Andy Oakes; *Music in a Foreign Language* Andrew Crumey (winner of the **Saltire Best First Book Award** in 1994). Welcomes submissions for original fiction and books suitable for its list but 'most people sending work in have no idea what kind of books Dedalus publishes and merely waste their efforts'. Author guidelines on website. Particularly interested in intellectually clever and unusual fiction. A letter about the author should always accompany any submission. No replies without s.a.e.
DIVISIONS/IMPRINTS **Original Fiction in Paperback**; **Contemporary European Fiction** 1992–2003; **Dedalus European Classics**; **Empire of the Senses**; **Literary Concept Books**.
Royalties paid annually.

Authors' Rating A small, quality publisher which actually recognises that good books can come from foreign language writers.

University of Delaware
See **Golden Cockerel Press Ltd**

JM Dent
See **The Orion Publishing Group Ltd**

André Deutsch Ltd
See **Carlton Publishing Group**

Digital Octopus
See **Octopus Publishing Group**

Digital Press
See **Elsevier Ltd**

Dinas
See **Y Lolfa Cyf**

Diva Books
See **Millivres Prowler Limited**

The Do-Not Press
16 Woodlands, London SE13 6TY
☎020 8698 7833 Fax 020 8698 7833
Email wh@thedonotpress.co.uk
Website www.thedonotpress.co.uk
Managing Director *Jim Driver*
Approx. Annual Turnover £150,000
FOUNDED 1994. *Publishes* general fiction and non-fiction. 18 titles in 2002. No unsolicited mss, synopses or ideas. IMPRINT **Bloodlines** Editorial Head *Carol de Salivate*. TITLES *Kiss It Away; No One Gets Hurt*.
Royalties paid annually.

John Donald Publishers Ltd
West Newington House, 10 Newington Road, Edinburgh EH9 1QS
☎0131 668 4371 Fax 0131 668 4466
Website www.birlinn.co.uk
Managing Director *Hugh Andrew*
Bought by **Birlinn Ltd** in 1999. *Publishes* academic and scholarly, archaeology, architecture, textbooks, guidebooks, local, and social history. About 20 titles a year. New books are published as an imprint of Birlinn Ltd.
Royalties paid annually.

Donhead Publishing Ltd
Lower Coombe, Donhead St Mary, Shaftesbury, Dorset SP7 9LY
☎01747 828422 Fax 01747 828522
Email jillpearce@donhead.com
Website www.donhead.com
Contact *Jill Pearce*
FOUNDED 1990 to specialise in publishing how-to books for building practitioners; particularly interested in architectural conservation material. *Publishes* building, architecture and heritage only. 6 titles a year. TITLES *Preserving Post-War Heritage; Stone Cleaning; Architecture 1900; Encyclopaedia of Architectural Terms; Cleaning Historic Buildings; Brickwork; Practical Stone Masonry; Conservation of Timber Buildings;*

Surveying Historic Buildings; English Heritage Directory of Building Limes; Heritage, Sands and Aggregates; Journal of Architectural Conservation (3 issues yearly). Unsolicited mss, synopses and ideas welcome.

Dorling Kindersley Ltd
Part of the Penguin Group, 80 Strand, London WC2R 0RL
☎020 7010 3000 Fax 020 7010 6060
Website www.dk.com

Chief Executive *Anthony Forbes Watson*
Managing Director *Andrew Welham*
Publisher *Christopher Davis*

FOUNDED 1974. Packager and publisher of illustrated non-fiction: cookery, crafts, gardening, health, travel guides, atlases, natural history and children's information and fiction. Launched a US imprint in 1991 and an Australian imprint in 1997. Acquired Henderson Publishing in 1995 and was purchased by Pearson plc for £311 million in 2000.

DIVISIONS
Adult: **Travel/Reference** Publisher *Douglas Amrine*; **General/Lifestyle** Publisher *John Roberts*. Children's: **Reference** Publisher *Miriam Farby*; **PreSchool/Primary** Publisher *Sophie Mitchell*. IMPRINTS **Ladybird**; **Ladybird Audio**; **Funfax**; **Eyewitness Guides**; **Eyewitness Travel Guides**. TITLES *BMA Complete Family Health Encyclopedia*; *RHS A–Z Encyclopedia of Garden Plants*; *Children's Illustrated Encyclopedia*; *The Way Things Work*. Unsolicited synopses/ideas for books welcome.

Authors' Rating The focus is on 'soft learning' products for the trade and education markets. Most titles are team efforts with writers and illustrators working closely with an in-house editor.

Doubleday
See **Transworld Publishers**

Ashley Drake Publishing Ltd
PO Box 733, Cardiff CF14 2YX
☎029 2056 0343 Fax 029 2056 1631
Email post@ashleydrake.com
Website www.ashleydrake.com

Managing Director *Ashley Drake*
Approx. Annual Turnover £100,000

FOUNDED 1995. *Publishes* academic, trade and Welsh-language books. 30 titles in 2003. No unsolicited mss; synopses and ideas for the Welsh Academic Press, St David's Press and

Scandinavian Academic Press imprints welcome. No scientific or computing books.

IMPRINTS
Welsh Academic Press English language academic, scholarly humanities and social sciences. **St David's Press** Sport, music, cookery and general trade. **Scandinavian Academic Press** Nordic studies including myth, legend and folklore. **Morgan Publishing** General trade. **Y Ddraig Fach** Welsh-language titles for children. **Gwasg Addysgol Cymru** Welsh-language educational titles.
Royalties paid annually.

Drake Educational Associates
St Fagans Road, Fairwater, Cardiff CF5 3AE
☎029 2956 0333 Fax 029 2956 0313

Managing Director *R.G. Drake*

Literacy, phonics and language development games and activities. Ideas and scripts in these fields welcome. Also resources for subject areas in the primary school and modern languages at KS2.

Dref Wen
28 Church Road, Whitchurch, Cardiff CF14 2EA
☎029 2061 7860 Fax 029 2061 0507
Email info.drefwen@btinternet.com

Chairman *R. Boore*
Managing Director *G. Boore*

FOUNDED 1970. *Publishes* Welsh language and bilingual children's books, Welsh and English educational books for Welsh learners.
Royalties paid annually.

Duckbacks
See **Gerald Duckworth & Co. Ltd**

Gerald Duckworth & Co. Ltd
61 Frith Street, London W1D 3JL
☎020 7434 4242 Fax 020 7434 4420
Email info@duckworth-publishers.co.uk
Website www.ducknet.co.uk

Chief Operations Officer *Gillian Hawkins*
Approx. Annual Turnover £2 million

FOUNDED 1898 by Gerald Duckworth. Original publishers of Virginia Woolf. Other early authors include Hilaire Belloc, John Galsworthy, D.H. Lawrence and George Orwell. Duckworth is a general trade publisher with eminent authors such as Beryl Bainbridge, D.J. Taylor and John Bayley in addition to a strong academic division. Acquired by **Penguin** in 2003.

IMPRINTS/DIVISIONS
Bristol Classical Press Classical texts and modern languages; **Chatham Publishing** Maritime history; **Duckworth Academic**;. **Duckworth General**; **Duckbacks**. No fiction. No unsolicited mss; synopses and sample chapters only. Enclose s.a.e. or return postage for response/return.

Royalties paid twice-yearly at first, annually thereafter.

Authors' Rating After losing out on backlist sales, Duckworth was put up for auction. The successful bidder was Peter Mayer, famous for rejuvenating Penguin in the 1980s. Better news for a much loved but not always well run publisher it is hard to imagine.

Duncan Petersen Publishing Limited
31 Ceylon Road, London W14 0PY
☎020 7371 2356   Fax 020 7371 2507
Email dp@appleonline.net

Director *Andrew Duncan*

FOUNDED 1986. Publisher and packager of childcare, business, antiques, birds, nature, atlases, walking and travel books. IMPRINT **Duncan Petersen** SERIES *Charming Small Hotel Guides*; *Charming Restaurant Guides*; *On Foot* (city walking guides). Unsolicited synopses and ideas for books welcome.

Fees paid.

Dunedin Academic Press Ltd
Hudson House, 8 Albany Street, Edinburgh EH1 3QB
☎0131 473 2397   Fax 01250 870937
Email mail@dunedinacademicpress.co.uk
Website www.dunedinacademicpress.co.uk

Managing Director *Anthony Kinahan*

FOUNDED 2001. *Publishes* academic and general non-fiction. 6 titles in 2002. Considerable experience in academic and professional publishing. Not interested in science other than earth sciences, fiction or children's. No unsolicted mss. Synopses and ideas welcome. Approach first in writing outlining proposal and identifying market.

Royalties paid annually.

Martin Dunitz Ltd
Taylor & Francis Group plc, 11 New Fetter Lane, London EC4P 4EE
☎020 7842 2001   Fax 020 7842 2306
Website www.dunitz.co.uk

Managing Director *Christopher Chesher*

Production Director *Susan Grant*

Acquired by the **Taylor & Francis Group plc** in 1999. *Publishes* specialist medical and dentistry atlases, texts, pocketbooks, slide atlases and CD-ROMs aimed at an international market. Particular areas of focus are psychiatry, neurology, cardiology, orthopaedics, dermatology, oncology and bone metabolism. The company won the Queen's Award for Export Achievement in 1991. 90–100 titles a year. Unsolicited synopses and ideas welcome but no mss.

Royalties paid twice-yearly.

Earthlight
See **Simon & Schuster UK Limited**

Earthscan Publications
See **Kogan Page Ltd**

Ebury Press
See **Random House Group Ltd**

Economist Books
See **Profile Books**

Eden
See **Transworld Publishers**

Edinburgh University Press
22 George Square, Edinburgh EH8 9LF
☎0131 650 4218   Fax 0131 662 0053
Website www.eup.ed.ac.uk

Chairman *Timothy Rix*
Managing Director *Timothy Wright*
Editorial Director *Jackie Jones*
Senior Editor *Nicola Carr*

Publishes academic and scholarly books (and journals): gender studies, geography, history – ancient, classical, medieval and modern, Islamic studies, linguistics, literary criticism, media and cultural studies; philosophy, politics, Scottish studies, theology and religious studies. About 100 titles a year.

Royalties paid annually.

Egmont Books Limited
239 Kensington High Street, London W8 6SA
☎020 7761 3500   Fax 020 7761 3510
Email <firstname>.<lastname>@ecb. egmont.com

Managing Director *Fiona Clarke*
Publishing Director *David Riley*
Fiction & Picture Books *Cally Poplak*

Part of the Egmont Group (Copenhagen), Egmont Books *publishes* children's picture books, fiction, non-fiction, licensed characters, baby and toddler books and home learning. About 500 titles a year. Synopses and sample chapters welcome; approach in writing with s.a.e. marked for the attention of 'The Reader'. 'We regret that we are unable to return unsolicited material without s.a.e.'

Royalties paid twice-yearly.

Authors' Rating Egmont has refined its list to focus more on really strong sellers. The emphasis now is on fiction and picture books. A sturdy backlist helps to keep the show on the fast track.

Eland Publishing Ltd

Third Floor, 61 Exmouth Market, Clerkenwell, London EC1R 4QL
☎020 7833 0762 Fax 020 7833 4434
Email info@travelbooks.co.uk
Website www.travelbooks.co.uk
Directors *Rose Baring, John Hatt, Barnaby Rogerson*
Approx. Annual Turnover £250,000

Travel re-print specialist, first established by travel writer and editor John Hatt in 1982. Backlist of 60 titles of classic world travel literature. TITLES *Naples '44* Norman Lewis; *Travels with Myself and Another* Martha Gelhorn. IMPRINTS **Sickle Moon** explorer narratives, history and anthropology. TITLES *Turkish Letters* Busbecq; *The Tuareg* Jeremy Keenan. **Baring & Rogerson** *Poetry of Place* pocket books. No unsolicited mss. Postcards and e-mails welcome.

Royalties paid annually.

Element

See **HarperCollins Publishers Ltd**

11:9

See **Neil Wilson Publishing Ltd**

Edward Elgar Publishing Ltd

Glensanda House, Montpellier Parade, Cheltenham, Gloucestershire GL50 1UA
☎01242 226934 Fax 01242 262111
Email info@e-elgar.co.uk
Website www.e-elgar.com
Chairman *Alex Ryan*
Managing Director *Edward Elgar*

FOUNDED 1986. International publisher in economics, the environment, public policy and social sciences. 276 titles in 2002. TITLES *Who's Who in Economics* (3rd ed.); *Handbook of Environmental and Resource Economics*; *Who's Who in the Management Sciences*. No unsolicited mss; synopses and ideas in the subject areas

listed above welcome. Approach by letter or e-mail; no telephone inquiries.

Royalties paid annually.

Elliot Right Way Books

Kingswood Buildings, Lower Kingswood, Tadworth, Surrey KT20 6TD
☎01737 832202 Fax 01737 830311
Email info@right-way.co.uk
Website www.right-way.co.uk
Managing Directors *A. Clive Elliot, Malcolm G. Elliot*

FOUNDED 1946 by Andrew G. Elliot. *Publishes* paperback how-to and educative titles on an unlimited variety of home reference, indoor and outdoor leisure pursuits, careers and business. Subjects include cookery, family financial and legal matters, public speaking, weddings, jokes, parenting, etiquette, English skills, driving, fishing, horse riding, drawing, music, puzzles, crosswords and quizzes, job seeking, running your own company.

IMPRINTS
Right Way Instructional paperbacks in B format for the most popular subjects; **Right Way Plus** Larger C format for more specialised subjects; **Clarion** B format for promotional/ultra low-price range. Unsolicited mss, synopses and ideas for books welcome.

Royalties paid annually.

Aidan Ellis Publishing

Whinfield, Herbert Road, Salcombe, South Devon TQ8 8HN
☎01548 842755 Fax 01548 844356
Email aidan@aepub.demon.co.uk
Website www.aepub.demon.co.uk
Partners/Editorial Heads *Aidan Ellis, Lucinda Ellis*

FOUNDED in 1971. *Specialises* in general trade books and non-fiction. TITLES *Eternity Regained* Marguerite Yourcenar – autobiography; *The Royal Gardens in Windsor Great Park* Charles Lyte; *Trees For Your Garden* Roy Lancaster; *Pesca* Ian B. Hart; *Presumed Dead* Eunice Chapman; *That's Rich!* Craig Rich – autobiography; *The Bird Table Book* Tony Soper. Ideas and synopses welcome (return postage, please).

Royalties paid twice-yearly.

Elm Publications/Training (wholly owned subsidiary of Elm Consulting Ltd)

Seaton House, Kings Ripton, Huntingdon, Cambridgeshire PE28 2NJ
☎01487 773254

Email sritchie@elm-training.co.uk
Website www.elm-training.co.uk
Managing Director *Sheila Ritchie*
FOUNDED 1977. *Publishes* textbooks, teaching
aids, educational resources and educational software in the fields of business and management
for adult learners. Books and teaching/training
resources are generally commissioned to meet
specific business, management and other syl-
labuses. 'We are actively seeking good training
materials for business/management, especially
tested and proven.' About 30 titles a year. Ideas
are welcome; first approach by post or e-mail
with outline, or by a brief telephone call.
Royalties paid annually.

Elsevier Ltd
The Boulevard, Langford Lane, Kidlington,
Oxford OX5 1GB
☎01865 843000 Fax 01865 843010
Website www.elsevier.com
Chief Operating Officer *Gavin Howe*
CEO, Science & Technology (Books &
  Journals) *Arie Jongejan*
Parent company **Reed Elsevier**, Amsterdam.
Now incorporates Pergamon Press and
Harcourt Publishers International. *Publishes*
academic and professional reference books, sci-
entific, technical and medical books, journals,
CD-ROMs and magazines.
DIVISION
Elsevier Health Sciences 32 Jamestown
Road, London NW1 7BY ☎020 7424 4200
Fax 020 7483 2293 Website www.elsevier-
health.com CEO Health Sciences (Books &
Journals) *Brian Nairn*; Managing Director
Dominic Vaughan Publishes scientific, technical,
medical books and journals.
  IMPRINTS **Academic Press; Architectural
Press; Baillière Tindall; Butterworth
Heinemann; Churchill Livingstone; Digital
Press; Elsevier; Elsevier Advanced
Technology; Focal Press; Gulf Professional
Press; JAI; Made Simple Books; Morgan
Kauffman; Mosby; Newnes; North-Holland;
Pergamon; W.B. Saunders**. No unsolicited
mss, but syopses and project proposals welcome.
Royalties paid annually.

Emissary Publishing
PO Box 33, Bicester, Oxfordshire OX26 4ZZ
☎01869 323447 Fax 01869 324096
Editorial Director *Val Miller*
FOUNDED 1992. *Publishes* mainly humorous
paperback books including the complete set of

Peter Pook novels; no poetry or children's.
Runs a biennial Humorous Novel Competition
in memory of the late Peter Pook and publishes
the winning novel (s.a.e. for details). No unsolicited mss or synopses.
Royalties paid twice-yearly.

Empiricus Books
See **Janus Publishing Company Ltd**

English Heritage (Publishing)
National Monuments Record Centre, Great
Western Village, Kemble Drive, Swindon,
Wiltshire SN2 2GZ
☎01793 414497 Fax 01793 414769
Email val.horsler@english-heritage.org.uk
Website www.english-heritage.org.uk
Head of Publishing *Val Horsler*
FOUNDED 1984 to publish English Heritage
guidebooks and a range of academic material
related directly to the work of the organisation,
together with a range of commercial co-publi-
cations. No unsolicited material.

Enitharmon Press
26B Caversham Road, London NW5 2DU
☎020 7482 5967 Fax 020 7284 1787
Email books@enitharmon.co.uk
Website www.enitharmon.co.uk
Director *Stephen Stuart-Smith*
FOUNDED 1967. An independent company with
an enterprising editorial policy, Enitharmon has
established itself as one of Britain's leading
poetry presses. Patron of 'the new and the
neglected', Enitharmon prides itself on the success of its collaborations between writers and
artists. *Publishes* poetry, literary criticism, fiction,
art and photography. TITLES *Jane Eyre* Paula
Rego; *Cenotaph of Snow* Michael Longley; *A
Renegade in Springtime* Michael Upward; *A Move
in the Weather* Anthony Thwaite; *The Two Roads
Taken* Dannie Abse. No unsolicited mss.
Royalties paid according to contract.

Epworth Press
c/o Methodist Publishing House, 4 John
Wesley Road, Werrington, Peterborough,
Cambridgeshire PE4 6ZP
☎01733 332202 Fax 01733 331201
Chairman *Dr John A. Newton, CBE*
Commissioning Editor *Dr Natalie K. Watson*
Publishes Christian books only: philosophy, the-
ology, biblical studies, pastoralia and social con-
cern. No fiction, poetry or children's. A series
based on the text of the *Revised Common
Lectionary*, entitled *Companion to the RCL*, was

launched in 1998 and the new series *Exploring Methodism* and *Thinking Things Through* continue. About 10 titles a year. TITLES *Nobodies to Somebodies* Anthony G. Reddie; *The Ministry of a Deacon* Ronnie Aitchison; *John Scott Lidgett, Archbishop of British Methodism?* Neil Dixon. Unsolicited mss considered but write to enquire in the first instance. Authors wishing to have their mss returned must send sufficient postage.
Royalties paid annually.

Euromonitor
60–61 Britton Street, London EC1M 5UX
☎020 7251 8024 Fax 020 7608 3149
Website www.euromonitor.com
Chairman *R.N. Senior*
Managing Director *T.J. Fenwick*
Approx. Annual Turnover £17 million
FOUNDED 1972. International business information publisher specialising in library and professional reference books, market reports, electronic databases, journals and CD-ROMs. *Publishes* business reference, market analysis and information directories only. About 200 titles a year.
DIVISIONS
Market Analysis *T. Kitchen, S. Holmes*; **Reference Books & Directories** *S. Hunter*. TITLES *Credit & Charge Cards: The International Market*; *European Marketing Handbook*; *European Directory of Trade and Business Associations*; *World Retail Directory and Sourcebook*.
Payment is generally by flat fee.

Europa Publications Ltd
See **Taylor & Francis Group plc**

Evans Brothers Ltd
2A Portman Mansions, Chiltern Street, London W1U 6NR
☎020 7487 0920 Fax 020 7487 0921
Email sales@evansbrothers.co.uk
Website www.evansbooks.co.uk
Managing Director *Stephen Pawley*
International Publishing Director *Brian Jones*
UK Publisher *Su Swallow*
Approx. Annual Turnover £4.5 million
FOUNDED 1908 by Robert and Edward Evans. Originally published educational journals, books for primary schools and teacher education. After rapid expansion into popular fiction and drama, both were sacrificed to a major programme of educational books for schools in East and West Africa. A UK programme was launched in 1986 followed by the acquisition

of Hamish Hamilton's non-fiction list for children in 1990. Acquired interests in Cherrytree Books and Zero to Ten in 1999. *Publishes* UK children's and educational books, and educational books for Africa, the Caribbean and Latin America. About 90 titles a year.
IMPRINTS **Cherrytree Books; Zero to Ten** trade under Zero to Ten Ltd at the Evans address above. Unsolicited mss, synopses and ideas for books welcome.
Royalties paid annually. *Overseas associates* in Kenya, Cameroon, Sierra Leone; Evans Bros (Nigeria Publishers) Ltd.

Everyman
See **The Orion Publishing Group Ltd**

Everyman Library
Gloucester Mansions, 140a Shaftesbury Avenue, London WC2H 8HD
☎020 7539 7600 Fax 020 7379 4060
Email books@everyman.uk.com
Publisher *David Campbell*
Approx. Annual Turnover £3.5 million
ESTABLISHED 1906. *Publishes* hardback classics of world literature, pocket poetry anthologies, children's books and travel guides. AUTHORS include Bulgakov, Bellow, Borges, Forster, Grass, Mann, Nabokov, Orwell, Rushdie, Updike and Waugh. No unsolicited mss.
Royalties paid annually.

University of Exeter Press
Reed Hall, Streatham Drive, Exeter, Devon EX4 4QR
☎01392 263066 Fax 01392 263064
Email uep@exeter.ac.uk
Website www.ex.ac.uk/uep/
Publisher *Simon Baker*
FOUNDED 1956. *Publishes* academic books: archaeology, classical studies, history, maritime studies, English literature (especially medieval), linguistics, European studies, modern languages and literature, film history, performance studies, Arabic studies and books on Exeter and the South West. About 30 titles a year. Proposals welcomed in the above subject areas.
Royalties paid annually.

Exley Publications Ltd
16 Chalk Hill, Watford, Hertfordshire WD19 4BG
☎01923 248328 Fax 01923 800440
Email editorial@exleypublications.co.uk
Website www.helenexleygiftbooks.com
Editorial Director *Helen Exley*

FOUNDED 1976. Independent family company. *Publishes* giftbooks, quotation anthologies and humour. About 35 titles a year. Only series ideas needed – no individual titles. No rhyming poetry, please.

Expert Books
See **Transworld Publishers**

Eyewitness Guides
See **Dorling Kindersley Ltd**

Faber & Faber Ltd
3 Queen Square, London WC1N 3AU
☎020 7465 0045 Fax 020 7465 0034
Website www.faber.co.uk

Chief Executive *Stephen Page*
Approx. Annual Turnover £13 million

Geoffrey Faber founded the company in the 1920s, with T.S. Eliot as an early recruit to the board. The original list was based on contemporary poetry and plays (the distinguished backlist includes Eliot, Auden and MacNeice). *Publishes* poetry and drama, children's, fiction, film, music, politics, biography.

DIVISIONS
Fiction Editor-in-Chief *Jon Riley* AUTHORS P.D. James, Peter Carey, Giles Foden, Michael Frayn, Kazuo Ishiguro, Barbara Kingsolver, Milan Kundera, Hanif Kureishi, John Lanchester, Patrick McCabe, John McGahern, Rohinton Mistry, Andrew O'Hagan, Jane Smiley; **Children's** *Suzy Jenvey* AUTHORS Philip Ardagh, Terry Deary, Russell Stannard; **Film** *Walter Donohue* and **Plays** *Peggy Paterson* AUTHORS Samuel Beckett, Alan Bennett, David Hare, Brian Friel, Patrick Marber, Harold Pinter, Tom Stoppard, Woody Allen, John Boorman, Joel and Ethan Coen, John Hodge, Martin Scorsese, Quentin Tarantino; **Music** *Belinda Matthews* AUTHORS Alfred Brendel, Humphrey Burton, Alexander Goehr, Nicholas Kenyon, Harvey Sachs, Elizabeth Wilson; **Poetry** *Paul Keegan* AUTHORS Simon Armitage, Douglas Dunn, Seamus Heaney, Ted Hughes, Tom Paulin; **Non-fiction** *Neil Belton, Julian Loose* AUTHORS John Carey, Simon Garfield, John Gray, Jan Morris, Francis Spufford, Jenny Uglow.
Royalties paid twice-yearly.

Authors' Rating Having cut the number of titles by a third, Faber is publishing fewer screenplays but is developing general non-fiction and children's books. Poetry, theatre, film and music remain the core subjects.

Facet Publishing
7 Ridgmount Street, London WC1E 7AE
☎020 7255 0590/0505 (text phone)
Fax 020 7255 0591
Email info@facetpublishing.co.uk
Website www.facetpublishing.co.uk

Managing Director *Janet Liebster*

Publishing arm of **CILIP: The Chartered Institute of Library and Information Professionals** (formerly the Library Association). *Publishes* library and information science, monographs, reference, IT training materials and bibliography aimed at library and information professionals. 25–30 titles a year.

IMPRINTS
Library Association Publishing; **Clive Bingley Books**; **Facet Publishing**. Over 200 titles in print, including *Walford's Guide to Reference Material* and *AACR2*. Unsolicited mss, synopses and ideas welcome provided material falls firmly within the company's specialist subject areas.
Royalties paid annually.

Fairleigh Dickinson University Press
See **Golden Cockerel Press**

Falmer Press
See **Taylor & Francis Group plc**

Fernhurst Books
Duke's Path, High Street, Arundel, West Sussex BN18 9AJ
☎01903 882277 Fax 01903 882715
Email sales@fernhurstbooks.co.uk
Website www.fernhurstbooks.co.uk

Chairman/Managing Director *Tim Davison*

FOUNDED 1979. For people who love watersports. *Publishes* practical, highly-illustrated handbooks on sailing and watersports. TITLES *Heavy Weather Crossing; First Aid Afloat; Simple Yacht Design; Staying Put! The Art of Anchoring; Helming to Win; The History of Surfing; Mirror Racing*. No unsolicited mss; synopses and ideas welcome.
Royalties paid twice-yearly.

David Fickling Books
See **Random House Group Ltd**

Findhorn Press Ltd
305A The Park, Findhorn, Moray IV36 3TE
☎01309 690582 Fax 01309 690036
Email books@findhorn.org
Website www.findhornpress.com

Directors *Karin Bogliolo, Thierry Bogliolo*
Approx. Annual Turnover £320,000

FOUNDED 1971. *Publishes* mind, body, spirit, New Age and healing. 14 titles in 2002. Unsolicited synopses and ideas welcome if they come within their subject areas. No children's books, fiction or poetry.
Royalties paid twice-yearly.

Firefly Publishing
See **Helter Skelter Publishing**

First & Best in Education Ltd
Unit K, Earlstrees Court, Earlstrees Road, Corby, Northamptonshire NN17 4HH
☎01536 399004 Fax 01536 399012
Email firstandbest9@themail.co.uk
Website www.firstandbest.co.uk

Publisher *Tony Attwood*
Editor *Anne Cockburn*

Publishers of over 1000 educational books of all types for all ages of children and for parents and teachers. All books are published as being suitable for photocopying and/or as electronic books. 'Looking for new authors of educational books all the time. No fiction, please.' TITLES *Raising Grades Through Study Skills; Business Sponsorship of Secondary Schools; Policy Documents for Day Nurseries and Nursery Units; Citizenship Through Assembly.* IMPRINTS **Multisensory Maths**; **School Improvement Reports**. In the first instance check the website or send s.a.e. for details of requirements and current projects to *Anne Cockburn*, Editorial Dept. at the address above.
Royalties paid twice-yearly.

First Authors
See **Vista House Ltd**

First Century Ltd
Suite 87, 407 Kings Road, London SW10 0BB
☎020 7644 3924
Email info@CromwellPublishers.co.uk *and* info@M&NPublishing.co.uk
Website www.CromwellPublisher.co.uk *and* www.MandNPublishing.co.uk
Also at: Vista House, 27 Greenhead Road, Huddersfield, West Yorkshire HD1 4EN
☎01484 545123

Managing Editor *R. Sharp*

Initial enquiries by e-mail or telephone. IMPRINTS **First Century** Fiction and non-fiction; **First Century Poetry**; **Cromwell** Fiction, non-fiction, biography and auto-biography; **Christian Publishing** Fiction, non-fiction, and poetry with a Christian underpinning; **M.&N. Publishing** Fiction and non-fiction. No erotica, politics or books for pre-school children.

Authors' Rating May ask authors to contribute towards costs of publication.

Fitzgerald Publishing
89 Ermine Road, Ladywell, London SE13 5JJ
☎020 8690 0597
Email fitzgeraldbooks@yahoo.co.uk

Managing Editor *Tim Fitzgerald*
General Editor *Andrew Smith*

FOUNDED 1974. *Specialises* in scientific studies of insects and spiders. 1–2 titles a year. TITLES *The Tarantula; Keeping Spiders and Insects in Captivity; Tarantulas of the USA; Scorpions of Medical Importance* (books) and *Earth Tigers – Tarantulas of Borneo; Desert Tarantulas* (TV/video documentaries). Unsolicited mss, synopses and ideas for books welcome. Also considers video scripts for video documentaries.

Fitzjames Press
See **Motor Racing Publications**

Fitzroy Dearborn
See **Taylor & Francis Group plc**

Fitzwarren Publishing
2 Orchard Drive, Aston Clinton, Aylesbury, Buckinghamshire HP22 5HR
☎01296 632627 Fax 01296 630028
Email pen2paper@btopenworld.com

Contact *Julie Stretton*

Publishes two or three books a year, mainly layman's handbooks on legal matters. All books published so far have followed a rigid 128-page format. TITLES *The E-Commerce Handbook; Landlord & Tenants Handbook; The Election Handbook; Licensing Handbook.* Welcomes written approaches and synopses from prospective authors, who, though not necessarily legally qualified, are expected to know their subject as well as a lawyer would.
Royalties paid twice-yearly.

Five Star
See **Serpent's Tail**

Flame
See **Hodder Headline Ltd**

Flamingo
See **HarperCollins Publishers Ltd**

Flicks Books

29 Bradford Road, Trowbridge, Wiltshire
BA14 9AN
☎01225 767728
Email flicks.books@dial.pipex.com
Publishing Director *Matthew Stevens*

FOUNDED 1986. Devoted solely to publishing
books on the cinema and related media. TITLES
Queen of the 'B's: Ida Lupino Behind the Camera
ed. Annette Kuhn; *By Angels Driven: The Films of
Derek Jarman* ed. Chris Lippard. Unsolicited mss,
synopses and ideas within the subject area are
welcome.
Royalties paid annually or twice-yearly.

Floris Books

15 Harrison Gardens, Edinburgh EH11 1SH
☎0131 337 2372 Fax 0131 347 9919
Email floris@floris.demon.co.uk
Managing Director *Christian Maclean*
Editors *Christopher Moore, Gale Winskill*
Approx. Annual Turnover £350,000

FOUNDED 1977. *Publishes* books related to the
Steiner movement, including The Christian
Community, as well as arts & crafts, children's
(including fiction with a Scottish theme), his-
tory, religious, science, social questions and
Celtic studies. No unsolicited mss. Synopses
and ideas for books welcome.
Royalties paid annually.

Focal Press

See **Elsevier Ltd**

Fodor's

See **Random House Group Ltd**

Folens Limited

Apex Business Centre, Boscombe Road,
Dunstable, Bedfordshire LU5 4RL
☎0870 609 1237 Fax 0870 609 1236
Email folens@folens.com
Website www.folens.com
Chairman *Dirk Folens*
Managing Director *Malcolm Watson*

FOUNDED 1987. Leading educational publisher. About 150 titles a year. IMPRINTS
Folens; **Belair**. Unsolicited mss, synopses and
ideas for educational books welcome.
Royalties paid annually.

Foulsham Publishers

The Publishing House, Bennetts Close,
Slough, Berkshire SL1 5AP
☎01753 526769 Fax 01753 535003
Chairman *R.S. Belasco*
Managing Director *B.A.R. Belasco*
Approx. Annual Turnover £2.2 million

FOUNDED 1819 and now one of the few
remaining independent family companies to survive takeover. *Publishes* non-fiction on most
subjects including lifestyle, travel guides, family
reference, cookery, diet, health, DIY, business,
self improvement, self development, astrology,
dreams, MBS. No fiction. IMPRINT **Quantum**
Mind, body and spirit titles. TITLES *Classic 1000
Cocktails; Old Moore's Almanack; Raphael's
Astrological Ephemeris*. Unsolicited mss, synopses
and ideas welcome. Around 60 titles a year.
Royalties paid twice-yearly.

Foundery Press

See **Methodist Publishing House**

Fountain Press

Newpro UK Ltd., Old Sawmills Road,
Faringdon, Oxfordshire SN7 7DS
☎01367 242411 Fax 01367 241124
Email sales@newprouk.co.uk
Publisher *C.J. Coleman*
Approx. Annual Turnover £800,000

FOUNDED 1923 when it was part of the
Rowntree Trust Social Service. Owned by the
British Electric Traction Group until 1982
when it was bought out by H.M. Ricketts.
Acquired by Newpro UK Ltd in July 2000.
Publishes mainly photography and natural his-
tory. About 10 titles a year. TITLES *Photography
and Digital 'Workshop'*; *Antique and Collectable
Cameras*; *Camera Manual* (series). Unsolicited
mss and synopses welcome.
Royalties paid twice-yearly.

Authors' Rating Highly regarded for production values, Fountain has the reputation for
involving authors in every stage of the publishing process.

Fourth Estate Ltd

77–85 Fulham Palace Road, London W6 8JB
☎020 8741 4414 Fax 020 8307 4466
Email general@4thestate.co.uk
Website www.4thestate.co.uk
Publishing Director *Nick Pearson*
Editorial Director *Courtney Hodell*
Approx. Annual Turnover £17 million

FOUNDED 1984. Acquired by **HarperCollins**
in July 2000, Fourth Estate has a strong reputation for literary fiction and up-to-the-minute
non-fiction. *Publishes* fiction, popular science,

current affairs, biography, humour, self-help, travel, reference. About 100 titles a year.

DIVISIONS **Literary Fiction/Non-fiction; General Fiction/Non-Fiction** TITLES *Unless* Carol Shields; *Silvertown* Melanie McGrath; *Moral Hazard* Kate Jennings; *Seal Wife* Kathryn Harrison; *The Lost King of France* Deborah Cadbury; *Genius* Harold Bloom; *The Chap Almanac* Vic Darkwood and Gustav Temple; *A Very English Deceit* Malcolm Balen; *Thirst* Nigel Slater. No unsolicited mss; synopses welcome.

Royalties paid twice-yearly.

Free Association Books Ltd

57 Warren Street, London W1T 5NR
☎020 7388 3182 Fax 020 7388 3187
Email fab57warrenst@yahoo.co.uk
Website www.fabooks.com

Managing Director/Publisher *T.E. Brown*

Publishes psychoanalysis and psychotherapy, psychology, cultural studies, sexuality and gender, women's studies, applied social sciences. TITLES *Reaching the Young Autistic Child* S. Janert; *Judo With Words* B. Berchan; *Psychoanalytic Psychotherapy Trainings – A Guide* R.M. Jones; *A Compendium of Lacanian Terms* Marks, Murphy and Glowinski. Always send a letter in the first instance accompanied by a book outline.

Royalties paid twice-yearly. *Overseas associates* ISBS, USA; Astam, Australia.

The Free Press

See **Simon & Schuster UK Ltd**

W.H. Freeman

Palgrave, Houndsmill, Basingstoke, Hampshire RG21 6XS
☎01256 329242 Fax 01256 330688

President *Elizabeth Widdicombe* (New York)
Sales & Marketing Director *Margaret Hewinson*

Following integration into the BFW (Bedford, Freeman, Worth) College Group, USA, Freeman now *publishes* academic educational and textbooks in biochemistry, biology and zoology, chemistry, geography and geology, mathematics and statistics, medical, natural history, neuroscience, palaeontology, physics. Freeman's editorial office is in New York (Basingstoke is a sales and marketing office only) but unsolicited mss can go through Basingstoke. Those which are obviously unsuitable will be sifted out; the rest will be forwarded to New York.

Royalties paid annually.

Samuel French Ltd

52 Fitzroy Street, London W1T 5JR
☎020 7387 9373 Fax 020 7387 2161
Email theatre@samuelfrench-london.co.uk
Website www.samuelfrench-london.co.uk

Chairman *Charles R. Van Nostrand*
Managing Director *Vivien Goodwin*

FOUNDED 1830 with the object of acquiring acting rights and publishing plays. *Publishes* plays only. About 50 titles a year. Unsolicited mss considered only after initial submission of synopsis and specimen scene. Such material should be addressed to the Performing Rights Department.

Royalties paid twice-yearly for books; performing royalties paid monthly, subject to a minimum amount.

Authors' Rating Thrives on the amateur dramatic societies who are forever in need of play texts. Editorial advisers give serious attention to new material but a high proportion of the list is staged before it goes into print. New writers are advised to try one-act plays, much in demand by the amateur dramatic societies but rarely turned out by established playwrights.

David Fulton (Publishers) Ltd

The Chiswick Centre, 414 Chiswick High Road, London W4 5TF
☎020 8996 3610 Fax 020 8996 3622
Email mail@fultonpublishers.co.uk
Website www.fultonpublishers.co.uk

Publishing Director *Christopher Glenniel*
Senior Commissioning Editors *Nina Stibbe, Helen Fairlie, Margaret Haigh*
Approx. Annual Turnover £2.4 million

FOUNDED 1987. *Publishes* non-fiction: books for teachers and teacher training at B.Ed and PGCE levels for early years, primary, secondary and virtually all aspects of special education; geography for undergraduates. Currently developing a range of curriculum materials (in book form, packs, on CD-ROM and/or disk) for use by teachers in the classroom. In 1995, David Fulton set up a Fulton Fellowship in Special Education (see entry under **Bursaries, Fellowships and Grants**). About 100 titles a year. No unsolicited mss; synopses and ideas for books welcome.

Royalties paid twice-yearly.

Funfax

See **Dorling Kindersley Ltd**

Gaia Books Ltd

66 Charlotte Street, London W1T 4QE
☎020 7323 4010 Fax 020 7323 0435
Email info@gaiabooks.com

Website www.gaiabooks.co.uk
Managing Director *Joss Pearson*
FOUNDED 1983. *Publishes* ecology, health, natural living, gardening, interiors, and mind, body & spirit, mainly in practical self-help illustrated reference form for Britain and the international market. About 12 titles a year. TITLES *Healing Drinks; The Feng Shui Kitchen; The Healing Energies of Earth; The Edible Container Garden; Pilates; The Fertility Plan*. Most projects are conceived in-house but outlines and mss with s.a.e. considered. 'From submission of an idea to project go ahead may take up to a year. Authors become involved with the Gaia team in the editorial, design and promotion work needed to create and market a book.'

Gairm Publications
29 Waterloo Street, Glasgow G2 6BZ
☎0141 221 1971 Fax 0141 221 1971
Chairman *Prof. Derick S. Thomson*
FOUNDED 1952 to publish the quarterly Gaelic periodical *Gairm* and soon moved into publishing other Gaelic material. Acquired an old Glasgow Gaelic publishing firm, Alexander MacLaren & Son, in 1970. *Publishes* a wide range of Gaelic and Gaelic-related books: dictionaries, grammars, handbooks, children's, fiction, poetry, biography, music and song. TITLES *The Companion to Gaelic Scotland; Derick Thomson's collection of poems, Meall Garbh/The Rugged Mountain*. Catalogue available.

Galaxy Children's Print
See entry under **BBC Audiobooks**

J. Garnet Miller
See **Cressrelles Publishing Co. Ltd**

Garnet Publishing Ltd
8 Southern Court, South Street, Reading, Berkshire RG1 4QS
☎0118 959 7847 Fax 0118 959 7356
Email enquiries@garnet-ithaca.demon.co.uk
Website www.garnet-ithaca.co.uk
Editorial Manager *Emma G. Hawker*
FOUNDED 1992 and purchased Ithaca Press in the same year. *Publishes* art, architecture, photography, archive photography, cookery, travel classics, travel, comparative religion, Islamic culture and history, foreign fiction in translation. Core subjects are Middle Eastern but list is rapidly expanding to be more general. About 30 titles a year.
IMPRINTS **Garnet Publishing** TITLES *The Story of Islamic Architecture; Traditional Greek Cooking; Jerusalem: Caught in Time* series.
Ithaca Press Specialises in post-graduate academic works on the Middle East, political science and international relations. About 20 titles a year. TITLES *The Making of the Modern Gulf States; The Palestinian Exodus; French Imperialism in Syria; Philby of Arabia*. Unsolicited mss not welcome – write with outline and ideas first plus current c.v.
Royalties paid twice-yearly. *Sister companies*: All Prints, Beirut; Garnet France, Paris.

Gay Men's Press
See **Millivres Prowler Limited**

Geddes & Grosset
David Dale House, New Lanark ML11 9DJ
☎01555 665000 Fax 01555 665694
Publishers *Ron Grosset, R. Michael Miller*
Approx. Annual Turnover £3 million
FOUNDED 1989. Publisher of children's and reference books. Unsolicited mss, synopses and ideas welcome. No adult fiction.

Geological Society Publishing House
Unit 7, Brassmill Enterprise Centre, Brassmill Lane, Bath BA1 3JN
☎01225 445046 Fax 01225 442836
Email dawn.angel@geolsoc.org.uk *or*
    angharad.hills@geolsoc.org.uk
Website www.bookshop.geolsoc.org.uk
Commissioning Editor *Angharad Hills*
Publishing arm of the Geological Society which was founded in 1807. *Publishes* post-graduate texts in the earth sciences. 25 titles a year. Unsolicited synopses and ideas welcome.

Stanley Gibbons Publications
5 Parkside, Christchurch Road, Ringwood, Hampshire BH24 3SH
☎01425 472363 Fax 01425 470247
Website www.stanleygibbons.com
Chairman *P. Fraser*
Editorial Head *H. Jefferies*
Long-established force in the philatelic world with over a hundred years in the business. *Publishes* philatelic reference catalogues and handbooks. About 15 titles a year. Reference works relating to other areas of collecting may be considered. TITLES *Stanley Gibbons British Commonwealth Stamp Catalogue; Stamps of the World*. Foreign catalogues include Japan and Korea, Portugal and Spain, Germany, Middle East, Balkans, China. Monthly publication:

Gibbons Stamp Monthly (see entry under **Magazines**). www.collectorcafe.com – internet site covering full range of collectables – editorial input always considered. Unsolicited mss, synopses and ideas welcome.
Royalties by negotiation.

Robert Gibson and Sons (Glasgow)
See **Hodder Gibson**

Gibson Square Books Ltd
15 Gibson Square, London N1 0RD
☎020 7689 4790 Fax 020 7689 7395
Email publicity@gibsonsquare.com
Website www.gibsonsquare.com
Chairman *Martin Rynja*

FOUNDED 2001. *Publishes* books with a strong biographical element based in some relevant way on personal experience. Must have high publicity value. IMPRINTS **Gibson Square** TITLES *The Chief* (biography of Randolph Hearst); *Preachers of Hate* Angus Roxburgh; *Who's a Dandy?* George Walden. **New Editions** TITLES *South from Ephesus* Brian Sewell; *A Small Boy and Others* Henry James; *Descent of Man* Charles Darwin. Welcomes unsolicited mss, synopses and ideas. Send self-addressed, franked, return envelope. No fiction or mind, body and spirit.
Royalties paid twice-yearly.

Ginn
See **Harcourt Education**

GMP (Gay Men's Press)
See **Millivres Prowler Limited**

Golden Cockerel Press Ltd
Unit 304, The Chandlery, 50 Westminster Bridge Rd, London SE1 7QY
☎020 7953 8770 Fax 020 7953 8738
Email aup.uk@btinternet.com
Directors *Tamar Lindesay, Andrew Lindesay*

FOUNDED 1980 to distribute titles for US-based Associated University Presses Inc., New Jersey. *Publishes* academic titles mostly: art, film, history, literary criticism, music, philosophy, sociology and special interest. About 120 titles a year.

IMPRINTS
AUP: **Bucknell University Press**; **University of Delaware**; **Fairleigh Dickinson University Press**; **Lehigh University Press**; **Susquehanna University Press**. Also: **Cygnus Arts** Non-academic books on the arts.

Authors' Rating Very much attuned to American interests with trans-Atlantic spelling and punctuation predominating. Some writers may find the process wearisome but those who persevere win through to a wider market.

Gollancz
See **The Orion Publishing Group Limited**

Gomer Press
Wind Street, Llandysul, Ceredigion SA44 4QL
☎01559 362371 Fax 01559 363758
Email gwasg@gomer.co.uk
Website www.gomer.co.uk
Chairman/Managing Director *J.H. Lewis*

FOUNDED 1892. *Publishes* adult fiction and non-fiction, children's fiction and educational material in English and Welsh. About 100 titles a year (65 Welsh; 35 English).
IMPRINTS **Gomer Press** *Bethan Mair, Gordon Jones, Keri Win Jones.* **Pont Books** *Mairwen Prys Jones.* No unsolicited mss, synopses or ideas.
Royalties paid twice-yearly.

The Good Web Guide Ltd
65 Bromfelde Road, London SW4 6PP
☎020 7720 8919 Fax 020 7738 5717
Email marketing@thegoodwebguide.com
Website www.thegoodwebguide.com
Chairman *David Teale*
Managing Director *Sarah Mahaffy*
Marketing Director *Nicky Granville*

FOUNDED 1999. *Publishes* guides to the best sites on the Internet, both as books and online. Subscription available giving full access to the website where reviews ae constantly updated and added to. 5 titles in 2002. No unsolicited mss; send synopsis/idea by post or e-mail. No fiction or children's books.
Royalties paid twice-yearly.

Gordon & Breach
See **Taylor & Francis Group plc**

Gower
See **Ashgate Publishing Ltd**

GPC Books
See **University of Wales Press**

Graham & Trotman
See **Kluwer Law International**

Graham & Whiteside Ltd
See **Gale** under **US Publishers**

Graham–Cameron Publishing & Illustration

The Studio, 23 Holt Road, Sheringham,
Norfolk NR26 8NB
☎01263 821333 Fax 01263 821334
Email <firstname>@graham-cameron-illustration.com

Also at: 59 Redvers Road, Brighton, E. Sussex
BN2 4BF ☎01273 385890

Editorial Director *Mike Graham-Cameron*
Art Director *Helen Graham-Cameron*
Marketing Manager *Duncan Graham-Cameron* (at Brighton address)

FOUNDED 1984 as a packaging operation. *Publishes* illustrated factual books for children, adults, institutions and business; also biography, education and social history. TITLES *Up From the Country; In All Directions; The Holywell Story; Let's Look at Dairying.* Has 37 contracted book illustrators concentrating on educational and children's books. *Absolutely no* unsolicited mss.
   Royalties paid annually.

Granada Media
See **Carlton Publishing Group**

Granta Books
2–3 Hanover Yard, Noel Road, London
N1 8BE
☎020 7704 9776 Fax 020 7354 3469
Website www.granta.com

Publisher *Gail Lynch*
Editorial Director *George Miller*

FOUNDED 1979. *Publishes* literary fiction and general non-fiction. About 35 titles a year. No unsolicited mss; synopses and sample chapters welcome.
   Royalties paid twice-yearly.

W. Green (Scotland)
See **Sweet & Maxwell Group**

Green Books
Foxhole, Dartington, Totnes, Devon
TQ9 6EB
☎01803 863260 Fax 01803 863843
Email edit@greenbooks.co.uk
Website www.greenbooks.co.uk

Chairman *Satish Kumar*
Publisher *John Elford*
Approx. Annual Turnover £300,000

FOUNDED in 1987 with the support of a number of Green organisations. Closely associated with *Resurgence* magazine. *Publishes* high-quality books on a wide range of Green issues, including economics, politics and the practical application of Green thinking. No fiction or books for children. TITLES *Forest Gardening* Robert A. de J. Hart; *Eco-Renovation* Edward Harland; *The Growth Illusion* Richard Douthwaite; *The Green Lanes of England* Valerie Belsey; *The Organic Directory* ed. Clive Litchfield. No unsolicited mss. Synopses and ideas welcome.
   Royalties paid twice-yearly.

Green Print
See **The Merlin Press Ltd**

Greenhill Books/ Lionel Leventhal Ltd
Park House, 1 Russell Gardens, London
NW11 9NN
☎020 8458 6314 Fax 020 8905 5245
Email Leventhal@greenhillbooks.com
Website www.greenhillbooks.com

Managing Director *Lionel Leventhal*

FOUNDED 1984 by Lionel Leventhal (ex-Arms & Armour Press). *Publishes* aviation, military and naval books, and its Napoleonic Library series. Synopses and ideas for books welcome. No unsolicited mss.
   Royalties paid twice-yearly.

Gresham Books Ltd
46 Victoria Road, Summertown, Oxford
OX2 7QD
☎01865 513582 Fax 01865 512718
Email greshambks@btinternet.com
Website www.gresham-books.co.uk

Managing Director *Paul A. Lewis*
Approx. Annual Turnover £350,000

A small specialist publishing house. *Publishes* hymn and service books for schools and churches, school histories, also craftbound choir and orchestral folders and Records of Achievement. TITLES include music and melody editions of *Hymns for Church and School*; *The School Hymnal; Praise and Thanksgiving.* No unsolicited material but ideas welcome.

Grisewood & Dempsey
See **Kingfisher Publications plc**

Grub Street
The Basement, 10 Chivalry Road, London
SW11 1HT
☎020 7924 3966/7738 1008
Fax 020 7738 1009
Email post@grubstreet.co.uk
Website www.grubstreet.co.uk

Managing Director *John Davies*

FOUNDED 1982. *Publishes* cookery, food and wine, health, military and aviation history books. About 20 titles a year. Unsolicited mss and synopses welcome in the above categories but please enclose return postage.
Royalties paid twice-yearly.

Guild of Master Craftsman Publications Ltd

166 High Street, Lewes, East Sussex BN7 1XU
☎01273 477374 Fax 01273 478606
Email pubs@thegmcgroup.com
Joint Managing Directors *J.A.J. Phillips, J.A.B. Phillips*
Approx. Annual Turnover £2 million
FOUNDED 1974. Part of G.M.C. Services Ltd. *Publishes* woodworking, craft, photography and gardening books, magazines and videos; also books on dolls' houses and miniatures. 40 titles in 2002. Unsolicited mss, synopses and ideas for books welcome. No fiction.
Royalties paid twice-yearly.

Guinness World Records Ltd

338 Euston Road, London NW1 3BD
☎020 7891 4567 Fax 020 7891 4501
Email info@guinnessrecords.com
Website www.guinnessworldrecords.com
Chief Operations Officer *Alistair Richards*
FOUNDED in 1954 to publish *The Guinness Book of Records*, published in 35 languages and the highest-selling copyright book in the world. The company's television shows have gained a global audience of more than 100 million and are broadcast in over 30 countries. In addition to *Guinness World Records* the company publishes the annual industry-standard volume *British Hit Singles*. In October 2002 Guinness World Records became part of HIT Entertainment Plc. Contact from prospective researchers, editors and designers welcome.

Gulf Professional Press

See **Elsevier Ltd**

Gullane Children's Books

Winchester House, 259–269 Old Marylebone Road, London NW1 5XJ
☎020 7616 7200 Fax 020 7616 7201
Editorial Director *Alison Ritchie*
FOUNDED 1994. Formerly David & Charles Children's Books; acquired by multimedia group, HIT Entertainment Plc in 2002.

Publishes board books, novelty books, picture books and gift collections for children of 0–12 years. Unsolicited mss will not be returned.
Royalties paid twice-yearly.

Gunsmoke Westerns

See entry under **BBC Audiobooks**

Gwasg Addysgol Cymru

See **Ashley Drake Publishing Ltd**

Gwasg Carreg Gwalch

12 Iard yr Orsaf, Llanrwst, Conwy LL26 0EH
☎01492 642031 Fax 01492 641502
Email books@carreg-gwalch.co.uk
Website www.carreg-gwalch.co.uk
Managing Editor *Myrddin ap Dafydd*
FOUNDED in 1980. *Publishes* Welsh language; English books of Welsh interest – history, folklore, guides and walks. 90 titles in 2002. Unsolicited mss, synopses and ideas welcome if of Welsh interest.
Royalties paid.

Gwasg Prifysgol Cymru

See **University of Wales Press**

Hachette-Livre

French publishing conglomerate which embraces **Orion Publishing Group, Octopus Publishing Group** and **Watts Publishing Group**. For further information, see entry under **European Publishers**.

Authors' Rating Almost unnoticed, at least by British pundits, French publisher Hachette has joined the league of UK conglomerates. With Orion, Octopus and Watts, the share of the illustrated market claimed by Hachette is over 25 per cent.

Peter Halban Publishers

22 Golden Square, London W1F 9JW
☎020 7437 9300 Fax 020 7437 9512
Email books@halbanpublishers.com
Website www.halbanpublishers.com
Directors *Peter Halban, Martine Halban*
FOUNDED 1986. Independent publisher. *Publishes* biography, autobiography and memoirs, history, philosophy, theology, politics, literature and criticism, Judaica and world affairs. 6–8 titles a year. No unsolicited material. Approach by letter in first instance.
Royalties paid twice-yearly for first two years, thereafter annually in December.

Robert Hale Ltd

Clerkenwell House, 45–47 Clerkenwell Green, London EC1R 0HT
☎020 7251 2661 Fax 020 7490 4958
Email enquire@halebooks.com

Chairman/Managing Director *John Hale*

FOUNDED 1936. Family-owned company. *Publishes* adult fiction (but not interested in category crime, romance or science fiction) and non-fiction. No specialist material (education, law, medical or scientific). Acquired **NAG Press Ltd** in 1993 with its list of horological, gemmological, jewellery and metalwork titles, and **J.A. Allen & Co.** in 1999 with its extensive list of horse and dog books (see entry). Over 250 titles a year. TITLES Non-fiction: *New Age Encyclopaedia* Belinda Whitworth; *Andrea Bocelli* Antonia Felix; *F.M. Halford and the Dry Fly Revolution* Tony Hayter; *Field Archery* Michael Hamlett-Wood; *Roger Moore: His Films and Career* Gareth Owen and Oliver Bayan. Fiction: *Methuselah's Children* Robert A. Heinlein; *The Silent Voyage* James Pattinson; *The Curious Conspiracy* Michael Gilbert. Unsolicited mss, synopses and ideas for books welcome.
Royalties paid twice-yearly.

Authors' Rating Smiled upon in a Society of Authors survey on author relations, Robert Hale has carved out a profitable niche for popular non-fiction.

Halsgrove

Halsgrove House, Tiverton Business Park, Lower Moor Way, Tiverton, Devon EX16 6SS
☎01884 243242 Fax 01884 243325
Email sales@halsgrove.com
Website www.halsgrove.com

Publisher *Simon Butler*

FOUNDED in 1990 and now the region's largest publishing and distribution group, specialising in books, video and audio tapes. Core interests remain in the South but now with offices in East Anglia and Derbyshire. *Publishes* local history (including the *Community History* series), cookery, biography and art, mainly in hardback. 130 titles in 2002. Also established a series of local interest magazines in southern England. No fiction or poetry. Unsolicited mss, synopses and ideas for books of regional interest welcome.
Royalties paid annually.

Hambledon and London

102 Gloucester Avenue, London NW1 8HX
☎020 7586 0817 Fax 020 7586 9970
Email office@hambledon.co.uk

Editorial Director *Martin Sheppard*
Commissioning Director *Tony Morris*

FOUNDED 1980 as The Hambledon Press. Winner of the **Sunday Times Award for Small Publishers** in 2001. *Publishes* history and biography. TITLES *Churchill: A Study in Greatness* Geoffrey Best; *The Ambassadors' Secret* John North; *Brunel: the Life and Times of Isambard Kingdom Brunel* Angus Buchanan; *Family Names and Family History* David Hey. No unsolicited mss; send preliminary letter. Synopses and ideas welcome.
Royalties paid twice-yearly. *Overseas distributor* Palgrave-Macmillan (USA and Canada).

Hamish Hamilton
See **Penguin Group (UK)**

Hamlyn Octopus
See **Octopus Publishing Group**

The Handsel Press
See **The Continuum International Publishing Group Limited**

Harcourt Education

Halley Court, Jordan Hill, Oxford OX2 8EJ
☎01865 311366 Fax 01865 314641
Website www.harcourteducation.co.uk

Chief Executive *John Philbin*

A member of the **Reed Elsevier Group plc**, Harcourt Education incorporates Heinemann Educational and Ginn in the UK; Greenwood Heinemann in the USA; Rigby Heinemann in Australia.

Heinemann Educational Fax 01865 314140 Managing Director *Bob Osborne*, Primary *Paul Shuter*, Secondary *Kay Symons*. Textbooks/literature/other educational resources for primary and secondary school and further education. Mss, synopses and ideas welcome.

Ginn & Co Fax 01865 314189 Managing Director *Paul Shuter*. Textbook/other educational resources for primary and secondary schools.
Royalties paid twice-yearly/annually, according to contract in all divisions.

Harlequin Mills & Boon Ltd

Eton House, 18–24 Paradise Road, Richmond, Surrey TW9 1SR
☎020 8288 2800 Fax 020 8288 2899
Website www.eharlequin.com *or* www.millsandboon.co.uk

Managing Director *Andrew Low*
Editorial Director *Karin Stoecker*

Approx. Annual Turnover £22 million

FOUNDED 1908. Owned by the Canadian-based Torstar Group. *Publishes* romantic fiction and historical romance. Over 600 titles a year.

IMPRINTS

Mills & Boon Modern Romance *Tessa Shapcott*; **Mills & Boon Tender Romance** *Bryony Green* (50–55,000 words) Contemporary romances with international settings, focusing on hero and heroine. **Mills & Boon Medical Romance** *Sheila Hodgson* (50–55,000 words) Modern medical practice provides a unique background to love stories. **Mills & Boon Historical Romance** *Linda Fildew* (75–80,000 words) Historical romances. **MIRA** *Linda Fildew* (minimum 100,000 words) Individual women's fiction. **Red Dress Ink** *Samantha Bell* (90–110,000 words) Contemporary women's fiction. **Mills & Boon Sensual Romance**, **Mills & Boon Blaze** and **Silhouette Superromance** titles are acquired through the Canadian office. **Silhouette Desire**, **Special Edition**, **Sensation** and **Intrigue** imprints are handled by US-based **Silhouette Books** (see entry under **US Publishers**). Please send query letter in the first instance. Tip sheets and guidelines for the Mills & Boon series available from the website or Harlequin Mills & Boon Editorial Dept. (please send s.a.e.).

Royalties paid twice-yearly.

Authors' Rating Sex has overtaken romance at M&B where the new Blaze imprint allows writers' erotic imagination to run riot. But the staple M&B romance is still going strong providing a good income for writers who can adapt to the clearly defined M&B formula. Just think, M&B has a network of 12,000 authors worldwide and every title scores six-figure sales. But be warned. M&B gets 2000 unsolicited manuscripts a year.

Harley Books

Martins, Great Horkesley, Colchester, Essex CO6 4AH
☎01206 271216 Fax 01206 271182
Email harley@keme.co.uk
Website www.harleybooks.com

Managing Director *Basil Harley*

FOUNDED 1983. Natural history publishers specialising in entomological and botanical books. Mostly definitive, high-quality illustrated reference works. TITLES *The Moths and Butterflies of Great Britain and Ireland; Dragonflies of Europe; The Aurelian Legacy: British Butterflies and their Collectors; The Liverwort Flora of the British Isles.*

Royalties paid twice-yearly in the first year, annually thereafter.

HarperCollins Publishers Ltd

77–85 Fulham Palace Road, London W6 8JB
☎020 8741 7070 Fax 020 8307 4440
Website www.harpercollins.co.uk
Also at: Westerhill Road, Bishopbriggs, Glasgow G64 2QT
☎0141 772 3200 Fax 0141 306 3119

CEO/Publisher *Victoria Barnsley*

HarperCollins is the second largest book publisher in the UK, with a wider range of books than any other publisher; from cutting-edge contemporary fiction to block-busting thrillers, from fantasy literature and children's stories to enduring classics. The wholly-owned division of News Corporation also *publishes* a selection of non-fiction including history, celebrity memoirs, biography, popular science, mind, body and spirit, dictionaries, maps and reference books. HarperCollins is also the third largest education publisher in the UK. Authors include many award-winning and international bestsellers such as Paulo Coelho, Josephine Cox, Michael Crichton, Barbara Erskine, Jonathan Franzen, Judith Kerr, Doris Lessing, Frank McCourt, Tony Parsons and Carol Shields. About 1500 titles a year.

GENERAL BOOKS DIVISION

Managing Director *Amanda Ridout* **HarperCollins (Trade)** Publishing Directors *Lynne Drew* (Fiction); *Michael Fishwick* (Non-fiction); *Arabella Pike* (Non-fiction); *Susan Watt* (Fiction/Non-fiction). IMPRINTS **Collins Crime** Publishing Director *Julia Wisdom*; **Collins Willow** Publishing Director *Michael Doggart* Sports titles; **Harper Entertainment** Managing Director *Trevor Dolby* Media-related books from film companions to autobiographies and TV tie-ins; **Voyager** Publishing Director *Jane Johnson* Science fiction/fantasy; **Special Projects & Estates** Publishing Director *David Brawn* Authors include Agatha Christie, J.R.R. Tolkien, C.S. Lewis.

Thorsons/Element Managing Director *Belinda Budge* Mind, body and spirit titles covering health, natural therapies, relationships and personal development.

Collins Children's (Children's Division) Managing Director *Sally Gritten*; Publishing Directors *Sue Buswell* (Picture Books & Properties); *Gillie Russell* (Fiction); Properties Director *Venetia Davie*. Quality picture books and book and tape sets for under-7s; fiction for age 6 up to young adult.

PerfectBound Global e-books available on four e-book platforms via 20 retail websites worldwide.

HarperCollins Audio (see entry under **Audio Books**).

COLLINS
Managing Director *Thomas Webster* IMPRINTS **Collins**; **Collins Gem**; **Collins New Naturalist Library**; **Times Books**; **Jane's** (Reference Division) Managing Director *Sarah Bailey* Publishing Director *Myles Archibald* Encyclopedias, guides and handbooks, phrase books and manuals on popular reference, art instruction, illustrated, cookery and wine, crafts, DIY, gardening, military, natural history, pet care, Scottish, pastimes.

Collins/Times Maps and Atlases (Cartographic Division) Publishing Directors *Juliet Lawler* (International titles); *Mike Cottingham* (UK titles) Maps, atlases, street plans and leisure guides.

Collins/Cobuild (Dictionaries Division) Publishing Director *Lorna Sinclair Knight* Bilingual and English dictionaries, English dictionaries for foreign learners.

Collins Education (Education Division) Managing Director *Jim Green* Books, CD-ROMs and online material for UK schools and colleges.

HARPERPRESS
Managing Director *Caroline Michel* Associate Publishers *Christopher Potter; Nicky Eaton* IMPRINTS **Flamingo** Publishing Director *Philip Gwyn Jones* Literary fiction/non-fiction; **Fourth Estate** (see entry).

Authors' Rating A front-runner among UK Publishers. HarperCollins is noted for strong marketing particularly of popular fiction and biography.

Harrap
See **Chambers Harrap Publishers Ltd**

Harvard University Press
Fitzroy House, 11 Chenies Street, London WC1E 7EY
☎020 7306 0603 Fax 020 7306 0604
Email info@HUP-MITpress.co.uk
Website www.hup.harvard.edu

Director *William Sisler*
General Manager *Ann Sexsmith*

European office of **Harvard University Press**, USA. *Publishes* academic and scholarly works in history, politics, philosophy, economics, literary criticism, psychology, sociology, anthropology, women's studies, biological sciences, classics, history of science, art, music, film, reference. All mss go to the American office: 79 Garden Street, Cambridge, MA 02138 (see entry under **US Publishers**).

The Harvill Press Ltd
See **Random House Group Ltd**

Haynes Publishing
Sparkford, Near Yeovil, Somerset BA22 7JJ
☎01963 440635 Fax 01963 440825
Email info@haynes-manuals.co.uk
Website www.haynes.co.uk

Chairman *John H. Haynes, OBE*
Approx. Annual Turnover £19.9 million

FOUNDED in 1960 by John H. Haynes. Family-run business. The mainstay of its programme has been the *Owners' Workshop Manual*, first published in the mid 1960s and still running off the presses today. Indeed the company maintains a strong bias towards motoring and transport titles. Acquired Sutton Publishing Ltd in March 2000. *Publishes* DIY service and repair manuals for cars, motorbikes and leisure plus other related topics under the Haynes imprint and a broad range of general non-fiction under the Sutton imprint.

AUTOMOTIVE DIVISION IMPRINT **Haynes** Editorial Director *Matthew Minter* Service and repair manuals; Editorial Director *Mark Hughes* Motoring, motor sport, cars, motorcycles, home, DIY and leisure titles. Unsolicited submissions welcome if they come within the subject areas covered.

GENERAL PUBLISHING DIVISION IMPRINT **Sutton Publishing Ltd** (see entry).

Royalties paid twice-yearly. *Overseas subsidiaries* Haynes Manuals Inc., California, USA, Editions Haynes S.A., France, Haynes Publishing Nordiska AB, Sweden.

Hazleton Publishing
3 Richmond Hill, Richmond, Surrey TW10 6RE
☎020 8948 5151 Fax 020 8948 4111
Email info@hazletonpublishing.com
Website www.hazletonpublishing.com

Chairman *R.F. Poulter*

Publisher of the leading Grand Prix annual *Autocourse*, now in its 52nd edition. *Publishes* high-quality motor sport titles including annuals. TITLES *Motocourse; Rallycourse*. About 13 titles a year. No unsolicited mss; synopses and ideas welcome. Interested in all motor sport titles.

Royalties Payment varies.

Headline
See **Hodder Headline Ltd**

William Heinemann
See **Random House Group Ltd**

Heinemann Educational
See **Harcourt Education**

Helicon Publishing Ltd
RM plc, New Mill House, 183 Milton Park,
Abingdon, Oxfordfordshire OX14 4SE
☎01235 826000 Fax 01235 823222
Email admin@helicon.co.uk
Website www.helicon.co.uk
General Manager *Michael Holyoke*
Approx. Annual Turnover £1 million

A division of Research Machines plc. Helicon
is a general reference database publisher for the
UK, US and Australian markets. Licenses qual-
ity reference content for online, print and CD-
ROM publications. TITLES include the flagship
single volume *Hutchinson 2002 Encyclopedia*
published under license from **Hodder
Headline**. CD-ROM TITLES include *The
Hutchinson Encyclopedia; The Hutchinson Science
Reference Suite; The Hutchinson History Reference
Suite; The Hutchinson Music Reference Suite.*

Christopher Helm
See **A.&C. Black (Publishers) Ltd**

Helm Information Ltd
The Banks, Mountfield, Nr Robertsbridge,
East Sussex TN32 5JY
☎01580 880561 Fax 01580 880541
Email amandahelm@helm-information.co.uk
Website www.helm-information.co.uk
Directors *Amanda Helm, Christopher Helm*
FOUNDED 1990. *Publishes* academic books for
students and university libraries. SERIES *The
Critical Assessments of Writers in English* (collected
criticism); *Literary Sources & Documents* (primary
source material on various themes/events/cul-
tural/aesthetic movements ranging from the
American Civil War to the Gothic Revival);
Sources & Documents in Art History (literary
sources of various movements in art); *The
Dickens Companions*. Will consider ideas and proposals provided they are relevant to the series
listed above.
Royalties paid annually.

Helter Skelter Publishing
4 Denmark Street, London WC2H 8LL
☎020 7836 1151 Fax 020 7240 9880

Email helter@skelter.demon.co.uk
Website www.helterskelterbooks.com
Contact *Sean Body*
FOUNDED 1995. *Publishes* music and film books
only. 15 titles a year. IMPRINTS **Helter Skelter
Publishing; Firefly Publishing**. Unsolicited
mss, synopses and ideas welcome.

Henderson Publishing
See **Dorling Kindersley Ltd**

Ian Henry Publications Ltd
20 Park Drive, Romford, Essex RM1 4LH
☎01708 749119 Fax 01708 736213
Managing Director *Ian Wilkes*
FOUNDED 1976. *Publishes* local history, transport history and Sherlockian pastiches. 8–10
titles a year. TITLES *Remember Chelmsford?;
Rainham Born and Bred; Dijaa Wanna Say
Sumpfing?* No unsolicited mss. Synopses and
ideas for books welcome.
Royalties paid twice-yearly.

The Herbert Press
See **A.&C. Black (Publishers) Ltd**

Hermes House
See **Anness Publishing Ltd**

Nick Hern Books
The Glasshouse, 49a Goldhawk Road,
London W12 8QP
☎020 8749 4953 Fax 020 8735 0250
Email info@nickhernbooks.demon.co.uk
Website www.nickhernbooks.co.uk
Chairman/Managing Director *Nick Hern*
FOUNDED 1988. Fully independent since 1992.
Publishes books on theatre and film: from how-
to and biography to plays and screenplays.
About 30 titles a year. No unsolicited
playscripts. Synopses, ideas and proposals for
other theatre material welcome. Not interested
in material unrelated to the theatre or cinema.

University of Hertfordshire Press
Learning and Information Services, Hatfield
Campus Learning Resources Centre, College
Lane, Hatfield, Hertfordshire AL10 9AB
☎01707 284681 Fax 01707 284666
Email W.A.Forster@herts.ac.uk
Website www.herts.ac.uk/UHPress
Contact *Bill Forster*
FOUNDED 1992. *Publishes* academic books on
gypsies, literature, regional and local history,
parapsychology. 12 titles in 2003. IMPRINTS

Interface Collection; Hertfordshire Publications; University of Hertfordshire Press. TITLES *We Are The Romany People* Ian Hancock; *Convict Theatres of Early Australia: 1788–1840* Robert Jordan; *Textual Shakespeare: Writing and the Word* Graham Holderness.

Hesperus Press Limited
4 Rickett Street, London SW6 1RU
☎020 7610 3331 Fax 020 7610 3337
Website www.hesperuspress.com
Managing Director/Publisher *Alessandro Gallenzi*

FOUNDED 2001. *Publishes* classic fiction in paperback. AUTHORS include Joseph Conrad, Edgar Allan Poe, Alexander Pope, Mark Twain, Anton Chekhov. 30 titles in 2002 including *The Diary of Adam and Eve* Mark Twain; *Life of Dante* Giovanni Boccaccio; *The Story of a Nobody* Anton Chekhov. The list for 2003 includes books by Oscar Wilde, Casanova, Balzac and Turgenev. Welcomes synopses and ideas for books. Approach in writing. No non-fiction.
Royalties paid annually.

High Stakes
See **Oldcastle Books Ltd**

Hippo
See **Scholastic Ltd**

Historic Military Press
See **SB Publications**

History Into Print
See **Brewin Books Ltd**

HMSO
See **TSO**

Hobsons Publishing
Challenger House, 42 Adler Street, London E1 1EE
☎020 7958 5000 Fax 020 7958 5001
Website www.hobsons.com
Chairman *Martin Morgan*
Group Managing Director *Christopher Letcher*

FOUNDED 1973. A division of Harmsworth Publishing Ltd, part of the Daily Mail & General Trust. *Publishes* course and career guides, under exclusive licence and royalty agreements for CRAC (Careers Research and Advisory Bureau); computer software; directories and specialist titles for employers, government departments and professional associations.

TITLES *Graduate Employment and Training; Degree Course Guides; The Which Degree Series; Which University* (CD-ROM); *The Postgrad Series: The Directory of Graduate Studies; The Directory of Further Education.*

Hodder & Stoughton
See **Hodder Headline Ltd**

Hodder Gibson
2a Christie Street, Paisley PA1 1NB
☎0141 848 1609 Fax 0141 889 6315
Email hoddergibson@hodder.co.uk
Website www.madaboutbooks.com
Managing Director *John Mitchell*

Part of the **Hodder Headline Group**. *Publishes* educational books specifically for Scotland. Combines the former **Robert Gibson and Sons (Glasgow)** with the Scottish branch of **Hodder Murray** (a merger of **John Murray** and **Hodder Stoughton Educational**). About 50 titles a year. Synopses/ideas preferred to unsolicited mss.
Royalties paid annually

Hodder Headline Ltd
338 Euston Road, London NW1 3BH
☎020 7873 6000 Fax 020 7873 6024
Website www.hodderheadline.co.uk
Group Chief Executive *Tim Hely Hutchinson*
Approx. Annual Turnover £130 million

Formed in June 1993 through the merger of Headline Book Publishing and Hodder & Stoughton. Headline was formed in 1986 and had grown dramatically, whereas Hodder & Stoughton was 125 years old with a diverse range of publishing. The company was acquired by WHSmith plc in 1999. Purchased **John Murray (Publishers) Ltd** in 2002 (see entry). About 2000 titles a year.

DIVISIONS
Headline Book Publishing Managing Director *Martin Neild*; **Non-fiction** Publishing Director *Val Hudson*; **Fiction** Publishing Director *Jane Morpeth*. *Publishes* commercial and literary fiction (hardback and paperback) and popular non-fiction including autobiography, biography, food and wine, gardening, history, popular science, sport and TV tie-ins. IMPRINTS **Headline**; **Review**. AUTHORS Kate Adie, Catherine Alliott, Lyn Andrews, Colin Bateman, Martina Cole, Janet Evanovich, Sophie Grigson, Wendy Holden, Ken Hom, Matthew Jukes, Faye and Jonathan Kellerman, Maggie O'Farrell, Sheila O'Flanagan, James Patterson.

Hodder & Stoughton General Managing Director *Jamie Hodder-Williams*; **Non-fiction** *Rowena Webb*; **Sceptre** *Carole Welch*; **Fiction** *Carolyn Mays*; **Audio** (See entry under **Audio Books**). *Publishes* commercial and literary fiction; biography, autobiography, history, self-help, humour, travel and other general interest non-fiction; audio. IMPRINTS **Hodder & Stoughton**, **Lir**; **Coronet**; **Flame**; **New English Library**; **Sceptre**; **Mobius**. AUTHORS Dickie Bird, Melvyn Bragg, John le Carré, Andrew Miller, Alex Ferguson, Charles Frazier, Elizabeth George, Amy Jenkins, Thomas Keneally, Stephen King, David Mitchell, Fiona Walker, Rosamunde Pilcher, Mary Stewart.

Hodder Children's Books Managing Director *Charles Nettleton*. IMPRINTS **Hodder Children's Books**; **Signature**; **Bite**; **Wayland**. AUTHORS David Almond, Enid Blyton, John Cunliffe, Lucy Daniels, Mick Inkpen, Emma Thomson, Hilary McKay, David Melling, Jenny Oldfield.

Hodder & Stoughton Religious Managing Director *Charles Nettleton*; Publishing Director *Judith Longman*; Bibles & Hodder Christian Books *David Moloney*. *Publishes* NIV Bibles, Christian books, autobiography, TV-tie-ins, gift books, self-help. IMPRINTS **Hodder & Stoughton**; **Hodder Christian Books**.

Hodder/Arnold Managing Director *Philip Walters*; Deputy Managing Director *Tim Gregson-Williams*. *Publishes* in the following areas: **Schoolbooks** *Lis Tribe*; **Consumer Education** *Katie Roden*; **Further Education/Higher Education Textbooks** *Mary Attree*; **Health Sciences** *Georgina Bentliff*; **Journals/Reference Books** *Mary Attree*. IMPRINTS **Hodder & Stoughton Educational**; **Teach Yourself**; **Hodder & Stoughton**; **Arnold** *John Murray* (Educational).

Hodder Gibson (see entry).

Authors' Rating The growth area is non-fiction where sales of biography and cookery titles are set to double over the next two years. An exciting relaunch of the famous but stuffy Teach Yourself list shows what can be done with a neglected backlist. But the biggest news is of a deal with Simon & Schuster US which will take Hodder Headline, now the UK's fourth largest trade publisher, into the American market. A recent Society of Authors survey of author/publisher relations gave the Headline imprint high marks.

Hodder/Arnold
See **Hodder Headline Ltd**

Honeyglen Publishing Ltd
56 Durrels House, Warwick Gardens, London W14 8QB
☎020 7602 2876 Fax 020 7602 2876
Directors *N.S. Poderegin, J. Poderegin*
FOUNDED 1983. A small publishing house whose output is 'extremely limited'. *Publishes* history, philosophy of history, biography and selective fiction. No children's or science fiction. TITLES *The Soul of India; A Child of the Century* Amaury de Riencourt; *With Duncan Grant in South Turkey* Paul Roche; *Vladimir, The Russian Viking* Vladimir Volkoff; *The Dawning* Milka Bajic-Poderegin; *Quicksand* Louise Hide. Unsolicited mss welcome.

Honno Welsh Women's Press
c/o U.T.C., King Street, Aberystwyth, Ceredigion SY23 2LT
☎01970 623150 Fax 01970 623150
Email post@honno.co.uk
Website www.honno.co.uk
Editor *Janet Thomas*
FOUNDED in 1986 by a group of women who wanted to create more opportunities for women in publishing. A co-operative operation which *publishes* fiction (adult and teenage) and children's books, all with a Welsh connection. Also publishes poetry, short story and autobiographical anthologies. About 6 titles a year. Welcomes mss and ideas for books from women only. All material must have a Welsh connection and be sent as hard copy, not by e-mail.
Royalties paid annually.

Horus Editions
See **Award Publications Limited**

House of Lochar
Isle of Colonsay, Argyll PA61 7YR
☎01951 200232 Fax 01951 200232
Email Lochar@colonsay.org.uk
Website www.houseoflochar.com
Chairman *Kevin Byrne*
Managing Director *Georgina Hobhouse*
Approx. Annual Turnover £95,000
FOUNDED 1995 on a tiny island, taking advantage of new technology and mains electricity and taking over some 20 titles from Thomas and Lochar. About 10 titles a year. *Publishes* mostly Scottish – history, topography, transport and fiction. IMPRINTS **House of Lochar** TITLES *The Clyde in Pictures; Alexander III; Ancient Scotland; The Clyde Puffer*. AUTHORS Neil Munro, Neill Gunn, John McPhee, Marion Campbell,

Ronald Williams. **Colonsay Books** TITLE *Summer in the Hebrides.* **West Highland Series** Mini walking guides. No poetry or books unrelated to Scotland or Celtic theme. Unsolicited mss, synopses and ideas welcome if relevant to subjects covered.
Royalties paid annually.

House of Stratus
Thirsk Industrial Park, Thirsk, North Yorkshire YO7 3BX
☎01845 527700 Fax 01845 527711
Email info@houseofstratus.com
Website www.houseofstratus.com
CEO *David Lane*

FOUNDED 1999. *Publishes* fiction and non-fiction. Backlist of over 1500 titles including C.P. Snow, Brian Aldiss, Nevil Shute and G.K. Chesterton. About 30 titles annually. Submissions should incorporate a synopsis, sample chapter and author c.v.
Royalties paid twice-yearly. Overseas offices in New York.

How To Books Ltd
3 Newtec Place, Magdalen Road, Oxford OX4 1RE
☎01865 793806 Fax 01865 248780
Email info@howtobooks.co.uk
Website www.howtobooks.co.uk
Publisher/Managing Director *Giles Lewis*
Commissioning Editor *Nikki Read*

An independent publishing house, FOUNDED in 1991. *Publishes* non-fiction reference books. How To titles are practical, accessible books that encourage their readers to improve their lives and develop their skills. How To authors must have first-hand experience of the subject about which they are writing and are given guidance in the development of their books. Subjects covered include business & management, home & family, career choices & career development, living & working abroad, personal finance, small business & self employment, study skills & student guides, creative writing.

Human Horizons
See **Souvenir Press Ltd**

Human Science Press
See **Kluwer Academic/Plenum Publishers**

Hunt & Thorpe
See **John Hunt Publishing Ltd**

John Hunt Publishing Ltd
46a West Street, New Alresford, Hampshire SO24 9AU
☎01962 736880 Fax 01962 736881
Email maria@johnhunt-publishing.com
Website www.johnhunt-publishing.com *and* www.o-books.net
Approx. Annual Turnover £1.5 million

Publishes children's and world religions as well as mind, body & spirit titles. About 25 a year. IMPRINTS **Hunt & Thorpe**; **John Hunt Publishing**; **Arthur James**; **O Books**. Unsolicited material welcome.

C. Hurst & Co.
38 King Street, London WC2E 8JZ
☎020 7240 2666 Fax 020 7240 2667
Email hurst@atlas.co.uk
Website www.hurstpub.co.uk
Chairman/Managing Director *Christopher Hurst*
Editorial Heads *Christopher Hurst, Michael Dwyer*

FOUNDED 1967. An independent company concerned with literacy, detail and visual aspects. *Publishes* contemporary history, politics, religion (not theology) and sociology. About 25 titles a year. TITLES *The Hungarians* Paul Lendvai; *Greece: The Modern Sequel; Serbia: the History behind the Name; Iceland's 1100 Years; Inside Al Qaeda: Global Network of Terror.* No unsolicited mss. Synopses and ideas welcome.
Royalties paid annually.

Hutchinson
See **Random House Group Ltd**

Hymns Ancient & Modern Ltd
St Mary's Works, St Mary's Plain, Norwich, Norfolk NR3 3BH
☎01603 612914 Fax 01603 624483
Email hymns@scm-canterburypress.co.uk
Chairman *Patrick Coldstream, CBE*
Chief Executive *G.A. Knights*
Publisher, SCM Canterbury Press *Christine Smith*
Publisher, RMEP *Mary Mears*
Approx. Annual Turnover £4.4 million

Publishes hymn books for churches, schools and other institutions. All types of liturgical and general religious books and material for religious and social education. Owns SCM-Canterbury Press Ltd controlling the IMPRINTS **SCM Canterbury Press** (see entry). **Religious and Moral Education Press (RMEP)** Religious, social and moral books for primary and secondary schools, assembly material and books for teachers and administrators. **G.J. Palmer & Sons Ltd** TITLES *Church Times* (see entry under **Magazines**); *The Sign* and *Home Words* – two monthly nationwide parish magazine inserts. Ideas welcome; no unsolicited mss.

Royalties paid annually.

Icon Books Ltd

Grange Road, Duxford, Cambridge CB2 4QF
☎01763 208008 Fax 01763 208080
Email info@iconbooks.co.uk
Website www.iconbooks.co.uk

Managing Director *Peter Pugh*
Editorial Director *Richard Appignanesi*
Publishing Director *Jeremy Cox*

FOUNDED 1992. SERIES *Introducing* Graphic introductions to key figures and ideas in the history of science, philosophy, psychology, religion and the arts. TITLE *Introducing Quantum Theory*. Publishes 'provocative and intelligent' non-fiction in science, politics and philosophy. TITLE *Why do People Hate America?* IMPRINT **Wizard Books** Children's fiction and non-fiction including SERIES *Fighting Fantasy* (adventure gamebooks). Submit synopsis only.

Royalties paid twice yearly. *Overseas associate* Totem Books, USA, distributed by National Book Network.

I.M.P. Fiction Ltd

PO Box 14691, London SE1 2ZA
☎01440 788561 Fax 01440 788562
Email info@impbooks.com
Website www.impbooks.com

Managing Director *Kaye Roach*

FOUNDED 1998. *Publishes* 'innovative new cutting-edge' fiction. No crime or science fiction. 2 titles in 2002. Approach in writing, enclosing biography, synopsis, first three chapters and s.a.e. Material will not be returned if postage and packing not provided.

Royalties paid twice-yearly.

The In Pinn

See **Neil Wilson Publishing Ltd**

Independent Music Press

PO Box 14691, London SE1 2ZA
☎020 7357 8007 Fax 020 7357 8608
Email info@impbooks.com
Website www.impbooks.com

Managing Director *Martin Roach*

FOUNDED 1992. *Publishes* music biography and

youth culture. No jazz or classical. TITLES include biographies of Travis, Stereophonics, Oasis, Prodigy and Ian Hunter's *Diary of a Rock 'n' Roll Star*. Approach by letter or e-mail, enclosing biography, synopsis, first three chapters and s.a.e. if return of work required. Material will not be returned if postage and packing not provided.

Royalties paid twice-yearly.

Independent Voices

See **Souvenir Press Ltd**

Informa

Informa House, 30–32 Mortimer Street, London W1W 7RE
☎020 7017 4600
Website www.informa.com

Managing Director *Lindsay Roberts*
Publishing Director *Fotini Liontou*
Legal Editor *Wendy Gill*

Part of LLP Professional Publishing, a trading division of Informa Publishing Group Ltd. *Publishes* a range of maritime, commerical, insurance, banking, intellectual property, medico-legal, academic newsletters, reports, books and magazines aimed at senior management and professional practices.

Inset Guide/Berlitz Publishing Co. Ltd

58 Borough High Stret, London SE1 1XF
☎020 7403 0284 Fax 020 7403 0290
Email publishing@berlitz.co.uk
Website www.berlitz.com

Managing Director *Jeremy Westwood*

FOUNDED 1970. Acquired by the Langenscheidt Publishing Group in February 2002. *Publishes* travel and language-learning products only: visual travel guides, phrasebooks and language courses. SERIES *Pocket Guides; Berlitz Complete Guide to Cruising and Cruise Ships; Phrase Books; Pocket Dictionaries; Business Phrase Books; Self-teach: Rush Hour Commuter Cassettes; Think & Talk; Berlitz Kids*. No unsolicited mss.

Inter-Varsity Press

38 De Montfort Street, Leicester LE1 7GP
☎0116 255 1754 Fax 0116 254 2044
Email ivp@uccf.org.uk
Website www.ivpbooks.com

Chairman *Ralph Evershed*
Chief Executive *Brian Wilson*

FOUNDED mid-1930s as the publishing arm of Universities and Colleges Christian Fellowship, it has expanded to wider Christian markets worldwide. *Publishes* Christian belief and lifestyle, reference and bible commentaries. About 50 titles a year. No secular material or anything which fails to empathise with orthodox Protestant Christianity.

IMPRINTS
IVP; **Apollos**; **Crossway** TITLES *The Bible Speaks Today; But Don't All Religions Lead to God?* Michael Green; *John Stott – A Global Ministry* Timothy Dudley-Smith. No unsolicited mss; synopses and ideas welcome.
Royalties paid twice-yearly.

Interface Collection
See **University of Hertfordshire Press**

International Thomson Publishing
See **Thomson Learning**

Intrigue
See **Harlequin Mills & Boon Ltd**

Isis Publishing
7 Centremead, Osney Mead, Oxford OX2 0ES
☎01865 250333 Fax 01865 790358
Website www.isis-publishing co.uk

Part of the Ulverscroft Group Ltd. *Publishes* large-print books – fiction and non-fiction – and unabridged audio books. Together with **Soundings** (see entry under **Audio Books**) produces around 4000 titles on audio tape and CD. AUTHORS Catherine Cookson, Stephen King, Terry Pratchett, Willy Russell. No unsolicited mss as Isis undertakes no original publishing.
Royalties paid twice-yearly.

Itchy Coo
See **Black & White Publishing Ltd**

Ithaca Press
See **Garnet Publishing Ltd**

IVP
See **Inter-Varsity Press**

Jacqui Small
See **Aurum Press Ltd**

JAI
See **Elsevier Ltd**

Arthur James
See **John Hunt Publishing Ltd**

Jane's Information Group
Sentinel House, 163 Brighton Road, Coulsdon, Surrey CR5 2YH
☎020 8700 3700 Fax 020 8763 1006
Email info@janes.co.uk
Website www.janes.com
Managing Director *Alfred Rolington*

FOUNDED 1898 by Fred T. Jane with the publication of *All The World's Fighting Ships*. Now part of the Woodbridge Company Limited. In recent years management has been focusing on growth opportunities in its core business and in enhancing the performance of initiatives like Jane's information available online and on CD-ROM. *Publishes* magazines and yearbooks on defence, aerospace, security and transport topics, with details of equipment and systems; plus directories and strategic studies. Also *Jane's Defence Weekly* (see entry under **Magazines**).

DIVISIONS
Magazines *Sean Howe* TITLES *Jane's Defence Weekly*; *Jane's International Defense Review*; *Jane's Airport Review*; *Jane's Defence Upgrades*; *Jane's Navy International*; *Jane's Islamic Affairs Analyst*; *Jane's Missiles and Rockets*. **Publishing for Defence, Aerospace, Transport** *Ian Kay* TITLES *Defence, Aerospace Yearbooks*. **Transport** TITLES *Transportation Yearbooks*. **Security** *John Boatman* TITLES *Jane's Intelligence Review*; *Foreign Report*; *Jane's Sentinel* (regional security assessment); *Police Review*. CD-ROM and electronic development and publication. Unsolicited mss, synopses and ideas for reference/yearbooks welcome.
Royalties paid twice-yearly. *Overseas associates* Jane's Information Group Inc., USA.

Janus Publishing Company Ltd
105–107 Gloucester Place, London W1U 6BY
☎020 7580 7664 Fax 020 7636 5756
Email publisher@januspublishing.co.uk
Managing Director *Sandy Leung*

Publishes fiction, human interest, memoirs, philosophy, mind, body and spirit, religion and theology, social questions, popular science, history, spiritualism and the paranormal, poetry and young adults. About 400 titles in print. IMPRINTS **Janus Books** Subsidy publishing; **Empiricus Books** Non-subsidy publishing. TITLES *The Anarchists in the Spanish Civil War; Nature of the Self; Healing Connections; Politics and Human Nature; Tales of French Corsairs and Revolutions; Child of the Thirties; Napoleon 1813.* Unsolicited mss welcome.
Royalties paid twice-yearly. Agents in the USA, Europe and Asia.

Authors' Rating Authors may be asked to cover their own productions costs but Janus seems to be moving into conventional publishing with its Empiricus imprint.

Jarrold Publishing

Whitefriars, Norwich, Norfolk NR3 1TR
☎01603 763300 Fax 01603 662748
Email publishing-sales@jarrold.com
Website www.jarrold-publishing.co.uk
Managing Director *Margot Russel-King*

Part of Jarrold & Sons Ltd, the printing and publishing company FOUNDED in 1770. *Publishes* UK tourism, travel, leisure, history and calendars. Material tends to be of a high pictorial content. About 30 titles a year. IMPRINTS **Pitkin**; **Unichrome**. Unsolicited mss, synopses and ideas welcome but before submitting anything, approach in writing to the editorial department.

Jensen Business Books
See **AMCD (Publishers) Ltd**

Jewish Chronicle Publications
See **Vallentine Mitchell**

Michael Joseph
See **Penguin Group (UK)**

Judith Handbooks
See **Studymates Limited**

Judith Handbooks
See **Studymates Limited**

Kahn & Averill

9 Harrington Road, London SW7 3ES
☎020 8743 3278 Fax 020 8743 3278
Email kahn@averill23.freeserve.co.uk
Managing Director *Mr M. Kahn*

FOUNDED 1967 to publish children's titles but now specialises in music titles. A small independent publishing house. *Publishes* music and general non-fiction. No unsolicited mss; synopses and ideas for books considered.
Royalties paid twice-yearly.

Karnak House

300 Westbourne Park Road, London W11 1EH
☎020 7243 3620 Fax 020 7243 3620
Email karnakhouse@aol.com
Managing Director *Amon Saba Saakana*

FOUNDED 1979. *Specialises* in African and Caribbean studies. *Publishes* anthropology, education, Egyptology, history, language and linguistics, literary criticism, music, prehistory. No poetry, humour or sport. About 12 titles a year. No unsolicited mss; send introduction or synopsis with one sample chapter. Synopses and ideas welcome.
Royalties paid twice-yearly. *Overseas subsidiaries* The Intef Institute, and Karnak House, Illinois, USA.

Kenilworth Press Ltd

Addington, Buckingham, Buckinghamshire MK18 2JR
☎01296 715101 Fax 01296 715148
Email editorial@kenilworthpress.co.uk
Website www.kenilworthpress.co.uk
Chairman/Managing Director *David Blunt*
Approx. Annual Turnover £500,000

FOUNDED in 1989 with the acquisition of Threshhold Books. The UK's principal instructional equestrian publisher, producing the official books of the British Horse Society, the famous *Threshold Picture Guides*, and a range of authoritative titles sold around the world. About 10 titles a year.

IMPRINT
Kenilworth Press TITLES *British Horse Society Manuals*; *Real Riding*; *Ride With Your Mind Essentials*; *Navicular Syndrome Explained*; *Threshold Picture Guides 1–46*. Unsolicited mss, synopses and ideas welcome but only for titles concerned with the care or riding of horses or ponies.
Royalties paid twice-yearly.

Kenyon–Deane
See **Cressrelles Publishing Co. Ltd**

Laurence King Publishing Ltd

71 Great Russell Street, London WC1B 3BP
☎020 7430 8850 Fax 020 7430 8880
Email enquiries@laurenceking.co.uk
Website www.laurenceking.co.uk
Chairman *Robin Hyman*
Managing Director *Laurence King*
Approx. Annual Turnover £5 million

FOUNDED in 1976 as a book packager under the name Calman & King Ltd, the Laurence King publishing division commenced operations in 1991. College and trade divisions were united in 2002 under Laurence King Publishing Ltd. *Publishes* illustrated books on art, architecture, graphic design, interior design, the decorative arts, film and religion. 40 titles in 2001. DIVISIONS **Professional & Trade** *Philip Cooper* TITLES *3D>2D: The Designers Republic;*

Experimental Houses. **College & Fine Art** *Lee Ripley-Greenfield* TITLES *A World History of Art*; *A History of Western Architecture.* Unsolicited material welcome; send synopsis by post.

Royalties paid twice-yearly.

Kingfisher Publications Plc

New Penderel House, 283–288 High Holborn, London WC1V 7HZ
☎020 7903 9999 Fax 020 7242 4979
Email sales@kingfisherpub.com

Managing Director *John Richards*

Formerly Larousse plc until 1997 when the company name changed to Kingfisher Publications Plc. FOUNDED 1994 when owners, Groupe de la Cité (also publishers of the Larousse dictionaries in France), merged their UK operations of Grisewood & Dempsey and **Chambers Harrap Publishers Ltd** (see entry). In 2002, Kingfisher officially became an imprint of **Houghton Mifflin Company** (see entry under US Publishers).

DIVISION

Kingfisher Non-fiction Publishing Director *Gill Denton* FOUNDED in 1973 by Grisewood & Dempsey Ltd. *Publishes* children's fiction and non-fiction in hardback and paperback: story books, rhymes and picture books, fiction and poetry anthologies, young non-fiction, activity books, general series and reference. No unsolicited mss accepted.

Royalties paid twice-yearly where applicable.

Jessica Kingsley Publishers Ltd

116 Pentonville Road, London N1 9JB
☎020 7833 2307 Fax 020 7837 2917
Email post@jkp.com
Website www.jkp.com

Managing Director and Publisher *Jessica Kingsley*
Editorial Director *Amy Lankester-Owen*

FOUNDED 1987. Independent publisher of books for professionals and academics on social and behavioural sciences, including special needs, arts therapies, child psychology, psychotherapy (including forensic psychotherapy), practical theology and social work. Over 100 titles a year. 'We are actively publishing and commissioning in all these areas. We welcome suggestions for books and proposals from prospective authors. Proposals should consist of an outline of the book, a contents list, assessment of the market and author's c.v., and should be addressed to *Jessica Kingsley* or *Amy Lankester-Owen*. Complete manuscript should not be sent.'

Royalties paid twice-yearly.

Kluwer Academic/ Plenum Publishers

241 Borough High Street, London SE1 1GB
☎020 7940 7490 Fax 020 7940 7495
Email mail@plenum.co.uk
Website www.wkap.nl

Managing Director *Dr Ken Derham*
Editor *Joanna Lawrence*

FOUNDED 1966. A division of **Kluwer Academic/Plenum Publishing**, New York. The London office is the editorial base for the company's UK and European operations. *Publishes* postgraduate, professional and research-level scientific, technical and medical textbooks, monographs, conference proceedings and reference books. About 200 titles (worldwide) a year.

IMPRINTS

Consultants Bureau; **Kluwer Academic/ Plenum Publishers**; **Plenum Press**; **Human Science Press**. Proposals for new publications will be considered, and should be sent to the editor.

Royalties paid annually.

Kluwer Law International

3rd Floor, 241 Borough High Street, London SE1 1GB
☎020 7940 8480 Fax 020 7940 8485

Publisher *Sian O'Neill*

FOUNDED 1995. Parent company: Wolters Kluwer Group. Kluwer Law International consists of three components: the law list of Graham & Trotman, Kluwer Law and Taxation and Martinus Nyhoff. *Publishes* international law. 200 titles a year. Unsolicited synopses and ideas for books on law at an international level welcome.

Royalties paid annually.

Knight Paperbacks Ltd
See **Caxton Publishing Group**

Kogan Page Ltd

120 Pentonville Road, London N1 9JN
☎020 7278 0433 Fax 020 7837 3768/6348
Email kpinfo@kogan-page.co.uk
Website www.kogan-page.co.uk *or* www.earthscan.co.uk

Managing Director *Philip Kogan*
Approx. Annual Turnover £8 million

FOUNDED 1967 by Philip Kogan to publish *The Industrial Training Yearbook*. In 1992 acquired Earthscan Publications. *Publishes* business and management reference books and monographs, education and careers, marketing, personal finance, personnel, small business, training and industrial relations, transport, plus journals. Further expansion is planned, particularly in the finance and high-tech, EC publications areas, yearbooks and directories, and international business reference. Has initiated a number of electronic publishing projects and provision of EP content. About 280 titles a year.

DIVISIONS
Kogan Page *Pauline Goodwin, Philip Mudd, Peter Chadwick*. **Earthscan Publications** *Jonathan Sinclair Wilson* Has close associations with the International Institute for Environment and Development and with the Worldwide Fund for Nature. *Publishes* Third World issues and their global implications, and general environmental titles, both popular and academic. About 50 titles a year. Unsolicited mss, synopses and ideas for books welcome. **Kogan Page Science** *Publishes* hi-tech engineering science monographs.
Royalties paid twice-yearly.

Authors' Rating The doyen of business books publishers, Philip Kogan is open to bright ideas for electronic publishing and for books that lend themselves to direct sales.

Kogan Page Science
See **Kogan Page Ltd**

Ladybird
See **Dorling Kindersley Ltd**

Landmark Publishing Ltd
Ashbourne Hall, Cokayne Avenue, Ashbourne, Derbyshire DE6 1EJ
☎01335 347349 Fax 01335 347303
Email landmark@clara.net
Website www.landmarkpublishing.co.uk
Chairman *Mr R. Cork*
Managing Director *Mr C.L.M. Porter*
Approx. Annual Turnover £450,000

FOUNDED in 1996. *Publishes* itinerary-based travel guides, and industrial and local history. 45 titles in 2003. No unsolicited mss; telephone in the first instance.
Royalties twice-yearly.

Larousse Plc
See **Kingfisher Publications Plc**

Lawrence & Wishart Ltd
99A Wallis Road, London E9 5LN
☎020 8533 2506 Fax 020 8533 7369
Email lw@lwbooks.co.uk
Website www.lwbooks.co.uk
Managing Director/Editor *Sally Davison*

FOUNDED 1936. An independent publisher with a substantial backlist. *Publishes* current affairs, cultural politics, economics, history, politics and education. 10 titles a year. TITLES *A New Modernity; Liberty or Death; The Struggle for Democracy in Britain 1780–1830; Rosa Luxemburg: An Intimate Portrait.*
Royalties paid annually, unless by arrangement.

The Learning Institute
Honeycombe House, Bagley, Wedmore, Somerset BS28 4TD
☎01934 713563 Fax 01934 713492
Email courses@inst.org
Website www.inst.org
Managing Director *Kit Sadgrove*

FOUNDED 1994 to publish home-study courses in vocational subjects such as garden design, writing and computing. *Publishes* subjects that show the reader how to work from home, gain a new skill or enter a new career. Interests include self-improvement, interior design, hobbies, parenting, health, careers, music and investment. TITLES *Diploma in Interior Design; Become a Garden Designer.* Author's guidelines sent on receipt of s.a.e. No unsolicited mss; send synopses and ideas only.
Royalties paid quarterly.

Learning World
See **Chrysalis Children's Books**

Lehigh University Press
See **Golden Cockerel Press Ltd**

Lennard Associates Ltd
Windmill Cottage, Mackerye End, Harpenden, Hertfordshire AL5 5DR
☎01582 715866 Fax 01582 715866
Email stephenson@lennardqap.co.uk
Chairman/Managing Director *Adrian Stephenson*

FOUNDED 1979. Publisher of sporting yearbooks; sponsored and commissioned projects only. YEARBOOKS *The Cricketers' Who's Who; PFA Footballers' Who's Who; Wooden Spoon Rugby World.* No unsolicited mss.
IMPRINTS **Lennard Publishing; Queen Anne Press**. Acquired the latter and most of its assets in 1992.
Payment Both fees and royalties by arrangement.

Charles Letts
See **New Holland Publishers (UK) Ltd**

Lionel Leventhal Ltd
See **Greenhill Books**

Dewi Lewis Publishing
8 Broomfield Road, Heaton Moor, Stockport
SK4 4ND
☎0161 442 9450 Fax 0161 442 9450
Email mail@dewilewispublishing.com
Website www.dewilewispublishing.com
Contacts *Dewi Lewis, Caroline Warhurst*
Approx. Annual Turnover £260,000
FOUNDED 1994. *Publishes* fiction, photography
and visual arts. 18 titles in 2002. TITLES *Industry
of Souls* Martin Booth (**Booker Prize** shortlist,
1998); *Wolfy and the Strudelbakers* Zvi Jagendorf
(**Booker Prize** longlist, 2001; **Sagittarius
Prize**, 2002); *Common Sense* Martin Parr; *New
York 1954–5* William Klein. Submissions: check
website.
Royalties paid twice-yearly.

LexisNexis Butterworths Tolley
See **Reed Elsevier Group plc**

John Libbey & Co. Ltd
PO Box 276, Eastleigh, Hampshire SO50 5YS
☎023 8065 0208 Fax 023 8065 0259
Email johnlibbey@aol.com
Website www.johnlibbey.com
Chairman/Managing Director *John Libbey*
FOUNDED 1979. *Publishes* medical books and
cinema/animation books and journals. *Specialises*
in epilepsy, neurology, nuclear medicine, nutri-
tion and obesity. Synopses and ideas welcome.
Overseas subsidiary John Libbey Eurotext Ltd,
France.

Librapharm Ltd
Gemini House, 162 Craven Road, Newbury,
Berkshire RG14 5NR
☎01635 522651 Fax 01635 36294
Website www.librapharm.com
Chairman *Mr M.W. Frost*
Managing Director *Dr P.L. Clarke*
Approx. Annual Turnover £1.5 million
FOUNDED 1995 as a partial buyout from
Kluwer Academic Publishers (UK) academic
list. *Publishes* medical and scientific books and
periodicals. IMPRINT **Petroc Press**. TITLES *The
Inner Consultation*; *Emergencies in General
Practice*; *Thinking About Patients*. Journals:
Primary Care Psychiatry; *Current Medical Research
and Opinion*; *Paediatric and Perinatal Drug
Therapy and Transpharma*. Unsolicited mss, syn-
opses and ideas for medical books welcome.
Royalties paid twice-yearly.

Library Association Publishing
See **Facet Publishing**

Frances Lincoln Ltd
4 Torriano Mews, Torriano Avenue, London,
NW5 2RZ
☎020 7284 4009 Fax 020 7267 5249
Email <firstname and initial of surname>@
frances-lincoln.com
Website www.franceslincoln.com
Managing Director *John Nicoll*
FOUNDED 1977. *Publishes* highly illustrated non-
fiction: gardening, art and interiors, health,
crafts, children's picture and information books;
and stationery. About 50 titles a year.
DIVISIONS **Adult Non-fiction** *Jo Christian*
TITLES *Chatsworth* Duchess of Devonshire; *Grow
Your Own Vegetables* Joy Larkom; **Children's
General Fiction and Non-fiction** *Janetta
Otter-Barry* TITLE *The Wanderings of Odysseus*
Rosemary Sutcliffe, illus. Alan Lee; **Stationery**
Anne Fraser TITLES *RHS Diary and Address Book*;
British Library Diary. Synopses and ideas for books
considered.
Royalties paid twice-yearly.

Linden Press
See **Open Gate Press**

Linford Romance/Linford Mystery/Linford Western
See **F.A. Thorpe (Publishing)**

Lion Publishing
Mayfield House, 256 Banbury Road, Oxford
OX2 7DH
☎01865 302750 Fax 01865 302757
Email enquiry@lion-publishing.co.uk
Website www.lion-publishing.co.uk
Managing Director *Paul Clifford*
Approx. Annual Turnover £6.77 million
FOUNDED 1971. A Christian book publisher,
strong on illustrated books for a popular international readership, with rights sold in over
100 languages worldwide. *Publishes* a diverse
list with Christian viewpoint the common
denominator. All ages, from board books for
children to multi-contributor adult reference,
educational, paperbacks and colour co-editions
and gift books.
DIVISIONS **Adult** *Laura Derico*; **Children's
and Giftlines** *Caroline Knight*. Unsolicited mss
accepted provided they have a positive
Christian viewpoint intended for a wide general and international readership.
Royalties paid twice-yearly.

Lir
See **Hodder Headline Ltd**

Little Tiger Press
An imprint of Magi Publications, 1 The Coda Centre, 189 Munster Road, London SW6 6AW
☎020 7385 6333 Fax 020 7385 7333
Email info@littletiger.co.uk
Website www.littletigerpress.com
Publisher *Monty Bhatia*
Editors *Ramona Reihill, Jude Evans*
Approx. Annual Turnover £4.5 million

Publishes children's picture and novelty books for ages 0–7. No texts over 1200 words. About 24 titles a year. Unsolicited mss, synopses and new ideas welcome, but please telephone first.
Royalties paid annually.

Little, Brown
See **Time Warner Books UK**

Liverpool University Press
4 Cambridge Street, Liverpool L69 7ZU
☎0151 794 2233 Fax 0151 794 2235
Website www.liverpool-unipress.co.uk
Managing Director/Editorial Head *Robin Bloxsidge*

LUP's primary activity is the publication of academic and scholarly books and journals but it also has a limited number of trade titles. Its principal focus is on the arts and social sciences, in which it is active in a variety of disciplines. 30–40 titles a year. TITLES *The Cannibal Hymn; Excavations on St Patrick's Isle; Peel; Isle of Man; Urban Visions; Public Sculpture of Warwickshire; Public Sculpture of the City of London; The Long Road to Peace in Northern Ireland; Knowledge and Learning in the Andes; Identity Parades; Northern Irish Culture and Dissident Subjects; HIV Stories; Breeding Superman; The Business of Music; Claude Simon: A Retrospective; Role Play and the World as Stage in the 'comedia'.*
Royalties paid annually.

Livewire Books for Teenagers
See **The Women's Press**

Lonely Planet Publications Ltd
72–82 Rosebery Avenue, London EC1R 4RW
☎020 7428 4800 Fax 020 7428 4828
Email go@lonelyplanet.co.uk
Website www.lonelyplanet.com
Owner *Lonely Planet (Australia)*
Editorial Head *Katharine Leck*
Approx. Annual Turnover £30 million

FOUNDED in 1973 by Tony and Maureen Wheeler to document a journey from London to Australia. Since then, Lonely Planet has grown into a global operation with headquarters in Melbourne and offices in Paris, California and London. *Publishes* travel guidebooks, phrasebooks, travel literature, pictorial books, city maps, regional atlases, diving and snorkelling, walking, cycling, wildlife, health, restaurant, pre-departure guidebooks. Also operates a commercial travel slide library called **Lonely Planet Images** (www.lonelyplanetimages.com). No unsolicited mss; synopses and ideas welcome.

Lorenz Books
See **Anness Publishing Ltd**

Lund Humphries
See **Ashgate Publishing Ltd**

The Lutterworth Press
PO Box 60, Cambridge CB1 2NT
☎01223 350865 Fax 01223 366951
Email publishing@lutterworth.com
Website www.lutterworth.com
Managing Director *Adrian Brink*

The Lutterworth Press dates back to the 18th century when it was founded by the Religious Tract Society. In the 19th century it was best known for its children's books and magazines, both religious and secular, including *The Boys' Own Paper.* Since 1984 it has been an imprint of **James Clarke & Co** (see entry). *Publishes* religious books for adults and children, adult non-fiction, children's fiction and non-fiction. TITLES *Socrates Café; Deviating Voices: Women and Orthodox Religious Traditions; Volunteering Abroad* Helen Grant and Sarita Bailur; *Psychology: A Complete GCSE Course* Geoffrey Shoesmith. First approach in writing with ideas.
Royalties paid annually.

M.&N. Publishing
See **First Century Ltd**

Macdonald & Co.
See **Time Warner Books UK**

McGraw-Hill Education
McGraw-Hill House, Shoppenhangers Road, Maidenhead, Berkshire SL6 2QL
☎01628 502500 Fax 01628 770224
Website www.mcgraw-hill.co.uk
Editorial Director *Melissa A. Rosati*

Owned by US parent company, FOUNDED in 1888. Began publishing in Maidenhead in

1965, having had an office in the UK since
1899. *Publishes* business, economics, computing, finance, accounting and engineering for
the academic, student and professional markets.
Acquired **Open University Press** in 2002 (see
entry). Around 100 titles a year. See website
for author's guide and how to submit new
book proposals.

Royalties paid twice-yearly.

Macmillan Publishers Ltd
The Macmillan Building, 4 Crinan Street,
London N1 9XW
☎020 7833 4000 Fax 020 7843 4640
Website www.macmillan.com

Chief Executive *Richard Charkin*
Approx. Annual Turnover £300 million
(Book Publishing Group)

FOUNDED 1843. Macmillan is one of the largest
publishing houses in Britain, publishing approximately 1400 titles a year. In 1995, Verlagsgruppe
Georg von Holtzbrinck, a major German publisher, acquired a majority stake in the Macmillan
Group. In 1996, Macmillan bought Boxtree, the
successful media tie-in publisher and, in 1997,
purchased the Heinemann English language
teaching list from Reed Elsevier.

DIVISIONS
Palgrave Macmillan Brunel Road,
Houndmills, Basingstoke, Hampshire RG21
6XS ☎01256 329242 Fax 01256 3479476
Managing Director *Dominic Knight*; **College**
Frances Arnold; **Scholarly & Reference** *Sam
Burridge*; **Journals** *David Bull*. *Publishes* text-
books, monographs and journals in academic
and professional subjects. Publications in both
hard copy and electronic format.

Macmillan Education Macmillan Oxford,
4 Between Towns Road, Oxford OX4
3PP ☎01865 405700 Fax 01865 405701
Email info@macmillan.com Website www.
macmillaneducation.com Executive Chairman
Christopher Paterson; Managing Director *Chris
Harrison*; Publishing Directors *Sue Bale* (ELT),
Alison Hubert (Education), *Ian Johnstone*
(Internet). *Publishes* a wide range of ELT titles
and educational materials for the international
education market from Oxford and through 30
subsidiaries worldwide.

Pan Macmillan 20 New Wharf Road,
London N1 9RR ☎020 7014 6000 Fax 020
7014 6001 Managing Director *David North*.
Publishes under **Macmillan, Pan, Picador,
Sidgwick & Jackson, Boxtree, Channel 4
Books, Macmillan Children's Books,
Campbell Books**.

IMPRINTS
Macmillan (FOUNDED 1843) Publishing
Director (fiction) *Maria Rejt*; Editorial
Directors (Fiction) *Imogen Taylor, Peter Lavery*.
Publishes commercial and literary fiction
including genre fiction, crime, thrillers, romantic, sci-fi, fantasy and horror. Editorial Director
(Non-fiction) *Georgina Morley*. *Publishes* autobiography, biography, business and industry,
economics, gift books, history, natural history,
travel, philosophy, politics and world affairs,
psychology, gardening and cookery, popular
science, trade reference titles.

Pan (FOUNDED 1947) Publishing Director
(Fiction) *Maria Rejt*; Editorial Directors
(Fiction) *Imogen Taylor, Peter Lavery*. *Publishes*
fiction: novels, detective fiction, sci-fi, fantasy
and horror. Editorial Director (Non-fiction)
Georgina Morley. *Publishes* serious and general
non-fiction: history, biography, science, sports
and games, film and theatre, travel, gardening
and cookery. IMPRINT **Tor**.

Picador (FOUNDED 1972) Publisher *Andrew
Kidd*, Senior Editorial Director *Ursula Doyle*.
Publishes literary international fiction and non-
fiction.

Sidgwick & Jackson (FOUNDED 1908)
Publishes popular non-fiction in hardback and
trade paperback with strong personality or
marketable identity, from celebrity and showbusiness to music and inspirational books. Also
military history list.

Boxtree (FOUNDED 1986) *Publishes* media
tie-in titles, including TV, film, music and
Internet, plus entertainment licences, pop cul-
ture, humour and event-related books. TITLES
*Dilbert; James Bond; Purple Ronnie; Viz; Wallace
& Gromit; The Onion*.

Channel 4 Books (FOUNDED 1998)
Publishes books that stand on their own merits
and not just the 'book of the series'. TITLES *Sex
and the City; A Place in the Sun; Six Feet Under;
Time Team*.

Macmillan Children's Books (New Wharf
Road address) Managing Director *Kate Wilson*;
Fiction, Non-Fiction, Poetry *Sarah Davies*;
Picture Books and Gift Books *Suzanne
Carnell*; **Campbell Books** *Camilla Reid*.
IMPRINTS **Macmillan, Pan, Campbell Books,
Young Picador**. *Publishes* novels, board books,
picture books, non-fiction (illustrated and non-
illustrated), poetry and novelty books in paper-
back and hardback. No unsolicited material.

Royalties paid annually or twice-yearly
depending on contract.

Authors' Rating The sale of the *Grove
Dictionary of Music* to OUP was a shock to the

system but leaves Palgrave Macmillan (noted publisher of the year by the Booksellers Association) to concentrate on its core subjects – politics, economics and social studies. On the trade side, Pan Macmillan has a strong front list of bestsellers but there are fewer titles published at the lower end of the scale. The aim is to raise new authors to stardom. The children's list has done particularly well.

Made Simple Books
See **Elsevier Ltd**

Mainstream Publishing Co. (Edinburgh) Ltd
7 Albany Street, Edinburgh EH1 3UG
☎0131 557 2959 Fax 0131 556 8720
Email editorial@mainstreampublishing.com
Website www.mainstreampublishing.com

Directors *Bill Campbell, Peter MacKenzie*
Approx. Annual Turnover £2.75 million

Publishes art, autobiography/biography, current affairs, health, sport, history, illustrated and fine editions, photography, politics and world affairs, popular paperbacks. Over 80 titles a year. TITLES *War of the Windsors* Stephen Prior; *Milestones in Murder* Hugh Jordan; *Harry's Game* Harry Gregg. Ideas for books considered, but they should be preceded by a letter, synopsis and s.a.e. or return postage.
Royalties paid twice-yearly.

Authors' Rating Strong on originality, Mainstream makes an impact far beyond the Scottish border. Keen on finding authors who 'can develop with us'.

Management Books 2000 Ltd
Forge House, Limes Road, Kemble, Cirencester, Gloucestershire GL7 6AD
☎01285 771441 Fax 01285 771055
Email m.b.2000@virgin.net
Website www.mb2000.com

Publisher *James Alexander*
Approx. Annual Turnover £500,000

FOUNDED 1993 to develop a range of books for executives and managers working in the modern world of business. 'Essentially, the books are working books for working managers, practical and effective.' *Publishes* business, management, self-development and allied topics as well as sponsored titles. About 30 titles a year. Unsolicited mss, synopses and ideas for books welcome.

Manchester United Books
See **Carlton Publishing Group**

Manchester University Press
Oxford Road, Manchester M13 9NR
☎0161 275 2310 Fax 0161 274 3346
Email mup@man.ac.uk
Website www.manchesteruniversitypress.co.uk

Publisher/Chief Executive *David Rodgers*
Head of Editorial *Matthew Frost*
Approx. Annual Turnover £2 million

FOUNDED 1904. MUP is Britain's third largest university press, with a list marketed and sold worldwide. Remit consists of occasional trade publications but mainly A-level and undergraduate textbooks and research monographs. *Publishes* in the areas of: literature, TV, film, theatre and media, history and history of art, design, politics, economics and international law. About 120 titles a year.

DIVISIONS **Humanities** *Matthew Frost*; **History/Art History** *Alison Whittle*; **Politics and Law** *Tony Mason*. Unsolicited mss welcome.
Royalties paid annually.

George Mann Books
PO Box 22, Maidstone, Kent ME14 1AH
☎01622 759591 Fax 01622 209193

Chairman/Managing Director *George Mann*

FOUNDED 1972. *Publishes* original non-fiction and selected reprints. Not considering new fiction for publication. 'Will only consider and respond to authors who, in the present publishing climate, are prepared to support *some of the costs* of publication. Unsolicited material not accompanied by return postage will neither be read nor returned.'
Royalties paid annually.

Manson Publishing Ltd
73 Corringham Road, London NW11 7DL
☎020 8905 5150 Fax 020 8201 9233
Email manson@man-pub.demon.co.uk
Website www.manson-publishing.co.uk

Chairman/Managing Director *Michael Manson*

FOUNDED 1992. *Publishes* scientific, technical, medical and veterinary. 10 titles in 2002. No unsolicited mss; synopses and ideas will be considered.
Royalties paid twice-yearly.

Marston House
Marston House, Marston Magna, Yeovil, Somerset BA22 8DH
☎01935 851331 Fax 01935 851372

Email alphaimage@marstonhouse.ndo.co.uk

Managing Director/Editorial Head
Anthony Birks-Hay

FOUNDED 1989. Publishing imprint of book packager Alphabet & Image Ltd. *Publishes* fine art, architecture, ceramics. 4 titles a year.
Royalties paid twice-yearly, or flat fee in lieu of royalties.

Martin Books
See **Simon & Schuster UK Ltd**

Kenneth Mason Publications Ltd
The Book Barn, Westbourne, Emsworth, Hampshire PO10 8RS
☎01243 377977 Fax 01243 379136

Chairman Kenneth Mason
Managing Director Piers Mason
Approx. Annual Turnover £500,000

FOUNDED 1958. *Publishes* diet, health, fitness, nutrition and nautical. No fiction. About 15 titles a year. IMPRINTS **Boatswain Press**; **Research Disclosure**. Initial approach by letter with synopsis only.
Royalties paid twice-yearly in first year, annually thereafter.

Kevin Mayhew Publishers
Buxhall, Stowmarket, Suffolk IP14 3BW
☎01449 737978 Fax 01449 737834
Email info@kevinmayhewltd.com
Website www.kevinmayhewltd.com

Chairman Kevin Mayhew
Managing Director Gordon Carter
Commissioning Editors Kevin Mayhew, Jonathan Bugden
Approx. Annual Turnover £4 million

FOUNDED in 1976. One of the leading sacred music and Christian book publishers in the UK. *Publishes* religious titles – liturgy, sacramental, devotional, also children's books and school resources. Unsolicited synopses and mss welcome; telephone prior to sending material, please.
IMPRINT **Palm Tree Press** Kevin Mayhew Bible stories, colouring/activity and puzzle books for children.
Royalties paid annually.

Melrose Press Ltd
St Thomas Place, Ely, Cambridgeshire CB7 4GG
☎01353 646600 Fax 01353 646601
Email tradesales@melrosepress.co.uk
Website www.melrosepress.co.uk

Chairman Richard A. Kay
Managing Director Nicholas S. Law
Approx. Annual Turnover £2 million

FOUNDED 1960. Took on its present name in 1969. *Publishes* biographical who's who reference only (not including *Who's Who*, which is published by **A.&C. Black**).

Mentor
See **Christian Focus Publications**

Mercat Press Ltd
10 Coates Crescent, Edinburgh EH3 7AL
☎0131 225 5324 Fax 0131 226 6632
Email enquiries@mercatpress.com
Website www.mercatpress.com

Directors Seán Costello, Tom Johnstone

The Press was FOUNDED in 1971 as an adjunct to former Scottish bookselling chain James Thin, becoming independent in 2002 following the collapse of the parent company. It began by publishing reprints of classic Scottish literature but now produces a wide range of new non-fiction titles. In 1992 the company acquired the bulk of the stock of Aberdeen University Press and the backlist expanded greatly as a result. In 1999 it took over some 60 titles from the Stationery Office's Scottish heritage list. New titles are added regularly. *Publishes* Scottish classics reprints and non-fiction of Scottish interest. This includes walking guides and historical and literary books. TITLES *A Sense of Belonging to Scotland* Andy Hall; *The Three Chimneys: Recipes and Reflections* Shirley Spear; *West Highland Way, Official Guide* Bob Aitken and Roger Smith; *25 Walks* series; *Jessie's Journey: Autobiography of a Traveller Girl* Jess Smith; *McLevy: The Edinburgh Detective* James McLevy. Unsolicited synopses of non-fiction Scottish interest books, preferably with sample chapters, are welcome. No new fiction or poetry.
Royalties paid annually.

The Merlin Press Ltd
PO Box 30705, London WC2E 8QD
☎020 7836 3020 Fax 020 7497 0309
Email info@merlinpress.co.uk
Website www.merlinpress.co.uk

Managing Director Anthony W. Zurbrugg

FOUNDED 1956. *Publishes* economics, history, philosophy, left-wing politics. No fiction. IMPRINTS **Merlin Press**; **Green Print**. TITLES *Socialist Register* (annual); *Ralph Miliband and the Politics of the New Left*; *Pit Women*. About 10 titles a year.
Royalties paid twice-yearly.

Merrell Publishers Ltd
42 Southwark Street, London SE1 1UN
☎020 7403 2047 Fax 020 7407 1333
Email mail@merrellpublishers.com
Website www.merrellpublishers.com
Managing Director *Hugh Merrell*
Approx. Annual Turnover £1.6 million
FOUNDED 1993. *Publishes* art, architecture,
design and photography. 24 titles in 2002. Un-
solicited synopses and ideas for books welcome.
Send c.v. and synopsis giving details of the
book's target markets and funding of illustrations.
   Royalties paid annually.

Methodist Publishing House
4 John Wesley Road, Werrington,
Peterborough, Cambridgeshire PE4 6ZP
☎01733 325002 Fax 01733 384180
Website www.mph.org.uk
Chair *Dudley Coates*
Chief Executive *Martin Stone*
Commissioning Editor *Natalie Stone*
Approx. Annual Turnover £2 million
FOUNDED 1800. Owned by the Methodist
Church. *Publishes* a wide range of books, mag-
azines and resources. Approx 20 titles a year.
Also *Flame* bi-monthly magazine. IMPRINTS
Epworth Press (see entry); **Foundery Press**
Unsolicited mss, synopses and ideas welcome;
send sample chapter and contents with cover-
ing letter.
   Royalties paid twice-yearly.

Methuen Publishing Ltd
215 Vauxhall Bridge Road, London
SW1V 1EJ
☎020 7798 1600 Fax 020 7233 9827
Email <name>@methuen.co.uk
Website www.methuen.co.uk
Managing Director *Peter Tummons*
Publishing Director *Max Eilenberg*
FOUNDED 1889. Methuen was owned by Reed
International until it was bought by Random
House in 1997 and then by a management buy-
out team in 1998. Acquired **Politico's
Publishing** in 2003. *Publishes* fiction and non-
fiction; travel, sport, drama, film, performing
arts, humour. DIVISIONS **General**; **Drama**;
Film; **Theatre**. No unsolicited mss; synopses
and ideas welcome. Prefers to be approached via
agents or a letter of inquiry. No first novels,
cookery books, personal memoirs.
   Royalties paid twice-yearly.

Metro Publishing
See **John Blake Publishing Ltd**

Michelin Travel Publications
Hannay House, 39 Clarendon Road, Watford,
Hertfordshire WD17 1JA
☎01923 205240 Fax 01923 205241
Website www.Viamichelin.co.uk
FOUNDED 1900 as a travel publisher. *Publishes*
travel guides, maps and atlases, children's I-Spy
books. 10 titles in 2002. Travel-related synopses and ideas welcome; no mss.

**Midland Publishing – An imprint
of Ian Allan Publishing Ltd**
4 Watling Drive, Hinckley, Leicestershire
LE10 3EY
☎01455 255490 Fax 01455 255495
Email midlandbooks@compuserve.com
Publisher *N.P. Lewis*
Publishes aviation, military and railways. No
wartime memoirs. No unsolicited mss; synopses and ideas welcome.
   Royalties paid quarterly.

Milet Publishing Limited
6 North End Parade, London W14 0SJ
☎020 7603 5477 Fax 020 7610 5475
Email info@milet.com
Website www.milet.com
Managing Directors *Sedat Turhan, Patricia
Billings*
FOUNDED 1995. *Publishes* children's picture
books in English and dual language; world litera-
ture for adults and language books. DIVISIONS
Children's, **English**; **Children's**, **Dual
Language** *Patricia Billings* TITLES *Pink Lemon;
I'm Afraid Too!* **World Literature**; **Language
Books** *Sedat Turhan* TITLE *Milet Picture
Dictionary*. Welcomes synopses and ideas for
books. Send proposal, outline or synopsis with
sample text and/or artwork, by post. 'Please
review existing titles on our website before submitting. We like bold, original stories and
artwork, universal and/or multicultural.'
   Royalties paid twice-yearly.

Harvey Miller Publishers
See **Brepols Publishers**

Miller's
See **Octopus Publishing Group**

Millivres Prowler Limited
Spectrum House, 32–34 Gordon House
Road, London NW5 1LP
☎020 7424 7400 Fax 020 7424 7401
Website www.gaymenspress.co.uk *or*

www.divamag.co.uk

Publisher (Books) *Helen Sandler*

Publishes about 24 titles of lesbian or gay interest each year as well as *Gay Times* and *Diva* magazines. IMPRINTS **Diva Books** Commissioning Editor *Helen Sandler* Literary and genre fiction and non-fiction with a lesbian slant. TITLES *The Ropemaker's Daughter* Virginia Smith; *Absent Kisses* Frances Gapper. Send first three chapters and synopsis with covering letter and s.a.e. No e-mail submissions. **GMP (Gay Men's Press)** Submission details as for Diva Books. TITLES *The Lodger* Drew Gummerson; *Bend Sinister* ed. Peter Burton. **Zipper Books; Red Hot Diva** Commissioning Editor *Kathleen Bryson* Explicit gay male and lesbian erotica, respectively. TITLES *The Masters File* Jack Dickinson; *Cherry* Charlotte Cooper. Contact commissioning editor for guidelines before sending material.

Mills & Boon
See **Harlequin Mills & Boon Ltd**

Mindfield
See **Camden Press Ltd**

MIRA
See **Harlequin Mills & Boon Ltd**

Mitchell Beazley
See **Octopus Publishing Group**

Mobius
See **Hodder Headline Ltd**

Modern English Publishing
32–34 Great Peter Street, London SW1P 2DB
☎020 7222 1155 Fax 020 7222 1551
Email info@esterbrooke.com

Director *Simon Collin*

FOUNDED 2002. *Publishes* books and magazines for teachers of English as a foreign language. About 10 titles a year.

Royalties paid twice-yearly.

Mojo Books
See **Canongate Books Ltd**

Monarch Books
Concorde House, Grenville Place, London NW7 3SA
☎020 8959 3668 Fax 020 8959 3678
Email monarch@angushudson.com

Editorial Director *Tony Collins*

An imprint of **Angus Hudson Ltd** (see entry under **UK Packagers**). *Publishes* an independent list of Christian books across a wide range of concerns. About 40 titles a year. IMPRINT **Monarch** Upmarket paperback list with Christian basis and strong social concern agenda including psychology, future studies, politics, mission, theology, leadership and spirituality. Unsolicited mss, synopses and ideas welcome.

Morgan Kauffman
See **Elsevier Ltd**

Morgan Publishing
See **Ashley Drake Publishing Ltd**

Mosby
See **Elsevier Ltd**

Motor Racing Publications
PO Box 1318, Croydon, Surrey CR9 5YP
☎020 8654 2711 Fax 020 8407 0339
Email mrp.books@virgin.net
Website www.motorracingpublications.co.uk

Chairman/Editorial Head *John Blunsden*

FOUNDED soon after the end of World War II to concentrate on motor-racing titles. Fairly dormant in the mid 1960s but was reactivated in 1968 by a new shareholding structure. John Blunsden later acquired a majority share and major expansion followed in the 1970s. About 6–8 titles a year. *Publishes* motor-sport history, classic and performance car collection and restoration, race track and off-road driving and related subjects.

IMPRINTS **Fitzjames Press; Motor Racing Publications** No unsolicited mss. Send synopses and ideas in specified subject areas in the first instance.

Royalties paid twice-yearly.

Mr Educator Handbooks
See **Studymates Limited**

Multi-Sensory Learning Ltd
Highgate House, Groom's Lane, Creaton, Northampton NN6 8NN
☎01604 505000 Fax 01604 505001
Email info@msl-online.net
Website www.msl-online.net

Senior Editor *Philippa Attwood*

Publishes materials and books related to dyslexia; the multi-sensory learning course for dyslexic pupils needing literacy skills development, plus numerous other items on assessment, reading, maths, music, etc. for dyslexics. Keen to locate authors able to write materials for dyslexic people and for teachers of dyslexics.

Murdoch Books UK Ltd
Ferry House, 51–57 Lacy Road, London
SW15 1PR
☎020 8355 1480 Fax 020 8355 1499
CEO *Amanda Roberts*
Publisher *Kay Scarlett*
Approx. Annual Turnover £6 million

Owned by Australian media group Murdoch
Magazines Pty Ltd. *Publishes* full-colour non-
fiction: homes and interiors, gardening, cookery, craft, cake decorating and DIY. About 46
titles a year. Synopses and ideas for books welcome; no unsolicited mss.
Royalties paid twice-yearly.

John Murray (Publishers) Ltd
338 Euston Road, London NW1 3BH
☎020 7873 6000 Fax 020 7873 6024
Website www.madaboutbooks.com
Managing Director *Roland Philipps*
FOUNDED 1768. Acquired by **Hodder
Headline** in May 2002. *Publishes* general trade
books. **Non-fiction** *Gordon Wise*; **Fiction**
Anya Serota. No unsolicited material; send pre-
liminary letter.
Royalties paid twice-yearly.

Authors' Rating Having sold out to Hodder
Headline, this august publisher has been given
an overdue shakeup. Though it is too early to
judge whether editorial policy will meet the
demands of more energetic marketing, bright
ideas are welcomed.

NAG Press Ltd
See **Robert Hale Ltd**

The National Archives
The National Archives, Kew, Surrey
TW9 4DU
☎020 8392 5271 Fax 020 8392 5266
Email jane.crompton@pro.gov.uk
Website www.nationalarchives.gov.uk
Publishing Manager *Jane Crompton*
Publishes books, guides and document packs
relating to the thousand years of historical
records held in The National Archives.
Specialist areas: family history, military history
and general history. TITLES *English Monarchs –
Treasures from The National Archives*; *The
Genealogists Internet* Peter Christian; *Lord Haw
Haw* Peter Martland; *Shot Down & On the Run*
Graham Pitchfork; *Elizabeth I: The Golden Age
of Glorianna* David Loades. Also publishes
Ancestors, a bi-monthly subscription magazine
of family history.

National Trust Publications
36 Queen Anne's Gate, London SW1H 9AS
☎020 7222 9251 Fax 020 7222 5097
Website www.nationaltrust.org.uk
Chairman *Charles Nunneley*
Director-General *Fiona Reynolds*
Publisher *Margaret Willes*

Publishing arm of The National Trust, FOUNDED
in 1895 by Robert Hunter, Octavia Hill and
Hardwicke Rawnsley to protect and conserve
places of historic interest and beauty. *Publishes*
gardening, cookery, handbooks, social history,
architecture, general interest and children's
books. TITLES *Literary Trails; The Art of Dress;
Flora Domestica; Living In Style; Vegetarian Recipes*.
No unsolicited material.
Royalties paid twice-yearly.

Nautical Data Ltd
The Book Barn, Westbourne, Emsworth,
Hampshire PO10 8RS
☎01243 389352 Fax 01243 379136
Email info@nauticaldata.com
Website www.nauticaldata.com
Managing Director *Piers Mason*
Approx. Annual Turnover £750,000

FOUNDED 1999. *Publishes* nautical almanacs,
pilots and nautical reference. 23 titles in 2002.
No unsolicited mss; synopses and ideas welcome. No fiction or non–nautical themes.
Royalties paid twice-yearly.

NCVO Publications
Regent's Wharf, 8 All Saints Street, London
N1 9RL
☎020 7713 6161 Fax 020 7713 6300
Website www.ncvo-vol.org.uk
Head of Marketing & Communications
Diane Lightfoot
Approx. Annual Turnover £140,000

FOUNDED 1928. Publishing imprint of the
National Council for Voluntary Organisations,
embracing former Bedford Square Press titles and
NCVO's many other publications. The list
reflects NCVO's role as the representative body
for the voluntary sector. *Publishes* directories,
good practice information on management and
trustee development, finance and employment
titles and information of primary interest to the
voluntary sector. TITLES *The Voluntary Agencies
Directory; The Good Trustee Guide; The Good
Campaigns Guide; The Good Financial Management
Guide; The Good Employment Guide; The Good
Management Guide; The Good Governance Action
Plan and The UK Voluntary Sector Almanac*. No

unsolicited mss as all projects are commissioned in-house.

Thomas Nelson & Sons Ltd
See **Nelson Thornes Limited**

Nelson Thornes Limited
Delta Place, 27 Bath Road, Cheltenham, Gloucestershire GL53 7TH
☎01242 267100 Fax 01242 221914
Email cservices@nelsonthornes.com
Website www.nelsonthornes.com

Managing Director *Oliver Gadsby*

FOUNDED in 2000 following the merger of Stanley Thornes (Publishers) Ltd and Thomas Nelson & Sons Ltd. Part of the Wolters Kluwer Group of companies. Educational publisher of printed and electronic product, from pre-school to Higher Education. Unsolicited mss, synopses and ideas for books welcome if appropriate to specialised lists.
Royalties paid annually.

Authors' Rating The second largest education publisher in the UK after Pearson, Nelson Thornes does best in health and science where it is helped by the dominant position in the market of its parent company, Wolters Kluwer.

New Beacon Books Ltd
76 Stroud Green Road, London N4 3EN
☎020 7272 4889 Fax 020 7281 4662

Chairman *John La Rose*
Managing Director *Sarah White*
Approx. Annual Turnover £120,000

FOUNDED 1966. *Publishes* fiction, history, politics, poetry and language, all concerning black people. No unsolicited material.
Royalties paid annually.

New Editions
See **Gibson Square Books Ltd**

New English Library
See **Hodder Headline Ltd**

New Holland Publishers (UK) Ltd
Garfield House, 86–88 Edgware Road, London W2 2EA
☎020 7724 7773
Fax 020 7258 1293 (editorial)
Email postmaster@nhpub.co.uk
Website www.newhollandpublishers.com

Managing Director *John Beaufoy*
Publishing Managers *Rosemary Wilkinson, Jo Hemmings*

Approx. Annual Turnover £6 million

FOUNDED 1956. Relaunched in 1987 as a publisher of illustrated books for the international market. In 1993, NH acquired Charles Letts Publishing Division list and four years later the then parent company (New Holland Struik Group, South Africa) acquired Southern Book Publishers, while their sister company (New Holland Australia) acquired the natural history and lifestyle divisions of Reed Australia. With its HQ in London, New Holland Publishers (UK) Ltd has now become the International Publishing Division of Johnnic Communications, one of Africa's leading publishing groups. NHP also has offices in Australia and New Zealand. *Publishes* non-fiction, practical and inspirational books in categories including cookery and food, crafts, DIY, fishing, gardening, interior design, mind, body and spirit, natural history, indoor and outdoor sports, travel, travel guides and general books. No unsolicited mss; synopses and ideas welcome.

Newnes
See **Elsevier Ltd**

Nexus
See **Virgin Books Ltd**

NFER-Nelson Publishing Co. Ltd
The Chiswick Centre, 414 Chiswick High Road, London W4 5TF
☎020 8996 8444 Fax 020 8996 3660
Website www.nfer-nelson.co.uk

General Manager *Tim Cornford*

FOUNDED 1981. Part of Granada Learning Ltd. *Publishes* educational and psychological tests and training materials. Main interest is in educational, clinical and occupational assessment and training material. Unsolicited mss welcome.
Royalties vary according to each contract.

Nia
See **The X Press**

Nightingale Books
See **Pegasus Elliot Mackenzie Publishers Ltd**

James Nisbet & Co. Ltd
Pirton Court, Prior's Hill, Pirton, Hitchin, Hertfordshire SG5 3QA
☎01462 713444 Fax 01462 713444

Chairman *E.M. Mackenzie-Wood*

FOUNDED 1810 as a religious publisher and

expanded into more general areas from around 1850 onwards. The first educational list appeared in 1926 but the company now concentrates on business studies with the education largely discontinued. About 5 titles a year. No fiction, leisure or religion. No unsolicited mss; synopses and ideas welcome.

Royalties paid twice-yearly.

NMS Publishing (a division of NMS Enterprises Ltd)

National Museums of Scotland, Chambers Street, Edinburgh EH1 1JF
☎0131 247 4026   Fax 0131 247 4012
Email l.taylor@nms.ac.uk
Website www.nms.ac.uk

Director *Lesley A. Taylor*
Approx. Annual Turnover £250,000

FOUNDED 1987 to *publish* non-fiction related to the National Museums of Scotland collections: academic and general; children's; archaeology, history, decorative arts worldwide, history of science, technology, natural history and geology, poetry. TITLES *John Logie Baird: a Life; Qianlong, A Great Emperor from the Forbidden City; Renaissance Decorative Painting in Scotland; Minerals of Scotland; William Spiers Bruce, Scottish Naturalist and Polar Explorer; Twa Tribes, Scots Among the Native Americans.* No unsolicited mss; only interested in synopses and ideas for books which are genuinely related to NMS collections and to Scotland in general.

Royalties paid twice-yearly.

No Exit Press
See **Oldcastle Books Ltd**

Nonesuch Press
See **Reinhardt Books Ltd**

North–Holland
See **Elsevier Ltd**

Northcote House Publishers Ltd

Horndon House, Horndon, Tavistock, Devon PL19 9NQ
☎01822 810066   Fax 01822 810034
Email northcote.house@virgin.net
Website www.northcotehouse.com

Managing Director *Brian Hulme*

FOUNDED 1985. *Publishes* a series of literary critical studies, in association with the British Council, *Writers and their Work*; education management, literary criticism, educational dance and drama. A new series of study aids for A-level students and undergraduates in English

literature is in preparation. 12 titles in 2002. 'Well-thought-out proposals, including contents and sample chapter(s), with strong marketing arguments welcome.'

Royalties paid annually.

W.W. Norton & Company Ltd

Castle House, 75–76 Wells Street, London W1T 3QT
☎020 7323 1579   Fax 020 7436 4553
Email office@wwnorton.co.uk

Managing Director *Alan Cameron*

Subsidiary of the US parent company FOUNDED in 1923. *Publishes* non-fiction and academic books.

Nottingham University Press

Manor Farm, Main Street, Thrumpton, Nottingham NG11 0AX
☎0115 983 1011   Fax 0115 983 1003
Email editor@nup.com
Website www.nup.com

Managing Editor *Dr D.J.A. Cole*
Approx. Annual Turnover £250,000

Initially concentrated on agricultural and food sciences titles but has now branched into new areas including engineering, lifesciences, medicine and law. TITLES *Global 2050; Lung Function Tests; Diet, Lipoproteins and Coronary Heart Disease; Nutrition of Sows and Boars; Writing and Presenting Scientific Papers.* **Castle Publications** TITLES *The Cricket Coach's Guide to Man Management; The Games Guide.*

Royalties paid twice-yearly.

O Books
See **John Hunt Publishing Ltd**

Oak
See **Omnibus Press**

Oberon Books

521 Caledonian Road, London N7 9RH
☎020 7607 3637   Fax 020 7607 3629
Email oberon.books@btinternet.com
Website www.oberonbooks.com

Publishing Director *James Hogan*
Managing Director *Charles D. Glanville*

A rapidly expanding company, Oberon *publishes* play texts (usually in conjunction with a production), theatre and dance books. *Specialises* in contemporary plays and translations of European classics. About 70 titles a year. IMPRINTS **Oberon Books; Absolute Classics.** Publishes over 300 writers and translators including Neil Bartlett, Richard Bean, Steven Berkoff, Ranjit

Bolt, John Bowen, Howard Brenton, Ken Campbell, Dario Fo, John Fosse, Pam Gems, Trevor Griffiths, Sir Peter Hall, Christopher Hampton, Giles Havergal, Rolf Hochhuth, Bernard Kops, Ash Kotak, Frederick Lonsdale, Adrian Mitchell, Stephen Mulrine, Meredith Oakes, John Osborne, Philip Osment, Julia Pascal, Michael Pennington, David Pownall, J.B. Priestley, Dennis Quilley, David Rudkin, Reza de Wet, John Whiting, Tennessee Williams. An extensive classics list included new translations of the complete works of Strindberg and recent performance (edited) versions of Shakespeare including *King Lear; Henry VIII; Romeo & Juliet; A Midsummer Night's Dream*. Also Chekhov, Molière, de Vega, etc.

Octagon Press Ltd
PO Box 227, London N6 4EW
☎020 8348 9392   Fax 020 8341 5971
Website www.octagonpress.com
Managing Director *George R. Schrager*
Approx. Annual Turnover £100,000

FOUNDED 1972. *Publishes* philosophy, psychology, travel, Eastern religion, translations of Eastern classics and research monographs in series. 4–5 titles a year. Unsolicited material not accepted. Enquiries in writing only.
Royalties paid annually.

Octopus Publishing Group
2–4 Heron Quays, London E14 4JP
☎020 7531 8400   Fax 020 7531 8650
Website www.octopus-publishing.co.uk
Chief Executive *Derek Freeman*
Approx. Annual Turnover £45 million (Group)

Formed following a management buyout of Reed Consumer Books from Reed Elsevier plc in 1998. Bought by French publishers Hachette-Livre in 2001 and acquired Cassell Illustrated and the lists of Ward Lock and Blandford Press.

Conran Octopus
Fax 020 7531 8627
Email info-co@conran-octopus.co.uk
Website www.conran-octopus.co.uk
Managing Director *Jane Aspden* Quality illustrated lifestyle books, particularly interiors, design, cookery, gardening and crafts TITLES *The Essential House Book* Terence Conran; *Fork to Fork* Monty Don; *Passion for Seafood* Gordon Ramsay; *New Retail* Rasshied Din.

Hamlyn Octopus
Email info-ho@hamlyn.co.uk

Website www.hamlyn.co.uk
Managing Director *Alison Goff* Popular non-fiction, particularly cookery, gardening, craft, sport, health, film and music TITLES *Larousse Gastronomique; Hamlyn All Colour Cookbook; Hamlyn Book of Gardening; Hamlyn Book of DIY & Decorating*.

Mitchell Beazley/Miller's
Fax 020 7537 0773
Email info-mb@mitchell-beazley.co.uk
Website www.mitchell-beazley.co.uk
Publisher/Managing Director *Jane Aspden* Quality illustrated reference books, particularly food and wine, gardening, interior design and architecture, antiques, general reference TITLES *Hugh Johnson's Pocket Wine Book; The New Joy of Sex; Miller's Antiques and Collectibles Price Guides*.

Philip's
Fax 020 7531 8460
Email george.philip@philips-maps.co.uk
Website www.philips-maps.co.uk
Managing Director *John Gaisford* World atlases, globes, astronomy, road atlases, encyclopaedias, thematic reference TITLES *Philip's Atlas of the World; Philip's Modern School Atlas; Philip's Guide to the Stars and Planets; Ordnance Survey Street Atlas; Philip's Millennium Encyclopaedia; Philip's Atlas of World History*.

Brimax
Fax 020 7531 8607
Email brimax@brimax.octopus.co.uk
Managing Director *Des Higgins* Mass-market board and picture books for children, age groups 1–10.

Bounty
Fax 020 7531 8607
Email bountybooksinfo-bp@bountybooks.co.uk
Managing Director *Alison Goff* Bargain and promotional books. New, repackaged and re-issued titles.

Cassell Illustrated
Fax 020 731 8624
Publishing Director *Polly Powell* Serious non-fiction covering a wide range of topics from history and cookery to fitness and art.

Digital Octopus
Fax 020 7537 0479
Contact *Derek Freeman* Digitally-formatted titles.

Octopus TV
Fax 020 7531 8469
Contact *Nick Salter* Television programmes from Octopus publications.
Royalties paid twice-yearly/annually, according to contract in all divisions.

Oldcastle Books Ltd

PO Box 394, Harpenden, Hertfordshire
AL5 1XJ
☎01582 761264   Fax 01582 761264
Email info@noexit.co.uk
Website www.noexit.co.uk *or*
  www.pocketessentials.com *or*
  www.highstakes.co.uk

Managing Director *Ion Mills*

FOUNDED 1985. *Publishes* crime/noir fiction, gambling non-fiction and 96pp mini-reference titles on film, ideas, history, music, etc. *No unsolicited mss.* Send synopses and ideas. IMPRINTS **No Exit Press** TITLES *Fierce Invalids Home from Hot Climates* Tom Robbins; *In the Hand of Dante* Nick Tosches; **High Stakes** TITLES *Fast Company* Jon Bradshaw; *Betting to Win* Prof Leighton V. Williams; **Pocketessentials** TITLES *Alfred Hitchcock; Vampire Films; Conspiracy Theories.*
Royalties paid annually.

Michael O'Mara Books Ltd

9 Lion Yard, Tremadoc Road, London
SW4 7NQ
☎020 7720 8643   Fax 020 7627 8953
Email <firstname.lastname>@
  michaelomarabooks.com
Website www.mombooks.com

Chairman *Michael O'Mara*
Managing Director *Lesley O'Mara*
Approx. Annual Turnover £5 million

FOUNDED 1985. Independent publisher. *Publishes* general non-fiction, royalty, history, humour, children's novelties, anthologies and reference. TITLES *Diana: Her True Story* Andrew Morton; *Eye of the Storm* Peter Ratcliffe; the 'Little Book' series, including *WAN2TLK?* IMPRINT **Buster Books** Children's titles. Unsolicited mss, synopses and ideas for books welcome.
Royalties paid twice-yearly.

Authors' Rating Master of the art of creating unlikely bestsellers. The text messaging bible, *WAN2TLK?*, which some thought a crazy idea, has sold more than a million copies. There is a welcome for bright ideas with gift appeal.

Omnibus Press

Music Sales Ltd, 8–9 Frith Street, London
W1D 3JB
☎020 7434 0066   Fax 020 7734 2246
Email chris.charlesworth@musicsales.co.uk
Website www.omnibuspress.com

Editorial Head *Chris Charlesworth*

FOUNDED 1971. Independent publisher of music books, rock and pop biographies, song sheets, educational tutors, cassettes, videos and software. A Division of the Music Sales Group of Companies.
  IMPRINTS **Amsco**; **Bobcat**; **Oak**; **Omnibus**; **Wise Publications**. Unsolicited mss, synopses and ideas for music-related titles welcome.
  Royalties paid twice-yearly.

Oneworld Publications

185 Banbury Road, Oxford OX2 7AR
☎01865 310597   Fax 01865 310598
Email info@oneworld-publications.com
Website www.oneworld-publications.com

Editorial Director *Juliet Mabey*

FOUNDED 1986. *Publishes* adult non-fiction across a range of subjects from world religions and social issues to psychology and philosophy. About 30 titles a year. SERIES include one on world religions (with authors such as Geoffrey Parrinder, Keith Ward, Klaus Klostermaier and John Hicks), concise encyclopedias on world religions and a series of short histories of countries. **Oneworld Philosophers** series was launched in 2001. TITLES *God: A Guide for the Perplexed* Keith Ward; *Palestine – Israeli Conflict: A Beginner's Guide.* No unsolicited mss; synopses and ideas welcome, but should be accompanied by s.a.e. for return of material and/or notification of receipt. No autobiographies, fiction, poetry or children's.
  Royalties paid annually.

Onlywomen Press Ltd

40 St Lawrence Terrace, London W10 5ST
☎020 8354 0796   Fax 020 8960 2817
Email onlywomenpress@aol.com
Website www.onlywomenpress.com

Editorial Director *Lilian Mohin*

FOUNDED 1974. *Publishes* feminist lesbian literature: fiction, poetry, literary criticism and political theory. Unsolicited mss and proposals welcome. Submissions must be accompanied by s.a.e. and explanatory letter.

OPC
See **Ian Allan Publishing Ltd**

Open Gate Press (incorporating Centaur Press 1954)

51 Achilles Road, London NW6 1DZ
☎020 7431 4391   Fax 020 7431 5129
Email books@opengatepress.co.uk

Managing Directors *Jeannie Cohen, Elisabeth Petersdorff*

FOUNDED in 1989 to provide a forum for psychoanalytic social and cultural studies. *Publishes*
psychoanalysis, philosophy, social sciences,
politics, literature, religion, animal rights, environment. SERIES *Psychoanalysis and Society.* Also
publishes a journal of psychoanalytic social
studies, *New Analysis.* IMPRINTS **Open Gate
Press**; **Centaur Press**; **Linden Press**. Since
the acquisition of Centaur Press, Open Gate
Press is continuing its work, in particular the
Kinship Library – a series on the philosophy,
politics and application of humane education.
No unsolicited mss.

Royalties paid twice-yearly.

Open University Press
McGraw-Hill House, Shoppenhangers Road,
Maidenhead, Berkshire SL6 2QL
☎01628 502500 Fax 01628 770224
Email enquiries@openup.co.uk
Website www.openup.co.uk
Managing Director *Simon Allen*
Approx. Annual Turnover £3 million

FOUNDED 1977 as an imprint independent of
the Open University's course materials.
Acquired by **McGraw Hill Education** in
2002. *Publishes* academic and professional
books in the fields of education, sociology,
health, psychology, women's studies, counselling, Higher Education. No economics or
anthropology. Not interested in anything outside the social sciences. About 100 titles a year.
No unsolicited mss; enquiries/proposals only.

Royalties paid annually.

Orbit
See **Time Warner Books UK**

Orchard Books
See **The Watts Publishing Group Ltd**

The Orion Publishing Group Limited
Orion House, 5 Upper St Martin's Lane,
London WC2H 9EA
☎020 7240 3444 Fax 020 7240 4822
Website www.orionbooks.co.uk/pub/
  index.htm
Chairman *Jean-Louis Lisimachio*
Chief Executive *Anthony Cheetham*
Group Managing Director *Peter Roche*
Approx. Annual Turnover £65 million

FOUNDED 1992 by Anthony Cheetham,
Rosemary Cheetham and Peter Roche.
Incorporates Weidenfeld & Nicolson, JM
Dent, Chapmans Publishers and Cassell.

DIVISIONS
Orion Managing Director *Malcolm Edwards*
IMPRINTS **Orion Fiction** Publishing Director
Jane Wood Hardcover fiction; **Orion Media**
Publishing Director *Trevor Dolby* Hardcover
non-fiction; **Orion Children's** Publisher
Fiona Kennedy Children's fiction/non-fiction;
Gollancz Editorial Directors *Simon Spanton, Jo
Fletcher* Science fiction and fantasy.
  Weidenfeld & Nicolson Managing
Director *To be appointed* IMPRINTS **Weidenfeld
Illustrated** Editor-in-Chief *Michael Dover*
Illustrated non-fiction; **Weidenfeld General**
Publishing Director *Richard Milner* General
non-fiction and literary fiction; **Phoenix Press**
Publishing Director *Ben Buchan* History;
Cassell Reference Publishing Director
Richard Milbank General reference; **Cassell
Military** Publishing Director *Ian Drury*
Military non-fiction; **Custom Publishing**
Managing Director *Mark Smith*.
Paperback Division Managing Director
Susan Lamb IMPRINTS **Orion**; **Phoenix**;
Everyman.

Authors' Rating Strong marketing and imaginative publishing leads to frequent appearances
for Orion titles in the bestseller lists.

Osprey Publishing Ltd
Elms Court, Chapel Way, Botley, Oxford
OX2 9LP
☎01865 727022 Fax 01865 727017/727019
Email info@ospreypublishing.com
Website www.ospreypublishing.com
Managing Director *William Shepherd*
Editor, Military History *Jane Penrose*
Editor, Aviation *Tony Holmes*

Publishes illustrated, military history and avia-
tion from around the world. FOUNDED 1969,
Osprey became independent from **Reed
Elsevier** in February 1998. 150 titles in 2002.
  MILITARY SERIES *Order of Battle; Men-at-
Arms; New Vanguard; Warrior; Fortress; Essential
Histories.* AVIATION SERIES *Aircraft of the Aces;
Combat Aircraft; Aviation Pioneers; Aviation Elite
Units.* No unsolicited mss; synopses and ideas
welcome.
  Royalties paid twice-yearly.

Peter Owen Ltd
73 Kenway Road, London SW5 0RE
☎020 7373 5628/7370 6093
Fax 020 7373 6760
Email admin@peterowen.com
Website www.peterowen.com
Chairman *Peter Owen*

Editorial Director *Antonia Owen*
FOUNDED 1951. *Publishes* biography, general
non-fiction, English-language literary fiction
and translations, history, literary criticism, the
arts. 'No genre or children's fiction; the company only rarely takes on first novels.'
AUTHORS Jane Bowles, Paul Bowles, Shusaku
Endo, Anna Kavan, Jean Giono, Anaïs Nin,
Jeremy Reed, Peter Vansittart. 35–40 titles a
year. Unsolicited synopses welcome for non-
fiction material; no highly illustrated books.
Please call in advance to admit fiction. Mss
should be preceded by a descriptive letter and
synopsis with s.a.e.
  Royalties paid twice-yearly. *Overseas associates*
worldwide.

Authors' Rating Peter Owen has been
described as 'a publisher of the old and idiosyncratic school'. He has seven Nobel prizewin-
ners on his list to prove it.

Oxford University Press
Great Clarendon Street, Oxford OX2 6DP
☎01865 556767 Fax 01865 556646
Email enquiry@oup.co.uk
Website www.oup.co.uk
Chief Executive *Henry Reece*
Approx. Annual Turnover £375 million
A department of Oxford University, OUP
started as the university's printing business and
developed into a major publishing operation in
the 19th century. *Publishes* academic works in
all formats (print and online): dictionaries, lexi-
cal and non-lexical reference, scholarly journals, student texts, schoolbooks, ELT materials,
music, bibles, paperbacks, and children's
books. Around 6000 titles a year.

DIVISIONS
Academic *I.S. Asquith* Academic and higher
education titles in major disciplines, dictionaries (acquired *The Grove Dictionary of Music* in
2003), non-lexical reference, journals and trade
books. OUP welcomes first-class academic
material in the form of proposals or accepted
theses.
  Education *K. Harris* National Curriculum
courses and support materials as well as children's literature.
  ELT *P.R. Mothersole* ELT courses and dictionaries for all levels.
  Royalties paid twice-yearly. *Overseas
branches/subsidiaries* Sister company in USA
with branches or subsidiaries in Argentina,
Australia, Brazil, Canada, China, East Africa,
India, Japan, Malaysia, Mexico, Pakistan,

Southern Africa, Spain and Turkey. Offices in
Chile, France, Greece, Italy, New Zealand,
Taiwan, Thailand and Uruguay.

Authors' Rating Increased investment in new
publishing includes the *New Dictionary of National
Biography*, one of the biggest projects of its kind
in contemporary publishing and, latterly, the
Grove Dictionary of Music, bought from
Macmillan. Following the acquisition of
Blackstone Press, OUP now rivals Butterworths
and Sweet & Maxwell as a leading law book
publisher. The ELT list continues to do well.

Palgrave Macmillan
See **Macmillan Publishers Ltd**

Palm Tree Press
See **Kevin Mayhew Publishers**

G.J. Palmer & Sons Ltd
See **Hymns Ancient & Modern Ltd**

Pan
See **Macmillan Publishers Ltd**

Paper Tiger
See **Chrysalis Books Group**

Paragon Large Print
See entry under **BBC Audiobooks**

Paragon Press Publishing/Paragon Summaries
See **Vista House Ltd**

Parthian
The Old Surgery, Napier Street, Aberteifi
(Cardigan) SA43 1ED
☎01239 612059 Fax 01239 612059
Email parthianbooks@yahoo.co.uk
Website www.parthianbooks.co.uk
Publisher *Richard Davies*
Fiction Editor *Gwen Davies*
Poetry Editor *Richard Gwyn*
FOUNDED 1993. *Publishes* contemporary Welsh
writing in English including novels, poetry and
drama, also translations from Welsh. Its list
includes many young writers. TITLES *In and
Out of the Goldfish Bowl* Rachel Trezise
(Winner of the Orange Futures Award); *Fuse*
Patrick Jones; *Diving Girls* Jo Mazelis (Winner
of the **Rhys Davies Trust** award); *Welsh Boys
Too* John Sam Jones (Winner of the American
Library Association Gay and Lesbian Honor

Book Award); *The Pterodactyl's Wing* poetry anthology edited by Richard Gwyn. Synopsis with first three sample chapters welcome. 'An idea of what we do is always an advantage.'

Royalties paid annually.

Paternoster Publishing

PO Box 300, Kingstown Broadway, Carlisle, Cumbria CA3 0QS
☎01228 554320 Fax 01228 593388
Website www.paternoster-publishing.com
Publishing Director *Mark Finnie*
Approx. Annual Turnover £2 million

A division of STL Ltd. IMPRINTS **Paternoster Press** FOUNDED 1936. Editorial Controller *Lucy Atherton Publishes* academic, religion and learned/church/life-related journals. Over 80 titles a year. TITLES *Complete Short Works of J.I. Packer; All's Well* R.T. Kendall. **Authentic Lifestyle** FOUNDED 1966. Editorial Controller *Nancy Lush Publishes* Christian books on evangelism, discipleship and mission. About 30 titles a year. TITLES *Operation World* Patrick Johnstone; publishing for Spring Harvest, Evangelical Alliance, Keswick Convention, Icthus, Operation Christmas Child. Unsolicited mss, synopses and ideas for books welcome.

Royalties paid twice-yearly.

Pavilion Books
See **Chrysalis Books Group**

Pavilion Children's Books
See **Chrysalis Children's Books**

Pearson Education

Edinburgh Gate, Harlow, Essex CM20 2JE
☎01279 623623 Fax 01279 431059
Website www.pearsoned-ema.com

The world's largest educational publisher was created by the merger of Addison Wesley Longman, Financial Times Management and **Simon & Schuster**'s educational list. *Publishes* across a wide range of curriculum subjects from primary students to professional practictioners. Unsolicited mss should be addressed to the appropriate department: **ELT** Lyn Kitteridge; **Schools** Chris Nott; **University and Professional level** Juliane Heinecke.

Royalties paid twice-yearly. *Overseas associates* worldwide.

Authors' Rating One of the world's largest educational publishers, Pearson must be grateful to books for making up the shortfall in press advertising.

Pegasus Elliot Mackenzie Publishers Ltd

Sheraton House, Castle Park, Cambridge CB3 0AX
☎01223 370012 Fax 01223 370040
Email editors@pegasuspublishers.com
Website www.pegasuspublishers.com
Senior Editor *D.W. Stern*
Editor *R. Sabir*

Publishes fiction and non-fiction, general interest, biography, autobiography, children's, history, humour, science fiction, poetry, travel, war, memoirs, crime and erotica, also Internet and e-books. IMPRINTS **Vanguard Press**; **Nightingale Books**; **Chimera** TITLES *Virgins are in Short Supply* Kevin Laffan; *And Hitler Stopped Play* George Cooper; *The Green Berets in Korea* Fred Hayhurst. Unsolicited mss, synopses and ideas considered if accompanied by return postage.

Royalties paid twice-yearly.

Authors' Rating Liable to ask authors to contribute to production costs.

Pen & Sword Books Ltd

47 Church Street, Barnsley, South Yorkshire S70 2AS
☎01226 734734 Fax 01226 734438
Email charles@pen-and-sword.co.uk
Website www.pen-and-sword.co.uk
Chairman *Sir Nicholas Hewitt*
Managing Director *Charles Hewitt*
Imprint Manager *Henry Wilson*

One of the leading military history publishers in the UK. *Publishes* non-fiction only, specialising in naval and aviation history, WW1, WW2, Napoleonic, autobiography and biography. Also publishes *Battleground* series for battlefield tourists. About 100 titles a year. IMPRINTS **Leo Cooper**; **Pen & Sword Aviation**; **Wharncliffe Publishing** (see entry). Unsolicited synopses and ideas welcome; no unsolicited mss.

Royalties paid twice-yearly.

Penguin Group (UK)

A Pearson Company, 80 Strand, London WC2R 0RL
☎020 7010 3000 Fax 020 7010 6060
Website www.penguin.co.uk
Group Chairman & Chief Executive *John Makinson*
CEO: Penguin UK, Dorling Kindersley Ltd *Anthony Forbes Watson*

Managing Director: Penguin *Helen Fraser*
Approx. Annual Turnover £121 million

Owned by Pearson plc. The world's best known book brand and for more than 60 years a leading publisher whose adult and children's lists include fiction, non-fiction, poetry, drama, classics, reference and special interest areas. Reprints and new work.

DIVISIONS
Penguin General Books Managing Director *Tom Weldon* Adult fiction and non-fiction is published in hardback under Michael Joseph, Viking and Hamish Hamilton imprints. Paperbacks come under the Penguin imprint. IMPRINTS **Viking/Penguin** Publisher *Juliet Annan* Publishing Director *Tony Lacey*; **Hamish Hamilton** Publishing Director *Simon Prosser*; **Michael Joseph/Penguin** Publishing Director *Louise Moore*. Does not accept unsolicited mss.

Penguin Press Managing Director *Stefan McGrath* Publishing Directors *Stuart Proffitt, Simon Winder* Academic adult non-fiction, reference, specialist and classics. IMPRINTS **Allen Lane**; **Penguin Reference** Publishing Director *Nigel Wilcockson*. No unsolicited mss.

Dorling Kindersley Ltd (see entry).

Frederick Warne Managing Director *Sally Floyer* Classic children's publishing and merchandising including *Beatrix Potter*™; *Flower Fairies*; *Orlando*. **Ventura** Publisher *Sally Floyer* Producer and packager of *Spot* titles by Eric Hill.

Ladybird (see **Dorling Kindersley Ltd**).

Puffin Managing Director *Francesca Dow* (poetry and picture books) Publishers *Rebecca McNally* (fiction), *Clare Hulton* (media and popular non-fiction). Leading children's paperback list, publishing in virtually all fields including fiction, non-fiction, poetry, picture books, media-related titles. No unsolicited mss; synopses and ideas welcome.

Penguin Audiobooks (see entry under **Audio Books**).

ePenguin Commissioning Editor *Jeremy Ettinghausen* e-books list launched in 2001.

Royalties paid twice-yearly. *Overseas associates* worldwide.

Authors' Rating After several years of acquisitions, Penguin is one of the world's biggest trade book publishers with an enviable list of bestsellers. Turning round Dorling Kindersley, the illustrated reference publisher, soaked up management and financial resources but Penguin is now well placed to exploit the next upswing in the market.

Peony Press
See **Anness Publishing Ltd**

PerfectBound
See **HarperCollins Publishers Ltd**

Pergamon
See **Elsevier Ltd**

Persephone Books
59 Lamb's Conduit Street, London
WC1N 3NB
☎020 7242 9292 Fax 020 7242 9272
Email sales@persephonebooks.co.uk
Website www.persephonebooks.co.uk
Managing Director *Nicola Beauman*

FOUNDED 1999. *Publishes* reprint fiction and non-fiction, mostly 'by women, for women and about women'. 8 titles a year. TITLES *Miss Pettigrew Lives for a Dog* Winifred Watson; *Kitchen Essays* Agnes Jekyll; *The Far Cry* Emma Smith; *The Priory* Dorothy Whipple. No unsolicited material.

Royalties paid twice-yearly

Petroc Press
See **Librapharm Ltd**

Phaidon Press Limited
Regent's Wharf, All Saints Street, London
N1 9PA
☎020 7843 1000 Fax 020 7843 1010
Email <name>@phaidon.com
Website www.phaidon.com
Chairman/Publisher *Richard Schlagman*
Managing Director *Andrew Price*
Deputy Publisher *Amanda Renshaw*
Editorial Director (New York) *Karen Stein*
Approx. Annual Turnover £21.2 million

Publishes quality books on the visual arts, including fine art, art history, architecture, design, photography, decorative arts, music and performing arts. Also produces videos. About 100 titles a year. DIVISIONS/SERIES (with Editorial Heads) **Architecture** *Ioan Baird*; **Design** *Emilia Terragni*; **Contemporary Art** *Gilda Williams*; **Photography** *Noel Daniel*; **Art and Academic** *Bernard Dod/David Anfan*. Unsolicited mss welcome but 'only a small amount of unsolicited material gets published'.

Royalties paid twice-yearly.

Authors' Rating Ah, those seductive art books. The quality of illustrations is superb and since language is a minor barrier to sales,

Phaidon is doing well on the Continent with subsidiaries in France and Germany.

Philip's
See **Octopus Publishing Group**

Phillimore & Co. Ltd
Shopwyke Manor Barn, Chichester, West Sussex PO20 2BG
☎01243 787636 Fax 01243 787639
Email bookshop@phillimore.co.uk
Website www.phillimore.co.uk
Chairman *Philip Harris*
Managing Director *Noel Osborne*
Approx. Annual Turnover £1.3 million

FOUNDED in 1897 by W.P.W. Phillimore, Victorian campaigner for local archive conservation in Chancery Lane, London. Became the country's leading publisher of historical source material and local histories. Somewhat dormant in the 1960s, it was revived by Philip Harris in 1968. *Publishes* British local and family history, including histories of institutions, buildings, villages, towns and counties, plus guides to research and writing in these fields. About 70 titles a year. No unsolicited mss; synopses/ideas welcome for local or family histories.
IMPRINT **Phillimore** *Noel Osborne* TITLES *Domesday Book; A History of Essex; Carlisle; The Haberdashers' Company; Channel Island Churches; Bolton Past; Warwickshire Country Houses.*
Royalties paid annually.

Phoenix Press
See **The Orion Publishing Group Ltd**

Piatkus Books
5 Windmill Street, London W1T 2JA
☎020 7631 0710 Fax 020 7436 7137
Email info@piatkus.co.uk
Website www.piatkus.co.uk
Managing Director *Judy Piatkus*
Approx. Annual Turnover £5.8 million

FOUNDED 1979 by Judy Piatkus. The company is customer-led and is committed to publishing fiction, both commercial and literary, and a wide range of non-fiction. *Specialises* in publishing books and authors 'who we feel enthusiastic and committed to as we like to build for long-term success as well as short-term!' *Publishes* fiction, biography and autobiography, history, popular culture, health, mind, body and spirit, popular psychology, self-help, history, science, business and management, cookery 'and other books that tempt us'. In 1996 launched a list of mass-market non-fiction and fiction titles. About 175 titles a

year (70 of which are fiction). Non-fiction general books IMPRINT **Portrait** launched autumn 2003.

DIVISIONS
Non-fiction *Judy Piatkus* TITLES *Optimum Nutrition for the Mind* Patrick Holford; *One Last Time* John Edwards; *10 Day MBA* Steven Silbiger; *How to Make Money from Your Property* Fiona Fullerton. **Fiction** *Gillian Green* TITLES *Chesapeake Blue* Nora Roberts; *The Dive from Clausen's Pier* Ann Packer; *Tricky Business* Dave Barry; *Twisted Minds* Hilary Norman. Piatkus is expanding its range of books and welcomes synopses and first three chapters.
Royalties paid twice-yearly.

Authors' Rating A thriving independent publisher takes another leap forward with Portrait, a new non-fiction list for 'popular culture, history, memoirs and sport'. Also strong on women's fiction.

Pica Press
See **A.&C. Black (Publishers) Ltd**

Picador/Young Picador
See **Macmillan Publishers Ltd**

Piccadilly Press
5 Castle Road, London NW1 8PR
☎020 7267 4492 Fax 020 7267 4493
Email books@piccadillypress.co.uk
Website www.piccadillypress.co.uk
Publisher/Managing Director *Brenda Gardner*
Approx. Annual Turnover £1.4 million

FOUNDED 1983. Independent publisher of children's and parental books. 28 titles in 2002. Welcomes approaches from authors 'but we would like them to know the sort of books we do. It is frustrating to get inappropriate material. They should check in their local libraries, bookshops or look at our website. We will send a catalogue (please enclose s.a.e.).' No adult or cartoon-type material.
Royalties paid twice-yearly.

Pictorial Presentations
See **Souvenir Press Ltd**

Pimlico
See **Random House Group Ltd**

Pitkin
See **Jarrold Publishing**

Plenum Publishers/Plenum Press
See **Kluwer Academic/Plenum Publishers**

Pluto Press Ltd
345 Archway Road, London N6 5AA
☎020 8348 2724 Fax 020 8348 9133
Email pluto@plutobooks.com
Website www.plutobooks.com
Managing Director *Roger Van Zwanenberg*
Publishing Director *Anne Beech*
FOUNDED 1970. Has developed a reputation
for innovatory publishing in the field of non-
fiction. *Publishes* academic and scholarly books
across a range of subjects including cultural
studies, politics and world affairs and more
general titles on key aspects of currrent affairs.
About 70 titles a year. Prospective authors are
encouraged to consult the website for guidelines on submitting proposals.

Pocket Books
See **Simon & Schuster UK Limited**

Pocketessentials
See **Oldcastle Books Ltd**

Point
See **Scholastic Ltd**

The Policy Press
Fourth Floor, Beacon House, Queen's Road,
Bristol BS8 1QU
☎0117 331 4054 Fax 0117 331 4093
Email tpp-info@bristol.ac.uk
Website www.policypress.org.uk
Managing Director *Alison Shaw*
Publishes policy studies work of regional, national
and international interest, in a variety of forms,
appropriate to differing policy audiences. The
Press publishes academic books, research mono-
graphs, student texts, readers, academic and prac-
titioner journals, research reports, practice guides
and general books on social issues.

Politico's Publishing
8 Artillery Row, London SW1P 1RZ
☎020 7931 0090 Fax 020 7828 8111
Email publishing@politicos.co.uk
Website www.politicos.co.uk/publishing
Chairman *John Simmons*
Managing Director *Iain Dale*
Publishing Director *Sean Magee*
Approx. Annual Turnover £325,000
FOUNDED 1998. Sister company to Politico's
Bookstore in Westminster. Acquired by
Methuen Publishing Ltd in April 2003.
Publishes political books. 25 titles in 2002.
TITLES *In My Own Time* Jeremy Thorpe; *Cherie*

Blair Linda McDougall; *Brief Encounters* Gyles
Brandreth. Unsolicited mss, synopses and ideas
welcome; telephone in the first instance.
Royalties paid annually.

Polity Press
65 Bridge Street, Cambridge CB2 1UR
☎01223 324315 Fax 01223 461385
Website www.polity.co.uk
FOUNDED 1984. All books are published in association with **Blackwell Publishers**. *Publishes*
archaeology and anthropology, criminology,
economics, feminism, general interest, history,
human geography, literature, media and cultural
studies, medicine and society, philosophy, politics, psychology, religion and theology, social
and political theory, sociology. Unsolicited synopses and ideas for books welcome.
Royalties paid annually.

Polygon/Polygon@Edinburgh
See **Birlinn Ltd**

Pont Books
See **Gomer Press**

Pop Universal
See **Souvenir Press Ltd**

Portland Press Ltd
59 Portland Place, London W1B 1QW
☎020 7637 5873 Fax 020 7323 1136
Email editorial@portlandpress.com
Website www.portlandpress.com
Chairman *Professor A.J. Turner*
Managing Director *Rhonda Oliver*
Managing Editor *Pauline Starley*
Approx. Annual Turnover £2.5 million
FOUNDED 1990 to expand the publishing activities of the Biochemical Society (1911). *Publishes*
biochemisty and medicine for graduate, postgraduate and research students. Expanding the
list to include schools and general readership. 5
titles in 2002. TITLES *Neuronal Signal Transduction
and Alzheimer's Disease; Virtual University?;
Educational Environments for the Future.* Unsolicited mss, synopses and ideas welcome. No fiction.
Royalties paid twice-yearly.

Portrait
See **Piatkus Books**

Prestel Publishing Limited
4 Bloomsbury Place, London WC1A 2QA
☎020 7323 5004 Fax 020 7636 8004

Email sales@prestel-uk.co.uk
Website www.prestel.com
Chairman *Jürgen Tesch*
FOUNDED 1924. *Publishes* art, architecture, photography, children's and general illustrated books. No fiction. Lead TITLES in 2002: *Blow Up: Inflatable Art, Architecture and Design; The Poetic Museum: Reviving Historic Collections; Gustav Klimt: Landscapes; African Masks; Xtreme Houses; Bridges that Changed the World*. Unsolicited mss, synopses and ideas welcome. Approach by post or e-mail.

Princeton University Press
See **University Presses of California, Columbia & Princeton Ltd**

Prion Books Ltd
Imperial Works, Perren Street, London NW5 3ED
☎020 7482 4248 Fax 020 7482 4203
Managing Director *Barry Winkleman*
Formerly a packaging operation but began publishing under the Prion imprint in 1987. Acquired by **Carlton Publishing Group** in February 2003. *Publishes* non-fiction: humour, popular culture, historical and literary reprints, beauty, food and drink, sex, psychology and health. About 40 titles a year. Synopses and ideas welcome only with s.a.e. and *not* by e-mail.
Royalties paid twice-yearly.

Authors' Rating A brave small publisher justly famed for its humour list. At the time of writing there is talk of a possible merger to strengthen its position in the market place.

Profile Books
58A Hatton Gardens, London EC1N 8LX
☎020 7404 3001 Fax 020 7404 3003
Email info@profilebooks.co.uk
Website www.profilebooks.co.uk
Managing Director *Andrew Franklin*
Approx. Annual Turnover £2.6 million
FOUNDED 1996. *Publishes* serious non-fiction including current affairs, history, politics, psychology, cultural criticism, business management and economics. Winner of the **Sunday Times Small Publisher of the Year Award** 1999/2000. AUTHORS include Alan Bennett, J.M. Coetzee, Francis Fukuyama and Peter Nichols.
  IMPRINTS **Profile Books** *Andrew Franklin*; **Economist Books** *Stephen Brough*. No unsolicited mss.
Royalties paid twice-yearly.

Authors' Rating Noted for author-friendly relations. Profile is now big in business books having bought the HarperCollins business list.

ProQuest Information and Learning Ltd
The Quorum, Barnwell Road, Cambridge CB5 8SW
☎01223 215512 Fax 01223 215513
Website www.proquest.co.uk
General Manager *Steven Hall*
Part of US company, ProQuest Information and Learning, the new name for Bell & Howell. *Publishes* humanities and literary databases on the Web, CD-ROM and microform. IMPRINT **Chadwyck-Healey**. TITLES *KnowUK; Literature Online; The English Poetry Database; Periodicals Contents Index; KnowEurope*. No unsolicited mss. Synopses and ideas welcome for reference works only.
  Royalties paid annually.

Psychology Press
See **Taylor & Francis Group plc**

Publishing House
Trinity Place, Barnstaple, Devon EX32 9HJ
☎01271 328892 Fax 01271 328768
Email publishinghouse@vernoncoleman.com
Website www.vernoncoleman.com
Managing Director *Vernon Coleman*
Publishing Director *Sue Ward*
Approx. Annual Turnover £750,000
FOUNDED 1989. Self-publisher of fiction, health, humour, animals, politics. Over 60 books published. TITLES *Mrs Caldicot's Cabbage War; England our England; Bodypower; Bilbury Chronicles; Second Innings; It's Never Too Late; How to Publish Your Own Book* all by Vernon Coleman. No submissions.

Puffin
See **Penguin Group (UK)**

Pushkin Press Ltd
123 Biddulph Mansions, Elgin Avenue, London W9 1HU
☎020 7266 9136 Fax 020 7266 9136
Email petra@pushkinpress.com
Website www.pushkinpress.com
Chairman *Melissa Ulfane*
Editorial Head *Petra Howard-Wuerz*
Approx. Annual Turnover £250,000
Publishes novels and essays in translation drawn

from the best of classic and contemporary European literature.

Royalties paid twice-yearly.

Authors' Rating English language writers who are short on ideas might do worse than raid this select list of translated European works for something fresh to say. A bold and imaginative venture.

Putnam Aeronautical Books
See **Chrysalis Books Group**

Quadrille Publishing Ltd
Alhambra House, 27–31 Charing Cross Road, London WC2H 0LS
☎020 7839 7117 Fax 020 7839 7118
Chairman *Sir David Cooksey*
Managing Director *Alison Cathie*
Editorial Director *Jane O'Shea*
FOUNDED in 1994 by four ex-directors of Conran Octopus, with a view to producing a small list of top-quality illustrated books. *Publishes* non-fiction, including cookery, gardening, interior design and decoration, craft, health. 38 titles in 2003. TITLES *Choosing Colours* Kevin McCloud; *Secrets* Gordon Ramsay; *RHS Lilies* Michael Jefferson Brown. Synopses and ideas for books welcome. No fiction or children's books.
Royalties paid twice-yearly.

Quantum
See **Foulsham Publishers**

Quartet Books
27 Goodge Street, London W1T 2LD
☎020 7636 3992 Fax 020 7637 1866
Chairman *Naim Attallah*
Managing Director *Jeremy Beale*
Publishing Director *Stella Kane*
Approx. Annual Turnover £1 million
FOUNDED 1972. Independent publisher. *Publishes* contemporary literary fiction including translations, popular culture, biography, music, history, politics and some photographic books. Unsolicited sample chapters with return postage welcome; no poetry, romance or science fiction. Submissions by disk or e-mail are not accepted.
Royalties paid twice-yearly.

Queen Anne Press
See **Lennard Associates Ltd**

Quiller Press (An imprint of Quiller Publishing Ltd)
Wykey House, Wykey, Shrewsbury, Shropshire SY4 1JA
☎01939 261616 Fax 01939 261606
Email info@quillerbooks.com
Managing Director *Andrew Johnston*
Specialises in sponsored books and publications sold through non-book trade channels as well as bookshops. *Publishes* architecture, biography, business and industry, collecting, cookery, DIY, gardening, guidebooks, humour, reference, sports, travel, wine and spirits. About 10 titles a year. TITLES *Camper and Nicholson* Ian Dear; *Great British Food* Heather Hay Ffrench; *The Dunlop Slazenger Story* Brian Simpson. Most ideas originate in-house; unsolicited mss only if the author sees some potential for sponsorship or guaranteed sales.
Royalties paid twice-yearly.

Radcliffe Medical Press Ltd
18 Marcham Road, Abingdon, Oxfordshire OX14 1AA
☎01235 528820 Fax 01235 528830
Email contact.us@radcliffemed.com
Website www.radcliffe-oxford.com
Managing Director *Andrew Bax*
Editorial Director *Gillian Nineham*
Approx. Annual Turnover £1.5 million
FOUNDED 1987. Medical publishers which began by specialising in books for general practice and health service management. *Publishes* clinical, management, health policy books, training materials and CD-ROMs. 80 titles in 2002. Unsolicited mss, synopses and ideas welcome. No non-medical or medical books aimed at lay audience.
Royalties paid twice-yearly.

Radcliffe Press
See **I.B. Tauris & Co. Ltd**

The Ramsay Head Press
9 Glenisla Gardens, Edinburgh EH9 2HR
☎0131 662 1915
Email conrad.wilson@genie.co.uk
Managing Director *Conrad Wilson*
FOUNDED 1968 by Norman Wilson, OBE. A small independent family publisher. *Publishes* biography, cookery, Scottish fiction and non-fiction, plus the biannual literary magazine *InScotland*. About 3–4 titles a year. TITLES *When It Works It Feels Like Play* Tessa Ransford; *Interesting Times, Poetry by David*

Simpson. Synopses and ideas for books of Scottish interest welcome.

Royalties paid twice-yearly.

The Random House Group Ltd

Random House, 20 Vauxhall Bridge Road, London SW1V 2SA
☎020 7840 8400 Fax 020 7233 6058
Email enquiries@randomhouse.co.uk
Website www.randomhouse.co.uk
Chief Executive/Chairman *Gail Rebuck*
Deputy Chairman *Simon Master*
Managing Director *Ian Hudson*

Random's increasing focus on trade publishing, both here and in the US, has been well rewarded, with sales continuing to grow over the last year. Random House Group Ltd is the parent company of three separate publishing divisions and of **Transworld** (see entry). The three divisions are: General Books, the Group's largest publishing division; Children's Books, and Ebury Press. General Books is divided into two operating groups, allowing hardcover editors to see their books through to publication in paperback. The literary imprints Jonathan Cape, Secker & Warburg, Yellow Jersey Press and Chatto & Windus work side by side with paperback imprints Vintage and Pimlico to form one group; trade imprints Century, William Heinemann and Hutchinson go hand-in-hand with Arrow to form the other group. Acquired The Harvill Press in March 2002.

IMPRINTS
Jonathan Cape Ltd ☎020 7840 8576 Fax 020 7233 6117 Publishing Director *Dan Franklin* Biography and memoirs, current affairs, fiction, history, photography, poetry, politics and travel. IMPRINT **Yellow Jersey.**

Secker & Warburg ☎020 7840 8649 Fax 020 7233 6117 Editorial Director *Geoff Mulligan* Principally literary fiction with some non-fiction.

Chatto & Windus Ltd ☎020 7840 8522 Fax 020 7233 6117 Publishing Director *Alison Samuel* Art, belles-lettres, biography and memoirs, current affairs, essays, fiction, history, poetry, politics, philosophy, translations and travel.

Century (including **Business Books**) ☎020 7840 8555 Fax 020 7233 6127 Managing Director *Richard Cable,* Publishing Director *Mark Booth* General fiction and non-fiction, plus business management, advertising, communication, marketing, selling, investment and financial titles.

The Harvill Press ☎020 7840 8400 Fax

020 7840 8664 Publisher *Christopher MacLehose,* Editorial Director *Margaret Stead* Literature in translation, English literature, quality thrillers, illustrated books and Africana, plus an occasional literature anthology.

William Heinemann ☎020 7840 8400 Fax 020 7233 6127 Publishing Director Non-fiction *Ravi Mirchandani,* Publishing Director Fiction *Andy McKillop* General non-fiction and fiction, especially history, biography, science, crime, thrillers and women's fiction.

Hutchinson ☎020 7840 8564 Fax 020 7233 7870 Publishing Director *Sue Freestone* General fiction and non-fiction including notably belles-lettres, current affairs, politics, travel and history.

Arrow ☎020 7840 8516 Fax 020 7233 6127 Publishing Director *Susan Sandon* Mass-market paperback fiction and non-fiction.

Pimlico ☎020 7840 8630 Fax 020 7233 6117 Publishing Director *Will Sulkin* Large-format quality paperbacks in the fields of history, biography, popular culture and literature.

Vintage ☎020 7840 8531 Fax 020 7233 6127 Publisher *Rachel Cugnoni* Quality paperback fiction and non-fiction. Vintage (FOUNDED 1990) has been described as one of the 'greatest literary success stories in recent British publishing'.

Random House Children's Books (at Transworld Publishers, 61–63 Uxbridge Road, London W5 5SA ☎020 8231 6800 Fax 020 8231 6767) Managing Director *Philippa Dickinson* IMPRINTS **Hutchinson** Publishing Director *Caroline Roberts*; **Jonathan Cape** Publishing Director *Tom Maschler,* **The Bodley Head**; **Hutchinson**; **Doubleday** Fiction Publisher *Penny Walker,* **David Fickling Books** Publishing Director *David Fickling,* Fiction Publisher *Annie Eaton*; **Corgi**; **Red Fox**.

Ebury Press ☎020 7840 8400 Fax 020 7840 8406 Publisher *Fiona MacIntyre* IMPRINTS **Ebury Press**; **Vermilion**; **Fodor's**. Art, antiques, biography, Buddhism, cookery, gardening, health and beauty, homes and interiors, personal development, spirituality, travel and guides, sport, TV tie-ins. About 150 titles a year. Unsolicited mss, synopses and ideas for books welcome.

Royalties paid twice-yearly for the most part.

Authors' Rating Way out in front of the fast-seller list, this high-powered publisher is ready to take a chance on new talent. Author relations are good according to a recent Society of Authors survey. Synopses and manuscripts may be passed on to freelance readers, but there is reasonable assurance that they are at least read.

Ransom Publishing Ltd

Rose Cottage, Howe Hill, Watlington, Oxfordshire OX49 5HB
☎01491 613711 Fax 01491 613733
Email jenny@ransom.co.uk
Website www.ransom.co.uk

Managing Director *Jenny Ertle*

FOUNDED 1995 by ex-McGraw-Hill publisher. Partnerships formed with, among others, Channel 4 and the ICL. *Publishes* educational and consumer multimedia, study packs and children's books. Over 40 CD-ROMs, most with educational support packs. TITLES include *The Early Learning* series; *The Little Monsters* series; *Whale of a Tale* series including maths, science, language and geography; *Tom Paint; The Castle Under Siege; The History of the Universe; The History of Life; Rivers* plus natural history CD-ROMs. Developing new children's educational book range pre-school and keystage 1. Only interested in submissions suitable for this.

Reader's Digest Association Ltd

11 Westferry Circus, Canary Wharf, London E14 4HE
☎020 7715 8000 Fax 020 7715 8181
Email gbeditorial@readersdigest.co.uk
Website www.readersdigest.co.uk

Managing Director *Andrew Lynam-Smith*
Editorial Head *Cortina Butler*

Editorial office in the USA (see entry under **US Publishers**). *Publishes* gardening, natural history, cookery, history, DIY, travel and word books. About 20 titles a year.

Reaktion Books

79 Farringdon Road, London EC1M 3JU
☎020 7404 9930 Fax 020 7404 9931
Email info@reaktionbooks.co.uk
Website www.reaktionbooks.co.uk

Managing Director *Michael R. Leaman*

FOUNDED in Edinburgh in 1985 and moved to London in 1987. *Publishes* art history, architecture, Asian studies, cultural studies, design, film, geography, history, photography and travel writing (*not* travel guides). About 30 titles a year. TITLES *An Encyclopedia of Stupidity* Matthijs van Boxser; *Forever Young: A Cultural History of Longevity* Lucian Boia; *Factory* Gillian Darley
  Royalties paid twice-yearly.

Reardon Publishing

56 Upper Norwood Street, Leckhampton, Cheltenham, Gloucestershire GL53 0DU
☎01242 231800

Email reardon@bigfoot.com
Website www.reardon.co.uk *or*
  www.cotswoldbookshop.com

Managing Editor *Nicholas Reardon*

FOUNDED in the mid-1970s. Family-run publishing house specialising in local interest and tourism in the Cotswold area. Member of the **Outdoor Writers Guild**. *Publishes* walking and driving guides, and family history for societies. 10 titles a year. TITLES *The Cotswold Way* (video); *The Cotswold Way Map; Cotswold Walkabout; Cotswold Driveabout; The Donnington Way; The Haunted Cotswolds.* Unsolicited mss, synopses and ideas welcome with return postage only. Also distributes for other publishers such as Ordnance Survey.
  Royalties paid twice-yearly.

Red Dress Ink
See **Harlequin Mills & Boon Ltd**

Red Fox
See **Random House Group Ltd**

Red Hot Diva
See **Millivres Prowler Ltd**

William Reed Directories

Broadfield Park, Crawley, West Sussex RH11 9RT
☎01293 613400 Fax 01293 610322
Email directories@william-reed.co.uk
Website www.william-reed.co.uk

Editorial Circulating Manager *Sulann Staniford*

William Reed Directories, a division of William Reed Publishing, was ESTABLISHED in 1990. Its portfolio includes 13 titles covering the food, drink, non-food, catering, retail and export industries. The titles are produced as directories, market research reports, exhibition catalogues and electronic publishing.

Reed Elsevier Group plc

25 Victoria Street, London SW1H 0EX
☎020 7222 8420 Fax 020 7227 5799
Website www.reedelsevier.com
Also at: 125 Park Avenue, 23rd Floor, New York, NY 10017, USA
☎001 212 309 5498 Fax 001 212 309 5480
Sara Burgerhartstraat 25, 1055 KV Amsterdam, The Netherlands
☎00 31 20 485 2434

Chief Executive Officer (UK) *Crispin Davis*

Reed Elsevier plc is a world-leading publisher

and information provider, operating in four core segments: science and medical, legal, education, business.

DIVISIONS **Harcourt Education** (see entry); **Elsevier** (see entry); **LexisNexis Butterworths Tolley** (formerly Butterworths) Halsbury House, 35 Chancery Lane, London WC2A 1EL ☎020 7400 2500 Fax 020 7400 2842 *Publishes* legal and accountancy textbooks, journals, law reports, CD-ROMs and online services; **Harcourt School Publishers** (see entry under **US Publishers**); **Reed Business** Quadrant House, The Quadrant, Sutton, Surrey SM2 5AS ☎020 8652 3500.

Regency House Publishing Limited

3 Mill Lane, Broxbourne, Hertfordshire EN10 7AZ
☎01992 479988 Fax 01992 479966
Email regencyhouse@btclick.com

Chairman *Brian Trodd*
Managing Director *Nicolette Trodd*
Approx. Annual Turnover £1 million

FOUNDED 1991. Publisher and packager of mass-market non-fiction. No fiction. No unsolicited material.
Royalties paid twice-yearly.

Reinhardt Books Ltd

Flat 2, 43 Onslow Square, London
SW7 3LR
☎020 7589 3751

Directors *Joan Reinhardt, Veronica Reinhardt*

FOUNDED in 1887 as H.F.L. (Publishers), it was acquired by Max Reinhardt in 1947, changing its name to the present one in 1987. First publication under the new name was Graham Greene's *The Captain and the Enemy*. Also publishes under the **Nonesuch Press** imprint. AUTHORS include Mitsumasa Anno, Alistair Cooke and Maurice Sendak. New books are no longer considered.
Royalties paid according to contract.

Religious & Moral Educational Press (RMEP)
See **Hymns Ancient & Modern Ltd**

Research Disclosure
See **Kenneth Mason Publications Ltd**

Review
See **Hodder Headline Ltd**

Richmond House Publishing Company Ltd

70 – 76 Bell Street, Marylebone, London NW1 6SP
☎020 7224 9666 Fax 020 7224 9688
Email sales@rhpco.co.uk
Website www.rhpco.co.uk

Managing Directors *Gloria Gordon, Spencer Block*

Publishes directories for the theatre and entertainment industries. TITLES *British Theatre Directory 2003*; *Artistes and Agents 2003*; *London Seating Plan Guide.* Synopses and ideas welcome.

Right Way/Right Way Plus
See **Elliot Right Way Books**

Robinson
See **Constable & Robinson Ltd**

Robson Books
See **Chrysalis Books Group**

RotoVision

Sheridan House, 112/116A Western Road, Hove, East Sussex BN3 1DD
☎01273 727268 Fax 01273 727269
Website www.rotovision.com

Managing Director *Ken Fund*
Publisher *Aidan Walker*

FOUNDED 1996. Rapidly-expanding visual arts publishers with a strong emphasis on education and inspiration. *Publishes* graphic design, photography, web design, advertising, film, architecture, practical art, lighting design, interiors, product design, packaging design. TITLES *World's Top Photographers: Wildlife*; *What Is Graphic Design?*; *The Total Beauty of Sustainable Products*; *Materials for Inspirational Design: Plastic*; *The Designer and the Grid*; *Screencraft: Directing*; *Up Against the Wall: International Poster Design*; *Stretch: The Art of Panoramic Photography.* No unsolicited mss; written synopses and ideas welcome. No phone calls, please. No academic or fiction.
Flat fee paid.

Roundhouse Publishing Group

Millstone, Limers Lane, Northam, North Devon EX39 2RG
☎01237 474474 Fax 01237 474774
Email roundhouse.group@ukgateway.net

Editorial Head *Alan Goodworth*

ESTABLISHED 1991. *Publishes* cinema and media-related titles. TITLES *The Bent Lens: A World Guide to Gay & Lesbian Films*; *Cinema of Oliver*

Stone; Cinema of Martin Scorsese. Represents and distributes a broad range of non-fiction publishing houses throughout the UK and Europe. No unsolicited mss.

Royalties paid twice-yearly.

Routledge

11 New Fetter Lane, London EC4P 4EE
☎020 7583 9855 Fax 020 7842 2298
Website www.routledge.com

Managing Director *Roger Horton*
Publishing Directors *Claire L'Enfant, Alan Jarvis, Mary MacInnes*
Approx. Annual Turnover £35.5 million (Group)

Formed in 1987 through an amalgamation of Routledge & Kegan Paul, Methuen & Co., Tavistock Publications, and Croom Helm. It subsequently acquired the Unwin Hyman academic list from **HarperCollins** (1991), *Who's Who* and historical atlases from **Dent/Orion** (1994), archaeology and ancient history titles from **Batsford** (1996), and the E & FN Spon imprint from ITP Science (1997). In 1998, Routledge became a subsidiary of **Taylor & Francis Group plc** (see entry). In 2001 Curzon Press combined with the imprint to form **Routledge Curzon** for Asian studies.

Publishes academic and professional books and journals in the social sciences, humanities, health sciences and the built environment for the international market. Subjects: addiction, anthropology, archaeology, architecture, Asian studies, biblical studies, the built environment, business and management, civil engineering, classics, heritage, construction, counselling, criminology, development and environment, dictionaries, economics, education, environmental engineering, geography, health, history, Japanese studies, journals, language, leisure studies and leisure management, linguistics, literary criticism, media and culture, Middle East, nursing, philosophy, politics, political economy, psychiatry, psychology, reference, social administration, social studies and sociology, therapy, theatre and performance studies, women's studies. No poetry, fiction, travel or astrology. About 900 titles a year. Send synopses with sample chapter and c.v. rather than complete mss.

Royalties paid annually and twice-yearly, according to contract.

Ryland Peters and Small Limited

Kirkman House, 12–14 Whitfield Street, London W1T 2RP
☎020 7436 9090 Fax 020 7436 9790
Email info@rps.co.uk

Website www.rylandpeters.com

Managing Director *David Peters*
Publishing Director *Alison Starling*

FOUNDED 1996. *Publishes* highly illustrated lifestyle books aimed at an international market, covering gardening, cookery, interior design and mind, body, spirit. No fiction. No unsolicited mss; synopses and ideas welcome.

Royalties paid twice-yearly.

Sage Publications

6 Bonhill Street, London EC2A 4PU
☎020 7374 0645 Fax 020 7374 8741
Website www.sagepub.co.uk

Managing Director *Stephen Barr*
Editorial Director *Ziyad Marar*

FOUNDED 1971. *Publishes* academic books and journals in humanities and the social sciences. Bought academic and professional books publisher Paul Chapman Publishing Ltd in 1998.

Royalties paid twice-yearly.

Saint Andrew Press

Church of Scotland, 121 George Street, Edinburgh EH2 4YN
☎0131 225 5722 Fax 0131 220 3113
Email standrewpress@cofscotland.org.uk
Website www.standrewpress.com *or* www.williambarclay.org

Head of Publishing *Ann Crawford*
Approx. Annual Turnover £225,000

FOUNDED in 1954. Owned by the Church of Scotland. *Publishes* religious, general reference, Scottish environmental and children's books aimed at the Christian trade and retail market in the UK and internationally. About 20 titles a year. Lead titles in 2001 included six *New Daily Study Bible* volumes by William Barclay (revised and updated, the series has sold over 10 million copies worldwide); *Outside Verdict* Harry Reid; *Wild Horses* Kenneth Steven. 'Saint Andrew Press is expanding and is actively seeking high-quality writing that is thought-provoking and, above all, helps readers to wrestle with the complexities of life today.' No unsolicited mss but proposals very welcome in synopsis form. Please approach in writing.

Royalties paid annually.

St David's Press

See **Ashley Drake Publishing Ltd**

St Pauls Publishing

187 Battersea Bridge Road, London SW11 3AS
☎020 7978 4300 Fax 020 7978 4370
Email editions@stpauls.org.uk

Publisher *Andrew Pudussery*

Publishing division of the Society of St Paul. Began publishing in 1914 but activities were fairly limited until around 1948. *Publishes* religious material mainly: theology, scripture, catechetics, prayer books and biography. Unsolicited mss, synopses and ideas welcome. About 30 titles a year.

Salamander Books
See **Chrysalis Books Group**

Sangam Books Ltd
57 London Fruit Exchange, Brushfield Street, London E1 6EP
☎020 7377 6399 Fax 020 7375 1230
Email sangambks@aol.com
Executive Director *Anthony de Souza*

Traditionally an educational publisher of school and college level textbooks. Also *publishes* art, India, medicine, science, technology, social sciences, religion, plus some fiction in paperback.

Saqi Books
26 Westbourne Grove, London W2 5RH
☎020 7221 9347 Fax 020 7229 7492
Email saqibooks@dial.pipex.com
Website www.saqibooks.com
Chairman/Managing Director *André Gaspard*

FOUNDED 1981, initially as a specialist publisher of books on the Middle East and Arab world but now includes Central Asia, South Asia and European fiction. *Publishes* fiction and non-fiction – academic and illustrated. 20 titles in 2002. Welcomes unsolicited material; approach by post or e-mail.
Royalties paid annually.

W.B. Saunders
See **Elsevier Ltd**

Savitri Books Ltd
See entry under **UK Packagers**

SB Publications
19 Grove Road, Seaford, East Sussex BN25 1TP
☎01323 893498 Fax 01323 893860
Email sales@sbpublications.swinternet.co.uk
Website www.sbpublications.swinternet.co.uk
Owner *Mrs Lindsay Woods*

FOUNDED 1987. *Specialises* in local history, including themes illustrated by old picture postcards and photographs; also travel, guides (town, walking) and railways. 20 titles a year.
IMPRINTS **Historic Military Press**; **Ben Gunn** TITLES *Dorset As She Wus Spoke; The Neat and Nippy Guide to Brighton; Sussex Memorabilia.* Also provides marketing and distribution services for local authors.
Royalties paid annually.

Scandinavian Academic Press
See **Ashley Drake Publishing Ltd**

Sceptre
See **Hodder Headline Ltd**

Scholastic Ltd
Villiers House, Clarendon Avenue, Leamington Spa, Warwickshire CV32 5PR
☎01926 887799 Fax 01926 883331
Website www.scholastic.co.uk
Chairman *M.R. Robinson*
Managing Director *Ian Ronald*
Approx. Annual Turnover £42 million

FOUNDED 1964. Owned by US parent company. *Publishes* children's fiction and non-fiction and education for primary schools.

DIVISIONS
Scholastic Children's Books *Richard Scrivener* Commonwealth House, 1–19 New Oxford Street, London WC1A 1NU ☎020 7421 9000 Fax 020 7421 9001 IMPRINTS **Scholastic Press** (hardbacks); **Hippo** (paperbacks); **Point** (paperbacks) TITLES *Horrible Histories; Goosebumps; Point Horror; His Dark Materials* trilogy by Philip Pullman.
  Educational Publishing *Anne Peel* (Villiers House address) Professional books and classroom materials for primary teachers, plus magazines such as *Child Education, Junior Education, Junior Focus, Infant Projects, Nursery Education; Literacy Time.*
  Scholastic Book Clubs *Miles Stevens Hoare* Windrush Park, Witney, Oxford OX29 0YT ☎01993 893456 Fax 01993 776813 SBC is the UK's number one Schools Book Club. Offering five age specific clubs, it provides 'the best books at great prices and supports teachers in the process'.
  School Book Fairs *Miles Stevens-Hoare* The Book Fair Division sells directly to children, parents and teachers in schools through 27,000 week-long book events held in schools throughout the UK.
Royalties paid twice-yearly.

Authors' Rating Another beneficiary of the Harry Potter phenomenon (via its children's book clubs), Scholastic also leads the intellectual sector of children's publishing with Philip Pullman who, by any literary standards, takes some beating. Fiction for 8 to 12-year-olds is seen as a growth sector. Noted for its author-friendly skills.

SCM Canterbury Press
9–17 St Albans Place, London N1 0NX
☎020 7359 8033 Fax 020 7359 0049
Email admin@scm-canterburypress.co.uk
Website www.scm-canterburypress.co.uk
Publishing Director *Christine Smith*
Approx. Annual Turnover £500,000

Part of **Hymns Ancient & Modern Ltd**. *Publishes* culturally-engaged theology, philosophy of religion, and religious ethics from an interdisciplinary and inter-faith perspective. About 35 titles a year. TITLES *The Meaning of Miracles; This is My Faith; Runcie: On Reflection.* No unsolicited mss or proposals considered.
Royalties paid annually.

Authors' Rating Leading publisher of religious ideas with well-deserved reputation for fresh thinking. At SCM, 'questioning theology is the norm'.

Scottish Cultural Press/ Scottish Children's Press
Unit 13d, Newbattle Abbey Business Annexe, Newbattle Road, Dalkeith EH22 3LJ
☎0131 660 6366 Fax 0131 660 6414
Email info@scottishbooks.com
Website www.scottishbooks.com
Directors *Avril Gray, Brian Pugh*

FOUNDED 1992. *Publishes* Scottish interest titles, including cultural literature, poetry, archaeology, local history. DIVISION **S.C.P. Children's Ltd** (trading as **Scottish Children's Press**) Children's fiction and non-fiction. Unsolicited mss, synopses and ideas welcome provided return postage is included, but always telephone before sending material, please.
Royalties paid.

Scribner
See **Simon & Schuster UK Limited**

Seafarer Books
102 Redwald Road, Rendlesham, Woodbridge, Suffolk IP12 2TE
☎01394 420789 Fax 01394 461314
Email info@seafarerbooks.com
Website www.seafarerbooks.com
Sole Proprietor *Patricia M. Eve*

FOUNDED 1968. *Publishes* sailing titles, with an emphasis on the traditional. AUTHORS Jack London, Erskine Childers, Adrian Seligman, Frank Mulville, Bjorn Larsson. No unsolicited mss; preliminary letter essential before making any type of submission.
Royalties paid twice-yearly.

Search Press Ltd
Wellwood, North Farm Road, Tunbridge Wells, Kent TN2 3DR
☎01892 510850 Fax 01892 515903
Email searchpress@searchpress.com
Website www.searchpress.com
Managing Director *Martin de la Bédoyère*
Commissioning Editor *Rosalind Dace*

FOUNDED 1970. *Publishes* full-colour art, craft, needlecrafts – papermaking and papercrafts, painting on silk, art techniques and embroidery. No unsolicited mss; synopsis with sample chapter welcome.
Royalties paid annually.

Secker & Warburg
See **Random House Group Ltd**

Seren
First Floor, 38–40 Nolton Street, Bridgend CF31 3BN
☎01656 663018 Fax 01656 649226
Email seren@seren.force9.co.uk
Website www.seren-books.com
Chairman *Cary Archard*
Managing Director *Mick Felton*
Approx. Annual Turnover £150,000

FOUNDED 1981 as a specialist poetry publisher but has now moved into general literary publishing with an emphasis on Wales. *Publishes* poetry, fiction, literary criticism, drama, biography, art, history and translations of fiction. About 25 titles a year.
DIVISIONS **Poetry** *Amy Wack* AUTHORS Owen Sheers, Tony Curtis, Sheenagh Pugh, Duncan Bush, Deryn Rees-Jones. **Drama** *Amy Wack* AUTHORS Edward Thomas, Charles Way, Lucinda Coxon. **Fiction, Art, Literary Criticism, History, Translations** *Mick Felton* AUTHORS Christopher Meredith, Leslie Norris, Richard John Evans.
IMPRINT **Border Lines Biographies** TITLES *Bruce Chatwin; Dennis Potter; Mary Webb; Wilfred Owen; Raymond Williams,* etc. Unsolicited mss, synopses and ideas for books welcome.
Royalties paid twice yearly.

Serpent's Tail

4 Blackstock Mews, London N4 2BT
☎020 7354 1949 Fax 020 7704 6467
Email info@serpentstail.com
Website www.serpentstail.com

Contact *Ben Cooper*
Approx. Annual Turnover £650,000

FOUNDED 1986. Winner of the **Sunday Times Small Publisher of the Year Award** (1989) and the Ralph Lewis Award for new fiction (1992). Serpent's Tail has introduced to British audiences a number of major internationally known writers. Noted for its strong emphasis on design and an eye for the unusual. *Publishes* contemporary fiction, contemporary gay fiction and non-fiction, including works in translation, crime, popular culture and biography. No poetry, romance or fantasy. About 40 titles a year.

IMPRINTS
Serpent's Tail TITLES *Fearless Jones* Walter Mosley; *Whatever* Michel Houellebecq; *This is Serbia Calling* Matthew Collin; *Pornocopia* Laurence O'Toole. **Five Star** TITLES *Nineteen Seventy Four* David Peace; *Always Outnumbered, Always Outgunned* Walter Mosley; *Beneath the Blonde* Stella Duffy. Send preliminary letter outlining proposal with a sample chapter and s.a.e. No unsolicited mss. Prospective authors unfamiliar with Serpent's Tail are advised to study the list before submitting anything.
Royalties paid annually.

Authors' Rating A publisher noted for originality which means doing what the conglomerates are unwilling or unable to do. An exciting fiction list much praised by its own and other publishers' authors.

Severn House Publishers

9–15 High Street, Sutton, Surrey SM1 1DF
☎020 8770 3930 Fax 020 8770 3850
Email info@severnhouse.com
Website www.severnhouse.com

Chairman *Edwin Buckhalter*
Editorial *Amanda Stewart*

FOUNDED 1974. A leader in library fiction publishing. *Publishes* hardback fiction: romance science fiction, horror, fantasy, crime. About 140 titles a year. No unsolicited material. Synopses/proposals preferred through *bona fide* literary agents only.
Royalties paid twice-yearly. *Overseas associate* Severn House Publishers Inc., New York.

Sheffield Academic Press

See **The Continuum International Publishing Group Limited**

Sheldon Press

See **Society for Promoting Christian Knowledge**

Sheldrake Press

188 Cavendish Road, London SW12 0DA
☎020 8675 1767 Fax 020 8675 7736
Email mail@sheldrakepress.demon.co.uk
Website www.sheldrakepress.demon.co.uk

Publisher *Simon Rigge*
Approx. Annual Turnover £250,000

FOUNDED in 1976 as a book packager and commenced publishing under its own imprint in 1991. *Publishes* illustrated non-fiction: history, travel, style, cookery and stationery. TITLES *The Victorian House Book; The Shorter Mrs Beeton; The Power of Steam; The Railway Heritage of Britain; Wild Britain; Wild France; Wild Spain; Wild Italy; Wild Ireland; Amsterdam: Portrait of a City* and Kate Greenaway stationery books. Synopses and ideas for books welcome, but not interested in fiction.

Shepheard-Walwyn (Publishers) Ltd

Suite 604, The Chandlery, 50 Westminster Bridge Road, London SE1 7QY
☎020 7721 7666 Fax 020 7721 7667
Email books@shepheard-walwyn.co.uk
Website www.shepheard-walwyn.co.uk

Managing Director *Anthony Werner*
Approx. Annual Turnover £150,000

FOUNDED 1972. 'We regard books as food for the mind and want to offer a wholesome diet of original ideas and fresh approaches to old subjects.' *Publishes* general non-fiction in three main areas: Scottish interest; gift books in calligraphy and/or illustrated; history, political economy, philosophy. About 5 titles a year. Synopses and ideas for books welcome.
Royalties paid twice-yearly.

The Shetland Times Ltd

Gremista, Lerwick, Shetland ZE1 0PX
☎01595 693622 Fax 01595 694637
Email publishing@shetland-times.co.uk
Website www.shetland-books.co.uk

Managing Director *Robert Wishart*
Publications Manager *Charlotte Black*

FOUNDED 1872 as publishers of the local newspaper. Book publishing followed thereafter plus publication of monthly magazine, *Shetland Life*. *Publishes* anything with Shetland connections – local and natural history, music, crafts, maritime. Prefers material with a Shetland theme/connection.

Royalties paid annually.

Shire Publications Ltd
Cromwell House, Church Street, Princes Risborough, Buckinghamshire HP27 9AA
☎01844 344301 Fax 01844 347080
Email shire@shirebooks.co.uk
Website www.shirebooks.co.uk
General Manager *Sue Ross*

FOUNDED 1962. *Publishes* original non-fiction paperbacks. About 25 titles a year. No unsolicited material; send introductory letter with detailed outline of idea.

Royalties paid annually.

Authors' Rating You don't have to live in the country to write books for Shire but it helps. With titles like *Church Fonts, Haunted Inns* and *Discovering Preserved Railways* there is a distinct rural feel to the list. Another way of putting it, to quote owner John Rotheroe, Shire specialises in 'small books on all manner of obscure subjects'.

Short Books
15 Highbury Terrace, London N5 1UP
☎020 7226 1607 Fax 020 7226 4169
Website www.theshortbookco.com
Contacts *Rebecca Nicolson, Aurea Carpenter*

FOUNDED 2001. *Publishes* informative, entertaining non-fiction (20,000 – 80,000 words). 21 titles in 2003. Lists include biographies – novella-length portraits of the co-stars of history; journalism – essays, investigations and reportage by authors including Paul Theroux, Francis Wheen and John Sutherland; children's books – lively biographies of intriguing figures from the past. No fiction as yet but will consider.

Sickle Moon
See **Eland Publishing Ltd**

Sidgwick & Jackson
See **Macmillan Publishers Ltd**

Sigma Press
5 Alton Road, Wilmslow, Cheshire SK9 5DY
☎01625 531035 Fax 01625 531035
Email info@sigma.press
Website www.sigmapress.co.uk

Chairman/Managing Director *Graham Beech*

FOUNDED in 1980 as a publisher of technical books, Sigma Press now publishes mainly in the leisure area. *Publishes* outdoor, local heritage, myths and legends, sports, dance and exercise. Approx. 20 titles in 2002. No unsolicited mss; synopses and ideas welcome. No poetry or novels required.

DIVISION **Sigma Leisure** TITLES *Holiday Walks in the Loire Valley*; *Leap into Legend* (biography); *Lonesome Rhodes* (biography); *Northumbria Church Walks*; *Discovering Manchester*.

Royalties paid twice-yearly.

Signature
See **Hodder Headline Ltd**

Silhouette
See **Harlequin Mills & Boon Ltd**

Simon & Schuster UK Limited
Africa House, 64–78 Kingsway, London WC2B 6AH
☎020 7316 1900 Fax 020 7316 0331
CEO/Managing Director *Ian S. Chapman*
Publishing Director *Suzanne Baboneau*
Publishers, Non-fiction *Helen Gummer, Andrew Gordon* (also **The Free Press**)
Publishers, Fiction *Suzanne Baboneau, Kate Lyall-Grant, Darren Nash* (**Earthlight**)
Scribner *Tim Binding, Ben Ball*

FOUNDED 1986. Sister company of the leading American company. *Publishes* hardback (**Simon & Schuster**) and paperback (**Pocket Books**) commercial and literary fiction, including science fiction and fantasy under its **Earthlight** imprint and non-fiction, including autobiography, biography, sport, mind, body & spirit, humour, travel and other general interest non-fiction. The recently launched **The Free Press** *publishes* serious non-fiction, including popular science, politics, history and current business. Literary international fiction and non-fiction is published under the **Scribner** imprint.

DIVISION **Martin Books** Director *Janet Copleston* Specialises in bespoke publishing and branded editions, and the Simon & Schuster UK cookery list.

Royalties paid twice-yearly.

Authors' Rating Editorially independent of its American counterpart, Simon & Schuster continues to grow in reputation as a powerhouse for new work. The latest initiative is the

Free Press imprint, 'a forum for original thinking', appealing to a general readership.

Skoob Russell Square
10 Brunswick Centre, off Bernard Street,
London WC1N 1AE
☎020 7278 8760 Fax 020 7278 3137
Email books@skoob.com
Website www.skoob.com
Editorial *M. Lovell*

Publishes literary guides, cultural studies, esoterica/occult, poetry, new writing from the Orient. No unsolicited mss, synopses or ideas. TITLES *Skoob Directory of Secondhand Bookshops*; *Perspectives on Post-Colonial Literature* D.C.R.A. Goonetilleke; *The Space of City Trees* Arthur Yap.

Smith Gryphon Ltd
See **John Blake Publishing Ltd**

Colin Smythe Ltd
PO Box 6, Gerrards Cross, Buckinghamshire
SL9 8XA
☎01753 886000 Fax 01753 886469
Email sales@colinsmythe.co.uk
Website www.colinsmythe.co.uk
Managing Director *Colin Smythe*
Approx. Annual Turnover £2.7 million

FOUNDED 1966. *Publishes* Anglo-Irish literature, drama; criticism and history. About 10 titles a year. No unsolicited mss. Also acts as literary agent for a small list of authors including Terry Pratchett.
  Royalties paid annually/twice-yearly.

Society for Promoting Christian Knowledge (SPCK)
Holy Trinity Church, Marylebone Road,
London NW1 4DU
☎020 7643 0382 Fax 020 7643 0391
Website www.spck.org.uk
Director of Publishing *Simon Kingston*

FOUNDED 1698, SPCK is the third oldest publisher in the country.

IMPRINTS
SPCK Editorial Director *Joanna Moriarty* Theology, academic, liturgy, prayer, spirituality, biblical studies, educational resources, mission, pastoral care, gospel and culture, worldwide. **Sheldon Press** Editor *Liz Marsh* Popular medicine, health, self-help, psychology. **Azure** Senior Editor *Alison Barr* General spirituality.
  Royalties paid annually.

Authors' Rating Religion with a strong social edge.

Southwater
See **Anness Publishing Ltd**

Souvenir Press Ltd
43 Great Russell Street, London WC1B 3PA
☎020 7580 9307/8 & 7637 5711/2/3
Fax 020 7580 5064
Chairman/Managing Director *Ernest Hecht*

Independent publishing house. FOUNDED 1951. *Publishes* academic and scholarly, animal care and breeding, antiques and collecting, archaeology, autobiography and biography, business and industry, children's, cookery, crafts and hobbies, crime, educational, fiction, gardening, health and beauty, history and antiquarian, humour, illustrated and fine editions, magic and the occult, medical, military, music, natural history, philosophy, poetry, psychology, religious, sociology, sports, theatre and women's studies. About 55 titles a year. Souvenir's Human Horizons series for the disabled and their carers is one of the most preeminent in its field and recently celebrated 28 years of publishing for the disabled.

IMPRINTS/SERIES
Condor; **Human Horizons**; **Independent Voices**; **Pictorial Presentations**; **Pop Universal**; **The Story-Tellers**. TITLES *The New Drawing on the Right Side of the Brain* Betty Edwards; *Arabian Flavours: Recipes and Tales of Arab Life* Salah Jamal; *People Before Profit* Charles Derber; *The Womb In Which I Lay* Pauline Perry; *The Third Sex, Kathoey: Thailand's Ladyboys* Richard Totman. Unsolicited mss considered but initial letter of enquiry and outline always required in the first instance.
  Royalties paid twice-yearly.

Authors' Rating The last of the marvellously eccentric independent publishers (just look at the state of his office), Ernest Hecht has proved time and again that he has an eye for the bestseller but his success owes as much to his love of the outrageous and a quirky sense of fun.

SPCK
See **Society for Promoting Christian Knowledge**

Special Interest Model Books
Stanley House, 3 Fleets Lane, Poole, Dorset
BH15 3AJ
☎01202 649930 Fax 01202 649950
Email chrlloyd@globalnet.co.uk

Contact *Chris Lloyd*

Publishes aviation, engineering, leisure and hobbies, modelling, electronics, health, craft, wine and beer making, woodwork. Send synopses rather than completed mss.

Royalties paid twice-yearly.

Speechmark Publishing Ltd

Telford Road, Bicester OX26 4LQ

☎01869 244644 Fax 01869 320040

Email info@speechmark.net

Website www.speechmark.net

Chairman and Managing Director *Ian Franklin*

Publishing Manager *Sarah Miles*

Approx. Annual Turnover £1.5 million

FOUNDED 1979. Formerly known as Winslow Publishing, Speechmark *publishes* practical books and *ColorCards* for health, education and special needs practitioners and students. 20 titles in 2002. Unsolicited mss, synopses and ideas welcome. Approach by letter or e-mail.

Royalties paid annually.

Spellmount Ltd

The Old Rectory, Staplehurst, Kent TN12 0AZ

☎01580 893730 Fax 01580 893731

Email enquiries@spellmount.com

Website www.spellmount.com

Managing Director *Jamie Wilson*

Approx. Annual Turnover £500,000

FOUNDED 1983. *Publishes* history and military history. About 30 titles a year. Synopses/ideas for books in these specialist fields welcome, enclosing return postage.

Royalties paid biannually for two years, then annually.

Spiro Press

17–19 Rochester Row, London SW1P 1LA

☎0870 164 8900 Fax 0870 165 8989

Website www.spiropress.com

Head of Publishing *Carl Upsall*

Commissioning Editor *Susannah Lear*

Approx. Annual Turnover (Publishing Division) £1.6 million

Spiro Press, formerly The Industrial Society Publishing, is part of the Capita Group and has been publishing for over 20 years. *Specialises* in business, management, self-development, human resources – books, manuals and special reports. TITLES *Inspirational Leadership – Henry V and the Muse of Fire*; *Business 2010*; *Why Innovation Fails*. SERIES *Fast Track*. Unsolicited mss, synopses and ideas welcome. No fiction or illustrated non-fiction.

Royalties paid twice-yearly.

E & FN Spon

See **Routledge**

SportsBooks Limited

PO Box 422, Cheltenham GL50 2YN

☎0870 071 3965 Fax 0870 075 0888

Email randall@sportsbooks.ltd.uk

Website www.sportsbooks.ltd.uk

Chairman & Managing Director *Randall Northam*

Approx. Annual Turnover £100,000

FOUNDED 1995. *Publishes* sports books including biographies, statistical and practical. 5 titles in 2002. TITLES *The Body Bible* Peta Bee; *Sweet Fighting Man* Melanie Lloyd. No unsolicited mss. Snyopses and ideas welcome. Approach by letter or e-mail. IMPRINT **BMM** *Editorial Head* Mark Jones.

Springer-Verlag London Limited

Sweetapple House, Catteshall Road, Godalming, Surrey GU7 3DJ

☎01483 418800 Fax 01483 415144

Email postmaster@svl.co.uk

Website www.springer.co.uk *or* www.springer.de

Managing Director *John Watson*

Editorial Director *Beverley Ford*

Approx. Annual Turnover £5 million

The UK subsidiary of BertelsmannSpringer of Germany. *Publishes* science, technical and medical books and journals. About 150 titles a year, plus journals. Specialises in computing, engineering, medicine, mathematics, statistics, astronomy. All UK published books are sold through Springer's German and US companies as well as in the UK. Not interested in social sciences, fiction or school books but academic and professional science and amateur astronomy mss or synopses welcome.

Royalties paid annually.

Stainer & Bell Ltd

PO Box 110, 23 Gruneisen Road, London N3 1DZ

☎020 8343 3303 Fax 020 8343 3024

Email post@stainer.co.uk

Website www.stainer.co.uk

Managing Directors *Carol Y. Wakefield, Keith M. Wakefield*

Publishing Director *Nicholas Williams*

Approx. Annual Turnover £82,000

FOUNDED 1907 to publish sheet music. *Publishes* music and religious subjects related to hymnody. Unsolicited synopses/ideas for books welcome. Send letter enclosing brief précis.

Royalties paid annually.

Harold Starke Publishers Ltd

Pixey Green, Stradbroke, Near Eye, Suffolk IP21 5NG

☎01379 388334   Fax 01379 388335

Email red@eclat.force9.co.uk

Directors *Naomi Galinski*

Publishes adult non-fiction, medical and reference. No unsolicited mss.

Royalties paid annually.

The Stationery Office

See **TSO**

The Story-Tellers

See **Souvenir Press Ltd**

Straightline Publishing Ltd

29 Main Street, Bothwell, Glasgow G71 8RD

☎01698 853000   Fax 01698 854208

Director *Frank Docherty*
Editor *Colin Calder*

FOUNDED 1989. *Publishes* magazines and directories – trade and technical – books of local interest. TITLES *Cabletalk*; *enterprisingglasgow*. No unsolicited material.

Royalties paid annually.

Studymates Limited

PO Box 2, Bishops Lydeard, Somerset TA4 3YE

☎01823 432002   Fax 01823 430097

Email info@studymates.co.uk

Website www.studymates.co.uk *or*
www.mr.educator.com *or*
www.studymatesusa.com

Managing Editor *Graham Lawler, MA*

FOUNDED 1998 as part of International Briefings Ltd and taken over by education expert Graham Lawler in July 2000. Studymates are academic titles for students at university or college. Two new lists were launched in 2002 – **Studymates Professional**, for the professional person to improve their knowledge in the workplace and **Judith Handbooks**, problem-solving books for women that deal with emotional and day-to-day practical issues. A third list is planned for 2004 – **Mr Educator Handbooks** for under-16s. Books both for children, e.g. *Literacy Poems*, and

for adults about educating children. Ideas first in writing; authors are asked to follow the layout of the author kit available on the website.

Summersdale Publishers Ltd

46 West Street, Chichester, West Sussex PO19 1RP

☎01243 771107   Fax 01243 786300

Email submissions@summersdale.com

Website www.summersdale.com

Directors *Stewart Ferris, Alastair Williams*
Editor *Elizabeth Kershaw*

Approx. Annual Turnover £1 million

FOUNDED 1990. *Publishes* travel literature and guides, fiction, biography, martial arts, self-help, cookery, humour and gift books. 50–60 titles a year. TITLES *La Bella Vita* Vida Adamoli; *The Lonely Sea and the Sky* Sir Francis Chichester; *Empire of the Soul* Paul William Roberts. No unsolicited mss; synopses and ideas welcome.

Royalties paid.

Susquehanna University Press

See **Golden Cockerel Press**

Sussex Academic Press

PO Box 2950, Brighton, East Sussex BN2 5SP

☎01273 699533   Fax 01273 621262

Email edit@sussex-academic.co.uk

Website www.sussex-academic.co.uk

Managing Director *Anthony Grahame*

Approx. Annual Turnover £225,000

FOUNDED 1994. Academic publisher. 30 titles in 2002. DIVISION/IMPRINT **Sussex Academic** TITLES *Art, Crime & Madness; Dugald Stewart – The Pride and Ornament of Scotland; Human Rights & Religion*. **Alpha Press** TITLES *First and Last Editions – England's Second-Hand Bookshops; The Christian Jesus – Faith in the Finding*. No unsolicited material; send letter of inquiry in the first instance.

Royalties paid annually.

Sutton Publishing Ltd

Phoenix Mill, Thrupp, Stroud, Gloucestershire GL5 2BU

☎01453 731114   Fax 01453 731117

Email publishing@sutton-publishing.co.uk

Managing Director *Jeremy Yates-Round*
Senior Commissioning Editors *Jaqueline Mitchell* (Biography); *Christopher Feeney* (General History); *Jonathan Falconer* (Military); *Simon Fletcher* (Local History)

FOUNDED   1978.   Acquired   by   **Haynes**

Publishing in March 2000. *Publishes* academic, archaeology, biography, countryside, history, military, aviation, regional interest, local history. About 200 titles a year. Send synopses rather than complete mss.
Royalties paid twice-yearly.

Authors' Rating Having started as a regional publisher, Sutton has branched out with a strong list of general non-fiction.

Swan Hill Press (An imprint of Quiller Publishing Ltd)
Wykey House, Wykey, Shrewsbury, Shropshire SY4 1JA
☎01939 261616 Fax 01939 261606
Email info@quillerbooks.com
Managing Director *Andrew Johnston*

Specialises in practical books on all country and field sports activities. *Publishes* books on fishing, shooting, gundog training, falconry, equestrian, deer, cookery. About 15 titles a year. Unsolicited mss must include s.a.e.
Royalties paid twice-yearly.

Sweet & Maxwell Group
100 Avenue Road, London NW3 3PF
☎020 7393 7000 Fax 020 7393 7010
Email customerservices@sweetandmaxwell.
co.uk
Website www.sweetandmaxwell.co.uk
Managing Director *Peter Lake*

FOUNDED 1799. Part of the Thomson Corporation. *Publishes* materials in all media; looseleaf works, journals, law reports, CD-ROMs and online. Over 1100 products, including 180 looseleafs, 80 periodicals, more than 40 digital products and online information services, and 200 new titles each year. Not interested in non-legal material. The legal and professional list is varied and contains academic titles as well as treatises and reference works in the legal and related professional fields.
IMPRINTS **Sweet & Maxwell**; **W. Green (Scotland)**; **Thomson Round Hall (Ireland)**. Ideas welcome. Writers with legal/ professional projects in mind are advised to contact the Legal Business Unit at the earliest possible stage in order to lay the groundwork for best design, production and marketing of a project.
Royalties and fees paid according to contract.

Tango Books
See **Sadie Fields Productions Ltd** under **UK Packagers**

Taschen UK Ltd
13 Old Burlington Street, London W1S 3AJ
☎020 7437 4350 Fax 020 7437 4360
Website www.taschen.com

UK office of the German photographic, art and architecture publisher. Editorial office in Cologne (see entry under **European Publishers**).

I.B. Tauris & Co. Ltd
6 Salem Road, London W2 4BU
☎020 7243 1225 Fax 020 7243 1226
Email mail@ibtauris.com
Website www.ibtauris.com
Chairman/Publisher *Iradj Bagherzade*
Managing Director *Jonathan McDonnell*

FOUNDED 1984. Independent publisher. *Publishes* general non-fiction and academic in the fields of international relations, current affairs, history, politics, cultural, media and film studies, Middle East studies. Joint projects with Cambridge University Centre for Middle Eastern Studies, Institute for Latin American Studies and Institute of Ismaili Studies.
Distributes The New Press (New York) outside North America and Philip Wilson Publishers worldwide. IMPRINTS **Tauris Parke Books** Illustrated books on architecture, travel, design and culture. **Tauris Parke Paperbacks** Trade titles, including art and art history. **British Academic Press** Academic monographs. **Radcliffe Press** Colonial history and biography. Unsolicited synopses and book proposals welcome.
Royalties paid twice-yearly.

Authors' Rating Imprint Radcliffe Press may require authors to contribute towards costs of publication.

Tavistock Publications
See **Routledge**

Taylor & Francis Group plc
11 New Fetter Lane, London EC4P 4EE
☎020 7583 9855 Fax 020 7842 2298
Website www.tandf.co.uk
Chairman *Robert Kiernan*
Chief Executive *David Smith*
Approx. Annual Turnover £150 million

FOUNDED 1798 with the launch of *Philosophical Magazine* which has been in publication ever since (now a solid state physics journal). The Group is now a public company but with strong academic connections among the major shareholders. **Falmer Press** joined the group in 1979 and it doubled its size in the late 1980s with the acquisition of Crane Russak in 1986 and Hemisphere Publishing Co in 1988 (now called Taylor & Francis Asia Pacific). In 1995, acquired Lawrence Erlbaum Associates Ltd, renamed **Psychology Press**, and Brunner/Mazel in 1997, adding to the growing list of psychology publications. In 1996, **UCL Press Ltd** was purchased, adding further to its portfolio of publications in science and humanities. In 1997, Garland Publishing Inc., New York, and in 1998 Routledge Publishing Holdings Ltd, including Carfax Publishing and E & FN Spon were acquired. **Europa Publications Ltd**, the reference book publisher covering international affairs, politics and economics and **Martin Dunitz Ltd** (see entry) were added in 1999. Acquired the international journals division of Scandinavian University Press in 2000, adding over 60 academic journals, followed in 2001 by **Gordon & Breach** and **Curzon Press** (see **Routledge**). Most recently acquired **Fitzroy Dearborn** in 2002, BIOS in January 2003 and CRC including Parthenon in March 2003. *Publishes* scientific, technical, education titles at university, research and professional levels. About 2000 titles a year. Unsolicited mss, synopses and ideas welcome.

Royalties paid yearly. *Overseas offices* Taylor & Francis Inc., Philadelphia, PA and New York; Taylor & Francis Asia Pacific, Singapore; Taylor & Francis AS, Norway and Sweden.

Authors' Rating One of those companies that barely registers with authors until they look at some of the famous imprints that are gathered under the corporate umbrella. Very much into higher education and reference, further expansion is predicted, particularly in the US where Taylor & Francis has acquired CRC Press, a science, engineering and medical publisher.

Teach Yourself
See **Hodder Headline Ltd**

Telegraph Books
1 Canada Square, Canary Wharf, London E14 5DT
☎020 7538 6826 Fax 020 7538 6064
Website www.telegraphbooksdirect.co.uk
Owner *Telegraph Group Ltd*
Publisher *Morven Knowles*
Approx. Annual Turnover £3 million

Concentrates on Telegraph branded books in association/collaboration with other publishers. Also runs Telegraph Books Direct, a direct

mail, phone-line bookselling service and off-the-page sales for other publishers' books. *Publishes* general non-fiction: journalism, business and law, personal finance, health, gardening, guides, sport, puzzles and games. About 50 titles a year. Only interested in books if a Telegraph link exists. No unsolicited material.

Royalties paid twice-yearly.

Texere Publishing Ltd
71–77 Leadenhall Street, London EC3A 3DE
☎020 7204 3644 Fax 020 7208 6701
Email david_wilson@etexere.com
Website www.etexere.co.uk
Owner *Texere LLC, New York*
Chairman *Myles Thompson*
Publisher *David Wilson*

FOUNDED 2000 when it purchased the **Orion** business list. Small publishing house that focuses on finance, business, economics, investment and current affairs, at both professional and trade level, particularly topics with a global appeal and including technology/science crossover into business and finance. No fiction. 22 titles in 2002. Unsolicited material welcome; telephone or e-mail *David Wilson* in the first instance.

Royalties paid twice-yearly.

Thames and Hudson Ltd
181A High Holborn, London WC1V 7QX
☎020 7845 5000 Fax 020 7845 5050
Email mail@thameshudson.co.uk
Website www.thamesandhudson.com
Managing Director *Thomas Neurath*
Editorial Head *Jamie Camplin*
Approx. Annual Turnover £24 million

Publishes art, archaeology, architecture and design, biography, fashion, garden and landscape design, graphics, history, illustrated and fine editions, mythology, music, photography, popular culture, style, travel and topography. 200 titles a year. SERIES *World of Art; New Horizons; StyleCity; Hip Hotels; Most Beautiful Villages; Earth From the Air.* TITLES *David Hockney: Secret Knowledge; Sensation; The Shock of the New; Contemporary Natural; Colour and Culture; The Book of Kells; The Mind in the Cave; The Eco-Design Handbook; Fashion Illustration Now; Ancient Egypt: The Great Discoveries; The Seventy Architectural Wonders of Our World.* Send preliminary letter and outline before mss.

Royalties paid twice-yearly.

Authors' Rating Quality illustrated books on art and design. The World of Art series, a huge range of modestly priced, scholarly books, is probably the best of its kind. Financial success rests on producing the sort of books that easily carry over to other languages.

Thomson Learning

High Holborn House, 50–51 Bedford Row, London WC1R 4LR
☎020 7067 2500 Fax 020 7067 2600
Website www.thomsonlearning.co.uk
CEO (Worldwide) *Ron Schlosser*
CEO (Thomson Learning EMEA) *Charles Iossi*
Publishing Director (Thomson Learning EMEA) *Emma Mitchell*

FOUNDED 1993. Formerly International Thomson Publishing, part of the Thomson Corporation and as such has offices worldwide with the UK office being reported to by Copenhagen (for Europe), Turkey (Middle East) and South Africa. *Publishes* education. TITLES *Management and Cost Accounting* Drury; *Strategy – Process, Content, Contact* DeWit and Meyer. Unsolicited material aimed at students is welcome but telephone in the first instance to check out the idea.

Royalties vary according to contract.

Thomson Round Hall
See **Sweet & Maxwell Group**

Stanley Thornes (Publishers) Ltd
See **Nelson Thornes Limited**

F.A. Thorpe (Publishing)

The Green, Bradgate Road, Anstey, Leicester LE7 7FU
☎0116 236 4325 Fax 0116 234 0205
Chairman *David Thorpe*
Group Chief Executive *Robert Thirlby*
Approx. Annual Turnover £6 million

FOUNDED in 1964 to supply large print books to libraries. Part of the Ulverscroft Group Ltd. *Publishes* fiction and non-fiction large print books. No educational, gardening or books that would not be suitable for large print. 453 titles in 2002. DIVISIONS **Charnwood**; **Ulverscroft**. IMPRINTS **Linford Romance**; **Linford Mystery**; **Linford Western**. No unsolicited material.

Thorsons
See **HarperCollins Publishers Ltd**

Time Warner Books UK

Brettenham House, Lancaster Place, London WC2E 7EN
☎020 7911 8000 Fax 020 7911 8100
Email uk@TimeWarnerBooks.com
Website www.TimeWarnerBooks.co.uk
Chief Executive *David Young*
Publisher *Ursula Mackenzie*
Approx. Annual Turnover £40 million

FOUNDED 1988 as Little, Brown & Co. (UK). Part of AOL Time Warner. Began by importing its US parent company's titles and in 1990 launched its own illustrated non-fiction list. Two years later the company took over former Macdonald & Co. *Publishes* hardback and paperback fiction, literary fiction, crime, science fiction and fantasy; and general non-fiction including true crime, biography and autobiography, cinema, gardening, history, humour, travel, crafts and hobbies, reference, cookery, wines and spirits.

IMPRINTS
Little, Brown *Ursula Mackenzie, Barbara Boote, Hilary Hale, Tara Lawrence* Hardback fiction and general non-fiction; **Abacus** *Richard Beswick* Literary fiction and non-fiction paperbacks; **Atom** *Ben Sharpe* Young adult/teen paperbacks; **Orbit** *Tim Holman* Science fiction and fantasy; **Time Warner** *Barbara Boote, Hilary Hale* Mass-market fiction and non-fiction hardbacks and paperbacks; **X Libris** *Sarah Shrubb* Women's erotica; **Virago** (see entry). Approach in writing in the first instance. No unsolicited mss.

Royalties paid twice-yearly.

Authors' Rating A quality publisher that manages to cover an impressive range of new writing. Much praised by authors for friendly efficiency.

Times Books
See **HarperCollins Publishers Ltd**

Titan Books

144 Southwark Street, London SE1 0UP
☎020 7620 0200 Fax 020 7620 0032
Email editorial@titanmail.com
Managing Director *Nick Landau*
Editorial Director *Katy Wild*

FOUNDED 1981. Now a leader in the publication of graphic novels and film and television tie-ins. *Publishes* comic books/graphic novels, film and television titles. About 150 titles a year.

IMPRINT **Titan Books** TITLES *Batman; Buffy the Vampire Slayer; Farscape: The Illustrated Season 4 Companion; The Simpsons; Star Wars; Superman; Transformers; 2000 AD; 100% Jackie*

Chan; *You Can Be a Movie Extra*; *Wallace & Gromit*. No unsolicited fiction or children's books. Ideas for film and TV titles considered; send synopsis/outline with sample chapter. No e-mail submissions. Author guidelines available.

Royalties paid twice-yearly.

TOR
See **Macmillan Publishers Ltd**

Transworld Publishers, A division of the Random House Group Ltd
61–63 Uxbridge Road, London W5 5SA
☎020 8579 2652 Fax 020 8579 5479
Email info@transworld-publishers.co.uk
Website www.booksattransworld.co.uk

Managing Director *Larry Finlay*
Publisher *Patrick Janson-Smith*
Deputy Publisher *Bill Scott-Kerr*
Senior Publishing Director *Francesca Liversidge*
Approx. Annual Turnover £72 million

FOUNDED 1950. A subsidiary of **Random House, Inc.**, New York, which in turn is a wholly-owned subsidiary of **Bertelsmann AG**, Germany. *Publishes* general fiction and non-fiction, gardening, sports and leisure. No unsolicited mss.

IMPRINTS
Bantam *Francesca Liversidge*; **Bantam Press** *Sally Gaminara*; **Corgi & Black Swan** *Bill Scott-Kerr*; **Doubleday** *Marianne Velmans*; **Eden** *Katrina Whone*; **Expert Books** *Gareth Pottle*. AUTHORS Kate Atkinson, Charlotte Bingham, Bill Bryson, Lee Child, Catherine Cookson, Jilly Cooper, Ben Elton, Nicholas Evans, Frederick Forsyth, Robert Goddard, Germaine Greer, Joanne Harris, Stephen Hawking, D.G. Hessayon, John Irving, Sophie Kinsella, Anne McCaffrey, Andy McNab, John O'Farrell, Terry Pratchett, Gerald Seymour, Danielle Steel, Joanna Trollope.

Royalties paid twice-yearly. *Overseas associates* Random House Australia Pty Ltd; Random House New Zealand; Random House (Pty) Ltd (South Africa).

Authors' Rating Brings quality to the mass market.

Travel Publishing Ltd
7A Apollo House, Calleva Park, Aldermaston, Berkshire RG7 8TN
☎0118 981 7777 Fax 0118 982 0077
Email travel_publishing@msn.com
Website www.travelpublishing.co.uk

Directors *Peter Robinson, Chris Day*

FOUNDED in 1997 by two former directors of **Reed Elsevier plc**. *Publishes* travel, accommodation, food, drink and specialist shops guides to Britain and Ireland. Over 40 titles in print. SERIES **Hidden Places**; **Hidden Inns**; **Country Living Rural Guides** (in conjunction with *Country Living* magazine; **Golfers Guides**; **Off the Motorway**. Welcomes unsolicited material; send letter in the first instance.

Royalties paid twice-yearly.

Treehouse Children's Books Ltd
2nd Floor, The Old Brewhouse, Lower Charlton Trading Estate, Shepton Mallet, Somerset BA4 5QE
☎01749 330529 Fax 01749 330544
Email richard.powell4@virgin.net

Co-Directors *Richard Powell, David Bailey*
Approx. Annual Turnover £1 million

FOUNDED 1992. *Publishes* children's pre-school novelty books. No mss. Illustrations, synopses and ideas for books welcome; write in the first instance.

Fees paid; no royalties.

Trentham Books Ltd
Westview House, 734 London Road, Stoke-on-Trent, Staffordshire ST4 5NP
☎01782 745567/844699 Fax 01782 745553
Website www.trentham-books.co.uk

Directors *Dr Gillian Klein, Barbara Wiggins*
Approx. Annual Turnover £1 million

Publishes education (nursery, school to higher), social sciences, intercultural studies, gender studies and law for professional readers *not* for children and parents. Also academic and professional journals. No fiction, biography or poetry. Over 30 titles a year. Unsolicited mss, synopses and ideas welcome if relevant to their interests. Material only returned if adequate s.a.e. sent.

Royalties paid annually.

Trident Press Ltd
Empire House, 175 Piccadilly, London W1J 9TB
☎020 7491 8770 Fax 020 7491 8664
Email admin@tridentpress.com
Website www.tridentpress.com

Managing Director *Peter Vine*
Approx. Annual Turnover £550,000

FOUNDED 1997. *Publishes* TV tie-ins, natural history, travel, geography, underwater/marine life,

history, archaeology, culture and fiction. DIVISIONS **Fiction/General Publishing** *Paula Vine;* **Natural History** *Peter Vine.* TITLES *Red Sea Sharks; The Elysium Testament; BBC Wildlife Specials; UAE in Focus.* No unsolicited mss; synopses and ideas welcome, particularly TV tie-ins. Approach in writing or *brief* communications by e-mail, fax or telephone.
Royalties paid annually.

Trotman & Co. Ltd
2 The Green, Richmond, Surrey TW9 1PL
☎020 8486 1150 Fax 020 8486 1161
Website www.trotmanpublishing.co.uk
Managing Director *Toby Trotman*
Editorial Director *Mina Patria*
Approx. Annual Turnover £3 million
Publishes general careers books, higher education guides, teaching support material, employment and training resources. About 50 titles a year. TITLES *Degree Course Offers; The Student Book; UCAS/Trotman Complete Guides; Students' Money Matters; Shine* magazine supporting the Connexions Card. Unsolicited material welcome. Also active in the educational resources market, producing recruitment brochures.
Royalties paid twice-yearly.

TSO (The Stationery Office)
St Crispins, Duke Street, Norwich, Norfolk NR3 1PD
☎01603 622211 Fax 01603 694313
(Editorial)
Website www.tso.co.uk
Chief Executive *Iain Burns*
Approx. Annual Turnover £250 million
Formerly HMSO, which was FOUNDED 1786. Became part of the private sector in October 1996. 11,000 new titles each year with 50,000 titles in print. Publisher of material sponsored by Parliament, government departments and other official bodies. Also commercial publishing in the following broad categories: business and professional, environment, transport, education and law.

Twenty First Century Publishers Ltd
Braunton Barn, Kiln Lane, Isfield, East Sussex TN22 5JG
☎01892 522802
Email TFCP@connectfree.co.uk
Website www.twentyfirstcenturypublishers.com
Chairman *Fred Piechoczek*

Approx. Annual Turnover £120,000
FOUNDED 2002. *Publishes* general fiction, financial thrillers and crime. 5 titles in 2002. TITLES *Means to an End; Ramona; The Signature of a Voice* (all by Johnny John Heinz); *Tarnished Copper* Geoffrey Sambrook; *Over a Barrel* Peter Driver. Welcomes submissions by e-mail: manuscripts@connectfree.co.uk (contact Fred Piechoczek). Send brief synopsis in the body of the e-mail with extracts from the book in a file attachment (two to three chapters from anywhere in the book). No non-fiction or children's.
Royalties paid twice-yearly.

20/20
See **The X Press**

UCL Press Ltd
See **Taylor & Francis Group Plc**

Ulverscroft
See **F.A. Thorpe (Publishing)**

Unichrome
See **Jarrold Publishing**

University Presses of California, Columbia & Princeton Ltd
1 Oldlands Way, Bognor Regis, West Sussex PO22 9SA
☎01243 842165 Fax 01243 842167
Email lois@upccp.demon.co.uk

Publishes academic titles only. US-based editorial offices. Over 200 titles a year. Enquiries only.

Usborne Publishing Ltd
83–85 Saffron Hill, London EC1N 8RT
☎020 7430 2800 Fax 020 7430 1562
Email mail@usborne.co.uk
Website www.usborne.com
Managing Director *Peter Usborne*
Publishing Director *Jenny Tyler*
Approx. Annual Turnover £20 million
FOUNDED 1973. *Publishes* non-fiction, fiction, computer books, puzzle books and music for children, young adults and pre-school. Some titles for parents. Up to 200 titles a year. Non-fiction books are written in-house to a specific format and therefore unsolicited mss are not normally welcome. Ideas which may be developed in-house are sometimes considered. Fiction for children will be considered. Keen to hear from new illustrators and designers.
Royalties paid twice-yearly.

Authors' Rating A children's publisher that finds favour with parents who can learn a thing or two from an imaginative non-fiction list. But fiction too is growing – up to 30 titles a year.

Vallentine Mitchell/ Jewish Chronicle Publications

Crown House, 47 Chase Side, Southgate, London N14 5BP
☎020 8920 2100 Fax 020 8447 8548
Email info@vmbooks.com
Website www.vmbooks.com
Chairman *Frank Cass*

Publishes books of Jewish interest: history, philosophy and heritage, Holocaust studies. An imprint of **Frank Cass & Co Ltd**.

Vanguard Press
See **Pegasus Elliot Mackenzie Publishers Ltd**

Vega
See **Chrysalis Books Group**

Ventura
See **Penguin Group (UK)**

Vermilion
See **Random House Group Ltd**

Verso
6 Meard Street, London W1F 0EG
☎020 7437 3546 Fax 020 7734 0059
Website www.versobooks.com
Chairman *George Galfalvi*
Managing Director *Gavin Everall*
Approx. Annual Turnover £2 million

Formerly New Left Books which grew out of the *New Left Review*. *Publishes* politics, history, sociology, economics, philosophy, cultural studies, feminism. TITLES *The Prophet Armed: Trotsky 1879–1921* Isaac Deutscher; *The Trial of Henry Kissinger* Christopher Hitchens; *The New Rulers of the World* John Pilger; *An Act of State: The Execution of Martin Luther King* William Pepper; *The Clash of Fundamentalism* Tariq Ali; *Innocent in the House* Andy McSmith; *The Holocaust Industry* Norman Finkelstein. No unsolicited mss; synopses and ideas for books welcome.

Royalties paid annually. *Overseas office* in New York.

Authors' Rating Dubbed by the *Bookseller* as 'one of the most successful small independent publishers'.

Viking
See **Penguin Group (UK)**

Vintage
See **Random House Group Ltd**

Virago Press
Time Warner Books, Brettenham House, Lancaster Place, London WC2E 7EN
☎020 7911 8000 Fax 020 7911 8100
Website www.virago.co.uk
Publisher *Lennie Goodings*
Senior Editor *Antonia Hodgson*
Editor, Virago Modern Classics *Jill Foulston*
Approx. Annual Turnover £2.5 million

FOUNDED in 1973 by Carmen Callil, Virago *publishes* fiction and non-fiction books of quality by women. Approximately 50 new books a year in the areas of autobiography, biography, fiction, history, politics, psychology and women's issues. IMPRINTS **Virago Modern Classics** 20th-century reprints; AUTHORS Margaret Atwood, Maya Angelou, Gail Anderson-Dargatz, Nina Bawden, Jennifer Belle, Sarah Dunant, Marilyn French, Michèle Roberts, Natasha Walter, Sarah Waters. Send synopsis and sample chapter and return postage with all unsolicited material.

Royalties paid twice-yearly.

Virgin Books Ltd
Thames Wharf Studios, Rainville Road, London W6 9HT
☎020 7386 3300 Fax 020 7386 3360
Email info@virgin-books.co.uk
Website www.virgin.com/books
Managing Director *K.T. Forster*
Approx. Annual Turnover £10 million

The Virgin Group's book publishing company. *Publishes* non-fiction, reference and large-format illustrated books on lifestyle, health, music, sport, biography, crime, film, TV and current affairs. No poetry, short stories, individual novels, children's books.

DIVISIONS **Non-fiction** IMPRINT **Virgin** Editorial Director *Caroline Thorne*; Sports Editorial Director *Jonathan Taylor*; Commissioning Editor/Scout (esp. Music) *Stuart Slater*. **Fiction** IMPRINTS **Virgin**; **Black Lace** Senior Editor *Kerri Sharp* Erotic fiction 'written by women for women'; **Nexus** Editor *Paul Copperwaite* Erotic fiction.

DISTRIBUTION British School of Motoring (BSM); **Independent Music Press (IMP)**.

Royalties paid twice-yearly.

Authors' Rating Black Lace is attracting huge

interest from authors eager to turn out raunchy titles but expect a long waiting time for any response to submissions.

Vista House Ltd
Suite 676, 37 Store Street, London
WC1W 7QF
☎020 7644 4816
Email editorial@vistahouse.net
Website www.vistahouse.net
Also at: Vista House, 27 Greenhead Road, Huddersfield, West Yorkshire HD1 4EN
☎01484 427200
Managing Editor *R. Sharp*
Publishing Director *H.L. Byram, M.Ed., BA(Hons)*

FOUNDED 1998. IMPRINTS **Paragon Press Publishing** Fiction & non-fiction. Includes the *Wizard Spell* series for young children; **Paragon Summaries** Educational series for secondary and tertiary education. Initial enquiries by e-mail or telephone. Submission guidelines on website (www.paragonpress-publishing.com); **Vista House** Fiction and non-fiction; biography and memoirs; **Vista Originals** Books on subjects away from the beaten track; **Vista Africa** Books and text-books about and for Africa south of the Sahara; **First Authors** Offers a range of publishing services, including self-publishing programmes (www.first-authors.co.uk).

Authors' Rating May ask authors to con-tribute towards costs of publication.

The Vital Spark
See **Neil Wilson Publishing Ltd**

Voyager
See **HarperCollins Publishers Ltd**

University of Wales Press
10 Columbus Walk, Brigantine Place, Cardiff CF10 4UP
☎029 2049 6899 Fax 029 2049 6108
Email press@press.wales.ac.uk
Website www.wales.ac.uk/press
Director *Susan Jenkins*
Deputy Director *Richard Houdmont*
Approx. Annual Turnover £500,000

FOUNDED 1922. *Publishes* academic and schol-arly books in English and Welsh in four core areas: history, Welsh and Celtic Studies, Euro-pean Studies, religion and philosophy. 60 titles in 2002.

IMPRINTS **GPC Books**; **Gwasg Prifysgol Cymru**; **University of Wales Press** TITLES *Theatre in Madrid and Barcelona, 1892–1936* David George; *Consuming Narratives – Gender and Monstrous Appetite in the Middle Ages and Renaissance* eds. Elizabeth Herbert McAvoy and Teresa Watts; *John Rawls: Towards a Just World Order* Patrick Hayden; *Making Sense of Wales* Graham Day. Unsolicited mss consid-ered. See website for further guidance.
Royalties paid annually.

Walker Books Ltd
87 Vauxhall Walk, London SE11 5HJ
☎020 7793 0909 Fax 020 7587 1123
Email editorial@walker.co.uk
Website www.walkerbooks.co.uk
Publisher *Jane Winterbotham*
Editors *Deirdre McDermott* (picture books), *Caroline Royds* (fiction, non-fiction and gift books), *Denise Johnstone-Burt* (picture books, board and novelty), *Lorraine Taylor* (character, audio, stationery and merchandising)
Approx. Annual Turnover £31.7 million

FOUNDED 1979. *Publishes* illustrated children's books, children's fiction and non-fiction. About 300 titles a year. TITLES *Maisy* Lucy Cousins; *Where's Wally?* Martin Handford; *Five Minutes' Peace* Jill Murphy; *Can't You Sleep, Little Bear?* Martin Waddell and Barbara Firth; *Guess How Much I Love You* Sam McBratney and Anita Jeram; *Eagle Strike* Anthony Horowitz. Unsolicited mss welcome.
Royalties paid twice-yearly.

Authors' Rating One of the most exciting children's lists. Much praised for author rela-tions.

Wallflower Press
5 Pond Street, Hampstead, London NW3 2PN
☎020 7431 6622 Fax 020 7435 6522
Email info@wallflowerpress.co.uk
Website www.wallflowerpress.co.uk
Editorial Director *Yoram Allon*
Chief Editor *Del Cullen*
Approx. Annual Turnover £150,000

FOUNDED 1999. *Publishes* academic and popu-lar film studies and related media and cultural studies. Over 20 titles a year. SERIES **Short Cuts** Introductory undergraduate books; **Director's Cuts** Studies on significant inter-national film-makers. Unsolicited mss, syn-opses and proposals welcome. No fiction or academic material not related to the moving image.
Royalties paid annually.

Ward Lock
See **Octopus Publishing Group**

Ward Lock Educational Co. Ltd
BIC Ling Kee House, 1 Christopher Road, East Grinstead, West Sussex RH19 3BT
☎01342 318980 Fax 01342 410980
Email wle@lingkee.com
Website www.wardlockeducational.com
Owner *Ling Kee (UK) Ltd*
FOUNDED 1952. *Publishes* educational books (primary, middle, secondary, teaching manuals) for all subjects, specialising in maths, science, geography, reading and English and currently focusing on Key Stages 1 and 2.

Frederick Warne
See **Penguin Group (UK)**

Franklin Watts
See **The Watts Publishing Group Ltd**

The Watts Publishing Group Ltd
96 Leonard Street, London EC2A 4XD
☎020 7739 2929 Fax 020 7739 6487
Email <gm>@wattspub.co.uk
Website www.wattspublishing.co.uk
Managing Director *Marlene Johnson*
Part of Groupe Lagardere. *Publishes* children's non-fiction, reference, information, gift, fiction, picture and novelty. About 300 titles a year.
IMPRINTS **Franklin Watts** *Philippa Stewart* Non-fiction and information; **Orchard Books** *Ann-Janine Murtagh* Fiction, picture and novelty books. Unsolicited mss, synopses and ideas for books welcome.
Royalties paid twice-yearly. *Overseas associates* in Australia and New Zealand.

Wayland
See **Hodder Headline Ltd**

Weidenfeld & Nicolson
See **The Orion Publishing Group Ltd**

Welsh Academic Press
See **Ashley Drake Publishing Ltd**

West Highland Series
See **House of Lochar**

Westworld International Ltd
Unit 3, 25 Putney Hill, London SW15 6BE
☎020 8788 2455
Email editor@westworldinternational.com
Website www.westworldinternational.com

Chairman/Editorial Head, Fiction *Paul Smith*
Managing Director/Editorial Head, Biography *Stephen Smith*
Approx. Annual Turnover £200,000
FOUNDED 1996. *Publishes* mass-market biography and fiction in paperback. 3 titles in 2002. Welcomes unsolicited material; contact by e-mail with short synopsis. 'We are only interested in fiction or true life stories.'
Royalties paid twice-yearly. *Overseas associate* Westworld Germany Inc.

Wharncliffe Publishing
47 Church Street, Barnsley, South Yorkshire S70 2AS
☎01226 734222 Fax 01226 734438
Email enquiries@wharncliffebooks.co.uk
Website www.wharncliffebooks.co.uk
Chairman *Sir Nicholas Hewitt*
Managing Director *Charles Hewitt*
Imprint Manager *Barbara Bramall*
An imprint of **Pen & Sword Books Ltd**. Wharncliffe is the book and magazine publishing arm of an old-established, independently owned newspaper publishing and printing house. *Publishes* local history throughout the UK, focusing on nostalgia and old photographs. SERIES *Aspects*. No unsolicited mss; synopses and ideas welcome.
Royalties paid twice-yearly.

Which? Books/ Consumers' Association
2 Marylebone Road, London NW1 4DF
☎020 7770 6000 Fax 020 7770 7660
Website www.which.net
Director *Sheila McKechnie*
Head of Publishing *Kim Lavely*
Head of Which? Books *Robert Gray*
FOUNDED 1957. Publishing arm of the Consumers' Association, a registered charity. *Publishes* non-fiction: information, reference and how-to books on travel, gardening, health, personal finance, consumer law, food, careers, DIY. All titles offer direct value or utility to the UK consumer. 25–30 titles a year.
IMPRINT **Which? Books** TITLES *The Good Food Guide*; *The Good Skiing and Snowboarding Guide*; *The Which? Hotel Guide*; *The Which? Wine Guide*; *Wills and Probate*; *Be Your Own Financial Adviser*. No unsolicited mss; send synopses and ideas only.
Royalties, if applicable, paid twice-yearly.

Whitaker Information Services

Woolmead House West, Bear Lane, Farnham,
Surrey GU9 7LG
☎01252 742500 Fax 01252 742501
Website www.whitaker.co.uk
Chief Executive *Jonathan Nowell*

FOUNDED in 1858 by bookseller Joseph
Whitaker. Acquired by BPI, American subsidiary of the Dutch group VNU, in 1999.
Published *Whitaker's Almanac* from 1868 until
the title was sold to the Stationery Office in
1997. Provides a range of services for the book
trade including the **ISBN Agency**, BookBank,
SourceData, Teleordering and Book Scan. Also
new Web services: LibWeb (for libraries);
PubWeb (for publishers) and WhitakerWeb (for
booksellers). *Publishes* bibliographic reference
products. TITLES *Whitaker's Books in Print*;
Directory of Publishers (*The Red Book*).

Whittet Books Ltd

Hill Farm, Stonham Road, Cotton,
Stowmarket, Suffolk IP14 4RQ
☎01449 781877 Fax 01449 781898
Email annabel@whittet.dircon.co.uk
Website www.whittetbooks.com
Managing Director *Annabel Whittet*

Publishes natural history, pets, poultry, horses,
domestic livestock, rural interest. Unsolicited
mss, synopses and ideas for books welcome.
Royalties paid twice-yearly.

Whurr Publishers Ltd

19B Compton Terrace, London N1 2UN
☎020 7359 5979 Fax 020 7226 5290
Email info@whurr.co.uk
Website www.whurr.co.uk
Chairman/Managing Director *Colin Whurr*
Approx. Annual Turnover £1 million

FOUNDED in 1987. *Publishes* speech and language therapy, nursing, psychology, psychotherapy, audiology, special education
including dyslexia, ADHD, autism and Downs
syndrome. No fiction and general trade books.
60 titles in 2002. Unsolicited mss, synopses and
ideas welcome within their specialist fields
only. 'Whurr Publishers believes authors can
be best served by a small, specialised company
combining old-fashioned service with the latest
publishing technology.'
Royalties paid twice-yearly.

Whydown Books Limited

Sedlescombe, East Sussex TN33 0RN
☎01580 830877 Fax 01424 870083

Email readerspost@whydownbooks.com
Website www.whydownbooks.com
Chairman *Dick Nesbitt-Dufort*
Managing & Finance Director *Chris Martin*
Editorial Head *Pamela Richards*

FOUNDED 2002. *Publishes* biography, fiction,
general interest with an emphasis on writers
with first-hand experience of distant places and
dangerous events. TITLES *Spies and Lovers*
Adrian Hill; *Black Lysander* John Nesbitt-
Dufort. No academic, children's or poetry at
present. No unsolicited mss. Synopses and
ideas welcome. Approach by letter or e-mail
with idea and writing history.
Royalties paid twice-yearly

Wild Goose Publications

Iona Community, 4th Floor, The Savoy
Centre, 140 Sauchiehall Street, Glasgow
G2 3DH
☎0141 332 6292 Fax 0141 332 1090
Email admin@ionabooks.com
Website www.ionabooks.com
Editorial Head *Sandra Kramer*
Approx. Annual Turnover £200,000

The publishing house of the Iona Community,
established in the Celtic Christian tradition of
St Columba, *publishes* books, tapes and CDs on
holistic spirituality, social justice, political and
peace issues, healing, innovative approaches to
worship, song and material for meditation and
reflection.

Wiley Europe Ltd

Atrium, Southern Gate, Chichester,
West Sussex PO19 8SQ
☎01243 779777 Fax 01243 775878
Website www.wileyeurope.com
Managing Director *Dr John Jarvis*
Publishing Directors *Mike Davis, Stephen
Smith*
Approx. Annual Turnover £57 million

FOUNDED 1807. US parent company. *Publishes*
professional, reference trade and text books,
scientific, technical and biomedical.

DIVISIONS
Architecture *Maggie Toy*; **Business** *Sarah
Stevens*; **Business/Management** *Steve Hardman*;
Chemistry & Earth Sciences *Sally Wilkinson*;
Computing *Gaynor Redvers-Mutton*; **Finance**
Samantha Whittaker; **General Interest** Sally
Smith; **Management/Marketing** *Claire
Plimmer*; **Psychology** *Vivien Ward*; **Major
Reference Works** *David Hughes*; **Medicine &**

Life Sciences *Deborah Dixion*; **Technology & Engineering** *Ann-Marie Halligan*.
Royalties paid annually.

Authors' Rating With an ever growing list of scientific, technical and medical books, Wiley is among the top educational and professional publishers. Academic authors are attracted by the American connection. Online publishing is set to increase.

Neil Wilson Publishing Ltd
Suite 303, The Pentagon Centre, 36 Washington Street, Glasgow G3 8AZ
☎0141 221 1117 Fax 0141 221 5363
Email info@nwp.sol.co.uk
Website www.nwp.co.uk *or* www.11-9.co.uk
Managing Director/Editorial Director
   Neil Wilson
11:9 Editorial Administrator *Morven Dooner*
Approx. Annual Turnover £300,000

FOUNDED 1992. *Publishes* Scottish interest and history, biography, humour and hillwalking, whisky; also cookery. About 10–15 titles a year. NWP manages the **11:9** fiction imprint for new Scottish writing, launched in 2000, which was financed under the New Directions Lottery fund, distributed by the Scottish Arts Council. In addition, three non-fiction IMPRINTS were launched in 2000: **The In Pinn** Outdoor pursuits; **The Angels' Share** Whisky, drink and food-related subjects; **The Vital Spark** Humour. Unsolicited mss, synopses and ideas welcome. No politics, academic or technical.
   Royalties paid twice-yearly.

Philip Wilson Publishers Ltd
7 Deane House, 27 Greenwood Place, London NW5 1LB
☎020 7284 3088 Fax 020 7284 3099
Email pwilson@philip-wilson.co.uk
Website www.philip-wilson.co.uk
Chairman *Philip Wilson*

FOUNDED 1976. *Publishes* art, art history, antiques and collectables. About 15 titles a year.

Wimbledon Publishing Company
75–76 Blackfriars Road, London SE1 8HD
☎020 7401 8855 Fax 020 7928 9226
Email editor@wpcpress.com
Website www.wpcpress.com
Managing Director *Kamaljit Sood*
General Manager *Noel McPherson*

FOUNDED in 1992 as a publisher of school texts, going on to launch **Anthem Press**, an academic and general interest imprint focusing on history, politics, economics, international affairs, literature and culture.
   IMPRINTS **Anthem Press** *Tom Penn, Caroline Broughton*; **WPC Education** *K. Sood*. Welcomes mss, synopses and ideas for books.
   Royalties paid annually. *Partner organisation* Stylus Publishing LLC, Sterling, VA, US.

Windhorse Publications
11 Park Road, Moseley, Birmingham B13 8AB
☎0121 449 9696 Fax 0121 449 9191
Email info@windhorsepublications.
   fsworld.co.uk
Website www.windhorsepublications.com
Chairman/Editorial Head *Jnanasiddhi*
Approx. Annual Turnover £250,000

FOUNDED 1977. *Publishes* meditation and Buddhism and biographies of Buddhists. Associated with the FWBO, a worldwide Buddhist movement. 9 titles in 2002. TITLE *Come and See for Yourself: the Buddhist Guide to Saving the Planet* Ayya Khema. Unsolicited mss, synopses and ideas welcome; approach by letter or e-mail in the first instance.
   Royalties paid quarterly.

Windsor Large Print
See entry under **BBC Audiobooks**

Wise Publications
See **Omnibus Press**

WIT Press
Ashurst Lodge, Ashurst, Southampton, Hampshire SO40 7AA
☎023 8029 3223 Fax 023 8029 2853
Email marketing@witpress.com
Website www.witpress.com
Owner *Computational Mechanics International Ltd, Southampton*
Chairman *Professor C.A. Brebbia*
Managing Director/Editorial Head *Lance Sucharov*

FOUNDED in 1980 as Computational Mechanics Publications to publish engineering analysis titles. Changed to WIT Press to reflect the increased range of publications. *Publishes* scientific and technical, mainly at postgraduate level and above, including architecture, environmental engineering, bioengineering. 50 titles in 2002. TITLES *The Sustainable City; Spatial Statistics Through Applications; Air Quality Management; Hybrid Vehicle Propulsion*. Unsolicited mss, synopses and ideas welcome; approach by post or e-mail. No non-scientific or technical material or lower level (school- and college-level texts).

Royalties paid annually. *Overseas subsidiary* Computational Mechanics, Inc., Billerica, USA.

Wizard Books
See **Icon Books Ltd**

Woburn Press
See **Frank Cass & Co Ltd**

Oswald Wolff Books
See **Berg Publishers**

The Women's Press
34 Great Sutton Street, London EC1V 0LQ
☎020 7251 3007 Fax 020 7608 1938
Website www.the-womens-press.com
Managing Director *Charlotte Gascoigne*
Approx. Annual Turnover £1 million

Part of the Namara Group. First title published in 1978. *Publishes* women only: quality fiction and non-fiction. Fiction usually has a female protagonist and a woman-centred theme. International writers and subject matter encouraged. Non-fiction: books for and about women generally; gender politics, race politics, disability, feminist theory, health and psychology, literary criticism. About 50 titles a year.

IMPRINTS
Women's Press Classics; **Livewire Books for Teenagers** Fiction and non-fiction series for young adults. Synopses and ideas for books welcome. No mss without previous letter, synopsis and sample material.
Royalties paid twice-yearly.

Authors' Rating An example of how to make niche publishing work. But many are those who wish to join the list and more than average patience may be needed by those who send in proposals.

Woodhead Publishing Ltd
Abington Hall, Abington, Cambridge CB1 6AH
☎01223 891358 Fax 01223 893694
Email wp@woodhead-publishing.com
Website www.woodhead-publishing.com *or* www.WoodheadFoodNet.com
Chairman *Alan Jessup*
Managing Director *Martin Woodhead*
Approx. Annual Turnover £1.3 million

FOUNDED 1989. *Publishes* engineering, materials technology, textile technology, finance and investment, food technology, environmental science. TITLES *Welding International* (journal); *Reinforced Plastics Durability*; *Meat Science 6e*; *Base Metals Handbook*; *Foreign Exchange Options*. About 50 titles a year. Website www.WoodheadFoodNet.com launched in 2002. Contains 50 e-books on food science, technology and nutrition.

DIVISIONS **Woodhead Publishing** *Martin Woodhead;* **Abington Publishing** (in association with the Welding Institute) *Francis Dodds.* Unsolicited material welcome.
Royalties paid annually.

Wordsmill & Tate Publishers
88 Kingsway, Holborn, London WC2B 6AA
☎020 7841 2715 Fax 020 7841 1001
Email <name>@ wordsmill.com
Website www.wordsmill.com
Commissioning Editor *Matthew Tate*
Editorial Coordinator *Jane Barrington*

Independent publisher *specialising* in hardback and paperback general fiction and non-fiction, biography, autobiography, memoirs, children's and history. No poetry, erotica or cookery. About 35–40 titles a year. Unsolicited material welcome with return postage. First time authors should send synopis and sample chapters only.
Royalties paid twice-yearly.

Authors' Rating Liable to ask authors to contribute towards costs of production.

Wordsworth Editions Ltd
8B East Street, Ware, Hertfordshire SG12 9HG
☎01920 465167 Fax 01920 462267
Email enquiries@wordsworth-editions.com *or* dennishart@wordsworth-editions.com (Editorial)
Website www.wordsworth-editions.co.uk
Directors *M.C.W. Trayler, E.G. Trayler*
Approx. Annual Turnover £4 million

FOUNDED 1987. *Publishes* classics of English and world literature, reference books, poetry, children's classics, military history. Recently launched a new series of myth, legend and folklore books. About 75 titles a year. No unsolicited mss.

WPC Education
See **Wimbledon Publishing Company**

X Libris
See **Time Warner Books UK**

The X Press

PO Box 25694, London N17 6FP
☎020 8801 2100 Fax 020 8885 1322
Email vibes@xpress.co.uk

Editorial Director *Dotun Adebayo*
Marketing Director *Steve Pope*

LAUNCHED in 1992 with the cult bestseller *Yardie*, The X Press is the leading publisher of Black-interest fiction in the UK. Also *publishes* general fiction and children's fiction. 28 titles in 2002. IMPRINTS **The X Press** TITLES *Yardie; Baby Father.* **Nia** TITLE *In Search of Satisfaction.* **20/20** TITLE *Curvy Lovebox.* Send mss rather than synopses or ideas (enclose s.a.e.). No poetry.
Royalties paid annually.

Authors' Rating A small company that has done an inestimable service by introducing Black writers to the publishing mainstream. Popular fiction is the mainstay but the list also covers reprints of classic Black fiction.

Y Ddraig Fach

See **Ashley Drake Publishing Ltd**

Y Lolfa Cyf

Talybont, Ceredigion SY24 5AP
☎01970 832304 Fax 01970 832782
Email ylolfa@ylolfa.com
Website www.ylolfa.com/

Managing Director *Garmon Gruffudd*
General Editor *Lefi Gruffudd*
Approx. Annual Turnover £800,000

FOUNDED 1967. Small company which publishes mainly in Welsh; has its own four-colour printing and binding facilities. *Publishes* Welsh language publications; Celtic language tutors; English language books for the Welsh and Celtic tourist trade. About 50 titles a year. Expanding slowly. TITLES *My Kingdom of Books* Richard Booth; *The Welsh Learner's Dictionary* Heini Gruffudd; *The Fight for Welsh Freedom* Gwynfor Evans; *Celtic Vision* John Merion Morris. IMPRINT **Dinas** Part-author-subsidised imprint for non-mainstream books of Welsh interest in English and Welsh. Write first with synopses or ideas.
Royalties paid twice-yearly.

Yale University Press (London)

47 Bedford Square, London WC1B 3DP
☎020 7079 4900 Fax 020 7079 4901

Managing Director *John Nicoll*

FOUNDED 1961. Owned by US parent company. *Publishes* academic and humanities. About 200 titles (worldwide) a year. Unsolicited mss and synopses welcome if within specialised subject areas.
Royalties paid annually.

Authors' Rating A publisher with a marvellous talent for turning out scholarly books which appeal to the general reader. Academic writers who want to reach a wider audience take note.

Roy Yates Books

Smallfields Cottage, Cox Green, Rudgwick, Horsham, West Sussex RH12 3DE
☎01403 822299 Fax 01403 823012

Chairman/Managing Director *Roy Yates*
Approx. Annual Turnover £120,000

FOUNDED 1990. *Publishes* children's books only. No unsolicited material as books are adaptations of existing popular classics suitable for translation into dual-language format.
Royalties paid quarterly.

Yellow Jersey

See **Random House Group Ltd**

Zambezi Publishing

PO Box 221, Plymouth, Devon PL2 2YJ
☎01752 367300 Fax 01752 350453
Email info@zampub.com
Website www.zampub.com

Chair *Sasha Fenton*
Managing Director *Jan Budkowski*

FOUNDED 1999. *Publishes* non-fiction: mind, body and spirit, New Age, self-help. 10 titles in 2002. IMPRINT **Zambezi Publishing** *Sasha Fenton* TITLES *Chinese Divinations; Fortune Telling by Tarot Cards; Astrology ... On the Move!* No unsolicied mss or ideas for books; send synopsis and sample chapter by mail. Brief e-mail communication acceptable but *no* attachments, please.
Royalties paid twice-yearly.

Zastrugi Books

PO Box 2963, Brighton, East Sussex BN1 6AW
☎01273 566369 Fax 01273 566369/562720

Chairman *Ken Singleton*

FOUNDED 1997. *Publishes* English-language teaching books only. No unsolicited mss; synopses and ideas for books welcome.
Royalties paid twice-yearly.

Zed Books Ltd

7 Cynthia Street, London N1 9JF
☎020 7837 4014 Fax 020 7833 3960

Email hosie@zedbooks.demon.co.uk
Website www.zedbooks.demon.co.uk
Approx. Annual Turnover £1.4 million
FOUNDED 1976. *Publishes* international and
Third World affairs, development studies,
women's studies, environmental studies, cultural studies, human rights and specific area
studies. No fiction, children's or poetry. About
60 titles a year.

DIVISIONS
Development & Environment *Robert
Molteno*; **Women's Studies**, **Cultural Studies**.
TITLES *The Development Dictionary* ed.

Wolfgang Sachs; *Staying Alive* Vandana Shiva;
The Autobiography of Nawal Nawal El Saadawi.
No unsolicited mss; synopses and ideas wel-
come though.
     Royalties paid annually.

Zero to Ten
See **Evans Brothers Ltd**

Zigzag
See **Chrysalis Children's Books**

Zipper Books
See **Millivres Prowler Limited**

Serial Killing

Book serialisations are big business for newspapers.
Brian MacArthur, Associate Editor of The Times,
reveals how authors can get in on the act

The publishing sensation of the year so far has been the £1.6 million paid for the memoirs of John Peel, the radio personality. Transworld will have to sell a lot of Peel in hardback and paperback to recoup that investment – but they will have factored into their calculations a tidy sum for a newspaper serialisation. Some papers may be willing to pay up to £200,000 for the serial rights, especially if Peel's book contains plenty of juicy anecdotes about celebrities and if there is at least one story which will make the front page. Both newspaper and publisher will then be happy. The newspaper will hope to sell more copies, an imperative in a marketplace where sales are declining year by year. It will also promote the serial on TV and/or radio which means that Transworld will launch the book in a blaze of publicity and will enter the bestseller lists.

The relationship between publishers and newspapers grows stronger by the year and the interest is not only in the big, blockbuster books. When *The Times* serialised Hodder's *The Thoughts of Marcus Aurelius* a while ago, five thousand copies of the book were sold from the 'puff' published at the end of the serialisation, amounting to almost the whole of the first print run. Newspapers now also sell the books they serialise. My guess, as the journalist who buys serialisations for *The Times,* is that newspapers spend at least £5 million a year, and almost certainly much more, on buying serials of extracts from books.

At least ten manuscripts or proof copies arrive on my desk each week accompanied by a letter selling their merits for serial or extract, often now after I have signed a confidentiality agreement swearing that the contents will not be revealed to anybody other than the reader and the editor. The reason is security. There is fierce rivalry between the tabloids and publishers fear that a paper that was unsuccessful in the auction for the book may be tempted to use what they have read for a 'spoiler' (as it is known in the trade), in which the rival newspaper launches its own serial, culled from cuttings and inside knowledge, to spoil the impact made by the successful newspaper.

The ideal book for a big serialisation, especially for *The Times*, will be a politician's or famous businessman's memoirs, or on a subject that interests the *Times2* tabloid features section or the Saturday Weekend section of the *Magazine*. Many of the books on offer aren't candidates. Those that are go to my main reader, Barry Turner, who sends back a report assessing whether the book will work for a newspaper and in which section of the paper. Within two months in 2003 we assessed fifty books, made bids for fifteen and bought ten.

They covered politics, religion, business, science, the Holocaust, Shakespeare, theatrical personalities, three books on the Clintons, many on health, family and lifestyle issues, the CIA and several on sport. All human life was there, but I have a budget and cannot buy every book that might seem suitable. Some of Turner's reports are withering and some will say that the book cannot be made into a serialisation without doing a serious injustice to the author. But that is not the end of the story. They can be reviewed in the books pages, we can ask the author to write his own two thousand words or ask for an interview, in which authors can explain what their books are about, all helpful to the authors and their publishers.

When there is a strongly favourable report, it will be discussed with the editor. If he is enthusiastic, we decide how much to bid and I then make an offer to the publisher. That isn't the end of the matter. Other newspapers will also have been making offers and there will be an auction until the paper with the biggest budget or the greatest determination is successful. On a few occasions my bids will be for more than £100,000, more for at least £50,000, but the majority of the books we buy we get for under £10,000 and some for under £1,000.

In 2002 *The Times* bought serials or extracts from forty books across a wide range of interests. The greatest sensations were the revelation by Edwina Currie of her affair with John Major and, in sport, the autobiography of Roy Keane, captain of Manchester United (and shared with *The News of the World*). Both made big headlines and increased sales of the paper. But we also did books on the Queen in her jubilee year, Margaret Thatcher, Rowan Williams, the new Archbishop of Canterbury, Alan Clark's final volume of diaries, Matthew Parris, John Birt and Sue Townsend, as well as autobiographies of David Attenborough and Nigel Hawthorne. *Times2* covered Steven Pinker and Oliver James, Sport did John McEnroe and Michael Atherton, and Business covered Enron, IBM and Vivendi. A slim volume on Irving Berlin's White Christmas made a nice extract for the Saturday Magazine.

Some books do achieve the aim of selling more newspapers – my fondest memories are of Sarah Bradford's biography of the Queen, Andrew Morton's revelation of Princess Diana's own role in his first book about her, the 'granny spy', and Edwina Currie. But most serials achieve the much simpler aim of being a 'good read' and adding to the entertainment or education offered by a newspaper to its readers. If you want to sell your writing to newspapers, the best tip is to study them thoroughly and to try to understand what makes them tick and what interests their editors. Think of news angles and news themes of the moment – and use an agent to try to sell them: they have the contacts on newspapers and know where best and to whom to send them.

Irish Publishers

International Reply Coupons (IRCs)
For return postage, IRCs are required (*not* UK postage stamps). These are available from post offices: letters, 60 pence; mss according to weight. For current postal rates from the Republic of Ireland to the UK see the website at www.letterpost.ie and click on 'Letterpost Services'.

An Gúm

Cúirt Fhreidric, Sr. Fhreidric Thuaidh, Baile Átha Cliath 1
☎00 353 1 889 2800 Fax 00 353 1 873 1140
Email angum@forasnagaeilge.ie
Senior Editor *Seosamh Ó Murchú*
Editor *Antain Mag Shamhráin*

FOUNDED 1926. Formerly the Irish language publications branch of the Department of Education and Science. Has now become part of the North/South Language Body, Foras na Gaeilge. *Publishes* educational, children's, young adult, music, lexicography and general. Little adult fiction or poetry. About 50 titles a year. Unsolicited mss, synopses and ideas for books welcome. Also welcomes reading copies of first and second level school textbooks with a view to translating them into the Irish language.
Royalties paid annually.

Anvil Books

45 Palmerston Road, Dublin 6
☎00 353 1 497 3628 Fax 00 353 1 496 8263
Managing Director *Rena Dardis*

FOUNDED 1964 with emphasis on Irish history and biography. IMPRINT **The Children's Press** was established in 1982. *Publishes* Irish history, biography (particularly 1916–22), folklore and children's fiction. No adult fiction, poetry, fantasy, short stories or full-colour books for children. About 7 titles a year. 'Because of promotional requirements, only books by Irish-based authors considered and only books of Irish interest.' Send synopsis only with IRCs (no UK stamps); unsolicited mss not returned.
Royalties paid annually.

Ashfield Press

See **Blackhall Publishing**

Atrium

See **Attic Press Ltd**

Attic Press Ltd

c/o Cork University Press, Crawford Business Park, Crosses Green, Cork, Co. Cork
☎00 353 21 432 1725 Fax 00 353 21 431 5329
Email S.Wilbourne@ucc.ie
Website www.corkuniversitypress.com
Publisher *Sara Wilbourne*

FOUNDED 1988. Began life in 1984 as a forum for information on the Irish feminist movement. *Publishes* non-fiction (history, women's studies, politics, biography). About 5 titles a year. Does not accept unsolicited proposals in adult fiction. IMPRINT **Atrium** General Interest.
Royalties paid twice-yearly.

Blackhall Publishing

27 Carysfort Avenue, Blackrock, Co. Dublin
☎00 353 1 278 5090 Fax 00 353 1 278 4446
Email blackhall@eircom.net
Website www.blackhallpublishing.com
Managing Director *Gerard O'Connor*
Commissioning Editor *Ruth Garvey*

Publishes business, management and law books. Main subject areas include accounting, finance, management, marketing and law books aimed at both students and professionals in the industry. TITLES *The Knowledge Tornado; The Management Compass; The Quantum Advantage; Why So Stupid?; Changing Healthcare Organisations.* IMPRINT **Ashfield Press** Irish-interest books, both fiction and non-fiction. Unsolicited mss and synopses welcome.
Royalties paid annually.

Blackwater Press

c/o Folens Publishers, Hibernian Industrial Estate, Greenhills Road, Tallaght, Dublin 24
☎00 353 1 413 7200 Fax 00 353 1 413 7280
Email john.o'connor@folens.ie
Chief Executive *Dirk Folens*
Managing Director *John O'Connor*

Part of Folens Publishers. *Publishes* political,

sports, fiction (*Margaret Burns*) and children's (*Deidre Whelan*).

Bradshaw Books

Tigh Filí, Thompson House, MacCurtain Street, Cork
☎00 353 21 450 9274   Fax 00 353 21 455 1617
Email admin@cwpc.ie
Website www.tighfili.com
Managing Director *Maire Bradshaw*
Literature Office *Liz Willows*

FOUNDED 1985. *Publishes* poetry, short stories, women's issues, spiritual, children's books. Organisers of the annual Cork Literary Review poetry competition. SERIES *Cork Literary Review*. Submit letter, synopsis, sample chapters and s.a.e.
Royalties not generally paid.

Brandon/Mount Eagle

Dingle, Co. Kerry
☎00 353 66 915 1463   Fax 00 353 66 915 1234
Website www.brandonbooks.com
Publisher *Steve MacDonogh*
Approx. Annual Turnover €445,000

FOUNDED in 1997. *Publishes* strong Irish fiction and some non-fiction. About 15 titles a year. Not seeking unsolicited mss.

Brookside

See **New Island**

Edmund Burke Publisher

Cloonagashel, 27 Priory Drive, Blackrock, Co. Dublin
☎00 353 1 288 2159   Fax 00 353 1 283 4080
Email deburca@indigo.ie
Website www.deburcararebooks.com
Managing Director *Eamonn De Búrca*
Approx. Annual Turnover €320,000

Small family-run business publishing historical and topographical and fine limited-edition books relating to Ireland. TITLES *History of the County of Mayo* Knox; *King Charles II Irish Army List* Dalton; *History of Dun Laoghaire Harbour* De Courcy Ireland; *Great Book of Irish Genealogies* 5 Vols.; *Irish Flower Garden Replanted* Nelson and Walsh; *The Three Candles, a Bibliographical Catalogue* de Búrca. Unsolicited mss welcome. No synopses or ideas.
Royalties paid annually.

Butterworth Ireland Limited

26 Upper Ormond Quay, Dublin 7
☎00 353 1 872 8514 (Law)/8524 (Tax)
Fax 00 353 1 873 1378
Website www.butterworths.ie

Chairman *Judy Vezmar (UK)*
Managing Editor, Law *Louise Leavy*
Managing Editor, Tax *David Hession*
List Development Editor *Ciarán Toland*

Subsidiary of LexisNexis Butterworths Tolley, London, (**Reed Elsevier** is the holding company). Leading publisher of Irish law and tax titles. *Publishes* solely law and tax books and electronic products. TITLES include *Kelly: The Irish Constitution*, 4th ed. Hogan & Whyte; *Butterworths Irish Companies Acts* MacCann *et al*; *Capital Acquistions Tax*, 2nd ed. Bohan & McCarthy; *The Law and Taxation of Trusts* Wylie & Keogan. Unsolicited mss, synopses and ideas welcome for titles within the broadest parameters of tax and law.
Royalties paid twice-yearly.

The Children's Press

See **Anvil Books**

Cló Iar-Chonnachta

Indreabhán, Connemara, Galway
☎00 353 91 593307   Fax 00 353 91 593362
Email cic@iol.ie
Website www.cic.ie
Chairman/Director *Micheál Ó Conghaile*
Editor *Róisín Ní Mhianáin*
Approx. Annual Turnover €320,000

FOUNDED 1985. *Publishes* fiction, poetry, plays, teenage fiction and children's, mostly in Irish, including translations. Also publishes cassettes of writers reading from their own works. 14 titles in 2002. TITLES *Sna Fir* Micheál ó Conghaile; *Breandán Ó hEithir, Iomramh Aonair* Liam Mac Con Iomaire; *Sruth Teangacha/Stream of Tongues* Gearóid Mac Lochlainn; *Ar Chreng i Làr na Farraige* Lillis ó Laoire; *Out in the Open* Cathal ó Searcaigh.
Royalties paid annually.

The Columba Press

55A Spruce Avenue, Stillorgan Industrial Park, Blackrock, Co. Dublin
☎00 353 1 294 2556   Fax 00 353 1 294 2564
Email sean@columba.ie (editorial) *or*
   info@columba.ie (general)
Website www.columba.ie
Chairman *Neil Kluepfel*
Managing Director *Seán O'Boyle*
Approx. Annual Turnover €1.02 million

FOUNDED 1985. Small company committed to growth. *Publishes* religious and counselling titles. 30 titles in 2002. (Backlist of 225 titles.) TITLES *The Glenstal Book of Icons* Gregory Collins OSB; *No Earthly Estate: God and Patrick*

Kavanagh Tom Stack. Unsolicited ideas and synopses rather than full mss preferred.
Royalties paid twice-yearly.

Cork University Press
Crawford Business Park, Crosses Green, Cork, Co. Cork
☎00 353 21 490 2980 Fax 00 353 21 431 5329
Email corkunip@ucc.ie
Website www.corkuniversitypress.com
Publisher *Sara Wilbourne*
FOUNDED 1925. Relaunched in 1992, the Press *publishes* academic and some trade titles. TITLES *The Field Day Anthology of Irish Writing – Volumes IV & V; Newgrange and the Bend of the Boyne; Irish Migrants in Bribin: 1815–1914.* Also two bi-annual journals: *Irish Review,* an interdisciplinary cultural review, and *The Irish Journal of Feminist Studies* . Unsolicited synopses and ideas welcome for textbooks, academic monographs, belles let-tres, illustrated histories and journals.
Royalties paid twice-yearly.

CJ Fallon Limited
Lucan Road, Palmerstown, Dublin 20
☎00 353 1 616 6400 Fax 00 353 1 616 6499
Email editorial@cjfallon.ie
Website www.cjfallon.ie
Owner *Adare Printing Group*
Managing Director *Henry McNicholas*
Editorial Head *Niall White*
FOUNDED 1927. Educational publishers for first and second level schools in Ireland. Unsolicited mss, synopses and ideas welcome; approach in writing in the first instance. No non-educa-tional material considered.
Royalties paid annually.

Flyleaf Press
4 Spencer Villas, Glenageary, Co. Dublin
☎00 353 1 280 6231 Fax 00 353 1 280 6231
Email Flyleaf@indigo.ie
Website www.flyleaf.ie
Managing Director *Dr James Ryan*
FOUNDED 1981. Concentrates on family history and Irish history as a background to family his-tory. No fiction. TITLES *Irish Records*; *Longford and its People*; *Tracing Your Kerry Ancestors*; *Tracing Your Dublin Ancestors.* Unsolicited mss, synopses and ideas for books welcome.
Royalties paid twice-yearly.

Four Courts Press Ltd
7 Malpas Street, Dublin 8
☎00 353 1 453 4668 Fax 00 353 1 453 4672
Email info@four-courts-press.ie

Website www.four-courts-press.ie
Chairman/Managing Director *Michael Adams*
Director *Martin Healy*
FOUNDED 1972. *Publishes* mainly scholarly books in the humanities. About 60 titles a year. Synopses and ideas for books welcome.
Royalties paid annually.

Gateway
See **Gill & Macmillan**

Gill & Macmillan
10 Hume Avenue, Park West, Dublin 12
☎00 353 1 500 9500 Fax 00 353 1 500 9599
Website www.gillmacmillan.ie
Managing Director *M.H. Gill*
Approx. Annual Turnover €11 million
FOUNDED 1968 when M.H. Gill & Son Ltd and Macmillan Ltd formed a jointly owned publish-ing company. *Publishes* biography/autobiogra-phy, history, current affairs, literary criticism (all mainly of Irish interest), guidebooks, cookery, popular fiction. Also educational textbooks for secondary and tertiary levels. About 100 titles a year. Contacts: *Hubert Mahony* (Educational); *Fergal Tobin* (General). IMPRINTS **Newleaf** *Eveleen Coyle* popular health, psychology, mind, body and spirit; **Gateway** Spirituality, cosmic issues, environment, alternative science. **Tivoli** *Alison Walsh* Popular fiction. Unsolicited syn-opses and ideas welcome.
Royalties paid subject to contract.

Goldcrest
See **Poolbeg Press Ltd**

Institute of Public Administration
57–61 Lansdowne Road, Dublin 4
☎00 353 1 240 3600 Fax 00 353 1 269 8644
Email Sales@ipa.ie
Website www.ipa.ie
Chairman *Stiofán de Búrca*
Director-General *John Cullen*
Publisher *Tony McNamara*
Approx. Annual Turnover €1 million
FOUNDED 1957 by a group of public servants, the Institute of Public Administration is the Irish public sector management development agency. The publishing arm of the organisation is one of its major activities. *Publishes* academic and profes-sional books and periodicals: history, law, poli-tics, economics and Irish public administration for students and practitioners. 18 titles in 2002. TITLES *Administration Yearbook & Diary; Criminal Justice in Ireland; Social Inclusion and the Legal*

System; Child Protection and Welfare; Alcohol, Drugs and Health Promotion. No unsolicited mss; synopses and ideas welcome. No fiction or children's publishing.

Royalties paid annually.

Irish Academic Press Ltd

44 Northumberland Road, Ballsbridge, Dublin 4
☎00 353 1 668 8244 Fax 00 353 1 660 1610
Email info@iap.ie
Website www.iap.ie
Chairman *Frank Cass* (London)
Managing Editor *Mike Milotte*
FOUNDED 1974. *Publishes* academic monographs and humanities. 17 titles in 2002. Unsolicited mss, synopses and ideas welcome.

Royalties paid annually.

Irish Management Institute (IMI)

Sandyford Road, Dublin 16
☎00 353 1 207 8400 Fax 00 353 1 295 5150
Email bill.carroll@imi.ie
Website www.imi.ie
Chief Executive *Barry Kenny*
Approx. Annual Turnover €15 million
FOUNDED 1952. The IMI, owned by its members, both corporate and individual, works to improve the practice of management. Offers managers a wide range of management development services. *Publishes* a quarterly newsletter, *Management Focus*. Other publications include the annual *Executive Salaries in Ireland*, periodic economic reports and management research and texts. Mss, synopses and ideas relevant to Irish management practice welcome.

Royalties paid annually.

The Lilliput Press

62–63 Sitric Road, Arbour Hill, Dublin 7
☎00 353 1 671 1647 Fax 00 353 1 671 1233
Email info@lilliputpress.ie
Website www.lilliputpress.ie
Chairman *Vincent Hurley*
Managing Director *Antony Farrell*
Approx. Annual Turnover €255,000
FOUNDED 1984. *Publishes* non-fiction: literature, history, autobiography and biography, ecology, essays; criticism; fiction and poetry. About 20 titles a year. TITLES *Images of Dublin*; *An Aran Keening*; *The Beautiful Changes*; *Lady Gregory's Toothbrush*; *Cats and Their Poets: Selected Prose of Patrick Kavanagh Unsolicited*; *Shackleton: An Irishman in Anatartica*. Mss, synopses and ideas welcome. No children's or sport titles.

Royalties paid annually.

Marino Books

See **Mercier Press Ltd**

Mercier Press Ltd

Douglas Village, Cork, Co. Cork
☎00 353 21 489 9858 Fax 00 353 21 489 9887
Email books@mercierpress.ie
Website www.mercierpress.ie
Chairman *George Eaton*
Managing Director *John F. Spillane*
FOUNDED 1944. One of Ireland's largest publishers with a list of approx 250 Irish interest titles. IMPRINTS **Mercier Press**; **Marino Books** Editorial Director *Mary Feehan* Children's, politics, history, folklore, biography, mind, body and spirit, current affairs, women's interest. TITLES *The Course of Irish History*; all of John B. Keane's works; *Beyond Prozac*; *It's a Long Way from Penny Apples*; *Ireland's Master Storyteller*. Unsolicited synopses and ideas welcome.

Royalties paid annually.

Merlin Publishing

16 Upper Pembroke Street, Dublin 2
☎00 353 1 676 4373 Fax 00 353 1 676 4368
Website www.merlin-publishing.com *or* drumshee.com
Managing Director *Chenile Keogh-Smyth*
Managing Editor *Aoife Barrett*
FOUNDED 2000. Member of **Clé**. *Publishes* film, music, art, biography, children's fiction, general non-fiction, history, photography, literature, literary studies and gift books. About 30 titles a year (mainly Irish interest). IMPRINT **Wolfhound Press** FOUNDED 1974. Fiction, children's and some non-fiction. TITLES *Famine*; *Eyewitness Bloody Sunday*; *Father Browne's Titanic Album*. Sample chapters of unsolicited mss (with synopses and s.a.e.) welcome but by post only. See Merlin website for submission guidelines and proposal form.

Mount Eagle

See **Brandon/Mount Eagle**

New Island

2 Brookside, Dundrum Road, Dundrum, Dublin 14
☎00 353 1 298 9937/298 3411
Fax 00 353 1 298 2783
Email brookside@iol.ie
Website www.newisland.ie
Managing Director/Editorial Head *Edwin Higel*
Editor *Emma Dunne*
FOUNDED 1990. *Handles* fiction, Irish non-

fiction, poetry and drama. 25 titles in 2002. Branching out into popular fiction and memoirs. IMPRINT **Brookside**. Unsolicited mss, synopses and ideas welcome. Send three chapters and synopsis by post.

Royalties paid twice-yearly

Newleaf
See **Gill & Macmillan**

The O'Brien Press Ltd
20 Victoria Road, Rathgar, Dublin 6
☎00 353 1 492 3333 Fax 00 353 1 492 2777
Email books@obrien.ie
Website www.obrien.ie
Managing Director/Publisher *Michael O'Brien*
Editorial Director *Íde Ní Laoghaire*
FOUNDED 1974. *Publishes* business, true crime, biography, music, travel, sport, Celtic subjects, food and drink, history, humour, politics, reference. Children's publishing – mainly fiction for every age from tiny tots to teenage. Illustrated fiction SERIES *Pandas* (5 years+); *Flyers* (6 years+); *Red Flag* (8 years+). Novels (10 years+) – contemporary, historical, fantasy. Some non-fiction – mainly historical, and art and craft, resource books for teachers. No poetry, adult fiction or academic. Unsolicited mss (sample chapters only), synopses and ideas for books welcome. Submissions will not be returned.
Royalties paid annually.

Oak Tree Press
19 Rutland Street, Cork, Co. Cork
☎00 353 21 431 3855 Fax 00 353 21 431 3496
Email info@oaktreepress.com
Website www.oaktreepress.com
Managing Director *Brian O'Kane*
FOUNDED 1992. Specialist publisher of business and professional books with a focus on small business start-up and development. Unsolicited mss and synopses welcome; send to the managing director, at the address above.
Royalties paid annually.

On Stream Publications Ltd
Currabaha, Cloghroe, Co. Cork
☎00 353 21 438 5798
Fax 00 353 21 438 5798
Email info@onstream.ie
Website www.onstream.ie
Chairman/Managing Director *Roz Crowley*
Approx. Annual Turnover €255,000
FOUNDED 1992. Formerly Forum Publications.

Publishes academic, fiction, cookery, wine, general health and fitness, local history, railways, photography and practical guides. About 3 titles a year. TITLES *Keeping Resources Human – A Practical Guide to Retaining Staff; The Book of Scarves: 100 Ideas; Dealing With Chronic Pain; Stirmixmash – A Cookbook for Young People.* Synopses and ideas welcome. No children's books.
Royalties paid annually.

Poolbeg Press Ltd
123 Grange Hill, Baldoyle, Dublin 13
☎00 353 1 832 1477 Fax 00 353 1 832 1430
Email poolbeg@poolbeg.com
Website www.poolbeg.com
Managing Director *Kieran Devlin*
Publisher *Paula Campbell*
FOUNDED 1976 to publish the Irish short story and has since diversified to include all areas of fiction (literary and popular), children's fiction and non-fiction, and adult non-fiction: history, biography and topics of public interest. About 70 titles a year. AUTHORS discovered and first published by Poolbeg include Marian Keyes, Sheila O'Flanagan, Cathy Kelly and Patricia Scanlan. 'Our slogan is Poolbeg.com – the Irish for Bestsellers!' Unsolicited mss, synopses and ideas welcome (mss preferred). No drama. IMPRINTS **Poolbeg** (paperback and hardback); **Poolbeg For Children**; **Goldcrest**; **Wren**.
Royalties paid twice-yearly.

Real Ireland Design Ltd
27 Beechwood Close, Boghall Road, Bray, Co. Wicklow
☎00 353 1 286 0799 Fax 00 353 1 282 9962
Managing Director *Desmond Leonard*
Producers of calendars, diaries, posters, greetings cards and books, servicing the Irish tourist industry. *Publishes* photography and tourism. About 2 titles a year. No fiction. Unsolicited mss, synopses and ideas welcome.
Royalties paid twice-yearly.

Royal Dublin Society
Science Section, Ballsbridge, Dublin 4
☎00 353 1 668 0866 Fax 00 353 1 660 4014
Email Annette.Macdonald@rds.ie
Website www.rds.ie
President *Michael Jacobs*
FOUNDED 1731 for the promotion of agriculture, science and the arts, and throughout its history has published books and journals towards this end. *Publishes* conference proceedings, biology

and the history of Irish science. TITLES *Agricultural Development for the 21st Century; The Right Trees in the Right Places; Agriculture & the Environment; Water of Life; Science, Technology & Realism; Science Centres for Ireland; Blueprint for a National Irish Science Centre; Science Education in Crisis;* occasional papers in *Irish Science & Technology* series.

Royalties not generally paid.

Royal Irish Academy

19 Dawson Street, Dublin 2
☎00 353 1 676 2570 Fax 00 353 1 676 2346
Email r.mcnicholl@ria.ie
Website www.ria.ie

Executive Secretary *Patrick Buckley*
Editor of Publications *Rachel McNicholl*

FOUNDED in 1785, the Academy has been publishing since 1787. Core publications are journals but more books published in last 15 years. *Publishes* academic, Irish interest and Irish language. About 7 titles a year. Welcomes mss, synopses and ideas of an academic standard.

Simon & Schuster/Town House
See **Town House Dublin**

Sitric Books

62–63 Sitric Road, Arbour Hill, Dublin 7
☎00 353 1 671 1682 Fax 00 353 1 671 1233

Chair *Vivienne Guinness*
Managing Director *Antony Farrell*

FOUNDED 2000. *Publishes* current affairs, biography and fiction. About 5 titles a year. TITLES *Mirror, Mirror: Confessions of A Plastic Surgery Addict; Snapshots; Overnight to Innsbruck.* Unsolicited mss, synopses and ideas welcome. No children's or sports titles.

Royalties paid annually.

Tír Eolas

Newtownlynch, Doorus, Kinvara, Co. Galway
☎00 353 91 637452 Fax 00 353 91 637452
Email info@tireolas.com
Website www.tireolas.com

Publisher/Managing Director *Anne Korff*

FOUNDED 1987. *Publishes* books and guides on ecology, archaeology, folklore and culture. TITLES *The Book of the Burren; The Shannon Floodlands; Not a Word of a Lie; The Book of Aran;*

Women of Ireland, A Biographic Dictionary; Kinvara, A Seaport Town on Galway Bay; A Burren Journal; The Shores of Connemara. Unsolicited mss, synopses and ideas for books welcome. No specialist scientific and technical, fiction, plays, school textbooks or philosophy.

Royalties paid annually.

Tivoli
See **Gill & Macmillan**

Town House Dublin

Trinity House, Charleston Road, Ranelagh, Dublin 6
☎00 353 1 497 2399 Fax 00 353 1 497 0927
Email books@townhouse.ie

Managing Director *Treasa Coady*

FOUNDED 1980. *Publishes* commercial fiction, art and archaeology, biography and environment. About 20 titles a year. TITLES *Love Like Hate Adore* Deirdre Purcell; *Mary, Mary* Julie Parsons; *Now is the Time* Sr. Stanislaus Kennedy; *Wild Wicklow* Richard Nairn and Miriam Crowley. IMPRINT **Simon & Schuster/TownHouse** FOUNDED 2001. *Publishes* Fiction and non-fiction. Unsolicited mss, synopses and ideas welcome. No children's books.

Royalties paid twice-yearly.

Veritas Publications

7–8 Lower Abbey Street, Dublin 1
☎00 353 1 878 8177 Fax 00 353 1 878 6507
Email publications@veritas.ie
Website www.veritas.ie

Director *Maura Hyland*
Managing Editor *Toner Quinn*

FOUNDED 1969 to supply religious textbooks to schools and later introduced a wide-ranging general list. Part of the Catholic Communications Institute. *Publishes* books on religious, ethical, moral, societal and social issues. 30 titles a year. Unsolicited mss, synopses and ideas for books welcome.

Royalties paid annually.

Wolfhound Press
See **Merlin Publishing**

Wren
See **Poolbeg Press Ltd**

Irish Literary Agents

The Book Bureau Literary Agency

7 Duncairn Avenue, Bray, Co Wicklow
☎00 353 1 276 4996
Fax 00 353 1 276 4834
Email thebookbureau@oceanfree.net
Contact *Geraldine Nichol*

Handles general and literary fiction. Special interest in women's fiction, crime and thrillers. Will suggest revision. Send preliminary letter, synopsis and first three chapters; return postage essential (/IRCs required when sending from UK or abroad). No reading fee. *Commission* Home 10%; Overseas 20%. Works with foreign associates.

Marianne Gunn O'Connor Literary Agency

(G.M.M.) Morrison Chambers, Suite 17, 32 Nassau St, Dublin 2
Email mariannegmm@eircom.net
Contact *Marianne Gunn O'Connor*

FOUNDED 1996. *Handles* literary and commercial fiction, non-fiction, biography, mind, body and spirit, health and children's fiction. CLIENTS include Niall Williams, Patrick McCabe, Morag Prunty, Suzanne Power, Andrew Proctor, Chris Binchy, Anita Notaro, Claire Kilroy, Vikram A. Chandra (one of India's leading political broadcasters), Julie Dam, Cecelia Ahern, Paddy McMahon. Send preliminary letter plus half page synopsis and first 50 pages. No reading fee. *Commission* Ireland, Home 10%; UK 15%; US & Translation 20%; Film & TV 20%. Translation rights handled by Vicki Satlow Literary Agency, Milan.

The Lisa Richards Agency

46 Upper Baggot Street, Dublin 4
☎00 353 1 660 3534 Fax 00 353 1 660 3545
Email fogrady@eircom.net
Contact *Faith O'Grady*

FOUNDED 1998. *Handles* fiction, including children's books, and general non-fiction. Approach with proposal and sample chapter for non-fiction, and 3–4 chapters and synopsis for fiction (s.a.e. essential). CLIENTS include June Considine, Judi Curtin, Denise Deegan, Terry Eagleton, Tar Heavey, Colm Keena, Martin Malone, Pauline McLynn, Sarah O'Brien, Hector O'hEochagain, Damian Owens, Homan Potterton, Kevin Rafter, Annie Sparrow. *Commission* Home 10%; UK 15%; US & Translation 20%; Film & TV 15%. *Overseas associate* **The Marsh Agency** for translation rights.

Jonathan Williams Literary Agency

Rosney Mews, Upper Glenageary Road, Glenageary, Co. Dublin
☎00 353 1 280 3482 Fax 00 353 1 280 3482
Contact *Jonathan Williams*

FOUNDED 1980. *Handles* general trade books: fiction, auto/biography, travel, politics, history, music, literature and criticism, gardening, cookery, sport and leisure, humour, reference, social questions, photography. Some poetry, business and children's, but less of a speciality. No plays, science fiction, mind, body and spirit, computer books, theology, multimedia, motoring, aviation. No reading fee 'unless the author wants a very fast opinion'. Initial approach by phone or letter. *Commission* Home 10%; US 20%; Translation 15%. *Overseas associates* Piergiorgio Nicolazzini Literary Agency, Italy; Lora Fountain Agency, France; Löcher & Lawrence, Germany.

An Easy Way to Lose Money

*Authors who pay to have their books published
often live to regret it. Barry Turner explains why.*

It says a lot for the myths and mystique of the book trade that writers still show surprise when they encounter a publisher who wants money up front. Publishers are supposed to pay authors, aren't they? Ideally, yes, but for those of us who are unable to meet the demands of the high-street purveyors of popular literature, there is another rank of publisher who, for a consideration, will put into print what might otherwise be lost to posterity. There is nothing wrong in this. The trouble comes if the author, having signed a hefty cheque, is led to expect that his book will be treated in the same way as all the other books coming onto the market. At this point he is liable to find himself out of luck. To pay for publication is no guarantee that a single copy will appear on the shelves of even the local bookshop. The satisfaction, such as it is, will be limited to seeing his work between hard covers and knowing that for one year at least there will be no difficulty in choosing Christmas presents.

For some authors this is enough. Others feel they have been conned, persuaded to part with money for services not rendered. Those unfortunates have landed at the sleazy end of what is known derisively as vanity publishing. The hook for the unwary author is a small ad in the literary pages. 'If your book deserves publication, write now to ...' 'American publisher seeks manuscripts for UK and USA ...' Those authors who take the bait do not have to wait long for a glowing response to their submission. No matter how illiterate, misconceived or downright boring the manuscript, the vanity merchant will offer praise and encouragement. The letter will also point out the mounting costs of book production – a terrible burden for a small idealistic company to bear. It is surely, therefore, only reasonable to invite the author, standing as he is on the brink of fame and fortune, to invest in his own success. What is missing and what is never admitted is that since the vanity publisher can make a profit without donating a penny of the company's money to the book, he has no incentive to sell it.

Reality is kept at bay until after the signing of the contract. This usually binds the author to pay 30 per cent of the fee upfront, 30 per cent on receipt of proofs, and the remainder upon publication. So much for the nitty-gritty part. The rest of the contract will positively glow with promise: what will be paid to the author for subsequent reprintings, subsidiary and foreign rights, and so on. He will also note with joy that the vanity publisher offers him royalties of up to 40 per cent of the retail price of his book's first printing, when he has been told that commercial publishers offer only 10–15 per cent. There are a couple of fallacies here. First, vanity books might sell in dozens, possibly hundreds – but never, with rare exceptions, in thousands. There have been some books that failed, to the author's dismay although not the publisher's, to sell a single copy. So the vanity house, having been paid to print, say, 1,500 copies of a book, is well protected against it selling more than a small proportion of the edition. In any case, in the unlikely event of royalties becoming payable, the author is merely receiving 40 per cent of his own money.

Other fairly standard clauses in a vanity contract include a quota of 'free' copies to the author; if he requires more, he has to pay for them. In reality, he is paying for them *twice*! The stock of unsold books usually remains the property of the publisher, so if there is a chance to remainder them later, he takes the proceeds. Then there is a fine-print definition of printing or publishing a book. In vanity-speak, this does not necessarily include the binding of a book. Unless otherwise directed, only a certain number of copies in an edition will actually be bound; the rest will remain as flat printed sheets until required, which is probably never. Of an edition of 1,500 copies, perhaps as few as 200 will emerge from the bindery. If these are sold and there are cash orders for more (including the author's cash order), the requisite number will be bound, but no more.

Another impressive-looking clause in a typical contract has the publisher offering to publish a second edition at his own expense – providing the entire original edition is sold first. As the clever combination of quantity and retail price will virtually ensure this will never happen, the offer is purely hypothetical.

The service a vanity house provides – which the author pays for – includes such things as editing, design, sending out review copies, marketing and sometimes advertising. These services sound better than they really are. It is almost impossible to improve a really bad idea or wretched writing, so no great effort is expended here. But the vanity client is really let down when the day of publication arrives. A former editor with a vanity publisher explains what happens. 'It is at this point, just as the book is about to be published, that the author's interest in its fate is at its most intense. Authors are keenly interested in the promotion and distribution of their books, and vanity authors especially so. It is the vanity author's only chance of recovering the thousands of pounds he has paid the publisher, and it is just here, when for the first time the circle broadens to include others in addition to the author and publisher that the fraud of vanity publishing becomes the most obvious. It is not now the author who must be convinced, but the reviewers, booksellers and the reading public.' Which is as unlikely as the vanity author winning the Booker Prize.

A vanity publisher will undertake to distribute a certain number of review copies, but this task is pretty academic; vanity books are invariably consigned to the wastebasket on sight, although the regional press might run notices if there is some local interest in the book. It is equally rare for a vanity book to be advertised and, if it is, it is usually an additional cost to the author.

Finally, and crucially, we arrive at the distribution and marketing operation. For most vanity books, neither exists. Again, unless the book reflects local interest or occupies some marketable niche – say, a book about hospital humour designed for sale at hospital gift shops or nearby bookstores – retailers will not be interested. Most vanity books are therefore sold through the vanity house's mail-order operation, with most of the work – circularizing friends, common interest groups – done by the author. In practice, unless the vanity house has an efficient and proven distribution and sales set-up, the author might as well take all the copies, because if they are going to be sold he is going to have to do it himself.

Despite the evidence, there are still writers who believe what they want to believe. That is why as soon as one vanity publisher goes out of business, another soon fills the gap. But for those who are prepared to take heed, the Society of Authors offers a few tips on what to look out for:

■ Do not take a flattering report on your manuscript at face value. The publisher may simply be motivated by a desire to do business at your expense.
■ Be suspicious of vague promises of quality production. Subsidized books are often tatty books.
■ Regard with suspicion promises to sell television and film rights, serialization and other money-making options. The chances of getting your money back from subsidiary rights are remote.
■ Be wary of cop-out clauses in the contract which enable the publisher to renege on his initial pitch. For example, if he tells you that he can sell 2,000 copies, do not believe him when he says it makes sense to try the market with a first print-run of 500 copies. Or rather, do believe him but do not expect him to reprint if the market does not respond.

There are a few vanity publishers who do a straightforward job without pretence, but they are the exception that proves the rule. However enticing the offer, the best advice is always to keep one hand on your wallet and the other on your chequebook.

Self-Publishing – A Good Idea?

Jude Garvey, Managing Editor of the Better Book Company, puts the case for literary DIY

It is a truth universally acknowledged that the chance of a first-time author being offered a contract by a mainstream publisher gets slimmer by the day. Commercial publishing is now a volatile and highly competitive business that regards taking on new authors as a high-risk venture. Some 25 years ago there were hundreds of small and medium-sized publishers who actively encouraged new writers and took a paternal interest in their progress. Few survive. The conglomerates moved in and those donnish, bow-tied gentlemen who would give a fledgeling author a glass of sherry, useful advice and perhaps a short-run contract were swept aside. This was one revolution that didn't improve the lot of the masses, if I can refer to authors in such terms. They have not, however, been deterred, but they have become increasingly disenchanted. Every week hundreds of hopeful authors despatch their work to the commercial houses and most of it is returned with the disheartening 'not for us' rejection slip. This is a great pity as many authors give up writing and much fine work never sees the light of day.

All is not lost, however. Over the last decade, authors have turned increasingly to self-publishing to get their work to its readership, and there have been some notable successes. Self-publishing – and I cannot emphasize this too strongly – is not vanity publishing. As the Society of Authors has pointed out, the expression 'vanity' publishing arose because some firms would send writers excessively flattering reports on their manuscripts: 'We don't accept just anything but your book really deserves publication' . . . that sort of thing. This would be followed by a request for a substantial contribution to the production costs, with the author being promised financial reward from royalties, i.e. a percentage of the cover price of any book sold. Self-publishing means what it says: the author is in control and can decide the cover design, the layout of the text, the use of colour, whether the work is to be produced as a hardback or paperback, the number of copies and how much is to be spent on marketing and distribution.

A company offering its services to self-publishing authors should at the very least provide a booklet setting out its working methods. But don't rely on this alone. Make an appointment to visit the company offices to meet the personnel with whom you might be working. If you can't visit then talk on the phone to someone senior and request a copy of a book that they have designed and produced which is similar to the one you have in mind. You might also ask for the opportunity to speak to a couple of authors they have worked with in the past. Of course, the self-publishing author who has an eye for design, is a computer 'whiz' and has a good grasp of marketing and PR can produce the book on a CD-ROM and take it to a local printer. This is sometimes done but what is absolutely essential is that the finished product looks professional and compares favourably with its commercial competitors. If it doesn't then it won't please anyone and all the work and cost will have been wasted.

Over the years, my company has produced and helped authors market their books in many genres: novels, biographies, poetry, children's stories, family and local histories, religion and instructional manuals. It is worth noting that over 50 per cent of our authors have ordered a reprint after selling the first run. The reason for this is that we always recommend a *minimum* first print run. This is for both economic and tactical reasons. First, with modern computer printing it is both easy and cheap to reprint as demand requires – so no reason to have hundreds of copies in the spare bedroom for a year – and second, once a sales pattern is established, re-orders (with any textual changes) can be run off with minimum wastage.

Cost is a vital factor when considering self-publishing. Be clear how you want your book to look – decide, for example, if colour for the cover or illustrations is necessary – and then ask for a cost estimate. Some case studies illustrate how this advice is put into practice. One of our authors wrote a biography of the novelist Elizabeth Goudge and provided an elegant photograph of the subject for the cover. Five hundred paperback copies cost £2,830 and cover price was set at £12.99. It was reviewed in *The Times* and reprinted. Another produced two novels, one with a Victorian theme, one based on Ancient Rome. Both have sold well, with the author being interviewed on radio and receiving coverage in local papers and magazines. Yet another has written two children's stories about the quirky adventures of a boy robot. Both have sold well and given her the confidence to approach mainstream publishers with her third manuscript and a good track record.

There is another very good example of how a self-published author can succeed. We have worked with a retired public school headmaster, designing and producing a first print of 100 copies of his autobiography. First, we organized press coverage and got photos and reviews in both local papers and regional magazines. A signing session was set up, with the full cooperation of his local library; a launch of his book at his old school, attended by both pupils and staff, went very well; and the book is now reprinting. The great thing about this particular example is the author is enjoying himself, old friends are getting in touch with him, he is meeting new people and he has made a profit on the adventure.

So why wait? Write your book, publish it, give it to friends and sell it to strangers. It is one of the most joyous experiences of the creative mind.

Audio Books

Assembled Stories
PO Box 5212, Grantham, Lincolnshire
NG33 5SR
☎01476 571333 Fax 01476 571333
Email assembledstories@hotmail.com
Website www.assembledstories.com

Managing Directors *Peter Joyce, Michael Joyce*

FOUNDED 1992. *Publishes* classic fiction on cassette and CD with all books read by Peter Joyce. 6 titles in 2002. TITLES *Idle Thoughts of an Idle Fellow* Jerome K. Jerome; *The Monkey's Paw* W.W. Jacobs; *The Beloved Vagabond* W.J. Locke. Ideas for cassettes welcome.

AudioBooksForFree.Com Limited
25 Green Lane, Amersham, Buckinghamshire
HP6 6AS
☎01494 431119 Fax 01494 583417
Email ToUs@AudioBooksForFree.Com
Website www.AudioBooksForFree.Com

Managing Director *Ruslan G. Fedorovsky*

FOUNDED 2000. *Publishes* fiction: thrillers, crime, science fiction only. 100 titles in 2002. AUTHORS Michael Hartland, James Herlihy, Jon Schiller, Patrick Walsh.

BBC Audiobooks
St James House, The Square, Lower Bristol
Road, Bath BA2 3SB
☎01225 878000 Fax 01225 310771
Email info@bbcaudiobooks.com
Also at: Windsor Bridge Road, Bath BA2 3AX
☎01225 878000 Fax 01225 422585

Owner *BBC Worldwide Ltd*
Managing Director *Paul Dempsey*

BBC Audiobooks consists of the following: **Cover to Cover Cassettes Ltd** incorporating *Harry Potter* and **Cover to Cover Classics**. Unabridged readings of classic or literary fiction. IMPRINTS **BBC Cover to Cover** Unabridged readings of classic and contemporary children's titles. Unsolicited work not accepted. **BBC Radio Collection** ESTABLISHED 1988. BBC Radio Collection releases material associated with BBC Radio and Television. Almost all releases sourced from BBC Radio and Television. Unsolicited work not accepted. TITLES *BBC Radio Shakespeare*; *Alan Bennett*; *This Sceptred Isle*; *Hancock*; *Steptoe*; *Round the Home*; *Agatha Christie*; *Sherlock Holmes*.

BBC Audiobooks also *publishes* for the library market; large print books, reprints and audio books under the **Chivers** name. Material published includes contemporary and classic fiction, non-ficton, biography and autobiography, children's books, crime, westerns. No unsolicted material. **Chivers** Audio & Book IMPRINTS **Windsor Hardcover Large Print**; **Paragon Softcover Large Print**; **Chivers Hardcover Large Print**; **Camden Softcover Large Print**; **Galaxy Children's Large Print**; **Gunsmoke Westerns**; **Black Dagger**; **Chivers Audio Books**; **Chivers Children's Audio Books**.

Bloomsbury Publishing
See entry under **UK Publishers**

Canongate Audio
See **Canongate Books** under **UK Publishers**

Chivers Audio Books
See **BBC Audiobooks**

Chrome Dreams
12 Seaforth Avenue, New Malden, Surrey
KT3 6JP
☎020 8715 9781 Fax 020 8241 1426
Email mail@chromedreams.co.uk
Website www.chromedreams.co.uk

Managing Director *Rob Johnstone*

A small record and music management company FOUNDED 1998 to produce audio-biographies of current rock and pop artists and legendary performers on CD and, more recently, books on the same subjects. Ideas for biographies welcome.

Corgi Audio
Transworld Publishers, A division of the Random House Group Ltd, 61–63 Uxbridge
Road, London W5 5SA
☎020 8579 2652 Fax 020 8231 6666

Managing Director *Larry Finlay*

Publishes fiction, autobiography, children's and

humour. TITLES *Discworld Series* Terry Pratchett; *Down Under* Bill Bryson and other travel writing.

Cover to Cover Cassettes Ltd
See **BBC Audiobooks**

CSA Word
6a Archway Mews, 241a Putney Bridge Road, London SW15 2PE
☎020 8871 0220 Fax 020 8877 0712
Email info@csatelltapes.demon.co.uk
Website www.csatelltapes.demon.co.uk
Managing Director *Clive Stanhope*
Audio Manager *Victoria Williams*

FOUNDED 1989. *Publishes* fiction, children's, short stories, poetry, travel, biographies. Over 100 titles to-date on cassette and CD. Tends to favour quality/classic/nostalgic/timeless literature. TITLES *Carry on Jeeves* P.G. Wodehouse; *Alfie* Bill Naughton; *Just William – Home for the Holidays* Richmal Crompton; *Sons and Lovers* D.H. Lawrence; *Room at the Top* John Braine; *Midwich Cuckoos* John Wyndham; *I Capture the Castle* Dodie Smith; *Classic Stories of the Old and New Testaments*.

CYP Children's Audio
The Fairway, Bush Fair, Harlow, Essex CM18 6LY
☎01279 444707 Fax 01279 445570
Email enquiries@cypmusic.co.uk
Website www.kidsmusic.co.uk
Managing Director *Mike Kitson*

FOUNDED 1978. *Publishes* children's audio material for those under 10 years of age; educational, entertainment, licensed characters (*Mr Men*; *Little Miss*; *Mopatop's Shop*; *Animal Stories*). Ideas for cassettes welcome. TV music and soundtrack production service available.

Faber.Penguin Audiobooks
80 Strand, London WC2R 0RL
☎020 7010 3000 Fax 020 7010 6060
Email audio@penguin.co.uk
Website www.penguin.co.uk
3 Queen Square, London WC1N 3AU
☎020 7465 0045 Fax 020 7465 0108
Head of Audio Publishing *Jeremy Ettinghausen*

A joint venture between **Penguin Books** and **Faber & Faber**. *Publishes* 5–10 titles per year, drawing on the strength of Faber's authors. AUTHORS include Ted Hughes, Philip Larkin, Garrison Keillor, Sylvia Plath, T.S. Eliot, Wendy Cope, William Golding, Seamus Heaney, Philip Ardagh.

57 Productions
See **Organisations of Interest to Poets**

Halsgrove
See entry under **UK Publishers**

HarperCollins AudioBooks
77–85 Fulham Palace Road, London W6 8JB
☎020 8741 7070 Fax 020 8307 4517 (adult) /8307 4291 (children's)
Website www.fireandwater.com
Managing Director *Amanda Ridout*

The HarperCollins audio list was launched in 1990

ADULT
Publisher *Rosalie George*. *Publishes* a wide range including popular and classic fiction, non-fiction, Shakespeare and poetry on cassette with many new titles on CD. 60 titles in 2002. TITLES *Billy* Pamela Stephenson; *Lord of the Rings* J.R.R. Tolkien; *Life of Pi* Yann Martel; *Man and Wife* Tony Parsons; *Prey* Michael Crichton; *Portrait of a Killer* Patricia Cornwell; Agatha Christie unabridged series.

CHILDREN'S DIVISION
Divisional Publishing Director *Sally Gritten*, Publisher *Rosalie George*. *Publishes* picture books/cassettes and story books/cassettes as well as single and double tapes and CDs for children aged 2–13 years. Fiction, songs, early learning, poetry, etc. 30 titles in 2002. AUTHORS C.S. Lewis, Roald Dahl, Dr Seuss, Lemony Snicket, J.R.R. Tolkien, Enid Blyton, Robin Jarvis, Ian Whybrow, Nick Butterworth, Judith Kerr.

Hodder Headline Audio Books
338 Euston Road, London NW1 3BH
☎020 7873 6000 Fax 020 7873 6024
Website www.hodder.co.uk
Publisher *Rupert Lancaster*

LAUNCHED 1994. *Publishes* fiction and non-fiction. Approx 30 titles in 2002. AUTHORS Tony Benn, Louis de Bernières, Dickie Bird, John LeCarré, Alex Ferguson, Joanne Harris, Stephen King, Ellis Peters, Rosamunde Pilcher, Terry Waite, Mary Wesley.

Isis Audio Books
See **Isis Publishing** under **UK Publishers**

Ladybird Audio
See **Dorling Kindersley Ltd** under **UK Publishers**

Laughing Stock Productions
81 Charlotte Street, London W1T 4PP
☎020 7637 7943   Fax 020 7436 1666
Managing Director *Colin Collino*
FOUNDED 1991. Issues a wide range of comedy
cassettes from family humour to alternative
comedy. 12–16 titles per year. TITLES *Red
Dwarf; Shirley Valentine* (read by Willy Russell);
*Rory Bremner; Peter Cook Anthology; Sean
Hughes; John Bird and John Fortune; Eddie Izzard.*

Macmillan Audio Books
20 New Wharf Road, London N1 9RR
☎020 7014 6040   Fax 020 7014 6141
Email a.muirden@macmillan.co.uk
Website www.panmacmillan.co.uk

Owner *Macmillan Publishers Ltd*
Audio Publisher *Alison Muirden*

FOUNDED 1995. *Publishes* adult fiction, non-
fiction and autobiography, focusing mainly on
lead book titles and releasing audio simultaneously with hard or paperback publication. Also
publishes children's audio titles including *The
Gruffalo* which won Children's Audio of the
Year at the 2002 **Spoken Word Awards**.

Naxos AudioBooks
18 High Street, Welwyn, Hertfordshire
AL6 9EQ
☎01438 717808   Fax 01438 717809
Email Naxos_Audiobooks@compuserve.com
Website www.naxosaudiobooks.com

Owner *HNH International, Hong Kong/
    Nicolas Soames*
Managing Director *Nicolas Soames*

FOUNDED 1994. Part of Naxos, the classical
budget CD company. Publisher of the Year in
the 2001 **Spoken Word Awards**. *Publishes*
classic and modern fiction, non-fiction, children's and junior classics, drama and poetry.
TITLES *Ulysses* Joyce; *King Lear* Shakespeare;
History of the Musical Fawkes; *Just So Stories*
Kipling.

Orion Audio Books (Division of the Orion Publishing Group Ltd)
Orion House, 5 Upper St Martin's Lane,
London WC2H 9EA
☎020 7240 3444   Fax 020 7379 6518
Email prw@orionbooks.co.uk
Website www.orionbooks.co.uk

Publisher *Pandora White*

Orion Audio has released over 200 titles since
it was FOUNDED in 1998. *Publishes* fiction, non-
fiction, humour, children's, poetry, science,
crime and thrillers. AUTHORS Penny Vincenzi,
Maeve Binchy, Ian Rankin, Robert Crais,
Michael Connelly, Francesca Simon (*Horrid
Henry* series), the Dave Pelzer trilogy, Vikram
Seth, Kevin Crossley-Holland, Anita Shreve.
Ideas for cassettes/CDs welcome.

Penguin Audiobooks
80 Strand, London WC2R 0RL
☎020 7010 3000   Fax 020 7010 6695
Email audio@penguin.co.uk
Website www.penguin.co.uk

Head of Audio Publishing *Jeremy Ettinghausen*

Launched in November 1993 and has rapidly
expanded since then to reflect the diversity of
Penguin Books' list. *Publishes* mostly fiction,
both classical and contemporary, non-fiction,
autobiography and an increasing range of children's titles under the **Puffin Audiobooks**
imprint. Approx. 70 titles a year. Contemporary
AUTHORS include: Zadie Smith, Barbara Vine,
Anne Fine, Eoin Colfer, John Mortimer, Roald
Dahl, Tom Clancy, Sue Townsend, Philip
Ridley, Nick Hornby.

Puffin Audiobooks
See **Penguin Audiobooks**

Random House Audiobooks
20 Vauxhall Bridge Road, London SW1V 2SA
☎020 7840 8400   Fax 020 7233 6127

Owner *The Random House Group Ltd.*
Managing Director *Richard Cable*
Manager *Georgia Marnham*

The audiobooks division of Random House
started early in 1991. Acquired the Reed
Audio list in 1997. *Publishes* fiction, non-fiction and self help. 23 titles in 2002. AUTHORS
include John Grisham, Stephen Fry, Stephen
Hawking, Sebastian Faulks, Peter Ackroyd,
Ruth Rendell, Ben Elton, Joanne Harris.

Rickshaw Productions
64 Fields Court, Warwick CV34 5HP
☎0780 3553214 Fax 01926 402490
Email rickprod@aol.com
Website www.rickshaw-audiobooks.com

Executive Producer *Ms L.J. Fairgrieve*

FOUNDED 1998. *Publishes* adult fiction and
non-fiction. Looking for unpublished writers
of any genre, particularly short stories (not
interested in children's stories). TITLES *The
Carved Pipe/The Tall Woman and Her Short
Husband* (read by Elizabeth Lindsay); *The
Halfway-House Hotel* by Richard James (Peter

Mimmack); *The Tailor of Salisbury* (Martin Jarvis). *The First Line of Defence – The Kent Castles* produced in association with English Heritage (Elizabeth Ryder); *Wednesdays and Other Stories* (writtten and read by Betty Smith).

Simon & Schuster Audio
Africa House, 64–78 Kingsway, London WC2B 6AH
☎020 7316 1900 Fax 020 7316 0332
Email rumana.haider@simonandschuster.co.uk
Website www.simonsays.co.uk
Audio Manager *Rumana Haider*

Simon & Schuster Audio began by distributing their American parent company's audio products. Moved on to repackaging products specifically for the UK market and in 1994 became more firmly established in this market with a huge rise in turnover. *Publishes* adult fiction, self help and business titles. TITLES *Animal Instincts* Alan Titchmarsh; *The Time Machine* H.G. Wells; *Popcorn* Ben Elton; *The 7 Habits of Highly Effective People* Stephen R. Covey; *Deja Dead* Kathy Reichs; *Lethal Seduction* Jackie Collins; *Ramses* Christian Jacq; *Rhinoceros* Colin Forbes; *Last Man Standing* David Baldacci.

SmartPass Ltd
15 Park Road, Rottingdean, Brighton, East Sussex BN2 7HL
☎01273 300742
Email jools@smartpass.co.uk
Website www.smartpass.co.uk
Managing Director *Phil Viner*

FOUNDED 1999. Family-run business. *Publishes* audio study guides, drama and analysis for GCSE English Literature set texts – novels, plays and poetry. TITLES include *Animal Farm* George Orwell; *A Kestrel for a Knave* Barry Hines; *Pride and Prejudice* Jane Austen; *Great Expectations* Charles Dickens; *Shakespeare: the works*; *War Poetry*. Welcomes ideas from authors who are teachers and from agents who represent these authors.

Smith/Doorstop Cassettes
The Poetry Business, The Studio, Byram Arcade, Huddersfield, West Yorkshire HD1 1ND
☎01484 434840 Fax 01484 426566
Email edit@poetrybusiness.co.uk
Website www.poetrybusiness.co.uk
Co-directors *Peter Sansom, Janet Fisher*

Publishes poetry, read and introduced by the writer. AUTHORS Carol Ann Duffy, Simon Armitage, Les Murray, Ian McMillan, Sujata Bhatt.

Soundings
Isis House, Kings Drive, Whitley Bay, Tyne & Wear NE26 2JT
☎0191 253 4155 Fax 0191 251 0662
Website www.isis-publishing.co.uk

FOUNDED in 1982. Part of the Ulverscroft Group Ltd. *Publishes* fiction and non-fiction; crime, romance. About 190 titles a year. AUTHORS include Angus McVicar, Barbara Cartland, Catherine Cookson, Joanne Harris, Olivia Manning, Derek Tangye, Lyn Andrews, Robert Ludlum, Susan Sallis, Mary Jane Staples, Alexander Fullerton, Patrick O'Brian, Pamela Oldfield.

Spokenbooks Audio
Ty'n Waun, Pencefn, Tregaron, SY25 6JF
Email spokenbooks@hotmail.com
Managing Director *Paul Ingrams*

ESTABLISHED 2002. Interested in titles with a Welsh interest: history, myth, legend, biography and social interest. Welcomes ideas from authors and agents.

British Poetry –
Just Like the British State

Peter Finch

These days, in the way it goes about its business, British poetry resembles the British state: it may prefer to lean towards the cooperative, caring left, but it's the hard-edged business-led right that drives the system. For the last ten years verse has been on the rise, consistently, all-embracingly. No longer. Sales have fallen. Has the slim volume with a single name on it finally had its day?

Neil Astley, outspoken MD at Bloodaxe Books, one of the UK's largest poetry independents, seems to think so. He cites a significant downturn in sales of single author poetry titles as evidence. He points to the higher discounts demanded by the book chains and their significant reduction in stockholding. He notes the way in which poetry is not marketed to the general consumer but rather at a coterie of informed intellectuals. What the general reader wants out of poetry is something that is relevant to their lives. What the general reader gets is information-rich obscurantism written mainly by white, middle-aged male intellectuals. This is an extremely general view, of course, but there's a touch of truth about it. 'Poetry today seems like the Church of England, bewildered at finding its ranks of pews empty, and asking what has gone wrong with everybody,' says Henry Shukman. Adrian Mitchell's prophetic 1964 remark, 'Most people ignore most poetry because most poetry ignores most people' rides again. Among commercial publishers the closure or reduction of the poetry list is the norm. OUP has passed its new poets to Carcanet; Chatto has cut back to the bone; Hutchinson, Dent, Secker, Macmillan and Gollancz have axed their lists; Sinclair-Stevenson has gone to dust.

However, the poetry anthology, the collection of works on a common theme, has perversely never had it so good. Driven by a combination of good marketing and relevant content, these books have become poetry's growth point. The *Poetry On the Underground* anthologies, published by Cassell, sell in their thousands because they contain short, significant, quality poems that many buyers have already sampled on the underground itself. Life-affirming anthologies, led by Neil Astley's *Staying Alive*, published by Bloodaxe, a collection of poetry 'directly relevant to everything going on in the world around us' have experienced remarkable sales. Backed up by her BBC2 series, Daisy Goodwin's *101 Poems Survival Guides* from HarperCollins, and similar collections of 'useful' verse have moved to the sales forefront. Elsewhere, it is the subject itself that has attracted readers. *The Poetry of Flowers, The Poetry of the Sea, The Poetry of the Great War, The Poetry of Childhood* are apparently much more appealing to readers than books which contain simply…

What? Well... *poetry*. Don't be general, be specific. In the marketplace this works.

As predicted by the conclusions of the Arts Council of England's research into the subject a few years back, the poem is finding new outlets. *Poetry On the Underground* was a forerunner. Poetry on the buses, on the walls of doctor's surgeries, on regional railways, in poster form in public places across the land are now expanding activities. Such schemes are cheap to run, celebrate the past as well as marking the present, and involve the whole local community. Local politicians like them. They are on the rise.

Poetry has also migrated in significant quantity to the Internet. Among print-based non-commercial small presses and little magazines there have been a number of cut-backs and casualties (especially *Thumbscrew*, Tim Kendall's excellent magazine from Oxford. But on the net, magazines, journals and individual one-poet sites have increased exponentially. Poetry has also begun to appear in much more dominant positions and in larger quantities in our broadsheet daily papers. The *Guardian* and the *Independent* publish daily poems, the Sundays use verse on a regular basis where they once only dabbled, and even the tabloid red-tops and local rags are testing the water. In the past year at least two dailies have run regular series on the way poetry works. Poetry may not be able to sell slim volumes but it is still a force, it seems.

Poetry's big annual media event remains National Poetry Day with its readers' poll for the nation's Favourite (*Poems of Celebration* was the most recent). Verse appears on the radio schedules, scattered like confetti throughout the listening day. The highlight is the awarding of the Forward prizes for best volume of poetry, best single poem and best newcomer. Verse has become newsworthy. Haiku are displayed on church railings. Sonnets appear in shop windows. New poetry on postcards gets handed out in supermarkets, on trains, in schools and libraries. Michael Horovitz, who was awarded the OBE for his services to poetry last year, runs another Poetry Olympics performance. No medals, just verse and spark. Did you miss all this? You couldn't have been looking. Last year even the business pages of the *Observer* chose to highlight the earnings of poets. Their conclusions? Verse won't do much to keep the wolf from the door.

Traditional forms are back too: sonnets, sestinas, things with metre and rhyme. A sonnet came second in the National Poetry Competition last year. And, as it was the 200th anniversary of Wordsworth's famous sonnet 'On Westminster Bridge', the Wordsworth Trust commissioned a whole raft of new versions. The BBC ran a poll as to which was best – the original, a modern rewrite and a text message version. The original won hands down.

On the circuits, live poetry continues its rise from back-room art to stage-front entertainment. The British Council, with help from the various national and regional Arts Councils, sends British poets to an ever-increasing number of foreign destinations. In exchange, foreign poets come to Britain to tour amid publicity thrash and rising hubbub, rather like the visiting jazz big bands of half a century ago. Recently, it's been Russian Women Poets; before that it was the Dutch, the Romanians and the Finns. The Poetry Society ran a *Respect Slam!* at the Oval House. Poets Twm Morys, Iwan Llwyd and others toured their *Seven Saints* verse performance to every town in Wales they could find which had the word 'Saint' in its name, and then went to Oxford and other places east of the border. In Scotland, schoolchildren sent poetry across the country using homing pigeons. The poetry reading is no longer an exclusive activity playing to a select few, it can reach everyone.

Overall, this doesn't sound quite like the bust the booksellers and publishers seem to think. Poetry still thrives in many quarters. What do the financial advisors say? Stick with the market, it'll bounce back. It won't be the market we once knew but it will be a market nonetheless.

What should you read?

The way in is first to discover what poetry actually is. To do this means putting some time in at the bookshop and the library. Be as open and catholic as you can in your selection. Ensure you check out the whole scene – the past, the present, mainstream English literature along with work in translation, the poets you find you like as well as those you find difficult. Appreciation will not come without effort. Stay the course.

Ask your bookshop for their recommendations. Check out Waterstones or Ottakers which both stock poetry titles. The on-line bookseller, Amazon, produces a browsable list. Most shops these days carry a basic stock, but if you need more then get hold of the Poetry Library's current list of shops with a specific interest in poetry or enquire at your local library.

Start with a recent anthology of contemporary verse. You'll be spoilt for choice here; the new millennium has encouraged a whole crop of century definers to rush into print. To get a broad view of what's going on, you should not only read Edna Longley's *Bloodaxe Book of Twentieth-Century Poetry*, Simon Armitage's and Robert Crawford's *British and Irish Poetry Since The War* (Penguin); Sean O'Brien's *The Firebox* (Picador); Michael Schmidt's *The Harvill Book of Twentieth-Century Poetry In English*; the latest annual *Forward Book of Poetry* (Faber) and Richard Caddel's and Peter Quartermain's *Other: British and Irish Poetry since 1970* (Wesleyan); but also Keith Tuma's *Anthology of Twentieth-Century British and Irish Poetry* (OUP); Todd Swift & Philip Norton's anthology of fusion poetry, *Short Fuse* (Rattapalax); Sarah-Jane Lovett's *Oral* (Sceptre); Lemn Sissay's *The Fire People – A Collection of Contemporary Black British Poets* (Payback Press); Neil Astley's *Staying Alive* (Bloodaxe), Jeni Couzyn's *The Bloodaxe Book of Contemporary Women Poets*; *Poems For the Millennium* (two volumes) edited by Jerome Rothenberg and Pierre Joris (California) and *Postmodern American Poetry,* a really splendid selection edited by Paul Hoover (Norton). This last title might be harder to find, but is worth the effort.

Fill in with a standard overview of poetry in English since Chaucer. John Gallas's *The Song Atlas: A Book of World Poetry* (Carcanet) is a good scattergun.

For a more balanced historical view try Christopher Rick's *The Oxford Book of English Verse* (OUP); Andrew Motion's *Here To Eternity* (Faber); Paul Keegan's *New Penguin Book of English Verse*; Helen Gardner's *New Oxford Book of English Verse* (OUP); the great *Norton Anthology of Poetry* or long-term standby *Palgrave's Golden Treasury* (OUP).

Progress to the literary magazine. Write off to a number of the magazine addresses which follow this article and ask the price of sample copies. Enquire about subscriptions. Expect to pay something, but it shouldn't break the bank. Buy – this is vital for little magazines, it is the only way in which they are going to survive. Check out the websites listed further on in this article. It is important that poets, particularly, read not only to familiarize themselves with what is currently fashionable and to increase their own facility for self-criticism, but to help support the activity in which they wish to participate.

Ok, I'm well read. What next?

Take a look at your own material. Are you personally convinced it's ready? If you are uncertain, then most likely that will be the view of everyone else. Check your text for glips and blips. Rework it. Root out any clichés or archaic poetry expressions such as 'O', 'doeth', 'bewilld'd' and the like. Drop any of what Peter Sansom calls 'spirit of the age' poetry words. Do without shards, lozenges, lambent patina, and stippled seagulls. Try and avoid shopping trolleys or tramps. If you work with rhyme attempt to avoid the obvious. Make sure any metre you may be using actually works. Try not to clank. If by this time your writing still sounds OK, then go ahead.

Publishing on the Internet

Although some people would still love it to be, the Internet is not a diversion. For the poet, or for that rare beast, the non-contributing poetry reader, the Web has now moved into high focus. No longer a simple extension of conventional print it is now an actual substitute which you ignore at your peril. Growth over the past few years has been nothing short of enormous. Not bad for a medium supposedly built originally as a military device. With the advent of cheap access, always-on, lightning-fast Broadband and complimentary webspace an increasing number of poetry enthusiasts, organizations and publishers have set up sites. Some poets have abandoned conventional print to operate solely online; others have launched without ever having known ink and paper. Cyberspace – the place where it all happens – is a mirror of the conventional world: the electronic repli-cates the real. Here are online books, magazines, historical and contemporary archives, reference works, creative tools, recordings, discussion forums and news round-ups. Many sites are dedicated entirely to poetry. Some of our national institutions, notably the BBC and the *Guardian*, have discovered that poetry makes ideal Web content and devote significant sections of their sites to verse. On the Internet poetry is a consumer staple. (For a list of websites, see page 125.)

Journals

Online magazines range from those which mirror their print-based cousins (and in some cases are simply direct copies) to those which are completely innovative, providing movement, video, sound and interactivity along with actual text. Some magazines (e-zines, online journals) offer playable recordings of their poets performing, others give space for readers to add criticism. More and more sites are opening chat rooms and forums where readers can exchange views. The difference between online and print-based magazines becomes more apparent when you discover that what you get when you call them up is not simply an enhanced version of the current issue but access to the entire back catalogue. All searchable, storable and, best of all, free.

Geography dissolves online. America is no further and no more costly to access than Britain. One of the great magazines, John Tranter's *Jacket,* is based in Australia. It's just as easy to read as George Simmers' *Snakeskin*, produced in Britain, Ethan Paquan's *Slope*, produced in the USA, or Rick Lupert's *Poetry Super Highway*, produced in Los Angeles. In fact, half the time, the user has no idea precisely where the site being accessed is physically based. Place ceases to matter, language takes over.

Online journals can range from the terrible to the terrific. For my money, the aforementioned *Jacket*, Joan Houlihan's *Perihelion,* Neil Rollinson's most professional *Boomerang,* Rupert Loydell's *Stride*, and Jennifer Ley's *Riding the Meridian* are some of the world's best. Not all magazines are English either. For an experience of strict metres have a look at *Cartref Cynghanedd ar y We* (*The Home of Cynghanedd* on the Web) although you'll need a Welsh-speaking guide to help you.

How do you contribute? As with all poetry ventures, read first. Will you fit in? If you think so, then send your poems by e-mail, either in the body of the e-mail or as an attached file. More than likely you'll get an instant answer. No more waiting around for six weeks before your poems return from traditional publishers, rejected and dog-eared. Online can be lightening fast.

Cyberspace is huge. Some of the sites which list online journals, such as Peter Howard's *Poetry Contacts* or Patrick Martin's *Poetry Resource* seem to go on for days. On the Web it is easy to put up more, so in terms of quality of content that often means less. As in the real world, not everything is even. Check the site's design. If thought has gone into it, then it's likely that consideration has been given to the content as well.

Home Pages

If you tire of contributing to the websites of others then why not start your own? A whole collection of verse online will present relatively little difficulty. Most

Internet Service Providers (ISPs) offer an amount of free webspace to users or, if you can put up with the adverts, you can claim a home for nothing at somewhere like Geocities. Building your own home page is certainly not beyond anyone capable of using a word processor. Many ISPs also provide free page-creation software. If you'd like to see the kind of thing that's possible, have a look at the site of poets Matthew Francis and Attila the Stockbroker, or for something more graphically challenging, Gwyneth Lewis's poetic voyage. You might also care to look at my own, *The Peter Finch Archive*. If you are reticent, get a fan to set up a site devoted to your works. This has happened to David Gascoyne, J.H. Prynne, Maya Angelou, Ivor Cutler, Benjamin Zephaniah and others. Most of us, however, seem to like the idea of self build. If you have a recording of yourself doing your stuff then get one jump ahead. Put that on the site too.

Hypertext

The Web has developed its own verse forms. Most of these straddle the boundaries between verse, sound and image, in much the same way that concrete poetry did fifty years ago. Many critics dismiss the new work as simply moving graphic art but protagonists see the world very differently. The subject is large and developing. Webartery will give you links to some of the leading practitioners. Look at the flash-driven examples on the BBC's poetry site as well as those created by poet and web-watcher Peter Howard.

Groups

To reduce the poet's traditional feeling of isolation the net presents a number of opportunities and world-wide poets, once they've got over the stunning breadth of net facilities, are usually hard to shut up. E-mail provides one vehicle. Here, bands of poets circulate their work, their criticisms and their views of world literature. Join a group (no cost, just ask) and you'll find a daily delivery of e-mails in your inbox. Some groups are moderated, which means that contributions are filtered by a controlling individual although most are free for alls. Discussion can range from the moronic to the stimulating. The British and Irish Poets Group established by Ric Caddel and Poetryetc, an outgrowth of the list begun by John Kinsella, are two worth trying.

A variant on e-mail discussion groups are usenet newsgroups. Newsgroups run through their own dedicated software (provided by your ISP as part of your subscription) and are open to contributions from anyone anywhere. Articles are delivered to your browser for consumption. If you want to contribute then type it, send it and it's done. The principal poetry newsgroups, rec.arts.poems and alt.arts.poetry.comments, offer pretty varied fare. They tend to be American dominated and standards of contribution are not always that high, but you can get an instant reaction to your latest poem. There are also masterclasses with established poets offering online advice. The BBC, Chadwyck-Healey and the

Poetry Society are some of the organizations which have offered virtual residencies with well-known bards.

Tools and resources

The net offers a multitude of these. There are online spell-checkers (in many languages), thesauri, an anagram creator, Shakespeare and Bible concordances and a rhyming dictionary. The archives of universities (particularly in America) offer the great poetry of the past in comprehensive quantity. Download facsimile editions of the *Germ* (the first ever poetry magazine established in 1850) or hear Seamus Heaney recite. Read the complete works of William Blake, find out what powered the Beat generation, discover how Thomas Hardy worked, check out the roots of modern verse. Not only can you find the texts themselves, but entire critical apparatuses, historical contexts, biographies, bibliographies, portraits, shoe sizes and the names of lovers for most of the greats. You can access information on poetry readings or look up the British Council site for data on literature festivals. For a glimpse of the broader picture check UNESCO's huge World Poetry Directory. Students revel in posting their dissertations and archives want their knowledge made available to everyone. Former UK journalist Martin Blyth offers a stimulating range of poetry reviews and opinion. Interested in a particular style? Haiku? Visual poetry? Traditional forms? They've all got their own sites. There has also been increasing interest recently in bad poetry – verse that is somehow so bad it transcends itself. William McGonagall was the forerunner but he's been joined by the Canadian 'Chaucer of Cheese', James McIntyre and American MFBP (Most Famous Bad Poet) Julia A. Moore. If your own verse is dreadful then you'll have friends on the Web.

E-commerce

Shopping on the Net is now the preferred method for buying specialist material. The big Internet bookshop, Amazon, offers searchable lists for the hunter of that difficult to obtain poetry title. Buying online is generally safe and swift although, as with all mail order, only as perfect as the van that brings the package to your door. The UK Poetry Book Society which acts as a poetry book club (see **Organizations of Interest to Poets)** is also taking advantage of Internet sales.

How to find it all

Use the search engines. The big ones – Google, Yahoo, Excite, AltaVista – can return enormous lists in response to keying in the word 'poetry'. I got 295,097 results out of AltaVista. It's much easier to log on to one of a number of poetry resource sites which run clickable lists of relevant pages. The Poetry Society, the Poetry Library and the *Poetry Review*'s 'web watcher', Peter Howard's home page, are worth consulting. Ted Slade's *Poetry Kit* provides a large amount of poetry information, competition lists and resources. And for a good worldwide look try *Pif Magazine's* pilot search.

Where next?

New ideas arrive all the time. The major online writing project, trAce, set up at Nottingham-Trent University with support from the Arts Council is signposting many of the ways Net writing can go. At the BBC website you can create your own works on screen using a virtual form of magnetic poetry more usually seen on the fronts of fridges. Peter Howard's *Poetry Page* site runs a number of online poetry generators and there's an easy to use couple at 'the hold com'. The user keys in basic vocabulary and the Java script does the rest. On the other hand, you may prefer to use your own creative engines. Log on now.

Some Web Addresses For Poets

Annedd y Cynganeddwyr	www.cynghanedd.com
Attila the Stockbroker	www.attilathestockbroker.com
BBC	www.bbc.co.uk/arts/poetry/ index.shtml
Martin Blyth	www.martinblyth.co.uk
Boomerang	www.boomeranguk.com
British Council Literature festivals	www.britishcouncil.org/arts/literature/ festivals
British Poets e-mail list	www.jiscmail.ac.uk/lists/ british-poets.html
Chadwyck-Healey Literature Online	lion.chadwyck.co.uk
Chaucer of Cheese	www.ocl.net/projects/poetrycontest/ links/links.html
Electronic Poetry Centre	wings.buffalo.edu/epc
Matthew Francis	www.7greenhill.freeserve.co.uk
Jacket (magazine)	www.jacketmagazine.com
John Kinsella	www.saltpublishing.com/kinsella.html
Gwyneth Lewis	www.gwynethlewis.com/voyage.shtml
Patrick Martin's Poetry Resource	www.pmpoetry.com
William McGonagall	www.mcgonagall-online.org.uk
Julia A. Moore	www.wmich.edu/english/txt/Moore
Nth Position (magazine)	www.nthposition.com
Perihelion (magazine)	webdelsol.com/Perihelion
Peter Finch Archive	www.peterfinch.co.uk
Peter Howard's Poetry Page	www.hphoward.demon.co.uk/poetry
Poetry Super Highway (magazine)	poetrysuperhighway.com/PoetLinks.html
Pif Magazine	www.pifmagazine.com
Poetry Book Society	www.poetrybooks.co.uk

Poetry Generators	www.the-hold.com/generate.html
Poetry Kit (magazine)	www.poetrykit.org
The Poetry Library	www.poetrylibrary.org.uk
The Poetry Society (UK)	www.poetrysoc.org.uk
Riding the Meridian (magazine)	www.heelstone.com/meridian
Slope (magazine)	www.slope.org
Snakeskin (magazine)	homepages.nildram.co.uk/~simmers
Stride	www.stridemagazine.co.uk
trAce	www.trace.ntu.ac.uk
Webartery	www.webartery.com
World Poetry Directory	www.unesco.org

WAP, SMS and Other Mobile Phone Wonders

WAP is the slow to load, cut-down version of the Internet used by some cell phones. Third generation mobiles with their much faster methods of data transfer should soon see it off. SMS are the ubiquitous text messages which have transformed the way some people write and spell. All these have been exploited by poets. Sponsored by Orange the *Guardian* has run a text poetry competition (www.guardian.co/textpoetry) which appears to have encouraged half of Britain to take part and at Tinywords (tinywords.com) you can get short poems delivered daily to your mobile. At www.wapdrive/basho you can idly browse haiku, or you can set up your own site for free at www.wapdrive.com/boomerang. Is this the future or a mere diversion along the route? Whichever your view the fact that it makes users reconsider the way language works is undeniable.

Commercial Publishers

It may come as a surprise but the number of commercial publishers who deal in poetry is actually quite small. Despite the apparent acceptability of verse, profit is more easily made elsewhere. Where once there was a multitude of mainstream poetry imprints there are now only three or four. With obvious exceptions, poetry is increasingly seen as the quality line which enhances a publisher's list. Despite a decade or more of poetry booms the stuff is still a commercial risk. Poetry sales overall are falling (although, as discussed earlier, the anthology, which gets much support from the bookshops, is holding its own) and slim volumes by single authors are difficult to shift. Poetry editors are almost always part-time or have other jobs within the publishing company and are often not allowed to publish what they would really like to.

The obvious exception to this approach is long-term market leader and envy of the whole business **Faber & Faber**. Here editor Paul Keegan presides over a poetry list which continues to be as important to the firm as when the poetry of T.S. Eliot inaugurated it more than seventy years ago. The best poetry transcends the limits of the traditional market, Faber believes. This is the imprint most poets would like to join. The greats of the twentieth century are here – Pound, Eliot, Plath, Hughes, Larkin. Seamus Heaney sold half-a-million copies when he won the Nobel prize. Wendy Cope's sales regularly number into five figures. The imprint is built on distinctively designed class and the roster of contemporary poets are some of the best we have – Simon Armitage, Derek Walcott, Don Paterson, Andrew Motion, Jo Shapcott, Hugo Williams, Paul Muldoon, Douglas Dunn. Faber publishes up to sixty poetry titles each year and runs a competition in conjunction with the booksellers, Ottakers. If you fancy your chances, then send a brief covering letter and a sample of your writing (six to ten poems) not forgetting an s.a.e., if you think this is where you'll fit in. The Faber website is at www.faber.co.uk.

Oxford University Press has transferred its contemporary list to Michael Schmidt at Carcanet. OUP is now a great historical poetry repository with some highly desirable titles. But new verse needs to be sent elsewhere.

A commercial editor with excellent taste is **Cape**'s Robin Robertson. His list is by no means all things to all people. John Burnside, Anne Carson, Mark Doty, Michael Longley, Sharon Olds, Peter Redgrove and Matthew Sweeney are typical. Roberston produces four to six titles annually – all single-poet books, no anthologies and with a few sourced from the other side of the Atlantic. Worth trying? Yes, but potential contributors should never waste anyone's time by not looking at the list first. Poetry at **Chatto & Windus**, another imprint of Random House, is in the hands of Rebecca Carter. Output is slightly lower than that at Cape and has recently included Bernard O'Donoghue, Ruth Padel and John Fuller. But unless supported by a strong recommendation from an established fellow practitioner, Carter does not want to see unsolicited manuscripts. Do read their handbook *52 Ways of looking at a Poem* by Ruth Padel, her *Independent on Sunday* articles anthologized.

Both **Chatto** and **Cape** preview examples from their lists in the poem for the day section of the Random House website at www.randomhouse.co.uk

The Harvill Press runs one of the smaller commercial poetry lists, publishing one or two new titles annually and has a particular interest in European translations. Central to its poetry publishing are the works of Paul Durcan, and a recent successes with Rutger Kopland. They also publish Michael Schmidt's fine anthology *The Harvill Book of Twentieth-Century Poetry In English*. Editor Euan Cameron will look at new manuscripts but the chances of being taken on are slim. New writers would be better off starting elsewhere.

Canongate (along with their imprint **Payback Press)** recycle Rabbie Burns and publish new work from Lemn Sissay, Alan Spence, Gil Scott-Heron and Gillian Ferguson.

Among the other commercial houses activity appears to be limited to nominal titles, anthologies or back-list obligations. **Orion** publishes Jeremy Reed and anthologies of love poetry. **Deutsch** prints John Hegley and Ogden Nash. **Duckworth** rolls on with William McGonagall. **Methuen** publishes Wole

Soyinka. **BBC Worldwide** churns out the Nation's Favourites and **Cassell** anthologizes the poems from the London Underground. **Hamish Hamilton** does John Updike. **John Murray** recycles Betjeman and prints anthologies of old chestnuts and travel verse. **Everyman** concentrates on work that's out of copyright – Dylan and R.S. Thomas and anthologies from the BBC series *Poetry Please*. **Boxtree** presents Purple Ronnie. Some specialist interests are dealt with at **Lion** (Christian verse) and **Windhorse** (Buddhist) – but it isn't a lot.

The Smaller Operators

Not all commercial publishing is vast and conglomerate. A few independents still exist and poetry occasionally occurs on their lists. Poet Jeremy Robson's **Robson Books** imprint publishes Vernon Scannell. Northern Ireland general publisher, **Blackstaff Press**, bring out one or two poetry titles annually, including Patrick Crotty's groundbreaking *Modern Irish Poetry*. Welsh family firm **Gwasg Gomer** produces neat editions of Gillian Clarke, Janet Dube, John Barnie, Nigel Jenkins and others. Their *Borders*, a bi-lingual collection from Grahame Davies and Elin ap Hywel, introduces Welsh verse to a wider audience. Their website is at www.gomer.co.uk **Polygon**, (an imprint of **Birlinn Ltd**) continues to mix Gaelic with English and has at least half a dozen poets on the list including Donny O'Rourke, Roddy Gorman, Liz Lochhead and W.N. Herbert. They also publish *Pocket Books*, a series which mixes poetry with photography and *The Dream State: The New Scottish Poets*. Others in the field include **Gill & Macmillan** and **Y Lolfa**.

Universities

With the collapse of OUP's poetry publishing, contemporary interest activity among UK university presses is sparse: reprints and literary studies at **Cambridge**; the same at **Manchester**; at the **University of Wales Press,** who publish a splendid series of collected works from Welsh poets, you need to be dead. American university presses such as Nebraska, **Princeton, Louisiana**, **Wisconsin**, **Chicago**, **Harvard**, **Michigan**, North Carolina, **Washington**, **Alabama** and **California** along with **W.W. Norton** publish an increasing amount of verse but exclusively by Americans. No chances there. Wolfgang Görtschacher's **Poetry Salzburg** is an independent Anglophone operation run from the University of Salzburg is Austria. They publish six to ten titles annually, concentrating on translations from European minorities and collections from neglected British poets. Their magazine *Poetry Salzburg* samples Görtschacher's taste. Their website is at www.poetrysalzburg.com

Women

There were days when **Virago** was out front here, but no longer. Now part of Time Warner they more or less only publish poetry from novelists already on their lists – Margaret Atwood, Michele Roberts, Maya Angelou along with genre anthologies. There are no plans for expansion.

At the **Women's Press**, Virago's traditional competitor, the situation is much the same. They reissue Elizabeth Barrett Browning and keep Alice Walker in print. The **Onlywomen Press**, however, have kept an active interest in poetry publishing. Lilian Mohin, Onlywomen Press editor, publishes around three poetry titles annually. Works by Marilyn Hacker, Kate Foley, Paula Jennings, U.A. Fanthorpe and Sunjoto Namjoshi are typical offerings. Read their anthology *Not For The Academy: Lesbian Poets*. Generally, however, women poets are better served by the poetry specialists. More of them anon.

The Mass Market Paperback

This popular end of the market is where many poets imagine the best starting place to be. Paperback houses were originally founded to publish inexpensive reprints of hard-cover originals and, despite years of innovation and market posturing, to a large extent still fulfil this role. Being neither cheap nor (in sales terms) that popular, poetry does not really fit in here. Among the carousels at airports you do not see it. Look, for example, at the lists of the empires of **Arrow**, **Bantam**, **Corgi, Headline** and **Mills & Boon**, if you discount the inspirational, you won't find a book of verse between them. **Vintage**, to their credit, reprinted Iain Sinclair's poetry to back up sales of his novels. Elsewhere nothing, with two exceptions.

At **Penguin**, where things are always different, poetry has a significant role. With its unfailing commercial ear the imprint has correctly assessed the market for a niche for contemporary and traditional verse and systematically and successfully found it. Reprinting important volumes pioneered by less commercial poetry presses, originating historic and thematic anthologies, reviving classic authors and producing a multitude of translations en route, Penguin continues to provide an almost unrivalled introduction to the world of verse. But appearances aside, this is most certainly no place for the beginner. 'We publish almost no new or unknown poets. In fact we publish very little new poetry beyond a small circle of established poets. We concentrate on selecteds and general anthologies,' publishing director Tony Lacey told me. The company focuses on sure sellers such as James Fenton, Linton Kwesi Johnson, Geoffrey Hill, Tony Harrison and Roger McGough. The main thrust remains the re-packaging of Derek Mahon, Carol Ann Duffy and U.A. Fanthorpe, a good range of modern poets in translation along with larger collections from the likes of William Empson, Allen Ginsberg and John Ashbery. The company's poetry overview anthologies, the Simon Armitage and Robert Crawford edited *British and Irish Poetry Since the War*, Peter Forbes' *Scanning the Century,* and Paul Keegan's *New Penguin Book of English Poetry* are musts. Penguin also publishes a number of useful books about poetry including Ian Hamilton's *Against Oblivion,* short biographies of twentieth-century poets and James Fenton's *An Introduction to English*

Poetry, a book for readers and writers of English poetry on metre, genre, diction, etc. Despite these obvious winners, Lacey sees the whole market for verse as small, despite the hype. Penguin online is at www.penguin.com

Penguin's nearest rival, **Picador**, the literary paperbacker from **Pan Macmillan**, is exhibiting considerable vigour in its poetry publishing and is now widely regarded as one of the country's leading poetry publishers. Under the commanding eye of successful and non-metropolitan poet Don Paterson, it has moved into high gear putting out a stream of successful collections both from new poets such as Jacob Polley and Yusef Komunyakaa, along with established names such as Kathleen Jamie, Ian Duhig, Peter Porter, Carol Ann Duffy, Kate Clanchy, Michael Donaghy, American poet laureate Billy Collins and Sean O'Brien. With its reliable content, Picador is turning itself into a British reference point. Picador will bring out at least six new titles annually as well as anthologies. Recent examples include Sean O'Brien's critically acclaimed *The Firebox* and Carol Ann Duffy's anthology of love poems *Hand in Hand*. Worth trying here? 'Certainly: ten poems better than a full length manuscript, but establish some track record in the reputable journals first,' advises Paterson.

The Specialists

Despite a clear lack of success in the commercial market place poetry still gets published in quantity. But by whom? By the specialist independents. These are the small army of semi-commercial operations scattered across the country. They are run by poetry enthusiasts whose prime concern starts not with money but with the furtherance of their art. Often begun as classic small presses which outgrew the restraints of back-bedroom offices and under-the-stairs warehousing they are now a real force on the poetry scene. You can find these in Waterstones, you can see them in Blackwells and at Ottakers. Most (but not all) receive grant aid, without which their publishing programmes would be sunk. They are models of what poetry publishing should be – active, involving, alert and exciting. They promote their lists through readings, tours, websites and broadcasts and they involve their authors in the production and sales of their books. Never before have new poets been faced with so many publishing opportunities. And if there is any criticism then it is that too many books jam the market. Just how does the reader see through the flood? By reputation, I guess. Two specialists publishers have emerged well ahead of the pack – **Carcanet** and **Bloodaxe**. Along with **Faber** these two now dominate British poetry publishing.

Taking them alphabetically, Neil Astley's acclaimed **Bloodaxe Books** publishes thirty titles annually. Although doing less than it once did, the press still brings out more poetry books than any other British imprint. Picking up poets dropped by the commercial operators as well as discovering new ones, it is certainly one of poetry's best proving grounds. Based in Northumberland and founded in Newcastle in the late seventies, the press is unhindered by a past catalogue of classical wonders or an overly regional concern; it relentlessly pursues the new. Astley presents the complete service from thematic anthologies, world greats and selections to slim volumes by total newcomers. The press has its own range of excellent handbooks to the scene including *Getting Into Poetry* and *Writing Poems* along with an increasing range of volumes of criticism. Best poetry sellers are their anthologies: Neil Astley's own *Staying Alive: Real Poems For Unreal Times,* Edna Longley's *Bloodaxe Book of Twentieh-Century Poetry* and their decade-framing anthology *The New Poetry.* Bloodaxe relishes the chance to publish work from outside the standard English mainstream – Ireland, Scotland, and Wales are all well represented (with Menna Elfyn and John Rowland's *Bloodaxe Book of Modern Welsh Poetry* at the forefront), as are our more traditional UK outsiders such as J.H. Prynne. They also give prominence to major American, European and Commonwealth poets. Typical poets include Fleur Adcock, David Constantine, Helen Dunmore, Selima Hill, Jackie Kay, Peter Reading and Ken Smith. Bloodaxe will not go rusty with age. Newcomers are advised to send a sample rather than a full collection. 'If you don't read contemporary poetry we are unlikely to be interested in your work,' comments Astley. A simple way to taste the imprint's range is to try their two house anthologies *Poetry With An Edge* and *New Blood.* Look at their website: one of the best poetry sites on the Web, at www.bloodaxe.com

Carcanet Press, has been the consistent recipient of critical accolades – publishing four Nobel prize-winning authors and four Pulitzers helps. Although it is no longer exclusively a publisher of verse (Carcanet publishes limited amounts of fiction, criticism, biographies and letters) the press still gives poetry pre-eminence. In 1999, it took over the list of contemporary poets published by OUP. Carcanet currently has over 500 titles in print, sales reps in forty-two countries and a programme that brings out forty or so poetry titles annually. Managing director Michael Schmidt agrees with Auden's observation that most people who read verse read it for some reason other than the poetry. He fights the tide with his own mainstream journal *PN Review.* Carcanet has a policy of publishing serious quality. 'I am strongly aware of the anti-modernist slant in a lot of poetry publishing, and publish to balance this,' Schmidt comments. 'Most submissions we receive come from people ignorant of the list to which they are submitting. Nothing is more disheartening than to receive a telephone call asking whether Carcanet publishes poetry.' The press has a four-part editorial programme: to publish new writing, to dust down substantial but neglected figures of earlier centuries, to encourage the translation of poetry, and to publish poets' prose and work relating to modern poetry.   Typical of their list are Ian Macmillan, John Ashbery, Gillian Clarke, Eavan Boland, Edwin Morgan, Les Murray, Jorie Graham Peter Robinson and best-seller Elizabeth Jennings. Carcanet has an air of purpose about it. 'We avoid the technicolour and pyrotechnic media razzmatazz,' says Schmidt. Have a look at their website at www.carcanet.co.uk New poets are welcome to submit but consider both your own past performance as well as Carcanet's style before you go ahead. Send six to ten pages of work and expect to wait six weeks for a reply. Carcanet's *New*

Poetries and *Oxford Poets* series of anthologies give an idea where the taste of the press is going next.

Production standards among other specialists can be equally as good as Carcanet and Bloodaxe although annual output is substantially less.

Anvil Press Poetry, founded by Peter Jay in 1968, is now England's longest-standing independent poetry publisher. The poetry editor is Hamish Ironside. More than thirty years on, Anvil still publish their earliest poets – their very first book was by Harry Guest, while among the latest is Guest's *A Puzzling Harvest*, a collection of poems to tie in with his seventieth birthday. The best of new English language poets are constantly sought: Greta Stoddart and Julian Turner were both shortlisted for the Forward Best First Collection award in the last two years. In addition, Anvil has won a deserved reputation for publishing the best poetry in translation from around the world – Tagore, Seferis, Bei Dao, Lorca, Hikmet. Producing around a dozen titles a year, Anvil gives particular attention to typographical detail, jacket design and the quality of binding, making each publication exceptionally attractive. Potential contributors are strongly advised to read through Anvil's books first and, if still keen, send manuscripts as hard copy, with postage for return. For those who wish to familiarize themselves with the flavour of the Anvil list, Jay's acclaimed anthology, *The Spaces of Hope*, gives a perfect starting point. Their informative website is at www.anvilpresspoetry.com

Enitharmon Press represents quality, cares about presentation and operates 'at the unfashionable end' of the poetry publishing spectrum. Its books are produced to the highest of standards. Enitharmon has little interest in fashion. The press is, as poet Anne Stevenson put it, 'dedicated to a poetry of the human spirit in an age of rampant commercialism'. Owner Stephen Stuart-Smith continues a policy of publishing new, established and unjustly neglected poets with output now up to sixteen volumes annually. Typical of the list are Jane Duran, Myra Schneider, Alan Brownjohn, Kevin Crossley-Holland and Anthony Thwaite. The press has benefited from the surge in interest in the anthology and has brought out volumes covering women's views of their parents, the *Exeter Riddles*, Sean Street's *Radio Anthology* and Anna Adam's *London in Poetry and Prose*. 'It seems unlikely that many new names will be added to the list, as the bookshop chains are so resistant to poetry that only well-known poets get their books stocked.' Which is a pity. We need more from publishers like Stuart-Smith. Visit www.enitharmon.co.uk for more information and samples of some of its poets reading.

Tony Ward's **Arc Publications**, based in Lancashire, brings out around twenty poetry titles annually. 'We publish work that we believe important, innovative, and of outstanding quality,' Ward told me. The imprint has Jean Boase-Beier, Jo Shapcott and John Kinsella on board and maintains a backlist of in excess of 100 titles. Ivor Cutler, Katherine Gallagher, Michael Haslam, John Kinsella and their *Visible Poets* parallel-text translation series are top sellers. Unafraid to take risks, Arc's policy is to publish the best in contemporary poetry, in a reader-friendly medium without in any way compromising the standards of quality for which they have always been known and recognized. The Arc website is at www.arcpublications.co.uk Submissions from unpublished authors are not accepted. Poets should familiarize themselves with the list before sending anything and, unless accompanied by a publishing history and s.a.e. will not be considered. 'We do not wish to put writers off or dampen enthusiasm, but we have never yet accepted an unpublished author,' is the official line. You have been warned.

Ward has an excellent reputation as a printer to the poetry press community and does a splendid job also for David Tipton's **Redbeck Press**. Tipton, who came up the pamphlet route used by many a small press has now driven Redbeck into the top echelon. He publishes everything from Nick Toczek's performance pieces to *Katkist*, Jane Ramsden's anthology of poetry about cats. His star title of recent times has been Debjani Chatterjee's 200-page *Redbeck Anthology of British South Asian Poetry*. Other Redbeck poets include John Freeman, Jim Burns, Barry Tebb, Kim Taplin, Martin Hayes, Tulio Mora, Jenny Swann and Alan Dent. Non-centralist to the core.

Seren Books is a Welsh-based literary house publishing novels, art books, short fiction, biographies and critical texts. Started by Cary Archard as an offshoot of the magazine *Poetry Wales* the imprint still maintains a solid interest in verse, publishing at least six new single author volumes annually. In receipt of public sponsorship, the bias towards work from Wales and the border regions is both admirable and inevitable. Poetry editor Amy Wack reads *everything* submitted but admits she has only ever accepted one unsolicited manuscript in her entire tenure. Poets should read more, she says. Editions are quality productions with plenty of attention paid to design inside and out. Typical recent poets include Paul Henry, best-seller Owen Sheers, Samantha Rhydderch and Sheenagh Pugh, and they've had success with *Birdsong,* an anthology of bird poetry. Their major best-seller is Dannie Abse's *Twentieth Century Anglo-Welsh Poetry*. A good press sampler is their anthology *Oxygen – New Poets from Wales*. They have also published their own guide to the scene, *The Poetry Business*.

Rupert Loydell's **Stride** has gathered a good reputation for catholic taste and running risks. After thirty-three issues in hard-copy his eponymous magazine is now available on the Web at www.stridemagazine.co.uk This is an excellent sample of Stride's taste with an eclectic mix of verse, criticism and feature. Based in the south-west output is less than it used to be, at 'six to twenty' volumes annually. The backlist runs to more than 200 titles ranging from the totally unknown to the famous. Stride perfectly fills the gap between the avant-garde and the user-friendly. No one else is operating in this area. 'Our books are as likely to discuss free jazz, techno music or drug culture as marvel at the effect of sunlight on water, question ideas of belief or explore the intricacies of languages and the visual arts; as likely to use collage and cut-up as reinvent the sonnet; more likely to challenge and excite than send you to sleep', is the official line. The press runs individual collections, criticism, interviews, and some excellent alternative anthologies. Stride responds to submissions swiftly, invariably within three weeks and often within three days. Successes include Martin Stannard and Charles Wright with their best sales coming from their anthologies *The Gift, New Writing for the NHS* and *Freedom to Breathe*, a collection of prose poetry. The continuing crisis in book-sales has, however, caused Stride to look at new methods of production including publishing on demand. Visit their website at www.stridebooks.com for up to date information. Their anthology, *Ladder To The Next Floor,* offers a sampler of how the press got where it is.

Peterloo Poets, based in Cornwall, represents poetry without frills, without fuss, without the Internet, and most definitely without the avant-garde. Run by Harry Chambers the press aims to publish quality work by new and neglected poets, some of them late starters (although if you have been flogging your stuff around the circuit for years and got nowhere then Chambers is unlikely to be your saviour); to co-publish with other reputable presses (notably a *Christmas Poems* collaboration with Enitharmon); and to establish a Peterloo list of volumes by a core of poets of proven worth. Heaney described Chambers as one of the 'great hearers and hearteners of the work being done in British and Irish Poetry'. Peterloo, which represents a stable centre for many people's idea of what poetry is, runs an active backlist of nearly 200 titles. Bestsellers include U.A. Fanthorpe whose *Collected Poems* was published in 2003, Elma Mitchell and Dana Gioia. Poets central to the list are William Scammell, David Sutton and John Whitworth. Recent additions include Valerie Laws. Peterloo, now in its twenty-seventh year runs its own £2,000 first prize poetry competition, and insists that prospective contributors to the press have had at least six poems published in reputable magazines. Send a full manuscript accompanied by an s.a.e. large enough to carry your manuscript back to you. Chambers currently takes a couple of months to reply and the Peterloo list is full to the year 2004.

Michael Hulse, a former editor at Stand, runs **Leviathan**, a publisher with high production standards. His editorial team includes John Kinsella and Anne Michaels. They publish five or so titles annually of British and American work alongside classics and poetry from around the world, in English or translation. Poets include Kit Wright, Jackie Wills, Roger Finch, Peter Goldsworthy, Giles Goodland and Stephanos Papadopoulous. *Leviathan* magazine offers samples of Hulse's taste. Their website is at www.rattapallax.com/leviathan/index.htm In difficult financial times this is a brave venture.

John Kinsella and Chris Hamilton-Emery have now established a Cambridge base for the international Australian-born **Salt**. Both the press and the journal of the same name have solid left-wing leanings and an interest in contemporary poetics. The press has a contemporary modernist backlist, often centered around the poetryetc e-mail list, which includes Rod Mengham, J.H. Prynne, Fay Zwicky, Andrew Duncan, Paul Hoover, Peter Larkin and Drew Milne. Their British interests will be driven by the flourishing of innovative poetry here.

There are other presses with less prodigious outputs but whose editions are still up there with the best of them. In Northumberland Margaret and Peter Lewis's **Flambard Press** has stuck the course. Begun in 1990 it now publishes around five or six or so titles annually in the Bloodaxe style. With aid from Northern Arts the press is interested in new and neglected poets especially from the north and the Borders. Gerard Benson, Wanda Barford, Gladys Mary Coles, Joolz and Amanda White are typical poets. Their website is at www.flambardpress.co.uk Gladys Mary Coles has developed her **Headland Publications** into a regular Peterloo clone and is now producing an increasing number of fine books. Her interest centres on north-west England and Wales with her **Headland Wales** series. Typical poets include John Barnie, Roger Elkin, Huw Jones, Richard Poole, Brian Wake and Alison Chisholm. Ken Edwards' **Reality Street Editions** specializes in 'linguistically innovative writing by women and men on both sides of the Atlantic.' Publishing a small number of single-author volumes, translations and ground-breaking anthologies the press takes new poetry seriously. Typical authors include Barbara Guest, Cris Cheek, Anslem Hollo's anthology of Finnish poetry, and Denise Riley. Reality Street has also published book/CD packages. Their website is at www.realitystreet.co.uk Currently, however, they are not accepting new manuscripts. Nicholas Johnson's **Etruscan Books** carries the flame for British avant-garde poetry and performance with a terrific series of readers, chapbooks and multi-contributor volumes along with a first-class anthology of contemporary material, *Foil*. If anyone is pushing the edge out then Johnson is, and he's doing it with style. Output is backed up by poetry tours and festival appearances. His published poets include Bob Cobbing, John Hall, Ed Dorn, Helen Macdonald, Wendy Mulford, Sean Rafferty, Maggie O'Sullivan, Bill Griffiths and Tom Pickard.

Paul Beasley's poetry agency (see **Organisations of Interest to Poets**) **57 Productions**, represents performance poetry heartland and, realizing that most of his material works better on audio, has concentrated on editions on cassette and CD. Recent successes have included a double Adrian Mitchell as well as performances by Jackie Kay, Gillian Clarke and Benjamin Zephaniah. Listen to their multi-artist *Poetry in Performance* CDs for a good taster.

In Huddersfield Janet Fisher and Peter Sansom run **Smith/Doorstop** the poetry imprint of their enterprising **Poetry Business** (see **Organisations of Interest to Poets**). The press produces five books and six pamphlets annually. Dorothy Nimmo, Gerard Benson, Dennis Casling, Susan Utting and Michael Laskey are typical authors. Smith/Doorstop also runs an annual poetry pamphlet competition (with publication as one of the prizes) as well as producing poetry on cassette. Its *Contemporary Poems* edited by Peter Sansom and Lesley Jeffries offers a good critical introduction to the scene. Its magazine is *The North*. The website is at www.poetrybusiness.co.uk With strong North American connections Jessie Lendennie runs **Salmon Publishing** from the Cliffs of Moher, Co. Clare, in Ireland. The press has been in business for twenty-one years and despite a reduction in Irish Arts Council support continues to publish some of the best designed titles in the West. An Irish connection is pretty useful when trying here, although Salmon does look at material from further afield. Typical poets include Adrienne Rich, Rita Ann Higgins, Marvin Bell, Linda

McCarriston, James Simmons and Mary O'Malley. Its anthology of contemporary Irish women poets, *The White Page/An Bhileog Bhan*, is a terrific achievement. Salmon has an excellent website at www.salmonpoetry.com which includes discussion, advice, events listings, sound files and a complete bookshop. And if the poetry is not flowing you can book in to a Salmon Creative Writing Workshop costing £100 for the weekend.

Peepal Tree is the largest independent publisher of Caribbean and black British poetry. Founded in 1986 it now produces around twelve poetry titles annually. Typical poets include Kwame Dawes, Dorothea Smartt, Raman Mundair, David Dabydeen and Anthony Kellman. Editor Jeremy Poynting and assistant Emma Smith read over 1,000 submissions annually and are not known for their speedy responses. Telephone or e-mail to submissions@peepaltreepress.com for submission guidelines before sending anything. You can view the Peepal Tree catalogue at www.peepaltreepress.com

A recent start-up is Edward Mackinnon's Nottingham-based **Shoestring Press**. An outgrowth from an episode of self-publishing the press now brings out excellent editions of Anela Leighton, David Tipton, John Tranter and David Holderness's translations from the Anglo-Saxon. Check out Shoestring's website at www.shoestringpress.co.uk Peter Fallon's **Gallery Press** in Co. Meath continues to produce substantial collections from the likes of Derek Mahon, Medbh McGuckian and Richard Murphy. Edinburgh's **Luath Press**, from the heart of Burns country, has spawned an increasing poetry roster which includes Alistair Findlay, Des Dillon and Tom Atkinson's splendid anthology of *Poems To Be Read Out Loud*. Its website it at www.luath.co.uk

In Wales, Lewis Davies's **Parthian Books** under poetry editor Richard Gwyn continues to increase its output. Typical poets include Ifor Thomas, Patrick Jones, Lloyd Robson, Lynne Rees, Rhian Sadaat and Landeg White. Its anthology *The Pterodactyl's Wing* is a collection of the best of Welsh poetry.

As technology continues to make life easier for publishers it becomes harder to draw the line between the poetry specialists and the classic small presses. Maybe by now such a division does not exist at all.

The traditional outlets

Poetry has a place in our national press, but traditionally a small one. The *Independent* and the *Guardian* feature verse from time to time as do some of the serious Sunday heavies. The *Times Literary Supplement* and the *London Review of Books* give space on a regular basis, but they do have their favourites. Among other journals the situation is fluid. Poetry gets in when someone on the staff shows an interest. See if you can find your targets along the shelves at W.H. Smith. Local newspapers and freesheets occasionally devote pages to contributions from readers, mostly dire doggerel and largely unpaid, although it *is* publication. If your paper doesn't do this, try sending in. Much of this might sound quite reassuring for the poet but the truth is that were poetry to cease to exist overnight these publications would continue to operate without a flicker. Who, other than the poets, would notice?

The regional anthologies

Running in parallel with the high-ground literary approach to much of the poetry world are empires largely unknown to the taste-makers and ignored by the critics. The biggest, Ian and Tracy Walton's **Forward Press** in Peterborough, now turns over two million pounds annually, has almost 5,500 titles in print, and reckons to account for the highest proportion of all *new* verse published in Britain. Depressed with 'twenty years of not being able to enjoy poetry' because it was inevitably obscure, the couple have moved from back kitchen to three-storey office block in the service of 750,000 active British verse scribblers. 'A high proportion of the thousands of letters we receive tell us that many people find poetry over-complex and difficult to understand' runs one of its brochures. For more than a decade since it was founded **Forward Press** has enthusiastically promoted an 'accessible, sincere poetry which everyone can relate to.' Although they have printed poems by the likes of Carol Ann Duffy, Simon Armitage and Gavin Ewart the higher realms are not for them. Publishing under a number of imprints including **Poetry Now**, **Anchor Books**, **Young Writers** and **Triumph House**, the operation receives thousands of contributions annually. Poets are sourced in the main through editorial copy in regional newspapers. The contributors flow in in their hundreds. 'It is a bit like amateur dramatics,' Ian told me, 'anyone can take part.'

Forward's outstanding success is built on its approachability. The Waltons and their team of young editors include as many as 160 poems in each anthology. No entry fee is asked. Submissions under thirty lines are preferred. Costs are kept down by using in-house printing equipment – a Ryobi digital press – coupled to serviceable bindings. If you want to see your work in print, and for most contributors this is the whole raison d'être for writing, then you have to buy a copy. For many poets this will be their first appearance in book form and chances are they will purchase more than a single copy. This is not a traditional vanity operation. No one is actually being ripped off, nor are the publishers raking in exorbitant profits. Page for page their titles are not much more expensive than those of Cape or Faber and are cheaper than the output of some little presses. However, distribution is patchy – not that many Forward titles make the shelves of our national chains, although efforts have been made. As with many small presses, interested parties are encouraged to buy direct. All published poets are entered for free into the Top 100 Poets of the Year Award which consists of a share of £10,000, the first prize standing at £3,000. Forward's critics claim that quality is being neglected in exchange for quantity. Dumb down your criteria for inclusion, cram the poems in, sell more copies. Undoubtedly the genuine literary achievement of appearing in one of Forward's books is questionable. But in mitigation it must be said that for some writers this will be their much-needed beginning (Angela Macnab and Sally Spedding, for example) but for others it is the only success they are ever going to get.

In addition to their schools and regional collections, Forward runs three magazines, *Poetry Now*, *Scribbler!* and *Wordsmith* (for young writers), a print and design service for self-publishers, **New Fiction**, an imprint for short story writers, and **Spotlight** – a joint publishing venture which showcases a dozen new poets a time. Its **Writers' Bookshop** imprint publishes a most useful series of reference books including subject and genre guides, directories and handbooks. Forward offers the complete poetry life. If *A Treasured Moment, Perception of Life, Inspire to Rhyme, In High Spirits, Message from Within* and *From A Distance* sound like your scene, send for the group's information pack (Remus House, Peterborough, PE2 9JX), ring them on 01733 898105, fax them on 01733 313524, check their website, www.forwardpress.co.uk, or e-mail your request (james@forwardpress.co.uk). You'll find no dubious accommodation-address dealing here, but on the other hand, few literary giants either.

Envious of Forward's success at catching the hearts and minds of most of the UK's poetry hobbyists a good number of rival empire builders have risen in their wake. Regional poetry anthologies, best of Britain collections, compendiums of English, Scottish, Irish and Welsh verse abound. Contributions are sourced through notices on library walls, local free-sheets, local radio and through direct mail. These operations vary from the glossy to a number of pathetically produced and, one hopes, short-lived incarnations based in the non-metropolitan sticks. No actual rip-off occurs and contributors get in whether they purchase or not, but if you want to see your work then you must buy and the books can cost upwards of thirty pounds. Before agreeing to contribute check the press's output. Do not submit blindly, research their backlist. It is what Faber would demand of you. The rule applies to the whole poetry scene.

The small press and the little magazine

Small publishing ventures have been with us since the dawn of print. And today, from a technical point of view, things are easier to manage than ever. Access to decent printers and the computers that drive them are commonplace. Word processing and publishing software comes as standard. Costs are down. For the past decade small press and little magazine publishing has seen a golden age. In America last year an heiress left $100 million to the literary journal *Poetry*, which will ensure that magazine's continuation in perpetuity.

Recently, however, there have been signs of change. For the first time ever the number of new start-ups has sunk below the number of closures. We've lost *Thumbscrew, Gentle Reader, Upstart!, Pause, As Well As, The Burning Bush, Still, Breathe, Konfluence, JuJu* and others and replacements have been scarce. The reasons? Many, but out front is the Web. Increasingly, small publishers are turning to the place where there are no distribution difficulties and size just doesn't matter. This does not mean that the traditional little magazine is dead. Far from it. All things are relative. Small poetry publishing in hardcopy form is still a powerful force.

Little magazines sell to non-traditional markets rarely finding space on book-shop shelves, where they are regarded as unshiftable nuisances. They go hand to hand among friends, at slams, readings, concerts, creative writing classes, literary functions, via subscriptions and are liberally exchanged among all those concerned. The network is large. The question remains: is anyone out there not directly concerned with the business of poetry actually reading it? But that is another story.

Statistically, the small presses and the little magazines are the largest British publishers of new poetry both in terms of range and circulation. They operate in a bewildering blur of shapes and sizes everywhere from Brighton to Birmingham, Aberystwyth to Aberdeen.

This country's best poetry magazines all began as classic littles. Between them *PN Review, Ambit, Orbis* (now relaunched under the editorship of Carole Baldock), *Poetry Review*, Craig Raine's *Arete, The Rialto, Acumen, The North, Smiths Knoll, The Paper, Envoi*, and *Leviathan Quarterly* do not have even half the circulation of journals like *Shooting Times* and *Practical Fishkeeping* – which says a lot about the way society values its poetry. Nonetheless, taken as a group, they will get to almost everyone who matters; they represent poetry as a whole. Read them and you will get some idea of where the cutting edge is. In the second division, in terms of kudos, lie the regional or genre specialists such as *Raw Edge* (new writing from the west Midlands), *The New Welsh Review, Poetry Wales, Poetry Ireland, Chapman* (Scotland's quality literary magazine), *Krax* (humorous verse), *Poetry Scotland, Mslexia* (for women who write), *Poetry Church* and *Time Haiku*. All these magazines are well produced, sometimes with the help of grants, and all represent a specific point of view. In Wales there is *Barddas* for poets using strict metres and in Scotland *Lallans* for poets working in Lowland Scots. The vast majority of small magazines, however, owe no allegiance. From quality round-ups like *Magma*, Sligo's *Flaming Arrows, Smoke, Tears In The Fence, Poetry Nottingham International*, former Rialto editor John Wakeman's splendid *SHOp*, the enormously long-lived *Iota*, and *Obsessed With Pipework* (high-wire poetry), general literary magazines such as the *Reader* and annuals, such as the excellent *Tabla*, to irregulars like the *Yellow Crane* (interesting new poems), *Roundyhouse* (bards from both sides of the border), *Pulsar* (poems from the Ligden Poetry Society), *Poetry Life* (Britain's sharpest), *Anon* (your work judged by what it says rather than your name), the *Interpreter's House* (the best prose and verse that the editor can get), the anarchic *Page 84* and *Skald* (always happy to receive poetry). Some like the *Penniless Press* are for the poor of pocket and the rich of mind, *Fire* goes for length and the otherwise unpublishable. If you can't find a magazine that suits you and your style then you can't be writing poetry. On the other hand, if you are really sure you are, then start your own.

Among the small presses there is a similar range, although these days slightly less choice than there once was. Philip Hoy's **Waywiser Press** publishes Peter

Dale, Al Alvarez, Anthony Hecht and other safe hands. Despite the withdrawal of its grant David Perman continues the conventional **Rockingham Press** with three or four new books annually. **Feather Books** publishes Christian verse, Alan Halsey's **West House Books** publishes the innovative Geraldine Monk, Bill Griffiths, Kelvin Corcoran, Ric Caddel and others. **Worple** seeks the unrecognized with an international feel – it publishes the unjustly ignored, those starting out as well as those seeking to consolidate. Janet Murch and Bob Mee's **Ragged Raven Press** follows the middle classes. With aid from Northern Arts, **Biscuit Publishing** publishes some excellent Tynesiders, as does fellow Independent Northern Publishers member **Arrowhead Books**. **Y Lolfa** publishes unofficial bards. Peter Manson's **Object Permanence** sporadically publishes the innovative. For the new writer these kinds of presses are the obvious place to try first. Indeed it is where many have. Who first put out T.S. Eliot's? A small publisher. Dannie Abse, Peter Redgrove, James Fenton and Dylan Thomas – the same. R.S. Thomas, Ezra Pound and Edgar Allen Poe didn't even get that far – they published themselves.

Poetry for Children

The thing to remember here is that children rarely buy poetry for themselves, nor are there poetry magazines aimed at them. On the other hand, there are a great number of children's poets out there – Duffy, McGough, Henri and Patten would be much lesser authors if they'd ignored the under-eighteens. The schools system regularly pays poets to read to their classes and teach their children. Macmillan, Faber, Penguin, Oxford, Walker and a few other publishers run specialist children's poetry lists. The market switches between the traditional and the hilarious – *See You Later, Escalator* chosen by John Foster is a typical title. If you have appropriate work send in a few samples marked for the attention of the children's poetry editor. But do not imagine this market to be easy nor a place where you can unload your adult failures. Kids do not suffer fools gladly. For more information check with the Poetry Society who publish a number of poetry in schools checklists along with a handbook.

Cash

Despite a small number very high-value awards (£75,000 plus) made by various government agencies to the select few, a lot of writers new to the business are surprised to learn that their poetry will not make them much money. For most, being a poet is not really much of an occupation. You get better wages delivering papers. There will be the odd twenty pounds from the better-heeled magazine, perhaps even as much as sixty or so from those periodicals lucky enough to be in receipt of a grant, but generally it will be free copies of the issues concerned, thank-you letters and little more. Poets with collections published by a subsidised, specialist publisher can expect a couple of hundred as an advance on royalties. Those using the small presses can look forward to a handful of complimentary copies. On the Internet published poets usually get nothing at all (although there are some exceptions, see *Pif*, for example). The truth is that poetry itself is undervalued. You can earn money writing about it, reviewing it, lecturing on it, teaching it or, certainly, by giving public performances (£150 standard here, £1,000 plus if you are Roger McGough, much more if you are Seamus Heaney. A good many poets are now actually making a living this way by mixing readings with creative writing residencies). But at bottom, most things in the poetry business will earn better money than the verse itself. This isn't capitalism, this is art.

Readings

Since the great Beat Generation, Albert Hall reading in 1964, there has been an ever-expanding phenomenon of poets on platforms, reading or reciting their stuff to an audience that can be anywhere between raptly attentive and fast asleep. Jaci Stephen, writing in the *Daily Mirror*, reckons readings to be like jazz. 'Both involve a small group of people making a lot of noise, and then, just when you think it's all over, it carries on.' But I believe there can be a magic in the spoken poem. Not everything, certainly. But when it's good it can be sublime. Yet for some writers the whole thing has devolved so far as to become a branch of the entertainment industry or, in the case of poetry slams (see **Competitions**, below), an opportunity to show off in front of friends. Whichever way you view it, it is certainly an integral and increasingly important part of the business and one in which the beginner is going to need to engage sooner or later. Begin by attending and see how others manage. Watch out for local events advertised at your local library, ring your local arts board or check www.liveliterature.net, the Arts Council of England's listings service, in Wales look at www.academi.org Poets with big reputations can often turn out to be lousy performers while many an amateur can really crack it out. Don't expect to catch every image as you listen. Readings are not places for total comprehension but rather for glancing blows. Treat it as fun, and it will be. If you are trying things yourself for the first time, make sure you've brought your books along to sell, stand upright, drop the shoulders, gaze at a spot at the back of the hall and blow.

Music

Poetry has made many inroads into the music business. There was a time when this meant Spike Milligan standing up and spouting in front of a jazz band or a middle of the road brass playing behind John Betjeman, but no longer. There are quite a number of poets now working with musicians, starting bands or mixing in pre-recorded backing tracks. The advent of rap, hip-hop and the ready use of the speech sample as a component part of dance beats has turned the public ear. Dub poets – such as Linton Kwesi Johnson – have long used reggae as a backdrop for their words and the likes of Americans Sonja Sohn, Saul Williams and Dana Bryant have been softening up the cool crowd with their funk-backed hooks. This is certainly a non-traditional approach well away from poetry's conventional involvement with literature and with books. Go to the clubs (and the events mounted by *Apples & Snakes* in London) to hear more and expect what you find to be nothing like what you expected. Poetry keeps moving. Thank the Lord for that.

Competitions and awards

Poetry competitions have been the vogue for decades now with the most unlikely organizations sponsoring them. The notion here is that anonymity ensures fairness. Entries are made under pseudonyms so that if your name does happen to be Andrew Motion, then this won't help you much. Results seem to bear this out. The big competitions run biennially by the **Arvon Foundation**, with the help of commercial sponsors, the **Academi**'s *Cardiff International* and the **Poetry Society**'s *National* attract an enormous entry and usually throw up quite a number of complete unknowns among the winners. And why do people bother? Cash prizes can be large – thousands – but it costs at least a few pounds a poem to enter, and often much more than that. If it is cash you want, then Lotto scratch-cards are a better bet. And there has been a trend for winners to come from places like Cape Girardeau, Missouri and Tibooburra, Australia. The odds are getting longer. Who won the last Arvon? I don't remember. But if you do fancy a try, then it is a pretty innocent activity. You tie up a poem for a few months and you spend a little money. Winners' tips include reading the work of the judges to see how they do it, submitting non-controversial middle of the road smiling things, and doing this just before the closing date so you won't have to wait too long. Try two or three of your best. Huge wodges are costly and will only convince the judges of your insecurity. Have a look at *The Ring Of Words* (Sutton Publishing), an excellent historical anthology of Arvon winners and runners-up. To find contests to enter read the small magazines, write to your regional arts council, browse *The New Writer, Poetry London, Writer's News* or the listings in *Orbis* magazine, look on the notice board at your local library, or write for the regularly updated list from **The Poetry Library** in London (see **Organisations of Interest to Poets**).

Combining both competition and reading is the **Poetry Slam**. Here all-comers are given the opportunity to strut their stuff for around three closely timed minutes before a usually, not all that literary crowd. Points are awarded much in the same style as those for ice skating. You get them for a combination of performance and audience reaction Scatology and street-wise crowd pleasing are more likely to get you through the rounds than closely-honed work. The events, which involve much shouting, can be a lot of fun.

Poetry **Awards** are slightly different. These are usually made for published books and convention generally requires your publisher to make the nomination rather than yourself. These glittering prizes are increasing both in value and impact. Both the annual T.S. Eliot and Forward Prizes are now worth £10,000 a time with the poetry section of the Whitbread Book Award not far behind. To win one of these your book needs to be pretty hot.

Radio and TV

Centring on National Poetry Day the BBC continue to poll the nation for their favourite poems. Classic poems, Children's Poems, Love poems, Twentieth-Century Poems, Comic Poems, Poetry of Journeys and Poems of Celebration have all been listed. BBC2 has made a centrepiece of Daisy Goodwin's *The Essential Poems* which concentrates on the great and the good with the verse mostly read by actors rather than poets. Nevertheless the television broadcaster's enthusiasm is slight; coverage for poetry on screen has always been scant – it is so hard to make verse visually appealing. Some producers have tried, notably Peter Symes with Tony Harrison and Ian Macmillan at BBC2. Film maker Brian Hill has produced a number of collaborations with Simon Armitage for Channel Four and there have been a number of poets featured on Channel Four's *Learning* series. Digital TV, however, with its almost insatiable appetite for material is potentially a much better market. On the new BBC networks they have already tried televised poetry slams. BBC4's *Readers and Writers Roadshow* has done its bit. Poetry can also occasionally be found sandwiched between the music on MTV but inevitably only that by the media-promoted bards.

Most poetry on air actually sticks with radio. The BBC's website (www.bbc.co.uk/arts/poetry/index.shtml) collects a great deal of information on the Corporation's poetry interests including clickable links that enable you to listen to the entire programme again should you have missed it when it first went out. Sue Roberts edits some poetry programmes from Manchester including *Word On The Street*, a new contemporary strand presented by Jackie Kay and an annual on-air poetry festival. Viv Beeby at Bristol is keen to make drama out of classic poetry as well as commissioning new work and making on-location broadcasts such as Ian Macmillan in *Maine Voices*. Also at Bristol, Sara Davies looks after Radio 4's regular long-running Sunday 4.30 spot with *Poetry Please* (a listeners request show which uses only published material) and other programmes include Katrina Porteous writing about Hadrian's Wall and a series of radio poems from Maura Dooley, Paul Farley and others.

Fiona Mclean produces poetry for Radio 3 including a series of *Poetry Proms* (co-produced with Sara Davies) featuring the work of poets such as Ken Smith, Selima Hill and Mimi Khalvati commissioned to write new works around the theme of a Proms concert. Julian May produces the exciting new genrehopping *The Verb* which is fronted by Ian Macmillan and has included poetry and sound pieces by Dana Bryant, Alice Oswald, Jackie Kay, Kate Clanchy and others. Julian is keen to hear new work that uses 'language in all its forms'. Poets have also been commissioned for the *Sunday Feature*, *Drama on 3* and *Between the Ears*. Radio 3's nightly culture slot, *Night Waves*, features readings and reviews of published work. Radio 1 puts poetry into some of its evening slots, showcasing poets who have high street-cred. BBC World has commissioned poets (including Andrew Motion, Paul Muldoon, Fleur Adcock and Jackie Kay) to rewrite famous lyric verse. Independent radio is trying verse as fillers.

Poetry on radio is a large but difficult market. The BBC are pretty definite about having no remit to use 'unpublished or amateur verse'. Programme ideas should always be directed to a programme-making department at the BBC rather than to Radio 4 or Radio 3 themselves. If you are determined to put your verse on air then local and regional radio offer better possibilities. Try sending in self-produced readings on cassette (if you are any good at it) or topical poetry which regional magazine programmes could readily use. Don't expect to be paid much.

Starting up

Probably the best place will be locally. Find out through the library, your regional arts council or browse the Internet to find which writers groups gather in your area and attend them. There you will meet others of a like mind, encounter whatever locally produced magazines there might be and get a little direct feedback on your work. 'How am I doing?' is a big question for the emerging poet and although criticism is not all that hard to come by, do not expect it from all sources. Magazine editors, for example, will rarely have the time to offer advice. It is also reasonable to be suspicious of that offered by friends and relations – they will no doubt be only trying to please. Writers' groups present the best chance for poets to engage in honest mutual criticism. But if you'd prefer a more detached, written analysis of your efforts and are willing to pay a small sum, then you could apply to *Prescription*, the service operated nationally by the Poetry Society (22 Betterton Street, London WC2H 9BU), to the service run by The Academi in Wales (see **Organisations of Interest to Poets**) or to those run on an area basis by your regional arts council. There are also a number of non-subsidized critical services which you will find advertised in writers' magazines.

Read: if it's all a mystery to you, try Tony Curtis' *How to Study Modern Poetry* (Macmillan); Matthew Sweeney's and John Hartley Williams' *Teach Yourself Writing Poetry* (Teach Yourself); John Whitworth's *Writing Poetry* (A&C Black) or my own *The Poetry Business* (Seren). How real poets actually work can be discovered by reading C.B. McCully's *The Poet's Voice and Craft* (Carcanet) or *How Poets Work* (Seren). After all this, if you still think it's appropriate, try sending in.

How to do it

Increase your chances of acceptance by following simple, standard procedure:

- Type or print on a single side of A4 paper, single-spaced with double between stanzas, exactly as you'd wish your poem to appear when printed.
- Give the poem a title, clip multi-page works together, include your name and address at the foot of the final sheet. Avoid files, plastic covers, stiffeners and fancy clips of any sort.
- Keep a copy, make a record of what you send where and when, leave a space to note reaction.
- Send in small batches – six is a good number – with a brief covering letter saying who you are. Leave justification, apology and explanation for your writers' group.
- Include a self-addressed, stamped envelope of sufficient size for reply and/or return of your work.
- Be prepared to wait some weeks for a response. Don't pester. Be patient. Most magazines will reply in the end.
- Never send the same poem to two places at the same time (and this includes e-zine vs. hard copy. The jury is still out on whether or not the inclusion of a poem on your own personal website actually counts as publication). If you've entered the poem for a competition then make sure you never simultaneously send it elsewhere.
- If you are thinking of sending your submission electronically *check* first. Most journals and publishers in the *Writer's Handbook* survey have said that they refuse to accept materials sent this way.
- Send your best. Work which fails to fully satisfy even the author is unlikely to impress anyone else.

Where?

Try the list which follows this article. This is by no means the whole British small press scene but only those where potential contributors might stand a chance. Even here, do not expect unrelenting positive responses: magazines get overstocked, editors change, addresses shift, policy alters, operators run out of steam. Be prepared to hunt around and for a lot of your work to come back. You can help improve things by buying copies. Send in an s.a.e asking how much. The total market is vast and if you want to go further than the *Writer's Handbook* listings then you could consult the following: the *Small Press Guide* (which only covers journals – Writers' Bookshop, Remus House, Coltsfoot Drive, Woodston, Peterborough PE2 9JX), *Light's List of Literary Magazines* which contains both British and US addresses (John Light, Photon Press, The Lighthouse, 37 The Meadows, Berwick upon Tweed, Northumberland TD15

1NY), or Len Fulton's *Directory of Poetry Publishers* (Dustbooks) – the main American directory.

Scams and cons

With poetry overpopulated by participants, it is not surprising that the con artist should make an appearance. There are plenty of people out there taking money off beginner writers and offering very little in return. Faced with legal action the traditional vanity anthology, once the staple of the trickster, is now in retreat. Nonetheless variations and embellishments on the approach resurface steadily. These include offers to put your poetry to music setting you off on the road to stardom, readings of your verse by actors with deep voices to help you break into the local radio market (there isn't one) and further requests for cash to have entries on you appear in leather-bound directories of world poets, (everyone appears, including your uncle). There are bogus competitions where entry fees bear no relation to final prize money (or such prize money turns out never to be forthcoming) and the advertised 'publication of winners in anthology form' often means shelling out more for what will turn out to be a badly printed abomination crammed full of weak work. Poets should look very carefully at anything which offers framed certificates, scrolls or engraved wall hangings. They should also be wary of suggestions that they have come high in the State of Florida's Laureateship Contest (or some such like) and have been awarded a calligraphed testimonial. Presentation usually occurs at a three-day festival held in one of the most expensive hotels. To get your bit of paper you need to stay for all three days and it is you who has to settle the bill. If you try your luck at a no-entry-fee, advertised in the Sunday papers international competition don't be too surprised to find you've made it through round one – that happens to everyone. The scam starts with round two when they start to ask you for money.

How do you spot the tricksters? They change their names and addresses at will. They bill themselves as Foundations, Societies, Libraries, National Associations, Guilds. They sound so plausible. If you have the slightest suspicion then check with the Poetry Society (see **Organisations of Interest to Poets**). Some of the scams operated in the poetry competition field have a warning website devoted to exposing them. Look at www.windpub.org/literary.scams/ilp.htm for a full view. In the poetry world genuine advertisements for contributions are rare. And if anyone asks you for money then forget it. It is not the way things should be done.

The next step

Once you have placed a few poems you may like to consider publishing a booklet. There are as many small presses around as there are magazines. Start with the upmarket professionals by all means – Jonathan Cape, Faber & Faber –

but be prepared for compromise. The specialists and the small presses are swifter and more open to new work.

If all else fails you could do it yourself. Blake did, so did Walt Whitman. Modern technology puts the process within the reach of us all and if you can put up a shelf, there is a fair chance you will be able to produce a book to go on it. Read my *How to Publish Yourself* (Allison & Busby). Remember that publishing the book may be as hard as writing it, but marketing and selling it is quite something else. See Alison Baverstock's *Marketing Your Book: An Author's Guide* (A&C Black) if you really want to get ahead.

The listings

None of the lists of addresses which follow are exhaustive. Publishers come and go with amazing frequency. There will always be the brand-new press on the look-out for talent and the projected magazine desperate for contributions. For up to the minute information check with some of the **Organisations of Interest to Poets** (see page 170). Poetry has a huge market. It pays to keep your ear to the ground. The magazines and presses listed here have all been active during the past eighteen months and most (although be warned, *not all*) have indicated a willingness to look at new work. Those with a positive disinterest in receiving unsolicited work have been excluded. In all cases check before sending. Ask to see a catalogue or a sample copy. Good luck.

Poetry Presses

Abbey Press
Abbey Grammar School, Courtney Hill,
Newry, Co Down BT34 2ED
☎028 3026 3142
Email molly71freeman@aol.com
Website www.geocities.com/abbeypress

Poetry, anthologies and works of literary criticism.

Akira Press
5 Blackhorse Lane, London E17 6DS
☎08700 503161
Email info@akirapress.co.uk
Website www.akirapress.co.uk

Contact *Beverley Jones-Joseph*

Hip Hop Rappers and Dancehall Reggae DJs.

Anvil Press Poetry Ltd
Neptune House, 70 Royal Hill, London
SE10 8RF
☎020 8469 3033   Fax 020 8469 3363
Email anvil@anvilpresspoetry.com
Website www.anvilpresspoetry.com

Contact *Peter Jay*

Contemporary British poetry and poetry in translation. See entry under **UK Publishers**.

Arc Publications
Nanholme Mill, Shaw Wood Road,
Todmorden, Lancs OL14 6DA
☎01706 812338   Fax 01706 818948
Email arc.publications@virgin.net
Website www.arcpublications.co.uk

Contact *Tony Ward*

Contemporary poetry from new and established writers both in the UK and abroad. See entry under **UK Publishers**.

Arrowhead Press
70 Clifton Road, Darlington, Co Durham
DL1 5DX
Email editor@arrowheadpress.co.uk
Website www.arrowheadpress.co.uk

Quality books and pamphlets of contemporary poetry.

Au Quai
8 Richmond Road, Staines, Middlesex
TW18 2AB

Email vennel@hotmail.com
Website www.indigogroup.co.uk/llpp/
   vennel.html

Contact *Richard Price*

Modern Scottish poetry; poetry in translation; poetry that takes its bearings from modernism. See also **Vennel Press** and **Southfields** presses.

BB Books
Spring Bank, Longsight Road, Copster Green,
Blackburn, Lancs BB1 9EU
☎01254 249128

Contact *Dave Cunliffe*

Post-Beat poetics and counterculture theoretic. Iconoclastic rants and anarchic psycho-cultural tracts. See also **Global Tapestry Journal**.

Big Little Poem Books
3 Park Avenue, Melton Mowbray,
Leicestershire LE13 0JB

Contact *Robert Richardson*

Effective contemporary approaches to the lyric and epigram. See also **Door – To – Everywhere** press.

Biscuit Publishing
Box 123, Washington, Newcastle upon Tyne
NE37 2YE

Bloodaxe Books Ltd
Highgreen, Tarset, Northumberland
NE48 1RP
☎01434 240500   Fax 01434 240505
Email editor@bloodaxebooks.co.uk
Website www.bloodaxebooks.com

Contact *Neil Astley*

Britain's leading publisher of new poetry. No submissions by e-mail attachments. See entry under **UK Publishers**.

Bradshaw Books
Thompson House, Maccurtain Street, Cork
Republic of Ireland
☎00 353 21 450 9274   Fax 00 353 21 455 1617
Email admin@cwpc.ie
Website www.tighfili.com

Contact *Tigh Fili*

Canna Press
10 Severn Road, Canton, Cardiff CF11 9NB
Email canna@care4free.net
Contact *Phil Maillard*
Works of Chris Torrance.

Carcanet Press
4th Floor, Alliance House, 28–34 Cross Street,
Manchester M2 7AQ
☎0161 834 8730 Fax 0161 832 0084
Email pnr@carcanet.u-net.com
Website www.carcanet.co.uk
Contact *Michael Schmidt*
Major poetry publisher. See entry under **UK Publishers**.

Chapman Publishing
4 Broughton Place, Edinburgh EH1 3RX
☎0131 557 2207 Fax 0131 556 9565
Email editor@chapman-pub.co.uk
Website www.chapman-pub.co.uk
Contact *Joy Hendry*
Scottish writing. See entry under **UK Publishers**.

The Collective Press
Penlanlas Farm, Llantilio Pertholey, Y-fenni,
Gwent NP7 7HN
☎01873 856350 Fax 01873 859559
Email jj@jojowales.co.uk
Website www.welshwriters.com
Contact *John Jones*
Non-profit promoter and publisher of contem-
porary poetry.

Community of Poets and Artists Press
Thyme Cottage, Bogshole Lane, Whitstable,
Kent CT5 3AT
☎01227 281806
Email bennetta.artco@virgin.net
Website www.artistspress.co.uk
Contact *Philip Bennetta*
Dedicated to making artists' books, hand-sewn
poetry collections and limited editions.

Corbie Press
57 Murray Street, Montrose, Angus DD10 8JZ
Contact *Neil Mathers*
Scottish & European literature, art, philosophy,
some poetry. See also **Epoch Magazine**.

Crystal Serenades
PO Box 17, Treorchy, Rhondda Cynon Taff
CF42 6YL
☎07730 899698
Email kelly@crystalserenades.co.uk
Website www.crystalserenades.co.uk
Contact *Kelly Burnell*
Undiscovered literary and artistic talents.

Dagger Press
1 Portland Street, Diglis, Worcester WR1 2NL
☎07986 792443
Email brian_morse@lineone.net
Contact *Brian Morse*
Poetry pamphlets, new and established poets.

Day Dream Press
39 Exmouth Street, Swindon, Wilts SN1 3PU
☎01793 523927
Contact *Kevin Bailey*
See also **HQ, Haiku Quarterly**.

Diamond Twig
5 Bentinck Road, Newcastle upon Tyne
NE4 6UT
☎0191 273 5326
Email diamond.twig@virgin.net
Website www.diamondtwig.co.uk
Contacts *Ellen Phethean & Others*
New writing by women in the north of
England.

Disseminate
23 Caestory Avenue, Raglan, Usk,
Monmouthshire NP15 2EH
Contact *Peter Huggins*

Door – To – Everywhere
3 Park Avenue, Melton Mowbray,
Leicestershire LE13 0JB
Contact *Robert Richardson*
Poem card series – imagination first. See also
Big Little Poem Books press.

Driftwood Publications
5 Timms Lane, Freshfield, Merseyside L37 7DW
☎01704 833911 Fax 0151 524 0216
Email janet.speedy@btinternet.com
Contact *Brian Wake*
New work by new and established poets more
suited to the page than the stage.

Enitharmon Press
26B Caversham Road, London NW5 2DU
☎020 7482 5967 Fax 020 7284 1787
Email books@enitharmon.co.uk
Website www.enitharmon.co.uk

Contact *Stephen Stuart-Smith*

Poetry and criticism. See entry under **UK Publishers**.

Erran Publishing
43 Willow Road, Carlton, Notts NG4 3BH
Email erranpublishing@hotmail.com
Website www.poetichours.homestead.com

Contact *Nick Clark*

Non-profit supporter of Third World charities. See also **Poetic Hours** magazine.

Essence Press
8 Craiglea Drive, Edinburgh EH10 5PA
Email jaj@essencepress.co.uk
Website www.essencepress.co.uk

Contact *Julie Johnstone*

Handbound editions of poetry, poetry postcards – interest in concrete poetry and nature. See also **Island** magazine.

Etruscan Books
28 Fowler's Court, Fore Street, Buckfast, Devon TQ11 0AA
☎01364 643128

Contact *Nicholas Johnson*

Modernist, sound, visual poetry, Gaelic, lyric poetry, US/UK poets.

Feather Books
PO Box 438, Shrewsbury, Shropshire SY3 0WN
☎01743 872177 Fax 01743 872177
Email john@waddysweb.freeuk.com
Website www.waddysweb.freeuk.com

Contact *Rev. J. Waddington-Feather*

Quarterly magazine of Christian poetry and prayers. See also **The Poetry Church** magazine and entry under **Small Presses**.

Firebird Press
104 Argyle Gardens, Upminster, Essex RM14 3EU
Website www.homestead.com/firebirdpress

Contact *Pamela Constantine*

Furthering a renaissance of the perennial values which make life meaningful and worthwhile. See also **Rebirth**, **Romantic Renaissance** and **The Solar Flame** magazines.

Flambard
Stable Cottage, East Fourstones, Hexham, Northumberland NE47 5DX
☎01434 674360 Fax 01434 674178

Website www.flambardpress.co.uk

Contact *Peter Elfed Lewis*

Concentrates on poetry but also publishes fiction, expecially literary and crime.

Forward Press
Remus House, Coltsfoot Drive, Woodston, Peterborough PE2 9JX
☎01733 898105 Fax 01733 313524
Email james@forwardpress.co.uk
Website www.forwardpress.co.uk

Contact *Ian Walton*

General poetry and short fiction anthologies. See also **Triumph House** press and **Poetry Now** magazine.

Four Quarters Press
7 The Towers, Stevenage, Herts SG1 1HE
Email chessmaster@ntlworld.com

Contact *Eric Ratcliffe*

Free ranging non-materialist poetry, non-profit, charity.

Glass Head Press
72 Doncaster Road, Mexborough, S. Yorks S64 0NA
Contact *Ian Parks*

Limited edition poetry pamphlets.

Green Arrow Publishing
2 Chambers Cottages, Underlyn Lane, Marden, Tonbridge, Kent TN12 9BD
☎07967 315270
Email greenarrow588882@aol.com

Contact *John Dench*

See also **Scriptor** magazine.

Headland Publications
Ty Coch, Galltegfa, Ruthin, Denbighshire LL15 2AR
☎0151 625 9128 Fax 0151 625 9128

Contact *Gladys Mary Coles*

Fine editions of poetry; anthologies.

Hippopotamus Press
22 Whitewell Road, Frome, Somerset BA11 4EL
☎01373 466653 Fax 01373 466653

Contact *Roland John*

First collections of verse from those with a track record in the magazines. See also **Outposts** magazine.

Honno Welsh Women's Press
Editorial Office, UTC, King Street,
Aberystwyth, Ceredigion SY23 2LT
☎01970 623150 Fax 01970 623150
Email post@honno.co.uk
Website www.honno.co.uk

Contact *Janet Thomas*

The Welsh women's press – novels, childrens fiction, short stories, poetry and autobiographical anthologies. See entry under **UK Publishers**.

Hub Editions
Longholm, East Bank, Wingland, Sutton Bridge, Spalding, Lincs PE12 9YS

Contact *Colin Blundell*

Good poetry, experimental writing, philosophy, real haiku, challenges to status quo.

JazzClaw
36 Wolfe Road, Norwich, Norfolk NR1 4HT
☎01603 499784
Email jazzclaw@lycos.co.uk
Website www.geocities.com/lifestylecentre/searle.html

Contact *David Searle*

Avant-garde poetry and prose, surrealism, erotica, dark themes, experimental. See also **Searle Publishing** press.

The King's England Press
Cambertown House, Commercial Road, Goldthorpe, Rotherham, S. Yorks S63 9BL
☎01709 270258 Fax 01709 897787
Email steve@kingsengland.demon.co.uk
Website www.kingsengland.com

Contact *Steve Rudd*

Children's books including poetry.

KT Publications
16 Fane Close, Stamford, Lincs PE9 1HG
☎01780 754193

Contact *Kevin Troop*

Still looking for 'the perfect work'. See also **The Third Half** magazine.

Mariscat Press
3 Mariscat Road, Glasgow G41 4ND
☎0141 423 7291
Email mariscatpress@hotmail.com

Contact *Hamish Whyte*

Currently publishing poetry pamphlets only.

Masque Publishing
PO Box 4194, Worthing, West Sussex BN11 2GT

Contact *Lisa Stewart*

Prints small collections of poetry. See also **Decanto** magazine.

Menard Press
8 The Oaks, Woodside Avenue, London N12 8AR

Contact *Anthony Rudolf*

Poetry, mainly translations and prose.

The Moving Finger
PO Box 4867, Birmingham B3 3HD

Contact *Dave Reeves*

See also **Raw Edge** magazine.

New Hope International
20 Werneth Avenue, Gee Cross, Hyde, Cheshire SK14 5NL
Email nhi@clara.net
Website www.nhi.clara.net/nhihome.htm

Contact *Gerald England*

Poetry booklet publisher. Query before submitting.

Oasis Books
12 Stevenage Road, London SW6 6ES
☎020 7736 5059

Contact *Ian Robinson*

Pamphlets of poetry and prose. Contact before submitting material. See also **Oasis** magazine.

Object Permanence
Flat 3/2, 16 Ancroft Street, Glasgow G20 7HU
Website www.objectpermanence.co.uk

Contact *Peter Manson*

The Old Stile Press
Catchmays Court,, Llandogo, Nr Monmouth, Monmouthshire NP25 4TN
☎01291 689226
Website www.oldstilepress.com

Contacts *Frances & Nicolas McDowall*

Fine, hand-printed books with text and images.

The One Time Press
Model Farm, Linstead Magna, Halesworth, Suffolk IP19 0DT
☎01986 785422
Email pw@onetimepress.com
Website www.onetimepress.com

Contact *Peter Wells*

Poetry of the forties in limited editions. Illustrated.

Original Plus
Flat 3, 18 Oxford Grove, Ilfracombe, Devon EX34 9HQ
☎01271 862708
Email smithsssj@aol.com
Website members.aol.com/smithsssj/ index.html

Contact *Sam Smith*

Requires something extra – another language or markedly original. See also **The Journal** magazine.

Othername Press
14 Rosebank, Rawtenstall, Rossendale BB4 7RD

Poetry and surrealism.

Oversteps Books
Oversteps, Froude Road, Salcombe, S. Devon TQ8 8LH
☎01548 843713 Fax 01548 843713
Email anne@oversteps.fsnet.co.uk

Contact *Anne Born*

Small poetry press publishing a couple of books a year.

Parthian Books
The Old Surgery, Napier Street, Cardigan SA43 1ED
☎029 2034 1314 Fax 029 2034 1314
Email parthianbooks@yahoo.co.uk
Website www.parthianbooks.co.uk

Contact *Richard Davies*

New Welsh writing.

Partners
289 Elmwood Avenue, Feltham, Middlesex TW13 7QB
Email partners_writing_group@hotmail.com
Website www.homestead.com/partners_ writing_group

Contact *Ian Deal*

Competitions and poetry pamphlets. See also **A Bard Hair Day**, **Imagenation**, **Poet Tree**, **Seventh Sense** and **The Word Life Journal** magazines.

Peepal Tree Press Ltd
17 King's Avenue, Leeds, W. Yorks LS1 1ND
☎0113 245 1703 Fax 0113 246 8368

Email hannah@peepal.demon.co.uk

Contact *Jeremy Poynting*

Best in Caribbean and south Asian writing from around the world. See entry under **Small Presses**.

Pen&Inc
School of English & American Studies, University of East Anglia, Norwich, Norfolk NR4 7TJ
☎01603 592783 Email info@penandinc.co.uk
Website www.penandinc.co.uk

Contact *Katri Skala*

A small press supported by the Regional Arts Lottery programme. See also **Pretext** magazine and **Reactions** press.

Peterloo Poets
The Old Chapel, Sand Lane, Calstock, Cornwall PL18 9QX
☎01822 833473 Fax 01822 833989
Email poets@peterloo.fsnet.co.uk

Contact *Harry Chambers*

Contemporary English poetry.

Pigasus Press
13 Hazely Combe, Arreton, Isle of Wight PO30 3AJ
☎01983 865668
Email pigasus.press@virgin.net
Website freespace.virgin.net/pigasus.press/ index.htm

Contact *Tony Lee*

Science fiction poetry in irregular themed anthologies.

Pipers' Ash Ltd
Pipers Ash, Church Road, Christian Malford, Chippenham, Wilts SN15 4BW
☎01249 720563 Fax 0870 056 8916
Email pipersash@supamasu.com
Website www.supamasu.com

Contact *Mr A. Tyson*

See entry under **Small Presses**.

Planet
PO Box 44, Aberystwyth SY23 3ZZ
☎01970 611255 Fax 01970 611197
Email planet.enquiries@planetmagazine.org.uk
Website www.planetmagazine.org.uk

Contact *John Barnie*

Fiction, poetry, current affairs, arts and environment. See also **Planet** magazine and entry under **Small Presses**. .

Poems in the Waiting Room
PO Box 488, Richmond TW9 4SW
Email leelda@globalnet.co.uk
Contact *Michael Lee*
Pamphlets for medical waiting rooms.

Poetry Now Young Writers
Remus House, Coltsfoot Drive, Woodston,
Peterborough, Cambs PE2 9JX
☎01733 890066 Fax 01733 313524
Email forward_press@compuserve.com
Website www.forwardpress.co.uk
Contact *Steve Twelvetree*
Publishers of children's poetry. See also
Scribbler! magazine.

Poetry Wednesday
25 Griffiths Road, West Bromwich
B71 2EH
☎07950 591455
Contact *Geoff Stevens*
See also **The Firing Squad** and **Purple Patch**
magazines.

Poets Anonymous
70 Aveling Close, Purley, Surrey
CR8 4DW
Email poets@poetsanon.org.uk
Website www.poetsanon.org.uk
Contact *Peter L. Evans*
Anthologies & collections of predominately
south London poets. See also **Poetic Licence**
magazine.

QQ Press
York House, 15 Argyle Terrace, Rothesay,
Isle of Bute PA20 0BD
Contact *Alan Carter*
Collections of poetry plus poetry anthologies.
See also **Quantum Leap** magazine.

Ragged Raven Press
1 Lodge Farm, Snitterfield, Stratford upon
Avon, Warwickshire CV37 0LR
☎01789 730358 Fax 01789 730320
Email raggedravenpress@aol.com
Website www.raggedraven.co.uk
Contacts *Bob Mee, Janet Murch*
Poetry. See also **Iota** magazine.

Raka Publications
Flat 7, Kingsbury Court, 194 Gravelly Hill,
Erdington, Birmingham B23 7PE
Email rakabooks@iemail.com

Raunchland Publications
18 Canon Lynch Court, Dunfermline, Fife
KY12 8AU
Email raunchland@hotmail.com
Website www.raunchland.co.uk
Contact *John Mingay*
Limited edition poetry/graphics booklets and
online publications.

Reactions
School of English & American Studies,
University of East Anglia, Norwich, Norfolk
NR4 7TJ
☎01603 592783
Email info@penandinc.co.uk
Website www.penandinc.co.uk
Contact *Katri Skala*
Annual poetry anthology – welcomes new
poets. See also **Pretext** magazine and
Pen&Inc press.

Red Candle Press
Rose Cottage, Threeholes Bridge, Wisbech,
Cambs PE14 9JR
Email rep@poetry7.fsnet.co.uk
Website www.members.tripod.com/
  redcandlepress
Contact *M.L. McCarthy*
Traditionalist poetry press. See also **Candel-
abrum Poetry Magazine**.

Rive Gauche Publishing
69 Lower Redland Road, Bristol BS6 6SP
☎0117 974 5106
Email twinset69@hotmail.com
Contact *P.V.T. West*
Poetry by women writing and performing in
Bristol.

Route Publishing
School Lane, Glasshoughton, Castleford,
W. Yorks WF10 4QH
☎01977 603028 Fax 01977 512819
Email info@route-online.com
Website www.route-online.com
Contact *Ian Daley*
Short fiction and poetry. See entry under
Small Presses.

Salt Publishing
PO Box 937, Great Wilbraham, Cambridge
CB1 5JX
Email cemery@saltpublishing.com
Website www.saltpublishing.com

Contacts *John Kinsella & Others*
International poetry and poetics. See also **Salt**
magazine.

Searle Publishing
36 Wolfe Road, Norwich, Norfolk NR1 4HT
☎01603 499784
Email mailbag@searlepublishing.co.uk
Website www.searlepublishing.co.uk
Contact *David Searle*

Run by writers for writers – unsolicited mss
welcome. See also **JazzClaw** press.

Seren
1st & 2nd Floors, 38–40 Nolton Street,
Bridgend CF31 3BN
☎01656 663018 Fax 01656 649226
Email seren@seren.force9.co.uk
Website www.seren-books.com
Contact *Mick Felton*

Poetry, fiction, lit crit, biography, essays. See
entry under **UK Publishers** and **Poetry
Wales** magazine.

Sixties Press
89 Connaught Road, Sutton, Surrey SM1 3RJ
☎020 8286 0419
Contact *Barry Tebb*

Small press concentrating on poetry and novellas. See also **Literature and Psychoanalysis**
magazine.

Smith/Doorstop Books
The Studio, Byram Arcade, Westgate,
Huddersfield, W. Yorks HD1 1ND
☎01484 434840 Fax 01484 426566
Email edit@poetrybusiness.co.uk
Website www.poetrybusiness.co.uk
Contact *Peter Sansom*

Contemporary books, pamphlets and audio
cassettes (see entry under **Audio Books**). See
also **The North** magazine.

Smoke
The Windows Project, 1st Floor, Liver
House, 96 Bold Street, Liverpool L1 4HY
☎0151 709 3688
Contact *Dave Ward*

Poetry graphics, short prose – 24pp – biannual.
See also **The Windows Project** press.

Southfields
8 Richmond Road, Staines, Middlesex
TW18 2AB

Email vennel@hotmail.com
Website www.indigogroup.co.uk/llpp/
  vennel.html
Contact *Richard Price*

Modern Scottish poetry that takes its bearings
from modernism. See also **Vennel** and **Au
Quai** presses.

Starborn Books
Glanrhydwilym, Llandissilio, Clinderwen,
Pembrokeshire SA66 7QH
☎01437 563562 Fax 01239 613754
Email sales@starbornbooks.co.uk
Website www.starbornbooks.co.uk
Contact *Phil Forder*

Children's books, song books, poetry and local
interest.

Stride Publications
11 Sylvan Road, Exeter, Devon EX4 6EW
Email editor@stridebooks.co.uk
Website www.stridebooks.co.uk
Contact *Rupert Loydell*

Innovative poetry, experimental fiction, essays
and interviews. See entry under **Small
Presses**.

Summer Palace Press
Cladnageerach, Kilbeg, Kilcar, Co Donegal
Republic of Ireland
☎00 353 733 8448 Fax 00 353 733 8448
Contacts *Kate & Joan Newman*

First collections of poetry, 64 pages, beautiful
books.

Survivors' Poetry Scotland
4C4 Templeton Centre, Templeton Street,
Glasgow G40 1DA
☎0141 556 4554 Fax 0141 400 8442
Email sps@spscot.co.uk
Website www.spscot.co.uk

For survivors of the mental health system. See
entry under **Organisations of Interest to
Poets**.

Tabla
Dept of English, University of Bristol,
3–5 Woodland Road, Bristol BS8 1TB
Fax 0117 928 8860
Email stephen.james@bristol.ac.uk
Website www.bristol.ac.uk/tabla
Contact *Dr Stephen James*

Publisher of the annual *Tabla Book of New
Verse*.

Talking Pen Press
12 Derby Crescent, Moorside, Consett,
Co Durham DH8 8DZ
Website www.newwritingnorth.com

Contact *Steve Urwin*

See also **Moodswing** magazine.

Thumbscrew Press
PO Box 657, Oxford OX2 6PH
Email tim.kendall@bristol.ac.uk
Website www.bristol.ac.uk/thumbscrew

Contact *Tim Kendall*

Pamphlets by new and established poets.

Triumph House
Remus House, Coltsfoot Drive, Woodston,
Peterborough PE2 9JX
☎01733 898102 Fax 01733 313524
Email triumphhouse@forwardpress.co.uk
Website www.forwardpress.co.uk

Contact *Sarah Andrew*

A Christian poetry imprint publishing many
anthologies annually.

United Press Ltd
Admail 3735, London EC1B 1JB
☎0870 240 6190 Fax 0870 240 6191
Email mail@upltd.co.uk
Website www.upltd.co.uk

Contact *Peter Quinn*

Publishes poetry and prose including national
poetry anthology.

Vennel Press
8 Richmond Road, Staines, Middlesex
TW18 2AB
Email vennel@hotmail.com
Website www.indigogroup.co.uk/llpp/
    vennel.html

Contact *Richard Price*

Modern Scottish poetry; poetry that takes its
bearings from modernism. See also **Au Quai**
and **Southfields** presses.

Wanda Publications
Word And Action, 75 High Street,
Wimborne, Dorset BH21 1HS
☎01202 889669
Email wanda@wordandaction.com

Contact *Jane Peters*

Poetry, stories, local history and world of
instant theatre.

Waterloo Press
51 Waterloo Road, Hove, East Sussex
BN3 1AN
☎01273 202876
Email dr.jenner@virgin.net

Contact *Simon Jenner*

Poetry and periodical publisher. Plese phone
for submissions. See also **Eratica** magazine.

Waywiser Press
9 Woodstock Road, London N4 3ET
☎020 8374 5526 Fax 020 8374 5736
Email waywiserpress@aol.com
Website www.waywiser-press.com

Contact *Philip Hoy*

Specialises in modern poetry in English. See
also **Between the Lines** magazine.

Wendy Webb Books
9 Walnut Close, Tavernham, Norwich,
Norfolk NR8 6YN
Email wwbuk@yahoo.co.uk
Website www.webbw.freeserve.co.uk

Contact *Wendy Webb*

The Windows Project
First Floor, Liver House, 96 Bold Street,
Liverpool L1 4HY
☎0151 709 3688

Contact *David Ward*

See also **Smoke** magazine.

Worple Press
12 Havelock Road, Tonbridge, Kent TN9 1JE
☎01732 367466
Email theworpleco@aol.com

Contacts *Amanda Knight & Peter Carpenter*

Contemporary UK and international poetry,
anthologies of new writing, essays and interviews.

Writers' Own Publications
121 Highbury Grove, Clapham, Bedford
MK41 6DU
☎01234 365982

Contact *Mrs E.M. Pickering*

Booklets of 22–36 poems by a single author.

Poetry Magazines

Aalst
Tartan Ink Press, PO Box 588, Doncaster
DN5 8YZ
Email aalst@tartanink.co.uk
Website www.btinternet.com/~tartanink/
   aalst/contact.html

Acumen
6 The Mount, Higher Furzeham, Brixham,
Devon TQ5 8QY
☎01803 851098 Fax 01803 851098
Contact *Patricia Oxley*

Good poetry, intelligent articles and wide-ranging reviews. See also **The Long Poem Group Newsletter**.

Aireings
Dean Head Farm, Scotland Lane, Leeds,
W. Yorks LS18 5HU
Contact *Jean Barker*

40-page poetry magazine published since 1980.
Leans towards women's work.

Ambit
17 Priory Gardens, London N6 5QY
☎020 8340 3566
Website www.ambit.co.uk
Contact *Martin Bax*

Poetry, fiction, art, reviews – established and emerging writers.

Anon
67 Learmouth Grove, Edinburgh EH4 1BL
☎020 7226 2657
Email mike@volta1.fsworld.co.uk
Website www.blanko.org.uk/anon
Contacts *Mike Stocks*

Poems selected anonymously.

Aquarius
Flat 4, Room B, 116 Sutherland Avenue,
London W9 2QP
Contact *Eddie S. Linden*

Literary magazine – prose and poetry.

Areopagus
101 Maytree Close, Winchester SO22 4JF
Fax 0870 134 6384

Email jareo@bigfoot.com
Website www.churchnet.org.uk/
   areopagus/index.html
Contact *Julian Barritt*

A Christian-based arena for creative writers.

Arete
8 New College Lane, Oxford OX1 3BN
☎01865 289193 Fax 01895 289194
Email craig.raine@new.ox.ac.uk
Website www.aretemagazine.com
Contact *Craig Raine*

Fiction, poetry, reportage, reviews.

Awen
38 Pierrot Steps, 71 Kursaal Way, Southend
on Sea, Essex SS1 2UY
Contact *David John Tyrer*

Poetry and vignette-length fiction of any style/
genre. See also **Bard**, **Garbaj** and **Monomyth**
magazines.

Banipal
PO Box 22300, London W13 8ZQ
☎020 8568 9747 Fax 020 8568 8509
Email editor@banipal.co.uk
Website www.banipal.co.uk
Contact *Margaret Obank*

Modern Arab literature in translation.

Bard
38 Pierrot Steps, 71 Kursaal Way, Southend
on Sea, Essex SS1 2UY
Contact *David John Tyrer*

Flyer-style poetry magazine. See also **Awen**,
Garbaj and **Monomyth** magazines.

A Bard Hair Day
289 Elmwood Avenue, Feltham, Middlesex
TW13 7QB
Email partners_writing_group@hotmail.com
Website www.homestead.com/
   partners_writing_group
Contact *Ian Deal*

General poetry magazine. See also **Partners**
press, **Imagenation**, **Poet Tree**, **Seventh
Sense** and **The Word Life Journal** magazines.

Barddas
Pen Rhiw, 71 Fford Pentrepoeth, Treforys,
Swansea SA6 6AE
☎01792 792829 Fax 01792 792829
Email alanllwyd@barddas.freeserve.co.uk

Contact *Alan Llwyd*

A magazine dedicated to Welsh language poetry.

Between the Lines
9 Woodstock Road, London N4 3ET
☎020 8374 5526 Fax 020 8374 5736
Email waywiserpress@aol.com
Website www.waywiser-press.com

Contact *Philip Hoy*

Interviews with poets. See also **Waywiser
Press**.

Black Mountain Review
PO Box 9, Ballyclare, Co Antrim BT39 0JW

Black Rose
PO Box 5461, Dublin 12, Republic of Ireland

Contact *David R. Running*

Horror and supernatural fiction.

Blue Badge Poetry Supplement
PO Box 184, South Ockenden, Essex
RM15 5WT

Contact *D.M. Heath*

Free biannual poetry mag for those whose life
has been touched by disability. See also **Reveal**
magazine.

Borderlines
Nant Y Brithyll, Llangynyw, Welshpool,
Powys SY21 0JS
☎01938 810263

Contacts *Dave Bingham & Kevin Bamford*

Open poetry magazine with no axe to grind.
Published by the Anglo-Welsh Poetry Society.

Braquemard
48 Clifton Street, Hull HU2 9AP
Email braquemard@hotmail.com
Website www.braquemard.fsnet.co.uk

Contact *David Allenby*

Forty pages of excellent poetry, prose and artwork.

Brittle Star
32b Gloucester Drive, London N4 2LN
☎020 8802 1507
Email brittlestar@versify.co.uk

Contact *Jo Homan*

Poetry, short stories and articles on contemporary poetry.

The Brobdignagian Times
96 Albert Road, Cork, Republic of Ireland

Contact *Giovanni Malito*

Poetry, very short fiction, cover art.

Buzz Words
Calvers Farm, Thelveton, Diss, Norfolk
IP21 4NG
Email zoeking@calversfarm.fsnet.co.uk
Website www.buzzwordsmagazine.co.uk

Contact *Zoe King*

Small magazine with an international flavour –
new and established writers of fiction and poetry.

Cadenza
PO Box 1768, Rugby CV21 4ZA
☎01788 334302 Fax 01788 334702
Email jo.good@ntlworld.com
Website www.qwfmagazine.co.uk

Contact *Jo Good*

Poetry and prose – mainstream but stretches
the emotional/linguistic envelope.

Candelabrum Poetry Magazine
Rose Cottage, Threeholes Bridge, Wisbech,
Cambs PE14 9JR
Email rep@poetry7.fsnet.co.uk
Website www.members.tripod.com/
   redcandlepress

Contact *M.L. McCarthy*

Formalist poetry mag for people who like
poetry rhythmic and shapely. See also **Red
Candle Press**.

Cannon Fodder
Laurel Cottage, 13 Ditton Hill, Surbiton,
Surrey KT6 5JB
Email reverendpike@hotmail.com

Contact *G. Rivka*

DIY publication seeking contributions from
writers/poets/artists – and female poets, in particular.

Cannon's Mouth
22 Margaret Grove, Harborne, Birmingham
B17 9JH
☎01952 277872

Carillon Magazine
19 Godric Drive, Brinsworth, Rotherham,
South Yorkshire S60 5AN
☎01709 371413

Email grippon@carillonmag.org.uk
Website www.carillonmag.org.uk
Contact *Graham Rippon*

Triannual magazine offering eclectic prose and poetry. Stories and articles up to 1200 words. Poetry up to forty lines. Unsolicited material welcome. See website for submission guidelines. 'The magazine that pays its writers.'

Chanticleer Magazine
2fl, 1 Alva Street, Edinburgh EH2 4PH
☎0131 226 3245
Contact *Richad Livermore*

Ideas and poetry – aims to challenge the mainstream on behalf of aesthetic values.

Chapman
4 Broughton Place, Edinburgh EH1 3RX
☎0131 557 2207 Fax 0131 556 9565
Email editor@chapman-pub.co.uk
Website www.chapman-pub.co.uk
Contact *Joy M. Hendry*

The best in Scottish and international writing, well-established writers and the up-and-coming. See entries under **UK Publishers** and **Magazines**.

The Coffee House
Charnwood Arts, Loughborough Library,
31 Granby Street, Loughborough, Leics
LE11 3DU
☎01509 822558 Fax 01509 822559
Email charnwood-arts@ndirect.co.uk
Website www.charnwood-arts.org.uk
Contact *Deborah Tyler-Bennett*

A meeting place for the arts, poetry, prose and visual artwork.

Current Accounts
16–18 Mill Lane, Horwich, Bolton, Lancs
BL6 6AT
Email rodriesco@cs.com

Poetry, short fiction, articles – magazine of the Bank Street Writers' Group.

Cyphers
3 Selskar Terrace, Ranelagh, Dublin 6,
Republic of Ireland Fax 00 353 1 497 8866
Contact *Eilean Ní Chuilleanain*

Irish literary magazine: poetry, prose, reviews.

Dandelion Arts Magazine
24 Frosty Hollow, East Hunsbury, Northants
NN4 0SY
☎01604 701730 Fax 01604 701730

Contact *Jacqueline Gonzalez-Marina*

International arts magazine – modern poetry, articles, stories and interviews.

The Dark Horse
3b Blantyre Mill Road, Bothwell,
S. Lanarkshire G71 8DD
Email gjctdh@freename.co.uk
Contact *Gerry Cambridge*

Poetry.

The David Jones Journal
The David Jones Society, 48 Sylvan Way,
Sketty, Swansea SA2 9JB
☎01792 206144 Fax 01792 205305
Email anne.price-owen@sihe.ac.uk
Website www.sihe.ac.uk/davidjones
Contact *Anne Price-Owen*

Articles, poetry, information, reviews and inspired works.

Decanto
PO Box 4194, Worthing, West Sussex
BN11 2GT
Contact *Lisa Stewart*

Non-conformist poetry magazine – any style considered, not just contemporary. See also **Masque Publishing** press.

Dial 174
21 Mill Road, Watlington, King's Lynn,
Norfolk PE33 0HH
☎01553 811949
Contact *Joseph Hemmings*

Poetry, short storie, articles, travelogues, artwork, etc.

Dream Catcher
9 Berkeley Square, Lincoln LN6 8BN
☎01522 882238
Website www.openingline.co.uk/magazines/
   dreamcatcher
Contact *Paul Sutherland*

Poetry, prose, b&w photographs, from national & international contributors.

Earthlove
PO Box 11219, Paisley PA1 2WH
Contact *Tracy Patrick*

Poetry magazine for the environment.

Eastern Rainbow
17 Farrow Road, Whaplode Drove, Spalding,
Lincs PE12 0TS

☎01406 330242
Email p_rance@yahoo.co.uk
Contact *Paul Rance*

Focuses on 20th century culture via poetry, prose and art. See also **Peace and Freedom** magazine.

Echoes of Gilgamesh
18 Craighead Way, Barrhead, Glasgow
G78 2RS
☎0141 881 9065
Email paul@mcdonagh18.freeserve.co.uk
Website www.gilgamesh.fsworld.co.uk/
Contact *Paul McDonagh*

Quarterly long poem magazine.

Eclipse
Linden Cottage, 45 Burton Road, Little Neston, Cheshire CH64 4AE
Contact *Elizabeth Boyd*

Bi-monthly poetry mag – which welcomes new poets.

The Engine
3 Ardgreenan Drive, Belfast BT4 3FQ
☎028 9065 9866 Fax 028 9032 2767
Email clitophon@yahoo.com
Contact *Paul Murphy*

Zine of poetry, reviews and short stories.

Envoi
44 Rudyard Road, Biddulph Moor, Stoke-on Trent ST8 7JN
☎01782 517892
Contact *Roger Elkin*

Poetry, sequences, features, reviews, competitions.

Epoch Magazine
57 Murray Street, Montrose, Angus
DD10 8JZ
Contact *Neil Mathers*

Scottish and European literature, art, philosophy, some poetry. See also **Corbie Press**.

Equinox
134 Joy Lane, Whitstable, Kent CT5 4ES
Contact *Barbara Dordi*

Twice-yearly journal of contemporary poetry illustrated with original artwork in colour. New writers published alongside new work from nationally known poets.

Eratica
Waterloo Press (Hove), 51 Waterloo Road, Hove, E. Sussex BN3 1AN
☎01273 202876
Email dr.jenner@virgin.net
Contact *Simon Jenner*

Annual journal with colour plates – focus on poetry, strong on music and art.

Fabric
93 Holmedeane Avenue, London SE24 9LD
Email fabricpoems@hotmail.com
Contact *M. Hogan*

Poetry published biannually.

Fan the Flames
c/o Brickhouse C S, The Barns, Sheepcote Lane, Silver End, Witham, Essex CM8 3PJ
Email editor@fantheflames.co.uk
Website www.fantheflames.co.uk
Contact *Emma Reed*

Poetry and prose quarterly, distributed throughout the UK and abroad.

Federation Magazine
Burslem School of Art, Queen Street, Stoke-on-Trent ST6 3EJ
☎01792 822327
Email thefwwcp@tiscali.co.uk
Website www.thefwwcp.org.uk
Contact *Tim Diggles*

Articles, reviews and news for people working in community publishing.

Fire
Field Cottage, Old Whitehill, Tackley, Kidlington, Oxon OX5 3AB
☎01869 331300 Website www.poetical.org
Contact *Jeremy Hilton*

Poetry: alternative, unfashionable, experimental, spiritual, demotic; occasional experimental prose.

The Firing Squad
25 Griffiths Road, West Bromwich B71 2EH
☎07950 591455
Contact *Geoff Stevens*

Protest poetry broadsheet. See also **Purple Patch** magazine.

First Time
The Snoring Cat, 16 Marianne Park, Dudley Road, Hastings, E. Sussex TN35 5PU
☎01424 423105 Fax 01424 428855

Contact *Josephine Austin*

Biannual magazine designed to encourage first-time poets.

Flaming Arrows
Sligo-Leitrim Arts, V E C, Riverside, Sligo, Republic of Ireland
☎00 353 71 45844 Fax 00 353 71 43093

Contact *Leo Regan*

Poetry of the spirit: mystical, metaphysical, grounded in the senses. Worldwide.

Folding Poems
Dingle Cottage, Newmarket Road, Combeston, Cambridge CB4 0AP

The Frogmore Papers
18 Nevill Road, Lewes, E. Sussex BN7 1PF
Website www.frogmorepress.co.uk

Contact *Jeremy Page*

Founded 1983. Biannual. Poetry, prose and artwork.

Gabriel
27 Headingley Court, North Grange Road, Leeds, W. Yorks LS6 2QC

Contact *Thelma Laycock*

Annual Christian poetry magazine.

Garbaj
38 Pierrot Steps, 71 Kursaal Way, Southend on Sea, Essex SS1 2UY

Contact *D.S. Davidson*

Humourous/non-pc poetry, vignette-length fiction, fake news, etc. See also **Awen**, **Bard** and **Monomyth** magazines.

Glass Beads
PO Box 36103, London SW1 4GQ
Email ruvi@well.com

Contact *Ruvi Simmons*

Global Tapestry Journal
Spring Bank, Longsight Road, Copster Green, Blackburn, Lancs BB1 9EU
☎01254 249128

Contact *Dave Cunliffe*

Global Bohemia, post-Beat and counterculture orientation. See also **BB Books** press.

Green Queen
BM Box 5700, London WC1N 3XX

Contact *Elsa Wallace*

Occasional magazine, Green issues, lesbian & gay fiction, articles, poetry.

Harlequin
PO Box 23392, Edinburgh EH7 5GL
Website www.geocities.com/harlequinmag

How Do I Love Thee?
1 Blue Ball Corner, Water Lane, Winchester, Hants SO23 0ER
Email adrian.abishop@virgin.net
Website freespace.virgin.net/poetry.life

Contact *Adrian Bishop*

The magazine for love poetry. See also **Poetry Life** magazine.

HQ Poetry Magazine (Haiku Quarterly)
39 Exmouth Street, Swindon, Wilts SN1 3PU
☎01793 523927

Contact *Kevin Bailey*

General poetry mag with slight bias towards imagistic/haikuesque work. See also **Day Dream Press**.

Imagenation
289 Elmwood Avenue, Feltham, Middx TW13 7QB
Email partners_writing_group@hotmail.com
Website www.homestead.com/partners_
    writing_group

Contact *Ian Deal*

Poetry and artwork magazine. See also **Partners** press, **A Bard Hair Day**, **Poet Tree**, **Seventh Sense**, **The Word Life Journal** magazines.

Imagine
The Enterprise Park, Barrack Street, Tallow, Co. Waterford Republic of Ireland
Email tallowwriter@eircom.net

Tallow writers.

Inclement
White Rose House, 8 Newmarket Road, Fordham, Ely, Cambs CB7 5LL

Contact *Michelle Foster*

All forms and styles of poetry.

The Interpreter's House
10 Farrell Road, Wootton, Beds MK43 9DU

Contact *Merryn Williams*

Poems and stories up to 2500 words; new and established writers.

Iota
1 Lodge Farm, Snitterfield, Stratford upon Avon, Warwickshire CV37 0LR
☎01789 730358   Fax 01789 730320
Email iotapoetry@aol.com
Website www.iotapoetry.co.uk
Contacts *Bob Mee & Janet Murch*

Poetry, reviews; long and short poems welcome. No epics. See also **Ragged Raven Press**

Irish Pages
The Linen Hall Library, 17 Donegall Square North, Belfast BT1 5GB
Email irishpages@yahoo.com
Contact *Chris Agee*

Outstanding writing from Ireland and overseas: poetry, short fiction, essays, etc.

Island
8 Craiglea Drive, Edinburgh EH10 7PA
Email jaj@essencepress.co.uk
Website www.essencepress.co.uk
Contact *Julie Johnstone*

A distinctive space for writing inspired by nature and exploring our place within the natural world. See also **Essence Press**.

The Journal
Flat 3, 18 Oxford Grove, Ilfracombe, Devon EX34 9HQ
☎01271 862708
Email smithsssj@aol.com
Contact *Sam Smith*

Poems in translation alongside poetry written in English. See also **Original Plus** press.

Krax
63 Dixon Lane, Wortley, Leeds, W. Yorks LS12 4RR
Contact *Andy Robson*

Light-hearted, contemporary poetry, short fiction and graphics.

Lallans
Scots Language Society, A K Bell Library, York Place, Perth PH2 8AP
☎01738 440199
Contact *John Law*

The literary magazine for writing in Scots.

Leviathan Quarterly
Bear Hays Farm, Brookhay Lane, Fradley, Litchfield WS13 8RG
☎01543 411161   Fax 01543 410679
Email claire.brodmann@btinternet.com
Contacts *Michael Hulse*

Publishes fiction, essays, poetry, art and criticism.

Liar Republic
7/8 Trinity Chare, Quayside, Newcastle upon Tyne NE1 3DF
☎0191 296 6787   Fax 0191 296 6787
Email psummers@liarincltd.fsnet.co.uk
Contact *Paul Summers*

State of the nation through fiction, journalism, poetry, visual art and reviews.

Lilith the Liverbird
75 Melbury Road, Huyton, Liverpool L14 8UR
Email liverpoolpoet@blueyonder.co.uk
Website www.geocities.com/lillithpink
Contact *Lynn Owen*

Women writers living life on Merseyside.

Linear B Publishing
PO Box 17162, Edinburgh EH11 2WT
☎0131 314 4471   Fax 0131 334 5353
Email linear26@hotmail.com
Contact *Jamie Kelly*

Literary fiction, poetry.

Links
Bude Haven, 18 Frankfield Rise, Tunbridge Wells, Kent TN2 5LF
Email linksmag@supanet.com
Contact *Bill Headdon*

Poetry magazine committed to quality writing and reviews.

Linkway
The Shieling, The Links, Burry Port, Carmarthenshire SA16 0HU
Contact *Fay C. Davies*

A publication for writers and friends – a general interest magazine for the whole family.

Literature and Psychoanalysis
89 Connaught Road, Sutton, Surrey SM1 3RJ
☎020 8286 0419
Contact *Barry Tebb*

New poems, reviews, articles on literary and psychoanalytical matters. See also **Sixties Press**.

London Magazine
30 Thurloe Place, London SW7 2HQ
Email editorial@londonmagazine.ukf.net
Website www.londonmagazine.ukf.net

Contact *Sebastian Barker*

Art and literature, memoirs and reviews.

The Long Poem Group Newsletter
6 The Mount, Higher Furzeham, Brixham,
S. Devon TQ5 8QY
☎01803 851098   Fax 01803 851098
Email pwoxley@aol.com
Website www.bath.ac.uk/~exxdgdc

Contact *William Oxley*

Eight pages devoted to debating the long poem
in our time. See also **Acumen** magazine.

M(onkey) K(ettle)
PO Box 4616, Kiln Farm, Milton Keynes
MK12 6XZ
Email monkeykettle@hotmail.com
Website www.monkeykettle.co.uk

Contact *Matthew Taylor*

Quarterly poetry, prose, photos, articles in
Milton Keynes and further afield.

Magma
43 Keslake Road, London NW6 6DH
Email magmapoems@aol.com
Website www.champignon.net/magma

Contact *David Boll*

New poetry plus poetry reviews and interviews.

Modern Poetry in Translation
MPT, School of Humanities, King's College
London, Strand, London WC2R 2LS
☎020 7848 2360   Fax 020 7848 2145
Website www.kcl.ac.uk/mpt

Contact *Norma Rinsler*

Poems from everywhere, translated into English.

Monomyth
38 Pierrot Steps, 71 Kursaal Way, Southend
on Sea, Essex SS1 2UY

Contact *David John Tyrer*

Poetry, prose and articles; all genres, styles and
lengths considered. New writers welcome. See
also **Awen**, **Bard** and **Garbaj** magazines.

Moodswing
12 Derby Crescent, Moorside, Consett,
Co. Durham DH8 8DZ
☎01207 505724

Contact *Steve Urwin*

Short poems, short prose, light/dark psycho-
logically charged. See also **Talking Pen** press.

Mslexia
PO Box 656, Newcastle upon Tyne NE99 1PZ
☎0191 281 9772 Fax 0191 281 9445
Email postbag@mslexia.demon.co.uk
Website www.mslexia.co.uk

For women who write. See entry under
Magazines.

Multi – Storey
PO Box 62, Levenshulme, Manchester
M19 1TH
Email stuff@multistorey.co.uk
Website www.multistorey.co.uk

Contact *Finella Davenport*

Biannual literary magazine.

Neon Highway
35 Glebe Road, Skelmersdale, Lancs WN8 9JP

Contact *Alice Lenkiewicz*

Innovative and experimental poetry/arts magazine.

Never Bury Poetry
Bracken Clock, Troutbeck Close, Hawkshaw,
Bury, Lancs BL8 4LJ
☎01204 884080
Email nbpoetry@zen.co.uk
Website www.nbpoetry.care4free.net

Contact *Jean Tarry*

Quarterly founded 1989. International reputation. Each issue has a different theme.

The New Caudron
19 The Sandhills, Wirral CH46 3ST
☎0151 678 1105   Fax 0151 678 1965
Email luna.cantos@virgin.net
Website www.thenewcauldron.co.uk

Contact *Anita Luna-Cantos*

Short stories, articles, poetry, competitions, letters, special features.

New Welsh Review
PO Box 170, Aberystwyth, Ceredigion
SY23 1WZ
☎01970 626230
Email nwr@welshnet.co.uk

Contact *Francesca Rhydderch*

Vibrant literary which showcases the best new
writing from Wales – also includes features and
reviews. See entry under **Magazines**.

Nomad
Survivors Press, 4 C4 Templeton Centre, 62 Templeton Street, Glasgow G40 1DA
☎0141 556 4554 Fax 0141 556 4695
Email sps@spscot.co.uk
Website www.spscot.co.uk

Contact *Gerry Loose*

Poetry and creative writing by survivors of the mental health system, of abuse or addictions.

Norfolk Poets and Writers
9 Walnut Close, Taverham, Norwich, Norfolk NR8 6YN
☎0798 917 4076
Email wwbuk@yahoo.co.uk
Website www.webbw.freeserve.co.uk

Contact *Wendy Webb*

Tips for writers, postcard magazines, brief poems and mini stories.

The North
The Studio, Byram Arcade, Huddersfield, W. Yorks HD1 1ND
☎01484 434840 Fax 01484 426566
Email edit@poetrybusiness.co.uk
Website www.poetrybusiness.co.uk

Contacts *Peter Sansom & Janet Fisher*

Contemporary poetry and articles, extensive reviews.

Oasis
12 Stevenage Road, London SW6 6ES
☎020 7736 5059

Contact *Ian Robinson*

Poetry, short fiction, essays, reviews, etc. See also **Oasis Books** press.

Obsessed With Pipework
41 Buckley's Green, Alvechurch, Birmingham B48 7NG
☎0121 445 2110 Email flare.stack@virgin.net

Contact *Charles Johnson*

Quarterly seeking new high-wire poems 'to surprise and delight' – any length, exploratory, not predictable, please.

Orbis
17 Greenhow Avenue, West Kirby, Wirral CH48 5EL
☎0151 625 1446
Email carolebaldock@hotmail.com

Contact *Carole Baldock*

An independent international quarterly of poetry and prose with many reader-friendly features.

Ore
Creative Writing, Cardiff University, School of English, Communication and Philosophy, PO Box 94, Cardiff CF10 3XB
☎029 2087 5310 Fax 029 2087 4647
Email youngj1@cardiff.ac.uk

Contact *Jennifer Young*

Innovation and quality in all genres, including poetry, fiction, creative non-fiction, scriptwriting, performance poetry.

Other Poetry
29 Western Hill, Durham DH1 4RL
☎0191 386 4058
Website www.otherpoetry.com

Contact *Michael Standen & Others*

Thrice-yearly 60 – 70 poems per issue. Process of selection involves all four editors. Token payment.

Outposts
22 Whitewell Road, Frome, Somerset BA11 4EL
☎01373 466653 Fax 01373 466653

Contact *Roland John*

Longest-surviving independent poetry magazine in the UK. See also **Hippopotamus Press**.

Page 84's Pseudo-Chaotic Magazines
P E F Productions, 196 High Road, London N22 8HH
Email page84direct@yahoo.co.uk
Website www.page84.ht.com

Contact *Mr Page 84*

Poetry, anti-poetry, aphorism, comment and artwork mag showing work of Page 84 and guest artists.

Panda
46 First Avenue, Clase, Swansea SA6 7LL
☎01792 414837 Fax 01792 414837
Email esmond.j@ntlworld
Website www.geocities.com/slap_dash/
  Quarterly_poetry.html

Contact *Esmond Jones*

Poetry and prose.

Peace and Freedom
17 Farrow Road, Whaplode Drove, Spalding, Lincs PE12 0TS
☎01406 330242
Email p_rance@yahoo.co.uk

Website uk.vgeocities.com/p_rance/pandf.htm

Contact *Paul Rance*

Poetry/prose/art mag – humanitarian, environmental, animal welfare. See also **Eastern Rainbow** magazine.

Peer Poetry International
26 (wh) Arlington House, Bath Street, Bath BA1 1QN
☎01225 445298
Email peerpoetryintl@tiny.com.uk
Website www.publish-your-poetry.com

Contact *Paul Amphlett*

All kinds of poetry.

The Penniless Press
100 Waterloo Road, Ashton, Preston, Lancs PR2 1EP
☎01772 736421

Contact *Alan Dent*

Quarterly for the poor pocket and the rich mind. Poetry, fiction, essays, reviews.

Pennine Ink Magazine
The Gallery, Mid-Pennine Arts, Yorke Street, Burnley, Lancs BB11 1HD
☎01282 703657
Email biglamp@projectoneoone.demon.co.uk
Website www.openingline.co.uk/
   openingline/version1/magazines/pennineink

Contact *Laura Sheridan*

Quality poetry reflecting traditional and modern trends.

Pennine Platform
Frizingley Hall, Frizingley Road, Bradford, W. Yorks BD9 4LD
☎01274 541015

Contact *Nicholas Nielby*

Poetry with reviews and critical articles.

Pitch
17 Castle Street, Carlisle, Cumbria CZ3 8TP
Website www.bookscumbria.com

Contact *Jacob Polley*

Planet
PO Box 44, Aberystwyth SY23 3ZZ
☎01970 611255 Fax 01970 611197
Email planet.enquiries@planetmagazine.org.uk
Website www.planetmagazine.org.uk

Contact *John Barnie*

The Welsh Internationalist – current affairs, arts, environment. See also **Planet** press.

PN Review
The Writing School, Manchester Metropolitan University, Geoffrey Manton Building, Rosamond Street West, Manchester M15 6LL
☎0161 834 8730 Fax 0161 832 0084
Email pnr@carcanet.u-net.com
Website www.carcanet.co.uk

Contact *Michael Schmidt*

See **Carcanet Press** under **UK Publishers**.

PN Spark
Remus House, Coltsfoot Drive, Woodston, Peterborough, Cambs PE2 9JX
☎01733 898101 Fax 01733 313524
Email poetrynow@forwardpress.co.uk
Website www.forwardpress.co.uk

Newsletter with challenging workshops, poetry news and competitions.

Poet Tree
289 Elmwood Avenue, Feltham, Middlesex TW13 7QB

Contact *Ian Deal*

General poetry and short story magazine. **Partners** press, **A Bard Hair Day**, **Imagenation**, **Seventh Sense**, **The Word Life Journal** magazines.

Poetic Hours
43 Willow Road, Carlton, Notts NG4 3BH
Email erranpublishing@hotmail.com
Website www.poetichours.homestead.com

Contact *Nick Clark*

Non-profit supporter of Third World charities. See also **Erran Publishing**.

Poetic Licence
70 Aveling Close, Purley, Surrey CR8 4DW
Email poets@poesanon.org.uk
Website www.poetsanon.org.uk

Contact *Peter L. Evans*

Original unpublished poems and drawings. See also **Poets Anonymous** press.

The Poetry Church
Feather Books, PO Box 438, Shrewsbury, Shropshire SY3 0WN
☎01743 872177 Fax 01743 872177
Email john@waddysweb.freeuk.com
Website www.waddysweb.freeuk.com

Contact *Rev. J. Waddington-Feather*

Quarterly magazine of Christian poetry and prayers. See **Feather Books** under **Small Presses**.

Poetry Cornwall/ Bardhonyeth Kernow

1 Station Hill, Redruth, Cornwall TR15 2PP
Email les.merton@tesco.net

Contact *Les Merton*

Poetry from Cornwall including Kernow and dialect.

Poetry Express

Diorama Arts Centre, 34 Osnaburgh Street, London NW1 3ND
☎020 7916 5317 Fax 020 7916 0830
Email survivor@survivorspoetry.org.uk
Website www.groups.msn.com/survivorspoetry

Contact *Alison Combs*

Quarterly newsletter from Survivors' poetry.

Poetry Ireland News

Bermingham Tower, Upper Yard, Dublin Castle, Dublin 2 Republic of Ireland
☎00 353 1 671 4632 Fax 00 353 1 671 4634
Email poetry@iol.ie
Website www.poetryireland.ie

Contact *Paul Lenehan*

Bi-monthly newsletter. See also **Poetry Ireland Review** magazine.

Poetry Ireland Review/ Eigse Eireann

Bermingham Tower, Upper Yard, Dublin 2 Republic of Ireland
☎00 353 1 671 4632 Fax 00 353 1 671 4634
Email poetry@iol.ie
Website www.poetryireland.ie

Contact *Eva Bourke*

Quarterly journal of poetry and reviews.

Poetry Life

1 Blue Bell Corner, Water Lane, Winchester, Hants SO23 0ER
Email adrian.abishop@virgin.net
Website freespace.virgin.net/poetry.life

Contact *Adrian Bishop*

Publishing the best of modern poetry. See also **How Do I Love Thee?** magazine.

Poetry London

1a Jewel Road, London E17 4QU
Email editors@poetrylondon.co.uk
Website www.poetrylondon.co.uk

Contact *Pascale Petit*

Poetry, listings, reviews, features and information. Accepts unsolicited mss.

Poetry Nottingham International

PO Box 6740, Nottingham NG5 1QG

Contact *Julie Lumsden*

Poetry, articles, letters, features, reviews, 48–56 pages, quarterly.

Poetry Now

Remus House, Coltsfoot Drive, Woodston, Peterborough, Cambs PE2 9JX
☎01733 898101 Fax 01733 313524
Email poetrynow@forwardpress.co.uk
Website www.forwardpress.co.uk

Contact *Natalie Nightingale*

Incorporating *Rhyme Arrival* magazine – communicating across the barriers.

Poetry People

Remus House, Coltsfoot Drive, Woodston, Peterborough, Cambs PE2 8JX
☎01733 898101 Fax 01733 313524
Email poetrynow@forwardpress.co.uk
Website www.forwardpress.co.uk

Newsletter of poetry news and views.

Poetry Review

Poetry Society, 22 Betterton Street, London WC2H 9BX
☎020 7420 9883 Fax 020 7240 4818
Email poetryreview@poetrysoc.com
Website www.poetrysoc.com

Contacts *Robert Potts & David Herd*

A quarterly forum on the state of poetry.

Poetry Salzburg Review

Dept of English and American Studies, University of Salzburg, Akademiestr. 24, A – 5020 Salzburg Austria
Email wolfgang.goertschacher@sbg.ac.uk
Website www.poetrysalzburg.com

Contact *Wolfgang Görtschacher*

Poetry magazine, formerly *The Poet's Voice*. Published with the University of Salzburg.

Poetry Scotland

3 Spittal Street, Edinburgh EH3 9DY
☎0131 229 7252
Website www.poetryscotland.co.uk

Contact *Sally Evans*

All-poetry broadsheet with Scottish emphasis.

Poetry Wales

1st & 2nd Floors, 38–40 Nolton Street, Bridgend CF31 3BN
☎01656 663018 Fax 01656 649226

Email poetrywales@seren.force9.co.uk
Website www.seren-books.com

Contact *Robert Minhinnick*

Poetry, criticism, essays, from Wales and further afield. See also **Seren** under **UK Publishers**.

Poets Cornered
28 Victoria Street, Brighton, E. Sussex
BN1 3FQ

Contact *Gemma Boyd*

PQR – Poetry Quarterly Review
Coleridge Cottage, Nether Stowey, Somerset
TA5 1NQ
☎01278 732662 Email pqrrev@aol.com

Contacts *Derrick Woolf & Tilla Brading*

In-depth reviews of mainstream/small-press poetry – no unrequested poetry, please.

Premonitions
13 Hazely Combe, Arreton, Isle of Wight
PO30 3AJ
☎01983 865668
Email pigasus.press@virgin.net

Contact *Tony Lee*

Magazine of sf-horror stories and horror stories, with genre poetry and art. See also **Pigasus Press**.

Presence
12 Grovehall Avenue, Leeds, W. Yorks
LS11 7EX
Email martin.lucas@talk21.com
Website freespace.virgin.net/haiku.presence

Contact *Martin Lucas*

Haiku, senryu, tanka, renku and related poetry in English.

Pretext
School of English & American Studies,
University of East Anglia, Norwich, Norfolk
NR4 7TJ
☎01603 592783 Email info@penandinc.co.uk
Website www.penandinc.co.uk

Contact *Katri Skala*

New fiction and poetry – essays on the world of writing. See also **Reactions** and **Pen&Inc** presses.

Pulsar
34 Lineacre Close, Grange Park, Swindon,
Wilts SN5 6DA
☎01793 875941 Email david.pike@virgin.net
Website www.pulsarpoetry.com

Contact *David Pike*

Hard hitting/inspirational poetry – quarterly.

Purple Patch
25 Griffiths Road, West Bromwich B71 2EH
☎07950 591455

Contact *Geoff Stevens*

Poetry mag founded 1976 – includes reviews and gossip column. See also **The Firing Squad** magazine.

Quantum Leap
York House, 15 Argyle Terrace, Rothesay,
Isle of Bute PA20 0BD

Contact *Alan Carter*

User-friendly magazine – encourages new writers – all types of poetry. See also **QQ Press**.

Raw Edge
PO Box 4867, Birmingham B3 3HD

Contact *Dave Reeves*

New writing, free from outlets in the West Midlands Arts area. Writers with a regional connection only. See also **The Moving Finger** press.

The Reader
University of Liverpool, Abercromby Square,
Liverpool L69 7ZR
Email readers@thereader.co.uk
Website www.thereader.co.uk

Contact *Jane Davis*

Literary magazine, new fiction, poetry, essays, book recommendations and reviews. See entry under **Magazines**.

Rebirth
104 Argyle Gardens, Upminster, Essex
RM14 3EU
Website www.homestead.com/firebirdpress

Contact *Pamela Constantine*

International journal of the new renaissance movement. See also **Firebird Press**, **Romantic Renaissance** and **The Solar Flame** magazines.

Recovery
Community Arts Workshop, Community Art
Gallery, Avenue Road, Leamington Spa,
Warwickshire CV31 3PP
☎01564 783425
Email paullockwood@care4free.net

Contact *Paul Lockwood*

Expressions of people recovering from, or living with, mental health problems.

Red Poets' Society
PO Box 661, Wrexham LL11 1QU
☎01978 366735 Fax 01978 366735
Email mv.jones@virgin.net
Contact *Mike Jenkins*
Radical Welsh poetry magazine.

The Remedy
Renegade Writers, 80 Brooklands Road, Spring Bank West, Hull HU5 5AE
Email renegadewriters@hotmail.com

Reveal
PO Box 184, South Ockendon, Essex RM15 5WT
Contact *D.M. Heath*
The more sensuous and heartfelt pen. See also **Blue Badge Poetry Supplement**.

The Review
4 Algar House, Webber Row, London SE1 8QT
Email thereview@hotmail.com
Website www.thereview.freeserve.co.uk
Contact *Raul Peschiera*

The Rialto
PO Box 309, Aylsham, Norwich, Norfolk NR11 6LN
Website www.therialto.co.uk
Contact *Michael Mackmin*
Excellent poetry in a clear environment.

Rising
80 Cazenove Road, Stoke Newington, London N16 6AA
Email timmywells@hotmail.com
Contact *Tim Wells*
The readers' wives of poetry mags.

Romantic Renaissance
104 Argyle Gardens, Upminster, Essex RM14 3EU
Website www.homestead.com/firebirdpress
Contact *Pamela Constantine*
Journal of the new renaissance movement. See also **Firebird Press**, **Rebirth** and **The Solar Flame** magazines.

Roundyhouse
3 Crown Street, Port Talbot SA13 1BG

Email srjones@alunbooks.co.uk
Contact *Sally R. Jones*
Poems and articles on poetry. Reviews. Eclectic approach.

The Rue Bella
2fl, 15 Warrender Park Terrace, Edinburgh EH19 1EG
☎0131 229 3883
Website www.ruebella.co.uk
Contact *Nigel Bird*
Poetry – new writers.

Sable
PO Box 33504, London E9 7YE
Email hotspotwriters@compuserve.com
Contact *Kadija Sesay*
120-page litmag for writers of colour – poetry, fiction, memoirs, etc.

Salt
PO Box 937, Great Wilbraham, Cambridge CB1 5JX
Email cemery@saltpublishing.com
Website www.saltpublishing.com
Contact *John Kinsella & Others*
International journal of poetry and poetics. See also **Salt Publishing** press.

Scribbler!
Remus House, Coltsfoot Drive, Woodston, Peterborough, Cambs PE2 9JX
☎01733 890066 Fax 01733 313524
Email scribbler@forwardpress.co.uk
Website www.youngwriters.co.uk
Contact *Steve Twelvetree*
Primary school magazine showcasing children's work. See also **Poetry Now Young Writers** press.

Scriptor
2 Chambers Cottages, Underlyn Lane, Marden, Tonbridge, Kent TN12 9BD
☎07967 315270
Email greenarrow588882@aol.com
Contact *John Dench*
Poetry, short stories, essays from the UK. See also **Green Arrow Publishing** press.

Seam
10 Collingwood Road, South Woodham Ferrers, Chelmsford, Essex CM3 5YB
Contact *Frank Dullaghan*
New poetry by established and new poets.

Seventh Sense
289 Elmwood Avenue, Feltham, Middlesex
TW13 7QB
Email partners_writing_group@hotmail.com
Website www.homestead.com/partners_
  writing_group

Contact *Ian Deal*

Dedicated to the ongoing spiritual quest. See
also **Partners** press, **Imagenation**, **A Bard
Hair Day**, **Poet Tree** and **The Word Life
Journal** magazines.

Shearsman
58 Velwell Road, Exeter, Devon EX4 4LD
☎01392 434511 Fax 01392 434511
Email editor@shearsman.com
Website www.shearsman.co.uk

Contact *Tony Frazer*

Mainly poetry, some prose, some reviews.
Poetry in the modernist tradition.

The Shop: A Magazine Of Poetry
Skeagh, Schull, Co Cork Republic of Ireland
Email wakeman@iol.ie

Contact *John Wakeman*

International but with emphasis on Irish poetry.

Skald
2 Greenfield Terrace, Hill Street, Menai
Bridge, Ynys Mon LL59 5AY
☎01248 716343
Email submissions@skald.co.uk
Website www.centralslate.omnia.co.uk/Skald

Contact *Zoe Skoulding*

Poetry and artwork, English and Welsh.

Smiths Knoll
49 Church Road, Little Glemham,
Woodbridge, Suffolk IP13 0BJ
Email royblackman@ukonline.co.uk

Contacts *Roy Blackman & Michael Laskey*

Surprising, honest, well-crafted poems. No
e-mail submissions.

Smoke
The Windows Project, 96 Bold Street,
Liverpool L1 4HY
☎0151 709 3688

Contact *Dave Ward*

Poetry, graphics, short prose – 24pp – biannual.

The Solar Flame
104 Argyle Gardens, Upminster, Essex
RM14 3EU

Website www.homestead.com/firebirdpress

Contact *Pamela Constantine*

Journal of the emerging spiritual and cultural
renaissance. See also **Firebird Press**, **Rebirth**
and **Romantic Renaissance** magazines.

Solo Survivors
37 Micklehill Drive, Shirley, Solihull,
W. Midlands B90 2PU
☎0121 745 4381
Email johnalanhirst@ukonline.co.uk
Website www.johnalanhirst.com

Contact *John Hirst & Others*

A quarterly bound, 60-page poetry and art
magazine for sufferers but not expressly so.

South
PO Box 5369, Poole, Dorset BH14 0XN
Email south@martinblyth.co.uk
Website www.martinblyth.co.uk

Poetry magazine from the southern counties of
England that welcomes poets from across the
world.

Spiked
63 Newmarket Street, Norwich, Norfolk
NR2 2DP
☎01603 629899
Email editors@spiked-magazine.co.uk
Website www.spiked-magazine.co.uk

Contact *Thea Abbott*

Ideas, literature and the arts for Norfolk.

Stand
School of English, University of Leeds, Leeds,
W. Yorks LS2 9JT
☎ 0113 233 4794 Fax 0113 233 4791
Email stand@leeds.ac.uk
Website saturn.vcu.edu/~dlatane/stand.html

Contact *Jon Glover*

Quarterly magazine of poetry, fiction, reviews
and cultural criticism.

Staple
35 Carr Road, Walkley, Sheffield S6 2WY
Email e.barrett@shu.ac.uk

Contact *Ann Atkinson*

Poetry, short fiction, articles. Three issues a
year.

The Stinging Fly
PO Box 6016, Dublin 8 Republic of Ireland
Email stingingfly@hotmail.com
Website www.stingingfly.org

Contact *Declan Meade*

Dublin's literary magazine. New Irish and international writing, Poetry, short fiction, author interviews and book reviews.

Tangled Hair

Snapshot Press, PO Box 132, Crosby, Liverpool L23 8XS

Contact *John Barlow*

Tanka.

Tears in the Fence

38 Hod View, Stourpaine, Nr Blandford Forum, Dorset DT11 8TN
☎01258 456803 Fax 01258 454026
Email esp@euphony.net
Website www.wanderingdog.co.uk

Contact *David Caddy*

A magazine looking for the unusual, perceptive, risk-taking, lived and visionary literature.

Temenos Academy Review

PO Box 203, Ashford, Kent TN25 5ZT
☎01233 813663
Email stephen.overy@ashfordtelecom.net

Contact *Grevel Lindop*

10th Muse

33 Hartington Road, Southampton, Hants SO14 OEW
Email andyj@noplace.screaming.net

Contact *Andrew Jordan*

Poetry, prose and graphics, ideally combining lyricism and the pastoral with experimental techniques.

The Third Half

16 Fane Close, Stamford, Lincs PE9 1HG
☎01780 754193

Contact *Kevin Troop*

Searches for good poetry and fiction.

Time Haiku

Basho-an, Kings Head Hill, London E4 7JG

Contact *Dr Erica Facey*

Haiku magazine aimed at experts and beginners.

The Unruly Sun

The Rising Arts Centre, 30 Silver Street, Reading, Berks RG1 2ST
Email unrulysubmissions@hotmail.com
Website www.unrulysun.co.uk

Contact *Jennifer Hoskins & Others*

Irregular poetry magazine – will consider anything contemporary.

Urthona

9a Auckland Road, Cambridge CB2 8DW
☎01223 472417 Fax 01223 566568
Email urthona.mag@virgin.net
Website www.urthona.com

Contact *Shantigarbha*

Art & Buddhism. Builds bridges between Buddhism and Western culture.

Wasafiri

Dept of English, Queen Mary College, University of London, Mile End Road, London E1 4SN
☎020 7882 3120 Fax 020 7882 3120
Email wasafiri@qmw.ac.uk
Website www.wasafiri.org

Contact *Susheila Nasta*

Literary journal of African, Asian, Caribbean and black British writing. See entry under **Magazines**.

The Word Life Journal

289 Elmwood Avenue, Feltham, Middlesex TW13 7QB
Website www.homestead.com/partners_
    writing_group

Contact *Ian Deal*

Poetry magazine dedicated to the ongoing romantic renaissance. See also **Partners** press, **A Bard Hair Day**, **Imagenation**, **Poet Tree** and **Seventh Sense** magazines.

Wordsmith

Remus House, Coltsfoot Drive, Woodston, Peterborough, Cambs PE2 9JX
☎01733 890066 Fax 01733 313524
Email wordsmith@forwardpress.co.uk
Website www.forward-press.co.uk

Contact *Lynsey Hawkins*

Publishers of poetry for teenagers.

The Yellow Crane

20 Princes Court, The Walk, Roath, Cardiff CF2 3AU

Contact *J. Brookes*

Interesting new poems from S. Wales and beyond.

Organisations of Interest to Poets

A survey of some of the societies, groups and other bodies which may be of interest to practising poets. Organisations not listed should send details to the Editor for inclusion in future editions.

Academi – The Welsh National Literature Promotion Agency and Society for Writers

3rd Floor, Mount Stuart House, Mount Stuart Square, Cardiff Bay, Cardiff CF10 5FQ
☎029 2047 2266 Fax 029 2049 2930
Email post@academi.org
Website www.academi.org

North West Wales Office: Ty Newydd, Llanystumdwy, Cricieth, Gwynedd LL52 0LW

West Wales Office: Dylan Thomas Centre, Somerset Place, Swansea SA1 1RR

Chief Executive *Peter Finch*

The writers' organisation of Wales with special responsibility for literary activity, writers' residencies, writers on tour, festivals, writers' groups, readings, tours, exchanges and other development work. **Yr Academi Gymreig/The Welsh Academy** operates the Arts Council of Wales franchise for Wales-wide literature development. It has offices in Cardiff and fieldworkers based in North West, North East and West Wales. *Publishes* the Lottery-funded *Encyclopedia of Wales*, the Welsh-medium literary magazine *Taliesin*, the *Academi English-Welsh Dictionary*, co-publisher of *The New Welsh Review* along with a number of other projects. The Academi sponsors a range of annual contests including the John Tripp Award For Spoken Poetry and the prestigious **Cardiff International Poetry Competition**. Publishes *A470* a bi-monthly literary information magazine.

Apples & Snakes

Battersea Arts Centre, Lavender Hill, London SW11 5TN
☎020 7924 3410 Fax 020 7924 3763
Email info@applesandsnakes.org
Website www.applesandsnakes.org

Director *Geraldine Collinge*

Set up in 1982 as a platform for poetry which would be popular, relevant, cross-cultural and accessible to the widest possible range of people, A&S aims to stretch the boundaries of poetry in education and in performance. Currently undergoing an extensive programme of expansion, bringing performance poetry to new places and new audiences across England.

Arts Councils

See section on **Arts Councils and Regional Offices**, page 574.

The Arvon Foundation

See entry under **Writers' Courses, Circles and Workshops**

The British Haiku Society

Lenacre Ford, Woolhope, Hereford HR1 4RF
☎01432 860328
Website www.britishhaikusociety.org

General Secretary *David Walker*

FORMED in 1990. Promotes the appreciation and writing within the British Isles of haiku, senryu, tanka, haibun and renga by way of tutorials, workshops, exchange of poems, critical comment and information. The Society runs a haiku library and administers the annual James W. Hackett Award, the prestigious **Sasakawa** prize and the Nobuyuki Yuasa International Haibun in English Contest. *Publishes The Haiku Kit* teaching pack and the quarterly journal, *Blithe Spirit*.

The Eight Hand Gang

5 Cross Farm, Station Road, North Fearnhead, Warrington WA2 0QG
Secretary *John F. Haines*

An association of SF poets. *Publishes Handshake*, a single-sheet newsletter of SF poetry and information available free in exchange for an s.a.e.

57 Productions

57 Effingham Road, Lee Green, London SE12 8NT
☎020 8463 0866 Fax 020 8463 0866
Email paul57prods@yahoo.co.uk
Website www.57productions.com

Contact *Paul Beasley*

Specialises in the promotion of poetry and its production through an agency service, a programme of events and a series of audio publications. Services are available to event promoters, festivals, education institutions and the media. Poets represented include Jean 'Binta' Breeze, Adrian Mitchell, John Cooper Clarke and Lemn Sissay. 57 Productions' series of audio cassettes, CDs and Poetry in Performance compilations offer access to some of the most exciting poets working in Britain today.

The Football Poets
4 The Retreat, Butterow, Stroud, Gloucestershire
☎01453 7573766
Email crispin@ctmuk.freeserve.co.uk *and* dave@footballpoets.org
Website www.footballpoets.org
Performance *Crispin Thomas*
Secretary *Dave Cockcroft*

The Football Poets exist to promote and encourage the writing and performing of football poetry. FOUNDED in 1995, they appear regularly at festivals and venues around the country. They also provide comprehensive and entertaining football poetry workshops in schools and communities. Their website is a fast and entertaining mix of literature and soccer poetry from around the world. Anyone may contribute.

The Poet's House/Teach na hÉigse
Clonbarra, Falcarragh, Co. Donegal, Republic of Ireland
☎00 353 74 65470 Fax 00 353 74 65471
Email phouse@iol.ie
Director *Janice Fitzpatrick Simmons*

Set in the heart of the Donegal Gaeltacht, the centre offers a year-long residential MA aong with three ten-day summer courses (to apply send three poems). During each session there are three resident and six visiting poets. Recent poets have included Peter Sirr, Paul Durcan, Michael Longley, Menna Elfyn, Frank Ormsby and Medbh McGuckian.

The Poetry Book Society
Book House, 45 East Hill, London SW18 2QZ
☎020 8870 8403 Fax 020 8870 0865
Website www.poetrybooks.co.uk
Director *Chris Holifield*

For readers, writers, students and teachers of poetry. FOUNDED in 1953 by T.S. Eliot and funded by the Arts Council, the PBS is a unique membership organisation and book club providing up-to-date and comprehensive information about poetry from publishers in the UK and Ireland. Members receive the quarterly *PBS Bulletin* packed with articles by poets, poems, news, listings and access to discounts of at least 25% off featured titles. These range from modern classics to contemporary works. The transactional website has over 1000 titles available at discount to members. There are three membership packages – two of which include a number of new books specially selected by the Society's panel of experts along with, at both primary and secondary levels, a special package for teachers. Subscriptions start at £10. The PBS also runs the annual **T.S. Eliot Prize** for the best collection of new poetry.

The Poetry Business
The Studio, Byram Arcade, Westgate, Huddersfield, West Yorkshire HD1 1ND
☎01484 434840 Fax 01484 426566
Email edit@poetrybusiness.co.uk
Website www.poetrybusiness.co.uk
Directors *Peter Sansom, Janet Fisher*

FOUNDED in 1986, the Business *publishes The North* magazine and books, pamphlets and cassettes under the **Smith/Doorstop** imprint. It runs an annual competition and organises monthly writing Saturdays. Send an s.a.e. for full details.

Poetry Can
Unit 11, Kuumba Project, 20–23 Hepburn Road, Bristol BS2 8UD
☎0117 942 6976 Fax 0117 944 1478
Email lucy@poetrycan.demon.co.uk
Website www.poetrycan.demon.co.uk
Administrator *Jemimah Kuhfeld*

FOUNDED in 1995, Poetry Can is a poetry development agency working across the Bristol and Bath areas It organises events and projects, supports the creative and professional development of poets and *publishes* a bi-monthly bulletin of poetry news and activity.

Poetry Ireland/Eigse Eireann
Bermingham Tower, Upper Yard, Dublin Castle, Dublin, Republic of Ireland
☎00 353 1 671 4632 Fax 00 353 1 671 4634
Email poetry@iol.ie
Website www.poetryireland.ie
Education ☎00 353 671 4216
Writers in Schools scheme
  ☎00 353 1 674 9860
Director *Joseph Woods*

The national organisation for poetry in Ireland, with its four core activities being readings, publications, education and an information and resource service. Organises readings by Irish and international poets countrywide. Through its website, telephone, post and public enquiries, Poetry Ireland operates as a clearing house for everything pertaining to poetry in Ireland. Operates the Writers in Schools scheme.

Publishes Poetry Ireland News, a bi-monthly newsletter containing information on events, competitions and opportunities. *Poetry Ireland Review* is published quarterly and is the journal of record for poetry in Ireland; current editor: *Michael Smith*. The organisation also produces occasional publications, most recently, *Watching the River Flow, a Century in Irish Poetry*. As a member of the International Translation Network, it has produced 12 dual-language titles by foreign poets.

The Poetry Library

Royal Festival Hall, Level 5, London
SE1 8XX
☎020 7921 0943/0664
Fax 020 7921 0939
Email info@poetrylibrary.org.uk
Website www.poetrylibrary.org.uk

FOUNDED by the Arts Council in 1953. A collection of 45,000 titles of modern poetry since 1912, from Georgian to Rap, representing all English-speaking countries and including translations into English by contemporary poets. Two copies of each title are held, one for loan and one for reference. A wide range of poetry magazines and ephemera from all over the world are kept along with casettes, records and videos for consultation, with many available for loan. There is a children's poetry section with teacher's resource collection.

An information service compiles lists of poetry magazines, competitions, publishers, groups and workshops which are available from the Library on receipt of a large s.a.e. or direct from the website. It also has a noticeboard for lost quotations through which it tries to identify lines or fragments of poetry which have been sent in by other readers.

General enquiry service available. Membership is free but proof of identity and address are essential to join. Open 11.00 am to 8.00 pm, Tuesday to Sunday. The Library's website is one of the best poetry resources on the Net.

Beside the Library is *The Voice Box*, a performance space especially for literature. For details of current programme ring 020 7921 0971.

Poetry London

1a Jewel Road, London E17 4QU
Email editors@poetrylondon.co.uk
Website www.poetrylondon.co.uk

Contacts *Andy McAllister* (listings), *Pascale Petit* (poetry editor), *Scott Verner* (reviews)

Published three times a year, *Poetry London* includes poetry by new and established writers, reviews of recent collections and anthologies, articles on issues relating to poetry, and an encyclopædic listings section of virtually everything to do with poetry in the capital and elsewhere in the UK.

The Poetry School

1a Jewel Road, London E17 4QU
☎020 8223 0401 Fax 020 8223 0401
Email programme@poetryschool.com
Website www.poetryschool.com

Administrator *Jacqueline Gabbitas*

Funded by London Arts, the School offers a wide range of courses and workshops on writing and reading poetry and is open to anyone regardless of experience or formal qualifications. Tutors include Graham Fawcett, Stephen Knight, Peter Jay, Selima Hill, Carole Satyamurti and Mimi Khalvati. The School provides a forum for practitioners to share experiences, develop skills and extend appreciation of the traditional and innovative aspects of their art. There are masterclasses on the Poet's Method, with visiting poets such as Marilyn Hacker, Jorie Graham, Gillian Clarke and Don Paterson.

The Poetry Society

22 Betterton Street, London WC2H 9BX
☎020 7240 9881/Membership Dept: 020 7384 3261 Fax 020 7240 4818
Email info@poetrysociety.org.uk
Website www.poetrysociety.org.us

Chair *Richard Price*
Director *Jules Mann*

FOUNDED in 1909 which ought to make it venerable, the Society exists to help poets and poetry thrive in Britain. In the past decade it has undergone a renaissance, reaching out from its Covent Garden base to promote the national health of poetry in a range of imaginative ways. Membership costs £35 for individuals. *Poetry News* membership is £15. Current activities include:

● Quarterly, redesigned magazine of new verse, views and criticism, *Poetry Review*.
● Quarterly newsletter, *Poetry News*.

- Promotions, events and cooperation with Britain's many literature festivals, poetry venues and poetry publishers.
- Competitions and awards, including the annual **National Poetry Competition** with a £5000 first prize.
- A manuscript diagnosis service, *The Poetry Prescription*, which gives detailed reports on submissions. Reduced rates for members.
- Seminars, fact sheets, training courses, ideas packs.
- Provides information and advice, publishes books, posters and resources for schools and libraries. Education membership costs £50/£30 which includes free poetry anthologies, lesson plans and a subscription to Poems on the Underground. Publications include *The Poetry Book For Primary Schools* and *Jumpstart Poetry for the Secondary School*, colourful poetry posters for Keystages 1, 2, 3 and 4. Many of Britain's most popular poets – including Michael Rosen, Roger McGough and Jackie Kay – contribute, offering advice and inspiration. (The Society's education website is at www.poetryclass.net)
- The Poetry Café serving snacks and drinks to members, friends and guests, part of The Poetry Place, a venue for many poetry activities – readings, poetry clinic, workshops and poetry launches. This space is available for bookings (☎020 7420 9887).

Recent projects include *Poetry Places*, a national programme of residencies, placements and projects.

Point

Ithaca, Apdo. 125, E–03590 Altea, Spain
☎00 34 96 584 2350
Fax 00 34 96 688 2767
Email elpoeta@point-editions.com
Website www.point-editions.com
Also at: Schapenstraat 157, B–1750 Lennik, Belgium
Director *Germain Droogenbroodt*

FOUNDED as POetry INTernational in 1984, Point is based in Spain and Belgium. A multilingual publisher of contemporary verse from *established* poets, the organisation has brought out more than 60 titles in at least eight languages, including English. Editions run the original work alongside a verse translation into Dutch made in cooperation with the poet. The organisation's website features the world's best-known and unknown poets in English, Spanish and Dutch. Point also co-organises an annual international poetry festival.

Scottish Poetry Library

5 Crichton's Close, Canongate, Edinburgh EH8 8DT
☎0131 557 2876
Email inquiries@spl.org.uk
Website www.spl.org.uk
Director *Robyn Marsack*

A comprehensive reference and lending collection of work by Scottish poets in Gaelic, Scots and English, plus the work of British and international poets. Stock includes books, tapes, videos, news cuttings and magazines. Borrowing is free to all. Services include a postal lending scheme, for which there is a small fee, a mobile library that can visit schools and other centres by arrangement, exhibitions, bibliographies, publications, information and promotion in the field of poetry. Also available is an online catalogue and computer index to poetry and poetry periodicals. The membership scheme costs £20 annually. Members receive a newsletter and other benefits and support the library.

Second Light

9 Greendale Close, London SE22 8TG
Email dilys_wood@lineone.net
Director *Dilys Wood*

A network of over 300 women poets, established and lesser known, aged from late thirties upwards. Aims to develop and promote women's poetry especially among those who began writing or publishing poetry late. *Publishes* a newsletter, runs an annual poetry competition, holds residential workshops, readings and cooperates with established poetry publishers to produce anthologies of women's work.

Slam! Productions

20 Coxwell Street, Cirencester, Gloucestershire GL7 2BH
☎01285 640470
Email slam@scarum.freeserve.co.uk
Website www.author.co.uk/slam
Directors *Marcus Moore, Sara-Jane Arbury*

'Spoken word, written word, anywhere, everywhere' with two writers who put a positive charge in live literature by organising quirky and original events such as Slam!Fests!, Spontaneity Days and Living Room Poetry performances, hosting UK poetry slams and running *word*shops for schools and adults. Also produce *SPIEL*, a monthly e-mail newsletter. Specialist in breathing new life into literature.

Survivors' Poetry

Diorama Arts Centre, 34 Osnaburgh Street,
London NW1 3ND
☎020 7916 5317 Fax 020 7916 0830
Email survivors@survivorspoetry.org.uk

A unique national literature organisation promoting poetry by survivors of mental distress through workshops, readings and performances to audiences all over the UK. It was FOUNDED in 1991 by four poets with first-hand experience of the mental health system. Survivors' community outreach work provides training and performance workshops and publishing projects. *Survivors* work with those who have survived mental distress and those who empathise with their experience.

Survivors' Poetry Scotland

4 C4 Templeton Centre, 62 Templeton Street, Glasgow G40 1DA
☎0141 556 4554 Fax 0141 400 8442
Email sps@spscot.co.uk
Website www.spscot.co.uk

Project Manager *Charlotte Barker*
Administrator *Catherine Davidson*
Managing Editor *Gerry Loose*

Promotes poetry by suvivors of mental distress through a poetry magazine, *Nomad*, which appears three times a year; writing workshops and performance evenings.

Tŷ Newydd

Llanystumdwy, Cricieth, Gwynedd LL52 0LW
☎01766 522811 Fax 01766 523095
Email tynewydd@dial.pipex.com

Website www.tynewydd.org
Director *Sally Baker*

Run by the Taliesin Trust, an independent, Arvon-style residential writers centre established in the one-time home of Lloyd George in North Wales. The programme (in both Welsh and English) has a regular poetry content. (See also **Writers' Courses, Circles and Workshops**.) Fees start at £100 for weekends and £320 for week-long courses. Among the many tutors to-date have been: Gillian Clarke, U.A. Fanthorpe, Roger McGough, Carol Ann Duffy, Liz Lochhead, Peter Finch and Paul Henry. Send for the centre's descriptive leaflets and programme of courses.

The Virtual Writing School

Manchester Metropolitan University, Dept. of English, Geoffrey Manton Building, Rosamond Street West, off Oxford Road, Manchester M15 6LL
☎0161 247 1735
Email h.watson@mmu.ac.uk
Website www.mmu.ac.uk/h-ss/eng

Contact *Heather Watson*

Manchester Metropolitan University's creative writing courses under Michael Schmidt (see also **Writers' Courses, Circles and Workshops**) offer a virtual poetry strand with tutors Simon Armitage, Carol Ann Duffy, Sophie Hannah, Michael Schmidt, Jeffrey Wainwright and others. The qualification is a MA/PgDip. Enquire early as places are strictly limited. The school also offers virtual novel writing.

Small Presses

Aard Press
c/o Aardverx, 31 Mountearl Gardens, London
SW16 2NL
Managing Editors *D. Jarvis, Dawn Redwood*
FOUNDED 1971. *Publishes* artists' bookworks,
experimental/visual poetry, 'zines, eonist literature, topographics, ephemera and international mail-art documentation. Very small
editions. No unsolicited material or proposals.
Royalties not paid. No sale-or-return deals.

Abbey Press
Abbey Grammar School, Courtenay Hill,
Newry, Co. Down BT34 2ED
☎028 3026 3142 Fax 028 3026 2514
Also at: 12 The Pines, Jordanstown,
Newtonabbey, Co. Antrim BT37 0SE
☎028 9086 0230
Editor *Adrian Rice*
Administrator *Mel McMahon*
FOUNDED in 1997, Abbey Press is a fast grow-
ing literary publisher with a strong poetry list.
Also *publishes* biography, memoirs, fiction, his-
tory, politics, Irish language, academic and art.
Lists currently full.

AK Press/AKA Books
PO Box 12766, Edinburgh EH8 9YE
☎0131 555 5165 Fax 0131 555 5215
Email ak@akedin.demon.co.uk
Website www.akuk.com
Managing Editor *Alexis McKay*
AK Press grew out of the activities of AK
Distribution which distributes a wide range of
radical (anarchist, feminist, etc.) literature
(books, pamphlets, periodicals, magazines),
both fiction and non-fiction. *Publishes* anarchist
politics and history, situationism in both book
and pamphlet form. About 12 titles a year.
Proposals and synopses welcome if they fall
within AK's specific areas of interest.
Royalties paid.

Akros Publications
33 Lady Nairn Avenue, Kirkcaldy, Fife
KY1 2AW
☎01592 651522
Publisher *Duncan Glen*

FOUNDED 1965. *Publishes* poetry collections,
pamphlets and anthologies; literary essays and
studies; local histories. About 10 titles a year.
Also publishes *Z20* poetry magazine No unsolicited mss. No fiction.
Royalties paid twice-yearly.

Allardyce, Barnett, Publishers
14 Mount Street, Lewes, East Sussex BN7 1HL
☎01273 479393 Fax 01273 479393
Website www.abar.net
Publisher *Fiona Allardyce*
Managing Editor *Anthony Barnett*
FOUNDED 1981. *Publishes* art, literature and
music. About 3 titles a year. IMPRINT **Allardyce
Book**. Unsolicited mss and synopses cannot be
considered.

Alphard Press
See **ignotus press**

Anglo-Saxon Books
Frithgarth, Thetford Forest Park, Hockwold
cum Wilton, Norfolk IP26 4NQ
☎01842 828430 Fax 01842 828332
Email tony@asbooks.co.uk
Website www.asbooks.co.uk
Managing Editor *Tony Linsell*
FOUNDED 1990 to promote a greater awareness
of and interest in early English history, lan-
guage and culture. *Publishes* Anglo-Saxon his-
tory, culture, language. About 5 titles a year.
Please phone before sending mss.
Royalties paid at standard rate.

Apex Publishing Ltd
PO Box 7445, Colchester, Essex CO4 9UA
☎0870 242 0938 Fax 0870 242 0938
Email enquiry@apexpublishing.co.uk
Website www.apexpublishing.co.uk
Managing Editor *Susan Kidby*
FOUNDED 2002. Subsidy publishing company
for unknown and established authors. *Publishes*
poetry, self-help, non-fiction, fiction, sci-fi, history, humour, fine art, art history, education and
textbooks, economics, crime, children's books,
biography, autobiography, academic, women's
interests, medical and philosophy. 4 titles in
2002. Welcomes unsolicited mss, synopses and

ideas for books. Approach in writing to the address above.

Royalties paid.

Archive Publishing

Wren Cottage, Ford Lane, Morton,
Lincolnshire PE10 0RQ
☎01778 571444 Fax 01778 571494
Website www.archivepublishing.co.uk

Managing Editor *Ian Thorp*

FOUNDED 2002. *Publishes* new, existing (out of print) or arcane material in the following areas: mind, body and spirit; transpersonal psychology; mysticism; spirituality; health & healing; Eastern and Western traditions; astrology and landscape; life guidance; science and transformation; the centre, self or soul within. 10 titles in 2003. Welcomes unsolicited synopses and ideas for books. Approach by telephone or e-mail in the first instance.

Royalties negotiable based on sales.

Athelney

1 Providence Street, King's Lynn, Norfolk
PE30 5ET Fax 01842 828332

Managing Editor *John Cooper*

FOUNDED 2000. *Publishes* nationalism in general; English nationalism in particular. Unsolicited outlines/contents page/first chapter welcome. Please enclose return postage.

Royalties paid at standard rate.

M.&M. Baldwin

24 High Street, Cleobury Mortimer,
Kidderminster DY14 8BY
☎01299 270110 Fax 01299 270110
Email mb@mbaldwin.free-online.co.uk

Managing Editor *Dr Mark Baldwin*

FOUNDED 1978. *Publishes* local interest/history, WW2 codebreaking and inland waterways books. Up to 5 titles a year. Unsolicited mss, synopses and ideas for books welcome (not general fiction).

Royalties paid.

Bardon Enterprises

6 Winter Road, Southsea, Hampshire
PO4 9BT
☎07752 873831 Fax 023 9287 4900
Email info@bardon-enterprises.co.uk
Website www.bardon-enterprises.co.uk

Managing Director *W.B. Henshaw*

FOUNDED 1996. *Publishes* music, art, biography, poetry, academic books and sheet music. Total publications: 22 books; 200 pieces of music.

Unsolicited mss, synopses and ideas welcome. Short run editions. 'Cost free publishing.'

BB Books

See entry under **Poetry Presses**

The Better Book Company Ltd

Warblington Lodge, The Gardens,
Warblington, Near Havant, Hampshire
PO9 2XH
☎023 9248 1160 Fax 023 9249 2819
Email editors@better-book.co.uk

Managing Editor *James Jude Garvey*

FOUNDED 1996. *Publishes* fiction, histories, memoirs, poetry, religious, scientific, company histories. 80 titles in 2002. Offers a complete editorial, design, printing and marketing service to self-publishing authors in all genre. A free booklet, *A Complete Guide to Self-Publishing* is available on request.

Between the Lines

9 Woodstock Road, London N4 3ET
☎020 8374 5526 Fax 020 8374 5736
Email btluk@aol.com
Website www.interviews-with-poets.com

Editorial Board *Peter Dale, Philip Hoy,*
J.D. McClatchy

FOUNDED 1998. *Publishes* extended interviews with leading contemporary poets. To-date, twelve volumes published (featuring W.D. Snodgrass, Michael Hamburger, Anthony Thwaite, Anthony Hecht, Donald Hall, Thom Gunn, Richard Wilbur, Seamus Heaney, Donald Justice, Ian Hamilton, Charles Simic and John Ashberry). Poets to be featured in forthcoming volumes include Mark Strand and Peter Dale. Each volume includes a career sketch, a comprehensive bibliography, a representative selection from the poets' critics and reviewers, an uncollected poem and photograph. A new series featuring three poets to a volume will be launched in 2003. The first two will feature Dana Gioia, Dick Davies, Timothy Steele, Rachel Hadas, Michael Donaghy and John Burnside.

The Bewildered Publishing Company Ltd

Argoed Hall, Tregaron, Ceredigion SY25 6JR
☎01974 298070 Fax 01974 298708
Email argoed.hall@btinternet.com

Publisher *John Wilson*

FOUNDED in 1999 'to provide a direct route to the book market for authors with an uncon-

ventional approach to writing and publishing'. *Publishes* humorous paperbacks. No unsolicited material; initial inquiry by telephone, e-mail or letter.
Royalties not paid.

Big Engine Co Ltd
PO Box 185, Abingdon, Oxfordshire OX14 1GR
☎01235 204011 Fax 01235 204012
Email info@bigengine.co.uk
Website www.bigengine.co.uk
Managing Editor *Ben Jeapes*

FOUNDED 2000 'to give new writers exposure and to re-issue deserving out of print titles'. *Publishes* science fiction and fantasy. 6 titles in 2002. No unsolicited mss. Synopses and ideas welcome by letter or e-mail.
Royalties paid twice-yearly

Black Cat Books
See **Neil Miller Publications**

BlackAmber Books Ltd
PO Box 10812, London SW7 4ZG
☎020 7373 3178 Fax 020 7373 3178
Email information@blackamber.com
Website www.blackamber.com
Publisher *Rosemarie Hudson*

FOUNDED 1998. Home of 'the best writing emanating from the vibrant, mostly young, immigrant-descended population'. A collection point for British and European Black and Asian literature. 'Gives an outlet for the creative voice of European racial minorities, demonstrating their strengths and place in a multicultural world.'

The Book Castle
12 Church Street, Dunstable, Bedfordshire LU5 4RU
☎01582 605670 Fax 01582 662431
Email bc@book-castle.co.uk
Website www.book-castle.co.uk
Managing Editor *Paul Bowes*

FOUNDED 1986. *Publishes* non-fiction of local interest (Bedfordshire, Hertfordshire, Buckinghamshire, Oxfordshire, Northamptonshire, the Chilterns). 12 titles a year. About 100 titles in print. Unsolicited mss, synopses and ideas for books welcome.
Royalties paid.

Book-in-Hand Ltd
20 Shepherds Hill, London N6 5AH
☎020 8341 7650 Fax 020 8341 7650

Contact *Ann Kritzinger*

Print production service for self-publishers. Includes design and editing suggestions to give customers a greater chance of selling in the open market.

Bookmarque Publishing
26 Cotswold Close, Minster Lovell, Oxfordshire OX29 0SX
☎01993 775179
Email john@bookmarque.fsbusiness.co.uk
Managing Editor *John Rose*

FOUNDED 1987. Publishing business with aim of filling gaps in motoring history of which it is said 'there are many'. *Publishes* motoring history, motor sport and 'general' titles. About 8 titles a year. All design and typesetting of books done in-house. Unsolicited mss and synopses welcome on motoring titles. S.a.e. required for reply or return of material or for advice on publishing your work.
Royalties paid.

Brantwood Books
PO Box 144, Orpington, Kent BR6 6LZ
☎01689 833117 Fax 01689 833117
Email philip45other@yahoo.co.uk
Editor *Philip Turner*

FOUNDED 1997. *Publishes* highly illustrated, limited edition print runs of specialist cinema titles, ranging from Russian cinema architecture to 36-page illustrated guides to British, North American and worldwide cinema circuit histories.

DIVISIONS **Brantwood Books** and **Outline Publications** UK/US cinema circuit and film studio histories; **Brantwood Biographical** Biographies of movie moguls, producers and directors; **Brantwood Miniature Life** Series of outline biographies of popular movie stars; **Brantwood Technical** Screen, film and camera/projection topics. Consideration given to ideas which can be adapted to a 32-page format; initial approach in writing, please.

Brilliant Publications
1 Church View, Sparrow Hall Farm, Edlesborough, Dunstable, Bedfordshire LU6 2ES
☎01525 229720 Fax 01525 229725
Email sales@brilliantpublications.co.uk
Website www.brilliantpublications.co.uk
Publisher *Priscilla Hannaford*

FOUNDED 1993. *Publishes* resource books for teachers, parents and others working with 0–13-

year-olds. About 10–15 titles a year. SERIES *How to Dazzle at ...* (9–13-year-olds, special needs); *How to be Brilliant at ...* (7–11-year-olds); *How to Sparkle at ...* (5–7-year-olds); *Activities* (3–5-year-olds). Submit synopsis and sample pages in the first instance. All the books have black and white insides and many can be photocopied. Potential authors are strongly advised to look at the format of existing books before submitting synopses.

Royalties paid twice-yearly.

The Brodie Press

Email thebrodiepress@hotmail.com
Website www.thebrodiepress.co.uk

Managing Editors *Tom Sperlinger, Hannah Sheppard, James Bainbridge, Rhiannon Davies*

FOUNDED 2002. *Publishes* poetry, literary fiction and anthologies. TITLE *The Liver Birds Anthology. The Brodie Poets* Series launched in 2003. Send synopses and proposals by e-mail in the first instance.

Cambridge Publishing and Printing Ltd

PO Box 163, SG14 1XN
☎0845 644 3859 Fax 0709 200 2268
Email info@cambridgeprinting.com
Website www.cambridgeprinting.com

Managing Director *Roland Miller*
Editorial Head *Fred Foot*

FOUNDED 2000. *Publishes* mainly but not exclusively, autobiographies, academic, children's, fiction, film and tv, health and fitness, history, humanities and social sciences, non-fiction, poetry, popular reference science fiction and fantasy, travel and tourism, women's issues. About 20 titles a year. 25 years knowledge of producing Talking Tapes/CDs. Publishers of more than 100 e-books. Unsolicited mss, synopses and ideas welcome if accompanied by s.a.e.

Royalties paid annually.

Charlewood Press

7 Weavers Place, Chandlers Ford, Eastleigh, Hampshire SO53 1TU
☎023 8026 1192 Email gponting@clara.net
Website www.home.clara.net/gponting/index-page11.html

Managing Editors *Gerald Ponting, Anthony Light*

FOUNDED 1987. Publishes local history books and walks booklets on Hampshire and adjacent counties, especially around the Fordingbridge area. Mss in this field considered.

Chrysalis Press

7 Lower Ladyes Hills, Kenilworth, Warwickshire CV8 2GN
☎01926 855223 Fax 01926 748202
Email brimagb@netscape.net

Managing Editor *Brian Boyd*

FOUNDED 1994. *Publishes* fiction, literary criticism and biography. No unsolicited mss.

Royalties paid.

CK Publishing

151 Brookfield Road, Cheadle, Cheshire SK8 1EY
☎0161 491 6074
Email editor@ckpublishing.co.uk
Website www.ckpublishing.co.uk

Managing Editor *Calum Kerr*

Publishes novels. Unsolicited mss welcome; no synopses or ideas. S.a.e. essential.

Royalties paid.

Claridge Press

Horsell's Farmhouse, Sunday Hill, Brinkworth, Wiltshire SN15 5AS
☎01666 510327 Fax 01666 510607

Managing Editor *Sophie Jeffreys*

FOUNDED 1987. *Publishes* non-fiction, philosophy, history and politics. 3 titles in 2002. No unsolicited mss; synopses and ideas for books welcome. Approach in writing.

Royalties paid.

Clinamen Press Ltd

Unit B, Aldow Enterprise Park, Blackett Street, Manchester M12 6AE
☎0161 272 7639 Fax 0161 272 6807
Email benstebbing@clinamen.net
Website www.clinamen.co.uk

Director *Ben Stebbing*

FOUNDED 1998. *Publishes* philosophy, literary criticism, cultural studies, photography, travel literature, fiction and art theory. No unsolicited mss; two sample chapters with covering letter welcome. See also **the-phone-book.com** under **Electronic Publishing & Other Services**.

CNP Publications
See **Lyfrow Trelyspen**

Columbia Publishing Wales Limited

Glen More, 6 Cwrt y Camden, Brecon, Powys LD3 7RR
☎01874 625270 Fax 01874 625270
Email dng@columbiawales.fsnet.co.uk

Website www.columbiapublishing.co.uk
Managing Editor *Dafydd Gittins*
FOUNDED 2000. *Publishes* fiction and non-fiction – books, film and music (mainly pop and rock). Subjects suitable for film or television. 2 titles in 2002. No unsolicited mss. Synopses and ideas welcome; approach by letter or e-mail in the first instance.
Royalties paid.

Copperfield Books
Hillbrook House, Lyncombe Vale Road, Bath BA2 4LS
☎01225 442835 Fax 01225 319755
Email sales@www.darcybook.com
Website www.darcybook.com
Director *Jean Brushfield*
Publishes paperback fiction and general non-fiction. No unsolicited mss; 'we only commission books to our own specification'.

The Cosmic Elk
68 Elsham Crescent, Lincoln LN6 3YS
☎01522 820922
Email cosmicelk@zoom.co.uk
Website pages.zoom.co.uk/cosmicelk/cosmicelk.htm
Contact *Heather Hobden*
FOUNDED 1988. *Publishes* easily updated books on science, history and the history of science. Websites designed and maintained, with or without associated printed books. 'New authors always welcome. Full information can be found on our website or contact by e-mail.'

Crescent Moon Publishing and Joe's Press
PO Box 393, Maidstone, Kent ME14 5XU
☎01622 729593
Email jrobinson@crescentmoon.org.uk
Website www.crescentmoon.org.uk
Managing Editor *Jeremy Robinson*
FOUNDED 1988 to publish critical studies of figures such as D.H. Lawrence, Thomas Hardy, André Gide, Walt Disney, Rilke, Leonardo da Vinci, Mark Rothko, C.P. Cavafy and Hélène Cixous. *Publishes* literature, criticism, media, art, feminism, painting, poetry, travel, guidebooks, cinema and some fiction. Literary magazine, *Passion*, launched February 1994. Quarterly. *Pagan America*, twice-yearly anthology of American poetry. About 15–20 titles per year. Do not send whole mss. Unsolicited synopses and ideas welcome but approach in writing first and send an s.a.e. *Royalties* negotiable.

Critical Vision
See **Headpress**

Crossbridge Books
345 Old Birmingham Road, Bromsgrove B60 1NX
☎0121 447 7897 Fax 0121 445 1063
Email crossbridgebooks@btinternet.com
Website www.crossbridgebooks.com
Managing Director *Eileen Mohr*
FOUNDED 1995. *Publishes* Christian books for adults and children. 1–2 titles a year including Trevor Dearing's latest books. No unsolicited mss; telephone in the first instance. No New Age or books not biblically Christian. IMPRINT **Mohr Books**.
Royalties paid twice-yearly.

Crown House Publishing
Crown Buildings, Bancyfelin, Carmarthen SA33 5ND
☎01267 211345 Fax 01267 211882
Email books@crownhouse.co.uk
Website www.crownhouse.co.uk
Managing Director *David Bowman*
Acquisitions Editor *Helen Kinsey*
FOUNDED 1998. *Publishes* titles in the areas of psychology, education, Neuro-Linguistic Programming (NLP), personal growth, therapy, business, health and hypnosis. The aim of our list is to both demystify the latest psychological advances, particularly in the fields of NLP and hypnosis. Crown House provide professional therapists, consultants and trainers with books detailing the latest cutting-edge developments in their field. Approx. 20 titles a year.
Royalties paid twice-yearly.

Culva House Publications
10 The Carrs, Sleights, Whitby, North Yorkshire YO21 1RR
☎01947 810819
Email alan@culvahouse.co.uk
Website www.culvahouse.co.uk
Managing Editor *Alan Whitworth*
FOUNDED in 1986 as a part-time self-publishing venture and grew into a full-time business in 2000. *Publishes* architecture and local history; biography. Unsolicited material welcome; approach by letter or e-mail.
Royalties paid.

Day Books
Orchard Piece, Crawborough, Charlbury, Oxfordshire OX7 3TX

☎01608 811196 Fax 01608 811196
Email diaries@day-books.com
Website www.day-books.com
Managing Editor *James Sanderson*

FOUNDED in 1997 to *publish* a series of great diaries from around the world, one of the most recent being *Inside Stalin's Russia*. Unsolicited mss, synopses and ideas welcome. Include return postage if return of material is required.

Delancey Press Ltd
4 Delancey Passage, London NW1 7NN
☎020 7387 3544 Fax 020 7383 5314
Email delanceypress@aol.com
Website www.delanceypress.com
Managing Editor *Tatiana von Saxe Wilson*

FOUNDED 2000. *Publishes* fiction, children's and humour. Not interested in academic books. Welcomes unsolicited mss, synopses and ideas sent by mail. Overseas subsidiaries in association with **The Book Guild Ltd**.
  Royalties paid twice-yearly.

Diagonal
See **Headpress**

The Dragonby Press
15 High Street, Dragonby, Scunthorpe, North Lincolnshire DN15 0BE
☎01724 840645 Email rah.williams@virgin.net
Website freespace.virgin.net/rah.williams/
Managing Editor *Richard Williams*

FOUNDED 1987 to publish affordable bibliography for reader, collector and dealer. About 3 titles a year. Unsolicited mss, synopses and ideas welcome for bibliographical projects only.
  Royalties paid.

Dramatic Lines
PO Box 201, Twickenham TW2 5RQ
☎020 8296 9502 Fax 020 8296 9503
Email mail@dramaticlinespublishers.co.uk
Website www.dramaticlines.co.uk
Managing Editor *John Nicholas*

FOUNDED to promote drama for young people. Publications with a wide variety of theatrical applications including classroom use and school assemblies, drama examinations, auditions, festivals, theatre group performance and musicals. Unsolicited drama-related mss, proposals and synopses welcome; enclose s.a.e.
  Royalties paid.

Education Now Publishing Cooperative Ltd
113 Arundel Drive, Bramcote Hills, Nottingham NG9 3FQ
☎0115 925 7261 Fax 0115 925 7261
Website www.educationnow.gn.apc.org
Managing Editors *Dr Roland Meighan,*
  Philip Toogood

A non-profit research and writing group set up in reaction to 'the totalitarian tendencies of the 1988 Education Act'. Its aim is to widen the terms of the debate about education and its choices. *Publishes* reports on positive educational initiatives such as flexi-schooling, mini-schooling, small schooling, home-based education and democratic schooling. 4–5 titles a year. No unsolicited mss or ideas. Enquiries only.
  Royalties generally not paid.

Educational Heretics Press
113 Arundel Drive, Bramcote Hills, Nottingham NG9 3FQ
☎0115 925 7261 Fax 0115 925 7261
Website www.edheretics.gn.apc.org
Directors *Janet & Roland Meighan*

Non-profit venture which aims to question the dogmas of schooling in particular and education in general, and establish the logistics of the next learning system. No unsolicited material. Enquiries only.
  Royalties not paid but under review.

EKO Publishing
Nant Yr Hafod Cottage, Llandegla, Wrexham, Denbighshire LL11 3BG
☎01978 790442
Email indesigneko@aol.com
Managing Editor *Brian W. Burnett*

FOUNDED 1996 to publish modern, lively books and magazines in and about Esperanto. Unsolicited mss, synopses and ideas welcome.
  Royalties paid.

Enable Enterprises
PO Box 1974, Coventry CV3 1YF
☎0800 358 8484 Fax 0870 133 23347
Email writers@enableenterprises.com
Website www.enableenterprises.com
Managing Director *Simon Stevens*

Enable Enterprises provides a wide range of accessibilty and disability services including publications on relevant issues. It welcomes unsolicited material related to accessibility and disability issues.

Fand Music Press

The Barony, 16 Sandringham Road,
Petersfield, Hampshire GU32 2AA
☎01730 267341 Fax 01730 267341
Email Paul@fandmusic.com
Website www.fandmusic.com

Managing Editor *Peter Thompson*

FOUNDED in 1989 as a sheet music publisher,
Fand Music Press has expanded its range to
include CD recordings and books on music.
Recently started publishing poetry and short
stories. 10 titles a year. No unsolicited mss.
Write with ideas in the first instance.

Feather Books

PO Box 438, Shrewsbury, Shropshire
SY3 0WN
☎01743 872177 Fax 01743 872177
Email john@waddysweb.freeuk.com
Website www.waddysweb.freeuk.com

Managing Director *Rev. John Waddington-Feather*

Directors *David Grundy, Tony Reavill*

FOUNDED 1980 to publish writers' group work.
All material has a strong Christian ethos. *Publishes*
poetry (mainly, but not exclusively, religious);
Christian mystery novels (the Revd. D.I. Blake
Hartley series); Christian children's novels; seasonal poetry collections and *The Poetry Church*
quarterly magazine. 20 titles a year. Produces
poetry, drama and music CD/cassettes. No
unsolicited mss, synopses or ideas. All correspondence to include s.a.e., please.

Fern House

19 High Street, Haddenham, Ely,
Cambridgeshire CB6 3XA
☎01353 740222
Email info@fernhouse.com
Website www.fernhouse.com

Managing Editor *Rodney Dale*

FOUNDED 1995. *Publishes* non-fiction with a
bias towards biography, reference and technology. 2 titles in 2002. Unsolicited synopses and
ideas 'are unlikely to strike a chord'. Please
avoid sending large e-mail attachments.
Royalties paid.

Five Leaves Publications

PO Box 81, Nottingham NG5 4ER
☎0115 969 3597
Email info@fiveleaves.co.uk
Website www.fiveleaves.co.uk

Contact *Ross Bradshaw*

FOUNDED 1995 (taking over the publishing
programme of Mushroom Bookshop), producing 6–8 titles a year. *Publishes* fiction, poetry,
social history, politics and Jewish interest.
Titles normally commissioned.
Royalties and fees paid.

Flambard

Stable Cottage, East Fourstones, Hexham,
Northumberland NE47 5DX
☎01434 674360 Fax 01434 674178
Website www.flambardpress.co.uk

Managing Editor *Peter Lewis*

FOUNDED 1990. *Publishes* poetry and literary
fiction including crime. 8 titles in 2002.
Welcomes unsolicted mss but essential to send
preliminary letter with details of author and
either a sample of 10 poems or a synopsis plus
2–3 chapters. *Royalties* paid.

Flame Books Ltd

PO Box 2177, Stafford ST17 4WJ
Email submit@flamebooks.com
Website www.flamebooks.com

FOUNDED 2003. *Publishes* literary fiction, both
novels and short stories for sale solely through
their website. 5 titles planned for 2003. No
unsolicited synopses or ideas but mss welcome
– see website for further information.
Royalties paid; 'at least 10% of retail price'.

Forth Naturalist & Historian

University of Stirling, Stirling FK9 4LA
☎01259 215091 Fax 01786 464994
Email lindsay.corbett@stir.ac.uk
Website www.stir.ac.uk/departments/natural
sciences/Forth_naturalist/index.htm

Also at: 30 Dunmar Drive, Alloa,
Clackmannanshire FK10 2EH

Honorary Secretary *Lindsay Corbett*

FOUNDED 1975 by the collaboration of Stirling
University members and the Central Regional
Council to promote interests and publications
on central Scotland. Aims to provide a 'valuable local studies educational resource for mid-
Scotland schools, libraries and people'. Runs an
annual symposium: Man and the Landscape
('Weather/Climate – living with change' in
2002). *Publishes* naturalist, historical and environmental studies and maps, including 1890s
maps 25″ to the mile – 24 of central Scotland
areas/places with historical notes. Over 20
selected papers from the annual *The Forth
Naturalist & Historian* (Vol. 25 in 2002) are
published in pamphlet form. Welcomes papers,
mss and ideas relevant to central Scotland.
Royalties not paid.

Foxbury Press
1 Step Terrace, Winchester, Hampshire
SO22 5BW
☎01962 864037
Managing Editor *Robert Cross*
FOUNDED in 1982 as part of St Paul's
Bibliographies which was subsequently sold to
Oak Knoll Press. *Publishes* bibliography and
history. 2 titles in 2002. Welcomes synopses
and ideas for books in the subject areas listed
above; approach by mail.
Royalties paid twice-yearly.

Frontier Publishing
Windetts, Kirstead, Norfolk NR15 1EG
☎01508 558174
Email frontier.pub@macunlimited.net
Website www.frontierpublishing.co.uk
Managing Editor *John Black*
FOUNDED 1983. *Publishes* travel, photography,
sculptural history and literature. 2–3 titles a
year. No unsolicited mss; synopses and ideas
welcome.
Royalties paid.

Galactic Central Publications
Imladris, 25A Copgrove Road, Leeds, West
Yorkshire LS8 2SP
Email philsp@compuserve.com
Website www.philsp.com
Managing Editor *Phil Stephensen-Payne*
FOUNDED 1982 in the US. *Publishes* science fic-
tion bibliographies. About 4 titles a year. All
new publications originate in the UK.
Unsolicited mss, synopses and ideas welcome.

Glosa Education Organisation
PO Box 18, Richmond, Surrey TW9 2GE
Website www.glosa.org
Managing Editor *Wendy Ashby*
FOUNDED 1981. *Publishes* textbooks, dictionar-
ies and translations for the teaching, speaking
and promotion of Glosa (an international, aux-
iliary language); also a newsletter, *Plu Glosa
Nota*, and journal, *PGN*. Unsolicited mss and
ideas for Glosa books welcome.

Grant Books
The Coach House, New Road, Cutnall
Green, Droitwich, Worcestershire WR9 0PQ
☎01299 851588 Fax 01299 851446
Email golf@grantbooks.co.uk
Website www.grantbooks.co.uk
Managing Editor *H.R.J. Grant*

FOUNDED 1978. *Publishes* golf-related titles only:
course architecture, history, biography, etc., but
no instructional material. New titles and old,
plus limited editions. About 6 titles a year.
Unsolicited mss, synopses and ideas welcome.
Royalties paid.

Great Northern Publishing
PO Box 202, Scarborough, North Yorkshire
YO11 3GE
☎01723 581329 Fax 01723 581329
Email books@greatnorthernpublishing.co.uk
Website www.greatnorthernpublishing.co.uk
Senior Editor *Diane Crowther*
Small, independent, award-winning, family-
owned company FOUNDED in 1999. Publishers
of books, magazines and journals. Also provides full book and magazine production
services to individuals, businesses, charities,
museums and other small publishers. *Publishes*
non-fiction (mainly military), and occasionally
fiction in most genres but no romance, religious, political, feminist, new-age, medical or
children's books. Publishers of *The Great War*
and *Jade* (erotic art and literature) magazines.
Mail order and Internet-based bookshop stock-
ing selected titles alongside its own. Website
gives submission guidelines and current publishing requirements. No unsolicited mss; send
letter in the first instance.
Royalties paid twice-yearly.

Grevatt & Grevatt
9 Rectory Drive, Newcastle upon Tyne
NE3 1XT
Email grevatt@softhome.net
Website grevatt-grevatt.freeservers.com/
   index.htm
Chairman/Editorial Head *Dr S.Y. Killingley*
FOUNDED 1981. Alternative publisher of works
not normally commercially viable. Three books
have appeared with financial backing from professional bodies. *Publishes* academic titles and
conference reports, particularly language, linguistics and religious studies. Some poetry also. No
unsolicited mss. Synopses and ideas should be
accompanied by s.a.e. Offers typesetting, editing
and other services; s.a.e. with enquiries.
Royalties paid annually (after first 500 copies).

GSSE
11 Malford Grove, Gilwern, Abergavenny,
Monmouthshire NP7 0RN
☎01873 830872
Email GSSE@zoo.co.uk
Website www.gsse.org.uk

Owner/Manager *David P. Bosworth*

Publishes books and booklets describing classroom practice (at all levels of education and training). Ideas welcome – particularly from practising teachers, lecturers and trainers describing how they use technology in their teaching.
Royalties paid by arrangement.

Happy House
3b Castledown Avenue, Hastings, East Sussex TN34 3RJ
☎01424 434778
Email HappyHouse@themail.co.uk

FOUNDED 1992 as a self-publishing venture for a Dave Arnold/Martin Honeysett collaboration of poetry and cartoons.

Haunted Library
Flat 1, 36 Hamilton Street, Hoole, Chester, Cheshire CH2 3JQ
☎01244 313685 Fax 01244 313685
Email pardos@globalnet.co.uk
Website www.users.globalnet.co.uk/~pardos/GS.html

Managing Editor *Rosemary Pardoe*

FOUNDED 1979. *Publishes* the *Ghosts and Scholars M.R. James Newsletter* two or three times a year, featuring articles, news and reviews (no fiction).
Royalties not paid.

Headpress
40 Rossall Avenue, Radcliffe, Manchester M26 1JD
☎0161 796 1935 Fax 0161 796 1935
Email info.headpress@zen.co.uk
Website www.headpress.com

Managing Editor *David Kerekes*

FOUNDED 1991. *Publishes Headpress* journal, devoted to the strange and esoteric, and *Creeping Flesh*, a journal devoted to horror and fantasy cinema. No fiction or poetry. IMPRINTS **Critical Vision**; **Diagonal** Unsolicited material welcome; send letter and outline in the first instance.
Royalties and flat fees paid.

Heart of Albion Press
2 Cross Hill Close, Wymeswold, Loughborough, Leicestershire LE12 6UJ
☎01509 880725 Fax 01509 881715
Email albion@indigogroup.co.uk
Website www.hoap.co.uk

Managing Editor *R.N. Trubshaw*

FOUNDED 1990 to publish local history.

Publishes folklore and mythology. Synopses relating to these subjects welcome.
Royalties negotiable.

Hilmarton Manor Press
Calne, Wiltshire SN11 8SB
☎01249 760208 Fax 01249 760379
Email mailorder@hilmartonpress.co.uk

Chairman/Managing Director *Charles Baile de Laperriere*

Publisher of fine art dictionaries and art reference only. Editor and publisher of *Who's Who In Art* (31st edition).
Royalties paid.

ignotus press
BCM-Writer, London WC1N 3XX
☎01530 831916 Fax 01530 831916
Email ignotuspress@aol.com
Website www.ignotuspress.com

Publisher *Suzanne Ruthven*

'We are looking for positive, forward-looking material (fiction and non-fiction) on all aspects of western ritual magic, mysteries, spiritual development, traditional and hereditary witchcraft and other paths which demonstrate the writer's grasp of both traditional and contemporary esoteric practice. No New Age idealism, fantasy, pseudo-spirituality or neo-Hammer House of Horror fiction.' Send s.a.e. for authors' guidelines before submitting material for consideration.
IMPRINTS **Moonraker Books** (fiction); **Alphard Press** (self-help and lifestyle).
Royalties paid.

Infinity Junction
PO Box 64, Neston DO, Cheshire CH64 0WB
Email infin-info@infinityjunction.com
Website www.infinityjunction.com
Managing Editor *Neil Gee*

Established originally as an internet outlet for self-published books, Infinity Junction became a publisher in 2001, releasing 2 titles, including an anthology of short stories. 'Authors are strongly advised to read the information on the website before contacting us. We cannot undertake to read unsolicited mss.'

Inner Sanctum Publications
75 Greenleaf Gardens, Polegate, East Sussex BN26 6PQ
☎01323 484058
Email innersanctum@clara.co.uk
Website www.innersanctum@clara.co.uk
Managing Editor *Mary Hession*

FOUNDED in 1999 to *publish* spiritual books. Unsolicited mss, synopses and ideas welcome; approach in writing in the first instance.
Royalties not paid.

Intellect
PO Box 862, Bristol BS99 1DE
☎0117 958 9910 Fax 0117 958 9911
Email info@intellectbooks.com
Website www.intellectbooks.com
Chairman *Masoud Yazdani*
Managing Director *Robin Beecroft*

A multidisciplinary publisher for both individual and institutional readers. Tracks newest developments in digital creative media – art, film, television, theatre design, etc. – and examines distinct theories in education, language, gender study and international culture through scholarly articles. Also publishes in AI, computer science and human–computer interaction in books, journals and website.
Royalties paid.

Iolo
38 Chaucer Road, Bedford MK40 2AJ
☎01234 301718/07909 934866
Fax 01234 301718
Email newplays@dedwyddjones.screaming.net
Managing Director *Dedwydd Jones*

Publishes Welsh theatre-related material and campaigns for a Welsh National Theatre. Ideas on Welsh themes welcome; approach in writing.

Ivy Books
351 Woodstock Road, Oxford OX2 7NX
Manager *A. Hardy*

Small press concentrating on academic works.

Ivy Publications
72 Hyperion House, Somers Road, London SW2 1HZ
☎020 8671 6872 Fax 020 8671 3391
Proprietor *Ian Bruton-Simmonds*

FOUNDED 1989. *Publishes* educational, science, fiction, philosophy, children's, travel, literary criticism, history, film scripts. No unsolicited mss; send two pages, one from the beginning and one from the body of the book, together with synopsis (one paragraph) and s.a.e. No cookery, gardening or science fiction.
Royalties paid annually.

The Jupiter Press
The Coach House, Gatacre, Claverley, Nr Wolverhampton WV5 7AW

☎01746 710694 Fax 01746 710158
Email gordon@jupiterpress.fsnet.co.uk
Website www.jupiter-press.com
Managing Editor *Gordon Thomas Drury*

FOUNDED 1995. Looking for niche market and information publications, also quiz and game subjects. Interested in clairvoyance and esoteric subjects. Synopses and ideas welcome. Send idea and sample chapter. Unsolicited mss welcome 'but may request a reader's fee'. Requires books for series entitled *How To Make Money At* ....
Royalties paid.

Kittiwake
3 Glantwymyn Village Workshops,
Nr Machynlleth, Montgomeryshire SY20 8LY
☎01650 511314 Fax 01650 511602/eFax: 0870 132 7404
Email david@perrocarto.co.uk
Website perrocarto.co.uk
Managing Editor *David Perrott*

FOUNDED 1986. *Publishes* guidebooks only, with an emphasis on careful design/production. Unsolicited mss, synopses and ideas for guidebooks welcome. Specialist research, writing, cartographic and electronic publishing services available. *Royalties* paid.

The Lindsey Press
Unitarian Headquarters, 1–6 Essex Street, Strand, London WC2R 3HY
☎020 7240 2384 Fax 020 7240 3089
Email ga@unitarian.org.uk
Convenor *Kate Taylor*

ESTABLISHED at the end of the 18th century as a vehicle for disseminating liberal religion. Adopted the name of The Lindsey Press at the beginning of the 20th century (after Theophilus Lindsey, the great Unitarian Theologian). *Publishes* books reflecting liberal religious thought or Unitarian denominational history. Also worship material – hymn books, collections of prayers, etc. No unsolicited mss; synopses and ideas welcome.
Royalties not paid.

Logaston Press
Logaston, Woonton, Almeley, Herefordshire HR3 6QH
☎01544 327344
Managing Editors *Andy Johnson, Ron Shoesmith*

FOUNDED 1985. *Publishes* guides, archaeology, social history, rural issues and local history for Wales, the Welsh Border and West Midlands. 10–15 titles a year. Unsolicited mss, synopses and ideas welcome. Return postage appreciated. *Royalties* paid.

Luath Press Ltd
543/2 Castlehill, The Royal Mile, Edinburgh EH1 2ND
☎0131 225 4326 Fax 0131 225 4324
Email gavin.macdougall@luath.co.uk
Website www.luath.co.uk
Managing Editor *G.H. MacDougall*

FOUNDED 1981. *Publishes* mainly books with a Scottish connection. Current list includes guidebooks, walking and outdoor, history, folklore, politics and global issues, cartoons, fiction, poetry, biography, food and drink, environment, music and dance, sport and *On the Trail Of* and *The Quest For* SERIES. About 20–30 titles a year. Unsolicited mss, synopses and ideas welcome; 'committed to publishing well-written books worth reading'.
Royalties paid.

Lyfrow Trelyspen
The Roseland Institute, Gorran, St Austell, Cornwall
☎01726 843501 Fax 01726 843501
Email trelispen@care4free.net
Managing Editor *Dr James Whetter*

FOUNDED 1975. *Publishes* works on Cornish history, biography, essays, etc. 1–2 titles a year. Also **CNP Publications** which *publishes* the quarterly journal *The Cornish Banner/An Baner Kernewek*. Unsolicited mss, synopses and ideas welcome.
Royalties not paid.

The Maia Press
82 Forest Road, London E8 3BG
☎020 7249 3711/3718
Email info@maiapress.com
Website www.maiapress.com
Contact *Maggie Hamand, Jane Havell*

FOUNDED 2002. *Publishes* fiction by known and new writers. 6 titles a year. No unsolicited mss, write with CV and synopsis only. S.a.e essential.
Royalties paid twice-yearly.

Maypole Editions
65 Mayfair Avenue, Ilford, Essex IG1 3DQ
☎020 8252 3937
Contact *Barry Taylor*

Publisher of plays and poetry in the main. 2–3 titles a year. Unsolicited mss welcome provided return postage is included. Poetry always welcome for collected anthologies and should be

approximately 30 lines of tight verse, broadly covering social concerns, ethnic minority issues, feminist incident, romance generally, travel and lyric rhyming verse. No politics except evenly comparative. The biannual collected anthology is designed as a small press platform for first-time poets who might not otherwise get into print, and a permanent showcase for those already published who want to break into the mainstream. Catalogue £1, plus A5 s.a.e. 'Please be patient when sending work because of the huge volume of submissions.' Exempt Charity Status.

Meadow Books
35 Stonefield Way, Burgess Hill, West Sussex RH15 8DW
☎01444 239044
Website www.historyofnursing.homestead.com
Managing Director *C. O'Neill*

FOUNDED 1990. Published *A Picture of Health* and *More Pictures of Health*.

Mercia Cinema Society
19 Pinder's Grove, Wakefield, West Yorkshire WF1 4AH
☎01924 372748
Email mervyn.gould@virgin.net
Managing Editor *Paul Smith*

FOUNDED 1980 to foster research into the history of picture houses. *Publishes* books and booklets on the subject, including cinema circuits and chains. Books are often tied in with specific geographical areas. Unsolicited mss, synopses and ideas.
Royalties not paid.

Meridian Books
40 Hadzor Road, Oldbury, West Midlands B68 9LA
☎0121 429 4397
Managing Editor *Peter Groves*

FOUNDED 1985 as a small home-based enterprise following the acquisition of titles from Tetradon Publications Ltd. *Publishes* walking and regional guides. 4–5 titles a year. Unsolicited mss, synopses and ideas welcome if relevant. Send s.a.e. if mss to be returned.
Royalties paid.

Mermaid Turbulence
Annaghmaconway, Cloone, Leitrim Republic of Ireland
☎00 353 71 96 36134 Fax 00 353 71 96 36134
Managing Director *Mari-aymone Djeribi*

FOUNDED in 1993 with the first issue of *element* – an international literary journal. *Publishes* essays, fiction, poetry, cookery, children's and artists' books. 7 titles in 2003. Unsolicited mss, synopses and ideas welcome. No pulp fiction. Approach in writing, enclosing international reply coupon. Mss will not be returned (recycled) unless an s.a.e. with Irish stamps is provided.

Royalties paid annually.

Merton Priory Press Ltd

67 Merthyr Road, Whitchurch, Cardiff CF14 1DD
☎029 2052 1956 Fax 029 2062 3599
Email merton@dircon.co.uk
Website www.merton.dircon.co.uk

Managing Director *Philip Riden*

FOUNDED 1993. *Publishes* academic and mid-market history, especially local, industrial and transport history; also memoirs and autobiographies. About 6 titles a year. Full catalogue available.

Royalties paid twice-yearly.

Neil Miller Publications

Ormonde House, 49 Ormonde Road, Hythe, Kent CT21 6OW
Also at: 4 Rue D'Equiire Bergueneuse, Pas de Calais, France 62134

Managing Editor *Neil Miller*

FOUNDED 1994. *Publishes* novels and short story anthologies under its **Miller Publications** imprint. Accepts collections of short stories on fantasy, adventure mystery, horror, detective, romance and tales with a twist. Under **Black Cat Books** imprint *publishes* non-fiction – war memoirs, true tales, biographies, history and comedy. 191 new authors published. Evaluation and critique service available. Send s.a.e. for details. 'We seek short story writers, in any genre. We read all tales that are sent in. No unsolicited/unrequested mss, please.'

Millers Dale Publications

7 Weavers Place, Chandlers Ford, Eastleigh, Hampshire SO53 1TU
☎023 8026 1192
Email gponting@clara.net
Website www.home.clara.net/gponting/
    index-page10.html

Managing Editor *Gerald Ponting*

FOUNDED 1990. *Publishes* books on local history related to central Hampshire. Also books related to slide presentations by Gerald Ponting. Ideas for local history books on Hampshire considered.

Minority Rights Group

379 Brixton Road, London SW9 7DE
☎020 7978 9498 Fax 020 7738 6265
Email minority.rights@mrgmail.org
Website www.minorityrights.org

Head of Publishing *Angela Warren*

FOUNDED in the late 1960s, MRG works to raise awareness of minority issues worldwide. *Publishes* books, reports and educational material on minority rights. 8–10 titles a year.

Modern Books Publishing

18 Wellington Street, Hertford, Hertfordshire SG14 3AW
☎01992 552040
Email editors@modbooks.co.uk

Editorial Head *Jonathan Miller*
Managing Editor *Mark Daniels*

FOUNDED 2002. *Publishes* fiction, non-fiction, biography, autobiography, astronomy, academic, humour, literature, romance, popular fiction, historical, world issues, environment, crime, science fiction, fantasy, political and philosophical. About 5–7 titles a year.

Royalties paid annually.

Mohr Books

See **Crossbridge Books**

Moonraker Books

See **ignotus press**

Morton Publishing

PO Box 23, Gosport, Hampshire PO12 2XD
Website www.mortonpublishing.com

Managing Editor *Nik Morton*

FOUNDED 1994. *Publishes* fiction – genre novellas (eg crime, science fiction, fantasy, horror, western), max. 20,000 words; short story anthologies – max. 4000 words per story. Unsolicited synopses and ideas for books welcome; enclose s.a.e. Also offers literary agent service of guidance and advice (fees on application).

Royalties paid annually.

Need2Know

Remus House, Coltsfoot Drive, Woodston, Peterborough PE2 9JX
☎01733 898103 Fax 01733 313524
Website www.forwardpress.co.uk

Managing Editor *James Feeke*

FOUNDED 1995 'to fill a gap in the market for

self-help books'. Need2Know is an imprint of **Forward Press** (see entry under **Poetry Presses**). *Publishes* contemporary health and lifestyle issues. No unsolicited mss. Call in the first instance.

Payment Advance plus 15% royalties.

Nimbus Press

18 Guilford Road, Leicester LE2 2RB
☎0116 270 6318 Fax 0116 270 6318
Email publisher@nimbuspress.co.uk
Website www.nimbuspress.co.uk
Managing Editor *Clifford Sharp*
Editor *Justin Moulder*

FOUNDED 1991. *Publishes* mind, body and spirit books from an open and inclusive perspective, Christian drama and humour. About 4 titles a year.

Royalties paid.

Norvik Press Ltd

School of Language, Linguistics & Translation Studies, University of East Anglia, Norwich, Norfolk NR4 7TJ
☎01603 593356 Fax 01603 250599
Email norvik.press@uea.ac.uk
Website www.uea.ac.uk/llt/norvik_press
Managing Editors *Janet Garton, Michael Robinson*

Small academic press. *Publishes* the journals *Scandinavica* and *Swedish Book Review* and books related to Scandinavian literature. About 4 titles a year. Interested in synopses and ideas for books within its *Literary History and Criticism* series. No unsolicited mss.

Royalties paid.

The Nostalgia Collection

Silver Link Publishing Ltd, The Trundle, Ringstead Road, Great Addington, Kettering, Northamptonshire NN14 4BW
☎01536 330588 Fax 01536 330588
Email sales@nostalgiacollection.com
Website www.nostalgiacollection.com
Managing Editor *Peter Townsend*

FOUNDED 1985 in Lancashire, changed hands in 1990 and now based in Northamptonshire. Small independent company specialising in nostalgia titles including illustrated books on towns and cities, villages and rural life, rivers and inland waterways, industrial heritage, railways, trams, ships and other transport subjects. *Publishes* post-war nostalgia on all aspects of social history under the **Past and Present Publishing** imprint. *Fees* paid.

Nyala Publishing

4 Christian Fields, London SW16 3JZ
☎020 8764 6292 Fax 020 8764 6292/0115 981 9418
Email nyala.publish@geo-group.co.uk
Website www.geo-group.co.uk
Editorial Head *J.F.J. Douglas*

FOUNDED 1996. Publishing arm of Geo Group. *Publishes* biography, travel and general non-fiction. No unsolicited mss; synopses and ideas considered. Also offers a wide range of printing and publishing services. 'Quality low-cost printing a speciality.'

Royalties paid twice-yearly.

Orpheus Publishing House

4 Dunsborough Park, Ripley Green, Ripley, Guildford, Surrey GU23 6AL
☎01483 225777 Fax 01483 225776
Email orpheuspubl.ho@btinternet.com
Managing Editor *J.S. Gordon*

FOUNDED 1996. *Publishes* 'well-researched and properly argued' books in the fields of occult science, esotericism and comparative philosophy/religion. 'Keen to encourage good (but sensible) new authors.' In the first instance, send maximum 3-page synopsis with s.a.e.

Royalties by agreement.

Outline Publications

See **Brantwood Books**

Packard Publishing Limited

Forum House, Stirling Road, Chichester, West Sussex PO19 7DN
☎01243 537977 Fax 01243 537977
Email info@packardpublishing.co.uk
Website www.packardpublishing.com
Chairman/Managing Director *Michael Packard*

FOUNDED in 1977 to distribute overseas publishers' lists in biology, biochemistry and ecology. *Publishes* academic & professional: school/university interface, postgraduate – mainly in land management and applied ecology; agriculture, forestry, nature conservation, rural studies, landscape architecture and garden design; some languages (French, Arabic). SERIES Instructional books on garden and landscape design, and monographs or critical biographies in garden and landscape design and history. No unsolicited mss. Synopses and ideas in relevant areas welcome. Telephone first.

Royalties paid twice-yearly in first year, then annually.

Palladour Books
23 Eldon Street, Southsea, Hampshire
PO5 4BS
☎02392 826935   Fax 02392 826395
Email palladour@powellj33.freeserve.co.uk
Managing Editors *Jeremy Powell, Anne Powell*
FOUNDED 1986. Started with a twice-yearly
issue of catalogues on the literature and poetry
of World War I. Occasional catalogues on
World War II poetry have also been issued. No
unsolicited mss.
Royalties not paid.

Panacea Press Limited
86 North Gate, Prince Albert Road, London
NW8 7EJ
☎020 7722 8464   Fax 020 7586 8187
Email ebrecher@panaceapress.net
Managing Editor *Erwin Brecher, PhD*
FOUNDED as a self-publisher but now open for
non-fiction from other authors. Material of
academic value considered provided it com-
mands a wide general market. No unsolicited
mss; synopses and ideas welcome. Approach by
fax or letter. No telephone calls.
Royalties paid annually.

Paradise Press
80 College Road, Isleworth, Middlesex
TW7 5DS
☎020 8568 3777
Email prdsprss@netscape.net

FOUNDED 1995. Considers only high quality
lesbian and gay fiction workshopped through
Gay Authors Workshop.

Parapress Ltd
The Basement, 9 Frant Road, Tunbridge
Wells, Kent TN2 5SD
☎01892 512118   Fax 01892 512118
Email office@parapress.co.uk
Website www.parapress.co.uk
Managing Editor *Elizabeth Imlay*
Production and Promotion *James Ewing*
FOUNDED 1993. *Publishes* animals, autobiogra-
phy, biography, comedy, history, literary criti-
cism, military and naval, music, self-help, sports.
Some self-publishing. About 6 titles a year.

Partnership Publishing Ltd
2 Crown Street, Wellington, Telford,
Shropshire TF1 1LP
☎01952 415334   Fax 01952 245077
Email info@publish.uk.ws
Managing Director *Steve Rooney*

TITLES *Bus and Coach Professional*; *Professional
Recovery*; *MOT Professional*; *Oakengates & District
News*; *Wellington News*; *Dawley, Madeley,
Broseley News*; *Vehicle Salvage Professional*. Offers
full magazine publication services, including
design and production, editorial and advertising
sales service.

Past and Present Publishing
See **The Nostalgia Collection**

Paupers' Press
27 Melbourne Road, West Bridgford,
Nottingham NG2 5DJ
☎0115 981 5063   Fax 0115 981 5063
Email stan2727uk@aol.com
Website members.aol.com/stan2727uk/
  pauper.htm
Managing Editor *Colin Stanley*
FOUNDED 1983. *Publishes* extended essays in
booklet form (about 15,000 words) on literary
criticism and philosophy. 'Sometimes we stray
from these criteria and produce full-length
books, but only to accommodate an exceptional
ms.' About 6 titles a year. Limited hardback editions of bestselling titles. No unsolicited mss but
synopses and ideas for books welcome.
Royalties paid.

Peepal Tree Press Ltd
17 King's Avenue, Leeds, West Yorkshire
LS6 1QS
☎0113 245 1703   Fax 0113 245 9616
Email info@peepaltreepress.com
Website www.peepaltreepress.com
Managing Editor *Jeremy Poynting*
FOUNDED 1985. *Publishes* fiction, poetry, drama
and academic studies. *Specialises* in Caribbean,
Black British and south Asian writing. About 18
titles a year. In-house printing and finishing facil-
ities. AUTHORS include **Forward Poetry
Prize**-winner Kwame Dawes. 'Please send an
A5 s.a.e. with a 38p stamp for a copy of our sub-
mission guidelines.' Write or phone for a free
catalogue. *Royalties* paid.

The Penniless Press
100 Waterloo Road, Ashton, Preston,
Lancashire PR2 1EP
Editor *Alan Dent*

Publishes quarterly magazine with literary,
philosophical and artistic content, including
reviews of poetry, fiction, non-fiction and
drama. Prose of up to 3000 words welcome.
No mss returned without s.a.e.
Payment Free copy of magazine.

Pipers' Ash Ltd
'Pipers' Ash', Church Road, Christian Malford, Chippenham, Wiltshire SN15 4BW
☎01249 720563 Fax 0870 0568916
Email pipersash@supamasu.com
Website www.supamasu.com
Managing Editor *Mr A. Tyson*

FOUNDED 1976. The company's publishing activities include individual collections of contemporary short stories, science fiction short stories, poetry, plays, short novels, local histories, children's fiction, philosophy, biographies, translations and general non-fiction. 18 titles a year. Synopses and ideas welcome; 'new authors with potential will be actively encouraged'. Offices in New Zealand and Australia.
Royalties paid annually.

Planet
PO Box 44, Aberystwyth, Ceredigion SY23 3ZZ
☎01970 611255 Fax 01970 611197
Email planet.enquiries@planetmagazine.org.uk
Website www.planetmagazine.org.uk
Managing Editor *John Barnie*

FOUNDED 1975 and relaunched in 1985 as publisher of the arts and current affairs magazine *Planet: The Welsh Internationalist* and branched out into book publishing in 1995. All books so far have been commissioned. Unsolicited synopses and ideas welcome.
Royalties paid.

Playwrights Publishing Co.
70 Nottingham Road, Burton Joyce, Nottinghamshire NG14 5AL
☎0115 931 3356
Email playwrightspublishingco@yahoo.com
Website geocities.com/
  playwrightspublishingco
Managing Editors *Liz Breeze, Tony Breeze*

FOUNDED 1990. *Publishes* one-act and full-length plays. Unsolicited scripts welcome. No synopses or ideas. Reading fees: £15 one act; £30 full length (waived if evidence of professional performance).
Royalties paid.

Pomegranate Press
Dolphin House, 51 St Nicholas Lane, Lewes, Sussex BN7 2JZ
☎01273 470100 Fax 01273 470100
Email sussexbooks@aol.com
Managing Editor *David Arscott*

FOUNDED in 1992 by writer/broadcaster David Arscott, who also administers the **Sussex Book Club**. *Specialises* in books about Sussex. IMPRINT **Pomegranate Practicals** How-to books.
Royalties paid twice-yearly.

David Porteous Editions
PO Box 5, Chudleigh, Newton Abbot, Devon TQ13 0YZ
☎01626 853310 Fax 01626 853663
Email editorial@davidporteous.com
Website www.davidporteous.com
Publisher *David Porteous*

FOUNDED 1992 to produce high quality colour illustrated books on hobbies and leisure for the UK and international markets. *Publishes* crafts, hobbies, art techniques and needlecrafts. No poetry or fiction. 3–4 titles a year. Unsolicited mss, synopses and ideas welcome if return postage included.
Royalties paid twice-yearly.

Power Publications
1 Clayford Avenue, Ferndown, Dorset BH22 9PQ
☎01202 875223 Fax 01202 875223
Email sales@powerpublications.co.uk
Contact *Mike Power*

FOUNDED 1989. *Publishes* local interest, pub walk guides and mountain bike guides. 2–3 titles a year. Unsolicited mss, synopses and ideas welcome. *Royalties* paid.

Praxis Books
Crossways Cottage, Walterstone, Herefordshire HR2 0DX
☎01873 890695
Email author@rebeccatope.fsnet.co.uk
Website www.rebeccatope.com
Proprietor *Rebecca Smith*

FOUNDED 1992. *Publishes* reissues of the works of Sabine Baring-Gould, memoirs, diaries and local interest. 19 titles to date. Unsolicited mss accepted with s.a.e. No fiction, children's or humour. Editing service available. Funding negotiable. 'I am most likely to accept work with a clearly identifiable market.'

Primrose Hill Press Ltd
Stratton Audley Park, Bicester, Oxfordshire OX27 9AB
☎01869 278000 Fax 01869 277820
Email info@primrosehillpress.co.uk
Website www.primrosehillpress.co.uk
Managing Director *W.E. Butler*

FOUNDED in 1997, having taken over the stock

and projects in progress of Silent Books Ltd. *Publishes* general art titles, wood engraving, poetry, book studies, books on bookplates, bibliography, book design and books for the gift market, 'all high quality productions'. No fiction. About 12 titles a year. Unsolicited mss, synopses and ideas welcome.

QueenSpark Books
49 Grand Parade, Brighton, East Sussex BN2 2QA
☎01273 571710   Fax 01273 571710
Email info@queensparkbooks.org.uk
Website www.queensparkbooks.org.uk

A community writing and publishing group run mainly by volunteers who work together to write and produce books. Since the early 1970s they have published 70 titles, mainly featuring the lives of local people. No fiction or poetry. Writing workshops and groups held on a regular basis. New members welcome.

Raby Books
The Coach Houe, Eggleston Hall, Eggleston, Barnard Castle, County Durham DL12 0AG
☎01833 650583   Fax 01833 650681

Advertising Manager *Rebecca Dobson*

FOUNDED 2001. *Publishes* mainly biographies and memoirs. 20 titles in 2002. Welcomes unsolicited mss, synopses and ideas. Please write in the first instance.
Royalties paid quarterly.

Radikal Phase Publishing House Ltd
Willow Court, Cordy Lane, Underwood, Nottinghamshire NG16 5FD
☎01773 764288   Fax 01773 764282
Email sales@radikalbooks.com
Website www.radikalbooks.com

Joint Managing Directors *Philip Gardiner,*
  Kevin Marks

FOUNDED 2001. *Publishes* radical revelation and technical electrical books. IMPRINTS **William Ernest** *Kevin Marks*; **Radikal Phase** *Philip Gardiner.* Welcomes unsolicited material; approach in writing in the first instance.
Royalties paid twice-yearly.

The Riverside Press
PO Box 388A, Surbiton, Surrey KT7 0ZT
☎020 8339 0945   Fax 020 8339 0945
Email ed@good-writing-matters.co.uk
Website www.good-writing-matters.co.uk

Managing Editor *Michael Russell*

FOUNDED 1998 to publish short-run titles from new writers. Mainly fiction but also special interest non-fiction. Editorial support service provided. No unsolicited mss. Send synopses/ideas and three chapters only with covering letter.

The Robinswood Press
30 South Avenue, Stourbridge, West Midlands DY8 3XY
☎01384 397475   Fax 01384 440443
Email info@robinswoodpress.com
Website www.robinswoodpress.com

Managing Editor *Christopher J. Marshall*

FOUNDED 1985. *Publishes* education, particularly teacher resources, SEN, including the Spotlight and Lifeboat Read and Spell ranges. Also collaborative publishing, e.g. with Camphill Foundation. About 12–15 titles a year. Unsolicited mss, synopses and ideas welcome.
Royalties paid.

Romer Publications
PO Box 10120, NL–1001 EC Amsterdam, The Netherlands
☎00 31 20 676 9442   Fax 00 31 20 676 9442
Email harrymelkman@hotmail.com

Managing Editor *Hubert de Brouwer*

FOUNDED 1986. *Publishes* critical reflection on origins and legitimacy of established institutions; law and history. Unsolicited mss, synopses and ideas within the areas covered welcome.
Royalties paid.

Route
School Lane, Glasshoughton, Castleford, West Yorkshire WF10 4QH
☎01977 603028   Fax 01977 512819
Email books@route-online.com
Website www.route-online.com

Books Coordinator *Ian Daley*

FOUNDED 1986. *Publishes* contemporary fiction (novels and short stories). No local history, children's, autobiography, poetry, reference or nostalgia. Unsolicited mss discouraged; authors should send for fact sheet first. Write or ring for free catalogue.
Royalties paid.

St James Publishing
Suite 213 Parkway House, Sheen Lane, East Sheen, London SW14 8LS
☎0870 870 8797   Fax 0870 870 8798

Managing Editors *Linda Smith, David Smith*

FOUNDED 1995 to provide teaching materials with spiritual substance for St James

Independent Schools: 'Good Books for Fine Minds'. Also many workbooks and texbooks for the study of English and mathematics. No unsolicited mss, synopses or ideas.

SAKS Publications

PO Box 33504, London, E9 7YE
Email hotspotwriters@compuserve.com

Publisher *Kadija George*

FOUNDED 1996. *Publishes Sable* literary magazine for writers of African/Caribbean/Asian descent. Includes poetry, prose, memoirs, travel narratives and reviews.

Serif

47 Strahan Road, London E3 5DA
☎020 8981 3990 Fax 020 8981 3990
Email stephen@serif.demon.co.uk

Managing Editor *Stephen Hayward*

FOUNDED 1993. *Publishes* cookery, Irish and African studies and modern history; no fiction. Ideas and synopses welcome; no unsolicited mss. *Royalties* paid.

Sherlock Publications

6 Bramham Moor, Hill Head, Fareham, Hampshire PO14 3RU
☎01329 667325
Email sherlock.publications@btinternet.com

Managing Editor *Philip Weller*

FOUNDED to supply publishing support to a number of Sherlock Holmes societes. *Publishes* Sherlock Holmes and other Conan Doyle studies only. About 14 titles a year. No unsolicited mss; synopses and ideas welcome.
Royalties not paid.

Shield Publications

PO Box 5, Low Fell, Gateshead NE9 7YS
☎0191 4823222

Managing Editor *Norman L. Middlemiss*

FOUNDED 1977. *Publishes* nautical books only – the *Merchant Fleet* series (44 vols.). 2 titles in 2002. Unsolicited mss and fleet lists welcome.
Royalties paid.

SINAP

See **Skrev Press**

Skrev Press

15 Pwllhai, Cardigan SA43 1DB
☎01239 613683
Email editor@skrev-press.com
Website www.skrev-press.com

Managing Editor *Daithidh MacEochaidh*

FOUNDED 2002. *Publishes Texts' Bones*, a journal of avant garde short fiction (four issues a year). IMPRINT **SINAP** *publishes* collections of short stories, novellas and novels under 80,000 words. Skrev also runs an annual themed short story competition with hard publication offered as the prize. Welcomes unsolicited mss, synopses and ideas. Initial approach by e-mail or letter with description. See website for further details.

Spacelink Books

115 Hollybush Lane, Hampton, Middlesex TW12 2QY
☎020 8979 3148
Website www.spacelink.fsworld.co.uk

Managing Director *Lionel Beer*

FOUNDED 1967. Named after a UFO magazine published in the 1960/70s. *Publishes* non-fiction titles connected with UFOs, Fortean phenomena and paranormal events. No unsolicited mss; send synopses and ideas. Publishers of *TEMS News* for the Travel and Earth Mysteries Society. Distributors of a wide range of related titles and magazines.
Royalties and fees paid according to contract.

Stenlake Publishing

54–58 Mill Square, Catrine, Ayrshire KA5 6RD
☎01290 552233
Email david@stenlake.co.uk
Website www.stenlake.co.uk

Publishes illustrated local history, railways, shipping, aviation and industrial. 49 titles in 2002. Unsolicited mss, synopses and ideas welcome if accompanied by s.a.e. Freelance writers with experience in above fields also sought for specific commissions.
Royalties or fixed fee paid.

Stone Flower Limited

PO Box 1513, Ilford IG1 3QU
Email stoneflower10622@aol.com

Managing Editor *L.G. Norman*

FOUNDED 1989. *Publishes* biography, law, humour and general fiction. Will consider mss, synopses and ideas only if sent with s.a.e. or IRC. Approach in writing in the first instance. 'No anthropomorphism, please.'

Stride

11 Sylvan Road, Exeter, Devon EX4 6EW
Email editor@stridebooks.co.uk
Website www.stridebooks.co.uk

Managing Editor *Rupert Loydell*

FOUNDED in 1982 as a magazine and booklet series. Since the mid-1980s, the press has published paperback editions of imaginative new writing. *Publishes* poetry, prose-poems, criticism, reviews, interviews, arts (particularly experimental music). No unsolicited submissions required at this time.

Royalties sometimes paid; free copies usually.

Superscript

404 Robin Square, Newtown, Powys
SY16 1HP
☎01588 650452
Email drjbford@yahoo.co.uk
Chairman *Geoff Dench*
Editor *Julie Ford*

FOUNDED 2002. An imprint of the Big Tent consortium. 'The fastest publisher in the West – topical titles can be on the market within 6–8 weeks of perfect typescript.' *Publishes* literary, philosophical and political fiction, autobiography and wartime memoirs, humanities and social sciences. 2 titles in 2002. All suitable ideas, synopses or mss are submitted to the Editorial Board who are looking for 'well-crafted material that exposes injustice, challenges stereotypes and promotes human dignity'. Will also consider new editions of out-of-print titles at author's request. Initial enquiries by letter, telephone or e-mail to the Editor.

Royalties vary with each contract.

Tamarind Ltd

PO Box 52, Northwood, Middlesex
HA6 1UN
☎020 8866 8808 Fax 020 8866 5627
Email info@tamarindbooks.co.uk
Website www.tamarindbooks.co.uk
Managing Editor *Verna Wilkins*

FOUNDED 1987 to publish picture books which give a high, positive profile to Black children. They feature regularly on the SATs List for National Curriculum, on BBC Words and Pictures, CBBC and Balamory. Regularly chosen among the Best Books of the Year. All titles sold into both trade and educational markets. Age range: 2–12.

Tarquin Publications

Stradbroke, Diss, Norfolk IP21 5JP
☎01379 384218 Fax 01379 384289
Email enquiries@tarquin-books.demon.co.uk
Website www.tarquin-books.demon.co.uk
Managing Editor *Gerald Jenkins*

FOUNDED 1970 as a hobby which gradually grew and now *publishes* mathematical, cut-out models, teaching and pop-up books. Other topics covered if they involve some kind of paper cutting or pop-up scenes. 5 titles in 2003. No unsolicited mss; letter with 1–2 page synopses welcome.

Royalties paid.

Tartarus Press

Coverley House, Carlton-in-Coverdale,
Leyburn, North Yorkshire DL8 4AY
☎01969 640399 Fax 01969 640399
Email tartarus@pavilion.co.uk
Website www.tartaruspress.com
Proprietor *Raymond Russell*
Editor *Rosalie Parker*

FOUNDED 1987. *Publishes* fiction, short stories, reprinted classic supernatural fiction and reference books. About 12 titles a year. 'Please do not send submissions. We cater to a small, collectable market; we solicit the fiction we publish.'

Tindal Street Press Ltd

217 The Custard Factory, Gibb Street,
Birmingham B9 4AA
☎0121 773 8157/8 Fax 0121 693 5525
Email emma@tindalstreet.co.uk
Website www.tindalstreet.co.uk
Managing Editor *Emma Hargrave*

FOUNDED in 1998 to publish contemporary original fiction from the English regions. *Publishes* original fiction only – novels and short story anthologies. No local history, memoirs or poetry. 6 titles in 2002. Approach with a letter, synopsis and three chapters and include s.a.e. for return of ms.

Royalties paid.

Tuckwell Press Ltd

The Mill House, Phantassie, East Linton,
East Lothian EH40 3DG
☎01620 860164 Fax 01620 860164
Email tuckwellpress@sol.co.uk
Website www.tuckwellpress.co.uk
Managing Director *John Tuckwell*

FOUNDED 1995. *Publishes* history, archaeology, literature, ethnology, biography, architecture, gardening history, genealogy, palaeography, with a bias towards Scottish and academic texts, also north of England. 170 titles in print. No unsolicited mss but synopses and ideas welcome if relevant to subjects covered.

Royalties paid annually.

Wakefield Historical Publications

19 Pinder's Grove, Wakefield, West Yorkshire
WF1 4AH
☎01924 372748
Email kate@airtime.co.uk
Managing Editor *Kate Taylor*

FOUNDED 1977 by the Wakefield Historical
Society to publish well-researched, scholarly
works of regional (namely West Riding) historical significance. 1–2 titles a year. Unsolicited mss,
synopses and ideas for books welcome.
Royalties not paid.

Watling Street Publishing Ltd

The Glen, Southrop, Nr Lechlade,
Gloucestershire GL7 3NY
☎01367 850558
Email watlingst@btinternet.com
Managing Director *John Monk*
Editorial Head *Christine Kidney*
Approx. Annual Turnover £20,000

FOUNDED 2001. *Publishes* non-fiction titles on
London and its history; children's and adult. 6
titles in 2002. No unsolicited mss. Ideas and
synopses welcome. Approach in writing or by
e-mail with a one-page proposal. 'Not interested in anything not related to London.'

Waywiser Press

9 Woodstock Road, London N4 3ET
☎020 8374 5526 Fax 020 8374 5736
Email waywiserpress@aol.com
Website www.waywiser-press.com

Editor *Philip Hoy*

FOUNDED 2001. *Specialises* in publishing new
poetry, but will also be publishing books
belonging to different genres from time to time.
No unsolicited mss, but will consider synopses,
short extracts, ideas. Approach in writing only
with s.a.e.
Royalties paid.

Whitchurch Books Ltd

67 Merthyr Road, Whitchurch, Cardiff
CF14 1DD
☎029 2052 1956 Fax 029 2062 3599
Email whitchurchbooks@btopenworld.com
Managing Director *Gale Canvin*

FOUNDED 2002. *Publishes* local interest, particularly local history. 2 titles in 2002. Welcomes
unsolicited mss, synsopses and ideas on relevant
subjects. Approach first by phone or in writing.
Royalties twice-yearly.

White Ladder Press

Great Ambrook, Near Ipplepen, Devon
TQ12 5UL
☎01803 813343 Fax 01803 813928
Email enquiries@whiteladderpress.com
Website www.whiteladderpress.com

Publishers *Roni Jay, Richard Craze*

FOUNDED 2002. *Publishes* non-fiction books
which present a new angle on everyday living.
Welcomes synopses and ideas by mail or
e-mail. Not interested in fiction or children's
titles.
Royalties paid twice-yearly.

Whittles Publishing

Roseleigh House, Latheronwheel, Caithness
KW5 6DW
☎01593 741240 Fax 01593 741360
Email info@whittlespublishing.com
Website www.whittlespublishing.com
Managing Editor *Dr Keith Whittles*

Publisher in civil and structural engineering and
geomatics disciplines plus nautical/maritime
and nature writing. Unsolicited mss, synopses
and ideas welcome on appropriate themes.
Royalties paid annually.

William Ernest

See **Radikal Phase Publishing House Ltd**

Witan Books

Cherry Tree House, 8 Nelson Crescent, Cotes
Heath, via Stafford ST21 6ST
☎01782 791673
Managing Editor *Jeff Kent*

FOUNDED in 1980 for self-publishing and commenced publishing other writers in 1991.
Publishes general books, including biography,
education, environment, geography, history,
politics, popular music and sport. 1 or 2 titles a
year. Unsolicited mss, synopses and ideas welcome (include s.a.e.)
Royalties paid.

Worple Press

12 Havelock Road, Tonbridge, Kent
TN9 1JE
☎01732 368958
Email theworpleco.@aol.com
Managing Editors *Peter Carpenter, Amanda
Knight*

FOUNDED 1997. Independent publisher specialising in poetry, art and alternative titles. 4 titles a
year. Write or phone for catalogue and flyers.
Royalties paid.

Writers' Bookshop

Remus House, Coltsfoot Drive, Woodston, Peterborough, Cambridgeshire PE2 9JX
☎01733 898103 Fax 01733 313524
Email james@forwardpress.co.uk
Website www.forwardpress.com

Managing Editor *James Feeke*

Writers' Bookshop is an imprint of **Forward Press** (see entry under **Poetry Presses**). *Publishes* writers' aids in the form of directories and how-to guides. Best-known annual title is the *Small Press Guide*. For further information and an author brief, call *James Feeke*.

Zymurgy Publishing

Hoults Estate, Walker Road, Newcastle upon Tyne NE6 2HL
☎0191 276 2425 Fax 0191 276 2425
Email martin.ellis@alibris.com
Website zymurgypublishing.com

Chairman *Martin Ellis*

FOUNDED 2000. *Publishes* adult non-fiction, ranging from full colour illustrated hardbacks to mass market paperbacks. Synopses and ideas for books welcome but no unsolicited mss. Contact by telephone or e-mail.

Royalties paid twice-yearly.

Electronic Publishing and Other Services

ABCtales
PO Box 34203, London NW5 1FX
☎020 7209 2607 Fax 020 7209 2594
Email mail@abctales.com
Website www.abctales.com
Owner *Burgeon Creative Ideas Ltd*
Editor *Mark Brown*

FOUNDED by A. John Bird, MBE, co-founder of the *Big Issue* magazine, Tony Cook and Gordon Roddick. ABCtales is a free website dedicated to publishing and developing new writing. Content is predominantly short stories and poetry but includes interviews and lifestyle features, photo essays, reviews (games, websites, film, music) and competitions. Anyone can upload creative writing to the website.

Authors OnLine
See entry under **UK Publishers**

BeWrite Books
363 Badminton Road, Nibley, Bristol
BS37 5JF
☎00 334 9335 9531 (editorial base in France)
Fax 00 334 9341 3509
Email info@bewrite.net
Website www.bewrite.net
Managing Director *Cait Myers*
Editorial Director *Neil Marr*

A multi-genre publishing house FOUNDED in 1999 and especially geared toward the encouragement and publication in electronic and print formats of first-time authors. Unsolicited mss and synopses welcome (e-mail only). 'All offers promptly acknowledged, decisions made quickly and draft manuscript-to-publication time shorter than most other publishing houses.'
  Royalties paid quarterly (no advance).

Books 4 Publishing
Lasyard House, Underhill Street, Bridgnorth, Shropshire WV16 4BB
☎0870 777 3339 Fax 01746 761298
Email editor@books4publishing.com
Website www.books4publishing.com
Owner *Corvedale Publishing Ltd*
Managing Director *Mark Horton-Oliver*

FOUNDED 2000. *Specialises* in helping new and unpublished authors gain recognition for their work by displaying synopses and up to 5000 words on the Books 4 Publishing website and promoting to publishers and agents. Mss, synopses and ideas welcome; initial enquiries by e-mail or post.

Chameleon HH Publishing
The Quarry House, East End, Witney, Oxfordshire OX29 6QA
☎01993 880223 Fax 01993 880236
Email marion@chameleonhh.co.uk and
  david@chameleonhh.co.uk
Website www.chameleonhh.co.uk
Directors *David Hall, Marion Hazzledine*

FOUNDED 1997. CD-ROM and Web publishers on behalf of commercial publishers, institutes, associations and government bodies. Produces web-updateable CDs – CD and DVD duplication, plus all artwork undertaken. Also digitisation of videos. Welcomes unsolicited mss for electronic publishing from self-publishers. Consulting and advice on CD-ROM and Web publishing.

Claritybooks.com
Colt Farm, Bromley Green Road, Ashford, Kent TN26 2EQ
Email editor@claritybooks.com
Website www.claritybooks.com

Publishes in a copyright protected, encrypted electronic format. Specialises in selling to users of hand-held computers/PDAs, Tablet PCs and laptops. Will consider all fiction and non-fiction categories from literary to genre, whether full length, novella or short stories. Particularly interested in book-length collected short stories. Professional/business 'how-to' books, good health/beauty/relationship guides, computing instruction. Children's books (not illustrated), especially structured readers, young fiction including virtual reality/alternative ending. Educational study guides, tie-ins with current exam syllabi. Humourous works. Observational/commentary on modern sexual politics, working life and times. Licence limited to e-book sales via Internet only. Author retains all other rights. No charges to authors. All communication by e-mail (no attachments). State target market and brief description of work. Authors may be invited to submit sample work either electronically or on paper according to preference (send s.a.e.).

Context Limited
Grand Union House, 20 Kentish Town Road, London NW1 9NR
☎020 7267 8989 Fax 020 7267 1133
Email postmaster@context.co.uk
Website www.context.co.uk
FOUNDED 1986. Electronic publisher of UK and European legal and offical information on CD-ROM, online and the Internet.

Deunant Books
PO Box 25, Denbigh LL16 5ZQ
☎01745 870259 Fax 01745 870259
Email mail@deunantbooks.com
Website www.deunantbooks.com
Managing Director *Les Broad*
FOUNDED 2001. Internet e-book publisher in English and Welsh of art, biography, children's, comedy, fiction, philosophy, poetry, science fiction, short story compendia, theology, travel. 26 titles in 2002. Welcomes written works incorporating sound and video: contact by phone, post or e-mail. 'All will be replied to personally.' No technical manuals that need regular updates.
Royalties paid quarterly.

Fledgling Press Limited
7 Lennox Street, Edinburgh EH4 1QB
☎0131 332 6867
Email info@fledglingpress.co.uk
Website www.fledglingpress.co.uk
Director *Zander Wedderburn*
FOUNDED 2000. Internet publisher, aiming to be 'a launching pad for new authors. Special interest in authentic writing about the human condition, including autobiography, diaries, poetry and fictionalised variations on these.' Monthly competition (www.canyouwrite.com) with prizes for short pieces. Also free books and reports in the areas of shiftwork and working time. Send mss and other details by e-mail from the website or by post. Currently £20 fee for mounting accepted work. Links into short-run book production.

The Good Web Guide Ltd
See entry under **UK Publishers**

New Authors Showcase
Barrie James Literary Agency, Rivendell, Kingsgate, Torquay, Devon TQ2 8QA
☎01803 326617

Email mail@newauthors.org.uk
Website www.newauthors.org.uk
Contact *Barrie E. James*
FOUNDED 1997. Internet site for new writers and poets to display their work to publishers. *No unsolicited mss.* First approach should be by sending s.a.e. or e-mail.

NoSpine.com
26 Sunningdale Way, Bletchley MK3 7SB
Email info@nospine.com
Website www.nospine.com
Managing Director *Andrew Gardner*
An electronic self-publishing venture 'designed by authors for authors'. NoSpine accepts electronic mss and arranges sales and distribution in return for a commission on each sale. Authors retain complete control over their work, full copyright, and set their own sale prices of which they retain 80%. 'We are not a vanity publisher, nor a subsidy publisher. No author ever pays us a penny: in effect we are a writers' cooperative.' All new submissions are refereed by the founding authors to screen out unacceptable or illegal material.

Online Originals
Priory Cottage, Wordsworth Place, London NW5 4HG
☎020 7267 4244
Website www.onlineoriginals.com
Managing Director *David Gettman*
Commissioning Editor *Dr Christopher Macann*
Publishes book-length works on the Internet only. Acquires global electronic rights (including print-on-demand and digital reading) in literary fiction, intellectual non-fiction, drama, fiction for young readers (ages 8–16). No poetry, fantasy, how-to, self-help, picture books, cookery, hobbies, crafts or local interest. 12 titles in 2002. TITLES *The Returning* John Potter; *An End to Anxiety* Claude Ducot; *Quintet* Frederick Forsyth. Unsolicited mss, synopses and ideas for books welcome. *All* authors must have Internet access. Unique peer-review, automated submissions system, accessed via the website address above. Submissions or enquiries on paper or diskette will be discarded.
Royalties paid annually (50% royalties on standard price of £6 or $9).

PerfectBound
See **HarperCollins Publishers Ltd** under **UK Publishers**

Puff Adder Books
35A Lower Park Road, Brightlingsea, Colchester, Essex CO7 0JX
☎01206 303607
Email books@puff-adder.com
Website www.puff-adder.com
Publisher *Karen Scott*
Managing Editor *Diana Hayden*

FOUNDED 2001. *Publishes* literary fiction, writers' guides, general non-fiction, poetry and children's fiction. Approx 40 titles a year. Also operate resource websites for writers (see **Author-Network**; **New Writers Consultancy** and **Writers' Circles** under **Useful Websites at a Glance**). Welcomes unsolicited material; send query letter and synopsis by e-mail in the first instance.
Royalties 45%.

StoryZone Ltd
Ryman's Cottages, Little Tew, Oxfordshire OX7 4JJ
☎0845 458 8408
Email contact@storyzone.co.uk
Website www.storyzone.co.uk

Online children's story library. The website makes available new and published stories by professional writers aimed at children between the ages of 4 and 10. Maximum length 1000 word, with illustrations. Minimum subscription: £5 for 5 stories.

the-phone-book.com
Unit B, Aldow Enterprise Park, Blackett Street, Manchester M12 6AE
☎0161 272 7639 Fax 0161 272 6807 3727
Email editor@the-phone-book.com
Website www.the-phone-book.com

FOUNDED 2001. *Publishes* ultra-short fiction of less than 150 words online to website and WAP site.

Triple Hitter
See entry under **Useful Websites at a Glance**.

WritersServices
See entry under **Useful Websites at a Glance**

Sign Here, Please

Contract jargon and how to cope with it

A book contract is essentially boring except for the part which deals with money. So let us start with that while never forgetting that the small print deserves close attention. Tedium now could make or save money later.

The mega-deals make headlines but are not typical. An established writer may celebrate £20,000 plus but a first-time novelist is lucky to get more than £1,000, while educational and academic writers may settle for a few hundred. A reasonable advance for all but the top names is a sum equivalent to 60 per cent of the estimated royalties payable on the first edition. The advance should be non-returnable, except when the author fails to deliver a manuscript by the due date, or if it is not in line with what was agreed with the publisher. Usually, it is split three ways, part on signature of contract, part on delivery of the manuscript and part on publication.

What proportion of the advance will be due on signature? Ideally one-third (or more if you can present a good case) with the remaining two-thirds due on delivery and publication respectively. If you have a contract for several books, check whether all of the advance money will be added together and sit against future royalties from all books, or whether each book will be separately accounted for against its portion of the advance. Make sure the contract is clear on this point.

A popular misconception is that if an advance is not recovered by royalties on sales, in other words if there is an unearned advance, the publisher is bound to lose money. But the correlation between royalties and profit is not precise. A typical royalty is 10 per cent of the sale price of the book; a publisher's margin may be 15 or 20 per cent after overheads and trade discounts are taken into account. It is possible, therefore, for an unearned advance to be absorbed into costs with the publisher still coming out at a profit. It all depends on the size of the advance, the level of sales and the publisher's margin over fixed costs. There are too many variables to produce a general rule. Just do not be too quick to assume that the publisher loses out.

Another unsafe assumption is that advances are bound to be higher if negotiated by an agent. This may be so for best-selling authors who put their work up for auction but down the scale there may not be much room for manoeuvre. Where an agent really proves his worth is in knowing the pitfalls of a publishing contract and helping his client to avoid them.

Much is written about royalties and what you can expect. In addition to the *Writer's Handbook*, both the Society of Authors and the Writers' Guild have a helpful advisory service for members, which can be used to gauge the fairness of an offer. Royalties – like the advance – are usually the first items to be agreed, even before there is sight of a contract, so find out as much as you can before saying yes. The rest of the contract follows the agent-publisher boilerplate, if there is one, with exceptional items held open for negotiation. It is likely that you can improve a contract significantly with some research and a little negotiation. No serious publisher is going to withdraw an offer to publish if you do not agree by return. Indeed, everyone expects that there will have to be some movement between an opening offer and the terms of a final signed contract. What is needed is an understanding of what it is reasonable to ask and what makes a changed offer worth accepting.

The writer who handles his own affairs is not entirely alone. After years of vigorous campaigning, the writers' unions have negotiated Minimum Terms Agreements (MTA) with several leading publishers. A copy of the standard MTA, which can be obtained from either the Society of Authors or the Writers' Guild (free of charge to members who send a stamped, addressed envelope), is a useful benchmark against which to judge a publisher's offer, though the standard MTA is to some extent a counsel of perfection. When it comes to signing on the dotted line, you may feel you have had to give way on a few points, but if the general principles of the MTA are followed, the chances of securing a reasonable deal are much enhanced.

Before looking at some of the major subsidiary rights deals it's worth stating an obvious truism that 'no two books are perceived equally'. One book hits its target market without any great effort on the part of publisher or author while another is declared out of print and appears now and then in one of those 'What I wish I had published' columns in the trade press, but which no one seems eager to reissue despite singing its praises. Yet another title appeals to the US market and the right to publish it there is sold for a small fortune, while many others, despite everyone's best efforts, slip further down the list of available titles at each passing book fair. What follows is a few guiding principles to deals which may, in the right circumstances, be relevant to your book.

Serial rights

For the right book, serialisation in a national newspaper can be one of the most lucrative rights to be exercised (see page 100). Serialisation of extracts prior to the book's publication (first serial rights) is more lucrative than any press follow-up (second serial rights). Obviously the book must strike some chord with the newspaper – either from a similarity in philosophy, or because its subject would be of more than passing interest to its readers. Most agents jealously guard these rights but when they are controlled by the publisher the following splits in revenue are typical: first serial rights may be divided as high as 90:10 in the author's favour, while second serial rights are usually 75:25. The days of the political memoir and its accompanying big-money newspaper serial deal may have passed but there is still a sale to targeted markets both in the UK and overseas. Fees can range from a few hundred pounds to a hundred thousand plus. Anything that throws new light on people or events in the news will command higher fees. But don't expect to get the money by the first post. The contract may well specify that any earnings on serialisation must be set against the advance.

US rights

This has always been seen as the most important market for many books, yet there is still no easy route to achieving success in the US. In an ideal world, the US publisher will pay an advance and royalty to the UK publisher which is then shared with the author. A successful author – if not represented by an agent – might receive 85 per cent of this income, while a less well-known writer might receive around 60 per cent. Often, though, this is not the whole story. One publishing firm might have a successful track record of selling rights in the US and offer no more than 75 per cent of these proceeds to its authors. On the other hand, a newly formed company with no obvious connections might happily offer 85 per cent though with no realistic chance that these rights will be sold. If pressed to grant these rights to a publisher, there is nothing to be lost by asking about its experience in the US market. But don't forget that 60 or 75 per cent of something is better than holding on to the rights and then not exploiting them.

There are other deals where printed copies are sold to a US publisher at a fixed price. Under this type of arrangement, a book priced at £18 in the UK might be sold for around £5 with consequently little return for the publisher or the author. These situations are very similar to the co-edition market for illustrated books. Why do it, then? It's not the first choice but it is a way to present books to the US market and to try to build up recognition of both publisher and author. The author can expect 7.5 to 10 per cent of the publisher's income from this type of deal, the sums varying according to whether bound or unbound copies are sold.

Translation rights

A large market in Spanish and German-speaking countries for rights to works in English is frequently overlooked by authors. Deals tend to be on an advance and royalty basis, though small companies in emerging markets may try for a flat fee. An author can expect 75 to 80 per cent of any proceeds. Some agents and publishers use local agents for translation deals which means more commission deducted from any sums due to the author. Working alone, translation can be a leap of faith for an author who has no knowledge of overseas publishers, but a little research on the company's website, or a query to a local online writers' discussion group, can pay dividends.

Electronic verbatim text rights

The current theory is that this will one day be a lucrative source of income, although events have not seen this borne out so far. Most publishers now expect to be granted some form of electronic text right when they acquire a book and it pays to do some research on how near they are to exploiting these rights. There is little point in either an author or publisher controlling rights which they are not capable of exploiting fully.

Only a few years ago, it looked as though content providers (authors and publishers) would be able to license their works to websites and make a small fortune from such sales. Today, this idea seems to have vanished as most of the Internet's sites do not require any payment and the received wisdom is that this so-called 'free distribution' model is here to stay. Not everyone agrees, though. Leading newspapers are beginning to charge users to access areas of their sites. If anything the recent downturn in fortunes of this new economy might persuade site owners that a combination of free and paid access is the only way to survive. Then there are the large portal sites such as Yahoo! which can only survive by offering users content on a wide variety of subjects. Many of these portal sites will not pay for content while some expect the publisher to pay to make the material available. The argument is that it is a form of marketing for the publisher and there should be money available in a marketing budget for this showcasing. In these cases, there is precious little return for authors unless it is from increased book sales, although there should be the chance of commissions from content teams attached to a site. This market may be static at present but as sites are redesigned and new ones form it is likely that it will take off again. Those writers who have bothered to keep up to date with such developments will be in a good position to be first in with their work.

For further reading and research investigate the websites of some of the US talent unions, e.g. www.nwu.org or www.asja.org The Society of Authors' quarterly journal *The Author* often analyses current issues in authors' contracts, supplementing the material contained in its Quick Guide series of booklets. Though written from the point of view of a publisher's rights department, Lynette Owen's book *Selling Rights* (Routledge, 2001) contains a wealth of background information that helps to put offered terms into economic perspective.

Useful Websites at a Glance

Many of these and other useful websites for writers can be found in *The Internet for Writers* by Nick Daws (ISBN 1-84025-308-8), one of a series of books published by Internet Handbooks; *The Incredibly Indispensible Web Directory* by Clive and Bettina Zietman, published by Kogan Page (ISBN 0-7494-3617-4); *thegoodwebguide for Writers* by Paul Chronnell, published by The Good Web Guide Limited (ISBN 1-0903282-38-1)

AbeBooks
www.abebooks.co.uk
The merging of AbeBooks and JustBooks in February 2002 has resulted in a second-hand and antiquarian online bookshop with over 35 million titles offered by nearly 10,000 book-sellers worldwide.

**Academi (Welsh Academy/
Yr Academi Gymreig)**
www.academi.org
News of events, publications and funding for Welsh-based literary events. (See entry under **Professional Associations**.)

Alibris
www.alibris.com
Used, foreign, rare and out-of-print books online.

Alliance of Literary Societies
www.sndc.demon.co.uk/als.htm
Details of societies and events. (See entry under **Professional Associations**.)

Amazon Bookshop
www.amazon.co.uk
A wide range of online shopping, including books, music, videos and electronics. Access to more than 1.5 million UK published titles.

Ancestry
www.ancestry.com
Family history information – databases, articles and other sources of genealogical data.

The Arts Council of England
www.artscouncil.org.uk
Includes information on funding applications, publications and the National Lottery. (See entry under **Arts Councils and Regional Offices**.)

Arvon Foundation
www.arvonfoundation.org
Information on the three Arvon centres in the UK. (See entry under **Writers' Courses, Circles and Workshops**.)

Association for Scottish Literary Studies
www.asls.org.uk
The educational charity promoting the lan-guages and literature of Scotland. (See entry under **Professional Associations**.)

Association of Authors' Agents (AAA)
www.agentsassoc.co.uk
UK agents' organisation including list of current members. (See entry under **Professional Associations**.)

Association of Authors' Representatives (AAR)
www.aar-online.org
US agents' organisation including list of current members. (See entry under **Professional Associations**.)

Authors' Licensing and Collecting Society (ALCS)
www.alcs.co.uk
Details of membership, news, publications, legal issues and rights, plus links to related sites. (See entry under **Professional Associations**.)

Author-Network
www.author-network.com
Writers' resource site, operated by **Puff Adder Books**.

Author-Publisher Network
www.author.co.uk
Services for writers, information network, newsletter and online magazine. (See entry under **Professional Associations**.)

BBC
www.bbc.co.uk
Access to all BBC departments and services.

bibliofind
www.bibliofind.com
Over 20 million second-hand and rare books, periodicals and ephemera for sale online via Amazon.com.

BOL
www.bol.com
Internet shopping, including books and music; a database of over 1.5 million titles.

Book2Book
www.book2book.co.uk
Established by a group of publishers, book-sellers, website developers and trade journalists to provide up-to-date news, features and useful information for the book trade.

Booktrust
www.booktrust.org.uk
Book information service, guide to prizes and awards, links to other book organisations, fact-sheets for writers. (See entry under **Professional Associations**.)

British Association of Picture Libraries and Agencies (BAPLA)
www.bapla.org.uk
Free telephone referrals available from the BAPLA database through this website. (See entry under **Professional Associations**.)

British Centre for Literary Translation
www.literarytranslation.com
A joint website with the British Council containing workshops by leading translators, contacts and networks, and listings of translation conferences, seminars and events. (See entry under **Professional Associations**.)

British Council
www.britishcouncil.org
Information on the Council's English Language services, education programmes, science and health links, and information exchange. (See entry under **Professional Associations**.)

British Film Institute (bfi)
www.bfi.org.uk
Information on the services offered by the Institute. (See entry under **Professional Associations**.)

British Library
www.bl.uk
Reader service enquiries, access to main catalogues, information on collections, links to the various Reading Rooms and exhibitions. (See related entries under **Library Services**.)

Children's Writing Resource Center
www.write4kids.com
US website for children's writers', whether published or beginners. Includes special reports, advice, chat links, news on the latest bestsellers and links to related sites.

CILIP
www.cilip.org.uk
The professional body for librarians and information professionals. (See entry under **Professional Associations**.)

Complete Works of William Shakespeare
www-tech.mit.edu/Shakespeare/works.html
Access to the text of the complete works with search facility, quotations and discussion pages.

Copyright Licensing Agency Ltd (CLA)
www.cla.co.uk
Copyright information, customer support and information on CLA services. (See entry under **Professional Associations**.)

Crime Writers' Association (CWA)
www.thecwa.co.uk
Website of the professional crime writers' association. (See entry under **Professional Associations**.)

Daily Mirror
www.mirror.co.uk
The *Daily Mirror* newspaper online.

Dictionary of Slang
dictionaryofslang.co.uk
A guide to slang 'from a British perspective'. Research information; search facility.

The Eclectic Writer
www.eclectics.com/writing/writing.html
US website offering a selection of articles on advice for writers on topics such as 'Proper Manuscript Format', 'Electronic Publishing', 'How to Write a Synopsis' and 'Motivation'. Also a Character Chart for fiction writers and an online discussion board.

Electronic Telegraph
www.telegraph.co.uk
The Daily Telegraph online – one of the first UK national newspapers to establish itself on the web.

Encyclopædia Britannica
www.eb.com
A subscription access to the entire Encyclopædia Britannica database as well as Merriam-Webster's Collegiate Dictionary and the Britannica Book of the Year. (A 30-day free trial is available.) EB online also gives links to more than 130,000 sites selected, rated and reviewed by Britannica editors.

The English Association
www.le.ac.uk/engassoc
News, publications, conference and membership information. (See entry under **Professional Associations**.)

Federation of Worker Writers and Community Publishers (FWWCP)
www.thefwwcp.org.uk
Links to members of the FWWCP, the Federation magazine, information on membership. (See entry under **Professional Associations**.)

Film Angel
www.filmangel.co.uk
Established in March 2000 by Hammerwood Films to create a shop window for writers and would-be film angels alike. Writers submit a short synopsis which can be displayed for a pre-determined period, for a fee, while would-be angels are invited to finance a production of their choice.

Filmmaker Store
www.filmmakerstore.com
Scriptwriting resources, listings and advice.

Financial Times
www.ft.com
Financial Times online.

Great Books Online
www.bartleby.com
An ever-expanding list of great books published online for reference, free of charge.

The Guardian
www.guardian.co.uk
Website of *The Guardian* and *The Observer* newspapers online.

Guide to Grammar and Style
www.andromeda.rutgers.edu/~jlynch/Writing
A guide to grammar and style which is organised alphabetically, plus articles and links to other grammatical reference sites.

Hansard
www.parliament.the-stationery-office.co.uk/
   pa/cm/cmhansrd.htm
The official record of debates and written answers in the House of Commons. The transcript of each day's business appears at noon on the following weekday.

House of Commons Research Library
www.parliament.uk/commons/lib/research/
   rpintro.htm
Gives access to the text of research reports prepared for MPs on a wide range of current issues.

HTML Writers Guild
www.hwg.org
US organisation offering resources, support, representation and education for web authors. (See entry under **Professional Associations**.)

The Independent
www.independent.co.uk
The Independent newspaper online.

Ingenta
www.ingenta.com
Established in 1998, Ingenta is the largest online academic research service in the UK. Formed through a public/private partnership with the University of Bath, the site offers 'free searching of millions of academic and professional articles from thousands of journals online'.

Institute of Linguists
www.iol.org.uk
Discussion forum, news on regional societies, job opportunities, 'Find a Linguist' service, and The Linguist magazine. (See entry under **Professional Associations**.)

Institute of Translation and Interpreting (ITI)
www.iti.org.uk
Website of the professional association of translators and interpreters, with the ITI Directory, publications, training and membership information. (See entry under **Professional Associations**.)

International Movie Database
www.imdb.com
Essential resource for film buffs and researchers with search engine for cast lists, screenwriters, directors and producers; film and television news, awards, film preview information, video releases.

Internet Bookshop
www.bookshop.co.uk
Online bookshop with 1.4 million UK and US titles.

Internet Classics Archive
classics.mit.edu
Includes 441 works of classical literature by 59 different authors. Mostly Greek and Roman works with some Chinese and Persian. All are in English translation.

Journalism UK
www.journalismuk.co.uk
A website for UK-based journalists who write for text-based publications. Includes links to newspapers, magazines, e-zines, news sources plus information on jobs, training and organisations.

**The Library Association
(See CILIP)**

**Mr William Shakespeare
and the Internet**
daphne.palomar.edu/Shakespeare
Guide to scholarly Shakespeare resources on the Internet.

National Union of Journalists (NUJ)
www.nuj.org.uk
Represents those journalists who work in all sectors of publishing, print and broadcasting. (See entry under Professional Associations.)

New Writers Consultancy
www.new-writers-consultancy.com
Advice for writers and critiques, offered by Diana Hayden and Karen Scott of **Puff Adder Books**.

New Writing North
www.newwritingnorth.com
Essentially for writers based in the north of England but also a useful source of advice and guidelines.

Novel Advice Newsletter
www.noveladvice.com
A free US journal aimed at the fiction writer; full text of current and past issues online.

PEN
www.pen.org.uk
Website of the English Centre of International PEN. News of events, membership details. (See entry under **Professional Associations**.)

PlaysOnTheNet
www.playsonthenet.com
Information and help for new playwrights. Launched in association with **Oneword Radio** in January 2002, the site offers the chance to get involved, whether as a writer or someone who enjoys reading and listening to new plays. The site features new works that can be downloaded.

Poets and Writers Online
www.pw.org
A US site containing publishing advice, a directory of writers, online bookstore, literary links, news, articles on aspects of writing, grants and awards.

Producers Alliance for Cinema and Television (PACT)
www.pact.co.uk
Publications, jobs in the industry, production companies, membership details. (See entry under **Professional Associations**.)

Publishers Association
www.publishers.org.uk
Information about the Association and careers in publishing; also 'Getting Published' pages. (See entry under **Professional Associations**.)

Relax With a Book
www.relaxwithabook.com
Reviews, author interviews and competitions online.

Royal Society of Literature
www.rslit.org
Information on lectures, discussions and readings; membership details and prizes. (See entry under **Professional Associations**.)

Science Fiction Foundation Collection
www.liv.ac.uk/~asawyer/sffchome.html
The research library of the Science Fiction Foundation, based at the University of Liverpool. Includes links to the Foundation, the John Wyndham archive, the Foundation's journal and other SF collections and associations. (See entry under **Library Services**.)

Scottish Arts Council
www.sac.org.uk
Information on funding and events; 'Image of the Month' and 'Poem of the Month'. (See entry under **Arts Councils and Regional Offices**.)

Scottish Book Trust
www.scottishbooktrust.com
Information on the Trust's activities and a link to their Book Information Service. (See entry under **Professional Associations**.)

Scottish Library Association
www.slainte.org.uk
Links to various services and major Scottish websites and information on people, organisations, libraries, events and resources of Scottish interest. (See entry under **Professional Associations**.)

Scottish Publishers Association
www.scottishbooks.org
Links to websites of members of the Association, information on activities and publications. (See entry under **Professional Associations**.)

Screenwriters and Playwrights Home Page
www.teleport.com/~cdeemer/scrwriter.html
A website resource for scriptwriters, maintained by US screenwriter Charles Deemer. Links to a discussion forum and 'Screenwright', an electronic screenwriting course.

Screenwriters Online
screenwriter.com/insider/news.html
Described as the 'only professional screenwriter's site run by major screenwriters who get their scripts and screenplays made into movies'. Contains screenplay analysis, expert articles and The Insider Report.

Self Publishing
www.SelfPublishing.co.uk
Established to allow writers to advertise their books on the Internet. Mostly of appeal to self-published authors but open to everyone by publishing a 'taster' of one chapter of a novel or equivalent for other books.

Society for Freelance Editors and Proofreaders (SFEP)
www.sfep.org.uk
Basic information about the Society. (See entry under **Professional Associations**.)

Society of Authors
www.societyofauthors.org
Includes FAQs for new writers, diary of events, membership details, links to publishers' and other societies' websites. (See entry under **Professional Associations**.)

Society of Indexers
www.socind.demon.co.uk
Indexing information for publishers and authors, 'Electronic Indexers Available' pages. Membership information. (See entry under **Professional Associations**.)

South Bank Centre, London
www.sbc.org.uk
Links to the Royal Festival Hall, the Hayward Gallery and Poetry Library; news of literature events.

The Sun
www.thesun.co.uk
Website of *The Sun* newspaper.

The Times
www.thetimes.co.uk
Website of *The Times* newspaper.

trAce Online Writing Centre
www.trace.ntu.ac.uk
Based at Nottingham Trent University, trAce is an online centre for writers and readers worldwide to share and critique their work, discuss favourite books and talk. Also holds occasional (live) conferences and workshops. Links to a wide range of sites for writers.

Triple Hitter
www.triplehitter.net
Website dedicated to 'aiding aspiring writers in obtaining their big break' by showcasing their work free of charge. Includes various interviews, links and helpful hints.

UK Children's Books Directory
www.ukchildrensbooks.co.uk
A directory of the online world of children's books.

The Arts Council of Wales
www.ccc-acw.org.uk
Information on publications, council meetings, the arts in Wales. Links to other arts websites. (See entry under **Arts Councils and Regional Offices**.)

The Web Writer
www.geocities.com/Athens/Parthenon/8390/
  TOC.htm
A site for writers who want to write for publication on the Web. Information and advice
includes getting online, choosing a computer,
saving money on your PC, dealing with
Windows, software information, researching
online, how to build a website, writing for the
Web, website issues.

Webster Dictionary/Thesaurus
www.m-w.com/home.htm
Merriam-Webster Online. Includes a search
facility for words in the *Webster Dictionary* or
Webster Thesaurus; word games, 'Word of the
Day' and Language Info Zone.

Welsh Academy - see Academi

**Welsh Books Council (Cyngor Llyfrau
Cymru)**
www.cllc.org.uk and www.gwales.com
Information about books from Wales, editorial
and design services, 'Wales Book Day'. (See
entry under **Professional Associations**.)

The Word Pool
www.wordpool.co.uk
Children's book review site with information
on writing for children and a thriving discussion group for children's writers.

Word Pool Design
www.wordpooldesign.co.uk
Web design for writers, illustrators and pub-

lishers. 'Friendly advice and help from people
who understand the world of books.'

WordCounter
www.wordcounter.com

Highlights the most frequently used words in a
given text. Use as a guide to see what words
are overused.

Writers' Guild of Great Britain
www.writersguild.org.uk
A wide range of information including rates of
pay, articles on topics such as copyright, news,
writers' resources and industry regulations. (See
entry under **Professional Associations**.)

**Writers, Artists and their Copyright
Holders (WATCH)**
www.watch-file.com
Database of copyright holders in the UK and
North America. (See entry under **Professional
Associations**.)

Writers' Circles
www.writers-circles.com
Offers free pages to writers' circles. Listings and
information. Operated by **Puff Adder Books**.

Writernet
www.writernet.org.uk
Formerly New Playwrights Trust. Information,
advice and guidance for writers on all aspects of
the live and recorded performance.

WritersNet
www.writers.net
A directory of writers, editors, publishers and
literary agents.

WritersServices
www.WritersServices.com
Established in 2000 by Chris Holifield, former
deputy managing director and publisher at
Cassell. Offers factsheets, book reviews, advice,
links and other resources for writers including
editorial services, contract vetting and self-publishing. (Enquiries to: info@writersservices.com)

UK Packagers

Aladdin Books Ltd
28 Percy Street, London W1T 2BZ
☎020 7323 3319 Fax 020 7323 4829
Managing Director *Charles Nicholas*

FOUNDED in 1979 as a packaging company but with joint publishing ventures in the UK and USA. *Commissions* children's fully illustrated, non-fiction reference books. About 40 titles a year. IMPRINTS **Aladdin Books** *Bibby Whittaker* Children's reference; **Nicholas Enterprises** *Charles Nicholas* Adult non-fiction; **The Learning Factory** *Charles Nicholas* Early learning concepts 0–4 years. TITLES *Encyclopedia of Awesome Dinosaurs; The Atlas of Animals.* Will consider synopses and ideas for children's non-fiction with international sales potential only. No fiction.
Fees usually paid instead of royalties.

The Albion Press Ltd
Spring Hill, Idbury, Oxfordshire OX7 6RU
☎01993 831094 Fax 01993 831982
Chairman/Managing Director *Emma Bradford*

FOUNDED 1984. *Commissions* illustrated trade titles, particularly children's. About 4 titles a year. TITLES *From a Distance* Jane Ray and Julie Gold; *The Little Mermaid and Other Fairy Stories* Isabelle Brent. Unsolicited synopses and ideas for books not welcome.
Royalties paid; fees paid for introductions and partial contributions.

Alphabet & Image Ltd
See **Marston House** under **UK Publishers**

Amber Books Ltd
Bradleys Close, 74–77 White Lion Street, London N1 9PF
☎020 7520 7600 Fax 020 7520 7606/7
Email enquiries@amberbooks.co.uk
Website www.amberbooks.co.uk
Managing Director *Stasz Gnych*
Rights Director *Sara Ballard*
Publishing Manager *Charles Catton*

FOUNDED 1989. *Commissions* military, aviation, transport, sport, combat, survival and fitness, cookery, lifestyle, naval history, crime and general reference. 120 titles in 2002. No fiction. IMPRINT **Brown Books**. No unsolicited material.
Fees paid.

Andromeda Children's Books
See **Pinwheel Limited**

Archival Facsimiles Limited
The Old Bakery, 52 Crown Street, Banham, Norwich, Norfolk NR16 2HW
☎01953 887277 Fax 01953 888361
Email erskpres@aol.com
Website www.erskine-press.com
Chief Executive *Crispin de Boos*

FOUNDED 1986. Specialist private publishers for individuals and organisations. Produces scholarly reprints and limited editions for academic/business organisations in Europe and the USA, ranging from leather-bound folios of period print reproductions to small illustrated booklets. Under the **Erskine Press** imprint *publishes* books on Antarctic exploration, general interest autobiographies and medical related 'Patient's Guides' (*Hip & Knee Replacement; Chronic Fatigue Syndrome*). No unsolicited mss. Ideas welcome.
Royalties paid twice-yearly.

AS Publishing
73 Montpelier Rise, London NW11 9DU
☎020 8458 3552 Fax 020 8458 0618
Managing Director *Angela Sheehan*

FOUNDED 1987. *Commissions* children's illustrated non-fiction. No unsolicited synopses or ideas for books, but approaches welcome from experienced authors, editors and illustrators in this field.
Fees paid.

BCS Publishing Ltd
2nd Floor, Temple Court, 109 Oxford Road, Cowley, Oxford OX4 2ER
☎01865 770099 Fax 01865 770050
Email bcs-publishing@dial.pipex.com
Managing Director *Steve McCurdy*
Approx. Annual Turnover £200,000

Commissions general interest non-fiction for the international co-edition market.

Bender Richardson White

PO Box 266, Uxbridge, Middlesex UB9 5BD
☎01895 832444 Fax 01895 835213
Email brw@brw.co.uk

Partners *Lionel Bender, Kim Richardson, Ben White*

FOUNDED 1990 to produce illustrated non-fiction for children, adults and family reference for publishers in the UK and abroad. 40 titles in 2002. Unsolicited material not welcome.
Fees paid.

Book House

See **Salariya Book Company Ltd**

Book Packaging and Marketing

1 Church Street, Blakesley, Towcester, Northamptonshire NN12 8RA
☎01327 861300 Fax 01327 861300
Email martin@marixevans.freeserve.co.uk

Contact *Martin F. Marix Evans*

FOUNDED 1989. Essentially a project management service, handling books demanding close designer/editor teamwork or complicated multi-contributor administration, for publishers, business 'or anyone who needs one'. Mainly illustrated adult non-fiction including military, travel, historical, home reference and coffee-table books. No fiction or poetry. 5–8 titles a year. Proposals considered but rarely come to fruition; most books are bespoke by publishers. Additional writers are sometimes required for projects in development. TITLES *The Fall of France 1940*; *Contemporary Photographers*, 3rd ed.; *The Vital Guide to Major Battles of World War II*; *Encyclopedia of the Boer War*; *The Military Heritage of Britain and Ireland*; *Passchendaele and the Battle of Ypres*; *American Voices of World War I*.
Payment Authors contract direct with client publishers; fees paid on first print usually and royalties on reprint but this depends on publisher.

Breslich & Foss Ltd

Unit 2.1A, Union Court, 20–22 Union Road, Clapham, London SW4 6JP
Email sales@breslichfoss.com

Directors *Paula Breslich, K.B. Dunning*
Approx. Annual Turnover £650,000

Packagers of adult non-fiction titles, including interior design, crafts, gardening, health and children's non-fiction and picturebooks. Unsolicited mss welcome but synopses preferred. Include s.a.e. with all submissions.
Royalties paid twice-yearly.

Brown Books

See **Amber Books Ltd**

Brown Wells and Jacobs Ltd

Forresters Hall, 25–27 Westow Street, London SE19 3RY
☎020 8771 5115 Fax 020 8771 9994
Email postmaster@popking.demon.co.uk
Website www.bwj.org

Managing Director *Graham Brown*

FOUNDED 1979. *Commissions* non-fiction, novelty, pre-school and first readers, natural history and science. About 40 titles a year. Unsolicited synopses and ideas for books welcome.
Fees paid.

Cameron & Hollis

PO Box 1, Moffat, Dumfriesshire DG10 9SU
☎01683 220808 Fax 01683 220012
Email info@cameronbooks.co.uk
Website www.cameronbooks.co.uk

Directors *Ian A. Cameron, Jill Hollis*
Approx. Annual Turnover £400,000

Commissions contemporary art, film, design, collectors' reference, natural history, decorative arts, architecture and children's non-fiction. About 6 titles a year.
Payment varies with each contract.

Compendium Publishing Ltd

See entry under **UK Publishers**

Roger Coote Publishing

Gissing's Farm, Fressingfield, Eye, Suffolk IP21 5SH
☎01379 588044 Fax 01379 588055
Email rgc@ndirect.co.uk

Director *Roger Goddard-Coote*

FOUNDED 1993. Packager of children's and adult non-fiction for trade, school and library markets. About 40 titles a year. No fiction. Include s.a.e. for return.
Fees paid; no royalties.

Diagram Visual Information Ltd

195 Kentish Town Road, London NW5 2JU
☎020 7482 3633 Fax 020 7482 4932
Email diagramvis@aol.com

Managing Director *Bruce Robertson*

FOUNDED 1967. Producer of library, school, academic and trade reference books. About 10 titles a year. Unsolicited synopses and ideas for books welcome.
Fees paid; no payment for sample material/submissions for consideration.

Direct Image Publishing

Beckside, Lindale, Grange over Sands,
Cumbria LA11 6NA
☎015395 33443 Fax 015395 35794
Email elaine@directimageprod.demon.co.uk
Website www.directimageprod.co.uk
Co-directors *Chris Ware, Elaine Ware*

A sub-division of Direct Image Productions
Ltd. FOUNDED in 1992 to support video training programmes. Two key areas: outdoor education; complimentary therapies. Builds training programmes and publishes teachers' resource material, usually as part of a video and book package. No unsolicited mss; approach with letter and outline of idea in the first instance.
Payment One-off fee paid.

Duncan Petersen Publishing Limited

See entry under **UK Publishers**

Eddison Sadd Editions

St Chad's House, 148 King's Cross Road,
London WC1X 9DH
☎020 7837 1968 Fax 020 7837 2025
Email reception@eddisonsadd.co.uk
Managing Director *Nick Eddison*
Editorial Director *Ian Jackson*
Approx. Annual Turnover £2.5 million

FOUNDED 1982. Produces a wide range of popular illustrated non-fiction – mind, body, spirit and complementary therapies are particular strengths – with books published in 30 countries. Ideas and synopses are welcome but titles must have international appeal.
Royalties paid twice yearly; flat fees paid when appropriate.

Erskine Press

See **Archival Facsimiles Limited**

Expert Publications Ltd

Sloe House, Halstead, Essex CO9 1PA
☎01787 474744 Fax 01787 474700
Email expert@lineone.net
Chairman *Dr. D.G. Hessayon*

FOUNDED 1993. Produces the *Expert* series of books by Dr. D.G. Hessayon. Currently 23 titles in the series, including *The Flower Expert*; *The Evergreen Expert*; *The Vegetable & Herb Expert*; *The Flowering Shrub Expert*; *The Container Expert*. No unsolicited material.

Haldane Mason Ltd

PO Box 34196, London NW10 3YB
☎020 8459 2131 Fax 020 8728 1216
Email info@haldane.mason.co.uk

FOUNDED 1994. *Commissions* adult and children's illustrated non-fiction and some young children's fiction. Adult list consists mainly of mind, body and spirit plus alternative health books under the Neals' Yard Remedies banner; children's age range 0–11. 20 titles in 2002. Unsolicited synopses and ideas welcome; approach in writing in the first instance. No adult fiction.
Fees paid.

Angus Hudson Ltd

Concorde House, Grenville Place, Mill Hill,
London NW7 3SA
☎020 8959 3668 Fax 020 8959 3678
Email coed@angushudson.com
Managing Director *Nicholas Jones*
Approx. Annual Turnover £3.5 million

FOUNDED 1977. Leading packager of religious co-editions. *Commissions* Christian books for all ages and co-editioning throughout the world. About 150 titles a year. Publishes under Candle Books and **Monarch Books** (see entry under **UK Publishers**) imprints. Prototype dummies complete with illustrations welcome for consideration. Synopses for text books welcome; no unsolicited mss, please.
Royalties paid.

The Ilex Press Limited

The Old Candlemakers, West Street, Lewes,
East Sussex BN7 2NZ
☎01273 487440 Fax 01273 487441
Email [surname]@ilex-press.com
Managing Director *Sophie Collins*

FOUNDED 1999. Sister company of **The Ivy Press Limited**. *Commissions* titles on digital art, design and photography as well as on all aspects of website design and graphics software. No fiction. Unsolicited synopses and ideas welcome; send a *brief* idea outline (3 or 4 pages) and a letter.
Fees paid.

The Ivy Press Limited

The Old Candlemakers, West Street, Lewes,
East Sussex BN7 2NZ
☎01273 487440 Fax 01273 487441
Email [surname]@ivypress.co.uk
Managing Director *Sophie Collins*

FOUNDED 1996. Sister company of **The Ilex**

Press Limited. *Commissions* illustrated non-fiction books covering subjects such as art, health, self-help, mind, body and spirit, and general reference. No fiction. 60 titles in 2002. Unsolicited synopses and ideas welcome; send a *brief* idea outline (3 or 4 pages) and a letter.
Fees paid.

The Learning Factory
See **Aladdin Books Ltd**

Lexus Ltd
60 Brook Street, Glasgow G40 2AB
☎0141 556 0440 Fax 0141 556 2202
Email peterterrell@ukonline.co.uk
Managing/Editorial Director *P.M. Terrell*
FOUNDED 1980. Compiles bilingual reference, language and phrase books. About 5 titles a year. TITLES *Rough Guide Phrasebooks; Harrap Study Aids; Hugo's Phrase Books; Oxford Italian Pocket Dictionary; Langenscheidt Chinese, Japanese, Korean* and *Vietnamese Dictionaries; Impact Specialist Bilingual Glossaries; Oxford Student's Japanese Learner.* No unsolicited material. Books are mostly commissioned. Freelance contributors employed for a wide range of languages.
Payment generally flat fee.

Lionheart Books
10 Chelmsford Square, London NW10 3AR
☎020 8459 0453 Fax 020 8451 3681
Email Lionheart.Brw@btinternet.com
Senior Partner *Lionel Bender*
Partner *Madeleine Samuel*
A design/editorial packaging team. Titles are primarily commissioned from publishers. Highly illustrated non-fiction for children aged 8–14, mostly natural history, history and general science. About 20 titles a year.
Payment generally flat fee.

Market House Books Ltd
2 Market House, Market Square, Aylesbury, Buckinghamshire HP20 1TN
☎01296 484911 Fax 01296 437073
Website www.mhbref.com
Directors *Dr Alan Isaacs, Dr John Daintith, Peter Sapsed*
FOUNDED 1970. Formerly Laurence Urdang Associates. Compiles dictionaries, encyclopedias and reference. About 15 titles a year. TITLES *Oxford Concise Medical Dictionary; Oxford Dictionary for Science Writers and Editors; Oxford Dictionary of Business; Oxford Dictionary of Nursing;*
Oxford Dictionary of Finance and Banking; Bloomsbury Thesaurus; Larousse Thematica (6 volume encyclopedia); *Collins English Dictionary; The Macmillan Encyclopedia; Grolier Bibliographical Encyclopedia of Scientists* (10 vols); *Penguin Biographical Dictionary of Women; New Penguin Dictionary of the Theatre; The Macmillan Dictionary of Philosophy; The Macmillan Dictionary of Phrase and Fable.* Unsolicited material not welcome as most books are compiled in-house.
Fees paid.

Marshall Editions Ltd
See **Quarto Publishing**

Monkey Puzzle Media Ltd
Gissing's Farm, Fressingfield, Eye, Suffolk IP21 5SH
☎01379 588044 Fax 01379 588055
Email rgc@ndirect.co.uk
Chairman/Managing Director *Roger Goddard-Coote*
Editorial Director *Edwina Conner*
FOUNDED 1998. Packager of adult and children's non-fiction for trade, school, library and mass markets. About 80 titles a year. No fiction or textbooks. Synopses and ideas welcome. Include s.a.e. for return.
Fees paid; no royalties.

Mike Moran Productions Ltd
33 Warner Road, Ware, Hertfordshire SG12 9JL
☎01920 466003 Fax 01920 466003
Email Mike.Moran@moran19.fsnet.co.uk
Website www.mikemoranphotography.co.uk
Chairman/Managing Director *Mike Moran*
Packager and publisher. TITLES *MM Publisher Database; MM Printer Database* (available in UK, European and international editions).

Nicholas Enterprises
See **Aladdin Books Ltd**

Orpheus Books Limited
2 Church Green, Witney, Oxfordshire OX28 4AW
☎01993 774949 Fax 01993 700330
Email info@orpheusbooks.com
Website www.orpheusbooks.com
Chairman *Nicholas Harris*
FOUNDED 1993. *Commissions* children's non-fiction. 12 titles in 2002. No unsolicited material.
Fees paid.

Pinwheel Limited/ Andromeda Children's Books

Station House, 8–13 Swiss Terrace, London
SW6 7LU
☎020 7586 5100 Fax 020 7483 1999
Email sales@pinwheel.co.uk
Website www.pinwheel.co.uk
Publishing Director *Linda Cole*

Pinwheel was FOUNDED in 1995 and bought by
Andromeda Oxford Ltd in 1999. Andromeda
Children's Books are now published alongside
Pinwheel in a combined catalogue with separate
lists. Pinwheel *commissions* children's novelty
books, first information, and non-fiction titles
for the under-fives. Andromeda *publishes* early
information titles, packs for pre-school and fiction
for ages up to 11. Welcomes synopses and
ideas for books; approach by e-mail.
    Fees paid instead of royalties.

Playne Books Limited

Chapel House, Trefin, Haverfordwest,
Pembrokeshire SA62 5AU
☎01348 837073 Fax 01348 837063
Email playne.books@virgin.net
Editorial Director *Gill Davies*
Design & Production *David Playne*

FOUNDED 1987. *Commissions* early learning
titles for young children – fun ideas with an
educational slant and novelty books. Also
highly illustrated and practical books on any
subject. Synopses and ideas by prior arrangement
only. Vanity publications considered.
    Royalties paid 'on payment from publishers'.
Fees sometimes paid instead of royalties.

PRC Publishing Ltd

64 Brewery Road, London N7 9NT
☎020 7697 3000 Fax 020 7697 3001
Email jmessham@chrysalisbooks.co.uk
Website www.chrysalisbooks.co.uk
Head of PRC Publishing Ltd *Joanne Messham*
Commissioning Editor *Martin Howard*

PRC Publishing is the packaging division of
Chrysalis Books (see entry under **UK
Publishers**). *Publishes* a wide array of subjects
including architecture, history and natural history,
lifestyle, art, hobbies and crafts, welfare
and transport. Up to 50 new titles worldwide.

Mathew Price Ltd

The Old Glove Factory, Bristol Road,
Sherborne, Dorset DT9 4HP
☎01935 816010 Fax 01935 816310

Email mathewp@mathewprice.com
Chairman/Managing Director *Mathew Price*
Approx. Annual Turnover £500,000
Commissions full-colour novelty picture books
and fiction for young children plus children's
non-fiction for all ages. TITLES *Nature Hide &
Seek: Jungles; Nature Hide & Seek: Woods and
Forests.*
    Fees sometimes paid instead of royalties.

Quarto Publishing

The Old Brewery, 6 Blundell Street, London
N7 9BH
☎020 7700 6700 Fax 020 7700 4191
Website www.quarto.com
Chairman *Laurence Orbach*

FOUNDED 1976. Britain's largest book packager.
Acquired Marshall Editions in 2002.
Commissions illustrated non-fiction, including
painting, graphic design, how-to, lifestyle,
visual arts, history, cookery, gardening, crafts.
Publishes under the Apple imprint. Unsolicited
synopses/ideas for books welcome.
    Payment Flat fees paid.

Regency House Publishing Limited

See entry under **UK Publishers**

Sadie Fields Productions Ltd

4C/D West Point, 36–37 Warple Way,
London W3 0RG
☎020 8996 9970 Fax 020 8996 9977
Email sales@tangobooks.co.uk
Directors *David Fielder, Sheri Safran*

FOUNDED 1981. Children's books with international
co-edition potential: pop-ups, three-dimensional,
novelty, picture and board books,
1500 words maximum. About 30 titles a year.
Approach with preliminary letter and sample
material in the first instance. *Publishes* in the
UK under the **Tango Books** imprint.
    Royalties based on a per-copy-sold rate and
paid in stages.

Salariya Book Company Ltd

25 Marlborough Place, Brighton, East Sussex
BN1 1UB
☎01273 603306 Fax 01273 693857
Email salariya@salariya.com
Website www.salariya.com *and*
    www.book-house.co.uk
Managing Director *David Salariya*

FOUNDED 1989. Children's information books –

fiction, history, art, music, science, architecture, education and picture books. *Publishes* under its IMPRINT **Book House** Publisher *David Salariya* Highly illustrated non-fiction in all subjects for children, from pre-school to teenage.

Payment by arrangement.

Savitri Books Ltd
25 Lisle Lane, Ely, Cambridgeshire
CB7 4AS
☎01353 654327 Fax 01353 654327
Email munni@savitribooks.demon.co.uk

Managing Director *Mrinalini S. Srivastava*
Approx. Annual Turnover £200,000

FOUNDED 1983 and since 1998, Savitri Books has also become a publisher in its own right (textile crafts). Keen to work 'very closely with authors/illustrators and try to establish long-term relationships with them, doing more books with the same team of people'. *Commissions* illustrated non-fiction, crafts and nature. About 7 titles a year. Unsolicited synopses and ideas for books 'very welcome'.

Sheldrake Press
188 Cavendish Road, London SW12 0DA
☎020 8675 1767 Fax 020 8675 7736
Email mail@sheldrakepress.demon.co.uk
Website www.sheldrakepress.demon.co.uk

Publisher *Simon Rigge*
Approx. Annual Turnover £100,000

Publishes illustrated non-fiction: history, travel, style, cookery and stationery. TITLES *The Shorter Mrs Beeton; The Victorian House Book; The Power of Steam; The Railway Heritage of Britain; Wild Britain; Wild France; Wild Spain; Wild Italy; Wild Ireland; Amsterdam: Portrait of a City* and Kate Greenaway stationery books. Synopses and ideas for books welcome, but not interested in fiction.

Fees or royalties paid.

Small Packages
20 Carisbrooke Road, London E17 7EF
☎020 8520 6073
Email mail@smallpackage.co.uk
Website www.smallpackage.co.uk

Partners *Adam Hibbert, Clare Hibbert*

FOUNDED 2002. *Publishes* children's illustrated non-fiction for trade, school and library markets, UK and co-editions. A mix of project management commissions and packaging. No unsolicted mss.

Flat *fees* paid.

Stonecastle Graphics Ltd/ Touchstone
Old Chapel Studio, Plain Road, Marden, Tonbridge, Kent TN12 9LS
☎01622 832590 Fax 01622 832592
Email touchstone@touchstone.ndirect.co.uk
Website www.touchstonedesign.co.uk *or*
     www.stonecastle-graphics.co.uk

Partner *Paul Turner*
Partner/Editorial Head *Sue Pressley*
Approx. Annual Turnover £300,000

FOUNDED 1976. Formed additional design/packaging partnership, Touchstone, in 1983. *Commissions* illustrated non-fiction general books – motoring, health, sport, leisure, home interest and popular culture. 20 titles in 2002. TITLES *The Ultimate History of Fast Cars/Fast Bikes; Hundreds of Fun Things to Do and Make; Magic and Card Tricks; Learn to Draw Anything; Out of the Flames; The Mountains of Mourne.* Unsolicited synopses and ideas for books welcome. *Fees* paid.

Templar Publishing
Pippbrook Mill, London Road, Dorking, Surrey RH4 1JE
☎01306 876361 Fax 01306 889097
Email editorial@templarco.co.uk
Website www.templarco.co.uk

Managing Director/Editorial Head
     Amanda Wood
Approx. Annual Turnover £10 million

FOUNDED 1981. A division of The Templar Company plc. *Commissions* quality novelty and gift books, picture books and children's illustrated non-fiction. 100 titles a year. Synopses and ideas for books welcome. 'We are particularly interested in picture book mss and ideas for new novelty concepts.'

Royalties by arrangement.

Toucan Books Ltd
Third Floor, 89 Charterhouse Street, London EC1M 6HR
☎020 7250 3388 Fax 020 7250 3123

Managing Director *Ellen Dupont*
Approx. Annual Turnover £1.2 million

FOUNDED 1985. *Specialises* in international co-editions and fee-based editorial, design and production services. *Commissions* illustrated non-fiction only. About 20 titles a year. Unsolicited synopses and ideas for books welcome. No fiction or non-illustrated titles.

Royalties paid twice-yearly; fees paid in addition to or instead of royalties.

Touchstone
See **Stonecastle Graphics Ltd**

David West Children's Books
7 Princeton Court, 55 Felsham Road, Putney,
London SW15 1AZ
☎020 8780 3836 Fax 020 8780 9313
Email dww@btinternet.com
Website www.davidwestchildrensbooks.com

FOUNDED 1992. *Commissions* children's illustrated reference books. No fiction or adult books.Unsolicited ideas and synopses welcome; approach in writing in the first instance.
  Fees and royalties paid annually.

Wordwright Publishing
8 St Johns Road, Saxmundham, Suffolk
IP17 1BE
☎01728 604204 Fax 01728 604029
Email wordwright@clara.co.uk
Contact *Charles Perkins*

FOUNDED by ex-editorial people 'so good writing always has a chance with us'. *Commissions* illustrated non-fiction: social history and comment, military history, women's issues, sport. *Specialises* in military and social history, natural history, science, art, cookery, and gardening. About 6–8 titles a year. Unsolicited synopses/ideas (a paragraph or so) welcome for illustrated non-fiction.
  Payment usually fees but royalties (twice-yearly) paid for sales above a specified number of copies.

Working Partners Ltd
1 Albion Place, London W6 0QT
☎020 8748 7477 Fax 020 8748 7450
Email enquiries@workingpartnersltd.co.uk
Chairman *Ben Baglio*
Managing Director *Chris Snowdon*
Creative Director *Rod Ritchie*
Editorial Director *Deborah Smith*

Specialises in quality mass-market fiction for leading children's publishers including Bloomsbury, HarperCollins, Hodder, Macmillan, Orchard, Random House, Scholastic. First chapter books to young adult. No picture books. Welcomes approaches from writers. Contact *Deborah Smith* on deborahsmith@workingpartnersltd.co.uk
  Payment Both fees and royalties by arrangement.

Zoë Books Ltd
15 Worthy Lane, Winchester, Hampshire
SO23 7AB
☎01962 851318
Email enquiries@zoebooks.co.uk
Website www.zoebooks.co.uk
Managing Director *Imogen Dawson*
Director *Bob Davidson*

FOUNDED 1990. *Specialises* in full-colour information and reference books for schools and libraries worldwide. Does *not* publish picture books or fiction. No freelance work available. Unsolicited material not considered.
  Fees paid.

Book Clubs

David Arscott's Sussex Book Club

Dolphin House, 51 St Nicholas Lane, Lewes, Sussex BN7 2JZ
☎01273 470100 Fax 01273 470100
Email sussexbooks@aol.com

FOUNDED January 1998. *Specialises* in books about the county of Sussex. Represents all the major publishers of Sussex books and offers a wide range of titles. Free membership without obligation to buy.

Artists' Choice

PO Box 3, Huntingdon, Cambridgeshire PE28 0QX
☎01832 710201 Fax 01832 710488
Website www.artists-choice.co.uk

Specialises in books for the amateur artist at all levels of ability.

Baker Books

Manfield Park, Cranleigh, Surrey GU6 8NU
☎01483 267888 Fax 01483 267409
Email bakerbooks@dial.pipex.com
Website www.bakerbooks.co.uk

Book clubs for schools: Rainbow for ages 2–5 and Funfare, ages 5–11. Two issues per term operated in the UK and overseas.

BCA (Book Club Associates)

Greater London House, Hampstead Road, London NW1 7TZ
☎020 7760 6500 Fax 020 7760 6901

With two million members, BCA is Britain's largest book club organisation. Consists of over 20 book and software clubs as well as bol.com. These include: Ancient & Medieval History Book Club, The Arts Guild, The Book Club of Ireland, Books For Children, Computer Books Direct, Discovery, The English Book Club, Escape (female fiction), Fantasy Science Fiction, History Guild, Home Software World, Just Good Books, Mango, Military and Aviation Book Society, Mind, Body & Spirit, Mystery and Thriller Club, Quality Paperbacks Direct, Railway Book Club, Taste, TSP, World Books.

Bibliophile Books

5 Thomas Road, London E14 7BN
☎020 7515 9222 Fax 020 7538 4115
Email orders@bibliophilebooks.com
Website www.bibliophilebooks.com

New books covering a wide range of subjects at discount prices. Write, phone or fax for free catalogue issued 10 times a year.

Cygnus Books

PO Box 15, Llandeilo, Carmarthenshire SA19 6YX
☎01550 777701 Fax 01550 777569
Email enquiries@cygnus-books.co.uk
Website www.cygnus-books.co.uk

'Books for your next step in spirituality and complementary health care. See website for over 1000 hand-picked titles.' Also publishes *The Cygnus Review* magazine which features 50–60 reviews on new mind, body and spirit titles each month.

The Folio Society

44 Eagle Street, London WC1R 4FS
☎020 7400 4222 Fax 020 7400 4242
Email enquiries@foliosoc.co.uk
Website www.foliosoc.co.uk

Fine editions of classic fiction, history and memoirs; also some children's classics.

Letterbox Library

71–73 Allen Road, London N16 8RY
☎020 7503 4801 Fax 020 7503 4800
Website www.letterboxlibrary.com

Children's book cooperative. Hard and soft-cover, non-sexist and multi-cultural books for children from one to teenage.

Poetry Book Society

See entry under **Organisations of Interest to Poets**

Readers' Union Ltd

Brunel House, Forde Close, Newton Abbot, Devon TQ12 2DW
☎01626 323200 Fax 01626 323318

Eight book clubs, all dealing with specific interests: Country Review, The Craft Club,

Craftsman Society, Equestrian Society, The Gardeners Society, Needlecrafts with Cross Stitch, Focal Point, Puzzles Plus.

Scholastic Book Clubs
See **Scholastic Ltd** under **UK Publishers**

Writers' News Bookshelf
PO Box 168, Wellington Street, Leeds, West Yorkshire LS1 1RF
☎0113 238 8333 Fax 0113 238 8330
Email janet.davison@writersnews.co.uk
Specialises in books for writers.

UK Literary Agents and Scouts

★ = Members of the **Association of Authors' Agents**

Sheila Ableman Literary Agency
122 Arlington Road, London NW1 7HP
☎020 7485 3409 Fax 020 7485 3409
Email sheila@ableman.freeserve.co.uk

Contact *Sheila Ableman*

FOUNDED 1999. *Handles* non-fiction including history, science, biography and autobiography. *Specialises* in TV tie-ins and celebrity ghost writing. No poetry, children's, cookery, gardening or sport. Unsolicited mss welcome. Approach in writing with publishing history, c.v., synopsis, three chapters and s.a.e. for return. No reading fee. *Commission* Home 15%; US & Translation 20%.

The Agency (London) Ltd★
24 Pottery Lane, Holland Park, London W11 4LZ
☎020 7727 1346 Fax 020 7727 9037
Email info@theagency.co.uk

Contacts *Stephen Durbridge, Leah Schmidt, Sebastian Born, Julia Kreitman, Bethan Evans, Hilary Delamere, Katie Haines, Ligeia Marsh*

FOUNDED 1995. *Handles* writers and rights for TV, film, theatre, radio scripts and children's fiction. Only existing clients for adult fiction or non-fiction. Send letter with s.a.e. No reading fee. *Commission* Home 10%; US by arrangement.

Gillon Aitken Associates Ltd★
29 Fernshaw Road, London SW10 0TG
☎020 7351 7561 Fax 020 7376 3594
Email reception@aitkenassoc.demon.co.uk

Contacts *Gillon Aitken, Clare Alexander, Lesley Shaw* (also film/TV)
Associated Agents *Anthony Sheil, Mary Pachnos*

FOUNDED 1977. *Handles* fiction and non-fiction. No plays, scripts or children's fiction unless by existing clients. Send preliminary letter, with half-page synopsis and first 30 pp of sample material, and adequate return postage, in the first instance. No reading fee. CLIENTS include Caroline Alexander, John Banville, Pat Barker, Nicholas Blincoe, Gordon Burn, John Cornwell, Josephine Cox, Sarah Dunant, Susan

Elderkin, Sebastian Faulks, Helen Fielding, John Fowles, Germaine Greer, Mark Haddon, Susan Howatch, Liz Jensen, John Keegan, Pete McCarthy, V.S. Naipaul, Jonathan Raban, Piers Paul Read, Michèle Roberts, Nicholas Shakespeare, Gillian Slovo, Matt Thorne, Colin Thubron, Sally Vickers, A.N. Wilson, Robert Wilson. *Commission* Home 10%; US 15%; Translation 20%; Film/TV 10%.

Michael Alcock Management★
Clerkenwell House, 45/47 Clerkenwell Green, London EC1R OHT
☎020 7837 8137 Fax 020 7837 8787
Email Alcockmgt@aol.com

Contacts *Michael Alcock, Anna Power*

FOUNDED 1997. A division of Johnson & Alcock Ltd. *Handles* general non-fiction including current affairs, biography and memoirs, history, lifestyle, health and personal development; literary and commercial mainstream fiction. No unsolicited mss; approach by letter in the first instance giving details of writing and other media experience, plus synopsis. For fiction send first three chapters as well. S.a.e. essential for response. No reading fee. CLIENTS include Tamsin Blanchard, Barbara Currie, Tom Dixon, Yehudi Gordon, Mark Griffiths, Joanna Hall, Lisa Hilton, Lynne Robinson, Barnaby Rogerson, Barry Turner, Lowri Turner. *Commission* Home 15%; US and Translation 20%. *Overseas Associates* **Andrew Nurnberg Associates**.

Darley Anderson Literary, TV & Film Agency★
Estelle House, 11 Eustace Road, London SW6 1JB
☎020 7385 6652 Fax 020 7386 5571
Email enquiries@darleyanderson.com
Website www.darleyanderson.com

Contacts *Darley Anderson, Lucie Whitehouse* (foreign rights) *Elizabeth Wright* (women's fiction/love stories/'tear-jerkers'), *Carrie Neilson* (TV/film, children's books), *Julia Churchill* (US/non-fiction), *Rosi Bridge* (finance).

Run by an ex-publisher with a knack for spotting talent and making great deals – many for six and seven figure advances. *Handles* commercial fiction and non-fiction; children's fiction; also selected scripts for film and TV. No academic books or poetry. *Special interests* Fiction: all types of thrillers, crime/mystery and young male fiction. All types of American and Irish novels. All types of women's fiction. Sagas, chick-lit, contemporary and literary. Also comic fiction. Non-fiction: celebrity autobiographies, biographies, sports books, 'true life' women in jeopardy, revelatory history and science, popular psychology, self-improvement, diet, health, beauty, fashion, animals, humour/cartoons, gardening, cookery, inspirational and religious. Send letter, synopsis and first three chapters; return postage/s.a.e. essential. Disk and e-mailed submissions cannot be considered.

CLIENTS Liz Allen, Richard Asplin, Anne Baker, Catherine Barry, Paul Carson, Caroline Carver, Lee Child, Kira Cochrane, Martina Cole, John Connolly, Margaret Dickinson, Rose Doyle, Joan Jonker, Astrid Longhurst, Rani Manicka, Carole Matthews, Lesley Pearse, Lynda Page, Allan Pease, Adrian Plass, Carmen Reid, Mary Ryan, Rebecca Shaw, Peter Sheridan, Kwong Kuen Shan, Linda Taylor, Elizabeth Waite. *Commission* Home 15%; US & Translation 20%; TV/Film/Radio 20%.

Overseas associates APA Talent and Literary Agency (LA/Hollywood); Liza Dawson Literary Agency (New York); and leading foreign agents throughout the world.

Anubis Literary Agency
6 Birdhaven Close, Lighthorne Heath, Warwickshire CV35 0BE
☎01926 642588 Fax 01926 642588
Contacts *Steve Calcutt, Maggie Heavey*

FOUNDED 1994. *Handles* genre fiction in the following categories: science fiction, fantasy, horror thrillers and crime. No other material considered. In the first instance send 50 pages along with a (one-page) synopsis (s.a.e. essential). No telephone calls. No reading fee. CLIENTS include Lesley Asquith, Georgie Hale, Anthea Ingham, Tim Lebbon, Adam Roberts, Steve Savile, Brett A. Savory, Zoe Sharp. *Commission* Home 15%; US & Translation 20%. Works with the **Marsh Agency** on translation rights.

Artellus Limited
30 Dorset House, Gloucester Place, London NW1 5AD
☎020 7935 6972 Fax 020 7487 5957

Chairman *Gabriele Pantucci*
Director *Leslie Gardner*
Associate *Darryl Samaraweera*

FOUNDED 1986. Full-length and short mss. *Handles* crime, science fiction, historical, contemporary and literary fiction; non-fiction: art history, current affairs, biography, general history, science. No reading fee. Will suggest revision. Return postage essential. Works directly in the USA and with agencies in Europe, Japan and Russia. *Commission* Home 10%; Overseas 12½–20%.

Author Literary Agents
53 Talbot Road, Highgate, London N6 4QX
☎020 8341 0442/07989 318245 (mobile)
Fax 020 8341 0442
Email agile@authors.co.uk
Contact *John Havergal*

FOUNDED 1997. New writing for book publishers and screen producers; also markets strong new content and design ideas for calendar, gift, greeting, game, toy, stationery and other markets. Send half-to-one-page outline, and first chapter writing sample. S.a.e. essential for reply. *Commission* Writing: Home 15%; Overseas & Translation 25%; Digital and other non-writing media: publishing 25%; advertising one-third.

The Bell Lomax Agency
James House, 1 Babmaes Street, London SW1Y 6HF
☎020 7930 4447 Fax 020 7925 0118
Email agency@bell-lomax.co.uk
Executives *Eddie Bell, Pat Lomax, Paul Moreton, June Bell*

ESTABLISHED 2002. *Handles* quality fiction and non-fiction, biography, children's, business and sport. No unsolicited mss without preliminary letter. No scripts. No reading fee.

Lorella Belli Literary Agency★
54 Hartford House, 35 Tavistock Crescent, Notting Hill, London W11 1AY
☎020 7727 8547 Fax 0870 787 4194
Email lorella@lorellabelliagency.com
Website www.lorellabelliagency.com
Contact *Lorella Belli*

FOUNDED 2002. *Handles* full length ficiton (from literary to genre) and general non-fiction. Particularly interested in first novelists, journalists, multi-cultural and international writing, books on or about Italy and/or in Italian. Welcomes approaches from new authors. Send outline plus two chapters for non-fiction, and short synopsis plus first thee chapters for fiction. S.a.e. essential. No reading fee. Revision suggested where appropriate. CLIENTS include Sean Bidder, Scott Capurro, Annalisa Coppolaro-Nowell, Sean Coughlan, Nino Filastro, Dario Fo (winner of the 1997 Nobel Prize for Literature), Jacopo Fo, Emily Giffin, Nisha Minhas, Rupert Steiner, Marcello Vannucci, Diana Winston. *Commission* Home 15%; US & Translation 20%. Works in conjunction with leading associate agencies in most countries. *Represents* The Imprint Agency (New York) and Studio Nabu Literary Agency (Italy).

Frances Bissell Agency

2 Carlingford Road, Hampstead, London NW3 1RX
☎020 7435 3536 Fax 020 7794 9359
Email febissell@msn.com

Contact *Frances Bissell*

FOUNDED 2001. *Handles* full length general fiction, both literary and commercial. Not interested in short stories, poetry or non-fiction. No unsolicitied mss; approach by telephone in the first instance. *Commission* Home 10–15%; US & Translation 20%.

Blake Friedmann Literary Agency Ltd★

122 Arlington Road, London NW1 7HP
☎020 7284 0408 Fax 020 7284 0442
Email <firstname>@blakefriedmann.co.uk
Website www.blakefriedmann.co.uk

Contacts *Carole Blake* (books), *Julian Friedmann* (film/TV), *Conrad Williams* (original scripts/radio), *Isobel Dixon* (books)

FOUNDED 1977. *Handles* all kinds of fiction from genre to literary; a varied range of specialised and general non-fiction, plus scripts for TV, radio and film. No poetry, juvenile, science fiction or short stories (unless from existing clients). *Special interests* commercial women's fiction, literary fiction, upmarket non-fiction. Unsolicited mss welcome but initial letter with synopsis and first two chapters preferred. Letters should contain as much information as possible on previous writing experience, aims for the future, etc. No reading fee. CLIENTS include Ted Allbeury, Jane Asher, Marcelle Bernstein, Joanna Briscoe, Elizabeth Chadwick, Barbara Erskine, Maeve Haran, Ken Hom, Paul Johnston, Glenn Meade, Lawrence Norfolk, Joseph O'Connor, Michael Ridpath, Tim Sebastian. *Commission* Books: Home 15%; US & Translation 20%. Radio/TV/Film: 15%. *Overseas associates* throughout Europe, Asia and the US.

David Bolt Associates

12 Heath Drive, Send, Surrey GU23 7EP
☎01483 721118 Fax 01483 721118

Contact *David Bolt*

FOUNDED 1983. *Handles* fiction and general non-fiction. No books for small children or verse (except in special circumstances). No scripts. *Special interests* fiction, African writers, biography, history, military, theology. Preliminary letter with s.a.e. essential. Reading fee for unpublished writers. Terms on application. CLIENTS include Chinua Achebe, David Bret, Joseph Rhymer, Colin Wilson. *Commission* Home 10%; US & Translation 19%.

BookBlast Ltd

PO Box 20184, London W10 5AU
☎020 8968 3089 Fax 020 8932 4087
Website www.bookblast.com

Contact *Address material to the Company*

HANDLES fiction and non-fiction. No scripts, horror, crime, children's, science fiction, fantasy, poetry, health, cookery, gardening, short stories, academic or articles. No unsolicited mss. No submissions on disk, by fax or e-mail. Preliminary letter, synopsis, biographical information and s.a.e. essential, also names of agents and publishers previously contacted. Film, TV and radio rights mainly sold in works by existing clients. No reading fee. 'We are taking on very few clients.' *Commission* Home 12%; US & Translation 20%; TV & Radio 15%; Film 20%.

Alan Brodie Representation Ltd (incorporating Michael Imison Playwrights Ltd)

211 Piccadilly, London W1J 9HF
☎020 7917 2871 Fax 020 7917 2872
Email info@alanbrodie.com
Website www.alanbrodie.com

Contacts *Alan Brodie, Sarah McNair, Ali Howarth*

FOUNDED 1989. *Handles* theatre, film and TV scripts. No books. Preliminary letter plus professional recommendation and c.v. essential. No reading fee but s.a.e. required. *Commission* Home 10%; Overseas 15%.

Rosemary Bromley Literary Agency

Avington, Near Winchester, Hampshire SO21 1DB
☎01962 779656 Fax 01962 779656
Email juvenilia@clara.co.uk

Contact *Rosemary Bromley*

FOUNDED 1981. *Handles* non-fiction. Also scripts for TV and radio. No poetry or short stories. *Special interests* natural history, leisure, biography and cookery. No unsolicited mss. No fax, telephone or e-mail enquiries. Send preliminary letter with full details. Enquiries unaccompanied by return postage will not be answered. CLIENTS include Elisabeth Beresford, Linda Birch, Teresa Collard, estate of Fanny Cradock, Glenn Hamilton, Cathy Hopkins, Keith West, John Wingate. *Commission* Home 10%; US 15%; Translation 20%.

Jenny Brown Associates

42 The Causeway, Edinburgh EH15 3PZ
☎0131 620 1556 Fax 0131 620 1556
Email jenny-brown@blueyonder.co.uk
Website www.jennybrownassociates.com

Contact *Jenny Brown*

FOUNDED 2002. *Handles* literary and mainstream fiction, non-fiction and children's. Not interested in science fiction, fantasy or academic. Welcomes unsolicited mss, synopses and ideas. Approach in writing with letter, synopsis and first two chapters. Include c.v. and s.a.e. CLIENTS include Des Dillon, Diana Hendry, Anne Macleod, Janet Morgan, Tom Pow, Suhayl Saadi, Christopher Whyte. *Commission* Home 10%; US & Translation 20%. Works with **The Marsh Agency**.

Felicity Bryan★

2A North Parade, Banbury Road, Oxford OX2 6LX
☎01865 513816 Fax 01865 310055

Agents *Felicity Bryan, Catherine Clarke*
Contact *Michele Topham*

FOUNDED 1988. *Handles* fiction of various types and non-fiction with emphasis on history, biography, science and current affairs. No scripts for TV, radio or theatre. No crafts, how-to, science fiction or light romance. No unsolicited mss. Best approach by letter. No reading fee. CLIENTS include Karen Armstrong, Simon Blackburn, Humphrey Carpenter, John Charmley, Liza Cody, Artemis Cooper, A.C. Grayling, Angela Huth, Diarmaid MacCulloch, Sue MacGregor, James Naughtie, John Julius Norwich, Gemma O'Connor, Iain Pears, Rosamunde Pilcher, Matt Ridley, Miriam Stoppard, Roy Strong, John Sulston. *Commission* Home 10%; US & Translation 20%. *Overseas associates* Andrew Nurnberg, Europe; several agencies in US.

Brie Burkeman★

14 Neville Court, Abbey Road, London NW8 9DD
☎0709 223 9113 Fax 0709 223 9111
Email brie.burkeman@mail.com

Contact *Brie Burkeman*

FOUNDED 2000. *Handles* commercial and literary full-length fiction and non-fiction. Film, TV, theatre scripts. No academic, text, poetry, short stories, musicals or short films. No reading fee but return postage essential. Unsolicited e-mail attachments will be deleted without opening. Also independent film and TV consultant to literary agents. *Commission* Home 15%; Overseas 20%.

Juliet Burton Literary Agency

2 Clifton Avenue, London W12 9DR
☎020 8762 0148 Fax 020 8743 8765
Email julietburton@virgin.net

Contact *Juliet Burton*

FOUNDED 1999. *Handles* fiction and non-fiction. *Special interests* crime and women's fiction. No plays, film scripts, articles, poetry or academic material. No reading fee. Approach in writing in the first instance; send synopsis and two sample chapters with s.a.e. No e-mail submissions. No unsolicited mss. *Commission* Home 10%; US & Translation 20%.

Campbell Thomson & McLaughlin Ltd★

1 King's Mews, London WC1N 2JA
☎020 7242 0958 Fax 020 7242 2408

Contacts *John McLaughlin, Charlotte Bruton*

FOUNDED 1931. *Handles* fiction and general non-fiction, excluding children's. No plays, film/TV scripts, articles, short stories or poetry. No unsolicited mss or synopses. Preliminary letter with s.a.e. essential. No reading fee. *Overseas associates* Fox Chase Agency, Pennsylvania; Raines & Raines, New York.

Capel & Land Ltd★

29 Wardour Street, London W1D 6PS
☎020 7734 2414 Fax 020 7734 8101
Email robert@capelland.co.uk

Contacts *Georgina Capel, Tristram Hunt, Diana Souhami, Simon Sebag Montefiore, Paul Burke, John Gimlette*

FOUNDED 2000. *Handles* fiction and non-fiction. Also film, TV, theatre and radio scripts. No children's or illustrated books. Send sample chapters and synopsis with covering letter in the first instance. No reading fee. CLIENTS

Kunal Basu, Julie Burchill, Andrew Greig, Henry Porter, Andrew Roberts, Louis Theroux, Lucy Wadham. *Commission* Home, US & Translation 15%.

Casarotto Ramsay and Associates Ltd
National House, 60–66 Wardour Street, London W1V 3HP
☎020 7287 4450 Fax 020 7287 9128
Email agents@casarotto.uk.com
Website www.casarotto.uk.com

Film/TV/Radio *Jenne Casarotto, Tracey Hyde, Charlotte Kelly, Jodi Shields, Chris Cope, Elinor Burns*
Stage *Tom Erhardt, Mel Kenyon*

Handles scripts for TV, theatre, film and radio. No unsolicited material without preliminary letter. CLIENTS include: **Theatre** Alan Ayckbourn, Caryl Churchill, Christopher Hampton, David Hare, Sarah Kane estate, Mark Ravenhill. **Film** Laura Jones, Neil Jordan, Nick Hornby, Shane Meadows, Purvis & Wade, Lynne Ramsay. **TV** Paul Abbott, Howard Brenton, Amy Jenkins, Susan Nickson, Jessica Stevenson. *Commission* Home 10%. *Overseas associates* worldwide.

Celia Catchpole
56 Gilpin Avenue, London SW14 8QY
☎020 8255 7200 Fax 020 8288 0653
Contact *Celia Catchpole*

FOUNDED 1996. *Handles* children's books – artists and writers. No TV, film, radio or theatre scripts. No poetry. No unsolicited mss. *Commission* Home 10% (writers) 15% (artists); US & Translation 20%. Works with associate agents abroad.

Chapman & Vincent*
The Mount, Sun Hill, Royston, Hertfordshire SG8 9AT
☎01763 245005 Fax 01763 243033
Email info@chapmanvincent.co.uk
Contacts *Jennifer Chapman, Gilly Vincent*

A small agency whose clients come mainly from personal recommendation. The agency looks after only a limited number of predominantly non-fiction writers and is not actively seeking clients but happy to consider really original work. Does not handle poetry, thrillers, adventure, children's books or genre fiction. Please do not telephone or submit by fax or e-mail. Write with two sample chapters and enclose s.a.e. CLIENTS include George Carter, Leslie Geddes-Brown, Sara George,

Rowley Leigh, Dorit Peleg. *Commission* Home 15%; US & Europe 20%.

Mic Cheetham Literary Agency
11–12 Dover Street, London W1S 4LJ
☎020 7495 2002 Fax 020 7495 5777
Website www.miccheetham.com
Contact *Mic Cheetham*

ESTABLISHED 1994. *Handles* general and literary fiction, crime and science fiction, and some specific non-fiction. No film/TV scripts apart from existing clients. No children's, illustrated books or poetry. No unsolicited mss. Approach in writing with publishing history, first two chapters and return postage. No reading fee. CLIENTS include Iain Banks, Carol Birch, Anita Burgh, Laurie Graham, Toby Litt, Ken MacLeod, China Miéville, Antony Sher, Janette Turner Hospital. *Commission* Home 10%; US & Translation 20%. Works with **The Marsh Agency** for all translation rights.

Judith Chilcote Agency*
8 Wentworth Mansions, Keats Grove, London NW3 2RL
☎020 7794 3717
Email judybks@aol.com
Contact *Judith Chilcote*

FOUNDED 1990. *Handles* commercial fiction, TV tie-ins, health and nutrition, sport, cinema, self-help, popular psychology, biography and autobiography and current affairs. No academic, science fiction, children's, short stories, film scripts or poetry. *No approaches by e-mail.* Send letter with c.v., synopsis, three chapters and s.a.e. for return. No reading fee. *Commission* Home 15%; Overseas 20–25%.

Teresa Chris Literary Agency
43 Musard Road, London W6 8NR
☎020 7386 0633
Contact *Teresa Chris*

FOUNDED 1989. *Handles* crime, general, women's, commercial and literary fiction, and non-fiction: history, biography, health, cookery, lifestyle, sport and fitness, gardening, etc. *Specialises* in crime fiction and commercial women's fiction. No scripts. Film and TV rights handled by co-agent. No poetry, short stories, fantasy, science fiction or horror. Unsolicited mss welcome. Send query letter with first two chapters plus two-page synopsis (*s.a.e. essential*) in first instance. No reading fee. CLIENTS include Stephen Booth, Susan Clark, Tamara McKinley, Marguerite Patten, Danuta Reah, Kate Tremayne. *Commission* Home

10%; US 15%; Translation 20%. *Overseas associates* Thompson & Chris Literary Agency, USA; representatives in most other countries.

Mary Clemmey Literary Agency★
6 Dunollie Road, London NW5 2XP
☎020 7267 1290 Fax 020 7267 1290
Contact *Mary Clemmey*
FOUNDED 1992. *Handles* fiction and non-fiction – high-quality work with an international market. No science fiction, fantasy or children's books. TV, film, radio and theatre scripts from existing clients only. No unsolicited mss. Approach by letter only in the first instance giving a description of the work (include s.a.e.). No reading fee. US & Canadian clients: The Bukowski Agency, **Frederick Hill Bonnie Nadell Inc.**, Lynn C. Franklin Associates Ltd, The Miller Agency, **Roslyn Targ**, Weingel-Fidel Agency Inc. *Commission* Home 10%; US & Translation 20%. *Overseas Associate* Elaine Markson Literary Agency, New York.

Clissitt Michie Agency Ltd
2 Sarum House, 55 Portobello Road, London W11 3DF
☎020 7727 3794 Fax 020 7727 3794
Email info@cmagency.co.uk
Website www.cmagency.co.uk
Contacts *Sappho Clissitt* (books), *Annie Michie* (scripts)
FOUNDED 2002. *Handles* general fiction and non-fiction, film and TV scripts. No theatre or radio scripts, no popular science, science fiction, technical or business books. CLIENTS include film scriptwriters Louis Mellis and David Scinto. Unsolicited mss welcome. Send covering letter, synopsis, approx first 50 pages and s.a.e. *Commission* Home (books) 15%, (film) 10%; US (books) 20%, (film) 13%; Translation 20%

Jonathan Clowes Ltd★
10 Iron Bridge House, Bridge Approach, London NW1 8BD
☎020 7722 7674 Fax 020 7722 7677
Contacts *Ann Evans, Chloe Loyd, Lisa Whadcock*
FOUNDED 1960. Pronounced 'clewes'. Now one of the biggest fish in the pond, and not really for the untried unless they are true high-flyers. Fiction and non-fiction, plus scripts. No textbooks or children's. *Special interests* situation comedy, film and television rights. No unsolicited mss; authors come by recommendation or by successful follow-ups to preliminary

letters. CLIENTS include David Bellamy, Bill Dare, Len Deighton, Elizabeth Jane Howard, David Lawrence, Doris Lessing, David Nobbs, Gillian White and the estate of Kingsley Amis. *Commission* Home & US 15%; Translation 19%. *Overseas associates* **Andrew Nurnberg Associates**; Sane Töregard Agency.

Elspeth Cochrane Personal Management
14/2 Second Floor, South Bank Commercial Centre, 140 Battersea Park Road, London SW11 4NB
☎020 7622 0314 Fax 020 7622 5815
Email info@ecpma.com
Website www.ecpma.com
Contact *Elspeth Cochrane*
FOUNDED 1960. *Handles* fiction, non-fiction, biographies, screenplays. Subjects have included Richard Burton, Marlon Brando, Sean Connery, Clint Eastwood, Lord Olivier. Also scripts for all media, with special interest in drama. No unsolicited mss. Preliminary letter, synopsis and s.a.e. is essential in the first instance. CLIENTS include Royce Ryton, Robert Tanitch. *Commission* 12½% ('the percentage is negotiable, as is the sum paid to the writer').

Rosica Colin Ltd
1 Clareville Grove Mews, London SW7 5AH
☎020 7370 1080 Fax 020 7244 6441
Contact *Joanna Marston*
FOUNDED 1949. *Handles* all full-length mss, plus theatre, film, television and sound broadcasting but few new writers being accepted. Preliminary letter with return postage essential; writers should outline their writing credits and whether their mss have previously been submitted elsewhere. May take 3–4 months to consider full mss; synopsis preferred in the first instance. No reading fee. *Commission* Home 10%; US 15%; Translation 20%.

Conville & Walsh Limited★
118–120 Wardour Street, London W1V 3LA
☎020 7287 3030 Fax 020 7287 4545
Email <firstname>@convilleandwalsh.com
Directors *Clare Conville, Patrick Walsh* (book rights), *Sam North* (film/TV rights), *Peter Tallack* (popular science)
ESTABLISHED in 2000 by Clare Conville (ex-**A.P. Watt**) and Patrick Walsh (ex-**Christopher Little Literary Agency**). *Handles* literary and commercial fiction plus serious and narrative non-fiction. Clare Conville also represents many

successful children's authors. Particularly interested in first novelists plus scientists, historians and journalists. CLIENTS Marina Benjamin, John Burningham, Kate Cann, Helen Castor, Tom Conran, Michael Cordy, Mike Dash, Professor John Emsley, Steve Erikson, Katy Gardner, Christopher Hart, Dermot Healy, James Holland, Tom Holland, Sebastian Horsley, David Huggins, Guy Kennaway, Manjit Kumar, P.J. Lynch, Hector Macdonald, Mark Mason, Harland Miller, Joshua Mowll, Jacqui Murhall, Ruth Padel, D.B.C. Pierre, Rebecca Ray, Patrick Redmond, Candace Robb, Mark Sanderson, Saira Shah, Tahir Shah, Nicky Singer, Simon Singh, Doron Swade, Dr Richard Wiseman, Adam Wishart, Isabel Wolff and the estate of Francis Bacon. *Commission* Home 15%; US & Translation 20%.

Jane Conway-Gordon★

1 Old Compton Street, London W1D 5JA
☎020 7494 0148 Fax 020 7287 9264

Contact *Jane Conway-Gordon*

FOUNDED 1982. Works in association with **Andrew Mann Ltd**. *Handles* fiction and general non-fiction. No poetry or science fiction. Unsolicited mss welcome; preliminary letter and return postage essential. No reading fee. *Commission* Home 15%; US & Translation 20%. *Overseas associates* McIntosh & Otis, Inc., New York; plus agencies throughout Europe and Japan.

Rupert Crew Ltd★

1A King's Mews, London WC1N 2JA
☎020 7242 8586 Fax 020 7831 7914
Email rupertcrew@compuserve.com
(correspondence only)

Contacts *Doreen Montgomery, Caroline Montgomery*

FOUNDED 1927. International representation, handling volume and subsidiary rights in fiction and non-fiction properties. No plays or poetry, journalism or short stories. Preliminary letter and return postage essential. No reading fee. *Commission* Home 15%; Elsewhere 20%.

Curtis Brown Group Ltd★

Haymarket House, 28/29 Haymarket, London SW1Y 4SP
☎020 7396 6600 Fax 020 7396 0110
Email cb@curtisbrown.co.uk
Also at: 37 Queensferry Street, Edinburgh EH2 4QS
☎0131 225 1286/1288 Fax 0131 225 1290

Chairman *Paul Scherer*

Group Managing Director *Jonathan Lloyd*
Directors *Mark Collingbourne* (Finance), *Fiona Inglis* (MD, Australia)
Books, London *Jonathan Lloyd, Jonny Geller, Hannah Griffiths, Ali Gunn, Camilla Hornby, Anthea Morton-Saner, Peter Robinson, Vivienne Schuster, Jonathan Pegg*
Books, Edinburgh *Giles Gordon*
Foreign Rights *Diana Mackay, Carol Jackson, Kate Cooper*
Film/TV/Theatre *Nick Marston* (MD, Media Division), *Ben Hall, Joe Phillips*
Presenters/Comedians/Actors *Sue Freathy, Julian Beynon, Jacquie Drewe, Maxine Hoffman, Sarah Spears, Sarah MacCormick, Kate Staddon*

Long-established literary agency, whose first sales were made in 1899. Merged with John Farquharson, forming the Curtis Brown Group Ltd in 1989. Also represents directors, designers and presenters. *Handles* a wide range of subjects including fiction, general non-fiction, children's books and associated rights (including multimedia) as well as film, theatre, TV and radio scripts. Outline for non-fiction and short synopsis for fiction with two or three sample chapters and autobiographical note. No reading fee. Return postage essential. *Commission* Home 10%; US & Translation 20%. *Overseas associates* in Australia, Canada and the US.

Judy Daish Associates Ltd

2 St Charles Place, London W10 6EG
☎020 8964 8811 Fax 020 8964 8966

Contacts *Judy Daish, Sara Stroud, Tracey Elliston*

FOUNDED 1978. Theatrical literary agent. *Handles* scripts for film, TV, theatre and radio. No books. Preliminary letter essential. No unsolicited mss.

Caroline Davidson Literary Agency

5 Queen Anne's Gardens, London W4 1TU
☎020 8995 5768 Fax 020 8994 2770

Contacts *Caroline Davidson, Emma Barker*

FOUNDED 1988. *Handles* fiction and non-fiction, including archaeology, architecture, art, astronomy, biography, design, fitness, gardening, health, history, medicine, natural history, reference, science. Finished, polished first novels positively welcomed. No occult, short stories, children's, plays or poetry. Writers should send an initial letter giving details of the project and/or book proposal, including the first 50 pages of their novel if a fiction writer, together with c.v. and return postage. Submissions without the latter are not considered or returned. CLIENTS Susan Aldridge, Peter Barham, Nigel Barlow, Stuart Clark, Andrew Dalby, Emma Donoghue, Andy Engel, Chris Greenhalgh, Tom Jaine, Huon Mallalieu, Linda Sonntag. *Commission* US, Home, Commonwealth, Translation 12½%; occasionally more (20%) if sub-agents are involved.

Merric Davidson Literary Agency

12 Priors Heath, Goudhurst, Cranbrook, Kent TN17 2RE
☎01580 212041 Fax 01580 212041
Email authors@mdla.co.uk

Contacts *Merric Davidson, Wendy Suffield*

FOUNDED 1990. *Handles* fiction. No scripts. No academic, short stories or articles. No unsolicited mss. Send preliminary letter with synopsis and biographical details. S.a.e. essential for response. No reading fee. CLIENTS include Alys Clare, Francesca Clementis, Murray Davies, Harold Elletson, Alison Habens, Frankie Park, Mark Pepper, Simon Scarrow. *Commission* Home 10%; US 15%; Translation 20%.

Felix de Wolfe

Garden Offices, 51 Maida Vale, London W9 1SD
☎020 7289 5770 Fax 020 7289 5731
Email info@felixdewolfe.com

Contact *Felix de Wolfe*

FOUNDED 1938. *Handles* quality fiction only, and scripts. No non-fiction or children's. No unsolicited mss. No reading fee. CLIENTS include Jan Butlin, Robert Cogo-Fawcett, Jeff Dowson, Carolina Giametta, Brian Glover, Sheila Goff, Aileen Gonsalves, John Kershaw, Bill MacIlwraith, Angus Mackay, Gerard McLarnon, Braham Murray, Julian Slade, Malcolm Taylor, David Thompson, Paul Todd, Dolores Walshe. *Commission* Home 12½%; US 20%.

The Dench Arnold Agency

24 D'Arblay Street, London W1F 8EH
☎020 7437 4551 Fax 020 7439 1355
Website www.dencharnold.co.uk

Contacts *Elizabeth Dench, Michelle Arnold*

FOUNDED 1972. *Handles* scripts for TV and film. Unsolicited mss will be read, but a letter with sample of work and c.v. (plus s.a.e.) is preferred. CLIENTS include Peter Chelsom. *Commission* Home 10–15%. *Overseas associates* include: William Morris/Sanford Gross and C.A.A., Los Angeles.

Dorian Literary Agency (DLA)★

Upper Thornehill, 27 Church Road, St Marychurch, Torquay, Devon TQ1 4QY
☎01803 312095 Fax 01803 312095

Contact *Dorothy Lumley*

FOUNDED 1986. *Handles* general fiction, specialising in popular fiction: women's (from romance, historicals to contemporary); crime (from historical to noir and thrillers); science fiction, fantasy (but cautious about humorous/soft fantasy, i.e. unicorns), dark fantasy and horror. Adult and young adult but no children's under 10, poetry or drama. Introductory letter with outline and 1–3 chapters (with return postage/s.a.e.) only, please. No enquiries or submissions by fax or e-mail. No reading fee. CLIENTS include Gillian Bradshaw, Stephen Jones, Brian Lumley, Amy Myers, Rosemary Rowe, Lyndon Stacey. *Commission* Home 10–12½% for new clients; US 15%; Translation 20–25%. Works with agents in most countries for translation.

Toby Eady Associates Ltd

9 Orme Court, London W2 4RL
☎020 7792 0092 Fax 020 7792 0879
Email toby@tobyeady.demon.co.uk *or* jessica@tobyeady.demon.co.uk
Website www.tobyeadyassociates.co.uk

Contacts *Toby Eady, Jessica Woollard*

Handles fiction, and non-fiction. Approach by personal recommendation. No film/TV scripts or poetry. *Special interests* China, Middle East, Africa, India. CLIENTS INCLUDE Nada Awar Jarrar, Julia Blackburn, Mark Burnell, Robert Carter, Bernard Cornwell, Rana Dasgupta, Fadia Faqir, Xiaolu Guo, Liu Hong, Wei Hui, Francesca Marciano, Rachel Seiffert, Ann Wroe, John Carey, Jung Chang, Kuki Gallmann, Julia Lovell, Robert Macfarlane, Ma Jian, Kanan Makiya, Linda Polman, Fiammetta Rocco, Deborah Scroggins, Xinran Xue. *Commission* Home 15%; Elsewhere 20%. *Overseas associates* USA: Ed Breslin; France: La Nouvelle Agence; Germany: Mohrbooks; Holland: Jan Michael; Italy, Spain, Portugal and Scandinavia: The Buckman Agency; China: Joanne Wang.

Eddison Pearson Ltd

6 Swains Lane, London N6 6QU
☎020 7700 7763 Fax 020 7700 7866
Email enquiries@eddisonpearson.com

Contact *Clare Pearson*

FOUNDED 1995. *Handles* children's books and

scripts, literary fiction and non-fiction, poetry. Please enquire in writing, enclosing s.a.e. E-mail enquiries also welcome. No unsolicited mss; send a brief sample of work in the first instance. No reading fee. *Commission* Home 10%; US & Translation 15%.

Edwards Fuglewicz★

49 Great Ormond Street, London
WC1N 3HZ
☎020 7405 6725 Fax 020 7405 6726

Contacts *Ros Edwards, Helenka Fuglewicz*

FOUNDED 1996. *Handles* fiction and commercial fiction; not children's, science fiction, horror or fantasy); non-fiction: biography, history, popular culture. No unsolicited mss or e-mail submissions. *Commission* Home 15%; US & Translation 20%.

Faith Evans Associates★

27 Park Avenue North, London N8 7RU
☎020 8340 9920 Fax 020 8340 9410

FOUNDED 1987. Small agency. *Handles* fiction and non-fiction. No scripts. New clients by personal recommendation only; no unsolicited mss or phone calls, please. CLIENTS include Melissa Benn, Shyam Bhatia, Madeleine Bourdouxhe, Eleanor Bron, Carolyn Cassady, Caroline Conran, Helen Falconer, Alicia Foster, Midge Gillies, Ed Glinert, Cate Haste, Jim Kelly, Helena Kennedy, Seumas Milne, Tom Paulin, Sheila Rowbotham, the estate of Lorna Sage, Rebecca Stott, Hwee Hwee Tan, Harriet Walter, Elizabeth Wilson. *Commission* Home 15%; US & Translation 20%. *Overseas associates* worldwide.

Lisa Eveleigh Literary Agency★

3rd Floor, 11/12 Dover Street, London
W1S 4LJ
☎020 7399 2803 Fax 020 7399 2801
Email Eveleigh@dial.pipex.com

Contact *Lisa Eveleigh*

FOUNDED 1996. *Handles* literary and commercial fiction and non-fiction and children's books. No plays, scripts or poetry, science fiction or horror. Send synopsis with covering letter and c.v. rather than full mss. No reading fee but return postage essential. Please restrict e-mail contact to preliminary letter only. CLIENTS include Christina Balit, Philip Casey, Paul Heiney, Lisa Kopper, Irma Kurtz, Jonathan Meres, Libby Purves, Lori Reid, Grace Wynne-Jones. *Commission* Home 15%; US & Translation 20%.

Famous Pictures & Features Agency

See entry under **Picture Libraries**

John Farquharson★

See **Curtis Brown Group Ltd**

Film Rights Ltd

See **Laurence Fitch Ltd**

Laurence Fitch Ltd

Mezzanine, Quadrant House, 80–82 Regent Street, London W1B 5AU
☎020 7734 9911
Email information@laurencefitch.com
Website www.laurencefitch.com

Contact *Brendan Davis*

FOUNDED 1952, incorporating the London Play Company (1922) and in association with Film Rights Ltd (1932). *Handles* children's and horror books, scripts for theatre, film, TV and radio only. No unsolicited mss. Send synopsis with sample scene(s) in the first instance. No reading fee. CLIENTS include Carlo Ardito, Hindi Brooks, John Chapman & Ray Cooney, Dave Freeman, John Graham, Robin Hawdon, Glyn Robbins, Lawrence Roman, John Rooney, Gene Stone, the estate of Dodie Smith, Edward Taylor. *Commission* UK 10%; Overseas 15%. *Overseas associates* worldwide.

Jill Foster Ltd

9 Barb Mews, Brook Green, London W6 7PA
☎020 7602 1263 Fax 020 7602 9336
Email agents@jflagency.com

Contacts *Jill Foster, Alison Finch, Simon Williamson*

FOUNDED 1976. *Handles* scripts for TV, drama and comedy. No fiction, short stories or poetry. No unsolicited mss; approach by letter in the first instance. No approaches by e-mail. No reading fee. CLIENTS include Ian Brown, Nick Doughty, Jan Etherington and Gavin Petrie, Phil Ford, Rob Gittins, Jenny Lecoat, Peter Tilbury, Susan Wilkins. *Commission* Home 12½%; Books, US & Translation 15%.

Fox & Howard Literary Agency

4 Bramerton Street, London SW3 5JX
☎020 7352 8691 Fax 020 7352 8691

Contacts *Chelsey Fox, Charlotte Howard*

FOUNDED 1992. A small agency, specialising in non-fiction, that prides itself on 'working closely with its authors'. *Handles* biography, history and popular culture, reference, business, mind, body and spirit, health. No unsolicited mss; send letter and synopsis with s.a.e. for response. No reading fee. *Commission* Home 15%; US & Translation 20%.

French's

78 Loudoun Road, London NW8 0NA
☎020 7483 4269 Fax 020 7722 0754

Contact *Mark Taylor*

FOUNDED 1973. *Handles* fiction and non-fiction; and scripts for all media, especially novels and screenplays. No religious or medical books. No unsolicited mss. 'For unpublished authors we offer a reading service at £70 per ms, exclusive of postage.' Interested authors should write in the first instance. *Commission* Home 10%.

Futerman, Rose & Associates*

Heston Court Business Estate, 19 Camp Road, Wimbledon, London SW19 4UW
☎020 8947 0188 Fax 020 8605 2162
Email guy@futermanrose.co.uk
Website www.futermanrose.co.uk

Contact *Guy Rose*

FOUNDED 1984. *Handles* scripts for film and TV. Commercial fiction and non-fiction with film potential; biography and show business, teenage fiction. No unsolicited mss. Send preliminary letter with a brief resumé, detailed synopsis and s.a.e. CLIENTS include Frank Dickens, Iain Duncan Smith, Royston Ellis, Charles Fourie, Russell Warren Howe, Sue Lenier, John McVicar, Angela Meredith, Valerie Grosvenor Myer, Yvonne Ridley, Gordon Thomas, Simon Woodham, Michael Walker, Paul Rattigan, Mark White, Frederick E. Smith, Michael O'Reilly, Adam Robinson. *Commission* 15–20%. *Overseas associates* worldwide.

Jüri Gabriel

35 Camberwell Grove, London SE5 8JA
☎020 7703 6186 Fax 020 7703 6186

Contact *Jüri Gabriel*

Handles quality fiction and non-fiction and (almost exclusively for existing clients) film, TV and radio rights. Jüri Gabriel worked in television, wrote books for 20 years and is chairman of **Dedalus** publishers. No short stories, articles, verse or books for children. Unsolicited mss ('two-page synopsis and three sample chapters in first instance, please') welcome if accompanied by return postage and letter giving sufficient information about author's writing experience, aims, etc. CLIENTS include Diana Constance,

Miriam Dunne, Pat Gray, Robert Irwin, John Lucas, David Madsen, Richard Mankiewicz, David Miller, Andy Oakes, John Outram, Dr Stefan Szymanski, Frances Treanor, Dr Terence White, Dr Robert Youngson. *Commission* Home 10%; US & Translation 20%.

Eric Glass Ltd

25 Ladbroke Crescent, London W11 1PS
☎020 7229 9500 Fax 020 7229 6220
Email eglassltd@aol.com

Contact *Janet Glass*

FOUNDED 1934. *Handles* fiction, non-fiction and scripts for publication or production in all media. No poetry, short stories or children's works. No unsolicited mss. No reading fee. CLIENTS include Marc Camoletti, Charles Dyer and the estates of Rodney Ackland, Jean Cocteau, Philip King, Robin Maugham, Beverley Nichols, Jack Popplewell, Jean-Paul Sartre, Arthur Schnitzler. *Commission* Home 15%; US & Translation 20%. *Overseas associates* in the US, Australia, France, Germany, Greece, Holland, Italy, Japan, Poland, Scandinavia, South Africa, Spain.

David Godwin Associates

55 Monmouth Street, London WC2H 9DG
☎020 7240 9992 Fax 020 7395 6110
Email assistant@davidgodwinassociates.co.uk
Website www.davidgodwinassociates.co.uk

Contact *David Godwin*

FOUNDED 1996. *Handles* literary and general fiction, non-fiction, biography. No scripts, science fiction or children's. No reading fee. Send covering letter with first three chapters and s.a.e. for response. *Commission* Home 10%; Overseas 20%.

Annette Green Authors' Agency

1 East Cliff Road, Tunbridge Wells, Kent TN4 9AD
☎01892 514275 Fax 01892 518124
Email annettekgreen@aol.com

Contact *Address material to the Company*

FOUNDED 1998. *Handles* literary and general fiction and non-fiction, upmarket popular culture, science, music, film, history, biography and memoirs. No dramatic scripts or poetry. Letter, synopsis, sample chapters and s.a.e. essential. No reading fee. CLIENTS include Nick Barlay, Bill Broady, Emma Gold, Justin Hill, Max Kinnings, Maria McCann, Ian Marchant, Professor Charles Pasternak, Owen Sheers, Elizabeth Woodcraft. *Commission* Home 15%; US & Translation 20%.

Christine Green Authors' Agent★

6 Whitehorse Mews, Westminster Bridge
Road, London SE1 7QD
☎020 7401 8844 Fax 020 7401 8860
Email christine@christinegreen.co.uk
Website www.christinegreen.co.uk

Contact *Christine Green*

FOUNDED 1984. *Handles* fiction (general and
literary) and general non-fiction. No scripts,
poetry or children's. No unsolicited mss; initial
letter and synopsis preferred. No reading fee
but return postage essential. *Commission* Home
10%; US & Translation 20%.

Louise Greenberg★

The End House, Church Crescent, London
N3 1BG
☎020 8349 1179 Fax 020 8343 4559
Email louisegreenberg@msn.com

Contact *Louise Greenberg*

FOUNDED 1997. *Handles* full-length literary fic-
tion and serious non-fiction only. No telephone
approaches. No reading fee. S.a.e. essential.
Commission Home 10%; US & Translation 20%.
Dramatic associate **Micheline Steinberg
Playwrights**.

Greene & Heaton Ltd★

37 Goldhawk Road, London W12 8QQ
☎020 8749 0315 Fax 020 8749 0318

Contacts *Carol Heaton, Judith Murray, Antony
Topping, Linda Davis* (children's)

A medium-sized agency with a broad list of
clients. *Handles* all types of fiction and non-
fiction. No original scripts for theatre, film or
TV. No reply to unsolicited submissions without
s.a.e. and/or return postage. CLIENTS include
Mark Barrowcliffe, Bill Bryson, Jan Dalley,
Marcus du Sautoy, Hugh Fearnley-Whittingstall,
Michael Frayn, P.D. James, Mary Morrissy, C.J.
Sansom, William Shawcross, Sarah Waters.
Commission Home 10–15%; US & Translation
20%. *Overseas Associates* worldwide.

Gregory & Company, Authors' Agents★ (formerly Gregory & Radice)

3 Barb Mews, London W6 7PA
☎020 7610 4676 Fax 020 7610 4686
Email info@gregoryandcompany.co.uk
Website www.gregoryandcompany.co.uk

Contact *Jane Gregory*
Editorial *Broo Doherty*
Rights *Anna Valdinger, Claire Morris*

FOUNDED 1987. *Handles* all kinds of fiction and
general non-fiction. *Special interest* fiction – literary, commercial, women's fiction, crime,
suspense and thrillers. 'We are particularly
interested in books which will also sell to publishers abroad.' No original plays, film or TV
scripts (only published books are sold to film
and TV). No science fiction, fantasy, poetry,
academic or children's books. No reading fee.
Editorial advice given to own authors. No
unsolicited mss; send a preliminary letter with
c.v., synopsis, first three chapters and future
writing plans (plus return postage). Short submissions by fax or e-mail. *Commission* Home
15%; US, Translation, Radio/TV/Film 20%. Is
well represented throughout Europe, Asia and
US.

David Grossman Literary Agency Ltd

118b Holland Park Avenue, London W11 4UA
☎020 7221 2770 Fax 020 7221 1445

Contact *Material should be addressed to the
Submissions Dept.*

FOUNDED 1976. *Handles* full-length fiction and
general non-fiction – good writing of all kinds
and anything healthily controversial. No verse
or technical books for students. No original
screenplays or teleplays (only works existing in
volume form are sold for performance rights).
Generally works with published writers of fiction only but 'truly original, well-written novels from beginners' will be considered. Best
approach by preliminary letter giving full
description of the work and, in the case of fiction, with the first 50 pages. All material must
be accompanied by return postage. No
approaches or submissions by fax or e-mail. No
unsolicited mss. No reading fee. *Commission*
Rates vary for different markets. *Overseas associates* throughout Europe, Asia, Brazil and the
US.

The Rod Hall Agency Limited

3 Charlotte Mews, London W1T 4DZ
☎020 7637 0706 Fax 020 7637 0807
Email office@rodhallagency.com
Website www.rodhallagency.com

Contacts *Rod Hall, Clare Barker,
Charlotte Mann*

FOUNDED 1997. *Handles* drama for film, TV
and theatre. Does not represent writers of
episodes for TV series where the format is provided but represents originators of series.
CLIENTS include Simon Beaufoy (*The Full
Monty*), Jeremy Brock (*Mrs Brown*), Liz

Lochhead (*Perfect Days*), Martin McDonagh (*The Beauty Queen of Leenane*). Introductory letter required with brief description of the work to be considered together with c.v. No reading fee. *Commission* Home 10%; US 15%; Translation 20%.

Margaret Hanbury Literary Agency★

27 Walcot Square, London SE11 4UB
☎020 7735 7680 Fax 020 7793 0316
Email maggie@mhanbury.demon.co.uk

Contact *Margaret Hanbury*

Personally run agency representing quality fiction and non-fiction. No plays, scripts, poetry, children's books, fantasy, horror. No unsolicited approaches at present. CLIENTS include J.G. Ballard, Simon Callow, George Alagiah, Judith Lennox, Jane Glover Jordan. *Commission* Home 15%; Overseas 20%.

Roger Hancock Ltd

4 Water Lane, London NW1 8NZ
☎020 7267 4418 Fax 020 7267 0705
Email info@rogerhancock.com

FOUNDED 1960. *Special interests* comedy drama and light entertainment. Scripts only. No books. Unsolicited mss not welcome. Initial phone call required. No reading fee. *Commission* Home 10%; Overseas 15%.

Antony Harwood Limited

405 Riverbank House, 1 Putney Bridge Approach, London SW6 3JD
☎020 7384 9209 Fax 020 7384 9206
Email mail@antonyharwood.com

Contacts *Antony Harwood, James Macdonald Lockhart*

FOUNDED 2000. *Handles* fiction and non-fiction. Send letter and synopsis with return postage in the first instance. No reading fee. CLIENTS Peter F. Hamilton, Alan Hollinghurst, A.L. Kennedy, Douglas Kennedy, Chris Manby, George Monbiot, Tim Parks. *Commission* Home 10%; US & Translation 20%.

A.M. Heath & Co. Ltd★

79 St Martin's Lane, London WC2N 4RE
☎020 7836 4271 Fax 020 7497 2561

Contacts *Bill Hamilton, Sara Fisher, Sarah Molloy, Victoria Hobbs*

FOUNDED 1919. *Handles* fiction, general non-fiction and children's. No dramatic scripts, poetry or short stories. Preliminary letter and synopsis essential. No reading fee. CLIENTS include Joan Aiken, Christopher Andrew, Bella Bathurst, Anita Brookner, Helen Cresswell, Patricia Duncker, Geoff Dyer, Katie Fforde, Lesley Glaister, Graham Hancock, Hilary Mantel, Hilary Norman, Susan Price, John Sutherland, Adam Thorpe, Barbara Trapido. *Commission* Home 10–15%; US & Translation 20%; Film & TV 15%. *Overseas associates* in the US, Europe, South America, Japan and the Far East.

Rupert Heath Literary Agency

The Beeches, Furzedown Lane, Amport, Hampshire SP11 8BW
☎01264 771899 Fax 020 7691 9331
Email enquiries@rupertheath.com

Contact *Rupert Heath*

FOUNDED 2000. *Handles* literary and general fiction and non-fiction, including history, biography and autobiography, current affairs, popular science, the arts and some popular culture. No scripts or poetry. Approach with e-mail or letter (sample chapter and s.a.e.). E-mail submission preferred. No reading fee. *Commission* Home 15%; US & Translation 20%. *Overseas associates* worldwide.

Henser Literary Agency

174 Pennant Road, Llanelli, Carmarthenshire SA14 8HN
☎01554 753520
Email henserliteraryagency@btopeworld.com

Contact *Steve Henser*

FOUNDED 2002. *Handles* mystery, mainstream, literary fiction, fantasy, science fiction. Also film, TV, radio and theatre scripts. No horror. *Specialises* in translations from Japanese into English – especially literary fiction. CLIENTS include John Campbell, Mary Matsumoto. No unsolicited mss, synopses or ideas as not looking for additional clients at this time. *Commission* Home 15%; Foreign & Translation 20%.

David Higham Associates Ltd★

5–8 Lower John Street, Golden Square, London W1F 9HA
☎020 7434 5900 Fax 020 7437 1072
Email dha@davidhigham.co.uk
Website www.davidhigham.co.uk

Scripts *Nicky Lund, Georgina Ruffhead, Gemma Hirst*
Books *Anthony Goff, Bruce Hunter, Jacqueline Korn, Caroline Walsh, Veronique Baxter*

FOUNDED 1935. *Handles* fiction, general non-fiction (biography, history, current affairs, etc.) and children's books. Also scripts. Preliminary letter with synopsis essential in first instance.

No reading fee. CLIENTS include John le Carré, Jonathan Dimbleby, Stephen Fry, Jane Green, James Herbert, Jeremy Paxman, Jacqueline Wilson. *Commission* Home 15%; US & Translation 20%.

Vanessa Holt Ltd★
59 Crescent Road, Leigh-on-Sea, Essex SS9 2PF
☎01702 473787 Fax 01702 471890
Email vanessa@holtlimited.freeserve.co.uk
Contact *Vanessa Holt*

FOUNDED 1989. *Handles* general fiction, non-fiction and non-illustrated children's books. No scripts, poetry, academic or technical. *Specialises* in crime fiction, commercial and literary fiction, and particularly interested in books with potential for sales abroad and/or to TV. No unsolicited mss. Approach by letter in first instance; s.a.e. essential. No reading fee. *Commission* Home 15%; US & Translation 20%; Radio/TV/Film 15%. Represented in all foreign markets.

Kate Hordern Literary Agency
18 Mortimer Road, Clifton, Bristol BS8 4EY
☎0117 923 9368 Fax 0117 973 1941
Email katehordern@blueyonder.co.uk
Contact *Kate Hordern*

FOUNDED 1999. *Handles* quality literary and commercial fiction including women's, suspense and genre fiction; also general non-fiction. No children's books. Approach in writing in the first instance with details of project. New clients taken on very selectively. Synopsis required for fiction; proposal/chapter breakdown for non-fiction. Sample chapters on request only. S.a.e. essential. No reading fee. CLIENTS Richard Bassett, Jeff Dawson, James Gray, Will Randall. *Commission* Home 15%; US & Translation 20%. *Overseas associates* Carmen Balcells Agency, Spain; Synopsis Agency, Russia and various agencies in Asia.

Valerie Hoskins Associates
20 Charlotte Street, London W1T 2NA
☎020 7637 4490 Fax 020 7637 4493
Email vha@vhassociates.co.uk
Contacts *Valerie Hoskins, Rebecca Watson*

FOUNDED 1983. *Handles* scripts for film, TV and radio. *Special interests* feature films, animation and TV. No unsolicited scripts; preliminary letter of introduction essential. No reading fee. *Commission* Home 12½%; US 20% (maximum).

Tanja Howarth Literary Agency★
19 New Row, London WC2N 4LA
☎020 7240 5553 Fax 020 7379 0969
Email tanja.howarth@virgin.net
Contact *Tanja Howarth*

FOUNDED 1970. Interested in taking on both fiction and non-fiction from British writers. No children's books, plays or poetry, but all other subjects considered providing the treatment is intelligent. *No unsolicited mss.* Also an established agent for foreign literature, particularly from the German language. *Commission* Home 15%; Translation 20%.

ICM
Oxford House, 76 Oxford Street, London W1D 1BS
☎020 7636 6565 Fax 020 7323 0101
Email admin@icmlondon.co.uk
Contacts *Sue Rodgers, Jessica Sykes, Cathy King, Greg Hunt, Hugo Young, Michael McCoy, Duncan Heath, Paul Lyon-Maris*

FOUNDED 1973. *Specialises* in scripts for film, theatre, TV and radio. No reading fee. *Commission* 10%. *Overseas associates* ICM, New York/Los Angeles.

ICM Books
International Creative Management Ltd, 4–6 Soho Square, London W1D 3DZ
☎020 7432 0800 Fax 020 7432 0808
Contact *Kate Jones*

Handles fiction and non-fiction; no plays or scripts. Send letter and sample chapters only in the first instance. No reading fee. *Overseas associate* International Creative Management Inc., 40 West 57th Street, New York, NY 10019, USA.

IMG Literary UK
The Pier House, Strand on the Green, Chiswick, London W4 3NN
☎020 8233 5000 Fax 020 8233 5001
IMG Literary US, 825 Seventh Avenue, Ninth Floor, New York, NY 10009
☎001 212 489 5400 Fax 001 212 246 1118
Chairman *Mark H. McCormack*
Agents *Sarah Wooldridge* (UK), *Mark Reiter, Lisa Queen, P.J. Mark* (US)

Handles celebrity books, commercial fiction, non-fiction, sports-related and how-to business books. No theatre, children's, poetry or academic books. *Commission* Home & US 20%; Elsewhere 25%.

Michael Imison Playwrights Ltd
See **Alan Brodie Representation Ltd**

Intercontinental Literary Agency★
33 Bedford Street, London WC2E 9ED
☎020 7379 6611 Fax 020 7379 6790
Email ila@ila-agency.co.uk
Contacts *Nicki Kennedy, Sam Edenborough*
FOUNDED 1965. *Handles* translation rights only
for, among others, the authors of **PFD**,
London; **LAW Ltd**, London; Harold Matson
Co. Inc., New York.

International Literary Representation & Management LLC
186 Bickenhall Mansions, Bickenhall Street,
London W1U 6BX
☎020 7224 1748 Fax 020 7224 1802
Email info@yesitive.com
Website www.yesitive.com
Vice President for Europe *Peter Cox*
European office of US agency. Represents
authors with major international potential.
Submissions considered only if the guidelines
given on the website have been followed. Do
not send unsolicited mss by post. No radio or
theatre scripts. No reading fee. CLIENTS Martin
Bell, OBE, Brian Clegg, Brian Cruver, Senator
Orrin Hatch, Barbara Jacobs, Commodore
Scott Jones, USN, Michael J. Nelson, David
Soul, Michelle Paver, Saxon Roach. *Commission* by agreement.

International Scripts
1A Kidbrooke Park Road, Blackheath,
London SE3 0LR
☎020 8319 8666 Fax 020 8319 0801
Contacts *Bob Tanner, Pat Hornsey, Jill Lawson*
FOUNDED 1979 by Bob Tanner. *Handles* most
types of books (non-fiction and fiction) and
scripts for most media. No poetry, articles or
short stories. Preliminary letter plus s.a.e.
required. CLIENTS include Jane Adams, Zita
Adamson, Ashleigh Bingham, Simon Clark,
Cory Daniells, Paul Devereux, Dr James
Fleming, Ed Gorman, Julie Harris, Robert A.
Heinlein, Anna Jacobs, Anne Jones, Richard
Laymon, Nick Oldham, Christine Poulson,
Mary Ryan, John and Anne Spencer, Janet
Woods, *Commission* Home 15%; US &
Translation 20%. *Overseas associates* include
Ralph Vicinanza, USA; Thomas Schlück,
Germany; Eliane Benisti, France.

Barrie James Literary Agency/New Authors Showcase
See **New Authors Showcase** under
Electronic Publishing and Other Services

Janklow & Nesbit (UK) Ltd
29 Adam & Eve Mews, London W8 6UG
☎020 7376 2733 Fax 020 7376 2915
Email queries@janklow.co.uk
Contacts *Tif Loehnis, Claire Paterson*
FOUNDED 2000. *Handles* fiction and non-
fiction; commercial and literary. No unsolicited mss. Send full outline (non-fiction), synopsis and three sample chapters (fiction) plus
informative covering letter and return postage.
(See also **Janklow & Nesbit Associates**, New
York, under **US Agents**.)

John Johnson (Authors' Agent)★
Clerkenwell House, 45/47 Clerkenwell
Green, London EC1R 0HT
☎020 7251 0125 Fax 020 7251 2172
Email johnjohnson@btinternet.com
Contacts *Andrew Hewson*
FOUNDED 1956. A division of Johnson & Alcock
Ltd. *Handles* general fiction and non-fiction. No
science fiction, technical or academic material.
Scripts from existing clients only. No unsolicited
mss; send a preliminary letter and s.a.e. first.
No reading fee. *Commission* Home 10%; US
15–20%; Translation 20%.

Jane Judd Literary Agency★
18 Belitha Villas, London N1 1PD
☎020 7607 0273 Fax 020 7607 0623
Contact *Jane Judd*
FOUNDED 1986. *Handles* general fiction and
non-fiction: women's fiction, crime, thrillers, literary fiction, humour, biography, investigative
journalism, health, women's interests and travel.
'Looking for good contemporary women's fiction but not Mills & Boon-type.' No scripts, academic, gardening, short stories or DIY.
Approach with letter, including synopsis, first
chapter and return postage. Initial telephone call
helpful in the case of non-fiction. CLIENTS
include Andy Dougan, David Winner, Jill
Mansell, Jonathon Porritt, Rosie Rushton,
Manda Scott, Cliff Goodwin. *Commission* Home
10%; US & Translation 20%.

Juvenilia
Avington, Near Winchester, Hampshire
SO21 1DB
☎01962 779656 Fax 01962 779656

Email juvenilia@clara.co.uk

Contact *Rosemary Bromley*

FOUNDED 1973. *Handles* young/teen fiction and picture books; non-fiction and scripts for TV and radio. No poetry or short stories unless part of a collection or picture book material. No unsolicited mss. Send preliminary letter with full details of work and biographical outline in first instance. Preliminary letters unaccompanied by return postage will not be answered. Enquiries by phone, fax or e-mail will not be answered. CLIENTS include Paul Aston, Elisabeth Beresford, Linda Birch, Denis Bond, Terry Deary, Ann Evans, Gaye Hicyilmaz, Tony Maddox, Phil McMylor, Anna Perara, Elizabeth Pewsey, Fran and John Pickering, Saviour Pirotta, Eira Reeves, Kelvin Reynolds, James Riordan, Peter Riley, Susan Rollings, Malcolm Rose, Cathy Simpson, Keith West. *Commission* Home 10%; US 15%; Translation 20%.

Tamar Karet Literary Agency

56 Priory Road, Crouch End, London N8 7EX

☎020 8340 6460 Fax 020 8348 8638

Email tamar@btinternet.com

Contact *Tamar Karet*

FOUNDED in 2001 by publisher with particular experience of fiction, social affairs and illustrated books. *Specialises* in fiction, travel, leisure, health, cookery, biography, history, social affairs and politics. No academic, children's, poetry, science fiction, horror, militaria or scripts. No unsolicited mss; no submissions by e-mail. Send synopsis and sample with s.a.e. *Commission* Home 15%; US & Translation 20%.

Michelle Kass Associates*

36–38 Glasshouse Street, London W1B 5DL

☎020 7439 1624 Fax 020 7734 3394

Contacts *Michelle Kass, Resham Naqvi*

FOUNDED 1991. *Handles* literary fiction and film primarily. Approach with telephone call in the first instance. No reading fee. *Commission* Home 10%; US & Translation 15–20%.

Frances Kelly*

111 Clifton Road, Kingston upon Thames, Surrey KT2 6PL

☎020 8549 7830 Fax 020 8547 0051

Contact *Frances Kelly*

FOUNDED 1978. *Handles* non-fiction, including illustrated: biography, history, art, self-help, food & wine, complementary medicine and therapies, finance and business books; and academic non-fiction in all disciplines. No scripts except for existing clients. No unsolicited mss. Approach by letter with brief description of work or synopsis, together with c.v. and return postage. *Commission* Home 10%; US & Translation 20%.

Paul Kiernan

PO Box 120, London SW3 4LU

Contact *Paul Kiernan*

FOUNDED 1990. *Handles* mainly fiction, also scripts for TV, film, radio and theatre (but TV and film scripts from book-writing clients only). No unsolicited mss. Preferred approach is by letter or personal introduction. Letters should include synopsis and brief biography. No reading fee. CLIENTS include K. Banta, Lord Chalfont, Ambassador Walter J.P. Curley, Sir Paul Fox. *Commission* Home 15%; US 20%.

Knight Features

20 Crescent Grove, London SW4 7AH

☎020 7622 1467 Fax 020 7622 1522

Email peter@knightfeatures.co.uk

Contacts *Peter Knight, Samantha Ferris, Gaby Martin, Ann King-Hall, Andrew Knight*

FOUNDED 1985. *Handles* motor sports, cartoon books, puzzles, business, history, factual and biographical material. No poetry, science fiction or cookery. No unsolicited mss. Send letter accompanied by c.v. and s.a.e. with synopsis of proposed work. CLIENTS include David Kerr Cameron, Frank Dickens, Gray Jolliffe, Angus McGill, Chris Maslanka, Barbara Minto. *Commission* dependent upon authors and territories. *Overseas associates* United Media, US; Auspac Media, Australia.

L&M

Milton House, Milton Street, Waltham Abbey, Essex EN9 1EZ

☎01992 711511/614527

Fax 01992 711511/614527

Email TriciaSumner@email.msn.com

Contact *Tricia Sumner*

FOUNDED 1995. *Specialises* in literary fiction, theatre, TV, radio and film. *Special interests* in multicultural, gay, feminist and anti-establishment writing. No new authors taken on except by recommendation. No unsolicited mss. CLIENTS Marion Baraitser, Kathleen Kiirik Bryson, John R. Gordon, Barry Grossman, Angela Lanyon, Catherine Muschamp, Roland Moore, Jeremy Rayner. *Commission* Home 15%; Overseas 20–25%.

LAW Ltd (Lucas Alexander Whitley)★

14 Vernon Street, London W14 0RJ
☎020 7471 7900 Fax 020 7471 7910
Email <firstname>@lawagency.co.uk

Contacts *Mark Lucas, Julian Alexander, Araminta Whitley, Philippa Milnes-Smith (children's), Alice Saunders, Celia Hayley, Lucinda Cook, Peta Nightingale, Helen Mulligan*

FOUNDED 1996. *Handles* full-length commercial and literary fiction, non-fiction and children's books. No plays, poetry, textbooks or fantasy. Film and TV scripts handled for established clients only. Unsolicited mss considered; send brief covering letter, short synopsis and two sample chapters. S.a.e. essential. No e-mailed submissions. *Commission* Home 15%; US & Translation 20%. *Overseas associates* worldwide.

Cat Ledger Literary Agency★

20–21 Newman Street, London W1T 1PG
☎020 7861 8226 Fax 020 7861 8001

Contact *Cat Ledger*

FOUNDED 1996. *Handles* non-fiction: popular culture – film, music, sport, travel, humour, biography, politics; investigative journalism; fiction (non-genre). No scripts. No children's, poetry, fantasy, science fiction, romance. No unsolicited mss; approach with preliminary letter, synopsis and s.a.e. No reading fee. *Commission* Home 10%; US & Translation 20%.

Barbara Levy Literary Agency★

64 Greenhill, Hampstead High Street, London NW3 5TZ
☎020 7435 9046 Fax 020 7431 2063

Contacts *Barbara Levy, John Selby*

FOUNDED 1986. *Handles* general fiction, non-fiction, and film and TV rights. No unsolicited mss. Send detailed preliminary letter in the first instance. No reading fee. *Commission* Home 10%; US 20%; Translation by arrangement, in conjunction with **The Marsh Agency**. *US associate* Arcadia Ltd, New York.

Limelight Management★

33 Newman Street, London W1T 1PY
☎020 7637 2529 Fax 020 7637 2538
Email limelight.management@virgin.net

Contacts *Fiona Lindsay, Linda Shanks*

FOUNDED 1991. *Handles* general non-fiction: cookery, gardening, antiques, interior design, wine, art and crafts and health. No fiction, TV, film, radio or theatre. *Specialises* in illustrated books. Unsolicited mss welcome; send preliminary letter (s.a.e. essential). No reading fee. *Commission* Home 15%; US & Translation 20%.

The Christopher Little Literary Agency★

10 Eel Brook Studios, 125 Moore Park Road, London SW6 4PS
☎020 7736 4455 Fax 020 7736 4490
Email <firstname>@christopherlittle.net

Contacts *Christopher Little, Kellee Nunley, Emma Schlesinger*

FOUNDED 1979. *Handles* commercial and literary full-length fiction and non-fiction. No poetry, plays, science fiction, fantasy, textbooks, illustrated children's or short stories. Film scripts for established clients only. No unsolicited submissions. *Commission* Home 15%; US, Canada, Translation, Audio, Motion Picture 20%.

London Independent Books

26 Chalcot Crescent, London NW1 8YD
☎020 7706 0486 Fax 020 7724 3122

Proprietor *Carolyn Whitaker*

FOUNDED 1971. A self-styled 'small and idiosyncratic' agency. *Handles* fiction and non-fiction reflecting the tastes of the proprietor. All subjects considered (except computer books and young children's), providing the treatment is strong and saleable. Scripts handled only if by existing clients. *Special interests* boats, travel, travelogues, commercial fiction, science fiction and fantasy. No unsolicited mss; letter, synopsis and first two chapters with return postage the best approach. No reading fee. *Commission* Home 15%; US & Translation 20%.

The Andrew Lownie Literary Agency★

17 Sutherland Street, London SW1V 4JU
☎020 7828 1274 Fax 020 7828 7608
Email lownie@globalnet.co.uk
Website www.andrewlownie.co.uk

Contact *Andrew Lownie*

FOUNDED 1988. *Specialises* in non-fiction, especially history, biography, current affairs, military history, UFOs, reference and packaging celebrities and journalists for the book market. No poetry, short stories or science fiction. Formerly a journalist, publisher and himself the author of 12 non-fiction books, Andrew Lownie's CLIENTS include Theo Aronson, Juliet Barker, the Joyce Cary estate, Tom

Devine, Peter Evans, Jonathan Fryer, Laurence Gardner, Timothy Good, Robert Holden, Gloria Hunniford, Robert Jobson, Leo McKinstry, Julian Maclaren-Ross estate, Patrick MacNee, Norma Major, Sir John Mills, Nick Pope, John Rae, Richard Rudgley, Desmond Seward, Andrew Wheatcroft, Alan Whicker, Lawrence James, editors of the *Oxford Classical Dictionary* and *Cambridge Guide to Literature in English*. Approach with letter, synopsis, sample chapter and s.a.e. Translation rights handled by **The Marsh Agency**. *Commission* Worldwide 15%.

Lucas Alexander Whitley
See **LAW Ltd**

Lutyens and Rubinstein★
231 Westbourne Park Road, London W11 1EB
☎020 7792 4855 Fax 020 7792 4833
Partners *Sarah Lutyens, Felicity Rubinstein*
Submissions *Susannah Godman*

FOUNDED 1993. *Handles* adult fiction and non-fiction books. No TV, film, radio or theatre scripts. Unsolicited mss accepted; send introductory letter, c.v., two chapters and return postage for all material submitted. No reading fee. *Commission* Home 15%; US & Translation 20%.

Duncan McAra
28 Beresford Gardens, Edinburgh EH5 3ES
☎0131 552 1558 Fax 0131 552 1558
Email duncanmcara@hotmail.com
Contact *Duncan McAra*

FOUNDED 1988. *Handles* fiction (literary fiction) and non-fiction, including art, architecture, archaeology, biography, military, travel and books of Scottish interest. Preliminary letter, synopsis and sample chapter (including return postage) essential. No reading fee. *Commission* Home 10%; Overseas 20%.

Bill McLean
Personal Management Ltd
23B Deodar Road, London SW15 2NP
☎020 8789 8191
Contact *Bill McLean*

FOUNDED 1972. *Handles* scripts for all media. No books. No unsolicited mss. Phone call or introductory letter essential. No reading fee. CLIENTS include Dwynwen Berry, Graham Carlisle, Pat Cumper, Jane Galletly, Patrick Jones, Tony Jordan, Bill Lyons, John Maynard,

Michael McStay, Les Miller, Ian Rowlands, Jeffrey Segal, Richard Shannon, Ronnie Smith, Barry Thomas, Garry Tyler, Frank Vickery, Laura Watson, Mark Wheatley. *Commission* Home 10%.

Eunice McMullen
Children's Literary Agent Ltd
Low Ibbotsholme Cottage, Off Bridge Lane, Troutbeck Bridge, Windermere, Cumbria LA23 1HU
☎01539 448551 Fax 01539 442289
Email eunicemcmullen@totalise.co.uk
Contact *Eunice McMullen*

FOUNDED 1992. *Handles* all types of children's material in particular picture books. Has 'an excellent' list of picture book authors and illustrators. *No unsolicited scripts*. Telephone enquiries only. CLIENTS include Wayne Anderson, Reg Cartwright, Jason Cockcroft, Ross Collins, Siobhan Dodds, Richard Fowler, Charles Fuge, Susie Jenkin-Pearce, Angela McAllister, David Melling, Sue Porter, Susan Winter, David Wood. *Commission* Home 10%; US 15%; Translation 20%.

Andrew Mann Ltd★
1 Old Compton Street, London W1D 5PH
☎020 7734 4751 Fax 020 7287 9264
Email manscript@onetel.net.uk
Contacts *Anne Dewe, Tina Betts, Sacha Elliot*

FOUNDED 1975. *Handles* fiction, general non-fiction and film, TV, theatre, radio scripts. No unsolicited mss. Preliminary letter, synopsis and s.a.e. essential. No reading fee. *Commission* Home 15%; US & Translation 20%. *Overseas associates* various.

Sarah Manson Literary Agent
6 Totnes Walk, London N2 0AD
☎020 883 3050
Email smliteraryagent.@aol.com
Contact *Sarah Manson*

FOUNDED 2002. *Handles* quality fiction for children and young adults. Brief e-mail enquiry or preliminary letter with s.a.e. No reading fee. *Commission* Home 10%; Overseas & Translations 20%.

Manuscript ReSearch
PO Box 33, Bicester, Oxfordshire OX26 4ZZ
☎01869 323447 Fax 01869 324096
Contact *Graham Jenkins*

FOUNDED 1988. *Handles* only scripts suitable for film/TV outlets. Preferred first approach from new contacts is by letter with brief outline and s.a.e. *Commission* Home 10%; Overseas 20%.

Marjacq Scripts Ltd
34 Devonshire Place, London W1G 6JW
☎020 7935 9499 Fax 020 7935 9115
Email subs@marjacq.com
Website www.marjacq.com

Contact *Mark Hayward*

Handles fiction and non-fiction, literary and commercial as well as film, TV, radio scripts. No fantasy, horror or poetry. New work welcome; send brief letter, synopsis and approx first 50 pages plus s.a.e. No reading fee. *Commission* Home 10%; Overseas 20%.

The Marsh Agency Ltd★
11/12 Dover Street, London W1S 4LJ
☎020 7399 2800 Fax 020 7399 2801
Email enquiries@marsh-agency.co.uk
Website www.marsh-agency.co.uk

Contacts *Paul Marsh, Daisy Meyrick*

FOUNDED 1994. International rights specialists selling English and foreign language writing. No TV, film, radio or theatre. Submissions by e-mail preferred, synopsis and sample chapters. CLIENTS include several British and American agencies and publishers, and some individual authors. See also **Paterson Marsh Ltd**.

Martinez Literary Agency
60 Oakwood Avenue, Southgate, London N14 6QL
☎020 8886 5829

Contacts *Mary Martinez, Francoise Budd*

FOUNDED 1988. *Handles* high-quality fiction, children's books, arts and crafts, interior design, alternative health/complementary medicine, autobiography, biography, popular music, sport and memorabilia books. Not accepting any new writers. *Commission* Home 15%; US, Overseas & Translation 20%; Performance Rights 20%.

MBA Literary Agents Ltd★
62 Grafton Way, London W1T 5DW
☎020 7387 2076 Fax 020 7387 2042
Email <firstname>@mbalit.co.uk

Contacts *Diana Tyler, John Richard Parker, Meg Davis, Laura Longrigg, David Riding*

FOUNDED 1971. *Handles* fiction and non-fiction, TV, film, radio and theatre scripts. No unsolicited mss. Works in conjunction with agents in most countries. Also UK representative for **Writers House, Inc**, the Donald Maass Agency, Fran Collin Literary Agency, Martha Millard Literary Agency, Montreal-Contacts/the Rights Agency and the JABberwocky Agency. CLIENTS include Campbell Armstrong, A.L. Barker, estate of Harry Bowling, Jeffrey Caine, Glenn Chandler, Andrew Cowan, Patricia Finney, Maggie Furey, Sue Gee, Joanna Hines, B.S. Johnson estate, Robert Jones, Anne McCaffrey, Paul Magrs, Susan Oudot, Sir Roger Penrose, Anne Perry, Gervase Phinn, Christopher Russell, Jim Shields, Iain Sinclair, Steve Strange, Mark Wallington, Richard Weston, Patrick Wilde, Paul Wilson, Valerie Windsor, The Chap Magazine. *Commission* Home 15%; Overseas 20%; Theatre/TV/Radio 10%; Film 10–20%.

Christy Moore Ltd
See **Sheil Land Associates Ltd**

William Morris Agency (UK) Ltd★
52/53 Poland Street, London W1F 7LX
☎020 7534 6800 Fax 020 7534 6900
Website www.wma.com

Managing Director *Stephanie Cabot*

London office FOUNDED 1965. Worldwide theatrical and literary agency with offices in New York, Beverly Hills and Nashville and associates in Sydney. *Handles* fiction, general non-fiction, TV and film scripts. Mss for books including s.a.e. with preliminary letter to Book Department. No reading fee. *Commission* TV 10%; UK Books 15%; US Books & Translation 20%.

Michael Motley Ltd
The Old Vicarage, Tredington, Tewkesbury, Gloucestershire GL20 7BP
☎01684 276390 Fax 01684 297355

Contact *Michael Motley*

FOUNDED 1973. *Handles* only full-length mss (i.e. 60,000+). No short stories or journalism. No science fiction, horror, poetry or original dramatic material. New clients by referral only: no unsolicited material considered. No reading fee. *Commission* Home 10%; US 15%; Translation 20%. *Overseas associates* in all publishing centres.

Judith Murdoch Literary Agency★
19 Chalcot Square, London NW1 8YA
☎020 7722 4197

Contact *Judith Murdoch*

FOUNDED 1993. *Handles* full-length fiction only. No thrillers, science fiction/fantasy, children's, poetry or short stories. No unsolicited mss; approach in writing only enclosing first two chapters and brief synopsis. Return postage/s.a.e. essential. No reading fee. CLIENTS include Meg Hutchinson, Lisa Jewell, Pamela Jooste. Translation rights handled by **The Marsh Agency**. *Commission* Home 15%; US & Translation 20%.

The Narrow Road Company
182 Brighton Road, Coulsdon, Surrey
CR5 2NF
☎020 8763 9895 Fax 020 8763 9329
Email coulsdon@narrowroad.co.uk
Contacts *Richard Ireson, Isabella Summers, James Ireson*

FOUNDED 1986. Part of the Narrow Road Group. Theatrical literary agency. *Handles* scripts for TV, theatre, film and radio. No novels or poetry. No unsolicited mss; approach by letter with c.v. Interested in writers with some experience and original ideas. CLIENTS include Vanessa Brooks, Steve Gooch, David Halliwell, Brian Marshall, Andy Smith.

William Neill-Hall Ltd
Old Oak Cottage, Ropewalk, Mount Hawke, Truro, Cornwall TR4 8DW
☎01209 891427 Fax 01209 891427
Email wneill-hall@msn.com
Contact *William Neill-Hall*

FOUNDED 1995. *Handles* general non-fiction, religion. No TV, film, theatre or radio scripts; no fiction or poetry. *Specialises* in religion and current affairs. No unsolicited mss. Approach by phone or letter. Enclose return postage. No reading fee. CLIENTS Mary Batchelor, George Carey, Richard Foster, Selwyn Hughes, Juliet Janvrin, Jennifer Rees Larcombe, Eugene Peterson, David Pytches, Mary Pytches, Philip Yancey. *Commission* Home 10%; US 15%; Translation 20%.

The Maggie Noach
Literary Agency★
22 Dorville Crescent, London W6 0HJ
☎020 8748 2926 Fax 020 8748 8057
Email m-noach@dircon.co.uk
Contact *Maggie Noach*

FOUNDED 1982. Pronounced 'no-ack'. *Handles* a wide range of well-written books including general non-fiction, especially biography, commercial fiction and non-illustrated children's books for ages 7–12. No scientific, academic or specialist non-fiction. No poetry,

plays, short stories or books for the very young. Recommended for promising young writers but *very* few new clients taken on as it is considered vital to give individual attention to each author's work. Unsolicited mss not welcome. Approach by letter (*not by telephone or e-mail*), giving a brief description of the book and enclosing a few sample pages. Return postage essential. No reading fee. *Commission* Home 15%; US & Translation 20%.

Andrew Nurnberg Associates Ltd★
Clerkenwell House, 45–47 Clerkenwell Green, London EC1R 0QX
☎020 7417 8800 Fax 020 7417 8812
Email all@nurnberg.co.uk
Directors *Andrew Nurnberg, Sarah Nundy, D. Roger Seaton, Vicky Mark*

FOUNDED in the mid-1970s. *Specialises* in foreign rights, representing leading authors and agents. Branches in Moscow, Bucharest, Budapest, Prague, Sofia, Warsaw, Riga, Beijing, Shanghai and Taipei. *Commission* Home 15%; US & Translation 20%.

Alexandra Nye
'Craigower', 6 Kinnoull Avenue, Dunblane, Perthshire FK15 9JG
☎01786 825114
Contact *Alexandra Nye*

FOUNDED 1991. *Handles* fiction and topical non-fiction. *Special interests* literary fiction and history. Unsolicited mss welcome (s.a.e. essential for return). Preliminary approach by letter, with synopsis, preferred. Reading fee for supply of detailed report. CLIENTS include Dr Tom Gallagher, Harry Mehta, Robin Jenkins. *Commission* Home 10%; US 20%; Translation 15%.

David O'Leary Literary Agents
10 Lansdowne Court, Lansdowne Rise, London W11 2NR
☎020 7229 1623 Fax 020 7727 9624
Email d.o'leary@virgin.net
Contact *David O'Leary*

FOUNDED 1988. *Handles* fiction, both popular and literary, and non-fiction. Areas of interest include thrillers, history, popular science, Russia and Ireland (history and fiction). No poetry or science fiction. No unsolicited mss but happy to discuss a proposal. Ring or write in the first instance. No reading fee. CLIENTS include David Crackanthorpe, James Kennedy, Nick Kochan, Jim Lusby, Derek Malcolm, Ken Russell. *Commission* Home & US 10%. *Overseas associates*

Lennart Sane, Scandinavia/Spain/South America; Tuttle Mori, Japan.

Deborah Owen Ltd★

78 Narrow Street, Limehouse, London
E14 8BP
☎020 7987 5119/5441 Fax 020 7538 4004

Contacts *Deborah Owen*

FOUNDED 1971. Small agency specialising in representing authors direct around the world. *Handles* international fiction and non-fiction (books which can be translated into a number of languages). No new authors. CLIENTS Amos Oz and Delia Smith. *Commission* Home 10%; US & Translation 15%.

Owen Robinson Literary Agents

20 Tolbury Mill, Bruton, Somerset BA10 0DY
☎01749 812836 Fax 01749 812008
Email jpr@owenrobinson.netlineuk.net
(enquiries only)

Contact *Justin Robinson*

FOUNDED 1998. *Handles* fiction and non-fiction. No plays, film scripts, poetry or short stories. No reading fee. No unsolicited mss. Approach in writing with s.a.e. in the first instance; send synopsis and three sample chapters subsequently. CLIENTS include Paul Garrison, Michael Holt, Sarah Lawson, Chrissie Loveday, Roger Nichols, Alistair Owen, Ann Taylor. *Commission* Home 10%; US & Translation 15–20%. Works with agents overseas.

Paterson Marsh Ltd★

11/12 Dover Street, London W1S 4LJ
☎020 7399 2800 Fax 020 7399 2801
Email steph@patersonmarsh.co.uk
Website www.patersonmarsh.co.uk

Contacts *Mark Paterson* (☎01206 825433; email mark@markpaterson.co.uk), *Paul Marsh, Stephanie Ebdon*

Formerly Mark Paterson & Associates, FOUNDED 1961. World rights representatives of authors and publishers handling many subjects, with specialisation in psychoanalysis and psychotherapy. CLIENTS range from Balint, Bion, Casement and Ferenczi, through to Freud and Winnicott; plus Hugh Brogan, Peter Moss and the estates of Sir Arthur Evans, Hugh Schonfield and Dorothy Richardson. No fiction, scripts, poetry, children's, articles, short stories or 'unsaleable mediocrity'. No unsolicited mss, but preliminary letter and synopsis with s.a.e. welcome. *Commission* 20% (including sub-agent's commission).

John Pawsey

60 High Street, Tarring, Worthing, West Sussex BN14 7NR
☎01903 205167 Fax 01903 205167

Contact *John Pawsey*

FOUNDED 1981. Experience in the publishing business has helped to attract some top names here, but the door remains open for bright, new ideas. *Handles* non-fiction: biography, politics, current affairs, popular culture, travel, sport, business and music; also fiction: crime, thrillers, suspense or 'genuine originals' but not science fiction, fantasy and horror. *Special interests* sport and biography. No children's, drama scripts, poetry, short stories, journalism or academic. Preliminary letter with s.a.e. essential. No reading fee. CLIENTS include David Rayvern Allen, Jennie Bond, Elwyn Hartley Edwards, William Fotheringham, Dan Hale, Patricia Hall, Dr David Lewis, Kathryn Spink. *Commission* Home 10–15%; US & Translation 19–25%. *Overseas associates* in the US, Japan, South America and throughout Europe.

Maggie Pearlstine Associates Ltd★

31 Ashley Gardens, Ambrosden Avenue, London SW1P 1QE
☎020 7828 4212 Fax 020 7834 5546
Email post@pearlstine.co.uk

Contact *Maggie Pearlstine*

FOUNDED 1989. Small, selective agency. *Handles* general non-fiction and fiction. *Special interest:* history, current affairs, biography and health. No children's, poetry, horror, science fiction, short stories or scripts. Seldom takes on new authors. Prospective clients should write an explanatory letter and enclose s.a.e. and the first chapter only. No submissions accepted by fax, e-mail or from abroad. No reading fee. CLIENTS Debbie Beckerman, John Biffen, Matthew Baylis, Kate Bingham, Menzies Campbell, Robin Cook, Frank Dobson, Kim Fletcher, Roy Hattersley, Rachel Holmes, Charles Kennedy, Mark Leonard, Eleanor Mills, Claire Macdonald, Dr Raj Persaud, Prof. Lesley Regan, Hugo Rifkind, Winifred Robinson, Jackie Rowley, Henrietta Spencer-Churchill, Prof. Alan Stewart, Jack Straw, Prof. Robert Winston. Translation rights handled by **Gillon Aitken Associates Ltd**. *Commission* Home 12½% (fiction), 10% (non-fiction); US & Translation 20%; TV, Film & Journalism 20%.

Peters Fraser & Dunlop Group Ltd
See **PFD**

PFD★

Drury House, 34–43 Russell Street, London WC2B 5HA
☎020 7344 1000
Fax 020 7836 9539/7836 9541
Email postmaster@pfd.co.uk
Website www.pfd.co.uk

Joint Chairmen *Anthony Jones, Tim Corrie*
Managing Director *Anthony Baring*
Books *Caroline Dawnay, Michael Sissons, Pat Kavanagh, Charles Walker, Rosemary Canter, Robert Kirby, Simon Trewin, James Gill*
Serial *Pat Kavanagh, Carol MacArthur*
Film/TV *Anthony Jones, Tim Corrie, Norman North, Charles Walker, St. John Donald, Rosemary Scoular, Natasha Galloway, Jago Irwin, Louisa Thompson, Lynda Mamy*
Actors *Maureen Vincent, Dallas Smith, Lindy King, Ruth Young, Lucy Brazier, Kathryn Fleming*
Theatre *Kenneth Ewing, St John Donald, Nicki Stoddart, Rosie Cobbe*
Children's *Rosemary Canter*
Multimedia *Rosemary Scoular*

FOUNDED 1988 as a result of the merger of A. D. Peters & Co. Ltd and Fraser & Dunlop, and was later joined by the June Hall Literary Agency. *Handles* all sorts of books including fiction and children's, plus scripts for film, theatre, radio and TV material. Prospective clients should write 'a full letter, with an account of what he/she has done and wants to do and enclose, when possible, a detailed outline and sample chapters'. Screenplays and TV scripts should be addressed to the 'Film & Script Dept.' Enclose s.a.e. No reading fee. The Children's Dept. accepts unsolicited written material in the form of a covering letter, brief plot summary and one paragraph only of text; submissions from illustrators also welcome. CLIENTS include Julian Barnes, Alan Bennett, Alain de Botton, A.S. Byatt, estate of C.S. Forester, Nicci Gerrard, Robert Harris, Nick Hornby, Clive James, Russell Miller, estate of Nancy Mitford, John Mortimer, Andrew Motion, Douglas Reeman, Ruth Rendell, Anthony Sampson, Gerald Seymour, Tom Stoppard, Emma Thompson, Joanna Trollope, estate of Evelyn Waugh. *Commission* Home 10%; US & Translation 20%.

Pollinger Limited★

9 Staple Inn, Holborn, London WC1V 7QH
☎020 7404 0342 Fax 020 7242 5737
Email info@pollingerltd.com
Website www.pollingerltd.com

Chairman *Paul Woolf*
Managing Director *Lesley Pollinger*
Adult List *Lesley Pollinger, Cordelia Feldman*
Permissions/Foreign Rights *Katy Loffman*
Children's List *Linda Jennings*
Consultant *Gerald Pollinger*

FOUNDED 2002. A successor of Laurence Pollinger Limited (founded 1958) and Pearn, Pollinger & Higham. *Handles* all types of general trade adult and children's fiction and non-fiction books; intellectual property development, illustrators/photographers. CLIENTS include Roy Apps, Derrry Brabbs, Michael Coleman, Teresa Driscou, Catherine Fisher, Philip Gross, Gene Kemp, Gary Latham, Nisha Minhas, Gary Paulsen, Nicholas Rhea and Sue Welford. Also the estates of H.E. Bates, Vera Chapman, Louis Bromfield, Erskine Caldwell, D.H. Lawrence, W.H. Robinson, Malcolm Saville, Clifford D. Simak and other notables. Unsolicited material considered *only* if preceded by letter or e-mail. *Commission* Home 15%; Translation 20%. Overseas theatrical, and media associates.

Shelley Power Literary Agency Ltd★

13 rue du Pré Saint Gervais, 75019 Paris, France
☎00 33 1 42 38 36 49
Fax 00 33 1 40 40 70 08
Email shelley.power@wanadoo.fr

Contact *Shelley Power*

FOUNDED 1976. Shelley Power works between London and Paris. This is an English agency with London-based administration/accounts office and the editorial office in Paris. *Handles* general commercial fiction, quality fiction, business books, self-help, true crime, investigative exposés, film and entertainment. No scripts, short stories, children's or poetry. Preliminary letter with brief outline of project (plus return postage as from UK or France) essential. 'We do not consider submissions by e-mail.' No reading fee. *Commission* Home 10%; US & Translation 19%.

Elizabeth Puttick Literary Agency★

46 Brookfield Mansions, Highgate Hill West, London N6 6AT
☎020 8340 6383 Fax 020 8340 6384
Email agency@puttick.com
Website www.puttick.com

Contact *Liz Puttick*

FOUNDED 1995. *Handles* general non-fiction (including illustrated books) with special interest in self-help, mind, body, spirit, health and fitness, lifestyle, business. Also interested in narrative non-fiction, biography, history, philosophy, science, humour, and popular culture. No fiction, poetry, scripts, drama or children's books. Preliminary enquiries and c.v. by post or e-mail. No reading fee, but s.a.e. essential. CLIENTS include William Bloom, Simon Buxton, Howard Charing, Cornel Chin, Ann-Marie Gallagher, Ross Heaven, Nirmala Heriza, Steve Nobel, Emma Restall Orr, Ed and Deb Shapiro, John Timperely. *Commission* Home 15%; US & Translation 20%. Works with associates in the US and with the **Marsh Agency** for translation rights.

PVA Management Limited
Hallow Park, Worcester WR2 6PG
☎01905 640663 Fax 01905 641842
Email books@pva.co.uk
Managing Director *Paul Vaughan*

FOUNDED 1978. *Handles* non-fiction only. Please send synopsis and sample chapters together with return postage. *Commission* 15%.

Real Creatives Worldwide
14 Dean Street, London W1D 3RS
☎020 7437 4188
Email realcreatives@aol.com
Contacts *Mark Maco, Malcolm Rasala, Simon Boyes, James Allen, Ian Mennear*

FOUNDED 1984. *Specialises* in drama, science, technology, factual and entertainment. Represents Hollywood TV/film writers and directors, as well as designers, editors, producers and composers. 'Send letter or e-mail requesting a writer's submission agreement covering libel, defamation, plagiarism, etc.' Reading fee: £25. Has a production arm making motion pictures, television etc.

Rogers, Coleridge & White Ltd★
20 Powis Mews, London W11 1JN
☎020 7221 3717 Fax 020 7229 9084
Contacts *Deborah Rogers, Gill Coleridge, Patricia White, David Miller, Zoe Waldie*
Foreign Rights *Ann Warnford-Davis, Laurence Laluyaux, Stephen Edwards*

FOUNDED 1967. *Handles* fiction, non-fiction and children's books. No poetry, plays or technical books. No unsolicited mss, please and no submissions by fax or e-mail. Rights representative in UK and translation for several New York agents. *Commission* Home 10%; US & Translation 20%. *Overseas associate* Melanie Jackson Agency, New York.

Frederick Rosschild Security
PO Box 155, Great Yarmouth, Norfolk NR31 8GY
Contact *Submissions Department*

FOUNDED 1994. *Handles* all types of fiction and non-fiction. Adult and children's books. Full-length novels, sagas, short stories and political mss accepted. No plays or poetry. *Specialises* in debut writers. Initial contact should be by letter accompanied by an A5 envelope and £5 for a copy of *The Guide for New Writers* which also contains terms and conditions. No telephone calls. (NB Office **closed** between 30 November and 1st March each year.) *Commission* Home 10%; Foreign 20%. Fees for arranging translations from most languages on request. (This includes American English into UK English.) Cheques or POs should be made out to Frederick Rosschild Security.

Uli Rushby-Smith Literary Agency
72 Plimsoll Road, London N4 2EE
☎020 7354 2718 Fax 020 7354 2718
Contact *Uli Rushby-Smith*

FOUNDED 1993. *Handles* fiction and non-fiction, commercial and literary, both adult and children's. Film and TV rights handled in conjunction with a sub-agent. No plays or poetry. Approach with an outline, two or three sample chapters and explanatory letter in the first instance (s.a.e. essential). No disks. No reading fee. *Commission* Home 15%; US & Translation 20%. Represents UK rights for **Curtis Brown**, New York (children's), 2.13.61 USA, Penguin (Canada), Penguin (South Africa), the Alice Toledo Agency (NL) and Columbia University Press.

The Saddler Literary Agency
9 Curzon Road, London W5 1NE
☎020 8998 4868 Fax 020 8998 8851
Email john@saddler.fsnet.co.uk
Contact *John Saddler*

FOUNDED March 2001. John Saddler has been senior editor of **Black Swan**, an editorial director of **Fourth Estate**, publishing director of **Flamingo** and, until 2000, was publisher of Anchor Books, the literary imprint of **Transworld Publishers**. *Handles* fiction and non-fiction. No science fiction or fantasy. Send preliminary letter with synopsis and return postage in the first instance. No reading fee. *Commission* Home 10%; US & Translation 20%.

Rosemary Sandberg Ltd
6 Bayley Street, London WC1B 3HB
☎020 7304 4110 Fax 020 7304 4109
Email rosemary@sandberg.demon.co.uk

Contact *Rosemary Sandberg*

FOUNDED 1991. In association with **Ed Victor Ltd**. *Handles* children's picture books and novels. *Specialises* in children's writers and illustrators. No unsolicited mss as client list is currently full. *Commission* 10%.

The Sayle Literary Agency★
Bickerton House, 25–27 Bickerton Road, London N19 5JT
☎020 7263 8681 Fax 020 7561 0529

Proprietor *Rachel Calder*

Handles fiction, crime and general. Nonfiction: current affairs, social issues, travel, biographies, historical. No plays, poetry, children's, textbooks, technical, legal or medical books. No unsolicited mss. Preliminary letter essential, including a brief biographical note and a synopsis plus two or three sample chapters. Return postage essential. No reading fee. CLIENTS Stephen Amidon, Pete Davies, Margaret Forster, Georgina Hammick, Phillip Knightley, Denise Mina, Malcolm Pryce, Kate Pullinger, Ronald Searle, Gitta Sereny, Stanley Stewart, William Styron, Mary Wesley. *Commission* Home 15%; US & Translation 20%. *Overseas associates* Dunow & Carlson Literary Agency; Darhansoff, Verrill and Feldman; Anne Edelstein Literary Agency, USA; translation rights handled by **The Marsh Agency**; film rights by **Sayle Screen Ltd**.

Sayle Screen Ltd
11 Jubilee Place, London SW3 3TD
☎020 7823 3883 Fax 020 7823 3363
Email info@saylescreen.com
Website www.saylescreen.com

Agents *Jane Villiers, Matthew Bates, Toby Moorcroft, Cathy Kehoe*

Specialises in writers and directors for film and television. Also deals with theatre and radio. Works in association with the **Sayle Literary Agency** representing film and TV rights in novels and non-fiction. No unsolicited material without preliminary letter. CLIENTS include Shelagh Delaney, Marc Evans, Margaret Forster, Rob Green, Mark Haddon, Christopher Monger, Paul Morrison, Gitta Sereny, Sue Townsend. No unsolicited material without preliminary letter.

The Sharland Organisation Ltd
The Manor House, Manor Street, Raunds, Northamptonshire NN9 6JW
☎01933 626600 Fax 01933 624860
Email tsoshar@aol.com

Contacts *Mike Sharland, Alice Sharland*

FOUNDED 1988. *Specialises* in national and international film and TV negotiations. Also negotiates multimedia, interactive TV deals and computer game contracts. Arranges and negotiates speaking engagements for major authors. *Handles* scripts for film, TV, radio and theatre; also nonfiction. Markets books for film and handles stage, radio, film and TV rights for authors. No scientific, technical or poetry. No unsolicited mss. Preliminary enquiry by letter or phone essential. *Commission* Home 15%; US & Translation 20%. *Overseas associates* various.

Sheil Land Associates Ltd★
(incorporating **Richard Scott Simon Ltd 1971** and **Christy Moore Ltd 1912**)
43 Doughty Street, London WC1N 2LH
☎020 7405 9351 Fax 020 7831 2127
Email info@sheilland.co.uk

Agents, UK & US *Sonia Land, Luigi Bonomi, Vivien Green, Amanda Preston*
Film/Theatrical/TV *John Rush, Roland Baggot*
Foreign *Amelia Cummins, Vanessa Forbes*

FOUNDED 1962. *Handles* full-length general, commercial and literary fiction and non-fiction, including: social politics, business, history, military history, gardening, thrillers, crime, romance, fantasy, drama, biography, travel, cookery and humour, UK and foreign estates. Also theatre, film, radio and TV scripts. Welcomes approaches from new clients either to start or to develop their careers. Preliminary letter with s.a.e. essential. No reading fee. CLIENTS include Peter Ackroyd, Vineet Bhatia, Melvyn Bragg, Stephanie Calman, Catherine Cookson estate, Anna del Conte, Elizabeth Corley, Seamus Deane, Alan Drury, Erik Durschmied, Alan Garner, Robert Green, Bonnie Greer, Susan Hill, Richard Holmes, HRH The Prince of Wales, John Humphries, Mark Irving, Simon Kernick, James Long, Richard Mabey, Colin McDowell, Patrick O'Brian estate, Esther Rantzen, Pam Rhodes, Jean Rhys estate, Richard and Judy, Martin Riley, Colin Shindler, Tom Sharpe, Martin Stephen, Brian Sykes, Jeffrey Tayler, Alan Titchmarsh, Rose Tremain, Phil Vickery, John Wilsher, Toby Young. *Commission* Home 15%; US & Translation 20%.

Overseas associates **Georges Borchardt, Inc.** (Richard Scott Simon). UK representatives for **Farrar, Straus & Giroux, Inc.** US film and TV representation: CAA, APA, and others.

Caroline Sheldon Literary Agency★

Thorley Manor Farm, Thorley, Yarmouth, Isle of Wight PO41 0SJ
☎01983 760205

Also at: 71 Hillgate Place, London W8 7SS

Contact *Caroline Sheldon*

FOUNDED 1985. *Handles* adult fiction, in particular women's, both commercial and literary novels. Also full-length children's fiction. No non-fiction, TV/film scripts unless by book-writing clients. Send letter with all relevant details of ambitions and first four chapters of proposed book (enclose large s.a.e.). No reading fee. *Commission* Home 10%; US & Translation 20%.

Dorie Simmonds Agency★

67 Upper Berkeley Street, London W1H 7QX
☎020 7486 9228 Fax 020 7486 8228
Email dhsimmonds@aol.com

Contact *Dorie Simmonds*

Handles a wide range of subjects including general non-fiction and commercial fiction, children's books and associated rights. Specialities include contemporary personalities and historical biographies. Outline required for non-fiction; a short synopsis for fiction with 2–3 sample chapters, and a c.v. with writing experience/publishing history. No reading fee. Return postage essential. *Commission* Home & US 15%; Translation 20%.

Jeffrey Simmons

10 Lowndes Square, London SW1X 9HA
☎020 7235 8852 Fax 020 7235 9733

Contact *Jeffrey Simmons*

FOUNDED 1978. *Handles* biography and autobiography, cinema and theatre, fiction (both quality and commercial), history, law and crime, politics and world affairs, parapsychology and sport (but not exclusively). No science fiction/fantasy, children's books, cookery, crafts, hobbies or gardening. Film scripts handled only if by book-writing clients. *Special interests* personality books of all sorts and fiction from young writers (i.e. under 40) with a future. Writers become clients by personal introduction or by letter, enclosing a synopsis if possible, a brief biography, a note of any previously published books, plus a list of any publishers and agents

who have already seen the mss. *Commission* Home 10–15%; US & Foreign 15%.

Richard Scott Simon Ltd
See **Sheil Land Associates Ltd**

Sinclair-Stevenson

3 South Terrace, London SW7 2TB
☎020 7581 2550 Fax 020 7581 2550

Contact *Christopher Sinclair-Stevenson*

FOUNDED 1995. *Handles* biography, current affairs, travel, history, fiction, the arts. No scripts, children's, academic, science fiction/fantasy. Send synopsis with s.a.e. in the first instance. No reading fee. CLIENTS include Jennifer Johnston, J.D.F. Jones, Ross King, Christopher Lee, Andrew Sinclair and the estates of Alec Guinness, John Cowper Powys and John Galsworthy. *Commission* Home 10%; US 15%; Translation 20%. *Overseas associate* T.C. Wallace Ltd, New York. Translation rights handled by **David Higham Associates**.

Robert Smith Literary Agency Ltd★

12 Bridge Wharf, 156 Caledonian Road, London N1 9UU
☎020 7278 2444 Fax 020 7833 5680
Email robertsmith.literaryagency@virgin.net

Contact *Robert Smith*

FOUNDED 1997. *Handles* non-fiction; biography, health and nutrition, cookery, lifestyle, showbusiness and true crime. No scripts, fiction, poetry, academic or children's books. No unsolicited mss. Send a letter and synopsis in the first instance. No reading fee. CLIENTS Carol Clerk, Stewart Evans, Neil and Christine Hamilton, James Haspiel, Chris Hutchins, Roberta Kray, Norman Parker, Mike Reid, Professor Bill Rubinstein, Keith Skinner, Douglas Thompson. *Commission* Home 15%; US & Translation 20%. *Overseas associate* Thomas Schlück Literary Agency (Germany).

Elaine Steel

110 Gloucester Avenue, London NW1 8HX
☎020 8348 0918 Fax 020 8341 9807
Email ecmsteel@aol.com

Contact *Elaine Steel*

FOUNDED 1986. *Handles* scripts, screenplays and books. No technical or academic. Initial phone call preferred. CLIENTS include Les Blair, Anna Campion, Michael Eaton, Pearse Elliott, Gwyneth Hughes, Brian Keenan, Troy Kennedy Martin, Rob Ritchie, Albie Sachs, Ben Steiner. *Commission* Home 10%; US & Translation 20%.

Abner Stein★

10 Roland Gardens, London SW7 3PH
☎020 7373 0456 Fax 020 7370 6316

Contact *Arabella Stein*

FOUNDED 1971. Mainly represents US agents and authors but *handles* some full-length fiction and general non-fiction. No scientific, technical, etc. No scripts. Send letter and outline in the first instance rather than unsolicited mss. *Commission* Home 10%; US & Translation 20%.

Micheline Steinberg Associates

Fourth Floor, 104 Great Portland Street, London W1W 6PE
☎020 7631 1310 Fax 020 7631 1146
Email info@steinplays.com

Contacts *Micheline Steinberg, Ginny Sennett*

FOUNDED 1988. *Specialises* in plays for stage, TV, radio and film. Best approach by preliminary letter (with s.a.e.). Dramatic associate for **Pollinger Limited**. *Commission* Home 10%; Elsewhere 15%.

Shirley Stewart Literary Agency

3rd Floor, 21 Denmark Street, London WC2H 8NA
☎020 7836 4440 Fax 020 7836 3482

Director *Shirley Stewart*

FOUNDED 1993. *Handles* literary fiction and non-fiction. No scripts, children's, science fiction, fantasy or poetry. Will consider unsolicited material; send letter with two or three sample chapters in the first instance. S.a.e. essential. Submissions by fax or on disk not accepted. No reading fee. *Commission* Home 10%; US & Translation 20%. *Overseas associate* **Curtis Brown Ltd**, New York.

The Susijn Agency

3rd Floor, 64 Great Titchfield Street, London W1W 7QH
☎020 7580 6341 Fax 020 7580 8626
Email info@thesusijnagency.com
Website www.thesusijnagency.com

Contacts *Laura Susijn, Charles Buchan*

FOUNDED April 1998. *Specialises* in selling rights worldwide in literary fiction and non-fiction. Preliminary letter, synopsis and first two chapters preferred. No reading fee. Also represents non-English language authors and publishers for UK, US and translation rights worldwide. *Commission* Home 15%; US & Translation 15–20%.

The Tennyson Agency

10 Cleveland Avenue, Wimbledon Chase, London SW20 9EW
☎020 8543 5939 Fax 020 8543 5939
Email agency@tenagy.co.uk
Website www.tenagy.co.uk

Contact *Christopher Oxford*

FOUNDED 2001. *Specialises* in theatre, radio, television and film scripts. Other material considered on an ad hoc basis; humanities bias. No short stories, children's, poetry, travel, military/historical, academic or sport. No unsolicited material; send introductory letter with résumé and proposal/ outline of work. No reading fee. CLIENTS Vivienne Allen, Alastair Cording, Iain Grant, Julian Howell, Philip Hurd-Wood, Joanna Leigh, John Ryan, Walter Saunders, Diana Ward. *Commission* Home 12½–15%; Overseas 17½–20%.

Lavinia Trevor Literary Agency★

The Glasshouse, 49A Goldhawk Road, London W12 8QP
☎020 8749 8481 Fax 020 8749 7377

Contact *Lavinia Trevor*

FOUNDED 1993. *Handles* general fiction (literary and commercial) and non-fiction, including popular science. No fantasy, science-fiction, poetry, academic, technical or children's books. No TV, film, radio, theatre scripts. Approach with a preliminary letter, a brief autobiography and first 50–100 typewritten pages. S.a.e. essential. No reading fee. *Commission* rate by agreement with author.

Jane Turnbull★

13 Wendell Road, London W12 9RS
☎020 8743 9580 Fax 020 8749 6079
Email jane.turnbull@btinternet.com

Contact *Jane Turnbull*

FOUNDED 1986. *Handles* fiction and non-fiction. No science fiction, romantic fiction, children's literature or plays. *Specialises* in biography, history, current affairs, health and diet. No unsolicited mss. Approach with letter in the first instance. No reading fee. Translation rights handled by **Gillon Aitken Associates Ltd**. *Commission* Home 10%; US & Foreign 20%.

Ed Victor Ltd★

6 Bayley Street, Bedford Square, London WC1B 3HE
☎020 7304 4100 Fax 020 7304 4111

Contacts *Ed Victor, Graham Greene, Maggie Phillips, Sophie Hicks, Lizzy Kremer*

FOUNDED 1976. *Handles* a broad range of material including children's books but leans towards the more commercial ends of the fiction and non-fiction spectrums. No poetry, scripts or academic. Takes on very few new writers. No unsolicited mss. After trying his hand at book publishing and literary magazines, Ed Victor, an ebullient American, found his true vocation. Strong opinions, very pushy and works hard for those whose intelligence he respects. Loves nothing more than a good title auction. CLIENTS include Eoin Colfer, Frederick Forsyth, A.A. Gill, Josephine Hart, Jack Higgins, Erica Jong, Nigella Lawson, Kathy Lette, Allan Mallinson, Anne Robinson and the estates of Douglas Adams, Raymond Chandler, Dame Iris Murdoch, Sir Stephen Spender and Irving Wallace. *Commission* Home & US 15%; Translation 20%.

Robin Wade Literary Agency

1 Cormorant Lodge, Thomas More Street, London E1W 1AU
☎020 7488 4171 Fax 020 7488 4172
Email rw@rwla.com
Website www.rwla.com

Contact *Robin Wade*
Associate *Jo Kitching*

FOUNDED 2001. *Handles* general fiction and non-fiction including children's books. No scripts, poetry, plays or short stories. Send detailed synopsis and two specimen chapters by e-mail with a brief biography. No reading fee. *Commission* Home 10%; Overseas & Translation 20%. 'Fees negotiable if a contract has already been offered.'

Cecily Ware Literary Agents

19C John Spencer Square, London N1 2LZ
☎020 7359 3787 Fax 020 7226 9828
Email info@cecilyware.com

Contacts *Cecily Ware, Gilly Schuster, Warren Sherman*

FOUNDED 1972. Primarily a film and TV script agency representing work in all areas: drama, children's, series/serials, adaptations, comedies, etc. No unsolicited mss or phone calls. Approach in writing only. No reading fee. *Commission* Home 10%; US 10–20% by arrangement.

Watson, Little Ltd★

Capo Di Monte, Windmill Hill, London NW3 6RJ
☎020 7431 0770 Fax 020 7431 7225
Email enquiries@watsonlittle.com

Contacts *Sheila Watson, Mandy Little, Sugra Zaman*

Handles fiction, commercial women's fiction, crime and literary fiction. Non-fiction *special interests* include history, science, popular psychology, self-help, business and general leisure books. Also children's fiction and non-fiction. No short stories, poetry, TV, play or film scripts. Not interested in purely academic writers. No unsolicited mss. Informative preliminary letter and synopsis with return postage essential. *Commission* Home 15%; US 24%; Translation 19%. *Overseas associates* worldwide. *Film & TV associates* **The Sharland Organisation Ltd**; Hurley Lowe Management.

A.P. Watt Ltd★

20 John Street, London WC1N 2DR
☎020 7405 6774 Fax 020 7831 2154
Email apw@apwatt.co.uk
Website www.apwatt.co.uk

Directors *Caradoc King, Linda Shaughnessy, Derek Johns, Georgia Garrett, Nick Harris, Natasha Fairweather*
Associate *Joanna Frank*

FOUNDED 1875. The oldest-established literary agency in the world. *Handles* full-length typescripts, including children's books, screenplays for film and TV. No poetry, academic or specialist works. No unsolicited mss accepted. CLIENTS include Trezza Azzopardi, Quentin Blake, Marika Cobbold, Helen Dunmore, Nicholas Evans, Giles Foden, Esther Freud, Janice Galloway, Martin Gilbert, Nadine Gordimer, Linda Grant, Colin and Jacqui Hawkins, Reginald Hill, Michael Holroyd, Michael Ignatieff, Mick Jackson, Philip Kerr, Dick King-Smith, India Knight, John Lanchester, Alison Lurie, Jan Morris, Jill Murphy, Andrew O'Hagan, Susie Orbach, Tony Parsons, Caryl Phillips, Philip Pullman, Jancis Robinson, Jon Ronson, Elaine Showalter, Zadie Smith, Graham Swift, Colm Toibin, Fiona Walker and the estates of Wodehouse, Graves and Maugham. *Commission* Home 10%; US & Translation 20%.

Josef Weinberger Plays

12–14 Mortimer Street, London W1T 3JJ
☎020 7580 2827 Fax 020 7436 9616
Email general.info@jwmail.co.uk
Website www.josef-weinberger.com

Contact *Michael Callahan*

Josef Weinberger is both agent and publisher of scripts for the theatre. No unsolicited mss; introductory letter essential. No reading fee.

CLIENTS include Ray Cooney, John Godber, Peter Gordon, Debbie Isitt, Arthur Miller, Sam Shepard, John Steinbeck. *Overseas representatives* in the US, Canada, Australia, New Zealand, India, South Africa and Zimbabwe.

John Welch, Literary Consultant & Agent

Mill Cottage, Calf Lane, Chipping Camden, Gloucestershire GL55 6JQ
☎01386 840237 Fax 01386 840568
Email johnwelch@waitrose.com

Contact *John Welch*

FOUNDED 1992. *Handles* military and naval history, aviation and history. No fiction, poetry, children's books or scripts for radio, TV, film or theatre. Already has a full hand of authors so no new authors being considered at present. CLIENTS include Alexander Baron, Michael Calvert, Patrick Delaforce, Timothy Jenkins, Sybil Marshall, Ewart Oakeshott, Norman Scarfe, Anthony Trew, Peter Trew, David Wragg. *Commission* Home 10%.

Dinah Wiener Ltd★

12 Cornwall Grove, Chiswick, London W4 2LB
☎020 8994 6011 Fax 020 8994 6044

Contact *Dinah Wiener*

FOUNDED 1985. *Handles* fiction and general non-fiction: auto/biography, popular science, cookery. No scripts, children's or poetry. Approach with preliminary letter in first instance, giving full but brief c.v. of past work and future plans. Mss submitted must include s.a.e. and be typed in double-spacing. CLIENTS include T.J. Armstrong, Valerie-Anne Baglietto, Malcolm Billings, Hugh Brune, Guy Burt, Victoria Corby, David Deutsch, Robin Gardiner, Jenny Hobbs, Mark Jeffery, Tania Kindersley, Michael Lockwood, Sarah Mason, Daniel Snowman, Peta Tayler, Mitchell Tonks, Rachel Trethewey, Marcia Willett. *Commission* Home 15%; US & Translation 20%.

Rebecca Winfield Writers' Agent

84 Cowper Road, London W7 1EJ
☎020 8567 6738 Fax 020 8567 6738
Email rebecca.winfield@btopenworld.com

Contact *Rebecca Winfield*

FOUNDED 2003. *Handles* quality fiction and non-fiction: romance, historical fiction, drama, humour, biography, social politics and narrative non-fiction. No science fiction, fantasy, horror or poetry. Send letter, synopsis and no more than three sample chapters in the first instance together with s.a.e. for return of material. Submissions on disk or by e-mail not accepted. No reading fee. Also provides rights consultancy service to literary agents. *Commission* Home 15%; US & Translation 20%.

The Wylie Agency (UK) Ltd

17 Bedford Square, London WC1B 3JA
☎020 7908 5900 Fax 020 7908 5901
Email mail@wylieagency.co.uk

Handles fiction and non-fiction. No scripts or children's books. Approach in writing with three sample chapters, synopsis and s.a.e./return postage. No reading fee. *Commission* Home 10%; US 15%; Translation 20%.

LITERARY SCOUTS

Literary scouts gather information from UK agents, publishers and editors on behalf of foreign clients. They only work with material that is already commissioned or being handled by an agent. They do **not** accept unsolicited material and do **not** deal directly with writers.

Louise Allen-Jones

40 Lillieshall Road, Clapham Old Town, London SW4 0LP
☎020 7720 2453 Fax 020 7498 1818
Email laj@bookscout.demon.co.uk

Contact *Louise Allen-Jones*

Scouts for Econ Ullstein List, Germany; The English Agency, Japan; Bruna, Signet, Signature and de Boekerij 'M', The Netherlands; Kinneret-Zmora, Israel; The Film Council, UK.

Badcock & Rozycki Literary Scouts

1 Old Compton Street, London W1D 5JA
☎020 7734 7997 Fax 020 7734 6886

Contacts *June Badcock* (june@badcock-rozycki.co.uk), *Barbara Rozycki* (barbara@badcock-rozycki.co.uk), *Claire Holt* (claire@badcock-rozycki.co.uk)

Scouts for Wilhelm Heyne Verlag, Marion von Schröder Verlag and Diana Verlag, Germany; Unieboek BV and Prometheus/Bert Bakker, The Netherlands; RCS Libri Group, Italy; Editions Jean-Claude Lattès, France; Ediciones Salamandra, Spain; Ellinika Grammata, Greece; Werner Söderström Osakeyhtiö, Finland; Forum, Sweden; NW Damm & Son A/S, Norway; Egmont Lademann A/S, Denmark; Edda Media, Iceland.

Anne Louise Fisher and Suzy Lucas

29 D'Arblay Street, London W1F 8EP
☎020 7494 4609 Fax 020 7494 4611
Email annelouise@alfisher.co.uk

Contacts *Anne Louise Fisher, Suzy Lucas*

Scouts for Doubleday Inc., Broadway Books and Nan A. Talese, US; Librarie Plon-Perrin-Orban and Pocket and Havas Poche, France; Karl Blessing Verlag, Berlin Verlag and Siedler Verlag, Germany; Arnoldo Mondadori Editore and Oscar Mondadori, Italy; Albert Bonniers Bokförlag, Sweden; Otava, Finland; Gyldendal Norsk Forlag, Norway; Mouria, The Netherlands; Plaza y Janés, Grijalbo, Editorial Debate, Editorial Lumen and Mondadori Iberica, Spain; Patakis Publications, Greece.

Koukla Maclehose

Arundel House, 3 Westbourne Road, London N7 8AR
☎020 7607 1336 Fax 020 7609 7775
Email koukla@btpenworld.com

Contact *Koukla Maclehose*

Scouts for Tammi, Finland; Wählström & Widstrand, Sweden; Pax, Norway; Rosinante, Denmark; Meulenhoff and Arena, The Netherlands; Hanser, Zsolnay, Sans Souci and Nagel & Kimche, Germany; Gallimard and Denoël, France; Einaudi, Italy; Anagrama, Spain; Asa, Portugal; Psichogios, Greece; Keter, Israel.

Folly Marland

6 Elmcroft Street, London E5 0SQ
☎020 8986 0111 Fax 020 8986 0111
Email fmarland@pobox.com

Contact *Folly Marland*

Scout for Scherz Verlag, Germany; Uitgeverij Het Spectrum, The Netherlands; Sony Magazines, Japan; Livani, Greece.

Rosalind Ramsay

195 Lavender Hill, London SW11 5TB
☎020 7978 7444 Fax 020 7924 5455
Email ros@rosramsay.com *or*
    saskia@rosramsay.com
Website www.rosramsay.com

Contacts *Rosalind Ramsay, Saskia Welman*

Scouts for Kiepenheuer & Witsch, Germany; Sperling & Kupfer, Italy; Ambo Anthos, The Netherlands; Norstedts, Sweden; Kadokawa, Japan; Hed Arzi, Israel; Dioptra, Greece.

Heather Schiller

1 Waldegrave Road, Brighton, East Sussex BN1 6GR
☎01273 505477 Fax 01273 505477
Email heather.schiller@virgin.net

Contact *Heather Schiller*

Scout for BZZTÔH, The Netherlands; Cappelens, Norway; Piper, Germany; Lindhardt & Ringhof, Denmark.

Jane Southern

11 Russell Avenue, Bedford MK40 3TE
☎01234 400147 Fax 01234 400146
Email jane.southern@ntlworld.com

Contact *Jane Southern*

Scouts for Hoffmann und Campe Verlag, Germany; Bertelsmann Club, Germany; The House of Books, The Netherlands; Belfond, Presses de la Cité and France Loisirs, France.

Van Lear Limited

PO Box 21816, Parson's Green, London SW6 5ZU
☎020 7610 6165 Fax 020 7610 6045
Email evl@vanlear.co.uk

Contact *Liz Van Lear*

Scouts for Droemer Knaur Schneekluth, Germany; Planeta Group, Spain and Latin America; Richters, Sweden; Artist House, Japan; Oceanida, Greece; Dom Quixote, Portugal; il Saggiatore, Italy; Veen Bosch & Keuning, The Netherlands.

Kathy van Praag

53 St John Street, Oxford OX1 2LQ
☎01865 556753 Fax 01865 556753
Email kvanpraag@aol.com

Contact *Kathy van Praag*

Scout for Rowohlt Verlag, Germany; Distribuidora Record, Brazil.

National Newspapers

Departmental e-mail addresses are too numerous to include in this listing. They can be obtained from the newspaper's main switchboard or the department in question

The Business

292 Vauxhall Bridge Road, London
SW1V 1SS
☎020 7961 0000
Owner *Barclay Brothers*
Editor-in-Chief *Andrew Neil*
Circulation 94,991

LAUNCHED in February 1998. National newspaper dedicated to business, finance and politics. No unsolicited material. All ideas must be discussed with the department's editor in advance.

Political Editor *Andrew Porter*
City Editor *Robert Bailhache*

Daily Express

Ludgate House, 245 Blackfriars Road, London
SE1 9UX
☎020 7928 8000 Fax 020 7620 1654
Website www.express.co.uk
Owner *Northern & Shell Media/Richard Desmond*
Editor *Chris Williams*
Circulation 945,076

Under owner Richard Desmond, publisher of *OK!* magazine, the paper features a large amount of celebrity coverage. The general rule of thumb is to approach in writing with an idea; all departments are prepared to look at an outline without commitment. Ideas welcome but already receives many which are 'too numerous to count'.

News Editor *David Leigh*
Diary (Hickey Column) *Kathryn Spencer*
Features Editor *Heather O'Connor*
City Editor *Stephen Kahn*
Political Editor *Patrick O'Flynn*
Sports Editor *Bill Bradshaw*
Planning Editor (News Desk) should be circulated with copies of official reports, press releases, etc., to ensure news desk cover at all times.

Saturday magazine. **Editor** *Martin Smith* Payment negotiable.

Daily Mail

Northcliffe House, 2 Derry Street,
Kensington, London W8 5TT
☎020 7938 6000 Fax 020 7937 3251
Owner *Associated Newspapers/Lord Rothermere*
Editor *Paul Dacre*
Circulation 2.41 million

In-house feature writers and regular columnists provide much of the material. Photo-stories and crusading features often appear; it's essential to hit the right note to be a successful *Mail* writer. Close scrutiny of the paper is strongly advised. Not a good bet for the unseasoned. Accepts news on savings, building societies, insurance, unit trusts, legal rights and tax.

News Editor *Tony Gallagher*
City Editor *Alex Brummer*
'Money Mail' Editor *Tony Hazell*
Political Editor *David Hughes*
Education Correspondent *Sarah Harris*
Diary Editor *Nigel Dempster*
Features Editor *Leaf Kalfayan*
Literary Editor *Jane Mays*
Sports Editor *Colin Gibson*
Femail Lisa Collins

Weekend: Saturday supplement. **Editor** *Heather McGlone*

Daily Mirror

1 Canada Square, Canary Wharf, London
E14 5AP
☎020 7293 3000 Fax 020 7293 3409
Website www.mirror.co.uk
Owner *Trinity Mirror plc*
Editor *Piers Morgan*
Circulation 1.93 million

No freelance opportunities for the inexperienced, but strong writers who understand what the tabloid market demands are always needed.

Deputy Editor *Des Kelly*
News Editor *Conor Hanna*
Features Editor *Peter Willis*
Political Editor *James Hardy*
Business Editor *Clinton Manning*

Education Editor *Dorothy Lepkowska*
Showbusiness Diary Editor *Kevin O'Sullivan*
Sports Editor *Dean Morse*

M magazine: Saturday supplement 'for young women'. **Editor-in-Chief** *Tina Weaver*

Daily Record

One Central Quay, Glasgow G3 8DA
☎0141 309 3000 Fax 0141 309 3340
Website www.record-mail.co.uk

Owner *Trinity Mirror plc*
Editor *Peter Cox*
Circulation 504,615

Mass-market Scottish tabloid. Freelance material is generally welcome.

News Editor *Tom Hamilton*
Features Editor *Trevor Ward*
Business Editor *Colin Calder*
Political Editor *Paul Sinclair*
Associate Sports Editor *Alan Thomson*
Magazine Editor *Angela Dewar*

Scotland Means Business Quarterly business magazine, launched March 2002. **Editor** *Magnus Gardham*

Daily Sport

19 Great Ancoats Street, Manchester
M60 4BT
☎0161 236 4466 Fax 0161 236 4535
Website www.dailysport.co.uk

Owner *Sport Newspapers Ltd*
Editor *David Beevers*
Circulation 200,000

Tabloid catering for young male readership. Unsolicited material welcome; send to News Editor.

News Editor *Nick Appleyard*
Sports Editor *Marc Smith*

Lads Mag monthly glossy magazine. **Editor** *Mark Harris*.

Daily Star

Ludgate House, 245 Blackfriars Road, London SE1 9UX
☎020 7928 8000 Fax 020 7922 7960

Owner *Richard Desmond*
Editor *Peter Hill*
Circulation 849,598

In competition with *The Sun* for off-the-wall news and features. Freelance opportunities available.

Deputy Editor *Hugh Whittow*

Features Editor *Dawn Neesom*
Sports Editor *Jim Mansell*

Daily Star Sunday

Ludgate House, 245 Blackfriars Road, London SE1 9UX
☎020 7928 8000

Owner *Richard Desmond*
Editor *Hugh Whittow*
Circulation 463,633

New Sunday, LAUNCHED in September 2002 in direct competition with **News of the World** and **The People**.

Star World: Showbiz magazine.

The Daily Telegraph

1 Canada Square, Canary Wharf, London E14 5DT
☎020 7538 5000 Fax 020 7513 2506
Website www.telegraph.co.uk

Owner *Conrad Black*
Editor *Charles Moore*
Circulation 930,822

Unsolicited mss not generally welcome – 'all are carefully read and considered, but only about one in a thousand is accepted for publication'. As they receive about 20 weekly, this means about one a year. Contenders should approach the paper in writing, making clear their authority for writing on that subject. No fiction.

Home Editor *Fiona Barton* Tip-offs or news reports from *bona fide* journalists. Must phone the news desk in first instance. Maximum 200 words. *Payment* minimum £40 (tip).

Arts Editor *Sarah Crompton*
City Editor *Neil Collins*
Political Editor *George Jones*
Diary Editor *Charlie Methvin* Always interested in diary pieces.
Education *John Clare*
Environment *Charles Clover*
Features Editor *Richard Preston* Most material supplied by commission from established contributors. New writers are tried out by arrangement with the features editor. Approach in writing. Maximum 1500 words.
Literary Editor *Kate Summerscale*
Sports Editor *David Welch* Occasional opportunities for specialised items.
Style Editor *Rachel Forder*
Payment by arrangement.

Daily Telegraph Weekend: Saturday colour supplement. **Editor** *Rachel Simhon*

Financial Times

1 Southwark Bridge, London SE1 9HL
☎020 7873 3000 Fax 020 7873 3076
Email <firstname>.<lastname>@ft.com
Website www.ft.com

Owner *Pearson*
Editor *Andrew Gowers*
Circulation 470,617

FOUNDED 1888. UK and international coverage of business, finance, politics, technology, management, marketing and the arts. All feature ideas must be discussed with the department's editor in advance. Not snowed under with unsolicited contributions – they get less than any other national newspaper. Approach by e-mail with ideas in the first instance.

News Editor *Edward Carr*
Features Editor *To be appointed*
Arts Editor *Peter Aspden*
Financial Editor *Jane Fuller*
Literary Editor *Jan Dalley*
Diary Editor *Sundeep Tucker*
Education *Jim Kelly*
Environment *Vanessa Houlder*
Political Editor *James Blitz*
Sports Correspondent *David Owen*

Weekend FT **Editor** *Chrystia Freeland*

How to Spend It Monthly magazine. **Editor** *Gillian de Bono*

The Guardian

119 Farringdon Road, London EC1R 3ER
☎020 7278 2332 Fax 020 7837 2114
Website www.guardian.co.uk

Owner *The Scott Trust*
Editor *Alan Rusbridger*
Circulation 398,778

Of all the nationals *The Guardian* probably offers the greatest opportunities for freelance writers, if only because it has the greatest number of specialised pages which use freelance work. But mss must be directed at a specific slot.

News Editor *Andrew Culf* No opportunities except in those regions where there is presently no local contact for news stories.

Home News *Harriet Sherwood*
Arts Editor *Dan Glaister*
Literary Editor *Claire Armitstead*
Financial Editor *Paul Murphy*
City Editor *Julia Finch*
Life *Emily Wilson* Thursday supplement published in association with *Nature*. Science technology, medicine, environment and other issues. Incorporates **Online** science and computing. Computing/communications (Internet) articles should be addressed to *Jack Schofield*; science articles to *Tim Radford*. Mss on disk or by e-mail (neil.mcintosh@guardian.co.uk).

Diary Editor *Matthew Norman*
Education Editor *Will Woodward* Expert pieces on modern education welcome.
Environment *John Vidal*
Features Editor *Ian Katz* Receives up to 50 unsolicited mss a day; these are passed on to relevant page editors.
Guardian Society *David Brindle* Focuses on social change – the forces affecting us, from environment to government policies. Top journalists and outside commentators.
Media Editor *Janine Gibson* Nine pages a week, plus 'New Media'. Outside contributions are considered. All aspects of modern media, advertising and PR. Background insight important. Best approach is by e-mail (janine.gibson@guardian.co.uk)
Political Editor *Mike White*
Sports Editor *Ben Clissitt*
Women's Page *Clare Margetson* Runs three days a week. Unsolicited ideas used if they show an appreciation of the page in question. Maximum 800–1000 words. Write, e-mail (clare.margetson@guardian.co.uk) or fax on 020 7239 9935.

The Guardian Weekend: glossy Saturday issue. **Editor** *Katharine Viner*.

The Guide *Tim Lusher*

The Herald (Glasgow)

200 Renfield Street, Glasgow G2 3PR
☎0141 302 7000 Fax 0141 302 7070
Website www.theherald.co.uk

Owner *Gannet UK Ltd*
Editor *Mark Douglas-Home*
Circulation 90,217

One of the oldest national newspapers in the English-speaking world, The Herald, which dropped its 'Glasgow' prefix in February 1992, was bought by Scottish Television in 1996. Lively, quality, national Scottish daily broadsheet. Approach with ideas in writing or by phone in first instance.

News Editor *Magnus Llewelin*
Arts Editor *Keith Bruce*
Business Editor *Robert Powell*
Diary *Ken Smith*
Education *Liz Buie*
Sports Editor *Donald Cowey*
Herald Magazine *Kathleen Morgan*

The Independent

Independent House, 191 Marsh Wall, London
E14 9RS
☎020 7005 2000 Fax 020 7005 2999
Website www.independent.co.uk

Owner *Independent Newspapers*
Editor *Simon Kelner*
Circulation 225,630

FOUNDED 1986. Particularly strong on its arts/
media coverage, with a high proportion of
feature material. Theoretically, opportunities
for freelancers are good. However, unsolicited
mss are not welcome; most pieces originate in-
house or from known and trusted outsiders.
Ideas should be submitted in writing.

News Editor *Michael Ellison*
Features *Adam Leigh*
Arts Editor *Ian Irvine*
Business Editor *Jeremy Warner*
Education *Richard Garner*
Environment *Michael McCarthy*
Literary Editor *Boyd Tonkin*
Political Editor *Andrew Grice*
Sports Editor *Paul Newman*
Travel Editor *Simon Calder*

The Independent Magazine: Saturday supplement. **Editor** *Laurence Earle*

The Information **Editor** *Jo Ellison*

Independent on Sunday

Independent House, 191 Marsh Wall, London
E14 9RS
☎020 7005 2000 Fax 020 7005 2999
Website www.independent.co.uk/sindy/
sindy.html

Owner *Independent Newspapers*
Editor *Tristan Davies*
Circulation 223,504

FOUNDED 1986. Regular columnists contribute
most material but feature opportunites exist.
Approach with ideas in first instance.

News Editor *Robert Mendick*
Focus Editor *Cole Moreton*
Arts Editor *Marcus Field*
Comment Editor *Catherine Pepinster*
Business Editor *Jason Nissé*
Literary Editor *Suzi Feay*
Environment *Geoffrey Lean*
Political Editor *Andy McSmith*
Sports Editor *Neil Morton*
Travel Editor *Jackie Hunter*

Talk of the Town **Editor** *Ian Irvine.*

The Sunday Review supplement. **Editor** *Andrew
Tuck*

International Herald Tribune

6 bis, rue des Graviers, 92521 Neuilly, Paris,
France
☎0033 1 4143 9300 Fax 0033 1 4143 9338
Email iht@iht.com
Website www.iht.com

Executive Editor *Walter Wells*
Deputy Editors *Katherine Knorr, Robert Marino*
Circulation 225,000

Published in France, Monday to Saturday, and
circulated in Europe, the Middle East, North
Africa, the Far East and the USA. General news,
business and financial, arts and leisure. Uses regular freelance contributors. Contributor policy can
be found on the website at: www.iht.com/con-
tributor.htm

The Mail on Sunday

Northcliffe House, 2 Derry Street,
Kensington, London W8 5TS
☎020 7938 6000 Fax 020 7937 3829

Owner *Associated Newspapers/Lord Rothermere*
Editor *Peter Wright*
Circulation 2.38 million

Sunday paper with a high proportion of newsy
features and articles. Experience and judge-
ment required to break into its band of regular
feature writers.

News Editor *Paul Field*
Financial Editor *Lisa Buckingham*
Diary Editor *Nigel Dempster*
Features Editor/Women's Page *Sian
James*
Books *Marilyn Warnick*
Political Editor *Simon Walters*
Sports Editor *Malcolm Vallerius*

Night & Day **Editor** *Christena Appleyard*

Review **Editor** *Jim Gillespie*

You – The Mail on Sunday Magazine: colour
supplement. Many feature articles, supplied
entirely by freelance writers. **Editor** *Sue Peart.*
Features Editor *Rosalind Lowe*

Morning Star

William Rust House, 52 Beachy Road, Bow,
London E3 2NS
☎020 8510 0815 Fax 020 8986 5694
Email morsta@geo2.poptel.org.uk

Owner *Peoples Press Printing Society*
Editor *John Haylett*
Circulation 9,000

Not to be confused with the *Daily Star*, the

Morning Star is the farthest left national daily. Those with a penchant for a Marxist reading of events and ideas can try their luck, though feature space is as competitive here as in the other nationals.

News Editor *Dan Coysh*
Features & Arts Editor *Richard Bagley*
Political Editor *Mike Ambrose*
Foreign Editor *Brian Denny*
Sports Editor *Mark Barber*

News of the World

1 Virginia Street, London E98 1NW
☎020 7782 1000   Fax 020 7583 9504
Website www.newsoftheworld.co.uk
Owner *News International plc/Rupert Murdoch*
Editor *Andy Coulson*
Circulation 3.89 million

Highest circulation Sunday paper. Freelance contributions welcome. News and features editors welcome tips and ideas.

Deputy Editor *Neil Wallis*
News Editor *Greg Miskin*
Features Editor *Gary Thompson*
Business/City Editor *Peter Prendergast*
Political Editor *Ian Kirby*
Sports Editor *Mike Dunn*
Sunday Magazine: colour supplement.
Editor *Judy McGuire*. Showbiz interviews and strong human-interest features make up most of the content, but there are no strict rules about what is 'interesting'. Unsolicited mss and ideas welcome.

The Observer

119 Farringdon Road, London EC1R 3ER
☎020 7278 2332   Fax 020 7713 4250
Email editor@observer.co.uk
Website www.observer.co.uk
Owner *Guardian Newspapers Ltd*
Editor *Roger Alton*
Circulation 455,482

FOUNDED 1791. Acquired by Guardian Newspapers from Lonrho in May 1993. Occupies the middle ground of Sunday newspaper politics. Unsolicited material is not generally welcome, 'except from distinguished, established writers'. Receives far too many unsolicited offerings already. No news, fiction or special page opportunities. The newspaper runs annual competitions which change from year to year. Details are advertised in the newspaper.

Executive Editor, News *Andy Malone*
Arts Editor *Jane Ferguson*

Review Editor *Louise France*
Comment Editor *Mike Holland*
City Editor *Richard Wachman*
Business Editor *Frank Kane*
Personal Finance Editor *Maria Scott*
Science Editor *Robin McKie*
Education Editor *Martin Bright*
Environment Correspondent *Mark Townsend*
Literary Editor *Robert McCrum*
Travel Editor *Jeannette Hyde*
Sports Editor *Brian Oliver*

The Observer Magazine: glossy arts and lifestyle supplement. **Editor** *Allan Jenkins*

The Observer Sport Monthly: glossy magazine supplement launched in 2000. **Editor** *Matthew Tench*

The Observer Food Monthly: launched summer 2001. **Editor** *Nicola Jeal*

The Observer Music Monthly: launched in 2003. **Editor** *Caspar Llewellyn Smith*

The People

1 Canada Square, Canary Wharf, London E14 5AP
☎020 7293 3000   Fax 020 7293 3887
Website www.people.co.uk
Owner *Trinity Mirror plc*
Editor *Mark Thomas*
Circulation 1.1 million

Slightly up-market version of *The News of the World*. Keen on exposés and big-name gossip. Interested in ideas for investigative articles. Phone in first instance.

News Editor *Ian Edmondson*
Features Editor *Dawn Alford*
Political Editor *Nigel Nelson*
Sports Editor *Lee Clayton*
Travel Associate Editor *Trisha Harbord*

The People Magazine. **Editor** *Kerry Parnell*
Approach by phone with ideas in first instance.

Scotland on Sunday

Barclay House, 108 Holyrood Road, Edinburgh EH8 8AS
☎0131 620 8620   Fax 0131 620 8491
Website www.scotlandonsunday.com
Owner *Scotsman Publications Ltd*
Editor *John McLellan*
Circulation 84,899

Scotland's top-selling quality broadsheet. Welcomes ideas rather than finished articles.

News Editor *Peter Laing*
Features Editor *Catherine Deveney*
Scotland on Sunday Magazine: colour supplement. Features on personalities, etc. **Editor** *Lee Randall*

The Scotsman

Barclay House, 108 Holyrood Road, Edinburgh EH8 8AS
☎0131 620 8620
Fax 0131 620 8616 (Editorial)
Website www.scotsman.com
Owner *Scotsman Publications Ltd*
Editor *Iain Martin*
Circulation 70,324

Scotland's national newspaper. Many unsolicited mss come in, and stand a good chance of being read, although a small army of regulars supply much of the feature material not written in-house. See website for contact details.
News Editor *David Lee*
Business Editor *Nick Beveans*
Education *Seonag MacKinnon*
Features Editor *Charlotte Ross*
Book Reviews *David Robinson*

The Sun

1 Virginia Street, London E98 1SN
☎020 7782 4000 Fax 020 7782 4108
Email <firstname>.<lastname>@the-sun.co.uk
Website www.the-sun.co.uk
Owner *News International plc/Rupert Murdoch*
Editor *Rebekah Wade*
Circulation 3.53 million

Highest circulation daily. Populist outlook; very keen on gossip, pop stars, TV soap, scandals and exposés of all kinds. No room for non-professional feature writers; 'investigative journalism' of a certain hue is always in demand, however.
Head of News *Graham Dudman*
Head of Features *Sean Carlisle*
Head of Sport *Steve Waring*
Woman's Editor *Sharon Hendry*
Fashion Editor *Erica Davies*

Sunday Express

Ludgate House, 245 Blackfriars Road, London SE1 9UX
☎020 7928 8000 Fax 020 7620 1654
Website www.express.co.uk
Owner *Northern & Shell Media/Richard Desmond*
Editor *Martin Townsend*

Circulation 959,363

The general rule of thumb is to approach in writing with an idea; all departments are prepared to look at an outline without commitment. Ideas welcome but already receives many which are 'too numerous to count'.
News Editor *Jim Murray*
Features Editor *Giulia Rhodes*
Business Editor *Richard Phillips*
Political Editor *Julia Hartley-Brewer*
Sports Editor *Scott Wilson*

S: Sunday supplement on celebrities, homes, food and health. **Editor** *Louise Robinson* No unsolicited mss. All contributions are commissioned. Ideas in writing only. *Enjoy*: Sunday showbiz and travel supplement.
Payment negotiable.

Sunday Herald

200 Renfield Street, Glasgow G2 3PR
☎0141 302 7800 Fax 0141 302 7815
Email editor@sundayherald.com
Website www.sundayherald.com
Owner *Scottish Media Group (SMG)*
Editor *Andrew Jaspan*
Circulation 58,708

Also at: 10 George Street, Edinburgh EH2 2DU
☎0131 200 8100 Fax 0131 200 8088
LAUNCHED February 1999. Scottish seven-section broadsheet.
Deputy Editor *Richard Walker*
News Editor *David Milne*
Political Editor *Douglas Fraser*
Sports Editor *David Dick*
Entertainment Editor *Andrew Burnet*
Magazine Editor *Jane Wright*

Sunday Mail

One Central Quay, Glasgow G3 8DA
☎0141 309 3000 Fax 0141 309 3587
Website www.sundaymail.co.uk
Owner *Trinity Mirror plc*
Editor *Allan Rennie*
Circulation 611,140

Popular Scottish Sunday tabloid.
News Editor *Jim Wilson*
Features Editor *Susie Cormack*

7Days: weekly supplement. **Editor** *Liz Steele*

Mailsport Monthly: monthly magazine. **Editor** *George Cheyne*

Entertainment Mail: monthly magazine. **Editor** *Billy Sloane*

Sunday Mirror

1 Canada Square, Canary Wharf, London
E14 5AP
☎020 7293 3000
Fax 020 7293 3939 (news desk)
Website www.sundaymirror.co.uk

Owner *Trinity Mirror*
Editor *Tina Weaver*
Circulation 1.62 million

In general terms contributions are welcome, though the paper patiently points out it has more time for those who have taken the trouble to study the market. Initial contact in writing preferred, except for live news situations. No fiction.

News Editor *Euan Stretch* The news desk is very much in the market for tip-offs and inside information. Contributors would be expected to work with staff writers on news stories. Approach by telephone or fax in the first instance.

Finance *Anna Day*
Features Editor *Nicky Dawson* 'Anyone who has obviously studied the market will be dealt with constructively and courteously.' Cherishes its record as a breeding ground for new talent.

Sports Editor *To be appointed*

M Celebs: colour supplement. **Editor** *Mel Brodie*

Sunday Post

2 Albert Square, Dundee DD1 9QJ
☎01382 223131 Fax 01382 201064
Email mail@sundaypost.com
Website www.sundaypost.com

Owner *D.C. Thomson & Co. Ltd*
Editor *David Pollington*
Circulation 562,900

Contributions should be addressed to the editor.

Sunday Post Magazine: monthly colour supplement. **Editor** *Maggie Dun*

Sunday Sport

19 Great Ancoats Street, Manchester
M60 4BT
☎0161 236 4466 Fax 0161 236 4535
Website www.sundaysport.co.uk

Owner *David Sullivan*
Editor *Paul Carter*
Circulation 186,641

FOUNDED 1986. Sunday tabloid catering for a particular sector of the male 15–35 readership. As concerned with 'glamour' (for which, read:

'page 3') as with human interest, news, features and sport. Unsolicited mss are welcome; receives about 90 a week. Approach should be made by phone in the case of news and sports items, by letter for features. All material should be addressed to the news editor.

News Editor *Nick Appleyardie* Off-beat news, human interest, preferably with photographs.

Showbiz Editor *Debbie Manley* Regular items: showbiz, television, films, pop music and gossip.

Sports Editor *Marc Smith* Hard-hitting sports stories on major soccer clubs and their personalities, plus leading clubs/people in other sports. Strong quotations to back up the news angle essential.

Payment negotiable and on publication.

The Sunday Telegraph

1 Canada Square, Canary Wharf, London
E14 5DT
☎020 7538 5000 Fax 020 7538 6242
Website www.telegraph.co.uk

Owner *Conrad Black*
Editor *Dominic Lawson*
Circulation 721,076

Right-of-centre quality Sunday paper which, although traditionally formal, has pepped up its image to attract a younger readership. Unsolicited material from untried writers is rarely ever used. Contact with idea and details of track record.

News Editor *Richard Ellis*
Features Editor *Anna Murphy*
City Editor *Robert Peston*
Political Editor *Colin Brown*
Education Editor *Martin Bentham*
Arts Editor *Susannah Herbert*
Environment Editor *David Harrison*
Literary Editor *Miriam Gross*
Diary Editor *Tim Walker*
Sports Editor *Jon Ryan*

Sunday Telegraph Magazine: colour supplement. **Editor** *Lucy Tuck*

The Sunday Times

1 Pennington Street, London E98 1ST
☎020 7782 5000 Fax 020 7782 5658
Website www.sunday-times.co.uk

Owner *News International plc/Rupert Murdoch*
Editor *John Witherow*
Circulation 1.4 million

FOUNDED 1820. Tendency to be anti-establishment, with a strong crusading investigative tradition. Approach the relevant editor with an idea in writing. Close scrutiny of the style of each section of the paper is strongly advised before sending mss. No fiction. All fees by negotiation.

News Editor *Charles Hymas* Opportunities are very rare.

News Review Editor *Eleanor Mills* Submissions are always welcome, but the paper commissions its own, uses staff writers or works with literary agents, by and large. The features sections where most opportunities exist are *Style* and *The Culture*.

Culture Editor *Helen Hawkins*
Business Editor *William Lewis*
City Editor *Paul Durman*
Education Editor *Geraldine Hackett*
Science/Environment *Jonathan Leake*
Literary Editor *Caroline Gascoigne*
Sports Editor *Alex Butler*
Style Editor *Tiffany Darke*

Sunday Times Magazine: colour supplement. **Editor** *Robin Morgan* No unsolicited material. Write with ideas in first instance.

Sunday Times Travel Magazine: monthly supplement. **Editor** *Brian Schofield*

The Times
1 Pennington Street, London E98 1TT
☎020 7782 5000 Fax 020 7488 3242
Website www.thetimes.co.uk

Owner *News International plc/Rupert Murdoch*
Editor *Robert Thomson*
Circulation 642,637

Generally right (though features can range in tone from diehard to libertarian). *The Times* receives a great many unsolicited offerings. Writers with feature ideas should approach by letter in the first instance. No fiction.

Deputy Editor *Ben Preston*
News Editor *John Wellman*
Features Editor *Anne Barrowclough*
Associate Editor *Brian MacArthur*
City/Financial Editor *Patience Wheatcroft*
Diary Editor *Jack Malvern*
Arts Editor *Sarah Vine*
Literary Editor *Erica Wagner*
Political Editor *Phil Webster*
Sports Editor *David Chappell*
Weekend Editor *Jane Wheatley*

The Times Magazine: Saturday supplement. **Editor** *Gill Morgan*

Times 2 Editor *Sandra Parsons*

Regional Newspapers

ENGLAND

Berkshire

Reading Evening Post
8 Tessa Road, Reading, Berkshire RG1 8NS
☎0118 918 3000 Fax 0118 959 9363
Email editorial@reading-epost.co.uk
Owner *Guardian Media Group*
Editor *Andy Murrill*
Circulation 20,568

Unsolicited mss welcome; one or two received every day. Fiction rarely used. Interested in local news features, human interest, well-researched investigations. Special sections include holidays & travel (Monday); food page; children's page (Tuesday); style page (Wednesday); business (Wednesday & Friday); motoring and motor-cycling; gardening; rock music (Friday).

Cambridgeshire

Cambridge Evening News
Winship Road, Milton, Cambridge
CB4 6PP
☎01223 434434 Fax 01223 434415
Owner *Cambridge Newspapers Ltd*
Editor *Colin Grant*
Circulation 36,540

News Editor *John Deex*
Business Editor *Jenny Chapman*
Sports Editor *Chris Gill*

Cheshire

**Chronicle Newspapers
(Chester & North Wales)**
Chronicle House, Commonhall Street,
Chester CH1 2AA
☎01244 340151 Fax 01244 340165
Email eric.langton@cheshirenews.co.uk
Website www.iccheshireonline.co.uk
Owner *Trinity Mirror Plc*
Editor-in-Chief *Eric Langton*

All unsolicited feature material will be considered.

Cleveland

Hartlepool Mail
New Clarence House, Wesley Square,
Hartlepool TS24 8BX
☎01429 274441 Fax 01429 869024
Email post@hartmail.demon.co.uk
Website www.hartlepooltoday.co.uk
Owner *Johnston Press Plc*
Editor *Paul Napier*
Circulation 21,604

News Editor *Gavin Ledwith*
Sports Editor *Roy Kelly*

Cumbria

News & Star
Newspaper House, Dalston Road, Carlisle,
Cumbria CA2 5UA
☎01228 612600 Fax 01228 612601
Owner *Cumbrian Newspaper Group Ltd*
Editor *Keith Sutton*
Circulation 25,375

Deputy Editor *Nick Turner*
Sports Editor *Mike Gardner*
Women's Page *Jane Loughran*

North West Evening Mail
Abbey Road, Barrow in Furness, Cumbria
LA14 5QS
☎01229 821835 Fax 01229 840164
Email news@nwemail.co.uk
Website www.nwemail.co.uk
Owner *Robin Burgess*
Editor *Stephen Brauner*
Circulation 20,815

All editorial material should be addressed to the editor.
Sports Editor *Leo Clarke*

Derbyshire

Derby Evening Telegraph
Northcliffe House, Meadow Road, Derby
DE1 2DW
☎01332 291111 Fax 01332 253027
Owner *Northcliffe Newspapers Group Ltd*
Editor *Mike Norton*

Circulation 53,571

Weekly business supplement.

News Editor *Michael Hill* (newsdesk@derbytelegraph.co.uk)

Features Editor/Women's Page *Sarah Newton* (sarahnewton@derbytelegraph.co.uk)

Sports Editor *Dave Parkinson* (sports@derbytelegraph.co.uk)

Motoring Editor *Bob Maddox*

Devon

Evening Herald

17 Brest Road, Derriford Business Park, Derriford, Plymouth, Devon PL6 5AA
☎01752 765500 Fax 01752 765527
Email news@westcountrypublications.co.uk
Website www.thisisplymouth.co.uk

Owner *Northcliffe Newspapers Group Ltd*
Editor *Alan Qualtrough*
Circulation 42,510

All editorial material to be addressed to the editor or the **News Editor** *John Casey*.

Express & Echo

Heron Road, Sowton, Exeter, Devon EX2 7NF
☎01392 442211
Fax 01392 442294/442287 (editorial)
Email echonews@expressandecho.co.uk
Website www.thisisexeter.co.uk

Owner *Westcountry Publications Limited*
Editor *Steve Hall*
Circulation 25,359

Weekly supplements: *Business Week; Property Echo; Wheels; Weekend Echo.*

Head of Content *Sue Kemp*
Features Editor/Women's Page *Richard Best*
Sports Editor *Richard Davies* (Fax 01392 442416)

Herald Express

Harmsworth House, Barton Hill Road, Torquay, Devon TQ2 8JN
☎01803 676000
Fax 01803 676228 (editorial)
Email editor@thisissouthdevon.co.uk
Website www.thisissouthdevon.co.uk

Owner *Northcliffe Newspapers Group Ltd*
Editor *B. Hanrahan*
Circulation 30,174

Drive scene, property guide, *On The Town*—leisure and entertainment guide, Monday sports, special pages, rail trail, Saturday surgery, nature and conservation column, dance scene, shop scene, The Business. Supplements: *Gardening* (weekly); *Visitors Guide* and *Antiques & Collectables* (fortnightly); *Devon Days Out* (every Saturday in summer and at Easter and May Bank Holidays). Unsolicited mss generally not welcome. All editorial material should be addressed to the editor in writing.

Sunday Independent

Burrington Way, Plymouth, Devon PL5 3LN
☎01752 206600 Fax 01752 206164

Owner *Newsquest*
Editor *Nikki Rowlands*
Circulation 29,000

Tabloid Sunday covering the whole of the West Country from Bristol to Weymouth and Land's End. News stories/tips, news features. All editorial should be addressed to the editor. *Payment* by arrangement.

Western Morning News

17 Brest Road, Derriford Business Park, Derriford, Plymouth, Devon PL6 5AA
☎01752 765500 Fax 01752 765535
Website www.thisisplymouth.co.uk

Owner *Northcliffe Newspapers Group Ltd*
Editor *Barrie Williams*
Circulation 45,915

Unsolicited mss welcome, but must be of topical and local interest and addressed to the **News Editor** *Emma Corlett*.
Sports Editor *Rick Cowdery*

Dorset

Daily Echo

Richmond Hill, Bournemouth, Dorset BH2 6HH
☎01202 554601 Fax 01202 299543

Owner *Newsquest Media Group Ltd (a Gannett company)*
Editor *Neal Butterworth*
Circulation 45,000

FOUNDED 1900. Has a strong news and features content and invites specialist articles, particularly on unusual subjects, either contemporary or historical, but only with a local angle or flavour. Special review sections each day, including sport, property, entertainment and culture, heritage, motoring, gardening, the environment and the coastline. Also *Saturday Magazine* and monthly *Society* glossy magazine. All editorial material should be addressed to the **Editor** *Neal Butterworth. Payment* on publication.

Dorset Evening Echo

Fleet House, Hampshire Road, Granby
Industrial Estate, Weymouth, Dorset DT4 9XD
☎01305 830930 Fax 01305 830956

Owner *Newsquest Media Group Ltd (a Gannett company)*
Editor *David Murdock*
Circulation 20,430

Farming, by-gone days, films, arts, showbiz, brides, children's page, motoring, property, weekend leisure and entertainment including computers and gardening.
  News Editor *Paul Thomas*
  Sports Editor *Paul Baker*

Co Durham

The Northern Echo

Priestgate, Darlington, Co. Durham DL1 1NF
☎01325 381313 Fax 01325 380539
Email echo@nne.co.uk
Website www.thisisthenortheast.co.uk

Owner *Newsquest (North East) Ltd (a Gannett company)*
Editor *Peter Barron*
Circulation 60,522

FOUNDED 1870. Freelance pieces welcome but telephone first to discuss submission.
  News Editor *Nigel Burton* Interested in reports involving the North East or North Yorkshire. Preferably phoned in.
  Features Editor *Nick Morrison* Background pieces to topical news stories relevant to the area. Must be arranged with the features editor before submission of any material.
  Business Editor *Mike Parker*
  Sports Editor *Nick Loughlin*
  Payment and length by arrangement.

Essex

Evening Echo

Newspaper House, Chester Hall Lane,
Basildon, Essex SS14 3BL
☎01268 522792 Fax 01268 469281

Owner *Newsquest Media Group (a Gannett company)*
Editor *Martin McNeill*
Circulation 40,000

Relies almost entirely on staff and regular outside contributors, but will very occasionally consider material sent on spec. Approach the editor in writing with ideas. Although the paper is Basildon-based, its largest circulation is in the Southend area.

Evening Gazette (Colchester)

Oriel House, 43–44 North Hill, Colchester,
Essex CO1 1TZ
☎01206 506000 Fax 01206 508274
Email newsdesk@thisisessex.co.uk
Website www.thisisessex.co.uk

Owner *Newsquest (Essex)*
Editor *Irene Kettle*
Circulation 26,725

Monday – Friday daily newspaper servicing north and mid-Essex including Colchester, Harwich, Clacton, Braintree, Witham, Maldon and Chelmsford. Unsolicited mss not generally used. Relies heavily on regular contributors.
  Features Editor *Iris Clapp*

Gloucestershire

The Citizen

St John's Lane, Gloucester GL1 2AY
☎01452 424442 Fax 01452 420664 (Editorial)

Owner *Northcliffe Newspapers Group Ltd*
Editor *Ian Mean*
Circulation 31,540

All editorial material to be addressed to the **Head of Content** *Matt Holmes*.

Gloucestershire Echo

1 Clarence Parade, Cheltenham,
Gloucestershire GL50 3NY
☎01242 271900 Fax 01242 271848

Owner *Northcliffe Newspapers Group Ltd*
Editor *Anita Syvret*
Circulation 24,808

All material, other than news, should be addressed to the editor.
  News Editor *Tanya Gledhill*

Hampshire

The News

The News Centre, Hilsea, Portsmouth,
Hampshire PO2 9SX
☎023 9266 4488 Fax 023 9267 3363
Email newsdesk@thenews.co.uk
Website www.portsmouth.co.uk

Owner *Portsmouth Printing & Publishing Ltd*
Editor *Mike Gilson*
Circulation 73,577

Unsolicited mss not generally accepted. Approach by letter.
  News Editor *Colin McNeill*
  Features Editor *John Millard* General subjects

of S.E. Hants interest. Maximum 600 words. No fiction.

Sports Editor *Colin Channon* Sports background features. Maximum 600 words.

The Southern Daily Echo

Newspaper House, Test Lane, Redbridge, Southampton, Hampshire SO16 9JX
☎023 8042 4777 Fax 023 8042 4770
Website www.thisishampshire.net

Owner *Newsquest PLC*
Editor *Ian Murray*
Circulation 60,343

Unsolicited mss 'tolerated'. Approach the editor in writing with strong ideas; staff supply almost all the material.

Kent

Kent Messenger

6 & 7 Middle Row, Maidstone, Kent ME14 1TG
☎01622 717880 Fax 01622 715225
Email sirwin@thekmgroup.co.uk
Website www.kentonline.co.uk

Owner *Kent Messenger Group*
Editorial Director *Simon Irwin*
Circulation 62,171

Very little freelance work is commissioned.

Medway Messenger

395 High Street, Chatham, Kent ME4 4PQ
☎01634 830600 Fax 01634 829484
Email medwaytoday@thekmgroup.co.uk

Owner *Kent Messenger Group*
Editor *Bob Dimond*

Published Mondays and Fridays with the free *Medway Extra* on Wednesday.

Business Editor *Trevor Sturgess*
Community Editor *David Jones*
Sports Editor *Mike Rees*

Lancashire

Bolton Evening News

Newspaper House, Churchgate, Bolton, Lancashire BL1 1DE
☎01204 522345 Fax 01204 365068
Email bennewsdesk@boltoneveningnews.co.uk
Website www.thisisbolton.co.uk

Owner *Newsquest Media Group Ltd (a Gannett company)*
Editor *Steve Hughes*
Circulation 35,800

Business, children's page, travel, local services, motoring, fashion and cookery.

News Editor *John Horne*
Features Editor/Women's Page *Angela Kelly*

The Gazette (Blackpool)

PO Box 20, Avroe House, Avroe Crescent, Blackpool, Lancashire FY4 2DP
☎01253 400888 Fax 01253 361870

Owner *Johnston Press plc*
Editor *David Helliwell*
Circulation 36,024
Managing Director *Philip Welsh*
Associate Editor *Neil Hepburn*

Unsolicited mss welcome in theory. Approach in writing with an idea. Supplements: *The Result* (sport, Monday); *Eve* (women, Tuesday); *Wheels* (motoring, Wednesday); *Property* (Thursday); *The Weekend* (entertainment, Friday); *Life!* magazine (entertainment & leisure, Saturday); *Jobs Plus* (jobs and careers supplement, Saturday).

Lancashire Evening Post

Olivers Place, Eastway, Fulwood, Preston, Lancashire PR2 9ZA
☎01772 254841 Fax 01772 880173
Website www.prestontoday.net

Owner *Johnston Press plc*
Editor *Simon Reynolds*
Circulation 44,876

Unsolicited mss are not generally welcome; many are received and not used. All ideas in writing to the editor.

Lancashire Evening Telegraph

Newspaper House, High Street, Blackburn, Lancashire BB1 1HT
☎01254 678678 Fax 01254 680429
Website www.thisislancashire.co.uk

Owner *Newsquest Media Group Ltd (a Gannett company)*
Editor *Kevin Young*
Circulation 37,936

News stories and feature material with an East Lancashire flavour (a local angle, or written by local people) welcome. Approach in writing with an idea in the first instance. No fiction.

News Editor *Andrew Turner*
Features Editor *John Anson*

Oldham Evening Chronicle

PO Box 47, Union Street, Oldham, Lancashire OL1 1EQ
☎0161 633 2121 Fax 0161 652 2111
Email editorial@oldham-chronicle.co.uk

Owner *Hirst Kidd & Rennie Ltd*
Editor *Jim Williams*
Circulation 28,285

Motoring, food and wine, women's page, business page.
   News Editor *Mike Attenborough*
   Women's Page *Janice Barker*

Leicestershire
Leicester Mercury
St George Street, Leicester LE1 9FQ
☎0116 251 2512 Fax 0116 253 0645
Website www.thisisleicestershire.co.uk
Owner *Northcliffe Newspapers Group Ltd*
Editor *Nick Carter*
Circulation 96,760

   News Editor *Mark Charlton*
   Features Editor *Alex Dawon*

Lincolnshire
Grimsby Telegraph
80 Cleethorpe Road, Grimsby,
N.E. Lincolnshire DN31 3EH
☎01472 360360 Fax 01472 372257
Email newsdesk@grimsbytelegraph.co.uk
Owner *Northcliffe Newspapers Group Ltd*
Editor *Michelle Lalor*
Circulation 41,094

Sister paper of the *Scunthorpe Evening Telegraph*. Unsolicited mss generally welcome. Approach in writing. No fiction. Weekly supplements: *Business Telegraph*; *Homes and Gardens*; *Drive* (motoring); *Sports Telegraph* (Saturday). All material to be addressed to the **News Editor** *D. Atkin*. Particularly welcomes hard news stories – approach in haste by telephone.
   Special Publications Editor *B. Farnsworth*

Lincolnshire Echo
Brayford Wharf East, Lincoln LN5 7AT
☎01522 820000 Fax 01522 804493
Email editor@lincolnshireecho.co.uk
Owner *Northcliffe Newspapers Group Ltd*
Editor *Michael Sassi*
Circulation 27,926

Best buys, holidays, motoring, dial-a-service, restaurants, sport, leisure, home improvement, record reviews, gardening corner, stars. All editorial material to be addressed to the editor.

Scunthorpe Evening Telegraph
4–5 Park Square, Scunthorpe, N. Lincolnshire DN15 6JH

☎01724 273273 Fax 01724 273101
Owner *Northcliffe Newspapers Group Ltd*
Editor *Jon Grubb*
Circulation 23,005

All correspondence should go to the **Assistant Editor** *Jane Manning*.

Greater London
Evening Standard
Northcliffe House, 2 Derry Street, London W8 5EE
☎020 7938 6000 Fax 020 7937 2648
Website www.thisislondon.com
Owner *Associated Newspapers/Lord Rothermere*
Editor *Veronica Wadley*
Circulation 406,561

Long-established evening paper, serving Londoners with both news and feature material. Genuine opportunities for London-based features. Produces a weekly colour supplement, *ES The Evening Standard Magazine*, a weekly listings magazine *MetroLife* and regular weekly supplements: *Just the Job* (Monday) and *Homes & Property* (Wednesday).
   Joint Deputy Editors *Andrew Bordiss, Ian MacGregor*
   Executive Editors *Anne McElvoy, Philip Evans*
   Assistant Editor (Features) *Guy Eaton*
   Assistant Editor (Arts) *Norman Lebrecht*
   Assistant Editor (Sport) *Simon Greenberg*
   News Editor *Ian Walker*
   Editor, *ES* *Catherine Ostler*
   Editor, *MetroLife* *Mark Booker*

Greater Manchester
Manchester Evening News
164 Deansgate, Manchester M60 2RD
☎0161 832 7200 Fax 0161 834 3814
Website www.manchesteronline.co.uk
Owner *Manchester Evening News Ltd*
Editor *Paul Horrocks*
Circulation 159,638

One of the country's major regional dailies. Initial approach in writing preferred. No fiction. *Personal Finance* (Mon); *Health* (Tues); *Homes & Property* (Wed); *Small Business* (Thurs); *Lifestyle* (Fri/Sat); *Holidays* (Sat).
   News Editor *Ian Wood*
   Features Editor *Maggie Henfield* Regional news features, personality pieces and showbiz profiles considered. Maximum 1200 words.

Sports Editor *Peter Spencer*
Women's Page *Diane Cooke*
Payment based on house agreement rates.

Merseyside

Daily Post

PO Box 48, Old Hall Street, Liverpool
L69 3EB
☎0151 227 2000 Fax 0151 236 4682
Website www.icliverpool.co.uk

Owner *Trinity Mirror Plc*
Editor *Jane Wostenholme*
Circulation 62,398

Unsolicited mss welcome. Receives about six a day. Approach in writing with an idea. No fiction. Local, national/international news, current affairs, profiles – with pictures. Maximum 800–1000 words.

Features Editor *Jane Haase*
News Editor *Andrew Edwards*
Sports Editor *Richard Williamson*
Women's Page *Susan Lee*

Liverpool Echo

PO Box 48, Old Hall Street, Liverpool
L69 3EB
☎0151 227 2000 Fax 0151 236 4682
Email letters@liverpoolecho.co.uk

Owner *Liverpool Daily Post & Echo Ltd*
Editor *Mark Dickinson*
Circulation 143,436

One of the country's major regional dailies. Unsolicited mss welcome; initial approach with ideas in writing preferred.

News Editor *Andrew Edwards*
Features Editor *Jane Haase*
Sports Editor *John Thompson*
Women's Editor *Susan Lee*

Norfolk

Eastern Daily Press

Prospect House, Rouen Road, Norwich,
Norfolk NR1 1RE
☎01603 628311 Fax 01603 623872
Website www.EDP24.co.uk

Owner *Archant Regional*
Editor *Peter Franzen*
Circulation 73,933

Most pieces by commission only. Supplements: *Centro* (daily); education (Tuesday); motoring, business, property pages, agriculture, employment (all weekly); *Event* full-colour magazine

(Friday); Saturday full colour magazine.

Deputy Editor *James Ruddy*
Assistant Editor (News) *Paul Durrant*
Features Editor *Mark Nicholls*
Sports Editor *David Thorpe*
Magazine Editor *Steve Snelling*

Evening News

Prospect House, Rouen Road, Norwich,
Norfolk NR1 1RE
☎01603 628311 Fax 01603 219060
Email david.bourn@archant.co.uk
Website www.eveningnews24.co.uk

Owner *Archant Ltd*
Editor *David Bourn*
Circulation 31,559

Includes special pages on local property, motoring, children's page, pop, fashion, arts, entertainments and TV, gardening, local music scene, home and family.

Assistant Editor *Tim Williams*
(tim.williams@archant.co.uk)
Deputy Editor *Roy Strowger*
(roy.strowger@archant.co.uk)
Features Editor *Derek James*
(derek.james@archant.co.uk)

Northamptonshire

Chronicle and Echo

Upper Mounts, Northampton NN1 3HR
☎01604 467000 Fax 01604 467190

Owner *Northamptonshire Newspapers*
Editor *Mark Edwards*
Circulation 26,213

Unsolicited mss are 'not necessarily unwelcome but opportunities to use them are rare'. Approach in writing with an idea. No fiction. Supplements: *Sports Chronicle* (Monday); *Property Week* (Wednesday); *What's On Guide* (Thursday); *Weekend Motors* (Friday).

News Editor *Richard Edmondson*
Features Editor/Women's Page *Sarah Freeman*
Sports Editor *Steve Pitts*

Evening Telegraph

Newspaper House, Ise Park, Rothwell Road,
Kettering, Northamptonshire NN16 8GA
☎01536 506100 Fax 01536 506195
Email etnewsdesk@northantsnews.co.uk
Website www.northantsnews.com

Owner *Johnston Press Plc*
Circulation 33,346
Managing Editor *David Penman*

Northamptonshire Business Guide (weekly); *Entertainment Guide* and *Jobs* supplements (Thursday); and *Home & Garden* – monthly lifestyle supplement including gardening, films, eating out, etc.
News Editor *Nick Tite*
Sports Editor *Ian Davidson*

Nottinghamshire
Evening Post Nottingham
Castle Wharf House, Nottingham NG1 7EU
☎0115 948 2000 Fax 0115 964 4032
Owner *Northcliffe Newspapers Group Ltd*
Editor *Graham Glen*
Circulation 78,191

Unsolicited mss occasionally used. Good local interest only. Maximum 800 words. No fiction. Send ideas in writing.
News Editor *Claire Catlow*
Deputy Editor *Marc Astley*
Sports Editor *Tim Walters*

Oxfordshire
Oxford Mail
Osney Mead, Oxford OX2 0EJ
☎01865 425262 Fax 01865 425554
Email nqonews@nqo.com
Website www.thisisoxfordshire.co.uk
Owner *Newsquest (Oxfordshire) Ltd*
Editor *Jim McClure*
Circulation 28,673

Unsolicited mss are considered but a great many unsuitable offerings are received. Approach in writing with an idea, rather than by phone. No fiction. All fees negotiable.

Shropshire
Shropshire Star
Ketley, Telford, Shropshire TF1 5HU
☎01952 242424 Fax 01952 254605
Owner *Shropshire Newspapers Ltd*
Editor *Sarah-Jane Smith*
Circulation 85,654

No unsolicited mss; approach the editor with ideas in writing in the first instance. No news or fiction.
Head of Features *Sharon Walters, Carl Jones*
Limited opportunities; uses mostly in-house or syndicated material. Maximum 1200 words.
Sports Editor *Dave Ballinger*

Somerset
The Bath Chronicle
Windsor House, Windsor Bridge Road, Bath BA2 3AU
☎01225 322322 Fax 01225 322291
Website www.thisisbath.com
Owner *BUP Plc*
Editor *David Gledhill* (editor@bathchron.co.uk)
Circulation 15,341
Local news and features especially welcomed. (news@bathchron.co.uk)
Deputy Editor *John McCready*
News Editor *Paul Wiltshire*
Features Editor *Graham Parker*
Sports Editor *Tony Harrison*

Evening Post
Temple Way, Bristol BS99 7HD
☎0117 934 3000 Fax 0117 934 3575
Email mail@epost.co.uk
Website www.epost.co.uk
Owner *Bristol United Press plc*
Editor *Mike Lowe*
Circulation 61,673
News Editor *Kevan Blackadder*
Features Editor *Bill Davis*
Sports Editor *Chris Bartlett*

Western Daily Press
Temple Way, Bristol BS99 7HD
☎0117 934 3000 Fax 0117 934 3574
Email WDEditor *or* WDNews *or* WDFeats@bepp.co.uk
Website www.westpress.co.uk
Owner *Bristol Evening Post & Press Ltd*
Editor *Terry Manners*
Circulation 51,192
Sports Editor *Bill Beckett*
Women's Page *Cathy Smith* (Features Production)

Staffordshire
Burton Mail
65–68 High Street, Burton upon Trent, Staffordshire DE14 1LE
☎01283 512345 Fax 01283 515351
Email editorial@burtonmail.co.uk
Owner *Burton Daily Mail Ltd*
Editor *Paul Hazeldine*
Circulation 17,309
Fashion, health, wildlife, environment, nostalgia, financial/money (Monday); consumer (Tuesday); women's world, rock (Wednesday); prop-

erty (Thursday); motoring, farming, what's on (Friday); what's on, leisure (Saturday).

News *Andrew Parker*
Sports Editor *Rex Page*
Women's Page *Emma Atkin*
Features *Killoran Wills*

The Sentinel/Sentinel Sunday
Sentinel House, Etruria, Stoke on Trent, Staffordshire ST1 5SS
☎01782 602525 Fax 01782 280781 (Sentinel)/201167 (Sentinel Sunday)
Website www.thisisstaffordshire.co.uk
Owner *Staffordshire Sentinel Newspapers Ltd*
Editor-in-Chief *Sean Dooley*
Circulation 79,258 (Sentinel)

Weekly sports final supplement. All material should be sent to the **Head of Content** *Martin Tideswell*.

Suffolk
East Anglian Daily Times
Press House, 30 Lower Brook Street, Ipswich, Suffolk IP4 1AN
☎01473 230023 Fax 01473 324776
Email EADT@ecng.co.uk
Website www.eadt.co.uk
Owner *Archant Ltd*
Editor *Terry Hunt*
Circulation 41,925

FOUNDED 1874. Unsolicited mss generally not welcome; three or four received a week and almost none are used. Approach in writing in the first instance. No fiction. Supplements: Sport (Monday); Business (Tuesday); Jobs (Wednesday); Property (Thursday); Motoring (Friday); Magazine (Saturday).

News Editor *Aynsley Davidson* Hard news stories involving East Anglia (Suffolk, Essex particularly) or individuals resident in the area are always of interest.

Features *Julian Ford* Mostly in-house, but will occasionally buy in when the subject is of strong Suffolk/East Anglian interest. Photo features preferred (extra payment). Special advertisement features are regularly run. Some opportunities here. Maximum 1000 words.

Sports Editor *Nick Garnham*
Women's Page *Victoria Hawkins*

Evening Star
30 Lower Brook Street, Ipswich, Suffolk IP4 1AN
☎01473 230023 Fax 01473 324850

Owner *Archant Ltd*
Editor *Nigel Pickover*
Circulation 28,322

News Editor *Colin Adwent*
Sports Editor *Mike Horne*

East Sussex
The Argus
Argus House, Crowhurst Road, Hollingbury, Brighton, East Sussex BN1 8AR
☎01273 544544 Fax 01273 505703
Email simonb@theargus.co.uk
Website www.thisisbrightonandhove.co.uk
Owner *Newsquest (Sussex) Ltd*
Editor-in-Chief *Simon Bradshaw*
Circulation 45,071

News Editor *Simon Freeman*
Sports Editor *Chris Giles*

Teesside
Evening Gazette
Borough Road, Middlesbrough, Teesside TS1 3AZ
☎01642 234242 Fax 01642 232014
Owner *Trinity Mirror plc*
Editor *Steve Dyson*
Circulation 60,316

Special pages: health, education, family, business, property, entertainment, leisure, motoring, recruitment.

News Editor *Jim Horsley*
Features Editor/Women's Page *Kathryn Armstrong*
Business *Helen Logan*
Sports Editor *Allan Boughey*
Councils *Sandy McKenzie*
Education *Lyndsey Emmett*
Consumer *Michelle Ruane*
Health *Helen Sturdy*
Crime *Mike Underwood*

Tyne & Wear
Evening Chronicle
Thomson House, Groat Market, Newcastle upon Tyne, Tyne and Wear NE1 1ED
☎0191 232 7500 Fax 0191 232 2256
Email ec.news@ncjmedia.co.uk
Website www.icnewcastle.co.uk
Owner *Trinity Mirror Plc*

Editor *Paul Robertson*
Circulation 94,677

Receives a lot of unsolicited material, much of which is not used. Family issues, gardening, pop, fashion, cooking, consumer, films and entertainment guide, home improvements, motoring, property, angling, sport and holidays. Approach in writing with ideas.
   News Editor *Mick Smith*
   Features Limited opportunities due to full-time feature staff.
   Sports Editor *Paul New*
   Women's Interests *Kay Jordan*

Gazette
Chapter Row, South Shields, Tyne & Wear NE33 1BL
☎0191 455 4661 Fax 0191 456 8270
Website www.southtynesidetoday.co.uk

Owner *Northeast Press Ltd*
Editor *John Szymanski*
Circulation 21,791

   News Editor *Gary Welford*
   Sports Editor *John Cornforth*
   Women's Page *Caroline Sword*

The Journal
Thomson House, Groat Market, Newcastle upon Tyne, Tyne & Wear NE1 1ED
☎0191 232 7500
Fax 0191 232 2256/201 6044
Email jnl.newsdesk@ncjmedia.co.uk
Website www.the-journal.co.uk

Owner *Trinity Mirror Plc*
Editor *Gerard Henderson*
Circulation 45,059

Daily platforms include farming and business.
   Deputy Editor *Graham Pratt*
   Sports Editor *Kevin Dinsdale*
   Arts & Entertainment Editor *David Whetstone*
   Environment Editor *Tony Henderson*
   Business Editor *Iain Laing*

Sunday Sun
Newcastle Chronicle & Journal Ltd, Thomson House, Groat Market, Newcastle upon Tyne, Tyne & Wear NE1 1ED
☎0191 201 6330 Fax 0191 201 6180
Email peter.montellier@ncjmedia.co.uk

Owner *Trinity Mirror Plc*
Editor *Peter Montellier*

Circulation 91,937

All material should be addressed to the appropriate editor (phone to check), or to the editor.
   Sports Editor *Dylan Younger*

Sunderland Echo
Echo House, Pennywell, Sunderland, Tyne & Wear SR4 9ER
☎0191 501 5800 Fax 0191 534 4861
Email andrew.smith@northeast-press.co.uk

Owner *Johnston Press Plc*
Editorial Director *Andrew Smith*
Circulation 50,593

All editorial material to be addressed to the **News Editor** *Patrick Lavelle* (echo.news@northeast-press.co.uk).

Warwickshire
Coventry Evening Telegraph
Corporation Street, Coventry CV1 1FP
☎024 7663 3633 Fax 024 7655 0869
Email news@coventry-telegraph.co.uk
Website www.IcCoventry.co.uk

Owner *Trinity Mirror Plc*
Editor *Alan Kirby*
Circulation 66,152

Unsolicited mss are read, but few are published. Approach in writing with an idea. No fiction. All unsolicited material should be addressed to the editor. Maximum 600 words for features.
   News Editor *John West*
   Features Editor *Steve Chilton*
   Sports Editor *Rob Madill*
   Women's Page *Steve Chilton*
   Payment negotiable.

Leamington Spa Courier
32 Hamilton Terrace, Leamington Spa, Warwickshire CV32 4LY
☎01926 457755 Fax 01926 451690
Email editorial@leamingtoncourier.co.uk
Website www.leamingtononline.co.uk

Owner *Central Counties Newspapers*
Editor *Martin Lawson*
Circulation 12,084

One of the Leamington Spa Courier Series which also includes the *Warwick Courier* and *Kenilworth Weekly News*. Unsolicited feature articles considered, particularly matter with a local angle. Telephone with idea first.
   News Editor *Calista Lewis*

West Midlands

Birmingham Evening Mail
PO Box 78, Weaman Street, Birmingham
B4 6AT
☎0121 236 3366   Fax 0121 233 0271

Owner *Trinity Mirror Plc*
Editor *Roger Borrell*
Circulation 114,346

Freelance contributions are welcome, particularly topics of interest to the West Midlands and Women's Page pieces offering original and lively comment.

   Deputy Editor *Colin Clark*
   Features Editor *Alison Handley*
   Women's Page *Diane Parkes*

Birmingham Post
28 Colmore Circus, Queensway, Birmingham
B4 6AX
☎0121 234 5419   Fax 0121 234 5667

Owner *Trinity Mirror Plc*
Publisher & Editor *To be appointed*
Circulation 17,238

One of the country's leading regional newspapers. Freelance contributions are welcome. Topics of interest to the West Midlands and pieces offering lively, original comment are particularly welcome.

   Head of News *Phil Brown*
   Head of Features *Lisa Piddington*

Express & Star
Queen Street, Wolverhampton, West
Midlands WV1 1ES
☎01902 313131   Fax 01902 319721

Owner *Midlands News Association*
Editor *Adrian Faber*
Circulation 169,766

   Deputy Editor *Keith Harrison*
   Assistant Editors *Roy Williams, Graham
     Barfoot*
   Head of News *Mark Drew*
   Features Editor *Dylan Evans*
   Business Editor *Jim Walsh*
   Sports Editor *Steve Gordos*
   Women's Editor *Anne-Laure Domenichini*
   Lifestyle Editor *Deanna Delamotta*

Sunday Mercury (Birmingham)
28 Colmore Circus, Queensway, Birmingham
B4 6AZ
☎0121 236 3366   Fax 0121 234 5877
Email sundaymercury@mrn.co.uk

Owner *Trinity Mirror Plc*
Editor *David Brookes*

Circulation 91,592

   Head of Content *Tony Larner*
   Assistant Editor (Sport) *Lee Gibson*

Wiltshire

Evening Advertiser
100 Victoria Road, Swindon, Wiltshire
SN1 3BE
☎01793 528144   Fax 01793 542434
Email editor@newswilts.co.uk
Website www.thisiswiltshire.co.uk

Owner *Newsquest (Wiltshire) Ltd*
Editor *Simon O'Neill*
Circulation 24,016

Copy and ideas invited. 'All material must be strongly related or relevant to the town of Swindon or the county of Wiltshire.' Little scope for freelance work. Fees vary depending on material.

   Deputy Editor *Pauline Leighton*
   News Editor *Jim Wildman*
   Sports Editor *Neville Smith*

Worcestershire

Evening News
Berrow's House, Hylton Road, Worcester
WR2 5JX
☎01905 748200   Fax 01905 748009

Owner *Newsquest (Midlands South) Ltd*
Editor *Stewart Gilbert*
Circulation 21,480

Local events (Tuesday); jobs/careers (Wednesday); property (Thursday); showbiz/what's on, motoring/Pulse pop page (Friday); holidays/what's on (Saturday).

   Deputy Editor *Mark Higgitt*
   News Editor *Sala Lloyd*
   Features Editor *Mike Pryce*
   Consumer Page *Melanie Hill*
   Sports Editor *Paul Ricketts*

Yorkshire

The Doncaster Star
40 Duke Street, Doncaster, South Yorkshire
DN1 3EA
☎01302 344001   Fax 01302 768340
Email rob.hollingworth@rim.co.uk

Owner *Sheffield Newspapers Ltd*
Editor/News Editor *Rob Hollingworth*
Circulation 8,312

All editorial material to be addressed to the editor.

Sports Editor *Steve Hossack*

Evening Courier
PO Box 19, King Cross Street, Halifax, West Yorkshire HX1 2SF
☎01422 260200 Fax 01422 260341
Website www.halifaxtoday.co.uk

Owner *Johnston Press Plc*
Editor *John Furbisher*
Circulation 25,636

News Editor *John Kenealy*
Features Editor *William Marshall*
Sports Editor *Ian Rushworth*
Women's Page *Diane Crabtree*

Evening Press
PO Box 29, 76–86 Walmgate, York YO1 9YN
☎01904 653051 Fax 01904 612853
Email newsdesk@ycp.co.uk
Website www.thisisyork.co.uk

Owner *Newsquest Media Group (a Gannett company)*
Editor *Elizabeth Page*
Circulation 41,557

Unsolicited mss not generally welcome, unless submitted by journalists of proven ability. *Business Press Pages* (Tuesday); *Property Press* (Thursday); *Friday Night Fever* – what's on (Friday); *8 Days* TV supplement (Saturday).

News Editor *Fran Clee*
Picture Editor *Martin Oates*
Sports Editor *Martin Jarred*
Payment negotiable.

Huddersfield Daily Examiner
Queen Street South, Huddersfield, West Yorkshire HD1 2TD
☎01484 430000 Fax 01484 437789

Owner *Trinity Mirror Plc*
Editor *Roy Wright*
Circulation 32,510

Home improvement, home heating, weddings, dining out, motoring, fashion, services to trade and industry.

News Editor *Neil Atkinson*
Features Editor *Andrew Flynn*
Sports Editor *John Gledhill*
Women's Page *Hilarie Stelfox*

Hull Daily Mail
Blundell's Corner, Beverley Road, Hull, East Yorkshire HU3 1XS
☎01482 327111 Fax 01482 584353
Email news@hulldailymail.co.uk

Website www.thisishull.co.uk

Owner *Northcliffe Newspapers Group Ltd*
Editor *John Meehan*
Circulation 74,724

Content Editor *Tracy Fletcher*
Features Editors *Lucy Smith, Matt Stephenson*

Scarborough Evening News
17–23 Aberdeen Walk, Scarborough, North Yorkshire YO11 1BB
☎01723 363636 Fax 01723 383825
Email editorial@scarboroughveningnews.co.uk
Website www.scarboroughtoday.co.uk

Owner *Yorkshire Regional Newspapers Ltd*
Editor *Ed Asquith*
Circulation 15,347

Special pages include property (Monday); motoring (Tuesday/Friday).

Deputy Editor *Sue Wilkinson*
News Editor *Neil Pickford*
Sports Editor *Charles Place*
All other material should be addressed to the editor.

The Star
York Street, Sheffield, South Yorkshire S1 1PU
☎0114 276 7676 Fax 0114 272 5978

Owner *Sheffield Newspapers Ltd*
Editor *Peter Charlton*
Circulation 71,785

Unsolicited mss not welcome, unless topical and local.

News Editor *Bob Westerdale* Contributions only accepted from freelance news reporters if they relate to the area.
Features Editor *John Highfield* Very rarely requires outside features, unless on specialised subject.
Sports Editor *Martin Smith*
Women's Page *Jo Davison*
Payment negotiable.

Telegraph & Argus (Bradford)
Hall Ings, Bradford, West Yorkshire BD1 1JR
☎01274 729511 Fax 01274 723634
Website www.thisisbradford.co.uk

Owner *Newsquest Media Group Ltd (a Gannett company)*
Editor *Perry Austin-Clarke*
Circulation 48,312

No unsolicited mss – approach in writing with samples of work. No fiction.

Assistant Editor (News) *To be appointed*

Local features and general interest. Showbiz pieces. 600–1000 words (maximum 1500).

Yorkshire Evening Post

Wellington Street, Leeds, West Yorkshire LS1 1RF
☎0113 243 2701 Fax 0113 238 8536
Email eped@ypn.co.uk

Owner *Johnson Press*
Editor *Neil Hodgkinson*
Circulation 84,944

Evening sister of the *Yorkshire Post.*
News Editor *Gilian Haworth*
Features Editor *Anne Pickles*
Sports Editor *Phil Rostron*
Women's Page *Jayne Dawson*

Yorkshire Post

Wellington Street, Leeds, West Yorkshire LS1 1RF
☎0113 243 2701 Fax 0113 238 8537
Email yp.editor@ypn.co.uk

Owner *Johnston Press*
Editor *Rachel Campey*
Circulation 64,648

A serious-minded, quality regional daily with a generally conservative outlook. Three or four unsolicited mss arrive each day; all will be considered but initial approach in writing preferred. All submissions should be addressed to the editor. No fiction, poetry or family histories. **Features Editor** *Mick Hickling* Open to suggestions in all fields (though ordinarily commissioned from specialist writers).
Deputy Editor *John Furbisher*
Sports Editor *Bill Bridge*
Women's Page *Jill Armstrong*

NORTHERN IRELAND

Belfast News Letter

46–56 Boucher Crescent, Belfast BT12 6QY
☎028 9068 0000 Fax 028 9066 4412

Owner *Century Newspapers Ltd*
Editor *Nigel Wareing*
Circulation 31,182

Weekly supplements: *Farming Life*; *Business News Letter*; *Female Times*; *The Guide*; *Sports Ulster.*
News Editors *Ric Clark, Steven Moore*
Features Editor *Geoff Hill*
Sports Editor *Brian Millar*
Fashion & Lifestyle/Property Editor *Sandra Chapman*

Business Editor *Adrienne McGill*
Agricultural Editor *David McCoy*

Belfast Telegraph

Royal Avenue, Belfast BT1 1EB
☎028 9026 4000 Fax 028 9055 4506/4540

Owner *Independent News & Media (UK)*
Editor *Edmund Curran*
Circulation 109,629

Weekly business, property and recruitment supplements.
Deputy Editor *Jim Flanagan*
News Editor *Paul Connolly*
Features Editor *John Caruth*
Sports Editor *John Laverty*
Business Editor *Nigel Tilson*

The Irish News

113/117 Donegall Street, Belfast BT1 2GE
☎028 9032 2226 Fax 028 9033 7505

Owner *Irish News Ltd*
Editor *Noel Doran*
Circulation 50,115

All material to appropriate editor (phone to check), or to the news desk.
Head of Content *Fiona McGarry*
Sports Editor *Thomas Hawkins*
Arts Editor/Women's Page *Joanna Braniff*

Sunday Life

124–144 Royal Avenue, Belfast BT1 1EB
☎028 9026 4300 Fax 028 9055 4739
Email betty.arnold@belfasttelegraph.co.uk
Website www.sundaylife.co.uk

Owner *Independent News & Media (UK)*
Editor/General Manager *Martin Lindsay*
Circulation 92,396

Deputy Editor *Martin Hill*
Sports Editor *Jim Gracey*

SCOTLAND

The Courier and Advertiser

80 Kingsway East, Dundee DD4 8SL
☎01382 223131 Fax 01382 454590
Email courier@dcthomson.co.uk
Website www.thecourier.co.uk

Owner *D.C. Thomson & Co. Ltd*
Editor *Bill Hutcheon*
Circulation 85,981

Circulates in East Central Scotland. Features occasionally accepted on a wide range of subjects, particularly local/Scottish interest –

including finance, insurance, agriculture, motoring, modern homes, lifestyle and fitness. Maximum length, 500 words.

News Editor *Arliss Rhind*
Features Editor/Women's Page *Shona Lorimer*
Sports Editor *Graeme Dey*

Daily Record (Glasgow)
See **National Newspapers**

Evening Express (Aberdeen)
PO Box 43, Lang Stracht, Mastrick, Aberdeen AB15 6DF
☎01224 690222 Fax 01224 699575
Email d.martin@ajl.co.uk
Owner *Northcliffe Newspapers Group Ltd*
Editor *Donald Martin*
Circulation 60,032

Circulates in Aberdeen and the Grampian region. Local, national and international news and pictures, sport. Family platforms include *What's On, Counter* (consumer news), *Eating Out Guide, Family Days Out.* Unsolicited mss welcome 'if on a controlled basis'.

News Editor *Richard Prest* Freelance news contributors welcome.
Payment negotiable.

Evening News
Barclay House, 108 Holyrood Road, Edinburgh EH8 8AS
☎0131 620 8620 Fax 0131 620 8696
Website www.edinburghnews.com
Owner *Scotsman Publications Ltd*
Editor *Ian Stewart*
Circulation 71,224

FOUNDED 1873. Circulates in Edinburgh, Fife, Central and Lothian. Coverage includes: entertainment, gardening, motoring, shopping, fashion, health and lifestyle, showbusiness. Occasional platform pieces, features of topical and/or local interest. Unsolicited feature material welcome. Approach the appropriate editor in writing.

News Editor *Jim Morrison*
Sports Editor *Martin Dempster*
Payment NUJ/house rates.

Evening Telegraph
80 Kingsway East, Dundee DD4 8SL
☎01382 223131 Fax 01382 454590
Email general@eveningtelegraph.co.uk
Website www.eveningtelegraph.co.uk
Owner *D.C. Thomson & Co. Ltd*

Editor *Alan Proctor*
Circulation 27,853

Circulates in Tayside, Dundee and Fife. All material should be addressed to the editor.

Evening Times
200 Renfield Street, Glasgow G2 3PR
☎0141 302 7000 Fax 0141 302 6677
Email times@eveningtimes.co.uk
Owner *S.M.G.*
Editor *Charles McGhee*
Circulation 95,562

Circulates in Glasgow and the west of Scotland. Supplements: *Job Search; Homes etc; Drive times; Extra times; Times Out; Times Out Weekend Extra.*

News Editor *Hugh Boag*
Features Editor *Grace McLean*
Sports Editor *David Stirling*

Greenock Telegraph
2 Crawfurd Street, Greenock PA15 1LH
☎01475 726511 Fax 01475 783734
Owner *Clyde & Forth Press Ltd*
Managing Editor *Steward Peterson*
Circulation 19,243

Circulates in Greenock, Port Glasgow, Gourock, Kilmacolm, Langbank, Bridge of Weir, Inverkip, Wemyss Bay, Skelmorlie, Largs. Unsolicited mss considered 'if they relate to the newspaper's general interests'. No fiction. All material to be addressed to the editor.

The Herald/Sunday Herald (Glasgow)
See **National Newspapers**

Paisley Daily Express
14 New Street, Paisley PA1 1YA
☎0141 887 7911 Fax 0141 887 6254
Email pde@s-un.co.uk
Owner *Scottish & Universal Newspapers Ltd*
Editor *Jonathan Russell*
Circulation 10,924

Circulates in Paisley, Linwood, Renfrew, Johnstone, Elderslie, Neilston and Barrhead. Unsolicited mss welcome only if of genuine local (Paisley) interest. The paper does not commission work and will consider submitted material. Maximum 1000–1500 words. All submissions to the editor.

News Editor *Anne Dalrymple*
Sports Reporters *Michelle Evans, Matt Vallance*

The Press and Journal
PO Box 43, Lang Stracht, Mastrick, Aberdeen
AB15 6DF
☎01224 690222 Fax 01224 663575

Owner *Northcliffe Newspapers Group Ltd*
Editor *Derek Tucker*
Circulation 94,080

A well-established daily that circulates in
Aberdeen, Grampians, Highlands, Tayside,
Orkney, Shetland and the Western Isles. Most
material is commissioned but will consider ideas.
    News Editor *Fiona McWhirr* Wide variety
of hard or off-beat news and features relating
especially, but not exclusively, to the north of
Scotland.
    Sports Editor *Alex Martin*
    Women's Page *Victoria Banks*
    Your Life *Sonja Cox* Saturday lifestyle
tabloid pullout. Features food, fashion, travel,
books, arts and lifestyle.
    Payment by arrangement.

Scotland on Sunday (Edinburgh)
See **National Newspapers**

The Scotsman (Edinburgh)
See **National Newspapers**

Sunday Mail (Glasgow)
See **National Newspapers**

Sunday Post (Dundee)
See **National Newspapers**

WALES

Daily Post
PO Box 202, Vale Road, Llandudno Junction,
Conwy LL31 9ZD
☎01492 574455 Fax 01492 574433
Email alistairmachray@dailypost.co.uk

Owner *Trinity Mirror Plc*
Editor in Chief *Alastair Machray*
Circulation 41,815

    Features Editor *Mark Brittain*
    News Editor *Maria Breslyn*
    Sports Editor *Jonathan McEvoy*

Evening Leader
Mold Business Park, Wrexham Road, Mold,
Clwyd CH7 1XY
☎01352 707707 Fax 01352 752180

Owner *North Wales Newspapers*
Editor-in-Chief *Richard Williams*

Circulation 28,227

Circulates in Wrexham, Flintshire, Deeside
and Chester. Special pages/features: motoring,
travel, arts, women's, children's, photography,
local housing, information and news for the
disabled, music and entertainment.
    Assistant Editor *Barrie Jones*
    Features Editor *Debra Greenhouse*
    Sports Editor *Nick Harrison*

South Wales Argus
Cardiff Road, Maesglas, Newport, Gwent
NP20 3QN
☎01633 810000 Fax 01633 777202
Website www.thisisgwent.co.uk

Owner *Newsquest*
Editor *Gerry Keighley*
Circulation 30,626

Circulates in Newport, Gwent and surrounding areas.
    News Editor *Alison Gow*
    Sports Editor *Carson Wishart*

South Wales Echo
Thomson House, Havelock Street, Cardiff
CF10 1XR
☎029 2022 3333 Fax 029 2058 3624
Website www.icwales.com

Owner *Trinity Mirror Plc*
Editor *Alastair Milburn*
Circulation 61,757

Circulates in South and Mid Glamorgan and
Gwent.
    Head of News & Design *Nick Machin*
    Head of Features & Development *Neil*
        Cammies
    Head of Sport *Carl Difford*

South Wales Evening Post
Adelaide Street, Swansea, West Glamorgan
SA1 1QT
☎01792 510000 Fax 01792 514697
Email postbox@swwp.co.uk
Website www.thisissouthwales.co.uk

Owner *Northcliffe Newspapers Group Ltd*
Editor *Spencer Feeney*
Circulation 59,440

Circulates throughout south west Wales.
    News Editor *Peter Slee*
    Features Editor *To be appointed*
    Sports Editor *David Evans*

Wales on Sunday
Thomson House, Havelock Street, Cardiff
CF10 1XR
☎029 2022 3333 Fax 029 2058 3725

Owner *Trinity Mirror plc*
Editor *Tim Gordon*
Circulation 62,286

LAUNCHED 1989. Tabloid with sports supplement. Does not welcome unsolicited mss.
News Editor *Laura Kemp*
Show Biz/Features Editor *Rachel Mainwaring*
Sports Editor *Nick Rippington*

The Western Mail

Thomson House, Havelock Street, Cardiff CF10 1XR
☎029 2058 3583 Fax 029 2058 3652
Website www.icwales.com

Owner *Trinity Mirror Plc*
Editor *Alan Edmunds*
Circulation 46,732

Circulates in Cardiff, Merthyr Tydfil, Newport, Swansea and towns and villages throughout Wales. Mss welcome if of a topical nature, and preferably of Welsh interest. No short stories or travel. Approach in writing to the editor. 'Usual subjects already well covered, e.g. motoring, travel, books, gardening. We look for the unusual.' Maximum 1000 words. Opportunities also on women's page. Supplements: *Saturday Magazine*; *Education*; *WM*; *Box Office*; *Welsh Homes*; *Business*; *Sport*; *Motoring*.
Assistant Editor *Mark Tattersall*
Head of News *Duncan Higgitt*
Sports Editor *Philip Blanche*
Features Editor *Ceri Gould*

CHANNEL ISLANDS

Guernsey Press & Star

Braye Road, Vale, Guernsey, Channel Islands GY1 3BW
☎01481 240240 Fax 01481 240235
Email newsroom@guernsey-press.com
Website www.guernsey-press.com

Owner *Guiton Group*
Editor *Richard Digard*
Circulation 16,301

Special pages include children's and women's interest, gardening and fashion.
News Editor *James Falla*
Sports Editor *Rob Batiste*
Features Editor *Suzanne Heneghan*

Jersey Evening Post

PO Box 582, Jersey, Channel Islands JE4 8XQ
☎01534 611611 Fax 01534 611622
Email editorial@jerseyeveningpost.com
Website www.thisisjersey.com

Owner *Jersey Evening Post Ltd*
Editor *Chris Bright*
Circulation 23,017

Special pages: gardening, motoring, property, boating, technology, young person's (16–25), women, food and drink, personal finance, rock reviews, health, business.
News Editor *Sue Le Ruez*
Features Editor *Elaine Hanning*
Sports Editor *Ron Felton*

Magazines

Abraxas

57 Eastbourne Road, St Austell, Cornwall
PL25 4SU
☎01726 64975 Fax 01726 64975
Email palnew7@hotmail.com
Website www.AbraxasMagazine.com

Owner *Paul Newman*
Editors *Paul Newman, Pamela Smith-Rawnsley*

FOUNDED 1991. QUARTERLY incorporating
the *Colin Wilson Newsletter*. Unsolicited mss
welcome after a study of the magazine. Initial
approach by phone or letter/e-mail preferred.

Features Essays, translations and reviews.
Welcomes provocative, lively articles on little-
known literary figures and new slants on psychology, existentialism and ideas. Maximum
length 2000 words. *Payment* nominal, if at all.

Fiction One story per issue. Maximum
2000 words. Favours compact, obsessional stories.

Poetry Double-page spread – slight penchant for the surreal but open to most styles.
Payment free copy of magazine.

Acclaim

See **The New Writer**

Accountancy

100 London Road, Kingston Upon Thames,
Surrey KT2 6SR
☎020 8247 1387 Fax 020 8247 1424

Owner *Croner CCH*
Editor *Chris Quick*
Circulation 53,681

FOUNDED 1889. MONTHLY. Written ideas
welcome.

Features *Lesley Bolton* Accounting/tax/
business-related articles of high technical content aimed at professional/managerial readers.
Maximum 2000 words.
Payment by arrangement.

Accountancy Age

32–34 Broadwick Street, London W1A 2HG
☎020 7316 9236/Features: 020 7316 9032
Fax 020 7316 9250
Email accountancy_age@vnu.co.uk
Website www.accountancyage.com

Owner *VNU Business Publications*

Editor *Damian Wild*
News Editor *Gavin Hinks* (020 7316 9242)
Circulation 77,806

FOUNDED 1969. WEEKLY. Unsolicited mss
welcome. Ideas may be suggested in writing
provided they are clearly thought out.

Features *Michelle Perry* Topics right across
the accountancy, business and financial world.
Maximum 2000 words.
Payment negotiable.

Ace Tennis Magazine

9–11 North End Road, London W14 8ST
☎020 7605 8000 Fax 020 7602 2323
Email Nigel.Billen@acemag.co.uk

Owner *Tennis GB*
Editor *Nigel Billen*
Circulation 49,064

FOUNDED 1996. MONTHLY specialist tennis
magazine. News (250 words max.) and features
(2000 words max.). No unsolicited mss; send
feature synopses by e-mail in the first instance.
No tournament reports.
Payment £200 per 1000 words.

Active Life

221–223 High Street, Berkhamsted,
Hertfordshire HP4 1AD
☎01442 289600 Fax 01442 879903

Owner *Computer Publishing*
Editor *Paul Jacques*

FOUNDED 1990. MONTHLY magazine aimed at
over-50s. General consumer interests including
travel, finance, property and leisure. Opportunities for freelancers in all departments,
including fiction. Approach in writing with
synopsis of ideas. Authors' notes available on
receipt of s.a.e.

Acumen

See under **Poetry Magazines**

Aeroplane

IPC Media Ltd., King's Reach Tower,
Stamford Street, London SE1 9LS
☎020 7261 5849 Fax 020 7261 5269
Email aeroplane_monthly@ipcmedia.com
Website www.aeroplanemonthly.com

Owner *IPC Country & Leisure Media Ltd*

Editor *Michael Oakey*
Circulation 34,500

FOUNDED 1973. MONTHLY. Historic aviation and aircraft preservation from its beginnings to the 1960s. No post-1960 aircraft types; no poetry. Will consider news items and features written with authoritative knowledge of the subject, illustrated with good quality photographs.

News *Tony Harsmworth* Maximum 500 words. **Features** *Michael Oakey* Maximum 3000 words. *Payment* £60 per 1000 words; £10–40 per picture used. Approach by letter in the first instance.

African Affairs

Dept of Politics, University of Newcastle upon Tyne, 40–42 Great North Road, Newcastle upon Tyne NE1 7RL
☎0191 222 6000 Fax 0191 222 5609
Email tim.kelsall@ncl.ac.uk

Owner *Royal African Society*
Editors *Tim Kelsall, Stephen Ellis*
Circulation 2250

FOUNDED 1901. QUARTERLY. learned journal publishing articles on recent political, social and economic developments in sub-Saharan countries. Also included are historical studies that illuminate current events in the continent. Unsolicited mss welcome. Maximum 8000 words.

No payment.

Air International

PO Box 100, Stamford, Lincolnshire PE9 1XQ
☎01780 755131 Fax 01780 757261
Email malcolm.english@keypublishing.com

Owner *Key Publishing Ltd*
Editor *Malcolm English*

FOUNDED 1971. MONTHLY. Civil and military aircraft magazine. Unsolicited mss welcome but initial approach by phone or in writing preferred.

AirForces Monthly

PO Box 100, Stamford, Lincolnshire PE9 1XQ
☎01780 755131 Fax 01780 757261
Email edafm@keypublishing.com

Owner *Key Publishing Ltd*
Editor *Alan Warnes*
Circulation 25,787

FOUNDED 1988. MONTHLY. Modern military aircraft magazine. Unsolicited mss welcome but initial approach by phone or in writing preferred.

Amateur Gardening

Westover House, West Quay Road, Poole, Dorset BH15 1JG
☎01202 440840 Fax 01202 440860

Owner *IPC Media*
Editor *Tim Rumball*
Circulation 66,312

FOUNDED 1884. WEEKLY. New contributions are welcome especially if they are topical and informative. All articles/news items should be supported by colour pictures (which may or may not be supplied by the author).

Features Topical and practical gardening articles. Maximum 1000 words.

News Compiled and edited in-house generally but all stories welcomed.

Payment negotiable.

Amateur Photographer

IPC Media Ltd., King's Reach Tower, Stamford Street, London SE1 9LS
☎020 7261 5100/0870 444 5000 (switchboard) Fax 020 7261 5404
Email amateurphotographer@ipcmedia.com

Owner *IPC Media*
Editor *Garry Coward-Williams*
Circulation 30,600

FOUNDED 1884. WEEKLY. For the competent amateur with a technical interest. Freelancers are used but writers should be aware that there is ordinarily no use for words without pictures.

Amateur Stage

Hampden House, 2 Weymouth Street, London W1W 5BT
☎020 7636 4343 Fax 020 7636 2323
Email cvtheatre@aol.com

Owner *Platform Publications Ltd*
Editor *Charles Vance*

Some opportunity here for outside contributions. Topics of interest include amateur premières, technical developments within the amateur forum and items relating to landmarks or anniversaries in the history of amateur societies. Approach in writing only (include s.a.e. for return of mss).

No payment.

Ancestors

See **The National Archives** under **UK Publishers**

Angler's Mail

IPC Media Ltd., King's Reach Tower, Stamford Street, London SE1 9LS
☎020 7261 5778 Fax 020 7261 6016

Email anglersmail@ipcmedia.com
Owner *IPC Media*
Editor *Tim Knight*
Circulation 46,466

FOUNDED 1965. WEEKLY. Angling news and matches. Interested in pictures, stories and tip-offs. No features. Approach the news desk by telephone.
Payment £10–40 per 200 words; pictures, £20–40.

Animal Action
Wilberforce Way, Southwater, Horsham, West Sussex RH13 9RS
☎0870 010 1181 Fax 0870 753 0048
Email publications@rspca.org.uk
Website www.rspca.org.uk

Owner *RSPCA*
Editor *Michaela Miller*
Circulation 80,000

BI-MONTHLY. RSPCA youth membership magazine. Articles (pet care, etc.) are written in-house. Good-quality animal photographs welcome.

Animalprints
Worthing Animal Aid, 56 Cissbury Gardens, Worthing, West Sussex BN14 0DZ
☎01903 877144
Email WorthingAnimalAid@btinternet.com

Owner *Worthing Animal Aid*
Editor *Lilian Taylor*
Circulation 500

FOUNDED 1999. QUARTERLY magazine that aims to advance the animal movement. Welcomes contributions that are well researched, subtly thought provoking and have the potential for stimulating discussion. Approach in writing. *Payment* Complimentary copies of relevant issue.

The Antique Dealer and Collectors' Guide
PO Box 805, Greenwich, London SE10 8TD
☎020 8691 4820 Fax 020 8691 2489
Email antiquedealercollectorsguide@
  ukbusiness.com
Website www.antiquecollectorsguide.co.uk

Owner *Statuscourt Ltd*
Publisher *Philip Bartlam*
Circulation 12,500

FOUNDED 1946. TEN ISSUES YEARLY. Covers all aspects of the antiques and fine art worlds. Unsolicited mss welcome.
Features Practical but readable articles on the history, design, authenticity, restoration and market aspects of antiques and fine art. Maximum 2000 words. *Payment* rates by arrangement.
News Items on events, sales, museums, exhibitions, antique fairs and markets. Maximum 300 words.

Antiques & Art Independent
PO Box 1945, Comely Bank, Edinburgh EH4 1AB
☎07000 268478
Email antiquesnews@hotmail.com
Website www.antiquesnews.co.uk

Owner *Gallery UK Ltd*
Publisher/Editor *Tony Keniston*
Circulation 21,000

FOUNDED 1997. BI-MONTHLY. Up-to-date information for the British antiques and art trade, circulated to dealers and collectors throughout the UK. News, photographs, gossip and controversial views on all aspects of the fine art and antiques world welcome. Articles on antiques and fine arts themselves are not featured. Approach in writing with ideas.

Apollo Magazine
1 Castle Lane, London SW1E 6DR
☎020 7233 6640 Fax 020 7630 7791
Email editorial@apollomag.com

Owner *The Spectator (1828) Ltd*
Editor *David Ekserdjian*
Publisher *Kimberly Fortier*

FOUNDED 1925. MONTHLY. Specialist articles on art and antiques, exhibition and book reviews, exhibition diary, information on dealers and auction houses. Unsolicited mss welcome. Interested in specialist, usually new research in fine arts, architecture and antiques.

Architects' Journal
151 Rosebery Avenue, London EC1R 4GB
☎020 7505 6700 Fax 020 7505 6701
Website www.ajplus.co.uk

Owner *Emap Construct*
Editor *Isabel Allen*
Circulation 16,441

WEEKLY trade magazine dealing with all aspects of the industry. No unsolicited mss. Approach in writing with ideas.

Architectural Design
John Wiley & Sons, 4th Floor, International House, Ealing Broadway Centre, London W5 5DB
☎020 8326 3800 Fax 020 8326 3801

Owner *John Wiley & Sons Ltd*
Editor *Helen Castle*

Senior Production Editor *Mariangela Palazzi-Williams*
Circulation 5,000

FOUNDED 1930. BI-MONTHLY. Sold as a book as well as a journal, *AD* charts theoretical and topical developments in architecture. Format consists of 128pp, the first part dedicated to a theme compiled by a specially commissioned guest-editor; the back section (AD+) carries series and more current one-off articles. Unsolicited mss not welcome generally, though journalistic contributions will be considered for the back section.

The Architectural Review
151 Rosebery Avenue, London EC1R 4GB
☎020 7505 6725 Fax 020 7505 6701
Website www.arplus.com

Owner *Emap Construct*
Editor *Peter Davey*
Circulation 23,925

MONTHLY professional magazine dealing with architecture and all aspects of design. No unsolicited mss. Approach in writing with ideas.

Arena
Endeavour House, 189 Shaftesbury Ave, London WC2H 8JG
☎020 7437 9011 (switchboard)

Owner *Emap élan East*
Editor *Anthony Noguera*
Circulation 31,712

Style and general interest magazine for men. Intelligent feature articles and profiles.

Features Fashion, lifestyle, film, television, politics, business, music, media, design, art, architecture and sport.

Art Monthly
4th Floor, 26 Charing Cross Road, London WC2H 0DB
☎020 7240 0389 Fax 020 7497 0726
Email info@artmonthly.co.uk
Website www.artmonthly.co.uk

Owner *Britannia Art Publications*
Editor *Patricia Bickers*
Circulation 6000

FOUNDED 1976. TEN ISSUES YEARLY. News and features of relevance to those interested in modern and contemporary visual art. Unsolicited mss welcome. Contributions should be addressed to the deputy editor, accompanied by s.a.e.

Features Always commissioned. Interviews and articles of up to 2000 words on art theory, individual artists, contemporary art history and issues affecting the arts (e.g. funding and arts education). Exhibition reviews of 750–1000 words; book reviews of 750–1000 words.
News Brief reports (250–300 words) on art issues.
Payment negotiable.

The Art Newspaper
70 South Lambeth Road, London SW8 1RL
☎020 7735 3331 Fax 020 7735 3332
Email feedback@theartnewspaper.com
Website www.theartnewspaper.com

Owner *Umberto Allemandi & Co. Publishing*
Editor *Anna Somers Cocks*
Circulation 22,000

FOUNDED 1990. MONTHLY. Tabloid format with hard news on the international art market, news, museums, exhibitions, archaeology, conservation, books and current debate topics. Length 250–2000 words. No unsolicited mss. Approach with ideas in writing. Commissions only.
Payment £120 per 1000 words.

The Artist
Caxton House, 63–65 High Street, Tenterden, Kent TN30 6BD
☎0158076 3673 Fax 0158076 5411
Website www.theartistmagazine.co.uk

Owner/Editor *Sally Bulgin*
Circulation 20,000

FOUNDED 1931. MONTHLY. Art journalists, artists, art tutors and writers with a good knowledge of art materials are invited to write to the editor with ideas for practical and informative features about art, materials, techniques and artists.

Artscene
Dean Clough Industrial Park, Halifax, West Yorkshire HX3 5AX
☎01422 322527 Fax 01422 322518
Email artscene@btconnect.com

Owner *Yorkshire Arts*
Editor *Victor Allen*
Circulation 25,000

FOUNDED 1973. MONTHLY. Listings magazine for Yorkshire and Humberside. No unsolicited mss. Approach by phone with ideas.

Features Profiles of artists (all media) and associated venues/organisers of events of interest. Topical relevance vital. Maximum length 1500 words. *Payment* £100 per 1000 words.
News 'Artscene strives to bring journalistic values to arts coverage' – all arts 'scoops' in the region are of interest. Maximum length 500 words. *Payment* £100 per 1000 words.

Asian Times

Unit 2, 65 Whitechapel Road, London
E1 1DU
☎020 7650 2000 Fax 020 7650 2001
Website www.ethnicmedia.co.uk

Owner *Ethnic Media Group*
Coordinating Editor *Ishara de Silva*
Circulation 28,525

FOUNDED 1983. WEEKLY community paper for the Asian community in Britain. Interested in relevant general, local and international issues. Approach in writing with ideas for submission.

Athletics Weekly

83 Park Road, Peterborough, Cambridgeshire
PE1 2TN
☎01733 898440 Fax 01733 898441
Email results@athletics-weekly.co.uk
Website www.athleticsweekly.com

Owner *Descartes Publishing*
Editor *Jason Henderson*
Circulation 14,000

FOUNDED 1945. WEEKLY. Covers track and field, road, fell, cross-country, race walking, athletic features and sports politics.
News *Steve Landells* Maximum 400 words.
Features *Tony Ward* Maximum 2000 words. Approach in writing.
  Payment negotiable.

Attitude

Northern & Shell Tower, City Harbour, 4 Selsdon Way, London E14 9GL
☎020 7308 5261 Fax 020 7308 5384
Email attitude@nasnet.co.uk

Owner *Northern & Shell plc*
Editor *Adam Mattera*
Deputy Editor *Matthew Todd*
Circulation 60,000

FOUNDED 1994. MONTHLY. Style magazine aimed primarily, but not exclusively, at gay men. Celebrity, fashion and cultural coverage. Brief summaries of proposed features, together with details of previously published work, should be sent by post or e-mail only. 'It sounds obvious, but anyone wanting to contribute to the magazine should read it first.'

The Author

84 Drayton Gardens, London SW10 9SB
☎020 7373 6642

Owner *The Society of Authors*
Editor *Fanny Blake*
Manager *Kate Pool*
Circulation 8500

FOUNDED 1890. QUARTERLY journal of the **Society of Authors**. Most articles are commissioned.

Auto Express

30 Cleveland Street, London W1T 4JD
☎020 7907 6200 Fax 020 7907 6234
Email editorial@autoexpress.co.uk
Website www.autoexpress.co.uk

Owner *Dennis Publishing*
Editor *David Johns*
News & Features Editor *Richard Yarrow*
Circulation 95,000

FOUNDED 1989. WEEKLY consumer motoring title with news, drives, tests, investigations, etc. **Features** Welcomes ideas. No fully-written articles – features will be commissioned if appropriate and good enough. Maximum 2000 words. *Payment* £350 per 1000 words. **News** News stories and tip-offs welcome. Fillers, 150 words max.; leads, 300 words. Approach by e-mail.

Autocar

60 Waldegrave Road, Teddington, Middlesex
TW11 8LG
☎020 8943 5630 Fax 020 8267 5759
Email autocar@haynet.com
Website www.autocarmagazine.co.uk

Owner *Haymarket Magazines Ltd*
Editor *Steve Fowler*
Circulation 70,000

FOUNDED 1895. WEEKLY. All news stories, features, interviews, scoops, ideas, tip-offs and photographs welcome. *Payment* negotiable.
  News *Phil McNamara*

Aviation News

HPC, Drury Lane, St Leonards on Sea, East Sussex TN38 9BJ
☎01424 720477 Fax 01424 443693
Email editor@aviation-news.co.uk
Website www.aviation-news.co.uk

Owner *Hastings Printing Company*
Editor *Barry C. Wheeler*
Circulation 21,000

FOUNDED 1939. MONTHLY review of aviation for those interested in military, commercial and business aircraft and equipment – old and new. Will consider articles on military and civil aircraft, airports, air forces, current and historical subjects. No fiction. **Features** 'New writers always welcome and if the copy is not good enough it is returned with guidance attached.' Maximum 5000 words. **News** Items are always considered from new sources. Maximum 300 words. *Payment* negotiable.

B Magazine
64 North Row, London W1K 7LL
☎020 7150 7020 Fax 020 7150 7677
Email letters@bmagazine.co.uk
Website www.hf-uk.com
Owner *Hachette Filipacchi (UK) Ltd*
Editor *Gina Johnson*
Circulation 192,945

MONTHLY glossy magazine aimed at women in their mid-twenties. Will consider real-life stories, emotional issues and celebrity features. Ideas for features should be sent to *Viki Wilson*. No short stories or opinion pieces. Approach in writing or by e-mail.

Baby & You
Highbury – WV, 53–79 Highgate Road, London NW5 1TW
☎020 7331 1068 Fax 020 7331 1108
Email amanda.burney@highburywv.com
Owner *Highbury House Communications Plc*
Editor *Amanda Burney*

MONTHLY parenting title that focuses on issues affecting the family as a whole.

Balance
Diabetes UK, 10 Parkway, London NW1 7AA
☎020 7424 1000 Fax 020 7424 1001
Email balance@diabetes.org.uk
Owner *Diabetes UK*
Editor *Martin Cullen*
Circulation 250,000

FOUNDED 1935. BI-MONTHLY. Unsolicited mss are not accepted. Writers may submit a brief proposal in writing. Only topics relevant to diabetes will be considered.
Features Medical, diet and lifestyle features written by people with diabetes or with an interest and expert knowledge in the field. General features are mostly based on experience or personal observation. Maximum 1500 words. *Payment* NUJ rates.
News Short pieces about activities relating to diabetes and the lifestyle of people with diabetes. Maximum 150 words.

The Banker
149 Tottenham Court Road, London W1P 9LL
☎020 7896 2507 Fax 020 7896 2586
Website www.thebanker.com
Owner *FT Business*
Editor *Stephen Timewell*
Circulation 30,000

FOUNDED 1926. MONTHLY. News and features on banking, finance and capital markets world-wide and technology.

BBC Gardeners' World Magazine
Woodlands, 80 Wood Lane, London W12 0TT
☎020 8433 3959 Fax 020 8433 3986
Email adam.pasco@bbc.co.uk
Owner *BBC Worldwide Publishing Ltd*
Editor *Adam Pasco*
Circulation 295,271

FOUNDED 1991. MONTHLY. Gardening advice, ideas and inspiration. No unsolicited mss. Approach by phone or in writing with ideas – interested in features about exceptional small gardens. Also interested in any exciting new gardens showing good design and planting ideas as well new plants and the stories behind them. 'The magazine aims to be the first to bring news of new trends and developments, and always welcomes ideas from contributors.'

BBC Good Food
Woodlands, 80 Wood Lane, London W12 0TT
☎020 8433 2000 Fax 020 8433 3931
Email goodfood.magazine@bbc.co.uk
Owner *BBC Worldwide Publishing Ltd*
Editor *Orlando Murrin*
Circulation 342,375

FOUNDED 1989. MONTHLY food and drink magazine with television and radio links. No unsolicited mss.

BBC Good Homes Magazine
Woodlands, 80 Wood Lane, London W12 0TT
☎020 8433 2391 Fax 020 8433 2691
Website www.bbcgoodhomes.com
Owner *BBC Worldwide Publishing Ltd*
Editor *Celia Woolfrey*
Circulation 116,468

FOUNDED 1998. MONTHLY. Interiors, gardening, property, home shopping. No non-homes related features, fiction or puzzles. **Features** *Gill Smith* Readers' homes; property features from specialists. Approach by letter with cuttings.

BBC History Magazine
Room A1050, Woodlands, 80 Wood Lane, London W12 0TT
☎020 8433 2433 Fax 020 8433 2931
Email bbchistory@galleon.co.uk
Website www.historymagazine.co.uk

Owner *BBC Worldwide Publishing Ltd*
Editor *Greg Neale*
Circulation 52,000

FOUNDED 2000. MONTHLY. General news and features on British and international history, with books and CD reviews, listings of history events, TV and radio history programmes and regular features for those interested in history and current affairs. Winner, British Society of Magazine Editors *Editor of the Year Award*, 2002, for general interest and current affairs titles. Will consider submissions from academic or otherwise expert historians/archaeologists and occasionally, from historically literate journalists who include expert analysis and historiography with a well-told narrative. Ideas for regular features are welcome. Also publishes cartoons, a monthly quiz and crossword. 'We cannot guarantee to acknowledge all unsolicited mss immediately.' **Features** should be pegged to anniversaries or forthcoming books/TV programmes, current affairs topics, etc. 750–3000 words. **News** 400–500 words. Send short letter or e-mail with synopsis, giving appropriate sources, pegs for publication dates, etc. *Payment* negotiable.

BBC Homes & Antiques

Woodlands, 80 Wood Lane, London
W12 0TT
☎020 8433 3490 Fax 020 8433 3867
Website www.bbcworldwide.com/antiques

Owner *BBC Worldwide Publishing Ltd*
Editor *Mary Carroll*
Circulation 150,454

FOUNDED 1993. MONTHLY traditional home interest magazine with a strong bias towards antiques and collectables. Opportunities for freelancers are limited; most features are commissioned from regular stable of contributors. No fiction, health and beauty, fashion or general showbusiness. Approach with ideas by phone or in writing.

Features *Caroline Wheater* At-home features: inspirational houses – people-led items. Pieces commissioned on recce shots and cuttings. Celebrity features: 'at homes or favourite things'. Send cuttings of relevant published work. Max. 1500 words. Guidelines available on request.

Special Pages Regular feature – 'Memories'. Maximum 800 words.
Payment negotiable.

BBC Music Magazine

Room A1004, Woodlands, 80 Wood Lane, London W12 0TT
☎020 8433 2000 Fax 020 8433 3292

Email music.magazine@bbc.co.uk
Website www.bbcmusicmagazine.com

Owner *BBC Worldwide Publishing Ltd*
Editor *Helen Wallace*
Circulation 78,707 (worldwide)

FOUNDED 1992. MONTHLY. All areas of classical music. Not interested in unsolicited material. Approach with ideas by e-mail or fax.

BBC Top Gear Magazine

Woodlands, 80 Wood Lane, London
W12 0TT
☎020 8433 3716 Fax 020 8433 3754
Website www.topgear.com

Owner *BBC Worldwide Publishing Ltd*
Editor *Kevin Blick*
Circulation 150,000

FOUNDED 1993. MONTHLY companion magazine to the popular TV series. No unsolicited material as most features are commissioned.

BBC Wildlife Magazine

Broadcasting House, Whiteladies Road, Bristol BS8 2LR
☎0117 973 8402 Fax 0117 946 7075
Email wildlife.magazine@bbc.co.uk

Owner *BBC Worldwide Publishing Ltd*
Editor *Rosamund Kidman Cox*
Circulation 50,811

FOUNDED 1963 (formerly *Wildlife*, née *Animals*). MONTHLY. Unsolicited mss generally not welcome.

Features Most features commissioned from writers with expert knowledge of wildlife or conservation subjects. Maximum 2500 words. *Payment* £200–450.

News Most news stories commissioned from known freelancers. Maximum 400 words. *Payment* £80–120

Bee World

IBRA, 18 North Road, Cardiff CF10 3DT
☎029 2037 2409 Fax 029 2066 5522
Email mail@ibra.org.uk
Website www.ibra.org.uk

Owner *International Bee Research Association*
Editor *Dr P.A. Munn*
Circulation 1700

FOUNDED 1919. QUARTERLY. High-quality factual journal, including peer-reviewed articles, with international readership. Features on apicultural science and technology. Unsolicited mss welcome but authors should write to the editor for guidelines before submitting material.

Bella

H. Bauer Publishing, Academic House,
24–28 Oval Road, London NW1 7DT
☎020 7241 8000 Fax 020 7241 8056
Owner *H. Bauer Publishing*
Editor-in-Chief *Rebecca Fleming*
Circulation 427,885

FOUNDED 1987. WEEKLY. Women's magazine
specialising in real-life, human interest stories.

Features *Sue Ricketts* Contributions welcome for some sections of the magazine: readers' letters, 'Blush with Bella'.

Fiction *Linda O'Byrne* Maximum
1000–1200 words. Send s.a.e. for guidelines.

Best

National Magazine House, 72 Broadwick
Street, London W1F 9EP
☎020 7439 5000 Fax 020 7312 4175
Email best@natmags.co.uk
Owner *National Magazine Company*
Editor *Louise Court*
Circulation 416,074

FOUNDED 1987. WEEKLY women's magazine.
Multiple features, news, short stories on all
topics of interest to women. Important for
would-be contributors to study the magazine's
style which differs from many other women's
weeklies. Approach in writing with s.a.e.

Features *Helen Garston, Charlotte Seligman*
Maximum 1500 words. No unsolicited mss.

Fiction *Pat Richardson* Short story slot – maximum 1000 words. Send s.a.e. for guidelines.

Payment negotiable.

Best of British

Ian Beacham Publishing, Bank Chambers,
27a Market Place, Market Deeping,
Lincolnshire PE6 8EA
☎01778 342814
Email mail@british.fsbusiness.co.uk
Website www.bestofbritishmag.co.uk
Owner *Ian Beacham Publishing*
Editor-in-Chief *Ian Beacham*

FOUNDED 1994. MONTHLY magazine celebrating all things British, both past and present.
Emphasis on nostalgia – memories from the
1940s, 1950s and 1960s. Study of the magazine
is advised in the first instance. All preliminary
approaches should be made in writing.

Best Solutions

IBIS, 38 Broad Street, Earls Barton,
Northamptonshire NN6 0ND
☎01604 466500 Fax 01604 466480

Email info@bestsolutions.org.uk
Website www.bestsolutions.org.uk
Editor *Graham White*

FOUNDED 1996. QUARTERLY 32pp business to
business consultancy magazine. No unsolicited
mss. Interested in business solution articles
(1000 words). Approach in writing.

The Big Issue

1–5 Wandsworth Road, London SW8 2LN
☎020 7526 3200 Fax 020 7526 3201
Email editorial@bigissue.com
Website www.bigissue.com
Editor-in-Chief *A. John Bird*
Editor *Matt Ford*
Circulation 122,679

FOUNDED 1991. WEEKLY. An award-winning
campaigning and street-wise general interest
magazine sold in London, the Midlands, the
North East and South of England. Separate
regional editions sold in Manchester, Scotland,
Wales and the South West.

Features Interviews, campaigns, comment,
opinion and social issues reflecting a varied and
informed audience. Balance includes social
issues but mixed with arts and cultural features.
Freelance writers used each week – commissioned from a variety of contributors. Best
approach in the first instance is to e-mail or
post synopses with examples of work to assistant editor, *Lorna Russell*. Maximum 1500
words. *Payment* £160 for 1000 words.

News *Judy Kerr* Hard-hitting exclusive stories
with emphasis on social injustice aimed at
national leaders.

Arts *Lorna Russell* Interested in interviews
and analysis ideas. Reviews written in-house.
Send synopses to arts editor.

Bird Life Magazine

RSPB, The Lodge, Sandy, Bedfordshire
SG19 2DL
☎01767 680551 Fax 01767 683262
Email derek.niemann@rspb.org.uk
Owner *Royal Society for the Protection of Birds*
Editor *Derek Niemann*
Circulation 90,000

FOUNDED 1965. BI-MONTHLY. Bird, wildlife
and nature conservation for 8–12 year-olds
(RSPB Wildlife Explorer members). No unsolicited mss. No 'captive/animal welfare'
articles.

Features Unsolicited material rarely used.

News News releases welcome. Approach in
writing in the first instance.

Bird Watching

Emap Active, Bretton Court, Peterborough
PE3 8DZ
☎01733 264666 Fax 01733 465376
Email david.cormack@emap.com

Owner *Emap Active*
Editor *David Cromack*
Circulation 20,466

FOUNDED 1986. MONTHLY magazine for bird-watchers at all levels of experience. Offers practical advice on where and when to see birds, how to identify them, product reviews (particularly binoculars and telescopes), extensive bird sightings, news and general articles.

Features Interested in authoritative articles on bird behaviour and bird watching/sites in the UK. Please send synopsis, not the whole piece. Maximum 1000 words. *Fees* negotiable.

News UK news pre-eminent, preferably with pictures. Maximum 350 words. *Fees* negotiable.

Birds

RSPB, The Lodge, Sandy, Bedfordshire
SG19 2DL
☎01767 680551 Fax 01767 683262
Email rob.hume@rspb.org.uk

Owner *Royal Society for the Protection of Birds*
Editor *R.A. Hume*
Circulation 613,500

QUARTERLY magazine which covers not only wild birds but also other wildlife and related conservation topics. No interest in features on pet birds or 'rescued' sick/injured/orphaned ones. Content refers mostly to RSPB work so opportunities for freelance work on other subjects are limited but some freelance submissions are used in most issues. Phone or e-mail to discuss.

Birdwatch

3D/F Leroy House, 436 Essex Road, London
N1 3QP
☎020 7704 9495 Fax 020 7704 2767
Email editorial@birdwatch.co.uk
Website www.birdwatch.co.uk

Owner *Solo Publishing*
Editor *Dominic Mitchell*
Circulation 15,000

FOUNDED 1992. MONTHLY magazine featuring illustrated articles on all aspects of birds and birdwatching, especially in Britain. No unsolicited mss. Approach in writing with synopsis of 100 words maximum. Annual **Birdwatch Bird Book of the Year** award (see entry under **Prizes**).

Features *Dominic Mitchell* Unusual angles/personal accounts, if well-written. Articles of an educative or practical nature suited to the readership. Maximum 2000 words.

Fiction *Dominic Mitchell* Very little opportunity although occasional short story published. Maximum 1500 words.

News *David Mairs* Very rarely use external material.

Payment £50 per 1000 words.

Bizarre

9 Dallington Street, London EC1V 0BQ
☎020 7687 7000 Fax 020 7687 7096
Email bizarre@ifgmags.com
Website www.bizarremag.com

Owner *I Feel Good Ltd*
Editor *Ben Raworth*
Circulation 105,620

FOUNDED 1997. MONTHLY magazine featuring amazing stories and images from around the world. No fiction, poetry, illustrations, short snippets.

Features *Ben Raworth* Maximum 2000 words. No unsolicited mss. Send synopsis by post or e-mail.

Payment negotiable.

Black Beauty & Hair

2nd Floor, Culvert House, Culvert Road, Battersea, London SW11 5HD
☎020 7720 2108 Fax 020 7498 3023
Email info@blackbeautyandhair.com
Website www.blackbeautyandhair.com

Owner *Hawker Consumer Publications Ltd*
Editor *Irene Shelley*
Circulation 21,499

BI-MONTHLY with one annual special: *The Hairstyle Book* in October; and a *Bridal Supplement* in the April/May issue. Black hair and beauty magazine with emphasis on authoritative articles relating to hair, beauty, fashion, health and lifestyle. Unsolicited contributions welcome.

Features Beauty and fashion pieces welcome from writers with a sound knowledge of the Afro-Caribbean beauty scene plus bridal features. Minimum 1000 words.

Payment £100 per 1000 words.

Bliss Magazine

Endeavour House, 189 Shaftesbury Avenue, London WC2H 8JG
☎020 7208 3478 Fax 020 7208 3591
Email christina.reeves@ecm.emap.com

Owner *Emap élan*

Editor *Helen Johnston*
Circulation 260,102

FOUNDED 1995. MONTHLY teenage lifestyle magazine for girls. No unsolicited mss; 'call the assistant editor (*Annabel Brog*) with an idea and then send it in.'

News *Katie Masters* Worldwide teenage news. Maximum 200 words. *Payment* £50–100.

Features Real life teenage stories with subjects willing to be photographed. Reports on teenage issues. Maximum 2000 words. *Payment* £350.

The Book Collector

PO Box 12426, London W11 3GW
☎020 7792 3492 Fax 020 7792 3492
Email info@thebookcollector.co.uk
Website www.thebookcollector.co.uk

Owner *The Collector Ltd*
Editor *Nicolas J. Barker*

FOUNDED 1950. QUARTERLY magazine on bibliography and the history of books, book-collecting, libraries and the book trade.

Book World Magazine

2 Caversham Street, London SW3 4AH
☎020 7351 4995 Fax 020 7351 4995

Owner *Christchurch Publishers Ltd*
Editor *James Hughes*
Circulation 5500

FOUNDED 1980. MONTHLY news and reviews for serious book collectors, librarians, antiquarian and other booksellers. No unsolicited mss. Interested in material relevant to literature, art and book collecting. Send letter in the first instance.

Bookdealer

Suite F22, Park Hall Estate, 40 Martell Road, West Dulwich, London SE21 8EN
☎020 8761 5570 Fax 020 8761 5570

Editor *Barry Shaw*

WEEKLY trade paper which acts almost exclusively as a platform for people wishing to buy or sell rare/out-of-print books. Twelve-page editorial only; occasional articles and book reviews by regular freelance writers.

Books

39 Store Street, London WC1F 7DS
☎020 7692 2900 Fax 020 7419 2111

Editor *Liz Thomson*
Circulation 80,000

Formerly *Books and Bookmen*. Free consumer magazine dealing chiefly with features about authors and reviews of books. Carries few commissioned pieces.

Payment negotiable.

The Bookseller

Endeavour House, 5th Floor, 189 Shaftesbury Avenue, London WC2H 8TJ
☎020 7420 6006 Fax 020 7420 6103
Website www.theBookseller.com

Owner *VNU Entertainment Media*
Editor *Nicholas Clee*

Trade journal of the publishing and book trade – the essential guide to what is being done to whom. Trade news and features, including special features, company news, publishing trends, bestseller data, etc. Unsolicited mss rarely used as most writing is either done in-house or commissioned from experts within the trade. Approach in writing first.

Features *Jenny Bell*
News *Joel Rickett*

Boxing Monthly

40 Morpeth Road, London E9 7LD
☎020 8986 4141 Fax 020 8986 4145
Email bm@boxing-monthly.demon.co.uk
Website www.boxing-monthly.co.uk

Owner *Topwave Ltd*
Editor *Glyn Leach*
Circulation 30,000

FOUNDED 1989. MONTHLY. International coverage of professional boxing; previews, reports and interviews. Unsolicited material welcome. Interested in small hall shows and grass-roots knowledge. No big fight reports. Approach in writing in the first instance.

Boyz

2nd Floor, Medius House, 63–69 New Oxford Street, London WC1A 1DG
☎020 7845 4300 Fax 020 7845 4309
Email hudson@boyz.co.uk

Editor *David Hudson*
Circulation 55,000

FOUNDED 1994. WEEKLY entertainment and features magazine aimed at a gay readership covering clubs, fashion, TV, films, music, theatre, celebrities and the UK gay scene in general. Unsolicited mss are looked at but not often used.

Brides

Vogue House, Hanover Square, London W1S 1JU
☎020 7499 9080 Fax 020 7152 3369

Owner *Condé Nast Publications Ltd*

Editor *Liz Savage*
Circulation 66,016

BI-MONTHLY. Much of the magazine is produced in-house, but a good, relevant feature on cakes, jewellery, music, flowers, etc. is always welcome. Maximum 1000 words. Prospective contributors should telephone with an idea in the first instance.

British Birds

The Banks, Mountfield, Robertsbridge,
East Sussex TN32 5JY
☎01580 882039 Fax 01580 882038
Email editor@britishbirds.co.uk
Editor *Dr R. Riddington*
Circulation 6,000

FOUNDED 1907. MONTHLY ornithological journal. Features main papers on topics such as behaviour, distribution, ecology, identification and taxonomy; annual *Report on Rare Birds in Great Britain* and *Rare Breeding Birds in the UK*; sponsored competition for Bird Photograph of the Year. Unsolicited mss welcome from ornithologists.

Features Well-researched, original material relating to Western Palearctic birds welcome.

News *Adrian Pitches* Items ranging from conservation to humour. Maximum 200 words. Email adrian.pitches@care4free.net

Payment for photographs, drawings, paintings and main papers.

British Chess Magazine

The Chess Shop, 44 Baker Street, London
W1U 7RT
☎020 7486 8222 Fax 020 7486 3355
Email bcmchess@compuserve.com
Website www.bcmchess.co.uk
Director/Editor *John Saunders*

FOUNDED 1881. MONTHLY. Emphasis on tournaments, the history of chess and chess-related literature. Approach in writing with ideas. Unsolicited mss not welcome unless from qualified chess experts and players.

British Medical Journal

BMA House, Tavistock Square, London
WC1H 9JR
☎020 7387 4499 Fax 020 7383 6418
Email editor@bmj.com
Website www.bmj.com
Owner *British Medical Association*
Editor *Professor Richard Smith*

One of the world's leading general medical journals.

British Philatelic Bulletin

Royal Mail, 148 Old Street, London
EC1V 9HQ
☎020 7250 2038 Fax 020 7250 2389
Owner *Royal Mail*
Editor *John Holman*
Circulation 25,000

FOUNDED 1963. MONTHLY bulletin giving details of forthcoming British stamps, features on older stamps and postal history, and book reviews. Welcomes photographs of interesting, unusual or historic letter boxes.

Features Articles on all aspects of British philately. Maximum 1500 words.

News Reports on exhibitions and philatelic events. Maximum 500 words. Approach in writing in the first instance.

Payment £45 per 1000 words.

British Railway Modelling

The Maltings, West Street, Bourne,
Lincolnshire PE10 9PH
☎01778 391176 Fax 01778 425437
Email johne@warnersgroup.co.uk
Website www.brmodelling.com
Owner *Warners Group Publications Plc*
Managing Editor *David Brown*
Editor *John Emerson*
Circulation 20,855

FOUNDED 1993. MONTHLY. A general magazine for the practising modeller. No unsolicited mss but ideas are welcome. Interested in features on quality models, from individual items to complete layouts. Approach in writing.

Features Articles on practical elements of the hobby, e.g. locomotive construction, kit conversions, etc. Layout features and articles on individual items which represent high standards of the railway modelling art. Maximum length 6000 words (single feature). *Payment* up to £60 per published page.

News News and reviews containing the model railway trade, new products, etc. Maximum length 1000 words. *Payment* up to £60 per published page.

Broadcast

33–39 Bowling Green Lane, London
EC1R 0DA
☎020 7505 8045 Fax 020 7505 8050
Owner *Emap Communications*
Editor *Conor Dignam*
Circulation 14,297

FOUNDED 1960. WEEKLY. Opportunities for

freelance contributions. Write to the relevant editor in the first instance.

Features *Katy Elliott/David Wood* Any broadcasting issue. Maximum 1500 words.

News *Colin Robertson* Broadcasting news. Maximum 350 words.

Payment £200 per 1000 words.

Brownie

17–19 Buckingham Palace Road, London SW1W 0PT

☎020 7834 6242 Fax 020 7828 5791

Email MarionT@girlguiding.org.uk

Website www.girlguiding.org.uk

Owner *The Guide Association*

Editor *Marion Thompson*

Circulation 16,500

FOUNDED 1962. MONTHLY. Aimed at Brownie members aged 7–10.

Articles Crafts and simple make-it-yourself items using inexpensive or scrap materials.

Fiction Brownie content an advantage. No adventures involving unaccompanied children in dangerous situations – day or night. Maximum 650 words.

Payment £50 per 1000 words pro rata.

The Burlington Magazine

14–16 Duke's Road, London WC1H 9SZ

☎020 7388 1228 Fax 020 7388 1230

Email editorial@burlington.org.uk

Website www.burlington.org.uk

Owner *The Burlington Magazine Publications Ltd*

Managing Director *Kate Trevelyan*

Acting Editors *Richard Shone, Bart Cornelis*

FOUNDED 1903. MONTHLY. Unsolicited contributions welcome on the subject of art history provided they are previously unpublished. All preliminary approaches should be made in writing.

Exhibition Reviews Usually commissioned, but occasionally unsolicited reviews are published if appropriate. Maximum 1000 words.

Articles Maximum 4500 words. *Payment* £140 (maximum).

Shorter Notices Maximum 2000 words. *Payment* £80 (maximum).

Business Brief

PO Box 582, Five Oaks, St Saviour, Jersey JE4 8XQ

☎01534 611600 Fax 01534 611610

Email mspeditorial@msppublishing.com

Owner *MSP Publishing*

Editor *Peter Body*

Circulation 6,000

FOUNDED 1989. MONTHLY magazine covering business developments in the Channel Islands and how they affect the local market. Styles itself as the magazine for business people rather than just a magazine about business. Interested in business-orientated articles only; 750 words maximum. Approach the editor by telephone initially. *Payment* negotiable.

Business Traveller

Nestor House, Playhouse Yard, London EC4V 5EX

☎020 7778 0000 Fax 020 7778 0022

Website www.businesstraveller.com

Owner *Perry Publications*

Editor-in-Chief *Julia Brookes*

Circulation 42,000

MONTHLY. Consumer publication. Opportunities exist for freelance writers but unsolicited contributions tend to be about leisure travel rather than business travel. Would-be contributors are advised to study the magazine or the website first. Approach in writing with ideas.

Payment varies.

Camcorder User

Highbury – WV, 53–79 Highgate Road, London NW5 1TW

☎020 7331 1000 Fax 020 7331 1242

Email rob.hull@highburywv.com

Website www.camuser.co.uk

Owner *Highbury WV*

Editor *Robert Hull*

Circulation 15,000

FOUNDED 1988. MONTHLY magazine dedicated to camcorders, with features on creative technique, shooting advice, new equipment, accessory round-ups and interesting applications on location. Unsolicited mss, illustrations and pictures welcome. *Payment* negotiable.

Campaign

22 Bute Gardens, London W6 7HN

☎020 8267 4683 Fax 020 8267 4914

Email campaign@haynet.com

Website www.brandrepublic.com

Owner *Haymarket Publishing Ltd*

Editor *Caroline Marshall*

Circulation 17,700

FOUNDED 1968. WEEKLY. Lively magazine serving the advertising and related industries. Freelance contributors are best advised to write in the first instance.

Features Articles of 1500–2000 words.
News Relevant news stories of up to 320 words.
Payment negotiable.

Camping and Caravanning
Greenfields House, Westwood Way,
Coventry, Warwickshire CV4 8JH
☎024 7669 4995 Fax 024 7669 4886
Owner *The Camping and Caravanning Club*
Editor *Nick Harding*
Circulation 157,571

FOUNDED 1901. MONTHLY. Interested in journalists with camping and caravanning knowledge. Write with ideas for features in the first instance.

Features Outdoor pieces in general, plus items on specific regions of Britain. Maximum 1200 words. Illustrations to support text essential.

Canal and Riverboat
PO Box 618, Norwich, Norfolk NR7 0QT
☎01603 708930 Fax 01603 708934
Email bluefoxfilms@netscapeonline.co.uk
Website www.canalandriverboat.com
Owner *A.E. Morgan Publications Ltd*
Editor *Chris Cattrall*
Circulation 20,000

Covers all aspects of waterways, narrow boats and cruisers. Contributions welcome. Make initial approach in writing.

Features Waterways, narrow boats and motor cruisers, cruising reports, practical advice, etc. Unusual ideas and personal comments are particularly welcome. Maximum 2000 words. Articles should be supplied in PC Windows format disk. *Payment* around £33 per page.

News Items of up to 300 words welcome on the Inland Waterways System, plus photographs if possible. *Payment* £15.

Car Mechanics
Kelsey Publishing Ltd, PO Box 13,
Westerham, Kent TN16 3WT
☎01733 771392 Fax 01733 203749
Email carmechanics@kelsey.co.uk
Owner *Kelsey Publishing*
Editor *Peter Simpson*
Circulation 35,000

MONTHLY. Practical guide to maintenance and repair of post-1978 cars for DIY and the motor trade. Unsolicited mss, with good-quality colour prints or transparencies, 'at sender's risk'. Ideas preferred. Initial approach by letter or phone welcome and strongly recommended, 'but please read a recent copy first for style. We are not interested in cartoons.'

Features Good, technical, entertaining and well-researched material welcome, especially anything presenting complex matters clearly and simply.

Payment by arrangement ('but generous for the right material').

Caravan Life
Warners Group Publications plc, The Maltings,
West Street, Bourne, Lincolnshire PH10 9PH
☎01778 391165 Fax 01778 425437
Email mikelec@warnersgroup.co.uk
Editor *Michael Le Caplain*
Circulation 17,000

FOUNDED 1987. Magazine for experienced caravanners and enthusiasts providing practical and useful information and product evaluation. Opportunities for caravanning, relevant touring and travel material, also monthly reviews of the best tow cars, all with good-quality colour photographs.

Caravan Magazine
IPC Media Ltd., Focus House, Dingwall Avenue, Croydon, Surrey CR9 2TA
☎020 8774 0600 Fax 020 8774 0939
Email caravan@ipcmedia.com
Website www.caravan.com
Owner *IPC Media*
Editor *Steve Rowe*
Circulation 17,744

FOUNDED 1933. MONTHLY. Unsolicited mss welcome. Approach in writing with ideas. All correspondence should go direct to the editor.

Features Touring with strong caravan bias, technical/DIY features and how-to section. Maximum 1500 words.

Payment by arrangement.

Caribbean Times
Unit 2, 65 Whitechapel Road, London E1 1DU
☎020 7650 2000 Fax 020 7650 2001
Website www.ethnicmedia.co.uk
Owner *Ethnic Media Group*
Editor *Ron Shillingford*
Circulation 25,190

FOUNDED 1981. WEEKLY community paper for the African and Caribbean communities in Britain. Interested in general, local and international issues relevant to these communities. Approach in writing with ideas for submission.

Cat World

Avalon Court, Star Road, Partridge Green,
West Sussex RH13 8RY
☎01403 711511 Fax 01403 711521
Email editor@catworld.co.uk
Website www.catworld.co.uk

Owner *Ashdown Publishing Ltd*
Editor *Jo Rothery*
Circulation 20,000

FOUNDED 1981. MONTHLY. Unsolicited mss
welcome but initial approach in writing preferred. No poems or fiction.

Features Lively, first-hand experience features on every aspect of the cat. Breeding features and veterinary articles by acknowledged
experts only. Preferred length 750 or 1700
words. Accompanying pictures should be good
quality and sharp.

News Short, concise, factual or humorous
items concerning cats. Maximum 100 words.

Submissions on disk (MS Word) if possible,
with accompanying hard copy and s.a.e. for
return or by e-mail.

The Catholic Herald

Lamb's Passage, Bunhill Row, London
EC1Y 8TQ
☎020 7588 3101 Fax 020 7256 9728
Email editorial@catholicherald.co.uk
Website www.catholicherald.co.uk

Editor *Dr William Oddie*
Deputy Editor *Luke Coppen*
Literary Editor *Damian Thompson*
Circulation 22,000

WEEKLY. Interested mainly in straight Catholic
issues but also in general humanitarian matters,
social policies, the Third World, the arts and
books.
Payment by arrangement.

CCC Magazine

IPC Focus Network, Focus House, Dingwall
Avenue, Croydon, Surrey CR9 2TA
☎020 8774 0946 Fax 020 8774 0935
Email ccc@ipcmedia.com

Owner *IPC Media*
Editor *Steve Kirk*
Circulation 25,000

FOUNDED 1963. MONTHLY. Unsolicited mss
welcome but prospective contributors are
advised to make initial contact in writing.

Features Technical articles on current
motorsport and unusual sport-orientated road
cars. Length by arrangement.
Payment negotiable.

Chapman

4 Broughton Place, Edinburgh EH1 3RX
☎0131 557 2207 Fax 0131 556 9565
Email editor@chapman-pub.co.uk
Website www.chapman-pub.co.uk

Owner/Editor *Joy Hendry*
Circulation 2000

FOUNDED 1970. Scotland's quality literary
magazine. Features poetry, short works of fiction, criticism, reviews and articles on theatre,
politics, language and the arts. Unsolicited
material welcome if accompanied by s.a.e.
Approach in writing unless discussion is
needed. Priority is given to full-time writers.

Features Topics of literary interest, especially Scottish literature, theatre, culture or
politics. Maximum 5000 words.

Fiction Short stories, occasionally novel
extracts if self-contained. Maximum 6000
words. *Payment* by negotiation.

Special Pages Poetry, both UK and non-
UK in translation (mainly, but not necessarily,
European). *Payment* by negotiation.

Chat

IPC Media Ltd., King's Reach Tower,
Stamford Street, London SE1 9LS
☎020 7261 6570 Fax 020 7261 6534
Website www.ipcmedia.com/pubs/chat.htm

Owner *IPC Connect*
Editor *Paul Merrill*
Circulation 552,800

FOUNDED 1985. WEEKLY general interest
women's magazine. Unsolicited mss considered; approach in writing with ideas. Not
interested in contributors 'who have never
bothered to read *Chat* and therefore don't
know what type of magazine it is'.

Features *Anna Kingsley* Human interest and
humour. Maximum 1000 words. *Payment* up
to £1500 maximum.

Chemist & Druggist

Sovereign House, Sovereign Way, Tonbridge,
Kent TN9 1RW
☎01732 377487 Fax 01732 367065
Email chemdrug@cmpinformation.com
Website www.dotpharmacy.com

Owner *CMP Information*
Editor *Patrick Grice*
Assistant Editor *Charles Gladwin*
Circulation 14,798

FOUNDED 1859. WEEKLY news magazine for
community pharmacies.

Features Practices, politics, professional

matters, clinical articles and business advice. Contact by phone or e-mail to discuss features ideas.

News Contact Assistant Editor with news articles relating to local pharmacy matters, local pharmaceutical industry events and pharmacists in the news. Maximum 200 words. *Payment* standard rates.

Child Education

Scholastic Ltd, Villiers House, Clarendon Avenue, Leamington Spa, Warwickshire CV32 5PR
☎01926 887799 Fax 01926 883331
Website www.scholastic.co.uk

Owner *Scholastic Ltd*
Editor *Jeremy Sugden*
Circulation 25,000

FOUNDED 1923. MONTHLY magazine aimed at teachers of children aged 4–7 years. Practical articles from teachers about education for this age group are welcome. Maximum 900 words. Approach in writing with synopsis.

Choice

First Floor, 2 King Street, Peterborough, Cambridgeshire PE1 1LT
☎01733 555123 Fax 01733 427500
Email editorial@choice-magazine.com

Publisher *Choice Publishing Ltd*
  Editor *Norman Wright*
Circulation 90,000

MONTHLY full-colour, lively and informative magazine for people aged 50 plus which helps them get the most out of their lives, time and money after full-time work.

Features Real-life stories, hobbies, interesting (older) people, British heritage and countryside, involving activities for active bodies and minds, health, relationships, book/entertainment reviews. Unsolicited mss read (s.a.e. for return of material); write with ideas and copies of cuttings if new contributor. No phone calls, please.

Rights/Money All items affecting the magazine's readership are written by experts. Areas of interest include pensions, state benefits, health, finance, property, legal.

Payment by arrangement.

Christian Herald

Christian Media Centre, Garcia Estate, Canterbury Road, Worthing, West Sussex BN13 1EH
☎01903 821082 Fax 01903 821081
Email news@christianherald.org.uk
Website www.christianherald.org.uk

Owner *Christian Media Centre Ltd*
Editor *Russ Bravo*
Circulation 15,000

WEEKLY. Evangelical, inter-denominational newspaper for committed Christians. News, bible-based comment and incisive features. No poetry. Contributors' guidelines available.

Payment Christian Media rates.

Church Music Quarterly

Cleveland Lodge, Westhumble, Dorking, Surrey RH5 6BW
☎01306 872800 Fax 01306 887260
Email cmq@rscm.com
Website www.rscm.com

Owner *Royal School of Church Music*
Editor *Esther Jones*
Circulation 16,500

QUARTERLY.   Contributions   welcome. Telephone in the first instance.

Features Articles on church music or related subjects considered. Maximum 2000 words.

Payment £60 per page.

Church of England Newspaper

20–26 Brunswick Place, London N1 6DZ
☎020 7417 5800 Fax 020 7216 6410
Email cen@parlicom.com
Website www.churchnewspaper.com

Owner *Parliamentary Communications Ltd*
Editor *Colin Blakely*
Circulation 9,500

FOUNDED 1828. WEEKLY. Almost all material is commissioned but unsolicited mss are considered.

Features *Emma Garrow* Preliminary enquiry essential. Maximum 1200 words.

News *Claire Shelley* Items must be sent promptly and should have a church/Christian relevance. Maximum 200–400 words.

Payment negotiable.

Church Times

33 Upper Street, London N1 0PN
☎020 7359 4570 Fax 020 7226 3073
Email news@churchtimes.co.uk *or* features@churchtimes.co.uk
Website www.churchtimes.co.uk

Owner *Hymns Ancient & Modern*
Editor *Paul Handley*
Circulation 32,553

FOUNDED 1863. WEEKLY. Unsolicited mss considered.

Features *Prudence Fay* Articles and pictures (any format) on religious topics. Maximum

2000 words. *Payment* £120 per 1000 words.

News *Helen Saxbee* Occasional reports (commissions only) and up-to-date photographs.

Payment by arrangement.

Classic Bike

EMAP Automotive, Media House, Lynchwood, Peterborough Business Park, Peterborough, Cambridgeshire PE2 6EA
☎01733 468465 Fax 01733 468466
Email classic.bike@emap.com

Owner *Emap Active Ltd*
Editor *Brian Crichton*
Circulation 50,000

FOUNDED 1978. MONTHLY. Mainly pre-1972 classic motorcycles with a heavy bias to British marques. Approach in writing.

News Genuine news with good illustrations, if possible, suitable for a global audience. Maximum 400 words.

Features British motorcycle industry inside stories, technical features 'that can be understood by all', German, Spanish and French machine features, people. Maximum 2000 words.

Special Pages How-to features, oddball machines, stunning pictures, features with a fresh slant.

Payment £100–125 per 1000 words, plus pictures.

Classic Boat

Focus House, Dingwall Avenue, Croydon, Surrey CR9 2TA
☎020 8744 0603 Fax 020 8744 0943
Email cb@ipcmedia.com
Website www.classicboat.co.uk

Owner *IPC Media*
Editor *Dan Houston*
Circulation 16,264

FOUNDED 1987. MONTHLY. Traditional boats and classic yachts, old and new; maritime history. Unsolicited mss, particularly if supported by good photos, are welcome. Sail and power boat pieces considered. Approach in writing with ideas. Interested in well-researched stories on all nautical matters. News reports welcome. Contributor's notes available (send s.a.e.).

Features Boatbuilding, boat history and design, events, yachts and working boats. Material must be well-informed and supported where possible by good-quality or historic photos. Maximum 3000 words. Classic is defined by excellence of design and construction – the boat need not be old and wooden! *Payment* £75–100 per published page.

News New boats, restorations, events, boatbuilders, etc. Maximum 500 words. *Payment* according to merit.

Classic Cars

Media House, Peterborough Business Park, Lynchwood, Peterborough PE2 6EA
☎01733 468219 Fax 01733 468888
Email classic.cars@emap.com

Owner *Emap Automotive Ltd*
Editor *Martyn Moore*
Circulation 54,493

FOUNDED 1973. TWELVE ISSUES YEARLY. International classic car magazine containing entertaining and informative articles about classic cars, events and associated personalities. Contributions welcome. *Payment* negotiable.

Classical Guitar

1 & 2 Vance Court, Trans Britannia Enterprise Park, Blaydon on Tyne NE21 5NH
☎0191 414 9000 Fax 0191 414 9001
Email classicalguitar@ashleymark.co.uk
Website www.classicalguitarmagazine.com

Owner *Ashley Mark Publishing Co.*
Editor *Colin Cooper*

FOUNDED 1982. MONTHLY.

Features *Colin Cooper* Usually written by staff writers. Maximum 1500 words. *Payment* by arrangement.

News *Thérèse Wassily Saba* Small paragraphs and festival concert reports welcome. *No payment.*

Reviews *Tim Panting* Concert reviews of up to 250 words are usually written by staff reviewers.

Classical Music

241 Shaftesbury Avenue, London WC2H 8TF
☎020 7333 1742 Fax 020 7333 1769
Email classical.music@rhinegold.co.uk
Website www.rhinegold.co.uk

Owner *Rhinegold Publishing Ltd*
Editor *Keith Clarke*

FOUNDED 1976. FORTNIGHTLY. A specialist magazine using precisely targeted news and feature articles aimed at the music business. Most material is commissioned but professionally written unsolicited mss are occasionally published. Freelance contributors may approach in writing with an idea but should familiarise themselves beforehand with the style and market of the magazine.

Payment negotiable.

Classics

Berwick House, 8–10 Knoll Rise, Orpington,
Kent BR6 0PS
☎01689 887200 Fax 01689 876438
Email classics@splpublishing.co.uk
Owner *Highbury – SPL Publishing Ltd*
Editor *Tim Morgan*

FOUNDED 1997. MONTHLY how-to magazine
for classic car owners, featuring everything
from repairing and restoring to buying, selling
and enjoying all types of cars from the 1950s to
1980s. Includes vehicle comparison tests, price
guide, practical advice and technical know-
how from experts and owners, plus hundreds
of readers' free ads.

Features Illustrated features on classic car
maintenance, repair and restoration with strong
technical content and emphasis on DIY.

News All classic car related news stories and
topical photos.

Climber

Warners Group Publications plc, West Street,
Bourne, Lincolnshire PE10 9PH
☎01778 391117
Email grettar@warnergroup.co.uk
Website www.climber.co.uk
Owner *Warners Group Publications plc*
Editor *Bernard Newman*

FOUNDED 1962. MONTHLY. Features articles
and news on climbing and mountaineering in
the UK and abroad. No unsolicited mss.

Club International

2 Archer Street, London W1D 7AW
☎020 7292 8000 Fax 020 7734 5030
Email swiftly@pr-org.co.uk *or* claireb@pr-
org.co.uk
Owner *Paul Raymond*
Editor *Robert Swift*
Circulation 180,000

FOUNDED 1972. MONTHLY. Features and short
humorous items aimed at young male readership aged 18–30.

Features Maximum 1000 words.
Shorts 200–750 words.
Payment negotiable.

Co-op Traveller

Wrap Communications Ltd, The Bake House,
J304 TBBC, 100 Clements Road, London
SE16 4DG
☎020 7231 0707 Fax 020 7231 1232
Email info@wrapcom.com
Website www.wrapcom.com

Owner *United Co-op Travel Division/Wrap
Communications*
Editor *Ciaran Jennings*
Circulation 150,000

FOUNDED 2001. TWO ISSUES YEARLY. Magazine
for Co-op Travel customers. Travel articles and
travel-related news for the independent traveller.
No unsolicted material; approach by telephone,
fax, letter or e-mail in the first instance.

Features Ideas for exciting travel features,
including destinations, accommodation, activities etc. Maximum 1000 words. *Payment* negotiable.

News Stories that reveal fascinating facts for
holidaymakers, including interesting products,
new destinations and developments in the
travel market. Maximum 300 words. *Payment*
negotiable.

Coin News

Token Publishing Ltd, Orchard House,
Duchy Road, Heathpark, Honiton, Devon
EX14 1YD
☎01404 46972 Fax 01404 44788
Email info@tokenpublishing.com
Website www.tokenpublishing.com
Owners *J.W. Mussell, Carol Hartman*
Editor *J.W. Mussell*
Circulation 10,000

FOUNDED 1964. MONTHLY. Contributions welcome. Approach by phone in the first instance.

Features Opportunity exists for well-
informed authors 'who know the subject and
do their homework'. Maximum 2500 words.
Payment £25 per 1000 words.

Company

National Magazine House, 72 Broadwick
Street, London W1F 9EP
☎020 7439 5000 Fax 020 7312 3797
Email company@natmags.co.uk
Website www.company.co.uk
Owner *National Magazine Co. Ltd*
Editor *Sam Baker*
Circulation 330,373

MONTHLY. Glossy women's magazine appealing to the independent and intelligent young
woman. A good market for freelancers: 'We
look for great newsy features relevant to young
British women'. Keen to encourage bright,
new, young talent, but uncommissioned material is rarely accepted. Feature outlines are the
only sensible approach in the first instance.
Maximum 1500–2000 words. Features to
Lindsay Frankel, **Features Editor**.
Payment £250 per 1000 words.

Compass Sport

Ballencrieff Cottage, Ballencrieff Toll,
Bathgate, West Lothian EH48 4LD
☎01506 632728   Fax 01506 635444
Email editor@compasssport.com
Website www.compasssport.com

Owner *Pages Editorial & Publishing Services*
Editor *Suse Coon*

BI-MONTHLY orienteering magazine covering all
disciplines of the sport including mountain
marathons, mountain bike O, ski O and trail O.
Includes profiles and articles on relevant topics,
with subsections on fixtures, junior news and
mountain marathons which are compiled by
sub-editors. Letters, puzzles and competition.
Phone or e-mail to discuss content and timing.
   Payment by arrangement.

Computer Arts

30 Monmouth Street, Bath BA1 2BW
☎01225 442244   Fax 01225 732295
Email ca.mail@futurenet.co.uk
Website www.computerarts.co.uk

Owner *The Future Network*
Editor *Vicki Atkinson*

FOUNDED 1999. MONTHLY. The world of
computer arts – 3D, web design, photoshop,
digital video. No unsolicited mss. Interested in
tutorials, profiles, tips, software and hardware
reviews. Approach by post or e-mail.

Computer Weekly

Quadrant House, The Quadrant, Sutton,
Surrey SM2 5AS
☎020 8652 3122   Fax 020 8652 8979
Email computer.weekly@rbi.co.uk
Website www.cw360.com

Owner *Reed Business Information*
Editorial Director *Karl Schneider*
Editor *To be appointed*
Circulation 143,000

FOUNDED 1966. Freelance contributions welcome.
   Features *Ross Bentley* Always looking for
good new writers with specialised industry
knowledge. Max. 1800 words.
   News *Lindsay Clark* Some openings for
regional or foreign news items. Max. 300 words.
   Payment negotiable.

Computing, The IT Newspaper

32–34 Broadwick Street, London W1A 2HG
☎020 7316 9000   Fax 020 7316 9160
Email computing@vnu.co.uk
Website www.computing.co.uk

Owner *VNU Business Publications Ltd*
Editor in Chief *Colin Barker*
   Editor *Mike Gubbins*
Circulation 110,000

FOUNDED 1973. WEEKLY newspaper for IT
professionals. Unsolicited technical articles
welcome. Please enclose s.a.e. for return.
   News *Bryan Glick*
   Payment up to £350 per 1000 words.

Condé Nast Traveller

Vogue House, Hanover Square, London
W1S 1JU
☎020 7499 9080   Fax 020 7493 3758
Email cntraveller@condenast.co.uk
Website www.cntraveller.co.uk

Owner *Condé Nast Publications*
Editor *Sarah Miller*
Circulation 82,000

FOUNDED 1997. MONTHLY travel magazine.
Proposals rather than completed mss preferred.
Approach in writing in the first instance. No
unsolicited photographs. 'The magazine has a
no freebie policy and no writing can be
accepted on the basis of a press or paid-for trip.'

Conservative Heartland

The Spectator (1828) Ltd, 56 Doughty Street,
London WC1N 2LL
☎020 7440 9240   Fax 020 7831 6468
Email editor@heartlandmag.co.uk

Owner *The Conservative Party*
Editor *Martin Van der Weyer*
Circulation 244,000

FOUNDED 1999. TWO ISSUES YEARLY. Conservative Party magazine. Lifestyle articles,
political comment and information. No unsolicited material; approach by telephone or
e-mail with idea in the first instance.

Contemporary Review

PO Box 1242, Oxford OX1 4FJ
☎01865 201529   Fax 01865 201529
Email editorial@contemporaryreview.co.uk
Website www.contemporaryreview.co.uk

Owner *Contemporary Review Co. Ltd*
Editor *Dr Richard Mullen*

FOUNDED 1866. MONTHLY. Covers international affairs and politics, literature and the
arts, history and religion. No fiction. Maximum 3000 words.
   Literary Editor *Dr James Munson* Monthly
book section with reviews which are always
commissioned.
   Payment £5 per page.

Cosmogirl!

National Magazine House, 72 Broadwick Street, London W1F 9EP
☎020 7439 5000 Fax 020 7439 5400
Email cosmogirl.mail@natmags.co.uk
Website www.cosmogirl.co.uk
Owner *National Magazine Co. Ltd*
Editor *Celia Duncan*
Circulation 142,073

FOUNDED 2001. MONTHLY glossy magazine for 'fun, fearless teens'. Fashion, beauty advice and boys. **Features** *Miranda Eason* Interested in ideas; send synopsis by mail – no finished articles.

Cosmopolitan

National Magazine House, 72 Broadwick Street, London W1F 9EP
☎020 7439 5000 Fax 020 7439 5016
Email cosmo.mail@natmags.co.uk
Website www.cosmopolitan.co.uk
Owner *National Magazine Co. Ltd*
Editor-in-Chief *Lorraine Candy*
Deputy Editor *Nina Ahmad*
Circulation 463,058

MONTHLY. Designed to appeal to the mid-twenties, modern-minded female. Popular mix of articles, with emphasis on relationships and careers, and hard news. No fiction. Will rarely use unsolicited mss but always on the look-out for 'new writers with original and relevant ideas and a strong voice'. Send short synopsis of idea to Features Editor *Charlotte Northedge*. All would-be writers should be familiar with the magazine.
Payment about £250 per 1000 words.

Counselling at Work

Association for Counselling at Work, BACP, 1 Regent Place, Rugby, Warwickshire CV21 2PJ
☎0870 443 5252
Email acw@bacp.co.uk
Owner *British Association for Counselling and Psychotherapy*
Editor *Ian Macwhinnie*
Circulation 1600

FOUNDED 1993. QUARTERLY official journal of the Association for Counselling at Work, a Division of BACP. Looking for well-researched articles (500–2400 words) about *any* aspect of workplace counselling. Mss from those employed as counsellors or in welfare posts are particularly welcome. Photographs accepted. No fiction or poetry. Send A4 s.a.e.

for writer's guidelines and sample copy of the journal. *No payment.*

Country Homes and Interiors

IPC Media Ltd., King's Reach Tower, Stamford Street, London SE1 9LS
☎020 7261 6451 Fax 020 7261 6895
Owner *IPC Media*
Editor *Deborah Barker*
Circulation 103,169

FOUNDED 1986. MONTHLY. The best approach for prospective contributors is with an idea in writing as unsolicited mss are not welcome.
Features *Jean Carr* Monthly personality interviews of interest to an intelligent, affluent readership (women and men), aged 25–44. Maximum 1200 words.
Houses *Arabella St John Parker* Country-style homes with excellent design ideas. Length 1000 words.
Payment negotiable.

Country Life

IPC Media Ltd., King's Reach Tower, Stamford Street, London SE1 9LS
☎020 7261 7058 Fax 020 7261 5139
Website www.countrylife.co.uk
Owner *IPC Media*
Editor *Clive Aslet*
Circulation 43,491

ESTABLISHED 1897. WEEKLY. *Country Life* features articles which relate to architecture, countryside, wildlife, rural events, sports, arts, exhibitions, current events, property and news articles of interest to town and country dwellers. Strong informed material rather than amateur enthusiasm. 'We regret we cannot be liable for the safe custody or return of any solicited or unsolicited materials.'
Payment variable, depending on word length and picture size.

Country Living

National Magazine House, 72 Broadwick Street, London W1F 9EP
☎020 7439 5000 Fax 020 7439 5093
Website www.countryliving.co.uk
Owner *National Magazine Co. Ltd*
Editor *Susy Smith*
Circulation 164,079

Magazine aimed at both country dwellers and town dwellers who love the countryside. Covers people, conservation, wildlife, houses (gardens and interiors) and rural businesses. No unsolicited mss.

Country Smallholding

Archant Publishing, Fair Oak Close, Exeter Airport Business Park, Clysts Honiton, Nr Exeter, Devon EX5 2UL
☎01392 447766 Fax 01392 446841
Email editorial.csh@archant.co.uk
Website www.countrysmallholding.com
Owner *Archant Publishing*
Editor *Diane Cowgill*
Circulation 17,000

FOUNDED 1975. MONTHLY magazine for small farmers, smallholders, practical landowners and for anyone looking for a new home in the country. Articles welcome on organic growing, keeping poultry, livestock and other animals, crafts, cookery, herbs, building and energy. Articles should be detailed and practical, based on first-hand knowledge and experience. Approach in writing or by e-mail.

Country Walking

Bretton Court, Bretton, Peterborough, Cambridgeshire PE3 8DZ
☎01733 282614 Fax 01733 282654
Email country.walking@emap.com
Owner *Emap Plc*
Editor *Jonathan Manning*
Circulation 48,000

FOUNDED 1987. MONTHLY magazine featuring coutnry walk ideas, features related to flora, fauna, country crafts, history and heritage, pubs and landscape photography. News, gear tests and profiles of celebrity walkers also feature. Special monthly pull-out section of 27 detailed walking routes. Original high quality photography and ideas for features considered, although very few unsolicited mss accepted. Approach by letter or e-mail.

Features *Perry Cleveland-Peck* **Special Pages** 'Down your way' section of walk routes, including outline map and step-by-step directions. Accurately and recently researched walk and fact file including photographs and points of interest en route. Please contact *Trevor Rickwood* for guidelines (unsolicited submissions generally not accepted for this section).
Payment not negotiable.

The Countryman

23 Sheep Street, Burford, Oxfordshire OX18 4LS
Email burford@countrymanmagazine.co.uk
Website www.countrymanmagazine.co.uk
Owner *Countryman Publishing Ltd*
Editor *David Horan*
Circulation 27,683

FOUNDED 1927. MONTHLY. Unsolicited mss with s.a.e. welcome; about 120 received each week. Contributors are strongly advised to study the magazine's content in the first instance. Articles supplied with top quality illustrations (colour transparencies, archive b&w prints and line drawings) are far more likely to be used. Maximum article length 1200 words.

The Countryman's Weekly (incorporating Gamekeeper and Sporting Dog)

Yelverton, Devon PL20 7PE
☎01822 855281 Fax 01822 855372
Email cmansweekly@aol.com
Publisher *Vic Gardner*
Managing Director *Kelly John*

FOUNDED 1895. WEEKLY. Unsolicited material welcome.
Features On any country sports topic. Maximum 1000 words.
Payment rates available on request.

County

26C High Street, Watlington, Oxfordshire OX49 5PY
☎01491 614040 Fax 01491 614041
Email sales@countymagazine.com
Website www.countymagazine.com
Owners *Mr and Mrs Watts*
Editor *Mrs Ashlyn Watts*
Circulation 50,000

FOUNDED 1986. QUARTERLY lifestyle magazine featuring homes, interiors, gardening, fashion and beauty, motoring, leisure and dining. Welcomes unsolicited mss. All initial approaches should be made in writing.

The Cricketer International

Ridge Farm, Lamberhurst, Kent TN3 8ER
☎01892 893000 Fax 01892 893010
Email editorial@cricketer.co.uk
Website www.cricketer.com
Owner *Ben G. Brocklehurst*
Editor *Peter Perchard*
Circulation 30,000

FOUNDED 1921. MONTHLY. Unsolicited mss considered. Ideas in writing only. No initial discussions by phone. All correspondence should be addressed to the editor.

Crimewave

5 Martins Lane, Witcham, Ely, Cambridgeshire CB6 2LB
☎01353 777931

Email ttapress@aol.com
Website www.ttapress.com

Owner *TTA Press*
Editor *Andy Cox*

FOUNDED 1998. QUARTERLY B5 colour magazine of crime fiction. 'The UK's only magazine specialising in crime short stories, publishing the very best from across the spectrum.' Every issue contains stories by authors who are household names in the crime fiction world but room is found for lesser known and unknown writers. *Taking Care of Frank* by Antony Mann (Crimewave 2) and *Prussian Snowdrops* by Marion Arnott (Crimewave 4) won the **CWA/ Macallan Short Story Dagger** award in 1999 and 2001 respectively. Submissions welcome (not via e-mail) with appropriate return postage. Potential contributors are advised to study the magazine. Contracts exchanged upon acceptance. *Payment* on publication.

Cumbria and Lake District Magazine

Stable Courtyard, Broughton Hall, Skipton, North Yorkshire BD23 3AZ
☎01756 701381 Fax 01756 701326
Email editorial@dalesman.co.uk
Website www.dalesman.co.uk

Owner *Dalesman Publishing Co. Ltd*
Editor *Terry Fletcher*
Circulation 15,742

FOUNDED 1951. MONTHLY. County magazine of strong regional and countryside interest, focusing on the Lake District. Unsolicited mss welcome. Maximum 1500 words. Approach in writing, by phone or e-mail with feature ideas. *Payment* negotiable.

Cutting Teeth

c/o Fringe Gallery, PO Box 3906, Glasgow G45 9YE
☎0141 634 2603 Fax 0141 631 1484
Email cuttingteeth@fringemedia.co.uk
Website www.fringemedia.co.uk

Editor *Lynne Mackenzie*

THREE ISSUES YEARLY. New Scottish writing by established and previously unpublished writers. Interested in unpublished poetry, short stories (maximum 3000 words) and reviews. Initial approach by e-mail.

Cycle Sport

IPC Media Ltd., Focus House, Dingwall Avenue, Croydon CR9 2TA
☎020 8774 0828 Fax 020 8686 0947

Email cycling@ipcmedia.com
Website www.cyclesport.co.uk

Owner *IPC Media*
Managing Editor *Robert Garbutt*
  Deputy Editor *Marguerite Lazell*
Circulation 20,667

FOUNDED 1993. MONTHLY magazine dedicated to professional cycle racing. Unsolicited ideas for features welcome.

Cycling Weekly

IPC Media Ltd, Focus House, Dingwall Avenue, Croydon, Surrey CR9 2TA
☎020 8774 0811 Fax 020 8774 0952
Email cycling@ipcmedia.com
Website www.cyclingweekly.co.uk

Owner *IPC Media*
Editor *Robert Garbutt*
Circulation 28,204

FOUNDED 1891. WEEKLY. All aspects of cycle sport covered. Unsolicited mss and ideas for features welcome. Approach in writing with ideas. Fiction rarely used.

Features Cycle racing, coaching, technical material and related areas. Maximum 2000 words. Most work commissioned but interested in seeing new work. *Payment* around £60–120 per 1000 words (quality permitting).

News Short news pieces, local news, etc. Maximum 300 words. *Payment* £15 per story.

The Dalesman

Stable Courtyard, Broughton Hall, Skipton, North Yorkshire BD23 3AZ
☎01756 701381 Fax 01756 701326
Email editorial@dalesman.co.uk
Website www.dalesman.co.uk

Owner *Dalesman Publishing Co. Ltd*
Editor *Terry Fletcher*
Circulation 48,298

FOUNDED 1939. Now the biggest-selling regional publication of its kind in the country. MONTHLY magazine with articles of specific Yorkshire interest. Unsolicited mss welcome; receives approximately ten per day. Initial approach in writing, by phone or e-mail. Maximum 1500 words.
  Payment negotiable.

Dance Theatre Journal

Laban, Creekside, London SE8 3DZ
☎020 8691 8600 Fax 020 8691 8400
Email dtj@laban.org
Website www.laban.org

Owner *Laban*

Editor *Ian Bramley*
Circulation 2000

FOUNDED 1982. QUARTERLY. Interested in features on every aspect of the contemporary dance scene, particularly issues such as the funding policy for dance, critical assessments of choreographers' work and the latest developments in the various schools of contemporary dance. Unsolicited mss welcome. Length 1000–3000 words.

Dance Today!

The Dancing Times Ltd, Clerkenwell House, 45–47 Clerkenwell Green, London EC1R 0EB
☎020 7250 3006 Fax 020 7253 6679
Email dancetoday!@dancing-times.co.uk
Website www.dancing-times.co.uk

Owner *The Dancing Times Ltd*
Editor *Sylvia Boerner*
Circulation 2500

FOUNDED 1956 as *Ballroom Dancing Times*. Relaunched as *Dance Today!* in 2001. MONTHLY magazine for anyone interested in dance, particularly social dance. Unsolicited contributions welcome; send c.v. with sample work by post or e-mail.

The Dancing Times

45–47 Clerkenwell Green, London EC1R 0EB
☎020 7250 3006 Fax 020 7253 6679
Email editorial@dancing-times.co.uk
Website www.dancing-times.co.uk

Owner *The Dancing Times Ltd*
Editor *Mary Clarke*

FOUNDED 1910. MONTHLY. Freelance suggestions welcome from specialist dance writers and photographers only. Approach in writing.

Darts World

81 Selwood Road, Croydon, Surrey CR0 7JW
☎020 8650 6580 Fax 020 8654 4343
Email dartsworld@blueyonder.co.uk
Website www.dartsworld.com

Owner *World Magazines Ltd*
Editor *A.J. Wood*
Circulation 18,780

Features Single articles or series on technique and instruction. Maximum 1200 words.
Fiction Short stories with darts theme. Maximum 1000 words.
News Tournament reports and general or personality news required. Maximum 800 words.
Payment negotiable.

Day by Day

Woolacombe House, 141 Woolacombe Road, Blackheath, London SE3 8QP
☎020 8856 6249

Owner *Loverseed Press*
Editor *Patrick Richards*
Circulation 25,000

FOUNDED 1963. MONTHLY. News commentary and digest of national and international affairs, with reviews of the arts (books, plays, art exhibitions, films, opera, musicals) and county cricket and Test reports among regular slots. Unsolicited mss welcome (s.a.e. essential). Approach in writing with ideas. Contributors are advised to study the magazine in the first instance. (Specimen copy £1.) UK subscription: £12.50; Europe £17; RoW £19.

News *Ronald Mallone* Interested in themes connected with non-violence and social justice only. Maximum 600 words.
Features No scope for freelance contributions here.
Poems *Michael Gibson* Short poems in line with editorial principles considered. Maximum 20 lines.
Payment negotiable.

Dazed & Confused

112 Old Street, London EC1V 1BD
☎020 7336 0766 Fax 020 7336 0966
Email dazed@confused.co.uk
Website www.confused.co.uk

Owner *Waddell Ltd*
Editor *Callum McGoch*
Circulation 80,000

FOUNDED 1992. MONTHLY. Cutting edge fashion, music, art interviews and features. No unsolicited material. Approach in writing with ideas in the first instance.

Decanter

First Floor, Broadway House, 2–6 Fulham Broadway, London SW6 5UE
☎020 7610 3929 Fax 020 7381 5282
Email editorial@decanter.com
Website www.decanter.com

Editor *Amy Wislocki*
Circulation 35,000

FOUNDED 1975. Glossy wines magazine. Feature ideas welcome – send to editor by e-mail or fax. No fiction.
News/Features All items and articles should concern wines, food and related subjects. *Payment* £230 per 1000 words.

Derbyshire Life and Countryside
Heritage House, Lodge Lane, Derby
DE1 3HE
☎01332 347087 Fax 01332 290688
Email editorials@hhgroup.co.uk
Owner *B.C. Wood*
Editor *Vivienne Irish*
Circulation 11,702
FOUNDED 1931. MONTHLY county magazine for Derbyshire. Unsolicited mss and photographs of Derbyshire welcome, but written approach with ideas preferred.

Descent
51 Timbers Square, Cardiff CF24 3SH
☎029 2048 6557 Fax 029 2048 6557
Email descent@wildplaces.co.uk
Owner *Wild Places Publishing*
Editor *Chris Howes*
Assistant Editor *Judith Calford*
FOUNDED 1969. BI-MONTHLY magazine for cavers and mine enthusiasts. Submissions welcome from freelance contributors who can write accurately and knowledgeably on any aspect of caves, mines or underground structures.
    Features General interest articles of under 1000 words welcome, as well as short foreign news reports, especially if supported by photographs/illustrations. Suitable topics include exploration (particularly British, both historical and modern), expeditions, equipment, techniques and regional British news. Maximum 2000 words.
    Payment on publication according to page area filled.

Desire
1a Fentiman Road, London SW8 1LD
☎020 7820 8844 Fax 020 7820 9944
Website www.desire.co.uk
Owner *Moondance Media Ltd*
Editor *Ian Jackson*
FOUNDED 1994. FIVE ISSUES YEARLY. Britain's only erotic magazine for both women and men, celebrating sex and sensuality with a mix of features, reviews, interviews, photography, reports and erotic fantasy. For a sample copy of the magazine plus contributors' guidelines and rates, please enclose four loose first class stamps.

Director
116 Pall Mall, London SW1Y 5ED
☎020 7766 8950 Fax 020 7766 8840
Email director-ed@iod.com
Editor *Joanna Higgins*
Circulation 50,000
1991 Business Magazine of the Year. Published by Director Publications Ltd. for members of the Institute of Directors. Wide range of features from political and business profiles and management thinking to employment and financial issues. Also book reviews. Regular contributors used. Send letter with synopsis/published samples rather than unsolicited mss. Strictly no 'lifestyle' writing.
    Payment negotiable.

Disability Now
6 Market Road, London N7 9PW
☎020 7619 7323 Fax 020 7619 7331
Email editor@disabilitynow.org.uk
Website www.disabilitynow.org.uk
Publisher *SCOPE*
Editor *Mary Wilkinson*
Circulation 25,399
FOUNDED 1984. Leading MONTHLY newspaper for disabled people in the UK – people with a wide range of physical disabilities, as well as their families, carers and relevant professionals. Freelance contributions welcome. No fiction. Approach in writing.
    Features Covering new initiatives and services, personal experiences and general issues of interest to a wide national readership. Maximum 1000 words. Disabled contributors welcome.
    News Maximum 300 words.
    Special Pages Possible openings for cartoonists.
    Payment by arrangement.

Disabled Motorist
DDMC, Cottingham Way, Thrapston, Northamptonshire NN14 4PL
☎01832 734724 Fax 01832 733816
Email ddme@ukonline.co.uk
Website www.ukonline.co.uk/ddmc
Owner *Disabled Drivers' Motor Club*
Editor *Lesley Browne*
Circulation 18,000
MONTHLY publication of the Disabled Drivers' Motor Club, an organisation which aims to promote and protect the interests and welfare of disabled people and help and encourage them in gaining increased mobility. Various discounts available for members; membership costs £10 p.a. (single), £15 (joint). The magazine includes information for members plus members' letters. Approach in writing with ideas. Unsolicited mss welcome.

Diva, lesbian life and style

Spectrum House, 32–34 Gordon House Road, London NW5 1LP
☎020 7424 7400   Fax 020 7424 7401
Email edit@divamag.co.uk
Website www.divamag.co.uk
Owner *Millivres Prowler Ltd*
Editor *Gillian Rodgerson*

FOUNDED 1994. MONTHLY journal of lesbian news and culture. Welcomes news, features, short fiction and photographs. No poetry. Contact the news editor with news items and *Gillian Rodgerson* with features, fiction and photographs. Approach in writing in the first instance.

Dog World

Somerfield House, Wotton Road, Ashford, Kent TN23 6LW
☎01233 621877   Fax 01233 645669
Website www.dogworld.co.uk
Owner *Dog World Ltd*
Editor *Simon Parsons*
Circulation 26,000

FOUNDED 1902. WEEKLY newspaper for people who are seriously interested in pedigree dogs. Unsolicited mss occasionally considered but initial approach in writing preferred.
  Features Well-researched historical items or items of unusual interest concerning dogs. Maximum 1000 words. Photographs of unusual 'doggy' situations occasionally of interest. *Payment* up to £50; photos £15.
  News Freelance reports welcome on court cases and local government issues involving dogs.

Dogs Monthly

Ascot House, High Street, Ascot SL5 7HG
☎01344 628269   Fax 01344 622771
Email admin@rtc-associates.freeserve.co.uk
Website www.dogsmonthly.co.uk
Owner *Mr D. Cavill*
Editor *Ruth Chapman*
Circulation 17,000

FOUNDED 1983. MONTHLY magazine suitable for serious dog owners whose dog is more than just a pet.
  Features Articles on breeds, topical news, but 'not interested in articles from the dog's point of view'. Approach the editor first by e-mail. Maximum length for features, news, fiction or other articles: 2000 words. *Payment* £35 per published page for illustrated articles.

Eastern Eye

Unit 2, 65 Whitechapel Road, London E1 1DU
☎020 7650 2000   Fax 020 7650 2001
Website www.ethnicmedia.co.uk
Owner *Ethnic Media Group*
Editor *Amar Singh*
Circulation 40,000

FOUNDED 1989. WEEKLY community paper for the Asian community in Britain. Interested in relevant general, local and international issues. Approach in writing with ideas for submission.

The Ecologist

Unit 18, Chelsea Wharf, 15 Lots Road, London SW10 0QJ
☎020 7351 3578   Fax 020 7351 3617
Email editorial@theecologist.org
Website www.theecologist.org
Owner *Ecosystems Ltd*
Editor *Zac Goldsmith*
Managing Editor *Harry Ram*
Circulation 20,000

FOUNDED 1970. MONTHLY. Unsolicited mss welcome but best approach is a brief (one-side, A4) proposal to the editor, outlining experience and background and summarising suggested article. Writers should study the magazine for style before submission.
  Features Radical approach to political, economic, social and environmental issues, with an emphasis on rethinking the basic assumptions that underpin modern society. Articles of between 500 and 3000 words.
  Payment £160 per first 1000 words, £100 per 1000 thereafter.

The Economist

25 St James's Street, London SW1A 1HG
☎020 7830 7000   Fax 020 7839 2968
Website www.economist.com
Owner *Pearson/individual shareholders*
Editor *Bill Emmott*
Circulation 144,019 (UK)

FOUNDED 1843. WEEKLY. Worldwide circulation. Approaches should be made in writing to the editor. No unsolicited mss.

The Edge

65 Guinness Buildings, Hammersmith, London W6 8BD
☎020 7460 9444
Email davec@theedge.abelgratis.co.uk
Website www.theedgeabelgratis.co.uk
Editor *Dave Clark*

QUARTERLY. Reviews and features: film (indie, arts), books, popular culture. Fiction: modern crime/horror/SF/erotica/slipstream. Sample issue £4 post-free (cheques payable to 'The Edge'). Writers' guidelines available on website, for s.a.e. or by e-mail.

Payment up to £60 per 1000 words.

Edinburgh Review

22A Buccleuch Place, Edinburgh EH8 9LN
☎0131 651 1415
Email edinburgh.review@ed.ac.uk
Publisher *Centre for the History of Ideas in Scotland*
Circulation 750

FOUNDED 1969. THREE ISSUES YEARLY. Articles and fiction on Scottish and international literary, cultural and philosophical themes. Unsolicited contributions are welcome (1600 are received each year), but prospective contributors are strongly advised to study the magazine first. Allow up to six months for a reply.

Features Interest will be shown in accessible articles on philosophy and its relationship to literature or visual art.

Fiction Scottish and international. Maximum 6000 words.

Electrical Times

Highbury Business Communications, Ann Boleyn House, 9–13 Ewell Road, Cheam, Surrey SM3 8BZ
☎020 8722 6000 Fax 020 8722 6095
Email b.evett@highburybiz.com
Owner *Highbury Business Communications*
Managing Editor *Bill Evett*
Circulation 14,476

FOUNDED 1891. MONTHLY. Aimed at electrical contractors, designers and installers. Unsolicited mss welcome but initial approach preferred.

Elle

32 Kingly Street, London W1B 5QQ
☎020 7025 5200 Fax 020 7025 5407
Owner *Hachette Filipacchi*
Editor *Sarah Bailey*
Deputy Editor *Margi Conklin*
Features Editor *Rachael Philipps*
Circulation 210,861

FOUNDED 1985. MONTHLY fashion glossy. Prospective contributors should approach the relevant editor in writing in the first instance, including cuttings.

Features Maximum 2500 words.

Hot List Short articles on hot trends, events, fashion and beauty. Maximum 500 words.

Payment about £300 per 1000 words.

Embroidery

PO Box 42B, East Molesley, Surrey KT8 9BB
☎020 8341 9721 Fax 020 8341 9721
Email pleonard@embroiderersguild.com
Website www.embroiderersguild.com
Owner *Embroiderers' Guild*
Editor *Polly Leonard*
Circulation 12,000

FOUNDED 1933. BI-MONTHLY. Features articles on historical and foreign embroidery, and contemporary artists' work with illustrations. Covers all forms of textile art, historical and contemporary. Also reviews. Unsolicited material welcome. Maximum 2500 words.

Payment negotiable.

Empire

4th Floor, Mappin House, 4 Winsley Street, London W1W 8HF
☎020 7436 1515 Fax 020 7343 8703
Email empire@emap.com
Website www.empireonline.co.uk
Owner *Emap East*
Editor *Colin Kennedy*
Circulation 164,500

FOUNDED 1989. Launched at the Cannes Film Festival. MONTHLY guide to the movies which aims to cover the world of films in a 'comprehensive, adult, intelligent and witty package'. Although most of *Empire* is devoted to films and the people behind them, it also looks at the developments and technology behind television and dvds plus music, multimedia and books. Wide selection of in-depth features and stories on all the main releases of the month, and reviews of over 100 films and videos. Contributions welcome but approach in writing first.

Features Behind-the-scenes features on films, humorous and factual features.

Payment by agreement.

The Engineer

50 Poland Street, London W1F 7AX
☎020 7970 4106 Fax 020 7970 4189
Website www.e4engineering.com
Owner *Centaur Communications*
Editor *Sean Brierley*
Circulation 41,000

FOUNDED 1856. FORTNIGHTLY news magazine for technology and innovation.

Features Most outside contributions are

commissioned but good ideas are always welcome. Maximum 2000 words.

News Scope for specialist regional free-lancers, and for tip-offs. Maximum 500 words.

Technology Technology news from specialists, and tip-offs. Maximum 500 words.

Payment by arrangement.

The English Garden

Romsey Publishing, Jubilee House, 2 Jubilee Place, London SW3 3QT

☎020 7751 4899 Fax 020 7751 4848

Email englishgarden@romseypublishing.com

Website www.theenglishgarden.co.uk

Owner *Romsey Publishing Ltd*
Editor *Julia Watson*
Circulation 95,917

FOUNDED 1996. MONTHLY. Features on beautiful gardens with practical ideas on design and planting. No unsolicited mss.

Features *Janine Wookey* Maximum 1000–1200 words. Approach in writing in the first instance; send synopsis of 150 words with strong design and planting ideas, feature proposals, or sets of photographs of interesting gardens.

English Nature Magazine

English Nature, Northminster House, Peterborough, Cambridgeshire PE1 1UA

☎01733 455191 Fax 01733 455436

Email gordon.leel@english-nature.org.uk

Website www.english-nature.org.uk

Owner *English Nature*
Editor *Gordon Leel*
Circulation 16,000

FOUNDED 1992. BI-MONTHLY magazine which explains the work of English Nature, the government adviser on wildlife and conservation policies. No unsolicited material.

The Erotic Review

EPS, 4th Floor, 1 Maddox Street, London W1S 2PZ

☎020 7439 8999 Fax 020 7437 3528

Email editrice@theeroticreview.co.uk

Website www.theeroticreview.co.uk

Owner *The Erotic Review Limited*
Editor *Rowan Pelling*
Circulation 30,000

FOUNDED 1997. MONTHLY erotic literary magazine containing articles, humour, fiction, poetry and art work. Unsolicited material welcome, but please read magazine first. No pornography. Approach in writing in the first instance enclosing a brief sample of work and s.a.e.

Features Esoteric, humorous or real-life experiences. Maximum 2000 words. *Payment* £40–100. **Fiction** Erotic short stories. Maximum 2000 words. *Payment* £50–100.

ES (Evening Standard magazine)

See entry under **Regional Newspapers**

Esquire

National Magazine House, 72 Broadwick Street, London W1F 9EP

☎020 7439 5000 Fax 020 7439 5675

Owner *National Magazine Co. Ltd*
Editor *Simon Tiffin*
Circulation 68,075

FOUNDED 1991. MONTHLY. Quality men's general interest magazine. No unsolicited mss or short stories.

Essentials

IPC Media Ltd., King's Reach Tower, Stamford Street, London SE1 9LS

☎020 7261 6970 Fax 020 7261 5262

Owner *IPC Media*
Editor *Karen Livermore*

FOUNDED 1988. MONTHLY women's interest magazine. Unsolicited mss (not originals) welcome if accompanied by s.a.e. Initial approach in writing preferred. Prospective contributors should study the magazine thoroughly before submitting anything. No fiction.

Features Maximum 2000 words (double-spaced on A4).

Payment negotiable, but minimum £100 per 1000 words.

Essex Life & Countryside

G13 Dugard House, Peartree Road, Stanway, Colchester, Essex CO3 5JX

☎01206 571364 Fax 01206 366982

Owner *Archant Life*
Editor *Carmen Konopka*
Submissions to: PO Box 6657, Bishop's Stortford CM23 4WB
Circulation 10,000

FOUNDED 1952. MONTHLY. Unsolicited material of Essex interest welcome. Features must include colour photos. No general interest material.

Features Countryside, culture and crafts in Essex. Maximum 1400 words.

Payment £25 per page.

The Essex Magazine

See **The Journal Magazines**

Eve
BBC Worldwide, Room AG200, 80 Wood
Lane, London W12 0TT
☎020 8433 3767 Fax 020 8433 3359
Email eve@bbc.co.uk
Owner *BBC Worldwide Publishing Ltd*
Editor *Jane Bruton*
Deputy Editor *Lucy Dunn*
Features Editor *Victoria Woodhall*
Circulation 121,157

FOUNDED 2000. MONTHLY. Wide-ranging
general interest – aimed at the intelligent 30+
woman. No unsolicited material. Send introductory letter, *recent* writings and outlines for
ideas aimed at a specific section. It is essential
that would-be contributors familiarise themselves with the magazine.

Eventing
See **Horse and Hound**

Evergreen
PO Box 52, Cheltenham, Gloucestershire
GL50 1YQ
☎01242 537900 Fax 01242 537901
Editor *R. Faiers*
Circulation 75,000

FOUNDED 1985. QUARTERLY magazine featuring articles and poems about Britain. Unsolicited contributions welcome.
Features Britain's natural beauty, towns and
villages, nostalgia, wildlife, traditions, odd customs, legends, folklore, crafts, etc. Length
250–2000 words.
Payment £15 per 1000 words; poems £4.

Executive Woman
2 Chantry Place, Harrow, Middlesex HA3 6NY
☎020 8420 1210 Fax 020 8420 1691
Email info@execwoman.com
Website www.execwoman.com
Owner *Saleworld*
Editor *Angela Giveon*
Circulation 85,000

FOUNDED 1987. BI-MONTHLY magazine for
female executives in the corporate field and
female entrepreneurs.
Features New and interesting business issues
and 'Women to Watch'. Health and conferenc-
ing, profiles, technology, beauty, fashion, training and arts items. 600–1200 words.
Legal/Financial Opportunities for lawyers/
accountants to write on issues in their field.
Maximum 600 words.
Payment negotiable.

The Face
3rd Floor, Endeavour House, 189 Shaftesbury
Avenue, London WC2H 8JG
☎020 7520 6400 Fax 020 7520 6450
Email editorial@theface.co.uk
Owner *Emap East*
Editor *Neil Stevenson*
Circulation 42,242

FOUNDED 1980. Magazine of the style generation, concerned with who's what and what's
cool. Profiles, interviews and stories. No fiction. Acquaintance with the 'voice' of *The Face*
is essential before sending mss on spec.
Features New contributors should write to
the features editor *Charles Davies* with their
ideas. Maximum 3000 words.
Diary No news stories.

Fairgame Magazine
The Baltic Business Centre, Gateshead, Tyne
and Wear NE8 3DA
☎0191 442 4001 Fax 0191 442 4002
Website www.fairgamemagazine.com
Editor *Jennifer O'Neill*
Circulation 15,000

FOUNDED 2003. BI-MONTHLY magazine for
women football players. Contributions welcome.
Features *Claire Foy* International reports,
player and team profiles, interviews, diet, health
and fitness, tactics, training advice, play improvement, fund-raising. 1500 words maximum.
News *Wilf Frith* Match reports, team news,
transfers, injuries, results and fixtures. 600
words maximum.

Family Circle
IPC Media Ltd., King's Reach Tower,
Stamford Street, London SE1 9LS
☎020 7261 5000 Fax 020 7261 5929
Email <firstname>_<lastname>@
ipcmedia.com
Owner *IPC Media*
Editor *Julie Barton-Breck*
Circulation 180,134

FOUNDED 1964. MONTHLY. Little scope for
freelancers as most material is produced in-
house. Unsolicited material is rarely used, but it
is considered. Prospective contributors are best
advised to e-mail ideas to the relevant editor.
Features *Emma Burstall*
Style *Justine Brennan*
Food and Wine *Heather Mairs*
Payment by arrangement.

Family Tree Magazine

61 Great Whyte, Ramsey, Huntingdon,
Cambridgeshire PE26 1HJ
☎01487 814050 Fax 01487 711361
Email lesboon@family-tree.co.uk
Website www.family-tree.co.uk

Owner *ABM Publishing Ltd*
Editor *Sue Fearn*
Circulation 45,000

FOUNDED 1984. MONTHLY. News and features
on matters of genealogy. Not interested in own
family histories. Approach in writing with
ideas. All material should be addressed to *Sue
Fearn.*

Features Any genealogically related subject.
Maximum 2400 words. No puzzles or fictional
articles.

Payment £40 per 1000 words (news and
features).

Fancy Fowl

The Publishing House, Station Road,
Framlingham, Suffolk IP13 9EE
☎01728 622030 Fax 01728 622031
Email ff@prestige.typo.co.uk

Owner *TP Publications*
Editor *Liz Fairbrother*
Circulation 3000

FOUNDED 1979. MONTHLY. Devoted entirely to
poultry, waterfowl, turkeys, geese, pea fowl, etc.
– management, breeding, rearing and exhibition.
Outside contributions of knowledgeable, technical poultry-related articles and news welcome.
Maximum 1000 words. Approach by letter.
Payment negotiable.

Farmers Weekly

Quadrant House, Sutton, Surrey SM2 5AS
☎020 8652 4911 Fax 020 8652 4005
Email farmers.weekly@rbi.co.uk
Website www.fwi.co.uk

Owner *Reed Business Information*
Editor *Stephen Howe*
Circulation 78,629

WEEKLY. 1996 Business Magazine of the Year.
For practising farmers and those in the ancillary
industries. Unsolicited mss considered.

Features A wide range of material relating
to farmers' problems and interests: specific sections on arable and livestock farming, farm life,
practical and general interest, machinery and
business.

News General farming news.
Payment negotiable.

Fast Car

Berwick House, 8–10 Knoll Rise, Orpington,
Kent BR6 0PS
☎01689 887200 Fax 01689 838844
Email fastcar@splpublishing.co.uk
Website www.fastcar.co.uk

Owner *Highbury – SPL Publishing*
Editor *Gez Jones*
Circulation 120,347

FOUNDED 1987. THIRTEEN ISSUES YEARLY.
Lad's magazine about perfomance tuning and
modifying cars. Covers all aspects of this youth
culture including the latest street styles and
music. Features cars and their owners, product
tests and in-car entertainment. Also includes a
free reader ads section.

Features Innovative ideas in line with the
above and in the *Fast Car* writing style. Generally
four pages in length. No Kit-car features, race
reports or road test reports of standard cars. Copy
should be as concise as possible. *Payment* negotiable.

News Any item in line with the above.

FHM

Mappin House, 4 Winsley Street, London
W1W 8HF
☎020 7436 1515 Fax 020 7343 3000
Email general@fhm.co.uk
Website www.fhm.co.uk

Owner *Emap Plc*
Editor *David Davies*
Circulation 620,226

FOUNDED in 1986 as a free fashion magazine,
FHM evolved to become more male oriented
but without much public acclaim until Emap
bought the title in 1994. Since then it has
become the best-selling men's magazine in the
world covering all areas of men's lifestyle. Published MONTHLY with 18 international editions
worldwide. No unsolicited mss. Synopses and
ideas welcome by e-mail. *Payment* negotiable.

Field, The

IPC Media Ltd., King's Reach Tower,
Stamford Street, London SE1 9LS
☎020 7261 5198 Fax 020 7261 5358
Email lbeatrice_gray@ipcmedia.com
Website www.thefield.co.uk

Owner *IPC Media*
Editor-in-Chief *Jonathan Young*
Circulation 33,718

FOUNDED 1853. MONTHLY magazine for those
who are serious about the British countryside
and its pleasures. Unsolicited mss (and trans-

parencies) welcome but initial approach should be made in writing or by phone on 020 7261 6225.

Features Exceptional work on any subject concerning the countryside. Most work tends to be commissioned.

Payment varies.

Film Review

Visual Imagination Ltd, 9 Blades Court, Deodar Road, London SW15 2NU
☎020 8875 1520   Fax 020 8875 1588
Email filmreview@visimag.com
Website www.visimag.com

Owner *Visual Imagination Ltd*
Editor *Neil Corry*
Circulation 50,000

FOUR WEEKLY. Reviews, profiles, interviews and special reports on films. Unsolicited material considered. *Payment* negotiable.

First Down

175 Tottenham Court Road, London W1T 7NU
☎020 7323 1988   Fax 020 7637 0862
Email firstdown@indmags.co.uk
Website www.first-down.co.uk

Owner *Independent Magazines (UK) Ltd*
Editor *Keith Webster*
Circulation 16,500

FOUNDED 1986. WEEKLY American football tabloid paper. Features and news. Welcomes contributions; approach by e-mail or in writing.

Fishing News

Telephone House, 69–77 Paul Street, London EC2A 4LQ
☎020 7017 4531   Fax 020 7017 4536
Email tim.oliver@informa.com
Website www.fishingnews.co.uk

Owner *Informa Group Plc*
Editor *Tim Oliver*
Circulation 11,400

FOUNDED 1913. WEEKLY. All aspects of the commercial fishing industry in the UK and Ireland. No unsolicited mss; telephone inquiry in the first instance. Maximum 600 words for news and 1500 words for features. *Payment* £100 per 1000 words.

The Fix

5 Martins Lane, Witcham, Ely, Cambridgeshire CB6 2LB
☎01353 777931
Email ttapress@aol.com
Website www.ttapress.com

Owner *TTA Press*
Editor *Andy Cox*

FOUNDED 1994. BI-MONTHLY. Features detailed contributors' guidelines of international short story publications, plus varied articles, news, views, reviews and interviews.

Features Unsolicited articles welcome on any aspect of short story publishing: market information, writing, editing, illustrating, interviews and reviews. All genres. Submissions should include adequate return postage. 'Please study the magazine: this will greatly enhance your chances of acceptance.'

Flight International

Quadrant House, The Quadrant, Sutton, Surrey SM2 5AS
☎020 8652 3882   Fax 020 8652 3840
Email flight.international@rbi.co.uk
Website www.flightinternational.com

Owner *Reed Business Information*
Editor *Murdo Morrison*
Circulation 52,222

FOUNDED 1909. WEEKLY. International trade magazine for the aerospace industry, including civil, military and space. Unsolicited mss considered. Commissions preferred – phone with ideas and follow up with letter. E-mail submissions encouraged.

Features *Murdo Morrison* Technically informed articles and pieces on specific geographical areas with international appeal. Analytical, in-depth coverage required, preferably supported by interviews. Maximum 1800 words.

News *Andrew Doyle* Opportunities exist for news pieces from particular geographical areas on specific technical developments. Maximum 350 words.

Payment NUJ rates.

Flora International

The Fishing Lodge Studio, 77 Bulbridge Road, Wilton, Salisbury, Wiltshire SP2 0LE
☎01722 743207   Fax 01722 743207

Publisher/Editor *Maureen Foster*
Circulation 16,000

FOUNDED 1974. BI-MONTHLY magazine for flower arrangers and florists. Unsolicited mss welcome. Approach in writing with ideas. Not interested in general gardening articles.

Features Fully illustrated, preferably with b&w photos or illustrations/colour transparencies. Flower arranging, flower arrangers' gardens and flower crafts. Floristry items written with practical knowledge and well illustrated are particularly welcome. Maximum 1000 words.

Profiles/Reviews Personality profiles and book reviews.

Payment £50 per 1000 words plus additional payment for suitable photographs.

FlyPast
PO Box 100, Stamford, Lincolnshire PE9 1XQ
☎01780 755131 Fax 01780 757261
Email flypast@keypublishing.com
Owner *Key Publishing Ltd*
Editor *Ken Ellis*
Circulation 48,157

FOUNDED 1981. MONTHLY. Historic aviation and aviation heritage, mainly military, Second World War period up to c.1970. Unsolicited mss welcome.

Focus
See **British Science Fiction Association** under **Professional Associations**

Focus
Origin Publishing, 14th Floor, Tower House, Fairfax Street, Bristol BS1 3BN
☎0117 927 9009 Fax 0117 934 9008
Website www.originpublishing.co.uk
Owner *Origin Publishing*
Editor *Emma Bayley*
News Editor *Graham Southorn*
Circulation 50,000

FOUNDED 1992. MONTHLY. Popular science and discovery. Welcomes *relevant* summaries of original feature ideas by e-mail.

For Women
Fantasy Publications, 4 Selsdon Way, London E14 9EL
☎020 7308 5090
Email ecoldwell@nasnet.co.uk
Editor *Liz Beresford*
Circulation 60,000

FOUNDED 1992. SIX-WEEKLY magazine of erotic and sex interest for women – health and sex, erotic fiction and erotic photography. No homes and gardens articles. Approach in writing in the first instance. Send e-mail or s.a.e. for submission guidelines.

Fiction *Elizabeth Coldwell* Erotic short stories. Maximum 3000 words. *Payment* £150 total.

Fortean Times: The Journal of Strange Phenomena
PO Box 2409, London NW5 4NP
☎020 7687 7002 Fax 020 7687 7099
Email david.sutton@ifgmags.com
Website www.forteantimes.com
Editor *David Sutton*
Circulation 30,000

FOUNDED 1973. MONTHLY. Accounts of strange phenomena and experiences, curiosities, mysteries, prodigies and portents. Unsolicited mss welcome. Approach in writing with ideas. No fiction, poetry, rehashes or politics.

Features Well-researched and referenced material on current or historical mysteries, or first-hand accounts of oddities. Maximum 3000 words, preferably with good relevant photos/illustrations.

News Concise copy with full source references essential.

Payment negotiable.

Foundation: The International Review of Science Fiction
c/o Middlesex University, White Hart Lane, London N17 8HR
Email farah3@mdx.ac.uk
Website www.sf-foundation.org
Owner *Science Fiction Foundation (reg. Charity 1041052)*
Editor *Dr Farah Mendlesohn*

THRICE-YEARLY publication devoted to the critical study of science fiction.
Payment None.

France Magazine
Cumberland House, Oriel Road, Cheltenham, Gloucestershire GL50 1BB
☎01242 216050 Fax 01242 216074
Email editorial@francemag.com
Website www.francemag.com
Owner *Archant (Life South) Ltd*
Editor *Philip Faiers*
Circulation 54,216

FOUNDED 1989. BI-MONTHLY magazine containing all things of interest to Francophiles – in English. Approach in writing in the first instance.

Freelance Market News
Sevendale House, 7 Dale Street, Manchester M1 1JB
☎0161 228 2362, ext 210 Fax 0161 228 3533
Email fmn@writersbureau.com
Editor *Angela Cox*

MONTHLY. News and information on the freelance writers' market, both inland and overseas. Includes market information, competitions, seminars, courses, overseas openings, etc. Short articles (700 words maximum). Unsolicited contributions welcome.

Payment by negotiation.

The Freelance
See **National Union of Journalists** under **Professional Associations and Societies**

FT Expat
4th Floor, 149 Tottenham Court Road, London W1P 9LL
☎020 7896 2000 Fax 020 7896 2229
Email hugh.fasken@ft.com
Website www.FTExpat.com
Owner *Financial Times Business*
Managing Editor *Hugh Fasken*
Circulation 50,000

FOUNDED January 2001. MONTHLY magazine aimed at British and non-British expatriates and international investors. Unsolicited mss considered, if suitable to the interests of the readership.

Features Up to 1200 words on finance, property, employment opportunities and other topics likely to appeal to readership, such as living conditions in countries with substantial expatriate populations.

Payment negotiable.

Garden Answers
Bretton Court, Bretton, Peterborough, Cambridgeshire PE2 8DZ
☎01733 264666 Fax 01733 282695
Owner *Emap Active Publications Ltd*
Editor *Nicola Dela-Croix*
Circulation 98,412

FOUNDED 1982. MONTHLY. 'It is unlikely that unsolicited manuscripts will be used, as articles are usually commissioned and must be in the magazine style.' Prospective contributors should approach the editor in writing. Interested in hearing from gardening writers on any subject, whether flowers, fruit, vegetables, houseplants or greenhouse gardening.

Garden News
Bretton Court, Bretton, Peterborough, Cambridgeshire PE3 8DZ
☎01733 264666 Fax 01733 282695
Owner *Emap Active Publications Ltd*
Editor *Sarah Page*
Circulation 52,031

FOUNDED 1958. Britain's biggest-selling, full-colour gardening WEEKLY. News and advice on growing flowers, fruit and vegetables, plus colourful features on all aspects of gardening

especially for the committed gardener. News and features welcome, especially if accompanied by top-quality photos or illustrations. Contact the editor before submitting any material.

The Garden, Journal of the Royal Horticultural Society
RHS Publications, 4th Floor, Churchgate New Road, Peterborough, Cambridgeshire PE1 1TT
Email thegarden@rhs.org.uk
Website www.rhs.org.uk
Owner *The Royal Horticultural Society*
Editor *Ian Hodgson*
Circulation 306,003

FOUNDED 1866. MONTHLY journal of the Royal Horticultural Society. Covers all aspects of the art, science and practice of horticulture and garden making. 'Articles must have depth and substance.' Approach by letter with a synopsis in the first instance. Maximum 2500 words.

Gardens Illustrated
BBC Worldwide, Woodlands, 80 Wood Lane, London W12 0TT
☎020 8433 1352 Fax 020 8433 2680
Website www.gardensillustrated.com
Owner *BBC Worldwide Publishing Ltd*
Editor *Clare Foster*
Circulation 32,120

FOUNDED 1993. TEN ISSUES YEARLY. 'Britain's most distinguished garden magazine' with a world-wide readership. The focus is on garden design, with a strong international flavour. Unsolicited mss are rarely used and it is best that prospective contributors approach the editor with ideas in writing, supported by photographs.

Gay Times
Unit M, Spectrum House, 32–34 Gordon House Road, London NW5 1LP
☎020 7424 7400 Fax 020 7424 7401
Website www.prowler.co.uk
Owner *Millivres Prowler Group*
Editor *Vicky Powell*
Circulation 65,000

Covers all aspects of gay life, plus general interest likely to appeal to the gay community, art reviews and news. Regular freelance writers used. *Payment* negotiable.

Gibbons Stamp Monthly
Stanley Gibbons, 5 Parkside, Christchurch Road, Ringwood, Hampshire BH24 3SH
☎01425 472363 Fax 01425 470247
Email hjefferies@stanleygibbons.co.uk

Website www.gibbonsstampmonthly.com
Owner *Stanley Gibbons Ltd*
Editor *Hugh Jefferies*
Circulation 22,000

FOUNDED 1890. MONTHLY. News and features. Unsolicited mss welcome. Make initial approach in writing, by telephone or e-mail to avoid disappointment.

Features *Hugh Jefferies* Unsolicited material of specialised nature and general stamp features welcome. Maximum 3000 words but longer pieces can be serialised. *Payment £40–50 per 1000 words.*

News *Michael Briggs* Any philatelic news item. Maximum 500 words. *No payment.*

Girl About Town
Independent House, 191 Marsh Wall, London E14 9RS
☎020 7005 5550 Fax 020 7005 5777
Website www.londoncareers.net
Owner *Independent Magazines*
Editor-in-Chief *Bill Williamson*
News/Style Pages *Laura Atkinson*
Circulation 85,000

FOUNDED 1972. Free WEEKLY magazine for women aged 18 to 45. Unsolicited mss may be considered. No fiction.

Features Standards are 'exacting'. Commissions only. Some chance of unknown writers being commissioned. Maximum 1500 words.
Payment negotiable.

Glamour
6–8 Old Bond Street, London W1S 4PH
☎020 7499 9080 Fax 020 7491 2551
Website www.glamour.com
Owner *Condé Nast*
Editor *Jo Elvin*
Circulation 537,474

FOUNDED 2001. Handbag-size glossy women's magazine – fashion, beauty and celebrities. No unsolicited mss; send ideas for features in synopsis form to the Features Editor *Miranda Levy*.

Gliding and Motorgliding International
281 Queen Edith's Way, Cambridge CB1 9NH
☎01223 247725
Email bryce.smith@virgin.net
Website www.glidingmagazine.com
Owner *Soaring Society of America*
Editor *Gillian Bryce-Smith*

FOUNDED November 1998 for international gliding and motorgliding enthusiasts. Few opportunities for freelance writers. Now on the Internet as the first gliding magazine to be electronic only. *No payment.*

Golf Monthly
IPC Media Ltd., King's Reach Tower, Stamford Street, London SE1 9LS
☎020 7261 7237 Fax 020 7261 7240
Email golfmonthly@ipcmedia.com
Website golf-monthly.co.uk
Owner *IPC Media*
Editor *Jane Carter*
Circulation 74,413

FOUNDED 1911. MONTHLY. Player profiles, golf instruction, general golf features and columns. Not interested in instruction material from outside contributors. Unsolicited mss welcome. Approach in writing with ideas.
Features Maximum 1500–2000 words.
Payment by arrangement.

Golf Weekly
Bushfield House, Orton Centre, Peterborough, Cambridgeshire PE2 5UW
☎01733 288035 Fax 01733 288025
Email golf.weekly@emap.com
Owner *Emap Active Publications Ltd*
Editor *Peter Masters*
Circulation 20,000

FOUNDED 1890. WEEKLY. Unsolicited material welcome from full-time journalists only. 'Always looking for photographic and written news contributions.' For features, approach in writing in first instance; for news, e-mail, fax or phone.
Features Maximum 1500 words.
News Maximum 300 words.
Payment negotiable.

Golf World
Bushfield House, Orton, Peterborough, Cambridgeshire PE2 5UW
☎01733 237111 Fax 01733 288025
Website www.emapgolf.com
Owner *Emap Active Publications Ltd*
Editor *Neil Pope*
Circulation 57,581

FOUNDED 1962. MONTHLY. No unsolicited mss. Approach in writing with ideas.

The Golf
Focus House, Dingwall Avenue, Croydon, Surrey CR9 2TA
☎020 8774 0799 Fax 020 8774 0937
Email thegolfmag@ipcmedia.com
Website www.thegolf.co.uk

Owner *IPC Media*
Editor *Mike Pye*
Circulation 35,000

FOUNDED 1995. MONTHLY. Features on Volkswagen Golfs and other VAG cars. Articles on tuning, styling, performance, technical and potential feature cars. 'Not interested in anything to do with the game of golf.' Submissions should be made directly to the editor. Articles must show excellent specialist knowledge of the subject matter. *Payment* by negotiation.

Good Holiday Magazine

27A High Street, Esher, Surrey KT10 9RL
☎01372 468140   Fax 01372 470765
Email info@goodholidayideas.com
Editor *John Hill*
Circulation 100,000

FOUNDED 1985. QUARTERLY aimed at better-off holiday-makers rather than travellers. Worldwide destinations including Europe and domestic. No unsolicited material but approach in writing or by e-mail with ideas and/or synopsis.

Payment negotiable.

Good Housekeeping

National Magazine House, 72 Broadwick Street, London W1F 9EP
☎020 7439 5000   Fax 020 7439 5591
Email
<firstname>.<lastname>@natmags.co.uk
Website www.natmags.co.uk
Owner *National Magazine Co. Ltd*
Editor-in-Chief *Lindsay Nicholson*
Circulation 407,032

FOUNDED 1922. MONTHLY glossy. No unsolicited mss. Write with ideas in the first instance to the appropriate editor.

Features *Kerry Fowler* Most work is commissioned but original ideas are always welcome. No ideas are discussed on the telephone. Send short synopsis, plus relevant cuttings, showing previous examples of work published. No unsolicited mss.

Health *Julie Powell*. Submission guidelines as for features; no unsolicited mss.

Good Motoring

Station Road, Forest Row, East Sussex RH18 5EN
☎01342 825676   Fax 01342 824847
Email gem@roadsafety.org.uk
Website www.roadsafety.org.uk
Owner *Guild of Experienced Motorists*
Editor *Derek Hainge*
Circulation 52,000

FOUNDED 1932. QUARTERLY motoring, road safety and travel magazine. Occasional general features. 1500 words maximum. Prospective contributors should approach in writing only.

Good News

50 Loxwood Avenue, Worthing, West Sussex BN14 7RA
☎01903 824174   Fax 01903 824174
Owner *Good News Fellowship*
Editor *Donald Banks*
Circulation 30,000

FOUNDED 2001. MONTHLY evangelistic newspaper which welcomes contributions. No fiction. Send for sample copy of writers' guidelines in the first instance. No poetry or children's stories.

News Items of up to 500 words (preferably with pictures) 'showing God at work, and human interest photo stories. "Churchy" items not wanted. Testimonies of how people have come to personal faith in Jesus Christ and the difference it has made are always welcome. They do not need to be dramatic!'

Women's Page Relevant items of interest welcome.

Payment negotiable.

Good Ski Guide

3rd Floor, The Interchange, Oval Road, London NW1 7DZ
☎020 7267 5000
Email info@goodskiguide.com
Website www.goodskiguide.com
Owner *Profile Media Group plc*
Editor *Owen Jones*
Circulation 50,000

FOUNDED 1976. FIVE ISSUES YEARLY. Unsolicited mss welcome from writers with a knowledge of skiing and ski resorts. Prospective contributors are best advised to make initial contact in writing as ideas and work need to be seen before any discussion can take place. *Payment* negotiable.

GQ

Vogue House, Hanover Square, London W1S 1JU
☎020 7499 9080   Fax 020 7495 1679
Website www.gq-magazine.co.uk
Owner *Condé Nast Publications Ltd*
Editor *Dylan Jones*
Circulation 123,502

FOUNDED 1988. MONTHLY. Men's style magazine. No unsolicited material. Write or fax with an idea in the first instance.

Granta
2–3 Hanover Yard, Noel Road, London
N1 8BE
☎020 7704 9776 Fax 020 7704 0474
Email editorial@granta.com
Website www.granta.com

Editor *Ian Jack*
Deputy Editor *Sophie Harrison*

QUARTERLY magazine of new writing, including fiction, memoirs, reportage and photography published in paperback book form. Highbrow, diverse and contemporary, with a thematic approach. Unsolicited mss (including fiction) considered. A lot of material is commissioned. Vital to read the magazine first to appreciate its very particular fusion of cultural and political interests. No reviews or news articles. No poetry. Access the website for submission guidelines. *Payment* negotiable.

The Great Outdoors
See **TGO**

The Great War
PO Box 202, Scarborough, North Yorkshire
YO11 3GE
☎01723 581329 Fax 01723 581329
Email books@greatnorthernpublishing.co.uk
Website www.greatnorthernpublishing.co.uk

Owner *Great Northern Publishing*
Editor *Mark Marsay*

FOUNDED 2001. BI-MONTHLY subscription magazine published in A5 format. 'The little magazine dedicated to the Great War and to those who perished and those who returned.'

Features articles and stories from the perspective of those who served (men and women of all nationalities) and their families: diaries; anecdotes; letters; postcards; poetry; unit histories; events; incidents and memorials, etc. No fiction. New material welcome but contact the editor prior to sending material. See website for submission guidelines. Sample copy £4.50.

Guardian Weekend
See under **National Newspapers (The Guardian)**

Guiding magazine
17–19 Buckingham Palace Road, London
SW1W 0PT
☎020 7834 6242 Fax 020 7828 5791
Email guiding@girlguiding.org.uk
Website www.girlguiding.org.uk

Owner *The Guide Association*

Editor *Victoria Wheater*
Circulation 61,000

FOUNDED 1914. MONTHLY. Unsolicited mss welcome provided topics relate to the Movement and/or women's role in society. Ideas in writing appreciated in first instance. No nostalgic, 'when I was a Guide', pieces, please.

Activity Ideas Interesting, contemporary ideas and instructions for activities for girls aged 5 to 18+ to do during unit meetings – crafts, games (indoor/outdoor), etc.

Features Topics relevant to today's girls and young women. 650 words.

News Items likely to be of interest to members. Maximum 100–150 words.

Payment £70 per 1000 words.

H&E Naturist
Burlington Court, Carlisle Street, Goole,
East Yorkshire DN14 5EG
☎01405 769712/764206 Fax 01405 763815
Email he@btconnect.com
Website www.healthandefficiency.co.uk

Owner *New Freedom Publications Ltd*
Editor *Mark Nisbet*
Circulation 20,000

FOUNDED 1898. MONTHLY naturist magazine. **Features** Will consider short features on social nudism, longer features on nudist holidays and nudist philosophy. 90% of every issue is by freelance contributors. 1000–1500 words. **News** 'We are always on the lookout for national and international nudist news stories.' 250–500 words. No soft porn, 'sexy' stories or sleazy photographs. Approach by post, e-mail or telephone.

Hair
IPC Media Ltd., King's Reach Tower,
Stamford Street, London SE1 9LS
☎020 7261 6975 Fax 020 7261 7382

Owner *IPC Media*
Editor *Lisa Allen*
Circulation 174,227

FOUNDED 1977. BI-MONTHLY hair and beauty magazine. No unsolicited mss, but always interested in good photographs. Approach with ideas in writing.

Features Fashion pieces on hair trends and styling advice. Maximum 1000 words.

Payment negotiable.

Hairflair
Hairflair Magazines Ltd, Freebournes House,
Freebournes Road, Witham, Essex CM8 3US
☎01376 534504 Fax 01376 534546

Owner *Hairflair Magazines Ltd*

Editor *Claire Moffatt*
Circulation 60,000

FOUNDED 1982. BI-MONTHLY. Original and interesting hair and beauty-related features written in a young, lively style to appeal to a readership aged 16–35 years. Unsolicited mss not welcome, although freelancers are used.
   Features Hair and beauty. Maximum 2500 words.
   Payment negotiable.

Harpers & Queen

National Magazine House, 72 Broadwick Street, London W1F 9EP
☎020 7439 5000 Fax 020 7439 5506

Owner *National Magazine Co. Ltd*
Editor *Lucy Yeomans*
Circulation 88,521

MONTHLY. Up-market glossy combining the stylish and the streetwise. Approach in writing (not phone) with ideas.
   Features *Harriet Green* Ideas only in the first instance.
   News Snippets welcome if very original.
   Payment negotiable.

Health & Fitness Magazine

Highbury wViP, 53–79 Highgate Road, London NW5 1TW
☎020 7331 1184 Fax 020 7331 1108
Website www.hfonline.co.uk

Owner *Highbury WV*
Editor *Mary Comber*
Circulation 65,000

FOUNDED 1983. MONTHLY. Target reader: active, health-conscious women aged 25–40.
Features news and articles on nutrition, exercise, healthy eating, holistic health and well-being. Will consider ideas; approach in writing in the first instance.

Health Education

The Health Education Unit, Research and Graduate School of Education, University of Southampton, Southampton SO17 1BJ
☎023 8059 3707
Email skw@soton.ac.uk
Website www.emeraldinsight.com

Owner *Emerald*
Editor *Dr Katherine Weare*
Circulation 2000

FOUNDED 1992. SIX ISSUES YEARLY. Health education journal with an emphasis on schools and young people. Professional readership.

Heat

Endeavour House, 189 Shaftesbury Avenue, London WC2H 8JG
☎020 7437 9011 Fax 020 7859 8670
Email heat@emap.com

Owner *Emap Entertainment*
Editor *Mark Frith*
Circulation 554,644

FOUNDED January 1999. WEEKLY entertainment magazine dealing with TV, film and radio information, fashion and features, with an emphasis on celebrity interviews and news. Targets 18– to 40 year-old readership, male and female. Articles written both in-house and by trusted freelancers. No unsolicited mss.

Hello!

Wellington House, 69–71 Upper Ground, London SE1 9PQ
☎020 7667 8700 Fax 020 7667 8716
Website www.hellomagazine.com

Owner *Hola! (Spain)*
Editor *Ronnie Whelan*
Commissioning Editor *Linda Newman*
Circulation 546,952

WEEKLY. Owned by a Madrid-based publishing family, *Hello!* has grown faster than any other British magazine since its launch here in 1988. The magazine has editorial offices both in Madrid and London. Major colour features plus regular news pages. Although much of the material is provided by regulars, good proposals do stand a chance. Approach the commissioning editor with ideas in the first instance. No unsolicited mss.
   Features Interested in celebrity-based features, with a newsy angle, and exclusive interviews from generally unapproachable personalities.
   Payment by arrangement.

Here's Health

Greater London House, Hampstead Road, London NW1 7EJ
☎020 7874 0200 Fax 020 7347 1897
Email rebecca.speechley@emap.com
Website www.thorsons.com/hereshealth

Owner *Emap Esprit*
Editor *Colette Harris*
Circulation 37,502

FOUNDED 1956. MONTHLY. Full-colour magazine dealing with alternative medicine, nutrition, natural health, wholefoods, supplements, organics and the environment. Prospective contributors should bear in mind that this is a specialist magazine with a pronounced bias towards alternative/complementary medicine, using expert contributors on the whole. No completed articles. Contact Features Editor *Lisa Howells* with ideas in the first instance. *Payment* negotiable.

Hi-Fi News
Focus House, Dingwall Avenue, Croydon, Surrey CR9 2TA
☎020 8774 0846 Fax 020 8774 0940
Email hi-finews@ipcmedia.com
Owner *IPC Media*
Editor *Steve Harris*
Circulation 18,415

FOUNDED 1956. MONTHLY. Write in the first instance with suggestions based on knowledge of the magazine's style and subject. All articles must be written from an informed technical or enthusiast viewpoint. *Payment* negotiable, according to technical content.

High Life
37–43 Sackville Street, London W1S 3EH
☎020 7534 2400 Fax 020 7534 2555
Email high.life@cedarcom.co.uk
Website www.cedarcom.co.uk
Owner *Cedar Communications*
Editor *Mark Jones*
Circulation 194,204

FOUNDED 1973. MONTHLY glossy. British Airways in-flight magazine. Almost all the content is commissioned. No unsolicited mss. Few opportunities for freelancers.

History Today
20 Old Compton Street, London W1D 4TW
☎020 7534 8000 Fax 020 7534 8008
Email p.furtado@historytoday.com
Website www.historytoday.com
Owner *History Today Trust for the Advancement of Education*
Editor *Peter Furtado*
Circulation 29,269

FOUNDED 1951. MONTHLY. General history and archaeology worldwide, history behind the headlines. Serious submissions only; no 'jokey' material. Approach by post or e-mail.

Home
Highbury-SPL, Berwick House, 8–10 Knoll Rise, Orpington, Kent BR6 0PS
☎01689 887200 Fax 01689 896847
Email jwooderson@splpublishing.co.uk
Owner *Highbury House Communications*

Editor *Sarah Giles*
Circulation 58,421

MONTHLY magazine with ideas, information and inspiration for the home. Features include style, design, home products, gardens and cookery. Synopses and ideas welcome; approach in writing. No health and lifestyle articles.

Home & Country
104 New Kings Road, London SW6 4LY
☎020 7731 5777 Fax 020 7736 4061
Owner *National Federation of Women's Institutes*
Editor *Susan Seager*
Circulation 50,000

FOUNDED 1919. MONTHLY. Official full-colour journal of the Federation of Women's Institutes, containing articles on a wide range of subjects of interest to women. Strong environmental country slant with crafts and cookery plus gardening appearing every month. Unsolicited mss, photos and illustrations welcome. *Payment* by arrangement.

Home & Family
Mary Sumner House, 24 Tufton Street, London SW1P 3RB
☎020 7222 5533 Fax 020 7222 1591
Owner *MU Enterprises Ltd*
Editor *Jill Worth*
Circulation 60,000

FOUNDED 1976. QUARTERLY. Unsolicited mss considered. No fiction or poetry. Features on family life, social problems, marriage, Christian faith, etc. Maximum 1000 words.
Payment 'modest'.

Homes & Gardens
IPC Media Ltd., King's Reach Tower, Stamford Street, London SE1 9LS
☎020 7261 5000 Fax 020 7261 6247
Website www.homesandgardens.com
Owner *IPC Media*
Editor *Isobel McKenzie-Price*
Circulation 157,981

FOUNDED 1919. MONTHLY. Almost all published articles are specially commissioned. No fiction or poetry. Best to approach in writing with an idea, enclosing snapshots if appropriate.

Horse
Room 2303, IPC Country & Leisure Media Ltd, King's Reach Tower, Stamford Street, London SE1 9LS
☎020 7261 7969 Fax 020 7261 7979

Email jaki-bell@ipcmedia.com
Website www.ipcmedia.com
Owner *IPC Media*
Editor *Jaki Bell*
Circulation 36,000

FOUNDED 1997. MONTHLY magazine aimed at people who ride regularly and are committed to learning more about current issues in the equestrian world such as riding concepts, veterinary developments and horse care as well as offering practical advice. Regular contributors provide a lot of reader interaction. Articles on leading equestrian celebrities. Send examples of published work with c.v. to the editor.

Horse and Hound

IPC Media Ltd., King's Reach Tower, Stamford Street, London SE1 9LS
☎020 7261 6315 Fax 020 7261 5429
Email jenny_sims@ipcmedia.com
Owner *IPC Media*
Editor *Lucy Higginson*
Circulation 67,100

FOUNDED 1884. WEEKLY. The oldest equestrian magazine on the market. Contains regular veterinary advice and instructional articles, as well as authoritative news and comment on fox hunting, international and national showjumping, horse trials, dressage, driving and endurance riding. Also weekly racing and point-to-points, breeding reports and articles. Regular books and art reviews, and humorous articles and cartoons are frequently published. Plenty of opportunities for freelancers. Unsolicited contributions welcome.

Also publishes a sister monthly publication, *Eventing*, which covers the sport of horse trials comprehensively; **Editor** *Kate Green*.

Payment NUJ rates.

Horse and Rider

Haslemere House, Lower Street, Haslemere, Surrey GU27 2PE
☎01428 651551 Fax 01428 654108
Email djm@djmurphy.co.uk
Website www.horseandridermagazine.co.uk
Owner *D.J. Murphy (Publishers) Ltd*
Editor *Alison Bridge*
Assistant Editor *Danielle Pascoe*
Circulation 46,000

FOUNDED 1949. MONTHLY. Adult readership, largely horse-owning. News and instructional features, which make up the bulk of the magazine, are almost all written in-house or commissioned. New contributors and unsolicited articles are occasionally used. Approach the editor in writing with ideas.

Hotline

The River Group, Victory House, Leicester Square, London WC2H 7BZ
☎020 7306 0304
Email jgardiner@riverltd.co.uk
Editor *Joe Gardiner*
Circulation 4 million (readership)

FOUNDED 1997. QUARTERLY on-board magazine for Virgin trains. UK travel-based features. Ideas and outlines by post welcome.

House & Garden

Vogue House, Hanover Square, London W1S 1JU
☎020 7499 9080 Fax 020 7629 2907
Website www.condenast.co.uk
Owner *Condé Nast Publications Ltd*
Editor *Susan Crewe*
Circulation 148,544

FOUNDED 1947. MONTHLY. Most feature material is produced in-house but occasional specialist features are commissioned from qualified freelancers, mainly for the interiors, wine and food sections and travel.

Features *Liz Elliot* Suggestions for features, preferably in the form of brief outlines of proposed subjects, will be considered.

House Beautiful

National Magazine House, 72 Broadwick Street, London W1F 9EP
☎020 7439 5000 Fax 020 7439 5625
Owner *National Magazine Co. Ltd*
Editor *Sarah Whelan*
Circulation 107,019

FOUNDED 1989. MONTHLY. Lively magazine offering sound, practical information and plenty of inspiration for those who want to make the most of where they live. Over 100 pages of easy-reading editorial. Regular features about decoration, DIY, food, gardening and home finance. Approach in writing with synopses or ideas in the first instance.

i-D Magazine

124 Tabernacle Street, London EC2A 4SA
☎020 7490 9710 Fax 020 7251 2225
Email editor@i-dmagazine.co.uk
Website www.i-dmagazine.com
Owner *Levelprint*
Editor *Avril Mair*
Circulation 66,000

FOUNDED 1980. MONTHLY lifestyle magazine for both sexes with a fashion bias. International. Very hip. Does not accept unsolicited contributions but welcomes new ideas from the fields of fashion, music, clubs, art, film, technology, books, sport, etc. No fiction or poetry. 'We are always looking for freelance non-fiction writers with new or unusual ideas.' A different theme each issue – past themes have included Green politics, taste, films, sex, love and loud dance music – means it is advisable to discuss feature ideas in the first instance.

Ideal Home

IPC Media Ltd., King's Reach Tower, Stamford Street, London SE1 9LS
☎020 7261 6505 Fax 020 7261 6697

Owner *IPC Media*
Editor *Jane Parbury*
Circulation 277,105

FOUNDED 1920. MONTHLY glossy. Unsolicited feature ideas are welcome only if appropriate to the magazine. Prospective contributors wishing to submit ideas should do so in writing to the editor. No fiction.

Features Furnishing and decoration of houses, kitchens or bathrooms; interior design, soft furnishings, furniture and home improvements, lifestyle and readers' homes. Length to be discussed with editor.

Payment negotiable.

The Illustrated London News

20 Upper Ground, London SE1 9PF
☎020 7805 5562 Fax 020 7805 5911
Email iln@ilng.co.uk
Website www.ilng.co.uk

Owner *James Sherwood*
Editor *Alison Booth*
Circulation 47,547

FOUNDED 1842. BIANNUAL: Christmas and Summer issues, plus the occasional special issue to coincide with particular events. Although the *ILN* covers issues concerning the whole of the UK, its emphasis remains on the capital and its life. Travel, wine, restaurants, events, cultural and current affairs are all covered. There are few opportunities for freelancers but all unsolicited mss are read (receives about five a week). The best approach is with an idea in writing to the editor. Particularly interested in articles relating to events and developments in contemporary London, and about people working in the capital. All features are illustrated, so ideas with picture opportunities are particularly welcome.

Image Magazine

Upper Mounts, Northampton NN1 3HR
☎01604 467000 Fax 01604 467190
Email image@northantsnews.co.uk

Owner *Northamptonshire Newspapers Ltd*
Editor *Ruth Supple*
Circulation 12,000

FOUNDED 1905. MONTHLY general interest regional magazine. No unsolicited mss. Approach by phone or in writing with ideas. No fiction.

Features Local issues, personalities, businesses, etc., of Northamptonshire, Bedfordshire, Buckinghamshire interest. Maximum 500 words. *Payment* negotiable.

News No hard news as such, just monthly diary column.

Other Regulars on motoring, fashion, beauty, lifestyle, travel and horoscopes. Maximum 500 words.

In Britain

Jubilee House, 2 Jubilee Place, London SW3 3TQ
☎020 7751 4800 Fax 020 7751 4848
Email inbritain@romseypublishing.com

Editor *Andrea Spain*
Circulation 47,000

FOUNDED in the 1930s. BI-MONTHLY. Travel magazine of the British Tourist Authority. Not much opportunity for unsolicited work – approach (by e-mail) with ideas and samples. Words and picture packages preferred (good quality transparencies only).

In Style

IPC Media Ltd., Kings Reach Tower, Stamford Street, London SE1 9LS
☎020 7261 5000 Fax 020 7261 6664
Email <firstname>_<lastname>@ ipcmedia.com

Owner *IPC Media*
Editor *Louise Chunn*
Senior Editors (Features) *Cath Rapley, Polly Williams*
Fashion Editor *Tamsin Doe*
Circulation 172,245

LAUNCHED March 2001. MONTHLY. UK edition of US fashion, beauty, celebrity and lifestyle magazine. Unsolicited material welcome; send by e-mail to individual editors.

Independent Magazine

See under **National Newspapers (The Independent)**

Inspirations

Highbury-SPL Publishing, Berwick House, 8–10 Knoll Rise, Orpington, Kent BR6 0PS
☎01689 887200   Fax 01689 896847

Owner *Highbury-SPL Publishing Ltd*
Editor *Andrée Frieze*
Circulation 61,000

Homes and interiors covering decorating, design, house features, makeovers, cookery, property, DIY advice and gardens. Will consider unsolicited synopses on these subjects.

Insurance Age

Informa House, 30–32 Mortimer Street, London W1W 7RE
☎020 7017 4129   Fax 020 7436 8392
Website www.insuranceage.com

Owner *Informa*
Editor *Joanna Malvern*
Circulation 22,050

FOUNDED 1979. MONTHLY publication circulated to insurance brokers. Covers general insurance (*not* life and pensions). No unsolicited mss. Interested in exclusive stories linked to the insurance broker market, risk managers, loss adjusters and claims managers.
   News *Jon Guy* Max. 400 words.
   Features *Michelle Worvell* Max. 1200 words. *Payment* negotiable.

The International Erotic Review

Diverse Publications, Unit 556, 3 Courthill House, 60 Water Lane, Wilmslow, Cheshire SK9 5BB
Email diversepublications@yahoo.co.uk

Owner *Diverse Publications Ltd*
Editors *Robin Barratt, Inna Zabrodskaya*
Circulation 25,000

FOUNDED 2003. QUARTERLY publication focusing on erotic art, poetry, photography and fiction. 'From India to Russia, from the UK to South Africa and Asia, we will be discussing and exploring the full range of erotic art and writing from a variety of countries and cultures.' Unsolicited contributions welcome, particularly from outside the UK – prose, fiction or poetry, up to 5000 words. Also monochrome or colour photographic portfolios. Absolutely *no* pornography.

International Rugby News

175 Tottenham Court Road, London W1T 7NU
☎020 7323 1944   Fax 020 7323 1943
Email sports@indmags.co.uk
Website www.rugbynews.net

Owner *Independent Magazines Ltd*
Editor *Graeme Gillespie*
Circulation 44,000

FOUNDED 1987. Contains news, views and features on the UK and the world rugby scene, with special emphasis on clubs, schools, fitness and coaching. Welcomes unsolicited material. Approach the editor in writing. *Payment* negotiable.

Interzone: Science Fiction & Fantasy

217 Preston Drove, Brighton, East Sussex BN1 6FL
☎01273 504710
Website www.sfsite.com/interzone

Owner/Editor *David Pringle*
Circulation 10,000

FOUNDED 1982. MONTHLY magazine of science fiction and fantasy. Unsolicited mss are welcome 'from writers who have a knowledge of the magazine and its contents'. S.a.e. essential for return.
   Fiction 2000–6000 words. *Payment* £30 per 1000 words.
   Features Book/film reviews, interviews with writers and occasional short articles. Length by arrangement. *Payment* negotiable.

Investors Chronicle

Maple House, 149 Tottenham Court Road, London W1T 7LB
☎020 7896 2525   Fax 020 7896 2054
Email matthew.vincent@ft.com *or* rosie.carr@ft.com
Website www.investorschronicle.co.uk

Owner *Pearson*
Editor *Matthew Vincent*
Deputy Editor *Rosie Carr*
Circulation 50,524

FOUNDED 1860. WEEKLY. Opportunities for freelance contributors in the survey section only. All approaches should be made in writing. Over forty surveys are published each year on a wide variety of subjects, generally with a financial, business or investment emphasis. Copies of survey list and synopses of individual surveys are obtainable from the surveys editor.
   Payment negotiable.

Irish Pages

The Linen Hall Library, 17 Donegall Square North, Belfast BT1 5GB
☎028 90 321 707
Email irishpages@yahoo.co.uk
Website www.irishpages.org

Editor *Chris Agee*
Circulation 1200

FOUNDED 2002. BI-ANNUAL non-partisan, non-sectarian journal publishing writing from Ireland and abroad. **Features** Poetry, short fiction, essays, non-fiction, memoirs, nature-writing, translated work, literary journalism and other autobiographical, historical and scientific writing of literary distinction. Irish language and Ulster Scots writing are published in the original with English translations. Equal editorial attention is given to established, emergent and new writers. Send submissions to the editor by post.

IRRV Valuer

Wrap Communications Ltd, The Bake House, J304 TBBC, 100 Clements Road, London SE16 4DG
☎010 7231 0707 Fax 020 7231 1232
Email info@wrapcom.com
Website www.wrapcom.com

Owner *Institue of Revenues, Rating and Valuation/Wrap Communications*
Managing Editor *Kate Miller*
Circulation 1322

FOUNDED 2001. Six BI-MONTHLY issues yearly for property valuation professionals. Well-qualified commentary, analysis and news covering issues affecting valuers, including reforms, legislation and technology. Small amount of appropriate lifestyle coverage. No unsolicited material; approach by telephone, fax, letter or e-mail in the first instance.
Features Ideas for stories must be well sourced and informed. Maximum 1000 words. *Payment* negotiable. **News** Stories relevant to property professionals. Maximum 300 words. *Payment* negotiable.

It's Hot! Magazine

Room A1151, BBC Worldwide, Woodlands, 80 Wood Lane, London W12 0TT
☎020 8433 2447 Fax 020 8433 2763
Email itshot@bbc.co.uk

Owner *BBC Worldwide*
Editor *Peter Hart*
Features *Kelly Wilks*
Circulation 103,000

FOUNDED 2002. MONTHLY magazine aimed at celebrity-mad 9–13–year-old girls, featuring music, film & TV gossip. Interested in exclusive celebrity interviews relevant to their market, and quizzes. Approach the editor with ideas by e-mail (peter.hart@bbc.co.uk) but 'please read the magazine first for style'. *Payment* negotiable.

J17

Endeavour House, 189 Shaftesbury Avenue, London WC2H 8JG
☎020 7208 3408 Fax 020 7208 3590

Owner *Emap élan Publications*
Editor *Anne-Louise Weatherley*
Deputy Editor *Donna Armstrong*
Circulation 143,308

FOUNDED 1983. MONTHLY. News, articles and quizzes of interest to girls aged 13–17. Ideas are sought in all areas. Prospective contributors should send ideas to the deputy editor.
Beauty *Lara Williamson*
Features/News *Chantelle Horton*
Payment by arrangement.

Jade

PO Box 202, Scarborough, North Yorkshire YO11 3GE
☎01723 581329 Fax 01723 581329
Email books@greatnorthernpublishing.co.uk
Website www.greatnorthernpublishing.co.uk

Owner *Great Northern Publishing*
Editors *Diane Crowther, Mark Marsay*

FOUNDED 2002. BI-MONTHLY magazine in A5 format. 'The erotic art and literature magazine for discerning adults.' Features new and established photographers, artists and writers in all erotic genres from around the world. No editorial articles, features or advice columns. Contributors should consult the website for submission guidelines and contact the editors prior to sending material. Sample copy £4.50 (NB contains strong adult content).

Jane's Defence Weekly

Sentinel House, 163 Brighton Road, Coulsdon, Surrey CR5 2YH
☎020 8700 3700 Fax 020 8763 1007
Email jdw@janes.co.uk
Website www.janes.com

Owner *Jane's*
Editor *Clifford Beal*
Circulation 25,500

FOUNDED 1984. WEEKLY. No unsolicited mss. Approach in writing with ideas in the first instance.
Features Current defence topics (politics, strategy, equipment, industry) of worldwide interest. No history pieces. Max. 2000 words.

Jazz Journal International

3 & 3A Forest Road, Loughton, Essex IG10 1DR
☎020 8532 0456/0678 Fax 020 8532 0440

Owner *Jazz Journal Ltd*
Editor-in-Chief *Eddie Cook*
Circulation 8000+

FOUNDED 1948. MONTHLY. A specialised jazz magazine, for record collectors, principally using expert contributors whose work is known to the editor. Unsolicited mss not welcome, with the exception of news material (for which no payment is made). It is not a gig guide, nor a free reference source for students.

Jersey Now

PO Box 582, Five Oaks, St Saviour, Jersey, Channel Islands JE4 8XQ
☎01534 611743 Fax 01534 611610
Email mspeditorial@msppublishing.com

Owner *MSP Publishing*
Managing Editor *Peter Body*
Circulation 24,000

FOUNDED 1987. QUARTERLY lifestyle magazine for Jersey covering homes, gardens, the arts, Jersey heritage, motoring, boating, fashion and technology. Upmarket glossy aimed at an informed and discerning readership. Interested in Jersey-orientated articles only – 1200 words maximum. Approach the editor initially.
Payment negotiable.

Jewish Chronicle

25 Furnival Street, London EC4A 1JT
☎020 7415 1500 Fax 020 7405 9040
Email editorial@thejc.com
Website www.thejc.com

Owner *Kessler Foundation*
Editor *Edward J. Temko*
Circulation 50,000

WEEKLY. Unsolicited mss welcome if 'the specific interests of our readership are borne in mind by writers'. Approach in writing, except for urgent current news items. No fiction. Maximum 1500 words for all material.
Features *Gerald Jacobs*
Leisure/Lifestyle *Alan Montague*
Home News *Barry Toberman*
Foreign News *Joe Millis*
Supplements *Angela Kiverstein*
Payment negotiable.

Jewish Quarterly

PO Box 35042, London NW1 7XH
☎020 7284 1117 Fax 020 7284 1117

Publisher *Jewish Literary Trust Ltd*
Editor *Matthew Reisz*

FOUNDED 1953. QUARTERLY illustrated magazine featuring Jewish literature and fiction, politics, art, music, film, poetry, history, dance, community, autobiography, Hebrew, Yiddish, Israel and the Middle East, Judaism, interviews, Zionism, philosophy and holocaust studies. Features a major books and arts section. Unsolicited mss welcome but letter or phone call preferred in first instance.

Jewish Telegraph

Jewish Telegraph Group of Newspapers, 11 Park Hill, Bury Old Road, Prestwich, Manchester M25 0HH
☎0161 740 9321 Fax 0161 740 9325
Email editor@jewishtelegraph.com
Website www.jewishtelegraph.com

Editor *Paul Harris*
Circulation 16,000

FOUNDED 1950. WEEKLY publication with local, national and international news and features. (Separate editions published for Manchester, Leeds, Liverpool and Glasgow.) Unsolicited features on Jewish humour and history welcome.

The Journal Magazines (Norfolk, Suffolk, Cambridgeshire)/The Essex Magazine

The Old County School, Northgate Street, Bury St Edmunds, Suffolk IP33 1HP
☎01284 701190 Fax 01284 701680
Email pippa@acornmagazines.co.uk

Owner *Acorn Magazines Ltd*
Editor *Pippa Bastin*
Circulation 12,000 each

FOUNDED 1990. MONTHLY magazines covering items of local interest – history, people, conservation, business, places, food and wine, fashion, homes and sport.
Features 750–1500 words maximum, plus pictures. Approach the editor by e-mail (see above) with ideas in the first instance.

Kerrang!

Mappin House, 4 Winsley Street, London W1N 7AR
☎020 7436 1515 Fax 020 7312 8910
Website www.kerrang.com

Owner *Emap Performance*
Editor *Ashley Bird*
Circulation 84,173

FOUNDED 1980. WEEKLY rock, punk and nu-metal magazine. 'Written by fans for fans.' Will consider ideas for features but not actively seeking new contributors unless expert in specialist fields such as Black metal and nu-metal.

The Lady

39–40 Bedford Street, London WC2E 9ER
☎020 7379 4717 Fax 020 7836 4620

Editor *Arline Usden*
Circulation 41,242

FOUNDED 1885. WEEKLY. Unsolicited mss are accepted provided they are not on the subject of politics or religion, or on topics covered by staff writers or special correspondents, i.e. fashion and beauty, health, cookery, household, gardening, finance and shopping.

Features Well-researched pieces on British and foreign travel, historical subjects or events; interviews and profiles and other general interest topics. Maximum 1200 words for illustrated two-page articles; 900 words for one-page features; 430 words for first-person 'Viewpoint' pieces. All material should be addressed to the editor with s.a.e. enclosed. Photographs supporting features may be supplied as colour transparencies or b&w prints. Telephone enquiries about features are not encouraged.

Land & Liberty

Wrap Communications Ltd, The Bake House, J304 TBBC, 100 Clements Road, London SE16 4DG
☎020 7231 0707 Fax 020 7231 1232
Email info@wrapcom.com
Website www.wrapcom.com

Owner *The Henry George Foundation/Wrap Communications*
Editor *Peter Gibb*
Circulation 2,500

FOUNDED 1894. FOUR ISSUES YEARLY for people interested in sustainable economics and political economy. Unique perspective with reports, analysis and comment on the core issues of political economy. No unsolicited material; approach by telephone, fax, letter or e-mail in the first instance.

Features Ideas for stories that explore how our common wealth should be used and to demonstrate this is the key to building the bridge of sustainability between the individual, the community and the environment. Must be well sourced and informed. Maximum 1000 words. *Payment* negotiable.

News Stories that reveal examples of good and bad practice in economic sustainability, including transport, environmental, political initiatives, resource rents, land ownership, etc. Maximum 300 words. *Payment* negotiable.

Land Rover World

Focus House, Dingwall Avenue, Croydon, Surrey CR9 2TA
☎020 8686 2599 Fax 020 8774 0937

Owner *IPC Media*
Editor *Luke Evans*
Circulation 30,000

FOUNDED 1994. MONTHLY. Incorporates *Practical Land Rover World* and *Classic Land Rover World*. Unsolicited material welcome, especially if supported by high-quality illustrations.

Features All articles with a Land Rover theme of interest. Potential contributors are strongly advised to examine previous issues before starting work.
Payment negotiable.

LG

Upper Mounts, Northampton NN1 3HR
☎01604 467043 Fax 01604 467190

Owner *Northamptonshire Newspapers Ltd*
Editor *Ruth Supple*
Circulation 6000

Formerly *Looking Good*, FOUNDED 1984. Relaunched in 2002 as *LG*, a QUARTERLY magazine aimed at women aged 18–30. Fashion and beauty, lifestyle, true life stories. Contributions occasionally considered but majority of work is done in-house.

Life&Soul Magazine

PO Box 8, 94 London Road, Headington, Oxford OX3 9FN
☎01865 423435 Fax 01865 423435
Email editor@lifeandsoul.com
Website www.lifeandsoul.com

Publisher *Karma Publishing Ltd*
Editor *Roy Stemman*
Circulation 3000

QUARTERLY. The only magazine in the world dealing with all aspects of reincarnation – from people who claim to recall their past lives spontaneously to those who have been regressed. It also examines other evidence for immortality, including near-death experiences, spirit communication and paranormal phenonema. Commissions only. No unsolicited mss.

Lincolnshire Life

County Life Ltd, PO Box 81, Lincoln LN1 1HD
☎01522 527127 Fax 01522 560035
Email editorial@lincolnshirelife.co.uk
Website www.lincolnshirelife.co.uk

Publisher *A.L. Robinson*

Executive Editor *Judy Theobald*
Circulation 10,000

FOUNDED 1961. MONTHLY county magazine featuring geographically relevant articles on local culture, history, personalities, etc. Maximum 1000–1500 words. Contributions supported by three or four good-quality photographs are always welcome. Approach in writing. *Payment* varies.

The Lincolnshire Poacher

County Life Ltd, PO Box 81, Lincoln LN1 1HD
☎01522 527127 Fax 01522 560035
Email editorial@lincolnshirelife.co.uk
Website www.lincolnshirelife.co.uk

Publisher *A.L. Robinson*
   Executive Editor *David Robinson*
Circulation 5000

QUARTERLY county magazine featuring geographically relevant but nostalgic articles on history, culture and personalities of Lincolnshire. Maximum 1000–1500 words. Contributions supported by three or four good-quality photographs/illustrations appreciated. Approach in writing. *Payment* varies.

The List

14 High Street, Edinburgh EH1 1TE
☎0131 558 1191 Fax 0131 557 8500
Email editor@list.co.uk
Website www.list.co.uk

Owner *The List Ltd*
Publisher *Robin Hodge*
Editor *Mark Fisher*
Circulation 17,500

FOUNDED 1985. FORTNIGHTLY. Events guide covering Glasgow and Edinburgh. Interviews and profiles of people working in film, theatre, music and the arts. Maximum 1200 words. No unsolicited mss. Phone with ideas. News material tends to be handled in-house. *Payment* £100.

Literary Review

44 Lexington Street, London W1F 0LW
☎020 7437 9392 Fax 020 7734 1844
Email litrev@dircon.co.uk
Website www.litreview.com

Editor *Nancy Sladek*
Circulation 15,000

FOUNDED 1979. MONTHLY. Publishes book reviews (commissioned), features and articles on literary subjects. Prospective contributors are best advised to contact the editor in writing. Unsolicited mss not welcome. Runs a monthly competition, the Literary Review Grand Poetry Competition, on a given theme. *Payment* 'minuscule'.

Living France Magazine

Cumberland House, Oriel Road, Cheltenham, Gloucestershire GL50 1BB
☎01242 216050 Fax 01242 216074
Email editorial@livingfrance.com
Website www.livingfrance.com

Owner *Archant Life*
Editor *Lucy-Jane Cypher*

FOUNDED 1989. MONTHLY. A Francophile magazine catering for those with a passion for France, French culture and lifestyle. Editorial covers all aspects of holidaying, living and working in France. Property section for those owning or wishing to buy a property in France. No unsolicited mss; approach in writing or by e-mail with an idea.

Loaded

IPC Media Ltd., King's Reach Tower, Stamford Street, London SE1 9LS
☎020 7261 5562 Fax 020 7261 5557
Email andrew_woods@ipcmedia.com

Owner *IPC Media*
Editor *Scott Manson*
Commissioning Editor *Andrew Woods*
Circulation 290,214

FOUNDED 1994. MONTHLY men's lifestyle magazine featuring music, sport, sex, humour, travel, fashion, hard news and popular culture. Will consider material which comes into these categories; approach the commissioning editor in writing or by e-mail in the first instance. No fiction or poetry.

Logos

5 Beechwood Drive, Marlow, Buckinghamshire SL7 2DH
☎01628 433871 Fax 01628 477577
Email logos-marlow@dial.pipex.com

Owner *Whurr Publishers Ltd*
Editor *Gordon Graham*
Associate Editor *Betty Graham*

FOUNDED 1990. QUARTERLY. Aims to 'deal in depth with issues which unite, divide, excite and concern the world of books', with an international perspective. Each issue contains 6–8 articles of between 3500–7000 words. 'Logos is a non-profit-making professional forum, not a scholarly journal.' Suggestions and ideas for contributions are welcome, and should be addressed to the editor. 'Guidelines for Contributors' available. Contributors write from their experience as authors, publishers, booksellers, librarians, etc.

Payment. Contributors receive 25 off-prints, a copy of the issue in which their article appears and a 50% concession on the subscription rate.

The London Magazine
32 Addison Grove, London W4 1ER
☎020 8400 5882 Fax 020 8994 1713
Email editorial@londonmagazine.ukf.net
Website www.londonmagazine.ukf.net

Owner *Christopher Arkell*
Editor *Sebastian Barker*
Circulation 1,200

FOUNDED originally in 1732 and relaunched in 2002. BI-MONTHLY review of literature and the arts. Publishes poems, short stories, features, memoirs, and book and performance reviews. Not interested in overtly political material or anything sent by e-mail or fax. No phone-calls. All submissions should be made by post with an s.a.e. to the editor. **Features** Maximum 5000 words. **Fiction** Maximum 5000 words. **Poems** 'Any length within reason'. *Payment* negotiable.

London Review of Books
28 Little Russell Street, London WC1A 2HN
☎020 7209 1101 Fax 020 7209 1102
Email edit@lrb.co.uk
Website www.lrb.co.uk

Owner *LRB Ltd*
Editor *Mary-Kay Wilmers*
Circulation 42,525

FOUNDED 1979. FORTNIGHTLY. Reviews, essays and articles on political, literary, cultural and scientific subjects. Also poetry. Unsolicited contributions welcome (approximately 50 received each week). No pieces under 2000 words. Contact the editor in writing. Please include s.a.e. *Payment* £150 per 1000 words; poems, £75.

Looking Good
See **LG**

Lothian Life
Ballencrieff Cottage, Ballencrieff Toll, Bathgate, West Lothian EH48 4LD
☎01506 632728 Fax 01506 635444
Email editor@lothianlife.co.uk
Website www.lothianlife.co.uk

Owner *Pages Editorial & Publishing Services*
Editor *Susan Coon*

QUARTERLY county magazine for people who live, work or have an interest in the Lothians. Includes three or four major features (1500 words) on successful people, businesses or initia-

tives. A local walk takes up the centre spread. Regular articles by experts on collectables, property, interior design, cookery and local gardening, plus news items, letters and a competition. Freelance writers used only for main features. Phone first to discuss content and timing.

Payment by arrangement.

Machine Knitting Monthly
PO Box 1479, Maidenhead, Berkshire SL6 8YX
☎01628 783080 Fax 01628 633250
Email rpa@surf3.net
Website www.machineknittingmonthly.co.uk

Owner *RPA Publishing Ltd*
Editor *Anne Smith*

FOUNDED 1986. MONTHLY. Unsolicited mss considered 'as long as they are applicable to this specialist publication. We have our own regular contributors each month but we're always willing to look at new ideas from other writers.' Approach in writing in the first instance.

Management Today
174 Hammersmith Road, London W6 7JP
☎020 7413 4956
Email management.today@haynet.com

Owner *Haymarket Business Publications Ltd*
Publishing Director *Rufus Olins*
Editor *Matthew Gwyther*
Circulation 93,394

General business topics and features. Ideas welcome. Send brief synopsis to the editor.

marie claire
13th Floor, King's Reach Tower, Stamford Street, London SE1 9LS
☎020 7261 5240 Fax 020 7261 5277
Email marieclaire@ipcmedia.com
Website www.ipcmedia.com

Owner *European Magazines Ltd*
Editor *Marie O'Riordan*
Circulation 400,038

FOUNDED 1988. MONTHLY. An intelligent glossy magazine for women, with strong international features and fashion. No unsolicited mss. Approach with ideas in writing or by e-mail (marieclaireideas@ipcmedia.com). No fiction.

Features *Charlotte Moore* Detailed proposals for feature ideas should be accompanied by samples of previous work.

Marketing Week
12–26 Lexington Street, London W1R 4HQ
☎020 7970 4000 Fax 020 7970 6721
Email stuart.smith@centaur.co.uk
Website www.mad.co.uk/publication/mw/

Owner *Centaur Communications*
Editor *Stuart Smith*
Circulation 41,000

WEEKLY trade magazine of the marketing industry. Features on all aspects of the business, written in a newsy and up-to-the-minute style. Approach with ideas in the first instance.
Features *Danny Parker Payment* negotiable.

Match

Bushfield House, Orton Centre, Peterborough, Cambridgeshire PE2 5UW
☎01733 237111   Fax 01733 288150
Email match.magazine@emap.com
Website www.matchmag.co.uk

Owner *Emap Active Ltd*
Editor *Simon Caney*
Deputy Editor *Ian Foster*

FOUNDED 1979. WEEKLY. The UK's biggest-selling football magazine aimed at 10–15 year-olds. All material is generated in-house by a strong news and features team. Work experience placements often given to trainee journalists and students; the majority of staff are recruited through this route. Approach in writing or by phone.

Match Angling Plus

Bushfield House, Orton Centre, Peterborough, Cambridgeshire PE2 5UW
☎01733 465705   Fax 01733 465658
Email steve.cole@emap.com

Owner *Emap Active*
Editor *Steve Cole*
Circulation 15,000

FOUNDED 1992. MONTHLY magazine aimed at match anglers and advanced pleasure anglers. Coarse fishing only.
Features only. Please send relevant articles, with or without pictures, by e-mail to the editor. Maximum 2500 words.

Matrix

See **British Science Fiction Association** under **Professional Associations**

Maxim

30 Cleveland Street, London W1T 4JD
☎020 7907 6410   Fax 020 7907 6439
Email editorial@maxim-magazine.co.uk

Owner *Dennis Publishing*
Editor *Tom Loxley*
Circulation 250,119

ESTABLISHED 1995. MONTHLY glossy men's lifestyle magazine featuring sex, travel, health, motoring and fashion. No fiction or poetry. Approach in writing in the first instance, sending outlines of ideas only together with examples of published work.

Mayfair

2 Archer Street, Piccadilly Circus, London W1D 7AW
☎020 7292 8000   Fax 020 7734 5030
Email mayfair@pr-org.co.uk
Website www.sexclub.co.uk

Owner *Paul Raymond Publications*
Editor *David Ryder*
Circulation 331,760

FOUNDED 1966. THIRTEEN ISSUES YEARLY. Unsolicited material accepted if pertinent to the magazine and *only* if accompanied by suitable illustrative material. Interested in features and humour aimed at men aged 18–80 in 800–1000 words. Punchy, bite-sized humour, top ten features, etc. 'Must make the editor laugh.' Also considers erotica.

Mayfair Times

27 John Adam Street, London WC2N 6HX
☎020 7839 2455   Fax 020 7839 3789
Email sjg@wetherell.co.uk

Owner *Mayfair Times Ltd*
Editor *Erik Brown*
Circulation 17,000

FOUNDED 1985. MONTHLY. Features on Mayfair of interest to residents, local workers, visitors and shoppers.

Medal News

Orchard House, Duchy Road, Heathpark, Honiton, Devon EX14 1YD
☎01404 46972   Fax 01404 44788
Email info@tokenpublishing.com
Website www.tokenpublishing.com

Owners *J.W. Mussell, Carol Hartman*
Editor *J.W. Mussell*
Circulation 7,000

FOUNDED 1989. MONTHLY. Unsolicited material welcome but initial approach by phone or in writing preferred.
Features 'Opportunities exist for well-informed authors who know the subject and do their homework.' Maximum 2500 words.
Payment £25 per 1000 words.

Media Week

Quantum House, 19 Scarbrook Road, Croydon, Surrey CR9 1LX
☎020 8565 4323   Fax 020 8565 4394
Website www.mediaweek.co.uk

Owner *Quantum Business Media*
Editor *Tim Burrowes*
Circulation 20,555

FOUNDED 1986. WEEKLY trade magazine. UK and international coverage on all aspects of commercial media. Approach in writing with ideas. See website for e-mail addresses.

Melody Maker
See **New Musical Express**

Men's Health
7–10 Chandos Street, London W1G 9AD
☎020 7291 6000 Fax 020 7291 6053
Website www.menshealth.co.uk

Owner *Rodale Press*
Editor *To be appointed*
Circulation 218,740

FOUNDED 1994. MONTHLY men's healthy lifestyle magazine covering health, fitness, nutrition, stress and sex issues. No unsolicited mss; will consider ideas and synopses tailored to men's health. No fiction, celebrities, sportsmen or extreme sports. Approach in writing in the first instance.

MiniWorld Magazine
Focus House, Dingwall Avenue, Croydon, Surrey CR9 2TA
☎020 8774 0600 Fax 020 8774 0937
Email miniworld@ipcmedia.co.uk
Website www.miniworld.co.uk

Owner *IPC Media*
Editor *Monty Watkins*
Circulation 37,000

FOUNDED 1991. MONTHLY car magazine devoted to the Mini. Unsolicited material welcome but prospective contributors are advised to contact the editor.

Features Maintenance, tuning, restoration, technical advice, classified, sport, readers' cars and social history of this cult car.

Payment negotiable.

Mizz
IPC Media Ltd., King's Reach Tower, Stamford Street, London SE1 9LS
☎020 7261 7358 Fax 020 7261 6032

Owner *IPC Media*
Editor *Sharon Christal*
Deputy Editor *Leslie Sinoway*
Circulation 129,654

FOUNDED 1985. FORTNIGHTLY magazine for the 10–14 year-old girl.

Features 'We have a full features team and thus do not accept freelance features.'
Fiction Maximum 1000 words.

Model Collector
IPC Focus Network, Focus House, Dingwall Avenue, Croydon, Surrey CR9 2TA
☎020 8774 0755 Fax 020 8774 0939
Email modelcollector@ipcmedia.com
Website www.modelcollector.com

Owner *AOL Time Warner/IPC Media*
Editor *David Jinks*
Circulation 20,000

FOUNDED 1987. THIRTEEN ISSUES YEARLY Britain's best selling die-cast magazine. From the latest models to classic 30's Dinkys. Interested in historical articles about particular models or ranges and reviews of the latest products. Photographs welcome. Not interested in radio controlled models or model railways.

Features Freelancers should contact the editor. Unsolicited material may be considered.

News Trade news welcome. Call *Lindsay Armrani* on 020 8774 0932 to discuss details.

Mojo
Mappin House, 4 Winsley Street, London W1W 8HF
☎020 7436 1515 Fax 020 7312 8296
Email mojo@ecm.emap.com

Owner *Emap-Metro*
Acting Editor *Paul Trynker*
Circulation 100,418

FOUNDED 1993. MONTHLY magazine containing features, reviews and news stories about rock music and its influences. Receives about five mss per day. No poetry, think-pieces on dead rock stars or similar fan worship.

Features Amateur writers discouraged except as providers of source material, contacts, etc. *Payment* negotiable.

News All verifiable, relevant stories considered.

Reviews Write to Reviews Editor *Jenny Bulley* with relevant specimen material.

Moneywise
RD Publications Ltd, 11 Westferry Circus, Canary Wharf, London E14 4HE
☎020 7715 8465 Fax 020 7715 8725
Website www.moneywise.co.uk

Owner *Reader's Digest Association*
Editor *David Ellis*
Circulation 105,000

FOUNDED 1990. MONTHLY. No unsolicited mss; initial approach in writing with c.v. preferred.

More!

Endeavour House, 189 Shaftesbury Avenue,
London WC2H 8JG
☎020 7208 3165 Fax 020 7208 3595
Email fran.lee@emap.com
Website www.moremagazine.co.uk

Owner *Emap élan Publications*
Editor *Alison Hall*
Features Director *Amanda Astill*
Editorial Enquiries *Fran Lee*
Circulation 246,261

FOUNDED 1988. FORTNIGHTLY women's magazine aimed at the working woman aged 16–24. Features on sex and relationships plus news. Most items are commissioned; approach features director with idea. Prospective contributors are strongly advised to study the magazine's style before submitting anything.

Mother and Baby

Greater London House, Hampstead Road,
London NW1 7EJ
☎020 7874 0200 Fax 020 7347 1888
Email motherandbaby@emap.com

Owner *Emap Esprit*
Editor *Dani Zur*
Circulation 84,871

FOUNDED 1956. MONTHLY. Welcomes suggestions for feature ideas about pregnancy, newborn basics, practical babycare, baby development and childcare subjects. Approaches may be made by telephone, e-mail or in writing to the **Features Editor** *Georgina Hersey.*

Motor Boat & Yachting

IPC Country & Leisure Media Limited,
King's Reach Tower, Stamford Street,
London SE1 9LS
☎020 7261 5333 Fax 020 7261 5419
Email mby@ipcmedia.com
Website www.mby.com

Owner *AOL Time Warner*
Editor *Tom Isitt*
Circulation 19,736

FOUNDED 1904. MONTHLY for those interested in motor boats and motor cruising.
Features *Tom Isitt* Cruising features and practical features especially welcome. Illustrations/photographs (mostly colour) are just as important as text. Maximum 3000 words. *Payment* from £100 per 1000 words or by arrangement.
News *Tom Isitt* Factual pieces. Maximum 200 words. *Payment* up to £50 per item.

Motor Caravan Magazine

Focus House, Dingwall Avenue, Croydon,
Surrey CR9 2TA
☎020 8774 0752 Fax 020 8774 0939
Email simon_collis@ipcmedia.com
Website www.motorcaravanmagazine.co.uk

Owner *IPC Media*
Editor *Simon Collis*
Circulation 15,000

FOUNDED 1986. MONTHLY consumer magazine delivering test reports, touring ideas and practical advice to motor caravanners. Unsolicited material welcome. Interested in holiday reports, interesting or unusual caravans, practical step-by-step motor caravanning features. Phone the editor or e-mail outlining basic ideas. Maximum 2500 words. *Payment* £60 a page.

Motor Cycle News

Media House, Lynchwood, Peterborough
Business Park, Peterborough PE2 6EA
☎01733 468000 Fax 01733 468028
Email MCN@emap.com
Website www.motorcylenews.com

Owner *Emap plc*
Editor *Adam Duckworth*
Circulation 150,000

FOUNDED 1955. WEEKLY. Interested in short news stories and features on motorcyles and motorcycle racing. No race reports. Contact relevant desks direct.

Motorcaravan Motorhome Monthly (MMM)

PO Box 88, Tiverton, Devon EX16 7ZN
Email mmeditor@warnersgroup.co.uk
Website www.mmmonline.co.uk

Owner *Warners Group Publications Plc*
Editor *Mike Jago*
Circulation 32,500

FOUNDED 1966. MONTHLY. 'There's no money in motorcaravan journalism but for those wishing to cut their first teeth ...' Unsolicited mss welcome if relevant, but ideas in writing preferred in first instance.
Features Caravan site reports. Maximum 500 words.
Travel Motorcaravanning trips (home and overseas). Maximum 2000 words.
News Short news items for miscellaneous pages. Maximum 200 words.
Fiction Must be motorcaravan-related and include artwork/photos if possible. Maximum 2000 words.
Special pages DIY – modifications to motorcaravans. Maximum 1500 words.

Owner Reports Contributions welcome from motorcaravan owners. Contact the editor for requirements. Maximum 2000 words.

Payment varies.

Ms London

Independent House, 191 Marsh Wall, London E14 9RS

☎020 7005 5959 Fax 020 7005 5999

Website www.londoncareers.net

Owner *Independent Magazines*
Editor-in-Chief *Bill Williamson*
Circulation 85,000

FOUNDED 1968. WEEKLY. Aimed at working women in London, aged 18–45. No unsolicited mss.

Features Content is varied and topical, ranging from celebrity interviews to news issues, fashion, health, careers, relationships and home-buying. Approach in writing only with ideas in the first instance, enclosing sample of published writing. Material should be London-angled, sharp or humorous and fairly sophisticated in content. Maximum 1500 words. *Payment* about £130 per 1000 words on publication.

News Handled in-house but follow-up feature ideas welcome.

Mslexia (For Women Who Write)

PO Box 656, Newcastle upon Tyne NE99 2XD

☎0191 261 6656 Fax 0191 261 6636

Email postbag@mslexia.demon.co.uk

Website www.mslexia.co.uk

Owner *Mslexia Publications Limited*
Editor *Debbie Taylor*
Circulation 10,000

FOUNDED 1997. QUARTERLY. Articles, advice, reviews, interviews, events for women writers plus new poetry and prose. Will consider fiction, poetry, features and letters but contributors *must* send for guidelines first.

Music Week

Ludgate House, 245 Blackfriars Road, London SE1 9UR

☎020 8742 2828 Fax 020 7579 4011

Owner *CMP Information*
Editor-in-Chief *Ajax Scott*
Circulation 13,900

Britain's only WEEKLY music business magazine. No unsolicited mss. Approach in writing with ideas.

Features Analysis of specific music business events and trends.

News Music industry news only.

Musical Opinion

2 Princes Road, St Leonards on Sea, East Sussex TN37 6EL

☎01424 715167 Fax 01424 712214

Email musicalopinion2@aol.com

Website www.musicalopinion.com

Owner *Musical Opinion Ltd*
Editor *Denby Richards*
Circulation 5000

FOUNDED 1877. QUARTERLY with four free supplements in intervening months. Classical music content, with topical features on music, musicians, festivals, etc., and reviews (concerts, festivals, opera, ballet, jazz, CDs, DVDs, videos, books and printed music). International readership. No unsolicited mss; commissions only. Ideas always welcome though; approach by phone, fax or e-mail, giving telephone number. It should be noted that topical material has to be submitted six months prior to events. Not interested in review material, which is already handled by the magazine's own regular team of contributors.

Payment negotiable.

My Weekly

80 Kingsway East, Dundee DD4 8SL

☎01382 223131 Fax 01382 452491

Email myweekly@dcthomson.co.uk

Owner *D.C. Thomson & Co. Ltd*
Editor *Harrison Watson*
Circulation 273,703

A traditional women's WEEKLY. D.C. Thomson has long had a policy of encouragement and help to new writers of promise. Ideas welcome. Approach in writing.

Features Particularly interested in human interest pieces (1000–1500 words) which by their very nature appeal to all age groups.

Fiction Three stories a week, ranging in content from the emotional to the off-beat and unexpected. 1000–4000 words.

Payment negotiable.

The National Trust Magazine

36 Queen Anne's Gate, London SW1H 9AS

☎020 7222 9251 Fax 020 7222 5097

Email enquiries@thenationaltrust.org.uk

Owner *The National Trust*
Editor *Gaynor Aaltonen*
Circulation 1.47 million

FOUNDED 1968. THREE ISSUES YEARLY. Conservation of historic houses, coast and countryside in England, Northern Ireland and Wales. No unsolicited mss. Approach in writing with ideas.

The Naturalist

c/o University of Bradford, Bradford, West
Yorkshire BD7 1DP
☎01274 234212 Fax 01274 234231
Email m.r.d.seaward@bradford.ac.uk

Owner *Yorkshire Naturalists' Union*
Editor *Prof. M.R.D. Seaward*
Circulation 5000

FOUNDED 1875. QUARTERLY. Natural history,
biological and environmental sciences for a professional and amateur readership. Unsolicited mss
and b&w illustrations welcome. Particularly
interested in material – scientific papers – relating
to the north of England.
No payment.

Nature

The Macmillan Building, 4–6 Crinan Street,
London N1 9XW
☎020 7833 4000 Fax 020 7843 4596
Email nature@nature.com
Website www.nature.com

Owner *Macmillan Magazines Ltd*
Editor *Philip Campbell*
Circulation 61,000

Covers all fields of science, with articles and
news on science and science policy only. Little
scope for freelance writers.

Needlecraft

30 Monmouth Street, Bath BA1 2BW
☎01225 442244 Fax 01225 732398
Email needlecraft@futurenet.co.uk

Owner *Future Publishing*
Editor *Debora Bradley*
Circulation 23,500

FOUNDED 1991. MONTHLY. Needlework projects with full instructions covering cross stitch,
needlepoint, embroidery, patchwork and quilt-
ing. Will consider ideas or sketches for projects
covering any of the magazine's topics. Initial
approaches should be made in writing.
Features on the needlecraft theme. Discuss
ideas before sending complete mss. Maximum
1000 words.
Payment negotiable.

New Beacon

105 Judd Street, London WC1H 9NE
☎020 7388 1266 Fax 020 8438 9092
Email beacon@rnib.org.uk
Website www.rnib.org.uk

Owner *Royal National Institute for the Blind*
Editor *Ann Lee*
Circulation 6000

FOUNDED 1917. MONTHLY (except August).
Published in print, braille and on tape, disk and
e-mail. Unsolicited mss welcome. Approach
with ideas in writing or by e-mail. Personal
experiences by writers who have sight difficulties (partial sight or blindness), and authoritative items by professionals or volunteers working in the field of sight difficulties welcome.
Maximum 1500 words.
Payment negotiable.

New Humanist

1 Gower Street, London WC1E 6HD
☎020 7436 1151
Email frank.jordans@newhumanist.org.uk

Owner *Rationalist Press Association*
Editor *Frank Jordans*
Circulation 5000

FOUNDED 1885. QUARTERLY. Unsolicited mss
welcome. No fiction.
Features Articles with a humanist perspective welcome in the following fields: religion
(critical), humanism, human rights, philosophy,
current events, literature, history and science.
2000 words. *Payment* nominal, but negotiable.
Book Reviews 750–1000 words, by
arrangement with the editor.

New Impact

Anser House, Courtyard Offices, 140 Oxford
Road, Marlow, Buckinghamshire SL7 2NT
☎01628 481581 Fax 01628 475570
Email curious@anserhouse.co.uk
Website www.anserhouse.co.uk

Owner *D.E. Sihera*
Editor *Elaine Sihera*
Features Editor *Sandhya Tharoor*
Circulation 10,000

FOUNDED 1993. BI-MONTHLY. Celebrates diversity, enterprise and achievement from a minority
ethnic perspective. Unsolicited mss welcome.
Interested in training, arts, features, personal
achievement, small business features, profiles of
personalities especially for a multicultural audience. Promotes the British Diversity Awards
each November and the Windrush Awards each
June, the Register of Diversity Managers among
employers and managing the diversity maze for
practitioners.
News Local training/business features –
some opportunities. Maximum length 550
words. *Payment* negotiable.
Features Original, interesting pieces with a
deliberate multicultural/diversity focus. Personal/
professional successes and achievements welcome. Max. 1000 words. *Payment* negotiable.

Fiction Short stories, poems – especially from minority writers. Not interested in romantic/sexual narratives. Maximum length 1500 words. *Payment* negotiable.

Special Pages Interviews with personalities – especially Asian, African Caribbean. Maximum length 1200 words. *Payment* negotiable.

New Internationalist
55 Rectory Road, Oxford OX4 1BW
☎01865 728181 Fax 01865 793152
Email ni@newint.org
Website www.newint.org/
Owner *New Internationalist Trust*
Co-Editors *Vanessa Baird, David Ransom, Katharine Ainger*
Circulation 80,000

Radical and broadly leftist in approach, but unaligned. Concerned with world poverty and global issues of peace and politics, feminism and environmentalism, with emphasis on the Third World. Difficult to use unsolicited material as they work to a theme each month and features are commissioned by the editor on that basis. The way in is to send examples of published or unpublished work; writers of interest are taken up.

New Musical Express
IPC Media Ltd., King's Reach Tower, Stamford Street, London SE1 9LS
☎020 7261 6472 Fax 020 7261 5185
Website www.nme.com
Owner *IPC Media*
Editor *Conor McNicholas*
Circulation 70,456

Britain's best-selling musical WEEKLY. Now incorporates *Melody Maker*. Freelancers used, but always for reviews in the first instance. Specialisation in areas of music (or film, which is also covered) is a help.

Reviews: LPs *Anthony Thornton* **Live** *Pat Long*. Send in examples of work, either published or specially written samples.

New Nation
Unit 2, 65 Whitechapel Road, London E1 1DU
☎020 7650 2000 Fax 020 7650 2001
Website www.ethnicmedia.co.uk
Owner *Ethnic Media Group*
Editor *Michael Eboda*
Circulation 30,000

FOUNDED 1996. WEEKLY community paper for the Black community in Britain. Interested in relevant general, local and international issues. Approach in writing with ideas for submission.

New Scientist
1st Floor, 151 Wardour Street, London W1F 8WE
☎020 8652 3500 Fax 020 7331 2772 (News)
Website www.newscientist.com
Owner *Reed Business Information Ltd*
Editor-in-Chief *Dr Alun Anderson*
Editor *Jeremy Webb*
Circulation 138,000

FOUNDED 1956. WEEKLY. No unsolicited mss. Approach with ideas – one A4–page synopsis – by fax or e-mail.

Features Commissions only, but good ideas welcome. Maximum 3500 words.

News *Matt Walker* Mostly commissions, but ideas for specialist news welcome. Maximum 1000 words.

Reviews *Maggie McDonald* Reviews are commissioned.

Opinion *Michael Bond* Unsolicited material welcome if of general/humorous interest and related to science. Maximum 1000 words.

Payment negotiable.

The New Shetlander
11 Mounthooly Street, Lerwick, Shetland ZE1 0BJ
☎01595 693816 Fax 01595 696787
Email shetland@zetnet.co.uk
Owner *Shetland Council of Social Service*
Editors *Brian Smith, Laureen Johnson*
Circulation 1900

FOUNDED 1947. QUARTERLY literary magazine containing short stories, essays, poetry, historical articles, literary criticism, political comment, arts and books. The magazine has two editors and an editorial committee who all look at submitted material. Interested in considering short stories, poetry, historical articles with a northern Scottish or Scandinavian flavour, literary pieces and articles on Shetland. As a rough guide, items should be between 1000 and 2000 words although longer mss are considered. Initial approach in writing, please.

Payment Complimentary copy.

New Statesman
Victoria Station House, 191 Victoria Street, London SW1E 5NE
☎020 7828 1232 Fax 020 7828 1881
Website www.newstatesman.co.uk
Publisher *Spencer Neal*
Editor *Peter Wilby*

Deputy Editor *Cristina Odone*
Circulation 26,000

WEEKLY magazine, the result of a merger (1988) of *New Statesman* and *New Society*. Coverage of news, book reviews, arts, current affairs, politics and social reportage. Unsolicited contributions with s.a.e. will be considered. No short stories.

Books *Jason Cowley*
Arts *Lisa Allardice*

New Theatre Quarterly

Oldstairs, Kingsdown, Deal, Kent CT14 8ES
☎01304 373448
Email simontrussler@lineone.net
Website www.uk.cambridge.org

Publisher *Cambridge University Press*
Editors *Clive Barker, Simon Trussler*

FOUNDED 1985 (originally launched in 1971 as *Theatre Quarterly*). Articles, interviews, documentation and reference material covering all aspects of live theatre. Recommend preliminary e-mail enquiry before sending contributions. No theatre reviews or anecdotal material.

New Welsh Review

PO Box 170, Aberystwyth, Ceredigion SY23 1W7
☎01970 626230   Fax 01970 626230
Email nwr@welshnet.co.uk

Owner *New Welsh Review Ltd*
Editor *Francesca Rhydderch*
Circulation 900

FOUNDED 1988. QUARTERLY Welsh literary magazine in the English language. Welcomes material of literary and cultural interest to Welsh readers and those with an interest in Wales. Approach in writing in the first instance.

   Features Maximum 3000 words. *Payment* £150 average.
   Fiction Maximum 5000 words. *Payment* £75 average.
   Reviews Maximum 800 words. *Payment* £40 average.

New Woman

Endeavour House, 189 Shaftesbury Avenue, London WC2H 8JG
☎020 7437 9011   Fax 020 7208 3585
Email lizzi.hosking@emap.com
Website www.newwoman.co.uk

Owner *Emap élan Ltd*
Editor *Sara Cremer*
Circulation 294,611

MONTHLY women's interest magazine. Winner of the PPA 'Magazine of the Year' award in 1998 and the BSME 'Editor of the Year' in 2001. Aimed at women aged 25–35. An 'entertaining, informative and intelligent' read. Main topics of interest include men, sex, love, health, careers, beauty and fashion. Uses mainly established freelancers but unsolicited ideas submitted in synopsis form will be considered. Welcomes ideas from male writers for humorous 'men's opinion' pieces.

   Features/News *Andrea Cottee* Articles must be original and look at subjects or issues from a new or unusual perspective.

The New Writer

PO Box 60, Cranbrook, Kent TN17 2ZR
☎01580 212626   Fax 01580 212041
Email editor@thenewwriter.com
Website www.thenewwriter.com

Publisher *Merric Davidson*
Editor *Suzanne Ruthven*
Poetry Editor *Abi Hughes-Edwards*

FOUNDED 1996. Published BI-MONTHLY following the merger between *Acclaim* and *Quartos* magazines. TNW continues to offer practical 'nuts and bolts' advice on poetry and prose but with the emphasis on *forward-looking* articles and features on all aspects of the written word that demonstrate the writer's grasp of contemporary writing and current editorial/publishing policies. Plenty of news, views, competitions, reviews and regional gossip in the Newsletter section; writers' guidelines available with s.a.e.

   Features Unsolicited mss welcome. Interested in lively, original articles on writing in its broadest sense. Approach with ideas in writing in the first instance. No material is returned unless accompanied by s.a.e. *Payment* £20 per 1000 words.
   Fiction Publishes short-listed entries from guest writers and subscriber-only submissions. *Payment* £10 per story.
   Poetry Unsolicited poetry welcome. Both short and long unpublished poems, providing they are original and interesting. *Payment* £3 per poem.

New Writing Scotland

Association for Scottish Literary Studies, c/o Department of Scottish History, 9 University Gardens, University of Glasgow G12 8QH
☎0141 330 5309   Fax 0141 330 5309
Email d.jones@scothist.arts.gla.ac.uk
Website www.asls.org.uk

Contact *Duncan Jones*

ANNUAL anthology of contemporary poetry and prose in English, Gaelic and Scots, produced by the **Association for Scottish Literary Studies** (see entry under **Professional Associations and Societies**). Will consider poetry, drama, short fiction or other creative prose but not full-length plays or novels, though self-contained extracts are acceptable. Contributors should be Scottish by birth or upbringing, or resident in Scotland. Maximum length of 3500 words is suggested. Send no more than two short stories and six poems. Submissions should be accompanied by two s.a.e.s (one for receipt, the other for return of mss). Mss, which must be sent by 31 January, should be typed, double-spaced, on one side of the paper only with the sheets secured at top left-hand corner. Provide covering letter with full contact details but do not put name or address on individual work(s). Prose pieces should carry an approximate word count.

newBOOKSmag

15 Scots Drive, Wokingham, Berkshire RG41 3XF
Email jo@newbooks.com
Website www.newbooksmag.com
Owner/Editor *Guy Pringle*
Circulation 15,000

FOUNDED 2000. BI-MONTHLY magazine for readers and reading groups with extracts from the best new fiction and free copies to be claimed. No unsolicited contributions.

Newcastle Life
See **North East Times**

19

IPC Media Ltd., King's Reach Tower, Stamford Street, London SE1 9LS
☎020 7261 6410 Fax 020 7261 7634
Owner *IPC Media*
Editor *Helen Bazvaye*
Circulation 118,001

FOUNDED 1968. MONTHLY women's magazine aimed at 18–25 year-olds. Aims for a 50/50 balance between fashion/lifestyle aspects and newsier, meatier material, e.g. women in prison, boys, abortion, etc. 40% of the magazine's feature material is commissioned, ordinarily from established freelancers. 'But we're always keen to see bold, original, vigorous writing from people just starting out.'
  Features *Laura Millar* Approach in writing with ideas.

North East Times

8 Landsdown Terrace, Gosforth, Newcastle upon Tyne NE3 1HN

☎0191 284 4495 Fax 0191 285 4176
Email alison.conlon@accentmagazines.co.uk
Owner *North East Times Ltd*
Editor *Alison Conlon*
Circulation 10,000

MONTHLY county magazine incorporating *Newcastle Life*. No unsolicited mss. Approach with ideas in writing. Not interested in any material that is not applicable to ABC1 readers.

The North
See **Poetry Magazines**

Now

IPC Media Ltd., King's Reach Tower, Stamford Street, London SE1 9LS
☎020 7261 6274
Owner *IPC Media*
Editor *Jane Ennis*
Circulation 630,212

FOUNDED 1996. WEEKLY magazine of celebrity gossip, news and topical features aimed at the working woman. Unlikely to use freelance contributions due to specialist content – e.g. exclusive showbiz interviews – but ideas will be considered. Approach in writing; no faxes.

Nursing Times

Greater London House, Hampstead Road, London NW1 7EJ
☎020 7874 0500 Fax 020 7874 0505
Owner *Emap Healthcare*
Editor *Rachel Downey*
Circulation 66,276

A large proportion of *Nursing Times'* feature content is from unsolicited contributions sent on spec. Pieces on all aspects of nursing and health care, both practical and theoretical, written in a lively and contemporary way, are welcome. Commissions also.
  Payment varies/NUJ rates apply to commissioned material from union members only.

OK! Magazine

Ludgate House, 245 Blackfriars Road, London SE1 9UX
☎020 7928 8000 Fax 020 7579 4607
Email <firstname>.<lastname>@express.co.uk
Owner *Northern & Shell Media/Richard Desmond*
Editor *Nic McCarthy*
Circulation 632,791

FOUNDED 1996. WEEKLY celebrity-based magazine. Welcomes interviews and pictures on well known personalities, and ideas for general features. Approach by phone or fax in the first instance.

Old Glory

Mortons Heritage Media, Newspaper House, Morton Way, Horncastle, Lincolnshire LN9 6JR
☎01507 529300 Fax 01507 529301
Email info@mortons.co.uk
Website www.oldglory.co.uk *or* www.classicmagazines.co.uk
Owner *Mortons Media Ltd*
Editor *Colin Tyson*

FOUNDED 1988. MONTHLY magazine covering all aspects of transport and industrial heritage both in the UK and overseas. Specialises in vintage vehicles and steam preservation. Unsolicited articles are welcome. Approach by letter addressed to the editor.
  Features Restoration projects from steam rollers to windmills. Maximum 1000 words.
  News Steam and transport rally reports. News concerning industrial and heritage sites and buildings.

The Oldie

65 Newman Street, London W1T 3EG
☎020 7436 8801 Fax 020 7436 8804
Email theoldie@theoldie.co.uk
Website www.theoldie.co.uk
Owner *Oldie Publications Ltd*
Editor *Richard Ingrams*
Circulation 30,000

FOUNDED 1992. MONTHLY general interest magazine with a strong humorous slant for the older person. Submissions welcome; enclose s.a.e. No poetry.

Opera

36 Black Lion Lane, London W6 9BE
☎020 8563 8893 Fax 020 8563 8635
Email editor@operamag.clara.co.uk
Website www.opera.co.uk
Owner *Opera Magazine Ltd*
Editor *John Allison*
Circulation 11,500

FOUNDED 1950. MONTHLY review of the current opera scene. Almost all articles are commissioned and unsolicited mss are not welcome. All approaches should be made in writing.

Opera Now

241 Shaftesbury Avenue, London WC2H 8TF
☎020 7333 1740 Fax 020 7333 1769
Email opera.now@rhinegold.co.uk

Website www.rhinegold.co.uk
Publisher *Rhinegold Publishing Ltd*
Editor-in-Chief *Ashutosh Khandekar*
Deputy Editor *Antonia Couling*

FOUNDED 1989. BI-MONTHLY. News, features and reviews aimed at those involved as well as those interested in opera. No unsolicited mss. All work is commissioned. Approach with ideas in writing.

Orbis

See **Poetry Magazines**

Organic Gardening

Sandvoe, North Roe, Shetland ZE2 9RY
☎01806 533319 Fax 01806 533319
Email organic.gardening@virgin.net
Editor *Gaby Bartai Bevan*
Circulation 20,000

FOUNDED 1988. MONTHLY. Articles and features on all aspects of gardening based on organic methods. Unsolicited material welcome; 800–2000 words for features and 100–300 for news items. Poetry not published. Prefers 'hands-on' accounts of projects, problems, challenges and how they are dealt with. Approach in writing.
  Payment by arrangement.

OS (Office Secretary) Magazine

First Floor, 63 High Street, Witney, Oxfordshire OX28 6HS
☎01993 775545 Fax 01993 778884
Owner *Peebles Media Group Ltd*
Editor *Louise Halkett*
Circulation 44,500

FOUNDED 1986. BI-MONTHLY. Features articles of interest to secretaries and personal assistants aged 25–60. No unsolicited mss.
  Features Informative pieces on technology and practices, office and employment-related topics. Length 1000 words. Approach with ideas by telephone or in writing.
  Payment by negotiation.

Palmtop User Magazine

Palmtop Publications, PO Box 188, Bicester, Oxfordshire OX26 6GP
☎01869 249287 Fax 01869 246043
Email editor@palmtop.co.uk
Website www.palmtop.co.uk
Owners *Mr S. Clack, Miss R.A. Rolfe*
Editor *Mr S. Clack*
Circulation 10,000

FOUNDED 1994. BI-MONTHLY users' magazine for hand-held computers. No unsolicited mss;

approach by telephone or e-mail in the first instance.

PC Format

Future Publishing, 30 Monmouth Street, Bath BA1 2BW
☎01225 442244 Fax 01225 732295
Email pcfmail@futurenet.co.uk
Website www.futurenet.co.uk

Owner *Future Publishing*
Publisher *Dave Taylor*
Acting Editor *Geoff Harris*
Circulation 76,337

FOUNDED 1991. FOUR-WEEKLY magazine covering everything for the consumer PC – games, hardware, Internet creativity. Welcomes feature ideas in the first instance; approach by telephone, e-mail or in writing.

People Management

Personnel Publications Limited, 17 Britton Street, London EC1M 5TP
☎020 7880 6200 Fax 020 7336 7635
Email editorial@peoplemanagement.co.uk
Website www.peoplemanagement.co.uk

Editor *Steve Crabb*
Circulation 107,648

FORTNIGHTLY magazine on human resources, industrial relations, employment issues, etc. Welcomes submissions but apply for 'Guidelines for Contributors' in the first instance. **Features** *Jane Pickard* **News** *Rima Manocha* **Law at Work** *Jill Evans*.

The People's Friend

80 Kingsway East, Dundee DD4 8SL
☎01382 462276/223131 Fax 01382 452491
Email peoplesfriend@dcthomson.co.uk

Owner *D.C. Thomson & Co. Ltd*
Editor *Margaret McCoy*
Circulation 397,080

The *Friend* is a fiction magazine, with two serials and several short stories each week. FOUNDED in 1869, it has always prided itself on providing 'a good read for all the family'. Stories should be about ordinary, identifiable characters with the kind of problems the average reader can understand and sympathise with. 'We look for the romantic and emotional developments of characters, rather than an over-complicated or contrived plot. We regularly use period serials and, occasionally, mystery/adventure.' Guidelines on request with s.a.e.

Short Stories Can vary in length from 1000 words or less to as many as 4000.

Serials Long-run serials of 10–15 instalments or more preferred. Occasionally shorter.
Articles Short fillers welcome.
Payment on acceptance.

Period Living & Traditional Homes

Mappin House, 4 Winsley Street, London W1W 8HF
☎020 7436 1515 Fax 020 7343 8710
Email period.living@emap.com

Owner *Emap East*
Editor *Sharon Parsons*
Deputy Editor *Andrew Lilwall-Smith*
Circulation 70,562

FOUNDED 1992. Formed from the merger of *Period Living* and *Traditional Homes*. Covers interior decoration in a period style, period house profiles, traditional crafts, renovation of period properties.

Payment varies according to length/type of article.

Personal Finance

Arnold House, 36–41 Holywell Lane, London EC2A 3SF
☎020 7827 5454 Fax 020 7827 0567

Owner *Charterhouse Communications plc*
Editor *Martin Fagan*
Circulation 50,000

ESTABLISHED 1994. MONTHLY finance magazine.

Features All issues relating to personal finance, particularly investment, insurance, banking, mortgages, savings, borrowing, health care and pensions. No corporate articles or personnel issues. Write to the editor with ideas in the first instance. No unsolicited mss. *Payment* £200 per 1000 words.

News All items written in-house.

The Philosopher

Centre for Lifelong Learning, Newcastle University, Newcastle upon Tyne NE1 7RU
Email thephilisophicalsociety@yahoo.co.uk
Website www.the-philosopher.co.uk

Owner *The Philosophical Society*
Editor *Martin Cohen*

FOUNDED 1913. BIANNUAL journal of the Philosophical Society of Great Britain with an international readership made up of members, libraries and specialist booksellers. Wide range of interests, but leaning towards articles that present philosophical investigation which is relevant to the individual and to society in our modern era. Accessible to the non-specialist.

Will consider articles and book reviews. Notes for Contributors available; send s.a.e., e-mail or see website.

As well as short philosophical papers, will accept:

News about lectures, conventions, philosophy groups. Ethical issues in the news. Maximum 1000 words.

Reviews of philosophy books (maximum 600 words); discussion articles of individual philosophers and their published works (maximum 2000 words).

Miscellaneous items, including graphics, of philosophical interest and/or merit.

Payment Free copies.

Piano

241 Shaftesbury Avenue, London WC2H 8TF
☎020 7333 1724 Fax 020 7333 1736
Email pianomagazine@mail.com
Website www.rhinegold.co.uk
Owner *Rhinegold Publishing*
Editor *Jeremy Siepmann*
Deputy Editor *Joanna Sallnow*
Circulation 11,000

FOUNDED 1993. BI-MONTHLY magazine containing features, profiles, technical information, news, reviews of interest to those with a serious amateur or professional concern with pianos or their playing. No unsolicited material. Approach with ideas in writing only.

Picture Postcard Monthly

15 Debdale Lane, Keyworth, Nottingham NG12 5HT
☎0115 937 4079 Fax 0115 937 6197
Email reflections@argonet.co.uk
Website www.postcardcollecting.co.uk
Owners *Brian & Mary Lund*
   Editor *Brian Lund*
Circulation 4000

FOUNDED 1978. MONTHLY. News, views, clubs, diary of fairs, sales, auctions, and well-researched postcard-related articles. Might be interested in general articles supported by postcards. Unsolicited mss welcome. Approach by phone or in writing with ideas.

Pilot

Archant Specialist, The Mill, Bearwalden Business Park, Wendens Ambo, Saffron Walden, Essex CB11 4GB
☎01799 544200 Fax 01799 544201
Email dave.calderwood@pilotweb.co.uk
Website www.pilotweb.co.uk
Owner *Archant Specialist plc*

Editor-in-Chief *Dave Calderwood*
Deputy Editor *Nick Bloom*
Circulation 22,308

FOUNDED 1968. MONTHLY magazine for private plane pilots. Much of the magazine is written by outside contributors – mostly regulars. Unsolicited mss welcome but ideas in writing preferred. Perusal of any issue of the magazine will reveal the type of material bought. 700 words of 'Advice to would-be contributors' sent on receipt of s.a.e. (mark envelope 'Advice'), or see the website for details.

Features Many articles are unsolicited personal experiences/travel accounts from pilots of private planes; good photo coverage is very important. Maximum 5000 words. *Payment* £30 for a photo with caption, £125 for article, £150–400 for a travel story.

News Contributions need to be as short as possible. See *Pilot Notes* and *Old-Timers* in the magazine.

Pink Paper

2nd Floor, Medius House, 63–69 New Oxford Street, London WC1A 1DG
☎020 7845 4300 Fax 020 7845 4309
Email editorial@pinkpaper.com
Editor *Tristan Reid-Smith*
Circulation 55,000

FOUNDED 1987. WEEKLY. Only national newspaper for lesbians and gay men covering politics, social issues, health, the arts and all areas of concern to lesbian/gay people. Unsolicited mss welcome. Initial approach by post with an idea preferred. Interested in profiles, reviews, in-depth features and short news pieces.

Payment by arrangement.

Planet: The Welsh Internationalist
See **Planet** under **Small Presses**

PN Review
See under **Poetry Magazines**

Poetry Ireland Review
See under **Poetry Magazines**

Poetry Review
See under **Poetry Magazines**

Poetry Scotland
See under **Poetry Magazines**

Poetry Wales
See under **Poetry Magazines**

Pony

D.J. Murphy (Publishers) Ltd, Haslemere House, Lower Street, Haslemere, Surrey GU27 2PE
☎01428 651551 Fax 01428 653888
Email pony@djmurphy.co.uk (text only)
Website www.ponymag.com
Owner *D.J. Murphy (Publishers) Ltd*
Editor *Janet Rising*
Assistant Editor *Zoe Cannon*
Circulation 33,074

FOUNDED 1948. Lively MONTHLY aimed at 10–16 year-olds. News, instruction on riding, stable management, veterinary care, interviews. Approach in writing with an idea.
Features welcome. Maximum 900 words.
News Written in-house. Photographs and illustrations (serious/cartoon) welcome.
Payment £65 per 1000 words.

Popular Crafts

Nexus House, Azalea Drive, Swanley, Kent BR8 8HU
☎01322 660070 Fax 01322 616319
Email debbie.moss@nexusmedia.com
Website www.popularcrafts.com
Owner *Highbury-Nexus*
Editor *Debbie Moss*
Circulation 32,000

FOUNDED 1980. MONTHLY. Covers crafts of all kinds. Freelance contributions welcome – copy needs to be lively and interesting. Approach in writing or by e-mail with an outline of idea and photographs.
Features Project-based under the following headings: Homecraft; Needlecraft; Popular Craft; Kidscraft; News and Columns. Any craft-related material including projects to make, with full instructions/patterns supplied in all cases; profiles of crafts people and news of craft group activities or successes by individual persons; articles on collecting crafts; personal experiences and anecdotes. *Payment* on publication.

PR Week

174 Hammersmith Road, London W6 7JP
☎020 8267 4429 Fax 020 8267 4509
Website www.prweek.com
Owner *Haymarket Business Publications Ltd*
Editor *Kate Nicholas*
Circulation 18,200

FOUNDED 1984. WEEKLY. Contributions accepted from experienced journalists. Approach in writing with an idea.
News *Gidon Freeman*
Payment negotiable.

Practical Boat Owner

Westover House, West Quay Road, Poole, Dorset BH15 1JG
☎01202 440820 Fax 01202 440860
Website www.pbo.co.uk
Owner *IPC Media*
Editor *Sarah Norbury*
Circulation 52,800

FOUNDED 1967. MONTHLY magazine of practical information for cruising boat owners. Receives about 1500 mss per year. Interested in hard facts about gear, equipment, pilotage and renovation, etc. from experienced yachtsmen.
Features Technical articles about maintenance, restoration, modifications to cruising boats, power and sail up to 45ft, or reader reports on gear and equipment. European pilotage articles and cruising guides. Approach in writing with synopsis in the first instance.
Payment negotiable.

Practical Caravan

60 Waldegrave Road, Teddington, Middlesex TW11 8LG
☎020 8267 5629 Fax 020 8267 5725
Email practical.caravan@haynet.com
Website www.practicalcaravan.com
Owner *Haymarket Magazines Ltd*
Editor *Carl Rodgerson*
Circulation 47,037

FOUNDED 1967. MONTHLY. Contains caravan reviews, travel features, investigations, products, park reviews. Unsolicited mss welcome on travel relevant only to caravanning/touring vans. No motorcaravan or static van stories. Approach with ideas by phone or letter.
Features Must refer to caravanning, towing. Written in friendly, chatty manner. Features with pictures/transparencies welcome but not essential. Maximum length 2000 words. *Payment* negotiable.

Practical Fishkeeping

Bretton Court, Bretton, Peterborough, Cambridgeshire PE3 8DZ
☎01733 264666 Fax 01733 465246
Email karen.youngs@emap.com
Owner *Emap Active Publications Ltd*
Editor *Karen Youngs*
Circulation 25,000

MONTHLY. Practical articles on all aspects of fishkeeping. Unsolicited mss welcome. Approach in writing with ideas. Quality photographs of fish always welcome. No fiction or verse.

Practical Parenting

IPC Media Ltd., King's Reach Tower, Stamford Street, London SE1 9LS
☎020 7261 5058 Fax 020 7261 6542

Owner *IPC Media*
Editor-in-Chief *Sara Pates*
Circulation 56,501

FOUNDED 1987. MONTHLY. Practical advice on pregnancy, birth, babycare and childcare, 0–3 years. Submit ideas in writing with synopsis or send mss on spec. Interested in feature articles of up to 3000 words in length, and in readers' experiences/personal viewpoint pieces of between 750–1000 words. All material must be written for the magazine's specifically targeted audience and in-house style. *Payment* negotiable.

Practical Photography

Bretton Court, Bretton, Peterborough, Cambridgeshire PE3 8DZ
☎01733 264666 Fax 01733 465246
Email practical.photography@emap.com

Owner *Emap Active Publications Ltd*
Editor *William Cheung*

THIRTEEN ISSUES YEARLY All types of photography, particularly technique-orientated pictures. No unsolicited mss. Preliminary approach may be made by e-mail. Always interested in new, especially unusual, ideas.

Features Anything relevant to the world of photography, but not 'the sort of feature produced by staff writers'. Features on technology, digital imaging techniques and humour are three areas worth exploring. Bear in mind that there is a three-month lead-in time. Maximum 2000 words.

Payment varies.

Practical Wireless

Arrowsmith Court, Station Approach, Broadstone, Dorset BH18 8PW
☎01202 659910 Fax 01202 659950
Email <name>@pwpublishing.ltd.uk
Website www.pwpublishing.ltd.uk

Owner *P.W. Publishing*
Editor *Rob Mannion*
Circulation 20,000

FOUNDED 1932. MONTHLY. News and features relating to amateur radio, radio construction and radio communications. Unsolicited mss welcome. Author's guidelines available (send s.a.e.). Approach by phone or e-mail with ideas in the first instance. Only interested in hearing from people with a thorough knowledge of radio. Copy (typed only) should be supported where possible by artwork, either illustrations, diagrams or photographs.

Payment £54–70 per page.

Practical Woodworking

Nexus Media, Nexus House, Azalea Drive, Swanley, Kent BR8 8HU
☎0101923 286421 Fax 01332 616319
Email practical.woodworking@ nexusmedia.com
Website www.getwoodworking.com

Owner *Nexus Media Ltd*
Editor *Mark Chisholm*

FOUNDED 1965. MONTHLY. Contains articles relating to woodworking – projects, techniques, new products, tips, letters, etc. Unsolicited mss welcome. No fiction. Approach with ideas in writing, by phone or e-mail.

Features Projects, techniques, etc. *Payment* £60–75 per published page.

Prediction

Focus House, Dingwall Avenue, Croydon, Surrey CR9 2TA
☎020 8774 0600 Fax 020 8774 0939
Website www.predictionmagazine.co.uk

Owner *IPC Media*
Editor *Tania Ahsan*
Circulation 35,000

FOUNDED 1936. MONTHLY. Covering astrology and mind, body, spirit topics. Unsolicited material in these areas welcome (about 200–300 mss received every year). Writers' guidelines available on request.

Astrology Pieces should be practical and of general interest. Charts and astro data should accompany them, especially if profiles.

Features Articles on divination, shamanism, alternative healing, psychics and other supernatural phenonema considered. Please read a recent copy of the magazine before sending unsolicited material.

Pregnacy & Birth

Greater London House, Hampstead Road, London NW1 7EJ
☎020 7347 1885 Fax 020 7347 1888
Email lucy.dimbylow@emap.com

Owner *Emap Esprit*
Editor *Elena Dalrymple*
Circulation 53,700

MONTHLY magazine covering all aspects of pregnancy from health to fashion. Regularly commissions features from health journalists. Freelancers should approach by post in the first instance. *Payment* varies.

<

Press Gazette

Quantum House, 19 Scarbrook Road, Croydon, Surrey CR9 1LX
☎020 8565 4200   Fax 020 8565 4395
Email pged@pressgazette.co.uk
Owner *Quantum*
Editor *Ian Reeves*
Deputy Editor *Jon Slattery*
Circulation 9500

WEEKLY magazine for all journalists – in regional and national newspapers, magazines, broadcasting and online – containing news, features and analysis of all areas of journalism, print and broadcasting. Unsolicited mss welcome; interested in profiles of magazines, broadcasting companies and news agencies, personality profiles, technical and current affairs relating to the world of journalism. Approach with ideas by phone, e-mail, fax or in writing.

Pride

Hamilton House, 55 Battersea Bridge Road, London SW11 3AX
☎020 7228 3110   Fax 020 7228 3129
Email info@pride.com
Owner *Carl Cushnie Junior*
Editor *Amina Taylor*
Circulation 40,000

FOUNDED 1991. MONTHLY lifestyle magazine for Black women with features, beauty, arts and fashion. Approach in writing or by e-mail with ideas.

Features Issues pertaining to the Black community. 'Ideas and solicited mss are welcomed from new freelancers.' Maximum 2000 words. **Fiction** Publishes the occasional short story. Maximum 3000 words. **Health, Beauty and Lifestyle** *Sherry Dickson* Freelancers used for short features. Maximum 1000 words.

Prima

National Magazine House, 72 Broadwick Street, London W1F 9EP
☎020 7439 5000
Email prima@natmags.co.uk
Website www.natmags.co.uk
Owner *National Magazine Company*
Editor *Maire Fahey*
Circulation 325,042

FOUNDED 1986. MONTHLY women's magazine.

Features Coordinator *Ruth Devine* Mostly practical and written by specialists, or commissioned from known freelancers. Unsolicited mss not welcome.

Private Eye

6 Carlisle Street, London W1D 3BN
☎020 7437 4017   Fax 020 7437 0705
Email strobes@private-eye.co.uk
Owner *Pressdram*
Editor *Ian Hislop*
Circulation 201,299

FOUNDED 1961. FORTNIGHTLY satirical and investigative magazine. Prospective contributors are best advised to approach the editor in writing. News stories and feature ideas are always welcome, as are cartoons. All jokes written in-house. *Payment* in all cases is 'not great', and length of piece varies as appropriate.

Professional Nurse

Emap Healthcare, Greather London House, Hampstead Road, London NW1 7EJ
☎020 7874 0385   Fax 020 7874 0386
Email pn@emap.com
Owner *Emap Healthcare*
Editor *Carolyn Scott*
Deputy Editor *Amanda Clark*
Circulation 21,000

MONTHLY magazine offering clinical papers, research, opinion and reviews for nurses working in hospitals and in the community.

Features Articles about the health service written by nurses preferably. Approach deputy editor by e-mail. Max. 1500 words. *Payment* £50.

Clinical Papers written by nurses. Approach editor by e-mail. Maximum 3000 words. *Payment* £75.

Prospect

2 Bloomsbury Square, London WC1A 2AQ
☎020 7255 1344 (editorial)/020 7255 1281 (publishing)   Fax 020 7255 1279
Email editorial@prospect-magazine.co.uk *or* publishing@prospect-magazine.co.uk
Website www.prospect-magazine.co.uk
Owner *Prospect Publishing Limited*
Editor *David Goodhart*
Circulation 20,500

FOUNDED 1995. MONTHLY. Essays, reviews and research on current/international affairs and cultural issues. No news features. Unsolicited contributions welcome, although more useful to approach in writing with ideas in the first instance.

Psychic News

The Coach House, Stansted Hall, Stansted, Essex CM24 8UD
☎01279 817050   Fax 01279 817051

Email pn@snu.org.uk
Website www.snu.org.uk
Owner *Psychic Press 1995 Ltd*
Editor *Lyn Guest de Swarte*
Circulation 40,000

FOUNDED 1932. *Psychic News* is the world's only WEEKLY spiritualist newspaper. It covers subjects such as psychic research, hauntings, ghosts, poltergeists, spiritual healing, survival after death, and paranormal gifts. Unsolicited material considered.

Publishing News
39 Store Street, London WC1E 7DS
☎020 7692 2900 Fax 020 7419 2111
Email mailbox@publishingnews.co.uk
Website www.publishingnews.co.uk

Editor *To be appointed*

WEEKLY newspaper of the book trade. Hardback and paperback reviews and extensive listings of new paperbacks and hardbacks. Interviews with leading personalities in the trade, authors, agents and features on specialist book areas.

Q
Mappin House, 4 Winsley Street, London W1W 8HF
☎020 7436 1515 Fax 020 7312 8247
Website www.q4music.com
Owner *Emap Performance*
Editor *Paul Rees*
Circulation 180,215

FOUNDED 1986. THIRTEEN ISSUES YEARLY. Glossy aimed at educated popular music enthusiasts of all ages. Few opportunities for freelance writers. Unsolicited mss are strongly discouraged. Prospective contributors should approach in writing only.

Quartos Magazine
See **The New Writer**

QWF Magazine
PO Box 1768, Rugby CV21 4ZA
☎01788 334302 Fax 01788 334702
Email jo@qwfmagazine.co.uk
Website www.qwfmagazine.co.uk

Editor *Jo Good*

BI-MONTHLY small press magazine. FOUNDED in 1994, as a showcase for the best in women's short story writing – original and thought-provoking. Only considers stories that are previously unpublished and of less than 4000 words; articles must be less than 1000 words and of interest to the writer. Include covering letter,

s.a.e. and brief biography with mss. Also runs script appraisal service and regular short story competitions. For further information and detailed guidelines for contributors please access the website or contact the editor at the address above.

Racecar Engineering
Focus House, Dingwall Avenue, Croydon CR9 2TA
☎020 8774 0946 Fax 020 8774 0935
Email racecar@ipcmedia.com
Website www.racecar-engineering.co.uk
Owner *IPC Media*
Editor *Charles Armstrong-Wilson*
Deputy Editor *Gemma Briggs*
Circulation 15,000

FOUNDED 1990. MONTHLY. In-depth features on motorsport technology plus news and products. Interested in receiving news and features from freelancers. **Features** Informed insight into current motorsport technology. 3000 words maximum. **News** New cars, products or business news relevant to motorsport. No items on road cars or racing drivers. 500 words maximum. Call or e-mail to discuss proposal.

Racing Post (incorporating The Sporting Life)
1 Canada Square, Canary Wharf, London E14 5AP
☎020 7293 3000 Fax 020 7293 3758
Email editor@racingpost.co.uk
Website www.racingpost.co.uk
Owner *Trinity Mirror Plc*
Editor *Chris Smith*

FOUNDED 1986. DAILY horse racing paper with some general sport. In 1998, following an agreement between the owners of *The Sporting Life* and the *Racing Post*, the two papers merged.

Radio Times
80 Wood Lane, London W12 0TT
☎020 8433 3400 Fax 020 8433 3160
Email radio.times@bbc.co.uk
Website www.radiotimes.com
Owner *BBC Worldwide Limited*
Editor *Jill Hudson*
Circulation 1.16 million

WEEKLY. UK's leading broadcast listings magazine. The majority of material is provided by freelance and retained writers, but the topicality of the pieces means close consultation with editors is essential. Very unlikely to use unsolicited material. Detailed BBC, ITV, Channel

4, Channel 5 and satellite television and radio listings are accompanied by feature material relevant to the week's output.
Payment by arrangement.

Rail
Bretton Court, Bretton, Peterborough, Cambridgeshire PE3 8DZ
☎01733 264666 Fax 01733 282720

Owner *Emap Active Publications Ltd*
Managing Editor *Nigel Harris*
Circulation 30,000

FOUNDED 1981. FORTNIGHTLY magazine dedicated to modern railway. News and features, and topical newsworthy events. Unsolicited mss welcome. Approach by phone with ideas. Not interested in personal journey reminiscences. No fiction.

Features By arrangement with the editor. All modern railway British subjects considered. Maximum 2000 words. *Payment* varies/negotiable.

News Any news item welcome. Maximum 500 words. *Payment* varies (up to £100 per 1000 words).

Railway Gazette International
Quadrant House, Sutton, Surrey SM2 5AS
☎020 8652 8608 Fax 020 8652 3738
Website www.railwaygazette.com

Owner *Reed Business Information*
Editor *Murray Hughes*

FOUNDED 1835. MONTHLY magazine written for senior railway managers and engineers worldwide. 'No material for railway enthusiast publications.' Telephone to discuss ideas in the first instance.

The Railway Magazine
IPC Media Ltd., King's Reach Tower, Stamford Street, London SE1 9LS
☎020 7261 5533/5821 Fax 020 7261 5269
Email railway@ipcmedia.com
Website www.ipcmedia.com

Owner *IPC Media*
Editor *Nick Pigott*
Circulation 33,132

FOUNDED 1897. MONTHLY. Articles, photos and short news stories of a topical nature, covering modern railways, steam preservation and railway history welcome. Maximum 2000 words, with sketch maps of routes, etc., where appropriate. Unsolicited mss welcome. No poetry.
Payment negotiable.

The Rambler
2nd Floor, Camelford House, 87–90 Albert Embankment, London SE1 7TW
☎020 7339 8500 Fax 020 7339 8501
Email ramblers@london.ramblers.org.uk

Owner *Ramblers' Association*
Editor *Christopher Sparrow*
Circulation 130,000

QUARTERLY. Official magazine of the Ramblers' Association, available to members only. Unsolicited mss welcome. S.a.e. required for return.

Features Freelance features are invited on any aspect of walking in Britain. Length 450–650 words, preferably with good photographs. No general travel articles.

Reader's Digest
11 Westferry Circus, Canary Wharf, London E14 4HE
☎020 7715 8000 Fax 020 7715 8716
Website www.readersdigest.co.uk

Owner *Reader's Digest Association Ltd*
Editor-in-Chief *Katherine Walker*
Circulation 1 million

Although in theory, a good market for general interest features of around 2500 words very few are ever accepted. However, 'a tiny proportion' comes from freelance writers, all of which are specially commissioned. Opportunities exist for short humorous contributions to regular features – 'Life's Like That', 'Humour in Uniform'. Issues a helpful booklet called 'Writing for Reader's Digest', available by post at £4.50.
Payment up to £200.

The Reader
Reader Office, 19 Abercromby Square, Liverpool L69 7ZG
Email readers@thereader.co.uk
Website www.thereader.co.uk

Editor *Jane Davis*
Circulation 1200

FOUNDED 1997. BIANNUAL. Poetry, short fiction, literary articles and essays, thought, reviews, recommendations. Contributions from internationally lauded and new voices. Welcomes articles/essays about reading, maximum 2000 words. *Payment* up to £50. Recommendations for good reading, maximum 1000 words. *Payment* £30 approx. Short stories, maximum 2500 words. *Payment* £50 approx. No theoretical style literary discourses. Approach in writing.

Real Countryside
The Old Town Hall, 367 Kennington Road, London SE1 4PT

☎020 7582 5432   Fax 020 7793 8484
Owner *Countryside Alliance*
Editors *Nigel Henson, Henny Goddard*
Circulation 60,000

FOUNDED 1996. QUARTERLY magazine on country sports and conservation issues. No unsolicited mss.

Record Collector
43–45 St Mary's Road, Ealing, London W5 5RQ
☎020 8579 1082   Fax 020 8566 2024
Email andy.davis@dpgmags.co.uk
Website www.recordcollectormag.com
Owner *Diamond Publishing Ltd*
Editor *Andy Davis*

FOUNDED 1979. MONTHLY. Detailed, well-researched articles welcome on any aspect of record collecting or any collectable artist in the field of popular music (1950s–1990s), with complete discographies where appropriate. Unsolicited mss welcome. Approach with ideas by phone or e-mail. *Payment* negotiable.

Red
16–18 Berners Street, London W1T 3LN
☎020 7664 6506   Fax 020 7664 6522
Email ruth.adams@hf-uk.com
Website www.redmagazine.co.uk
Owner *Hachette Filipacchi UK Ltd*
Editor *Trish Halpin*
Circulation 192,005

FOUNDED 1998. MONTHLY magazine aimed at the 30–something woman. Will consider ideas sent in 'on spec' but tends to rely on regular contributors.

Report
ATL, 7 Northumberland Street, London WC2N 5RD
☎020 7930 6441   Fax 020 7782 1618
Owner *Association of Teachers and Lecturers*
Editor *Heather Pinnell*
Circulation 160,000

FOUNDED 1978. TEN ISSUES YEARLY during academic terms. Contributions welcome. All submissions should go directly to the editor. Articles should be no more than 800 words and must be of practical interest to the classroom teacher and F.E. lecturers.

Right Now!
PO Box 2085, London W1A 5SX
☎0845 601 3243   Fax 0845 601 3243
Email rightnow@compuserve.com
Website www.right-now.org
Owner *Right Now! Press Ltd*
Editor *Derek Turner*
Circulation 3000

FOUNDED 1993. QUARTERLY right-wing conservative commentary. Welcomes well-documented disputations, news stories and features about British heritage ('the more politically incorrect, the better!'). No fiction or poems. Initial approach in writing.
   No payment.

Rugby World
IPC Media Ltd., 23rd Floor, King's Reach Tower, Stamford Street, London SE1 9LS
☎020 7261 6830   Fax 020 7261 5419
Website www.rugbyworld.com
Owner *IPC Media*
Editor *Paul Morgan*
Circulation 38,500

FOUNDED 1960. MONTHLY. Features of special rugby interest only. Unsolicited contributions welcome but s.a.e. essential for return of material. Prior approach by phone or in writing preferred.

Runner's World
7–10 Chandos Street, London W1M 0AD
☎020 7291 6000   Fax 020 7291 6080
Email rwedit@rodale.co.uk
Website www.runnersworld.co.uk
Owner *Rodale Press*
Editor *Steven Seaton*
Circulation 561,208

FOUNDED 1979. MONTHLY magazine giving practical advice on all areas of distance running including products and training, travel features, news and cross-training advice. Personal running-related articles, famous people who run or off-beat travel articles are welcome. No elite athlete or training articles. Approach with ideas in writing in the first instance.

Running Fitness
2nd Floor, Arcade Chambers, Westgate Arcade, Peterborough, Cambridgeshire PE1 1PY
☎01733 347559   Fax 01733 352749
Website www.running-fitness.com
Owner *Kelsey Publishing*
Editor *Paul Larkins*
Circulation 26,000

FOUNDED 1985. MONTHLY. Instructional articles on running, fitness, and lifestyle, plus running-related activities and health.

Features Specialist knowledge an advantage. Opportunities are wide, but approach with ideas in first instance.

News Opportunities for people stories, especially if backed up by photographs.

Sable
See **SAKS Publications** under **Small Presses**

Safeway The Magazine
Redwood, 7 Saint Martin's Place, London WC2N 4HA
☎020 7747 0788 Fax 020 7747 0799
Editor *Jennifer Newton*
Circulation 1.8 million
FOUNDED 1996. MONTHLY in-store magazine covering food and recipes, beauty, health, shopping, gardens, travel and features. Regular freelancers are employed and although outside material is rarely used ideas will be considered for beauty, health, travel and features. Approach in writing in the first instance.

Saga Magazine
Saga Publishing Ltd, The Saga Building, Enbrook Park, Folkstone, Kent CT20 3SE
☎01303 771523 Fax 01303 776699
Website www.saga.co.uk
Owner *Saga Publishing Ltd*
Editor *Emma Soames*
Circulation 1.19 million
FOUNDED 1984. MONTHLY magazine that sets out to celebrate the role of older people in society, reflecting their achievements, promoting their skills, protecting their interests, and campaigning on their behalf. A warm personal approach, addressing the readership in an upbeat and positive manner. It has a hard core of celebrated commentators/writers (e.g. Keith Waterhouse, Alexander Chancellor, Angela Rippon) as regular contributors. Articles mostly commissioned or written in-house but exclusive celebrity interviews welcome if appropriate/relevant. Length 1000–1200 words (maximum 1600).

Sailing Today
4 Chapel Row, Bath BA1 1HN
☎01225 470074 Fax 01225 313325
Email feedback@sailingtoday.co.uk
Owner *Madforsport Ltd*
Editor *John Goode*
FOUNDED 1997. MONTHLY practical magazine for cruising sailors. *Sailing Today* covers owning and buying a boat, equipment and products for sailing and is about improving readers' skills, boat maintenance and product tests. Most articles are commissioned but will consider practical features and cruise stories with photos. Approach by telephone or in writing in the first instance.

Sainsbury's The Magazine
20 Upper Ground, London SE1 9PD
☎020 7633 0266 Fax 020 7401 9423
Owner *New Crane Publishing*
Editor *Sue Robinson*
Consultant Food Editor *Delia Smith*
Circulation 340,017
FOUNDED 1993. MONTHLY featuring a main core of food and cookery with features, health, beauty, fashion, home, gardening and news. No unsolicited mss. Approach in writing with ideas only in the first instance.

The Salisbury Review
33 Canonbury Park South, London N1 2JW
☎020 7226 7791 Fax 020 7354 0383
Email salisbury-review@easynet.co.uk
Website www.salisbury-review.co.uk
Managing Editor *Merrie Cave*
Consulting Editors *Roger Scruton, Sir Richard Body, Dennis O'Keeffe*
Circulation 1700
FOUNDED 1982. QUARTERLY magazine of conservative thought. Editorials and features from a right-wing viewpoint. Unsolicited material welcome.
Features Maximum 4000 words.
Reviews Maximum 1000 words.
No payment.

Scotland in Trust
28 Charlotte Square, Edinburgh EH2 4ET
☎0131 243 9300 Fax 0131 243 9397
Email igale@nts.org.uk
Owner *National Trust for Scotland*
Editor *Iain Gale*
Circulation 138,878
FOUNDED 1983. THREE ISSUES YEARLY. Magazine containing heritage/conservation features. No unsolicited mss.

Scotland on Sunday Magazine
See under **National Newspapers (Scotland on Sunday)**

The Scots Magazine
D.C. Thomson & Co., 2 Albert Square, Dundee DD1 9QJ
☎01382 223131 Fax 01382 322214
Email mail@scotsmagazine.com

Website www.scotsmagazine.com
Owner *D.C. Thomson & Co. Ltd*
Editor *John Methven*
Circulation 55,000

FOUNDED 1739. MONTHLY. Covers a wide field of Scottish interests ranging from personalities to wildlife, climbing, reminiscence, history and folklore. Outside contributions welcome; 'staff delighted to discuss in advance by letter or e-mail'.

The Scottish Farmer

SMG Magazines, 200 Renfield Street, Glasgow G2 3PR
☎0141 302 7700 Fax 0141 302 7799
Email <firstname>.<lastname>@smg.plc.uk
Owner *SMG Magazines*
Editor *Alasdair Fletcher*
Circulation 22,000

FOUNDED 1893. WEEKLY. Farmer's magazine covering most aspects of Scottish agriculture. Unsolicited mss welcome. Approach with ideas in writing, by fax or e-mail.

Features *Alasdair Fletcher* Technical articles on agriculture or farming units. 1000–2000 words.

News *John Duckworth* Factual news about farming developments, political, personal and technological. Maximum 800 words.

Weekend Family Pages Rural and craft topics.

Scottish Field

Special Publications, Craigcrook Castle, Craigcrook Road, Edinburgh EH4 3PE
☎0131 312 4550 Fax 0131 312 4551
Email editor@scottishfield.co.uk
Owner *Oban Times*
Editor *Archie Mackenzie*

FOUNDED 1903. MONTHLY. Scotland's quality lifestyle magazine. Unsolicited mss welcome but writers should study the magazine first.

Features Articles of general interest on Scotland and Scots abroad with good photographs or, preferably, colour slides. Approx 1000 words.

Payment negotiable.

Scottish Home & Country

42A Heriot Row, Edinburgh EH3 6ES
☎0131 225 1724 Fax 0131 225 8129
Email magazine@swri.demon.co.uk
Owner *Scottish Women's Rural Institutes*
Editor *Liz Ferguson*
Circulation 12,000

FOUNDED 1924. MONTHLY. Scottish or rural-related issues, health, travel and general interest. Unsolicited mss welcome. Commissions are rare and tend to go to established contributors only.

Scottish Rugby Magazine

First Press Publishing, 1 Central Quay, Glasgow G3 8DA
☎0141 309 1400 Fax 0141 248 1099
Email editor@scottishrugby.co.uk
Senior Editor *Alex Macleod*
Circulation 19,200

FOUNDED 1990. MONTHLY. Features, club profiles, etc. Approach with ideas by e-mail or in writing.

ScottishGolf

ScottishGolf, Gateway East, Technology Park, Dundee DD2 1SW
☎01382 429084 Fax 01382 429001
Email editor@scottishgolf.com
Website www.scottishgolf.com
Owner *ScottishGolf*
Editor *Martin Vousden*
Circulation 40,000

FOUNDED mid-1980s. MONTHLY (March to November). Features and results of Scottish and world golf. No unsolicited mss. Approach in writing with ideas.

Scouting Magazine

Gilwell House, Gilwell Park, Chingford, London E4 7QW
☎020 8433 7100 Fax 020 8433 7103
Email scouting.magazine@scout.org.uk
Website www.scoutbase.org.uk *or* www.scouts.org.uk
Owner *The Scout Association*
Editor *Anna Sorensen*
Circulation 20,000+

MONTHLY magazine for adults connected to or interested in the Scout Movement. Interested in Scouting-related submissions only.

Payment by negotiation.

Screen

Gilmorehill Centre for Theatre, Film and Television, University of Glasgow, Glasgow G12 8QQ
☎0141 330 5035 Fax 0141 330 3515
Email screen@arts.gla.ac.uk
Website www.screen.arts.gla.ac.uk
Publisher *Oxford University Press*
Editors *Annette Kuhn, John Caughie, Simon Frith, Karen Lury, Jackie Stacey, Sarah Street*

Editorial Assistant *Caroline Beven*
Circulation 1200

QUARTERLY refereed academic journal of film and television studies for a readership ranging from undergraduates to screen studies academics and media professionals. There are no specific qualifications for acceptance of articles. Straightforward film reviews are not normally published. Check the magazine's style and market in the first instance.

Screen International
33–39 Bowling Green Lane, London EC1R 0DA
☎020 7505 8056 Fax 020 7505 8117
Email leo.barraclough@media.emap.com
Website www.screendaily.com
Owner *Emap Communications*
Managing Editor *Leo Barraclough*

International trade paper of the film, video and television industries. Expert freelance writers are occasionally used in all areas. No unsolicited mss. Approach with ideas in writing or by e-mail.
Features *Louise Tutt*
Payment negotiable on NUJ basis.

Screentrade Magazine
Screentrade Media Ltd, PO Box 144, Orpington, Kent BR6 6LZ
☎01689 833117 Fax 01689 833117
Email philip45other@yahoo.co.uk
Owner *Screentrade Media Ltd*
Editor *Philip Turner*
Circulation 3000+

FOUNDED 2002. QUARTERLY journal for British and European exhibitors and film distributors.
Features items on cinema management, technical, cinema building history, nostalgia, showmanship, book reviews and other managerial matters. Also film and producer/director opinions. Some film reviews but no 'film star' interviews. Most contributions are from within the industry. Items on the state of cinema exhibition, film distribution, cinema architecture, interviews with key industry personnel frequently undertaken. 1500–3000 words. **News** Topical items (if substantiated) welcome. Events coverage (e.g. festivals) from an exhibitor's viewpoint preferred.

Scriptwriter Magazine
2 Elliott Square, London NW3 3SU
☎020 7586 4853 Fax 020 7586 4853
Email julian@scriptwritermagazine.com

Website www.scriptwritermagazine.com
Owner *Scriptease Ltd*
Editor *Julian Friedmann*
Circulation 1500

LAUNCHED November 2001. Six issues per year. Magazine for professional scriptwriters covering all aspects of the business and craft of writing for the small and large screen. Interested in serious, in-depth analysis; maximum 1500–3500 words. E-mail with synopsis sample material and c.v.
Payment £20 per 1000 words.

Sea Breezes
Mannin Media Group Ltd, Media House, Cronkbourne, Isle of Man IM4 4SB
☎01624 696566 Fax 01624 661655
Email seabreezes@manninmedia.co.im
Website www.seabreezes.co.im
Owner *Print Centres*
Editor *Captain A.C. Douglas*
Circulation 17,000

FOUNDED 1919. MONTHLY. Covers virtually everything relating to ships and seamen. Unsolicited mss welcome; they should be thoroughly researched and accompanied by relevant photographs. No fiction, poetry, or anything which 'smacks of the romance of the sea'.
Features Factual tales of ships, seamen and the sea, Royal or Merchant Navy, sail or power, nautical history, shipping company histories, epic voyages, etc. Length 1000–4000 words. 'The most readily acceptable work will be that which shows it is clearly the result of first-hand experience or the product of extensive and accurate research.'
Payment £14 per page (about 800 words).

She Magazine
National Magazine House, 72 Broadwick Street, London W1F 9EP
☎020 7439 5000 Fax 020 7312 3981
Website www.natmags.co.uk
Owner *National Magazine Co. Ltd*
Editor *Eve Cameron*
Circulation 183,017

Glossy MONTHLY for the thirty-something woman, addressing her needs as an individual, a partner and a parent. Talks to its readers in an intelligent, humorous and sympathetic way.
Features should be about 1200 words long. Approach with ideas in writing or e-mail **Features Editor** *Cayte Williams* (cayte.williams@natmags.co.uk). No unsolicited material.
Payment negotiable.

Ships Monthly
IPC Country & Leisure Media Ltd,
222 Branston Road, Burton-upon-Trent,
Staffordshire DE14 3BT
☎01283 542721   Fax 01283 546436
Email shipsmonthly@ipcmedia.com

Owner *IPC Country & Leisure Media Ltd*
Editor *Iain Wakefield*
Circulation 22,000

FOUNDED 1966. MONTHLY A4 format magazine for ship enthusiasts and maritime professionals. News, photographs and illustrated articles on all kinds of ships – mercantile and naval, sail and steam, past and present. No yachting. Most articles are commissioned; prospective contributors should telephone in the first instance.

Shoot Monthly Magazine
IPC Media Ltd., King's Reach Tower,
Stamford Street, London SE1 9LS
☎020 7261 6287   Fax 020 7261 6019
Email shoot@ipcmedia.com

Owner *IPC Media*
Editor *Colin Mitchell*
Circulation 30,000

FOUNDED 1969. MONTHLY football magazine. No unsolicited mss. Present ideas for news, features or colour photo-features to the editor by letter or e-mail.
Features Hard-hitting, topical and off-beat.
News Items welcome, especially exclusive gossip and transfer speculation.
Payment negotiable.

Shooting and Conservation
BASC, Marford Mill, Rossett, Wrexham
LL12 0HL
☎01244 573000   Fax 01244 573001

Owner *The British Association for Shooting and Conservation (BASC)*
Editor *Jeffrey Olstead*
Circulation 120,000

SIX ISSUES PER YEAR. Good articles and stories on shooting, conservation and related areas may be considered although most material is produced in-house. Maximum 1500 words.
Payment negotiable.

Shooting Times & Country Magazine
IPC Media Ltd., King's Reach Tower,
Stamford Street, London SE1 9LS
☎020 7261 6180   Fax 020 7261 7179
Email robert_gray@ipcmedia.com

Owner *IPC Media*
Editor *Robert Gray*
Circulation 27,040

FOUNDED 1882. WEEKLY. Covers shooting, fishing and related countryside topics. Unsolicited mss considered.
Payment negotiable.

Shout Magazine
D.C. Thomson & Co., Albert Square,
Dundee, Tayside DD1 9QJ
☎01382 223131   Fax 01382 200880
Email shout@dcthomson.co.uk

Owner *D.C. Thomson Publishers*
Editor *Maria T. Welch*
Circulation 111,069

FOUNDED 1993. FORTNIGHTLY. Pop music, quizzes, emotional, beauty, fashion, soap features.
Fiction *Maria Welch* Supernatural/spooky stories welcome. Approach by telephone in the first instance. Maximum 1500 words. *Payment* £100.

Shout!
PO Box YR46, Leeds, West Yorkshire
LS9 6XG
☎0113 248 5700   Fax 0113 295 6097
Email shout.magazine@ntlworld.com
Website www.shout.connectfree.co.uk

Owner/Editor *Mark Michalowski*
Circulation 7000

FOUNDED 1995. MONTHLY lesbian/gay and bisexual news, views, arts and scene for Yorkshire; lgb health and politics. Interested in reviews of Yorkshire lgb events, happenings, news, analysis – 300 to maximum 1000 words. No fiction, fashion or items with no reasonable relevance to Yorkshire and the north.
Payment £40 per 1000 words.

Showing World
The Publishing House, Station Road,
Framlingham, Suffolk IP13 9EE
☎01728 622030   Fax 01728 622931
Email todaymagazine@btopenworld.com

Owner *T.P. Publications*
Editor *Charlotte Knight*
Circulation 3000

FOUNDED 1991. Features every aspect of showing horses and ponies, including natives, miniatures and donkeys. Knowledgeable and how-to-do-it articles welcome. Photos essential.
Payment negotiable.

Shropshire Magazine
77 Wyle Cop, Shrewsbury, Shropshire
SY1 1UT
☎01743 362175
Owner *Shropshire Newspapers Ltd*
Editor *Sarah-Jane Smith*
FOUNDED 1950. MONTHLY. Unsolicited mss welcome but ideas in writing preferred.
Features Personalities, topical items, historical (e.g. family) of Shropshire; also general interest: homes, weddings, antiques, etc. Maximum 1000 words.
Payment negotiable 'but modest'.

Sight & Sound
British Film Institute, 21 Stephen Street, London W1T 1LN
☎020 7255 1444 Fax 020 7436 2327
Website www.bfi.org.uk/sightandsound
Owner *British Film Institute*
Editor *Nick James*
FOUNDED 1932. MONTHLY. Topical and critical articles on international cinema, with regular columns from the USA and Europe. Length 1000–5000 words. Relevant photographs appreciated. Also book, film and video release reviews. Approach in writing with ideas.
Payment by arrangement.

The Sign
See **Hymns Ancient & Modern Ltd** under **UK Publishers**

Ski and Board
The White House, 57–63 Church Road, Wimbledon, London SW19 5SB
☎020 8410 2000 Fax 020 8410 2001
Email s&b@skiclub.co.uk
Website www.skiclub.co.uk
Owner *Ski Club of Great Britain*
Editor *Arnie Wilson*
FOUNDED 1903. FOUR ISSUES YEARLY. Features from established ski/snowboard writers only.

The Skier and Snowboarder Magazine
Mountain Marketing Ltd., PO Box 386, Sevenoaks, Kent TN13 1AQ
☎0845 310 8303 Fax 01732 779266
Email skierandsnowboarder@hotmail.com
Publisher *Mountain Marketing Ltd*
Editor *Frank Baldwin*
Circulation 30,000
Official magazine to the World Ski and Snowboard Association, UK. SEASONAL. From July to May. FIVE ISSUES YEARLY. Outside contributions welcome.
Features Various topics covered, including race reports, resort reports, fashion, equipment update, dry slope, school news, new products, health and safety. Crisp, tight, informative copy of 800 words or less preferred.
News All aspects of skiing news covered.
Payment negotiable.

Slimming
Greater London House, Hampstead Road, London NW1 7EJ
☎020 7347 1854 Fax 020 7347 1863
Email claire.selsby@emap.com
Owner *Emap Esprit*
Editor *Rashmi Madan*
Circulation 106,029
FOUNDED 1969. ELEVEN ISSUES YEARLY. Leading magazine about slimming, diet and health. Opportunities for freelance contributions on general health (diet-related); psychology related to health and fitness; celebrity interviews. It is best to approach with an idea in writing or by e-mail.
Payment negotiable.

Smallholder
Hook House, Wimblington March, Cambridgeshire PE15 0QL
☎01354 741182 Fax 01354 741182
Email edit@smallholder.co.uk
Website www.smallholder.co.uk
Owner *Newsquest*
Editor *Liz Wright*
Circulation 20,000
FOUNDED 1982. MONTHLY. Outside contributions welcome. Send for sample magazine and editorial schedule before submitting anything. Follow up with samples of work to the editor so that style can be assessed for suitability. No poetry or humorous but unfocused personal tales.
Features New writers always welcome, but must have high level of technical expertise – 'not textbook stuff'. Illustrations and photos welcomed and paid for. Length 750–1500 words.
News All agricultural and rural news welcome. Length 200–500 words.
Payment negotiable ('but modest').

Smash Hits
Mappin House, Winsley Street, London W1W 8HF
☎020 7436 1515 Fax 020 7636 5792

Email letters@smashhits.net
Website www.smashhits.net
Owner *Emap Performance*
Editor *Lisa Smosarski*
Circulation 145,174

FOUNDED 1978. FORTNIGHTLY. Top of the mid-teen market. Unsolicited mss are not accepted, but prospective contributors may approach in writing with ideas.

Sneak Magazine

Mappin House, 4 Winsley Street, London W1W 8HF
☎020 7436 1515 Fax 020 7312 8229
Email michelle.garnett@emap.com
Website www.sneakmagazine.com
Owner *EMAP*
Editor *Jennifer Cawthron*
Circulation 100,000

FOUNDED 2002. WEEKLY magazine for teenagers providing gossip and entertainment. Unsolicited material welcome.
Features *Leo Roberts* **News** *Kate Taylor* **Fiction** *Louise Christie.* Approach by e-mail.

Snooker Scene

Cavalier House, 202 Hagley Road, Edgbaston, Birmingham B16 9PQ
☎0121 454 2931 Fax 0121 452 1822
Owner *Everton's News Agency*
Editor *Clive Everton*
Circulation 16,000

FOUNDED 1971. MONTHLY. No unsolicited mss. Approach in writing with an idea.

The Spectator

56 Doughty Street, London WC1N 2LL
☎020 7405 1706 Fax 020 7242 0603
Email editor@spectator.co.uk
Website www.spectator.co.uk
Owner *The Spectator (1828) Ltd*
Editor *Boris Johnson*
Deputy Editor *Stuart Reid*
Circulation 60,776

FOUNDED 1828. WEEKLY political and literary magazine. Prospective contributors should write in the first instance to the relevant editor. Unsolicited mss welcome, but no 'follow up' phone calls, please.
Books *Mark Amory*
Payment nominal.

The Sporting Life

See **Racing Post**

Springboard – Writing To Succeed

8 Landrock Road, London N8 9HP
☎020 8340 8356
Email springboardmag@aol.com
Owner/Editor *Fiona Mallin-Robinson*
Circulation 100

FOUNDED 1990. QUARTERLY. *Springboard* provides articles, news, market information, competition/folio news directed at helping writers to achieve success. Competitions in every issue to encourage new and established writers. Unsolicited short stories and poetry are invited but writers are advised to read the magazine before submitting pieces to the editor. No unsolicited articles please.

Staffordshire Life

The Publishing Centre, Derby Street, Stafford ST16 2DT
☎01785 257700 Fax 01785 253287
Email editor@staffordshirelife.co.uk
Owner *The Staffordshire Newsletter*
Editor *Philip Thurlow-Craig*
Circulation 20,000

FOUNDED 1982. ELEVEN ISSUES YEARLY. Full-colour county magazine devoted to Staffordshire, its surroundings and people. Contributions welcome. Approach in writing with ideas.
Features Maximum 1200 words.
Fashion Copy must be supported by photographs.
Payment NUJ rates.

The Stage (incorporating Television Today)

Stage House, 47 Bermondsey Street, London SE1 3XT
☎020 7403 1818 Fax 020 7357 9287
Email editor@thestage.co.uk
Website www.thestage.co.uk
Owner *The Stage Newspaper Ltd*
Editor *Brian Attwood*
Circulation 41,500

FOUNDED 1880. WEEKLY. No unsolicited mss. Prospective contributors should write with ideas in the first instance.
Features Preference for middle-market, tabloid-style articles. 'Puff pieces', PR plugs and extended production notes will not be considered. Maximum 800 words. Profiles: 1200 words.
News News stories from outside London are always welcome. Maximum 300 words.
Payment £100 per 1000 words.

Stamp Magazine

Focus House, Dingwall Avenue, Croydon
CR9 2TA
☎020 8774 0772 Fax 020 8774 0939
Email steve_fairclough@ipcmedia.com

Owner *IPC Media*
Editor *Steve Fairclough*
Circulation 12,000

FOUNDED 1934. MONTHLY news and features
on the world of stamp collecting from the past
to the present day. Interested in articles by
experts on particular countries or themes such
as subject matter illustrated on stamps – dogs,
politics, etc. Approach in writing.

News *Deborah Lees* News of latest stamp
issues or industry news. Maximum 500 words.

Features *Steve Fairclough* Any features welcome on famous stamps, rarities, postmarks,
postal history, exhibitions, postcards, personal
collections, auctions. Must be illustrated with
colour images ('we can arrange for photography of original stamps'). Maximum 2500
words, or 5000 for two-part expert piece.

Payment negotiable.

Stand Magazine

See under **Poetry Magazines**

Staple

See under **Poetry Magazines**

Steam Railway Magazine

Bretton Court, Bretton, Peterborough,
Cambridgeshire PE3 8DZ
☎01733 264666 Fax 01733 282720
Email steam.railway@emap.com

Owner *Emap Active Limited*
Editor *Tony Streeter*
Circulation 32,255

FOUNDED 1979. FOUR-WEEKLY magazine targeted at all steam enthusiasts interested in the
modern preservation movement. Unsolicited
material welcome. News reports, photographs,
steam-age reminiscences. Approach in writing
or by e-mail.

The Strad

Orpheus Publications, SMG Plc, 3
Waterhouse Square, 138–142 Holborn,
London EC1N 2NY
☎020 7882 1040 Fax 020 7882 1020
Email thestrad@orpheuspublications.com
Website www.thestrad.com

Owner *SMG Plc*
Editor *Naomi Sadler*
Circulation 17,500

FOUNDED 1890. MONTHLY for classical string
musicians, makers and enthusiasts. Unsolicited
mss accepted occasionally 'though acknowl-
edgement/return not guaranteed'.

Features Profiles of string players, teachers,
luthiers and musical instruments, also relevant
research. Maximum 2000 words.

Reviews *Ariane Todes, Naomi Sadler.*
Payment £150 per 1000 words.

Suffolk and Norfolk Life

The Publishing House, Framlingham, Suffolk
IP13 9EE
☎01728 622030 Fax 01728 622031

Owner *Today Magazines Ltd*
Editor *Kevin Davis*
Circulation 17,000

FOUNDED 1989. MONTHLY. General interest,
local stories, historical, personalities, wine,
travel, food. Unsolicited mss welcome.
Approach by phone or in writing with ideas.
Not interested in anything which does not
relate specifically to East Anglia.

Features *Kevin Davis* Maximum 1500 words,
with photos.

News *Kevin Davis* Maximum 1000 words,
with photos.

Special Pages *William Locks* Study the magazine for guidelines. Maximum 1500 words.

Payment £35–50.

Sugar Magazine

17 Berners Street, London W1T 3LN
☎020 7664 6440 Fax 020 7703 3409

Owner *Hachette Filipacchi (UK)*
Editor *To be appointed*
Editorial Director *Lysanne Currie*
Circulation 321,258

FOUNDED 1994. MONTHLY. Everything that
might interest the teenage girl. No unsolicited
mss. Will consider ideas or contacts for real-life
features. No fiction. Approach in writing in
the first instance.

Sunday Post Magazine

See under **National Newspapers (Sunday
Post, Dundee)**

Sunday Times Magazine

See under **National Newspapers (The
Sunday Times)**

SuperBike Magazine

IPC Media, Focus House, Dingwall Avenue,
Croydon, Surrey CR9 2TA
☎020 8774 0600 Fax 020 8774 0951

Website www.ipcmedia.com
Owner *IPC Media*
Publisher *Keith Foster*
Editor *Kenny Pryde*
Circulation 73,122

FOUNDED 1977. MONTHLY. Dedicated to all that is best and most exciting in the world of high-performance motorcycling. Unsolicited mss, synopses and ideas welcome.

Sussex Life

Baskerville Place, 28 Teville Road, Worthing, West Sussex BN11 1UG
☎01903 218719   Fax 01903 820193
Email ian@sussexlife.co.uk
Website www.sussexlife.com

Owner *Archant Life*
Editor *Ian Trevett*
Circulation 42,000

FOUNDED 1965. MONTHLY. Sussex and general interest magazine. Regular supplements on education, fashion, homes and gardens. Interested in investigative, journalistic pieces relevant to the area and celebrity profiles. Unsolicited mss, synopses and ideas in writing welcome. Minimum 500 words.

Swimming Magazine

Harold Fern House, Derby Square, Loughborough, Leicestershire LE11 5AL
☎01509 618766   Fax 01509 618768

Owner *Amateur Swimming Association*
Editor *P. Hassall*
Circulation 20,000

FOUNDED 1923. MONTHLY about competitive swimming and associated subjects. Unsolicited mss welcome.

Features Technical articles on swimming, water polo, diving or synchronised swimming. Length and payment negotiable.

The Tablet

1 King Street Cloisters, Clifton Walk, London W6 0QZ
☎020 8748 8484   Fax 020 8748 1550
Email thetablet@tablet.co.uk
Website www.thetablet.co.uk

Owner *The Tablet Publishing Co Ltd*
Editor *John Wilkins*
Circulation 22,466

FOUNDED 1840. WEEKLY. Quality international Roman Catholic magazine featuring articles — political, social, cultural, theological or spiritual – of interest to concerned Christian laity and clergy. Unsolicited material welcome

(1500 words) if relevant to magazine's style and market. All approaches should be made in writing. *Payment* from about £75.

Take a Break

Academic House, 24–28 Oval Road, London NW1 7DT
☎020 7241 8000   Fax 020 7241 8052
Email tab.features@bauer.co.uk

Owner *H. Bauer Publishing Ltd*
Editor *John Dale*
Circulation 1.15 million

FOUNDED 1990. WEEKLY. True-life feature magazine. Approach with ideas in writing.

News/Features Always on the look-out for good, true-life stories. Maximum 1200 words. *Payment* negotiable.

Fiction Sharp, succinct stories which are well told and often with a twist at the end. All categories, provided it is relevant to the magazine's style and market. Maximum 1000 words. *Payment* negotiable.

Tate – International Arts and Culture

Condé Nast, Vogue House, 1 Hanover Square, London W1S 1JU
☎020 7499 9080   Fax 020 7152 3899
Email tate@condenast.co.uk
Website www.tate.org.uk/magazine

Owner *Condé Nast/Tate*
Editor *Robert Violette*
Circulation 90,000

RELAUNCHED 2002. BI-MONTHLY visual arts magazine aimed at a broad readership with articles ranging from historic to cutting-edge. Interested in reviews and interviews. Please send material by post.

Tatler

Vogue House, Hanover Square, London W1S 1JU
☎020 7499 9080   Fax 020 7409 0451
Website www.tatler.co.uk

Owner *Condé Nast Publications Ltd*
Editor *Geordie Greig*
Circulation 84,018

Up-market glossy from the Condé Nast stable. New writers should send in copies of either published work or unpublished material; writers of promise will be taken up. The magazine works largely on a commission basis: they are unlikely to publish unsolicited features, but will ask writers to work to specific projects.

Features Director *Vassi Chamberlain*

TGO (The Great Outdoors)
SMG Magazines, 200 Renfield Street,
Glasgow G2 3PR
☎0141 302 7700 Fax 0141 331 6948
Email smg.mags@smg.plc.uk

Owner *SMG Ltd*
Editor *Cameron McNeish*
Circulation 22,000

FOUNDED 1978. MONTHLY. Deals with walking, backpacking and wild country topics. Unsolicited mss are welcome.

Features Well-written and illustrated items on relevant topics. Maximum 2500 words. Colour photographs only, please.
News Short topical items (or photographs). Maximum 300 words.
Payment £200–400 for features; £50–100 for news.

that's life!
Academic House, 24–28 Oval Road, London
NW1 7DT
☎020 7241 8000 Fax 020 7241 8008
Email <firstname>.<lastname>@bauer.co.uk

Owner *H. Bauer Publishing Ltd*
Editor *Jo Checkley*
Circulation 597,170

FOUNDED 1995. WEEKLY. True-life stories, puzzles, health, homes, parenting, cookery and fun.
Features *Andreina Cordani* Maximum 1600 words. *Payment* £750.
Fiction *Emma Fabian* 1200 words. *Payment* £300.

The Third Alternative
5 Martins Lane, Witcham, Ely,
Cambridgeshire CB6 2LB
☎01353 777931
Email ttapress@aol.com
Website www.ttapress.com

Owner *TTA Press*
Editor *Andy Cox*

FOUNDED 1993. Quarterly A4 colour magazine of horror, fantasy, science fiction and cross-genre fiction, plus interviews, profiles, comment, cinema and artwork. Publishes talented newcomers alongside famous authors. Unsolicited mss welcome if accompanied by s.a.e. or e-mail address for overseas submissions (no length restriction, but no novels or serialisations). Queries and letters welcome via e-mail but submissions as hard copy only. Potential contributors are advised to study the magazine. Contracts are exchanged upon acceptance; payment is upon publication.

Winner of several British Fantasy Awards. The magazine is supported by **Eastern Arts** and the **Arts Council of England**.

This England
PO Box 52, Cheltenham, Gloucestershire
GL50 1YQ
☎01242 537900 Fax 01242 537901

Owner *This England Ltd*
Editor *Roy Faiers*
Circulation 200,000

FOUNDED 1968. QUARTERLY, with a strong overseas readership. Celebration of England and all things English: famous people, natural beauty, towns and villages, history, traditions, customs and legends, crafts, etc. Generally a rural basis, with the 'Forgetmenots' section publishing readers' recollections and nostalgia. Up to one hundred unsolicited pieces received each week. Unsolicited mss/ideas welcome. Length 250–2000 words. *Payment* £25 per 1000 words.

Time
Brettenham House, Lancaster Place, London
WC2E 7TL
☎020 7499 4080 Fax 020 7322 1259
Email edit-office@timemagazine.com
Website www.timeeurope.com

Owner *AOL Time Warner*
Editor (Europe, Middle East, Africa) *Eric Pooley*
Circulation 597,038 (Europe)

FOUNDED 1923. WEEKLY current affairs and news magazine. There are few opportunities for freelancers on *Time* as almost all the magazine's content is written by staff members from various bureaux around the world. No unsolicited mss.

Time Out
Universal House, 251 Tottenham Court Road, London W1T 7AB
☎020 7813 3000 Fax 020 7813 6001
Website www.timeout.com

Publisher *Lesley Gill*
Editor *Laura Lee Davies*
Circulation 86,000

FOUNDED 1968. WEEKLY magazine of news and entertainment in London.
Features *Jessica Cargill Thompson* 'Usually written by staff writers or commissioned, but it's always worth submitting an idea by post if particularly apt to the magazine.' 1000 words.
Consumer Section *Neil McLennan* Fashion, shopping, travel, design, property. *Payment* negotiable.

The Times Educational Supplement

Admiral House, 66–68 East Smithfield,
London E1W 1BX
☎020 7782 3000 Fax 020 7782 3200
Email editor@tes.co.uk *or*
newsdesk@tes.co.uk *or* friday@tes.co.uk
Website www.tes.co.uk

Owner *News International*
Editor *Bob Doe*
Circulation 120,000

FOUNDED 1910. WEEKLY. New contributors
are welcome and should fax or e-mail ideas on
one sheet of A4 for news, features or reviews to
the editor.

Opinion *Jeremy Sutcliffe* 'Platform': a weekly
slot for a well-informed and cogently argued
viewpoint. Maximum 1200 words. 'Another
Voice': a shorter comment on an issue of the
day by non–education professionals. Maximum
700 words.

Governors *Karen Thornton* Weekly pages
on practical issues for school governors and
managers. Maximum 800 words.

Research Focus *David Budge*

Further Education *Ian Nash* Includes post-
16 education and training in colleges, work and
the wider community. Aimed at everyone
from teachers/lecturers to leaders and opinion
formers in lifelong learning. News, features,
comment and opinion on all aspects of college
life welcome. Length from 350 words (news)
to 1000 maximum (features).

Friday A weekly magazine with *The TES*
which focuses on whole school issues, good
practice, teaching as a career and the work/life
balance:

Features *Sarah Bayliss* Unsolicited features
are rarely accepted but ideas are welcome
accompanied by cuttings and/or c.v. Length
from 1000–2000 words. Strong storylines are
expected.

Books *Geraldine Brennan*
Arts *Heather Neill*
Resources *Yolanda Brooks*

Talkback *Jill Craven* Short, first person
pieces, maximum 650 words, are welcome for
consideration. Humour from teachers is encouraged, especially for the 'Thank God it's
Friday' column.

Online (Computers in Education) *Merlin John*
A magazine devoted to information and com-
munications technology appearing with *The
TES* six times a year.

TES Teacher *Joyce Arnold* The weekly magazine for classroom teachers appearing with *The*

TES focusing on what individual teachers do
in the classroom to teach pupils and subjects.
Specific subject section each week. Maximum
800 words.

Special Issues Occasional pull-out magazines
on topics including newly qualified teachers
(*Fiona Flynn*), business links (*Ian Nash*), school
visits – *Going Places* – (*Yolanda Brooks*).

The Times Educational Supplement Scotland

Scott House, 10 South St Andrew Street,
Edinburgh EH2 2AZ
☎0131 557 1133 Fax 0131 558 1155
Email scoted@tes.co.uk
Website www.tes.co.uk/scotland

Owner *TSL Education Ltd*
Editor *Neil Munro*
Circulation 9000

FOUNDED 1965. WEEKLY. Unsolicited mss welcome.

Features Articles on education in Scotland.
Maximum 1000 words.

News Items on education in Scotland.
Maximum 600 words.

The Times Higher Education Supplement

Admiral House, 66–68 East Smithfield,
London E1W 1BX
☎020 7782 3000 Fax 020 7782 3300
Email editor@thes.co.uk
Website www.thes.co.uk

Owner *News International*
Editor *John O'Leary*
Circulation 26,000

FOUNDED 1971. WEEKLY. Unsolicited mss are
welcome but most articles and almost all book
reviews are commissioned. 'In most cases it is
better to write or e-mail, but in the case of
news stories it is all right to phone.'

Books *Andrew Robinson*
Features *Mandy Garner* Most articles are
commissioned from academics in higher education.

News *Mary Cook* Freelance opportunities
very occasionally.

Science *Steve Farrar*
Science Books *Andrew Robinson*
Foreign *David Jobbins*
Payment by negotiation.

The Times Literary Supplement

Admiral House, 66–68 East Smithfield,
London E1W 1BX
☎020 7782 3000 Fax 020 7782 3100

Website www.the-tls.co.uk
Owner *TSL Education Ltd*
Editor *Peter Stothard*
Circulation 35,000

FOUNDED 1902. WEEKLY review of literature. Contributors should approach in writing and be familiar with the general level of writing in the *TLS*.

Literary Discoveries *Alan Jenkins*
Poems *Mick Imlah*
News News stories and general articles concerned with literature, publishing and new intellectual developments anywhere in the world. Length by arrangement. *Payment* by arrangement.

Titbits

2 Caversham Street, London SW3 4AH
☎020 7351 4995 Fax 020 7351 4995
Owner *Sport Newspapers Ltd*
Editor *James Hughes*
Circulation 150,000

FOUNDED 1895. MONTHLY. Consumer magazine for men covering show business and general interests. Ideas in writing welcome. Maximum 3000 words. News, features, particularly photofeatures (colour), and fiction. Always send letter or telephone first. *Payment* negotiable.

Today's Fishkeeper

TRMG, Winchester Court, 1 Forum Place, Hatfield, Hertfordshire AL10 0RN
☎01707 273999 Fax 01707 269333
Email derek@trmg.co.uk
Website www.trmg.co.uk
Owner *TRMG*
Editor *Derek Lambert*
Circulation 20,000

FOUNDED 1924. MONTHLY. Covers all aspects of aquarium and pondkeeping: conservation, herpetology (study of reptiles and amphibians), news, reviews and aquatic plant culture. Unsolicited mss welcome. Ideas should be submitted in writing or by e-mail first.
Features Good opportunities for writers on any of the above topics or related areas. 1000–1500 words, plus illustrations. **News** Very few opportunities. *Payment* negotiable.

Today's Golfer

Bushfield House, Orton Centre, Peterborough, Cambridgeshire PE2 5UW
☎01733 237111 Fax 01733 288014
Owner *Emap Active Ltd*

Editor *Paul Hamblin*
Associate Editor *John McKenzie*
Circulation 101,000

FOUNDED 1988. MONTHLY. Golf instruction, features, player profiles and news. Most features written in-house but unsolicited mss will be considered. Approach in writing with ideas. Not interested in instruction material from outside contributors.
Features/News *Kevin Brown* Opinion, player profiles and general golf-related features.

Top of the Pops Magazine

Room A1136, Woodlands, 80 Wood Lane, London W12 0TT
☎020 8433 3910 Fax 020 8433 2694
Website www.beeb.com/totp
Owner *BBC Worldwide Publishing Ltd*
Editor *Corinna Shaffer*
Circulation 246,241

FOUNDED 1995. MONTHLY teenage pop music magazine with a lighthearted and humorous approach. No unsolicited material apart from pop star interviews.

Total Film

99 Baker Street, London W1U 6FP
☎020 7317 2600 Fax 020 7317 0275
Email totalfilm@futurenet.co.uk
Owner *Future Publishing*
Editor *Matt Mueller*
Circulation 86,000

FOUNDED 1997. MONTHLY reviews-based movie magazine. Interested in ideas for features, not necessarily tied in to specific releases, and humour items. No reviews or interviews with celebrities/directors. Approach by post or e-mail.

Total Vauxhall

A&S Publishing Co. Ltd, 35 St Michaels Square, Gloucester GL1 1HX
☎01452 317790 Fax 01452 415817
Email info@totalvauxhall.co.uk
Website www.totalvauxhall.co.uk
Owner *A&S Publishing Co. Ltd*
Editor *Jon Walsh*
Circulation 20,000

FOUNDED 2001. MONTHLY independent magazine aimed at 18–25 year-old readers focusing on the Vauxhall brand. Articles on new motor sport and mostly modified cars, also Opel, Holden and other GM related products. Ideas for features and news welcome. No fiction. Phone beforehand for style, word count, timing and other requirements. *Payment* negotiable.

Traditional Woodworking
151 Station Street, Burton on Trent,
Staffordshire DE14 1BG
☎01283 742950 Fax 01283 742957
Email enquiries@twonline.co.uk

Owner *Waterways World*
Editor *Alison Bell*

FOUNDED 1988. MONTHLY. Features workshop projects, techniques, reviews of the latest woodworking tools and equipment, general articles on woodworking and furniture making. Supplements: *Power Tool Quarterly* and *Power Tool Guide*.

Features Technical features and furniture projects welcome. The latter must include drawings and cutting lists. A photograph of the piece is required before commissioning. Approach in writing in the first instance. *Payment* negotiable.

Trail
Bretton Court, Bretton, Peterborough,
Cambridgeshire PE3 8DZ
☎01733 264666 Fax 01733 282653
Website www.trailmag.com

Owner *Emap Active Publishing Ltd*
Editor *Guy Proctor*
Circulation 36,450

FOUNDED 1990. MONTHLY. Gear reports, where to walk and practical advice for the hillwalker and long distance walker. Inspirational reads on people and outdoor/walking issues. Health, fitness and injury prevention for high level walkers and outdoor lovers. Approach by phone or in writing in the first instance.

Features *Matthew Swaine* Very limited requirement for overseas articles, 'written to our style'. Ask for guidelines. Maximum 2000 words.

Limited requirement for guided walks articles. Specialist writers only. Ask for guidelines. 750–2000 words (depending on subject).

Payment £100 per 1000 words.

Traveller
45–49 Brompton Road, London SW3 1DE
☎020 7589 0500 Fax 020 7581 1357
Website www.traveller.org.uk

Owner *Wexas International*
Editor *Jonathan Lorie*
Deputy Editor *Amy Sohanpaul*
Circulation 37,000

FOUNDED 1970. QUARTERLY.
Features High quality, personal narratives of remarkable journeys. Articles should be off-beat, adventurous, authentic. No mainstream destinations. For guidelines, see website. Articles may be accompanied by professional quality, original slides. Freelance articles considered. Maximum 1200 words. Initial contact by e-mail.

Payment £150 per 1000 words.

Trout Fisherman
EMAP Active Ltd, Bushfield House, Orton Centre, Peterborough, Cambridgeshire PE2 5UW
☎01733 237111 Fax 01733 465820
Email mark.sutcliffe@emap.com

Owner *Emap Active Ltd*
Editor *Mark Sutcliffe*
Circulation 42,000

FOUNDED 1977. MONTHLY instructive magazine on trout fishing. Most of the articles are commissioned, but unsolicited mss and quality colour transparencies welcome.

Features Maximum 2500 words.
Payment varies.

TVTimes
IPC Media Ltd., King's Reach Tower,
Stamford Street, London SE1 9LS
☎020 7261 7000 Fax 020 7261 7777

Owner *IPC Media*
Editor *Mike Hollingsworth*
Circulation 566,855

FOUNDED 1955. WEEKLY magazine of listings and features serving the viewers of independent television, BBC, satellite and radio. Freelance contributions by commission only. No unsolicited contributions.

Ulster Tatler
39 Boucher Road, Belfast BT12 6UT
☎028 9068 1371 Fax 028 9038 1915
Email ulstertat@aol.com
Website www.ulstertatler.com

Owner/Editor *Richard Sherry*
Circulation 15,000

FOUNDED 1965. MONTHLY. Articles of local interest and social functions appealing to Northern Ireland's ABC1 population. Welcomes unsolicited material; approach by phone or in writing in the first instance.

Features *Noreen Dorman* Max. 1500 words.
Fiction *Richard Sherry* Max. 3000 words.

The Universe
St James's Buildings, Oxford Street,
Manchester M1 6FP
☎0161 236 8856 Fax 0161 236 8892

Email joe.kelly@the-universe.com
Website www.totalcatholic.com
Owner *Gabriel Communications Ltd*
Editor *Joe Kelly*
Circulation 60,000

Occasional use of new writers, but a substantial network of regular contributors already exists. Interested in a very wide range of material: all subjects which might bear on Christian life. Fiction not normally accepted.
Payment negotiable.

Vector
See **British Science Fiction Association** under **Professional Associations**

The Vegan
Donald Watson House, 7 Battle Road, St Leonards on Sea, East Sussex TN37 7AA
☎01424 427393 Fax 01424 717064
Email editor@vegansociety.com
Website www.vegansociety.com
Owner *Vegan Society*
Editor *Rick Savage*
Circulation 5000

FOUNDED 1944. QUARTERLY. Deals with the ecological, ethical and health aspects of veganism. Unsolicited mss welcome. Maximum 2000 words.
Payment negotiable.

Verbatim The Language Quarterly
PO Box 156, Chearsley, Aylesbury, Buckinghamshire HP18 0DQ
☎01844 208474
Email verbatim.uk@tesco.net
Website www.verbatimmag.com
Owner *Word, Inc.*
Editor *Erin McKean*

FOUNDED in 1974 by Laurence Urdang. QUARTERLY journal devoted to what is amusing, interesting and engaging about the English language and languages in general. Will consider unsolicited material but write for writer's guidelines in the first instance. For a sample copy of the magazine, send 50p (stamp or IRC).
Payment ranges from £20–300, 'depending on length, wit and other merit'.

Vogue
Vogue House, Hanover Square, London W1S 1JU
☎020 7499 9080 Fax 020 7408 0559
Email voguemail@aol.com
Website www.vogue.co.uk
Owner *Condé Nast Publications Ltd*
Editor *Alexandra Shulman*
Circulation 202,108

Condé Nast Magazines tend to use known writers and commission what's needed, rather than use unsolicited mss. Contacts are useful.
    Features *Jo Craven* Upmarket general interest rather than 'women's'. Good proportion of highbrow art and literary articles, as well as travel, gardens, food, home interest and reviews.

The Voice Newspaper
Blue Star House, 234–244 Stockwell Road, London SW9 9UG
☎020 7737 7377 Fax 020 7274 8994
Email newsdesk@the-voice.co.uk
Website www.voice-online.co.uk
Managing Director *Linda McCalla*
Group Editor *Deidre Forbes*
Circulation 40,000

FOUNDED 1982. Leading WEEKLY newspaper for black Britons. Includes news, features, arts, sport and a comprehensive job section. Also produces a monthly glossy women's supplement and a fortnightly youth magazine. Open to ideas for news and features on sports, community events and the arts. *Payment* negotiable.

Voyager
PSP Communications, 15 Craven Street, London WC2N 5AD
☎020 7747 9390 Fax 020 7839 5955
Email daskadavis@pspcom.com
Website www.pspcom.com
Owner *PSP Communications*
Editor *Daska Davis*
Circulation 36,000

TEN ISSUES PER YEAR. In-flight magazine of bmi british midland. Lifestyle features and profiles, plus British Midland information. No unsolicited mss. Approach in writing with ideas in the first instance. No destination travel articles.

The War Cry
101 Newington Causeway, London SE1 6BN
☎020 7367 4900 Fax 020 7367 4710
Email warcry@salvationarmy.org.uk
Website www.salvationarmy.org.uk/warcry
Owner *The Salvation Army*
Editor *Major Nigel Bovey*
Circulation 65,000

FOUNDED 1879. WEEKLY magazine containing Christian comment on current issues. Unsolicited mss welcome if appropriate to contents. No fiction or poetry. Approach by phone with ideas.

News relating to Christian Church or social issues. Maximum length 500 words. *Payment* £20 per article.

Features Human interest articles aimed at the 'man/woman-in-the-street'. Maximum length 500 words. *Payment* £20 per article.

Wasafiri
Dept of English & Drama, Queen Mary College, University of London, Mile End Road, London E1 4NS
☎020 7882 3120 Fax 020 7882 3120
Email wasafiri@qmw.ac.uk
Website www.wasafiri.org

Editor *Susheila Nasta*
Managing Editor *Richard Dyer*
Reviews Editor *Mark Stein*

TRI-ANNUAL literary journal of African, Asian, Black British and Caribbean culture. Short stories, poetry, reviews, interviews, criticism and cross cultural debate, film and literature. Illustrations in b&w. Send double-spaced mss, in duplicate, with s.a.e. No e-mail submissions. *Payment* negotiable.

The Water Gardener
Winchester Court, 1 Forum Place, Hatfield, Hertfordshire AL10 0RN
☎01707 273999 Fax 01707 276555
Email watergardener@trmg.co.uk
Website www.trmg.co.uk

Owner *TRMG*
Editor *Christina Guthrie*

FOUNDED 1994. MONTHLY. Everything relevant to water gardening. Will consider photonews items and features on aspects of the subject; write with idea in the first instance. Maximum 2000 words. *Payment* by negotiation.

Waterways World
151 Station Street, Burton on Trent, Staffordshire DE14 1BG
☎01283 742950 Fax 01283 742957
Email suzanne.willday@wwonline.co.uk

Owner *Waterways World Ltd*
Editor *Hugh Potter*
Circulation 22,408

FOUNDED 1972. MONTHLY magazine for inland waterway enthusiasts. Unsolicited mss welcome, provided the writer has a good knowledge of the subject. No fiction.

Features *Hugh Potter* Articles (preferably illustrated) are published on all aspects of inland waterways in Britain and abroad, including

recreational and commercial boating on rivers and canals.

News *Chris Daniels* Maximum 500 words. *Payment* £42 per 1000 words.

Web User
IPC Media, Room 0305, King's Reach Tower, Stamford Street, London SE1 9LS
☎020 7261 5168 Fax 020 7261 7878
Email letters@web-user.co.uk
Website www.web-user.co.uk

Owner *IPC Media/AOL Time Warner*
Editor *Richard Clark*
Circulation 70,508

FOUNDED 2001. FORTNIGHTLY best-seller Internet magazine for all users of the Internet. No unsolicited material; send e-mail or letter of enquiry in the first instance.

Wedding and Home
IPC Media Ltd., King's Reach Tower, Stamford Street, London SE1 9LS
☎020 7261 7471 Fax 020 7261 7459
Email weddingandhome@ipcmedia.com
Owner *IPC Media*
Editor *Kate Barlow*
Circulation 51,813

FOUNDED 1985. BI-MONTHLY offering ideas and inspiration for women planning their wedding. Most features are written in-house or commissioned from known freelancers. Unsolicited mss are not welcome, but approaches may be made in writing.

Weekly News
D.C. Thomson & Co. Ltd., Albert Square, Dundee DD1 9QJ
☎01382 223131 Fax 01382 201390
Email d.burness@dcthomson.co.uk
Owner *D.C. Thomson & Co. Ltd*
Editor *David Burness*
Circulation 128,000

FOUNDED 1855. WEEKLY. Newsy, family-orientated magazine designed to appeal to the busy housewife. 'We receive a lot of unsolicited articles and there is great loss of life among them.' Usually commissions, but writers of promise will be taken up. Series include showbiz, royals and television. Limited general interest fiction. *Payment* negotiable.

What Car?
60 Waldegrave Road, Teddington, Middlesex TW11 8LG
☎020 8267 5688 Fax 020 8267 5750
Email whatcar@haynet.com

Website www.whatcar.co.uk

Owner *Haymarket Motoring Publications Ltd*
Editor *Rob Aherne*
Circulation 153,164

MONTHLY. The car buyer's bible, *What Car?* concentrates on road test comparisons of new cars, news and buying advice on used cars, as well as a strong consumer section. Some scope for freelancers. Testing is only offered to the few, and general articles on aspects of driving are only accepted from writers known and trusted by the magazine. No unsolicited mss.

Payment negotiable.

What Hi-Fi? Sound & Vision

38–42 Hampton Road, Teddington, Middlesex TW11 0JE
☎020 8943 5000 Fax 020 8267 5019
Email whathifi@haynet.com
Website www.whathifi.com

Owner *Haymarket Magazines Ltd*
Managing Director *Kevin Costello*
Editor *Andy Clough*
Circulation 76,000

FOUNDED 1976. MONTHLY. Features on hi-fi and home cinema. No unsolicited contributions. Prior consultation with the editor essential.

Features General or more specific on hi-fi and home cinema pertinent to the consumer electronics market.

Reviews Specific product reviews. All material is now generated by in-house staff. Freelance writing no longer accepted.

What Investment

Arnold House, 36–41 Holywell Lane, London EC2A 3SF
☎020 7827 5454 Fax 020 7827 0567

Owner *Charterhouse Communications*
Editor *Sally Wright*
Circulation 37,000

FOUNDED 1982. MONTHLY. Features articles on a variety of savings and investment matters. All approaches should be made in writing.

Features Length 1200–1500 words (maximum 2000).

Payment NUJ rates minimum.

What Mortgage

Arnold House, 36–41 Holywell Lane, London EC2A 3SF
☎020 7827 5454 Fax 020 7827 0567
Email hiliary.osborne@charterhouse-communications.co.uk
Website www.whatmortgageonline.co.uk

Owner *Charterhouse Communications*
Editor *Hilary Osborne*
Circulation 25,000

FOUNDED 1982. MONTHLY magazine on property purchase and finance. No unsolicited material; prospective contributors may make initial contact with ideas either by telephone or in writing.

Features Up to 1500 words on related topics are considered. Particularly welcome are new angles, ideas or specialities relevant to mortgages.

Payment £200 per 1000 words.

What Satellite and Digital TV

Highbury – WV, 53–79 Highgate Road, London NW5 1TW
☎020 7331 1000 Fax 020 7331 1241
Email wvwhatsat@wvip.co.uk
Website www.wotsat.com

Owner *Highbury – WV*
Editor *Alex Lane*
Circulation 65,000

FOUNDED 1986. MONTHLY including news, technical information, equipment tests, programme background, listings. Contributions welcome; phone first.

Features *Alex Lane* Unusual installations and users. In-depth guides to popular/cult shows. Technical tutorials.

News *Alex Lane* Industry and programming. 250 words maximum.

What's New in Building

Ludgate House, 245 Blackfriars Road, London SE1 9UY
☎020 7921 8228 Fax 020 7921 8247
Email mpennington@cmpinformation.com

Owner *CMP Information*
Editor *Mark Pennington*
Circulation 29,000

MONTHLY. Specialist magazine covering new products for building. Unsolicited mss not generally welcome. The only freelance work available is rewriting press release material. This is offered on a monthly basis of 25–50 items of about 150 words each.

Payment £5.25 per item.

What's On in London

180–182 Pentonville Road, London N1 9JP
☎020 7278 4393 Fax 020 7837 5838
Email whatson@gxn.co.uk
Website www.whatsoninlondon.co.uk

Owner *S.D. Shaw*
Editor *Michael Darvell*

Circulation 40,000

FOUNDED 1935. WEEKLY entertainment-based guide and information magazine. Features, listings and reviews. Always interested in well-thought-out and well-presented mss. Articles should have London/Home Counties connection, except during the summer when they can be of much wider tourist/historic interest, relating to unusual traditions and events. Approach the editor by telephone in the first instance.

Features *Graham Hassell*
Art *Fisun Güner*
Cinema *Rachel Holdsworth*
Pop Music *John Coleman*
Classical Music *Michael Darvell*
Theatre *Oliver Jones*
Events *Andrew Williams*
Payment by arrangement.

Wild Times

RSPB, The Lodge, Sandy, Bedfordshire SG19 2DL
☎01767 680551 Fax 01767 683262
Email derek.niemann@rspb.org.uk

Owner *Royal Society for the Protection of Birds*
Editor *Derek Niemann*

FOUNDED 1965. BI-MONTHLY. Bird, wildlife and nature conservation for under 8 year-olds (RSPB Wildlife Explorer members). No unsolicited mss. No 'captive/animal welfare' articles.

Features Unsolicited material rarely used.
News News releases welcome. Approach in writing in the first instance.

Wine Magazine

Quest Magazines Ltd., 6–14 Underwood Street, London N1 7JQ
☎020 7549 2572 Fax 020 7549 2550
Email wine@wilmington.co.uk
Website www.connectingdrinks.com

Owner *Wilmington Publishing*
Managing Editor *Catherine Lowe*
Circulation 35,000

FOUNDED 1983. MONTHLY. No unsolicited mss.

News/Features Wine, spirits, cigars, food and food/wine-related travel stories. Prospective contributors should approach in writing.

Wingbeat

RSPB, The Lodge, Sandy, Bedfordshire SG19 2DL
☎01767 680551 Fax 01767 683262
Email derek.niemann@rspb.org.uk

Owner *Royal Society for the Protection of Birds*
Editor *Derek Niemann*

FOUNDED 1965. BI-MONTHLY. Bird, wildlife and nature conservation for 14–18 year-olds (RSPB Wildlife Explorer members). No unsolicited mss. No 'captive/animal welfare' articles.

Features Unsolicited material rarely used.
News News releases welcome. Approach in writing in the first instance.

Wisden Cricket Monthly

c/o The New Boathouse, 136–142 Bramley Road, London W10 6SR
☎020 7565 3000 Fax 020 7565 3090
Email wcm@wisden.com

Owner *Wisden Cricket Magazines Ltd*
Editor *Stephen Fay*
Circulation 20,000

FOUNDED 1979. MONTHLY. Very few uncommissioned articles are used, but would-be contributors are not discouraged. Approach in writing. *Payment* varies.

Woman

IPC Media Ltd, King's Reach Tower, Stamford Street, London SE1 9LS
☎020 7261 7023 Fax 020 7261 5997

Owner *IPC Media*
Editor *Carole Russell*
Circulation 638,036

FOUNDED 1937. WEEKLY. Long-running, popular women's magazine which boasts a readership of over 2.5 million. No unsolicited mss. Most work commissioned. Approach with ideas in writing.

Features *Judy Yorke* Maximum 1250 words.
Books *Carole Russell*

Woman and Home

IPC Media Ltd., King's Reach Tower, Stamford Street, London SE1 9LS
☎020 7261 5176 Fax 020 7261 7346

Owner *IPC Media*
Editor *Sue James*
Circulation 271,887

FOUNDED 1926. MONTHLY. No unsolicited mss. Prospective contributors are advised to write with ideas, including photocopies of other published work or details of magazines to which they have contributed. S.a.e. essential for return of material. Most freelance work is specially commissioned.

Woman's Own

IPC Media Ltd., King's Reach Tower, Stamford Street, London SE1 9LS
☎020 7261 5500 Fax 020 7261 5346

Owner *IPC Media*
Editor *Elsa McAlonan*

Features Editor *Jackie Hatton*
Circulation 519,388

FOUNDED 1932. WEEKLY. Prospective contributors should contact the features editor *in writing* in the first instance before making a submission. No unsolicited fiction.

Woman's Realm

Merged with *Woman's Weekly* in 2001.

Woman's Weekly

IPC Media Ltd., King's Reach Tower, Stamford Street, London SE1 9LS
☎0870 444 5000 Fax 020 7261 6322

Owner *IPC Media*
Editor *Gilly Sinclair*
Deputy Editor *Geoffrey Palmer*
Circulation 504,531

FOUNDED 1911. Mass-market women's WEEKLY.

Features Inspiring, positive human interest stories, especially first-hand experiences, of up to 1200 words. Freelancers used regularly but tend to be experienced magazine journalists. Synopses and ideas should be submitted in writing.

Fiction *Gaynor Davies* Short stories 1000–2500 words; serials 12,000–30,000 words. Guidelines for serials: 'a strong emotional theme with a conflict not resolved until the end'; short stories should have warmth and originality.

Women's Health

Highbury – WV, 53–79 Highgate Road, London NW5 1TW
☎020 7331 1000 Fax 020 7331 1108
Email womenshealth@wvip.co.uk

Owner *Highbury House Communications*
Editor *Tracey Smith*
Circulation 100,000

FOUNDED 1998. MONTHLY lifestyle magazine with a health twist, taking an irreverant approach. Aimed at ABC1 women of 25–39. No unsolicited mss. Will consider ideas for items with interesting angles on fitness and beauty plus alternative health and food. Approach in writing or by e-mail in the first instance.

Woodworker

Nexus House, Azalea Drive, Swanley, Kent BR8 8HU
☎01322 660070 Fax 01322 616319
Website www.getwoodworking.com

Owner *Highbury Nexus Special Interests*

Editor *Mark Ramuz*
Circulation 45,000

FOUNDED 1901. MONTHLY. Contributions welcome; approach with ideas in writing.

Features Articles on woodworking with good photo support appreciated. Maximum 2000 words. *Payment* £100 per 1000 words.

News Stories and photos (b&w) welcome. Maximum 300 words. *Payment* £10–25 per story.

World Fishing

Nexus House, Azalea Drive, Swanley, Kent BR8 8HU
☎01322 660070 Fax 01322 616324
Email adrian.tatum@nexusmedia.com

Owner *Nexus Media Ltd*
Editor *Adrian Tatum*
Circulation 5769

FOUNDED 1952. MONTHLY. Unsolicited mss welcome; approach by phone or in writing with an idea.

News/Features of a technical or commercial nature relating to the commercial fishing and fish processing industries worldwide (the magazine is read in 116 different countries). Maximum 1500 words.
Payment by arrangement.

The World of Interiors

Vogue House, Hanover Square, London W1S 1JU
☎020 7499 9080 Fax 020 7493 4013
Email interiors@condenast.co.uk
Website www.worldofinteriors.co.uk

Owner *Condé Nast Publications Ltd*
Editor *Rupert Thomas*
Circulation 64,287

FOUNDED 1981. MONTHLY. Best approach by fax or letter with an idea, preferably with reference snaps or guidebooks.

Features *Rupert Thomas* Most feature material is commissioned. 'Subjects tend to be found by us, but we are delighted to receive suggestions of interiors, archives, little-known museums, collections, etc. unpublished elsewhere, and are keen to find new writers.'

World Ski and Wintersports Guide

27a High Street, Esher, Surrey KT10 9RL
☎01372 468140 Fax 01372 470675
Email info@goodholidayideas.com

Editor *John Hill*
Circulation 65,000

FOUNDED 2002. BI-ANNUAL desitination guide for skiers and winter sports enthusiasts covering the top 100 ski and winter sports resorts. No unsolicited mss. Approach with ideas and/or synopsis in writing or by e-mail.

Payment negotiable.

World Soccer

IPC Media Ltd., King's Reach Tower, Stamford Street, London SE1 9LS
☎020 7261 5737 Fax 020 7261 7474
Email world_soccer@ipcmedia.com
Website www.worldsoccer.com

Owner *IPC Media*
Editor *Gavin Hamilton*
Circulation 52,547

FOUNDED 1960. MONTHLY. Unsolicited material welcome but initial approach by e-mail or in writing. News and features on world soccer.

Writers' Forum incorporating World Wide Writers

PO Box 3229, Bournemouth, Dorset BH1 1ZS
☎01202 589828 Fax 01202 587758
Email writintl@globalnet.co.uk
Website www.worldwidewriters.com

Owner *Writers International Ltd*
Editor *John Jenkins*
Deputy Editor *Mary Hogarth*

FOUNDED 1993. TEN ISSUES YEARLY. Magazine covering all aspects of the craft of writing. Well written articles welcome. Write to the editor in the first instance.

Writers Forum Short Story Competition Prizes range from £150–250 with an annual trophy and a cheque for £1000 for the best story of the year. Entrance fee: non-subscribers, £10; subscribers, £6. Winners published in every issue.

Writers' Forum Poetry Competition First prize £100, runners up £25. Entrance fee: £5 for one poem or £7 for two. Winners published in every issue.

Writers' News/Writing Magazine

PO Box 168, Wellington Street, Leeds, West Yorkshire LS1 1RF
☎0113 238 8333 Fax 0113 238 8330

Owner *Warners Group Publications plc*
Editor *Derek Hudson*
Circulation 17,000(WN)/37,000(WM)

FOUNDED 1989. MONTHLY/BI-MONTHLY magazines containing news and advice for writers. *Writers' News* is exclusive to mail-order members who also receive *Writing Magazine*, a full-colour glossy publication, which is available on newsstands. No poetry or general items on 'how to become a writer'. Receive 1000 mss each year. Approach in writing.

News Exclusive news stories of interest to writers. Maximum 350 words.

Features How-to articles of interest to professional writers. Maximum 1500 words.

Yachting Monthly

IPC Media Ltd., King's Reach Tower, Stamford Street, London SE1 9LS
☎020 7261 6040 Fax 020 7261 7555
Email paul_gelder@ipcmedia.com
Website www.yachtingmonthly.com

Owner *IPC Media*
Editor *Paul Gelder*
Circulation 37,083

FOUNDED 1906. MONTHLY magazine for yachting and cruising enthusiasts – not racing. Unsolicited mss welcome, but many are received and not used. Prospective contributors should make initial contact in writing.

Features A wide range of features concerned with maritime subjects and cruising under sail; well-researched and innovative material always welcome, especially if accompanied by colour transparencies. Maximum 2250 words.

Payment £80–110 per 1000 words.

Yachting World

IPC Media Ltd., King's Reach Tower, Stamford Street, London SE1 9LS
☎020 7261 6800 Fax 020 7261 6818
Email yachting_world@ipcmedia.com
Website www.yachting-world.com

Owner *IPC Media*
Editor *Andrew Bray*
Circulation 35,807

FOUNDED 1894. MONTHLY with international coverage of yacht racing, cruising and yachting events. Will consider well researched and written sailing stories. Preliminary approaches should be by phone for news stories and in writing for features.

Payment by arrangement.

Yorkshire Women's Life Magazine

PO Box 113, Leeds, West Yorkshire LS8 2WX
☎0113 262 1409

Publisher/Editor *Dawn Maria France*

FOUNDED 2001. THREE ISSUES YEARLY. Features of interest to women along with regional, national, international news and lifestyle articles. Past issues have covered anorexia nervosa, dealing with a monster boss, new female contraceptive. 'It is important to study the style of the magazine before submitting material. Send A4 s.a.e. with 41p stamp for copy of submission guidelines. Unsolicited mss and new writers actively encouraged; approach in writing in the first instance with s.a.e.'

You & Your Wedding
National Magazine Company, 72 Broadwick Street, London W1F 9EP
☎020 7439 5000 (Editorial)
Fax 020 7439 2985
Owner *NatMags Specialist Media (AIM) Ltd*
Editor *Carole Hamilton*
Circulation 62,145

FOUNDED 1985. BI-MONTHLY. Anything relating to weddings, setting up home, and honeymoons. No unsolicited mss. Ideas may be submitted in writing only, especially travel features. No phone calls.

You – The Mail on Sunday Magazine
See under **National Newspapers (The Mail on Sunday)**

Young Writer
Glebe House, Weobley, Hereford HR4 8SD
☎01544 318901 Fax 01544 318901
Email editor@youngwriter.org
Website www.youngwriter.org
Editor *Kate Jones*

Describing itself as 'The Magazine for Children with Something to Say', *Young Writer* is issued three times a year, at the back-to-school times of September, January and April. A forum for young people's writing – fiction and non-fiction, prose and poetry – the magazine is an introduction to independent writing for young writers aged 5–18.
Payment from £20 to £100 for freelance commissioned articles (these can be from adult writers).

Your Cat Magazine
Roebuck House, 33 Broad Street, Stamford, Lincolnshire PE9 1RB
☎01780 766199 Fax 01780 766416
Email suebpgroup@talk21.com
Website www.yourcat.co.uk
Owner *Bourne Publishing Group*

Editor *Sue Parslow*

FOUNDED 1994. MONTHLY magazine giving practical information on the care of cats and kittens, pedigree and non-pedigree, plus a wide range of general interest items on cats. Will consider 'true life' cat stories (maximum 900 words) and quality fiction. Send synopsis in the first instance. 'No articles written as though by a cat.'

Your Dog Magazine
Roebuck House, 33 Broad Street, Stamford, Lincolnshire PE9 1RB
☎01780 766199 Fax 01780 766416
Owner *BPG (Stamford) Ltd*
Editor *Sarah Wright*
Circulation 26,000

FOUNDED 1995. MONTHLY. Practical advice for pet dog owners. Will consider practical features and some personal experiences (no highly emotive pieces or fiction). Telephone in the first instance.
News Maximum 300–400 words.
Features Maximum 2500 words; limited opportunities.
Payment negotiable.

Your Home Magazine
The National Magazine Company, 72 Broadwick Street, London W1F 9EP
☎020 7439 5000 Fax 020 7439 5141
Website www.yourhomemagazine.co.uk
Owner *National Magazine Company*
Editor *Sue Rose*
Circulation 150,062

FOUNDED 1998. MONTHLY magazine offering makeovers and readers' homes. No unsolicited mss.

Your Horse
Bretton Court, Bretton, Peterborough, Cambridgeshire PE3 8DZ
☎01733 264666 Fax 01733 465200
Owner *Emap Active Ltd*
Editor *Amanda Stevenson*
Circulation 61,000

For people who live, breath and have fun around horses. Most writing produced in-house but well-targeted articles will always be considered.

Yours Magazine
Emap Esprit, Bretton Court, Bretton, Peterborough, Cambridgeshire PE3 8DZ
☎01733 264666 Fax 01733 465266

Owner *Emap Esprit*
Editor *Valery McConnell*
Circulation 368,006

FOUNDED 1973. MONTHLY plus four seasonal specials. Aimed at a readership aged 55 and over.

Features Unsolicited mss welcome but must enclose s.a.e. Maximum 1500 words.

News Short, newsy items of interest to readership welcome. Length 300–500 words.

Fiction One or two short stories used in each issue. Maximum 1500 words.

Payment negotiable.

Zest

National Magazine House, 72 Broadwick Street, London W1F 9EP
☎020 7439 5000 Fax 020 7312 3750
Email zest.mail@natmags.co.uk
Website www.zest.co.uk

Owner *National Magazine Company*
Editor *Alison Pylkkanen*
Deputy Editor *Rebecca Frank*

FOUNDED 1994. MONTHLY. Health, beauty, fitness, nutrition and general well-being. No unsolicited mss. Prefers ideas in synopsis form; approach in writing.

News Agencies

Associated Press Limited
12 Norwich Street, London EC4A 1BP
☎020 7353 1515
Fax 020 7353 8118 (Newsdesk)

Material is either generated in-house or by regulars. Hires the occasional stringer. No unsolicited mss.

Atlantic Syndication Ltd
17–18 Hayward's Place, Clerkenwell, London EC1R 0EQ
☎020 7566 0360   Fax 020 7566 0388
Email tyork@atlanticsyndication.com
Website www.atlanticsyndication.com

FOUNDED 1978. *Specialises* in worldwide newspaper syndication of photos, features and cartoons. Professional contributors only.

Dow Jones Newswires
10 Fleet Place, London EC4M 7QN
☎020 7842 9900   Fax 020 7842 9361

A real-time financial and business newswire operated by Dow Jones & Co., publishers of *The Wall Street Journal*. No unsolicited material.

Hayters Teamwork Sports Agency
6 Sharman Walk, Apperknowle, Sheffield, South Yorkshire S18 4BJ
☎01246 414767/07970 284848 (mobile)
Fax 01246 414767
Email Nicksport1@aol.com

Contact *Nick Johnson*

Provides written/broadcast coverage of sport in the South Yorkshire area.

National News Press and Photo Agency
4–5 Academy Buildings, Fanshaw Street, London N1 5LQ
☎020 7684 3000   Fax 020 7684 3030

Email news@nationalnews.co.uk

All press releases are welcome. Most work is ordered or commissioned. Coverage includes courts, tribunals, conferences, general news, etc. – words and pictures – as well as PR.

Press Association Ltd
292 Vauxhall Bridge Road, London SW1V 1AE
☎020 7963 7000/7830 (Newsdesk)
Fax 020 7963 7192 (Newsdesk)
Email copy@pa.press.net
Website www.pa.press.net

No unsolicited material. Most items are produced in-house though occasional outsiders may be used. A phone call to discuss specific material may lead somewhere 'but this is rare'.

Reuters
85 Fleet Street, London EC4P 4AJ
☎020 7250 1122

No unsolicited material.

Space Press NA
Bridge House, Blackden Lane, Goostrey, Cheshire CW4 8PZ
☎01477 533403/534440   Fax 01477 535756
Email Scoop2001@aol.com

Editor *John Williams*
Pictures *Emma Williams*

FOUNDED 1972. Press and picture agency covering Cheshire and the North West, North Midlands, including Knutsford, Macclesfield, Congleton, Crewe and Nantwich, Wilmslow, Alderley Edge, serving national, regional and local press, TV, radio, and digital picture transmission. A member of the National Association of Press Agencies (NAPA).

Television and Radio

For the latest information on broadcast rates for freelancers access the following websites: the National Union of Journalists 'Rates for the Job': www.gn.apc.org/media; the Producers Alliance for Cinema and Television: www.pact.co.uk; the Society of Authors: www.societyofauthors.org; and the Writers' Guild: www.writersguild.org.uk

BBC TV and Radio

Website www.bbc.co.uk

Director-General *Greg Dyke*

The structure of the BBC includes the following divisions: Television Division – responsible for the network television channels and for commissioning in most genres; Drama, Entertainment and Children's; Factual and Learning; Radio and Music; News; Sport; Nations and Regions; and the New Media division which develops the BBC's interactive television and online activities.

TELEVISION

BBC Television Centre, Wood Lane,
London W12 7RJ
☎020 8743 8000

Director, Television *Jana Bennett*
Controller, BBC1 *Lorraine Heggessey*
Controller, BBC2 *Jane Root*
Controller, Daytime *Alison Sharman*

Digital television
Controller, BBC Three *Stuart Murphy*
Controller, BBC Four *To be appointed*

BBC Three was launched February 2003, replacing BBC Choice. Broadcasts a wide range of entertainment aimed at a 25–34-year-old audience with programmes such as *Liquid News* – headline stories from the world of showbusiness. BBC Four, launched in March 2002, is devoted solely to the arts. Programmes include *Readers and Writers*, a weekly book programme.

RADIO

Broadcasting House, Portland Place, London
W1A 1AA
☎020 7580 4468

Director of Radio & Music *Jenny Abramsky*
Controller, Radio 1 *Andy Parfitt*
Executive Producer, Radio 1 *Maria Williams*
Controller, Radio 2 *James Moir* (retires end 2003)
Commissions & Schedules Manager,
    Radio 2 *Julian Grundy*

Controller, Radio 3 *Roger Wright*
Commissions & Schedules Manager,
    Radio 3 *David Ireland*
Controller, Radio 4 *Helen Boaden*

The following statement appears on the Radio 4 Commissioning website. 'If you wish to propose ideas to Radio 4 you will need to do so through an in-house department or a registered independent company'. For a list of these log on to www.bbc.co.uk/commissioning/structure/process_radio.shtml

Controller, Radio 5 Live *Bob Shennan*
Commissioning Editor, Radio 5 *Moz Dee*

Digital radio
BBC 1Xtra
BBC Five Live Sports Extra
BBC 6 Music
BBC 7 (comedy, drama and books)
BBC Asian Network

Drama, Entertainment and Children's Division

Director *Alan Yentob*

BBC *writersroom* finds and champions writers across all BBC platforms, running targeted schemes and workshops linked directly to production. It accepts, and assesses unsolicited scripts for film, single TV dramas, comedy and radio drama. Also runs *northern exposure* which focuses on new writing in the north of England, channelled through theatres in Liverpool, Manchester, Bradford, Leeds and Newcastle. To be considered for one of the schemes run by writersroom, send a sample full length drama script to: BBC writersroom, 1 Mortimer Street, London W1T 3JA. For guidelines on unsolicited scripts please log on to www.bbc.co.uk/writersroom or send a large s.a.e. to *Jessica Dromgoole*, New Writing Coordinator, BBC Drama, Entertainment and CBBC at the Mortimer Street address above. For details of TV and Radio Commissioning log on to www.bbc.co.uk/ commissioning

DRAMA

Controller, Drama Commissioning *Jane Tranter*

Controller, Continuing Drama Series *Mal Young*

Head of Drama Commissioning *Gareth Neame*

Head of Drama Serials *Laura Mackie*

Head of Development, Drama Series *Sarah Cullen*

Controller, Daytime Drama, Factual Entertainment & Entertainment on BBC One/Two: *Alison Sharman* (daytime.proposals@bbc.co.uk)

Head of Films *David Thompson*

Head of Development, Films *Tracey Scoffield*

Creative Director, New Writing *Kate Rowland*

Head of Radio Drama *Gordon House*

Executive Producer (Birmingham)/Editor, The Archers *Vanessa Whitburn*

Executive Producer (World Service Drama) *Marion Nancarrow*

ENTERTAINMENT

Controller, Commissioning Entertainment *Jane Lush*

Genre Executive *Jo McIlvenna*

Head of Comedy Entertainment, Television *Jon Plowman*

Producer *Bill Dare*

Head of Light Entertainment, Radio 4 *John Pidgeon*

Programmes produced range from *The Kumars* and *The Weakest Link* on television to *Loose Ends* and *The Now Show* on Radio 4. Virtually every comic talent in Britain got their first break writing one-liners for topical comedy weeklies. For information on those programmes requiring non-commissioned submissions, join the mailing list for *Writer's Newsletter* – contact: lianna.ross@bbc.co.uk

CBBC (CHILDREN'S)

Controller, CBBC *J. Nigel Pickard*

Head of Programmes *Dorothy Prior*

Head of Acquisitions *Theresa Plummer-Andrews*

Head of CBBC Drama *Elaine Sperber*

Head of Entertainment *Anne Gilchrist*

Head of CBBC News and Factual Programmes *Roy Milani*

Head of CBBC Pre-school *Clare Elstow*

Head of CBBC Education *Sue Nott*

Factual and Learning Division

Director, Factual TV & Learning *John Willis*

Controller, Factual TV *Glenwyn Benson*

Controller, Learning *To be appointed*

Commissioner, Arts & Culture *Franny Moyle*

Commissioner, Current Affairs & Investigations *Peter Horrocks*

Commissioner, Specialist Factual *Emma Swain*

Acting Commissioner, Documentaries & Contemporary Factual *Tom Archer*

Head of Independent Commissioning, Specialist Factual, Current Affairs and Arts *Adam Kemp*

Controller, Documentaries and Contemporary Factual *Anne Morrison*

Controller, Specialist Factual *Keith Scholey*

Head of Lifeskills TV *Seetha Kumar*

Executive Editor, Children's Education *Karen Johnson*

Development Executives *Michelle Matherson, Sara Brailsford* (genfact.proposals@bbc.co.uk)

Commissioner, New Media *Liz Cleaver*

Head of Interactive TV Programmes *Scott Gronmark*

News Division

Website www.bbc.co.uk/news or news.bbc.co.uk

BBC News is the world's largest news-gathering organisation, with 2000 journalists, 250 specialist correspondents and 57 bureaux around the world. There are four specialist units: world affairs; economics and business; politics; and social affairs. BBC News serves: BBC1, BBC2, BBC Three, Radios 1, 2, 3, 4 and 5 Live, BBC News 24, BBC Parliament, BBC World, BBC World Service, News Online, Ceefax.

Director, News *Richard Sambrook*

Deputy Director, News *Mark Damazer*

Head of Current Affairs *Peter Horrocks*

Head of Newsgathering *Adrian Van Klaveran*

Head of Interactive *Richard Deverell*

Head of Political Programmes *Fran Unsworth*

Head of Radio News *Stephen Mitchell*

Head of TV News *Roger Mosey*

Deputy Head of TV News *Rachel Attwell*

TELEVISION

Editor, 1 o'clock News *Chris Rybczynski*

Editor, 6 o'clock News *Jay Hunt*

Editor, 10 o'clock News *Mark Popescu*

Editor, Newsnight *George Entwhistle*

Editor, Breakfast News *Richard Porter*

Editor, Breakfast With Frost *Barney Jones*

Editor, Correspondent *Karen O'Conner*

Editor, World Service News Programmes *Alan Le Breton*

RADIO
Editor, Today *Kevin Marsh*
Editor, The World at One/World This Weekend/PM/Broadcasting House *Richard Clark*
Head of Five Live News *Ceri Thomas*
Editors, The World Tonight *Jenni Russell/ Prue Keely*

Ceefax
Room 7013, BBC Television Centre, Wood Lane, London W12 7RJ
☎020 8576 1801
Editor, Ceefax *Paul Brannan*

Subtitling
Room 1468, BBC White City, Wood Lane, London W12 7RJ
☎020 8752 7054/0141 339 8844 ext. 2128
A rapidly expanding service available via Ceefax page 888. Units based in both London and Glasgow.

Sport Division
Director, Sport *Peter Salmon*
Executive Editor, Football *Niall Sloane*
Head of Interactive *Andrew Thompson*

Sports news and commentaries across television and Radios 1, 4 and 5 Live, with the majority of output on Radio 5 Live. Regular programmes include *Sportsnight; Sports News* and *Sport on Five*.

BBC Religion
New Broadcasting House, Oxford Road, Manchester M60 1SJ
☎0161 200 2020 Fax 0161 244 3183
Head of Religion and Ethics *Alan Bookbinder*

Regular programmes for television include *Heaven & Earth; Songs of Praise; A Country Parish*. Radio output includes *Good Morning Sunday; Sunday Half Hour; Thought for the Day; The Daily Service*.

BBC Talent
Website www.bbc.co.uk/talent
The BBC's search for new talent covers a wide range of areas including TV and radio producers, presenters, filmmakers, sitcom and comedy writers. Access the website for further information.

BBC World Service
PO Box 76, Bush House, Strand, London WC2B 4PH
☎020 7240 3456 Fax 020 7557 1900
Website www.bbc.co.uk/worldservice
Director *Mark Byford*
Director, English Networks & News, BBCWS *Phil Harding*

The World Service broadcasts in English and 42 other languages. The English service is round-the-clock, with news and current affairs as the main component. With over 150 million listeners, excluding countries where research is not possible, it reaches a bigger audience than its five closest competitors combined. The World Service is increasingly available throughout the world on local FM stations, via satellite and online as well as through short-wave frequencies. Coverage includes world business, politics, people/events/opinions, development issues, the international scene, developments in science and technology, sport, religion, music, drama, the arts. BBC World Service broadcasting is financed by a grant-in-aid voted by Parliament amounting to £201 million for 2003/2004.

BBC writersroom
Website www.bbc.co.uk/writersroom
See **Drama, Entertainment and Children's Division**.

BBC Regions

BBC Northern Ireland
Broadcasting House, Ormeau Avenue, Belfast BT2 8HQ
☎028 9033 8000
Website www.bbc.co.uk/northernireland
Controller *Anna Carragher*
Head of Broadcasting *Tim Cooke*
Head of News & Current Affairs *Andrew Colman*
Editor, News Gathering *Michael Cairns*
Editor, Television News *Angelina Fusco*
Editor, Radio News *Kathleen Carragher*
Head of Drama *Robert Cooper*
Head of Entertainment, Events & Sport *Mike Edgar*
Editor, Entertainment *Alex Johnston*
Editor, Sport *Edward Smith*
Editor, Music Programmes *Declan McGovern*
Head of Factual and Learning *Bruce Batten*
Editor, Learning *Kieran Hegarty*
Editor, Radio Factual *Susan Lovell*

Editor, TV Factual *Deirdre Devlin*
Producer, Religion *Bert Tosh*
Editor, Political Programmes *Lena Ferguson*
Editor, Text Services *Eddie Fleming*
Editor, Network Development *Eamon Hardy*
Senior Producer Entertainment *Noleen Golding*
Managing Director, Foyle *Ana Leddy*
Head of Programme Operations *Stephen Beckett*

Regular television programmes include *Newsline 6.30* and a wide range of documentary, popular factual and entertainment programmes. Radio stations: BBC Radio Foyle and BBC Radio Ulster (see entries).

Television and film scripts should be sent to: *Susan Carson*, Development Co-ordinator Television, BBC Northern Ireland Drama, Room 3.07, Blackstaff House, Great Victoria Street, Belfast, BT2 7BB. (☎028 90 33 8498 Email tvdrama.ni@bbc.co.uk)

Radio scripts should be sent to: *Anne Simpson*, Manager Radio Drama at the same address.

BBC Scotland
Broadcasting House, Queen Margaret Drive, Glasgow G12 8DG
☎0141 338 2000
Website www.bbc.co.uk/scotland

Controller *John McCormick*
Controller, Network Development, Nations and Regions *Colin Cameron*
Head of Drama, Television *Barbara McKissack*
Head of Drama, Radio *Patrick Rayner*
Head of Comedy and Entertainment *Mike Bolland*
Head of Factual Programmes *Andrea Miller*
Executive Editor New Media *Julie Adair*
Head of Programmes, Scotland *Ken MacQuarrie*
Head of CBBC *Claire Mundell*
Editor, Education *Moira Scott*
Head of Radio *Maggie Cunningham*
Head of Gaelic *Donalda MacKinnon*
Head of News and Current Affairs *Blair Jenkins*
Head of Sport *Neil Fraser*
Commissioning Editor, Television *Ewan Angus*

Headquarters of BBC Scotland with centres in Aberdeen, Dundee, Edinburgh and Inverness. Regular and recent programmes include *Reporting Scotland*, *Sportscene* and *Monarch of the Glen* on television and *Good Morning Scotland* and *Fred Macaulay* on radio.

Aberdeen
Broadcasting House, Beechgrove Terrace, Aberdeen AB9 2ZT
☎01224 625233
Head of North *Andrew Jones*

News, plus some features, including the regular *Beechgrove Garden*. Second TV centre, also with regular radio broadcasting.

Dundee
Nethergate Centre, 66 Nethergate, Dundee DD1 4ER
☎01382 202481

News base only; contributors' studio.

Edinburgh
The Tun, Holyrood Road, Edinburgh EH8 8JF
☎0131 557 5677
Senior Producer, Arts & Features *Jane Fowler*

News, current affairs, arts and features.

Inverness
7 Culduthel Road, Inverness 1V2 4AD
☎01463 720720
Editor *Ishbel MacLennan*

News features for Radio Scotland.

Radio Nan Gaidheal
Rosebank, Church Street, Stornoway, Isle of Lewis PA87 2LS
☎01851 705000
Editor *Marion MacKinnon*

The Gaelic radio service serving most of Scotland.

BBC Wales
Broadcasting House, Llandaff, Cardiff CF5 2YQ
☎029 2032 2000 Fax 029 2055 2973
Website www.bbc.co.uk/wales
Controller *Menna Richards*
Head of Programmes (Welsh Language) *Keith Jones*
Head of Programmes (English Language) *Clare Hudson*
Head of News & Current Affairs *Aled Eurig*
Head of Drama *Matthew Robinson*
Commissioning Editor, Independents and 2W *Martyn Ingram*
Series Editor, Pobol y Cwm *Bethan Jones*
Editor, New Media *Iain Tweedale*

Headquarters of BBC Wales, with regional centres in Bangor, Aberystwyth, Carmarthen, Wrexham and Swansea. BBC Wales television produces up to 12 hours of English language programmes a week, 12 hours in Welsh for transmission on **S4C** and an increasing number of hours on network services. BBC2W, the digital channel, was launched in 2001. Regular programmes include *Wales Today; Newyddion* (Welsh-language daily news); *Week In Week Out, The Exchange* and *Pobol y Cwm* (Welsh-language soap) on television and *Good Morning Wales; Good Evening Wales; Post Cyntaf* and *Post Prynhawn* on Radio Wales and Radio Cymru.

Ideas for programmes should be submitted either by post to *Martyn Ingram,* Commissioning Editor Room 3021 at the address above or by e-mail to commissioning@bbc.co.uk

Bangor
Broadcasting House, Meirion Road, Bangor, Gwynedd LL57 2BY
☎01248 370880 Fax 01248 351443
Head of Centre *Marian Wyn Jones*

BBC Asian Network
BBC Pebble Mill, Epic House, Charles Street, Leicester LE1 3SH
☎0116 251 6688 Fax 0116 253 2004
Email asian.network@bbc.co.uk
Website www.bbc.co.uk/asiannetwork
Managing Editor *Vijay Sharma*

Commenced broadcasting in November 1996. Broadcasts to a Midlands audience during the day and nationwide coverage in the evening. Programmes in English, Bengali, Gujerati, Hindi, Punjabi and Urdu.

BBC Birmingham
Pebble Mill Road, Birmingham B5 7QQ
☎0121 432 8888 Fax 0121 432 8847
Website www.bbc.co.uk/birmingham
Head of Regional and Local Programmes *David Holdsworth*
Output Editor *Charles Watkin*

Home of the Pebble Mill Studio. Output for the network includes: TV – *Doctors; Countryfile; Top Gear; Dalziel and Pascoe; Gardener's World; Big Strong Boys; Trading Up.* Radio – *The Archers; Shake, Rattle and Roll; Farming Today; Late Night Currie; Ramblings With Clare Balding.*

BBC East Midlands (Nottingham)
East Midlands Broadcasting Centre, London Road, Nottingham NG2 4UU
☎0115 955 0500 Fax 0115 902 1983
Website www.bbc.co.uk/nottingham
Head of Regional Programming *Alison Ford*
Output Editor *Lisa Lambden*

BBC East (Norwich)
St Catherine's Close, All Saint's Green, Norwich, Norfolk NR1 3ND
☎01603 619331 Fax 01603 284455
Website www.bbc.co.uk/norfolk
Head of Regional Programming *Tim Bishop*
Output Editor *Dave Betts*

BBC Bristol
Broadcasting House, Whiteladies Road, Bristol BS8 2LR
☎0117 973 2211
Managing Editor *Jenny Lacey*
Head of General Factual & Learning *Tom Archer*
Head of Natural History Unit *Neil Nightingale*

BBC Bristol is the home of the BBC's Natural History Unit, producing programmes such as *Blue Planet; Life of Mammals; Wildlife on One; The Natural World* and *The Really Wild Show* for BBC1 and BBC2. It also produces natural history programmes for Radio 4 and Radio 5 Live. The Features department produces a wide range of television programmes, including *999; Antiques Roadshow; Bargain Hunt* and *Vets in Practice* in addition to radio programmes specialising in history, travel, literature and human interest features for Radio 4.

BBC London
35 Marylebone High Street, London W1U 4QA
☎020 7224 2424
Head of Regional Programming *Jane Mote*
Executive Editor *Mike MacFarlane* (Responsible for BBC London Live and Newsroom South East)
Editor, Newsgathering *Sandy Smith*

BBC North/BBC North West/ BBC North East & Cumbria
The regional centres at Leeds, Manchester and Newcastle make their own programmes on a bi-media approach, each centre having its own head of regional and local programmes.

BBC North (Leeds)
Broadcasting Centre, Woodhouse Lane, Leeds, West Yorkshire LS2 9PX
☎0113 244 1188
Head of Regional and Local Programmes *Colin Philpott*
Editor, Newsgathering *Jake Fowler*

Editor, Look North *Kate Watkins*
Assistant News Editors, Look North
Denise Wallace, Ned Thacker
Political Editor, North of Westminster
Len Tingle
**Senior Broadcast Journalist, North of
Westminster** *Rod Jones*
Weeklies Editor, Close Up North *Ian
Cundall*
Producers, Close Up North *Richard Taylor,
Paul Greenan*

BBC North West (Manchester)
New Broadcasting House, Oxford Road,
Manchester M60 1SJ
☎0161 200 2020
Head of Regional and Local Programmes
Martin Brooks
Editors, Newsgathering *Mike Bristow,
Michelle Mayman*
Output Editor *Tamsin O'Brien*
Producer, Northwest Tonight *Jim Clark*
Producer, Inside Out *Deborah van Bishop*
Producer, The Politics Show *Liam Fogarty*

**BBC North East & Cumbria
(Newcastle upon Tyne)**
Broadcasting Centre, Barrack Road,
Newcastle Upon Tyne NE99 2NE
☎0191 232 1313
Head of Regional and Local Programmes
Wendy Pilmer
Editor, Newsgathering *Andrew Hartley*
Executive Producer, Look North *Andrew
Lambert*

BBC South East (Tunbridge Wells)
The Great Hall, Mount Pleasant, Tunbridge
Wells, Kent TN1 1QQ
☎01892 670000
Head of Regional and Local Programmes
Laura Ellis (Responsible for BBC South East
[TV], BBC Radio Kent and BBC Southern
Counties Radio)
Editor, South East Today *Rod Beards*
Editor, Southern Counties Radio *Mike
Hapgood*
Editor, Radio Kent *Robert Wallace*
Editor, Newsgathering *Talya Roberson*
Producer, Inside Out *Linda Bell*

**BBC West/BBC South/
BBC South West**
The three regional television stations, BBC
West, BBC South and BBC South West pro-

duce the nightly news magazine programmes,
as well as regular 30-minute local current affairs
programmes and parliamentary programmes.
Each of the regions operates a comprehensive
local radio service as well as a range of correspondents specialising in subjects like health,
education, business, local government, home
affairs and the environment.

BBC West (Bristol)
Broadcasting House, Whiteladies Road, Bristol
BS8 2LR
☎0117 973 2211
Head of Regional and Local Programmes
Andrew Wilson (Responsible for BBC West
[TV], BBC Radio Bristol, BBC Somerset
Sound, BBC Radio Gloucestershire and
BBC Wiltshire Sound)
Output Editors *Jane Kinghorn, Stephanie
Marshall*
Series Producer, Inside Out *James
MacAlpine*

BBC South (Southampton)
Broadcasting House, Havelock Road,
Southampton, Hampshire SO14 7PU
☎023 8022 6201
Head of Regional and Local Programmes
Eve Turner (Responsible for BBC South
[TV], BBC Radio Berkshire, BBC Radio
Oxford and BBC Radio Solent)
Newsgathering Editor *Cathy Burnett*
Series Producer, Inside Out *Jane French*

BBC South West (Plymouth)
Broadcasting House, Seymour Road,
Mannamead, Plymouth, Devon PL3 5BD
☎01752 229201
Head of Regional and Local Programmes
Leo Devine (Responsible for BBC South
West [TV], BBC Radio Devon, BBC
Radio Cornwall, BBC Radio Guernsey and
BBC Radio Jersey)
News Editor *Simon Read*
Editor, Current Affairs *Simon Willis*

BBC Local Radio

BBC Local Radio
Room 2661, Broadcasting House, London
W1A 1AA
☎020 7580 4468
Website www.bbc.co/england

There are 39 local BBC radio stations in
England transmitting on FM and medium

wave. These present local news, information and entertainment to local audiences and reflect the life of the communities they serve. Each has its own newsroom which supplies local bulletins and national news service. Many have specialist producers. A comprehensive list of programmes for each is unavailable and would soon be out of date. For general information on programming, contact the relevant station direct.

BBC Radio Berkshire
PO Box 104.4, Reading, Berkshire RG94 8FH
☎0118 9464200 Fax 0118 9464555
Website www.bbc.co.uk/radioberkshire

Editor *Marianne Bell*

BBC Radio Bristol
PO Box 194, Bristol BS99 7QT
☎0117 974 1111 Fax 0117 923 9323
Email radio.bristol@bbc.co.uk
Website www.bbc.co.uk/radiobristol

Managing Editor *Jenny Lacey*

Wide range of feature material used.

BBC Radio Cambridgeshire
PO Box 96, 104 Hills Road, Cambridge
CB2 1LD
☎01223 259696 Fax 01223 460832
Email cambs@bbc.co.uk
Website www.bbc.co.uk/radiocambridgeshire

Editor *David Martin*

Commenced broadcasting in May 1982. Short stories are broadcast occasionally.

BBC Radio Cleveland
PO Box 95FM, Broadcasting House,
Newport Road, Middlesbrough, Cleveland
TS1 5DG
☎01642 225211 Fax 01642 211356
Email radio.cleveland@bbc.co.uk
Website www.bbc.co.uk/tees

Managing Editor *Andrew Glover*

Material used is mainly local to Teesside, Co. Durham and North Yorkshire, and is almost exclusively news and current affairs.

BBC Radio Cornwall
Phoenix Wharf, Truro, Cornwall TR1 1UA
☎01872 275421 Fax 01872 275045
Email radio.cornwall@bbc.co.uk
Website www.bbc.co.uk/radiocornwall

Editor *Pauline Causey*

On air from 1983 serving Cornwall and the Isles of Scilly. Broadcasts 117 hours of local pro-grammes weekly including news, phone-ins and specialist music. Martin Bailie's afternoon programme includes interviews with local authors and arts-related features on Cornish themes.

BBC Radio WM Coventry and Warwickshire
Holt Court, 1 Greyfriars Road, Coventry
CV1 2WR
☎024 7686 0086 Fax 024 7657 0100
Email coventry.warwickshire@bbc.co.uk
Website www.bbc.co.uk/
    coventrywarwickshire

Managing Editor *Keith Beech*

Commenced broadcasting in January 1990 as CWR. Shares programmes with sister station, BBC Radio WM. News, current affairs, public service information and community involvement, relevant to its broadcast area: Coventry and Warwickshire.

BBC Radio Cumbria
Annetwell Street, Carlisle, Cumbria CA3 8BB
☎01228 592444 Fax 01228 511195
Email radio.cumbria@bbc.co.uk
Website www.bbc.co.uk/cumbria

Editor *Nigel Dyson*

Occasional opportunities for plays and short stories are advertised on-air.

BBC Radio Cymru
Broadcasting House, Llandaff, Cardiff
CF5 2YQ
☎029 20 322018 Fax 029 20 322473
Email radio.cymru@bbc.co.uk
Website www.bbc.co.uk/radiocymru

Editor *Aled Glynne Davies*

Welsh language station serving Welsh speaking communities. Rich mix of news, music, sport, features, current affairs, drama, comedy, religion and education.

Writing Opportunities: **Drama** daily 10 minute soap *Eileen* and over nine further hours of new radio drama each year. **Comedy** occasional series during the year (for details of independent commissions see www.bbc.co.uk/wales/commissioning/

BBC Radio Derby
PO Box 104.5, Derby DE1 3HL
☎01332 361111 Fax 01332 290794
Email radio.derby@bbc.co.uk
Website www.bbc.co.uk/derby

Editor *Simon Cornes*

News, sport, information and entertainment.

BBC Radio Devon

PO Box 1034, Broadcasting House, Seymour
Road, Mannamead, Plymouth, Devon
PL3 5YQ
☎01752 260323 Fax 01752 234599
Email radio.devon@bbc.co.uk
Website www.bbc.co.uk/devon

Also at: Walnut Gardens, St David's Hill,
Exeter, Devon EX4 4DB
☎01392 215651

Managing Editor *John Lilley*
Head of Programmes *Ian Timms*
Head of News *Sarah Solftley*

On air since 1983. Programmes include *Douglas
Mounce with Show Time* – Sunday, 5.00 pm to
7.00 pm.

BBC Essex

198 New London Road, Chelmsford, Essex
CM2 9XB
☎01245 616000 Fax 01245 492983
Email essex@bbc.co.uk
Website www.bbc.co.uk/essex

Editor *Margaret Hyde*

Broadcasts local and regional programmes for
20 hours every day aimed at a mature audience.
Programmes are a mix of news, interviews,
expert contributors, phone-ins, sport and special interest such as gardening.

BBC Radio Foyle

8 Northland Road, Londonderry BT48 7GD
☎028 7137 8600 Fax 028 7137 8666
Website www.bbc.co.uk/northernireland

Managing Editor *Ana Leddy*
News Producers *Eimear O'Callaghan,
Paul McFadden*
Arts/Book Reviews *Colum Arbuckle*
Features *Michael Bradley*

Radio Foyle broadcasts about seven hours of
original material a day, seven days a week to
the north west of Northern Ireland. Other programmes are transmitted simultaneously with
Radio Ulster. The output ranges from news,
sport, and current affairs to live music recordings and arts reviews.

BBC Radio Gloucestershire

London Road, Gloucester GL1 1SW
☎01452 308585 Fax 01452 309491
Email radio.gloucestershire@bbc.co.uk
Website www.bbc.co.uk/radiogloucestershire

Managing Editor *Mark Hurrell*

News and information covering the large variety
of interests and concerns in Gloucestershire.

Leisure, sport and music, plus African Caribbean
and Asian interests. Regular book reviews and
interviews with local authors in the *Anna King
Show.*

BBC GLR

See **BBC London 94.9FM**

BBC GMR

PO Box 951, Oxford Road, Manchester
M60 1SD
☎0161 200 2000 Fax 0161 236 5804
Email gmr@bbc.co.uk
Website www.bbc.co.uk/gmr

Managing Editor *Steve Taylor*
News Editor *Mark Elliot*
Assistant Editor *Mike Shaft*

On air from 1970, originally as Radio
Manchester. Became BBC GMR in 1988. One
of the largest of the BBC local radio stations,
broadcasting news, current affairs, phone-ins,
help, advice and sport.

BBC Radio Guernsey

Broadcasting House, Bulwer Avenue,
St Sampson's, Guernsey, Channel Islands
GY2 4LA
☎01481 200600 Fax 01481 200361
Email radio.guernsey@bbc.co.uk
Website www.bbc.co.uk/radioguernsey

Managing Editor *Rod Holmes*

Opened with its sister station, BBC Radio
Jersey, in March 1982. Broadcasts 80 hours of
local programming a week.

BBC Hereford & Worcester

Hylton Road, Worcester WR2 5WW
☎01905 748485 Fax 01905 748006
Email bbchw@bbc.co.uk
Website www.bbc.co.uk/herefordworcester

Also at: 43 Broad Street, Hereford HR4 9HH
☎01432 355252 Fax 01432 356446

Managing Editor *James Coghill*

Has an interest in writers/writing with local
connections

BBC Radio Humberside

9 Chapel Street, Hull, North Humberside
HU1 3NU
☎01482 323232 Fax 01482 621403
Email radio.humberside@bbc.co.uk
Website www.bbc.co.uk/radiohumberside

Executive Editor *Helen Thomas*

On air since 1971. Occasionally broadcasts
short stories by local writers and holds com-

petitions for local amateur authors and play-wrights.

BBC Radio Jersey

18 Parade Road, St Helier, Jersey, Channel Islands JE2 3PL
☎01534 870000 Fax 01534 732569
Email jersey@bbc.co.uk
Website www.bbc.co.uk/radiojersey
Managing Editor *Denzil Dudley*
Assistant Editor *Matthew Price*

Local news, current affairs and community items.

BBC Radio Kent

The Great Hall, Mount Pleasant Road, Tunbridge Wells, Kent TN1 1QQ
☎01892 670000 Fax 01892 549118
Email radio.kent@bbc.co.uk
Website www.bbc.co.uk/radiokent
Managing Editor *Robert Wallace*

Occasional commissions are made for local interest documentaries and other one-off programmes.

BBC Radio Lancashire

Darwen Street, Blackburn, Lancashire BB2 2EA
☎01254 262411 Fax 01254 680821
Email radio.lancashire@bbc.co.uk
Website www.bbc.co.uk/radiolancashire
Editor *John Clayton*

Journalism-based radio station, interested in interviews with local writers. Contact *Caroline Mai* Daily Programmes Producer Monday to Friday (caroline.mai@bbc.co.uk)

BBC Radio Leeds

Broadcasting House, Woodhouse Lane, Leeds, West Yorkshire LS2 9PN
☎0113 244 2131 Fax 0113 242 0652
Email radio.leeds@bbc.co.uk
Website www.bbc.co.uk/radioleeds
Managing Editor *Richard Whittaker*

One of the country's biggest local radio stations, BBC Radio Leeds was also one of the first, coming on air in the 1960s as something of an experimental venture. The station is 'all talk', with a comprehensive news, sport and information service as the backbone of its daily output. BBC Radio Leeds has been a regular finalist for the title of Sony Regional Station of the Year. Has also won two Gold Sonys for best presentation.

BBC Radio Leicester

Epic House, Charles Street, Leicester LE1 3SH
☎0116 251.6688 Fax 0116 251 1463
Email radio.leicester@bbc.co.uk
Website www.bbc.co.uk/radioleicester
Editor *Liam McCarthy*

The first local station in Britain. Occasional interviews with local authors.

BBC Radio Lincolnshire

PO Box 219, Newport, Lincoln LN1 3XY
☎01522 511411 Fax 01522 511726
Email radio.lincolnshire@bbc.co.uk
Website www.bbc.co.uk/radiolincolnshire
Managing Editor *Charlie Partridge*

Unsolicited material considered only if locally relevant. Maximum 1000 words: straight narrative preferred, ideally with a topical content.

BBC London 94.9FM

35 Marylebone High Street, London W1U 4QA
☎020 7224 2000 Fax 020 7208 9661
Email londonlive@bbc.co.uk
Website www.bbc.co.uk/londonlive
Editor *David Robey*

Formerly Greater London Radio (GLR), launched in 1988, BBC London 94.9 broadcasts news, information, travel bulletins, sport and music to Greater London and the Home Counties. Dotun Adebayo's *Word for Word* explores and celebrates poetry, the spoken word and song lyrics every Sunday between 1.00 pm and 3.00 pm.

BBC Radio Manchester
See **BBC GMR**

BBC Radio Merseyside

55 Paradise Street, Liverpool L1 3BP
☎0151 708 5500 Fax 0151 794 0988
Email radio.merseyside@bbc.co.uk
Website www.bbc.co.uk/radiomerseyside *or* www.bbc.co.uk/liverpool
Editor *Mick Ord*

First Friday – a monthly poetry slot between 1.30 pm and 2.00 pm on the first Friday of every month in the Roger Phillips lunchtime programme. Merseyside writers can offer poetry by e-mailing roger.phillips@bbc.co.uk or send copies with name/address attached, to 'First Friday Poetry', c/o BBC Radio Merseyside at the address above. Only the poets used will be acknowledged and contacted.

BBC Radio Newcastle

Broadcasting Centre, Barrack Road,
Newcastle upon Tyne NE99 1RN
☎0191 232 4141
Email radio.newcastle@bbc.co.uk
Website www.bbc.co.uk/tyne *or*
  www.bbc.co.uk/wear

Editor *Sarah Drummond*
Senior Producer (Programmes) *Sarah Miller*

Commenced broadcasting in January 1971.
The BBC's eighth biggest local radio station in
England, Radio Newcastle reaches an audience
of 229,000.

BBC Radio Norfolk

Norfolk Tower, Surrey Street, Norwich,
Norfolk NR1 3PA
☎01603 617411 Fax 01603 633692
Email norfolk@bbc.co.uk
Website www.bbc.co.uk/radionorfolk

Editor *David Clayton*

Good local ideas and material welcome for
features/documentaries, but must relate
directly to Norfolk.

BBC Radio Northampton

Broadcasting House, Abington Street,
Northampton NN1 2BH
☎01604 239100 Fax 01604 230709
Email northampton@bbc.co.uk
Website www.bbc.co.uk/radionorthampton

Managing Editor *David Clargo*

Books of local interest are regularly featured.
Authors and poets are interviewed on merit.
Poems and short stories are reviewed occasionally, but not broadcast. Runs regular competitions for local writers.

BBC Radio Nottingham

London Road, Nottingham NG2 4UU
☎0115 955 0500 Fax 0115 902 1983
Email radio.nottingham@bbc.co.uk
Website www.bbc.co.uk/radionottingham

Editor *Mike Bettison*

Rarely broadcasts scripted pieces of any kind
but interviews with authors form a regular part
of the station's output.

BBC Radio Oxford

PO Box 95.2, Oxford OX2 7YL
☎08459 311444 Fax 08459 311555
Email radio.oxford@bbc.co.uk
Website www.bbc.co.uk/radiooxford
Managing Editor *Phil Ashworth*

Restored to its original name in 2000 having
been merged with BBC Radio Berkshire in
1995 to create BBC Thames Valley. The station
frequently carries interviews with local authors
and offers books as prizes.

BBC Radio Scotland (Dumfries)

Elmbank, Lover's Walk, Dumfries DG1 1NZ
☎01387 268008 Fax 01387 252568
Email dumfries@bbc.co.uk

Senior Producer *Willie Johnston*

Previously Radio Solway. The station mainly
outputs news bulletins (four daily) although the
station has become more of a production centre with programmes being made for Radio
Scotland as well as BBC Radio 2 and 5 Live.
Freelancers of a high standard, familiar with
Radio Scotland, should contact the producer.

BBC Radio Scotland (Orkney)

Castle Street, Kirkwall, Orkney KW15 1DF
☎01856 873939 Fax 01856 872908

Senior Producer *John Fergusson*

Regular programmes include *Around Orkney*
(weekday news programme) and *Bruck* (magazine programme).

BBC Radio Scotland (Selkirk)

Municipal Buildings, High Street, Selkirk
TD7 4JX
☎01750 21884 Fax 01750 22400

Senior Broadcaster *Ninian Reid*

Formerly BBC Radio Tweed. Local news bulletins.

BBC Radio Sheffield

Shoreham Street, Sheffield S1 4RS
☎0114 273 1177 Fax 0114 267 5454
Email radio.sheffield@bbc.co.uk
Website www.bbc.co.uk/radiosheffield
Managing Editor *Gary Keown*
Programmes Editor *Angus Morat*
News Editor *Michael Woodcock*

Writer interviews, writing-related topics and
readings on the Rony Robinson show at
9.00 am.

BBC Radio Shetland

Pitt Lane, Lerwick, Shetland ZE1 0DW
☎01595 694747 Fax 01595 694307
Senior Producer *Caroline Moyes*

Regular programmes include *Good Evening
Shetland*. An occasional books programme highlights the activities of local writers and writers'
groups.

BBC Radio Shropshire

2–4 Boscobel Drive, Shrewsbury, Shropshire
SY1 3TT
☎01743 248484   Fax 01743 237018
Email radio.shropshire@bbc.co.uk
Website www.bbc.co.uk/shropshire
Managing Editor *Tim Pemberton*

On air since 1985. Unsolicited literary material
rarely used, and then only if locally relevant.

BBC Radio Solent

Broadcasting House, Havelock Road,
Southampton, Hampshire SO14 7PW
☎023 8063 1311   Fax 023 8033 9648
Email radio.solent@bbc.co.uk
Website www.bbc.co.uk/radiosolent
Managing Editor *Mia Costello*

Broadcasting since 1970.

BBC Somerset Sound

Broadcasting House, Park Street, Taunton,
Somerset TA1 4DA
☎01823 348920   Fax 01823 332539
Email somerset.sound@bbc.co.uk
Website www.bbc.co.uk/radiobristol/
  somerset
Managing Editor *Jenny Lacey*
Assistant Editor *Simon Clifford*

Informal, speech-based programming, with
strong news and current affairs output and regular local-interest features, including local writing. Poetry and short stories on the *Adam
Thomas Programme*.

BBC Southern Counties Radio

Broadcasting Centre, Guildford, Surrey
GU2 5AP
☎01483 306306   Fax 01483 304952
Email southern.counties.radio@bbc.co.uk
Website www.bbc.co.uk/southerncounties
Also at: Broadcasting House, 40–42 Queens,
Brighton, East Sussex BN1 3XB
Managing Editor *Mike Hapgood*

Regular programmes include three individual
breakfast shows: *Breakfast Live in Brighton with
JoAnne Good/in Surrey with Ed Douglas/in Sussex
with John Radford*.

BBC Radio Stoke

Cheapside, Hanley, Stoke on Trent,
Staffordshire ST1 1JJ
☎01782 208080   Fax 01782 289115
Email radio.stoke@bbc.co.uk
Website www.bbc.co.uk/radiostoke
Editor *Sue Owen*

On air since 1968, one of the first eight 'experimental' BBC stations. Emphasis on news, current affairs and local topics. Music represents
one fifth of total output. Unsolicited material
of local interest is welcome – send to *Janine
Machin*.

BBC Radio Suffolk

Broadcasting House, St Matthew's Street,
Ipswich, Suffolk IP1 3EP
☎01473 250000   Fax 01473 210887
Email suffolk@bbc.co.uk *or*
radiosuffolk@bbc.co.uk
Website www.bbc.co.uk/radiosuffolk
Managing Editor *Gerald Main*

Strongly locally speech-based, dealing with
news, current affairs, community issues, the arts,
agriculture, commerce, travel, sport and leisure.
Programmes sometimes carry interviews with
writers.

BBC Thames Valley

See **BBC Radio Oxford**

BBC Three Counties Radio

1 Hastings Street, Luton, Bedfordshire
LU1 5XL
☎01582 637400   Fax 01582 401467
Email 3cr@bbc.co.uk
Website www.bbc.co.uk/3counties
Managing Editor *Mark Norman*

Encourages freelance contributions from the
community across a wide range of radio output, including interview and feature material.
Interested in local history topics (five minutes
maximum).

BBC Radio Ulster

Broadcasting House, Ormeau Avenue, Belfast
BT2 8HQ
☎028 9033 8000

Programmes broadcast from 6.30 am to midnight weekdays and from 6.55 am to midnight at
weekends. Radio Ulster has won seven Sony
awards in recent years. Programmes include:
Good Morning Ulster; *John Bennett*; *Gerry Anderson*;
Talk Back; *Just Jones*; *Evening Extra*; *On Your
Behalf*; *Your Place and Mine* and *Across the Line*.

BBC Radio Wales

Broadcasting House, Llandaff, Cardiff CF5 2YQ
☎029 2032 2000   Fax 029 2032 2674
Email radio.wales@bbc.co.uk
Website www.bbc.co.uk/radiowales
Editor *Julie Barton*
Editor, Radio Wales News *Geoff Williams*

Broadcasts news on the hour and half hour throughout weekday daytime programmes; hourly bulletins in the evenings and at weekends. Programmes include *Good Morning Wales*; *Roy Noble*; *Nicola Heywood Thomas* and *Kevin Hughes*. Access line number: 08700 100110.

BBC Radio Wiltshire
PO Box 1234, Trowbridge & Salisbury, Wiltshire
☎01793 513626 Fax 01793 513650
Email radio.wiltshire@bbc.co.uk
Website www.bbc.co.uk/england/radiowiltshire
Editor *Tony Worgon*

Regular programmes include: *Peter Heaton-Jones's Mid-Morning Show* (reviews and author interviews).

BBC Radio WM
PO Box 206, Birmingham B5 7SD
☎0121 432 2000 Fax 0121 472 3174
Email radio.wm@bbc.co.uk
Website www.bbc.co.uk/radiowm
Managing Editor *Keith Beech*

Commenced broadcasting in November 1970 as BBC Birmingham and has won four gold Sony awards in recent years. Speech-based station broadcasting to the West Midlands, South Staffordshire, North Worcestershire and North Warwickshire.

BBC Radio York
20 Bootham Row, York YO30 7BR
☎01904 641351 Fax 01904 610937
Email northyorkshire.radio@bbc.co.uk
Website www.bbc.co.uk/northyorkshire
Editor *Matt Youdale*

Stories only accepted in reponse to occasional short story competitions.

Independent Television

Anglia Television
Anglia House, Norwich, Norfolk NR1 3JG
☎01603 615151 Fax 01603 761245
Email angliatv@angliatv.co.uk
Website www.angliatv.com
Managing Director *Graham Creelman*
Controller of Programmes *Neil Thompson*
Controller of News *Guy Adams*

Anglia Television is a major producer of programmes for the ITV network, including *Trisha* (Trisha Goddard's chat show) and major documentaries. Network drama is produced by Anglia's parent company, Granada.

Border Television plc
Television Centre, Durranhill, Carlisle, Cumbria CA1 3NT
☎01228 525101 Fax 01228 541384
Website www.border-tv.com
Deputy Chairman *James Graham, OBE*
Controller of Programmes *Neil Robinson*

Border's programming concentrates on documentaries rather than drama. Most scripts are supplied in-house but occasionally there are commissions. Apart from notes, writers should not submit written work until their ideas have been fully discussed.

Carlton Television
Website www.carlton.com
Chief Executive, Carlton Channels *Clive Jones*
Director of Programmes, Carlton Productions *Steve Hewlett*

Carlton Television holds four of the 15 regional ITV licences: Carlton – the weekday broadcaster for the London region; Carlton Central Region – covering the east, west and south Midlands; Carlton West Country Region – covering the south west of England; HTV Wales and HTV West – covering the west of England. Network drama includes *The Vice; Dead Gorgeous; Margery and Gladys* and *Fortysomething*. See also **Carlton Productions** under **Film, TV and Radio Production Companies**.

Carlton Broadcasting, London Region
101 St Martin's Lane, London WC2N 4RF
☎020 7240 4000 Fax 020 7240 4171

Managing Director, Broadcasting *Colin Stanbridge*

**Carlton Broadcasting,
Carlton Central Region**
Gas Street, Birmingham B1 2JT
☎0121 643 9898 Fax 0121 634 4240
Website www.carlton.com/central
Managing Director, Carlton Broadcasting *Ian Squires*

Regular regional programmes include *Central Weekend* and *Asian Eye*.

**Carlton Broadcasting,
Carlton West Country Region**
Langage Science Park, Western Wood Way, Plymouth, Devon PL7 5BQ

☎01752 333333 Fax 01752 333444
Website www.carlton.com/westcountry
Managing Director *Mark Haskell*
Director of Programmes *Jane McCloskey*
Controller of News *Phil Carrodus*
Head of Current Affairs *Graham Smith*

Came on air in January 1993. News, current affairs, documentary and religious programming.

HTV Wales

The TV Centre, Culverhouse Cross, Cardiff CF5 6XJ
☎029 2059 0590 Fax 029 2059 7183
Website www.htvwales.co.uk

Controller/Director of Programmes *Elis Owen*

HTV West

Television Centre, Bath Road, Bristol BS4 3HG
☎0117 972 2722 Fax 0117 972 2400
Website www.htvwest.co.uk

Managing Director *Jeremy Payne*
Controller, HTV West & Director of Regional Programmes *Sandra Jones*

Channel 4

124 Horseferry Road, London SW1P 2TX
☎020 7396 4444 Fax 020 7306 8356
Website www.channel4.com

Director of Programmes *To be appointed*
Head of Film *Tessa Ross*
Head of Entertainment and Comedy, Controller of E4 *Danielle Lux*
Head of Features & Factual Entertainment *Ben Frow*

COMMISSIONING EDITORS
Head of Drama and Animation *Tessa Ross*
Head of Comedy *Caroline Leddy*
Head of Entertainment *John McHugh*
Director of Programmes, E4 *Murray Boland*
Head of Contemporary Factual Group & Documentaries *Peter Dale*
News, Current Affairs & Business *Dorothy Byrne*
Sport *David Kerr*
Multicultural Programmes *Yasmin Anwar*
Controller of Acquisition *June Dromgoole*

Channel 4 started broadcasting as a national channel in November 1982. It enjoys unique status as the world's only major public service broadcaster funded entirely by its own commercial activities. All programmes are commissioned from independent production companies and are

broadcast across the whole of the UK except those parts of Wales covered by S4C. Its FilmFour channel, launched in November 1998, is a premium pay-TV channel featuring modern independent cinema. A second digital channel, E4 was launched in January 2001, broadcasting a range of programmes similar to Channel 4.

Channel Television

Television Centre, La Pouquelaye, St Helier, Jersey, Channel Islands JE1 3ZD
☎01534 816816 Fax 01534 816817
Website www.channeltv.co.uk

Also at: Television House, Bulwer Avenue, St Sampsons, Guernsey, Channel Islands GY2 4LA
☎01481 241888 Fax 01481 241878

Managing Director *Michael Lucas*
Director of Programmes *Karen Rankine*
Director of Sales *Gordon De Ste Croix*
Director of Resources & Transmission *Kevin Banner*

Channel Television is the Independent Television broadcaster to the Channel Islands, serving 143,000 residents, most of whom live on the main islands, Jersey, Guernsey, Alderney and Sark. The station has a weekly reach of more than 94% with local programmes (in the region of five and a half hours each week) at the heart of the ITV service to the islands.

Five

22 Long Acre, London WC2E 9LY
☎020 7550 5555 Fax 020 7550 5554
Website www.channel5.co.uk

CEO *Jane Lighting*
Director of Programmes *Kevin Lygo*
Controller of Children's and Religious Programmes *Nick Wilson*
Senior Programme Controller *Chris Shaw*
Controller of Drama Programmes *Corinne Hollingworth*

Channel 5 Broadcasting Ltd won the franchise for Britain's third commercial terrestrial television station in 1995 and came on air at the end of March 1997. Regular programmes include *Family Affairs* (Monday to Friday soap opera) and *The Wright Stuff* (weekday morning chat show), plus documentaries, drama, films, children's programmes, sport and entertainment.

GMTV

The London Television Centre, Upper Ground, London SE1 9TT
☎020 7827 7000 Fax 020 7827 7249
Email talk2us@gmtv.co.uk

Website www.gmtv.co.uk
Managing Director *Paul Corley*
Director of Programmes *Peter McHugh*
Managing Editor *John Scammell*

Winner of the national breakfast television franchise. Jointly owned by Scottish Media Group, Carlton Communications, Walt Disney Company and Granada Group. GMTV took over from TV-AM on 1 January 1993, with live programming from 6.00 am to 9.25 am. Regular news headlines, current affairs, topical features, showbiz and lifestyle, sports and business, quizzes and competitions, travel and weather reports. Launched its digital service, GMTV2, in January 1999, with daily broadcasts from 6.00 am to 9.25 am. News reports, travel, health and lifestyle features, some simulcast with GMTV1. Children's programming on Saturdays.

Grampian Television Limited
Craigshaw Business Park, West Tullos,
Aberdeen AB12 3QH
☎01224 848848 Fax 01224 848800
Website www.grampiantv.co.uk
Managing Director *Derrick Thomson*
Head of News and Current Affairs *Henry Eagles*

Extensive regional news and reports including farming, fishing and sports, interviews and leisure features, various light entertainment, Gaelic and religious programmes, and live coverage of the Scottish political, economic and industrial scene. Serves the area stretching from Fife to Shetland. Regular programmes include *North Tonight*; *The People Show* and other varied genre shows strongly reflecting the regionality of the north of Scotland.

Granada Television
Quay Street, Manchester M60 9EA
☎0161 832 7211 Fax 0161 953 0283
Website www.granadamedia.com
Director of Programmes *John Whiston*
Director of Production *Claire Poyser*
Controller of Regional Programmes *Kieron Collins*
Controller of Drama *Carolyn Reynolds*
Controller of Current Affairs and Features *Jeff Anderson*
Controller of Documentaries, History and Science *Bill Jones*

Opportunities for freelance writers are not great but mss from professional writers will be considered. All mss should be addressed to the head of scripts. Regular programmes include *Coronation Street* and *Tonight*.

HTV Wales/ HTV West
See **Carlton Television**

ITN (Independent Television News Ltd)
200 Gray's Inn Road, London WC1X 8XZ
☎020 7833 3000 Fax 020 7430 4868
Email contact@itn.co.uk
Website www.itn.co.uk
Chief Executive *Mark Wood*
Editor-in-Chief *Richard Tait*
Editor, ITN News for ITV *David Mannion*
Editor, Channel 4 News *Jim Gray*
Editor, Channel 5 News *Gary Rogers*

Provider of the main national and international news for ITV, Channel 4 and Five, and radio news for IRN. Programmes on ITV: *Lunchtime News*; *Evening News*; *News at Ten*, plus regular news summaries, and three programmes a day at weekends. Programmes on Channel 4 include the in-depth news analysis programmes *Channel 4 News* and *The Big Breakfast News*. Programmes on Five: *5 News Early*; *5 News at Noon*; *5 News* plus regular updates. ITN also has operating control of *Euronews*, Europe's only pan-European broadcaster. Since August 2000, ITN broadcasts in its own right on ITN News Channel, a 24-hour news service available for television, video, audio and text format.

LWT (London Weekend Television)
The London Television Centre, Upper Ground, London SE1 9LT
☎020 7620 1620
Website www.itv.com/lwt
Executive Chairman *Charles Allen*
Managing Director *Christy Swords*
Director of Production *Claire Poyser*
Controller of Entertainment *Nigel Hall*
Controller of Drama *Michele Buck*
Controller of Arts *Melvyn Bragg*
Controller of Factual Programmes *Will Smith*
Deputy Director of Broadcasting *Geraldine Woods*

Makers of current affairs, entertainment and drama series. Provides a large proportion of ITV's drama and light entertainment, and also for BSkyB and Channel 4.

Meridian Broadcasting
Television Centre, Southampton, Hampshire SO14 0PZ
☎023 8022 2555 Fax 023 8033 5050
Email viewerliaison@meridiantv.com
Website www.meridiantv.com

Managing Director *Lindsay Charlton*
Controller of Regional Programmes *Mark Southgate*
Director of News *Andy Cooper*

Meridian's studios in Southampton provide a base for network and regional productions. Regular regional programmes include the award-winning news service, *Meridian Tonight*; *Countryways* and *Grass Roots*.

S4C

Parc Tŷ Glas, Llanishen, Cardiff CF14 5DU
☎029 2074 7444 Fax 029 2075 4444
Email s4c@s4c.co.uk
Website www.s4c.co.uk

Chief Executive *Huw Jones*
Director of Programmes *Huw Eirug*

The Welsh 4th Channel, established by the Broadcasting Act 1980, is responsible for a schedule of Welsh and English programmes on the Fourth Channel in Wales. Known as S4C, the analogue service is made up of about 34 hours per week of Welsh language programmes and more than 85 hours of English language output from Channel 4. S4C Digital broadcasts in Welsh exclusively for 80 hours per week. Ten hours a week of the Welsh programmes are provided by the BBC; the remainder are purchased from HTV and independent producers. Drama, comedy and documentary are all part of S4C's programming. Commissioning guidelines can be viewed on the website given above.

Scottish Television Ltd

200 Renfield Street, Glasgow G2 3PR
☎0141 300 3000 Fax 0141 300 3030
Website www.stv.co.uk

Managing Director, Scottish TV *Sandy Ross*
Head of Features & Entertainment *Agnes Wilkie*
Senior News Producer *Paul McKinney*
Head of Sport *Andrea Brownlie*
Head of General Factual Programmes *Jackie Brady*
Head of Drama *Eric Coulter*
Head of Children's Programmes *Elizabeth Partyka*

Scottish Television produces 16.5 hours of television a week for the central Scotland region and a number of network programmes. This is made up of news, current affairs and sport, and a wide-ranging portfolio of other programmes ranging from entertainment, documentary, religion, drama and children's such as *Taggart*; *I'm A Celebrity ... Get Me Out of Here* and *Squeak!*

Scottish Television together with Grampian and Scottish Screen have made a number of short films under the banner of New Found Land.

Teletext Ltd

Building 10, Chiswick Park, Chiswick High Road, London W4 5TS
☎0970 731 300 Fax 0870 731 3001
Website www.teletext.co.uk

Managing Director *Mike Stewart*
Editor-in-Chief *John Sage*

On 1 January 1993, Teletext Ltd took over the electronic publishing service for both ITV and Channel 4. Transmits a wide range of news pages and features, including current affairs, sport, TV listings, weather, travel, holidays, finance, games, competitions, etc. Also broadcasts on Five, digital terrestrial (Channel 9), digital cable TV and the Web and mobile services.

Tyne Tees Television

Television Centre, Newcastle upon Tyne NE1 2AL
☎0191 261 0181 Fax 0191 261 2302
Email tyne.tees@granadamedia.com
Website www.tynetees.tv

Managing Director *Margaret Fay*
Controller of Programmes *Graeme Thompson*
Head of New Media *Malcolm Wright*
Editor, Current Affairs and Features *Jane Bolesworth*
Managing Editor, News *Graham Marples*
Executive Producer & Head of Development, Yorkshire Tyne Tees Features *Mark Robinson*
Head of Regional Affairs *Norma Hope*
Head of Sport *Roger Tames*

Programming covers religion, politics, news and current affairs, regional documentaries, business, entertainment, sport and arts. Regular programmes include *North East Tonight with Mike Neville* and *Around the House* (politics). In 2003, Tyne Tees screened a series of eight new regional dramas – *Hot House* – showcasing north east writers and directors.

UTV (Ulster Television)

Havelock House, Ormeau Road, Belfast BT7 1EB
☎028 9032 8122 Fax 028 9024 6695

Director of UTV *Alan Bremner*
Head of News, Current Affairs and Sport *Rob Morrison*

Regular programmes on news and current

affairs, politics, sport, education, music, light entertainment, arts, health and local culture.

Yorkshire Television

The Television Centre, Leeds, West Yorkshire LS3 1JS
☎0113 243 8283 Fax 0113 244 5107
Website www.granadamedia.com

London office: Global House, 96–108 Great Suffolk Street, London SE1 0BE
☎020 7578 4304 Fax 020 7578 4320

Chairman *Charles Allen*
Managing Director *David Croft*
Director of Programmes, Yorkshire Tyne Tees Productions *John Whiston*
Controller of Drama, Yorkshire Tyne Tees Productions *Keith Richardson*
Controller of Drama, YTV *Carolyn Reynolds*
Controller of Comedy Drama and Drama Features *David Reynolds*

Part of Granada Media Group. Drama series, situation comedies, film productions and long-running series like *Emmerdale* and *Heartbeat*. Always looking for strong writing in these areas, but prefers to find it through an agent. Documentary/current affairs material tends to be supplied by producers; opportunities in these areas are rare but adaptations of published work as a documentary subject are considered. In theory, opportunity exists within series, episode material. Best approach is through a good agent.

Cable and Satellite Television

Artsworld

80 Silverthorne Road, London SW8 2XA
☎020 7819 1160 Fax 020 7819 1161
Email tv@artsworld.com
Website www.artsworld.com

Chief Executive *John Hambley*
Programme Controller *Alison Martin*

Satellite arts channel, launched in November 2000. Broadcasts from 7.00 pm to midnight (repeated from 2.00 pm to 7.00 pm the following day) via BSkyB. Programmes include the series, *Great Books*.

British Sky Broadcasting Ltd (BSkyB)

6 Centaurs Business Park, Grant Way, Isleworth, Middlesex TW7 5QD
☎020 7705 3000 Fax 020 7705 3030
Website www.sky.com

Chief Executive *Tony Ball*
Managing Director, Sky Networkds *Dawn Airey*
Chief Operating Officer *Richard Freudenstein*
Head of Sky News *Nick Pollard*
Managing Director, Sky Sports *Vic Wakeling*

Launched in 1989, British Sky Broadcasting gives over 15 million viewers (in 6.3 million households) access to movies, news, entertainment and sports channels, and interactive services on Sky digital. Launched in October 1998, Sky digital has more than 380 channels and offers a range of innovative interactive services. 2001 saw the introduction of the next-generation integrated digital satellite set-top box/personal video recorder, Sky+.

WHOLLY-OWNED SKY CHANNELS

Sky Premier
Blockbusting action, comedy and romance, featuring recent box office hits.

Sky MovieMax
Contemporary hit movies, embracing all genres, from Hollywood's major studios.

Sky Cinema
Classic and popular movies from 70 years of cinema, including seasons and retrospectives.

Sky News
Award winning 24-hours news service with hourly bulletins and expert comment.

Sky One/Sky One Mix
The most frequently watched non-terrestrial channel with the accent on entertainment for 16–34-year-olds.

Sky Sports 1/Sky Sports 2/Sky Sports 3/Sky Sports News/Sky Sports Extra
Over 30,000 hours of sport are broadcast every year across the five Sky Sports channels. Sky Sports 1, 2 and 3 are devoted to live events, support programmes and in-depth sports coverage seven days a week. Two further channels are available on Sky digital: Sky Sports News provides sports news and the latest results and information 24 hours a day; Sky Sports Extra carries additional sports programming including the award-winning live interactive coverage.

Sky Travel
Magazine shows, documentaries and teleshopping.

JOINT VENTURES
National Geographic; Nickelodeon; Nick Jr; The History Channel; Paramount Comedy Channel; QVC; MUTV; Music Choice Europe;

Granada Men & Motors; Granada Plus; Artsworld; Adventure One; The Biography Channel; Attheraces; Chelsea Digital Media.

CNBC Europe
10 Fleet Place, London EC4M 7QS
☎020 7653 9300 Fax 020 7653 9480
Email feedback@cnbceurope.com
Website www.cnbceurope.com
Managing Director *Rick Cotton*

A service of NBC and Dow Jones. 24-hour business and financial news service. Programmes include *Today's Business Europe; European Market Watch; Capital Ideas; Squawk Box.*

CNN International
Turner House, 16 Great Marlborough Street, London W1F 7HS
☎020 7693 1000 Fax 020 7693 1001
Website www.europe.cnn.com
Senior Vice President, CNN International Europe, Middle East, Africa & Editor, CNN.com Europe *Tony Maddox*

CNN, the leading global 24-hour news network, is available to one billion people worldwide via the 35 CNN branded TV, Internet, radio and mobile services produced by CNN News Group, an AOL Time Warner company. CNN has major production centres in Atlanta, New York, Los Angeles, London, Hong Kong and Mexico City. The London bureau, the largest outside the USA, is CNN's European headquarters and produces over 50 hours of programming per week. There are 7 live business and news programmes, including *News Biz Today; Business International; World News* and *World Business Today.* Weekly programmes include *Inside Europe,* a look at the cultural heritage of Europe and *International Correspondents,* a discussion programme featuring journalists and media figures.

MTV Networks Europe
180 Oxford Street, London W1D 1DS
☎020 7284 7777 Fax 020 7284 7788
Website www.mtv.co.uk
President & Chief Executive *Brent Hansen*

ESTABLISHED 1987. Europe's 24-hour music and youth entertainment channel, available on cable, via satellite and digitally. Transmitted from London in English across Europe.

NBC Europe
Unit 1/1, Harbour Yard, Chelsea Harbour, London SW10 0XD
☎020 7352 9205 Fax 020 7352 9628

Chairman *Patrick Cox*
Director of Programming *Bernhard Bertram*

24-hour European broad-based news, information and entertainment service in English, with additional programmes in German and advertisements in English and German.

Travel (Landmark Travel Channel)
66 Newman Street, London W1P 3LA
☎020 7636 5401 Fax 020 7636 6424
Website www.travelchannel.co.uk

Launched in February 1994. Broadcasts programmes and information on the world of travel. Destinations reports, lifestyle programmes plus food and drink, sport and leisure pursuits. Transmits from 7.00 am to 1.00 am throughout Europe and Africa.

National Commercial Radio

Classic FM
7 Swallow Place, London W1B 2AG
☎020 7343 9000 Fax 020 7344 2700
Website www.classicfm.com
Chief Executive *Ralph Bernard*
Managing Director/Programme Controller *Roger Lewis*
Managing Editor *Darren Henley*

Classic FM, Britain's largest national commercial radio station, started broadcasting in September 1992. Plays accessible classical music 24 hours a day and broadcasts news, weather, travel, business information, political/celebrity/general interest talks, features and interviews. Classic has gone well beyond its expectations, attracting 7 million listeners a week. Winner of the 'Station of the Year' Sony Award in 2000.

Digital One
20 Southampton Street, London WC2E 7QH
☎020 7288 4600
Email info@digitalone.co.uk
Website www.ukdigitalradio.com

The UK's only national commercial digital radio network. Backed by radio group GWR and cable supplier ntl, Digital One began broadcasting on 15 November 1999. Channels include **Classic FM**, **Virgin Radio**, **TalkSport** and **Oneword**.

Oneword
Landseer House, 19 Charing Cross Road, London WC2H 0ES
☎020 7976 3030 Fax 020 7930 9460

Website www.oneword.co.uk

Managing Director *Ben Budworth*
Programme Manager *Christina Captieux*

The first commercial radio station dedicated solely to the transmission of plays, books, comedy and reviews for those who are 'looking for a break from unrelenting music on the radio'. Broadcasts between 6.00 am and midnight daily on the Digital One network in the UK, on Sky Digital (channel 887), Freeview (channel 893), ntl (channel 893) in Europe and worldwide on the Internet. Programmes include *Between the Lines*, a twice-daily conversation by Paul Blezard with different authors. Winner of the 'Station of the Year' Sony Radio Awards in 2001 and 2002.

TalkSport

PO Box 1089, London SE1 8WQ
☎020 7959 7800
Website www.talksport.net

Programme Director *Mike Parry*

Commenced broadcasting in February 1995 as Talk Radio UK. Re-launched January 2000 as TalkSport, the UK's first sports radio station. Broadcasts 24 hours a day. News items can be e-mailed to *Mike Parry* via the website.

Virgin Radio

1 Golden Square, London W1F 9DJ
☎020 7434 1215 Fax 020 7494 1055
Website www.virginradio.co.uk

Chief Executive *John Pearson*
Programme Director *Paul Jackson*

Music-based station launched in 1973, bought by Chris Evans' Ginger Media Group in December 1997 and acquired by the Scottish Media Group in March 2000.

Independent Local Radio

96.3 Radio Aire/Magic 828

51 Burley Road, Leeds, West Yorkshire LS3 1LR
☎0113 283 5500 Fax 0113 283 5501
Website www.radioaire.co.uk

Programme Controller *Stuart Baldwin*

Music-based programming. 96.3 Radio Aire caters for the 15–34–year–old listener while Magic 828 aims at the 25–44 age group with easy favourites.

Beacon FM/Classic Gold WABC

267 Tettenhall Road, Wolverhampton, West Midlands WV6 0DQ

☎01902 461300 Fax 01902 461299
Email beaconfm@koko.com
Website www.koko.com

Programme Controller *Chris Pegg*

Part of the GWR Group plc. No outlets for unsolicited literary material.

Radio Borders

Tweedside Park, Tweedbank, Galashiels TD1 3TD
☎01896 759444 Fax 0845 345 7080
Website www.radioborders.com

Programme Controller *Danny Gallagher*
Head of News *Angeline McConville*

Music-based station with local and national news.

Breeze

See **Essex FM**

BRMB-FM 96.4/1152 Capital Gold

Nine Brindley Place, 4 Oozells Square, Birmingham B1 2DJ
☎0121 245 5000 Fax 0121 245 5245
Website www.brmb.co.uk

Programme Controller *Adam Bridge*
News Editor *Kevin Pashby*

Music-based stations; no outlets for writers. Part of Capital Radio Plc.

Broadland 102/Classic Gold Amber

47–49 Colegate, Norwich, Norfolk NR3 1DB
☎01603 630621
Fax 01603 671175 (newsroom)
Website www.koko.com

Programme Controller *Chris Marston*

Part of GWR Group plc. Popular music programmes and local news only.

1152 Capital Gold

See **BRMB-FM 96.4**

Capital Radio

30 Leicester Square, London WC2H 7LA
☎020 7766 6000 Fax 020 7766 6100
Website www.capitalfm.com

Group Programme Director *Keith Pringle*

Commenced broadcasting in October 1973 as the country's second commercial radio station (the first being LBC, launched a week earlier). Europe's largest commercial radio station. Main outlet is entertainment news bulletins, Monday to Thursday at 7.30 pm, called *Entertainment Capital*, covering pop music, films, TV and

London events. The vast majority of material is generated in-house.

Central FM Ltd
201–203 High Street, Falkirk FK1 1DU
☎01324 611164 Fax 01324 611168
Website www.centralfm.co.uk
Managing Director and Programme Controller*Tom Bell*

Broadcasts music, sport and local news to central Scotland, 24 hours a day.

Century FM
Century House, PO Box 100, Church Street, Gateshead NE8 2YY
☎0191 477 6666 Fax 0191 477 5660
Programme Controller *Giles Squire*

Music, talk, news and interviews, 24 hours a day.

CFM
PO Box 964, Carlisle, Cumbria CA1 3NG
☎01228 818964 Fax 01228 819444
Email cfmradio.com
Website www.cfmradio.com
Programme Controller *David Bain*
Head of Commercial Production *Peter White*
News Editor *Bill Macdonald*

Music, news and information station.

Channel 103 FM
6 Tunnell Street, St Helier, Jersey, Channel Islands JE2 4LU
☎01534 888103 Fax 01534 887799
Website www.channel103.com
Station Manager *Richard Johnson*

Music programmes, 24 hours a day.

Chiltern FM/Classic Gold Digital
Chiltern Road, Dunstable, Bedfordshire LU6 1HQ
☎01582 676200
Fax 01582 676241 (newsroom)
Website www.koko.com
Programme Controller, FM *Ian Walker*
Programme Controller, Classic Gold Digital *Don Douglas*

Part of the GWR Group plc. Music-based programmes, broadcasting 24 hours a day.

Classic Gold 1332 AM
See **102.7 Hereward FM**

Classic Gold 1359
See **Mercia FM**

Classic Gold 1521
See **102.7 Mercury FM**

Classic Gold 1557 Northamptonshire
See **Northants 96**

Classic Gold 666/954
Hawthorn House, Exeter Business Park, Exeter, Devon EX1 3QS
☎01392 444444 Fax 01392 354202
Programme Controller *Colin Slade*
Part of CGDL. No outlets for writers.

Classic Gold 774
See **Severn Sound FM**

Classic Gold Amber
See **Broadland 102**

Classic Gold GEM
See **96 TRENT FM**

Classic Gold Marcher
Marcher Sound Ltd., The Studios, Mold Road, Wrexham LL11 4AF
☎01978 752202 Fax 01978 722209
Website www.marchergold.co.uk
Programme Controller *Graham Ledger*

Occasional features and advisory programmes. Hour-long Welsh language broadcasts are aired weekdays at 6.00 pm.

Classic Gold WABC
See **Beacon FM**

Clyde 1/Clyde 2
Clydebank Business Park, Clydebank G81 2RX
☎0141 565 2200 Fax 0141 565 2265
Website www.clyde1.com or
www.clyde2.com
Managing Director *Paul Cooney*

Programmes usually originate in-house or by commission. All documentary material is made in-house. Good local news items always considered. There are three book programmes presented by Alex Dickson each week on Clyde 2 at 10.00 pm – 10.30 pm: *Authors* (Monday) features author interviews while *Hardback Bookcase* (Tuesday) and *Paperback Bookcase* (Wednesday) review latest titles.

Cool FM
See **Downtown Radio**

Downtown Radio/Cool FM

Newtownards, Co. Down, Northern Ireland
BT23 4ES
☎028 9181 5555 Fax 028 9181 5252
Email programmes@downtown.co.uk
Website www.downtown.co.uk

Managing Director *David Sloan*

Downtown Radio first ran a highly successful short story competition in 1988, attracting over 400 stories. The competition is now an annual event and writers living within the station's transmission area are asked to submit material during the winter and early spring. The competition is promoted in association with Eason Shops. For further information, write to *Derek Ray* at the station.

Essex FM/Breeze

Radio House, Clifftown Road, Southend on Sea, Essex SS1 1SX
☎01702 333711 Fax 01702 333686
Website www.koko.com

Programme Director *Jeff O'Brien*

Music-based stations. Part of the GWR Group plc. No real opportunities for writers' work as such, but will occasionally interview local authors of published books. Contact *Tracey Cooper*, Head of News.

Forth One/Forth 2

Forth House, Forth Street, Edinburgh EH1 3LF
☎0131 556 9255 Fax 0131 475 1221
Email richard@forthone.com *or*
scott@forth2.com
Website www.forthonline.co.uk

Controller, Forth One & Forth 2 *Nik Goodman*
Programme Producer, Radio Forth *Moira Millar*
News Editor *Paul Robertson*

News stories welcome from freelancers. Music-based programming.

FOX FM

Brush House, Pony Road, Cowley, Oxford OX4 2XR
☎01865 871000 Fax 01865 871037 (news)
Website www.foxfm.co.uk

Managing Director *Sam Walker*
Head of News *Huw James*

Owned by Capital Radio Plc. Music programmes. No outlet for creative writing.

Galaxy 102.2

See **100.7 Heart FM**

Gemini FM

Hawthorn House, Exeter Business Park, Exeter, Devon EX1 3QS
☎01392 444444 Fax 01392 354202
Website www.koko.com

Programme Controller *Kevin Kane*

Part of GWR Group plc. No outlets for writers.

GWR FM

PO Box 2000, 1 Passage Street, Bristol BS99 7SN
☎0117 984 3200 Fax 0117 984 3202
Website www.koko.com

Programme Controller *Paul Andrew*

Very few opportunities for writers. Almost all material originates in-house. Part of the GWR Group plc.

Hallam FM/Magic AM

Radio House, 900 Herries Road, Sheffield S6 1RH
☎0114 209 1000 Fax 0114 285 3159
Website www.hallamfm.co.uk

Programme Director *Anthony Gay*

Music, news and features, 24 hours a day.

100.7 Heart FM/Galaxy 102.2

1 The Square, 111 Broad Street, Birmingham B15 1AS
☎0121 695 0000 Fax 0121 695 0055
Email mail@heartfm.co.uk *or*
mail@galaxy1022.co.uk
Website www.heartfm.co.uk *or*
www.galaxy1022.co.uk

Managing Director *Paul Fairburn*
Programme Director, Heart FM *Alan Carruthers*
Programme Director, Galaxy *Neil Greenslade*

Heart FM commenced broadcasting music, regional news and information in September 1994. Galaxy broadcasts today's dance and soul, news and information.

102.7 Hereward FM/ Classic Gold 1332 AM

PO Box 225, Queensgate Centre, Peterborough, Cambridgeshire PE1 1XJ
☎01733 460460 Fax 01733 281444
Website www.koko.com

Programme Controller *Paul Green*

Part of GWR Group plc. Not usually any openings offered to writers as all material is compiled and presented by in-house staff.

FM 103 Horizon
Broadcast Centre, Crownhill, Milton Keynes,
Buckinghamshire MK8 0AB
☎01908 269111 Fax 01908 564893
Website www.koko.com

Programme Controller *Trevor Marshall*

Part of the GWR Group plc. Music and news.

Invicta FM/Capital Gold
PO Box 100, Whitstable, Kent CT5 3YR
☎01227 772004 Fax 01227 774450
Website www.invictafm.com

Programme Controller *Rebecca Trbojevich*

Music-based station, serving listeners in Kent.
Part of Capital Radio Plc.

Island FM
12 Westerbrook, St Sampsons, Guernsey,
Channel Islands GY2 4QQ
☎01481 242000 Fax 01481 249676
Website www.islandfm.guernsey.net

Managing Director *Nick Creed*

Music-based programming.

Isle of Wight Radio
Dodnor Park, Newport, Isle of Wight
PO30 5XE
☎01983 822557 Fax 01983 821690
Email mail@iwradio.co.uk
Website www.iwradio.co.uk

Managing Director *Andy Shier*
Programme Manager *Tom Stroud*

Part of the Radio Investments Limited Group,
Isle of Wight Radio is the island's only radio
station broadcasting local news, music and general entertainment including phone-ins and
interview based shows.

Key 103/Magic 1152
Castle Quay, Castlefield, Manchester
M15 4PR
☎0161 288 5000 Fax 0161 288 5001
Website www.key103.co.uk

Programme Director *Andrew Robson*

Music-based programming.

KM – FM
Berkeley House, 186 High Street, Rochester,
Kent ME1 1EY
☎01634 841111 Fax 01634 841122

Programme Director *Suzanne Fitzsimmons*

A wide range of music programming plus
news, views and local interest. Part of the Kent
Messenger Group.

LBC News 1152 AM
See **LBC Radio Ltd**

LBC Radio Ltd
The Chrysalis Building, Bramley Road,
London W10 6SP
☎020 7314 7300 Fax 020 7324 7373
Website www.lbc.co.uk

Programme Director *Steve Kyte*

LBC 97.3 FM is a talk-based station broadcasting
24 hours a day providing entertainment, interviews, celebrity guests, music, chat shows, local
interest, news and sport. **Editorial Director**
Jonathan Richards
    LBC News 1152 AM, the sister station of
LBC 97.3 FM, provides 24-hour rolling news.

105.4 FM Leicester Sound
6 Dominus Way, Meridian Business Park,
Leicester LE19 1RP
☎0116 256 1300 Fax 0116 256 1305

Programme Controller *Craig Boddy*

Part of GWR Group plc. Predominantly a
music station. Very occasionally, unsolicited
material of local interest – 'targeted at our particular audience' – may be broadcast.

Magic 1152 (Manchester)
See **Key 103**

Magic 1152AM
(Newcastle upon Tyne)
See **Metro Radio**

Magic 1161
See **Viking FM**

Magic 1548
See **Radio City Ltd**

Magic 828
See **96.3 Radio Aire**

Magic AM
See **Hallam FM**

Mercia FM/Classic Gold 1359
Mercia Sound Ltd., Hertford Place, Coventry
CV1 3TT
☎024 7686 8200 Fax 024 7686 8203

Programme Controller *Louis Clark*

Music-based station.

102.7 Mercury FM/ Classic Gold 1521

9 The Stanley Centre, Kelvin Way, Manor Royal, Crawley, West Sussex RH10 9SE
☎01293 519161 Fax 01293 560927
Email chris.rick@creation.com

Programme Controller *Chris Rick*

Mercury FM plays contemporary music targeting 15–34 years. Breeze 1521 AM plays hits from the 1960s to '90s, targeting 35 years-plus. Both services carry local, national and international news.

Metro Radio/Magic 1152AM

Swalwell, Newcastle upon Tyne NE99 1BB
☎0191 420 0971 (Metro)/420 3040 (Magic)
Fax 520191 488 8611
Website www.metroradio.co.uk

Programme Director *Tony McKenzie*

Very few opportunities for writers, but phone-in programmes may interview relevant authors.

Minster FM

PO Box 123, Dunnington, York YO1 5ZX
☎01904 488888 Fax 01904 488811
Website www.minsterfm.com

Joint Station Managers *Sarah Barry, John Harding*

Music, local news and sport.

Moray Firth Radio

PO Box 271, Scorguie Place, Inverness IV3 8UJ
☎01463 224433 Fax 01463 243224
Email gary.robinson@mfr.co.uk

Managing Director/Programme Controller *Gary Robinson*
Programme Organiser *Ray Atkinson*
Book Reviews *May Marshall*

Book reviews every Sunday morning at 7.00 am – 8.00 am.

Northants 96/Classic Gold 1557 Northamptonshire

19–21 St Edmunds Road, Northampton NN1 5DY
☎01604 795600 Fax 01604 795601
Email reception@northants96.musicradio.com
Website www.classicgolddigital.com *or* www.koko.com

Programme Controller *Richard Neale*

Music and news, 24 hours a day. Part of the GWR Group plc.

NorthSound Radio

45 King's Gate, Aberdeen AB15 4EL
☎01224 337000 Fax 01224 400003
Website www.northsound.co.uk

Managing Director *Adam Findlay*
Programme Controller *Fiona Stalker*

Features and music programmes 24 hours a day including, mid-morning (9.00 am – midday), *Northsound 2* feature programme.

Ocean Radio/Power 103.2 FM/ Capital Gold

Radio House, Whittle Avenue, Segensworth West, Fareham, Hampshire PO15 5SH
☎01489 589911 Fax 01489 589453
Email info@oceanradio.co.uk
Website www.oceanradiofm.com *or* www.powerfm.com *or* www.capitalgold.com

Programme Controller *Stuart Davis*

Music-based programming only. Part of Capital Radio Plc.

Orchard FM

Haygrove House, Shoreditch, Taunton, Somerset TA3 7BT
☎01823 338448 Fax 01823 321611
Email steve.bulley@musicradio.com
Website www.koko.com

Programme Director *Steve Bulley*

Music-based programming only. Part of the GWR Group plc.

Plymouth Sound Radio

Earl's Acre, Alma Road, Plymouth, Devon PL3 4HX
☎01752 227272 Fax 01752 275605
Website www.koko.com

Programme Controller *Gavin Marshall*

Music-based station. No outlets for writers. Part of the GWR Group plc.

Power 103.2 FM

See **Ocean Radio**

Premier Christian Radio

22 Chapter Street, London SW1P 4NP
☎020 7316 1300 Fax 020 7233 6706
Email premier@premier.org.uk
Website www.premier.org.uk

Managing Director *Peter Kerridge*

Broadcasts programmes that reflect the beliefs and values of the Christian faith, 24 hours a day on 1305, 1413, 1332 MW, Sky digital 873, ntl 886 and on the web.

Q103FM

PO Box 103, Vision Park, Chivers Way,
Histon, Cambridge CB4 9WW
☎01223 235255 Fax 01223 235161
Website www.koko.com

Programme Controller *Avis Lilly*

Part of GWR Group plc. Music and news.

Q96

65 Sussex Street, Kenning Park, Glasgow
G41 1DK
☎0141 429 9430 Fax 0141 429 9431
Email news@q-fm.com

Station Director *Esther Morton*
Programme Controller *Gary Burgess*

Music-based programming plus local information and news. Part of the Wireless Group.

Radio City Ltd/Magic 1548

Radio City Tower, St John's Beacon, 1
Houghton Street, Liverpool L1 1RL
☎0151 472 6800 Fax 0151 472 6821
Website www.radiocity.co.uk

Managing Director *Sean Marley*
Programme Director *Richard Maddock*

Opportunities for writers are very few and far
between as this is predominantly a music station.

Radio XL 1296 AM

KMS House, Bradford Street, Birmingham
B12 0JD
☎0121 753 5353 Fax 0121 753 3111

Managing Director *Arun Bajaj*

Asian broadcasting for the West Midlands, 24
hours a day. Broadcasts *Love Express* featuring
love stories and poems. Writers should send
material for the attention of *Faiza Mirza*.

Red Dragon FM/Capital Gold

Atlantic Wharf, Cardiff CF10 4DJ
☎029 2066 2066 Fax 029 2066 2060
Website www.reddragonfm.co.uk

Programme Controller *David Rees*
News Editor *Tracey Spurrier*

Acquired by Capital Radio in 1998. Music-
based programming only.

Red Rose Radio

PO Box 301, St Paul's Square, Preston,
Lancashire PR1 1YE
☎01772 477700 Fax 01772 477701
Website www.rockfm.co.uk

Programme Director *Brian Paige*

Music-based station. No outlets for writers.

Sabras Radio

Radio House, 63 Melton Road, Leicester
LE4 6PN
☎0116 261 0666 Fax 0116 266 7776
Email don@sabrasradio.com
Website www.sabrasradio.com

Programme Controller *Don Kotak*

Programmes for the Asian community, broadcasting 24 hours a day.

Severn Sound FM/ Classic Gold 774

Bridge Studios, Eastgate Centre, Gloucester
GL1 1SS
☎01452 313200 Fax 01452 313213
Website www.koko.com

Managing Director *Russ Wilcox*

Part of the GWR Group plc. Music and news.

SGR Ipswich

Alpha Business Park, Whitehouse Road,
Ipswich, Suffolk IP1 5LT
☎01473 461000 Fax 01473 741200
Website www.koko.com

Programme Controller *Chris Skinner*

Music-based programming. Part of the GWR
Group plc.

Signal One/Signal Two

Stoke Road, Shelton, Stoke on Trent,
Staffordshire ST4 2SR
☎01782 441300 Fax 01782 441301
Website www.signalone.co.uk

Programme Controller *Kevin Howard*

Music-based station. No outlets for writers.
Part of the Wireless Group.

Southern FM

PO Box 2000, Brighton, East Sussex
BN41 2SS
☎01273 430111 Fax 01273 430098
Website www.southernfm.com

Programme Controller *Tony Aldridge*
News Manager *Laurence King*

Music, news, entertainment and competitions.
Part of Capital Radio Plc.

Spectrum Radio

204–206 Queenstown Road, Battersea,
London SW8 3NR
☎020 7627 4433 Fax 020 7627 3409
Email enquiries@spectrumradio.net
Website www.spectrumradio.net

Managing Director *Toby Aldrych*

Programmes for a broad spectrum of ethnic groups in London.

Spire FM

City Hall Studios, Malthouse Lane, Salisbury, Wiltshire SP2 7QQ
☎01722 416644 Fax 01722 416688
Website www.spirefm.co.uk

Station Director *Ceri Herford*

Music, news current affairs, quizzes and sport. Won the Sony Award for the best local radio station in 1994 and 1996.

Star 107.5 FM

1st Floor, The West Suite, Cheltenham Film Studios, Arle Court, Hatherly Lane, Cheltenham, Gloucestershire GL51 6PN
☎01242 699555 Fax 01242 699666
Email mail@star1075.co.uk
Website www.star1075.co.uk

Programme Controller *Ian Timms*

Formerly 107.5 CAT FM. Music-based programmes, broadcasting 24 hours a day.

Sun FM 103.4

PO Box 1034, Sunderland, Tyne & Wear SR5 2YL
☎0191 548 1034 Fax 0191 548 7171
Website www.sun-fm.com

Programme Controller *Simon Grundy*

Music-based programmes only.

Sunrise Radio (Yorkshire)

Sunrise House, 30 Chapel Street, Bradford, West Yorkshire BD1 5DN
☎01274 735043 Fax 01274 728534
Email usha@sunriseradio.fm
Website www.sunriseradio.fm

Programme Controller, Chief Executive & Chairman *Usha Parmar*

Programmes for the Asian community in Bradford.

Sunshine 855

South Shropshire Communications Ltd., Unit 11, Burway Trading Estate, Bromfield Road, Ludlow, Shropshire SY8 1EN
☎01584 873795 Fax 01584 875900
Website www.sunshine855.co.uk

Operations Director *Mrs G. Murfin*

Music, news and information, broadcast 24 hours a day.

Swansea Sound 1170 MW

See **The Wave FM**

107.8FM Thames Radio

Brentham House, 45c High Street, Hampton Wick, Kingston upon Thames, Surrey KT1 4DG
☎020 8288 1300 Fax 020 8288 1312
Email info@thamesradio.com
Website www.thamesradio.com

Station Manager *Peter Stremes*
Programme Controller *Dave Owen*

Music-based programmes of current hits and classic pop.

96 Trent FM/Classic Gold GEM

29–31 Castle Gate, Nottingham NG1 7AP
☎0115 952 7000 Fax 0115 912 9302
Email admin@trentfm.creation.com
Website www.koko.com

Programme Controller, 96 Trent FM *Dick Stone*
Programme Controller, Classic Gold GEM *Don Douglas*

Part of the GWR Group plc.

2CR-FM/Classic Gold 828

5–7 Southcote Road, Bournemouth, Dorset BH1 3LR
☎01202 259259 Fax 01202 255244
Email newsbournemouth@creation.com
Website www.koko.com

Programme Controller *Craig Morris*

Wholly-owned subsidiary of the GWR Group plc. Serves Dorset and Hampshire. All reviews/topicality/press releases to the Programme Controller, 2CR-FM at the address above.

2-Ten FM/Classic Gold

PO Box 2020, Reading, Berkshire RG31 7FG
☎0118 945 4400
Fax 0118 928 8513 (admin)/8809 (news)
Website www.koko.com

Programme Controller *Tim Parker*

A subsidiary of the GWR Group plc. Music-based programming.

Vibe 101

1 Passage Street, Bristol BS2 0JF
☎0117 901 0101 Fax 0117 984 3202
Email caroline.cook@vibe101.co.uk
Website www.vibe101.co.uk

Programme Controller *Jason Staveley*

Dance music, 24 hours a day.

Viking FM/Magic 1161

Commercial Road, Hull, North Humberside
HU1 2SG
☎01482 325141 Fax 0845 585969
Website www.vikingfm.co.uk

Managing Director *Mike Bawden*
Programme Controller *Darrell Woodman*
News Co-ordinator *Jamie York*

Music-based programming. Part of the EMAP
Group.

The Wave FM/Swansea Sound 1170 MW

Victoria Road, Gowerton, Swansea
SA4 3AB
☎01792 511964 (FM)/511170 (MW)
Fax 01792 511965 (FM)/511171 (MW)
Email admin@thewave.co.uk *or*
    admin@swanseasound.co.uk
Website www.the wave.co.uk *or*
    swanseasound.co.uk

Station Director *Andy Griffiths*
Programme Manager *Steve Barnes*
News Editor *Emma Thomas*

Music-based programming on FM while
Swansea Sound is interested in a wide variety
of material, though news items must be of local
relevance. An explanatory letter, in the first
instance, is advisable.

Wessex FM

Radio House, Trinity Street, Dorchester,
Dorset DT1 1DJ
☎01305 250333 Fax 01305 250052

Website www.wessexfm.co.uk
Programme Controller *Stewart Smith*
Music, local news, information and features.

West Sound AM/West FM

Radio House, 54 Holmston Road, Ayr
KA7 3BE
☎01292 283662
Fax 01292 283665/262607 (news)
Website www.west-sound.co.uk *or*
www.westfmonline.co.uk

Programme Director *Alan Toomey*
Music-based broadcasting.

102.4 Wish FM

Orrell Road, Wigan WN5 8HJ
☎01942 761024 Fax 01942 777694
Programme Controller *Craig Beck*
Music-based programming plus news and
sport. Part of the Wireless Group.

Wyvern FM

5–6 Barbourne Terrace, Worcester
WR1 3JZ
☎01905 612212/746644 (newsroom)
Fax 01905 746637
Website www.koko.com

Programme Controller *Simon Monk*
Part of the GWR Group plc. Music-based programming.

Film, TV and Radio
Production Companies

Aardman
Gas Ferry Road, Bristol BS1 6UN
☎0117 984 8485 Fax 0117 984 8486
Website www.aardman.com
Head of Script Development *Mike Cooper*
Development Executive (Shorts & Series)
   Helen Brunsdon

FOUNDED 1972. Award-winning animation studio producing films, television series, videos, commercials and new media properties. OUTPUT includes: *Rex the Runt*; *Morph Files*; *Creature Comforts*; *Wallace and Gromit*; *Angry Kid*; *Chicken Run*; *The Presentators*. No unsolicited submissions.

Above The Title
Level 2, 10/11 St Georges Mews, London
NW1 8XE
☎020 7916 1984 Fax 020 7722 5706
Email mail@abovethetitle.com
Website www.abovethetitle.com
Contacts *Bruce Hyman, Helen Chattwell*

Producer of radio drama and documentary programmes. OUTPUT *The Irving Trial; Night Class; Rosalind* (all BBC R4). Unsolicited mss and ideas welcome. Approach in the first instance by e-mail. 'We encourage and support new writing in every way we can.'

Absolutely Productions Ltd
8th Floor, Alhambra House, 27–31 Charing Cross Road, London WC2H 0AU
☎020 7930 3113 Fax 020 7930 4114
Email info@absolutely-uk.com
Website www.absolutely-uk.com
Executive Producer *Gordon Kennedy*

TV and film production company specialising in comedy and entertainment. OUTPUT *Absolutely* series 1–4 (Ch4); *mr don and mr george* (Ch4); *Squawkietalkie* (comedy wildlife programme for Ch4); *The Preventers* (ITV); *Scotland v England* (Ch4); *Barry Welsh is Coming* (HTV); *The Jack Docherty Show* (Ch5); *The Morwenna Banks Show* (Ch5); *Stressed Eric* (BBC2); *Armstrong & Miller* (Paramount/Ch4); *The Creatives* (BBC2); *Trigger Happy* (Ch4); *The Announcement* (Dakota Entertainment).

Abstract Images
117 Willoughby House, Barbican, London
EC2Y 8BL
☎020 7638 5123
Email productions@abstract-images.co.uk
Contact *Howard Ross*

Television documentary and drama programming. Also theatre productions. OUTPUT includes *Balm in Gilead* (drama); *Road* (drama); *Bent* (drama); *God: For & Against* (documentary); *This Is a Man* (drama/doc). Encourages new writers; send synopsis in the first instance.

Acacia Productions Ltd
80 Weston Park, London N8 9Tb
☎020 8341 9392 Fax 020 8341 4879
Email acacia@dial.pipex.com
Website www.acaciaproductions.co.uk
Contact *J. Edward Milner*

Producer of award-winning television and video documentaries; also news reports, corporates and programmes for educational charities. No unsolicited mss. OUTPUT includes documentary series entitled *Last Plant Standing*; *A Farm in Uganda*; *Montserrat: Under the Volcano*; *Spirit of Trees* (8 progs.); *Vietnam: After the Fire*; *Macroeconomics – the Decision-makers*; *Greening of Thailand*; *A Future for Forests*.

Acrobat Television
107 Wellington Road North, Stockport, Cheshire SK4 2LP
☎0161 477 9090 Fax 0161 477 9191
Email info@acrobat-tv.co.uk
Contacts *David Hill, Annie Broom*

Corporate video producer. OUTPUT includes instructional video for the British Association of Ski Instructors; corporate videos for Neilson Sailing, Hepworth Building Products, The Simon Group and First Choice Ski. No unsolicited mss.

All Out Productions
40 Copperas Street, Manchester M4 1HS
☎0161 834 9955 Fax 0161 834 6978
Email mail@allout.co.uk
Website www.allout.co.uk

Contact *David Cook*

Producer of documentaries, features and current affairs programmes for radio. OUTPUT includes *Five Live Report* (BBC Five Live – weekly news documentary); *Lamacq Live* (BBC Radio One – music and social affairs). Ideas welcome but not mss. Approach by e-mail.

Anglo/Fortunato Films Ltd
170 Popes Lane, London W5 4NJ
☎020 8932 7676 Fax 020 8932 7491
Contact *Luciano Celentino*

Film, television and video producer/director of action comedy and psych-thriller drama. No unsolicited mss.

Ariel Productions Ltd
11 Albion Gate, Hyde Park Place, London
W2 2LF
☎020 7262 7726 Fax 020 7262 7726
Producer *Otto Plaschkes*

Feature film and television producer. OUTPUT includes *Georgy Girl; Hopscotch; In Celebration; Butley; Doggin' Around.* Encourages new writers through involvement with the **National Film and Television School** and Screen Laboratory. No unsolicited mss.

Arlington Productions Limited
Cippenham Court, Cippenham Lane,
Cippenham, Nr Slough, Berkshire SL1 5AU
☎01753 516767 Fax 01753 691785

Television producer. Specialises in popular international drama, with *occasional* forays into other areas. 'We have an enviable reputation for encouraging new writers but only accept unsolicited submissions via agents.'

The Ashford Entertainment Corporation Ltd
182 Brighton Road, Coulsdon, Surrey
CR5 2NF
☎020 8645 0667
Email info@ashford-entertainment.co.uk
Website www.ashford-entertainment.co.uk
Managing Director *Frazer Ashford*
Head of Production *Georgina Huxstep*

FOUNDED in 1996 by award-winning film and TV producer Frazer Ashford whose credits include *Great Little Trains* (Mainline Television for Westcountry/Ch4, starring the late Willie Rushton); *Street Life* and *Make Yourself at Home* (both for WTV). Produces theatrical films and television – drama, lifestyle and documentaries. Happy to receive ideas for documentaries but

submit a one-page synopsis only in the first instance, enclosing s.a.e. 'Be patient, allow up to four weeks for a reply. Be precise with the idea; specific details rather than vague thoughts. Attach a back-up sheet with credentials and supporting evidence, ie, can you ensure that your idea is feasible?'

Assembly Film and Television Ltd
Riverside Studios, Crisp Road, London
W6 9RL
☎020 8237 1075 Fax 020 8237 1071
Email judithmurrell@riversidestudios.co.uk
Contacts *William Burdett-Coutts, Judith Murrell*

Television documentary producer. OUTPUT includes the Prudential Awards for the Arts; the London Comedy Festival; Ch4's Black Season, *In Exile: Sitcom*; BAFTA award-winning *Black Books: Sitcom* and Jo Brand's *Hot Potatoes* for BBC1.

Beckmann Productions Ltd
Meadow Court, West Street, Ramsey, Isle of
Man IM8 1AE
☎01624 816585 Fax 01624 816589
Email beckmann@enterprise.net
Website www.beckmanngroup.co.uk
Contacts *Josephine White, Stuart Semark*

Isle of Man-based company. Video and television documentary. OUTPUT *Practical Guide to Europe* (travel series); *Maestro* (12-part series on classical composers); *Ivory Orphans; Ages in History.*

Big Heart Media
Flat 4, 6 Pear Tree Court, London
EC1R 0DW
☎020 7608 0352 Fax 020 7250 1138
Email info@bigheartmedia.com
Website www.bigheartmedia.com
Contacts *Colin Izod, Beth Newell*

Producers of drama and documetaries for television, radio and video. Ideas/outlines welcome by e-mail, but not unsolicted mss. 'We will respond as soon as we can. We're very keen to enourage new writing – particularly for radio drama.'

Black Coral Productions Ltd
2nd Floor, 241 High Street, London E17 7BH
☎020 8520 2830 Fax 020 8520 2358
Email bcp@coralmedia.co.uk
Website www.m4media.net
Contacts *Lazell Daley, Marcia Miller*

Committed to new writing, BCP is currently

developing a slate of drama and factual documentary programmes and is interested in television proposals geared towards UK and European broadcasters. Welcomes proposals and treatments and offers a script consultancy service for which a fee is payable. Please call for further information.

Blackwatch Productions Limited
752–756 Argyle Street, Anderston, Glasgow G3 8UJ
☎0141 222 2640/2641 Fax 0141 222 2646
Email info@blackwatchtv.com
Website www.blackwatchtv.com
Company Director Nicola Black
Head of Production Paul Gallagher
Head of Development Steve Carroll
Research & Development Officers Heidi
  Proven, Anne-Claire Pilley
Production Manager Amanda Keown

Film, television, video producer of drama and documentary programmes. OUTPUT includes *The Paranormal Peter Sellers; When Freddie Mercury Met Kenny Everett; Designer Vaginas; Bonebreakers; Luv Bytes;* and *Can We Can We Carry On, Girls?* for Ch4. Also coordinates *Mesh,* animation scheme. Does not welcome unsolicited mss.

Blue Heaven Productions Ltd
116 Great Portland Street, London W1W 6PJ
☎020 7436 5552 Fax 020 7436 0888
Contact Christine Benson

Film and television drama and occasional documentary. OUTPUT *The Ruth Rendell Mysteries; Crime Story: Dear Roy, Love Gillian; Ready When You Are/Screen Challenge* (three series for Meridian Regional); *The Man who Made Husbands Jealous* (Anglia Television Entertainment/Blue Heaven). Scripts considered but treatments or ideas preferred in the first instance. New writing encouraged.

Bona Lattie Productions
19 Dalgleish House, Scrimgeour Place, Dundee DD3 6TU
☎01382 225403 Fax 01382 229300
Email bonalattie@aol.com
Website www.bonalattie.co.uk
Contact Turan Ali

Producer of award-winning drama and documentary programmes for BBC Radio 4 with occasional TV and film projects. No unsolicted mss but send a one-paragraph summary by e-mail in the first instance. 'Writers new to BBC radio should expect to write a whole script on spec to win a commission.' Runs radio and TV drama training courses in the UK and internationally.

Bronco Films Ltd
The Producers Centre, 61 Holland Street, Glasgow G2 4NJ
☎0141 287 6817 Fax 0141 287 6817
Email broncofilm@btinternet.com
Website www.broncofilms.co.uk
Contact Peter Broughan

Film, television and video drama. OUTPUT includes *Rob Roy* (feature film) and *Young Person's Guide to Becoming a Rock Star* (TV series). No unsolicited mss.

Buccaneer Films
5 Rainbow Court, Oxhey, Hertfordshire WD19 4RP
☎01923 254000/07740 902095 (mobile)
Email michael@gosling.com
Contact Michael Gosling

Corporate video production and still photography specialists in education and sport. No unsolicited mss.

Caravel Film Techniques Ltd
The Great Barn Studios, Cippenham Lane, Slough, Berkshire SL1 5AU
☎01494 446662 Fax 01494 446662
Email Ajjcaraveltv.aol.com
Website www.caravelstudios.com
Contact Anita See

Film, video and TV: documentary, commercials and corporate. OUTPUT Promos for commercial TV, documentaries for BBC and ITV, sales and training material for corporate blue chip companies. No unsolicited scripts. Prepared to review mostly serious new writing.

Carlton Productions
35–38 Portman Square, London W1H 6NU
☎020 7486 6688 Fax 020 7486 1132
Website www.carlton.com
**Managing Director/Director of
  Programmes** Steve Hewlett
Director of Drama & Co-production
  Jonathan Powell

Makers of independently produced TV drama for ITV. OUTPUT *The Vice; Dead Gorgeous; Margery & Gladys; Pollyanna; Dirty Tricks; Blue Dove; Sweet Medicine; fortysomething.* 'We try to use new writers on established long-running series.' Scripts from experienced writers and agents only.

Carnival (Films & Theatre) Ltd

12 Raddington Road, Ladbroke Grove,
London W10 5TG
☎020 8968 0968 Fax 020 8968 0155
Email info@carnival-films.co.uk
Website www.carnival-films.co.uk

Contact *Brian Eastman*

Film, TV and theatre producer. OUTPUT Film: *The Mill on the Floss* (BBC); *Firelight* (Hollywood Pictures/Wind Dancer Productions); *Up on the Roof* (Rank/Granada); *Shadowlands* (Savoy/Spelling); *The Infiltrator* (Home Box Office); *Under Suspicion* (Columbia/Rank/LWT). Television: *As If* (Ch4/Columbia); *Lucy Sullivan is Getting Married* (ITV); *The Tenth Kingdom* (Sky/NBC); *Agatha Christie's Poirot* (ITV/LWT/A&E); *Every Woman Knows a Secret* and *Oktober* (both for ITV Network Centre); *The Fragile Heart* (Ch4); *Crime Traveller* (BBC); *Bugs 1–4* (BBC); *Anna Lee* (LWT); *All Or Nothing At All* (LWT); *Head Over Heels* (Carlton); *Jeeves & Wooster* I–IV (Granada); *Traffik* (Ch4); *Forever Green 1–3* (LWT); *Porterhouse Blue* (Ch4); *Blott on the Landscape* (BBC). Theatre: *What a Performance; Juno & the Paycock; Murder is Easy; Misery; Ghost Train; Map of the Heart; Shadowlands; Up on the Roof.*

Cartwn Cymru

Ben Jenkins Court, 19A High Street, Llandaf,
Cardiff CF5 2DY
☎029 2057 5999 Fax 029 2057 5919
Email production@cartwn-cymru.demon.co.uk

Contact *Naomi Jones*

Animation production company. OUTPUT *Toucan 'Tecs* (YTV/S4C); *Funnybones* and *Turandot: Operavox* (both for S4C/BBC); *Testament: The Bible in Animation* (BBC2/S4C); *The Miracle Maker* (S4C/BBC/British Screen/Icon Entertainment International); *Faeries* (HIT Entertainment plc for CITV); *Otherworld* (animated feature film for SAC Films, British Screen, Arts Council of Wales).

Celador

39 Long Acre, London WC2E 9LG
☎020 7240 8101 Fax 020 7845 6977
Email tvhits@celador.co.uk
Website www.celador.co.uk

Head of Entertainment *Colman Hutchinson*
Development Executives *Humphrey Barclay, Vanessa Haynes*
Head of Radio *Liz Anstee*

Producer of TV and radio comedy and light entertainment. OUTPUT *Who Wants to be a Millionaire; Winning Lines; Commercial Breakdown; Britain's Brainiest ...; All About Me; It's Been A Bad Week.* 'We are interested in original non-derivative sitcom scripts and entertainment formats. Some broadcast experience would be helpful. As a relatively small company our script-reading capacity is limited.'

Celador Films

39 Long Acre, London WC2E 9LG
☎020 7845 6998 Fax 020 7497 9541
Email IMackinnon@celador.co.uk
Website www.celador.co.uk

Head of Production and Development *Christian Colson*
Story Editor *Ivana MacKinnon*

Producer of feature films. OUTPUT *Dirty Pretty Things.* Currently developing work by Julian Fellowes and Neil Marshall. No unsolicited mss.

Celtic Films Ltd

21 Grafton Street, London W1S 4EU
☎020 7409 2080 Fax 020 7409 2383
Email celticfilms@aol.com

Contact *Stuart Sutherland*

Film and television drama producer. OUTPUT includes 14 feature-length *Sharpe* TV films for Carlton and *A Life for a Life – The True Story of Stefan Kiszko* TV film for ITV. Devised *Hornblower* series for ITV. Supports new writing and welcomes unsolicited mss.

Central Office of Information Film & Video

Hercules Road, London SE1 7DU
☎020 7261 8667 Fax 020 7261 8776

Head of Department *Jackie Huxley*

Film, video and TV: drama, documentary, commercials, corporate and public information films. OUTPUT includes government commercials and corporate information. No scripts. New writing commissioned as required.

Chameleon Television Ltd

Television House, 104 Kirkstall Road, Leeds,
West Yorkshire LS3 1JS
☎0113 244 4486 Fax 0113 243 1267
Email allen@chameleontv.com

Contacts *Allen Jewhurst, Kevin Sim, Anna Hall, Simon Wells*

Film and television drama and documentary producer. OUTPUT includes *The Reckoning* (USA/Ch4); *Dunblane* (ITV); *Foul Play* (Ch5); *College Girls* and *Ken Dodd in the Dock* (both for Ch4);

Divorces From Hell, New Voices and *Shipman* (all for ITV). Scripts not welcome unless via agents but new writing is encouraged.

Chatsworth Television Limited
97–99 Dean Street, London W1D 3TE
☎020 7734 4302 Fax 020 7437 3301
Email television@chatsworth-tv.co.uk
Website www.chatsworth-tv.co.uk
Managing Director *Malcolm Heyworth*

Drama, factual and entertainment television producer. Interested in contemporary and factually based series.

The Children's Film & Television Foundation Ltd
The John Maxwell Building, Elstree Film & TV Studios, Shenley Road, Borehamwood, Hertfordshire WD6 1JG
☎020 8953 0844 Fax 020 8207 0860
Email annahome@cftf.onyxnet.co.uk
Chief Executive *Anna Home*

Involved in the development and co-production of films for children and the family, both for the theatric market and for TV.

Cinécosse
North Meadows, Oldmeldurm, Aberdeenshire AB51 OGQ
☎01651 873311 Fax 01651 873300
Email admin@cinecosse.co.uk
Website www.cinecosse.co.uk
Contact *Graeme Mowat*

Television and video documentary and corporate productions. OUTPUT includes *Scotland's Larder* (Scottish/Grampian TV); safety and training videos for industry; tourism promotional and sales information. All scripts are commissioned; no unsolicited material.

Cinema Verity Productions Ltd
11 Addison Avenue, London W11 4QS
☎020 7460 2777 Fax 020 7371 3329
Contact *Verity Lambert*

Leading television drama producer whose credits include *She's Out* by Lynda la Plante; *Class Act* by Michael Aitkens; *May to December* (BBC series); *Running Late* by Simon Gray (Screen 1); *The Cazalets* adapt. of *The Cazalet Chronicle* by Elizabeth Jane Howard (BBC). No unsolicited mss.

Circus Films
See **Elstree (Production) Co. Ltd.**

Clarion Film & Television
Merton Abbey Mills, Water Mill Way, London SW19 2Rd
☎020 8545 2000 Fax 0709 203 0160
Email info@clariontv.com
Website www.clariontv.com
Director of Programming *Kieran Matthew*
Creative Director *Andrew Linton*
Managing Director *Richard Hannah*

Film & TV production house covering news and factual entertainment commissions, corporate video production and business TV. Own facilities including house animation studio and copyright clearance bureau. Creators of news and language series *The Spoken Word*. Will consider submissions for educational series, particularly if relevant to international market place (address to *Alina Rosenska*, Producer) but unable to return material.

Cleveland Productions
5 Rainbow Court, Oxhey, Near Watford, Hertfordshire WD19 4RP
☎01923 254000/07740 902095 (mobile)
Email michael@gosling.com
Contact *Michael Gosling*

Communications in sound and vision A/V production and still photography specialists in education and sport. No unsolicited mss.

Collingwood & Convergence Productions Ltd
10–14 Crown Street, Acton, London W3 8SB
☎020 8993 3666 Fax 020 8993 9595
Email info@crownstreet.co.uk
Producers *Christopher O'Hare, Terence Clegg, Tony Collingwood*
Head of Development *Helen Stroud*

Film and TV. Convergence Productions produces live action, drama documentaries; Collingwood O'Hare Entertainment specialises in children's animation. OUTPUT **Convergence**: *Theo* (film drama series); *Plastic Fantastic* (UK cosmetic surgery techniques, Ch5); *David Starkey's Henry VIII* (Ch4 historical documentary) and *On the Road Again* (BBC2 documentary travel series). **Collingwood**: *RARG* (award-winning animated film); *Captain Zed and the Zee Zone* (ITV); *Daisy-Head Mayzie* (Dr Seuss animated series for Turner Network and Hanna–Barbera); *Animal Stories* (animated poems, ITV network); *Eddy and the Bear* (CITV) and *The King's Beard* (CITV). Unsolicited mss not welcome 'as a general rule as we do not have the capacity to process the sheer weight of submissions this creates. We therefore tend to review material from individuals recommended to us through personal contact with agents or other industry professionals. We like to encourage new writing and have worked with new writers but our ability to do so is limited by our capacity for development. We can usually only consider taking on one project each year, as development/finance takes several years to put in place.'

The Comedy Unit
Glasgow TV & Film Studios, Glasgow Media Park, Craigmount Street, Glasgow G20 9BT
☎0141 305 6666 Fax 0141 305 6600
Email comedyunit@comedyunit.co.uk
Website www.comedyunit.co.uk
Contacts *April Chamberlain, Colin Gilbert*

Producers of comedy and entertainment for film television, video and radio. OUTPUT *Chewin' the Fat; Still Game; The Karen Dunbar Sketch Show; Spin on This; Watsons Wind Up* and *Perfect* (short film). Unsolicited mss welcome by post or e-mail.

Company of Wolves
19–23 Wells Street, London W1P 3FP
☎020 7344 8090 Fax 020 7344 8091
Email cofwolves@aol.com
Contact *Stephen Woolley*

Leading feature film producer. OUTPUT has included *End Of the Affair; Butcher Boy; Interview With the Vampire; Michael Collins; Crying Game; Mona Lisa; Company of Wolves.* Forthcoming productions: *The Actors* (comedy set in Dublin); *The Borgias*; and *Double Down* (thriller starring Nick Nolte). No unsolicited material.

Convergence Productions Ltd
See **Collingwood & Convergence Productions Ltd**

Cosgrove Hall Films
8 Albany Road, Chorlton–cum–Hardy, Manchester M21 0AW
☎0161 882 2500 Fax 0161 882 2555
Email animation@chf.co.uk
Contacts *Mark Hall, Iain Pelling*

Children's animation producer; film video and television. OUTPUT includes *Noddy* and *Rotten Ralph* (both for BBC); *Lavender Castle* by Gerry Anderson; *The Fox Busters; Animal Shelf; Rocky & the Dodos*; Alison Uttley's *Little Grey Rabbit* (all for children's ITV); Terry Pratchett's

Discworld (Ch4). 'We try to select writers on a project-by-project basis.' Hosted the **Writers' Guild** workshop in 1998.

Creative Channel Ltd
Channel TV, Television Centre, St Helier, Jersey, Channel Islands JE1 3ZD
☎01534 816873 Fax 01534 816889
Email david@channeltv.co.uk
Website www.channeltv.co.uk
Senior Producer *David Evans*

Producer of TV commercials and corporate material: information, promotional, sales, training and events coverage. CD and DVD production; promotional videos for all types of businesses throughout Europe. No unsolicited mss; new writing/scripts commissioned as required. Interested in hearing from local writers resident in the Channel Islands.

Creative Film Makers Ltd
Pottery Lane House, 34A Pottery Lane, London W11 4LZ
☎020 7229 5131 Fax 020 7229 4999
Contacts *Michael Seligman, Nicholas Seligman*

Corporate and sports documentaries, commercials and television programmes. OUTPUT *The World's Greatest Golfers*, plus various corporate and sports programmes for clients like Nestlé, Benson & Hedges, Wimpey, Bouygues. 'Always open to suggestions but have hardly ever received unsolicited material of any value.' Keen nevertheless to encourage new writers.

The Creative Partnership
13 Bateman Street, London W1D 3AF
☎020 7439 7762
Email sally@thecreativepartnership.co.uk
Website www.thecreativepartnership.co.uk
Contacts *Christopher Fowler, Jim Sturgeon*

'Europe's largest "one-stop shop" for advertising and marketing campaigns for the film and television industries.' Clients include most major and independent film companies. No scripts. 'We train new writers in-house, and find them from submitted c.v.s. All applicants must have previous commercial writing experience.'

Cricket Ltd
Medius House, 63–69 New Oxford Street, London WC1A 1EA
☎020 7845 0300 Fax 020 7845 0303
Email team@cricket-ltd.com
Website www.cricket-ltd.com

Head of Production (Film & Video)
Jonathan Freer

Film and video, live events and conferences, print and design. 'Communications solutions for business clients wishing to influence targeted external and internal audiences.'

CSA Telltapes
(trading as **CSA Word**)
6A Archway Mews, 241A Putney Bridge Road, London SW15 2PE
☎020 8871 0220 Fax 020 8877 0712
Email clive@csatelltapes.demon.co.uk
Website www.csatelltapes.demon.co.uk
Contacts *Victoria Williams, Clive Stanhope*

Producer of drama, documentaries and readings for radio. OUTPUT *Alfie Elkins & His Little Life* (drama for BBC World Service); *Lucky Man* (reading for BBC R4); *The Scarlet Pimpernel* (reading for BBC R2); *It's a Girl; Chat Snaps; Videotape – Two* (documentaries for BBC World Service Learning). Unsolicited mss and ideas welcome by post or e-mail. 'We encourage new drama and short story writing.'

Cutting Edge Productions Ltd
27 Erpingham Road, Putney, London SW15 1BE
☎020 8780 1476 Fax 020 8780 0102
Email norridge@globalnet.co.uk
Contact *Julian Norridge*

Corporate and documentary video and television. OUTPUT includes US series on evangelicalism, 'Dispatches' on US tobacco and government videos. No unsolicited mss; 'we commission all our writing to order but are open to ideas.'

Cwmni'r Castell Ltd
10 Garth Road, Colwyn Bay, Conwy LL29 8AF
☎01492 512349 Fax 01492 514235
Email cwmnicastell@aol.com
Contact *Elwyn Vaughan Williams*

Television light entertainment and corporate video producer.

Dakota Films Ltd
4 Junction Mews, London W2 1PN
☎020 7706 9407 Fax 020 7402 6111
Email info@dakota-films.demon.co.uk
Managing Director *Jonathan Olsberg*

Film and television drama. Feature films include: *Me Without You; Janice Beard 45wpm;* *Let Him Have It; Othello.* Currently developing a slate of films, including John Sayles' *Fade to Black* and John Duigan's *Head in the Clouds*, and a number of projects by new writers. Interested in working with new talent but does not consider unsolicited material.

Devlin Morris Productions Ltd
97b West Bow, Edinburgh EH1 2JP
☎0131 226 7728 Fax 0131 226 6668
Email contact@devlinmorris-prod.sol.co.uk
Contacts *Morris Paton, Vivien Devlin*

Independent media production house encompassing international arts and travel writing as well as a range of drama, radio, film and television projects.

Direct Image Productions Ltd
See **Direct Image Publishing** under **UK Packagers**

Diverse Production Limited
Gorleston Street, London W14 8XS
☎020 7603 4567 Fax 020 7603 2148
Website www.diverse.co.uk
Contacts *Roy Ackerman, Narinder Minhas*

Broadcast television production with experience in popular prime-time formats, strong documentaries (one-offs and series), investigative journalism, science, business and history films, travel series, arts and music, talk shows, schools and education. OUTPUT includes *Secret Lives; Omnibus; Cutting Edge; Equinox; Modern Times; Dispatches; Without Walls; Panorama; The Big Idea; Empires and Emperors* and *The Little Picture Show.*

DMS Films Ltd
369 Burnt Oak Broadway, Edgware, Middlesex HA8 5XZ
☎020 8951 6060 Fax 020 8951 6050
Email danny@argonaut.com
Producer *Daniel San*

Film drama producer. OUTPUT includes *Understanding Jane; Hard Edge; Strangers.* Unsolicited screenplays not welcome: phone, fax or e-mail synopsis or outline in first instance.

Double-Band Films
Crescent Arts Centre, 2–4 University Road, Belfast BT7 1NH
☎028 9024 3331 Fax 028 9023 6980
Email info@doublebandfilms.com
Website www.doublebandfilms.com

Contacts *Michael Hewitt, Dermot Lavery*

Documentary and drama programmes for film and television. Has specialised in documentary production for the past twelve years. OUTPUT *George Best's Body, Escobar's Own Goal* and *Maradona: Kicking the Habit* (all for Ch4); *Still Life* (short drama film). Currently working on a documentary about English and Argentinean football for Ch4.

Drake A-V Video Ltd

89 St Fagans Road, Fairwater, Cardiff CF5 3AE
☎029 2056 0333 Fax 029 2055 4909
Website www.drakeav.com

Contact *Ian Lewis*

Corporate A-V film and video, mostly promotional, training or educational. Scripts in these fields welcome. Design and installation of AV systems.

The Drama House Ltd

Coach Road Cottage, Little Saxham, Suffolk IP29 5LE
☎01284 810521 Fax 01284 811425
Email jack@dramahouse.co.uk
Website www.dramahouse.co.uk

Contact *Jack Emery*

Film and television producer. OUTPUT *Inquisition* (Five); *Little White Lies* (BBC1); *Breaking the Code* (BBC1); *Witness Against Hitler* (BBC1); *Suffer the Little Children* (BBC2). Send two-page synopsis only. All synopses read and returned if accompanied by s.a.e. Interested especially in new writers.

Charles Dunstan Communications Ltd

42 Wolseley Gardens, London W4 3LS
☎020 8994 2328 Fax 020 8994 2328

Contact *Charles Dunstan*

Producer of film, video and TV for documentary and corporate material. OUTPUT *Renewable Energy* for broadcast worldwide in *Inside Britain* series; *The Far Reaches* travel series; *The Electric Environment*. No unsolicited scripts.

Ruth Evans Productions

4 Offlands Cottages, Moulsford, Oxfordshire OX10 9HP
☎01491 651331
Email ruthgevans@msn.com

Contact *Ruth Evans*

Producer of features and documentaries for the World Service and BBC Radio 4. Unsolicited ideas and mss welcome by e-mail. New writing is 'to be encouraged'.

Excalibur Productions

Slack Top Farm, Heptonstall, West Yorkshire HX7 7HA
☎01422 843871 Fax 01422 843871

Contact *Jay Jones*

Most recent productions are medical documentaries including an investigation into diabetes control sponsored by Bayer Diagnostics, collaborative literary and cultural projects such as *The Boys From Savoy* with David Glass, and corporates for South Yorkshire Supertram and Datacolor International. Interested in ideas, scripts and possible joint development for broadcast, sell-through and experimental arts.

Fairline Productions Ltd

15 Royal Terrace, Glasgow G3 7NY
☎0141 331 0077 Fax 0141 331 0066
Email fairprods@aol.com

Contact *Leigh McMahon*

Television and video producer of documentary and corporate programmes and commercials. OUTPUT includes *Hooked*, a 15-part angling series (Discovery Channel) plus training and instructional videos for Forbo-Nairn Ltd, Royal Bank of Scotland, and Health & Safety Executive. No unsolicited scripts.

Farnham Film Company Ltd

34 Burnt Hill Road, Lower Bourne, Farnham, Surrey GU10 3LZ
☎01252 710313 Fax 01252 725855
Website www.farnfilm.com

Contact *Ian Lewis*

Television and film: children's drama and documentaries. Unsolicited mss usually welcome but prefers a letter to be sent in the first instance. Check website for current requirements.

Farrant Partnership

429 Liverpool Road, London N7 8PR
☎020 7700 4647 Fax 020 7697 0224
Email mail@farrant-partnership.com

Contact *James Farrant*

Corporate video productions, seminars, conferences.

Fast Films

Christmas House, 213 Chester Road, Castle Bromwich, Solihull, West Midlands B36 0ET
☎0121 749 7147/4144

Contact *Gavin Prime*

Film and television: comedy, entertainment and animation. No unsolicited mss.

Festival Film and Television Ltd

Festival House, Tranquil Passage, Blackheath, London SE3 0BJ

☎020 8297 9999 Fax 020 8297 1155

Email info@festivalfilm.com

Contacts *Ray Marshall, Matt Marshall*

Specialises in television drama. In the last ten years has produced the Catherine Cookson mini-series for ITV. Now made its first feature film *Mandancin'*. Looking primarily for commercial projects for both cinema and TV.

Features – should be 'feel good'/family or projects with 'heart'. No horror or violence.

TV – mainly looking for series or 2/3 parters. Prefers submissions through an agent. Unsolicited work must be professionally presented or it will be returned unread.

Festival Productions Limited

PO Box 70, Brighton BN1 1YJ

☎01273 669595 Fax 01273 669596

Email post@festivalradio.com

Website www.festivalradio.com

Managing Director *Steve Stark*

Producer of globally syndicated music shows, Sony Award winning radio campaigns, contemporary spoken word productions and a dedicated net radio service at www.totallyradio.com Unsolicited mss welcome by post or by e-mail.

Fiction Factory

14 Greenwich Church Street, London SE10 9BJ

☎020 8853 5100 Fax 020 8293 3001

Email radio@fictionfactory.co.uk

Website www.fictionfactory.co.uk

Creative Director *John Taylor*

Producer of drama and documentaries for radio. OUTPUT *What Maisie Knew* and *Crime and Punishment* (BBC R4 classic serials); *A Wild Ride to Dublin* and *After Scarborough* (new plays for R4); *The Thin Green Line* (feature series – R4); *What About The Family* (feature series – BBC World Service). Ideas considered if sent by e-mail. Mss only from agents or writers with a professional track record in the broadcast media. 'Selected mss are forwarded to us by an agency to whom we have previously referred unsolicted scripts.'

Film and General Productions Ltd

4 Bradbrook House, Studio Place, London SW1X 8EL

☎020 7235 4495 Fax 020 7245 9853

Contacts *Clive Parsons, Davina Belling*

Film and television drama. Feature films include *True Blue* and *Tea with Mussolini*. Also *Seesaw* (ITV drama), *The Greatest Store in the World* (family drama, BBC) and *The Queen's Nose* (children's series, BBC). Interested in considering new writing but subject to prior telephone conversation.

The Firedog Motion Picture Corporation Ltd

182 Brighton Road, Coulsdon, Surrey CR5 2NF

☎020 8516 2912

Email info@firedogfilms.co.uk

Website www.firedogfilms.co.uk

Managing Director *Frazer Ashford*
Head of Development *Jonathan Martin*

Member of the **Ashford Entertainment Group**. 'Happy to see film/drama ideas.' In the first instance, authors should send a one-page synopsis, their writing c.v. and a brief history/submission history of the project to-date.

Firehouse Productions

42 Glasshouse Street, London W1B 5DW

☎020 7439 2220 Fax 020 7439 2210

Email postie@firehouse.biz

Website www.firehouse.biz

Contacts *Julie-anne Edwards, Gavin Knight*

Corporate films and websites, commercials and DRTV. OUTPUT includes work for De Beers; BT, Video Arts and various agencies.

The First Film Company Ltd

38 Great Windmill Street, London W1D 7LU

☎020 7439 1640 Fax 020 7437 2062

Producers *Roger Randall-Cutler, Rob Cheek*

FOUNDED 1984. Cinema screenplays. All submissions should be made through an agent.

First Writes Theatre Company

Lime Kiln Cottage, High Starlings, Banham, Norwich NR16 2BS

☎01953 888525 Fax 01953 888974

Email ellen-don@first-writes.co.uk

Website www.first-writes.co.uk

Contacts *Don Taylor, Ellen Dryden*

Producer of numerous afternoon, Friday and Saturday plays, classic serials and comedy narrative series for BBC Radio 3, 4 and World Service. Welcomes unsolictied mss or ideas by post. 'As an independent company it is difficult to obtain commissions for new writers and in-house should be your first port of call. However, we are committed to producing new work by established writers.'

Flannel
21 Berwick Street, London W1F 0PZ
☎020 7287 9277 Fax 020 7287 7785
Email mail@flannel.net

Contact *Kate Haldane*

Producer of drama, documentaries and comedy for television and radio. OUTPUT includes *Women's Hour* (BBC R4); *The Hendersons' Christmas Party* (five-part Christmas drama – BBC R4). No unsolicited mss. 'Keen to encourage new writing, but must come via an agent. Particularly interested in 45–50 minute dramas for radio. Not in a position to produce plays for stage, but very happy to consider adaptations. Welcomes comedy with some track record.'

Flashback Television Limited
11 Bowling Green Lane, London EC1R 0BG
☎020 7490 8996 Fax 020 7490 5610
Email mailbox@flashbacktv.co.uk
Website www.flashbacktv.com

Contact *Tim Ball*

Producer of documentaries and factual entertainment since 1982. Opened regional operation Flashback Bristol in 2001. Recent credits include *Nigella Forever Summer* (Ch4); *Heavy Metal/Battle Stations* (A&E, Ch4) and *The 200 Year House* (Ch4).

Flick Features
3rd Floor, 179 Wardour Street, London W1F 8WY
☎020 7855 3636 Fax 020 7855 3697
Website www.flickmedia.co.uk

Contact *Esther Knight*

Producer of film drama, including *Conspiracy of Silence* (feature film). No unsolicited scripts.

Flicks Films Ltd
101 Wardour Street, London W1F 0UG
☎020 7734 4892 Fax 020 7287 2307
Website www.flicksfilms.com

Managing Director/Producer *Terry Ward*

Film and video: children's animated series and specials. OUTPUT *The Mr Men; Little Miss; Bananaman; The Pondles; Nellie the Elephant; See How They Work With Dig and Dug; Timbuctoo*. Scripts specific to their needs will be considered. 'Always willing to read relevant material.'

Focus Films Ltd
The Rotunda Studios, Rear of 116–118 Finchley Road, London NW3 5HT
☎020 7435 9004 Fax 020 7431 3562
Email focus@pupix.demon.co.uk

Contacts *David Pupkewitz, Malcolm Kohll* (Head of Development)

Film producer. OUTPUT *The Book of Eve* (Canadian drama); *The Bone Snatcher* (Horror, UK/Can/SA); *Julia's Ghost* (German co-production); *The 51st State* (feature film); *Secret Society* (comedy drama feature film); *Crimetime* (feature thriller); *Diary of a Sane Man; Othello*. Projects in development include *Barry; Dogwatch; Indibindie and 3*. No unsolicited scripts.

Mark Forstater Productions Ltd
27 Lonsdale Road, London NW6 6RA
☎020 7624 1123 Fax 020 7624 1124

Contact *Mark Forstater*

Active in the selection, development and production of material for film and TV. OUTPUT *Monty Python and the Holy Grail; The Odd Job; The Grass is Singing; Xtro; Forbidden; Separation; The Fantasist; Shalom Joan Collins; The Silent Touch; Grushko; The Wolves of Willoughby Chase; Between the Devil and the Deep Blue Sea; Doing Rude Things*. No unsolicited scripts.

FremantleMedia Ltd
1 Stephen Street, London W1T 1AL
☎020 7691 6000 Fax 020 7691 6100
Website www.fremantlemedia.com

Chief Executive *Tony Cohen*
Chief Executive, UK Production *Peter Fincham*

FremantleMedia, formerly known as Pearson Television, is the production arm of the RTL Group, Europe's largest TV and radio company. Acquired Thames Television in 1993 (producer of *The Bill*) and Grundy Worldwide (*Neighbours*) in 1995. Further acquisitions were Witzend Productions (*Lovejoy*) and Alomo Productions in 1996 and **TalkBack Productions** (see entry) in 2000. FremantleMedia produces more than 260 programmes in over 39 countries and territories a year.

Full Moon Productions
rue Fenelon, Salignac Eyvigues, Dordogne, 24590 France
☎00 33 553 29 94 06 Fax 00 33 825 17 60 28
Email fullmoonproductions@worldonline.fr
Website www.salignacfoundation.com

Contact *Barry C. Paton, BSc.*

Production and logistics management in France. 'We are keen to explore new and innovative drama production for broadcast and/or film. Our script advisors can assess projects. No unsolicited scripts initially, please.' Initial contact should be by letter or e-mail. Also runs training courses in video production and screenwriting.

Gabriela Productions Limited
51 Goldsmith Avenue, London W3 6HR
☎020 8993 3158 Fax 020 8993 8216
Email only4contact@yahoo.com

Contact *W. Starecki*

Film and television drama and documentary productions, including *Blooming Youth* and *Dog Eat Dog* for Ch4 and *Spider's Web* for Polish TV. Welcomes unsolicited mss.

Gaia Communications
Sanctuary House, 35 Harding Avenue, Eastbourne, East Sussex BN22 8PL
☎01323 734809/727183 Fax 01323 734809
Email mail@gaiacommunications.co.uk
Website www.gaiacommunications.co.uk

Producer *Robert Armstrong*
Script Editor *Loni Webb*

ESTABLISHED 1987. Video and TV corporate and documentary. OUTPUT *Discovering* (south east regional tourist and local knowledge series); *Holistic* (therapies and general information).

Gala Productions Ltd
25 Stamford Brook Road, London W6 0XJ
☎020 8741 4200 Fax 020 8741 2323
Email david@galaproductions.co.uk

Producer *David Lindsay*

TV commercials, promos, film and TV documentaries.

Noel Gay Television
Shepperton Studios, Studios Road, Shepperton, Middlesex TW17 0QD
☎01932 592569 Fax 01932 592172
Email charles.armitage@virgin.net

CEO *Charles Armitage*

OUTPUT: *The Fear* (BBC Choice); *Second Chance*

(Ch4); *Hububb* – Series 1–5 (BBC); *I-Camcorder* (Ch4); *Frank Stubbs Promotes* (Carlton/ITV); *10%ers* – Series 2 (Carlton/ITV); *Call Up the Stars* (BBC1); *Smeg Outs* (BBC video); *Red Dwarf* – 8xseries; *Dave Allen* (ITV); *Windrush* (BBC2). Joint ventures and companies include a partnership with Odyssey, a leading Indian commercials, film and TV producer, and the Noel Gay Motion Picture Company, whose credits include *Virtual Sexuality; Trainspotting* (with Ch4 and Figment Films); *Killer Tongue; Dog Soldiers; Fast Sofa*; and *Pasty Faces.* Associate NGTV companies are Grant Naylor Productions, **Rose Bay Film Productions** (see entry) and Pepper Productions. NGTV is willing to accept unsolicited material from writers but 1–2-page treatments only. No scripts, please.

Ginger Television
See **SMG & Ginger TV Productions Ltd**

Goldcrest Films International Ltd
65–66 Dean Street, London W1D 4PL
☎020 7437 8696 Fax 020 7437 4448
Email mailbox@goldcrest-films.com

Chairman *John Quested*
Contact *Abigail Walsh*

FOUNDED in the late 1970s. Formerly part of the Brent Walker Leisure Group but independent since 1990 following management buyout led by John Quested. The company's core activities are film production, post-production facilities and worldwide distribution. Scripts via agents only.

The Good Film Company
The Studio, 5–6 Eton Garages, Lambolle Place, London NW3 4PE
☎020 7794 6222 Fax 020 7794 4651
Email productions@goodfilms.co.uk
Website www.goodfilms.co.uk

Contact *Yanina Barry*

Commercials and pop videos. CLIENTS include Hugo Boss, Cadbury's, Wella, National Express Coaches, Camel Cigarettes, Tunisian Tourist Board. *No* unsolicited mss.

Granite Film & Television Productions Ltd
Vigilant House, 120 Wilton Road, London SW1V 1JZ
☎020 7808 7230 Fax 020 7808 7231

Contact *Simon Welfare*

Producer of television documentary programmes such as *Nicholas & Alexandra; Victoria*

& *Albert* and *Arthur C. Clarke's Mysterious Universe*. No unsolicited mss.

Green Umbrella Ltd
The Production House, 147a St Michaels Hill, Bristol BS2 8DB
☎0117 973 1729 Fax 0117 946 7432
Email postmaster@umbrella.co.uk
Website www.umbrella.co.uk

Film producers specialising in science and natural history documentaries. OUTPUT includes episodes for *The Natural World*, *Wildlife on One* and original series such as *Living Europe* and *Triumph of Life*. Unsolicited treatments relating to natural history and science subjects are welcome.

Greenwich Village Productions
14 Greenwich Church Street, London SE10 9BJ
☎020 8853 5100 Fax 020 8293 3001
Email info@greenwichvillage.tv
Website www.greenwichvillage.tv
Contact *John Taylor*

Producer of videos and television drama documentaries as well as arts features and educational programmes. OUTPUT *An Arundel Tomb* (video treatment of Philip Larkin's poem); *Pluckley – England's Haunted Village* and *The Mystery of Balham Priory* (drama documentaries). Welcomes ideas by e-mail. 'Mss only from agents or writers with a professional track record in the chosen medium. Selected mss are sent to us by an agency to whom we have previously referred unsolicted scripts from new writers.'

Hammer Film Productions Ltd
92 New Cavendish Street, London W1W 6XJ
☎020 7637 2322 Fax 020 7323 2307
Contact *Terry Ilott*

Television and feature films. Please do not send unsolicited scripts or treatments.

Hammerwood Film Productions
110 Trafalgar Road, Portslade, East Sussex BN41 1GS
☎01273 277333 Fax 01273 705451
Email filmangels@freenetname.co.uk
Website www.filmangel.co.uk
Contacts *Ralph Harvey, Petra Ginman*

Film, video and TV drama. OUTPUT *Boadicea – Queen of Death* (film; co-production with Pan-European Film Productions and Boudicca Film Productions Ltd); *Boudicca – A Celtic Tragedy* (TV series). In pre-production: *Road to Nirvana*

(Ealing-style comedy); *The Black Egg* (witchcraft in 17th century England); *The Ghosthunter, A Symphony of Spies* (true stories of WW2 espionage and resistance required); *Iceni* (documentary of the rebellion of AD61). 'Authors are recommended to access www.filmangel.co.uk (see **Useful Websites at a Glance**).'

Hartswood Films Ltd
Twickenham Studios, The Barons, St Margarets, Middlesex TW1 2AW
☎020 8607 8736 Fax 020 8607 8744
Email films.tv@hartswoodfilms.co.uk
Contact *Elaine Cameron*

Film and TV production for drama, comedy and documentary. OUTPUT *Men Behaving Badly* (BBC); *Border Cafe* (BBC); *Coupling* (BBC); *Me Again* (feature film).

Hat Trick Productions Ltd
10 Livonia Street, London W1F 8AF
☎020 7434 2451 Fax 020 7287 9791
Website www.hattrick.com
Contact *Denise O'Donoghue*

Television programmes. OUTPUT includes *Clive Anderson All Talk; Small Potatoes; The Wilsons; The Peter Principle; Whatever You Want; Confessions; Drop the Dead Donkey; Father Ted; Game On; Have I Got News For You; If I Ruled the World; Room 101; Whose Line Is It Anyway?; Clive Anderson Talks Back; Dicing with Debt.* The company's drama output includes: *A Very Open Prison; Boyz Unlimited; Crossing the Floor; Eleven Men Against Eleven; Gobble; Lord of Misrule; Mr White Goes to Westminster; Underworld; Sex 'n' Death.* Films: *The Suicidal Dog; Sleeping Dictionary; Bloody Sunday.*

Head to Head Communication Ltd
The Hook, Plane Tree Crescent, Feltham, Middlesex TW13 7AQ
☎020 8893 7766 Fax 020 8893 2777
Email amanda@hthc.co.uk
Contact *Amanda Anderson*

Producer of business and corporate communication programmes and events.

Healthcare Productions Limited
Unit 1.04 Bridge House, Three Mills, Three Mill Lane, London E3 3DU
☎020 8980 9444 Fax 020 8980 1901
Email penny@healthcareproductions.co.uk
Website www.healthcareproductions.co.uk
Contact *Penny Webb*

Television and video: documentary and drama.

Produces training and educational material, in text, video and CD-ROM, mostly health-related, social care issues, law and marriage.

Jim Henson Productions Ltd
30 Oval Road, Camden, London NW1 7DE
☎020 7428 4000 Fax 020 7428 4001
Website www.henson.com *and*
www.muppets.com

Contacts *Angus Fletcher, Sophie Finston*

Feature films and TV: family entertainment and children's. OUTPUT *Gulliver's Travels; Buddy; Muppet Treasure Island; The Muppet Christmas Carol; Muppets From Space; The Dark Crystal; Labyrinth; The Witches* (films); *Dinosaurs* (ABC); *Muppet Tonight* (BBC/Sky); *The Muppet Show* (ITV); *The Storyteller* (Ch4/BBC); *Dr Seuss; The Secret Life of Toys* (BBC); *The Animal Show* (BBC); *Mopatop's Shop* (ITV); *Brats of the Lost Nebula* (WB); *Farscape* (Sci-Fi/USA/BBC); *Bear in the Big Blue House* (Disney Channel/Ch5); *Jim Henson's Construction Site* (ITV); *The Hoobs* (Ch4); *Jack and the Beanstalk: The Untold Story* (CBS); *Telling Stories with Tomie de Paola* and *Donna's Day* (both for Odyssey); *The Fearing Mind* (Fox); *It's a Very, Merry Muppet Christmas* (NBC); *Good Boy!* (MGM); *Kermit's Swamp Years* (CTHV); *Animal Jam* (Discovery); *Bambaloo* (Seven Network). Scripts via agents only.

Heritage Media Limited
Castle Eden Studios, Castle Eden, County Durham TS27 4SD
☎01429 838885 Fax 01429 838775

Contact *Toby Horton*

Producer of audio publications and independent productions with a heritage/classic theme.

Heritage Theatre Ltd
8 Clanricarde Gardens, London W2 4NA
☎020 7243 2750 Fax 020 7792 8584
Email rm@heritagetheatre.com
Website www.heritagetheatre.com

Contact *Robert Marshall*

Video recordings of successful stage plays, sold to the public in VHS and DVD format. 'It is possible to negotiate agreements before the production is staged.'

John Holloway
53 Daybrook Road, Wimbledon, London SW19 3DJ
☎020 8542 7721
Email holliesx2@aol.com
Contact *John Holloway*

Corporate video and promotional articles. CLIENTS include the Post Office, IBM, British Gas, Freemans, Eastern Electricity, Customs & Excise.

Holmes Associates
The Studio, 37 Redington Road, London NW3 7QY
☎020 7813 4333 Fax 020 7916 9172
Email holmesassociates@blueyonder.co.uk
Contact *Andrew Holmes*

Prolific originator, producer and packager of documentary, drama and music television and films. See also **Open Road Films**. OUTPUT has included *Prometheus* (Ch4 'Film on 4'); *The Shadow of Hiroshima* (Ch4 'Witness'); *The House of Bernarda Alba* (Ch4/WNET/Amaya); *Piece of Cake* (LWT); *The Cormorant* (BBC/Screen 2); *John Gielgud Looks Back; Rock Steady; Well Being; Signals; Ideal Home?* (all Ch4); *Timeline* (with MPT, TVE Spain & TRT Turkey); *Seven Canticles of St Francis* (BBC2). Not currently producing TV drama/documentaries.

Hourglass Pictures Ltd
27 Prince's Road, Wimbledon, London SW19 8RA
☎020 8540 8786
Email productions@hourglass.co.uk
Website www.hourglass.co.uk

Directors *Martin and Jacqueline Chilcott*

Film and video; documentary and drama. OUTPUT BAFTA nominated scientific television documentaries and educational programming. Also current affairs, health and social issues.

Icon Films
4 West End, Somerset Street, Bristol BS2 8NE
☎0117 924 8535 Fax 0117 942 0386
Email info@iconfilms.co.uk
Website www.iconfilms.co.uk

Contact *Harry Marshall*

Film and TV documentaries. OUTPUT *Yeti, Hunt for the Wildman* (Ch4/TLC); *A Different Ball Game* (National Geographic); *Quest for the True Cross* (Ch4/Discovery). Specialises in documentaries. Open-minded to new filmmakers. Proposals welcome.

Ideal Image Ltd
Cherrywood House, Crawley Down Road, Felbridge, Surrey RH19 2PP
☎01342 300566
Contact *Alan Frost*

Producer of documentary and drama for film, video, TV and corporate clients. OUTPUT *The Pipeline; Beating the Market*. No unsolicited scripts.

Imari Entertainment Ltd

PO Box 158, Beaconsfield, Buckinghamshire HP9 1AY
☎01494 677147 Fax 01494 677147
Email info@imari-entertainment.com

Contacts *Jonathan Fowke, David Farey*

TV and video producer, covering all areas of drama and documentary. Also partner company, Imari Multi-media.

Isis Productions

106 Hammersmith Grove, London W6 7HB
☎020 8748 3042 Fax 020 8748 3046
Email isis@isis-productions.com
Website www.isisproductions.co.uk

Directors *Nick de Grunwald, Jamie Rugge-Price*
Production Coordinator *Catriona Lawless*

Formed in 1991, Isis Productions focuses on the production of music and documentary programmes. OUTPUT *Bernie Taupin* (ITV 'South Bank Show'); *Iron Maiden, Judas Priest* (Five 'Rock Classics'); Films on *Deep Purple, Metallica, Def Leppard, Lou Reed, Elton John, Elvis Presley, Sex Pistols* (ITV 'Classic Albums 3'); *Nosey Series 3* (Five – Children's); *The Genesis Songbook* (Five); *England's Other Elizabeth – Elizabeth Taylor* (BBC 'Omnibus').

Isolde Films Ltd

28 Narrow Street, London E14 8DQ
☎020 7702 8700 Fax 020 7702 8701

Contacts *Tony Palmer, Michela Antonello*

Film and TV: drama and documentary. OUTPUT *Wagner; Menuhin; Maria Callas; Testimony; In From the Cold; Pushkin; England, My England* (by John Osborne); *Kipling*. Unsolicited material is read, but please send a written outline first.

JAM Pictures and Jane Walmsley Productions

8 Hanover Street, London W1S 1YE
☎020 7290 2676 Fax 020 7290 2677
Email producers@jampix.com

Contacts *Jane Walmsley, Michael Braham*

JAM Pictures was FOUNDED in 1996 to produce drama for film, TV and stage. Projects include: *Son of Pocahontas* (TV film, ABC); *Rudy: the Rudy Giuliani Story* (TV film, USA Network);

One More Kiss (feature, directed by Vadim Jean); *Bad Blood* (UK theatre tour). Jane Walmsley Productions, formed in 1985 by TV producer, writer and broadcaster, Jane Walmsley, has completed award-winning documentaries and features such as *Hot House People* (Ch4). No unsolicited mss. 'Letters can be sent to us, asking if we wish to see mss; we are very interested in quality material.'

Keo Films.com

Studio 2B, 151–157 City Road, London EC1V 1JH
☎020 7490 3580 Fax 020 7490 8419
Email keo@keofilms.com
Website www.keofilms.com

Contact *Katherine Perry*

Television documentaries and factual entertainment. OUTPUT includes BBC's 'QED': *The Maggot Mogul* and *Sleeping it Off*; plus *A Cook on the Wild Side; TV Dinners; Beast of the Amazon; Big Snake* and *Jungle Trip* ('To the Ends Of the Earth' series); *River Cottage; Return to River Cottage; The Real Deal; Agia Napa Fantasy Island; Shadow People; River Cottage Forever; Brown Britain; Going To Extremes.* All for Ch4. No unsolicited mss.

Kingfisher Television Productions Ltd

Carlton Studios, Lenton Lane, Nottingham NG7 2NA
☎0115 964 5262 Fax 0115 964 5263

Contact *Tony Francis*

Broadcast television production.

Kismet Film Company

25A Old Compton Street, London W1D 5JW
☎020 7734 0099 Fax 020 7734 1222
Email kismetfilms@dial.pipex.com

Producer *Michele Camarda*
Head of Development *Mathias Loertscher*

Feature films. OUTPUT includes *Photographing Fairies; This Year's Love; Wonderland* and *Born Romantic*. Kismet can no longer accept unsolicited material. Involved in workshops such as PAL Writer's Workshop, **Equinoxe Screenwriting Workshops** and North by Northwest.

Kudos Film and Televison Limited

65 Great Portland Street, London W1W 7LW
☎020 7580 8686 Fax 020 7580 8787

Email reception@kudosproductions.co.uk

Head of Development *Claire Parker*
Head of Drama *Jane Featherstone*
Head of Film *Stephen Garrett*

Film and television; drama and documentaries such as *Among Giants* (feature); *Pure* (feature); *The Magician's House* and *Spooks* (BBC1 series) and *Psychos* (Ch4 series); *Confidence Lab* (BBC2 series). No unsolicited mss.

Lagan Pictures Ltd

21 Tullaghbrow, Tullaghgarley, Ballymena, Co Antrim BT42 2LY
☎028 2563 9479/077 9852 8797
Fax 028 2563 9479
Email laganpictures@tullaghbrow.
  freeserve.co.uk

Producer/Director *Stephen Butcher*

Film, video and TV: drama, documentary and corporate. OUTPUT *A Force Under Fire* (Ulster TV). In development: *Into the Bright Light of Day* (drama-doc); *The £10 Float* (feature film); *The Centre* (drama series). 'We are always interested in hearing from writers originating from or based in Northern Ireland or anyone with, preferably unstereotypical, projects relevant to Northern Ireland. We do not have the resources to deal with unsolicited mss, so please write with a brief treatment/synopsis in the first instance.'

Landseer Productions Ltd

140 Royal College Street, London NW1 0TA
☎020 7485 7333 Fax 020 7485 7573
Email mail@landseerfilms.com
Website www.landseerfilms.com

Directors *Derek Bailey, Ken Howard*

Film and video production: documentary, drama, music and arts. OUTPUT *Should Accidentally Fall* (BBC/Arts Council); *Nobody's Fool* ('South Bank Show' on Danny Kaye for LWT); *Swinger* (BBC2/Arts Council); *Auld Lang Syne* and *Retying the Knot – The Incredible String Band* (both for BBC Scotland); *Benjamin Zander* ('The Works', BBC2); *Zeffirelli* ('South Bank Show', LWT); *Death of a Legend – Frank Sinatra* ('South Bank Show' special); *Petula Clark* and *Bing Crosby* (both 'South Bank Show'); *Routes of Rock* (Carlton); *See You in Court* (BBC); *Nureyev Unzipped*, *Gounod's Faust*, *The Judas Tree*, *Ballet Boyz*, *4Dance* and *Bourne to Dance* (all for Ch4), Johnnie Ray ('South Bank Show'), *Proms in the park* (Belfast).

Lilyville Screen Entertainment Ltd

7 Lilyville Road, London SW6 5DP
☎020 7371 5940 Fax 020 7736 9431
Email tonycash@msn.com

Contact *Tony Cash*

Drama and documentaries for TV. OUTPUT *Poetry in Motion* (series for Ch4); 'South Bank Show': *Ben Elton* and *Vanessa Redgrave*; *Musique Enquête* (drama-based French language series, Ch4); *Landscape and Memory* (arts documentary series for the BBC); Jonathan Miller's production of the *St Matthew Passion* for the BBC; major documentary on the BeeGees for the 'South Bank Show'. Scripts with an obvious application to TV may be considered. Interested in new writing for documentary programmes.

London Scientific Films Ltd

Mill Studio, Crane Mead, Ware, Hertfordshire SG12 9PY
☎01920 444399
Email lsf@londonscientificfilms.co.uk

Contact *Mike Cockburn*

Film and video documentary and corporate programming. No unsolicited mss.

Lucida Productions

Lucida Studios, 14 Havelock Walk, London SE23 3HG
☎020 8699 5070

Contact *Paul Joyce*

Television and cinema: arts, adventure, current affairs, documentary, drama and music. OUTPUT has included *Motion and Emotion: The Films of Wim Wenders; Dirk Bogarde – By Myself; Sam Peckinpah – Man of Iron; Kris Kristofferson – Pilgrim; Wild One: Marlon Brando; Stanley Kubrick: 'The Invisible Man'; 2001: the Making of a Myth* (Ch4); *Mantrap – Straw Dogs,* the final cut (with Dustin Hoffman). Currently in development for documentary and drama projects.

LWT United Productions

London Television Centre, Upper Ground, London SE1 9LT
☎020 7620 1620

Controller of Drama *Michele Buck*

Television drama. OUTPUT *London's Burning*; *Night and Day*; *Hornblower*; *Walking on the Moon* by Martin Sadofski (drama-doc); *Touching Evil*; *Where the Heart Is*; *The Last Detective*; *William and Mary*.

Malone Gill Productions Ltd

27 Campden Hill Road, London W8 7DX
☎020 7937 0557 Fax 020 7376 1727
Email malonegill@aol.com

Contact *Georgina Denison*

Mainly documentary but also some drama.
OUTPUT includes *The Face of Russia* (PBS);
Vermeer ('South Bank Show'); *Highlanders*
(ITV); *Storm Chasers*; *Nature Perfected* and *The
Feast of Christmas* (all for Ch4); *The Buried
Mirror: Reflections on Spain and the New World* by
Carlos Fuentes (BBC2/Discovery Channel).
Approach by letter with proposal in the first
instance.

Mike Mansfield Television Ltd

41–42 Berners Street, London W1T 3NB
☎020 7580 2581 Fax 020 7580 2582
Email mikemantv@aol.com

Contact *Mr Hilary McLaren*

Television for BBC, ITV, Ch4 and Five.
OUTPUT includes *Viva Diva!* (Shirley Bassey
music special); *Jean Michel Jarre Pyramids New
Year*; *Gimme A Freak* (BBC Choice).

Jane Marshall Productions

The Coach-House, Westhill Road,
Blackdown, Leamington Spa, Warks
CV32 6RA
☎01926 831680 Fax 01926 313603
Email jane@jmproduction.freeserve.co.uk

Contact *Jane Marshall*

Producer of readings of published work both
fiction and non-fiction. No unsolicited mss.
Published work only.

Maverick Television

The Custard Factory, Gibb Street,
Birmingham B9 4AA
☎0121 771 1812 Fax 0121 771 1550
Email maverick@mavericktv.co.uk
Website www.mavericktv.co.uk

Contact *Clare Welch*

FOUNDED 1994. High quality and innovative
DVC programming in both documentary and
drama. Expanding into light entertainment and
more popular drama. OUTPUT includes *Trade
Secrets* (BBC2); *Picture This: Accidental Hero*
(BBC2); *Motherless Daughters*, *Highland
Bollywood: Black Bag*, *Health Alert: My Teenage
Menopause*, *Embarrassing Illnesses*, *Vee-TV* and
Home From Home (all for Ch4); *Long Haul*
(Scottish Screen/STV); *Learning to Love the
Grey* (BBC/OU).

Maya Vision International Ltd

43 New Oxford Street, London WC1A 1BH
☎020 7836 1113 Fax 020 7836 5169
Website www.mayavisionint.com

Contact *John Cranmer*

Film and TV: drama and documentary.
OUTPUT *Saddam's Killing Fields* (for
'Viewpoint', Central TV); *3 Steps to Heaven*
and *A Bit of Scarlet* (feature films for BFI/Ch4);
A Place in the Sun and *North of Vortex* (drama
for Ch4/Arts Council); *The Real History Show*
(Ch4); *In the Footsteps of Alexander the Great*
(BBC2 documentary); *Hitler's Search for the
Holy Grail* (Ch4 documentary); *Conquistadors*
(BBC2 documentary). Absolutely no unso-
licited material; commissions only.

MBP TV

Saucelands Barn, Coolham, Horsham,
West Sussex RH13 8QG
☎01403 741620 Fax 01403 741647
Email info@mbptv.com
Website www.mbptv.com

Contact *Phil Jennings*

Maker of film and video specialising in programmes covering equestrianism and the
countryside. No unsolicited scripts, but always
looking for new writers who are fully
acquainted with the subject.

Melendez Films

Suite 501, Triumph House, 189–191 Regent
Street, London W1B 4JY
☎020 7323 5273 Fax 020 7434 3131

Contact *Steven Melendez*

Independent producer working with TV
stations. Animated films aimed mainly at a family audience, produced largely for the
American market, and prime-time network
broadcasting. Also develops and produces feature films (eight so far). OUTPUT has included
Peanuts (TV specials); *The Lion, the Witch and
the Wardrobe*; *Babar the Elephant* (TV specials);
Dick Deadeye or Duty Done, a rock musical
based on Gilbert & Sullivan operattas. Synopses
only, please. Enclose s.a.e. for return.

Mendoza Productions

75 Wigmore Street, London W1U 1QD
☎020 7935 4674 Fax 020 7935 4417
Email debz@mendozafilms.com

Contacts *Wynn Wheldon, Debby Mendoza*

Commercials, title sequences (e.g. Alan
Bleasdale's *G.B.H.*); party political broadcasts.

Currently in pre-production on a feature-length comedy film. Unsolicited mss welcome but 'comedies only, please'. Material will not be returned without s.a.e. Involved with the **Screenwriters' Workshop**.

Mersey Television Company Ltd
Campus Manor, Childwall Abbey Road, Liverpool L16 0JP
☎0151 722 9122 Fax 0151 722 1969
Website www.merseytv.com
Chairman *Prof. Phil Redmond*

The best known of the independents in the north of England. Makers of television drama. OUTPUT *Brookside; Hollyoaks* (both for Ch4); *Grange Hill* (BBC)

Mission Pictures
23 Golden Square, London W1F 9JP
☎020 7734 6303 Fax 020 7734 6202
Email info@missionpictures.net
Contacts *Katie Goodson, Ed Rubin*

Feature films, including *Welcome to Sarajevo; Thunderpants; Gridlock'd; The Debt Collector; Splendor; A Texas Funeral; Some Voices; Very Annie-Mary; Gradiatress.* Likes to encourage young talent but cannot consider unsolicited mss.

Monty Funk Productions Ltd
95 Spencer Street, Birmingham B18 6DA
☎0121 523 1070 Fax 0121 523 1071
Email mail@montyfunk.com
Website www.montyfunk.com
Contacts *Peter Nash, David Corser*

Producer of corporate videos and drama and documentaries for radio. OUTPUT *A Place Called England* (folk night for BBC R3); *Soulsville USA* (documentary for BBC R4); *Not For King Or Country* (archive feature R4). No unsolited mss.

Moonstone Films Ltd
5 Linkenholt Mansions, Stamford Brook Avenue, London W6 0YA
☎020 8846 8511 Fax 0870 4017171
Email info@moonstonefilms.co.uk
Contact *Tony Stark*

Television: current affairs, science and history documentaries. OUTPUT *Arafat's Authority*, a critical look at the Palestinian authority in the West Bank and Gaza for BBC 'Correspondent' plus various Ch 4 news commissions. Unsolicited mss welcome.

Murf Media
1–3 Brockholes Lane, Brockholes, Yorkshire HD9 7ED
☎08707 481471
Email info@fmjock.com
Website www.fmjock.com
Contact *Brett Harley*

Producer of topical comedy for radio. Song parodies, spoof adverts and gags. 'We welcome all new writers and have freelance writers from all walks of life!' Please approach by e-mail.

MW Entertainments Ltd
48 Dean Street, London W1D 5BF
☎020 7734 7707 Fax 020 7734 7727
Email development@michaelwhite.co.uk
Contact *Michael White*

High-output company whose credits include *Widow's Peak; White Mischief; Nuns on the Run; Enigma; The Comic Strip Series.* Also theatre projects, including *Notre-Dame de Paris; Fame; Me and Mamie O'Rourke; She Loves Me; Crazy for You.* Contributions are passed by Michael White to a script reader for consideration.

Newgate Company
13 Dafford Street, Larkhall, Bath, Somerset BA1 6SW
☎01225 318335
Contact *Jo Anderson*

A commonwealth of established actors, directors and playwrights, Newgate originally concerned itself solely with theatre writing (at the Bush, Stratford, Roundhouse, etc.). However, in the course of development, several productions fed into a list of ongoing drama for BBC TV/Ch4. Looking to develop this co-production strand for film, television and radio projects with other 'Indies'.

Octopus TV
See **Octopus Publishing Group** under **UK Publishers**

Omnivision
Pinewood Studios, Iver Heath, Buckinghamshire SL0 0NH
☎01753 656329 Fax 01753 631146
Email info@omnivision.co.uk
Website www.omnivision.co.uk
Contacts *Christopher Morris, Steve Rowsell*

TV and video producers of documentary, corporate, news and sport programming. Also equipment and facilities hire. Interested in ideas; approach by letter or e-mail.

ON Communication
5 East St Helen Street, Abingdon, Oxford
OX14 5EG
☎01235 537400 Fax 01235 530581
Email ON@oncomms-tv.co.uk
Website www.oncomms-tv.co.uk

Contact *Jane May*

An independent production company FOUNDED in 1985 to produce high-quality factual programming, including science, current affairs, authored documentaries for television, as well as for corporate and heritage markets.

Open Media
The Mews Studio, 8 Addison Bridge Place, London W14 8XP
Email contact@openmedia.co.uk
Website www.openmedia.co.uk

Contact *Laura Cook*

Broadcast television: OUTPUT *After Dark; The Secret Cabaret; James Randi Psychic Investigator; Opinions; Is This Your Life?; Don't Quote Me; Brave New World; The Talking Show; Natural Causes; Equinox; Dispatches.*

Open Road Films
The Studio, 37 Redington Road, London NW3 7QY
☎020 7813 4333 Fax 020 7916 9172
Email openroadfilms@blueyonder.co.uk

Development Executive *Sophie Prideaux*
Producer *Andrew Holmes*

Company, formed by **Holmes Associates**, to produce low to medium budget British feature films. OUTPUT *Chunky Monkey; Ashes & Sand.* Four projects in development. Unsolicited drama/film scripts will be considered but may take some time for response.

Orlando TV Productions
Up-the-Steps, Little Tew, Chipping Norton, Oxfordshire OX7 4JB
☎01608 683218 Fax 01608 683364
Email orlando.tv@btinternet.com
Website www.orlandodigital.co.uk

Contact *Mike Tomlinson*

Producer of TV documentaries and digital multimedia content, with science subjects as a specialisation. OUTPUT includes programmes for *Horizon* and *QED* (BBC). Approaches by established writers/journalists to discuss proposals for collaboration are welcome.

Orpheus Productions
6 Amyand Park Gardens, Twickenham, Middlesex TW1 3HS
☎020 8892 3172 Fax 020 8892 4821
Email richard-taylor@blueyonder.co.uk

Contact *Richard Taylor*

Television documentaries and corporate work. OUTPUT has included programmes for BBC Current Affairs, Music and Arts, and the African-Caribbean Unit as well as documentaries for the Shell Film Unit and Video Arts. Unsolicited scripts are welcomed with caution. 'We have a preference for visually stirring documentaries with quality writing of the more personal and idiosyncratic kind, not straight reportage.'

Outcast Production
92 Buckhold Road, London SW18 4AP
Email andythewise@aol.com

Contact *Andreas Wisniewski*

Low-budget feature films. No unsolicited mss; send synopsis or treatment only. 'We are actively searching for and encouraging new writing.'

Ovation
One Prince of Wales Passage, 117 Hampstead Road, London NW1 3EF
☎020 7387 2342 Fax 020 7380 0404

Contact *John Plews*

Corporate video and conference scripts. Unsolicited mss not welcome. 'We talk to new writers from time to time.' Ovation also runs the fringe theatre, 'Upstairs at the Gatehouse' in Highgate, north London.

Oxford Scientific Films Ltd
Lower Road, Long Hanborough, Oxfordshire OX8 8LL
☎01993 881881 Fax 01993 882808
Email enquiries@osf.uk.com
Website www.osf.uk.com

Chief Executive *Claire Birks*
Directors *Sean Morris, Suzanne Aitzetmuller*

Established media company with specialist knowledge and expertise in award-winning natural history films and science-based programmes. Film, video and TV documentaries. Scripts welcome. Operates an extensive stills and film footage library specialising in wildlife and special effects (see entry under **Picture Libraries**).

Pacificus Productions
47 Addison Avenue, London W11 4QU
☎020 7603 6991 Fax 020 7603 6593
Email mail@pacificus.co.uk

Contacts *Clive Brill, Tom Treadwell*

Produced feature film *Before You Go* (directed by Lewis Gilbert) plus many dramas for BBC Radio 4. Encourages new writing with small development fund available. Approach by e-mail in the first instance with ideas and mss. Clive Brill is a regular tutor at **The Arvon Foundation**.

Barry Palin Associates Ltd

Unit 10 Princeton Court, 55 Felsham Road, London SW15 1AZ
☎020 8394 5660 Fax 020 8785 0440
Email mail@barrypalinassociates.com

Contact *Barry Palin*

Film, video and TV production for drama, documentary, commercials and corporate material. OUTPUT *Harmfulness of Tobacco* Anton Chekhov short story – BAFTA Best Short Film Award-winner (Ch4); Corporate: Philip Morris, York International, Republic Bank of New York.

Panther Pictures Ltd

3rd Floor, 16 Golden Square, London W1F 9JQ
☎07976 256 610 Fax 020 7734 8858
Website www.pantherpictures.co.uk

Contact *Robert Sutton*

Feature films, including *Inside/Out*, a US/UK/Canada/France co-production.

Paper Moon Productions

Wychwood House, Burchetts Green Lane, Littlewick Green, Nr. Maidenhead, Berkshire SL6 3QW
☎01628 829819 Fax 01628 825949
Email david@paper-moon.co.uk

Contact *David Haggas*

Broadcast documentaries and corporate communications. Recent OUTPUT includes *Bilbo & Beyond*, an affectionate glimpse into the life and work of the dedicated philologist and fantasy writer J.R.R. Tolkien.

Parallax Independent Ltd

7 Denmark Street, London WC2H 8LS
☎020 7836 1478 Fax 020 7497 8062
Website www.parallaxindependent.co.uk

Contact *Sally Hibbin*

Feature films/television drama. OUTPUT *Riff-Raff; Bad Behaviour; Raining Stones; Ladybird, Ladybird; I.D.; Land and Freedom; The Englishman Who Went up a Hill But Came Down a Mountain; Bliss; Jump the Gun; Carla's Song; The Governess; My Name Is Joe; Stand and Deliver; Dockers; Hold Back the Night; Bread and Roses; Princesa; The Navigators; Sweet Sixteen; Innocence; The Intendend; Blind Flight.*

Passion Pictures

3rd Floor, 33–34 Rathbone Place, London W1T 1TN
☎020 7323 9933 Fax 020 7323 9030
Email info@passion-pictures.com

Managing Director *Andrew Ruhemann*

Documentary and drama includes: *One Day in September* (Academy Award-winner for Best Feature Documentary, 2000); also commercials and music videos: Carphone Warehouse, Mini, Aero, Gorillaz, Coldplay and Robbie Williams. Unsolicited mss welcome.

Pathé Pictures

14–17 Kenthouse, Market Place, London W1W 8AR
☎020 7323 5151 Fax 020 7631 3568

Head of Development *Matthew Gannon*
Development Executive *Celine Haddad*
Development Assistant *Erol Arguden*

Produces 4–6 theatrical feature films each year. 'We are pleased to consider all material that has representation from an agent or production company.'

PBF Motion Pictures

The Little Pickenhanger, Tuckey Grove, Ripley, Surrey GU23 6JG
☎01483 225179 Fax 01483 224118
Email peter@pbf.co.uk

Contact *Peter B. Fairbrass*

Film, video and TV: drama, documentary, commercials and corporate. Also televised chess series and chess videos. No scripts; send one-page synopsis only in the first instance. 'Good scripts which relate to current projects will be followed up, otherwise not, as PBF do not have the time to reply to proposals which do not interest them. Only good writing stands a chance.'

Pearson Television

See **FremantleMedia Ltd**

Pelicula Films

59 Holland Street, Glasgow G2 4NJ
☎0141 287 9522 Fax 0141 287 9504

Contact *Mike Alexander*

Television producer. Maker of drama documentaries and music programmes for the BBC and Ch4. OUTPUT *As an Eilean (From the Island); The Trans-Atlantic Sessions 1 & 2; Nanci Griffith, Other Voices 2; Follow the Moonstone.*

Penumbra Productions Ltd
80 Brondesbury Road, London NW6 6RX
☎020 7328 4550 Fax 020 7328 3844
Email nazpenumbra@aol.com

Contact *H.O. Nazareth*

Film, video, TV and radio: drama and social issues documentaries. OUTPUT includes *Fugitive Pieces* (Radio 3 play); *Stories My Country Told Me* (BBC2, 'Arena'); *Repomen* (Ch4, 'Cutting Edge'). Send synopses only, preferably by e-mail. Keen to assist in the development of new writing but only interested in social issue-based material.

Photoplay Productions Ltd
21 Princess Road, London NW1 8JR
☎020 7722 2500 Fax 020 7722 6662
Email photoplay@compuserve.com

Contact *Patrick Stanbury*

Documentaries for film, television and video plus restoration of silent films and their theatrical presentation. OUTPUT includes *Cinema Europe: The Other Hollywood; Universal Horror; D.W. Griffith: Father of Film; Lon Chaney, Man of 1000 Faces* and the 'Channel 4 Silents' series of silent film restoration, including *The Wedding March* and *The Iron Mask.* Recently completed *The Tramp and the Dictator.* No unsolicited mss; 'we tend to create and write all our own programmes.'

Picardy Media Group
1 Park Circus, Glasgow G3 6AX
☎0141 333 1200 Fax 0141 332 6002
Email jr@picardy.co.uk
Website www.picardy.co.uk

Senior Producer *John Rocchiccioli*

Television and video: arts documentaries, training and promotional videos, education projects, multi-media productions, and TV and cinema commercials. Unsolicited mss welcome; 'keen to encourage new writing.'

Picture Palace Films Ltd
13 Egbert Street, London NW1 8LJ
☎020 7586 8763 Fax 020 7586 9048
Email info@picturepalace.com
Website www.picturepalace.com

Contacts *Malcolm Craddock, Katherine Hedderly*

FOUNDED 1971. Leading independent producer of film and TV drama. OUTPUT *Rebel Heart* (BBC1); *Extremely Dangerous* and *A Life for A Life* (both for ITV); *Sharpe's Rifles* (14 films for Carlton TV); *Little Napoleons* (comedy drama, Ch4); *The Orchid House* (drama serial, Ch4); *Tandoori Nights; 4 Minutes; When Love Dies* (all for Ch4); *Ping Pong* (feature film); *Acid House* (Picture Palace North). Material will only be considered if submitted through an agent.

Phil Pilley Productions
Ferryside, Felix Lane, Shepperton, Middlesex TW17 8NG
☎01932 702916 Fax 01932 702916
Email pilley@tinyworld.co.uk

Programmes for TV and video, mainly sports. Now specialising in sporting history books, particularly golf.

Planet 24 Productions Ltd
195 Marsh Wall, London E14 9SG
☎020 7345 2424 Fax 020 7345 9400
Email info@planet24.co.uk
Website www.planet24.com

Managing Director *Mary Durkan*

Television producer of light and factual entertainment, comedy, music, features and computer animation. Wholly owned subsidiary of Carlton Communications plc. OUTPUT *The Big Breakfast; The Word; The Messiah* (live recording); *Hotel Babylon; Gaytime TV; Delicious; Extra Time, Nothing But the Truth; Watercolour Challenge; Andi Meets ...; Richard Whiteley Unbriefed; The Richard Blackwood Show; A Family of My Own.*

Plantagenet Films Limited
Ard-Daraich Studio B, Ardgour, Nr Fort William, Inverness-shire PH33 7AB
☎01855 841384 Fax 01855 841384
Email plantagenetfilms@aol.com

Contact *Norrie Maclaren*

Film and television: documentary and drama programming such as *Dig* (gardening series for Ch4); various 'Dispatches' for Ch4 and 'Omnibus' for BBC. Keen to encourage and promote new writing; unsolicited mss welcome.

Portobello Pictures
PO Box 31579, London W11 3YA
☎020 7229 7420 Fax 020 7229 2072 5599

Contact *Eric Abraham*

Film drama, including Jan Sverak's *Dark Blue World* and *Kolya*; Jez Butterworth's *Mojo* and Tim Roth's *The War Zone*, plus BBC1's *Dalziel & Pascoe* (series 1–3).

Pozzitive Television
Paramount House, 162–170 Wardour Street, London W1F 8AB
☎020 7734 3258 Fax 020 7437 3130
Email pozzitive@pozzitive.demon.co.uk
Contact *David Tyler*

Producer of comedy and entertainment for television and radio. OUTPUT *Dinner Ladies; Coogan's Run; The 99p Challenge.* Unsolicited mss welcome. Send hard copy of full sample script. 'We read eveything submitted this way.'

Promenade Enterprises Limited
6 Russell Grove, London SW9 6HS
☎020 7582 9354 Fax 020 7587 1564
Email promenadeproductions@msn.com
Website www.promenadeproductions.com
Contact *Nicholas Newton*

Producer of drama for radio and theatre predominantly. Supports new writing but only accepts unsolicited mss via agents or producers.

Red Weather
Easton Business Centre, Felix Road, Easton, Bristol BS5 0HE
☎0117 941 5854 Fax 0117 941 5851
Email jayne@redweather.co.uk
Contact *Jayne Cotton*

Broadcast documentaries on arts and disability, corporate video and CD ROM for Water Aid, British Oxygen.

Renaissance Vision
256 Fakenham Road, Taverham, Norwich, Norfolk NR8 6QW
☎01603 260280 Fax 01603 864853
Email bfg@renvision.co.uk
Contact *B. Gardner*

Video: full range of corporate work (training, sales, promotional, etc.). Producers of educational and special-interest video publications. Willing to consider good ideas and proposals.

Renovators Productions Ltd
The Old Courthouse, 26A Church Street, Bishop's Stortford, Hertfordshire CM23 2LY
☎01279 501622 Fax 01279 501644
Email patrick.wallis@virgin.net

Contacts *Patrick Wallis, Barney Broom*

Film, television and video: drama, documentary, corporate and commercials. No unsolicited mss.

Richmond Films & Television Ltd
PO Box 33154, London NW3 4AZ
☎020 7722 6464 Fax 020 7722 6232
Email mail@richmondfilms.com
Contact *Development Executive*

Film and TV: drama and comedy. OUTPUT *Press Gang; The Lodge; The Office; Wavelength; Privates.* 'No unsolicited scripts. We will accept *two pages only* consisting of a brief treatment of your project (either screenplay or TV series) which includes its genre and its demographics. Please tell us also where the project has been submitted previously and what response you have had. *Your two pages will not be returned.*'

Rose Bay Film Productions
13 Austin Friars, London EC2N 2JX
☎020 7670 1609 Fax 020 8357 0845
Email info@rosebay.co.uk
Contacts *Matthew Steiner, Simon Usiskin*

Formats and TV production: entertainment and comedy. Unsolicited scripts (with s.a.e.) welcome.

Brenda Rowe Productions
42 Wellington Park, Clifton, Bristol BS8 2UW
☎0117 973 0390 Fax 0117 973 8254
Email br007b3169@blueyonder.co.uk
Contact *Brenda Rowe*

Produces observational, investigative, current affairs TV documentaries, and training and promotional videos for business organisations. Open to new work; unsolicited mss welcome.

RS Productions
119 Trewhitt Road, Newcastle upon Tyne NE6 5DY
☎0191 224 4301/07710 064632 (Mobile)
Fax 0191 224 4301
Email enquiries@rsproductions.co.uk
Website www.rsproductions.co.uk
Contact *Mark Lavender*

Feature films, television and new media: drama series/serials and singles. TV docs and series. Working with established and new talent.

Sands Films

119 Rotherhithe Street, London SE16 4NF
☎020 7231 2209 Fax 020 7231 2119
Website www.sandsfilms.co.uk

Contacts *Christine Edzard, Olivier Stockman*

Film and TV drama. OUTPUT *Little Dorrit; The Fool; As You Like It; A Dangerous Man; The Long Day Closes; A Passage to India; The Nutcracker; Seven Years in Tibet; The Children's Midsummer Night's Dream.* No unsolicited scripts.

Scala Productions Ltd

15 Frith Street, London W1D 4RE
☎020 7734 7060 Fax 020 7437 3248
Email scalaprods@aol.com

Contacts *Nik Powell*

Production company set up by ex-Palace Productions Nik Powell and Stephen Woolley, who have an impressive list of credits including *Company of Wolves; Absolute Beginners; Mona Lisa; Scandal; Crying Game; Backbeat; Neon Bible; 24:7; Little Voice; Divorcing Jack; Welcome to Woop Woop; The Lost Son; Fanny and Elvis; The Last September; Wild About Harry; Last Orders; A Christmas Carol – The Movie; Black and White; Leo; One Love; The Night We Called It A Day.* In development: *Boswell for the Defence; Brian Jone Project; The Queen & I; Surprising New Zealand; Ladies in Lavender; Meek; Train to Glory; Shang-a-Lang; Mort; Haroun and the Sea of Stories; Level; St Agnes' Stand; Johnny Bollywood; English Passenger; He Kills Coppers.*

Scope Productions Ltd

Keppie House, 147 Blythswood Street, Glasgow G2 4EN
☎0141 332 7720 Fax 0141 332 1049
Email laurakingwell@scopeproductions.co.uk
Website www.scopeproductions.co.uk

Corporate *Laura Kingwell*

Corporate film and video; broadcast documentaries and sport; TV commercials. Unsolicited, realistic scripts/ideas welcome.

Screen First Ltd

The Studios, Funnells Farm, Down Street, Nutley, East Sussex TN22 3LG
☎01825 712034 Fax 01825 713511
Email paul.madden@virgin.net

Contacts *M. Thomas, P. Madden*

Television dramas, documentaries, arts and animation programmes. Developing major drama series, feature films, animated specials and series. No unsolicited scripts.

Screen Ventures Ltd

49 Goodge Street, London W1T 1TE
☎020 7580 7448
Email sales@screenventures.com

Contacts *Christopher Mould, Naima Mould*

Film and TV sales and production: documentary, music videos and drama. OUTPUT *Life and Limb* (documentary, Discovery Health Channel); *Pavement Aristocrats* (SABC); *Woodstock Diary; Vanessa Redgrave* and *Genet* (both for LWT 'South Bank Show'); *Mojo Working; Burma: Dying for Democracy* (Ch4); *Dani Dares* (Ch4 series on strong women); *Pagad* (Ch4 news report).

Screenhouse Productions Ltd

Chapel Allerton House, 114 Garrogate Road, Leeds, West Yorkshire LS7 4NY
☎0113 266 8881 Fax 0113 266 8882
Email paul.bader@screenhouse.co.uk
Website www.screenhouse.co.uk

Contacts *Paul Bader, Barbara Govan*

Factual programmes, mainly popular science and history. Also new media. OUTPUT includes *Science Shack*, BBC2 series presented by Adam Hart-Davis; six series of *Local Heroes*, factual programmes about the greats of science; two series of *Hart-Davis on History*, a magazine series about local history and how to become involved in historical research (both for BBC2); two history series for BBC Knowledge, *History Quest* and *History Fix*. Contact with one-page outline of idea in the first instance.

Screenprojex.com – a division of Screen Production Associates Ltd

☎020 7287 1170 Fax 020 7287 1123
Email enquiries@screenprojex.com
Website screenprojex.com

Contacts *Doug Abbott, John Jaquiss, Julia Vickers*

Feature films: *The Fourth Man; The Case; Black Badge* (all in association with The Writers' Studio); *The Truth Game; Club Le Monde; Midnight Warriors; Strong Language; The Case; Holding On.* No unsolicited mss. Send preliminary letter outlining project and c.v.

September Films Ltd

Glen House, 22 Glenthorne Road, London W6 0NG
☎020 8563 9393 Fax 020 8741 7214
Email september@septemberfilms.com
Website www.septemberfilms.com

Head of Production *Elaine Day*

Head of Drama and Film Development
Nadine Mellor

Factual entertainment and documentary specialists expanding further into television drama and film. Feature film OUTPUT includes *Breathtaking*; *House of America*; *Solomon & Gaenor*.

Serendipity Picture Company
Media Centre, Emma-Chris Way,
Abbeywood Park, Bristol BS34 7JU
☎0117 906 6541 Fax 0117 906 6542
Email tony@serendipitypictures.com
Contacts *Tony Yeadon, Nick Dance*

Television and video; corporate and documentary programming. Encourages new writing and will consider scripts.

Seventh House Films
1 Hall Farm Place, Bawburgh, Norwich,
Norfolk NR9 3LW
☎01603 749068 Fax 01603 749069
Email caflo.dunn@virgin.net
Contacts *Clive Dunn, Angela Rule*

Documentary for film, video and TV on subjects ranging from arts to history and science to social affairs. OUTPUT *The Last Fling* (life for a paralysed jump-jockey); *Dark Miracle* (an investigation into a near nuclear disaster in East Anglia); *A Pleasant Terror* (life and ghosts of M.R. James); *Piano Pieces* (musical excursion exploring different aspects of the piano); *Rockin' the Boat* (memories of pirate radio); *White Knuckles* (on the road with a travelling funfair); *King Romance* (life of Henry Rider Haggard); *A Drift of Angels* (three women and the price of art); *Bare Heaven* (the life and fiction of L.P. Hartley); *A Swell of the Soil* (life of Alfred Munnings); *Light Out of the Sky* (the art and life of Edward Seago). 'We welcome programme proposals with a view to collaborative co-production. Always interested in original and refreshing expressions for visual media.'

Sianco Cyf
36 Y Maes, Caernarfon, Gwynedd
LL55 2NN
☎01286 676100/07831 726111 (Mobile)
Fax 01286 677616
Email post@sianco.tv
Contact *Siân Teifi*

Children's, youth and education programmes and children's drama.

SilentSound Films Ltd
Cambridge Court, Cambridge Road, Frinton
on Sea, Essex CO13 9HN
☎01255 676381 Fax 01255 676381
Email thj@silentsoundfilms.co.uk
Website www.silentsoundfilms.co.uk *or*
www.londonfoodfilmfiesta.co.uk
Contact *Timothy Foster*

Active in European film co-production with mainstream connections in the USA. Special interest in developing stage and film musicals and documentaries on the arts. Synopses considered via e-mail or post.

Siriol Productions
3 Mount Stuart Square, Butetown, Cardiff
CF10 5EE
☎029 2048 8400 Fax 029 2048 5962
Email enquiries@siriol.co.uk
Website www.siriolproductions.com
Contact *Andrew Offiler*

Animated series, mainly for children. OUTPUT includes *Meeow; Hilltop Hospital; The Hurricanes; Tales of the Toothfairies; Billy the Cat; The Blobs*, as well as the feature films, *Under Milkwood* and *The Princess and the Goblin*. Write with ideas and sample script in the first instance.

Skyline Productions
10 Scotland Street, Edinburgh EH3 6PS
☎0131 557 4580 Fax 0131 556 4377
Email leslie@skyline.uk.com
Producer/Writer *Leslie Hills*

Film and television drama and documentary. Encourages new writers but telephone first before sending material.

SMG & Ginger TV Productions Ltd
116 New Oxford Street, London WC1A 1HH
☎020 7663 2300
Website www.ginger.com
Also: SMG TV Productions (Glasgow),
200 Renfield Street, Glasgow G2 3PR
☎0141 300 3000
Managing Director *Jagdip Jagpal*
Head of Drama *Erina Rayner, Eric Coulter*
    (Glasgow)
Executive Producer for Drama *Judy Counihan*
Head of Development and Children's
    Elizabeth Partyka
Head of Factual Programming *John Farren,*
    Helen Alexander (Glasgow)

SMG (Scottish Media Group) TV Productions Ltd, which incorporates Ginger Television, makes programmes for the national television networks, including ITV, Ch4 and Sky. Specialises in drama, factual entertainment and children's programming. OUTPUT includes *Taggart; Rebus; Take Me; TFI Friday; Remembering Lockerbie; The Priory; How2.*

So Television Ltd
18 Hatfields, London SE1 8GN
☎020 7960 2000 Fax 020 7960 2095

Contact *Nina Gosling*

Producer of a daily entertainment comedy show for television. Developing comedy entertainment and comedy narrative. No unsolicited mss.

Specific Films
25 Rathbone Street, London W1T 1NQ
☎020 7580 7476 Fax 020 7494 2676
Email info@specificfilms.com

Contacts *Michael Hamlyn*

FOUNDED 1991. OUTPUT includes *Mr Reliable* (feature film co-produced by PolyGram and the AFFC); *The Adventures of Priscilla, Queen of the Desert*, co-produced with Latent Image (Australia) and financed by PolyGram and AFFC; *U2 Rattle and Hum*, full-length feature – part concert film/part cinema verité documentary; *Paws* (executive producer); *The Last Seduction 2* (Polygram); and numerous pop promos for major international artists.

Spellbound Productions Ltd
90 Cowdenbeath Path, Islington, London N1 0LG
☎020 7713 8066 Fax 020 7713 8067
Email phspellbound@hotmail.com

Contact *Paul Harris*

Specialises in feature films for cinema and drama for television. Keen to support and encourage new writing. Material will only be considered if in correct screenplay format and accompanied by s.a.e.

Spice Factory (UK) Ltd
81 The Promenade, Brighton, East Sussex BN10 8LS
☎01273 585275 Fax 01273 585304
Email info@spicefactory.co.uk

Contacts *Lucy Shuttleworth, Emily Kyriakides*

FOUNDED 1995. Film producers. OUTPUT *Pilgrim* (starring Ray Liotta); *Anazupta* (Lena Headey, Jason Fleming); *Mr In-Between* (Andrew Howard); *Plots With a View* (Christopher Walken, Brenda Blethyn, Alfred Molina, Lee

Evans); *Bollywood Queen* (Preeya Kallidas, James McAvoy, Ian McShane). No unsolicited material accepted.

'Spoken' Image Ltd
8 Hewitt Street, Manchester M15 4GB
☎0161 236 7522 Fax 0161 236 0020
Email multimedia@spoken-image.com

Contacts *Geoff Allman, Steve Foster*

Film, video and TV production for documentary and corporate material. Specialises in high-quality brochures and reports, CD-ROMs, exhibitions, conferences, film and video production for broadcast, industry and commerce.

Standish Films
320 Woodhouse Lane, Wigan, Lancashire WN6 7TD
Email mail@sirco.co.uk
Website www.sirco.co.uk/standishfilms.htm

Contact *Rosemary Allen*

Film, video and TV: documentary, drama, commercials and corporate, including dramatised training videos. Currently looking for feature film scripts with Anglo/American/European themes. 'Interested in supporting and encouraging new talent and experienced writers looking for new and imaginative ways to express their ideas.' No unsolicited material; send synopses and enquiries via e-mail. Check website for current needs.

Starz! – Film and Theatre Performing Arts
Christmas House, Chester Road, Castle Bromwich, Solihull B36 0ET
☎0121 749 7147

Creative Director *Gavin Prime*

Teaching disabled, disadvantaged and mainstream children. The only totally free theatre and film school of this type in England. Students range in age from eight to 19 and work in all ways connected to performing arts. This includes writing and showing them the structure of the business and how to try and get work accepted.

Tony Staveacre Productions
Channel View, Blagdon, North Somerset BS40 7TP
☎01761 462161 Fax 01761 462161
Email staving@dircon.co.uk

Contact *Tony Staveacre*

Producer of dramas and documentaries as well

as music, arts and comedy progammes. OUTPUT *The Wodehouse Notebooks* (BBC Radio 4); *Tango Maestro* (BBC Four); *The Very Thought of You* (theatre). Welcomes unsolicited mss by mail or e-mail. 'Go for it!'

Stirling Film & TV Productions Limited
137 University Street, Belfast BT7 1HP
☎028 9033 3848 Fax 028 9043 8644
Email anne@stirlingtelevision.co.uk
Contact *Anne Stirling*

Producer of broadcast and corporate programming – documentary, sport, entertainment and lifestyle programmes.

Storm Film Productions Ltd
32–34 Great Marlborough Street, London W1F 7JB
☎020 7439 1616 Fax 020 7439 4477
Email sophie.storm@btclick.com
Website www.stormfilms.tv
Contact *Nic Auerbach*

Producer of commercials for clients such as British Airways and Shell. Unsolicited mss welcome.

Straight Forward Film & Television Productions Ltd
Building 2, Lesley Office Park, 393 Hollywood Road, Belfast BT4 2LS
☎028 9065 1010 Fax 028 9042 3384
Email enquiries@sforward.prestel.co.uk
Contacts *John Nicholson, Ian Kennedy*

Northern Ireland-based production company specialising in documentary, feature and lifestyle series for both regional and network transmission. OUTPUT includes *We Shall Overcome* (winner of Best Documentary at 1999 Celtic Television Festival for BBC); *Conquering the Normans* (Ch4 Learning – history of Normans in Ireland); *Gift of the Gab* (Ch4 Learning – contemporary Irish writing); *Fire School* (BBC NI – training of a team of fire-fighters); *Fish Out of Water* (BBC NI – job swaps north and south of the Irish border); *Just Jones* (BBC Radio Ulster daily show); *Sportsweek* (BBC Radio Ulster); *School Challenge* (3rd series, BBC NI); *World Indoor Bowls* (BBC NI); *Awash With Colour* (series, BBC Daytime).

Strawberry Productions Ltd
36 Priory Avenue, London W4 1TY
☎020 8994 4494 Fax 020 8742 7675
Contact *John Black*

Film, video and TV: drama and documentary; corporate and video publishing.

Sunset + Vine Productions Ltd
30 Sackville Street, London W1S 3DY
☎020 7478 7300 Fax 020 7478 7403

Sports, children's and music programmes for television. No unsolicited mss. 'We hire freelancers only upon receipt of a commission.'

Sweetheart Films
15 Quennel Mansions, Weir Road, London SW12 0NQ
☎020 8673 3855
Producer *Karel Bata*

Low-to-medium-budget feature films. No unsolicited mss; 'an introductory letter with, perhaps, a treatment and short extract would receive consideration. Nothing too domestic. No TV series. Tip: study your craft!'

Table Top Productions
1 The Orchard, Chiswick, London W4 1JZ
☎020 8742 0507 Fax 020 8742 0507
Email alvin@tabletopproductions.com
Contact *Alvin Rakoff*

TV and film. OUTPUT *Paradise Postponed* (TV mini-series); *A Voyage Round My Father*; *The First Olympics 1896*; *Dirty Tricks*; *A Dance to the Music of Time*; *Too Marvellous for Words*. No unsolicited mss. Also Dancetime Ltd.

Talisman Films Limited
5 Addison Place, London W11 4RJ
☎020 7603 7474 Fax 020 7602 7422
Email email@talismanfilms.com
Contact *Richard Jackson*

Drama for film and TV: developing the full range of drama – TV series, serials and single films, as well as theatric features. 'We will only consider material submitted via literary agents.' Interested in supporting and encouraging new writing.

TalkBack Productions
20–21 Newman Street, London W1T 1PG
☎020 7861 8000 Fax 020 7861 8001
Email reception@talkback.co.uk
Chief Executive *Peter Fincham*
Managing Director *Sally Debonnaire*

TalkBack Productions is a **FremantleMedia** company. Specialises in comedy, comedy drama and drama; also feature lifestyle programmes. OUTPUT *Smith and Jones; Murder Most Horrid; The Day Today; Knowing Me*

Knowing You with Alan Partridge; I'm Alan Partridge; They Think It's All Over; Never Mind the Buzzcocks; Brass Eye; House Doctor; She's Gotta Have It; Grand Designs; Sword of Honour; In a Land of Plenty; Shooting the Past; 11 o'clock Show; Smack the Pony; Big Train; Los Dos Bros; Your Money or Your Life; Property Ladder; Would Like to Meet.

Tandem TV & Film Ltd
10 Bargrove Avenue, Hemel Hempstead, Hertfordshire HP1 1QP
☎01442 261576 Fax 01442 219250
Email info@tandemtv.com
Website www.tandemtv.com

Contact *Barbara Page*

Produces training videos, especially health and safety; construction and civil engineering documentaries; drama-doc life stories for satellite television; Christian church and charity documentary, training and promotional programmes. Welcomes unsolicited mss.

Taylor Made Broadcasts Ltd
PO Box 100, Woodstock, Oxon OX20 1XE
☎01608 67777
Email post@tmtv.co.uk

Contact *Helen Johnson*

Producer of corporate videos and documentaries for television and radio. OUTPUT includes *Gardeners' Question Time* (BBC Radio 4). No unsolicited mss.

Telemagination Ltd
Royalty House, 72–74 Dean Street, London W1V 6AE
☎020 7434 1551 Fax 020 7434 3344
Email mail@tmation.co.uk
Website www.telemagination.co.uk

Contact *Marion Edwards*

Producer of television animation. OUTPUT includes *The Animals of Farthing Wood; Noah's Island; The Last Polar Bears; Little Ghosts; Pongwiffy.* In production: *Metal Heads; Cramp Twins – Series 2.* No unsolicited material.

Teliesyn
Chapter Arts Centre, Market Road, Canton, Cardiff CF5 1QE
☎029 2030 0876 Fax 029 2030 0877
Email tv@teliesyn.demon.co.uk
Website www.teliesyn.co.uk

Contact *Chris Davies*

Film and video: produces drama, documentary, music and social action in English and Welsh.

Celtic Film Festival, BAFTA Cymru, Grierson and Indie award winner. OUTPUT *Llafur Cariad* (epic drama, S4C); *How Red Was My Valley* (documentary series on the Labour Party, BBC2W); *Suckerfish* (35mm short); *Navida Nuestra* (Christmas mass from Argentina, S4C); *Subway Cops and the Mole Kings* (Ch4). Will consider unsolicited scripts only if accompanied by synopsis and c.v. Encourages new writing wherever possible in close association with a producer.

Tern Television Productions Ltd
73 Crown Street, Aberdeen AB11 6EX
☎01224 211123 Fax 01224 211199
Email office@terntv.com
Website www.terntv.com
Also at: RWF House, 5 Renfield Street, Glasgow G2 5EZ ☎0141 270 2905

Contacts *David Strachan, Gwyneth Hardy* (Aberdeen), *Harry Bell* (Glasgow)

Broadcast, television and corporate video productions. Specialises in factual entertainment. Currently developing drama.

Testbed Productions
Fifth Floor, 14–16 Great Portland Street, London W1W 8QW
☎020 7436 0555 Fax 020 7436 2800
Email mail@testbed.co.uk
Website www.testbed.co.uk

Contacts *Viv Black, Nick Baker*

Producer of documentaries, light entertainment, factual and spoken word programmes for radio. OUTPUT *Feedback* and *Wireless Wise* (BBC Radio 4); *Horrible Histories* (comedy). Welcomes unsolicted mss by post. 'We read all that comes in.'

Testimony Films
12 Great George Street, Bristol BS1 5RS
☎0117 925 8589 Fax 0117 925 7608
Email stevehumphries@testimonyfilms. force9.co.uk

Contact *Steve Humphries*

TV documentary producer. Specialises in social history exploring Britain's past using living memory. OUTPUT includes *Hooked: History of Addictions* (Ch4 series); *A Secret World of Sex* (BBC series); *Some Liked It Hot* (ITV series). Welcomes ideas form those working life stories and oral history.

Theatre of Comedy Company
See **Theatre Producers**

Tiger Aspect Productions Ltd

5 Soho Square, London W1D 3QA
☎020 7434 0672 Fax 020 7287 1448
Email madelineaddy@tigeraspect.co.uk
Website www.tigeraspect.co.uk
Contact *Charles Brand*

Television producer for comedy, drama, documentary and entertainment. OUTPUT *Births, Marriages & Deaths; Kid in the Corner; Country House; Gimme Gimme Gimme; Harry Enfield & Chums; Howard Goodalls' Big Bangs; Playing the Field I, II & III; Streetmate I & II; Let Them Eat Cake; The Vicar of Dibley.* Only considers material submitted via an agent or from writers with a known track record.

Tintinna (Productions and Media Solutions)

Summerfield, Bristol Road, Chew Stoke, Somerset BS40 8UB
☎01275 333128 Fax 01275 332316
Email tintinna@aol.com
Contacts *W. Ian Bell, Sandy Bell*

Producer of history programmes, human interest features and documentaries for radio. OUTPUT includes *What If?, That's History* (BBC Radio 4); *Cuppa, Goldfish & Candy Floss* (BBC Radio 2). Most recently, *This Green Unpleasant Land* (BBC Radio 4). Welcomes unsolicited mss by e-mail but 'difficult to sell to network commissioners'.

Tonfedd Eryri

Hen Ysgol Aberpwll, Y Felinheli, Bangor, Gwynedd LL56 4JS
☎01248 671167 Fax 01248 671172
Email swyddfa@tonfedd-eryi.com
Contacts *Hefin Elis, Norman Williams*

Light entertainment, comedy, music and drama.

Touch Productions Ltd

The Malt House Studios, Donhead St Mary, Dorset SP7 9DN
☎01747 828030 Fax 01747 828004
Email erica@touchproductions.co.uk
Contacts *Erica Wolfe-Murray, Malcolm Brinkworth*

Over the past 15 years has produced 'investigative documentary films, history based films with a strong contemporary relevance, powerful observational series and innovative films that stretch the form.' Television documentaries such as *Life of a £10 Note; Afghan Warrior – the Life & Death of Abdul Haq; Falklands 20th*

Anniversary; OJ – The Untold Story; Simon Weston V; Siege Doctors (all for BBC); *The Good Life; The Surgery; Coast of Dreams; A French Affair; Watching the Detectives; Brown Babies* (all for Ch4); *Fame School* and *Fame School – the Graduates* (both for Meridian). Also has a drama section based on real-life stories and unsolicited mss are welcome.

Transatlantic Films Production and Distribution Company

Studio One, 3 Brackenbury Road, London W6 0BE
☎020 8735 0505 Fax 020 8735 0605
Email mail@transatlanticfilms.com
Website www.transatlanticfilms.com
Executive Producer *Revel Guest*

Producer of TV documentaries. OUTPUT *Belzoni* (Ch4 Schools); *Science of Sleep and Dreams, Science of Love* and *Extreme Body Parts* (all for Discovery Health); *Legends of the Living Dead* (Discovery Travel/S4C International); *2025* (Discovery Digital); *How Animals Tell the Time* (Discovery); *Trailblazers* (Travel Channel). No unsolicited scripts. Interested in new writers for 'the book of the series', e.g. for *Greek Fire* and *The Horse in Sport*, but not usually drama script writers.

TV Choice Ltd

PO Box 597, Bromley, Kent BR2 0YB
☎020 8464 7402 Fax 020 8464 7845
Email tvchoiceuk@aol.com
Website www.tvchoice.uk.com
Contact *Norman Thomas*

Produces a range of educational videos for schools and colleges on subjects such as history, geography, business studies and economics. No unsolicited mss; send proposals only.

Twentieth Century Fox Film Co

Twentieth Century House, 31–32 Soho Square, London W1D 3AP
☎020 7437 7766 Fax 020 7734 3187
Website www.fox.co.uk

London office of the American giant.

Twofour Productions Limited

Quay West Studios, Old Newnham, Plymouth, Devon PL7 5BH
☎01752 333900 Fax 01752 344224
Email enq@twofour.co.uk
Website www.twofour.co.uk
Managing Director *Charles Wace*
Director of Broadcasting *Jill Lourie*

Specialises in factual and leisure programming for network and regional television; corporate communications for national/international business and public sector; special interest videos for retail/mail order; and, through its subsidiary twofourtv, webcasting and Intrantet or Internet-based TV.

Tyburn Film Productions Limited

Cippenham Court, Cippenham Lane, Cippenham, Berkshire SL1 5AU
☎01753 516767 Fax 01753 691785

Feature films. Subsidiary of **Arlington Productions Limited**. No unsolicited submissions.

UBA Ltd

21 Alderville Road, London SW6 2EE
☎01984 623619 Fax 01984 623733
Email shawjshaw@aol.com *or* petershaw@btinternet.com
Contacts *Peter Shaw, Joanna Shaw*

Feature films and TV for an international market. OUTPUT *Windprints; The Lonely Passion of Judith Hearne* (co-production with HandMade Films Ltd); *Taffin; Castaway; Turtle Diary; Sweeney Todd; Keep the Aspidistra Flying.* In development: *Kinder Garden; Rebel Magic; No Man's Land.* Prepared to commission new writing whether adapted from another medium or based on a short outline/treatment. Concerned with the quality of the script (*Turtle Diary* was written by Harold Pinter) and breadth of appeal. 'Exploitation material' not welcome.

UK Film and TV Production Company Plc

3 Colville Place, London W1T 2BH
☎020 7255 1650
Contact *Henrietta Fudakowski*

Film and television. Currently looking for feature film or TV drama scripts, with a preference for stories with humour. Return postage and list of credits essential. Please phone before submitting material.

Vera Productions

66–68 Margaret Street, London W1W 8SR
☎020 7436 6116 Fax 020 7436 6117
Contact *Rachel Sutherland*

Produces television comedy such as *Alistair McGowan's Big Impression* and *Rory Bremner.*

Video Enterprises

12 Barbers Wood Road, High Wycombe, Buckinghamshire HP12 4EP
☎01494 534144/07831 875216 (Mobile)
Fax 01494 534145
Email videoenterprises@btconnect.com
Website www.videoenterprises.btconnect.com
Contact *Maurice R. Fleisher*

Video and TV, mainly corporate: business and industrial training, promotional material and conferences. No unsolicited material 'but always ready to try out good new writers'.

Brian Waddell Productions Ltd

Strand Studios, 5/7 Shore Road, Holywood, Co. Down BT18 9HX
☎028 9042 7646 Fax 028 9042 7922
Email strand@bwpltv.co.uk
Contacts *Brian Waddell*

Producer of a wide range of television programmes in leisure activities, the arts, music, children's, comedy, travel/adventure and documentaries. Currently developing two feature films.

Wall to Wall

8–9 Spring Place, London NW5 3ER
☎020 7485 7424 Fax 020 7267 5292
Website www.walltowall.co.uk
Chief Executive *Alex Graham*

Factual and drama programming. OUTPUT includes *A Rather English Marriage; Glasgow Kiss; Sex, Chips & Rock 'n' Roll; The 1940s House; Body Story* and *Neanderthal.* Drama ideas welcomed through established agents.

Jane Walmsley Productions
See **JAM Pictures**

Walnut Media Communications Ltd

Crown House, Armley Road, Leeds, West Yorkshire LS12 2EJ
☎08707 427070 Fax 08707 427080
Email mail@walnutmedia.com
Website www.walnutmedia.com
Contact *Geoff Penn*

Walnut Media provides business communications services to large corporate clients through a range of services such as video, live events and new media. Founded as the Walnut Partnership in 1984, the company has diversified from corporate video production in order to provide a more complete visual service.

Walsh Bros. Limited
4 The Heights, London SE7 8JH
☎020 8858 5870/8854 5557
Fax 020 8858 6870
Email walshbros@lycosmail.com
Producer/Director *John Walsh*
Producer/Head of Finance *David Walsh, ACA*
Producer/Head of Development *Maura Walsh*

Award-winning producer of drama documentaries and feature films. OUTPUT *Monarch* (feature film on the events on the eve of the death of King Henry VIII); *Trex* (factual series shooting in China, Mexico, Vancouver and Alaska); *Nu Model Armi* (documentary); *TUEX2* (shot in Romania, India, Iceland and Louisiana); *Boyz & Girlz*, (documentary series); *Cowboyz & Cowgirlz* (US sequel to the first hit series); *Ray Harryhausen* (profile of the work of Hollywood special effects legend); *The Comedy Store* (behind-the-scenes view of the birthplace of alternative comedy); *The Sceptic & The Psychic*; *The Sleeper* and *A State of Mind* (film dramas).

Warner Sisters Film & TV Ltd
The Cottage, Pall Mall Deposit, 124 Barlby Road, London W10 6BL
☎020 8960 3550 Fax 020 8960 3880
Email sisters@warnercine.com
Chief Executives *Lavinia Warner, Jane Wellesley, Dorothy Viljoen*

FOUNDED 1984. Drama and comedy. TV and feature films. OUTPUT includes *Selling Hitler; Rides; Life's a Gas; She-Play; A Village Affair; Dangerous Lady; Dressing for Breakfast; The Spy that Caught a Cold; The Bite; Jilting Joe; The Jump; Lady Audley's Secret; Do or Die*. Developing a wide range of projects including *The Letters* (feature film).

Paul Weiland Film Company
14 Newburgh Street, London W1F 7RT
☎020 7287 9875 Fax 020 7439 4256
Email action@paulweiland.com
Contact *Mary Francis*

Television commercials and pop promos.

Whistledown Productions Ltd
66 Southwark Bridge Road, London SE1 0AS
☎020 7922 1120 Fax 020 7261 0939
Contact *David Prest*

Producer of Sony Award Winning Landmark Series for BBC Radio 4 – *Evacuation, The Child Migrants*. Features and documentaries on wide range of social and historical subjects, contemporary series and popular culture. OUTPUT includes *Questions Questions* and *The Reunion* (Radio 4); music-based documentaries for Radio 2. 'We welcome contributions on contemporary issues for talks slots etc., but phone or e-mail first.'

Michael White Productions Ltd
See **MW Entertainments Ltd**

Windrush Productions Ltd
7 Woodlands Road, Moseley, Birmingham B13 4EH
☎0121 449 6439/07977 059378 (Mobile)
Fax 0121 449 6439
Email beboyyaa@hotmail.com
Contacts *Emma Jeffares, Pogus Caesar*

Television documentaries, including a multi-cultural series for Carlton TV *Xpress*. Also for Carlton produced and directed *Respect; An Eye on X; The A-Force* (BBC); *I'm Black in Britain* (Central TV) and the music film *Xpress Urself Thru Muzik*. Produces films, documentaries, pop promos, corporate videos for a range of clients. 'We encourage new writing, especially from the regions and seek scripts from writers interested in developing new Black fiction/comedy.'

Working Title Films Ltd
Oxford House, 76 Oxford Street, London W1D 1BS
☎020 7307 3000 Fax 020 7307 3001/2/3
Co-Chairmen (Films) *Tim Bevan, Eric Fellner*
Head of Development (Films) *Chris Clark*
Development Assistant *Luke Parker-Bowles*
Television *Simon Wright*

Feature films, TV drama; also family/children's entertainment and TV comedy. OUTPUT Films: *Bridget Jones's Diary; Captain Corelli's Mandolin; Ali G in da House; Notting Hill; Elizabeth; Plunkett & Macleane; The Borrowers; The Matchmaker; Fargo; Dead Man Walking; French Kiss; Four Weddings and a Funeral; The Hudsucker Proxy; The Tall Guy; Wish You Were Here; My Beautiful Laundrette*. Television: *More Tales of the City; The Borrowers I & II; Armisted Maupin's Tales of the City; News Hounds; Randall & Hopkirk Deceased; Doomwatch*. No unsolicited mss at present.

Worldview Pictures

Units 1&2, Leeds Place, off Tollington Park, London N4 3RQ
☎020 7916 4696 Fax 020 7916 4696
Email anyone@worldviewpictures.co.uk

Contacts *Stephen Trombley*

Documentaries and series for television, plus theatrical. OUTPUT *A Death in the Family*; *Project X*; *War and Civilization*; *Nuremberg*; *Raising Hell: The Life of A.J. Bannister*; *The Execution Protocol*; *Drancy: A Concentration Camp in Paris*; *The Lynchburg Story*; *99% Woman*.

Worthwhile Productions

16 Biddulph Road, London W6 1JB
☎020 7266 9166 Fax 020 7266 9166

Contact *Jeremy Wootliff*

Feature films, video; documentary, corporate and commercials. Unsolicited mss welcome.

Wortman Productions UK

48 Chiswick Staithe, London W4 3TP
☎020 8994 8886/07976 805976 (Mobile)
Email nevillewortman@beeb.net

Producer *Neville Wortman*

Co-producers with Polestar Pictures Ltd. Feature film and TV production for drama, documentary, entertainment and corporate. OUTPUT *House in the Country* John Julius Norwich (ITV series); *Tribute to Ellington* (jazz special); *Lost Ships* (maritime historical drama series; Discovery Channel); *The Assassination of Julius Caesar* (Discovery/History Channel/Five) In preparation: *Samuel's Last Summer* (feature film). Open to new writing, preferably through agents; single page outline, some pages of dialogue; s.a.e. for reply.

WT2

Oxford House, 76 Oxford Street, London W1D 1BS
☎020 7307 3000 Fax 020 7307 3004

Head of WT2 *Natascha Wharton*
Head of Development *Rachel Prior*
WT2 Assistant *Hannah Farrell*

Low budget film division of **Working Title Films**. Feature films only. OUTPUT *Billy Elliot; Long Time Dead; Ali G Indahouse; My Little Eye*. No unsolicited screenplays at present, but keen to encourage new writing via New Writers Scheme (Four-page outlines only) – contact *Hannah Farrell*.

Yoda Productions Ltd

30 Oak Corner, Beare Green, Dorking, Surrey RH5 4SG
☎01306 710472 Fax 01306 710472
Email gail@yodaproductions.co.uk

Contact *Gail Lowe*

Medical, scientific, technical marketing and promotional, training videos and multimedia. No unsolicited mss.

Zenith Entertainment Ltd

43–45 Dorset Street, London W1U 7NA
☎020 7224 2440 Fax 020 7224 3194
Email general@zenith-entertainment.co.uk

Script Editor *Alex Jones*

Feature films and TV drama. OUTPUT Films: Todd Haynes' *Velvet Goldmine; Wisdom of Crocodiles;* Nicole Holofcener's *Walking and Talking*. Television: *Hamish Macbeth; Rhodes; Bodyguards; The Uninvited; Bomber; 2000 Acres of Sky*. No unsolicited scripts.

Taking Off: A Writer's Diary

A regular contributor to The Writer's Handbook *on the trials and tribulations of the aspiring writer, Bob G. Ritchie reports on a year in which he finally made his breakthrough.*

January

Still not heard anything from *Doctors* about my story ideas. Nor from *EastEnders*. Reaching the final fifteen of last year's BBC Talent Competition was obviously no open sesame. Decide to approach *Family Affairs* while I'm waiting.

Meanwhile, in my other role as the country's authority on how to achieve not-quite-success as a writer, receive e-mail confirming commission for my article in *The Writer's Handbook 2004,* i.e. this one. In buoyant mood, finish outline of sample episode for new TV drama series, *Alternative Therapy.* Start to write draft but immediately have doubts about very first scene. Is a woman lying motionless on a kitchen table enough of a hook to stop viewers reaching for their remotes?

Helena e-mails from *EastEnders*: my *Casualty* script has reached the top of her pile. 'Bear with me and you will get a response.' When, though? When?

February

First rejection of the year: a *Family Affairs* script editor doesn't think it's worth giving me a trial. Furthermore, he doesn't think it's worth giving me any reasons. Oh, well, who watches Channel 5, anyway? In defiant mood finish first draft of *Alternative Therapy* then, with great effort of will, put it aside, resolving not to start rewrites for at least two weeks, as recommended in all good screenwriting books.

Half the country seems to be watching *Pop Idol*, while the other half think it's the end of civilization as we know it. Occurs to me a similar series could be made about would-be authors. *Writer Star!* A nationwide search for Britain's next Ian Rankins and Zadie Smiths. Will the hundreds of literary hopefuls grab Germaine? Move Melvyn? Fascinate Fay? Feel the heartbreak. See the tears. After suitably humiliating regional eliminators the best fifty go to London, where in five days they must write a fictional exploration of one of the major literary themes of the day: love, postmodern minimalism, football. Eventually ten are selected to go on to the final, conducted live on prime-time TV. Which is when it gets personal. Yes, they can all write, but do they have what it takes to be *writers?* Did they have lonely, miserable, violent childhoods or lifelong battles with drug abuse? Are the men ruggedly wasted, as if they have just spent a year working on a Siberian oil rig? Do the women look as sexy as Minette Walters? Who, in other words, has the write stuff?

March

Work on outline for a film: a robbery performed by OAPs. Very pleased with the structure, so decide to run it past Christopher Vogler's famous memo to Disney executives, the template many claim to be behind every successful movie. Let's see now, there are twelve stages in the Hero's Journey...

E-mail from one of the other Talent finalists to complain all his ideas for *Doctors* have been rejected. Can't help feeling a glow of schadenfreude: all the more room for mine.

E-mail from *Doctors*: all my ideas rejected.

Resolve to treat this as a learning experience, however. Set VCR for new series: will analyse in detail minimum of twenty episodes. If I can't crack relatively straightforward daily half-hour drama, what hope Hollywood?

Unbidden and definitely unwanted idea for a novel comes into my head. Now, what did I say last year about writing a novel? Stop it, just stop it.

E-mail from Helena at *EastEnders*: 'I've read your *Casualty* script ... Stories are clear and engaging ... Nice blend of drama with comedy and some very subtle shifts in tone ... Overall strong and confidently written episode.' And apparently I'm now on a 'long shortlist'. Whatever that is.

April

Phone call from editor of this handbook: how would I like to contribute a 'getting started' chapter to a forthcoming guide to writing for stage and screen? Takes me all of half a second to decide. I may not be the best qualified person, but I haven't noticed a lack of knowledge about a subject inhibiting other writers.

I mull over possible approaches to my commission. (What a lovely word, commission, such a comfortingly financial ring to it.) Should I fill it with anecdotes or lots of tick boxes? Should I be lighthearted or serious? Encouraging or discouraging? As part of research decide to attend seminar organized by the Writer's Guild. Theme of the evening ostensibly writing for different media, but actually it's just another excuse for writers to whinge. Resentment homes in on a popular target: TV script editors. Oh yes, we've all suffered at their hands.

'Now they're even being sent on scriptwriting courses,' complains one speaker, as if that were somehow cheating, 'so they know what to look out for.'

May

Wake in the early hours with more than the usual feeling of panic. What have I done? Oh yes. Have agreed to write two more chapters of forthcoming writer's guides. Only myself to blame, of course. Always been a bit of an innocent at working lunches. Like a lady of easy virtue, softened up by flattering words and a decent bottle of red, am soon ready to agree to any proposition put to me. So now I am to write not only advice on how to make a start as a dramatist, but also to interview key BBC drama executives and provide an overview of classic fictional detectives.

Feel surrounded by half-finished projects: first draft pilot episode of *Alternative Therapy* awaiting rewrites; rough plan of OAP caper film awaiting inspiration;

idea for novel awaiting research – yes, I know I said I wasn't going to write another novel, but this one's going to be good, trust me – 'getting started' chapter waiting for me to get started; new ideas for *Doctors* awaiting final polish ... .

June

To Broadcasting House to interview Kate Rowland, creative director of BBC New Writing. She tells me a lot I know already, but a lot I don't. Apparently one of the most common pits into which new writers fall is that of imitation. Her shelves are currently overflowing with feeble re-hashes of *The Royle Family*. Yes, it's changed the face of TV sitcom, but she and her team of script readers can see a bandwagon coming before anyone's even thought of jumping on it. Mentally search soul for signs of same crime, but honestly fail to find any. Hear no band, see no wagon.

Then to White City to interview Mal Young, the man whose name is at the end of the credits for most BBC drama series. His office has a huge TV pride of place, so have to conduct interview with *Can't Cook Won't Cook* flickering silently at my elbow. Doesn't start well. At the top of the questions I e-mailed beforehand I called him the Head of Drama Series. He takes out a pen and firmly puts a line through the first word: 'Actually, I'm the Controller of Drama Series.' Whoops.

July

Finally finish my 'getting started' chapter. Wittily subtitle the first paragraph, 'Step 1: Be related to a producer'.

Finish reading stack of crime novels (what is the collective noun: a suspicion?) as part of research for chapter on legendary detectives. Have been looking for common threads, but find few. Some concentrate on atmosphere, others on characterization. Some have plots more difficult to understand than quantum theory, others so simple even the police could have found the solution by page ten. All have one thing in common, though. Closure. Villain is always caught or killed. Reason prevails. Good triumphs. In that respect, at least, not so very different from an episode of *Doctors*.

Receive my transcribed interviews with Kate Rowland and Mal Young. Thankfully, the editor has broken up Mal's almost continuous monologue with the questions I would have asked if only I could have got a word in edgeways. Actually, rather chuffed with it. Good punchy stuff from Mal; lots of useful advice for aspiring writers. It even makes me sound as if I know what I'm talking about.

August

Going through writing crisis. After flirtation with world of soaps (or returning drama series, as Mal Young calls them), have come to realize I don't like them very much. Of course, failure to get anything accepted may be contributory factor. Have nothing but admiration for the writers: they must live and breathe the shows. Unfortunately can't honestly see myself ever feeling the same.

So, to Broadcasting House again – but wearily now – with three of last year's

Talent co-finalists to meet one of the script editors from *Doctors*. When we complain we've had all our ideas rejected and are ready to give up, she tells us a regular writer on the series owes them five scripts but his last nine ideas have been rejected too. We gather this bit of bad news is a script editor's way of being encouraging. So we plunge into a discussion of the dramatic possibilities of various medical conditions and I emerge three hours later full of renewed enthusiasm. I'll crack this bloody show if it's the last thing I do.

September
Phone rings. Laura. Yes? From the BBC. Pulse quickens. Gather she's calling from *EastEnders*. On behalf of Helena. Pulse changes up another gear. I've moved from the long shortlist to the short shortlist. I'm one of only twenty-four writers they're considering for their next shadow scheme – a training scheme for new *EE* writers. Pulse now at danger level. Take deep breath. Try to relax steely grip on phone. Would I like to come and have a chat?

Put phone down. Feel suffused with rosy glow – or is it high blood pressure? Drift into reverie of scriptwriting fame and fortune, only to have it come to a speedy end when recall haven't actually watched a single episode of *EE* for last three months. Also have embarrassing recollection of writing in this diary only a few weeks ago I couldn't care less about soaps any more.

Well, that was then.

'Tell us about yourself,' suggests Helena. The most predictable question but still the one I was most dreading. How to make thirty-five years of rejection slips sound like a well-planned learning curve? Luckily we soon move onto the show itself. Guiltily confess I don't watch it every night. Helena says that if I did they'd think I was a very sad person who should get out more.

Two nailbiting days pass before Helena calls. 'We'd like to invite you to attend the shadow scheme.' With what I consider to be admirable restraint the scream YESSSSS! happens only in my head.

October
To BBC Elstree for the two-day seminar part of the shadow scheme, led by *EE* veteran writer Tony Jordan. Soon discover most of the other eleven hopefuls already have reams of TV credits to their names. Feel a distinct amateur among all these professionals. Mood only lifts when I find myself next to a man who scripts *The Sooty Show*.

Spend the rest of the week reading three months' worth of story summaries to get to the point where the episode I'm to write starts. My script won't be used, but it is a real episode, scheduled for transmission mid-February. Word soon gets out. Strangers approach me in the supermarket to ask me what's going to happen. Smugly tell them I'm sworn to secrecy.

Five days later, back to Elstree to discuss my proposed scene breakdown with Helena and my script editor, Aamina. I pitch my ideas about how I see my episode being put together, where the focus is, the main story, characters' journeys, climaxes, pivotal scenes... Getting quite carried away by my own brilliance when interrupted by Aamina. Surely my emphasis is on the wrong story? And don't I give the viewers a big let-down at the end of my second story? And shouldn't I be making more of...?

Four hours later, drive out of car park feeling distinctly as if been run over by a bus. Who the hell do these script editors think they are?

November
Finish first draft of my episode. Then put it aside for two days in usual desperate attempt to lend distance. Even so, still reads depressingly like my own work. E-mail it to Aamina then try to spend next few days working on something else. Drive to review meeting feeling even more nervous than before my initial interview, but Aamina smiles warmly as she greets me in reception. Spirits lift even further when she opens by saying my script is 'really, really good' and lots of other flattering things I forget in the cloud of euphoria that quickly envelopes me. Aren't script editors wonderful?

Then she spends four hours telling me all the things I have to change.

Two days after e-mailing my second draft Helena phones. Surely too soon for feedback? I half-close ears in anticipation of bad news, so actual words go by in a bit of a blur. '...calling to congratulate you on your second draft ... what a good job you've done ... really like it ...' I decide it's safe to listen properly. 'Now it'll be handed to the series editor ... very much hope it will take you somewhere.' I try not to respond too excitedly, but obviously fail. She cautions, 'Don't give up the day job yet. The series editor will have a whole pile of scripts to read before she decides who to commission. Though she will almost certainly come back to me for an opinion, which in your case,' she assures me, 'will be a very strong recommendation.'

Hardly dare, but can't help thinking I might finally be on my way.

December
Celebrate with a pre-Christmas drinks party. The entire county now knows I am on the verge of writing for *EE*, but even I am beginning to tire of the sound of my own voice talking about it. With relief find myself chatting to a Hawthornden Prize-winner in the middle of his fifth novel. At last. Genuine literary talent. We talk about how difficult it is for new writers to get started. I confess to being disappointed no one has taken up my *Writer Star!* idea. 'With its start in the drab ordinary world and its subsequent trials, hope, despair and ultimate return with the elixir of fame and fortune, it is,' I tell him, 'a perfect example of Vogler's Hero's Journey. Does no one recognize a winning formula when they see it?'

'Never mind all that,' he says. 'Tell me what's going to happen in *EastEnders*.'

Theatre Producers

For latest minimum rates for writers of plays for Subsidised Repertory Theatres (not Scotland) access the following websites: Theatrical Management Association: www.tmauk.org; and the Writers' Guild: www.writersguild.org.uk

Actors Touring Company (ATC)

Alford House, Aveline Street, London
SE11 5DQ
☎020 7735 8311
Fax 020 7735 1031 attn. ATC
Email info@atc-online.com
Website www.atc-online.com
Artistic Director *Gordon Anderson*

Collaborates with writers on adaptation and/or translation work and unsolicited mss will be considered in this category as well as new writing. 'We endeavour to read mss but do not have the resources to do so quickly.' As a small-scale company, all plays must have a cast of six or less.

Almeida Theatre Company

The Almeida Theatre, Almeida Street, London N1 1TA
☎020 7288 4900 Fax 020 7288 4901
Website www.almeida.co.uk
Artistic Director *Michael Attenborough*

FOUNDED 1980. Now in its fourteenth year as a full-time producing theatre, presenting a year-round theatre and music programme in which international writers, composers, performers, directors and designers are invited to work with British artists on challenging new and classical works. Previous productions: *Galileo; Moonlight; The School for Wives; Hamlet; Who's Afraid of Virginia Woolf; Ivanov; Naked; The Judas Kiss; The Iceman Cometh; The Jew of Malta; Celebration; The Room; Richard II; Coriolanus; Lulu; The Shape of Things; King Lear, The Lady from the Sea.* No unsolicited mss: 'our producing programme is very limited and linked to individual directors and actors'.

Alternative Theatre Company Ltd

Bush Theatre, Shepherds Bush Green, London W12 8QD
☎020 7602 3703 Fax 020 7602 7614
Email info@bushtheatre.co.uk
Literary Manager *Nicola Wilson*

FOUNDED 1972. Trading as The Bush Theatre.

Produces nine new plays a year (principally British) including up to three visiting companies also producing new work: 'we are a writer's theatre'. Previous productions: *Kiss of the Spiderwoman* Manuel Puig; *Raping the Gold* Lucy Gannon; *The Wexford Trilogy* Billy Roche; *Love and Understanding* Joe Penhall; *This Limetree Bower* Conor McPherson; *Discopigs* Enda Walsh; *The Pitchfork Disney* Philip Ridley; *Caravan* Helen Blakeman; *Beautiful Thing* Jonathan Harvey; *Killer Joe* Tracy Letts; *Shang-a-Lang* Catherine Johnson; *Howie the Rookie* Mark O'Rowe; *The Glee Club* Richard Cameron; *Adrenalin ... Heart* Georgia Fitch. Scripts are read by a team of associates, then discussed with the management, a process which takes about four months. The theatre offers a small number of commissions, recommissions to ensure further drafts on promising plays, and a guarantee against royalties so writers are not financially penalised even though the plays are produced in a small house. Writers should send scripts (full-length plays only) with small s.a.e. for acknowledgement and large s.a.e. for return of script.

Birmingham Repertory Theatre

Centenary Square, Broad Street, Birmingham
B1 2EP
☎0121 245 2000 Fax 0121 245 2100
Website www.birmingham-rep.co.uk
Associate Director (Literary) *Ben Payne*
Literary Officer *Caroline Jester*

The Birmingham Repertory Theatre aims to provide a platform for the best work from new writers from both within and beyond the West Midlands region. The Rep is committed to a policy of integrated casting and to the production of new work which reflects the diversity of contemporary experience. The commissioning of new plays takes place across the full range of the theatre's activities: in the Main House, The Door (which is a dedicated new writing space) and on tour to community venues in the region. 'Writers are advised that the Rep is very unlikely to produce an unsolicited script. We usually assess unsolicited submissions on the basis of whether it indicates a writer with whom the theatre may be interested in working. The theatre runs a programme of writers' attachments every year in addition to its commissioning policy and maintains close links with *Stagecoach* (the regional writers' training agency) and the **MA in Playwriting Studies** at the University of Birmingham.' For more information contact the Literary Officer.

Black Theatre Co-op
See **NITRO**

Bootleg Theatre Company
23 Burgess Green, Bishopdown, Salisbury, Wiltshire SP1 3El
☎01722 421476
Email colin@thebootlegtheatrecompany. fsnet.co.uk

Contact *Colin Burden*

FOUNDED 1984. Tries to encompass as wide an audience as possible and has a tendency towards plays with socially relevant themes. A good bet for new writing since unsolicited mss are very welcome. 'Our policy is to produce new and/or rarely seen plays and anything received is given the most serious consideration.' Actively seeks to obtain grants to commission new writers for the company. Productions include: *Clubland* by Giles, Harris, Suthers and Mordell; *Hanging Hanratty* by Michael Burnham; *The Truth About Blokes* by Trevor Suthers; *Cool Blokes: Decent Suits* by Russell Mardell.

Borderline Theatre
Darlington New Church, North Harbour Street, Ayr KA8 8AA
☎01292 281010 Fax 01292 263825
Email enquiries@borderlinetheatre.co.uk
Website www.borderlinetheatre.co.uk

Producer *Eddie Jackson*

FOUNDED 1974. Borderline is one of Scotland's leading touring companies. Committed to new writing, it tours an innovative programme of new plays and radical adaptations/translations of classic texts in an accessible and entertaining style. Tours to main-house theatres and small venues throughout Scotland. Productions include the world premières of *The Angels' Share* by Chris Dolan; *The Prince and the Pilot* Anita Sullivan. Previous writers have included Dario Fo, Liz Lochhead and John Byrne. Borderline is also committed to commissioning and touring new plays for young people. Please contact the company before submitting synopsis or script.

Bristol Old Vic Theatre Company (Theatre Royal, New Vic Studio & Basement)
Theatre Royal, King Street, Bristol BS1 4ED
☎0117 949 3993 Fax 0117 949 3996
Email admin@bristol-old-vic.co.uk
Website www.bristol-old-vic.co.uk

Committed to the commissioning and production of new writing in the Theatre Royal (650 seats). Plays must have enough popular appeal to attract an audience of significant size. In the New Vic Studio (150 seats) up to four plays a year are produced. The theatre will read and report on unsolicited scripts, and asks for a fee of £15 per script to cover the payments to readers. 'We also seek to attract emerging talent to the Basement, a profit-share venue (50 seats) committed to producing one-act plays. Plays for the Basement will be read free of charge although no report can be provided.' In all cases, if return of script is required, please supply s.a.e.

Bush Theatre
See **Alternative Theatre Company Ltd**

Carnival (Films & Theatre) Ltd
See entry under **Film, TV and Radio Production Companies**

Guy Chapman Productions Ltd
37 Southampton Street, London WC2E 7HE
☎020 7379 7474 Fax 020 7379 8484
Email guy@g-c-a.co.uk

Contacts *Guy Chapman*

Performs to young audiences with innovative, experimental theatre. Productions include: *Love Upon the Throne*; *Shopping and Fucking*; *Crave*; *Disco Pigs*; *Resident Alien*; *Corpus Christi*; *New Boy*.

Chester Gateway Theatre Trust Ltd
Hamilton Place, Chester, Cheshire CH1 2BH
☎01244 318104 Fax 01244 317277
Email jasminehendry@gateway-theatre.org
Website www.chestergateway.co.uk

Chief Executive *Jasmine Hendry*

FOUNDED 1968. 440-seater main house and 120-seater Manweb Studio. Committed to producing two in-house productions a year and aims to present a varied programme of theatre, dance, music, opera and comedy. The Education and Access Department works in schools and the community, and a writers' group meets fortnightly. Each year the group presents rehearsed readings using professional actors and directors.

Citizens Theatre

Gorbals, Glasgow G5 9DS
☎0141 429 5561   Fax 0141 429 7374
Email info@citz.co.uk
Website www.citz.co.uk

General Manager *Anna Stapleton*

No formal new play policy. The theatre has a play reader but opportunities to do new work are limited.

Clwyd Theatr Cymru

Mold, Flintshire CH7 1YA
☎01352 756331   Fax 01352 701558
Email drama@celtic.co.uk
Website www.clwyd-theatr-cymru.co.uk

Literary Manager *William James*
   (william.james@clwyd-theatr-cymru.co.uk)

Clwyd Theatr Cymru produces a season of plays each year performed by a core ensemble, along with tours throughout Wales (in English and Welsh). Plays are a mix of classics, revivals, contemporary drama. Recent new writing includes: *The Rabbit* Meredydd Barker; *Journey of Mary Kelly* Siân Evans; *Rape of the Fair Country, Hosts of Rebecca* and *Song of the Earth* all adapt. Manon Eames; *Celf* by Yasmina Reza, *Damwain a Hap* by Dario Fo, both translated by Manon Eames; *Flora's War/Rhyfel Flora, Word for Word/Gair am Air* and *The Secret/Y Gyfrinach* by Tim Baker. Plays by Welsh writers or with Welsh themes will be considered.

Michael Codron Plays Ltd

Aldwych Theatre Offices, Aldwych, London WC2B 4DF
☎020 7240 8291   Fax 020 7240 8467

General Manager *Paul O'Leary* (Productions)

Michael Codron Plays Ltd manages the Aldwych Theatre in London's West End. The plays it produces don't necessarily go into the Aldwych but always tend to be big-time West End fare. Previous productions: *Bedroom Farce; Blue Orange; Copenhagen; The Invention of Love; Hapgood; Uncle Vanya; Rise and Fall of Little Voice; Arcadia; Dead Funny.* No particular rule of thumb on subject matter or treatment. The acid test is whether 'something appeals to Michael'. Straight plays rather than musicals.

Colchester Mercury Theatre Limited

Balkerne Gate, Colchester, Essex CO1 1PT
☎01206 577006   Fax 01206 769607
Email info@mercurytheatre.co.uk

Chief Executive *D. Evans*

Associate Director *Adrian Stokes*

Producing theatre with a wide-ranging audience. Unsolicited scripts welcome. The theatre has a free playwright's group for adults with a serious commitment to writing plays.

The Coliseum, Oldham

Fairbottom Street, Oldham, Lancashire OL1 3SW
☎0161 624 1731   Fax 0161 624 5318

Chief Executive *Kevin Shaw*

The policy of the Coliseum is to present high quality work that is unashamedly 'popular'. Has a special interest in new work that has a Northern flavour, however this does not rule out other plays. Unsolicited scripts are all read but will only be returned if a s.a.e. is included.

Contact Theatre Company

Oxford Road, Manchester M15 6JA
☎0161 274 3434   Fax 0161 274 0640
Email info@contact-theatre.org.uk

Artistic Director *John E. McGrath*

'In partnership with the BBC, we are investing in innovative approaches to the discovery of new writers – and new kinds of writing – for stage, screen, radio and new media.' In general, Contact works primarily with the 13–30 age group and is particularly interested in materials that relate to the lives and culture of young people. 'We welcome work from writers of all ages. Hearing from a variety of voices, from different cultures and backgrounds, is also important to us. We encourage concise pitches from writers – no more than 10 pages – including a summary and some sample pages.'

Crucible Theatre

55 Norfolk Street, Sheffield S1 1DA
☎0114 249 5999   Fax 0114 249 6003

Associate Director *Michael Grandage*
Literary Associates *Matthew Byam Shaw, Anna Mackmin*

'Most of the new work we present will be the result of commissions or a prolonged exchange of ideas and script development with writers in whom we have expressed an interest. However, we are interested in all new work and offer a free script reading service for unsolicited scripts. NB We do not offer readers' reports. Please ring or send s.a.e. for full details of script reading service.'

Cwmni Theatr Gwynedd

Deiniol Road, Bangor, Gwynedd LL57 2TL
☎01248 351707   Fax 01248 351915
Email theatr@theatregwynedd.co.uk

Contact *Artistic Director*

FOUNDED 1984. A mainstream company, performing in major theatres on the Welsh circuit. Welsh-language work only at present. Classic Welsh plays, translations of European repertoire and new work, including adaptations from novels. New Welsh work always welcome; works in English considered if appropriate for translation (i.e. dealing with issues relevant to Wales). 'We are keen to discuss projects with established writers and offer commissions where possible.'

Derby Playhouse

Eagle Centre, Derby DE1 2NF
☎01332 363271 Fax 01332 547200
Website www.derbyplayhouse.co.uk

Chief Executive *Karen Hebden*
Creative Producer *Stephen Edwards*

Derby Playhouse is interested in new work and has produced several world premières over the last year. 'We have a discrete commissioning budget but already have several projects under way. Due to the amount of scripts we receive, we now ask writers to send a letter accompanied by a synopsis of the play, a résumé of writing experience and any ten pages of the script they wish to submit. We will then determine whether we think it is suitable for the Playhouse, in which case we will ask for a full script.' Writers are welcome to send details of rehearsed readings and productions as an alternative means of introducing the theatre to their work.

Druid Theatre Company

Chapel Lane, Galway, Republic of Ireland
☎00 353 91 568660 Fax 00 353 91 563109
Email info@druidtheatre.com
Website www.druidtheatre.com

Contact *Literary Manager*

FOUNDED 1975. Based in Galway and playing nationally and internationally, the company operates a major programme for the development of new writing. While focusing on Irish work, the company also accepts unsolicited material from outside Ireland.

The Dukes

Moor Lane, Lancaster LA1 1QE
☎01524 598505 Fax 01524 598519

Chief Executive *Amanda Belcham*
Artistic Director *Ian Hastings*

FOUNDED 1971. The only producing house in Lancashire. Wide target market for cinema and theatre. Plays in a 320-seater end-on auditorium and in a 198-seater in-the-round studio. Host for Litfest – Lancaster's annual festival of literature. In the summer months open-air promenade performances are held in Williamson Park. Also, community based Youth Arts Centre.

Dundee Repertory Theatre

Tay Square, Dundee DD1 1PB
☎01382 227684 Fax 01382 228609
Email hwatson@dundeereptheatre.co.uk
Website www.dundeereptheatre.co.uk

Artistic Directors *Dominic Hill, James Brining*

FOUNDED 1939. Plays to a varied audience. Translations and adaptations of classics, and new local plays. Most new work is commissioned. Interested in contemporary plays in translation and in new Scottish writing. No scripts except by prior arrangement.

Eastern Angles Theatre Company

Sir John Mills Theatre, Gatacre Road,
Ipswich, Suffolk IP1 2LQ
☎01473 218202 Fax 01473 384999
Email admin@easternangles.co.uk
Website www.easternangles.co.uk

Artistic Director *Ivan Cutting*
General Manager *Jill Streatfeild*

FOUNDED 1982. Plays to a rural audience for the most part. New work only: some commissioned, some devised by the company, some researched documentaries. Unsolicited mss welcome from regional writers. 'We are always keen to develop and produce new writing, especially that which is germane to a rural area.'

Edinburgh Royal Lyceum Theatre

See **Royal Lyceum Theatre Company**

English Touring Theatre

25 Short Street, London SE1 8LJ
☎020 7450 1990 Fax 020 7450 1991
Email admin@englishtouringtheatre.co.uk
Website www.englishtouringtheatre.co.uk

Artistic Director *Stephen Unwin*

FOUNDED 1993. National touring company visiting middle-scale receiving houses and arts centres throughout the UK. Mostly mainstream. Largely classical programme, but with increasing interest to tour one modern English play per year. Strong commitment to education work. No unsolicited mss.

Finborough Theatre

118 Finborough Road, London SW10 9Ed
☎020 7244 7439 Fax 020 7835 1853
Website www.finboroughtheatre.co.uk

Artistic Director *Neil McPherson*

FOUNDED 1980. 'One of London's leading new writing venues' (*Time Out*). Presents revivals of neglected 20th century plays, music theatre and UK premières of foreign work, particularly from Ireland, the United States and Canada. The theatre is available for hire and the fee is sometimes negotiable to encourage interesting work, though unsolicted mss are no longer accepted. Premièred work by Chris Lee, Anthony Neilson, Naomi Wallace, Tony Marchant, Diane Samuels and Mark Ravenhill.

Robert Fox Ltd
6 Beauchamp Place, London SW3 1NG
☎020 7584 6855 Fax 020 7225 1638
Email rf@robertfoxltd.com
Contact *Robert Fox*

Producer and co-producer of work suitable for West End production. Previous productions: *Another Country; Chess; Lettice and Lovage; Burn This; When She Danced; The Ride Down Mount Morgan; The Importance of Being Earnest; The Seagull; Goosepimples; Vita & Virginia; The Weekend; Three Tall Women; Skylight; Who's Afraid of Virginia Woolf; Masterclass; A Delicate Balance; Amy's View; Closer; The Lady in the Van; The Caretaker; The Breath of Life.* Also Broadway productions and films including *Iris* and *The Hours*. Scripts, while usually by established playwrights, are always read.

Gate Theatre Company Ltd
11 Pembridge Road, London W11 3HQ
☎020 7229 5387 Fax 020 7221 6055
Artistic Director *Erica Whyman*

FOUNDED 1979. Plays to a mixed, London-wide audience, depending on production. Aims to produce British premières of plays which originate from abroad and translations of neglected classics. Most work is with translators. Runs a biennial Translation Award. Next due October 2003. Recent productions: *Ion* by Euripides, transl. by Stephen Sharkey; *Witness* by Cecilia Parkert, transl. by Kevin Halliwell. Positively encourages writers from abroad to send in scripts or translations. Most unsolicited scripts are read but it is extremely unlikely that new British plays will have any future at the theatre due to emphasis on plays translated from foreign languages. Please address submissions to 'Scripts'. Always enclose s.a.e. if play needs returning.

Graeae Theatre Company
Interchange Studios, Hampstead Town Hall Centre, 213 Haverstock Hill, London NW3 4QP
☎020 7681 4755 Fax 020 7681 4756
Email info@graeae.org
Website www.graeae.org
Minicom 020 7267 3167
Artistic Director *Jenny Sealey*
Executive Producer *Roger Nelson*

Europe's premier theatre company of disabled people, the company tours nationally and internationally with innovative theatre productions highlighting both historical and contemporary disabled experience. Graeae also runs Forum Theatre and educational programmes available to schools, youth clubs and day centres nationally, provides vocational training in theatre arts (including playwriting). Unsolicited scripts – from disabled writers – welcome. New work examining disability issues is commissioned.

Hampstead Theatre
Eton Avenue, Swiss Cottage, London NW3 3EU
☎020 7449 4200 Fax 020 7449 4201
Email literary@hampsteadtheatre.com
Website www.hampsteadtheatre.com
Literary Manager *Jeanie O'Hare*

A brand new Hampstead Theatre opened in 2003. The building is an intimate space with a flexible stage and an auditorium capable of expanding to seat 325. The artistic policy continues to be the production of British and international new plays and the development of important young writers. 'We are looking for writers who recognise the power of theatre and who have a story to tell. All plays are read and discussed. We give feedback to all writers with potential.' Writers produced at Hampstead include: Michael Frayn, Roy Williams, Shelagh Stephenson, Simon Block, Philip Ridley, Frank McGuinness, Rona Munro, Brad Fraser, Tim Firth and Abi Morgan.

Harrogate Theatre Company
Oxford Street, Harrogate, North Yorkshire HG1 1QF
☎01423 502710 Fax 01423 563205
Email staff.name@harrogatetheatre.demon.
  co.uk
Artistic Director *Hannah Chissick*

Produces four to five productions a year on the main stage, one of which may be a new play but is most likely to be commissioned. Annual mainstage Youth Theatre production may also be commissioned. Over the next two years it is planned to workshop and read new plays by local writers and possibly stage them in the studio.

Unsolicited scripts from outside Yorkshire are unlikely to receive a production or workshop. Please write with a brief synopsis initially.

Heritage Theatre Ltd
See entry under **Film, TV and Radio Production Companies**

The Hiss & Boo Company Ltd
1 Nyes Hill, Wineham Lane, Bolney, West Sussex RH17 5SD Fax 01444 882057
Email hissboo@msn.com
Website www.hissboo.co.uk
Contact *Ian Liston*

Particularly interested in new thrillers, comedy thrillers, comedy and melodrama – must be commercial full-length plays. Also interested in plays/plays with music for children. No one-acts. Previous productions: *The Shakespeare Revue; Come Rain Come Shine; Sleighrider; Beauty and the Beast; An Ideal Husband; Mr Men's Magical Island; Mr Men and the Space Pirates; Nunsense; Corpse!; Groucho: A Life in Revue; See How They Run; Christmas Cat and the Pudding Pirates; Pinocchio* and traditional pantos written by Roy Hudd for the company. 'We are keen on revue-type shows and compilation shows but *not* tribute-type performances.' No unsolicited scripts; no telephone calls. Send synopsis and introductory letter in the first instance.

Hull Truck Theatre Company
Spring Street, Hull HU2 8RW
☎01482 224800 Fax 01482 581182
Executive Director *Joanne Gower*

John Godber, of *Teechers, Bouncers, Up 'n' Under* fame, the artistic director of this high-profile Northern company since 1984, has very much dominated the scene in the past with his own successful plays. The emphasis is still on new writing but Godber's work continues to be toured extensively. Most new plays are commissioned. Previous productions: *Studs* and *Like a Virgin* by Gordon Steel; *Oft Out* Gill Adams and *Double Top* by Ron Rose. The company receives a large number of unsolicited scripts but cannot guarantee a quick response. Bear in mind the artistic policy of Hull Truck, which is 'accessibility and popularity'. In general they are not interested in musicals, or in plays with casts of more than eight.

Stephen Joseph Theatre
Westborough, Scarborough, North Yorkshire YO11 1JW
☎01723 370540 Fax 01723 360506

Website www.sjt.uk.com
Artistic Director *Alan Ayckbourn*
Literary Manager *Laura Harvey*

A two-auditoria complex housing a 165-seat end stage theatre/cinema (the McCarthy) and a 400-seat theatre-in-the-round (the Round). Positive policy on new work. For obvious reasons, Alan Ayckbourn's work features quite strongly but a new writing programme ensures plays from other sources are actively encouraged. Also runs a lunchtime season of one-act plays each summer. Writers are advised however that the SJT is very unlikely to produce an unsolicited script – synopses are preferred. Recent commissions and past productions include: *Larkin with Women* Ben Brown; *Amaretti Angels* Sarah Phelps; *Something Blue* Gill Adams; *The Star Throwers* Paul Lucas; *Man for Hire* Meredith Oakes; *Safari Party* Tim Firth; *Beautiful People* Neil Monaghan; *Bedtime Stories* Lesley Bruce; *Gameplan, Flatspin, Roleplay* and *House and Garden* Alan Ayckbourn. 'Writers are welcome to send details of rehearsed readings and productions as an alternative means of introducing the theatre to their work.' Submit to *Laura Harvey* enclosing an s.a.e. for return of mss.

Bill Kenwright Ltd
BKL House, 106 Harrow Road, London W2 1RR
☎020 7446 6200 Fax 020 7446 6222
Contact *Bill Kenwright*

Presents both revivals and new shows for West End and touring theatres. Although new work tends to be by established playwrights, this does not preclude or prejudice new plays from new writers. Scripts should be addressed to Bill Kenwright with a covering letter and s.a.e. 'We have enormous amounts of scripts sent to us although we very rarely produce unsolicited work. Scripts are read systematically. Please do not phone; the return of your script or contact with you will take place in time.'

Komedia
Gardner Street, North Lane, Brighton, East Sussex BN1 1UN
☎01273 647101 Fax 01273 647102
Email info@komedia.co.uk
Website www.komedia.co.uk
Contact *David Lavender*

FOUNDED in 1994, Komedia promotes, produces and presents new work. Mss of new plays welcome.

Leeds Playhouse
See **West Yorkshire Playhouse**

Leicester Haymarket Theatre

Belgrave Gate, Leicester LE1 3YQ
☎0116 253 0021   Fax 0116 251 3310
Website www.leicesterhaymarkettheatre.org
Artistic Directors *Paul Kerryson, Kully Thiarai*

Leicester Haymarket Theatre aims for a balanced programme of original and established works. It is a multi-cultural, racially integrated company with educational projects attached to all productions and areas of work. Recent productions include the première of *Bollywood Jane*; the second production of *The Cripple of Inishmaan* and a London season of two musicals *Rent* and *On Your Toes* starring Adam Cooper. There is also a full studio programme and thriving youth theatre.

Library Theatre Company

St Peter's Square, Manchester M2 5PD
☎0161 234 1913   Fax 0161 228 6481
Email ltc@libraries.manchester.gov.uk
Website www.libtheatreco.org.uk
Artistic Director *Chris Honer*

Produces new and contemporary work, as well as occasional classics. No unsolicited mss. Send outline of the nature of the script first. Encourages new writing through the commissioning of new plays and through a programme of rehearsed readings to help writers' development.

Live Theatre Company

7/8 Trinity Chare, Newcastle upon Tyne
NE1 3DF
☎0191 261 2694   Fax 0191 232 2224
Email info@live.org.uk
Website www.live.org.uk
Artistic Director *Max Roberts*
Executive Director *Jim Beirne*

FOUNDED 1973. Produces shows at its refurbished 200-seat venue, and also tours regionally and nationally. Company policy is to produce work that is rooted in the culture of the region, particularly for those who do not normally get involved in the arts. The company is particularly interested in promoting new writing. As well as full-scale productions the company organises workshops, rehearsed readings and other new writing activities. The company also enjoys a close relationship with **New Writing North** and is funded to support new writing through the BBC's *Northern Exposure Project*. Productions include: *Buffalo Girls* by Karin Young; *Two* Jim Cartwright; *Cabaret*, and an ambitious cycle of plays – *Twelve Tales of Tyneside* – which involved 12 writers; *Falling Together* Tom Hadaway; *Cooking With Elvis* Lee Hall; *Bones* Peter Straughan; *Laughter When We're Dead* Sean O'Brien and *ne1*; *Tales From the Backyard* Alan Plater and *Double Lives* Julia Darling and Sean O'Brien.

London Bubble
Theatre Company

3–5 Elephant Lane, London SE16 4JD
☎020 7237 4434   Fax 020 7231 2366
Email peth@londonbubble.org.uk
Website www.londonbubble.org.uk
Artistic Director *Jonathan Petherbridge*

Produces workshops, plays and events for a mixed audience of theatregoers and non-theatregoers, wide-ranging in terms of age, culture and class. Previous productions: *Gilgamesh; Sleeping Beauty; Growing People*. Unsolicited mss are received but 'our reading service is extremely limited and there can be a considerable wait before we can give a response'. Commissions approximately one new project a year, often inspired by a promenade site, specific community of interest or workshop group.

Lyric Theatre Hammersmith

King Street, London W6 0QL
☎020 8741 0824   Fax 020 8741 5965
Email enquiries@lyric.co.uk
Website www.lyric.co.uk
Artistic Director *Neil Bartlett*
Executive Director *Simon Mellor*

The main theatre stages an eclectic programme of new and revived classics. Interested in developing projects with writers, translators and adaptors. The Lyric does not accept unsolicited scripts. Its 110-seat studio focuses on work for children, young people and families.

MAC – The Centre for Birmingham

Cannon Hill Park, Birmingham B12 9QH
☎0121 440 4221   Fax 0121 446 4372
Email enquiries@mac-birmingham.org.uk
Website www.birminghamarts.org.uk/
   organisations/mac.asp
Director *Dorothy Wilson*

The base of the Geese Theatre Company, Sampad South Asian Arts, artSites, Sound it Out, 404 Productions and Caficché as well as a host of other arts/performance-related organisations based in Birmingham.

Manchester Library Theatre
See **Library Theatre Company**

Midland Arts Centre
See **MAC - The Centre for Birmingham**

New Vic Theatre
Etruria Road, Newcastle under Lyme,
Staffordshire ST5 0JG
☎01782 717954 Fax 01782 712885
Email admin@newvictheatre.org.uk
Artistic Director *Gwenda Hughes*

The New Vic is a purpose-built theatre-in-the-round. Plays to a fairly broad-based audience which tends to vary from one production to another. A high proportion are not regular theatre-goers and new writing has been one of the main ways of contacting new audiences. Synopses preferred to unsolicited scripts.

Newpalm Productions
26 Cavendish Avenue, London N3 3QN
☎020 8349 0802 Fax 020 8346 8257
Contact *Lionel Chilcott*

Rarely produces new plays (*As Is* by William M. Hoffman, which came from Broadway to the Half Moon Theatre, was an exception to this). National tours of productions such as *Peter Pan (The Musical); Noises Off, Seven Brides for Seven Brothers* and *Rebecca*, at regional repertory theatres, are more typical examples of Newpalm's work. Unsolicited mss, both plays and musicals, are, however, welcome; scripts are preferable to synopses.

NITRO
6 Brewery Road, London N7 9NH
☎020 7609 1331 Fax 020 7609 1221
Email btc@dircon.co.uk
Website www.nitro.co.uk
Artistic Director *Felix Cross*

FOUNDED 1978. Formerly Black Theatre Co-op. Plays to a mixed audience, approximately 65% female. Usually tours nationally twice a year. 'A music theatre company, we are committed in the first instance to new writing by Black British writers and work which relates to the Black culture and experience throughout the Diaspora.' Unsolicited mss welcome.

Northcott Theatre
Stocker Road, Exeter, Devon EX4 4QB
☎01392 223999 Fax 01392 223996
Website www.northcott-theatre.co.uk
Artistic Director *Ben Crocker*

FOUNDED 1967. The Northcott is the South-west's principal subsidised producing theatre, situated on the University of Exeter campus. Describes its audience as 'geographically diverse, with a core audience of AB1s (40–60 age range)'. Continually looking to broaden the base of its audience profile, targeting younger and/or non-mainstream theatregoers. Aims to develop, promote and produce quality new writing which reflects the life of the region and addresses the audience it serves. Generally works on a commission basis but occasionally options existing new work. Unsolicited mss welcome – current turnaround on script-reading service is approximately three months and no mss can be returned unless a correct value s.a.e. is included with the original submission.

Northern Stage
Newcastle Playhouse, Barras Bridge,
Newcastle upon Tyne NE1 7RH
☎0191 232 3366 Fax 0191 261 8093
Email directors@northernstage.com
Website www.northernstage.com
Artistic Director *Alan Lyddiard*
Executive Director *Caroline Routh*

A contemporary performance company whose trademarks are a strong visual and physical style, international influences, appeal to young people and strongly linked programmes of community work. As likely to produce devised work as conventional new writing. No unsolicited scripts.

Norwich Puppet Theatre
St James, Whitefriars, Norwich, Norfolk
NR3 1TN
☎01603 615564 Fax 01603 617578
Email norpuppet@hotmail.com
Website www.geocities.com/norwichpuppets
Artistic Director *Luis Boy*
General Manager *Ian Woods*

Plays to a young audience (aged 3–12) but developing shows for adult audiences interested in puppetry. All year round programme plus tours to schools and arts venues. Unsolicited mss welcome if relevant.

Nottingham Playhouse
Nottingham Theatre Trust, Wellington
Circus, Nottingham NG1 5AF
☎0115 947 4361 Fax 0115 947 5759
Artistic Director *Giles Croft*

Aims to make innovation popular, and present the best of world theatre, working closely with the communities of Nottingham and Nottinghamshire. Unsolicited mss will be read. It normally takes about six months, however, and 'we have never yet produced an unsolicited script. All our plays have to achieve a minimum of 60 per cent audiences in a 732-seat theatre. We have no studio.'

Nottingham Playhouse Roundabout Theatre in Education

Wellington Circus, Nottingham NG1 5AF
☎0115 947 4361 Fax 0115 953 9055
Email andrewb@nottinghamplayhouse.co.uk
Website www.roundabout.org.uk

Contact *Andrew Breakwell*

FOUNDED 1973. Theatre-in-Education company of the **Nottingham Playhouse**. Plays to a young audience aged 5–18 years of age. 'Most of our current work uses existing scripts but we try and commission at least one new play every year. We are committed to the encouragement of new writing as and when resources permit. With other major producers in the East Midlands we share the resources of the literary manager who is based at the Playhouse. See website for philosophy and play details. Please make contact before submitting scripts.'

N.T.C. Touring Theatre Company

The Playhouse, Bondgate Without, Alnwick, Northumberland NE66 1PQ
☎01665 602586 Fax 01665 605837
Email admin@ntc-touringtheatre.co.uk
Website www.ntc-touringtheatre.co.uk

Contact *Gillian Hambleton*
General Manager *Anna Flood*

FOUNDED 1978. Formerly Northumberland Theatre Company. A Northern Arts revenue funded organisation. Predominantly rural, small-scale touring company, playing to village halls and community centres throughout the Northern region, the Scottish Borders and countrywide. Productions range from established classics to new work and popular comedies, but must be appropriate to their audience. Unsolicited scripts welcome but are unlikely to be produced. All scripts are read and returned with constructive criticism within six months. Writers whose style is of interest may then be commissioned. The company encourages new writing and commissions when possible. Financial constraints restrict casting to a *maximum* of five.

Nuffield Theatre

University Road, Southampton, Hampshire SO17 1TR
☎023 8031 5500 Fax 023 8031 5511

Artistic Director *Patrick Sandford*
Script Executive *John Burgess*

Well known as a good bet for new playwrights, the Nuffield gets an awful lot of scripts. They do a couple of new main stage plays every season. Previous productions: *Exchange* by Yuri Trifonov (transl. Michael Frayn) which transferred to the Vaudeville Theatre; *The Floating Light Bulb* Woody Allen (British première); new plays by Claire Luckham: *Dogspot; The Dramatic Attitudes of Miss Fanny Kemble;* and by Claire Tomalin: *The Winter Wife*. Open-minded about subject and style, producing musicals as well as straight plays. Also opportunities for some small-scale fringe work. Scripts preferred to synopses in the case of writers new to theatre. All will, eventually, be read 'but please be patient. We do not have a large team of paid readers. We read everything ourselves.'

Octagon Theatre Trust Ltd

Howell Croft South, Bolton, Lancashire BL1 1SB
☎01204 529407 Fax 01204 380110

Executive Director *John Blackmore*

FOUNDED 1967. The Octagon Theatre has pursued a dynamic policy of commissioning new plays in recent years. These have been by both established writers such as Paul Abbott, Tom Elliott, Henry Livings and Les Smith as well as new and emerging writers through partnerships with organisations such as **North West Playwrights** and the national new writing company **Paines Plough**. Whilst there is no prescriptive 'house style' at the Octagon, the theatre is nevertheless keen to encourage the development of writers from the North West region, telling stories that will resonate with the local audience. The Associate Director, *Sue Reddish*, coordinates the new writing initiative at the Octagon and any unsolicited scripts are processed through North West Playwrights.

Orange Tree Theatre

1 Clarence Street, Richmond, Surrey TW9 2SA
☎020 8940 0141 Fax 020 8332 0369
Email admin@orange-tree.demon.co.uk
Website www.orangetreetheatre.co.uk

Artistic Director *Sam Walters*

One of those theatre venues just out of London which are good for new writing, both full-scale productions and rehearsed readings. Productions from September 2002: *The Road to Ruin* Thomas Holcroft; *Saint's Day* John Whiting; *Engaged* W.S. Gilbert; *The Beggar's Opera* Vaclav Havel;

a new play by Don Taylor; a new translation of *Bernarda Alba* Lorca and a Feydeau farce. Unsolicited mss are read, but patience (and s.a.e.) required.

Out of Joint
7 Thane Works, Thane Villas, London N7 7PH
☎020 7609 0207   Fax 020 7609 0203
Email ojo@outofjoint.co.uk
Website www.outofjoint.co.uk
Director *Max Stafford-Clark*
Producer *Graham Cowley*
Literary Manager *Jenny Worton*

FOUNDED 1993. Award-winning theatre company with new writing central to its policy. Produces new plays which reflect society and its concerns, placing an emphasis on education activity to attract young audiences. Welcomes unsolicited mss. Productions include: *Blue Heart* Caryl Churchill; *Our Lady of Sligo, The Steward of Christendom* and *Hinterland* Sebastian Barry; *Shopping and Fucking* and *Some Explicit Polaroids* Mark Ravenhill; *Rita, Sue and Bob Too* Andrea Dunbar; *A State Affair* Robin Soans; *Sliding with Suzanne* Judy Upton; *The Positive Hour* and *A Laughing Matter* April de Angelis.

Oxford Stage Company
Chertsey Chambers, 12 Mercer Street, London WC2H 9QD
☎02074 389941   Fax 02074 389941
Website www.oxfordstage.co.uk
Artistic Director *Dominic Dromgoole*

A middle-scale touring company producing established and new plays. At least one new play or new adaptation a year. Due to forthcoming projects not considering unsolicited scripts at present.

Paines Plough
4th Floor, 43 Aldwych, London WC2B 4DN
☎020 7240 4533   Fax 020 7240 4534
Email office@painesplough.com
Website www.painesplough.com
Artistic Director *Vicky Featherstone*
Associate Director *John Tiffany*
Literary Associate *Lucy Morrison*

Tours new plays nationally. Works with writers to develop their skills and voices through workshops, rehearsed readings and playwriting projects. Provides a supportive environment for commissioned writers to push themselves and challenge their craft. Will consider unsolicited material from UK writers (please send s.a.e. for return of script).

Palace Theatre, Watford
Clarendon Road, Watford, Hertfordshire WD17 1JZ
☎01923 235455 Fax 01923 819664
Email enquiries@watfordtheatre.co.uk
Website www.watfordtheatre.co.uk
Artistic Director *Lawrence Till*

An important part of artistic and cultural policy is the commissioning of new plays and translations. Recent new plays: *Elton John's Glasses* David Farr (1997 Writers' Guild Best Regional Play award); *The Talented Mr Ripley* Phyllis Nagy; *The Dark* Jonathan Holloway; *The Late Middle Classes* Simon Gray (1999 Barclays/TMA Best New Play Award); *Morning Glory* Sarah Daniels; *The True-Life Fiction of Mata Hari* Diane Samuels; *Full House* and *The Hairless Diva* (after Ionesco) John Mortimer; *Big Night Out at the Little Palace Theatre* Sandi Toksvig and Dillie Keane.

Perth Repertory Theatre Ltd
185 High Street, Perth PH1 5UW
☎01738 472700 Fax 01738 624576
Email info@perththeatre.co.uk
Website www.perththeatre.co.uk
Artistic Director *Michael Winter*
General Manager *Paul Hackett*

FOUNDED 1935. Combination of one- to four-weekly repertoire of plays and musicals, incoming tours and studio productions. Unsolicited mss are read when time permits, but the timetable for return of scripts is lengthy. New plays staged by the company are usually commissioned under the SAC scheme.

Plymouth Theatre Royal
See **Theatre Royal**

Polka Theatre for Children
240 The Broadway, Wimbledon, London SW19 1SB
☎020 8545 8320 Fax 020 8545 8365
Email info@polkatheatre.com
Website www.polkatheatre.com
Artistic Director *Annie Wood*
Executive Director *Stephen Midlane*
Director of New Writing *Richard Shannon*

FOUNDED in 1967 and moved into its Wimbledon base in 1979. Leading children's theatre committed to commissioning and producing new plays. Programmes are planned two years ahead and at least three new plays are commissioned each year. 'Many of our scripts are commissioned from established writers. We are, however, keen to develop work from writers new to children and young people's theatre. We run a new writing programme which includes master classes and workshops. Potential new writers' work is read and discussed on a regular basis; thus we constantly add to our pool of interesting and interested writers. This department is now headed by a new position, Director of New Writing.'

Praxis Theatre Company Ltd
24 Wykeham Road, London NW4 2SU
☎020 8203 1916 Fax 020 8203 1916
Email praxisco@globalnet.co.uk
Website www.users.globalnet.co.uk/~praxisco
Artistic Director *Sharon Kennet*

FOUNDED 1993. Performs to a mixed European audience, 'crossing the divide between text-based theatre and visual theatre'. No unsolicited mss. Previous productions and films: *Seed*; *My Brother Whom I Love*; *The Sacred Penman*; *She's Well Out of Order*; *Dot*.

Queen's Theatre, Hornchurch
Billet Lane, Hornchurch, Essex RM11 1QT
☎01708 456118 Fax 01708 452348
Email info@queens-theatre.co.uk
Website www.queens-theatre.co.uk
Artistic Director *Bob Carlton*

The Queen's Theatre is a 500-seat producing theatre in the London Borough of Havering and within the M25. ESTABLISHED in 1953, the theatre has been located in its present building since 1975 and produces up to nine in-house productions per year, including pantomime. The Queen's has re-established a permanent core company of actor/musicians under the artistic leadership of Bob Carlton. Aims to produce distinctive and accessible performances in an identifiable house style focused upon actor/musician shows but, in addition, embraces straight plays, classics and comedies. 'New play/musical submissions are welcome but should be submitted in treatment and not script form.' Each year there is a large-scale community play commissioned from a local writer culminating in a summer event beside the theatre. A new writers' group has been established, led currently by *David Eldridge*. Enquiries about joining should be directed to the education manager.

The Really Useful Group Ltd
22 Tower Street, London WC2H 9TW
☎020 7240 0880 Fax 020 7240 1204
Website www.reallyuseful.com

Commercial/West End theatre producer whose output has included *Jesus Christ Superstar*; *Sunset Boulevard*; *Joseph and the Amazing Technicolor Dreamcoat*; *Cats*; *Phantom of the Opera*; *Starlight Express*; *Daisy Pulls It Off*; *Lend Me a Tenor*; *Arturo Ui*; *The Beautiful Game*; *Whistle Down the Wind*; *Aspects of Love*; *Bombay Dreams*.

Red Ladder Theatre Company
3 St Peter's Buildings, York Street, Leeds, West Yorkshire LS9 8AJ
☎0113 245 5311 Fax 0113 245 5351
Email wendy@redladder.co.uk
Website www.redladder.co.uk
Artistic Director/Literary Manager *Wendy Harris*
Administrator *Janis Smyth*

FOUNDED 1968. Commissioning company touring 2–3 shows a year with a strong commitment to new work and new writers. Aimed at an audience of young people aged between 14–25 years who have little or no access to theatre. Performances held in youth clubs and similar venues where young people choose to meet. Recent productions: *After You* by Brendan Murray (2002); *Wize Buys* by Philip Osment, *Silent Cry* by Madani Younis, *Dreaming of Bones* by Damian Gorman (2003). The company is particularly keen to enter into a dialogue with writers with regard to creating new work for young people. Red Ladder is running an attachment scheme, *Outwrite In*, in partnership with BBC *northern exposure* for writers from or based in Bradford. E-mail the artistic director for more information at the address above.

Red Shift Theatre Company
TRG2 Trowbray House, 108 Weston Street, London SE1 3QB
☎020 7378 9787 Fax 020 7378 9789
Email mail@redshifttheatreco.co.uk
Website www.redshifttheatreco.co.uk
Contact *Jonathan Holloway, Artistic Director*
General Manager *Jess Lammin*

FOUNDED 1982. Small-scale touring company which plays to a theatre-literate audience. Unlikely to produce an unsolicited script as most work is commissioned. Welcomes contact with writers – 'we try to see their work' – and receipt of c.v.s and treatments. Occasionally runs workshops bringing new scripts, writers and actors together. These can develop links with a reservoir of writers who may feed the company. Interested in new plays with subject matter which is accessible to a broad audience and concerns issues of importance; also new translations and adaptations. Previous productions: *Nicholas Nickleby* and *The Love Child*.

Ridiculusmus

c/o Your Imagination, BAC, Lavender Hill,
London SW11 5TN
Email ridiculusmus@yourimagination.org
Website www.ridiculusmus.com

Artistic Directors *Jon Hough, David Woods*

FOUNDED 1992. Touring company which
plays to a wide range of audiences. Productions
have included adaptations of *Three Men In a
Boat; The Third Policeman; At Swim Two Birds*
and original work: *The Exhibitionists; Yes, Yes,
Yes* and *Say Nothing.* Unsolicited scripts not
welcome.

Royal Court Theatre

Sloane Square, London SW1W 8AS
☎020 7565 5050
Fax 020 7565 5002 (Literary office)
Website www.royalcourttheatre.com

Literary Manager *Graham Whybrow*

The Royal Court is a leading international
theatre producing up to 17 new plays each year
in its 400-seat proscenium theatre and 80-seat
studio. In 1956 its first director George Devine
set out to find 'hard-hitting, uncompromising
writers whose plays are stimulating, provocative
and exciting'. This artistic policy helped trans-
form post-war British theatre, with new plays by
writers such as John Osborne, Arnold Wesker,
John Arden, Samuel Beckett, Edward Bond and
David Storey, through to Caryl Churchill, Jim
Cartwright, Kevin Eylot and Timberlake
Wertenbaker. Since 1994 it has produced a new
generation of writers such as Joe Penhall,
Rebecca Prichard, Sarah Kane, Jez Butterworth,
Martin McDonagh, Mark Ravenhill, Ayub
Khan-Din, Conor McPherson, Roy Williams
and many other first-time writers. The Royal
Court has programmes for young writers and
international writers, and it is always searching
for new plays and new playwrights.

Royal Exchange
Theatre Company

St Ann's Square, Manchester M2 7DH
☎0161 833 9333 Fax 0161 832 0881
Website www.royalexchange.co.uk

Literary Manager *Sarah Frankcom*

FOUNDED 1976. The Royal Exchange has developed a new writing policy which it finds is
attracting a younger audience to the theatre. The
company has produced new plays by Simon
Stephens, Shelagh Stephenson, Brad Fraser,
Simon Burke, Jim Cartwright, Peter Barnes and
Owen McCafferty. Also English and foreign
classics, modern classics, adaptations and new
musicals. The Royal Exchange receives
500–2000 scripts a year. These are read by Sarah
Frankcom and a team of experienced readers.
Only a tiny percentage is suitable, but a number
of plays are commissioned each year.

Royal Lyceum Theatre Company

Grindlay Street, Edinburgh EH3 9AX
☎0131 248 4800 Fax 0131 228 3955

Artistic Director *Mark Thomson*
Administration Manager *Ruth Butterworth*
Administration Director *Sadie McKinlay*

FOUNDED 1965. Repertory theatre which plays
to a mixed urban Scottish audience. Produces
classic, contemporary and new plays. Would like
to stage more new plays, especially Scottish. No
full-time literary staff to provide reports on submitted scripts.

Royal National Theatre

South Bank, London SE1 9PX
☎020 7452 3333 Fax 020 7452 3350
Website www.nationaltheatre.org.uk

Literary Manager *Jack Bradley*

The majority of the National's new plays come
about as a result of direct commission or from
existing contacts with playwrights. There is no
quota for new work, though so far more than a
third of plays presented have been the work of
living playwrights. Writers new to the theatre
would need to be of exceptional talent to be successful with a script here, though the Royal
National Theatre Studio helps a limited number
of playwrights, through readings, workshops and
discussions. In some cases a new play is presented
for a shorter-than-usual run in the Cottesloe
Theatre. Scripts considered (send s.a.e).

Royal Shakespeare Company

Dramaturgy, Royal Shakespeare Theatre,
Waterside, Stratford upon Avon,
Warwickshire CV37 6BB
☎01789 412200
Website www.rsc.org.uk

Dramaturg *Paul Sirett*

The RSC is a classical theatre company based
in Stratford upon Avon. It has recently transformed itself to create the opportunity for different ensemble companies to work on distinct
projects that will open both in Stratford upon
Avon and at various venues around London.
The company also has an annual residency in
Newcastle upon Tyne and tours both nationally and internationally. As well as Shakespeare,
English classics and foreign classics in trans-

lation, new plays counterpoint the RSC's repertory, especially those which celebrate language. 'The dramaturgy department is pro-active rather than reactive and seeks out the plays and playwrights it wishes to commission. It will read all translations of classic foreign works submitted, or of contemporary works where the original writer and/or translator is known. It is unable to read unsolicited work from less established writers. It can only return scripts if an s.a.e. is enclosed with submission.'

7:84 Theatre Company Scotland

333 Woodlands Road, Glasgow G3 6NG
☎0141 334 6686 Fax 0141 334 3369
Email admin@784theatre.com
Website www.784theatre.com

Artistic Director *Gordon Laird*

FOUNDED 1973. One of Scotland's foremost touring theatre companies committed to producing work that addresses current social, cultural and political issues. Recent productions include commissions by Scottish playwrights such as Nicola McCartney (*Cave Dwellers*); Peter Arnott (*A Little Rain*); Stephen Greenhorn (*Dissent*); David Greig (*Caledonia Dreaming*) and the Scottish premières of Tony Kushner's *Angels in America* and Athol Fugard's *Valley Song*. 'The company is committed to a new writing policy that encourages and develops writers at every level of experience, to get new voices and strong messages on to the stage.' New writing development has always been central to 7:84's core activity and has included Summer Schools and the 7:84 Writers Group. The company continues to be committed to this work and its development. 'Happy to read unsolicited scripts.'

Shared Experience

The Soho Laundry, 9 Dufours Place, London W1F 7SJ
☎020 7434 9248 Fax 020 7287 8763
Email admin@setheatre.co.uk

Joint Artistic Directors *Nancy Meckler, Polly Teale*

FOUNDED 1975. Varied audience depending on venue, since this is a touring company. Recent productions have included: *Anna Karenina* (adapt. Helen Edmundson); *Mill on the Floss* (adapt. Helen Edmundson); *The Danube* Maria Irene Fornes; *Desire Under the Elms* Eugene O'Neill; *War and Peace* (adapt. Helen Edmundson); *The Tempest* William Shakespeare; *Jane Eyre* (adapt. Polly Teale); *I Am Yours* Judith Thompson; *The House of Bernarda Alba* (transl. Rona Munro); *Mother Courage* (transl. Lee Hall); *A* *Doll's House* (transl. Michael Meyer); *The Magic Toyshop* (adapt. Bryony Lavery); *The Clearing* Helen Edmundson; *A Passage to India* (adapt. Martin Sherman). No unsolicited mss. Primarily not a new writing company but 'we are interested in innovative new scripts'.

Sherman Theatre Company

Senghennydd Road, Cardiff CF24 4YE
☎029 2064 6901 Fax 029 2064 6902
Website www.shermantheatre.co.uk

Artistic Director *Phil Clark*

FOUNDED 1973. Theatre for Young People, with main house and studio. Encourages new writing; has produced 86 new plays in the last ten years. Previous productions include a David Wood adaptation of Roald Dahl's *James and the Giant Peach*, plays by Frank Vickery (*Pullin the Wool*); Helen Griffin (*Flesh and Blood*); Patrick Jones (*Everything Must Go*); Terry Deary (*Horrible Histories Crackers Christmas*); Mike Kenny (*Puff the Magic Dragon*); Brendan Murray (*Something Beginning With ...*); Roald Dahl (*The Enormous Crocodile*); Roger Williams (*Pop*); Arnold Wesker (*Break, My Heart*). The company has presented four seasons of six new plays live on stage and broadcast on BBC Radio Wales, and four series of one-act lunchtime plays on stage and then filmed for HTV Wales. Priority will be given to Wales-based writers.

Show of Strength

74 Chessel Street, Bedminster, Bristol BS3 3DN
☎0117 902 0235 Fax 0117 902 0196
Email sheila@showofstrength.freeserve.co.uk
Website www.showofstrength.org.uk

Artistic Director *Sheila Hannon*

FOUNDED 1986. Plays to an informal, younger than average audience. Aims to stage at least one new play each season with a preference for work from Bristol and the South West. Will read unsolicited scripts but a lack of funding means they are unable to provide written reports. OUTPUT *The Wills Girls* by Amanda Whittington (Director Alan Dossor); *Lags* by Ron Hutchinson; *Blue Murder, So Long Life: Nicholodeon* Peter Nichols. Also, rehearsed readings of new work.

Snap People's Theatre Trust

29 Raynham Road, Bishop's Stortford, Hertfordshire CM23 5PE
☎01279 461607 Fax 01279 506694
Email info@snaptheatre.co.uk
Website www.snaptheatre.co.uk

Contacts *Andy Graham, Mike Wood*

FOUNDED 1979. Plays to young people (5–11; 12–19), and for the under 25s. New writing, young people and new media are the priorities. Writers should make contact in advance of sending material. New writing is encouraged and should involve, be written for or by young people. 'Projects should reflect the writer's own beliefs, be thought-provoking, challenging and accessible. The writer should be able to work with designers, directors and musicians in the early stages to develop the text and work alongside other disciplines.'

Soho Theatre Company
21 Dean Street, London W1D 3NE
☎020 7287 5060 Fax 020 7287 5061
Email writers@sohotheatre.com
Website www.sohotheatre.com
Artistic Director *Abigail Morris*

Dedicated to new writing, the company has an extensive research and development programme consisting of a free script-reading service, workshops and readings. Also runs many courses for new writers. The company produces around four plays a year. Previous productions include: *Office* Shan Khan, winner of the 2000 Verity Bargate Award; *Angels and Saints* Jessica Townsend, joint winner of the 1998 Peggy Ramsay Award; *Jump Mr Malinoff Jump* Toby Whithouse, winner of the 1998 Verity Bargate Award; *Gabriel* Moira Buffini, winner of the 1996 LWT Award; *Be My Baby* Amanda Whittington; *Kindertransporte* Diane Samuels. Runs the **Verity Bargate Award**, a biennial competition (see entry under **Prizes**).

Sphinx Theatre Company
25 Short Street, London SE1 8LJ
☎020 7401 9993 Fax 020 7401 9995
Email sphinxtheatre@demon.co.uk
Website www.sphinxtheatre.co.uk
Artistic Director *Sue Parrish*
General Manager *Susannah Krakt-Levene*

FOUNDED 1973. Tours new plays by women nationally to small and mid-scale venues. Synopses and ideas are welcome.

The Steam Industry
c/o/ Finborough Theatre, 118 Finborough Road, London SW10 9ED
☎020 7244 7439 Fax 020 7835 1853
Email steamindustry@finboroughtheatre.freeserve.co.uk
Website www.steamindustry.co.uk
Artistic Director *Phil Willmott*

Artistic Director, Finborough Theatre
Neil McPherson

Since June 1994, the multi-awards-winning production company The Steam Industry has become known for its diverse and prolific productions of both new writing, radical adaptations of classic texts and musicals at many venues including the Finborough Theatre, BAC, The Bridewell, The Drill Hall and Riverside Studios. Unsolicited scripts are no longer welcome.

Talawa Theatre Company Ltd
3rd Floor, 23–25 Great Sutton Street, London EC1V 0DN
☎020 7251 6644 Fax 020 7251 5969
Email hq@talawa.com
Website www.talawa.com
Acting General Manager *Jonathan Lamede*

FOUNDED 1985. 'Aims to provide high quality productions that reflect the significant creative role that Black theatre plays within the national and international arena and also to enlarge theatre audiences from the Black community.' Previous productions include all-Black performances of *The Importance of Being Earnest* and *Antony and Cleopatra*; plus Jamaican pantomime *Arawak Gold; The Gods Are Not to Blame; The Road* Wole Soyinka; *Beef, No Chicken* Derek Walcott; *Flying West* Pearl Cleage; *Othello* William Shakespeare. Seeks to provide a platform for new work from up and coming Black British writers. Send synopsis in the first instance. Runs a black script development project. Talawa is funded by the London Arts Board.

Theatre Absolute
57–61 Corporation Street, Coventry CV1 1GQ
☎024 7625 7380 Fax 024 7655 0680
Email julia@theatreabsolute.co.uk
Website www.theatreabsolute.co.uk
Artistic Director/Writer *Chris O'Connell*
Producer *Julia Negus*

FOUNDED 1992. An independent theatre company which commissions, produces and tours new plays which are based on a strong narrative text and aimed at audiences aged 15 and upwards. Productions include: *Car*, winner of an Edinburgh Fringe First Award 1999 and a *Time Out* Live Award – Best New Play on the London Fringe 1999; and most recently, *Raw*, winner of a Fringe First Award 2001. Alongside the Belgrade Theatre, the company also runs The Writing House, a script development scheme.

Theatre of Comedy Company
210 Shaftesbury Avenue, London WC2H 8DP
☎020 7379 3345   Fax 020 7836 8181
Email info@toc.dltentertainment.co.uk
Chief Executive *Richard Porter*
Development Coordinator *David Costello*

FOUNDED 1983 to produce new work as well as classics and revivals. Interested in strong comedy in the widest sense – Chekhov comes under the definition as does farce. Also has a light entertainment division, developing new scripts for television, namely situation comedy and series.

Theatre Royal, Plymouth
Royal Parade, Plymouth, Devon PL1 2TR
☎01752 230347   Fax 01752 225892
Email d.prescott@theatreroyal.com
Website www.theatreroyal.com
Artistic Director *Simon Stokes*
Artistic Associate *David Prescott*

Stages small, middle and large-scale drama and music theatre. Commissions and produces new plays. Unsolicited scripts with s.a.e. are read and responded to. Send only one script at a time – by post only.

Theatre Royal Stratford East
Gerry Raffles Square, London E15 1BN
☎020 8279 1104   Fax 020 8534 8381
Email asohoye@stratfordeast.com
Website www.stratfordeast.com
New Writing Manager *Ashmeed Sohoye*

Lively East London theatre, catering for a very mixed audience, both local and London-wide. Produces plays, musicals, youth theatre and local community plays/events, all of which is new work. Special interest in Asian and Black British work, and contemporary London/UK stories. New initiatives include developing contemporary British musicals. Unsolicited scripts which are fully completed and have never been produced are welcome. Feedback is given only on scripts that closely meet the artistic remit.

Theatre Royal Windsor
Windsor, Berkshire SL4 1PS
☎01753 863444   Fax 01753 831673
Email info@theatreroyalwindsor.co.uk
Website www.theatreroyalwindsor.co.uk
Executive Producer *Bill Kenwright*
Executive Director *Mark Piper*

Plays to a middle-class, West End-type audience. Produces thirteen plays a year and 'would be disappointed to do fewer than two new

plays in a year; always hope to do half a dozen'. Modern classics, thrillers, comedy and farce. Only interested in scripts along these lines.

Theatre Workshop Edinburgh
34 Hamilton Place, Edinburgh EH3 5AX
☎0131 225 7942   Fax 0131 220 0112
Artistic Director *Robert Rae*

First ever professional producing theatre to fully include disabled actors in all its productions. Plays to a young, broad-based audience with many pieces targeted towards particular groups or communities. OUTPUT has included *D.A.R.E.* Particularly interested in issues-based work for young people and minority groups. Frequently engages writers for collaborative work and devised projects. Commissions a significant amount of new writing for a wide range of contexts, from large-scale community plays to small-scale professional productions. Favours writers based in Scotland, producing material relevant to a contemporary Scottish audience.

Tiebreak Theatre
Heartsease High School, Marryat Road,
Norwich, Norfolk NR7 9DF
☎01603 435209   Fax 01603 435184
Email info@tiebreak-theatre.com
Website www.tiebreak-theatre.com
Artistic Director *David Farmer*

FOUNDED 1981. Specialises in high-quality theatre for children and young people, touring schools, youth centres, small-scale theatres, museums and festivals. Productions: *Frog in Love; My Uncle Arly; Time and Tide; The Snow Egg; One Dark Night; Suitcase Full of Stories; Fast Eddy; Breaking the Rules; George Speaks; Frog and Toad; Singing in the Rainforest; The Invisible Boy; My Friend Willy; The Ugly Duckling.* New writing encouraged. Interested in low-budget, small-cast material only. School and educational material of special interest. 'Scripts welcome but please ring first to discuss any potential submission.'

The Torch Theatre
St Peter's Road, Milford Haven,
Pembrokeshire SA73 2BU
☎01646 694192   Fax 01646 698919
Email info@torchtheatre.co.uk
Website www.torchtheatre.org.uk
Artistic Director *Peter Doran*

FOUNDED 1977. Stages a mixed programme of in-house and middle-scale touring work. Unsolicited scripts will be read and guidance offered but production unlikely due to restricted funding. Please include s.a.e. for return of script and notes; mark clearly, 'FAO Peter Doran'. Torch Theatre Company productions include: *Dancing at Lughnasa; Neville's Island; The Woman in Black; Abigail's Party; Taking Steps; Blue Remembered Hills; A Prayer for Wings; Little Shop of Horrors; The Caretaker; One Flew Over the Cuckoo's Nest; One for the Road*, plus annual Christmas musicals.

Traverse Theatre
Cambridge Street, Edinburgh EH1 2ED
☎0131 228 3223 Fax 0131 229 8443
Email roxana@traverse.co.uk
Website www.traverse.co.uk
Artistic Director *Philip Howard*
Literary Director *Roxana Silbert*
International Literary Associate *Katherine Mendelsohn*
Literary Development Officer *Hannah Rye*
Literary Assistant *Neil Coull*

The Traverse is Scotland's only new writing theatre, with a particular commitment to producing new Scottish plays. However, it also has a strong international programme of work in translation and visiting companies. Previous productions: *Iron* Rona Munro; *Outlying Islands* David Greig; *Gagarin Way* Gregory Burke; *Wiping My Mother's Arse* Iain Heggie; *The Speculator* David Greig; *The Juju Girl* Aileen Ritchie; *Perfect Days* Liz Lochhead. Please address unsolicited scripts to *Neil Coull,* Literary Assistant.

Trestle Theatre Company
Birch Centre, Hill End Lane, St Albans, Hertfordshire AL4 0RA
☎01727 850950 Fax 01727 855558
Artistic Director *Toby Wilsher*
FOUNDED 1981. Physical, mask touring theatre company. Usually devised work but does work with writers to create new writing for physical/visual theatre. No unsolicited scripts.

Tricycle Theatre
269 Kilburn High Road, London NW6 7JR
☎020 7372 6611 Fax 020 7328 0795
Website www.tricycle.co.uk
Artistic Director *Nicolas Kent*
FOUNDED 1980. Plays to a very mixed audience, in terms of both culture and class. Previous productions: *Stones in his Pockets* Marie Jones; *The Stephen Lawrence Enquiry – The Colour of Justice* adapt. from the enquiry transcripts by Richard Norton-Taylor; *Nuremberg* adapt. from transcripts of the trials by Richard Norton-Taylor; *Joe Turner's Come and Gone, The Piano Lesson* and *Two Trains Runnin'* all by August Wilson; *Kat and the Kings* David Kramer. New writing welcome from women and ethnic minorities (particularly Black, Asian and Irish). Looks for a strong narrative drive with popular appeal, not 'studio' plays. Fee £12 per script. Supplies written reader's report. Can only return scripts if postage coupons or s.a.e. are enclosed with original submission.

Tron Theatre Company
63 Trongate, Glasgow G1 5HB
☎0141 552 3748 Fax 0141 552 6657
Email neil@tron.co.uk
Website www.tron.co.uk
Director *Neil Murray*
FOUNDED 1981. Plays to a broad cross-section of Glasgow and beyond, including international tours. Recent productions: *Our Bad Magnet* Douglas Maxwell; *Further Than the Furthest Thing* Zinnie Harris (co-production with the **Royal National Theatre**); *Shining Souls* Chris Hannan (co-production with V. Amp). Interested in ambitious plays by UK and international writers. No unsolicited mss.

Unicorn Theatre for Children
St Mark's Studios, Chillingworth Road, London N7 8QJ
☎020 7700 0702 Fax 020 7700 3870
Email admin@unicorntheatre.com
Website www.unicorntheatre.com
Artistic Director *Tony Graham*
Literary Manager *Carl Miller*
FOUNDED 1947, resident at the Arts Theatre from 1967 to 1999. Produces full-length professionally performed plays for children, aged 4–12, their teachers and families. Recent work includes *Merlin the Magnificent* by Stuart Paterson; *Great Expectations* by Charles Dickens, adapted by John Clifford; *Beauty and the Beast* by Charles Way and *Diary of an Action Man* by Mike Kenny (co-production with Graeae) Currently produces at London venues including the Pleasance Theatre, Regents Park Open Air Theatre, the Cochrane Theatre and on tour nationally and internationally. Moving to new Unicorn Children's Centre with two theatres on Bankside, London, in 2004. Does not produce unsolicited scripts but works with commissioned writers. Writers interested in working with the company should send details of relevant previous work and why they would like to write for Unicorn.

Upstairs at the Gatehouse
See **Ovation Productions** under **Film, TV and Radio Production Companies**

Charles Vance Productions
Hampden House, 2 Weymouth Street, London W1W 5BT
☎020 7636 4343 Fax 020 7636 2323
Email cvtheatre@aol.com
Contact *Charles Vance*

In the market for medium-scale touring productions and summer-season plays. Hardly any new work and no commissions but writing of promise stands a good chance of being passed on to someone who might be interested in it. Occasional try-outs for new work in the Sidmouth repertory theatre. Send s.a.e. for return of mss.

Warehouse Theatre
62 Dingwall Road, Croydon CR0 2NF
☎020 8681 1257 Fax 020 8688 6699
Email warehous@dircon.co.uk
Website www.warehousetheatre.co.uk
Artistic Director *Ted Craig*

South London's new writing theatre (adjacent to East Croydon railway station) seats 100–120 and produces up to six new plays a year. Also co-produces with, and hosts, selected touring companies who share the theatre's commitment to new work. Continually building upon a tradition of discovering and nurturing new writers, with activities including a monthly writers' workshop and the annual **International Playwriting Festival**. Also hosts youth theatre workshops and Saturday morning children's theatre. Previous productions: *Iona Rain* by Peter Moffat and *Fat Janet is Dead* by Simon Smith (both past winners of the International Playwriting Festival); *The Shagaround* Maggie Neville; *Coming Up* James Martin Charlton and M.G. 'Monk' Lewis; *The Castle Spectre* edited by Phil Willmott; *Dick Barton Special Agent*; *Dick Barton and the Curse of the Pharaoh's Tomb* and *Dick Barton: The Tango of Terror* Phil Willmott. Unsolicited scripts welcome but it is more advisable to submit plays through the theatre's International Playwriting Festival.

Watford Palace Theatre
See **Palace Theatre**

West Yorkshire Playhouse
Playhouse Square, Leeds, West Yorkshire LS2 7UP
☎0113 213 7800 Fax 0113 213 7250
Email alex.chisholm@wyp.org.uk
Website www.wyp.org.uk
Literary Manager *Alex Chisholm*

Committed to working with new writing originating from or set in the Yorkshire and Humberside region. New writing from outside the region is programmed usually where writer or company is already known to the theatre. The Playhouse runs workshops, courses and writers' events including Thursday Night Live, an open platform held at the theatre for local writers and performers. For more information contact the Literary Manager on 0113 213 7286 or e-mail to address above. Scripts should be submitted with s.a.e. for return.

Whirligig Theatre
14 Belvedere Drive, Wimbledon, London SW19 7BY
☎020 8947 1732 Fax 020 8879 7648
Email whirligig-theatre@virgin.net
Contact *David Wood*

One play a year in major theatre venues, usually a musical for primary school audiences and weekend family groups. Interested in scripts which exploit the theatrical nature of children's tastes. Previous productions: *The See-Saw Tree; The Selfish Shellfish; The Gingerbread Man; The Old Man of Lochnagar; The Ideal Gnome Expedition; Save the Human; Dreams of Anne Frank; Babe, the Sheep-Pig.*

Michael White Productions Ltd
See **MW Entertainments Ltd** under **Film, TV and Radio Production Companies**

White Bear Theatre Club
138 Kennington Park Road, London SE11 4DJ
Administration: 3 Dante Road, Kennington, London SE11 4RB
☎020 7793 9193 Fax 020 7793 9193
Contact *Michael Kingsbury*
Administrator *Julia Parr*

FOUNDED 1988. OUTPUT primarily new work for an audience aged 20–35. Unsolicited scripts welcome, particularly new work with a keen eye on contemporary issues, though not agit-prop. *Absolution* by Robert Sherwood was nominated by the Writers' Guild for 'Best Fringe Play' and *Spin* by the same author was the *Time Out* Critics' Choice in 2000. The theatre received the *Time Out* award for Best Fringe Venue in 2001 and a Peter Brook award for best up-and-coming venue. The Writers' Guild, sponsored by the Mackintosh Foundation, is

leading writer workshops and readings throughout the year.

Windsor Theatre Royal
See **Theatre Royal Windsor**

The Young Vic
66 The Cut, London SE1 8LZ
☎020 7922 8400 Fax 020 7922 8401
Email info@youngvic.org
Website www.youngvic.org
Artistic Director *David Lan*
Executive Director *Kevin Fitzmaurice*
FOUNDED 1970. The Young Vic is a theatre for everyone but, above all, for younger artists and
audiences. Produces revivals of classics – old
and new – as well as new plays and annual
events that embrace both young people and
adults. The main house is one of London's
most exciting spaces and seats up to 450. A
smaller, flexible space, the Young Vic Studio,
seats 80 and is used for research, experiment
and performance. Each main house production
is accompanied by an extensive programme of
Teaching Participation and Research aimed at
local schools and colleges. Under the Funded
Ticket Scheme 10% of the audience see productions for nothing or very little. Recent productions include *Doctor Faustus*; *The Daughter-
in-Law* and *Sleeping Beauty*.

Festivals

Aberdeen Arts Carnival
Aberdeen Arts Centre, 33 King Street,
Aberdeen AB24 5AA
☎01224 635208
Website www.aberdeenartscentre.org.uk

Venue Manager *Arthur Deans*

Performances – mainly by local amateurs and arts workshops in drama, music, art, dance and creative writing – take place each summer during the school holidays.

Aberystwyth Rich Text Literature Festival
Aberystwyth Arts Centre, Penglais,
Aberystwyth SY23 3DE
☎01970 622889/622883
Email lla@aber.ac.uk

FOUNDED 2000. Annual weekend festival held in October. Previous guest writers have included Robin Young, John Stoddart and Menna Elfyn.

The Aldeburgh Literary Weekend
44 High Street, Aldebugh, Suffolk IP15 5AB
☎01728 453581 Fax 01728 452389
Website www.aldeburghbookshop.co.uk

Festival Organisers *John and Mary James*

FOUNDED 2002. Held on the first weekend in March. The programme includes creative writing workshops, a literary dinner and lunch, and talks. Previous speakers have included Alan Bennett, Craig Brown, Richard Dawkins, Anthony Horovitz, P.D. James, Doris Lessing, Christopher Matthew, Matt Ridley, Alexander McCall Smith, Libby Purves and Sally Vickers.

Aldeburgh Poetry Festival
Reading Room Yard, The Street, Brockdish,
Diss, Norfolk IP21 4JZ
☎01379 668345 Fax 01379 668844
Email aldeburghpoetry.trust@virgin.net
Website www.aldeburghpoetryfestival.org

Festival Director *Naomi Jaffa*

Now in its fifteenth year, an annual international festival of contemporary poetry held on the first weekend of November in Aldeburgh, attracting large audiences. Regular features include a four-week residency leading up to the festival, poetry readings, children's event, workshops, public masterclass, lecture, performance spot and the festival prize for the year's best first collection (see entry under **Prizes**). Also full fringe programme.

Arthur Miller Centre Literary Festival at UEA
University of East Anglia, School of English and American Studies, Norwich NR4 8TJ
☎01603 592810
Email v.striker@uea.ac.uk

Contact *Val Striker*

FOUNDED 1991. Annual festival, held in the autumn

Arundel Festival
The Arundel Festival Society, 3 Castle Mews,
Tarrant Street, Arundel, West Sussex
BN18 9DG
☎01903 883690 Fax 01903 884243
Email arundelfestival@btopenworld.com
Website www.arundelfestival.co.uk

Festival Manager *Debbie Levenson*

Annual summer festival (22nd to 31st August in 2003). Events include small-scale theatre, open-air theatre in Arundel Castle, concerts with internationally known artists, jazz, visual arts and active fringe.

Aspects Literature Festival
North Down Borough Council, Town Hall,
The Castle, Bangor BT20 4BT
☎028 9127 8032 Fax 028 9127 1370

Festival Director *Kenneth Irvine*
Administrator and Arts Officer *Gail Prentice*

FOUNDED 1992. 'Ireland's Premier Literary Festival' is held at the end of September and celebrates the richness and diversity of living Irish writers with occasional special features on past generations. It draws upon all disciplines – fiction (of all types), poetry, theatre, non-fiction, cinema, song-writing, etc. It also includes a day of writing for young readers and sends writers to visit local schools during the festival. Highlights of recent festivals include appearances by Bernard MacLaverty, Marion Keyes, Alice Taylor, Frank Delaney, Seamus Heaney, Brian Keenan and Fergal Keane.

Bath Fringe Festival

The Bell, 103 Walcot Street, Bath BA1 5BW
☎01225 480079 Fax 01225 480079
Email admin@bathfringe.co.uk
Website www.bathfringe.co.uk

Contact *Wendy Matthews*

FOUNDED 1981. Complementing the international music festival, the Fringe presents theatre, poetry, jazz, blues, comedy, cabaret, street performance and more in venues, parks and streets of Bath during late May and early June.

Bath Literature Festival

Administration Office: Bath Festivals Trust,
5 Broad Street, Bath BA1 5LJ
☎01225 462231 Fax 01225 445551
Email info@bathfestivals.org.uk

Box Office: Bath Festivals Box Office,
2 Church Street, Abbey Green, Bath BA1 1NL.
☎01225 463362.
E-mail boxoffice@bathfestivals.org.uk

Festival Director *Nicola Bennett*
Artistic Director *Sarah LeFanu*

FOUNDED 1995. This annual festival (28 February to 7 March in 2004) programmes over 100 different literary events from debates and lectures to reader's groups, workshops and film venues throughout the city. In addition there are a number of events for children and young people. Previous featured writers include A.S. Byatt, Sebastian Faulks, Jackie Kay, Andrew Motion and Jacqueline Wilson.

Belfast Festival at Queen's

Festival House, 25 College Gardens, Belfast BT9 6BS
☎028 9066 7687 Fax 028 9066 3733
Email festival@qub.ac.uk
Website www.belfastfestival.com

Director *Stella Hall*

FOUNDED 1964. Annual three-week festival held in the autumn. Organised by Queen's University in association with the **Arts Council of Northern Ireland**, the festival covers a wide variety of events, including literature. Programme available in September.

Between the Lines –
Belfast Literary Festival

Crescent Arts Centre, 2–4 University Road, Belfast BT7 1NH
☎028 9024 2338 Fax 028 9024 6748
Email info@crescentarts.org
Website www.crescentarts.org

Artistic Director *Jo Baker*

FOUNDED 1998. Annual 7–10-day international event held in March. Features readings, workshops, open platforms, quizzes and performance. All genres covered: playwriting, prose, poetry, screenwriting, etc. and special events for children. Previous guests include David Lodge, Lemn Sissay, Sheila O'Flanagan, Matthew Sweeney, Medbh McGuckian, Conor O'Callaghan, Merlin Holland, Ciaran Carson. Telephone to join free mailing list.

Beyond the Border
International Storytelling Festival

St Donats Arts Centre, St Donats Castle, Vale of Glamorgan CF61 1WF
☎01446 799100 Fax 01446 799101
Email info@beyondtheborder.com
Website www.beyondtheborder.com

Festival Directors *David Ambrose, Ben Haggarty*

FOUNDED 1993. Annual event held over the first full weekend in July when storytellers from around the world gather in the grounds of a medieval cliff-top castle. Features formal and informal story sessions, ballad singing, storywalks, folk and world music, dance and a full programme of events for children.

Birmingham Book Festival

c/o Book Communications, Unit 116,
The Custard Factory, Gibb Street,
Birmingham B9 4AA
☎0121 246 2777/2770 Fax 0121 246 2771
Email info@bookcommunications.co.uk

Contacts *Helen Thomas, Jonathan Davidson*

FOUNDED 1999. Annual two-week-long festival held the last two weeks of October at various venues around Birmingham. Includes performances, lectures, discussion events and workshops.

Book Now!

The Arts Team, Orleans House Gallery,
Riverside, Twickenham TW1 3DJ
☎020 8891 0221 Fax 020 8744 0501
Email artsinfo@richmond.gov.uk
Website www.richmond.gov.uk

FOUNDED 1992. Annual festival which runs throughout the month of November, administered by the Arts Section of Richmond Council. Principal focus is on poetry and serious fiction, but events also cover biography, writing for theatre, children's writing. Programme includes readings, discussions, workshops, debates, exhibitions, schools events. Writers who appeared at past festivals include Beryl Bainbridge, Sally Beauman, Andrew Motion, A.S. Byatt, Penelope Lively, Benjamin Zephaniah, Roger McGough, Rose Tremain, John Mortimer, P.D. James, P.J. O'Rourke, Libby Purves, Mark Lawson and Tony Benn.

Bradford Book Festival

Central Library, Princes Way, Bradford, West Yorkshire BD1 1NN
☎01274 433915
Email paula.truman@bradford.gov.uk
Contact *Paula Truman*
FOUNDED 1999. Month-long festival organized by Bradford Libraries, held during May/June.

Brighton Festival

Festival Office, 12a Pavilion Buildings, Castle Square, Brighton, East Sussex BN1 1EE
☎01273 700747 Fax 01273 707505
Email info@brighton-festival.org.uk
Website www.brighton-festival.org.uk
Contact *General Manager*
FOUNDED 1966. For 24 days every May, Brighton hosts England's largest mixed arts festival. Music, dance, theatre, film, opera, literature, comedy and exhibitions. Literary enquiries will be passed to the literature officer. Deadline October for following May.

Bristol Poetry Festival

The Poetry Can, Unit 11, 20–23 Hepburn Road, Bristol BS2 8UD
☎0117 942 6976 Fax 0117 944 1478
Email festival@poetrycan.demon.co.uk
Website www.poetrycan.demon.co.uk
Festival Director *Colin Brown*
FOUNDED 1996. Annual festival taking place across the city every October. A celebration of the best in contemporary poetry, from readings and performances to cabaret and multimedia. Local, national and international poetry is showcased and explored in all its manifestations, with events for everyone including performances and workshops, competitions and commissions, public poetry interventions, community work and cross art form and digital projects. Telephone for further details.

Broadstairs Dickens Festival

10 Lanthorne Road, Broadstairs, Kent CT10 3NH
☎01843 861827 Fax 01843 861827
Website www.broadstairs.gov.uk/
  DickensFestivel.html

Organiser *Sylvia Hawkes*
FOUNDED 1937 to commemorate the 100th anniversary of Charles Dickens' first visit to Broadstairs in 1837, which he continued to visit until 1859. The Festival lasts for nine days in June and events include an opening gala concert, a parade, a performance of a Dickens play (*A Tale of Two Cities* in 2003), duels, melodramas, Dickens readings, a Victorian cricket match, Victorian bathing parties, talks, music hall, three-day Victorian country fair. Costumed Dickensian ladies in crinolines with top-hatted escorts promenade during the week.

Cambridge History Festival

Indicombe, West Buckland, Barnstaple EX32 0SE
☎01598 760367
Email info@histfest.com
Website www.histfest.com
Contacts *Derek Wilson, Ruth Wilson*

Annual three-day festival held in September in the heart of the university. The major networking event for all popular history enthusiasts – academics, historical novelists, popular historians, TV producers and presenters, museum and gallery staff. Varied programme includes talks, presentations, displays, discussions, concerts of period music, publishers' receptions, etc. Programmes available from April. Writers who have appeared include: David Starkey, Beryl Bainbridge, Louis de Bernières, Timothy West, Tracy Chevalier, Diarmaid MacCulloch, John Guy and Lindsey Davis.

Camelford Poetry Festival

The Indian King Arts Centre, Camelford, Cornwall PL32 9PG
☎01840 212111 Fax 01840 212111
Email indianking@btconnect.com
Website www.indianking.co.uk
Director *Helen Wood*
FOUNDED 1997 as the Jon Silkin Memorial Poetry Festival. Jon Silkin taught annual poetry workshops and readings to raise funds for the Centre, and the festival was held to honour his life and work. Held annually the weekend before Easter in Camelford, the central town in North Cornwall, in the Indian King, North Cornwall's only community arts centre. The festival includes workshops, poetry readings and performances, writing and literary walks, a dinner in memory of Jon Silkin on the Friday evening and a weekend long poetry cafe where visitors can book reading slots. The 2003 Festival was hosted by the performance group Late Shift. Previous

guests have included Fred d'Aguilar, Sara Jane Arbury, John Branfield, Ann Gray, John Greening, Philip Gross, Derrek Hines, Christopher Logue, William Oxley, Ian Parks, Fiona Sampson, Myra Schneider and Dilys Wood. Book for individual events or buy a weekend ticket.

Canterbury Festival
Christ Church Gate, The Precincts,
Canterbury, Kent CT1 2EE
☎01227 452853 Fax 01227 781830
Email info@canterburyfestival.co.uk

Festival Director *Mark Deller*

FOUNDED 1984. Annual two-week festival held in October (11th to 25th in 2003). A mixed programme of events including concerts in the cathedral by international artistes, opera, dance, drama, jazz and folk, visual arts open-house trail, community events and street theatre, talks and walks.

Centre for Creative & Performing Visiting Writers at UEA
University of East Anglia, School of English & American Studies, Norwich NR4 8TJ
☎01603 592810
Email v.striker@uea.ac.uk

Contact *Val Striker*

FOUNDED 1995. Annual event held in the spring.

The Cheltenham Festival of Literature
Town Hall, Imperial Square, Cheltenham,
Gloucestershire GL50 1QA
☎01242 263494 Fax 01242 256457
Email sarahsm@cheltenham.gov.uk
Website www.cheltenhamfestivals.co.uk

Festival Director *Sarah Smyth*

FOUNDED 1949. Annual festival held in October. The first purely literary festival of its kind, this festival has over the past decade developed from an essentially local event into the largest and most popular in Europe. A wide range of events including talks and lectures, poetry readings, novelists in conversation, exhibitions, discussions and a large bookshop.

Chester Literature Festival
8 Abbey Square, Chester CH1 2HU
☎01244 319985 Fax 01244 341200
Email freda@chesterfestivals.co.uk

Chairman *John Scrivener*

FOUNDED 1989. Annual festival always held commencing first weekend in October (2–24th in 2004). Events include international and nationally known writers, as well as events by local literary groups. There is a Literary Lunch, events for children, workshops, competitions. Free mailing list.

Children's Books Ireland – Annual Festival
See **Children's Books Ireland** under **Professional Associations and Societies**

Dartington Literary Festival
See **Ways With Words**

Derbyshire Literature Festival
c/o Arts Office, Derbyshire County Council, Libraries & Heritage Department, Alfreton Library, Severn Square, Alfreton, Derbyshire DE55 7BQ
☎01773 832497 Fax 01773 831359
Email ann.wright@derbyshire.gov.uk
Website www.derbyshire.gov.uk

Festival Organiser *Ann Wright*

FOUNDED 2000. The festival takes place throughout June every two years and covers the whole county. The festival programming includes all types of live literature event; performance poetry, theatre, talks, readers' groups, workshops, dramatized readings, signings, song, readings, storytelling and literary trails, as well as a number of cross-art form events. The festival takes place in libraries and many other community venues including heritage centres, industrial buildings, stately homes, parks and moors, churches and schools and is specifically designed to reach as many different communities and geographical areas in the county as possible.

Dorchester Festival
Dorchester Arts Centre, School Lane, The Grove, Dorchester, Dorset DT1 1XR
☎01305 266926 Fax 01305 266143
Website www.dorchester.org.uk

Contact *Artistic Director*

FOUNDED 1996. A biennial four-day festival over early May Bank Holiday weekend (next to be held in 2004) which includes performing, media and visual arts, with associated educational and community projects in the three weeks around the Festival. Includes a wide range of events, in many venues, for all age groups, including some literature and poetry.

The Daphne du Maurier Festival of Arts & Literature

Restormel Borough Council, Penwinnick Road, St Austell, Cornwall PL25 5DR
☎01726 223535
Website www.restormel.org.uk/daphne/

Annual festival, held in Fowey over ten days in May. Guests at the 2003 Festival included David Nobbs, Sally Beauman, Barry Norman, Clive James, Roy Hattersley, Ann Widdecombe and Libby Purves.

Dublin Writers' Festival

Dublin City Council Arts Office, 10 Cornmarket, Dublin 8 Republic of Ireland
☎00 353 1 872 2816 Fax 00 353 1 872 2933
Email info@dublinwritersfestival.com
Website www.dublinwritersfestival.com
Programme Director *Pat Boran*

Annual festival held in mid-June, including Bloomsday. Features readings, public interviews and discussions, along with a poetry slam and beginners' workshops. Major Irish and international poets and writers.

Dumfries and Galloway Arts Festival

Gracefield Arts Centre, 28 Edinburgh Road, Dumfries DG1 1JQ
☎01387 260447 Fax 01387 260447
Email dgartsfestival@ukgateway.net
Festival Organiser *Mrs Barbara Kelly*

FOUNDED 1980. Annual week-long festival held at the end of May with a variety of events including classical and folk music, theatre, dance, literary events, exhibitions and children's events.

Durham Literature Festival

Durham City Arts, Byland Lodge, Hawthorn Terrace, Durham City DH1 4TD
☎0191 301 8245 Fax 0191 301 8821
Email info@durhamcityarts.demon.co.uk
Festival Coordinator *Alison Lister*

FOUNDED 1989. Annual 2–3-week festival now held in September–October at various locations in the city. Performances plus workshops, cabaret, exhibitions and other events.

Edinburgh International Book Festival

Scottish Book Centre, 137 Dundee Street, Edinburgh EH11 1BG
☎0131 228 5444 Fax 0131 228 4333
Email admin@edbookfest.co.uk
Website www.edbookfest.co.uk
Director *Catherine Lockerbie*

FOUNDED 1983. The world's largest and most dynamic annual book event takes place over 17 days in Edinburgh each August. An extensive programme showcases the work of the world's top authors and thinkers to an audience of over 160,000 adults and children. Featuring workshops, readings, lectures and a high profile debate and discussion series.

'Everybody's Reading' – Leicester's Festival of Words

Leicester City Council, Arts and Leisure, Block A, New Walk Centre, Welford Place, Leicester LE1 6ZG
☎0116 252 7347
Email libraries@leicester.gov.uk
Literature Development Officer *Sarah Butler*

Annual celebration of words and reading held in June. A mixture of author events, workshops, profiles of community arts and spotlights on local writing held in a range of community/library/arts venues around the city.

Exeter Festival

Festival Office, Civic Centre, Exeter, Devon EX1 1JN
☎01392 265200 Fax 01392 265366
Email lesley.waters@exeter.gov.uk
Website www.exeter.gov.uk/festival
Contact *Festival Organiser*

FOUNDED 1980. Annual two-week summer festival with a variety of events including concerts, theatre, dance and exhibitions.

Fife Festival of Authors

Fife Council Libraries – Central Area, Libraries HQ, East Fergus Place, Kirkcaldy, Fife KY1 1XT
☎01592 412930
Email david.spalding@fife.gov.uk
Contact *David Spalding*

FOUNDED 1996. Annual festival running in March/April for adults and children. Aims to bring the best of modern writing to the public as well as stimulate and foster creative writing within the local communities. Author readings, poetry events, writing workshops, literary competitions and dramatic presentations feature in the programme.

Folkestone LiteratureFestival
The Metropole Galleries, The Leas,
Folkestone, Kent CT20 2LS
☎01303 244706
Email info@folkestonelitfest.com
Website www.folkestonelitfest.com
Festival Director *Nick Ewbank*

The Folkestone Literary Festival brings outstanding writers to this beautiful seaside town for a week packed with tours, discussions, talks and readings. September 2004.

Frome Festival
25 Market Place, Frome, Somerset BA11 1AH
☎01373 453889 Fax 01373 464912
Email fromefestival@ukonline.co.uk
Website www.fromefestival.co.uk
Festival Director *Martin Bax*

An annual festival held from the first Friday in July for ten days celebrating all aspects of visual and performing arts and entertainment and with a strong literary element. Features music, film, dance, drama and visual arts plus readings, talks and workshops. Previous literary guests have included nationally renowned writers as well as local authors.

Graham Greene Festival
See **Graham Greene Birthplace Trust** under **Literary Societies**

Greenwich + Docklands Festivals
6 College Approach, London SE10 9HY
☎020 8305 1818 Fax 020 8305 1188
Email info@festival.org
Website www.festival.org
Executive Director *Mathew Russell*
Artistic Director *Bradley Hemmings*

Greenwich + Docklands Festivals (GDF) is a festival and event-producing organisation working across east London in the boroughs of Greenwich, Tower Hamlets, Newham and more recently further afield. GDF's portfolio includes the International Festival, London's largest multi-artform festival; First Night, a celebration of the new year through the arts; and diversification, producing events for a wide range of contexts across London and beyond.

The Guardian Hay Festival
25 Lion Street, Hay-on-Wye HR3 5AD
☎01497 821217 Fax 01497 821066
Website www.hayfestival.co.uk
Festival Director *Peter Florence*

FOUNDED 1988. Annual May festival sponsored by *The Guardian*. Guests have included Paul McCartney, Bill Clinton, Salman Rushdie, Toni Morrison, Stephen Fry, Joseph Heller, Carlos Fuentes, Maya Angelou, Amos Oz, Arthur Miller.

Guildford Book Festival
c/o Tourist Information Centre, 15 Tunsgate, Guildford, Surrey GU1 3QT
☎01483 444334
Email book-festival-director@surrey.ac.uk
Website www.guildfordbookfestival.org.uk
Book Festival Director *Glenis Pycraft*

FOUNDED 1990. Patrons: Sandi Toksvig, Fay Weldon and Timothy West. Held annually, during October/November in a variety of venues throughout the ancient town of Guildford. This two-week festival includes events with celebrated and new writers workshops, poetry performances, children's events and competitions, First Novel Award, literary lunches and teas. Its appeal lies in its diversity and its aim is to involve, instruct and entertain all who care about literature. Past guest authors have included Germaine Greer, Antonio Carluccio, Wendy Cope, Penny Vincenzi and many others.

Hallam Literature Festival and Book Fair
School of Cultural Studies, Sheffield Hallam University, 32 Colegiate Crescent Campus, Sheffield S10 2BP
☎0114 225 2228 Fax 0114 225 4403
Festival Coordinator *E.A. Markham*

FOUNDED 1997. The third festival was held in association with *Mslexia* magazine. Events featured 'Poet to Poet', and 'Writing the Life' discussions, and guests included Michele Roberts, Sean O'Brien, Penny Faith and Gareth Creer.

Haringey Literature Festival
Haringey Arts Council, The Chocolate Factory, Clarendon Road, London N22 6XJ
☎020 8365 7500 Fax 020 8365 8686
Email dana@haringeyartscouncil.org
Festival Organiser *Dana Captainino*

FOUNDED 1995. Annual literature programme is a mixture of poetry and literature in the form of readings, discussions, workshops and masterclasses. Writers who have appeared at past festivals include: Diran Adebayo, Alex Wheatle, Michael Donaghy, Patience Agbebi, Fay Weldon, Jane Duran, John Hegley.

Harrogate Crime Writing Festival

1 Victoria Avenue, Harrogate, North Yorkshire GH1 1EQ
☎01423 562303   Fax 10423 521264
Email crime@harrogate-festival.org.uk
Website www.harrogate-festival.org.uk

Festival Coordinator *Jane Bradish-Ellames*

LAUNCHED 2003. Weekend of events at the end of July each year featuring the best of British and American crime writers. Events also include industry 'How to ...' sessions, social events and late night shows. Part of the Harrogate International Festival.

Harrogate International Festival

1 Victoria Avenue, Harrogate, North Yorkshire HG1 1EQ
☎01423 562303   Fax 01423 521264
Email info@harrogate-festival.org.uk
Website www.harrogate-festival.org.uk

Festival Director *William Culver-Dodds*
Festival Manager *Sharon Canavar*

FOUNDED 1966. Annual two-week festival at the end of July and beginning of August. Events include international symphony orchestras, chamber concerts, ballet, celebrity recitals, contemporary dance, opera, drama, jazz, comedy plus an international street theatre festival.

Hastings International Poetry Festival

'The Snoring Cat', 16 Marianne Park, Dudley Road, Hastings, East Sussex TN35 5PU

Contact *Josephine Austin*

FOUNDED 1968. Annual weekend poetry festival held in November in the Sussex Hall, White Rock Theatre, Hastings. Runs the Hastings National Poetry Competition; entry forms available from the address above.

The Hay Festival

See **The Guardian Hay Festival**

Hebden Bridge Arts Festival

New Oxford House, Albert Street, Hebden Bridge, West Yorkshire HX7 4AH
☎01422 842684
Email hbartsfestival@hotmail.com *or*
   enid@step9.freeserve.co.uk
Website www.hebdenbridge.co.uk/festival

Contact *Enid Stephenson*

FOUNDED 1994. Annual arts festival with increasingly strong adult and children's literature events. Previous guest writers include Roger McGough, Benjamin Zephaniah, Anne Fine, Juliet Barker, Jacqueline Wilson, Pete McCarthy, Ian McMillan, Adele Geras.

Hull Literature Festival

See **Humber Mouth**

Humber Mouth – Hull Literature Festival

City Arts Unit, Central Library, Albion Street, Kingston upon Hull HU1 3TF
☎01482 616961   Fax 01482 616827
Email humber.mouth@hullcc.gov.uk
Website www.humbermouth.org.uk

Contact *Maggie Hannan, City Arts Unit*

FOUNDED 1992. Hull's largest festival and one of the region's liveliest events. Features readings, talks, performances and workshops by writers and artists from around the world and from the city.

Ilkley Literature Festival

The Manor House, Ilkley, West Yorkshire LS29 9DT
☎01943 601210   Fax 01943 817079
Email admin@ilkleyliteraturefestival.org.uk
Website www.ilkleyliteraturefestival.org.uk

Director *Rachel Feldberg*

FOUNDED 1973. Major literature festival in the north with events running throughout the year. Large-scale annual festival each October. Recent guests: Louis de Bernières, John Simpson, A.S. Byatt, Carol Ann Duffy and Iain Banks. Telephone or e-mail to join free mailing list.

Imagine: Writers and Writing for Children

See **Royal Festival Hall Literature & Talks**

The International Festival of Mountaineering Literature

University of Leeds, Bretton Hall Campus, Wakefield, West Yorkshire WF4 4LG
☎0113 343 9022   Fax 0133 343 9148
Email tgifford@leeds.ac.uk
Website www.
   festivalofmountaineeringliterature.co.uk

Director *Terry Gifford*

FOUNDED 1987. Annual one-day festival held in March 2004 celebrating recent books, commissioning new writing, overviews of national literatures, debates of issues, book signings, discussion with Chair of Judges of the adjudication of the annual **Boardman Tasker Award** for the best mountaineering book of the year. Announces the winner of the festival writing competition run in conjunction with *High* magazine. Write to join free mailing list.

International Playwriting Festival
Warehouse Theatre, Dingwall Road,
Croydon CR0 2NF
☎020 8681 1257 Fax 020 8688 6699
Email warehous@dircon.co.uk
Website www.warehousetheatre.co.uk
Festival Administrator *Rose Marie Vernon*
FOUNDED 1985. Annual competition for full-length unperformed plays, judged by a panel of theatre professionals. Finalists given rehearsed readings during the festival week in November. Entries welcome from all parts of the world. Scripts plus two s.a.e.s (one script-sized) should reach the theatre by the end of June, accompanied by an entry form (available from the theatre). Previous winners produced at the theatre include: Kevin Hood *Beached*; Ellen Fox *Conversations with George Sandburgh After a Solo Flight Across the Atlantic*; Guy Jenkin *Fighting for the Dunghill*; James Martin Charlton *Fat Souls*; Peter Moffat *Iona Rain*; Dino Mahoney *YoYo*; Simon Smith *Fat Janet is Dead*; Dominic McHale *The Resurrectionists*; Philip Edwards *51 Peg*; Roumen Shomov *The Dove*; Maggie Nevill *The Shagaround*; Andrew Shakeshaft *Just Sitting*. Shares plays with its partner festival in Italy, the Premio Candoni Arta Terme.

Isle of Man Literature Festival
Isle of Man Arts Council, 10 Villa Marina Arcade, Douglas, Isle of Man IM1 2HN
☎01624 611316 Fax 01624 615423
Email dawn.maddrell@iomartscouncil.
dtl.gov.im
Contact *Arts Development Manager*
FOUNDED 1997. Annual festival of literature, poetry and music. The 2003 Festival takes place from 9th to 12th October.

Kent Literature Festival
See Folkestone Literary Festival

King's Lynn, The Fiction Festival
19 Tuesday Market Place, King's Lynn,
Norfolk PE30 1JW
☎01553 691661 (office hours) or 761919
Fax 01553 691779
Contact *Anthony Ellis*
FOUNDED 1989. Annual weekend festival held in March. Over the weekend there are readings and discussions, attended by guest writers of which there are usually eight. Guests at the 2003 festival included Beryl Bainbridge, Paul Bailey, Penelope Edric, Christopher Bigsby, Geoff Dyer and John Fuller.

King's Lynn, The Poetry Festival
19 Tuesday Market Place, King's Lynn,
Norfolk PE30 1JW
☎01553 691661 (office hours) or 761919
Fax 01553 691779
Contact *Anthony Ellis*
FOUNDED 1985. Annual weekend festival held at the end of September (26th to 28th in 2003), with guest poets (usually eight). Previous guests have included Carol Ann Duffy, Paul Durcan, Gavin Ewart, Peter Porter, Stephen Spender. Events include readings and discussion panels and the presentation of the King's Lynn Award; current Laureate is C.K. Stead.

Lancaster LitFest
26 Castle Park, Lancaster LA1 1YQ
☎01524 62166 Fax 01524 841216
Email andy.darby@litfest.org
Website www.litfest.org
FOUNDED 1978. Regional Literature Development Agency, organising workshops, readings, residencies, publications. Year-round programme of literature-based events and annual festival in October featuring a wide range of writers from the UK and overseas. Organises annual poetry competition with winners receiving cash prizes and anthology publication.

Leamington Festival
Warwick Arts Society, Pageant House, 2 Jury Street, Warwick CV34 4EW
☎01926 410747 Fax 01926 409050
Email admin@warwickarts.org.uk
Website www.warwickarts.org.uk
Festival Director *Richard Phillips*
LAUNCHED 2003, created from annual themed chamber music weekend in early May to embrace jazz and world music. Will in future contain literary events reflecting the theme of the annual Festival. Education programme and workshops will also be developed.

Ledbury Poetry Festival
Town Council Offices, Church Lane,
Ledbury, Herefordshire HR8 1DH
☎01531 634156
Email info@poetry-festival.com
Website www.poetry-festival.com
Contact *Charles Bennett*
FOUNDED 1997. Annual ten-day festival held in July. Includes readings, discussions, workshops,

exhibitions, music and walks. There are also writers in residence at local schools and residential homes, a national poetry competition and the Town Party. Past guests have included Andrew Motion, Benjamin Zephaniah, Simon Armitage, Roger McGough, John Hegley and Germaine Greer. Full programme available in May.

Leicester Literature Festival
See 'Everybody's Reading'

Lewes Live Literature
PO Box 2766, Lewes, East Sussex
BN7 2WF
☎01273 400560 Fax 01273 400560
Email info@leweslivelit.co.uk
Website www.leweslivlit.co.uk
Artistic Director *Mark Hewitt*

FOUNDED 1995. Year round literature organisation promoting Lewes Live Literature Festival (three day intensive late October/early November) and the LLL Spring Season (sometime April/May/June) as well as occasional projects outside these times. Areas of interest include poetry, fiction. non-fiction, art, art history, music, theatre, film, TV. Events include readings, performance, lectures, workshops, screenings of film and video, exhibitions.

Lichfield Festival
7 The Close, Lichfield, Staffordshire
WS13 7LD
☎01543 306270 Fax 01543 306274
Email lichfield.fest@lichfield-arts.org.uk
Website www.lichfieldfestival.org
Festival Director *Meurig Bowen*

FOUNDED 1982. Annual July festival with events taking place in the 13th century Cathedral, the new Lichfield Garrick Theatre, and various country churches and outdoor venues. Mainly music but a growing programme of literary events such as poetry, plays and talks.

City of London Festival
230 Bishopsgate, London EC2M 4HW
☎020 7377 0540 Fax 020 7377 1972
Email admin@colf.org
Website www.colf.org
Director *Kathryn McDowell*

FOUNDED 1962. Annual three-week festival held in June and July. Features over fifty classical and popular music events alongside poetry and prose readings, street theatre and open-air extravaganzas, in some of the most outstanding performance spaces in the world.

London New Play Festival
40/7 Altenburg Gardens, London SW11 1JW
☎07050 641959 Fax 07050 642929
Website www.lnpf.co.uk
Literary Manager *Julia Parr*
Education Director *Christopher Preston*

FOUNDED 1989. Annual festival of new plays held in venues around London each September, centring on a short play platform season held in the West End in association with Really Useful Theatres. LNPF specialises in developing and producing new plays, normally working with early career playwrights. As well as the annual festival, LNPF stages education and production programmes throughout the year. Full information can be found on the website. Script submissions should be sent to *Julia Parr* as above.

Lowdham Book Festival
4th Floor Arts, County Hall, West Bridgford, Nottinghamshire NG2 7QP
Email ross.bradshaw@nottsscc.gov.uk
Contact *Ross Bradshaw*

FOUNDED 1999. Annual week-long festival combining a village fête atmosphere with that of a major literature festival. Guests have included Carol Ann Duffy, Pete McCarthy, Ian McMillan, Alan Sillitoe, Jackie Kay, Sarah Harrison and Carole Blake. Talks on everything from St Kilda to the Jewish roots of rock 'n' roll. Free mailing list includes *County Lit* magazine.

Ludlow Festival
Castle Square, Ludlow, Shropshire SY8 1AY
☎01584 875070 (Admin)/872150 (Box Office)
Fax 01584 877673
Email info@ludlowfestival.co.uk
Website www.ludlowfestival.co.uk
Contact *Festival Administrator*

Now in its 44th year, the 2003 Festival ran to three weeks with two open-air Shakespeare production held at Ludlow Castle and a varied programme of events including recitals, opera, dance, popular and classical concerts, literary and historical lectures.

Manchester Festival of Writing
Manchester Central Library, St Peter's Square, Manchester M2 5PD
☎0161 234 1981
Email libbyt@libraries.manchester.gov.uk
Contact *Libby Tempest*

FOUNDED 1990. An annual event organised by Manchester Libraries and Commonword community publishers. It consists of a short programme of practical writing workshops on specific themes/genres run by well-known writers. Attendance at all workshops is free to Manchester residents.

Manchester Poetry Festival
3rd Floor, 24 Lever Street, Stevenson Square, Manchester M1 1D2
☎0161 236 5725 Fax 0161 236 5719
Email mpf@dial.pipex.com
Contact *Helen Riley*

Held in the autumn, Manchester Poetry Festival is the largest urban poetry festival outside of London. 2003 is the tenth birthday of the festival and saw an innovative and cutting-edge festival which brought nationally recognised poets to Manchester and supported local poets and groups.

Margate Poetry Festival
31 Addington Road, Margate, Kent
CT9 1NH
☎01843 224058
Contact *Doreen Perry*

FOUNDED 1997 the festival attracts people from all over the country and abroad and particularly encourages people with disabilities. Guest poets have included Jean Binta Breeze, Maggie Harris, Lionel Fanthorp, Ted Smith Ore, John Rice and Barbara Dordi.

Mere Literary Festival
Lawrence's, Old Hollow, Mere, Wiltshire
BA12 6EG
☎01747 860475/861211 (Tourist Information)
Contact *Adrienne Howell*

FOUNDED 1997. Annual festival held in the second week of October in aid of registered charity, The Mere & District Linkscheme. Events include readings, quiz, workshop, writer's lunch and talks. Finale is adjudication of the festival's writing competition (see entry under **Prizes**) and presentation of awards.

National Association of Writers' Groups (NAWG) Open Festival of Writing
The Arts Centre, Washington, Tyne & Wear
NE38 2AB
☎0191 416 9751
Email briannawgfestival@yahoo.co.uk
Website www.nawg.co.uk
Festival Administrator *Brian Lister*

FOUNDED 1997. Annual festival held at St Aidan's College, University of Durham in September or October. Three days of creative writing tuition covering poetry, short and long fiction, playwriting, journalism, TV sitcom and other subjects all led by professional writer-tutors. 36 workshops, 32 surgeries plus seminars and fringe events. Saturday gala dinner and awards ceremony. Full- or part-residential weekend, or single workshops only. Open to all, no qualifications or NAWG membership required.

National Eisteddfod of Wales
40 Parc Ty Glas, Llanishen, Cardiff
CF14 5WU
☎029 2076 3777 Fax 029 2076 3737
Website www.eisteddfod.org.uk

The National Eisteddfod, held in August, is the largest arts festival in Wales, attracting over 170,000 visitors during the week-long celebration of more than 800 years of tradition. Competitions, bardic ceremonies and concerts.

National Student Drama Festival
See **University of Hull** under **Writers' Courses, Circles and Workshops**

New Hall School Festival of Literature
New Hall School, Chelmsford CM3 3HS
Email publicity@newhallschool.co.uk
Website www.newhallschool.co.uk
Contact *Anne Sparrow*

FOUNDED 1992 the week-long festival is open to parents, staff and friends. The aim is to widen students' horizons and, during the week, students from other schools in the town are invited to join in an array of events.

Northern Children's Book Festival
Schools Library Service, Sandhill View Centre, Grindon Lane, Sunderland SR3 4EN
☎0191553 8866/7/8 Fax 0191 553 8869
Secretary *Eleanor Dowley*

FOUNDED 1984. Annual two-week festival during November. Events in schools and libraries for children in the North East region. One Saturday during the festival sees the staging of a large book event hosted by one of the local authorities involved.

Off the Page Literature Festival
County Library Support Services, Glaisdale Parkway, Nottingham NG8 4GP
☎0115 985 4242 Fax 0115 928 6400
Email alison.hirst@nottscc.gov.uk
Contact *Alison Hirst*

Author visits aimed at making authors accessible to readers. In 2003 the series takes place at Nottingham Central Library in November. Programme available from late summer/early autumn.

Off the Shelf Literature Festival

Central Library, Surrey Street, Sheffield
S1 1XZ
☎0114 273 4716/4400   Fax 0114 273 5009
Email off-the-shelf@pop3.poptel.org.uk
Website www.offtheshelf.org.uk
Festival Organisers *Maria de Souza, Susan Walker*

FOUNDED 1992. Annual two-week festival held during the last fortnight in October. Lively and diverse mix of readings, workshops, children's events, storytelling and competitions. Previous guests have included Bill Bryson, Doris Lessing, Benjamin Zephaniah, Terry Pratchett, Michael Palin, Carol Ann Duffy and Louis de Bernières.

Oxford Literary Festival

See *The Sunday Times* Oxford Literary Festival

Paddington International Poetry Festival

Uprise Arts, PO Box 33082, London
W9 3WA
☎010 7286 1880
Contact *Seema Gill*

FOUNDED in 1999 by the writer and painter Richard Heley, the main focus is on performance and slam poetry but the event also covers live painting, art exhibitions, plays and book launches.

Poetry Otherwise

Emerson College, Forest Row, East Sussex
RH18 5JX
☎01342 822238   Fax 01342 826055
Email mail@emerson.org.uk
Website www.emerson.org.uk *or*
   www.poetryotherwise.org
Director *Paul Matthews*

Held in August. A summer gathering of poets, writers and all lovers of language. Workshops, readings, talks, conversation, practice in the art of speaking poetry. Contributors have included Andrea Hollander Budy, John Freeman, Ashley Ramsden, Andie Lewenstein, Paul Matthews, Peter Abbs, Katherine Pierpoint, Fiona Owen. 'Wholesome food, wonderful Sussex countryside.'

ProudWords Writing Festival

PO Box 181, Newcastle upon Tyne NE6 5XG
☎07973 8949 12
Email pwcwf@hotmail.com
Website www.proudwords.org.uk
Contact *Mary Lowe*

FOUNDED 1998. The only writing festival in the UK to celebrate the diversity of literary talent that exists within the gay community. Held annually, a week long festival in June/July which includes workshops, bus trips, walking tours, readings, discussions and performances of both writing and music. ProudWords encourages participation, lively debate, an interest in literature-related activity and offers opportunities for gay people to express themselves in writing in a supportive, friendly atmosphere. Writers at past festivals include Jackie Kay, Julia Darling, Sarah Waters, Jake Arnott, P-P Hartness, Emma Donaghue, Paul Magrs, Stella Duffy, Julia Bell, Val McDermid, Chrissie Glazebrook and Cathal O Searcaigh. 'Lesbians, gay men and bisexuals are invited to Newcastle to discover for themselves the thriving writing culture that exists here.'

Purple Patch Poetry Convention

25 Griffiths Road, West Bromwich B71 2EH
Email ppatch66@hotmail.com
Contact *Geoff Stevens*

Held at the Barlow Theatre near Birmingham this event celebrates the strength of small press poets. It was intended to make it a biennial event but it has been held in 1999, 2001 and 2002. A similar event was organized by Oxford Back Room poets in Oxford in July 2003 and 'we hope to resume in 2004'. Purple Patch Convention is a three-day event of poetry readings, talks, workshops and discussions and admission charges are kept very low, payments to participants being low to non-existent. The Convention's aims are quality and an opportunity to participate. Poets at past festivals have included Ray Avery, R.G. Bishop, Tilla Brading, Gerald England, J.F. Haines, Brendan Hawthorne, Martin Holroyd, Mike Hoy, Eamer O'Keeffe Carolyn King, Paul McDonald, Bob Mee, Les Merton, Michael Newman, Simon Pitt, Andy Robson, Sam Smith and Steve Sneyd.

Royal Court Young Writers Programme

The Site, Royal Court Theatre, Sloane Square, London SW1W 8AS
☎020 7565 5050   Fax 020 7565 5001

Email ywp@royalcourttheatre.com

Website www.royalcourttheatre.com

Associate Director *Ola Animashawun*

Open to young people up to the age of 25. The YWP focuses on the process of playwriting by running a series of writers groups throughout the year at its base in Sloane Square. Additionally the YWP welcomes unsolicited scripts from all young writers from across the country. 'We are always looking for scripts for development and possible production (not film scripts).'

Royal Festival Hall
Literature & Talks
Performing Arts Department, Royal Festival Hall, London SE1 8XX

☎020 7921 0906 Fax 020 7928 2049

Email shoare@rfh.org.uk

Website www.sbc.org.uk

Head of Literature & Talks *Ruth Borthwick*

The Royal Festival Hall presents a year-round literature programme covering all aspects of writing. Regular series range from A Life Indeed! to Fiction International and there are two biennial festivals: Poetry International and Imagine: Writers and Writing for Children. Literature events are now programmed in the Voice Box, Purcell Room and Queen Elizabeth Hall. To join the free mailing list, phone 020 7921 0971 or e-mail Literature&Talks@rfh.org.uk

Rye Festival
PO Box 33, Rye, East Sussex TN31 7YB

☎01797 224982

Literary Director *Hilary Brooke*

FOUNDED 1972. Annual two-week September event, plus short winter series. Variety of events with strong emphasis on literature (nominated by the *Independent on Sunday* as one of ten best British festivals), classical and modern music, visual arts, workshops and masterclasses. Write or phone to join free mailing list.

Salisbury Festival
Festival Office, 75 New Street, Salisbury, Wiltshire SP1 2PH

☎01722 332241 Fax 01722 410552

Email info@salisburyfestival.co.uk

Website www.salisburyfestival.co.uk

Director *Trevor Davies*

FOUNDED 1972. Annual festival held at the end of May/beginning of June, including classical music, theatre, jazz and exhibitions.

The Scottish Book Town Festival
Book Town Officer, 26 South Main Street, Wigtown DG8 9EH

☎01988 402036 Fax 01988 402506

Email booktown-wigit@btinternet.com

Website www.wigtown-booktown.co.uk

Contact *Jennifer Bradley*

FOUNDED 1999. A rural literary festival which takes place annually at the end of September over three days in Wigtown town centre, many of the town's bookshops and the nearby Bladnoch Distillery. Authors' readings, including children's authors, debates, poety, music and film.

Southwell Poetry Festival
4th Floor Arts, County Hall, West Bridgford, Nottinghamshire NG2 7QP

Email ross.bradshaw@nottscc.gov.uk

Contact *Ross Bradshaw*

This festival returned in 2003 after a trial run in 2000.

Southwold Festival
See **Ways with Words**

StAnza: Scotland's Poetry Festival
Gilstonbrig, by Upper Largo, Fife KY8 5QW

☎01333 360491

Email stanza@st-andrews.ac.uk

Website www.stanzapoetry.org

Contact *Brian Johnstone*

The only regular festival dedicated to poetry in Scotland, StAnza is international in outlook. Held annually in the ancient university town of St Andrews, the festival is an opportunity to hear world class poets reading in exciting and atmospheric venues. The 2003 festival themes were Poetry and the Garden and Poetry and Song. The festival featured performance poetry, poetry in exhibition, workshops and children's poetry. StAnza 2003 was headlined by Carol Ann Duffy and the Poet Laureate, Andrew Motion, and other poets included Patience Agbabi, Michael Alexander, Moniza Alvi, John Burnside, Gael Turnbull and Colin Will. Tickets can be purchased from the Byre Theatre box office on 01334 475000.Free programmes can be ordered from Fife Council Arts Development on 01592 414714 or by e-mail to arts.development@fife.gov.uk.

Stoke Newington Festival
Old Town Hall, Stoke Newington Church Street, London N16 0JR

☎020 8356 6410 Fax 020 8356 6435

Email fiona@stokenewingtonfestival.co.uk

Website www.stokenewingtonfestival.co.uk

Programme Producer *Fiona Fieber*

FOUNDED 1993. Previous festivals, held over ten days in June, have featured WordontheStreet, a one-day programme of literature, text, spoken word and artistic interventions to do with the Word, held in Stoke Newington Church Street. Other literature events have featured Writers Surgery, Poetry Workout and Turkish Storytelling for Children.

Stratford-upon-Avon Poetry Festival

The Shakespeare Centre, Henley Street, Stratford-upon-Avon, Warwickshire CV37 6QW

☎01789 204016/292176 (Box office)

Fax 01789 296083

Email director@shakespeare.org.uk

Festival Director *Roger Pringle*

FOUNDED 1953. Annual festival held on Sunday evenings during July and August. Readings by poets and professional actors by invitation.

The Sunday Times Oxford Literary Festival

301 Woodstock Road, Oxford OX2 7NY

☎01865 514149 Fax 01865 514804

Email oxford.literary.festival@ntlworld.com

Directors *Sally Dunsmore, Angela Prysor-Jones*

FOUNDED 1997. Annual six-day festival held two weekends prior to Easter. Authors speaking about their books, covering a wide variety of writing: fiction, poetry, biography, travel, food, gardening, children's art. Previous guests have included William Boyd, Andrew Motion, Candia McWilliam, Beryl Bainbridge, Sophie Grigson, Jamie McKendrick, Bernard O'Donoghue, Philip Pullman and Korky Paul.

Swansea Festivals

Dylan Thomas Centre, Somerset Place, Swansea SA1 1RR

☎01792 463980 Fax 01792 463993

Email dylan.thomas@swansea.gov.uk

Website www.dylanthomas.org *and* www.dylanthomasfestival.com

Contact *David Woolley*

Wordplay (6th to 11th October): ninth annual festival of literature and arts for young people. The Dylan Thomas Celebration (27th October to 9th November) is two weeks of performances, talks, lectures, films, music, poetry, exhibitions and celebrity guests. A programme of events to mark the 50th anniversary of Dylan Thomas' death (9th November 1953) has been running throughout the year.

Swindon Festival of Literature

Lower Shaw Farm, Shaw, Swindon, Wiltshire SN5 5PJ

☎01793 771080 Fax 01793 771080

Email swindonlitfest@lowershawfarm.co.uk

Website www.swindonfestivaloliterature. co.uk

Festival Director *Matt Holland*

FOUNDED 1994. Annual festival held in May, starting with 'Dawn Chorus' at sunrise on May Day. Includes a wide range of authors, speakers, discussions, performances and workshops, plus the Clive Brain Memorial Lecture and the Swindon Performance Poetry Slam competition.

Tears in the Fence Festival

38 Hod View, Stourpaine, Blandford Forum, Dorset DT11 8TN

☎01258 456803

Email esp@euphony.net

Website www.wanderingdog.co.uk

Festival Director *David Caddy*

Festival Manager *Jonathan Ward*

FOUNDED 1995. Annual international poetry festival based in London with readings, talks, discussions and workshops continuing the work begun by the Wessex Poetry Festivals, 1995–2001. Previous guests have included Barry MacSweeney, Jon Silkin, Doug Oliver, Alice Notley, Fred Voss, Joan Jobe Smith, Irina Ratushinskaya, Michele Roberts, Edwin Morgan and Kim Taplin.

The Dylan Thomas Celebration

See **Swansea Festivals**

Warwick Festival

Warwick Arts Society, Pageant House, 2 Jury Street, Warwick CV34 4EW

☎01926 410747 Fax 01926 409050

Email admin@warwickarts.org.uk

Website www.warwickarts.org.uk

Festival Director *Richard Phillips*

FOUNDED 1980, this annual festival has had four names but the new format from 2003 means events only in Warwick town, using Warwick Castle and the historic buildings in the centre, plus new theatres The Dream Factory and Bridge House Theatre on the outskirts. Primarily a music festival but embraces drama, opera, dance, puppets, art exhibitions, poetry readings and other literary events. Extensive eduational programme including workshops.

Warwick Words

Warwick Events Group, Northgate, Warwick
CV34 4JL
☎01926 497000 Fax 01926 407606
Email admin@warwickarts.org.uk
Website www.WarwickLive.com

Launched 2002. Annual venture featuring both
living writers and those who have had connec-
tions with Warwick – Tolkien, Larkin and
Landor in particular. Also workshops and an
education programme. A weekend festival of
literature and spoken word for all the family.
Events at The Dream Factory, Bridge House
Theatre, St Mary's Church, the Lord Leycester
Hospital and other historic buildings around
Warwick over the first weekend in October.

Ways with Words

Droridge Farm, Dartington, Totnes, Devon
TQ9 6JQ
☎01803 867373 Fax 01803 863688
Email admin@wayswithwords.co.uk
Website www.wayswithwords.co.uk

Festival Director *Kay Dunbar*

Ways with Words runs a major literature festival at Dartington Hall in south Devon for ten
days in July each year. Features over 200 writers giving lectures, readings, interviews, discussions, performances, masterclasses and
workshops.

Also, Words by the Water, a Cumbrian literature festival held in Keswick. The 2003 festival ran from 18th to 23rd March. There is a
regular festival in held in Southwold, Suffolk
(dates for 2003 are 13th to 18th November).
Organises writing, reading and painting courses
in Italy.

Wellington Literary Festival

Civic Offices, Larkin Way, Tan Bank,
Wellington, Telford, Shropshire TF1 1LX
☎01952 222935 Fax 01952 222936
Email WellTownCl@aol.com
Website www.wellington-shropshire.gov.uk

Contact *Derrick Drew*

FOUNDED 1997. Annual festival held throughout October. Events include storytelling, writers' forum, 'Pints and Poetry', children's poetry
competition, story competition, theatre review
and guest speakers.

Wells Festival of Literature

25 Chamberlain Street, Wells, Somerset
BA5 2PQ
☎01749 670929
Website www.somersite.co.uk/wellsfest.htm

Contact *Pamela Egan*

FOUNDED 1992. Annual weekend-plus festival
held at the end of October. Main venue is the
historic, moated Bishop's Palace. A wide range
of speakers caters for different tastes in reading.
Recent guests include: Shirley Vickers, Beryl
Bainbridge, Libby Purves, Margaret Drabble,
Mary Warnock, William Dalrymple, Timothy
West. Short story and poetry competitions and
writing workshops are run in conjunction with
the Festival.

Wessex Poetry Festival

See **Tears in the Fence Festival**

Wonderful Words Book Festival

c/o Bude Library, The Wharf, Bude,
Cornwall EX23 8LQ
☎01288 359242
Website www.cornwall.gov.uk

Festival Organiser *Rebecca Rowland*

FOUNDED 1994. Biennial two-month festival
hosted throughout Cornwall. The next and sixth
Wonderful Words Book Festival will be hosted
in 2004. The festival has grown into a prestigious
event of writers' workshops, author talks, storytelling, discussions and literary walks. The 2002
festival was the largest to date and hosted 30
authors culminating in 64 events countywide.
Guest authors included Doris Lessing, Ruth
Rendell, Margaret Drabble, Bernice Rubens,
P.D. James, Clare Francis, Eric James, William
Dalrymple and Dick King-Smith.

WordontheStreet

See **Stoke Newington Festival**

Wordplay

See **Swansea Festivals**

Words by the Water

See **Ways with Words**

'Words Live' Literature Festival

London Borough of Harrow, Arts and Leisure
Service, Civic Centre, PO Box 22, Milton
House, Station Road, Harrow, Middlesex
HA1 2UW
☎020 8424 1076 Fax 020 8424 1817
Website www.Harrow.gov.uk

Festival Organiser *Arts Development Officer*

FOUNDED 1999. Annual two-week community
based literature festival held in March, combining readings from established authors with workshops and innovative literature development
activities for all ages. Previous guests have

442   FESTIVALS

included: Courttia Newland, Bernadine
Everisto, Alexie Sayle, Ian McEwan, Leslie
Glaister, Deborah Moggach, E.A. Markham,
Dotun Adebayo and Claire Rayner. The festival
is part of a year-long development programme.

Wordsworth Trust
The Wordsworth Trust, Dove Cottage,
Grassmere, Cumbria LA22 9SH
☎015394 35544 Fax 015394 35748
Email enquiries@wordsworth.org.uk
Website www.wordsworth.org.uk

Annual weekend festival at the end of January.
The programme is a mixture of lectures, surgeries and workshops on subjects touching on
Romanticism in all its forms. Although the
speakers are experts in their fields, the aim is to
reach out to a general public. Guests have
included Charles Saumerez Smith, Patrick Leigh
Fermor, Fiona MacCarthy, Paul Johnson,
Lucasta Miller and Nicolas Barker. Part of the
programme also comprises poetry readings by
writers in residence at The Wordsworth Trust,
including Paul Farley, Jacob Polley and Henry
Shukman.

European Publishers

Austria

Springer-Verlag KG
PO Box 89, A–1200 Vienna
☎00 43 1 3302415 Fax 00 43 1 3302426
Website www.springer.at
FOUNDED 1924. *Publishes* anthropology, architecture, art, business, chemistry, computer science, communications, electronics, economics, education, environmental studies, engineering, law, mathematics, dentistry, medicine, nursing, philosophy, physics, psychology, technology and general science.

Verlag Carl Ueberreuter GmbH
Postfach 306, A–1091 Vienna
☎00 43 1 404440 Fax 00 43 1 404445
Website www.ueberreuter.de
FOUNDED 1548. *Publishes* fiction and general non-fiction: art, biography, government, history, economics, political science, general science, health and nutrition, science fiction, fantasy, music and dance.

Paul Zsolnay Verlag GmbH
Postfach 142, A–1041 Vienna
☎00 43 1 50576610
Fax 00 43 1 505766110
Website www.zsolnay.at
FOUNDED 1923. *Publishes* biography, fiction, general non-fiction, history, poetry.

Belgium

Brepols Publishers NV
Begijnhof 67, 2300 Turnhout
☎00 32 14 448020 Fax 00 32 14 428919
FOUNDED 1796. *Publishes* academic – architecture, archaeology, art, interior design, Asian studies, history, language studies, linguistics, literature, literary criticism, essays, philosophy, religion.

Facet NV
Willem Linnigstr 13, 2060 Antwerp
☎00 32 3 2274028 Fax 00 32 3 2273792
FOUNDED 1986. *Publishes* children's books.

Uitgeverij Lannoo NV
Kasteelstr 97, B–8700 Tielt
☎00 32 51 424211 Fax 00 32 51 401152
Website www.lannoo.be
FOUNDED 1909. *Publishes* general non-fiction, art, architecture and interior design, cookery, biography, economics, gardening, health and nutrition, history, management, photography, self-help, poetry, government, political science, religion, travel.

Standaard Uitgeverij
Belgiëlei 147a, 2018 Antwerp
☎00 32 3 2857200 Fax 00 32 3 2857299
Website www.standard.com
FOUNDED 1919. *Publishes* education, fiction, poetry, humour.

Denmark

Forlaget Apostrof ApS
Postboks 2580, DK–2100 Copenhagen O
☎00 45 39 208420 Fax 00 45 39 208453
Website www.apostrof.dk
FOUNDED 1980. *Publishes* psychology and psychiatry.

Aschehoug Dansk Forlag A/S
PO Box 2179, DK–1017 Copenhagen K
☎00 45 33 305522 Fax 00 45 33 305822
Website www.aschehoug.dk
FOUNDED 1977. Part of the Egmont Group. *Publishes* fiction, biography, cookery, how-to, maritime, health and nutrition.

Blackwell Munksgaard
PO Box 2148, DK–1016 Copenhagen K
☎00 45 77 333333 Fax 00 45 77 333377
Website www.blackwellmunksgaard.com
FOUNDED 1917. *Publishes* dentistry, medicine, nursing, psychology, psychiatry, general science.

Borgens Forlag A/S
Valbygardsvej 33, DK–2500 Valby
☎00 45 36 153615 Fax 00 45 36 153616
Website www.borgens.dk
FOUNDED 1948. *Publishes* fiction, literature, literary criticism, general non-fiction, art,

astrology, child care, crafts, education, environmental studies, essays, games, hobbies, health and nutrition, how-to, humour, music, dance, occult, philosophy, poetry, psychology, psychiatry, religion.

Egmont Lademann A/S
Gerdasgade 37, DK–2500 Valby
☎00 45 36 156600 Fax 00 45 36 441162
Website www.egmont.com
FOUNDED 1954. *Publishes* general illustrated non-fiction, fiction, children's books and CD-ROMs.

Forum Publishers
Købmagergade 62, DK–1019 Copenhagen K
☎00 45 33 411830 Fax 00 45 33 411831
Website www.gyldendal.dk
FOUNDED 1940. Part of **Gyldendalske Boghandel-Nordisk Forlag A/S**. *Publishes* fiction, history, humour and mysteries.

GEC Gads Forlags Aktieselskab
Klosterstraede 9, DK–1157 Copenhagen K
☎00 45 33 150558 Fax 00 45 33 110800
FOUNDED 1855. *Publishes* general non-fiction, biological sciences, cookery, crafts, games, economics, education, English as a second language, environmental studies, gardening, history, mathematics, natural history, physics, plants, travel.

Gyldendalske Boghandel-Nordisk Forlag A/S
Klareboderne 3, DK–1001 Copenhagen K
☎00 45 33 755555 Fax 00 45 33 755556
Website www.gyldendal.dk
FOUNDED 1770. *Publishes* fiction, art, biography, dance, dentistry, education, history, how-to, medicine, music, poetry, nursing, philosophy, psychology, psychiatry, general and social sciences, sociology.

Hekla Forlag
Valbygaardsvej 33, DK–2500 Valby
☎00 45 36 153615 Fax 00 45 36 153616
FOUNDED 1979. *Publishes* general fiction and non-fiction.

Høst & Søn Publishers Ltd
PO Box 2212, DK–1018 Copenhagen K
☎00 45 33 382888 Fax 00 45 33 382898
FOUNDED 1836. *Publishes* fiction, crafts, environmental studies, games, hobbies, history, regional interests.

Lindhardt og Ringhof
Frederiksborggade 1, DK–1360 Copenhagen K
☎00 45 33 695000 Fax 00 45 33 695001
Website www.logr.dk
FOUNDED 1971. *Publishes* fiction and general non-fiction.

Nyt Nordisk Forlag Arnold Busck A/S
Købmagergade 49, DK–1150 Copenhagen K
☎00 45 33 733575 Fax 00 45 33 733576
Website www.nytnordiskforlag.dk
FOUNDED 1896. *Publishes* fiction, art, biography, dance, dentistry, history, how-to, music, philosophy, religion, medicine, nursing, psychology, psychiatry, general and social sciences, sociology.

Samlerens Forlag A/S
Købmagergade 62, DK–1019 Copenhagen K
☎00 45 33 411800 Fax 00 45 33 411801
FOUNDED 1942. *Publishes* essays, fiction, government, history, literature, literary criticism, political science.

Det Schønbergske Forlag
Landemaerket 5, DK–1119 Copenhagen K
☎00 45 33 733585 Fax 00 45 33 733586
Website www.nytnordiskforlag.dk
FOUNDED 1857. Part of **Nyt Nordisk Forlag Arnold Busck A/S**. *Publishes* art, biography, careers, fiction, history, humour, philosophy, poetry, psychology, psychiatry, travel

Spektrum Forlagsaktieselskab
Snaregade 4, DK–1205 Copenhagen K
☎00 45 33 147714 Fax 00 45 33 147791
FOUNDED 1990. *Publishes* general non-fiction.

Tiderne Skifter Forlag A/S
Købmagergade 62, DK–1019 Copenhagen K
☎00 45 33 411820 Fax 00 45 33 411821
Website www.tiderneskifter.dk
FOUNDED 1973. *Publishes* fiction, literature and literary criticism, essays, ethnicity, photography, behavioural sciences.

Finland

Gummerus Publishers
PO Box 749, SF–00101 Helsinki
☎00 358 9 584301 Fax 00 358 9 58430200
Website www.gummerus.fi
FOUNDED 1872. *Publishes* fiction and general non-fiction.

Karisto Oy
PO Box 102, SF–13101 Hämeenlinna
☎00 358 3 6161551 Fax 00 358 3 6161565
FOUNDED 1900. *Publishes* fiction and general non-fiction.

Kirjayhtymä Oy
Urho Kekkosen Katu 4–6E, SF–00100 Helsinki
☎00 358 9 6937641 Fax 00 358 9 69376366
Website www.kirjayhtyma.fi
FOUNDED 1958. *Publishes* fiction and general non-fiction.

Otava Publishing Co. Ltd
PO Box 134, SF–00121 Helsinki
☎00 358 9 19961 Fax 00 358 9 643136
Website www.otava.fi
FOUNDED 1890. *Publishes* fiction, general non-fiction, how-to.

Werner Söderström Osakeyhtiö (WSOY)
PO Box 222, SF–00121 Helsinki
☎00 358 9 61681 Fax 00 358 9 61683566
FOUNDED 1878. *Publishes* fiction, general non-fiction, education.

Tammi Publishers
PO Box 410, SF–00101 Helsinki
☎00 358 9 6937621 Fax 00 358 9 69376266
Website www.tammi.net
FOUNDED 1943. *Publishes* fiction, general non-fiction.

France

Editions Arthaud SA
26 rue Racine, F–75278 Paris Cedex 06
☎00 33 1 4051 3008 Fax 00 33 1 4325 0118
FOUNDED 1890. Imprint of **Flammarion SA**. *Publishes* art, history, literature, literary criticism, essays, sport, travel.

Editions Belfond
12 avenue d'Italie, F–75013 Paris
☎00 33 1 4544 3823 Fax 00 33 1 4544 9804
FOUNDED 1963. *Publishes* fiction, literature, literary criticism, essays, mysteries, romance, poetry, general non-fiction, art, biography, dance, health, history, how-to, music, nutrition.

Editions Bordas
89 blvd Auguste Blanqui, F–75013 Paris
☎00 33 1 4439 5445 Fax 00 33 1 4439 4350

FOUNDED 1946. *Publishes* education and general non-fiction.

Editions Calmann–Lévy–Stock SA
3 rue Auber, F–75009 Paris
☎00 33 1 4742 3833 Fax 00 33 1 4742 7781
FOUNDED 1836. *Publishes* fiction, science fiction, fantasy, biography, history, humour, economics, philosophy, psychology, psychiatry, social sciences, sociology, sport.

Editions Denoël Sàrl
9 rue du Cherche-Midi, F–75006 Paris
☎00 33 1 4439 7372 Fax 00 33 1 4439 7390
FOUNDED 1932. *Publishes* art, economics, fiction, science fiction, fantasy, government, history, philosophy, political science, psychology, psychiatry.

Librairie Arthème Fayard
75 rue des Saints-Pères, F–75006 Paris
Cedex 06
☎00 33 1 4549 8200 Fax 00 33 1 4222 4017
FOUNDED 1854. *Publishes* biography, fiction, history, dance, music, philosophy, religion, social sciences, sociology, general science, technology.

Flammarion SA
26 rue Racine, F–75278 Paris Cedex 06
☎00 33 1 4051 3008 Fax 00 33 1 4325 0118
FOUNDED 1875. *Publishes* general fiction and non-fiction, art, architecture, gardening, plants, interior design, literature, literary criticism, essays, medicine, nursing, dentistry, wine and spirits.

Editions Gallimard
5 rue Sébastien-Bottin, F–75328 Paris
Cedex 07
☎00 33 1 4954 4200 Fax 00 33 1 4544 9403
FOUNDED 1911. *Publishes* fiction, poetry, art, biography, dance, history, music, philosophy.

Editions Grasset & Fasquelle
61 rue des Saints-Pères, F–75006 Paris
☎00 33 1 4439 2200 Fax 00 33 1 4222 6418
Website www.edition-grasset.fr
FOUNDED 1907. *Publishes* fiction and general non-fiction, essays, literature, literary criticism, philosophy.

Hachette–Livre
43 quai de Grenelle, F–75905 Paris Cedex 15
☎00 33 1 4392 3000 Fax 00 33 1 4392 3030
FOUNDED 1826. *Publishes* fiction and general

non-fiction, architecture and interior design, art, economics, education, general engineering, government, history, language and linguistics, political science, philosophy, general science, self-help, social sciences, sociology, sport, travel.

Editions Robert Laffont, Nil, Fixot, Seghers, Julliard
24 ave Marceau, F–75381 Paris Cedex 08
☎00 33 1 5367 1400
Fax 00 33 1 5367 1414
Website www.laffont.fr

FOUNDED 1941. *Publishes* fiction and non-fiction; literature, literary criticism, essays, poetry, philosophy, self-help, psychology, psychiatry, general science, social sciences, sociology.

Librairie Larousse
21 rue de Montparnasse, F–75006 Paris
☎00 33 1 4439 4343
Fax 00 33 1 4439 4107

FOUNDED 1852. *Publishes* animals, pets, childcare, cookery, gardening, history, medicine, nursing, dentistry, music, dance, self-help, psychology, psychiatry, general science, social sciences, sociology, language arts, linguistics, technology.

Editions Jean–Claude Lattès
17 rue Jacob, F–75006 Paris
☎00 33 1 4441 7400   Fax 00 33 1 4325 3047
FOUNDED 1968. Part of **Hachette-Livre**. *Publishes* fiction, criminology, general non-fiction.

Magnard SA
20 rue Berbier-du-Mets, F–75647 Paris Cedex 13
☎00 33 1 4408 8585   Fax 00 33 1 4408 4979
FOUNDED 1933. *Publishes* education.

Michelin et Cie (Services de Tourisme)
46 ave de Breteuil, F–75324 Paris
☎00 33 1 4566 1234   Fax 00 33 1 4566 1163
FOUNDED 1900. *Publishes* travel.

Les Editions de Minuit SA
7 rue Bernard-Palissy, F–75006 Paris
☎00 33 1 4439 3920
Fax 00 33 1 4544 8236
FOUNDED 1942. *Publishes* fiction, essays, literature, literary criticism, philosophy, social sciences, sociology.

Fernand Nathan
9 rue Méchain, F–75014 Paris
☎00 33 1 4587 5000   Fax 00 33 1 4331 2169
Website www.nathan.fr

FOUNDED 1881. *Publishes* education, history, philosophy, psychology, psychiatry, general and social sciences, sociology.

Presses de la Cité
12 ave d'Italie, F–75627 Paris Cedex 13
☎00 33 1 4416 0500   Fax 00 33 1 4416 0505
Website www.pressesdelacite.com

FOUNDED 1947. Imprint of **Editions Belfond**. *Publishes* fiction and general non-fiction, science fiction, fantasy, horror, mysteries, thrillers, humour, romance, biography.

Presses Universitaires de France (PUF)
6 ave Reille, F–75685 Paris Cedex 14
☎00 33 1 5810 3100   Fax 00 33 1 5810 3182
Website www.puf.com

FOUNDED 1921. *Publishes* art, biography, dance, dentistry, government, general engineering, geography, geology, history, law, medicine, music, nursing, philosophy, psychology, psychiatry, religion, political science, social science, sociology.

Editions du Seuil
27 rue Jacob, F–75261 Paris
☎00 33 1 4046 5050   Fax 00 33 1 4046 4300
Website www.seuil.com

FOUNDED 1935. *Publishes* fiction, literature, literary criticism, essays, poetry, art, biography, dance, government, political science, history, how-to, music, photography, philosophy, psychology, psychiatry, religion, general and social sciences, sociology.

Les Editions de la Table Ronde
7 rue Corneille, F–75006 Paris
☎00 33 1 4046 7070   Fax 00 33 1 4046 7101
FOUNDED 1944. *Publishes* fiction and general non-fiction, biography, history, psychology, psychiatry, religion.

Librairie Vuibert
20 rue Babier-du-Mets, F–75647 Paris Cedex 13
☎00 33 1 4408 4900   Fax 00 33 1 4408 4939
Website www.vuibert.com

FOUNDED 1877. *Publishes* biological and earth sciences, chemistry, chemical engineering, economics, law, mathematics, physics.

Germany

Verlag C.H. Beck (OHG)

Postfach 400340, 80703 Munich
☎00 49 89 381890 Fax 00 49 89 38189398
Website www.beck.de

FOUNDED 1763. *Publishes* general non-fiction, anthropology, archaeology, art, dance, economics, essays, history, language arts, law, linguistics, literature, literary criticism, music, philosophy, social sciences, sociology, theology.

Bertelsmann

Verlagsgruppe Random House, Neumarkter Strasse 28, 81673 Munich
☎00 49 89 4136-0
Website www.randomhouse.de

FOUNDED 1835. Part of the Random House Group. *Publishes* fiction and general non-fiction, art, biography, government and political science.

Carlsen Verlag GmbH

Postfach 500380, 22703 Hamburg
☎00 49 40 398040 Fax 00 49 40 39804390
Website www.carlsen.de

FOUNDED 1953. *Publishes* fiction, humour and picture books.

Deutscher Taschenbuch Verlag GmbH & Co. KG (dtv)

Postfach 400422, 80704 Munich
☎00 49 89 38167-0 Fax 00 49 89 346428
Email info@dtv.de
Website www.dtv.de

FOUNDED 1961. *Publishes* fiction and general non-fiction; art, astronomy, biography, child care and development, cookery, computer science, dance, education, government, history, how-to, music, poetry, psychiatry, psychology, philosophy, political science, religion, medicine, dentistry, nursing, social sciences, literature, literary criticism, essays, humour, travel.

Econ-Verlag GmbH

Paul-Heyse-Strasse 28, 80336 Munich
☎00 49 89 5148-0 Fax 00 49 89 5148-2229
Website www.econ-verlag.de

FOUNDED 1950. *Publishes* general non-fiction and fiction, economics, general science.

S Fischer Verlag GmbH

Postfach 700355, 60553 Frankfurt am Main
☎00 49 69 60620 Fax 00 49 69 6062214
Website www.s-fischer.de

FOUNDED 1886. Part of the **Holtzbrinck** Group. *Publishes* fiction, general non-fiction, essays, literature, literary criticism.

Carl Hanser Verlag

Postfach 860420, 81631 Munich
☎00 49 89 998300 Fax 00 49 89 984809
Email info@hanser.de
Website www.hanser.de

Managing Director, Non-Fiction *Wolfgang Beisler*
Managing Director, Fiction *Michael Krüger*

FOUNDED in 1928 in Munich. *Publishes* international and German contemporary literature; classics, anthropology, non-fiction on social sciences and the arts; children's and juveniles; specialist books on engineering, natural science, plastics, computers and computer science, economics and management, dentistry. *Subsidiaries* **Paul Zsolnay Verlag**, Vienna; Sanssouci Verlag, Zurich; Verlag Nagel & Kimche, Zurich; Fachbuchverlag Leipzig, Leipzig; Hanser Gardner Publications, Cincinatti.

Wilhelm Heyne Verlag

Paul-Heyse-Strasse 28, 80336 Munich
☎00 49 89 5148-0 Fax 00 49 89 5148-2103
Website www.heyne.de

FOUNDED 1934. *Publishes* fiction, mystery, romance, humour, science fiction, fantasy, astrology, biography, cookery, film, history, how-to, occult, psychology, psychiatry, video.

Hoffmann und Campe Verlag GmbH

Postfach 130444, 20139 Hamburg
☎00 49 40 441880 Fax 00 49 40 44188-202
Website www.hoffmann-und-campe.de

FOUNDED 1781. *Publishes* fiction and general non-fiction; art, biography, dance, history, music, poetry, philosophy, psychology, psychiatry, general science, social sciences, sociology.

Verlagsgruppe Georg von Holtzbrinck GmbH

Gänsheidestrasse 26, 70184 Stuttgart
☎00 49 711 21500 Fax 00 49 711 2150100
Email info@holtzbrinck.com
Website www.holtzbrinck.com

FOUNDED 1948. One of the world's largest publishing groups with 12 book publishing houses and 40 imprints. Also publishes the newspapers, *Handelsblatt* and *Die Zeit*.

Hüthig GmbH & Co. KG

Postfach 102869, 69121 Heidelberg
☎00 49 6221 489-0 Fax 00 49 6221 489-279

Website www.huethig.de

FOUNDED 1925. Germany's fourth largest professional publisher.

Ernst Klett Verlag GmbH

Rotebühlstrasse 77, 70178 Stuttgart
☎00 49 711 6672-0
Fax 00 49 711 6672-2000
Website www.klett.de

FOUNDED 1897. *Publishes* education, geography, geology.

Langenscheidt Verlagsgruppe

Postfach 401120, 80711 Munich 40
☎00 49 89 36096-0 Fax 00 49 89 36096-376
Website www.langenscheidt.de

FOUNDED 1856. *Publishes* dictionaries, reference, maps, travel guides, how-to, language.

Gustav Lübbe Verlag GmbH

Postfach 200180, 51431 Bergisch Gladbach
☎00 49 2202 1210 Fax 00 49 2202 121928
Website www.lubbe.de

FOUNDED 1963. *Publishes* fiction and general non-fiction, archaeology, biography, history, how-to.

Propylän Verlag, Zweigniederlassung Berlin der Ullstein Buchverlage GmbH

Postfach 8030, 10888 Berlin
☎00 49 30 25913500
Fax 00 49 30 25913533

FOUNDED 1903. *Publishes* fiction and general non-fiction, romance, mysteries, architecture and interior design, art, biography, dance, film, video, education, essays, ethnology, geography, geology, government, health, history, how-to, humour, literature, literary criticism, maritime, military science, music, nutrition, poetry, political science, general science, social sciences, sociology, travel.

Rowohlt Taschenbuch Verlag GmbH

Postfach 1349, 21462 Reinbeck
☎00 49 40 72720 Fax 00 49 40 7272319
Website www.rowohlt.de

FOUNDED 1953. *Publishes* fiction and general non-fiction; archaeology, art, computer science, crafts, education, essays, games and hobbies, government, political science, history, literature, literary criticism, philosophy, psychology, psychiatry, religion, general science, social sciences, sociology.

Springer-Verlag GmbH & Co KG

Postfach 105280, 69042 Heidelberg
☎00 49 6221 4870
Fax 00 49 6221 487-8366
Website www.springer.de

FOUNDED 1842. *Publishes* agriculture, architecture and interior design, art, astronomy, behavioural sciences, business, biological sciences, chemical engineering, civil engineering, computer science, criminology, dentistry, economics, finance, geography, geology, government, health, nutrition, history, library and information sciences, management, marketing, mechanical engineering, electronics, electrical engineering, general engineering, earth sciences, environmental studies, law, mathematics, medicine, nursing, political science, philosophy, psychology, psychiatry, physics, general science, social sciences, sociology, technology.

Suhrkamp Verlag

Postfach 101945, 60019 Frankfurt am Main
☎00 49 69 756010
Fax 00 49 69 75601314
Website www.suhrkamp.de

FOUNDED 1950. *Publishes* fiction, poetry, biography, philosophy, psychology, psychiatry, general science.

Taschen GmbH

Hohenzollernring 53, 50672 Cologne
☎00 49 221 201800
Fax 00 49 221 254919
Email contact@taschen.com
Website www.taschen.com

FOUNDED 1980. *Publishes* photography, art, erotica, architecture and interior design.

K. Thienemanns Verlag

Blumenstr 36, 70182 Stuttgart
☎00 49 711 210550
Fax 00 49 711 2105539
Website www.thienemanns.de

FOUNDED 1849. *Publishes* fiction and general non-fiction.

WEKA Firmengruppe GmbH & Co KG

Postfach 1209, 86425 Kissing
☎00 49 8233 230
Fax 00 49 8233 237266

FOUNDED 1973. Germany's largest professional publisher.

Italy

Adelphi Edizioni SpA
Via S. Giovanni sul Muro 14, 20121 Milan
☎00 39 2 725731 Fax 00 39 2 89010337
Website www.adelphi.it
FOUNDED 1962. *Publishes* fiction, literature, literary criticism, essays, mysteries, poetry, anthropology, biography, history, mathematics, philosophy, physics, psychology, religion, general science.

Bompiana–RCS Libri
Via Mecenate 91, 20138 Milan
☎00 39 2 50951 Fax 00 39 2 5065361
Website www.rcslibri.it
FOUNDED 1929. *Publishes* fiction and general non-fiction, art, drama, theatre and general science.

Bulzoni Editore SRL (Le Edizioni Universitarie d'Italia)
Via Dei Liburni 14, 00185 Rome
☎00 39 6 4455207 Fax 00 39 6 4450355
FOUNDED 1969. *Publishes* fiction, literature, literary criticism, essays, art, drama, general engineering, film, law, language, linguistics, philosophy, general science, social sciences, sociology, theatre, video.

Nuova Casa Editrice Licinio Cappelli GEM srl
Via Farini 14, 40124 Bologna
☎00 39 51 239060 Fax 00 39 51 239286
Website www.cappellieditore.com
FOUNDED 1851. *Publishes* fiction, art, biography, drama, film, government, history, music, dance, poetry, medicine, nursing, dentistry, philosophy, political science, psychology, psychiatry, religion, general science, social sciences, sociology, theatre, video.

Garzanti Editore
Via Newton 18A, 20148 Milan
☎00 39 2 487941 Fax 00 39 2 48794292
FOUNDED 1861. *Publishes* fiction, literature, literary criticism, essays, art, biography, history, poetry, government, political science.

Giunti Publishing Group
Via Bolognese 165, 50139 Florence
☎00 39 55 66791 Fax 00 39 55 6679298
FOUNDED 1840. *Publishes* fiction, literature, literary criticism, essays, art, chemistry, chemical engineering, education, history, how-to, language arts, linguistics, mathematics, psychology, psychiatry, general science. Italian publishers of National Geographical Society books.

Ernesto Gremese Editore SRL
Via Virginia Agnelli 88, 00151 Rome
☎00 39 6 65740507 Fax 00 39 6 65740509
Website www.gremese.com
FOUNDED 1954. *Publishes* fiction, art, erotica, astrology, cookery, crafts, dance, drama, film, video, fashion, games, hobbies, essays, literature, literary criticism, health and nutrition, house and home, how-to, music, occult, sport, travel, theatre, television, radio, wine and spirits.

Longanesi & C
Corso Italia 13, 20122 Milan
☎00 39 2 8692640 Fax 00 39 2 72000306
Website www.longanesi.it
FOUNDED 1946. *Publishes* fiction, art, biography, dance, history, how-to, medicine, nursing, dentistry, music, philosophy, psychology, psychiatry, religion, general and social sciences, sociology.

Arnoldo Mondadori Editore SpA
Via Mondadori, 20090 Segrate (Milan)
☎00 39 2 75421 Fax 00 39 2 75422302
Website www.mondadori.com
FOUNDED 1907. *Publishes* fiction, mystery, romance, art, biography, dance, dentistry, history, how-to, medicine, music, poetry, philosophy, psychology, psychiatry, religion, nursing, general science, education.

Società Editrice Il Mulino
Str Maggiore 37, 40125 Bologna
☎00 39 51 256011 Fax 00 39 51 256034
Website www.mulino.it
FOUNDED 1954. *Publishes* economics, government, history, law, language arts, linguistics, philosophy, political science, psychology, psychiatry, social sciences, sociology.

Gruppo Ugo Mursia Editore SpA
Via Mellhiorre Gioia 45, 20124 Milan
☎00 39 2 6737 8500 Fax 00 39 2 6737 8605
FOUNDED 1922. *Publishes* fiction, poetry, art, biography, education, history, maritime, philosophy, religion, sport, general science, social sciences, sociology.

RCS Libri SpA
Via Mecenate 91, 20138 Milan
☎00 39 2 50951 Fax 00 39 2 5065361
Website www.rcslibri.it

FOUNDED 1945. *Publishes* art, crafts, dance, business, games, hobbies, history, music, medicine, nursing, dentistry, outdoor recreation, general science.

Società Editrice Internazionale – SEI
Corso Regina Margherita 176, 10152 Turin
☎00 39 11 52271 Fax 00 39 11 5211320
FOUNDED 1908. *Publishes* literature, literary criticism, essays, education, geography, geology, history, mathematics, philosophy, physics, religion, psychology, psychiatry.

Sonzogno
Via Mecenate 91, 20138 Milan
☎00 39 2 50951 Fax 00 39 2 5065361
Website www.rcslibri.it
FOUNDED 1818. *Publishes* fiction, mysteries, and general non-fiction.

Sperling e Kupfer Editori SpA
Via Durazzo 4, 20134 Milan
☎00 39 2 217211 Fax 00 39 2 21721277
FOUNDED 1899. *Publishes* fiction and general non-fiction, biography, economics, health, how-to, management, nutrition, general science, sport, travel.

Sugarco Edizioni SRL
Via Fermi 9, 21040 Carnago (Varese)
☎00 39 331 985511 Fax 00 39 331 985385
FOUNDED 1956. *Publishes* fiction, biography, history, how-to, philosophy.

Todariana Editrice
Via Gardone 29, 20139 Milan
☎00 39 2 56812953 Fax 00 39 2 55213405
FOUNDED 1967. *Publishes* fiction, poetry, science fiction, fantasy, literature, literary criticism, essays, language arts, linguistics, psychology, psychiatry, social sciences, sociology, travel.

The Netherlands
A.W. Bruna Uitgevers BV
Postbus 40203, 3504 AA Utrecht
☎00 31 30 247 0411 Fax 00 31 30 241 0018
FOUNDED 1868. *Publishes* fiction and general non-fiction; thrillers, suspense, mysteries, computer science, history, philosophy, psychology, psychiatry, general science, social sciences, sociology.

BZZTÔH Publishers
Laan van Meerdervoort 10,
2517 AJ The Hague
☎00 31 70 363 2934 Fax 00 31 70 363 1932
Website www.bzztoh.nl
FOUNDED 1970. *Publishes* fiction, mysteries, literature, literary criticism, essays, general non-fiction, animals, astrology, biography, cookery, dance, humour, music, philosophy, self-help, health and nutrition, occult, pets, religion (Buddhist, Hindhu, Jewish), romance, sport, travel, women's studies.

Elsevier Science BV
Sara Burgehartst. 25, 1055 KV Amsterdam
☎00 31 20 586 2911 Fax 00 31 20 485 2457
Website www.elsevier.nl
FOUNDED 1946. Parent company – Reed Elsevier. *Publishes* sciences (all fields), medicine, nursing, dentistry, economics, engineering (computer, chemical and general), mathematics, physics, technology.

Kluwer Academic Publishers
Postbus 17, 3300 AA Dordrecht
☎00 31 78 657 6000 Fax 00 31 78 657 6254
Website www.wkap.nl
FOUNDED 1889. *Publishes* education, medical, technical encyclopedias, trade books and journals, law, life sciences, humanities, social sciences, environmental sciences, engineering.

Uitgeversmaatschappij J. H. Kok BV
PO Box 5019, 8260 GA Kampen
☎00 31 38 339 2555 Fax 00 31 38 332 7331
FOUNDED 1894. *Publishes* fiction, poetry, history, religion, general science, social sciences, sociology.

M & P Publishing House
Postbus 170, 3990 DD Houten
☎00 31 30 637 7736 Fax 00 31 30 637 7764
FOUNDED 1974. *Publishes* general non-fiction.

J.M. Meulenhoff & Co BV
Postbus 100, 1000 AC Amsterdam
☎00 31 20 553 3500 Fax 00 31 20 625 8511
FOUNDED 1895. *Publishes* international co-productions, fiction and general non-fiction. Specialises in Dutch and translated literature.

Pearson Education Netherlands
Concertgebouwplein 25, 1071 LM Amsterdam
☎00 31 20 575 5800 Fax 00 31 20 664 5334

Website www.pearsoneducation.nl

FOUNDED 1942. *Publishes* education, business, computer science, economics, management, technology.

Uitgeverij Het Spectrum BV
Postbus 2073, 3500 GB Utrecht
☎00 31 30 265 0650 Fax 00 31 30 262 0850
FOUNDED 1935. *Publishes* science fiction, fantasy, literature, literary criticism, essays, mysteries, criminology, general non-fiction, computer science, history, astrology, occult, management, environmental studies, travel.

Unieboek BV
Postbus 97, 3990 DB Houten
☎00 31 30 637 7660 Fax 00 31 30 637 7600
FOUNDED 1891. *Publishes* fiction, general non-fiction, architecture and interior design, government, political science, literature, literary criticism, essays, archaeology, cookery, history.

Uniepers BV
Postbus 69, 1390 AB Abcoude
☎00 31 29 428 5111 Fax 00 31 29 428 3013
FOUNDED 1961. *Publishes* (mostly in co-editions) antiques, anthropology, archaeology, architecture and interior design, art, culture, dance, history, music, natural history.

Norway

H. Aschehoug & Co (W. Nygaard) A/S
Postboks 363, Sentrum, 0102 Oslo
☎00 47 22 400400 Fax 00 47 22 206395
Website www.aschehoug.no
FOUNDED 1872. *Publishes* fiction and general non-fiction, general science, social sciences, sociology.

J.W. Cappelens Forlag A/S
Postboks 350, Sentrum, 0101 Oslo
☎00 47 22 365000 Fax 00 47 22 365040
FOUNDED 1829. *Publishes* fiction, general non-fiction, religion.

N.W. Damm & Søn A/S
Fridtjof Nansenvei 14, 0055 Oslo
☎00 47 24 051000 Fax 00 47 24 051290
Website www.damm.no
FOUNDED 1843. Owned by the Egmont Group. *Publishes* general non-fiction, education, reference and translated fiction.

Ex Libris Forlag A/S
Postboks 2130, Grünerløkka, 0505 Oslo
☎00 47 22 809500 Fax 00 47 22 385160
FOUNDED 1982. *Publishes* cookery, health, nutrition, humour, human relations, publishing and book trade reference.

Gyldendal Norsk Forlag A/S
Postboks 6860, St Olavs Plass, 0130 Oslo
☎00 47 22 034100 Fax 00 47 22 034105
Website www.gyldendal.no
FOUNDED 1925. *Publishes* fiction, science fiction, fantasy, art, dance, biography, government, political science, history, how-to, music, social sciences, sociology, poetry, philosophy, psychology, psychiatry, religion.

Tiden Norsk Forlag
PO Box 8813, Youngstorget, 0028 Oslo
☎00 47 22 007100 Fax 00 46 22 426458
FOUNDED 1933. *Publishes* fiction, general non-fiction; essays, literature, literary criticism, science fiction, fantasy, management.

Portugal

Bertrand Editora Lda
Rua Anchieta 29–1, 1200 Lisbon
☎00 351 1 3468286 Fax 00 351 1 3479728
FOUNDED 1727. *Publishes* art, essays, literature, literary criticism, social sciences, sociology.

Editorial Caminho SARL
Al Santo Antonio dos Capuchos 6B, 1100 Lisbon
☎00 351 1 3152683 Fax 00 351 1 534346
FOUNDED 1977. *Publishes* fiction, government, political science.

Livraria Civilização (Américo Fraga Lamares & Ca Lda)
Rua Alberto Aires de Gouveia 27, 4000 Porto
☎00 351 2 20002286
FOUNDED 1921. *Publishes* fiction, art, economics, history, social sciences, political science, government, sociology.

Publicações Dom Quixote Lda
Rua Luciano Cordiero 116–2, 1098 Lisbon
☎00 351 21 538079 Fax 00 351 21 574595
FOUNDED 1965. *Publishes* fiction, poetry, education, history, philosophy, general science, social sciences, sociology.

Publicações Europa-América Lda
Estrada Nacional 249 (Lisboa-Sintra), Km 14,
2725–397 Mem Martins
☎00 351 21 926 7700
Fax 00 351 21 926 7771
FOUNDED 1945. *Publishes* fiction, poetry, art,
biography, dance, education, general engineering, history, how-to, music, philosophy, medicine, nursing, dentistry, psychology, psychiatry, general science, social sciences, sociology,
technology.

Gradiva–Publicações Lda
Rua Almeida e Sousa 21–r/c Esq,
1399 041 Lisbon
☎00 351 1 3974067 Fax 00 351 1 3953471
Website www.gravida.pt
FOUNDED 1981. *Publishes* fiction, literature,
literary criticism, essays, science fiction, fantasy,
romance, anthropology, Asian studies, astronomy, behavioural sciences. biological science,
communications, computer science, crafts,
earth sciences, education, games, hobbies,
economics, general engineering, geography,
geology, government, political studies, journalism, natural history, history, humour, environmental studies, human relations, management,
mathematics, philosophy, general science,
physics, psychology, psychiatry, social sciences,
sociology.

Livros Horizonte Lda
Rua Chagas 17 - 1 Dto, 1200 Lisbon
☎00 351 1 3466917 Fax 00 351 1 3326921
FOUNDED 1953. *Publishes* art, education, history, psychology, psychiatry, social sciences,
sociology.

Editorial Verbo SA
Rua Carlos Testa 1–2, 1000 Lisbon
☎00 351 1 3562131 Fax 00 351 1 3865396
FOUNDED 1959. *Publishes* education, history,
general science.

Spain
Alianza Editorial SA
Juan Ignacio Luca de Tena 15, 28027 Madrid
☎00 349 1 393 8888 Fax 00 349 1 320 7480
Website alianzaeditorial.es
FOUNDED 1965. *Publishes* fiction, poetry, art,
history, mathematics, dance, music, philosophy, government, political science, social sciences, sociology, general science.

Ediciones Anaya SA
Juan Ignacio Luca de Tena 15, 28027 Madrid
☎00 349 1 393 8600 Fax 00 349 1 742 6631
FOUNDED 1959. *Publishes* education.

Editorial Don Quijote
Compás del Porvenir 6, 41013 Seville
☎00 349 5 423 5080
FOUNDED 1981. *Publishes* fiction, literature, literary criticism, poetry, essays, drama, theatre,
history.

EDHASA (Editora y Distribuidora Hispano – Americana SA)
Av Diagonal 519–521, 08029 Barcelona
☎00 349 3 494 9720 Fax 00 349 3 419 4584
Website www.edhasa.es
FOUNDED 1946. *Publishes* fiction, literature,
literary criticism, essays, history.

Editorial Espasa–Calpe SA
Apdo de correos 547, Carreterade Irún Km
12, 200, 28049 Madrid
☎00 349 1 358 9689 Fax 00 349 1 358 8679
Website www.espasa.es
FOUNDED 1925. *Publishes* fiction, science fiction, fantasy, English as a second language,
general non-fiction, art, child care and development, cookery, biography, essays, history,
literature, literary criticism, self-help, social sciences, sociology.

Grijalbo Mondadori SA
Arago 385, 08013 Barcelona
☎00 349 3 476 7110 Fax 00 349 3 476 7119
Website www.grijalbo.com
FOUNDED 1962. *Publishes* fiction, general non-
fiction, architecture and interior design, gardening, plants, humour, literature, literary criticism, essays, poetry, human relations.

Grupo CEAC SA
Aragón 472, 08013 Barcelona
☎00 349 3 247 2424 Fax 00 349 3 231 5115
Website www.ceacedit.com
Publishes education, technology, science fic-
tion, fantasy.

Ediciónes Hiperión SL
Calle Salustiano Olózaga 14, 28001 Madrid
☎00 349 1 557 6015 Fax 00 349 1 435 8690
Website www.hiperion.com
FOUNDED 1976. *Publishes* literature, literary
criticism, essays, poetry, language arts, religion
(Islamic and Jewish).

Editorial Luis Vives (Edelvives)
C/Xaudaró 25, 28034 Madrid
☎00 349 1 334 4883
Fax 00 349 1 334 4892
FOUNDED 1890. *Publishes* education.

Editorial Molino
Calabria 166, 08015 Barcelona
☎00 349 3 226 0625
Fax 00 349 3 226 6998
Website www.editorialmolino.com
FOUNDED 1933. *Publishes* education, sport, fiction.

Pearson Educacion SA
Nunez de Balboa 120, 28006 Madrid
☎00 349 1 590 3432
Fax 00 349 1 590 3448
FOUNDED 1942. *Publishes* art, education, history, language arts, linguistics, medicine, nursing, dentistry, general science, psychology, psychiatry, philosophy.

Editorial Planeta SA
Córsega 273–277, 08008 Barcelona
☎00 349 3 228 5800
Fax 00 349 3 217 7140
Website www.planeta.com
FOUNDED 1952. *Publishes* fiction and general non-fiction.

Editorial Seix Barral SA
Provenza 260, 08008 Barcelona
☎00 349 3 496 7003
Fax 00 349 3 496 7004
Website www.seix-barral.es
FOUNDED 1945. Part of Grupo Planeta. Foreign language publisher of literature.

Tusquets Editores
Cesare Cantù 8, 08023 Barcelona
☎00 349 3 253 0400
Fax 00 349 3 417 6703
Website www.tusquets-editores.com
FOUNDED 1969. *Publishes* fiction, biography, essays, literature, literary criticism, general science.

Sweden

Albert Bonniers Förlag
PO Box 3159, S-103 63 Stockholm
☎00 46 8 696 8000   Fax 00 46 8 696 8361
FOUNDED 1837. *Publishes* fiction and general non-fiction.

Bokförlaget Bra Böcker AB
PO Box 890, S-20180 Malmo
☎00 46 40 665 4500
Fax 00 46 40 665 4622
Website www.bbb.se
FOUNDED 1965. *Publishes* fiction, geography, geology, history.

Brombergs Bokförlag AB
PO Box 12886, S-112 98 Stockholm
☎00 46 8 5626 2080
Fax 00 46 8 5626 2085
Website www.brombergs.se
FOUNDED 1973. *Publishes* fiction and general non-fiction.

Bokförlaget Forum AB
PO Box 70321, S-107 23 Stockholm
☎00 46 8 696 8440   Fax 00 46 8 696 8367
FOUNDED 1944. *Publishes* fiction and general non-fiction.

Bokförlaget Natur och Kultur
PO Box 27323, S-102 54 Stockholm
☎00 46 8 4538600   Fax 00 46 8 4538790
Email info@nok.se
Website www.nok.se
FOUNDED 1922. *Publishes* fiction and general non-fiction; biography, history, psychology, psychiatry and general science.

Norstedts Förlag
Box 2052, S-103 12 Stockholm
☎00 46 8 7698700   Fax 00 46 8 7698864
Website www.norstedt.se
FOUNDED 1823. *Publishes* fiction and general non-fiction.

Rabén och Sjögren Bokförlag
PO Box 2052, S-103 12 Stockholm
☎00 46 8 7698800   Fax 00 46 8 7698813
Website www.raben.se
FOUNDED 1942. *Publishes* general non-fiction.

Richters Egmont
Ostra Förstadsgatan 46, 205 75 Malmö
☎00 46 40 380600   Fax 00 46 40 933708
FOUNDED 1942. *Publishes* fiction.

B. Wählströms Bokförlag AB
Box 30022, S-104 25 Stockholm
☎00 46 8 6198600   Fax 00 46 8 6189761
Website www.wahlstroms.se
FOUNDED 1911. *Publishes* fiction and general non-fiction.

Switzerland

Arche Verlag AG, Raabe und Vitali
Postfach 112, CH-8030 Zurich
☎00 41 1 2522410 Fax 00 41 1 2611115
FOUNDED 1944. *Publishes* literature and literary criticism, essays, biography, fiction, poetry, music, dance, travel.

Diogenes Verlag AG
Sprecherstr 8, CH-8032 Zurich
☎00 41 1 2548511 Fax 00 41 1 2528407
Email info@diogenes.ch
Website www.diogenes.ch
FOUNDED 1952. *Publishes* fiction, essays, literature, literary criticism, mysteries, art, drama, theatre, philosophy.

Langenscheidt AG Zürich-Zug
Postfach 326, CH-8021 Zurich
☎00 41 1 2115000 Fax 00 41 1 2122149
Part of **Langenscheidt Group**, Germany. *Publishes* language arts and linguistics.

Larousse (Suisse) SA
c/o Acces-Direct, 3 Route du Grand-Mont, CH-1052 Le Mont-sur-Lausanne
☎00 41 21 335336
Publishes dictionaries, reference and textbooks. Part of **Librairie Larousse**, France.

Neptun-Verlag
Postfach 307, CH-8280 Kreuzlingen
☎00 41 72 727262 Fax 00 41 72 642023
FOUNDED 1946. *Publishes* history and travel.

Orell Füssli Verlag
Nuschelerstrasse 22, CH-8022 Zurich
☎00 41 1 2113630 Fax 00 41 1 4667412
Website www.orell-fuessli-verlag.ch
FOUNDED 1519. *Publishes* art, biography, economics, education, geography, geology, history, how-to.

Editions Payot Lausanne
CP 529, CH-1001 Lausanne
☎00 41 21 3290264
Fax 00 41 21 3290266
FOUNDED 1875. *Publishes* general non-fiction, anthropology, archaeology, architecture and interior design, dance, education, history, law, medicine, nursing, dentistry, music, philosophy, literature, literary criticism, essays, general science, social sciences and sociology.

Sauerländer AG
Laurenzenvorstadt 89, CH-5001 Aarau
☎00 41 64 8268626
Fax 00 41 64 8245780
Website www.sauerlaender.ch
FOUNDED 1807. *Publishes* education and general non-fiction.

Scherz Verlag AG
Theaterplatz 4–6, CH-3000 Berne 7
☎00 41 31 3277150
Fax 00 41 31 3277171
Website www.scherzverlag.ch
FOUNDED 1939. *Publishes* fiction and general non-fiction; biography, history, psychology, psychiatry, philosophy, parapsychology.

European Television Companies

Austria

ORF (Österreichisher Rundfunk)
Würzburggasse 30, A–1136 Vienna
☎00 43 1 87 8780 Fax 00 43 1 87 8782550
Website www.orf.at

Belgium

Radio-Télévision Belge de la Communauté Française (RTBF)
Boulevard Auguste Reyers 52, B–1044 Brussels
☎00 32 2 737 2111 Fax 00 32 2 737 2936
Website www.rtbf.be

Vlaamse Radio en Televisieomroep (VRT)
Omroepcentrum, Reyerslaan 52, B–1043 Brussels
☎00 32 2 741 3111 Fax 00 32 2 739 9351
Email info@vrt.be
Website www.vrt.be

Vlaamse Televisie Maatschappij (VTM) (cable)
Medialaan 1, B–1800 Vilvoorde
☎00 32 2 255 3211 Fax 00 32 2 252 5141
Email info@vtm.be
Website www.vtm.be

Denmark

Danmarks Radio–TV
TV-Byen, DK–2860 Søborg
☎00 45 35 20 3040 Fax 00 45 35 20 2644
Email dr@dr.dk
Website www.dr.dk

TV Danmark
Langebrogade 6A, DK–1411 Copenhagen K, Denmark
☎00 45 70 10 1010 Fax 00 45 32 69 9699
Email info@tvdanmark.dk
Website www.tvdanmark.dk

TV–2 Danmark
Rugaardsvej 25, DK–5100 Odense C
☎00 45 65 91 9191 Fax 00 45 65 91 3322
Website www.tv2.dk

Finland

MTV3 Finland
Ilmalantori 2, FIN–00240 Helsinki
☎00 358 9 15001 Fax 00 358 9 1500707
Website www.mtv3.fi

Yleisradio Oy (YLE)
PO Box 90, FIN–00024 Yleisradio
☎00 358 9 14801 Fax 00 358 9 14803215
Email fbc@yle.fi
Website www.yle.fi

France

Arte France (cable & satellite)
8 rue Marceau, 92785 Issy les Moulineaux Cedex 9
☎00 33 1 55 00 77 77
Fax 00 33 1 55 00 77 00
Website www.arte-tv.com

Canal + (pay TV)
85–89 quai André Citroën, 75711 Paris Cedex 15
☎00 33 1 44 25 10 00
Website www.cplus.fr

France 5
10–12 rue Horace-Vernet, 92785 Issy-les-Moulineaux Cedex 9
☎00 33 1 56 22 91 91
Fax 00 33 1 56 22 95 95
Website www.france5.fr

France Télévision (France 2/ France 3)
7 Esplanade Henri de France, 75907 Paris Cedex 15
☎00 33 1 56 22 42 42(France 2)/30 30 (France 3)
Website www.france2.fr *and* www.france3.fr

M6 (Métropole Télévision)
89 ave Charles de Gaulle, 92575 Neuilly-sur-Seine Cedex
☎00 33 1 41 92 66 66
Fax 00 33 1 41 92 66 10
Website www.m6.fr

RFO (Radio Télévision Française d'Outre-mer)

5 ave du Recteur Poincaré, 75016 Paris
☎00 33 1 42 15 71 00
Email rfo@rfo.fr
Website www.rfo.fr

TF1 (Télévision Française 1)

1 quai du Pont du Jour, 92656 Boulogne
☎00 33 1 41 41 12 34
Fax 00 33 1 41 41 28 40
Website www.tf1.fr

Germany

ARD – Das Erste

ARD Büro, Bertramstr 8, 60320 Frankfurt am Main
☎00 49 69 59 0607 Fax 00 49 69 15 52075
Website www.daserste.de

Arte Germany (cable & satellite)

Schützenstrasse 1, 76530 Baden–Baden
☎00 49 7221 9369–0
Website www.arte.de

ZDF (Zweites Deutsches Fernsehen)

Postfach 40 40, 55100 Mainz
☎00 49 61 31/701 Fax 00 49 61 31 702157
Email info@zdf.de
Website www.zdf.de

Republic of Ireland

Radio Telefís Éireann (RTE – RTE 1)

Donnybrook, Dublin 4
☎00 353 1 208 3111 Fax 00 353 1 208 3080
Website www.rte.ie

Teilefís na Gaelige

Baile na hAbhann, Co. na Gaillimhe
☎00 353 91 505050 Fax 00 353 91 505021
Website www.tg4.ie

Italy

RAI (RadioTelevisione Italiana)

Viale Mazzini 14, 00195 Rome
☎00 39 06 3878–1 Fax 00 39 06 372 5680
Website www.rai.it

Tele piu' (pay TV)

Via Piranesi 44/46, 20137 Milan

☎00 39 02 700 271 Fax 00 39 02 700 27201
Email infopiu@telepiu.it
Website www.telepiu.it

The Netherlands

AVRO (Algemene Omroep Vereniging)

Postbus 2, 1200 JA Hilversum
☎00 31 35 671 79 11 Fax 00 31 35 671 74 39
Website www.central.avro.nl/index.asp

IKON

Postbus 10009, 1201 DA Hilversum
☎00 31 35 672 72 72 Fax 00 31 35 621 51 00
Email ikon@ikon.nl
Website www.omroep.nl/ikon

NCRV (Nederlandse Christelijke Radio Vereniging)

Postbus 25000, 1202 HB Hilversum
☎00 31 35 671 99 11 Fax 00 31 35 671 92 85
Website www.info.omroep.nl/ncrv

NOS (Nederlandse Omroep Stichting)

Sumatralaan 45, 1217 GP Hilversum
☎00 31 35 677 92 22 Fax 00 31 35 677 4863
Website www.omroep.nl/nos/noshome/
index.html

NPS (Nederlandse Programma Stichting)

Postbus 29000, 1202 MA Hilversum
☎00 31 35 677 9333
Website www.omroep.nl/nps

TROS (Televisie en Radio Omroep Stichting)

Postbus 28300, 1202 LH Hilversum
☎00 31 35 671 57 15 Fax 00 31 35 671 53 16
Website www.omroep.nl/tros

VARA

Postbus 175, 1200 AD Hilversum
☎00 31 35 671 19 11 Fax 00 31 35 671 13 40
Email vara@vara.nl
Website www.omroep.nl/vara

VPRO

Postbus 11, 1200 JC Hilversum
☎00 31 35 671 29 11 Fax 00 31 35 671 25 41
Email info@vpro.nl
Website www.vpro.nl

Norway

NRK (Norsk Rikskringkasting), N–0340 Oslo
☎00 47 23 04 7000 Fax 00 47 23 04 7575
Email info@nrk.no
Website www.nrk.no

TVNorge
Biskop Gunnerus gate 6, N–0155 Oslo
☎00 47 21 02 2000 Fax 00 47 22 05 1000
Email tvnorge@tvnorge.no
Website www.tvnorge.no

TV2
Postboks 7222, N–5020 Bergen
☎00 47 55 90 8070 Fax 00 47 55 90 8090
Website www.tv2.no

Portugal

Radiotelevisão Portuguesa (RTP)
Avenida 5 de Outubro 197, 1050–054 Lisbon
☎00 351 21 794 7000
Website www.rtp.pt

TVI (Televisão Independente)
Rua Mário Castelhano 40, Queluz de Baixo,
2749–502 Barcarena
☎00 351 21 434 7500
Website www.tvi.pt

Spain

RTVE (RadioTelevision Española)
Edificio Prado del Rey, E–28223 Madrid
☎00 349 1 581 7238 Fax 00 349 1 581 7239
Website www.rtve.es

Sweden

Sveriges Television AB–SVT
Oxenstierngatan 26–34, S–105 10 Stockholm
☎00 46 8 784 0000 Fax 00 46 8 784 1500

Email information@svt.se
Website www.svt.se

TV4
Tegeluddsvägen 3, S–115 79 Stockholm
☎00 46 8 459 4000 Fax 00 46 8 459 4444
Website www.tv4.se

Switzerland

RTR (Radio e Televisiun Rumantscha) (Romansch language TV)
Via dal Teater 1, CH–7002 Cuira
☎00 41 81 255 7575 Fax 00 41 81 255 7500
Website www.rtr.ch

RTSI (Radiotelevisione svizzera di lingua Italiana) (Italian language TV)
Casella postale, CH–6903 Lugano
☎00 41 91 803 51 11 Fax 00 41 91 803 5355
Website www.rtsi.ch

SF DRS (Schweizer Fernsehen) (German language TV)
Fernsehenstrasse 1–4, CH–8052 Zurich
☎00 41 1 305 66 11 Fax 00 41 1 305 56 60
Email sfdrs@sfdrs
Website www.sfdrs.ch

SRG SSR idée suisse (Swiss Broadcasting Corp.)
Giacomettistr 3, CH–3000 Berne15
☎00 41 31 350 91 11 Fax 00 41 31 350 92 56
Website www.srg-ssr.ch

TSR (Télévision Suisse Romande)
Quai Ernest Ansermet 20,
CH–1211 Geneva 8
☎00 41 22 708 99 11
Fax 00 41 22 708 98 00
Website www.tsr.ch

US Publishers

Anyone corresponding with the big American publishers should know that following the terrorist attacks of 11 September 2001 they are very wary of any package or letter that looks in any way suspicious. Of course, this begs the question what is or what is not suspicious which is as difficult to answer as what makes or does not make a good novel. The best policy is to make an initial enquiry by e-mail.

International Reply Coupons (IRCs)
For return postage, send IRCs, available from post offices. Letters, 60 pence; mss according to weight. For current postal rates to the UK go to the United States Postal Service website at www.usps.com and click on 'Calculate Postage'.

ABC–CLIO
PO Box 1911, Santa Barbara, CA 93116–1911
☎001 805 968 1911 Fax 001 805 685 9685
Email sales@abc-clio.com
Website www.abc-clio.com
CEO *Ronald J. Boehm*
FOUNDED 1953. *Publishes* academic and reference, focusing on history and social studies; books and multimedia. No unsolicited mss; synopses and ideas welcome.
   Royalties paid annually. *UK subsidiary* **ABC-Clio Ltd**, Oxford.

Abingdon Press
PO Box 801, Nashville, TN 37202–0801
☎001 615 749 6290 Fax 001 615 749 6056
Website www.abingdon.org
Snr. VP/Editorial Director *Harriett Jane Olson*
Publishes non-fiction: religious (lay and professional), children's religious and academic texts. Over 100 titles a year. Approach in writing only with synopsis and samples; ms submission guidelines available on the website. IRCs essential.

Harry N. Abrams, Inc.
100 Fifth Avenue, New York, NY 10011
☎001 212 206 7715 Fax 001 212 645 8437
Website www.abramsbooks.com
Editor-in-Chief *Eric Himmel*
FOUNDED 1950. *Publishes* illustrated books: art, architecture, nature, entertainment and children's. No fiction. About 200 titles a year. Submit completed mss (no dot matrix), together with sample illustrations.

Academy Chicago Publishers
363 W. Erie Street, Chicago, IL 60610
☎001 312 751 7300 Fax 001 312 751 7306
Email info@academychicago.com
Website www.academychicago.com
President/Senior Editor *Anita Miller*
FOUNDED 1975. *Publishes* mainstream fiction; non-fiction: history, books for women. No romance, children's, young adult, religious, sexist or avant-garde. Send first three consecutive chapters with synopsis only, accompanied by IRCs.
   Royalties paid twice-yearly. *Distributed* in the UK and Europe by Gazelle, Lancaster.

Ace/Putnam
See **Penguin Putnam Inc.**

Adams Media Corporation
55 Littlefield Street, Avon, MA 02322
☎001 508 427 7100 Fax 001 508 427 6790
Website www.adamsmedia.com
Publishing Director *Gary M. Krebs*
FOUNDED 1980. *Publishes* general non-fiction: self-help, business, personal finance, relationships, parenting, psychology/self-improvement, reference, cooking and fitness. Send query letter with IRCs.

Addison Wesley

75 Arlington Street, Suite 300, Boston,
MA 02116
☎001 617 848 7500
Email <firstname>.<lastname>@
pearsoned.com
Website www.awl.com

Part of Pearson Education. *Publishes* academic textbooks, multimedia and learning programs in computer science, economics, finance, mathematics and statistics. See the website for submission guidelines.

University of Alabama Press

Box 870380, Tuscaloosa, AL 35487–0380
☎001 205 348 5180 Fax 001 205 348 9201

Director *Nicole Mitchell*

FOUNDED 1945. *Publishes* American history, Latin American history, American religious history; African-American and Native American studies, Judaic studies, theatre. Submissions are not invited in poetry, fiction or drama. About 50 titles a year.

Aladdin Books

See **Simon & Schuster Children's Publishing**

University of Alaska Press

PO Box 756240, University of Alaska,
Fairbanks, AK 99775–6240
☎001 907 474 5831 Fax 001 907 474 5502
Email fypress@uaf.edu
Website www.uaf.edu/uapress

Director *Claus. M. Naske*
Senior Editor *Carla Helfferich*
Acquisitions *Pam Odom*

Traces its origins back to 1927 but was relatively dormant until the early 1980s. *Publishes* scholarly works about Alaska and the North Pacific rim, with a special emphasis on circumpolar regions. 5–10 titles a year. No fiction or poetry.

DIVISIONS
Rasmuson Library Historical Translation Series; Oral Biography Series; Monograph Series; Classic Reprint Series; Lanternlight Library Informal non-fiction covering Northern interest. Unsolicited mss, synopses and ideas welcome.

Allen Lane The Penguin Press

See **Penguin Putnam Inc.**

Alyson Publications

6922 Hollywood Boulevard, Suite 1000,
Los Angeles, CA 90028
☎001 323 860 6065 Fax 001 323 467 0152
Email mail@alyson.com
Website www.alyson.com

Publisher *Greg Constante*
Senior Editor *Angela Brown*

FOUNDED 1980. *Publishes* fiction and non-fiction books of general interest to the gay and lesbian community. No unsolicited mss. Synopses and ideas for books welcome; initial contact by mail or e-mail.
Royalties paid twice-yearly.

AMACOM Books

1601 Broadway, New York, NY 10019–7406
☎001 212 586 8100 Fax 001 212 903 8083
Website www.amacombooks.org

President & Publisher *Harold V. Kennedy*

FOUNDED 1972. Owned by American Management Association. *Publishes* business books only, including general management, business communications, sales and marketing, finance, computers and information systems, career/personal growth skills, human resource management and training, research development, project management and manufacturing, quality/customer service titles. About 70 titles a year. Proposals welcome.
Royalties paid twice-yearly.

Anchor

See **Random House, Inc.**

Anvil

See **Krieger Publishing Co.**

Shaye Areheart Books

See **The Crown Publishing Group**

University of Arizona Press

355 S. Euclid Avenue, Ste. 103, Tucson,
AZ 85719–6654
☎001 520 621 1441 Fax 001 520 621 8899
Website www.uapress.arizona.edu

Director *Christine Szuter*

FOUNDED 1959. *Publishes* academic non-fiction, particularly with a regional/cultural link, plus Native-American and Hispanic literature. About 50 titles a year.

University of Arkansas Press

McIlroy House, 201 Ozark Avenue,
Fayetteville, AR 72701
☎001 479 575 3246 Fax 001 479 575 6044

Email uapress@carern.uark.edu
Website www.uapress.com

Director *Lawrence J. Malley*

FOUNDED 1980. *Publishes* scholarly monographs, poetry and general trade including
biography, etc. Particularly interested at present in scholarly works in history, politics and
literary criticism. About 30 titles a year.
Royalties paid annually.

ASM Press

1752 N. Street NW, Washington, DC 20036
Fax 001 202 942 9342
Email books@asmusa.org
Website www.asmpress.org

Managing Director *Jeff Hoffmeier*

FOUNDED 1899. The book publishing division
of the American Society for Microbiology.
Publishes monographs, texts, reference books
and manuals in microbiological sciences. Unsolicited mss, synopses and ideas welcome;
approach by mail or e-mail in the first instance.
No fiction.
Royalties paid annually.

Aspect

See **Warner Books Inc.**

Atheneum Books for Young Readers

See **Simon & Schuster Children's Publishing**

Atlantic Monthly Press

See **Grove/Atlantic Inc.**

Atria Books

See **Simon & Schuster Adult Publishing Group**

AUP (Associated University Presses)

AUP New Jersey titles are handled in the UK
by **Golden Cockerel Press** (see entry under
UK Publishers).

Avery Publishing Group, Inc.

375 Hudson Street, New York, NY 10014
☎001 212 366 2000 Fax 001 212 366 2643
Website www.penguinputnam.com

Publisher *John Duff*
Executive Editor *Laura Shepherd*

FOUNDED 1976. Imprint of **Penguin Putnam
Inc.** *Publishes* alternative and complementary
health care, nutrition, disease prevention, diet,
supplements, functional foods, mind/body

therapies, holistic healing. About 50 titles a
year. No unsolicited mss; synopses and ideas
welcome if accompanied by s.a.e./IRCs.
Royalties paid twice-yearly.

Avon Books

10 East 53rd Street, New York, NY 10022
☎001 212 207 7000 Fax 001 212 702 2525
Website www.harpercollins.com

Editor-in-Chief *Larry Ashmead*

FOUNDED 1941. An imprint of **HarperCollins
Publishers, Inc.** *Publishes* hardcover; trade
and mass-market paperback reprints and originals including fiction, non-fiction, adult, juvenile and young adult. 500 titles a year.
Submit query letter and sample chapter.

Baker Book House

PO Box 6287, Grand Rapids, MI 49516–6287
☎001 616 676 9185 Fax 001 616 676 9573
Website www.bakerbooks.com

President *Dwight Baker*
Director of Publications *Don Stephenson*

FOUNDED 1939. Began life as a used-book store
and began publishing in earnest in the 1950s, primarily serving the evangelical Christian market.
About 165 titles a year. Additional information
for authors on website.

DIVISIONS/IMPRINTS

Baker Books *Publishes* religious non-fiction
and fiction, Bible reference, professional (pas-
tors and church leaders) books, children's
books. About 80 titles a year. No unsolicited
proposals.

Baker Academic *Jim Kinney Publishes* col-
lege/seminary textbooks, religious reference
books, biblical studies monographs. About 30
titles a year. No unsolicited proposals.
Fleming H. Revell *Lonnie Hull Du Pont*
FOUNDED 1870. A family-owned business until
1978, Revell was one of the first Christian
publishers to take the step into secular publishing. Joined Baker Book House in 1992.
Publishes adult fiction and non-fiction for evangelical Christians. About 45 titles a year. No
unsolicited proposals. **Brazos Press** *Rodney
Clapp Publishes* academic and trade books in
theology, biblical studies, ethics, cultural criticism and spirituality (trade editions only).
About 15 titles a year. No unsolicited mss.
Chosen Books *Jane Campbell* FOUNDED 1971;
joined Baker Book House in 1992. *Publishes*
charismatic adult non-fiction for evangelical
Christians. About 10 titles a year. No unsolicited proposals.

Ballantine Books

1540 Broadway, 11th Floor, New York,
NY 10036 Fax 001 212 782 8439
Email bfi@randomhouse.com
Website www.randomhouse.com
President/Publisher *Gina Centrello*

FOUNDED 1952. A division of **Random House, Inc.** since 1973. *Publishes* fiction and non-fiction, science fiction.

DIVISIONS/IMPRINTS **Ballantine Books**; **Del Rey**; **Fawcett Books** Mystery; **Ivy** Romance; **Library of Contemporary Thought**; **Lucas Books**; **One World**; **Wellspring**. No unsolicited mss.

Banner Books

See **University Press of Mississippi**

Bantam Dell Publishing Group

1540 Broadway, New York, NY 10036
☎001 212 782 9000 Fax 001 212 302 7985
Website www.randomhouse.com/bantamdell
President/Publisher *Irwyn Applebaum*

FOUNDED 1945. The largest mass market paperback publisher in the USA. A division of **Random House, Inc.** *Publishes* general commercial fiction and non-fiction, young readers and children's.

DIVISIONS/IMPRINTS **Bantam Classics**; **Delacorte Press**; **Dell**; **Delta Books**; **Dial Press**; **DTP**; **Island Books**.

Barron's Educational Series, Inc.

250 Wireless Boulevard, Hauppauge,
NY 11788–3917
☎001 516 434 3311 Fax 001 516 434 3723
Email info@barronseduc.com
Website www.barronseduc.com
President *Manuel H. Barron*
Acquisitions Editor *Wayne Barr*

FOUNDED 1942. *Publishes* adult non-fiction, children's fiction and non-fiction, test preparation materials and language materials, cookbooks, pets, hobbies, sport, photography, health, business, law, computers, travel, business, art and painting. No adult fiction. 400 titles a year. Unsolicited mss, synopses and ideas for books welcome.
   Royalties paid twice-yearly.

Basic Books

See **Perseus Books Group**

Beacon Press

25 Beacon Street, Boston, MA 02108
☎001 617 742 2110 Fax 001 617 723 3097

Website www.beacon.org
Director *Helene Atwan*

FOUNDED 1854. *Publishes* general non-fiction. About 85 titles a year. Does not accept unsolicited mss. For further information, refer to website page.

Beech Tree Books

See **HarperCollins Publishers, Inc.**

Belknap Press

See **Harvard University Press**

Berkley Books

See **Penguin Putnam Inc.**

H.&R. Block

See **Simon & Schuster Adult Publishing Group**

BlueHen Books

See **Penguin Putnam Inc.**

Boulevard

See **Penguin Putnam Inc.**

Boyds Mills Press

815 Church Street, Honesdale, PA 18431
☎001 570 253 1164 Fax 001 570 253 0179
Website www.boydsmillspress.com
Publisher *Kent Brown Jr*
Manuscript Coordinator *Kathryn Yerkes*

A subsidiary of Highlights for Children, Inc. FOUNDED 1990 as a publisher of children's trade books. *Publishes* children's fiction, non-fiction and poetry. About 50 titles a year. Unsolicited mss, synopses and ideas for books welcome. No romance or fantasy novels.
   Royalties paid twice-yearly.

Bradford Books

See **The MIT Press**

Brassey's, Inc.

22841 Quicksilver Drive, Dulles, VA 20166
☎001 703 661 1548 Fax 001 703 661 1547
Email djacobs@booksintl.com
Website www.brasseysinc.com
Publisher *Don McKeon*

FOUNDED 1984 (acquired in 1999 by Books International of Dulles, Virginia). *Publishes* non-fiction titles on topics of history (especially military history), world and US affairs, US foreign policy, defence, intelligence, biography, transport (especially automobiles) and sports.

About 80 titles a year. No unsolicited mss; synopses and ideas welcome.

Royalties paid annually.

Brazos Press
See **Baker Book House**

Broadway Books
See **Doubleday Broadway Publishing Group**

University of California Press
2000 Center Street, Suite 303, Berkeley, CA 94704
☎001 510 642 4247 Fax 001 510 643 7127
Director *James H. Clark*

FOUNDED 1893. *Publishes* scholarly and scientific non-fiction; some fiction and poetry in translation. Preliminary letter with outline preferred.

Carolrhoda Books, Inc.
241 First Avenue North, Minneapolis, MN 55401
☎001 612 332 3344 Fax 001 612 332 7615
Submissions Editor *Rebecca Poole*

FOUNDED 1969. A division of the **Lerner Publishing Group**. *Publishes* children's: nature, biography, history, beginners' readers, world cultures, photo essays, historical fiction and picture books. Please send s.a.e. for author guidelines, making sure guideline requests are clearly marked on the envelope or they will be returned. 'We are *only* accepting submissions twice a year – from March 1–31 and October 1–31. Submissions postmarked with other dates will be returned unopened. Also, only submissions with s.a.e./IRCs will receive a response.'

Charlesbridge Publishing
85 Main Street, Watertown, MA 02472
☎001 617 926 0329 Fax 001 617 926 5720
Email books@charlesbridge.com
Website www.charlesbridge.com
Chairman *Brent Farmer*
Managing Editor, School Division *Elena Dworkin Wright*
Senior Editor, Trade Division *Dominic Barth*

FOUNDED 1980 as an educational publisher focused on a strategic approach to reading, writing, maths and science. *Publishes* children's educational programmes, non-fiction picture books and fiction for 3- to 12-year-olds. School division publishes mathematical fiction, *Maths Adventures*, in picture-book format and astronomy-related picture books. Complete mss or proposals welcome with self-addressed envelope and IRCs. Unsolicited mss are accepted but must be exclusive submissions. Responses are sent within three months.

University of Chicago Press
1427 East 60th Street, Chicago, IL 60637–2954
☎001 773 702 7700 Fax 001 773 702 9756
Email general@press.uchicago.edu
Website www.press.uchicago.edu
FOUNDED 1891. *Publishes* academic non-fiction only.

Children's Press
See **Scholastic Library Publishing**

Chosen Books
See **Baker Book House**

Chronicle Books LLC
85 Second Street, Sixth Floor, San Francisco, CA 94105
☎001 415 537 4200 Fax 001 415 437 4460
Email frontdesk@chroniclebooks.com
Website www.chroniclebooks.com
President/Publisher *Jack Jensen*

FOUNDED 1966. *Publishes* illustrated and non-illustrated adult trade and children's books as well as stationery and gift items. About 200 titles a year. Query or submit outline/synopsis and sample chapters and artwork. Guidelines for ms submissions on the website.

Royalties paid twice-yearly.

Clarkson Potter
See **The Crown Publishing Group**

Columbia University Press
61 West 62nd Street, New York, NY 10023
☎001 212 459 0600 Fax 001 212 459 3679
Website www.columbia.edu/cu/cup
Managing Director *William B. Strachan*
Editorial Director *Jennifer Crewe*
Approx. Annual Turnover $10 million

FOUNDED 1893. *Publishes* scholarly and general interest non-fiction, reference, translations of Asian literature. No fiction or poetry. 160 titles in 2002. Welcomes unsolicited material if the subject fits their programme (see website). Approach by regular mail only.

Royalties paid annually.

Contemporary Books
1 Prudential Plaza, Suite 900, Chicago, IL 60601
☎001 312 233 7500 Fax 001 312 233 7570

FOUNDED 1947. *Publishes* general adult non-fiction. About 400 titles a year. Submissions require s.a.e./IRCs for response.

Copper Beech Books
See **The Millbrook Press, Inc.**

Counterpoint Press
See **Perseus Books Group**

Crocodile Books, USA
See **Interlink Publishing Group, Inc.**

The Crown Publishing Group
299 Park Avenue, New York, NY 10171
☎001 212 572 2600   Fax 001 212 940 7408
Website www.randomhouse.com

FOUNDED 1933. Division of **Random House, Inc.** *Publishes* popular trade fiction and non-fiction.
IMPRINTS **Clarkson Potter** Editorial Director *Lauren Shakely* Illustrated books – cookery, gardening, style, decorating and design; **Crown Business** Editorial Director *Steve Ross* Business books; **Crown Publishers** Editorial Director *Steve Ross* General fiction and non-fiction; **Harmony Books** Editorial Director *Shaye Areheart* New Age, spirituality, religion, some fiction; **Shaye Areheart Books** Editorial Director *Shaye Areheart* Fiction; **House of Collectibles** Director *Dottie Harris* Antiques and collectibles; **Three Rivers Press** Executive Editor *Becky Cabaza* Non-fiction paperbacks.

Cumberland House Publishing
431 Harding Industrial Drive, Nashville, TN 37211
☎001 615 832 1171   Fax 001 615 832 0633
Email info@cumberlandhouse.com
Website www.cumberlandhouse.com

FOUNDED 1996. *Publishes* fiction, non-fiction, cookery and sports. Unsolicited mss, synopses and ideas welcome; approach by mail. No children's books or poetry.
Royalties paid annually.

Benjamin Cummings
1301 Sansome Street, San Francisco, CA 94111
☎001 415 402 2500   Fax 001 415 402 2591
Email question@aw.com
Website www.awl.com

Part of Pearson Education. *Publishes* academic textbooks, multimedia and learning programs in chemistry, health and life science. See the website for submission guidelines.

Currency
See **Doubleday Broadway Publishing Group**

Da Capo Press
See **Perseus Books Group**

DAW Books, Inc.
375 Hudson Street, 3rd Floor, New York, NY 10014–3658
☎001 212 366 2096/Submissions: 366 2095
Fax 001 212 366 2090
Email daw@penguinputnam.com
Website www.dawbooks.com
Publishers *Elizabeth R. Wollheim, Sheila E. Gilbert*
Submissions Editor *Peter Stampfel*

FOUNDED 1971 by Donald and Elsie Wollheim as the first mass-market publisher devoted to science fiction and fantasy. *Publishes* science fiction/fantasy, and some horror. No short stories, anthology ideas or non-fiction. Unsolicited mss, synopses and ideas for books welcome. About 36 titles a year.
Royalties paid twice-yearly.

Dearborn Financial Publishing, Inc.
155 N. Wacker Drive, Chicago, IL 60606–1719
☎001 312 836 4400   Fax 001 312 836 1021
Website www.dearborn.com
President *Eric Cantor*

FOUNDED 1967. A niche publisher serving the financial services industries. *Publishes* real estate, insurance, financial planning, securities, commodities, investments, banking, professional education, motivation and reference titles, investment reference and how-to books for the consumer (personal finance, real estate) and small business owner. About 200 titles a year. Unsolicited mss, synopses and ideas welcome.
Royalties paid twice-yearly.

Del Rey
See **Ballantine Books**

Delacorte Press
See **Bantam Dell Publishing Group**

Dell
See **Bantam Dell Publishing Group**

Delta Books
See **Bantam Dell Publishing Group**

Dial Books for Young Readers

345 Hudson Street, New York,
NY 10014–3657
☎001 212 366 2800

Queries *Submissions Coordinator*

FOUNDED 1961. A division of Penguin Putnam
Books for Young Readers. *Publishes* children's
books, including picture books, beginning
readers, fiction and non-fiction for middle
grade and young adults. 50 titles a year.
    IMPRINTS Hardcover only: **Dial Books for
Young Readers**; **Dial Easy-to-Read**. No
unsolicited mss accepted; query letters with
return postage only.
    Royalties paid twice-yearly.

Dial Press

See **Bantam Dell Publishing Group**

Dolphin Books

See **Doubleday Broadway Publishing
Group**

Doubleday Broadway Publishing Group

1540 Broadway, New York, NY 10036
☎001 212 782 9000 Fax 001 212 302 7985
Website www.randomhouse.com

President & Publisher *Stephen Rubin*

The Doubleday Broadway Publishing Group, a
division of **Random House, Inc.** was formed
by a merger of Doubleday and Broadway Books
in 1999. *Publishes* fiction and non-fiction.
    DIVISION/IMPRINTS **The Anchor Bible**;
Anchor Books; **Broadway Books**;
Currency; **DD Equestrian Library**; **Double
D Western**; **Doubleday**; **Doubleday
Activity Books**; **Doubleday Religious
Publishing**; **Dolphin Books**; **Foundation
Books**; **Galilee Books**; **Image Books**;
Loveswept; **Made Simple Books**; **Main
Street/Back List**; **New Jerusalem Bible**;
Nan A. Talese; **Outdoor Bible Series**;
Perfect Crime; **Spy Books**. No unsolicited
material.

Lisa Drew Books

See **Simon & Schuster Adult Publishing
Group**

DTP

See **Bantam Dell Publishing Group**

Thomas Dunne Books

See **St Martin's Press LLC**

Sanford J. Durst Publications

11 Clinton Avenue, Rockville Centre, New
York, NY 11570
☎001 516 766 4444 Fax 001 516 766 4520

Owner *Sanford J. Durst*

FOUNDED 1975. *Publishes* non-fiction: numis-
matic and related, philatelic, legal and art. Also
children's books. About 12 titles a year.
    Royalties paid twice-yearly.

Dushkin

See **The McGraw-Hill Companies, Inc.**

Dutton/Dutton's Children's Books

See **Penguin Putnam Inc.**

The Ecco Press

See **HarperCollins Publishers, Inc.**

William B. Eerdmans Publishing Co.

255 Jefferson Avenue SE, Grand Rapids,
MI 49503
☎001 616 459 4591 Fax 001 616 459 6540
Email sales@eerdmans.com
Website www.eerdmans.com

President *William B. Eerdmans Jr*
Vice President/Editor-in-Chief *Jon Pott*

FOUNDED 1911 as a theological and reference
publisher. Gradually began publishing in other
genres with authors like C.S. Lewis, Dorothy
Sayers and Malcolm Muggeridge on its lists.
Publishes religious: theology, biblical studies,
ethical and social concern, social criticism and
children's, religious history, religion and literature. DIVISIONS **Children's** *Judy Zylstra*;
Other *Jon Pott*. Unsolicited mss, synopses and
ideas welcome.
    Royalties paid twice-yearly.

M. Evans & Co., Inc.

216 East 49th Street, New York, NY 10017
☎001 212 688 2810 Fax 001 212 486 4544
Email editorial@mevans.com
Website www.mevans.com

President *George C. de Kay*

FOUNDED 1954 as a packager. Began publishing
in 1962. Best known for its popular psychology
and health books, with titles like *Dr Atkins' New
Diet Revolution*, *This is How Love Works*, *Bragging
Rights* and *Robert Crayhon's Nutrition Made
Simple*. *Publishes* general non-fiction and fiction.
About 30 titles a year. No unsolicited mss; query
first. Synopses and ideas welcome.
    Royalties paid twice-yearly.

Everyman's Library
See **Random House, Inc.**

Faber & Faber, Inc.
19 Union Square West, New York,
NY 10003
☎001 212 741 6900 Fax 001 212 633 9385
Editor *Denise Oswald*

FOUNDED 1976. An affiliate of **Farrar, Straus & Giroux, Inc.** *Publishes* primarily non-fiction books for adults with a focus on film, theatre, music, popular culture and literary and cultural criticism. Unsolicited mss accepted; please query first and include IRCs with letter.
Royalties paid twice-yearly.

Facts On File, Inc.
132 West 31st Street, New York, NY 10001
☎001 212 967 8800 Fax 001 212 967 9196
President *Mark McDonnell*
Publisher *Laurie E. Likoff*

Started life in the early 1940s with News Digest subscription series to libraries. Began publishing on specific subjects with the Facts On File imprint and developed its current reference and trade book programme in the 1970s. *Publishes* general trade, young adult trade and academic reference for the school and library markets. *Specialises* in single subject encyclopedias, atlases and biographical dictionaries. About 150 titles a year. No fiction, cookery or popular non-fiction.
DIVISIONS **General Reference** *Laurie Likoff*; **Academic Reference** *Owen Lancer*; **Adult Trade** *James Chambers*; **Young Adult & US History** *Nicole Bowen*; **Electronic Publishing** *James Housley*; **Literary Studies** *Anne Savarese*. Unsolicited synopses and ideas welcome; no mss. Send query letter in the first instance.
Royalties paid twice-yearly.

Farrar, Straus & Giroux, Inc.
19 Union Square West, New York,
NY 10003
☎001 212 741 6900 Fax 001 212 741 6973
Website www.fsgbooks.com

FOUNDED 1946. *Publishes* general fiction, non-fiction, juveniles. No unsolicited material.

Fawcett Books
See **Ballantine Books**

Frederick Fell Publishers, Inc.
2131 Hollywood Boulevard, Ste 305,
Hollywood, FL 33020
☎001 954 925 5242 Fax 001 954 925 5244
Email info@fellpub.com

Website www.fellpub.com
Chairman *Donald L. Lessne*
Managing Director *Barbara Newman*

FOUNDED 1943. *Publishes* trade non-fiction. 40 titles in 2001. Unsolicited mss, synopses and ideas welcome; send query letter with two chapters and table of contents in the first instance. No fiction.
Royalties twice-yearly.

Fireside
See **Simon & Schuster Adult Publishing Group**

First Avenue Editions
See **Lerner Publishing Group**

Fodor's Travel Publications
See **Random House, Inc.**

The Free Press
See **Simon & Schuster Adult Publishing Group**

Samuel French, Inc.
45 West 25th Street, New York,
NY 10010–2751
☎001 212 206 8990 Fax 001 212 206 1429
Email samuelfrench@earthlink.net
Website www.samuelfrench.com
Senior Editor *Lawrence Harbison*

FOUNDED 1830. *Publishes* plays in paperback: Broadway and off-Broadway hits, light comedies, mysteries, one-act plays and plays for young audiences. Unsolicited mss welcome. No synopses.
Royalties paid annually (books); twice-yearly (amateur productions); monthly (professional productions). *Overseas associates* in London, Toronto, Sydney and Johannesburg.

Gale (formerly Gale Group)
27500 Drake Road, Farmington Hills,
MI 48331
☎001 248 699 4253 Fax 001 248 699 8070
Email galeord@gale.com
Website www.gale.com
CEO *Allen Paschal*

FOUNDED 1954. A subsidiary of The Thomson Corporation, Gale is a world leader in e-information publishing. *Publishes* electronic reference material for libraries, schools and businesses. IMPRINTS **Blackbird Press**; **Charles Scribner & Sons**; **Five Star**; **Graham & Whiteside Ltd**; **Greenhaven Press**; **G.K. Hall & Co**; **KG Saur Verlag GmbH & Co KG**; **Kidhaven**

Press; **Lucent Books**; **Macmillan Reference USA**; **Primary Source Media**; **St James Press**; **Schirmer Reference**; **The Taft Group**; **Thorndike Press**; **Twayne Publishers**; **UXL**; **Wheeler Publishing**.

The Globe Pequot Press
PO Box 480, Guilford, CT 06437
☎001 203 458 4500   Fax 001 203 458 4601
Email info@globe-pequot.com
Website www.globe-pequot.com
President *Linda Kennedy*

FOUNDED 1947. *Publishes* regional and international travel, how-to, regional and outdoor recreation. Also publishes the *Insiders'* guides. About 250 titles a year. Unsolicited mss, synopses and ideas welcome, particularly for travel and outdoor recreation books.
   Royalties paid 'occasionally'.

Great Source Education Group
See **Houghton Mifflin Co.**

Greenhaven Press
See **Gale Group**

Greenwillow Books
See **HarperCollins Publishers, Inc.**

Griffin
See **St Martin's Press LLC**

Grolier Publishing
See **Scholastic Library Publishing**

Grosset & Dunlap/Grosset Putnam
See **Penguin Putnam Inc.**

Grove/Atlantic Inc.
841 Broadway, New York, NY 10003–4793
☎001 212 614 7850   Fax 001 212 614 7886
Website www.groveatlantic.com
President/Publisher *Morgan Entrekin*
Managing Editor *Michael Hornburg*

FOUNDED 1952. *Publishes* general fiction and non-fiction. IMPRINTS **Atlantic Monthly Press**; **Grove Press**.

Gulliver Green Books
See **Harcourt Trade Publishers**

Harcourt School Publishers
6277 Sea Harbor Drive, Orlando,FL 32887
☎001 407 345 2000   Fax 001 407 352 3445
Website www.harcourtschool.com
President/CEO *Stephen Gandy*

A division of Harcourt Inc., FOUNDED 1919. *Publishes* education materials – books, CD-ROMs, Internet and audio.

Harcourt Trade Publishers
(formerly **Harcourt Trade Division**)
525 'B' Street, Suite 1900, San Diego, CA 92101–4495
☎001 619 231 6616   Fax 001 619 699 6777
Website www.harcourtbooks.com
Managing Editor *Dan Farley*

A division of Harcourt Inc. *Publishes* fiction, poetry and non-fiction covering a wide range of subjects: biography, environment and ecology, history, travel, science and current affairs for children and young adults. About 175 titles a year.
   IMPRINTS **Greenlight Readers**; **Gulliver Green Books**; **Harcourt Young Classics**; **Harcourt Brace Young Classics**; **Harvest Books**; **Libros Viajeros**; **Magic Carpet Books**; **Odyssey Classics**; **Red Wagon Books**; **Silver Whistle Books**; **Voyager Books**; **Helen & Kurt Wolff Books**. No unsolicited mss.

Harlequin Historicals
See **Silhouette Books**

Harmony Books
See **The Crown Publishing Group**

HarperCollins Publishers, Inc.
10 East 53rd Street, New York, NY 10022
☎001 212 207 7000   Fax 001 212 207 6968
Website www.harpercollins.com
President/Chief Executive Officer *Jane Friedman*

FOUNDED 1817. Owned by News Corporation. *Publishes* general and literary fiction, general non-fiction, business, children's, reference and religious books. About 1700 titles a year. No unsolicited material.
   DIVISIONS/IMPRINTS **Adult Trade**; **HarperCollins/HarperCollins Children's Books**; **HarperResource** (reference); **HarperAudio**; **Avon Books** (see entry); **Beech Tree Books**; **Greenwillow Books**; **Hearst Books**; **Lothrop, Lee & Shepard**; **Mulberry Books**; **Quill**; **Regan Books**; **The Ecco Press**; **William Morrow**.
   SUBSIDIARY **Zondervan Publishing House** (see entry).

Harvard University Press
79 Garden Street, Cambridge, MA 02138–1499
☎001 617 495 2600   Fax 001 617 495 5898

Email <firstname>.<lastname>@harvard.edu
Website www.hup.harvard.edu
Director *William P. Sisler*
FOUNDED 1913. *Publishes* scholarly non-fiction
only: medical and scientific. IMPRINT **Belknap
Press**.

University of Hawai'i Press
2840 Kolowalu Street, Honolulu, HI 96822
☎001 808 956 8694   Fax 001 808 988 6052
Email pcrosby@hawaii.edu
Website www.uhpress.hawaii.edu
Chairman *William Hamilton*
Executive Editor *Patricia Crosby*
FOUNDED 1947. *Publishes* scholarly books pertaining to East Asia, Southeast Asia, Hawaii and
the Pacific. IMPRINT **Lattitude 20**. Unsolicited
mss; synopses and ideas welcome; approach by
mail. No poetry, children's books or any topics
other than Asia and the Pacific.
  Royalties paid twice-yearly.

Hearst Books
See **HarperCollins Publishers, Inc.**

HiddenSpring
See **Paulist Press**

Hill Street Press
191 E. Broad Street, Suite 209, Athens,
GA 30601–2848
☎001 706 613 7200   Fax 001 706 613 7204
Email info@hillstreetpress.com
Website www.hillstreetpress.com
Senior Editor *Patrick Allen*
FOUNDED 1998. *Publishes* books on the American South – fiction and non-fiction: literary his-
tory/criticism, memoirs, history, current issues,
cookery. No poetry, erotica, romance, children's
or young adults. Unsolicited material welcome;
approach in writing in the first instance.
  Royalties paid twice-yearly.

Hippocrene Books, Inc.
171 Madison Avenue, New York, NY 10016
☎001 212 685 4371   Fax 001 212 779 9338
Email hippocrene.books@verizon.net
Website www.hippocrenebooks.com
President/Editorial Director *George
  Blagowidow*
Foreign Language Editor *Caroline Gates*
Cookbook Editor *Anne McBride*
FOUNDED 1971. *Publishes* general non-fiction
and reference books. Particularly strong on for-
eign language dictionaries, language studies and

international cookbooks. No fiction. Send
brief summary, table of contents and one chapter for appraisal. S.a.e. essential for response.
For manuscript return include sufficient
postage cover (IRCs).

Holiday House, Inc.
425 Madison Avenue, New York, NY 10017
☎001 212 688 0085   Fax 001 212 421 6134
Vice President/Editor-in-Chief *Regina
  Griffin*
Publishes children's general fiction and non-
fiction (pre-school to secondary). About 50
titles a year. Send query letters only. IRCs for
reply must be included.

Henry Holt & Company Inc.
115 West 18th Street, New York, NY 10011
☎001 212 886 9200   Fax 001 212 633 0748
Website www.henryholt.com
President/Publisher *John Sterling*
Editor-in-Chief *Jennifer Barth*
**Executive Editor, Books for Young
  Readers** *Nina Ignatowicz*
**Associate Publisher, Books for Young
  Readers** *Laura Godwin*
FOUNDED in 1866, the company is one of the
oldest in the United States. Part of Holtzbrinck
Publishing Holdings. *Publishes* fiction, by both
American and international authors, biographies,
and books on history and politics, ecology and
psychology.   230 titles a year.   DIVISIONS/
IMPRINTS **Adult Trade**; **Books for Young
Readers**; **John Macrae Books** *John Macrae*;
Metropolitan Books *Sara Bershtel*; **Owl
Books**; **Times Books** *David Sobel*.

Houghton Mifflin Co.
222 Berkeley Street, Boston, MA 02116–3764
☎001 617 351 5000   Fax 001 617 351 1125
Website www.hmco.com
Contact *Submissions Editor*
FOUNDED 1832. Acquired by Vivendi in June
2001. *Publishes* literary fiction and general non-
fiction, including autobiography, biography
and history. Also school and college textbooks;
children's fiction and non-fiction. Average 100
titles a year. Unsolicited adult mss no longer
accepted. Send synopses, outline and sample
chapters for children's non-fiction; complete
mss for children's fiction. IRCs required with
all submissions/queries.
  DIVISIONS/SUBSIDIARIES **Houghton Mifflin
College Division**; **Houghton Mifflin
School Division**; **Houghton Mifflin Trade
& Reference Division**; **Great Source**

Education Group; **McDougal Littell Inc.;** **The Riverside Publishing Co.; Sunburst Technology** (multimedia and video).

House of Collectibles
See **The Crown Publishing Group**

HPBooks
See **Penguin Putnam Inc.**

University of Illinois Press
1325 South Oak Street, Champaign, IL 61820–6903
☎001 217 333 0950 Fax 001 217 244 8082
Email uipress@uillinois.edu
Website www.press.uillinois.edu
Editorial Director *Willis Regier*

Publishes non-fiction, scholarly and general, with special interest in Americana, women's studies, African–American studies, film, religion, American music and regional books. About 140–150 titles a year.

Image Books
See **Doubleday Broadway Publishing Group**

Indiana University Press
601 North Morton Street, Bloomington, IN 47404–3797
☎001 812 855 8817 Fax 001 812 855 8507
Email iupress@indiana.edu
Website www.indiana.edu/~iupress
Director *Peter-John Leone*

Publishes scholarly non-fiction in the following subject areas: African studies, anthropology, Asian studies, Afro-American studies, environment and ecology, film, folklore, history, Jewish studies, literary criticism, medical ethics, Middle East studies, military, music, paleontology, philanthropy, philosophy, politics, religion, semiotics, Russian and East European studies, Victorian studies, women's studies. Query in writing in first instance.

Interlink Publishing Group, Inc.
46 Crosby Street, Northampton, MA 01060
☎001 413 582 7054 Fax 001 413 582 7057
Email info@interlinkbooks.com
Website www.interlinkbooks.com
Publisher *Michel Moushabeck*

FOUNDED 1987. *Publishes* fiction, travel, children's, politics, cookbooks. *Specialises* in Middle East titles and ethnicity. IMPRINTS **Crocodile Books, USA** Editorial Head *Ruth Lane Moushabeck*; **Olive Branch Press** Editorial

Head *Phyllis Bennis*. See submission guidelines on the website before making an approach.
Royalties paid annually.

University of Iowa Press
100 Kuhl House, 119 West Park Road, Iowa, City IA 52242–1000
☎001 319 335 2000 Fax 001 319 335 2055
Email uipress@uiowa.edu
Website www.uiowapress.org
Director *Holly Carver*

FOUNDED 1969 as a small scholarly press publishing about five books a year. Now publishing about 35 a year in a variety of scholarly fields, plus local interest, short stories, creative non-fiction and poetry anthologies. No unsolicited mss; query first. Unsolicited ideas and synopses welcome.
Royalties paid annually.

Iowa State University Press
2121 State Avenue, Ames, IA 50010
☎001 515 292 0140 Fax 001 515 292 3348
Email vanhouten@iowastatepress.com
Website www.iowastatepress.com
Publishing Director *Gretchen Van Houten*

FOUNDED 1934 as an offshoot of the university's journalism department. Now a Blackwell Science company. *Publishes* reference books and textbooks on agriculture, aviation, food science, human dentistry, dietetics, journalism, and veterinary medicine. No fiction, trade books or poetry.
Royalties paid annually.

Irwin
See **The McGraw-Hill Companies, Inc.**

Island Books
See **Bantam Dell Publishing Group**

Ivy
See **Ballantine Books**

Jove
See **Penguin Putnam Inc.**

University Press of Kansas
2501 West 15th Street, Lawrence, KS 66049–3905
☎001 785 864 4154 Fax 001 785 864 4586
Email upress@ku.edu
Website www.kansaspress.ku.edu
Director *Fred M. Woodward*

FOUNDED 1946. Became the publishing arm for all six state universities in Kansas in 1976.

Publishes scholarly books in American history studies, legal studies, presidential studies, American studies, political philosophy, political science, military history and environmental. About 50 titles a year. Proposals welcome.
Royalties paid annually.

Kar-Ben Publishing
See **Lerner Publishing Group**

Jean Karl Books
See **Simon & Schuster Children's Publishing**

Kent State University Press
Kent OH 44242–0001
☎001 330 672 7913 Fax 001 330 672 3104
Director (Interim) *Will Underwood*
Editor-in-Chief *Joanna Hildebrand Craig*
FOUNDED 1965. *Publishes* scholarly works in history and biography, literary studies and general non-fiction with an emphasis on American studies. 25–30 titles a year. Queries welcome; no mss.
Royalties paid annually.

Kluwer Academic Publishers
101 Philip Drive, Assinippi Park, Norwell, MA 02061
☎001 781 871 6600 Fax 001 781 871 6528
Email kluwer@wkap.com
Website www.wkap.nl
CEO *Peter Hendriks*
Managing Editor *Claire Stanton*
FOUNDED 1972. *Publishes* scholarly scientific, technical, medical, business and professional books and journals. Over 300 titles a year. Queries only.
IMPRINTS **Kluwer Academic Publishers/ Plenum Publishers**.

Alfred A. Knopf
See **Random House, Inc.**

Krieger Publishing Co.
PO Box 9542, Melbourne, FL 32902–9542
☎001 321 724 9542 Fax 001 321 951 3671
Email info@krieger-pub.com
Website www.krieger-publishing.com
Chairman *Robert E. Krieger*
President *Donald E. Krieger*
Vice-President *Maxine D. Krieger*
FOUNDED 1970. *Publishes* science, education, ecology, humanities, history, mathematics, chemistry, space science, technology and en-

gineering. IMPRINTS/SERIES **Anvil; Exploring Community History; Open Forum; Orbit; Professional Practices; Public History**. Unsolicited mss welcome. Not interested in synopses/ideas or trade type titles.
Royalties paid yearly.

Lanternlight Library
See **University of Alaska Press**

Lattitude 20
See **University of Hawai'i Press**

Lehigh University Press
See **Golden Cockerel Press** under **UK Publishers**

Lerner Publishing Group
241 First Avenue North, Minneapolis, MN 55401
☎001 612 332 3344 Fax 001 612 332 7615
Email info@lernerbooks.com
Website www.lernerbooks.com
Chairman *Harry J. Lerner*
President & Publisher *Adam M. Lerner*
FOUNDED 1959. *Publishes* primarily children's non-fiction, fiction and curriculum material for readers of all grade levels. DIVISIONS/IMPRINTS Editorial Head *Mary Rodgers* **Lerner Publications; Carolrhoda Books; Lerner Sport; Lerner Classroom; First Avenue Editions; Kar-Ben Publishing** Editorial Heads *Judye Groner, Madeline Wikler*. No puzzle, work, song or text books, or plays. Submissions are accepted in the months of March and October *only*. Work received in any other month will be returned unopened. S.a.e./IRCs required for authors who wish to have their material returned. Please allow two to six months for a response. No phone calls.
Royalties paid twice-yearly.

Library of Contemporary Thought
See **Ballantine Books**

Little Simon
See **Simon & Schuster Children's Publishing**

Little, Brown and Company
Adult Trade Division: 1271 Avenue of the Americas, New York, NY 10020
☎001 212 522 8700 Fax 001 212 522 2067
Website www.twbookmark.com
CHILDREN'S BOOKS DIVISION: 3 Center Plaza, Boston, MA 02108–2084 ☎001 617 227 0730

Fax 001 617 263 2864

IMPRINT of the AOL Time Warner Book Group. FOUNDED 1837. *Publishes* fiction, non-fiction and children's. DIVISIONS **Adult Trade** VP/Publisher *Michael Pietsch*; **Children's Books** VP/Editor-in-Chief *Maria Modugno*. No unsolicited mss.

Living Language
See **Random House, Inc.**

Llewellyn Publications
PO Box 64383, St Paul,
MN 55164–0383
☎001 612 291 1970 Fax 001 612 291 1908
Email nancym@llewellyn.com
Website www.llewellyn.com

President/Publisher *Carl L. Weschcke*
Acquisitions Manager *Nancy J. Mostad*

Division of Llewellyn Worldwide Ltd. FOUNDED 1901. *Publishes* self-help and how-to: astrology, alternative health, tantra, Fortean studies, tarot, yoga, Santeria, dream studies, metaphysics, magic, witchcraft, herbalism, shamanism, organic gardening, women's spirituality, graphology, palmistry, parapsychology. Also fiction with an authentic magical or metaphysical theme. About 100 titles a year. Unsolicited mss welcome; proposals preferred. IRCs essential in all cases.

Lothrop, Lee & Shepard
See **HarperCollins Publishers, Inc.**

Louisiana State University Press
Baton Rouge LA 70803
☎001 225 578 6295 Fax 001 225 578 6461
Email lsupress@lsu.edu
Website www.lsu.edu/lsupress

Director *L.E. Phillabaum*

Publishes non-fiction: Southern history, American history, Southern literary criticism, American literary criticism, biography, political science, music (jazz) and Latin American studies. About 80 titles a year. Send IRCs for mss guidelines.

Love Inspired
See **Silhouette Books**

Lucas Books
See **Ballantine Books**

Lucent Books
See **Gale**

The Lyons Press Inc.
123 West 18th Street, Sixth Floor, New York NY 10011
☎001 212 620 9580 Fax 001 212 929 1836
Website www.lyonspress.com

Senior Vice-President *Tony Lyons*
Managing Editor *Richard Rothschild*

FOUNDED 1978. *Publishes* general fiction and non-fiction; outdoor, natural history, sports, gardening, cookery and art. About 180 titles a year. No unsolicited mss; synopses and ideas welcome.

Royalties paid twice-yearly.

McDougal Littell Inc.
See **Houghton Mifflin Co.**

Margaret K. McElderry Books
See **Simon & Schuster Children's Publishing**

McFarland & Company, Inc., Publishers
PO Box 611, Jefferson NC 28640
☎001 336 246 4460 Fax 001 336 246 5018
Email info@mcfarlandpub.com
Website www.mcfarlandpub.com

President/Editor-in-Chief *Robert Franklin*
Vice President *Rhonda Herman*
Senior Editor *Steve Wilson*
Editor *Virginia Tobiassen*

FOUNDED 1979. A library reference and upper-end speciality market press publishing scholarly books in many fields: international studies, performing arts, popular culture, sports, automotive history, women's studies, music and fine arts, chess, history and librarianship. *Specialises* in general reference. Especially strong in cinema studies. No fiction, poetry, children's, New Age or inspirational/devotional works. About 220 titles a year. No unsolicited mss; send query letter first. Synopses and ideas welcome; submissions by mail preferred.

Royalties paid annually.

The McGraw-Hill Companies, Inc.
1221 Avenue of the Americas, New York, NY 10020
☎001 212 512 2000
Website www.mcgraw-hill.com

President/CEO *Harold McGraw, III*

FOUNDED 1888. Parent of **McGraw-Hill Education** which has offices in the UK (see entry under **UK Publishers**. *Publishes* a wide range of educational, professional, business, science, engineering and computing books.

HIGHER EDUCATION/PROFESSIONAL DIVISIONS
McGraw-Hill Professional; McGraw-Hill Trade; McGraw-Hill/ Osborne Media; McGraw-Hill Higher Education; McGraw-Hill/Irwin; McGraw-Hill/Dushkin; McGraw-Hill/Primis Custom Publishing; McGraw-Hill/ Contemporary.

John Macrae Books
See **Henry Holt & Company Inc.**

Magic Attic Press
See **The Millbrook Press, Inc.**

University of Massachusetts Press
PO Box 429, Amherst, MA 01004–0429
☎001 413 545 2217 Fax 001 413 545 1226
Website www.umass.edu/umpress

Director *Bruce Wilcox*
Senior Editor *Clark Dougan*

FOUNDED 1964. *Publishes* scholarly, general interest, African-American, ethnic, women's and gender studies, cultural criticism, architecture and environmental design, literary criticism, poetry, philosophy, biography, history. Unsolicited mss considered but query letter preferred in the first instance. Synopses and ideas welcome. 40 titles a year.
Royalties paid annually.

Mentor
See **Penguin Putnam Inc.**

Meridian
See **Penguin Putnam Inc.**

Metropolitan Books
See **Henry Holt & Company Inc.**

The University of Michigan Press
PO Box 1104, Ann Arbor, MI 48106–1104
☎001 734 764 4388 Fax 001 734 615 1540
Email um.press@umich.edu
Website www.press.umich.ef

FOUNDED 1930. *Publishes* non-fiction, textbooks, literary criticism, theatre, economics, political science, history, classics, anthropology, law studies, gender studies, English as a second language.
Royalties paid twice-yearly.

The Millbrook Press, Inc.
2 Old New Milford Road, PO Box 335,
Brookfield, CT 06804
☎001 203 740 2220 Fax 001 203 740 2526

Website www.millbrookpress.com
School/Library Publisher *Jean Reynolds*
Publisher (Roaring Brook Press) *Simon Boughton*
Managing Editor *Colleen Seibert*

FOUNDED 1989. *Publishes* mainly non-fiction, children's and young adult, for trade, school and public library. About 180 titles a year. IMPRINTS **Copper Beech Books**; **Twenty-First Century Books**; **Magic Attic Press**; **Roaring Brook Press** Fiction.
Royalties paid twice-yearly.

Minotaur
See **St Martin's Press LLC**

University Press of Mississippi
3825 Ridgewood Road, Jackson,
MS 39211–6492
☎001 601 432 6205 Fax 001 601 432 6217
Email press@ihl.state.ms.us
Website www.upress.state.ms.us

Director *Seetha Srinivasan*
Editor-in-Chief *Craig Gill*

FOUNDED 1970. Non-profit book publisher partially supported by the eight State universities. *Publishes* scholarly and trade titles in literature, history, American culture, Southern culture, African-American, women's studies, popular culture, folklife, ethnic, performance, art and photography, and other liberal arts. About 60 titles a year.
IMPRINTS **Muscadine Books** *Craig Gill* Regional trade titles. **Banner Books** Paperback reprints of significant fiction and non-fiction. Send letter of enquiry, prospectus, table of contents and sample chapter prior to submission of full mss.
Royalties paid annually. *Represented* worldwide. UK representatives: **Roundhouse Publishing Group**.

University of Missouri Press
2910 LeMone Boulevard, Columbia,
MO 65201
☎001 573 882 7641 Fax 001 573 884 4498
Website www.system.missouri.edu/upress

Director *Beverly Jarrett*

FOUNDED 1958. *Publishes* academic: history, literary criticism, intellectual history and related humanities disciplines and short stories – usually four volumes a year. Best approach is by letter. Send one short story for consideration, and synopses for academic work. About 60 titles a year.

The MIT Press
5 Cambridge Ctr., Cambridge, MA 02142
☎001 617 253 5646 Fax 001 617 258 6779
Website www.mitpress.mit.edu
Editor-in-Chief *Laurence Cohen*
FOUNDED 1961. *Publishes* scholarly and professional, technologically sophisticated books, including computer science and artificial intelligence, economics, finance, architecture, cognitive science, neuroscience, environmental studies, linguistics and philosophy. IMPRINT **Bradford Books**.

The Modern Library
See **Random House, Inc.**

Monograph Series
See **University of Alaska Press**

William Morrow
See **HarperCollins Publishers, Inc.**

MTV Books
See **Pocket Books**

Mulberry Books
See **HarperCollins Publishers, Inc.**

Muscadine Books
See **University Press of Mississippi**

Mysterious Press
See **Warner Books Inc.**

NAL
See **Penguin Putnam, Inc.**

University of Nevada Press
MS 166, Reno, NV 89557–0076
☎001 775 784 6573 Fax 001 775 784 6200
Website www.nvbooks.nevada.edu
Director *Ronald Latimer*
Editor-in-Chief *Joanne O'Hare*
FOUNDED 1961. *Publishes* scholarly and popular books; serious fiction, Native American studies, natural history, Western Americana, Basque studies and regional studies. About 40 titles a year including reprints. Unsolicited material welcome if it fits in with areas published, or offers a 'new and exciting' direction.
Royalties paid twice-yearly.

University Press of New England
23 South Main Street, Hanover,
NH 03755–2055
☎001 603 643 7100 Fax 001 603 643 7117

Website www.upne.com
Director & Editor-in-Chief *Richard Abel*
Executive Editor *Phyllis Deutsch*
FOUNDED 1970. A scholarly book publisher sponsored by five institutions of higher education in the region: Brandeis, Dartmouth, Middlebury, Tufts and the University of New Hampshire. *Publishes* general and scholarly non-fiction and Hardscrabble Books fiction of New England. About 80 titles a year. Unsolicited material welcome.
Royalties paid annually. *Overseas associates:* Canada – University of British Columbia; UK, Europe, Middle East – University Presses Marketing; Australia, New Zealand, Asia & the Pacific – East-West Export Books.

University of New Mexico Press
1720 Lomas Boulevard NE, Albuquerque,
NM 87131–1591
☎001 505 277 2346 Fax 001 505 277 9270
Website www.unmpress.com
Director *Elizabeth C. Hadas*
Editor *Larry Durwood Ball*
FOUNDED 1929. *Publishes* scholarly and regional books. No fiction, how-to, children's, humour, self-help, technical or textbooks.

University of North Texas Press
PO Box 311336, Denton, TX 76203–1336
☎001 940 565 2142 Fax 001 940 565 4590
Email rchrisman@unt.edu
Website www.unt.edu/untpress
Director *Ronald Chrisman*
FOUNDED 1987. *Publishes* folklore, regional interest, contemporary, social issues, Texas history, military history, women's issues, multicultural. Publishes the Vassar Miller Poetry Prize winner each year. About 20 titles a year. No unsolicited mss; synopses and ideas welcome.
Royalties paid annually.

W.W. Norton & Company, Inc.
500 Fifth Avenue, New York,
NY 10110–0017
☎001 212 354 5500 Fax 001 212 869 0856
Website www.wwnorton.com
Vice-President/Managing Editor
Nancy K. Palmquist
FOUNDED 1923. *Publishes* fiction and non-fiction, college textbooks and professional books. About 300 titles a year.

Odyssey Classics
See **Harcourt Trade Division**

University of Oklahoma Press
1005 Asp Avenue, Norman,
OK 73019–6051
☎001 405 325 2000 Fax 001 405 325 4000
Website www.ou.edu/oupress
Director *John N. Drayton*
FOUNDED 1928. *Publishes* general scholarly
non-fiction only: American Indian studies, history of American West, classical studies, literary
theory and criticism, anthropology, archaeology, natural history, political science and
women's studies. About 100 titles a year.

Olive Branch Press
See **Interlink Publishing Group, Inc.**

One World
See **Ballantine Books**

Onyx
See **Penguin Putnam Inc.**

Open Forum
See **Krieger Publishing Co.**

Orbit
See **Krieger Publishing Co.**

Osborne Media
See **The McGraw-Hill Companies, Inc.**

Owl Books
See **Henry Holt & Company Inc.**

Palgrave
See **St Martin's Press LLC**

Pantheon Books
See **Random House, Inc.**

Paper Star
See **Penguin Putnam Inc**

Paragon House
2700 University Avenue, Suite 200, St Paul,
MN 55114–1016
☎001 651 644 3087 Fax 001 651 644 0997
Email paragon@paragonhouse.com
Website www.paragonhouse.com
Executive Director *Dr Gordon L. Anderson*
FOUNDED 1982. *Publishes* non-fiction: reference and academic. Subjects include history,
religion, philosophy, spirituality, Jewish interest, political science, international relations,
psychology.
Royalties paid twice-yearly.

Paulist Press
997 Macarthur Boulevard, Mahwah,
NJ 07430
☎001 201 825 7300 Fax 001 201 825 8345
Email sales@paulistpress.com
Website www.paulistpress.com
Owner *Missionary Society of St Paul the Apostle,
New York*
CSP/Publisher *Fr. Lawrence Boadt*
Managing Editor *Paul McMahon*
FOUNDED in 1866 by the Paulist Fathers as the
Catholic Publication Society. One of the largest
Catholic Publishing houses in the world, the
Paulist Press *publishes* religious, spiritual, theology
and children's religious books. 90 titles a year.
   IMPRINTS **Paulist Press** *Paul McMahon*
Spirituality, ministry resources, ethics and social
issues, ecumenical and inter-religious; *Chris
Bellitto* Theology and philosophy; *Susan O'Keefe*
Children's religious. **HiddenSpring** *Jan-Erik
Guerth* General religious trade books. Unsolici-
ted mss, synopses and ideas welcome; approach
through direct mail with IRCs for return postage
of material and/or letter. No New Age,
Evangelical Christian books.

Pelican Publishing Company
Box 3110, Gretna, LA 70054–3110
☎001 504 368 1175
Website www.pelicanpub.com
Editor-in-Chief *Nina Kooij*
Publishes general non-fiction: popular history,
cookbooks, travel, art, business, children's, editorial cartoon, architecture, golf, Scottish interest, collectibles guides and motivational. About
100 titles a year. Initial enquiries required for
all submissions.

Pelion Press
See **The Rosen Publishing Group, Inc.**

Penguin Putnam Inc.
375 Hudson Street, New York, NY 10014
☎001 212 366 2000 Fax 001 212 366 2666
Email online@penguinputnam.com
Website www.penguinputnam.com
President/CEO *David Shanks*
Penguin Putnam is a division of the Penguin
Group, which is owned by Pearson plc. The
Group is the second-largest trade book pub-
lisher in the world. *Publishes* fiction and non-
fiction in hardback and paperback; adult and
children's. About 2500 titles a year. No unso-
licited mss.
   PENGUIN GROUP IMPRINTS Hardback:

Dutton; **Viking**; **Viking Studio**; **Allen Lane The Penguin Press**; **DAW Books, Inc.** (see entry); Paperback: **Penguin**; **Plume**; **Signet/Signet Classics**; **Onyx**; **Roc**; **Topaz**; **Mentor**; **Meridian**. CHILDREN'S DIVISION: **Dial Books for Young Readers** (see entry); **Dutton's Children's Books**; **Viking Children's Books**; **Puffin**; **Grosset & Dunlap**; **NAL**; **Frederick Warne**.

PUTNAM BERKLEY IMPRINTS Hardback: **G.P. Putnam's Sons** (see entry); **Riverhead Books**; **BlueHen Books**; **Jeremy P. Tarcher**; **Avery** (see entry); **Grosset/Putnam**; **Ace/Putnam**; **Boulevard**; **Putnam**; **Price Stern Sloan**; Paperbacks: **Berkley Books**; **Jove**; **Perigee**; **Prime Crime**; **HPBooks**; Children's Division: **Philomel**; **Paper Star**; **Planet Dexter**.

Royalties paid twice-yearly.

University of Pennsylvania Press
4200 Pine Street, Philadelphia, PA 19104–4011
☎001 215 898 6261 Fax 001 215 898 0404
Website www.upenn.edu/pennpress

Director *Eric Halpern*

FOUNDED 1890. *Publishes* serious non-fiction: scholarly, reference, professional, textbooks and semi-popular trade. No original fiction or poetry. About 75 titles a year. No unsolicited mss but synopses and ideas for books welcome.
Royalties paid annually.

Perigee
See **Penguin Putnam Inc.**

Perseus Books Group
10 East 53rd Street, New York, NY 10022
☎001 212 207 7600 Fax 001 212 207 7635
Website www.perseusbooksgroup.com

President/CEO *Jack McKeown*

FOUNDED 1997. Subsidiary of Perseus Capital LLC. *Publishes* general, academic and professional. IMPRINTS **Basic Books** *John Donatich*; **Perseus Publishing** *David Goehring*; **Counterpoint Press** *Jack Schumacher*; **Perseus Press** *Don Fehr*; **Da Capo Press** *John Radziewicz*; **Westview Press** *Holly Hodder*; **Public Affairs** *Peter Osnos*. No unsolicited mss.

Philomel
See **Penguin Putnam Inc.**

Picador USA
See **St Martin's Press LLC**

Planet Dexter
See **Penguin Putnam Inc.**

Players Press
PO Box 1132, Studio City CA 91614–0132
☎001 818 789 4980

CEO *William-Alan Landes*

FOUNDED 1965 as a publisher of plays; now publishes across the entire range of performing arts: plays, musicals, theatre, film, cinema, television, costume, puppetry, plus technical theatre and cinema material. No unsolicited mss; synopses/ideas welcome. Send query letter.
Royalties paid twice-yearly. *Overseas subsidiaries* in Canada, Australia, Germany and the UK.

Plenum Publishers
See **Kluwer Academic Publishers**

Plume
See **Penguin Putnam Inc.**

Pocket Books
1230 Avenue of the Americas, New York, NY 10020
☎001 212 698 1260 Fax 001 212 698 1253
Website www.simonsays.com

Executive VP/Publisher *Louise Burke*

FOUNDED 1939. A division of **Simon & Schuster Adult Publishing Group**. *Publishes* trade paperbacks and hardcovers; mass-market, reprints and originals. IMPRINTS **Pocket Books/Pocket Star Books**; **Sonnet Books**; **MTV Books**.

PowerKids Press
See **The Rosen Publishing Group, Inc.**

Price Stern Sloan
See **Penguin Putnam Inc.**

Prime Crime
See **Penguin Putnam Inc.**

Princeton Review
See **Random House, Inc.**

Professional Practices
See **Krieger Publishing Co.**

Public Affairs
See **Perseus Books Group**

Public History
See **Krieger Publishing Co.**

Puffin
See **Penguin Putnam Inc**

G.P. Putnam's Sons (Children's)
345 Hudson Street, New York, NY 10014
☎001 212 366 2000
Website www.penguinputnam.com
President/Publisher *Nancy Paulsen*
Executive Editor *Kathy Dawson*
A children's book imprint of Penguin Putnam Books for Young Readers, a member of **Penguin Putnam Inc.** *Publishes* picture books, middle-grade fiction and young adult fiction.

Quill
See **HarperCollins Publishers, Inc.**

Rand McNally
PO Box 7600, Chicago, IL 60680
☎001 847 329 8100 Fax 001 847 673 0539
Website www.randmcnally.com
President/CEO *Mike Hehir*
FOUNDED 1856. *Publishes* world atlases and maps, road atlases of North America and Europe, city and state maps of the United States and Canada, educational wall maps, atlases and globes, plus children's products. Includes electronic multimedia products. IMPRINTS **Rand McNally for Kids**.

Random House, Inc.
1540 Broadway, New York, NY 10036
☎001 212 782 9000 Fax 001 212 726 0600
Website www.randomhouse.com
Chairman/Chief Executive Officer *Peter Olson*
FOUNDED 1925. The world's largest English-language general trade book publisher. A division of the Bertelsmann Book Group AG, one of the foremost media companies in the world. The reach of Random House, Inc. is global with subsidiaries and affiliated companies in Canada, the UK, Australia, New Zealand and South Africa. Through Random House International, the books published by the imprints of Random House, Inc. are sold in virtually every country in the world. Submissions via agents preferred.
DIVISIONS/IMPRINTS
Random House Adult Books; **Ballantine Books** (see entry); **Bantam Dell Publishing Group** (see entry); **Crown Publishing Group** (see entry); **Doubleday Broadway Publishing Group** (see entry). **Alfred A. Knopf** (including **Everyman's Library**, **Knopf, Pantheon Books, Schocken Books**, **Vintage** and **Anchor**) FOUNDED 1915. Fiction and non-fiction. **Random House**

Audio Publishing Group; Random House Children's Books (including **Random House Books for Young Readers, Alfred A. Knopf Books for Young Readers, Crown Books for Young Readers, Delacorte Press** and **Doubleday Books for Young Readers**); **Random House Large Print; Random House Value Publishing; Random House New Media; Fodor's Travel Publications; Living Language; Princeton Review; Random House Reference; Villard; The Modern Library**.
Royalties paid twice-yearly.

Rawson Associates
See **Simon & Schuster Adult Publishing Group**

Reader's Digest Association Inc
Reader's Digest Road, Pleasantville, NY 10570–7000
☎001 914 238 1000 Fax 001 914 238 4559
Website www.rd.com
Chairman/CEO *Thomas Ryder*
Publishes home maintenance reference, cookery, DIY, health, gardening, children's books; videos and magazines.

Red Wagon Books
See **Harcourt Trade Division**

Regan Books
See **HarperCollins Publishers, Inc.**

Fleming H. Revell
See **Baker Book House**

Riverhead Books
See **Penguin Putnam Inc.**

The Riverside Publishing Co.
See **Houghton Mifflin Co.**

Roaring Brook Press
See **The Millbrook Press, Inc.**

Roc
See **Penguin Putnam Inc.**

The Rosen Publishing Group, Inc.
29 East 21st Street, New York, NY 10010
☎001 212 777 3017 Fax 001 212 777 0277
Website www.rosenpublishing.com
President *Roger Rosen*
Associate Editor, PowerKids Press *Gina Strazzabosco-Hayn*

Editorial Director *Erin Hovanec*

FOUNDED 1950. *Publishes* non-fiction books
(supplementary to the curriculum, reference
and self-help) for a young adult audience.
Reading levels are years 7–12, 4–6 (books for
teens with literacy problems), and 5–9. Areas of
interest include careers, self-esteem, sexuality,
personal safety, science, sport, African studies,
Holocaust studies and a wide variety of other
multicultural titles. About 180 titles a year.

IMPRINTS **Pelion Press** Music titles;
PowerKids Press Non-fiction books for
Reception up to Year 4 that are supplementary
to the curriculum. Subjects include conflict resolution, character building, health, safety, drug
abuse prevention, history, self-help, religion and
multicultural titles. 144 titles a year. For all
imprints, write with outline and sample chapters.

Rutgers University Press

100 Joyce Kilmer Avenue, Piscataway,
NJ 08854–8099
☎001 732 445 7762 Fax 001 732 445 7039
Email arashap@rci.rutgers.edu
Website rutgerspress.rutgers.edu

Director *Marlie Wasserman*
Associate Director/Editor-in-Chief *Leslie
Mitchner*

FOUNDED 1936. *Publishes* scholarly books,
regional, social sciences and humanities.
Unsolicited mss, synopses and ideas for books
welcome. No original fiction or poetry. About
80 titles a year.
Royalties paid annually.

St Martin's Press LLC

175 Fifth Avenue, New York, NY 10010
☎001 212 674 5151 Fax 001 212 420 9314
Email inquiries@stmartins.com
Website www.stmartins.com

CEO (Holtzbrinck) *John Sargent*
President/Publisher (Trade Division)
Sally Richardson

FOUNDED 1952. A subsidiary of **Macmillan
Publishers** (UK), St Martin's Press made its
name and fortune by importing raw talent from
the UK to the States and has continued to buy
heavily in the UK. *Publishes* general fiction,
especially mysteries and crime; and adult non-
fiction: history, self-help, political science,
travel, biography, scholarly, popular reference,
college textbooks. All submissions via legitimate literary agents only.

IMPRINTS **Picador USA**; **Griffin** (Trade
paperbacks); **St Martin's Paperbacks** (Mass

market); **Thomas Dunne Books**; **Minotaur**;
Palgrave; **Truman Talley Books**.

Scarecrow Press Inc.

4720 Boston Way, Lanham MD 20706
☎001 301 459 3366 Fax 001 301 429 5747
Website www.scarecrowpress.com

Editorial Director/Associate Publisher
Shirley Lambert

FOUNDED 1950 as a short-run publisher of
library reference books. Acquired by **University
Press of America, Inc.** in 1995 which is now
part of Rowman and Littlefield Publishing
Group. *Publishes* reference, scholarly and monographs (all levels) for libraries. Reference books
in all areas except sciences, specialising in the
performing arts, music, cinema and library science. About 165 titles a year. Unsolicited mss
welcome but material will not be returned unless
requested and accompanied by return postage.
Unsolicited synopses and ideas for books welcome.
Royalties paid annually.

Schocken Books

See **Random House, Inc.**

Anne Schwartz Books

See **Simon & Schuster Children's
Publishing**

Scholastic Library Publishing

(formerly **Grolier Publishing**)
90 Sherman Turnpike, Danbury, CT 06816
☎001 203 797 3500
Website www.scholasticlibrary.com/
grolierdocs/home.html

President *Neil Goff*

FOUNDED 1895. Acquired by Scholastic, Inc.
in 2000. *Publishes* juvenile non-fiction, encyclopedias, speciality reference sets, children's
fiction and picture books. About 600 titles a
year. DIVISIONS/IMPRINTS **Children's Press**;
Grolier Educational; **Grolier Classroom
Publishing**; **Franklin Watts**.

Scott Foresman

1900 E Lake Avenue, Glenview, IL 60025
☎001 847 729 3000 Fax 001 847 729 8910
Email <firstname>.<lastname>@
scottforesman.com
Website www.scottforesman.com

President *Paul McFall*

FOUNDED 1896. *Publishes* elementary education materials. No unsolicited material.

Scribner
See **Simon & Schuster Adult Publishing Group**

Seven Stories Press
140 Watts Street, New York, NY 10013
☎001 212 226 8760 Fax 001 212 226 1411
Email info@sevenstories.com
Website www.sevenstories.com

CEO *Daniel Simon*

FOUNDED 1995. Named by *Publishers Weekly* in 2001 as the fastest growing independent publisher in America. *Publishes* fiction, literature, literary translations, memoirs, political non-fiction, health, history, current affairs. DIVISION **Siete Cuentos Editorial** *Juana Ponce de Leon.* No unsolicited mss; synopses and ideas from agents welcome or send query letter. No children's or business books.

Royalties paid twice-yearly. *Overseas subsidiaries:* Turnaround Publishing Services, UK; Tower Books, Australia; Hushion House, Canada.

Signet/Signet Classics
See **Penguin Putnam Inc.**

Silhouette Books
300 East 42nd Street, New York, NY 10017
☎001 212 682 6080 Fax 001 212 682 4539

Editorial Director *Tara Gavin*

FOUNDED 1979 as an imprint of Simon & Schuster and was acquired by a wholly owned subsidiary of Toronto-based Harlequin Enterprises Ltd in 1984. *Publishes* category, contemporary romance fiction and historical romance fiction only. Over 360 titles a year across a number of lines.

IMPRINTS **Silhouette Romance** *Mary Theresa Hussey;* **Silhouette Desire** *Joan Marlow Golan;* **Silhouette Special Edition** *Karen Taylor Richman;* **Silhouette Intimate Moments** *Leslie Wainger;* **Harlequin Historicals** *Tracy Farrell;* **Steeple Hill** *Tracy Farrell.* Imprint, launched in 1997, **Love Inspired** publishes a line of inspirational contemporary romances with stories designed to 'lift readers' spirits and gladden their hearts'. No unsolicited mss. Submit query letter in the first instance or write for detailed submission guidelines/tip sheets. See also **Harlequin Mills & Boon Ltd** under **UK Publishers**.

Royalties paid twice-yearly. *Overseas associates* worldwide.

Silver Whistle Books
See **Harcourt Trade Division**

Simon & Schuster Adult Publishing Group (Division of Simon & Schuster, Inc)
1230 Avenue of the Americas, New York, NY 10020
☎001 212 698 7000 Fax 001 212 698 7007
Website www.simonsays.com

President/Publisher *Carolyn K. Reidy*

Publishes fiction and non-fiction.

DIVISIONS
The Free Press VP & Senior Editor *Fred W. Hills;* **Fireside/Touchstone** VP & Editor-in-Chief *Trish Todd;* **Scribner** VP & Editor-in-Chief *Nan Graham;* **Simon and Schuster** Senior VP & Editor-in-Chief *Michael V. Korda;* **Trade Paperbacks** VP & Editor-in-Chief *Trish Todd;* **Pocket Books** (see entry).

IMPRINTS **Atria Books**; **H.&R. Block**; **Lisa Drew Books**; **Fireside**; **The Free Press**; **Rawson Associates**; **Scribner**; **Scribner Classics**; **Scribner Paperback Fiction**; **S&S Libros eñ Espanol**; **Simon & Schuster**; **Touchstone**. No unsolicited mss.

Royalties paid twice-yearly.

Simon & Schuster Children's Publishing
1230 Avenue of the Americas, New York, NY 10020
☎001 212 698 7200

President/Publisher *Kristina Peterson*
VP/Publisher, Hardcover & Paperback Imprints *Brenda Bowen*

A division of the Simon & Schuster Consumer Group. *Publishes* pre-school to young adult, picture books, hardcover and paperback fiction, non-fiction, trade, library and mass-market titles. About 480 titles a year.

IMPRINTS
Aladdin Books *Ellen Krieger* Picture books, paperback fiction and non-fiction reprints and originals, and limited series for ages pre-school to young adult; **Atheneum Books for Young Readers** *Ginee Seo* Picture books, hardcover fiction and non-fiction books across all genres for ages three to young adult. Two lines within this imprint are **Jean Karl Books** quality fantasy-fiction and **Anne Schwartz Books** distinct picture books and high-quality fiction; **Little Simon** *Robin Corey* Mass-market novelty books (pop-ups, board books, colouring & activity) and merchandise (book and audiocassette) for ages birth through eight; **Margaret K. McElderry Books** *Margaret K. McElderry, Emma Dryden* Picture books, hard-

cover fiction and non-fiction trade books for children ages three to young adult; **Simon & Schuster Books for Young Readers** *Steve Geck* Picture books, hardcover fiction and non-fiction for children ages three to young adult. **Simon Spotlight** *Jennifer Koch* New imprint devoted exclusively to children's media tie-ins and licensed properties.

For submissions to all imprints: send envelope (US size 10) for guidelines, attention: *Manuscript Submissions Guidelines.*

Simon Spotlight
See **Simon & Schuster Children's Publishing**

Sonnet Books
See **Pocket Books**

Southern Illinois University Press
PO Box 3697, Carbondale,
IL 62902–3697
☎001 618 453 2281 Fax 001 618 453 1221
Email jstetter@siu.edu
Website www.siu.edu/~siupress
Director *John F. Stetter*

FOUNDED 1956. *Publishes* scholarly and general interest non-fiction books and educational materials. 50 titles a year.
Royalties paid annually.

Stackpole Books
5067 Ritter Road, Mechanicsburg,
PA 17055
☎001 717 796 0411 Fax 001 717 796 0412
Website www.stackpolebooks.com
President *David Ritter*
Vice President/Editorial Director *Judith Schnell*

FOUNDED 1933. *Publishes* outdoor sports, fishing, nature, photography, military reference, history. About 80 titles a year.
Royalties paid twice-yearly.

Stanford University Press
1450 Page Mill Road, Palo Alto CA
94304–1124
☎001 650 723 9434 Fax 001 650 725 3457
Website www.sup.org
ManagingDirector *Geoffrey R.H. Burn*

FOUNDED 1925. *Publishes* non-fiction: scholarly works in all areas of the humanities, social sciences, history and literature, also professional lists in business, economics and law. About 120 titles a year. No unsolicited mss; query in writing first.

Steeple Hill
See **Silhouette Books**

Sterling Publishing Co. Inc.
387 Park Avenue South, 5th Floor, New York, NY 10016–8810
☎001 212 532 7160 Fax 001 212 213 2495
Website www.sterlingpub.com
President *Lincoln A. Boehm*
Executive Vice-President *Charles Nurnberg*
Editorial Director *John Woodside*

FOUNDED 1949. *Publishes* non-fiction: reference and information books, science, business, nature, arts and crafts, home improvement, history, photography, children's humour, complementary health, wine and food, sports, music, psychology, occult, woodworking, pets, hobbies, gardening, puzzles.

Sunburst Technology
See **Houghton Mifflin Co.**

Susquehanna University Press
See **Golden Cockerel Press** under **UK Publishers**

Syracuse University Press
621 Skytop Road, Suite 110, Syracuse,
NY 13244–5290
☎001 315 443 5534 Fax 001 315 443 5545
Acting Director *John Fruehwirth*

FOUNDED 1943. *Publishes* scholarly books in the following areas: contemporary Middle East studies, Middle East literature in translation, international affairs, Irish studies, Iroquois studies, women and religion, Jewish studies, medieval studies, religion and politics, television, geography. About 70 titles a year. Also co-publishes with a number of organisations such as the American University of Beirut. No unsolicited mss. Send query letter with IRCs.
Royalties paid annually.

Nan A. Talese
See **Doubleday Broadway Publishing Group**

Jeremy P. Tarcher
See **Penguin Putnam Inc**

Temple University Press
1601 N. Broad Street, 083–42, Philadelphia,
PA 19122–6099
☎001 215 204 8787 Fax 001 215 204 4719
Website www.temple.edu/tempress
Editor-in-Chief *Janet M. Francendese*

FOUNDED 1969. *Publishes* scholarly books. About 60 titles a year. Authors generally academics. Letter of inquiry with brief outline. Include fax/e-mail address.

University of Tennessee Press
110 Conference Center Bldg., Knoxville, TN 37996
☎001 865 974 3321 Fax 001 865 974 3724
Website www.utpress.org
Managing Editor *Stan Ivester*
FOUNDED in 1940. *Publishes* scholarly and regional non-fiction.
Royalties paid annually.

University of Texas Press
PO Box 7819, Austin TX 78713–7819
☎001 512 471 7233/Editorial: 471 4278
Fax 001 512 232 7178
Website www.utexas.edu/utpress/
Director *Joanna Hitchcock*
Assistant Director/Executive Editor-in-Chief *Theresa J. May*
Publishes scholarly and regional non-fiction: anthropology, architecture, classics, environmental studies, humanities, social sciences, geography, language studies, literary modernism; Latin American/Latino/Mexican American/Middle Eastern/Native American studies, natural history and ornithology, regional books (Texas and the southwest). Unsolicited material welcome in above subject areas only. About 90 titles a year and 12 journals.
Royalties paid annually.

Thorndike Press
See **Gale**

Three Rivers Press
See **The Crown Publishing Group**

Times Books
See **Henry Holt & Company Inc.**

Topaz
See **Penguin Putnam Inc.**

Touchstone
See **Simon & Schuster Adult Publishing Group**

Transaction Publishers Ltd
c/o Rutgers University, 35 Berrue Circle, Piscataway, NJ 08854–8042
☎001 732 445 2280 Fax 001 732 445 3138
Email ihorowitz@transactionpub.com

Website www.transactionpub.com
Chairman *I.L. Horowitz*
Managing Director *Mary E. Curtis*
FOUNDED 1962. Independent publisher of academic social scientific books, periodicals and serials.

Truman Talley Books
See **St Martin's Press LLC**

Twenty-First Century Books
See **The Millbrook Press, Inc.**

Tyndale House Publishers, Inc.
PO Box 80, Wheaton, IL 60189
☎001 630 668 8310 Fax 001 630 668 3245
Website www.tyndale.com
President *Mark D. Taylor*
FOUNDED 1962. Non-denominational religious publisher of around 300 titles a year for the evangelical Christian market. Books cover a wide range of categories from non-fiction to gift books, theology, doctrine, Bibles, children's and youth. Also produces video material, calendars and audio books for the same market. No poetry. No unsolicited mss. Synopses and ideas considered. Send query letter summarising contents of book and length. Include a brief biography, detailed outline and three sample chapters. IRCs essential for response or return of material. No audio cassettes, disks or video tapes in lieu of mss. Response time around 12–16 weeks. No phone calls or e-mail submissions. Send s.a.e. for submission guidelines.
Royalties paid annually.

University Press of America, Inc.
4720 Boston Way, Lanham, MD 20706
☎001 301 459 3366 Fax 001 301 459 2118
Website www.univpress.com
President/Publisher *James E. Lyons*
Director *Judith L. Rothman*
FOUNDED 1974. *Publishes* scholarly monographs, college and graduate level textbooks. No children's, elementary or high school. About 450 titles a year. Submit outline or request proposal questionnaire.
Royalties paid annually.

Viking/Viking Children's Books
See **Penguin Putnam Inc**

Villard
See **Random House, Inc.**

Vintage Books
See **Random House, Inc.**

University of Virginia Press
PO Box 400318, Charlottesville,
VA 22904–4318
☎001 434 924 3468 Fax 001 434 982 2655
Email upressvirginia@virginia.edu
Website www.upress.virginia.edu

Director *Penelope J. Kaiserlian*

FOUNDED 1963. *Publishes* academic books in humanities and social science with concentrations in American history, African-American studies, architecture, Victorian literature, Caribbean literature and ecocriticism. No unsolicited mss; will consider synopses and ideas for books if in their specific areas of concentration. Approach by mail for full proposal; e-mail for short inquiry. No fiction, children's, poetry or academic books outside interests specified above.
    Royalties paid annually.

Voyager Books
See **Harcourt Trade Division**

J. Weston Walch, Publisher
PO Box 658, Portland, ME 04104
☎001 207 772 2846 Fax 001 207 772 3105
Website www.walch.com

President *John Thoreson*
Editor-in-Chief *Susan Blair*

FOUNDED 1927. *Publishes* supplementary educational materials for middle and secondary schools across a wide range of subjects, including English/language arts, literacy, special needs, mathematics, social studies, science and school-to-career. Always interested in ideas from secondary school teachers who develop materials in the classroom. Proposal letters, synopses and ideas welcome.

Walk Worthy Press
See **Warner Books Inc.**

Walker & Co.
435 Hudson Street, New York, NY 10014
☎001 212 727 8300 Fax 001 212 727 0984

Contact *Submissions Editor*

FOUNDED 1959. *Publishes* mystery, children's and non-fiction. Please contact the following editors in advance before sending any material to be sure of their interest, then follow up as instructed:

Mystery *Michael Seidman* 65–70,000 words. Send first three chapters and two-page synopsis. **Trade Non-fiction** *George Gibson* Permission and documentation must be available with mss. Submit prospectus first, with sample chapters and marketing analysis. **Books for Young Readers** *Emily Easton* Fiction and non-fiction for all ages. Query before sending non-fiction proposals. Especially interested in young science and picture books, historical and contemporary fiction for middle grades and young adults. BFYR will consider unsolicited submissions.

Frederick Warne
See **Penguin Putnam Inc**

Warner Books Inc.
1271 Avenue of the Americas, New York,
NY 10020
☎001 212 522 7200 Fax 001 212 522 7991
Website www.twbookmark.com

Senior Vice-President/Publisher *Jamie Raab*
Associate Publisher *Les Pockell*

FOUNDED 1961. A subsidiary of Time Warner Book Group. *Publishes* fiction and non-fiction, audio books. About 250 titles a year.
    IMPRINTS **Aspect** *Jaime Levine*; **Mysterious Press** *Sara Ann Freed*; **Time Warner Audio Books**; **Warner Vision**; **Walk Worthy Press**; **Warner Faith**. No unsolicited mss.

Washington State University Press
PO Box 645910, Pullman, WA 99164-5910
☎001 509 335 3518 Fax 001 509 335 8568
Email wsupress@wsu.edu
Website www.wsu.edu/wsupress

Editor *Glen Lindeman*

FOUNDED 1928. *Publishes* hardcover originals, trade paperbacks and reprints. *Publishes* mainly on the history, prehistory, culture, politics and natural history of the Northwest United States (Washington, Idaho, Oregon, Montana, Alaska) and British Columbia, but works that focus on national topics or other regions may also be considered if they have a Northwest connection. Subjects include history, biography, cooking/food history, nature/environment, politics. 8–10 titles a year. Queries welcome.
    Royalties paid annually.

Franklin Watts
See **Scholastic Library Publishing**

Wellspring
See **Ballantine Books**

Westview Press
See **Perseus Books Group**

John Wiley & Sons, Inc.
605 Third Avenue, New York, NY 10158
☎001 212 850 6000 Fax 001 212 850 6088
Email info@wiley.com
Website www.wiley.com
Chief Executive Officer *William J. Pesce*

FOUNDED 1807. Acquired a major stake in
Oxford-based business publisher Capstone Publishing Ltd in 2000. *Publishes* professional and
trade print and electronic products in the following fields: culinary arts and hospitality, architec-
ture/design, business, accounting, psychology,
non-profit institution management, computers,
engineering and general interest. Educational
products: the sciences, mathematics, engineering, accounting, business, teacher education,
modern languages, religion. Scientific, technical
and medical publishers of journals, encyclopedias, available in print and electronic media.
About 1500 titles a year. No unsolicited mss.

The University of Wisconsin Press
1930 Monroe Street, 3rd Floor, Madison,
WI 53711–2059
☎001 608 263 1110 Fax 001 608 263 1120
Email uwiscpress@uwpress.wisc.edu
Website www.wisc.edu/wisconsinpress
Director *Robert A. Mandel*

FOUNDED 1936. *Publishes* scholarly, general
interest non-fiction and regional books about
Wisconsin and the mid-west. About 50 titles a
year. No unsolicited mss; proposals (sent by
mail) welcome. 'No unrevised dissertations, no
Festschrifts, no genre, no how-to.'

Zondervan Publishing House
5300 Patterson Avenue SE, Grand Rapids,
MI 49530
☎001 616 698 6900 Fax 001 616 698 3439
Website www.zondervan.com
President/Chief Executive *Bruce E.*
  Ryskamp

FOUNDED 1931. Subsidiary of **HarperCollins
Publishers, Inc.** *Publishes* Protestant religion,
Bibles, books, audio & video, computer soft-
ware, calendars and speciality items.

US Literary Agents

★ = Members of the **Association of Authors' Representatives, Inc.**

Altair Literary Agency★
PO Box 11656, Washington, DC 20008
☎001 202 237 8282
Email APedolsky *or*
 NSmith@AltairLiteraryAgency.com
Website www.AltairLiteraryAgency.com

Contacts *Andrea Pedolsky, Nicholas T. Smith*

FOUNDED 1996. *Handles* historical, pre-20th century, literary and women's related fiction; activity books for children; and non-fiction covering how-to, history, biography, women's issues, contemporary issues, autobiography, illustrated/photography, history of science. No true crime or memoirs. Send query letter and proposal for non-fiction; query letter and synopsis for fiction. Return postage essential. No reading fee. *Commission* Home 15%; Foreign 20%.

Miriam Altshuler Literary Agency★
53 Old Post Road North, Red Hook,
NY 12571
☎001 845 758 9408 Fax 001 845 758 3118
Email malalit@ulster.net

Contact *Sara McGhee*

FOUNDED 1994. *Handles* literary and commercial fiction; general non-fiction, psychology, biography. No romance, science fiction, mysteries, thrillers or self-help. Send query letter and synopsis in the first instance with return postage. No reading fee. *Commission* Home 15%; Foreign/Translation 20%.

Bart Andrews & Associates Inc
7510 Sunset Boulevard, Suite 100,
Los Angeles CA 90046–3418
☎001 310 271 9916

Contact *Bart Andrews*

FOUNDED 1982. General non-fiction: show business, biography and autobiography, film books, trivia, TV and nostalgia. No scripts. No fiction, poetry, children's or science. No books of less than major commercial potential. *Specialises* in working with celebrities on autobiographies. No unsolicited mss. 'Send a brilliant letter (with IRCs for response) extolling your manuscript's virtues. Sell me!' No reading fee. *Commission* Home & Translation 15%. *Overseas associate* **Abner Stein**, UK.

Malaga Baldi Literary Agency
204 West 84th Street, Suite 3C, New York,
NY 10024
☎001 212 579 5075 Fax 001 212 579 5078
Email MBALDI@aol.com

Contact *Malaga Baldi*

FOUNDED 1986. *Handles* quality fiction and non-fiction. No scripts. No westerns, men's adventure, science fiction/fantasy, romance, how-to, young adult or children's. Writers of fiction should send query letter describing the novel plus IRCs. Allow ten weeks *minimum* for response. For non-fiction, approach in writing with a proposal, table of contents and two sample chapters. No reading fee. *Commission* 15%. *Overseas associates* **Abner Stein**, UK; Japan Uni; Eliane Benisti, France; **Marsh Agency**.

The Balkin Agency, Inc.★
PO Box 222, Amherst, MA 01004
☎001 413 548 9835 Fax 001 413 548 9836
Email balkin@crocker.com

Contact *Richard Balkin*

FOUNDED 1973. *Handles* adult non-fiction only. No reading fee for outlines and synopses. *Commission* Home 15%; Foreign 20%.

Loretta Barrett Books, Inc.★
101 Fifth Avenue, New York NY 10003
☎001 212 242 3420 Fax 001 212 807 9579

Contacts *Loretta Barrett, Nick Mullendore*

FOUNDED 1990. *Handles* all non-fiction and fiction genres except children's, poetry, science fiction/fantasy. *Specialises* in women's fiction, history, spirituality. No scripts. Send query letter with biography and return postage only in the first instance. *Commission* Home 15%; Foreign 20%.

Meredith Bernstein Literary Agency, Inc.★
2112 Broadway, Suite 503A, New York,
NY 10023
☎001 212 799 1007 Fax 001 212 799 1145

Contacts *Meredith Bernstein, Elizabeth Cavanaugh*

FOUNDED 1981. *Handles* commercial and literary fiction, mysteries and non-fiction (women's issues, business, memoirs, health, current affairs, crafts). *Commission* Home & Dramatic 15%; Translation 20%. *Overseas associates* **Abner Stein**, UK; Lennart Sane, Holland, Scandinavia and Spanish language; Thomas Schluck, Germany; Bardon Chinese Media Agency; William Miller, Japan; Frederique Porretta, France; Agenzia Letteraria, Italy.

Bleecker Street Associates, Inc.★
532 LaGuardia Place #617, New York,
NY 10012
☎001 212 677 4492 Fax 001 212 388 0001

FOUNDED 1984. *Handles* fiction – women's, mystery, suspense, literary; non-fiction – history, women's interests, parenting, health, relationships, psychology, sports, sociology, current events, biography, spirituality, New Age, business. No poetry, children's, westerns, science fiction, professional, academic. Send query letter in the first instance. Will only respond if envelope and return postage enclosed. No phone calls, faxes or e-mails. No reading fee. *Commission* Home 15%; Foreign 25%.

The Blumer Literary Agency★
PO Box 20754, Park West Station,
New York, NY 10025–1516
☎001 212 749 8853 Fax 001 212 749 1603
Contact *Olivia Blumer*

FOUNDED 2002. *Handles* a broad range of commercial and literary fiction and non-fiction. Strong background in memoir, inspiration, commercial, literary fiction, illustrated and non-fiction. *Specialist subject*: cookery. No TV, film, radio or theatre scripts. No children's, science fiction and fantasy or romances. Send initial introductory letter via e-mail. No reading fee. *Commission* Home 15%; Foreign 20%; Translation 20%.

Reid Boates Literary Agency
PO Box 328, Pittstown, NJ 08867–0328
☎001 908 730 8523 Fax 001 908 730 8931
Contact *Reid Boates*

FOUNDED 1985. *Handles* general fiction and non-fiction. New clients by personal introduction only. *Commission* Home & Dramatic 15%; Translation 20%. *Overseas associates* worldwide.

Book Deals, Inc.★
244 Fifth Avenue, Suite 2164, New York,
NY 1001-7604
☎001 212 252 2701 Fax 001 212 591 6211
Email BookDeals@aol.com
Website www.BookDealsInc.com

President *Caroline Carney*

FOUNDED 1997. *Handles* health, finance, business, self-help, parenting, narrative non-fiction and literary fiction. No scripts, genre fiction, cookbooks, illustrated children's, coffee table books, travel guides, military history, paranormal experience. No unsolicited material; query letter welcome. No reading fee. *Commission* Home 15%; Foreign/Translation 20%.

Georges Borchardt, Inc.★
136 East 57th Street, New York, NY 10022
☎001 212 753 5785 Fax 001 212 838 6518

FOUNDED 1967. Works mostly with established/published authors. *Specialises* in fiction, biography, and general non-fiction of unusual interest. Unsolicited mss not read. *Commission* Home, UK & Dramatic 15%; Translation 20%. *UK associate* **Sheil Land Associates Ltd** (Richard Scott Simon), London.

Brandt & Hochman Literary Agents, Inc.★
1501 Broadway, New York, NY 10036
☎001 212 840 5760

Contacts *Carl D. Brandt, Gail Hochman, Marianne Merola, Charles Schlessiger*

FOUNDED 1914. *Handles* non-fiction and fiction. No poetry. No unsolicited mss. Approach by letter describing background and ambitions; include return postage. No reading fee. *Commission* Home & Dramatic 15%; Foreign 20%. *UK associate* **A.M. Heath & Co. Ltd**.

Pema Browne Ltd, Illustration and Literary Agents
HCR Box 104B, Neversink, NY 12765
☎001 818 340 4320 Fax 001 818 340 4320
Email ppbltd@earthlink.net
Website www.pemabrowneltd.com
Contacts *Pema Browne, Perry Browne*

FOUNDED 1966. ('Pema rhymes with Emma.') *Handles* mass-market mainstream and hardcover fiction: romance, business, children's picture books and young adult; non-fiction: how-to and reference. No unsolicited mss; send query letter with IRCs. No fax or e-mail queries. Also handles illustrators' work. No longer accepting screenplays. *Commission* Home 15%; Translation 20%; Overseas authors 20%.

Sheree Bykofsky Associates, Inc.★
16 West 36th Street, 13th Floor, New York,
NY 10018
☎001 212 244 4144

Email shereebee@aol.com
Contact *Sheree Bykofsky*

FOUNDED 1991. *Handles* adult fiction and non-fiction. No scripts. No children's, young adult, horror, science fiction, romance, westerns, occult or supernatural. No unsolicited mss. Send query letter first with brief synopsis or outline and writing sample (1–3 pp) for fiction. IRCs essential for reply or return of material. No phone calls. No reading fee. *Commission* Home 15%; UK (including sub-agent's fee) 25%.

Carlisle & Company LLC★
24 East 64th Street, New York, NY 10021
☎001 212 813 1881 Fax 001 212 813 9567
Email ep@carlisleco.com
Website www.carlisleco.com

Contacts *Michael V. Carlisle, Christy Fletcher, Emma Parry, Michelle Tessler*

FOUNDED 1998. *Handles* history, science, travel, narrative non-fiction, literary and category fiction. No scripts, children's, juvenile, romance, science fiction/fantasy, mysteries. No unsolicited mss. Query letter for fiction by mail or through website; proposal with query for non-fiction. No reading fee. *Commission* Home 15%; Foreign/Translation 20%. *Associates* Co-agents in every major territory.

Maria Carvainis Agency, Inc.★
1350 Avenue of the Americas, Suite 2905, New York, NY 10019
☎001 212 245 6365 Fax 001 212 245 7196
Email mca@mariacarvainisagency.com
President *Maria Carvainis*
Executive *Frances Kuffel*

FOUNDED 1977. *Handles* fiction: literary and mainstream, contemporary women's, mystery, suspense, historical, young adult novels; non-fiction: business, finance, women's issues, politics, film, memoirs, reportage, biography, medicine, psychology and popular science. No film scripts unless from writers with established credits. No science fiction. No faxed or e-mailed queries. No unsolicited mss; they will be returned unread. Queries only, with IRCs for response. No reading fee. *Commission* Domestic & Dramatic 15%; Translation 20%.

Martha Casselman, Literary Agent
PO Box 342, Calistoga, CA 94515
☎001 707 942 4341
Contact *Martha Casselman*

FOUNDED 1979. *Handles* non-fiction. No fiction at present. Main interest: food/cookery. No

scripts, children's, textbooks, poetry, coming-of-age fiction or science fiction. Especially interested in cookery with an appeal to the American market for possible co-publication in UK. Send queries and brief summary, with return postage. No mss. If you do not wish return of material, please state so. Also include, where applicable, any material on previous publications, reviews, brief biography. No proposals via fax. No reading fee. *Commission* Home 15%.

Castiglia Literary Agency★
1155 Camino del mar, #510, Del Mar, CA 92014
☎001 858 755 8761 Fax 001 858 755 7063
Email jaclagency@aol.com
Contacts *Julie Castiglia, Winifred Golden*

FOUNDED 1993. *Handles* fiction: literary, mainstream, ethnic; non-fiction: narrative, biography, science, health, parenting, memoirs, psychology, women's and contemporary issues. *Specialises* in science, biography and literary fiction. No scripts, horror or true crime. No unsolicited material; send query letter only in the first instance. No reading fee. *Commission* Home 15%; Foreign/Translation 25%.

The Catalog Literary Agency
PO Box 2964, Vancouver, WA 98668
☎001 360 694 8531
Contact *Douglas Storey*

FOUNDED 1986. *Handles* popular, professional and textbook material in all subjects, especially business, health, money, science, technology, computers, electronics and women's interests; also how-to, self-help, mainstream fiction and children's non-fiction. No genre fiction. No scripts, articles, screenplays, plays, poetry or short stories. No unsolicited mss. Query with an outline and sample chapters, and include IRCs. No reading fee. *Commission* 15%.

Linda Chester & Associates★
Rockefeller Center, 630 Fifth Avenue, New York, NY 10111
☎001 212 218 3350 Fax 001 212 218 3343
Email lcassoc@mindspring.com
Website www.lindachester.com

Contact *Joanna Pulcini, Associate*

FOUNDED 1978. *Handles* literary and commercial fiction and non-fiction in all subjects. No scripts, children's or textbooks. No unsolicited mss or queries. No reading fee for solicited material. *Commission* Home & Dramatic 15%; Translation 25%.

Clausen, Mays & Tahan Literary Agency

249 West 34th Street, Suite 605, New York, NY 10001

☎001 212 239 4343 Fax 001 212 239 5248

Email cmtassist@aol.com

Contacts *Stedman Mays, Mary M. Tahan*

Handles fiction and non-fiction work such as memoirs, biography, true crime, true stories, how-to, psychology, spirituality, relationships, style, health/nutrition, fashion/beauty, women's issues, humour and cookbooks. Some fiction. For fiction send synopsis and first 10 pages. For non fiction send query letter only. Include IRCs. *UK associate* **David Grossman Literary Agency Ltd**.

Ruth Cohen, Inc.*

PO Box 2244, La Jolla, CA 92038–2244

Contact *Ruth Cohen*

Handles mystery, women's literature, romance, fiction, young adult and children's books. No scripts. No unsolicited mss; send a brief, well thought-out synopsis, the opening ten pages (carefully edited) and return postage. No reading fee.

Frances Collin Literary Agent*

PO Box 33, Wayne, PA 19087–0033

☎001 610 254 0555 Fax 001 610 254 5029

Contact *Frances Collin*

FOUNDED 1948. Successor to Marie Rodell. *Handles* general fiction and non-fiction. No scripts. No unsolicited mss. Send query letter only, with IRCs for reply, for the attention of *Marsha Kear*. No reading fee. Rarely accepts non-professional writers or writers not represented in the UK. *Overseas associates* worldwide.

Don Congdon Associates, Inc.*

156 Fifth Avenue, Suite 625, New York, NY 10010–7002

☎001 212 645 1229 Fax 001 212 727 2688

Contacts *Don Congdon, Michael Congdon, Susan Ramer, Cristina Concepcion*

FOUNDED 1983. *Handles* fiction and non-fiction. No academic, technical, romantic fiction, or scripts. No unsolicited mss. Query letter with return postage in the first instance. No reading fee. *Commission* Home 15%; UK & Translation 19%. *Overseas associates* worldwide.

Cornerstone Literary Agency*

4500 Wilshire Boulevard, Los Angeles, CA 90010

☎001 323 930 6039 Fax 001 323 930 0407

Email info@cornerstoneliterary.com

Website www.cornerstoneliterary.com

Contact *Helen Breitwieser*

FOUNDED 1998. *Handles* literary and commercial fiction. *Specialises* in thrillers and commercial women's fiction. No scripts, children's, self-help, science fiction or fantasy. No unsolicited mss via mail, e-mail or fax; send query letter and one-page synopsis via fax or mail (enclosing return postage with latter). No reading fee. *Commission* Home 15%; Foreign/ Translation 20%.

Richard Curtis Associates, Inc.

171 East 74th Street, Second Floor, New York, NY 10021

☎001 212 772 7363 Fax 001 212 772 7393

Email info@curtisagency.com

Website www.curtisagency.com

Contact *Richard Curtis*

FOUNDED 1969. *Handles* genre and mainstream fiction, plus commercial non-fiction. No children's books or scripts.

Curtis Brown Ltd*

10 Astor Place, New York, NY 10003

☎001 212 473 5400

Book Rights *Laura Blake Peterson, Ellen Geiger, Peter L. Ginsberg, Emilie Jacobson, Ginger Knowlton, Marilyn E. Marlow, Maureen Walters, Mitchell Walters*

Film, TV Rights *Timothy Knowlton, Edwin Wintle*

Translation *Dave Barbor*

FOUNDED 1914. *Handles* general fiction and non-fiction. Also some scripts for film, TV and theatre. No unsolicited mss; queries only, with IRCs for reply. No reading fee. *Overseas associates* Representatives in all major foreign countries.

Joan Daves Agency

21 West 26th Street, New York, NY 10010–1003

☎001 212 685 2663 Fax 001 212 685 1781

Director *Jennifer Lyons*

FOUNDED 1952. See also **Writers House LLC**. Literary fiction and non-fiction. No romance or textbooks. No scripts. Send query letter in the first instance. 'A detailed synopsis seems valuable only for non-fiction work. Material submitted should specify the author's background, publishing credits and similar pertinent information.' No reading fee. *Commission* Home 15%; Dramatic/Film 15%; Foreign 20%.

Sandra Dijkstra Literary Agency★

PMB 515, 1155 Camino Del Mar, Del Mar,
CA 92104–3115
☎001 858 755 3115   Fax 001 858 794 2822

Contact *Babette Sparr*

FOUNDED 1981. *Handles* quality and commercial
non-fiction and fiction, including some genre
fiction. No scripts. No westerns, contemporary
romance or poetry. Willing to look at children's
projects. *Specialises* in quality fiction, mystery/
thrillers, narrative non-fiction, psychology, self-
help, science, health, business, memoirs, biography. 'Dedicated to promoting new and original
voices and ideas.' For fiction: send brief synopsis
(one page) and first 50 pages; for non-fiction:
send proposal with overview, chapter outline,
author biog, two sample chapters and profile of
competition. All submissions should be accompanied by IRCs. No reading fee. *Commission*
Home 15%; Translation 20%. *Overseas associates*
Abner Stein, UK; Ursula Bender, Agence
Hoffman, Germany; Licht & Burr, Scandinavia;
Luigi Bernabo, Italy; Sandra Bruna, Spain;
Caroline Van Gelderen, Netherlands; M. Kling
(La Nouvelle Agence), France; William Miller,
The English Agency, Japan.

Douglas & Kapelman Artists Inc★

393 West 49th Street, Suite G, New York,
NY 10019
☎001 212 445 0160   Fax 001 212 246 7138

Handles plays and musicals only – does not
handle books. No unsolicited material. No
reading fee.

Dunham Literary Inc★

156 Fifth Avenue, Suite 625, New York,
NY 10010
☎001 212 929 0994   Fax 001 212 929 0904
Website www.dunhamlit.com

Contacts *Jennie Dunham, Donna H. Lieberman*

FOUNDED 2000. *Handles* literary fiction and non-
fiction, New Age spirituality, mysteries and
children's (from picture books through young
adult). No scripts, romance, westerns, horror,
science-fiction/fantasy or poetry. No unsolicited
material. Send query letter (with return postage)
giving information on the author and ms. No
e-mail or faxed queries; see the website for further contact information. No reading fee. *Commission* Home 15%; Foreign/Translation 20%.
Overseas associate UK & Europe – **A.M. Heath
& Co. Ltd**. The Rhoda Weyr Agency is now a
division of Dunham Literary Inc.

Jane Dystel Literary Management★

One Union Square West, Suite 904,
New York, NY 10003
☎001 212 627 9100   Fax 001 212 627 9313
Website www.dystel.com

Contacts *Jane Dystel, Miriam Goderich, Stacey
Glick, Michael Bourret, Jim McCarthy*

FOUNDED 1991. *Handles* non-fiction and fiction. *Specialises* in politics, history, biography,
cookbooks, current affairs, celebrities, commercial and literary fiction. No reading fee.

Educational Design Services, Inc.

PO Box 253, Wantagh, NY 11793
☎001 718 539 4107/516 221 0995
Email linder.eds@juno.com *or*
eselzer@nyc.rr.com

President *Bertram Linder*
Vice President *Edwin Selzer*

FOUNDED 1979. *Specialises* in educational ma-
terial and textbooks for sale to school markets.
IRCs must accompany submissions. *Commission*
Home 15%; Foreign 25%.

Elek International Rights Agents (a subsidiary of **The Content Company, Inc.**)

5111 JFK Boulevard East, West New York,
NJ 07093
☎001 201 558 0323   Fax 001 201 558 0307
Email info@theliteraryagency.com
Website www.theliteraryagency.com

Contact *Juliet Gentite*

FOUNDED 1979. *Handles* adult non-fiction and
children's picture books. No scripts, fiction,
psychology, New Age, poetry, short stories or
autobiography. No unsolicited mss; send letter
of enquiry with IRCs for reply; include résumé,
credentials, brief synopsis. No reading fee.
Commission Home 15%; Dramatic & Foreign
20%.

Ethan Ellenberg Literary Agency★

548 Broadway, #5E, New York NY 10012
☎001 212 431 4554   Fax 001 212 941 4652
Email agent@ethanellenberg.com
Website www.ethanellenberg.com

Contacts *Ethan Ellenberg, Michael Psaltis*

FOUNDED 1984. *Handles* fiction: commercial,
genre, literary and children's; non-fiction: history, biography, business, science, health,
cooking, current affairs. No scripts, poetry or
short stories. *Specialises* in commercial fiction,
thrillers, suspense and romance. Prefers submissions by mail with return postage. For fiction

send synopsis and three chapters; for non-fiction send proposal and sample chapters, if available. No reading fee. Accepts e-mail submissions; for e-mail submissions send only query letter, no attachments. *Commission* Home 15%; Translation 20%.

Ann Elmo Agency, Inc.★
60 East 42nd Street, New York, NY 10165
☎001 212 661 2880/1 Fax 001 212 661 2883
Contacts *Lettie Lee, Mari Cronin, Andree Abecassis*

FOUNDED in the 1940s. *Handles* literary and romantic fiction, mysteries and mainstream; also non-fiction in all subjects, including biography and self-help. Some children's (8–12-year-olds). Query letter with outline of project in the first instance. No reading fee. *Commission* Home 15–20%. *Overseas associate* **John Johnson Ltd**, UK.

The Fogelman Literary Agency★
7515 Greenville Avenue, Suite 712, Dallas, TX 75231
☎001 214 361 9956 Fax 001 214 361 9553
Email FogLit@aol.com
Website www.fogelman.com
Also at: 919 Third Avenue, Suite 2700, New York, NY 10022
Contacts *Evan Fogelman, Linda Kruger, Helen Brown*

FOUNDED 1989. *Handles* non-fiction and fiction: romance (including historical and contemporary) and some mystery/suspense. No scripts, poetry, westerns, science fiction/fantasy or children's books. No unsolicited material. Published authors are welcome to call but unpublished authors should send query by e-mail or letter with return postage. No reading fee. *Commission* Home 15%; Foreign/Translation 10%. *Overseas associates* Thomas Schluck Agency; Shin Won Literary Agency; Bastei Lubbe Taschenbucher; Big Apple Tuttle-Mori Agency.

ForthWrite Literary Agency & Speakers Bureau
23852 W. Pacific Coast Highway, Suite 701, Malibu, CA 90265
☎001 310 456 5698 Fax 001 310 456 6589
Email agent@KellerMedia.com
Website www.KellerMedia.com
Contact *Wendy L. Keller*

FOUNDED 1988. *Specialises* in non-fiction: biography, business (marketing, finance, management and sales), alternative health, cookery, gardening, nature, popular psychology, history, self-help, home and health, crafts, computer, how-to, animal care by experts known in the field. Handles electronic, foreign (translation and distribution) and resale rights for previously published books. Send query letter with IRCs. No reading fee. *Commission* Foreign 20%.

Jeanne Fredericks Literary Agency, Inc.★
221 Benedict Hill Road, New Canaan, CT 06840
☎001 203 972 3011 Fax 001 203 972 3011
Email jfredrks@optonline.net
Contact *Jeanne Fredericks*

FOUNDED 1997. *Handles* quality adult non-fiction, usually of a practical and popular nature by authorities in their fields. *Specialises* in health, gardening, business, self-help, reference, careers. No fiction, juvenile, poetry, essays, politics, academic or textbooks. No unsolicited material; send query by e-mail (no attachments) or letter with return postage in the first instance. No reading fee. *Commission* Home 15%; Foreign 25% (with co-agent) or 20% (direct).

Robert A. Freedman Dramatic Agency, Inc.★
Suite 2310, 1501 Broadway, New York, NY 10036
☎001 212 840 5760
President *Robert A. Freedman*
Vice President *Selma Luttinger*

FOUNDED 1928 as Brandt & Brandt Dramatic Department, Inc. Took its present name in 1984. Works mostly with established authors. *Specialises* in plays, film and TV scripts. Unsolicited mss not read. *Commission* Dramatic 10%.

Max Gartenberg, Literary Agent
521 Fifth Avenue, Suite 1700, New York, NY 10175
☎001 212 292 4354 Fax 001 973 535 5033
Email gartenbook@att.net
Contact *Max Gartenberg*

FOUNDED 1954. Works mostly with established/published authors. *Specialises* in non-fiction and trade fiction. Query first. *Commission* Home & Dramatic 10%; 15% on initial sale, 10% thereafter; Foreign 15/20%.

Gelfman Schneider Literary Agents, Inc.★
250 West 57th Street, Suite 2515, New York NY 10107

☎001 212 245 1993 Fax 001 212 245 8678
Contacts *Deborah Schneider, Jane Gelfman*

FOUNDED 1919 (London), 1980 (New York). Formerly John Farquharson Ltd. Works mostly with established/published authors. *Specialises* in general trade fiction and non-fiction. No poetry, short stories or screenplays. No reading fee for outlines. Submissions must be accompanied by IRCs. *Commission* Home 15%; Dramatic 15%; Foreign 20%. *Overseas associate* **Curtis Brown Group Ltd**, UK. No e-mail queries please.

Sanford J. Greenburger Associates, Inc.★
15th Floor, 55 Fifth Avenue, New York, NY 10003
☎001 212 206 5600 Fax 001 212 463 8718
Website www.greenburger.com

Contacts *Heide Lange, Faith Hamlin, Beth Vesel, Theresa Park, Elyse Cheney, Daniel Mandel*

Handles fiction and non-fiction. No unsolicited mss. First approach with query letter, sample chapter and synopsis. No reading fee.

The Charlotte Gusay Literary Agency
10532 Blythe Avenue, Los Angeles, CA 90064
☎001 310 559 0831 Fax 001 310 559 2639
Email gusay1@aol.com
Website www.mediastudio.com/gusay

Contact *Charlotte Gusay*

FOUNDED 1988. *Handles* fiction, both literary and commercial, books to film and screenplays, plus non-fiction: children's and adult humour, parenting, gardening, women's and men's issues, feminism, psychology, memoirs, biography, travel. No science fiction, horror, short pieces or collections of stories. No unsolicited mss; send query letter first, then if your material is requested, send succinct outline and first three sample chapters for fiction, or proposal for non-fiction. No response without IRCs or self-addressed stamped envelope. No reading fee. *Commission* Home 15%; Dramatic 10%; Translation & Foreign 25%.

Joy Harris Literary Agency, Inc.★
156 Fifth Avenue, Suite 617, New York, NY 10010
☎001 212 924 6269 Fax 001 212 924 6609
Email gen.office@jhlitagent.com

Contacts *Joy Harris, Stephanie Abou, Leslie Daniels, Alexia Paul*

Handles adult non-fiction and fiction. No unsolicited mss. Query letter in the first instance. No reading fee. *Commission* Home & Dramatic 15%; Foreign 20%. *Overseas associates* Michael Meller, Germany; **Abner Stein**, UK; Roberto Santachiara, Italy; various Japanese agencies; **Andrew Nurnberg Associates**, rest of the territories.

John Hawkins & Associates, Inc.★
71 West 23rd Street, Suite 1600, New York, NY 10010
☎001 212 807 7040 Fax 001 212 807 9555
Email jha@jhaliterary.com
Website www.jhaliterary.com

Contacts *John Hawkins, William Reiss*

FOUNDED 1893. *Handles* film and TV rights. No unsolicited mss; send queries with 1–3-page outline and one-page c.v. IRCs necessary for response. No reading fee. *Commission* Apply for rates.

The Jeff Herman Agency, LLC
PO Box 1522, Stockbridge, MA 01262
☎001 413 298 0077 Fax 001 413 298 8188
Email jeff@jeffherman.com
Website www.jeffherman.com

Contact *Jeffrey H. Herman*

Handles all areas of non-fiction, textbooks and reference. No scripts. No unsolicited mss. Query letter with IRCs in the first instance. No reading fee. Jeff Herman publishes a useful reference guide to the book trade called *The Writer's Guide to Book Editors, Publishers & Literary Agents* (Prima). *Commission* Home 15%; Translation 10%.

Frederick Hill Bonnie Nadell Inc.
1842 Union Street, San Francisco, CA 94123
☎001 415 921 2910 Fax 001 415 921 2802

Contacts *Fred Hill, Bonnie Nadell, Irene Moore*

FOUNDED 1979. General fiction and non-fiction. No scripts. Send query letter detailing past publishing history if any. IRCs required. *Commission* Home & Dramatic 15%; Foreign 20%. *Overseas associate* **Mary Clemmey Literary Agency**, UK.

IMG Literary US
See entry under **UK Literary Agents**

Janklow & Nesbit Associates
445 Park Avenue, New York NY 10022
☎001 212 421 1700 Fax 001 212 980 3671

Partners *Morton L. Janklow, Lynn Nesbit*

Senior Vice-President *Anne Sibbald*
Agents *Tina Bennett, Luke Janklow, Richard Morris, Eric Simonoff*

FOUNDED 1989. *Handles* fiction and non-fiction; commercial and literary. No unsolicited mss. See also **Janklow & Nesbit (UK) Ltd** under **UK Literary Agents**.

JCA Literary Agency, Inc★
27 West 20th Street, Suite 1103, New York, NY 10011
☎001 212 807 0888 Fax 001 212 807 0461

Contacts *Jeff Gerecke, Tony Outhwaite, Peter Steinberg*

FOUNDED 1978. *Handles* general fiction and non-fiction. No scripts, poetry, science fiction/fantasy or children's books. No unsolicited mss; send query letter with return postage. No reading fee. *Commission* Home 15%; Foreign 20%. *Overseas associate* **Vanessa Holt Ltd**, UK.

Kidde, Hoyt & Picard★
333 East 51st Street, New York, NY 10022
☎001 212 755 9461/9465
Fax 001 212 223 2501

Chief Associate *Katharine Kidde*

FOUNDED 1981. *Specialises* in mainstream and literary fiction, mysteries, romantic fiction (historical and contemporary), and quality non-fiction in humanities and social sciences (biography, history, current affairs, the arts). No unsolicited mss. Query first, include return postage. No reading fee. *Commission* 15%.

Kirchoff/Wohlberg, Inc.★
866 United Nations Plaza, Suite 525, New York, NY 10017
☎001 212 644 2020 Fax 001 212 223 4387

Authors' Representative *Elizabeth Pulitzer-Voges*

FOUNDED 1930. *Handles* books for children and young adults, specialising in children's picture books. No adult material. No scripts for TV, radio, film or theatre. Send letter of enquiry with synopsis or outline and writing sample plus IRCs for reply or return. No reading fee.

Harvey Klinger, Inc.★
301 West 53rd Street, New York, NY 10019
☎001 212 581 7068 Fax 001 212 315 3823
Email havey@harveyklinger.com
Website harveyklinger.com

Contact *Harvey Klinger*

FOUNDED 1977. *Handles* mainstream fiction and non-fiction. Specialises in commercial and literary fiction, psychology, health and science. No scripts, poetry, computer or children's books. Welcomes unsolicited material; send by e-mail or post (no faxes). No reading fee. *Commission* Home 15%; Foreign 25%. *Overseas associates* in all principal countries.

The Knight Agency, Inc★
PO Box 550648, Atlanta, GA 30355
Fax 001 404 237 3439
Email knightagency@msn.com
Website www.knightagency.net

Contacts *Deidre Knight, Pamela Harty, Lisa Payne*

FOUNDED 1996. *Handles* romance and women's, literary, and commercial fiction; general non-fiction including business, finance, African American, religion, health. No scripts, horror, science fiction, action/adventure, mystery, short story or poetry collections. No unsolicited material. Prefers a well-written one-page query sent via e-mail (no attachments) or post. If sent by the latter, include return postage. No reading fee. *Commission* Home 15%; Foreign 20–25 %.

Paul Kohner, Inc.
9300 Wilshire Boulevard, Suite 555, Beverly Hills, CA 90212
☎001 310 550 1060 Fax 001 310 276 1083

Contacts *Pearl Wexler, Stephen Moore, Brian Dreyfuss*

FOUNDED 1938. *Handles* a broad range of books for subsidiary rights sales to film and TV. Few direct placements with publishers as film and TV scripts are the major part of the business. *Specialises* in true crime, biography and history. Non-fiction preferred to fiction for the TV market but anything 'we feel has strong potential' will be considered. No short stories, poetry, science fiction or gothic. Unsolicited material will be returned unread, if accompanied by s.a.e. Approach via a third-party reference or send query letter with professional résumé. No reading fee. *Commission* Home & Dramatic 10%; Publishing 15%.

Linda Konner Literary Agency★
10 West 15 Street, Suite 1918, New York, NY 10011
☎001 212 691 3419
Email ldkonner@cs.com

Contact *Linda Konner*

FOUNDED 1996. *Handles* non-fiction only, specialising in health, self-help, diet/fitness, pop psychology, relationships, parenting, personal finance. Also some pop culture/celebrities.

Books must be written by or with established experts in their field. No scripts, fiction, poetry or children's books. No unsolicited material; send one-page query with return postage. No reading fee. *Commission* Home 15%; Foreign 25%.

Peter Lampack Agency, Inc.

551 Fifth Avenue, Suite 1613, New York, NY 10176
☎001 212 687 9106
Email renboPLA@aol.com
Contact *Loren Soeiro*

FOUNDED in 1977. *Handles* commercial fiction: male action and adventure, contemporary relationships, historical, mysteries and suspense, literary fiction; also non-fiction from recognised experts in a given field, plus biographies, autobiographies. Also handles theatrical, motion picture, and TV rights from book properties. No original scripts or screenplays, series or episodic material. Best approach by letter in first instance. No reply without s.a.e. 'We will respond within three weeks and invite the submission of manuscripts which we would like to examine.' No reading fee. No unsolicited mss. *Commission* Home & Dramatic 15%; Translation & UK 20%.

The Lazear Agency, Inc./ Talkback, A Speaker's Bureau

800 Washington Avenue N., Suite 660, Minneapolis MN 55401
☎001 612 332 8640 Fax 001 612 332 4648
Contacts *Christi Cardenas, Jonathon Lazear, Wendy Lazear, Anne Blackstone, Julie Mayo*

FOUNDED 1984. *Handles* fiction: mysteries, suspense, young adult, commercial and literary; also commercial and serious non-fiction of all types; and children's books. No poetry or stage plays. Approach by letter, with description of mss, short autobiography and IRCs. No reading fee. Also book packaging division and select entertainment management. Talkback is the agency's speaker's bureau. *Commission* Home & Dramatic 15%; Translation 20%.

Sarah Lazin Books★

126 Fifth Avenue, Suite 300, New York, NY 10011
☎001 212 989 5757 Fax 001 212 989 1393
Contacts *Sarah Lazin, Paul Balzer*

Handles adult narrative non-fiction in pop culture, biography, social issues, music reference, photography, fiction. *Specialises* in music and biography. Send query letter with references

and writing sample. *Commission* Home 15%; Foreign 10%.

Lescher & Lescher Ltd★

47 East 19th Street, New York, NY 10003
☎001 212 529 1790 Fax 001 212 529 2716
Email rl@lescherltd.com *or* mc@lescherltd.com
Contacts *Robert Lescher, Mickey Choate*

ESTABLISHED 1966. *Handles* a broad range of serious non-fiction including current affairs, history, biography, memoir, government, politics, law, contemporary issues, sociology, psychology, popular culture, food and wine, literary and commercial fiction including mysteries and thrillers; some children's books. No poetry, science fiction, New Age, spiritual, romance. *Specialises* in wine books and cookbooks. No unsolicited manuscripts – please query first. No reading fee. *Commission* Home 10%; Foreign 20%.

Literary & Creative Artists Inc.★

3543 Albemarle Street NW, Washington, DC 20008–4213
☎001 202 362 4688 Fax 001 202 362 8875
Email muriel@lcadc.com
Website www.lcadc.com
Contacts *Muriel G. Nellis, Jane F. Roberts, Stephen Rowe*

FOUNDED 1981. *Specialises* in a broad range of general non-fiction and some literary fiction. No poetry, pornography, academic or educational textbooks. No unsolicited mss; query letter in the first instance. Include IRCs for response. No reading fee. *Commission* Home 15%; Dramatic 20%; Translation 20–25%.

Sterling Lord Literistic, Inc.

65 Bleecker Street, New York, NY 10012
☎001 212 780 6050 Fax 001 212 780 6095
Contacts *Philippa Brophy, Chris Calhoun*

FOUNDED 1979. *Handles* all genres, fiction and non-fiction, plus scripts for TV and film. No unsolicited mss. Prefers letter outlining all non-fiction. No reading fee. *Commission* Home 15%; UK & Translation 20%.

Barbara Lowenstein Associates

See **Lowenstein–Yost Associates Inc**

Lowenstein–Yost Associates Inc★

121 West 27th Street, Suite 601, New York, NY 10001
☎001 212 206 1630 Fax 001 212 727 0280
Website www.lowensteinyost.com

Agents *Barbara Lowenstein, Nancy Yost, Eileen Cope, Dorian Karchmar*

FOUNDED 1976. *Handles* fiction: literary and commercial, women's, mainstream, romance, mystery, thrillers. Non-fiction: narrative, health, business, women's issues, adventure travel, science, spirituality, psychology, social issues, ethnic and cultural issues, history, biography and the arts. No textbooks, westerns, science fiction, cookery or children's books. No reading fee. Fiction – send query letter, synopsis and first chapter; nonfiction – send query with proposal, if available, or overview. Include return postage. *Commission* Home 15%; Foreign/Translation 20%. *Overseas associates* in all major countries.

Donald Maas Literary Agency★

160 West 95th Street, Suite 113, New York, NY 10025
☎001 212 866 8200 Fax 001 212 866 8181
Email info@maasagency.com

Contacts *Donald Maas, Jennifer Jackson, Michelle Brummer (Overseas Associates)*

ESTABLISHED 1981. *Handles* all types of fiction and very select non-fiction. No scripts, children's, general/non-fiction (only interested in narrative non-fiction and non-fiction related to mystery and SF/fantasy fields). *Specialises* in mystery and science fiction/fantasy. Send query letter with concise one-page synopsis. Mss should only be sent on request. No reading fee. *Commission* Home 15%; Foreign/Translation 20%.

Gerard McCauley Agency Inc.

PO Box 844, New York, NY 1056
☎001 232 914 5700 Fax 001 232 814 1506
Email gerrymccauleyagency@earthlink.net

Contact *Gerard McCauley*

ESTABLISHED 1970. *Handles* history, public affairs, adult non-fiction. No scripts, fiction or children's books. No unsolicited material. Submission on recommendation only. No reading fee. *Commission* Home 15%; Foreign 20% with sub-agents receiving 10%; Translation 20%. *Overseas Associates* (sub-agents) in all foreign countries.

Carol Mann Agency★

55 Fifth Avenue, New York, NY 10003
☎001 212 206 5635 Fax 001 212 674 4809
Email carole@carolmannagency.com *or* jfitzgerald@carolmannagency.com *or* kim@carolmannagency.com

Contacts *Carol Mann, Jim Fitzgerald, Kim Goldstein, Leylha Ahuiley*

FOUNDED 1977. *Handles* literary fiction and narrative non-fiction, including psychology, biography, memoirs, history, pop culture, spirituality. No scripts or genre fiction. No unsolicited material; send query letter with return postage. No reading fee. *Commission* Home 15%; Foreign 20%.

Manus & Associates Literary Agency, Inc.★

375 Forest Avenue, Palo Alto, CA 94301
Email ManusLit@ManusLit.com
Website www.ManusLit.com

Also at: 445 Park Avenue, New York, NY 10022

Contacts *Janet Manus, Jillian Manus, Jandy Nelson, Stephanie Lee, Christian Cummings*

Handles commercial and literary fiction; non-fiction, including true crime, self-help, memoirs, history, pop culture and popular science. No scripts, science fiction/fantasy, westerns, romance, horror, poetry or children's books. No unsolicited mss. Fiction: send query letter and first 30 pages; non-fiction: query letter and proposal. Include return postage. No reading fee. *Commission* Home 15%; Foreign 25%.

The Evan Marshall Agency★

Six Tristam Place, Pine Brook, NJ 07058–9445
☎001 973 882 1122 Fax 001 973 882 3099
Email evanmarshall@TheNovelist.com
Website www.TheNovelist.com

Contact *Evan Marshall*

FOUNDED 1987. *Handles* general adult fiction. No unsolicited mss; send query letter first. *Commission* Home 15%; UK & Translation 20%.

Helen Merrill Ltd★

295 Lafayette Street, Suite 915, New York, NY 10012–2700
☎001 212 226 5015 Fax 001 212 226 5079
Email litasst@hmlartists.com

Contacts *Patrick Herold, Morgan Jenness, Beth Blickers*

FOUNDED 1974. *Handles* film and television scripts only. No unsolicited material. New clients through professional reference only.

Mews Books Ltd

c/o Sidney B. Kramer, 20 Bluewater Hill, Westport, CT 06880
☎001 203 227 1836 Fax 001 203 227 1144

Contacts *Sidney B. Kramer, Fran Pollak*
Email mewsbooks@aol.com (initial contact only; submission by regular mail)

FOUNDED 1970. *Handles* adult fiction and non-fiction, children's, pre-school and young adult. No scripts, short stories or novellas (unless by established authors). *Specialises* in cookery, medical, health and nutrition, scientific non-fiction, children's and young adult. Unsolicited material welcome. Presentation must be professional and should include summary of plot/characters, one or two sample chapters, personal credentials and brief on target market, all suitable for forwarding to a publisher. No reading fee. If material is accepted, agency asks $350 circulation fee (4–5 publishers), which will be applied against commissions (waived for published authors). Charges for photocopying, postage expenses, telephone calls and other direct costs. Principal agent is an attorney and former publisher (a founder of Bantam Books). Offers consultation service through which writers can get advice on a contract or on publishing problems. *Commission* Home 15%; Film & Translation 20%. *Overseas associate* **Abner Stein**, UK.

Doris S. Michaels
Literary Agency Inc.★
1841 Broadway, Suite 903, New York, NY 10023
☎001 212 265 9474 Fax 001 212 265 9480
Email infor@dsmagency.com
Website www.dsmagency.com

Contact *Doris Michaels*

Handles literary fiction that has a commercial appeal and strong screen potential and women's fiction; non-fiction: current affairs, biography and memoirs, self-help, business, history, health, classical music, sports, women's issues, computers and pop culture. No action/adventure, suspense, science fiction, romance, New Age, religion/spirituality, gift books, art books, fantasy, mysteries, thrillers, westerns, occult and supernatural, horror, historical fiction, poetry, children's literature, humour or travel books. Send query letter via e-mail with a one-page synopsis and include a short paragraph detailing credentials. No reading fee. *Commission* Home 15%.

Howard Morhaim
Literary Agency★
11 John Street, Suite 407, New York, NY 10038
☎001 212 529 4433 Fax 001 212 995 1112
Contact *Howard Morhaim*

FOUNDED 1979. *Handles* general adult fiction and non-fiction. No scripts. No children's or young adult material, poetry or religious. No

unsolicited mss. Send query letter with synopsis and sample chapters for fiction; query letter with outline or proposal for non-fiction. Include return postage. No reading fee. *Commission* Home 15%; UK & Translation 20%. *Overseas associates* worldwide.

Henry Morrison, Inc.
PO Box 235, Bedford Hills NY 10507
☎001 914 666 3500 Fax 001 914 241 7846

Contact *Henry Morrison*

FOUNDED 1965. *Handles* general fiction, crime and science fiction, and non-fiction. No scripts unless by established writers. Unsolicited material welcome but send query letter with outline (1–5 pp) in the first instance. No reading fee. *Commission* Home 15%; UK & Translation 25%.

Multimedia Product
Development, Inc.★
410 S. Michigan Avenue, Suite 724, Chicago, IL 60605
☎001 312 922 3063 Fax 001 312 922 1905
Email mpd@mpdinc.net
President *Jane Jordan Browne*
Agent *Danielle Egan Miller*

FOUNDED 1971. *Handles* commercial and literary fiction, and practical non-fiction with wide appeal. No scripts, science fiction or poetry. In the first instance, send query letter with return postage. No unsolicited material; no e-mail queries. No reading fee. *Commission* Home 15%; Foreign/Translation 20%. *Overseas associates* in Europe, Latin America, Japan and Asia.

The Jean V. Naggar
Literary Agency★
216 East 75th Street, New York, NY 10021
Contacts *Jean Naggar, Alice Tasman, Jennifer Weetz*

FOUNDED 1978. *Handles* strong mainstream fiction, literary fiction, memoir, biography, sophisticated self-help, popular science and psychology. No scripts. No unsolicited material; send query letter *only* with return postage initially. No reading fee. *Commission* Home 15%; Foreign 20%.

Ruth Nathan Agency
141 East 33rd Street, New York, NY 10016–4606
☎001 212 889 2696 Fax 001 212 481 1185
FOUNDED 1984. *Specialises* in illustrated books, fine art & decorative arts, historical fiction with

emphasis on Middle Ages, true crime, showbiz. Query first. No unsolicited mss. No reading fee. *Commission* 15%.

B.K. Nelson Literary Agency
84 Woodland Road, Pleasantville, NY 10570
☎001 914 741 1322 Fax 001 914 741 1324
Email bknelson4@cs.com
Website www.bknelson.com
Also at: 1565 Paseo Vida, Palm Springs, CA 92264
☎001 760 880 7800 Fax 001 760 778 0034
President *Bonita K. Nelson*
Vice President *Leonard 'Chip' Ashbach*
Editorial Director *John W. Benson*
FOUNDED 1979. *Specialises* in novels, business, self-help, how-to, political, autobiography, celebrity biography. Major motion picture and TV documentary success. No unsolicited mss. Letter of inquiry. Reading fee charged. *Commission* 20%. Lecture Bureau for Authors founded 1994; Foreign Rights Catalogue established 1995; BK Nelson Infomercial Marketing Co. 1996, primarily for authors and endorsements, and BKNelson, Inc. for motion picture production in 1998. Signatory to Writers Guild of America, West (WGAW).

New England Publishing Associates, Inc.★
Box 5, Chester, CT 06412
☎001 860 345 7323 Fax 001 860 345 3660
Email nepa@nepa.com
Website www.nepa.com
Contacts *Elizabeth Frost-Knappman, Edward W. Knappman, Kris Schiavi, Ron Formica, Victoria S. Harlow* (photo/research editor)
FOUNDED 1983. *Handles* non-fiction. *Specialises* in current affairs, history, science, women's studies, reference, psychology, politics, biography, true crime and literature. No textbooks or anthologies. No scripts, poetry or fiction. Unsolicited mss considered but query letter or phone call preferred first. No reading fee. *Commission* Home 15%. *Overseas associates* throughout Europe and Japan; Scott-Ferris, UK. Dramatic rights: Joel Gotlan Associates, Los Angeles.

Richard Parks Agency★
138 East 16th Street, Suite 5B, New York, NY 10003
☎001 212 254 9067 Fax 001 212 228 1786
Email rp@richardparksagency.com
Contact *Richard Parks*
FOUNDED 1989. *Handles* general trade fiction and

non-fiction: literary novels, mysteries and thrillers, commercial fiction, science fiction, biography, pop culture, psychology, self-help, parenting, medical, cooking, gardening, history, etc. No scripts. No technical or academic. No unsolicited mss. Fiction read by referral only. No reading fee. *Commission* Home 15%; UK & Translation 20%. *Overseas associates* **The Marsh Agency**; **Barbara Levy Literary Agency**.

James Peter Associates, Inc.★
PO Box 358, New Canaan, CT 06840
☎001 203 972 1070 Fax 001 203 972 1759
Email gene_brissie@msn.com
President *Eugene Brissie*
FOUNDED 1971. Non-fiction only. 'Many of our authors are historians, psychologists, physicians – all are writing trade books for general readers.' No scripts. No fiction or children's books. *Specialises* in history, popular culture, business, health, biography and politics. No unsolicited mss. Send query letter first with brief project outline, samples and biographical information. No reading fee. *Commission* 15%.

Alison J. Picard Literary Agent
PO Box 2000, Cotuit, MA 02635
☎001 508 477 7192 Fax 001 508 477 7192 (notify before faxing)
Email ajpicard@aol.com
Contact *Alison Picard*
FOUNDED 1985. *Handles* mainstream and literary fiction, contemporary and historical romance, children's and young adult, mysteries and thrillers; plus non-fiction. No short stories or poetry. Rarely any science fiction and fantasy. Particularly interested in expanding non-fiction titles. Approach with written query. No reading fee. *Commission* 15%. *Overseas associate* **A.M. Heath & Co. Ltd**, UK.

Pinder Lane & Garon-Brooke Associates Ltd★
159 West 53rd Street, Suite 14–E, New York, NY 10019
☎001 212 489 0880 Fax 001 212 489 7104
Email pinderl@interport.net
Owner Agents *Dick Duane, Robert Thixton*
Consulting Agent *Nancy Coffey*
FOUNDED 1951. Fiction and non-fiction. No category romance, westerns or mysteries. No unsolicited mss. First approach by query letter. No reading fee. *Commission* Home 15%; Dramatic 10–15%; Foreign 30%. *Overseas associates* **Abner Stein**, UK; Translation: Rights Unlimited.

PMA Literary & Film Management, Inc.

PO Box 1817, Old Chelsea Sta., New York, NY 10011
☎001 212 929 1222 Fax 001 212 206 0238
Email pmalitfilm@aol.com
Website www.pmalitfilm.com

President *Peter Miller*
Associate *Nathan Rice*

FOUNDED 1976. Commercial fiction and non-fiction. *Specialises* in books with motion picture and television potential, and in true crime. No poetry, pornography, non-commercial or academic. No unsolicited mss. Approach by letter with one-page synopsis. *Commission* Home 15%; Dramatic 10–15%; Foreign 20–25%.

The Aaron M. Priest Literary Agency★

708 Third Avenue, 23rd Floor, New York, NY 10017
☎001 212 818 0344 Fax 001 212 373 0417

Contact *Joy Ritchey, General Assistant*

FOUNDED 1974. *Handles* literary and commercial fiction. No scripts, children's fantasy or sci-fi. Submissions by mail only. No reading fee.

Susan Ann Protter Literary Agent★

110 West 40th Street, Suite 1408, New York, NY 10018
☎001 212 840 0480

Contact *Susan Ann Protter*

FOUNDED 1971. *Handles* general fiction, mysteries, thrillers, science fiction and fantasy; non-fiction: history, general reference, biography, science, health and parenting. No romance, poetry, westerns, religious, children's or sport manuals. No scripts. First approach with letter, including IRCs. No reading fee. *Commission* Home & Dramatic 15%. *Overseas associates* **Abner Stein**, UK; agents in all major markets.

Quicksilver Books, Literary Agents

50 Wilson Street, Hartsdale, NY 10530
☎001 914 946 8748

President *Bob Silverstein*

FOUNDED 1973. *Handles* literary fiction and mainstream commercial fiction: blockbuster, suspense, thriller, contemporary, mystery and historical; and general non-fiction, including self-help, psychology, holistic healing, ecology, environmental, biography, fact crime, New Age, health, nutrition, cookery, enlightened wisdom and spirituality. No scripts, science fiction and fantasy, pornographic, children's or romance. UK material being submitted must have universal appeal for the US market. Unsolicited material welcome but must be accompanied by IRCs for response, together with biographical details, covering letter, etc. No reading fee. *Commission* Home & Dramatic 15%; Translation 20%.

Reece Halsey North★

98 Main Street, #704, Tiburon, CA 94920
☎001 415 789 9191 Fax 001 415 789 9177
Email info@reecehalseynorth.com
Website www.kimberleycameron.com

Also: Reece Halsey Agency, 8733 Sunset Blvd. #101, Los Angeles, CA 90069
☎001 310 652 2409 Fax 001 310 652 7595

Contact (Tiburon) *Kimberley Cameron*
Contact (Los Angeles) *Dorris Halsey*

FOUNDED 1957. *Represents* literary and mainstream fiction, non-fiction. No scripts, poetry or children's books. No unsolicited material; send query letter with first 10 pages together with return postage. No e-mail submissions. No reading fee. *Commission* Home 15%; Foreign 20%.

Helen Rees Literary Agency★

123 N. Washington Street, 2nd Floor, Boston, MA 02114–2113
☎001 617 227 9014 Fax 001 617 227 8762
Email wwhelen@aol.com *or*
    joanmaz@aol.com *or*
    brifkind@mediaone.com *or*
    acoll10702@aol.com

Contact *Joan Mazmanian*
Associate *Ann Collette*

FOUNDED 1982. *Specialises* in books on health and business; also handles biography, autobiography and history; quality fiction. No scholarly or technical books. No scripts, science fiction, children's, poetry, photography, short stories, cooking. No unsolicited mss. no email queries or attachments. Send query letter with IRCs. No reading fee. *Commission* Home 15%; Foreign 20%.

Rights Unlimited, Inc.★

101 West 55th Street, Suite 2D, New York, NY 10019
☎001 212 246 0900 Fax 001 212 246 2114
Email bkurman@rightsunlimited.com

Contact *Bernard Kurman*

FOUNDED 1985. *Handles* adult fiction, non-fiction. No scripts, poetry, short stories, educational or literary works. Query letter with synopsis preferred in the first instance. No reading fee. *Commission* Home 15%; Translation 20%.

The Angela Rinaldi Literary Agency*

PO Box 7877, Beverly Hills, CA 90212–7877
☎001 310 842 7665 Fax 001 310 837 8143
Email arinaldilitagcy@aol.com

Contact *Angela Rinaldi*

FOUNDED 1993. *Handles* commercial and literary fiction; narrative non-fiction, practical and pro-active self-help. No scripts, cookery, science fiction, westerns, romance, poetry, children's/young adult. Send brief e-mail or query letter with return postage in the first instance. No reading fee. *Commission* Home 15%; Foreign 20%.

B.J. Robbins Literary Agency*

5130 Bellaire Avenue, North Hollywood, CA 91607
☎001 818 760 6602 Fax 001 818 760 6616
Email robbinsliterary@aol.com

Contacts *B.J. Robbins, Robert McAndrews*

FOUNDED 1992. *Handles* literary fiction, narrative and general non-fiction. No scripts, genre fiction, romance, horror, science fiction or children's books. Send covering letter with first three chapters or e-mail query in the first instance. No reading fee. *Commission* Home 15%; Foreign/Translation 10%. *Overseas associates* **Abner Stein** and **The Marsh Agency**, UK.

Linda Roghaar Literary Agency, Inc.*

133 High Point Drive, Amherst, MA 01002
☎001 413 256 1921 Fax 001 413 256 2636
Email LRoghaar@aol.com
Website www.LindaRoghaar.com

Contact *Linda L. Roghaar*

FOUNDED 1997. *Handles* fiction and non-fiction, specialising in religious titles. No science fiction or horror. Scripts through sub-agents. Send query by e-mail or letter with return postage (for fiction, include the first five pages). No reading fee. *Commission* Home 15%; Foreign/Translation rate varies.

The Rosenberg Group*

23 Lincoln Avenue, Marblehead, MA 01945
Website www.rosenberggroup.com

Contact *Barbara Collins Rosenberg*

FOUNDED 1998. *Handles* non-fiction (please see website for areas of interest), fiction, specialising in romance (single title and category) and

women's; non-fiction, specialising in college textbooks. No scripts, science fiction, true crime, inspirational fiction, children's and young adult. No unsolicited material; send query letter by post only. No reading fee. *Commission* Home 15%; Foreign 25%.

Rosenstone/Wender*

38 East 29th Street, 10th Floor, New York, NY 10016
☎001 212 725 9445 Fax 001 212 725 9447

Contacts *Phyllis Wender, Susan Perlman Cohen, Sonia E. Pabley*

FOUNDED 1981. *Handles* fiction, non-fiction, children's, and scripts for film, TV and theatre. No material for radio. No unsolicited mss. Send letter outlining the project, credits, etc. No reading fee. *Commission* Home 15%; Dramatic 10%; Foreign 20%. *Overseas associates* La Nouvelle Agence, France; Andrew Nurnberg, Netherlands; The English Agency, Japan; Mohrbooks, Germany; Ole Licht, Scandinavia.

Gail Ross Literary Agency*

1666 Connecticut Avenue, NW, Suite 500, Washington, DC 20009
☎001 202 328 3282 Fax 001 202 328 9162
Email jennifer@gailross.com
Website www.gailross.com

Contacts *Jennifer Manguera, Gail Ross*

FOUNDED 1998. *Handles* non-fiction, self-help, health, financial. No scripts, poetry, science fiction or children's books. No unsolicited mss; send query letter with sample material. No reading fee.

Jane Rotrosen Agency LLC*

318 East 51st Street, New York, NY 10022
☎001 212 593 4330 Fax 001 212 935 6985

Contacts *Meg Ruley, Andrea Cirillo, Annelise Robey, Kara Cesare, Peggy Gordijn*

Handles commercial fiction: romance, horror, mysteries, thrillers and popular non-fiction. No scripts, educational, professional or belles lettres. Query by referral only. No reading fee. *Commission* Home 15%; UK & Translation 20%. *Overseas associates* worldwide and film agents on the West Coast.

The Sagalyn Literary Agency*

7201 Wisconsin Avenue, Suite 675, Bethesda, MA 20814
☎001 301 718 6440 Fax 001 301 718 6444
Email agency@sagalyn.com
Website www.sagalyn.com

Contact *Ethan Kline*

FOUNDED 1980. *Handles* mostly upmarket nonfiction with some fiction. No screenplays, romance, science fiction/fantasy, children's literature. No unsolicited material. See website for submissions procedure. No reading fee.

Victoria Sanders & Associates LLC★

241 Avenue of the Americas, Suite 11H, New York, NY 10014
☎001 212 633 8811 Fax 001 212 633 0525
Email queriesvsa@hotmail.com
Website www.victoriasanders.com

Contacts *Victoria Sanders, Diane Dickensheid*

FOUNDED 1993. *Handles* general trade fiction and non-fiction, plus ancillary film and television rights. *Commission* Home & Dramatic 15%; Translation 20%.

Sandum & Associates

144 East 84th Street, New York, NY 10028
☎001 212 737 2011

Contact *Howard E. Sandum*

FOUNDED 1987. *Handles* all categories of general adult non-fiction, plus occasional fiction. No scripts. No children's, poetry or short stories. No unsolicited mss. Third-party referral preferred but direct approach by letter, with synopsis, brief biography and IRCs, is accepted. No reading fee. *Commission* Home & Dramatic 15%; Translation & Foreign 20%. *Overseas associate* Scott Ferris Associates.

Jack Scagnetti Talent & Literary Agency

5118 Vineland Avenue, Suite 102, North Hollywood, CA 91601
☎001 818 762 3871

Contact *Jack Scagnetti*

FOUNDED 1974. Works mostly with established/published authors. *Handles* non-fiction, fiction, film and TV scripts. No reading fees. *Commission* Home & Dramatic 10% (scripts), 15% (books); Foreign 15%.

Schiavone Literary Agency, Inc.

236 Trails End, West Palm Beach, FL 33413–2135
☎001 561 966 9294 Fax 001 561 966 9294
Email profschia@aol.com
Website www.freeyellow.com/members8/schiavone/index.html

Branch office (June/July/Aug. only):
3671 Hudson Manor Terrace, Suite 11H, Bronx, NY 10463 ☎/Fax 001 718 543 5093

President *James Schiavone*

FOUNDED 1996. *Handles* fiction and non-fiction (all genres). *Specialises* in biography, autobiography, celebrity memoirs. No poetry. No unsolicited mss; send query with brief biog-sketch, synopsis, outline and sample chapters (enclose IRCs). No reading fee. *Commission* Home 15%; Foreign & Translation 20%. *Overseas associates* in Europe.

Susan Schulman, A Literary Agency★

454 West 44th Street, New York, NY 10036
☎001 212 713 1633/4/5
Fax 001 212 581 8830
Email schulman@aol.com
Website www.susanschulmanagency.com

Submissions Editor (Books) *Christine Morin*
Submissions Editor (Plays) *Brian Leifert*

FOUNDED 1979. *Specialises* in non-fiction of all types but particularly in health and psychology-based self-help for men, women and families. Other interests include business, the social sciences, biography, language and international law. Fiction interests include contemporary fiction, including women's, mysteries, historical and thrillers 'with a cutting edge'. Always looking for 'something original and fresh'. No unsolicited mss. Query first, including outline and three sample chapters with IRCs. No reading fee. Represents properties for film and television, and works with agents in appropriate territories for translation rights. *Commission* Home & Dramatic 15%; Translation 20%. *Overseas associates* Plays: **Rosica Colin Ltd** and **The Agency Ltd**, UK; Children's books: Marilyn Malin, UK, Commercial fiction: Laura Morris, UK.

Scovil Chichak Galen Literary Agency, Inc.★

381 Park Avenue South, New York, NY 10016
☎001 212 679 8686 Fax 001 212 679 6710
Email mailroom@scglit.com

Contacts *Russell Galen, Anna M. Ghosh, Jack Scovil*

FOUNDED 1993. *Handles* all categories of books. No scripts. No unsolicited material; send query by e-mail or letter. No reading fee. *Commission* Home 15%; Foreign 20%.

Shapiro-Lichtman – Talent Agency

8827 Beverly Boulevard, Los Angeles, CA 90048
☎001 310 859 8877 Fax 001 310 859 7153
FOUNDED 1969. Works mostly with estab-

lished/published authors. *Handles* film and TV scripts. Unsolicited mss will not be read. *Commission* Home & Dramatic 10%; Foreign 20%.

The Shepard Agency
M&T Bank Building, Suite 3, 1525 Rte. 22, Brewster, NY 10509
☎001 203 790 4230; 203 790 1780
Fax 001 203 798 2924
Email shepardagcy@mindspring.com
Website home.mindspring.com/~shepardagcy
Contacts *Jean Shepard, Lance Shepard*

FOUNDED 1987. *Handles* non-fiction: business, food, self-help and travel; some fiction: adult, children's and young adult and the occasional script. No pornography. *Specialises* in business. Send query letter, table of contents, sample chapters and IRCs for response. No reading fee. *Commission* Home & Dramatic 15%; Translation 20%.

Bobbe Siegel Literary Agency
41 West 83rd Street, New York, NY 10024
☎001 212 877 4985   Fax 001 212 877 4985
Contacts *Bobbe Siegel*

FOUNDED 1975. Works mostly with established/published authors. *Specialises* in literary fiction, detective, suspense, historical, fantasy, biography, how-to, women's interest, fitness, health, beauty, sports, pop psychology. No scripts. No cookbooks, crafts, children's, short stories or humour. First approach with letter including IRCs for response. Will not accept queries via fax. No reading fee. Critiques given if the writer is taken on for representation. *Commission* Home 15%; Dramatic & Foreign 20%. (Foreign/Dramatic split 50/50 with sub-agent.) Also handles foreign rights for many US agents. *Overseas associates* in various countries, including **John Pawsey** in the UK.

Rosalie Siegel, International Literary Agency, Inc.★
1 Abey Drive, Pennington, NJ 08534
☎001 609 737 1007   Fax 001 609 737 3708
Email rsiegel@ix.netcom.com
Contact *Rosalie Siegel*

FOUNDED 1978. A one-woman, highly selective agency that takes on only a limited number of new projects. *Handles* fiction, non-fiction, especially narrative non-fiction, memoir, biography, history, current affairs, social history, psychology, botany, art history, zoology, neuroscience, social science and anthropology. *Specialises* in French

history and literature; Europe in general; American history, social history. No science fiction, photography, illustrated art books or children's. No unsolicited material; send query letter citing background, previously published books and brief description of current book. Include return postage. No reading fee. *Commission* Home 15%; Foreign 20%. *Overseas associate* **Louise Greenberg**, UK; plus associates worldwide.

Michael Snell Literary Agency
PO Box 1206, Truro, MA 02666–1206
☎001 508 349 3718
President *Michael Snell*
Vice President *Patricia Smith*

FOUNDED 1980. Adult non-fiction, especially science, business and women's issues. *Specialises* in business and computer books (professional and reference to popular trade how-to); general how-to and self-help on all topics, from diet and exercise to parenting, relationships, health, sex, psychology and personal finance, plus literary and suspense fiction. No unsolicited mss. Send outline and sample chapter with return postage for reply. No reading fee for outlines. Brochure available on how to write a book proposal. Author of *From Book Idea to Bestseller*, published by Prima. Rewriting, developmental editing, collaborating and ghostwriting services available on a fee basis. Send IRCs. *Commission* Home 15%.

Spectrum Literary Agency★
320 Central Park West, Ste. 1-D, New York, NY 10025
☎001 212 362 4323   Fax 001 212 362 4562
Website www.spectrumliterary agency.com
President and Agent *Eleanor Wood*
Agent *Lucienne Diver*

FOUNDED 1976. *Handles* science fiction, fantasy, mystery, suspense and romance. No scripts. Not interested in self-help, New Age, religious fiction/non-fiction, children's books, poetry, short stories, gift books or memoirs. Send query letter in first instance with s.a.e. Faxed or electronic submissions are not accepted. No reading fees. *Commission* Home 15%; Translation 20%.

The Spieler Agency
154 West 57th Street, Room 135, New York, NY 10019
☎001 212 757 4439   Fax 001 212 333 2019
Email SpielerLit@aol.com
The Spieler Agency/West, 4096 Piedmont Avenue, Oakland, CA 94611

☎001 510 985 1422 Fax 001 510 985 1323

Contacts *Joseph Spieler, John Thornton, Lisa M. Ross, Dierdre Mullane, Katya Balter* (NY); *Victoria Shoemaker* (Oakland)

FOUNDED 1980. *Handles* literary fiction and non-fiction. No how-to or genre romance. *Specialises* in history, science, ecology, social and political issues and business. No scripts. Approach in writing with IRCs. No reading fee. *Commission* Home 15%; Translation 20%. *Overseas associates* **Abner Stein**; **The Marsh Agency**, UK.

Philip G. Spitzer Literary Agency★
50 Talmage Farm Lane, East Hampton, NY 11937
☎001 631 329 3650 Fax 001 631 329 3651
Email spitzer516@aol.com

Contact *Philip Spitzer*

FOUNDED 1969. Works mostly with established/published authors. *Specialises* in general non-fiction and fiction – thrillers. No reading fee for outlines. *Commission* Home & Dramatic 15%; Foreign 20%.

Lyle Steele & Co. Ltd Literary Agents
511 East 73rd Street, Suite 6, New York, NY 10021
☎001 212 288 2981

President *Lyle Steele*

FOUNDED 1985. *Handles* general non-fiction and category fiction. Also North American rights to titles published by major English publishers. No scripts unless derived from books already being handled. No romance. No unsolicited mss: query with IRCs in first instance. No reading fee. *Commission* 10%. *Overseas associates* worldwide.

Steele–Perkins Literary Agency★
26 Island Lane, Canandaigua, NY 14424
☎001 716 396 9290 Fax 001 716 396 3579
Email pattiesp@aol.com

Contact *Pattie Steele-Perkins*

Handles mainstream women's fiction, romance. No scripts. Send query letter, synopsis, three chapters and return postage. No reading fee. *Commission* Home 15%.

Gloria Stern Agency (Hollywood)
12535 Chandler Boulevard, Suite 3, North Hollywood, CA 91607
☎001 818 508 6296 Fax 001 818 508 6296
Email wryter21@excite.com

Contact *Gloria Stern*

FOUNDED 1984. *Handles* film scripts, genre (romance, detective, thriller and sci-fi) and mainstream fiction; electronic media. Accepts interactive material, games and electronic data. 'No books containing gratuitous violence.' Approach with letter, biography and synopsis. Reading fee charged by the hour. *Commission* Home 15%; Offshore 20%.

Stimola Literary Studio★
210 Crescent Avenue, Leonia, NJ 07605
☎001 201 944 9886 Fax 001 201 944 9886
Email LtryStudio@aol.com

Contact *Rosemary B. Stimola*

FOUNDED 1997. *Handles* children's books – preschool through young adult – fiction and non fiction. Specialises in picture books, middle/young adult novels. No adult fiction. No unsolicited material; send query e-mail. No reading fee. *Commission* Home 15%; Foreign 20%.

Gunther Stuhlmann Author's Representative
PO Box 276, Becket, MA 01223
☎001 413 623 5170

Contact *Barbara Ward Stuhlmann*

FOUNDED 1954. *Handles* literary fiction, biography and serious non-fiction. 'At the present time we are not taking on any new clients.' No short stories, detective, romance, adventure, poetry, technical or computers. Query first with IRCs, including sample chapters and synopsis of project. No reading fee. *Commission* Home 10%; Foreign 15%; Translation 20%.

Roslyn Targ★
105 West 13th Street, 15 E, New York, NY 10011
☎001 212 206 9390 Fax 001 212 989 6233
Email roslyntarg@aol.com

Contact *Roslyn Targ*

FOUNDED 1970. *Handles* non-fiction, particularly biography, self-help, and literary fiction. No scripts or cookbooks. No unsolicited material; send query e-mail or letter describing the work. No reading fee. *Commission* Home 15%; Foreign 20%.

S(c)ott Treimel NY★
434 Lafayette Street, New York, NY 10003
☎001 212 505 8353 Fax 001 212 505 0664
Email st.ny@verizon.net

FOUNDED 1995. *Handles* children's books only – from concept/board books to teen fiction. No scripts. No unsolicited material. 'Not accepting anyone unless recommended by professional authors or editors.' No reading fee. *Commission* Home 15%; Foreign 20%.

2M Communications Ltd
121 West 27th Street, Suite 601, New York, NY 10001
☎001 212 741 1509 Fax 001 212 691 4460
Email morel@bookhaven.com
Website www.2mcommunications.com
Contact *Madeleine Morel*

FOUNDED 1982. *Handles* non-fiction only: everything from pop psychology and health to cookery books, biographies and pop culture. No scripts. No fiction, children's, computers or science. No unsolicited mss; send letter with sample pages and IRCs. No reading fee. *Commission* Home & Dramatic 15%; Translation 20%. *Overseas associates* Thomas Schluck Agency, Germany; Asano Agency, Japan; EAIS, France; Living Literary Agency, Italy; Nueva Agencia Literaria Internacional, Spain.

Van der Leun & Associates
32 Gramercy Park South #11L, New York, NY 10003
☎001 212 982 6165
Website www.publishersmarketplace.com/members/pvanderleun
Contact *Patricia Van der Leun*

FOUNDED 1984. *Handles* fiction and non-fiction. No scripts. No science fiction, fantasy or romance. *Specialises* in art and architecture, science, cookbooks, wine, reference, lifestyle, religious, biography and fiction. No unsolicited mss; query first, with letter and short biography. No reading fee. *Commission* 15%. *Overseas associates* **Abner Stein**, UK; Michelle Lapautre, France; English Agency, Japan; Carmen Balcells, Spain; Lucia Riff, South America; Susanna Zevi, Italy.

The Vines Agency, Inc.★
648 Broadway, Suite 901, New York, NY 10012
☎001 212 777 5522 Fax 001 212 777 5978
Email JV@vinesagency.com
Website www.vinesagency.com
Contacts *James C. Vines, Kate Payne*

FOUNDED 1995. *Handles* fiction – literary, women's, thrillers, love stories; narrative non-fiction, historical, biography, advice, how-to. No children's picture books or poetry. *Specialises* in women's fiction and thrillers. Unsolicited mss, synopses and sample chapters welcome. Send query with one-page letter and return postage.

No reading fee. *Commission* Home 15%; Foreign/Translation 25%. *Overseas associate* Baror International (foreign rights).

Wales Literary Agency, Inc.★
PO Box 9428, Seattle, WA 98109–0428
☎001 206 284 7114
Email waleslit@aol.com
Contacts *Elizabeth Wales, Meg Lemke, Adrienne Reed*

FOUNDED 1988. *Handles* quality fiction and non-fiction. No genre fiction, westerns, romance, science fiction or horror. Special interest in 'Pacific Rim', West Coast and Pacific Northwest stories. No unsolicited mss; send query letter with publication list and writing sample. No e-mail queries longer than one page and no attachments. No reading fee. *Commission* Home 15%; Dramatic & Translation 20%.

John A. Ware Literary Agency
392 Central Park West, New York, NY 10025
☎001 212 866 4733 Fax 001 212 866 4734
Contact *John Ware*

FOUNDED 1978. *Specialises* in non-fiction: biography, history, current affairs, investigative journalism, science, nature, inside looks at phenomena, medicine and psychology (academic credentials required). Also handles literary fiction, mysteries/thrillers, sport, oral history, Americana and folklore. Unsolicited mss not read. Send query letter first with IRCs to cover return postage. No reading fee. *Commission* Home & Dramatic 15%; Foreign 20%.

Waterside Productions, Inc.
2187 Newcastle Avenue, #204, Cardiff by the Sea, CA 92007
☎001 760 632 9190 Fax 001 760 632 9295
Website www.waterside.com
Contact *William Gladstone*

FOUNDED 1982. *Handles* non-fiction: computers and technology, science, business, sports, pop culture, New Age, etc. All types of multimedia. No unsolicited mss; send query letter. No reading fee. *Commission* Home 15%; Dramatic 20%; Translation 25%.

Watkins Loomis Agency, Inc.
133 East 35th Street, Suite 1, New York, NY 10016
☎001 212 532 0080 Fax 001 212 889 0506
Contact *Katherine Fausset*

FOUNDED 1904. *Handles* fiction and non-fiction. No scripts for film, radio, TV or theatre. No science fiction, fantasy or horror. No reading fee. No unsolicited mss. Approach in writing with enquiry or proposal and s.a.e. *Commission* Home 15%; UK & Translation 20%. *Overseas associates* **Abner Stein**; **The Marsh Agency**, UK.

Wecksler–Incomco
170 West End Avenue, New York,
NY 10023
☎001 212 787 2239 Fax 001 212 496 7035
Email jacinny@aol.com

Contacts *Sally Wecksler, Joann Amparan-Close*

FOUNDED 1971. *Handles* literary fiction and non-fiction: business, reference, biography, performing arts and heavily illustrated books; also some children's books. Send queries only. No unsolicited mss. No submissions by fax or e-mail; hard copy only. No reading fee. Foreign rights. *Commission* Home 15%; Translation & UK 20%.

Cherry Weiner Literary Agency
28 Kipling Way, Manalapan, NJ 07726
☎001 732 446 2096 Fax 001 732 792 0506
Email Cherry8486@aol.com

Contact *Cherry Weiner*

FOUNDED 1977. *Handles* all types of fiction: science fiction and fantasy, mainstream, romance, mystery, westerns. No submissions except through referral. No reading fee. *Commission* 15%. *Overseas associates* **Abner Stein**, UK; Thomas Schluck, Germany; International Editors Inc., Spain; Prava Prevodi Agency (Eastern Europe), Serbia; Elaine Benisti Agency, France; Borderline Literary Agency, Italy; Nucihan Kesim Literary Agency, Turkey; English Agency (Japan) Ltd; Alex Korzhenevski Agency, Russia; Renaissance Media – movie agent. Also dealing with various e-book publishers.

The Rhoda Weyr Agency
See **Dunham Literary Inc**

Wieser & Wieser, Inc.
25 East 21st Street, New York, NY 10010
☎001 212 260 0860

Contacts *Olga B. Wieser, Jake Elwell*

FOUNDED 1976. Works mostly with established/published authors. *Specialises* in literary and mainstream fiction, serious and popular historical fiction, and general non-fiction: business, finance, aviation, sports, travel and popular medicine. No poetry, children's, science fiction or religious. No unsolicited mss. First approach by letter with IRCs. No reading fee

for outlines. *Commission* Home & Dramatic 15%; Foreign 20%.

Ann Wright Representatives
165 West 46th Street, Suite 1105, New York,
NY 10036–2501
☎001 212 764 6770 Fax 001 212 764 5125

Contact *Dan Wright*

FOUNDED 1961. *Specialises* in material with strong film potential. *Handles* screenplays and novels, drama and fiction. No academic, scientific or scholarly. Approach by letter; no reply without IRCs. Include outline and credits only. 'Has reputation for encouraging new writers.' No reading fee. Signatory to the Writers Guild of America Agreement. *Commission* Literary 10–20%; Screenplays 10% of gross.

Writers House, LLC.★
21 West 26th Street, New York, NY 10010
☎001 212 685 2400 Fax 001 212 685 1781

Contacts *Albert Zuckerman, Amy Berkower, Merrilee Heifetz, Susan Cohen, Susan Ginsburg, Robin Rue, Simon Lipskar, Steven Malk, Jennifer Lyons, Jodi Reamer*

FOUNDED 1974. See also **Joan Daves Agency**. *Handles* all types of fiction, including children's and young adult, plus narrative non-fiction: history, biography, popular science, pop and rock culture as well as how-to, business and finance, and New Age. *Specialises* in popular and literary fiction, women's novels, thrillers and children's. No scripts. No professional or scholarly. For consideration of unsolicited mss, send one-page letter of enquiry, 'explaining why your book is wonderful, briefly what it's about and outlining your writing background'. No reading fee. *Commission* Home & Dramatic 15%; Foreign 20%. Albert Zuckerman is author of *Writing the Blockbuster Novel*, published by Little, Brown & Co. and Warner Paperbacks.

The Zack Company, Inc.★
243 West 70th Street, Suite 8D, New York,
NY 10023–4366
☎001 212 712 2400 Fax 001 212 712 9110
Website www.zackcompany.com

Contact *Andrew Zack*

FOUNDED 1996. *Handles* serious narrative non-fiction by qualified experts: history, particularly military, politics, current affairs, science and technology, biography, autobiography, memoirs, personal finance, parenting, health and medicine, business, relationships. Commercial fiction – thrillers, mysteries, crime, science fiction/fantasy. No women's fiction, westerns, gay or lesbian, scripts. See website for full listing of areas of representation and submission guidelines. No unsolicited material. For non-fiction, send query letter, résumé and 1–2 pages describing project; fiction – query letter should include publishing history (title, publisher and year), if any, and a 2–3 paragraph summary of the work. No reading fee. *Commission* Home 15% (published authors)/20% (new, unpublished); Foreign/Translation 20%.

US Media Contacts in the UK

ABC News Intercontinental Inc.
3 Queen Caroline Street, Mail Code 2303,
London W6 9PE
☎020 8222 5000 Fax 020 8222 5020
**Bureau Chief & Director of News
  Coverage, Europe, Middle East &
  Africa** *Marcus Wilford*

Alaska Journal of Commerce
16 Cavaye Place, London SW10 9PT
☎0702 092 4480 Fax 0702 092 4482
Bureau Chief *Robert Gould*

The Associated Press
12 Norwich Street, London EC4A 1BP
☎020 7353 1515 Fax 020 7353 8118
**Chief of Bureau/Managing Director,
  AP Ltd** *Barry Renfrew*

The Baltimore Sun
11 Kensington Court Place, London W8 5BJ
☎020 7460 2200 Fax 020 7460 2211
Bureau Chief *Ted Richissin*

Bloomberg Business News
City Gate House, 39–45 Finsbury Square,
London EC2A 1PQ
☎020 7330 7500 Fax 020 7392 6666
London Bureau Chief *Ed Roussel*

Boston Globe
34 West Heath Road, London NW3 7UR
☎020 7431 5797 Fax 020 7431 5807
Bureau Chief *Charles Sennott*

Business Week
1 Albemarle Street, London W1S 4DT
☎020 7491 8985 Fax 020 7409 7152
Bureau Chief *Stanley Reed*

Cable News Network Inc. (CNN)
Turner House, 16 Great Marlborough Street,
London W1P 1DF
☎020 7693 1000 Fax 020 7693 1552
Office Manager *Rosalind Jackman*

CBC Television and Radio
43/51 Great Titchfield Street, London
W1P 8DD
☎020 7412 9200 Fax 020 7412 9226
London Bureau Manager *Ann Macmillan*

CBS News
68 Knightsbridge, London SW1X 7LL
☎020 7581 4801 Fax 020 7581 4431
Vice President/Bureau Chief *John Paxson*

Chicago Tribune Press Service
169 Piccadilly, London W1J 9EH
☎020 7499 8769 Fax 020 7499 8781
Chief European Correspondent *Tom Huntley*

CNBC
10 Fleet Place, Limeburner Lane, London
EC4M 7QS
☎020 7653 9451 Fax 020 7653 9393
Executive Producer *Harry Fuller*

Dallas Morning News
☎020 8742 0495 Fax 020 8747 3131
European Bureau Chief *Gregory Katz*

Dow Jones Newswires
10 Fleet Place, Limeburner Lane, London
EC4M 7QN
☎020 7842 9900
Editor (Europe, Middle East, Africa)
  Gabriella Stern

Fairchild Publications of New York
20 Shorts Gardens, London WC2H 9AU
☎020 7240 0420 Fax 020 7240 0290
Bureau Chief *Samantha Conti*

Forbes Magazine
10 Rotherwick Road, London NW11 7DA
☎020 8455 0463 Fax 020 8455 0512
European Bureau Chief *Richard C. Morais*

Fox News Channel
6 Centaurs Business Park, Grant Way,
Isleworth, Middlesex TW7 5QD
☎020 7805 7143 Fax 020 7805 1111
Producer/Bureau Chief *Paul Tyson*

The Globe and Mail
43–51 Great Titchfield Street, London
W1W 7DA
☎020 7323 0449 Fax 020 7323 0428
European Correspondent *Alan Freeman*

International Herald Tribune
40 Marsh Wall, London E14 9TP
☎020 7510 5718 Fax 020 7987 3470
London Correspondent *Eric Pfanner*
(See entry under **National Newspapers**)

Los Angeles Times
150 Brompton Road, London SW3 1HX
☎020 7823 7315 Fax 020 7823 7308
Bureau Chief *John Daniszewski*

Market News International
Ocean House, 10–12 Little Trinity Lane,
London EC41 2AR
☎020 7634 1655 Fax 020 7236 7122
Bureau Chief *Gavin Friend*

National Public Radio
Room G–10 East Wing, Bush House, Strand,
London WC2B 4PH
☎020 7557 1087 Fax 020 7379 6486
Correspondent *Guy Raz*

NBC News Worldwide Inc.
4th Floor, 3 Shortlands, Hammersmith,
London W6 8HX
☎020 8600 6600 Fax 020 8600 6601
Bureau Chief *Chris Hampson*

The New York Times
66 Buckingham Gate, London SW1E 6AU
☎020 7799 5050 Fax 020 7799 2962
Chief Correspondent *Warren Hoge*

Newsweek
18 Park Street, London W1K 2HQ
☎020 7629 8361 Fax 020 7408 1403
Bureau Chief *Stryker McGuire*

People Magazine
Brettenham House, Lancaster Place, London
WC2E 7TL
☎020 7322 1134 Fax 020 7322 1125
Bureau Chief *Bryan Alexander*

Philadelphia Inquirer
2 Cranley Mews, London SW7 3BX
☎020 7460 6800 Fax 020 7460 6800
Bureau Chief *Andrea Gerlin*

Reader's Digest Association Ltd
11 Westferry Circus, Canary Wharf, London
E14 4HE
☎020 7715 8046 Fax 020 7715 8716
(See entries under **UK Publishers** and
Magazines)

Time Magazine
Brettenham House, Lancaster Place, London
WC2E 7TL
☎020 7499 4080 Fax 020 7322 1230
Bureau Chief *Jef McAllister*
(See entry under **Magazines**)

USA Today
69 New Oxford Street, London WC1A 1DG
☎020 7559 5859 Fax 020 7559 5895
Correspondent *Ellen Hale*

Voice of America
International Press Centre, 76 Shoe Lane,
London EC4A 3JB
☎020 7410 0960 Fax 020 7410 0966
Bureau Chief/Senior Editor *Al Pessin*

Wall Street Journal
10 Fleet Place, Limeburner Lane, London
EC4M 7RB
☎020 7842 9200 Fax 020 7842 9201
London Bureau Chief *James R. Hagerty*

Washington Post
18 Park Street, London W1Y 4HH
☎020 7629 8958 Fax 020 7629 8950
Bureau Chief *T.R. Reid*

US Writer's Courses

In general, courses are open to students from overseas, though of course in some cases the financial aid information varies for international students.

California

American Film Institute

2021 N. Western Avenue, Los Angeles, CA 90027
☎001 323 856 7628
Email jjackman@afi.com

Contact *J.J. Jackman, Admissions Manager*

Screenwriting at AFI focuses on narrative story-telling in an environment designed to stimulate the world of the professional screenwriter. Screenwriting fellows in the first year are immersed in the production process in order to learn how screenplays are visualised. Initially writing short screenplays – one of which will be the basis for a first year production – writers collaborate with producing and directing fellows to see their work move from page to screen. The remainder of the year is devoted to the completion of a feature-length screenplay. Second year fellows may write a feature-length screenplay, or develop materials for television, including biopics, television movies and spec scripts for sitcoms and one-hour dramas. They also have the opportunity to work closely with other disciplines by writing a second year thesis script.

California Institute for the Arts

MFA Writing Program, School of Critical Studies, 24700 McBean Parkway, Valencia, CA 91355
☎011 661 253 7701
Email writing@calarts.edu

Contact *Dwayne Moser, Program Coordinator*

The two-year MFA Writing Programme is rooted in principles of critical thought, experimentation and innovation. It is intended as an alternative to traditional programmes, with a founding premise that distinctions between creative and critical writing should be suspended. Students are encouraged to work across genres and often work in various multi-media forms in addition to their literary production.

Chapman University

Master of Fine Arts Degree, Office of Admissions, Orange, CA 92866
☎001 714 997 6711
Email shoover@chapman.edu

Contact *Saundra Hoover, Admissions*

Three-year Master of Fine Arts (MFA) degree in *Creativing Writing* includes courses in fiction writing, poetry and screenwriting as well as courses in world and comparative literature. Programme connected with the John Fowles Center for Creative Writing.

Saint Mary's College of California

MFA Program in Creative Writing, PO Box 4686, Moraga, CA 94575–4686
☎001 925 631 4762 Fax 001 925 631 4471
Email writers@stmarys-ca.edu

Programme Coordinator *Thomas Cooney*

Two-year MFA course in *Fiction, Playwriting* or *Poetry*. Students have the opportunity to gain knowledge of the world of publishing through internships in the College's in-house press, Momotombo Press and literary journal, *26*.

Strawberry Mansion Films

13586 Mahogany Place, Tustin, CA 92780
☎001 714 997 6586
Email axelrod@chapman.edu

Contact *Mark Axelrod*

One-day, three-day and five-day seminar/workshops in *Screenwriting*. A practising screenwriter, Mark Axelrod has conducted such programmes at the Escuela Internacional de Cine y TV in San Antonio de los Baños, Cuba (founded by García Márquez); the Goethe Institute, Santiago, Chile (with Antonio Skármeta – *Il Postino*) and the National Film School of Denmark, as well as the University of East Anglia in Norwich, Columbia College, Chicago, and the Film Stadium der Universität, Hamburg. Latest film books include: *Aspects of the Screenplay* and *Character and Conflict*.

Colorado

Colorado State University

Department of English, Creative Writing Program, Fort Collins, CO 80523–5601
☎001 970 491 6428 Fax 001 970 491 5601

Email english@lamar.colostate.edu
Website www.colostate.edu/Depts/English/
programs/mfa.htm
Contacts *Assistant to the Director of Creative Writing* or *Director of Creative Writing*

Three-year Master of Fine Arts (MFA) programme in creative writing with concentrations in fiction or poetry. The programme offers a balance of intimate and intensive writing and translation. Course work culminates in a thesis – a collection of poetry or short stories or a novel. Students have the opportunity to teach introductory creative-writing courses, intern with literary journals including the *Colorado Review* and be a part of a thriving community.

Florida
University of West Florida
Department of English and Foreign Languages, College of Arts and Sciences, 11000 University Parkway, Pensacola, FL 32514
☎001 850 474 2923 Fax 001 850 474 2935
Email English@uwf.edu
Website uwf.edu/english

BA in *English (Writing Specialization)*: students who choose to develop their creative writing skills or editing can take courses in poetry, fiction, creative non-fiction, magazine writing and editing, and feature writing. *MA in English (Creative Writing Specialization)*: workshop courses in the specialisation include fiction, creative non-fiction, poetry, editing, teaching creative writing and special topics in creative writing. Students also have the opportunity to work on the literary magazine *Bayou*.

Georgia
Georgia State University
Department of English, University Plaza, Atlanta, GA 30303
Email tmchaney@gsu.edu
Website www.gsu.edu/~wwweng/
Contact *Director of Creative Writing*

BA, MA, MFA and PhD programmes in *Creative Writing* – fiction or poetry.

Illinois
Southern Illinois University
Department of English, Carbondale, IL 62901–4503
☎001 618 453 6849 Fax 001 618 453 3253
Email crwr@siu.edu
Contact *Professor Beth Lordan*

Three-year MFA in *Creative Writing*. The programme accepts a maximum of eight students each year, so workshops are small and faculty members work closely with students.

Indiana
Taylor University
Department of English, 1025 West Rudisill Boulevard, Fort Wayne, IN 46807–2170
☎001 260 744 8647
Email DNHensley@TaylorU.edu
Contact *Dr Dennis E. Hensley*

One-day seminars on *Freelance Writing* and *Fiction Writing* held on Saturdays each spring and autumn. Taught by Dr Hensley, Director of the Professional Writing major at the University.

Louisiana
Louisiana State University
English Department, 213 Allen Hall, Baton Rouge, LA 70803
Website www.english.lsu.edu
Contacts *James Wilcox, Judy Kahn*

Master of Fine Arts (MFA) course with a focus in *Poetry, Fiction, Playwriting, Screenwriting* or *Creative Non-fiction*. Includes opportunity to edit literary journals.

Maryland
Goucher College
Welch Center for Graduate Studies, 1021 Dulaney Valley Road, Baltimore, MD 21204–2794
☎001 800 697 4646 Fax 001 410 337 6085
Email center@goucher.edu
Course Director *Patsy Sims* (☎001 800 697 4646)

The two-year MFA Program in *Creative Nonfiction* is a limited-residency course that allows students to complete most of the requirements off campus while developing their skill as non-fiction writers under the close supervision of a faculty mentor. Provides instruction in the following areas: the personal essay, memoir, literary journalism, travel/nature/science writing, biography/profiles, and narrative non-fiction.

Johns Hopkins University
The Writing Seminars, 3400 N. Charles Street, Baltimore, MD 21218
☎001 410 516 6286
Email regina@jhu.edu

One-year Master of Arts in *Creative Writing* – concentrates on fiction, poetry or science writing.

Minnesota

Minnesota State University, Moorhead

Graduate Studies Office, MSUM, Moorhead, MN 56563
☎001 218 236 4681
Email davisa@mnstate.edu
Website www.mnstate.edu/finearts

Programme Coordinator *Alan Davis*

MFA in *Creative Writing* (Fiction, Non-fiction, Playwriting, Poetry, Screenwriting). The programme offers the opportunity to take workshops, seminars and tutorials in chosen areas and to work with New Rivers Press (www. newriverspress.com). A limited number of teaching assistantships are available. Credits are also available each May through participation in the University's 'British Isles Tour'.

Missouri

University of Missouri–Columbia

Creative Writing Program, Department of English, 107 Tate Hall, Columbia, MO 65211-1500
☎011 573 884 7773
Email creativewriting@missouri.edu/~cwp
Website www.missouri.edu/~cwp

Contact *Sharon Fisher*

Creative Writing MA and PhD in English programmes in fiction, poetry and non-fiction.

New York

New York University

19 University Place, 2nd Floor, New York, NY 10003
Email creative.writing@nyu.edu
Website www.nyu.edu/gsas/program/cwp

Contact *Russell Carmony*
Director *Melissa Hammerle*

Offers MFA in *Creative Writing* and MA in *English* with focus in *Creative Writing* in poetry and fiction. Includes writing workshops and craft courses, literary outreach programmes, a public reading series, student readings, special literary seminars and student teaching opportunities. Publishes two literary journals: *Washington Square* and *Calabash*. Contact the department via e-mail.

North Carolina

University of North Carolina at Greensboro

MFA Writing Program, Department of English, 134 Melver Building, UNCG, PO Box 26170, Greensboro, NC 27402-6170
☎001 336 334 5459 Fax 001 336 334 3281
Email jlclark@uncg.edu
Website www.uncg.edu/eng/mfa

Contact *Jim Clark, Director*

BA and MFA degree programmes in *Creative Writing*: fiction and poetry.

BA in English with Concentration in Creative Writing (poetry, fiction) The university offers a writing concentration for undergraduate English majors. Courses in journalism, expository, technical and creative writing as well as publishing are available for a maximum of 15 s/hrs, with 21 s/hrs to be taken in literature courses. The student may plan a course of study suited to individual needs. A limited number of scholarships are available to undergraduates in creative writing.

MFA in Creative Writing (poetry, fiction) One of the oldest of its kind in the country, the MFA Writing Program at Greensboro is a two-year residency with an emphasis on providing students with studio time in which to study the writing of poetry or fiction with a flexibility that permits students to develop their particular talents through small classes in writing, literature and the arts.

University of North Carolina at Wilmington

Department of Creative Writing, 601 S. College Avenue, Wilmington, NC 28403–5938
☎001 910 962 7063 Fax 001 910 962 7461
Email mfa@uncw.edu
Website www.uncw.edu/writers

Chair *Mark Cox*

An intensive studio-academic programme in the writing of fiction, poetry and creative non-fiction leading to either the Master of Fine Arts or Bachelor of Fine Arts degree in *Creative Writing*. Courses include workshops in the three genres, screenwriting, special topics and forms courses as well as a range of courses in literature. Course work in publishing and editing is also offered in the Publishing Laboratory, a university press imprint which supports local, regional and national publishing projects.

Philadelphia

Seton Hill University

1 Seton Hill Drive, Greensburg, PA 15601
☎001 724 838 4221
Email gadmit@setonhill.edu
Website www.setonhill.edu

Contact *Jennell Krymowski*

The MA in Writing Popular Fiction programme at Seton Hill University allows students to earn a graduate degree by writing fiction that people *actually* read. Students attend week-long residencies in January and June and complete writing projects off-campus, working with a faculty mentor who is a published author in the chosen genre. Students can choose to specialise in science fiction, fantasy, horror, children's literature, romance or mystery. Programmes can be completed in 24 months.

Temple University

1024 Anderson Hall, Temple University, Philadelphia, PA 19122–6090
Email creatwrt@blue.temple.edu
Website www.temple.edu/english

Director of Creative Writing *Rachel Blau DuPlessis*

MA in *English/Creative Writing*. Two-year programme with workshops in poetry and fiction; one-on-one tutorials in poetry, fiction and translation; also graduate literature courses in genre.

Rhode Island

Rhode Island Brown University

Creative Writing, Box 1852, Providence, RI 02912
☎001 401 863 3260
Email Writing@brown.edu

Contact *Director of Creative Writing*

Two-year MFA in *Fiction, Poetry, Playwriting and Electronic Writing*. Students take three workshops, four electives and one independent study (through which they complete a thesis project).

Texas

University of Texas at Austin

Department of Radio-Television-Film, Austin, TX 78712
☎001 512 475 7399 (Admissions)
Website www.utexas.edu/ftp/coc/rtf

Four-year BSc course in *Radio-Television-Film* during which writing for film and television may be studied in the third and fourth years. At graduate level, a MA in *Screenwriting* is offered.

Commonwealth Publishers

Australia

ACER Press
Private Bag 55, Camberwell, Victoria 3124
☎00 61 3 9277 5555 Fax 00 61 3 9277 5500
Website www.acer.edu.au

FOUNDED 1930. *Publishes* Education, human relations, psychology, psychiatry.

Allen & Unwin Pty Ltd
PO Box 8500, St Leonards, Sydney, NSW 1590
☎00 61 2 8425 0100 Fax 00 61 2 9906 2218
Website www.allenandunwin.com

FOUNDED 1976. *Publishes* fiction, literature, literary criticism, essays; general non-fiction, art, Asian studies, behavioural sciences, business, cookery, earth sciences, economics, education, gay and lesbian, government, labour, political science, health and nutrition, history, industrial relations, general science.

Edward Arnold (Australia) Pty Ltd
PO Box 885, Kew, Victoria 3101
☎00 61 3 985 9011 Fax 00 61 3 985 9141

FOUNDED 1966. Part of Hodder & Stoughton (Australia) Pty Ltd. *Publishes* general non-fiction: accountancy, Asian studies, behavioural sciences, career development, computer science, cookery, geography, geology, government, political science, health and nutrition, law, mathematics, psychology and psychiatry, technology.

Blackwell Science Pty Ltd
PO Box 378, South Carlton, Victoria 3053
☎00 61 3 9347 0300 Fax 00 61 3 9347 5001

FOUNDED 1971. Part of Blackwell Science Ltd, UK. *Publishes* general science, medicine, nursing, dentistry, earth sciences, general engineering, computer science, mathematics, physical sciences, physics, psychology, psychiatry.

Currency Press Pty Ltd
PO Box 2287, Strawberry Hills, NSW 2012
☎00 61 2 9319 5877 Fax 00 61 2 9319 3649
Website www.currency.com.au

FOUNDED 1971. Performing arts publisher – drama, theatre, music, dance, film and video.

Dangaroo Press
PO Box 93, New Lambton, NSW 2305
☎00 61 2 4954 5938 Fax 00 61 2 4954 6531

FOUNDED 1978. *Publishes* general non-fiction, art, literature, literary criticism, essays, poetry, social sciences, sociology, women's studies.

E.J. Dwyer (Australia) Pty Ltd
Locked Bag 71, Alexandria, NSW 2015
☎00 61 2 9550 2355 Fax 00 61 2 9519 3218

FOUNDED 1904. *Publishes* self-help, marketing, social sciences, sociology, religion, theology.

Harcourt Australia Pty Ltd
Locked Bag 16, Marrickville NSW 2044
☎00 61 2 9517 8999 Fax 00 61 2 9517 2294

FOUNDED 1972. *Publishes* business, education, general science, medicine, nursing, dentistry, psychology, psychiatry, veterinary science, social sciences, sociology, mathematics.

HarperCollins Publishers (Australia) Pty Ltd
PO Box 321, Pymble, NSW 2073
☎00 61 2 9952 5445 Fax 00 61 2 9952 5544
Website www.harpercollins.com.au

FOUNDED 1872. Part of the HarperCollins Publishers Group. *Publishes* fiction and general non-fiction, biography, children's, gardening, humour, government, political science, regional interests, literature, literary criticism, essays, women's studies.

Hodder Headline Australia
Level 22, 201 Kent Street, Sydney, NSW 2000
☎00 61 2 8248 0800 Fax 00 61 2 8248 0810
Website www.hha.com.au

FOUNDED 1958. Owned by **Hodder Headline**, UK. *Publishes* general non-fiction and fiction (adult and children's), education.

Hyland House Publishing Pty Ltd
PO Box 122, Flemington, Victoria 3031
☎00 61 3 9376 4461 Fax 00 61 3 9376 4461

FOUNDED 1976. *Publishes* general non-fiction, Asian studies, biography, cookery, animals, pets, history, essays, fiction, gardening, literature, literary criticism.

LexisNexis Butterworths Australia Ltd
Tower 2, 475–495 Victoria Avenue, Chatswood, NSW 2067
☎00 61 2 9422 2222 Fax 00 61 2 9422 2444
Website www.lexisnexis.com.au
FOUNDED 1910. A division of Reed Elsevier. *Publishes* law.

Thomas C. Lothian Pty Ltd
Level 5, 132–136 Albert Road, South Melbourne, Victoria 3205
☎00 61 3 9694 4900 Fax 00 61 3 9645 0705
Website www.lothian.com.au
FOUNDED 1888. *Publishes* general non-fiction: business, health and nutrition, New Age, astrology, occult, self-help.

Macmillan Education Australia Pty Ltd
Locked Bag 1400, South Yarra, Victoria 3141
☎00 61 3 9825 1025 Fax 00 61 3 9825 1010
Website www.macmillan.com.au
FOUNDED 1896. Part of **Macmillan Publishers**, UK. *Publishes* accountancy, behavioural sciences, economics, education, geography, geology, government, political science, history, management, mathematics, physics, general science, social sciences, sociology.

McGraw-Hill
PO Box 239, Roseville, NSW 2069
☎00 61 2 9415 9899 Fax 00 61 2 9417 8872
Website www.mcgraw-hill.com.au
FOUNDED 1964. Owned by **McGraw-Hill Inc.**, USA. *Publishes* accountancy, education, health and nutrition, advertising, aeronautics, aviation, anthropology, architecture and interior design, art, behavioural sciences, chemistry, chemical engineering, child care and development, computer science, criminology, disability, earth sciences, economics, electronics, electrical engineering, general engineering, English as a second language, environmental studies, film and video, geography, geology, journalism, industrial relations, labour, language arts, linguistics, management, marketing, maritime, mathematics, mechanical engineering, medicine, nursing, dentistry, philosophy, photography, physics, psychology, psychiatry, sport, social sciences and sociology.

Melbourne University Press
PO Box 278, Carlton South, Victoria 3053
☎00 61 3 9342 0300 Fax 00 61 3 9342 0399
Website www.mup.unimelb.edu.au

FOUNDED 1922. *Publishes* general non-fiction, biography, essays, history, literature, literary criticism, natural history, psychology, psychiatry, travel.

Openbook Publishers
GPO Box 1368, Adelaide, SA 5001
☎00 61 8 8223 5468 Fax 00 61 8 8223 4552
Website www.openbook.com.au
FOUNDED 1913. *Publishes* religious and educational books.

Oxford University Press Australia and New Zealand
PO Box 2784Y, Melbourne, Victoria 3001
☎00 61 3 9934 9123 Fax 00 61 3 9934 9100
Website www.oup.com.au
FOUNDED 1908. Owned by **Oxford University Press**, UK. *Publishes* for the college, school and trade markets.

Pan Macmillan Australia Pty Ltd
Level 18, St Martin's Tower, 31 Market Street, Sydney, NSW 2000
☎00 61 2 9285 9100 Fax 00 61 2 9285 9190
Email panpublishing@www.macmillan.com.au
Website www.panmacmillan.com.au
FOUNDED 1983. Part of **Macmillan Publishers**, UK. *Publishes* fiction, essays, literature, literary criticism; general non-fiction, biography, health and nutrition, humour, self-help, travel.

Pearson Education Australia
LMB 507, Frenchs Forest, NSW 1640
☎00 61 3 9454 2200 Fax 00 61 3 9453 0089
Website www.awl.com.au
Australia's largest educational publisher.

Penguin Books Australia Ltd
PO Box 701, Hawthorn, Victoria 3124
☎00 61 3 9811 2400 Fax 00 61 3 9811 2620
Website www.penguin.com.au
FOUNDED 1946. *Publishes* general non-fiction and fiction; biography, cookery, humour, literature, literary criticism, essays, science fiction, fantasy, self-help, travel.

University of Queensland Press
PO Box 6042, St Lucia Queensland 4067
☎00 61 7 3365 2127 Fax 00 61 7 3365 7579
Website www.uqp.uq.edu.au
FOUNDED 1948. *Publishes* Aboriginal studies, reference, social and political issues; general non-fiction and fiction, literature, literary criti-

cism, essays, poetry, biography, history, sport, travel.

Random House Australia
20 Alfred Street, Milsons Point, NSW 2061
☎00 61 2 9954 9966 Fax 00 61 2 9954 4562
Email random@randomhouse.com.au
Website www.randomhouse.com.au

Subsidiary of **Bertelsmann AG**. *Publishes* fiction and non-fiction.

Reader's Digest (Australia) Pty Ltd
PO Box 4353, Sydney, NSW 2001
☎00 61 2 9690 6935
Fax 00 61 2 9690 6390

FOUNDED 1946. Associate company of **Reader's Digest Association, Inc.** (USA). Educational publisher.

Reed Educational Publishing Australia
PO Box 460, Port Melbourne, Victoria 3207
☎00 61 3 9245 7188 Fax 00 61 3 9245 7265
Website www.reededucation.com.au

FOUNDED 1982. *Publishes* art, chemistry, chemical engineering, environmental studies, geography, geology, health and nutrition, history, mathematics, physics.

Scholastic Australia Pty Limited
PO Box 579, Gosford, NSW 2250
☎00 61 2 4328 3555 Fax 00 61 2 4329 1106
Website www.scholastic.com.au

FOUNDED 1968. Educational publisher.

Science Press
54a Fitzroy Street, Marrickville, NSW 2204
☎00 61 2 9516 1122 Fax 00 61 2 9550 1915

FOUNDED 1945. Educational publisher.

Simon & Schuster Australia Pty Ltd
PO Box 507, East Roseville, NSW 2069
☎00 61 2 9415 9900 Fax 00 61 2 9417 3188

FOUNDED 1987. Part of **Simon & Schuster Inc.**, USA. *Publishes* general non-fiction.

University of Western Australia Press
35 Stirling Highway, Crawley, WA 6009
☎00 61 8 9380 3182 Fax 00 61 8 9380 1027
Website www.uwapress.uwa.edu.au

FOUNDED 1954. *Publishes* general non-fiction, essays, literature, literary criticism, science fiction, fantasy, history, social sciences, sociology, natural history, autobiography, women's studies.

John Wiley & Sons Australia Ltd
PO Box 1226, Milton Queensland 4064
☎00 61 7 3859 9755 Fax 00 61 7 3859 9715
Email brisbane@johnwiley.com.au
Website www.johnwiley.com.au

FOUNDED 1954. Owned by **John Wiley & Sons Inc.**, USA. *Publishes* general non-fiction and education books.

Canada

Canadian Scholars' Press, Inc
180 Bloor Street W, Suite 1202, Toronto, Ontario M5S 2V6
☎001 416 929 2774 Fax 001 416 929 1926
Email info@cspi.org
Website www.cspi.org

FOUNDED 1987. *Publishes* academic books in English and French.

Fenn Publishing Co Ltd
34 Nixon Road, Bolton, Ontario L7E 1W2
☎001 905 951 6600 Fax 001 905 951 6601
Website www.hbfenn.com

FOUNDED 1977. *Publishes* fiction and non-fiction, children's.

Fitzhenry & Whiteside Limited
195 Allstate Parkway, Markham, Ontario L3R 4T8
☎001 905 477 9700 Fax 001 905 477 9179
Email godwit@fitzhenry.ca
Website www.fitzhenry.ca

FOUNDED 1966. *Publishes* trade, reference and children's books; educational material.

Golden Books Publishing (Canada) Inc
73 Water Street N., No 501, Cambridge, Ontario N1R 5X2
☎001 519 623 3590 Fax 001 519 623 3598
Website www.goldenbooks.com

FOUNDED 1942. *Publishes* (in English and French) juvenile and adult books, Bibles.

Harcourt Canada Ltd
55 Horner Avenue, Toronto, Ontario M8Z 4X6
☎001 416 255 4491 Fax 001 416 255 4046
Website www.harcourtcanada.com

FOUNDED 1922. *Publishes* educational material.

HarperCollins Publishers Limited
55 Avenue Road, Suite 2900, Hazelton Lanes, Toronto, Ontario M5R 3L2

☎001 416 975 9334 Fax 001 416 975 9884
Website www.harpercanada.com
FOUNDED 1989. *Publishes* fiction and non-fiction, children's and religious.

Irwin Publishing
325 Humber College Blvd., Toronto, Ontario
M9W 7C3
☎001 416 798 0424 Fax 001 416 798 1384
Email irwin@irwin-pub.com
Website www.irwin-pub.com
FOUNDED 1945. *Publishes* (in English and French) education.

Lexis Nexis Butterworths Canada Ltd
75 Clegg Road, Markham, Ontario L6G 1A1
☎001 905 479 2665 Fax 001 905 479 2826
Website www.lexisnexis.ca
FOUNDED 1912. *Publishes* law books, CD-ROMs, journals, newsletters, law reports.

McClelland & Stewart Ltd
481 University Avenue, Suite 900, Toronto, Ontario M5G 2E9
☎001 416 598 1114 Fax 001 416 598 7764
Website www.mcclelland.com
FOUNDED 1906. *Publishes* fiction and non-fiction, poetry.

McGraw-Hill Ryerson Ltd
300 Water Street, Whitby, Ontario
L1N 9B6
☎001 905 430 5000 Fax 001 905 430 5020
Website www.mcgrawhill.ca
FOUNDED 1944. Subsidiary of McGraw-Hill Education. *Publishes* education and professional.

Nelson
1120 Birchmount Road, Scarborough, Ontario M1K 5G4
☎001 416 752 9100 Fax 001 416 752 9646
Website www.nelson.com
FOUNDED 1914. Division of Thomson Canada Ltd. Leading educational publisher. Also *publishes* professional and reference.

New Star Books Ltd
107–3477 Commercial Street, Vancouver, BC V5N 4E8
☎001 604 738 9429 Fax 001 604 738 9332
Email info@newstarbooks.com
Website www.NewStarBooks.com
FOUNDED 1974. *Publishes* social issues and current affairs, fiction, literature, history, inter-national politics, labour, feminist, gay and lesbian studies.

Oxford University Press, Canada
70 Wynford Drive, Don Mills, Onatario
M3C 1J9
☎001 416 441 2941 Fax 001 416 444 0427
Website www.oup.com/ca
FOUNDED 1904. Owned by **Oxford University Press**, UK. *Publishes* for college, school and trade markets.

Pearson Education Canada Inc.
PO Box 580, Don Mills, Ontario M3C 2T8
☎001 416 447 5101 Fax 001 416 443 0948
Website www.pearsoned.com
FOUNDED 1966. Fourth-largest educational publisher in Canada. *Publishes* in English and French.

Penguin Books Canada Limited
10 Alcorn Avenue Street, Suite 300, Toronto, Ontario M4V 3B2
☎001 416 925 2249 Fax 001 416 925 0068
Website www.penguin.ca
FOUNDED 1974. *Publishes* fiction and non-fiction books and audio cassettes.

Random House of Canada Ltd
One Toronto Street, Unit 300, Toronto, Ontario M5C 2V6
☎001 416 364 4449 Fax 001 416 364 6863
Website www.randomhouse.ca
FOUNDED 1944. *Publishes* fiction and non-fiction and children's.

Scholastic Canada Ltd
175 Hillmount Road, Markham, Ontario
L6C 1Z7
☎001 905 887 7323 Fax 001 905 887 1131
Website www.scholastic.ca
FOUNDED 1957. *Publishes* (in English and French) children's books and educational material.

Tundra Books
481 University Avenue, Suite 900, Toronto, Ontario M5G 2E9
☎001 416 598 4786 Fax 001 416 598 0247
FOUNDED 1967. Division of **McClelland & Stewart Ltd**. *Publishes* (in English and French) children's illustrated books.

John Wiley & Sons Canada Ltd
22 Worcester Road, Etobicoke, Ontario
M9W 1L1

☎001 416 236 4433   Fax 001 416 236 4447
Website www.wiley.com
FOUNDED 1968. Subsidiary of **John Wiley & Sons Inc.**, USA. *Publishes* professional, reference and textbooks.

India

Affiliated East West Press Pvt Ltd
104 Nirmal Tower, 26 Barakhamba Road,
New Delhi 110 001
☎00 91 11 331 5398   Fax 00 91 11 326 0538
FOUNDED 1962. *Publishes* aeronautics, aviation, agriculture, anthropology, biological sciences, chemistry, engineering (chemical, civil, electrical, mechanical), computer science, economics, electronics, mathematics, management, microcomputers, physical sciences, physics, general science, veterinary science, women's studies.

Arnold Heinman Publishers (India) Pvt Ltd
AB-9, 1st Floor, Safdaoung Enclave, New Delhi 110 029
☎00 91 11 688 3422   Fax 00 91 11 687 7571
FOUNDED 1969. Associate company of Edward Arnold (Publishers) Ltd, UK. *Publishes* fiction, poetry, essays, literature, literary criticism, art, general engineering, government, political science, philosophy, religion, medicine, nursing, dentistry, social sciences and sociology.

S. Chand & Co Ltd
PO Box 5733, New Delhi 110 055
☎00 91 11 367 2080   Fax 00 91 11 367 7446
FOUNDED 1917. *Publishes* art, business, economics, government, political science, medicine, nursing, dentistry, philosophy, social sciences, sociology, general science, technology.

Current Books
Round West, Trichur 680 001
☎00 91 487 335642   Fax 00 91 487 335660
FOUNDED 1952. *Publishes* fiction and general non-fiction.

General Book Depot
1691 Nai Sarak, Delhi 110 007
☎00 91 11 326 3695   Fax 00 91 11 294 0861
FOUNDED 1936. *Publishes* general non-fiction; business, career development, how-to, English as a second language, language arts, linguistics, self-help, travel.

HarperCollins Publishers India Pty Ltd
7/61 Ansari Road, Daryaganj,
New Delhi 110 002
☎00 91 11 327 8586   Fax 00 91 11 327 7294
FOUNDED 1991. *Publishes* fiction, poetry, biography and education.

Hind Pocket Books Private Ltd
18–19 Dilshad Garden G T Road,
Delhi 110 095
☎00 91 11 228 2467   Fax 00 91 11 228 2332
FOUNDED 1957. *Publishes* fiction and general non-fiction; biography, how-to and self-help.

Jaico Publishing House
121–125 Mahatma Gandhi Road,
Mumbai 400 023
☎00 91 22 267 6702   Fax 00 91 22 204 1673
Website www.jaicobooks.com
FOUNDED 1945. *Publishes* biography, behavioural sciences, language arts, linguistics, health and nutrition, cookery, law, criminology, astrology, occult, philosophy, religion, general engineering, economics, humour, history, government, political science, psychology, psychiatry.

Macmillan India Ltd
315/316 Raheja Chambers, 12 Museum Road, Bangalore 560 052
☎00 91 80 558 6563   Fax 00 91 80 558 8713
Email macmillan@aindia.com
Website www.macmillan-india.com
FOUNDED 1903. Part of **Macmillan Publishers**, UK. *Publishes* scientific and mathematical books and journals.

McGraw-Hill Publishing Company
No 7 West Patel Nagar, New Delhi 110 008
☎00 91 11 573 2841   Fax 00 91 11 573 2918
FOUNDED 1970. *Publishes* general engineering and science, business, social sciences, sociology and management.

Munshiram Manoharlal Publishers Pvt Ltd
PO Box 5715, New Delhi 110 055
☎00 91 11 367 1668   Fax 00 91 11 361 2745
FOUNDED 1952. *Publishes* art, architecture and interior design, anthropology, archaeology, astrology, occult, religion (Buddhist, Hindu, Islamic), philosophy, history, language arts and linguistics, music, dance, drama, theatre, Asian studies.

National Book Trust India
H–29, Green Park Extension,
New Delhi 110 016
☎00 91 11 664 9962 Fax 00 91 11 685 1795
FOUNDED 1957. *Publishes* human relations and foreign countries.

National Publishing House
23 Daryaganj, New Delhi 110 002
☎00 91 11 327 4161
FOUNDED 1950. *Publishes* human relations, ethnicity, social sciences, sociology.

Orient Paperbacks
1590 Madarsa Road, Kashmere Gate,
Delhi 110 006
☎00 91 11 386 2267 Fax 00 91 11 386 2935
Website www.orientpaperbacks.com
FOUNDED 1977. *Publishes* fiction and general non-fiction; business, career development, cookery, crafts, games, hobbies, humour, drama, theatre, health and nutrition, how-to, poetry, astrology, occult, self-help, sport.

Oxford University Press India
2/11 Ansari Road, Daryaganj,
New Delhi 110 002
☎00 91 11 202 1029 Fax 00 91 11 373 2312
FOUNDED 1912. Owned by **Oxford University Press**, UK. Academic publishers.

Rajpal & Sons
Madarasa Road, Kashmere Gate, Delhi 110 006
☎00 91 11 296 3904 Fax 00 91 11 296 7791
FOUNDED 1891. *Publishes* fiction, literature, literary criticism, essays, human relations, general science.

Vidyarthi Mithram Press
Baker Road, Kottayam 686 001
☎00 91 481 563 281 Fax 00 91 481 562 616
FOUNDED 1928. *Publishes* child care and development, cookery, drama and theatre, economics, biography, biological sciences, chemistry and chemical engineering, computer science.

A.H. Wheeler & Co Ltd
411 Surya Kiran Building, 19 K G Marg,
New Delhi 110 001
☎00 91 11 331 2629 Fax 00 91 11 335 7798
FOUNDED 1879. *Publishes* computer science, behavioural sciences, accountancy, advertising, business, career development, civil engineering, communications.

New Zealand

Auckland University Press
University of Auckland, 1–11 Short Street,
Auckland
☎00 64 9 373 7528 Fax 00 64 9 373 7465
Website www.auckland.ac.nz/aup
FOUNDED 1966. *Publishes* art, archaeology, biography, government, political science, history, social sciences, sociology, women's studies, essays, poetry, literature, literary criticism.

Butterworths New Zealand Ltd
PO Box 472, Wellington 1
☎00 64 4 385 1479 Fax 00 64 4 385 1598
Website www.butterworths.co.nz
FOUNDED 1914. *Publishes* law.

Canterbury University Press
University of Canterbury, Private Bag 4800,
Christchurch
☎00 64 3 364 2914 Fax 00 64 3 364 2044
Email mail@cup.canterbury.ac.nz
FOUNDED 1960. *Publishes* general non-fiction; biography, biological sciences, history, natural history.

The Caxton Press
PO Box 25088, Christchurch
☎00 64 3 366 8516 Fax 00 64 3 365 7840
FOUNDED 1935. *Publishes* general non-fiction; biography, gardening and plants.

HarperCollins Publishers (New Zealand) Ltd
31 View Road, Auckland
☎00 64 9 443 9400 Fax 00 64 9 443 9403
Website www.harpercollins.co.nz
FOUNDED 1888. *Publishes* fiction, art, history, humour, natural history, biography, cookery, plants, gardening, sport, travel, self-help.

Hodder Moa Beckett Publishers Ltd
PO Box 3858, Auckland
☎00 64 9 444 3640 Fax 00 64 9 444 3646
FOUNDED 1971. Owned by **Hodder Headline**, UK. *Publishes* fiction and general non-fiction, biography.

Huia Publishers
PO Box 17335, Karori, Wellington
☎00 64 4 473 9262 Fax 00 64 4 473 9265
Website www.huia.co.nz
FOUNDED 1991. *Publishes* Maori cultural his-

tory and language, children's books in Maori and English, histories of colonisation in New Zealand.

University of Otago Press
PO Box 56, Dunedin
☎00 64 3 479 8807 Fax 00 64 3 479 8385
Email university.press@otago.ac.nz
Website www.otago.ac.nz
FOUNDED 1958. *Publishes* fiction, essays, literature, literary criticism, poetry, art, history, education, biography, anthropology, natural history, environmental studies, photography, psychology, psychiatry, government and political science.

Oxford University Press
New Zealand
PO Box 11149, Ellerslie, Auckland 5
☎00 64 9 523 3134
Academic publishers.

Pearson Education New Zealand
Private Bag 102908, North Shore Mail Centre, Glenfield, Auckland 10
☎00 64 9 444 4968 Fax 00 64 9 444 4957
FOUNDED 1968. Educational publishers.

Penguin Books (NZ) Ltd
182–190 Wairau Road (Glenfield), Private Bag, Takapuna, Auckland 9
☎00 64 9 444 4965 Fax 00 64 9 444 1470
FOUNDED 1976. Owned by **Penguin UK**.

Reed Publishing (NZ) Ltd
Private Bag 34901, Birkenhead, Auckland 10
☎00 64 9 480 4950 Fax 00 64 9 419 4999
Website www.reed.co.nz
FOUNDED 1988. *Publishes* fiction and general non-fiction, biography, cookery, history, natural history, regional interests, travel.

Southern Press Ltd
R D 1, Porirua 6221
☎00 64 4 239 9068 Fax 00 64 4 239 9835
FOUNDED 1971. *Publishes* aviation, aeronautics, maritime, transport, technology, mechanical and civil engineering, archaeology.

Tandem Press
2 Rugby Road, Birkenhead, Auckland 10
☎00 64 9 480 1452 Fax 00 64 9 480 1455
FOUNDED 1990. *Publishes* fiction and general non-fiction; cookery, business, alternative, ethnicity, health and nutrition, photography, psy-

chology, psychiatry, self-help, women's studies.

Victoria University Press
PO Box 600, Wellington
☎00 64 4 496 6580 Fax 00 64 4 471 1701
Website www.vup.vuw.ac.nz
FOUNDED 1979. *Publishes* government, political science, essays, poetry, literature, literary criticism, drama, theatre, history, social sciences and sociology, anthropology, language and linguistics, law, architecture and interior design.

Viking Sevenseas NZ Ltd
PO Box 152, Paraparaumu 6150, Wellington
☎00 64 4 902 8240
FOUNDED 1957. *Publishes* natural history and ethnicity.

Bridget Williams Books Ltd
PO Box 5482, Wellington
☎00 64 4 473 8317 Fax 00 64 4 473 8417
FOUNDED 1990. *Publishes* general non-fiction, biography, government, political science, history, women's studies.

South Africa

Butterworths South Africa
PO Box 4, Mayville, Durban 4058
☎00 27 31 268 3111
Fax 00 27 31 268 3100
Website www.butterworths..co.za

Owned by Butterworth & Co. UK. *Publishes* general science, medicine, nursing and dentistry, economics, education, law.

Flesch Financial Publications (Pty) Ltd
PO Box 3473, Cape Town 8000
☎00 27 21 461 7472
Fax 00 27 21 461 3758
FOUNDED 1966. *Publishes* aviation, aeronautics, maritime, animals, pets, business.

Heinemann Educational
Publishers Southern Africa
PO Box 781940, Sandton, Johannesburg 21461
☎00 27 11 322 8600
Fax 00 27 11 322 8717
Website www.heinemann.co.za
FOUNDED 1986. Parent company: Reed Educational & Professional Publishing, UK. *Publishes* economics, education, English as a

second language, mathematics, mechanical engineering.

Maskew Miller Longman

PO Box 396, Cape Town 8000
☎00 27 21 531 7750
Fax 00 27 21 531 4877

FOUNDED 1893. *Publishes* education, language arts and linguistics, essays, literature, literary criticism.

University of Natal Press

PB X01, Scottsville, Pietermaritzburg 3209
☎00 27 331 260 5226
Fax 00 27 331 260 5599
Email books@press.unp.ac.za

FOUNDED 1947. *Publishes* essays, literature and literary criticism, natural history, history, women's studies.

Oxford University Press Southern Africa

PO Box 12119, N1 City 7463
☎00 27 21 595 4400
Fax 00 27 21 595 4430
Email oxford.za@oup.com
Website www.oup.com/za

FOUNDED 1915. Parent company: **Oxford University Press**, UK. *Publishes* academic, educational and general books.

Ravan Press (Pty) Ltd

PO Box 145, Randburg, Johannesburg 2125
☎00 27 11 789 7636 Fax 00 27 11 789 7653

FOUNDED 1972. Part of Hodder & Stoughton Educational South Africa. *Publishes* fiction and general non-fiction.

Shuter & Shooter (Pty) Ltd

PO Box 618, Ferndale 2160
☎00 27 11 792 8363 Fax 00 27 11 792 7024

FOUNDED 1925. *Publishes* general non-fiction; biography, history, ethnicity, general science, technology, social sciences, sociology.

Struik Publishers (Pty) Ltd

PO Box 1144, Cape Town 8000
☎00 27 21 517128 Fax 00 27 21 4624379

FOUNDED 1962. *Publishes* child care and development, cookery, gardening, plants, environmental studies, natural history.

Witwatersrand University Press

PO Wits, Johannesburg 2050
☎00 27 11 484 5907 Fax 00 27 11 484 5971
Website www.wirs.ac.za/wup.html

FOUNDED 1922. *Publishes* essays, literature and literary criticism, drama, theatre, history, business, anthropology, archaeology, natural history, religion (Jewish), medicine, nursing and dentistry.

Professional Associations

Academi (Yr Academi Gymreig)
3rd Floor, Mount Stuart House, Mount Stuart Square, Cardiff CF10 5FQ
☎029 2047 2266 Fax 029 2049 2930
Email post@academi.org
Website www.academi.org

North West Wales office: Tŷ Newydd, Llanystumdwy, Cricieth, Gwynedd LL52 0LW
☎01766 522817 Fax 01766 523095
Email academi.gog@dial.pipex.com

West Wales office: Dylan Thomas Centre, Somerset Place, Swansea SA1 1RR
☎01792 463980 Fax 01792 463993
Email academi.dylan.thomas@business.ntl.com

Chief Executive *Peter Finch*

Academi is the trading name of Yr Academi Gymreig, the national society of Welsh writers. The Society exists to promote the literature of Wales. Yr Academi Gymreig was FOUNDED in 1959 as an association of Welsh language writers. An English language section was established in 1968. Membership, for those who have made a significant contribution to the literature of Wales, is by invitation. Membership currently stands at 500. The Academi runs courses, competitions (including the **Cardiff International Poetry Competition**), conferences, tours by authors, festivals and represents the interests of Welsh writers and Welsh writing both inside Wales and beyond. Its publications include *Taliesin*, a quarterly literary journal in the Welsh language, *The Oxford Companion to the Literature of Wales*, *The Welsh Academy English-Welsh Dictionary* and a variety of translated works.

In 1998 the Academi won the franchise from the Arts Council of Wales to run the Welsh National Literature Promotion Agency. The new, much enlarged organisation now administers a variety of schemes including Writers on Tour, Writers Residencies and a number of literature development projects. It promotes an annual literary festival alternating between North and South Wales, runs its own programme of literary activity and publishes *A470*, a bi-monthly literature information magazine. The Academi is also in receipt of a lottery grant to publish the first Welsh National Encyclopedia. This is expected to be ready towards the end of 2004.

Those with an interest in literature in Wales can become an associate of the Academi (which carries a range of benefits). Rates are £15 p.a. (waged); £7.50 (unwaged).

ALCS
See **Authors' Licensing & Collecting Society**

Alliance of Literary Societies
22 Belmont Grove, Havant, Hampshire PO9 3PU
☎023 9247 5855 Fax 08700 560330
Email rosemary@sndc.demon.co.uk
Website www.sndc.demon.co.uk/als.htm
Honorary Secretary *Mrs Rosemary Culley*

FOUNDED 1974. Aims to help and support its 90+ member societies and, when necessary, to act as a pressure group. Produces a handbook which holds useful information that is deemed important for the successful running of a literary society. It also contains details of the member societies and events to publicise them to the ALS members and the wider public. In addition, the Alliance produces two newsletters and *The Open Book*, an annual publication.

Arts & Business (A&B)
Nutmeg House, 60 Gainsford Street, Butlers Wharf, London SE1 2NY
☎020 7378 8143 Fax 020 7407 7527
Email head.office@AandB.org.uk
Website www.AandB.org.uk
P.R. Manager *Jonathan Tuchner*

The purpose of Arts & Business (formerly the Association for Business Sponsorship of the Arts) is to help strengthen communities by developing creative and effective partnership between Business and the Arts. It provides a wide range of services to over 350 business members as well as to 700 arts organisations and museums through the Development Forum. The Arts & Business Skills Bank, Board Bank and mentoring schemes enable individual business people to share their skills with arts managers. On behalf of the Department for Culture, Media and Sport, it manages the Arts & Business New Partners Programme, an incentive programme for new and established sponsors of the arts. Arts & Business is working with forward-looking businesses to determine the future of business/arts partnerships. With the support of its President, HRH The Prince of Wales, it is exploring and developing new ways for business, the arts and society to interact. Arts & Business has 15 offices offering a range of services throughout the UK.

Arvon Foundation
See entry under **Writers' Courses, Circles and Workshops**

ASLS
See **Association for Scottish Literary Studies**

Association for Business Sponsorship of the Arts (ABSA)
See **Arts & Business**

Association for Scottish Literary Studies
c/o Department of Scottish History, 9 University Gardens, University of Glasgow, Glasgow G12 8QH
☎0141 330 5309 Fax 0141 330 5309
Email d.jones@scothist.arts.gla.ac.uk
Website www.asls.org.uk

Contact *Duncan Jones*
Subscription £34 (Individual);
£63 (Institutional)

FOUNDED 1970. ASLS is an educational charity promoting the languages and literature of Scotland. *Publishes* works of Scottish literature; essays, monographs and journals; and *Scotnotes*, a series of comprehensive study guides to major Scottish writers. Also produces *New Writing Scotland*, an annual anthology of contemporary poetry and prose in English, Gaelic and Scots (see entry under **Magazines**).

Association of American Correspondents in London
c/o Time Magazine, Brettenham House, Lancaster Place, London WC2E 7TL
☎020 7322 1084 Fax 020 7322 1230

Contact *Elizabeth Lea*
Subscription £90 (Organisations)

FOUNDED 1919 to serve the professional interests of its member organisations, promote social cooperation among them, and maintain the ethical standards of the profession. (An extra £30 is charged for each department of an organisation which requires separate listing in the Association's handbook and a charge of £10 for each

full-time editorial staff listed, up to a maximum of £120 regardless of the number listed.)

Association of American Publishers, Inc
71 Fifth Avenue, 2nd Floor, New York, NY 10003–3004, USA
☎001 212 255 0200 Fax 001 212 255 7007
Website www.publishers.org
Also at: 50 f Street, NW, Washington, DC 20001–1564
☎001 202 347 3375 Fax 001 202 347 3690

Contact *Judith Platt*

FOUNDED 1970. For information, visit the Association's website.

Association of Authors' Agents
A.P. Watt Ltd, 20 John Street, London WC1N 2DR
☎020 7405 6774 Fax 020 7831 2154
Email aaa@apwatt.co.uk
Website www.agentsassoc.co.uk

President *Derek Johns*
Membership £50 p.a.

FOUNDED 1974. Membership voluntary. The AAA maintains a code of practice, provides a forum for discussion and represents its members in issues affecting the profession. For a full list of members visit the AAA website.

Association of Authors' Representatives
PO Box 237201, Ansonia Station, New York, NY 10023, USA
☎001 212 252 3695
Email aarinc@mindspring.com
Website www.aar-online.org

Administrative Secretary *Leslie Carroll*

FOUNDED in 1991 through the merger of the Society of Authors' Representatives and the Independent Literary Agents Association. Membership of this US organisation is restricted to agents of at least two years' operation. Provides information, education and support for its members and works to protect their best interests.

Association of British Editors
See **Society of Editors**

Association of British Science Writers (ABSW)
23 Savile Row, London W1X 2NB
☎020 7439 1205 Fax 020 7973 3051
Email absw@absw.org.uk
Website www.absw.org.uk

Chairman *Pallab Ghosh*
Administrator *Barbara Drillsma*
Membership £35 p.a.; £30 (Associate);
£5 (Student)

ABSW has played a central role in improving the standards of science journalism in the UK over the last 40 years. The Association seeks to improve standards by means of networking, lectures and organised visits to institutional laboratories and industrial research centres. Puts members in touch with major projects in the field and with experts worldwide. A member of the European Union of Science Journalists' Associations, ABSW is able to offer heavily subsidised places on visits to research centres in most other European countries, and hosts reciprocal visits to Britain by European journalists. Membership open to those who are considered to be *bona fide* science writers/editors, or their film/TV/radio equivalents, who earn a substantial part of their income by promoting public interest in and understanding of science. Runs the administration and judging of the **Glaxo Science Writers' Awards**, for outstanding science journalism in newspapers, journals and broadcasting and, with The Wellcome Trust, awards bursaries for science undergraduates taking a science communication course.

Association of Canadian Publishers

110 Eglinton Avenue East, Suite 702,
Toronto, Ontario M4P 1J5, Canada
☎001 416 487 6116   Fax 001 416 487 8815
Email info@canbook.org
Website www.publishers.ca
Executive Director *John Pelletier*

FOUNDED 1971. ACP represents over 140 Canadian-owned book publishers countrywide from the literary, general trade, scholarly and education sectors. Aims to encourage the writing, publishing, distribution and promotion of Canadian books and to support the development of a 'strong, independent and vibrant Canadian-owned publishing industry'. The organisation's website has information on getting published and links to many of their member publishers' websites.

Association of Christian Writers

All Saints Vicarage, 43 All Saints Close,
Edmonton, London N9 9AT
☎020 8884 4348   Fax 020 8884 4348
Email admin@christianwriters.org.uk
Website www.christianwriters.org.uk
Administrator *Mrs Jenny Kyriacou*

Subscription Single: £20 (£17 Direct Debit);
Joint Husband/Wife: £23 (£20 DD);
Overseas: £27 (£24 DD on UK a/c)

FOUNDED in 1971 'to inspire and equip men and women to use their talents and skills with integrity to devise, write and market excellent material which comes from a Christian worldview. In this way we seek to be an influence for good and for God in this generation.' *Publishes* a quarterly magazine. Runs three training events each year, biennial conference, competitions, postal workshops, area groups, prayer support and manuscript criticism. Charity No. 1069839.

Association of Freelance Editors, Proofreaders & Indexers (Ireland)

Skeagh, Skibbereen, Co. Cork, Republic of Ireland
☎00 353 28 38259   Fax 00 353 28 38004
Email gloria@redbarn-publishing.ie
Contact *Gloria Greenwood*
Subscription €25 p.a.

The organisation was established in Ireland to protect the interests of its members and to provide information to publishers on freelancers working in the relevant fields. Membership is restricted to freelancers with experience and/or references (but does not test or evaluate the skills of members). New category of membership – Associate Member – available for trainees in proofreading/editing who are taking the Book House Training Centre correspondence courses in Proofreading and Copy-editing.

Association of Freelance Journalists

2 Glen Cottage, Brick Hill Lane, Ketley,
Telford, Shropshire TF2 6SB
Email afj_UK@Yahoo.com
Website www.afj.home-page.org
Official Patron *Dr Carl Chinn, PhD, MBE*
Founding President *Martin Scholes*
Subscription £30 p.a.

Offers membership to all who work in the field of journalism but especially local correspondents, stringers, freelance journalists, news photographers, those at the beginning of their careers or long established. Also welcomes those who make a modest income writing for the specialist press or who self-publish; who have written for a hobby but now wish to make a career of their writing. Members receive a regular newsletters a laminated press card, a free postal/e-mail advice service, the opportunity to network with other members (through the newsletter and a special Internet service) and editors who contact the

AFJ. There are discounts on products and services, including the AFJ writing course.

Association of Freelance Writers
Sevendale House, 7 Dale Street, Manchester M1 1JB
☎0161 228 2362, ext 210   Fax 0161 228 3533
Email fmn@writersbureau.com
Contact *Angela Cox*
Subscription £29 p.a.

FOUNDED in 1995 to help and advise new and established freelance writers. Members receive a copy of *Freelance Market News* each month which gives news, views and the latest advice and guidelines about publications at home and abroad. Other benefits include one free appraisal of prose or poetry each year, reduced entry to **The Writers Bureau** writing competition, reduced fees for writing seminars and discounts on books for writers.

Association of Golf Writers
1 Pilgrims Bungalow, Mulberry Hill, Chilham, Kent CT4 8AH
☎01227 732496   Fax 01227 732496
Email andyfarrell@compuserve.com
Honorary Secretary *Andy Farrell*

FOUNDED 1938. Aims to cooperate with golfing bodies to ensure best possible working conditions.

Association of Illustrators
81 Leonard Street, London EC2A 4QS
☎020 7613 4328   Fax 020 7613 4417
Email info@a-o-illustrators.demon.co.uk
Website www.theaoi.com
Contact *Membership & Publications Secretary*

FOUNDED 1973 to promote illustration, protect illustrators' rights, and encourage professional standards. The AOI is a non-profit-making trade association dedicated to its members, to protecting their interests and promoting their work. Talks, seminars, a journal, regional groups, legal and portfolio advice as well as a number of related publications such as *Rights, The Illustrator's Guide to Professional Practice*; *Survive, The Illustrator's Guide to a Professional Career* and *Images*, the only jury-selected annual of British illustration.

Association of Independent Libraries
Leeds Library, 18 Commercial Street, Leeds, West Yorkshire LS1 6AL
☎0113 245 3071
Chairman *Geoffrey Forster*

Secretary *Krystyna Smithers*

Established to 'further the advancement, conservation and restoration of a little-known but important living portion of our cultural heritage'. Members include the **London Library, Devon & Exeter Institution, Linen Hall Library** and **Plymouth Proprietary Library**.

Association of Learned and Professional Society Publishers
South House, The Street, Clapham, Worthing, West Sussex BN13 3UU
☎01903 871686   Fax 01903 871457
Email sec-gen@alpsp.org
Website www.alpsp.org
Secretary-General *Sally Morris*
Business Manager *Jill Tolson*
Editors, Learned Publishing *Robert Welham* (UK), Mike Spinella (USA)

Represents the community of not-for-profit publishers and those who work with them. Monitors national and international issues and represents members' interests to the wider world. Extensive programme of research, publications, eduation, training and development. Has an informative website and publishes a quarterly journal, *Learned Publishing* and a monthly electronic newsletter, *SLPSP Alert*. Approx. 240 members worldwide.

Association of Scottish Motoring Writers
c/o Scottish and Universal Newspapers, 5/15 Bank Street, Airdrie ML6 6AF
☎01236 748048   Fax 01236 748098
Email jmurdoch@s-un.co.uk
Secretary *John Murdoch*
Subscription £45 (Full); £25 (Associate)

FOUNDED 1961. Aims to co-ordinate the activities of, and provide shared facilities for, motoring writers resident in Scotland. Membership is by invitation only.

Australian Copyright Council
PO Box 1986, Strawberry Hills, NSW 2016, Australia
☎00 61 29318 1788   Fax 00 61 29698 3536
Email info@copyright.org.au
Website www.copyright.org.au
Contact *Customer Service*

FOUNDED 1968. The Council's activities and services include a range of publications, organising and speaking about copyright at seminars, research, consultancies and free legal advice.

Aims include assistance for copyright owners to exercise their rights effectively, raising awareness about the importance of copyright and seeking changes to the law of copyright.

Australian Publishers Association

60/89 James Street, Ultimo, NSW 2007, Australia
☎00 61 2 9281 9788
Email apa@publishers.asn.au
Website www.publishers.asn.au

Chief Executive *Susan Bridge*
Subscription Annual membership open to Australian publishers

FOUNDED 1948. The APA initiates programmes that contribute to the development of publishing in Australia, virgorously protects and furthers the interests of copyright owners, agents and licensees and actively represents members' interests to government and other organisations as appropriate. The Association encourages excellence in writing, editing, design, production, marketing and distribution of published works in Australia, protects freedom of expression and manages members' funds to further the interests of the industry.

Australian Society of Authors

PO Box 1566, Strawberry Hills, NSW 2012, Australia
☎00 61 2 9318 0877
Fax 00 61 2 9318 0530
Email asa@asauthors.org
Website www.asauthors.org

Executive Director *José Borghino*

FOUNDED 1963. The ASA aims to promote and protect the professional interests of Australian authors. Provides contract advice and assists authors on industry standards and practices. *Publishes Australian Author* magazine.

Authors' Club

40 Dover Street, London W1S 4NP
☎020 7499 8581 Fax 020 7409 0913

Secretary *Mrs Ann de La Grange*

FOUNDED in 1891 by Sir Walter Besant, the Authors' Club welcomes as members writers, agents, publishers, critics, journalists, academics and anyone involved with literature and the written word. Administers the **Authors' Club Best First Novel Award** and **Sir Banister Fletcher Award**, and organises regular talks and dinners with well-known guest speakers. Membership fee: apply to secretary.

Authors' Licensing & Collecting Society Limited (ALCS)

Marlborough Court, 14–18 Holborn, London EC1N 2LE
☎020 7395 0600 Fax 020 7395 0660
Email alcs@alcs.co.uk
Website www.alcs.co.uk

Subscription £10.00 incl. VAT (UK; free to members of **Society of Authors, Writers' Guild, NUJ, BAJ** and **CIOJ**); £10.00 (EU residents); £12.50 (Overseas)

FOUNDED 1977. The UK rights management society for writers and their successors, ALCS is a non-profit organisation whose principal purpose is to ensure that hard-to-collect revenues due to writers are efficiently collected and speedily distributed. Established to give assistance to writers through the protection and exploitation of collective rights, ALCS has distributed over £80m. in secondary royalties to writers since its creation.

ALCS represents all types of writer, fiction and non-fiction, including educational, research and academic authors, scriptwriters, playwrights, poets, editors and freelance journalists across the print and broadcast media. On joining, members give ALCS a mandate to administer on their behalf those rights which the law determines must be received or which are best handled collectively. Chief among these are: photocopying, cable retransmission (including the fees for BBC Prime and BBC World Service programming), rental and lending rights (but not British Public Lending Right), off-air recording, electronic rights, the performing right and public reception of broadcasts. The society is a prime resource and a leading authority on copyright matters and writers' collective interests. It maintains a watching brief on all matters affecting copyright both in Britain and abroad, making representations to UK government authorities and the EU. Visit the website or contact the office for application forms and further information.

BACB

See **British Association of Communicators in Business**

BAPLA (British Association of Picture Libraries and Agencies)

18 Vine Hill, London EC1R 5DZ
☎020 7713 1780 Fax 020 7713 1211
Email enquiries@bapla.org.uk
Website www.bapla.org

Everything you need to know about finding, buying and selling pictures. Established 1975.

BFC
See **British Film Commission**

The Bibliographical Society
c/o Institute of English Studies, Room 304,
Senate House, Malet Street, London
WC1E 7HU
☎020 7862 8679   Fax 020 7862 8720
Email secretary@bibsoc.org.uk
President D. Shaw
Honorary Secretary M. L. Ford
Subscription £33 p.a.

Aims to promote and encourage the study and
research of historical, analytical, descriptive and
textual bibliography, and the history of printing, publishing, bookselling, bookbinding and
collecting; to hold meetings at which papers
are read and discussed; to print and publish
works concerned with bibliography; to form a
bibliographical library. Awards grants and bursaries for bibliographical research. *Publishes* a
quarterly magazine called *The Library*.

Book Packagers Association
8 St John's Road, Saxmundham, Suffolk
IP17 1BE
☎01728 604204   Fax 01728 604029
Treasurer Charles Perkins
Subscription £150 p.a.; £75 (Associate);
£100 (Overseas)

Aims to provide members with a forum for the
exchange of information, to improve the image
of packaging and to represent the interests of
members. Activities include meetings, seminars
and the provision of standard contracts.

Booksellers Association
of the UK & Ireland Ltd
Minster House, 272 Vauxhall Bridge Road,
London SW1V 1BA
☎020 7802 0802   Fax 020 7802 0803
Email mail@booksellers.org.uk
Website www.booksellers.org.uk
Chief Executive Tim Godfray

FOUNDED 1895. The BA helps 3200 independent,
chain and multiple members to sell more books,
reduce costs and improve efficiency. It represents
members' interests to the UK Government,
European Commission, publishers, authors and
others in the trade as well as offering marketing
assistance, running training courses, conferences,
seminars and exhibitions. Together with **The
Publishers Association**, coordinates World
Book Day. *Publishes* directories, catalogues, surveys
and various other publications connected with the
book trade and administers the **Whitbread Book
Awards** and the **Samuel Johnson Prize for
Non-fiction**.

Booktrust
Book House, 45 East Hill, London
SW18 2QZ
☎020 8516 2977   Fax 020 8516 2978
Email info@booktrust.org.uk
Website www.booktrust.org.uk *and*
www.booktrusted.com
Director Chris Meade
Press & Publicity Helen Hayes

FOUNDED 1925. Booktrust, the independent
educational charity promoting books and reading, runs the Book Information Line giving
accurate facts about topical books and the book
world (☎0906 516 1193, weekdays 10 am to
1.00 pm; calls charged at £1.50 per minute).
Runs Booktrusted.com, their website for all
those who care what young people read which
includes details of Children's Book Week and
Booktrusted publications. Administers many
literary prizes such as the Orange and Booker,
creative reading projects like Breathtaker and
Bookscapes, and runs Bookstart, the acclaimed
national scheme which aims to supply a free
introductory bag of baby books to all babies at
their eight-month health check. Booktrust is to
launch the Booktrust Teenage Prize for fiction
only. Novels, short story collections and
graphic novels may be entered.

British Academy of Composers and Songwriters
2nd Floor, British Music House, 25–27
Berners Street, London W1T 3LR
☎020 7636 2929   Fax 020 7636 2212
Email info@britishacademy.com
Website www.britishacademy.com
Head of Membership Fergal Kilroy

The Academy represents the interests of music
writers of all genres, providing advice on professional and artistic matters. *Publishes* quarterly
magazine, *The Works*. Administers the annual
Ivor Novello Awards.

British Association of Communicators in Business (BACB)
Suite A, First Floor, The Auriga Building,
Davy Avenue, Knowhill, Milton Keynes
MK5 8HG
☎0870 121 7606   Fax 0870 121 7601
Email enquiries@cib.uk.com

Website www.cib.uk

Secretary General *Kathie Jones*

FOUNDED 1949. The Association aims to be the 'market leader for those involved in corporate media management and practice by providing professional, authoritative, dynamic, supportive and innovative services'.

British Association of Journalists

88 Fleet Street, London EC4Y 1PJ
☎020 7353 3003 Fax 020 7353 2310

General Secretary *Steve Turner*

Subscription National newspaper staff, national broadcasting staff, national news agency staff: £12.50 a month. Other seniors, including magazine journalists, PRs and freelances who earn the majority of their income from journalism: £7.50 a month. Journalists under 24: £5 a month.

FOUNDED 1992. Aims to protect and promote the industrial and professional interests of journalists.

British Association of Picture Libraries and Agencies

See **BAPLA**

British Centre for Literary Translation

University of East Anglia, Norwich, Norfolk NR4 7TJ
☎01603 592134/592785 Fax 01603 592737
Email bclt@uea.ac.uk
Website www.literarytranslation.com

Contact *Catherine Fuller*

FOUNDED 1989. Aims to promote literary translation and the status of the literary translator by working in the UK and overseas with translator associations and centres (e.g. European network of Translation Centres), cultural policy-makers, teachers and researchers of literary translation, arts organisations, publishers and the media, libraries and schools. PhD programme in literary translation. Coordinates activities, mostly in collaboration with other organisations, including a summer school, conferences (e.g. British Council seminars on literary translation) and seminars, workshops and readings. With European and other funding, BCLT runs a translator-in-residence programme for translators to spend one calendar month in Norwich. *Publishes* proceedings and reports of its activities where

possible, a journal *In Other Words* jointly with the **Translators Association**. Free mailing list.

British Copyright Council

Copyright House, 29–33 Berners Street, London W1T 3AB
☎01986 788122 Fax 01986 788847
Email copyright@bcc2.demon.co.uk

Contact *Janet Ibbotson*

Works for the national and international acceptance of copyright and acts as a lobby/watchdog organisation on behalf of creators, publishers and performers on copyright and associated matters. Publications include *Guide to the Law of Copyright and Rights in Performances in the UK*.

The British Council

10 Spring Gardens, London SW1A 2BN
☎020 7930 8466/7389 4268 (Press Office)
Fax 020 7839 6347
Website www.britishcouncil.org

Head of Literature *Margaret Meyer*

The British Council promotes Britain abroad. It provides access to British ideas, expertise and experience in education, the English language, literature and the arts, science and technology and governance. Works in 109 countries running a mix of offices, libraries, resource centres and English teaching operations.

British Equestrian Writers' Association

Priory House, Station Road, Swavesey, Cambridge CB4 5QJ
☎01954 232084 Fax 01954 231362
Email gnewsumn@aol.com

Contact *Gillian Newsum*

Subscription £15

FOUNDED 1973. Aims to further the interests of equestrian sport and improve, wherever possible, the working conditions of the equestrian press. Membership is by invitation of the committee. Candidates for membership must be nominated and seconded by full members and receive a majority vote of the committee.

British Film Commission (BFC)

10 Little Portland Street, London W1W 7JG
☎020 7861 7860 Fax 020 7861 7864
Email info@bfc.co.uk
Website www.bfc.co.uk

FOUNDED in 1991, the British Film Council is now a division of the Film Council. Its remit is to promote the UK as an international production centre by encouraging the use of British artists and technicians, technical services, facilities and locations, and to provide wide-ranging support to those filming and contemplating filming in the UK.

British Film Institute
21 Stephen Street, London W1T 1LN
☎020 7255 1444 Fax 020 7436 0439
Website www.bfi.org.uk
Chair *Anthony Minghella CBE*
Acting Director *Adrian Wootton*
24-hour *bfi* events line: 0870 240 4050

The **British Film Institute** was established in 1933 to promote greater understanding, appreciation and access to film and television culture. Its activities and services include preserving the world's largest collection of film and television material and running the National Film Theatre, the IMAX cinema, the Regus London Film Festival and the *bfi* National Library. It also releases films in cinemas and on video and publishes books and educational resources. Visit the website to find out more.

British Guild of Beer Writers
15 Sollershott West, Letchworth,
Hertfordshire SG6 3PU
☎01462 685844 Fax 01462 685783
Email beer@bremner.tv
Secretary *Barry Bremner*
Subscription £30 p.a.

FOUNDED 1988. Aims to improve standards in beer writing and at the same time extend public knowledge of beers and brewing. *Publishes* a directory of members with details of their publications and their particular areas of interest; this is then circulated to newspapers, magazines, trade press and broadcasting organisations. Also *publishes* a monthly newsletter, the *BGBW Newsletter*. As part of the plan to improve writing standards and to achieve a higher profile for beer, the Guild offers annual awards, The Gold and Silver Tankard Awards, to writers and broadcasters judged to have made the most valuable contribution towards this end in their work. Meetings are held regularly.

British Guild of Travel Writers
178 Battersea park Road, London SW11 4ND
☎020 7720 0990 Fax 020 7498 6153
Email bgtw@garlandintl.co.uk
Website www.bgtw.org
Chairman *Mary Johns*

Honorary Secretary *Melissa Shales*
Subscription £100 p.a.

The professional association of travel writers, broadcasters, photographers and editors which aims to serve its members' professional interests by acting as a forum for debate, discussion and 'networking'. The Guild *publishes* an annual Year Book and has a website giving full details of all its members and useful trade contacts, holds monthly meetings and has a monthly newsletter. Members are required to spend the majority of their working time on travel.

British Science Fiction Association
1 Long Row Close, Everdon, Daventry,
Northants NN11 3BE
☎01327 361661
Email bsfa@enterprise.net
Chair *Paul and Elizabeth Billinger*
Subscription £21 p.a. (reduction for unwaged)

FOUNDED originally in 1958 by a group of authors, readers, publishers and booksellers interested in science fiction. With a worldwide membership, the Association aims to promote the reading, writing and publishing of science fiction and to encourage SF fans to maintain contact with each other. *Publishes Matrix* bi-monthly newsletter with comment and opinions, news of conventions, etc. Contributions from members welcomed; *Vector* bi-monthly critical journal – reviews of books and magazines; *Focus* biannual magazine with articles, original fiction and letters column. Also offers postal writer's workshop. For further information, contact the Membership Secretary Estelle Roberts at 97 Sharp Street, Newland Avenue, Hull HU5 2AE or via email.

British Society of Comedy Writers
61 Parry Road, Ashmore Park,
Wolverhampton, West Midlands WV11 2PS
☎01902 722729 Fax 01902 722729
Email comedy@bscw.co.uk
Website www.bscw.co.uk
Contact *Ken Rock*

FOUNDED 1999. The Society aims to develop good practice and professionalism among comedy writers while bringing together the best creative professionals, and working to standards of excellence agreed with the light entertainment industry. Offers a network of industry contacts and a range of products, services and training initiatives including specialised workshops, an annual international conference, script assessment service and opportunities to visit international festivals.

British Society of Magazine Editors (BSME)

137 Hale Lane, Edgware, Middlesex HA8 9QP
☎020 8906 4664   Fax 020 8959 2137
Email bsme@cix.co.uk
Website www.bsme.com

Contact *Gill Branston*

Holds regular industry forums and events as well as an annual awards dinner.

Broadcasting Press Guild

Tiverton, The Ridge, Woking, Surrey GU22 7EQ
☎01483 764895   Fax 01483 765882
Email torin.douglas@bbc.co.uk

Membership Secretary *Richard Last*
Subscription £15 p.a.

FOUNDED 1974 to promote the professional interests of journalists specialising in writing or broadcasting about the media. Organises monthly lunches addressed by leading industry figures, and annual TV and radio awards. Membership by invitation.

BSME

See **British Society of Magazine Editors**

Bureau of Freelance Photographers

Focus House, 497 Green Lanes, London N13 4BP
☎020 8882 3315   Fax 020 8886 5174
Email info@thebfp.com

Membership Secretary *Emma Farrell*
Subscription £45 p.a. (UK); £60 p.a. (Overseas)

FOUNDED 1965. Assists members in selling their pictures through monthly *Market Newsletter*, and offers advisory, legal assistance and other services.

Campaign for Press and Broadcasting Freedom

Second Floor, 23 Orford Road, Walthamstow, London E17 9NL
☎020 8521 5932   Fax 020 8521 5932
Email freepress@cpbf.org.uk
Website www.cpbf.org.uk

Subscription £15 p.a. (concessions available); £25 p.a. (Institutions/ Organisations)

Broadly based pressure group working for more accountable and accessible media in Britain.

Advises on right of reply and takes up the issue of the portrayal of minorities. Members receive *Free Press* (bi-monthly), discounts on publications and news of campaign progress.

Canadian Authors Association

National Office: Box 419, 320 South Shores Road, Campbellford, ON K0L 1L0, Canada
☎001 705 653 0323 (866 216 6222 toll-free)
Fax 001 705 653 0593
Email canauth@redden.on.ca
Website www.CanAuthors.org

Administrator *Alec McEachern*

FOUNDED 1921. The CAA 'has expanded from a group of published authors concerned with protection of their own property to one that now includes those not yet published who want protection of what they might eventually produce and who need help producing it.' The Association has branches across the country providing support to local members in the form of advice, local contests, publications and writers' circles. *Publishes National Newsline* (quarterly) and *The Canadian Writer's Guide.*

Canadian Publishers' Council

250 Merton Street, Suite 203, Toronto, Ontario M4S 1B1, Canada
☎001 416 322 7011   Fax 001 416 322 6999
Email pubadmin@pubcouncil.ca
Website www.pubcouncil.ca

Executive Director, External Relations
Jacqueline Hushion

FOUNDED 1910. Trade association of English-language publishers which represents the domestic and international interests of member companies.

The Caravan Writers' Guild

2 Harbury Field Cottage, Harbury, Leamington Spa, Warwickshire CV33 8JN
☎01926 613186   Fax 01926 613186
Email caratesters@hotmail.com

Membership Officer *Adrian French*
Subscription £5 Joining fee plus £20 p.a.; Associates: £12.50

Guild for writers active in the specialist fields of caravan and camping journalism.

Careers Writers' Association

16 Caewal Road, Llandaff, Cardiff CF5 2BT
☎029 2056 3444   Fax 029 2065 8190
Email anne.goodman5@ntlworld.com
Website www.careerswriters.co.uk

Membership Secretary *Anne Goodman*

FOUNDED 1979. An association of professional careers writers whose work meets its high standards of accuracy and impartiality. It provides a network for members to exchange information and experience and holds meetings on topics of interest to its members. Forges links with organisations that share related interests and maintains regular contact with national education and training bodies, government agencies and publishers. 'The Association can provide a list of its members to organisations that require high standards of careers writing.' See website for details.

Chartered Institute of Journalists

2 Dock Offices, Surrey Quays Road, London SE16 2XU
☎020 7252 1187 Fax 020 7232 2302
Email memberservices@ioj.co.uk
Website www.ioj.co.uk
General Secretary *Christopher Underwood*
Subscription £190 p.a.; £16 (monthly)

FOUNDED 1884. The Institute is concerned with professional journalistic standards and with safeguarding the freedom of the media. It is open to writers, broadcasters and journalists (including self-employed) in all media. Affiliate membership (£120) is available to part-time or occasional practitioners and to overseas journalists who can join the Institute's International Division. Members also belong to the IOJ (TU), an independent trade union which protects, advises and represents them in their employment or freelance work; negotiates on their behalf and provides legal assistance and support. The IOJ (TU) is a certificated independent trade union which represents members' interests in the workplace, and the CIOJ is also a constituent member of the National Council for the Training of Journalists, the **British Copyright Council** and the Journalists Copyright Fund. Editor of the Institute's quarterly magazine is Rodney Bennett-England..

Children's Book Circle

c/o Egmont Bools Ltd, 239 Kensington High Street, London W8 6SA
☎020 7761 3699 Fax 020 7761 3740
Membership Secretary *Nicola Williamson*

The Children's Book Circle provides a discussion forum for anybody involved with children's books. Monthly meetings are addressed by a panel of invited speakers and topics focus on current and controversial issues. Administers the **Eleanor Farjeon Award**.

Children's Books Ireland

17 Lower Camden Street, Dublin 2, Republic of Ireland
☎00 353 1 872 5854 Fax 00 353 1 872 5854
Email info@childrensbooksireland.com.net
Website www.childrensbooksireland.com
Contact *Claire Ranson*
Subscription €25 p.a. (Individual);
€35 (Institutions); €15 (Students);
€45/US$40 (Overseas)

Aims to promote quality children's books and reading. Holds annual spring seminar, summer school and autumn conference for adults. Quarterly magazine, *Inis*. Annual children's book festival in October; Bisto/CBI Book of the Year Award. *Publishes Book Choice for Primary Schools; Book Choice for Post Primary Schools; The Big Guide 2: Irish Children's Books, What's The Story? The Reading Choices of Young People in Ireland.*

CILIP in Scotland

1st Floor, Building C, Brandon Gate, Leechlee Road, Hamilton M13 6AU
☎01698 458888 Fax 01698 283170
Email cilips@slainte.org.uk
Website www.slainte.org.uk
Director *Elaine Fulton*

CILIP in Scotland (Chartered Institute of Library and Information Professionals in Scotland) – formerly the Scottish Library Association – aims to bring together everyone engaged in or interested in library work in Scotland. The Association has over 2300 members, covering all aspects of library and information work. Its main aims are the promotion of library services and the qualifications and status of librarians.

CILIP: The Chartered Institute of Library and Information Professionals

7 Ridgmount Street, London WC1E 7AE
☎020 7255 0500 Fax 020 7255 0501
Email info@cilip.org.uk
Website www.cilip.org.uk
Chief Executive *Bob McKee*

The leading membership body for library and information professionals, formed in 2002 following the unification of the Library Association and the Institute of Information Scientists. **Facet Publishing** (successor to LA Publishing) produces 25–30 new titles each year and has over 200 in print from the LA's back catalogue. Further information from Marketing & External Relations, CILIP.

Circle of Wine Writers

166 Meadvale Road, London W5 1LS
☎020 8930 0181
Email administration@winewriters.org
Website www.winewriters.org

Administrator *Andrea Warren*
Membership £45 p.a.

FOUNDED 1960. Membership is open to all those professionally engaged in communicating about wines and spirits, with the exception of people primarily doing so for promotional purposes. Aims to improve the standard of writing, broadcasting and lecturing about wines, spirits and beers; to contribute to the growing knowledge and interest in wine; to promote wines and spirits of quality and to comment adversely on faulty products or dubious practices; to establish and maintain good relations with the news media and the wine trade; to provide members with a strong voice with which to promote their views; to provide a programme of workshops, meetings, talks and tastings.

Cleveland Arts

Third Floor, Melrose House, Melrose Street, Middlesbrough TS1 2HZ
☎01642 264651 Fax 01642 264955

Contact *Programme Manager (Literature)*

Cleveland Arts is an independent arts development agency working in the areas of Middlesbrough, Stockton on Tees, Hartlepool and Redcar & Cleveland. The company works in partnership with local authorities, public agencies, the business sector, schools, colleges, individuals and organisations to coordinate, promote and develop the arts – crafts, film, video, photography, music, drama, dance, literature, public arts, disability, Black arts, community arts.

Clé, The Irish Book Publishers' Association

43/44 Temple Bar, Dublin 2, Republic of Ireland
☎00 353 1 670 7393 Fax 00 353 1 670 7642
Email info@publishingireland.com
Website www.publishingireland.com

President *Fergal Tobin*
Executive Director *Orla Martin*

FOUNDED 1970 to promote Irish publishing, protect members' interests and train the industry.

Comedy Writers' Association UK

12 Erskine Road, Colwyn Bay, Conwy, North Wales LL29 8EU
☎0151 287 2982
Website www.cwauk.co.uk

Honorary President *Ken Dodd*
Chairman *Bob Orr*
Membership Secretary *Paul Oulton* (at address above)

FOUNDED 1981 to assist and promote the work of comedy writers, the Association has grown to become the largest group of independent comedy writers in the UK. Holds annual and one-day seminars. Members receive a monthly newsletter and regular market opportunities.

Comhairle nan Leabhraichean/ The Gaelic Books Council

22 Mansfield Street, Glasgow G11 5QP
☎0141 337 6211 Fax 0141 341 0515
Email fios@gaelicbooks.net
Website www.gaelicbooks.net

Chairman *Professor Donald E. Meek*
Director *Ian MacDonald*

FOUNDED 1968 and now a charitable company with its own bookshop. Encourages and promotes Gaelic publishing by giving grants to publishers and writers; providing editorial and word-processing services; retailing Gaelic books; producing a catalogue of all Gaelic books in print and answering enquiries about them; mounting occasional literary evenings and training courses.

Commercial Radio Companies Association

77 Shaftesbury Avenue, London W1D 5DU
☎020 7306 2603 Fax 020 7470 0062
Email info@crca.co.uk

Chairman *Lord Eatwell*
Chief Executive *Paul Brown, CBE*
Research and Communications Manager *Alison Winter*
Public Affairs Manager *Lisa Kerr*

The CRCA is the trade body for the independent radio stations. It represents members' interests to Government, the **Radio Authority**, trade unions, copyright organisations and other bodies.

Copyright Advice and Anti-Piracy Hotline

Clivemont House, 54 Clivemont Road, Maidenhead, Berkshire SL6 7BZ
☎0845 603 4567

Copyright Line Administrator *Keith Lowde*

FOUNDED 1999 to offer advice and information

to anyone who wants to use film, music and software copyrights. The Hotline also helps the public and law enforcement agencies to identify and report piracy, and the intellectual property industries to monitor infringements and co-ordinate their responses.

The Copyright Licensing Agency Ltd

90 Tottenham Court Road, London
W1T 4LP
☎020 7631 5555 Fax 020 7631 5500
Email cla@cla.co.uk
Website www.cla.co.uk

Chief Executive *Peter Shepherd*

The CLA is the UK's reproduction rights organization which looks after the interests of authors, publishers and artists in the photocopying and scanning of extracts from books, journals and periodicals. Founded in 1982 by the **Authors' Licensing and Collecting Society (ALCS)** and the **Publishers Licensing Society Ltd (PLS)** to promote and enforce intellectual property rights of British rightsholders both at home and abroad. The CLA also has close ties with the Design and Artists Copyright Society (DACS) which represents artists and illustrators. A not-for-profit organisation, the CLA licenses the use of copyright text by business, education and government and distributes fees collected via authors, publishers and artists collective societies. CLA is currently developing licences which will enable digitisation of existing print material The licence will enable users to scan and electronically send extracts from copyright works. Scanning and e-mail distribution is only available for UK works at present. Since its inception in 1982, CLA has distributed over £100 million.

Council for British Archaeology

Bowes Morrell House, 111 Walmgate, York
YO1 9WA
☎01904 671417 Fax 01904 671384
Email info@britarch.ac.uk
Website www.britarch.ac.uk

Information Officer *Jonathan Bateman*

FOUNDED 1944 to represent and promote archaeology at all levels. Its aims are to improve the public's awareness in and understanding of Britain's past; to carry out research; to survey, guide and promote the teaching of archaeology at all levels of education; to publish a wide range of academic, educational, general and bibliographical works (see **CBA Publishing** under **UK Publishers**).

Council of Academic and Professional Publishers

See **The Publishers Association**

Crime Writers' Association (CWA)

PO Box 273, Boreham Wood, Hertfordshire
WD6 2XA
Website www.thecwa.co.uk

Hon. Secretary *Liz Evans*
Membership Secretary *Rebecca Tope*
  (at Crossways Cottage, Walterstone,
  Herefordshire HR2 0DX)
Membership £45, £60 (Associate)

Full membership is limited to professional crime writers, but publishers, literary agents, booksellers, etc. who specialise in crime, are eligible for Associate membership. The Association has regional chapters throughout the country, including Scotland. Meetings are held regularly in central London, with informative talks frequently given by police, scenes of crime officers, lawyers, etc., and a weekend conference is held annually in different parts of the country. Produces a monthly newsletter for members called *Red Herrings* and presents various annual awards (see **Prizes**).

The Critics' Circle

c/o Catherine Cooper, 69 Marylebone Lane,
London W1U 2PH
☎020 7224 1410
Website www.criticscircle.org.uk

President *Charles Osborne*
Honorary General Secretary *Charles Hedges*
Subscription £18 p.a.

Membership by invitation only. Aims to uphold and promote the art of criticism (and the commercial rates of pay thereof) and preserve the interests of its members: professionals involved in criticism of film, drama, music and dance.

Cyngor Llyfrau Cymru

See **Welsh Books Council**

Department for Culture, Media and Sport

2–4 Cockspur Street, London SW1Y 5DH
☎020 7211 6000 Fax 020 7211 6270
Email toby.sargent@culture.gsi.gov.uk

Head of News *Paddy Feeny*

The Department for Culture, Media and Sport has responsibilities for Government policies relating to the arts, museums and galleries, public libraries, sport, gambling, broadcasting, Press standards, the built heritage, the film and music industries, tourism and the National Lottery. It funds the **Arts Council**, national museums and galleries, the **British Library**, the Public Lending Right and the Royal Commission on Historical Manuscripts. It is responsible within Government for the public library service in England, and for library and information matters generally, where they are not the responsibility of other departments.

Directory & Database Publishers Association

PO Box 23034, London W6 0RJ
☎020 8846 9707
Website www.directory-publisher.co.uk
Contact *Rosemary Pettit*
Subscription £120–1200 p.a.

FOUNDED 1970 to promote the interests of *bona fide* directory and database publishers and protect the public from disreputable and fraudulent practices. The objectives of the Association are to maintain a code of professional practice to safeguard public interest; to raise the standard and status of directory publishing throughout the UK; to promote business directories as a medium for advertising; to protect the legal and statutory interests of directory publishers; to foster bonds of common interest among responsible directory publishers and to provide for the exchange of technical, commercial and management information between members. Meetings, seminars, conference, newsletter, awards, exhibition, business support helpline.

Drama Association of Wales

The Old Library Building, Singleton Road, Splott, Cardiff CF24 2ET
☎029 2045 2200 Fax 029 2045 2277
Email aled.daw@virgin.net
Contact *Teresa Hennessy*

Runs a large playscript lending library; holds an annual playwriting competition (see entry under **Prizes**); offers a script-reading service (£15 per script) which usually takes three months from receipt of play to issue of reports. From plays submitted to the reading service, selected scripts are considered for publication of a short run (70–200 copies). Writers receive a percentage of the cover price on sales and a percentage of the performance fee.

Edinburgh Bibliographical Society

Edinburgh University Library, George Square, Edinburgh EH8 9LJ
Email p.freshwater@ed.ac.uk *or*
 warrenmcdougall@aol.com
Website www.edbibsoc.lib.ed.ac.uk
Honorary Treasurer *Peter B. Freshwater*
Honorary Secretary *Warren McDougall*
Subscription £10; £15 (Institution);
 £7 (Students)

FOUNDED 1890. Organises lectures on bibliographical topics and visits to libraries. *Publishes* an occasional journal called *Transactions*, which is free to members, and other occasional publications.

Educational Publishers Council

See **The Publishers Association**

Electronic Publishers' Forum

See **The Publishers Association**

The English Association

University of Leicester, University Road, Leicester LE1 7RH
☎0116 252 3982 Fax 0116 252 2301
Email engassoc@le.ac.uk
Website www.le.ac.uk/engassoc/
Chief Executive *Helen Lucas*

FOUNDED 1906 to promote understanding and appreciation of the English language and its literatures. Activities include sponsoring a number of publications and organising lectures and conferences for teachers, plus annual sixth-form conferences. Publications include *Year's Work in Critical and Cultural Theory, English, Use of English, English 4–11, Essays and Studies* and *Year's Work in English Studies*.

Federation of Entertainment Unions

1 Highfield, Twyford, Nr Winchester, Hampshire SO21 1QR
☎01962 713134 Fax 01962 713134
Email harris@interalpha.co.uk
Secretary *Steve Harris*

Plenary meetings six times annually and meetings of the Film and Electronic Media Committee six times annually on alternate months. Additionally, there are Training & European Committees. Represents the following unions: British Actors' Equity Association; Broadcasting Entertainment Cinematograph and Theatre Union; Musicians' Union; AEEU; **National Union of Journalists**; **The Writers' Guild of Great Britain**.

The Federation of Worker Writers and Community Publishers (FWWCP)

Burslem School of Art, Queen Street, Stoke on Trent ST6 3EJ
☎01782 822327 Fax 01782 822327
Email thefwwcp@tiscali.co.uk
Website www.thefwwcp.org.uk
Administrator/Coordinator *Tim Diggles*

The FWWCP is a federation of writing groups committed to writing and publishing based on working–class experience and creativity. The FWWCP is the membership's collective national voice and has for some time been given funding by the **Arts Council**. Founded in 1976, it comprises around 60 member groups, each one with its own identity, reflecting its community and membership.

These groups represent over 5000 people who regularly (often weekly) meet to offer constructive criticism, produce books and tapes, perform and share skills, offering creative and critical support. There are writers' workshops of long standing; adult literacy organisations; groups working mainly in oral and local history; groups and local networks of writers who come together to publish, train or perform; groups with a specific remit to further the aims of a section of the community such as the homeless or disabled.

Although diverse in nature, member organisations share the aim of making writing and publishing accessible to people and encourage them to take an active, cooperative and democratic role in writing, performing and publishing. The main activities include training days and weekends to learn and share skills, a quarterly magazine, a quarterly broadsheet of members' writing, a major annual festival of writing and networking between member organisations.

The FWWCP has published a number of anthologies and is willing to work with other organisations on publishing projects. Membership is open only to groups but individuals will be put in touch with groups which can help them, and become friends of the Federation. Contact the address above for an information leaflet.

Fellowship of Authors and Artists

PO Box 158, Hertford SG13 8FA
☎0870 747 2514 Fax 0870 747 2557
Email fellowship@compassion-in-business.co.uk
Website www.author-fellowship.co.uk
Contact *Graham Irwin*

FOUNDED in 2000 to promote and encourage the use of writing and all art forms as a means of therapy and self healing; to provide a valuable resource and meeting point for all interested parties including, but not limited to, writers, artists, counsellors and healers; to publish as web pages or e-books any suitable works that may help to support or promote the aims of the fellowship.

Film Council

10 Little Portland Street, London W1W 7JG
☎020 7861 7861 Fax 020 7861 7862
Email info@filmcouncil.org.uk
Website www.filmcouncil.org.uk

The UK's leading film body. Uses lottery money and government grants to encourage the development of new talent, skills and creative and technological innovation in UK film; help new and established filmmakers make distinctive British films; support the creation and growth of stable businesses in the film sector; provide access to finance and help the UK film industry to compete in the global marketplace. Also promotes enjoyment and understanding of the cinema and ensures that film's economic and creative interests are properly represented in public policy making.

Foreign Press Association in London

11 Carlton House Terrace, London SW1Y 5AJ
☎020 7930 0445 Fax 020 7925 0469
Email secretariat@foreign-press.org.uk
Website www.foreign-press.org.uk
General Manager *Bob Jenner*
Membership (incl. VAT) £145 p.a. (Full);
  £135 (Associate Journalists);
  £200 (Associate Non-Journalists)
FOUNDED 1888. Non-profit-making service association for foreign correspondents based in London, providing a variety of press–related services.

The Gaelic Books Council

See **Comhairle nan Leabhraichean**

The Garden Writers' Guild

c/o Institute of Horticulture, 14/15 Belgrave Square, London SW1X 8PS
☎020 7245 6943
Email gwg@horticulture.org.uk
Website www.gardenwriters.co.uk
Contact *Angela Clarke*
Subscription £45; (£40 to Institute of

Horticulture members); £55 (Associate members)

FOUNDED 1990. Aims to raise the quality of gardening communication, to help members operate efficiently and profitably, to improve liaison between garden communicators and the horticultural industry. Administers an annual awards scheme. Operates a mailing service and organises press briefing days.

Guild of Agricultural Journalists

Charmwood, 47 Court Meadow, Rotherfield, East Sussex TN6 3LQ
☎01892 853187 Fax 01892 853551
Email don.gomery@farmline.com
Website www.gaj.org.uk
Honorary General Secretary *Don Gomery*
Subscription £40 p.a.

FOUNDED 1944 to promote a high professional standard among journalists who specialise in agriculture, horticulture and allied subjects. Represents members' interests with representative bodies in the industry; provides a forum through meetings and social activities for members to meet eminent people in the industry; maintains contact with associations of agricultural journalists overseas; promotes education schemes and supports suitable entrants into agricultural journalism.

Guild of Editors

See **Society of Editors**

The Guild of Food Writers

48 Crabtree Lane, London SW6 6LW
☎020 7610 1180 Fax 020 7610 0299
Email gfw@gfw.co.uk
Website www.gfw.co.uk
Administrator *Christina Thomas*
Subscription £70

FOUNDED 1985. The objects of the Guild are to bring together professional food writers, including journalists, broadcasters and authors; to extend the range of members' knowledge and experience by arranging discussions, tastings and visits; and to encourage new writers through competitions and awards. The Guild aims to contribute to the growth of public interest in, and knowledge of, the subject of food and to campaign for improvements in the quality of food.

Guild of Motoring Writers

30 The Cravens, Smallfield, Surrey
RH6 9QS
☎01342 843294 Fax 01342 844093

Email sharon@scott-fairweather.freeserve.co.uk
Website www.newspress.co.uk/guild
General Secretary *Sharon Scott-Fairweather*
FOUNDED 1944. Represents members' interests and provides a forum for information exchange.

Horror Writers Association

UK Contact: 24 Pearl Road, Walthamstow, London E17 4QZ
Email hwa@horror.org
Website www.horror.org
US Contact: HWA Membership, PO Box 50577, Palo Alto, CA 94303, USA
☎001 650 322 4610
Contact (UK) *Jo Fletcher*

FOUNDED 1987. World-wide organisation of writers and publishers dedicated to promoting the interests of writers of horror and dark fantasy. *Publishes* a bi-monthly newsletter, issues e-mail bulletins, gives access to lists of horror agents, reviewers and bookstores; and keys to the 'Members Only' area of the HWA website. Presents the annual **Bram Stoker Awards** (see entry under **Prizes**).

HTML Writers Guild

Email membership-questions@hwg.org
Website www.hwg.org

FOUNDED in 1994 by a small group of HTML writers, the Guild is an international organisation for Internet designers with over 123,000 members world-wide and is open to anyone with an interest in the craft of web design. Provides extensive resources through the Guild website and mailing lists. Online classes to support members' efforts from the professional designer to the hobbyist designing a homepage. Various levels of membership available.

Independent Publishers Guild

PO Box 93, Royston, Hertfordshire
SG8 5GH Fax 01763 246293
Email sheila@ipg.uk.com
Website www.ipg.com
Secretary *Sheila Bounford*
Subscription £100 + VAT p.a.

FOUNDED 1962. Membership open to independent publishers, packagers and suppliers, i.e. professionals in allied fields. Regular meetings, annual conference, seminars, mailings and e-mail bulletin.

Independent Television Association

See **ITV Network Ltd**

Independent Theatre Council
12 The Leathermarket, Weston Street,
London SE1 3ER
☎020 7403 1727 Fax 020 7403 1745
Email admin@itc-arts.org
Website www.itc-arts.org
Secretary *Charlotte Jones*

The management association and representative
body for small/middle-scale theatres and touring theatre companies. Negotiates contracts and
has established standard agreements for theatre
professionals with Equity. The rights and fee
structure agreement, reached with WGGB in
1991, was updated in December 2002. Contact
Writer's Guild for details.

Institute of Copywriting
Honeycombe House, Bagley, Wedmore
BS28 4TD
☎01934 713563 Fax 01934 713492
Email copy@inst.org
Website www.inst.org/copy
Secretary *Lynn Hall*

FOUNDED 1991 to promote copywriters and
copywriting (writing publicity material). Maintains a code of practice. Membership is open to
students as well as experienced practitioners.
Runs training courses (see entry under **Writers'
Courses**). Has a list of approved copywriters.
Answers queries relating to copywriting. Contact
the Institute for a free booklet.

Institute of Linguists
Saxon House, 48 Southwark Street, London
SE1 1UN
☎020 7940 3100 Fax 020 7940 3101
Email info@iol.org.uk
Website www.iol.org.uk
Chief Executive Officer *Henry Pavlovich*
Marketing Manager *Stephen Eden*

FOUNDED 1910. Association for translators,
interpreters and trainers; examining body for languages at degree level and above for vocational
purposes; the National Register of Public Service
Interpreters is managed by NRPSI Limited, an
IoL subsidiary. Subscription rates on application.
The Institute's limited company, Language
Services Ltd, provides customised assessments of
language-oriented requirements, skills, etc.

Institute of Translation and Interpreting (ITI)
Fortuna House, South Fifth Street, Milton
Keynes, Buckinghamshire MK9 2EU
☎01908 325250 Fax 01908 325259

Email info@iti.org.uk
Website www.iti.org.uk
FOUNDED 1986. The ITI is an association of
translators and interpreters who aim to promote
the highest standards in their field. It has strong
corporate membership and runs professional
development courses and conferences. Membership is open to those with a genuine and proven
involvement in translation and interpreting
(including students). ITI's *Directory of Members*, its
bi-monthly *Bulletin* and other publications are
available from the Secretariat, which also offers a
free referral service for those in need of a professional translator/interpreter. ITI is a full and
active member of FIT (International Federation
of Translators).

Irish Book Publishers' Association
See **Clé**

Irish Copyright Licensing Agency Ltd
Irish Writers' Centre, 19 Parnell Square,
Dublin 1, Republic of Ireland
☎00 353 1 872 9202 Fax 00 353 1 872 2035
Email icla@esatlink.com
Executive Director *Samantha Holman*

FOUNDED 1992 to provide a scheme through
which rights holders can give permission, and
users of copyright material can obtain permission, to copy.

Irish Playwrights and Screenwriters Guild
Irish Writers' Centre, 19 Parnell Square,
Dublin 1, Republic of Ireland
☎00 353 1 872 1302 Fax 00 353 1 872 6282
Email moffats@indigo.ie
Website www.writerscentre.ie/IPSG.html
Contact *Sean Moffatt*
Subscription Details available on request

FOUNDED in 1969 to safeguard the rights of
scriptwriters for radio, stage and screen.

Irish Translators' & Interpreters' Association
Irish Writers' Centre, 19 Parnell Square,
Dublin 1, Republic of Ireland
☎00 353 1 285 9137 Fax 00 353 1 872 6282
Email translation@eircom.net
Website www.translatorsassociation.ie
Honorary Secretary *Miriam Lee*
Subscription €35 p.a. (Ordinary); €15
  (Students, Unwaged, Pensioners, Members
  of affiliated organisations); €80 (Corporate);

€55 (Professional – membership by application to Professional Membership Committee only)

FOUNDED 1986. The Association is for all translators: technical, commercial, literary and cultural, both written and spoken. It is also for those with an interest in translation such as teachers and students. Provides legal advice to members, issues a register of translators and *publishes* a quarterly newsletter, *Translation Ireland*.

Irish Writers' Union

Irish Writers' Centre, 19 Parnell Square, Dublin 1, Republic of Ireland
☎00 353 1 872 1302 Fax 00 353 1 872 6282
Email katherine@writerscentre.ie
Website www.ireland-writers.com

Chairman *Conor Kostick*
Secretary *Anthony P. Quinn*
Subscription €45 p.a.

FOUNDED 1986 to promote the interests and protect the rights of writers in Ireland.

ISBN Agency

Woolmead House, Bear Lane, Farnham, Surrey GU9 7LG
☎01252 742590 Fax 01252 742526
Email isbn@whitaker.co.uk
Website www.whitaker.co.uk/isbn.htm

ISBNs are product numbers used by all sections of the book trade for ordering and listing purposes. While ISBNs have no links to copyright and carry no form of legal protection for the book, they will enable your books to be listed on bibliographic databases and may therefore help sales. The UK Standard Book Numbering Agency is the national ISBN agency, responsible for assigning ISBN prefixes to publishers based in the UK or Republic of Ireland. Its services include advising publishers on the correct implementation of the ISBN system and maintaining a database of publishers and their prefixes, as well as providing technical advice and assistance to publishers and the booktrade on all aspects of ISBN usage. Applications for ISBNs for new publishers, help with calculating ISBNs and additional prefixes are all available from the Agency.

Isle of Man Authors

11 Christian Avenue, Ballastowell Gardens, Ramsey, Isle of Man IM8 2AU
☎01624 815634

Secretary *Mrs Beryl Sandwell*

Subscription £5 p.a.

An association of writers living on the Isle of Man, which has links with the **Society of Authors**.

ITI

See **Institute of Translation and Interpreting**

ITV Network Ltd.

200 Gray's Inn Road, London WC1X 8HF
☎020 7843 8000 Fax 020 7843 8158
Website www.itv.com

Director of Programmes *Nigel Pickard*

The ITV Network Ltd., wholly owned by the ITV companies, independently commissions and schedules the television programmes which are shown across the ITV network. As a successor to the Independent Television Association, it also provides a range of services to the ITV companies where a common approach is required.

IVCA (International Visual Communication Association)

19 Pepper Street, Glengall Bridge, London E14 9RP
☎020 7512 0571 Fax 020 7512 0591
Email info@ivca.org
Website www.ivca.org

Chief Executive *Wayne Drew*
Publications and Information Officer
    Louise Ange

The IVCA is a professional association representing the interests of the users and suppliers of visual communications. In particular it pursues the interests of producers, commissioners and manufacturers involved in the non-broadcast and independent facilities industries and also business event companies. It represents all sizes of company and freelance individuals, offering information and advice services, publications, a professional network, special interest groups, a magazine and a variety of events including the UK's Film and Video Communications Festival.

Learning on Screen (The Society for Screen Based Learning)

9 Bridge Street, Tadcaster, North Yorkshire LS24 9AW
☎01937 530520 Fax 01937 530520
Email josie.key@learningonscreen.u-net.com
Website www.learningonscreen.org.uk

Administrator *Josie Key*

Learning on Screen brings together individuals and organisations with a common interest in helping people to learn via any kind of screen be it television or computer. The Society is a meeting place, a skills forum and resource for all those who want to exploit screen-based media in their roles as managers, trainers, lecturers, teachers, producers and communicators in the field of education, training, government and commerce. Annual conference and production awards. New members welcome.

Lewes Live Literature
See entry under **Festivals**

The Library Association
See **CILIP: The Chartered Institute of Library and Information Professionals**

The Media Society
56 Roseneath Road, London SW11 6AQ
Contact *Peter Dannheisser*
Subscription £35 p.a.; £10 Entry fee
FOUNDED 1973. A registered charity which aims to provide a forum for the exchange of knowledge and opinion between those in public and political life, the professions, industry and education. Meetings (about 10 a year) usually take the form of luncheons and dinners in London with invited speakers. The society also acts as a 'think tank' and submits evidence and observations to royal commissions, select committees and review bodies.

Medical Journalists' Association
Fairfield, Cross in Hand, Heathfield,
East Sussex TN21 0SH
☎01435 868786 Fax 01435 865714
Email pigache@globalnet.co.uk
Website www.medicaljournalists.org.uk
Chairman *Peter Moore*
Honorary Secretary *Philippa Pigache*
Subscription £30 p.a.
FOUNDED 1967. Aims to improve the quality and practice of medical and health journalism and to improve relationships and understanding between medical and health journalists and the health and medical professions. Regular meetings with senior figures in medicine and medico politics; educational workshops on important subject areas or issues of the day; debates; awards for medical journalists from commercial sponsors, plus the MJA's own awards financed by members. *Publishes* a newsletter five times a year.

Medical Writers' Association
The Barn, Tonacliffe Road, Whitworth
OL12 8SJ
Contact *Dr David Brooks*
Subscription £30 p.a.; £40 (Joint)
FOUNDED in 1986 and expanding rapidly in membership and influence. Exists to promote and improve professional and lay writing activities within and for general practice. Open to doctors and other health professionals especially those working in the field of general practice; also to professional journalists writing on anything pertaining to general practice. Keen to develop input from interested parties who work mainly outside the profession. Regular workshops held around Britain. *Publishes* a twice-yearly journal (*The GP Writer*), anthologies and books from members, and a register of members and their writing interests.

Medical Writers' Group
The Society of Authors, 84 Drayton Gardens, London SW10 9SB
☎020 7373 6642 Fax 020 7373 5768
Email info@societyofauthors.org
Website www.societyofauthors.org/medical
Contact *Dorothy Sym*
FOUNDED 1980. A specialist group within the **Society of Authors** offering advice and help to authors of medical books.

Mystery Writers of America, Inc.
17 East 47th Street, 6th Floor, New York,
NY 10017, USA
☎001 212 888 8171 Fax 001 212 888 8107
Email mwa@mysterywriters.org
Website www.mysterywriters.org
Admin Director *Mary Beth Becker*
Subscription $95(US); $60 (Corresponding members)
FOUNDED 1945. Aims to promote and protect the interests of writers of the mystery genre in all media; to educate and inform its membership on matters relating to their profession; to uphold a standard of excellence and raise the profile of this literary form to the world at large. Holds an annual banquet at which the 'Edgars' are awarded (named after Edgar Allan Poe).

National Association for Literature Development
PO Box 140, Ilkley, West Yorkshire
LS29 6RH
☎01943 872546

Email steve@nald.org
Website www.nald.org

Coordinator *Steve Dearden*

NALD exists to enable literature professionals to talk to each other, develop their professional skills and make the case for increased investment in their work. Offers individual, organisational or corporate membership.

National Association of Writers Groups

The Arts Centre, Biddick Lane, Washington, Tyne & Wear NE38 2AB
☎01262 609228
Email mikediane@tesco.net
Website www.nawg.co.uk

Secretary *Diane Wilson*
Subscription £20 p.a. + £5 registration (Group); £10 p.a. (Individual)

FOUNDED 1995 with the object of furthering the interests of writers' groups throughout the UK. A registered charity, No: 1059047, NAWG is strictly non-sectarian and non-political. *Publishes* a bi-monthly newsletter, distributed to member groups; gives free entry to competitions for group anthologies, poetry, short stories, articles, novels and sketches; holds an annual open festival of writing with 36 workshops, seminars, individual surgeries led by professional, high-profile writers. Membership is open to all writers' groups and individual writers – there are no restrictions or qualifications required for joining; 140 groups are affiliated to-date.

National Association of Writers in Education

PO Box 1, Sheriff Hutton, York YO60 7YU
☎01653 618429
Email paul@nawe.co.uk
Website www.nawe.co.uk

Contact *Paul Munden*
Subscription £20 p.a. (Individual); £10 (Student); £60 (Institution); £30 (Overseas)

FOUNDED 1991. Aims to promote the contribution of living writers to education and to encourage both the practice and the critical appreciation of creative writing. Has over 500 members. Organises national conferences and training courses. A directory of over 1200 writers who work in schools, colleges and the community is available online. *Publishes* a magazine, *Writing in Education*, issued free to members three times per year.

National Campaign for the Arts

Pegasus House, 37–43 Sackville Street, London W1S 3EH
☎020 7333 0375 Fax 020 7333 0660
Email nca@artscampaign.org.uk
Website www.artscampaign.org.uk

Director *Victoria Todd*
Deputy Director *Anna Leatherdale*

FOUNDED 1984 to represent the cultural sector in Britain and to make sure that the problems facing the arts are properly put to Government, at local and national level. The NCA is an independent body relying on finance from its members. Involved in all issues which affect the arts: public finance, education, lottery funding for the arts, public entertainment licensing, the rights of artists, the place of the arts on the public agenda and structures for supporting culture. Membership open to all arts organisations and to individuals. Literature subscriptions available.

National Literacy Trust

Swire House, 59 Buckingham Gate, London SW1E 6AJ
☎020 7828 2435 Fax 020 7931 9986
Email contact@literacytrust.org.uk
Website www.literacytrust.org.uk *and* www.rif.org.uk

Director *Neil McClelland*

FOUNDED 1993. A registered charity (No: 1015539) which aims to make 'an independent, strategic contribution to the creation of a society in which all can enjoy the appropriate skills, confidence and pleasures of literacy to support their educational, economic, social and cultural goals.' Maintains an extensive website with literacy issues, research news and information on literacy practice nationwide; promotes and facilitates literacy partnerships; organises an annual conference, courses and training centres; *publishes* quarterly magazine, *Literacy Today* (the Educational Publishing Company, subscription £18). Organised and implemented the National Year of Reading 1998–99 and is coordinating the National Reading Campaign. It also incorporates Reading Is Fundamental, UK, which provides books free to children.

National Union of Journalists

Headland House, 308 Gray's Inn Road, London WC1X 8DP
☎020 7278 7916 Fax 020 7837 8143
Email acorn.house@nuj.org.uk
Website www.nuj.org.uk

General Secretary *Jeremy Dear*
Subscription £171 p.a. (Freelance) or 1% of

annual income if lower; or 0.5% if income less than £12,000 p.a.

Represents journalists in all sectors of publishing, print and broadcast. Responsible for wages and conditions agreements which apply across the industry. Provides advice and representation for its members, as well as administering unemployment and other benefits. *Publishes* various guides and magazines: *On-Line Freelance Directory, Fees Guide, The Journalist* and *The Freelance.*

New Playwrights Trust
See **Writernet**

New Producers Alliance (NPA)
9 Bourlet Close, London W1W 7BP
☎020 7580 2480   Fax 020 7580 2484
Email queries@npa.org.uk
Website www.newproducer.co.uk

The NPA is *the* national membership and training organisation for independent new filmmakers. It provides a forum and focus for over 800 members, ranging from students and first timers to highly experienced feature filmmakers and industry affiliates. Services include: producer training from 'entrance' to 'advanced' levels; seminars, masterclasses, business breakfasts, themed networking evenings and preview screenings; in addition the NPA supports its members at film festivals including Cannes and Edinburgh with events and industry receptions. Provides free advice services including Legal and Tax & Accounting; the NPA also *publishes* a monthly newsletter and online members directory included in the website. In 2003 the Alliance will be celebrating its tenth anniversary.

The New SF Alliance (NSFA)
c/o BBR, PO Box 625, Sheffield, South Yorkshire S1 3GY
Website www.bbr-online.com/catalogue
Contact *Chris Reed*

FOUNDED 1989. Committed to supporting the work of new writers and artists by promoting independent and small press publications worldwide. 'Helps with finding the right market for your material by providing a mail-order service which allows you to sample magazines, quickly and conveniently from a single address, to help you to find the ones best suited to your needs. What's more, you'll find useful information about many more outlets in the review pages of these magazines, whilst *Light's List* provides contact addresses for a whole host of small press publications, and the *BBR Directory* features

books, magazines and other independently-published items as they appear.'

New Writing North
7/8 Trinity Chare, Quayside, Newcastle upon Tyne NE1 3DF
☎0191 232 9991   Fax 0191 230 1883
Email mail@newwritingnorth.com
Website www.newwritingnorth.com
Director *Claire Malcolm*
Administrator *Silvana Michelini*

New Writing North is the literature development agency for the **Arts Council North East** region and offers many useful services to writers, organising events, readings and courses. NWN produces writing guides and has a website with literary news, events and opportunities. Administers the **Northern Rock Foundation Writer's Award** (see entry under **Bursaries, Fellowships and Grants**) and the Northern Writers' Awards, which include tailored development packages (mentoring and financial help). NWN has strong links with the post of Northern Literary Fellow. NWN also works to develop theatre writing and creative radio writing projects within the region.

The Newspaper Society
Bloomsbury House, 74–77 Great Russell Street, London WC1B 3DA
☎020 7636 7014   Fax 020 7631 5119
Email ns@newspapersoc.org.uk
Website www.newspapersoc.org.uk
Director *David Newell*

FOUNDED in 1836, the Newspaper Society is the voice of Britain's regional and local newspapers. It represents and promotes the interests of around 1300 regional daily and weekly, paid for and free, titles. The range of activities and services provided by the Society can be split into two broad areas: marketing and lobbying. Holds a series of conferences and seminars each year and runs the annual Local Newspaper Week.

NPA
See **New Producers Alliance**

NSFA
See **The New SF Alliance**

Outdoor Writers' Guild
PO Box 520, Bamber Bridge, Preston, Lancashire PR5 8LF
☎01772 696732   Fax 01772 696732

Secretary *Terry Marsh*
Subscription £60 p.a.

FOUNDED 1980 to promote, encourage and assist the development and maintenance of professional standards among those involved in all aspects of outdoor journalism. Membership is not limited to writers but includes other outstanding professional media practitioners in the outdoor world such as broadcasters, photographers, filmmakers, editors, publishers and illustrators. *Publishes* a quarterly journal, *Bootprint*, and an annual *Directory* (£35; free to members). Presents five Awards for Excellence plus other awards in recognition of achievement.

PACT (Producers Alliance for Cinema and Television)

45 Mortimer Street, London W1W 8HJ
☎020 7331 6000   Fax 020 7331 6700
Email enquiries@pact.co.uk
Website www.pact.co.uk
Chief Executive *John McVay*
Information Manager *David Alan Mills*

FOUNDED 1991. PACT is the trade association of the UK independent television and feature film production sector and is a key contact point for foreign producers seeking British co-production, co-finance partners and distributors. Works for producers in the industry at every level and operates a members' regional network throughout the UK with a divisional office in Scotland. Membership services include: a dedicated industrial relations unit; discounted legal advice; a varied calendar of events; business advice; representation at international film and television markets; a comprehensive research programme; various publications: a monthly magazine, an annual members' directory; affiliation with European and international producers' organisations; extensive information and production advice. Lobbies actively with broadcasters, financiers and governments to ensure that the producer's voice is heard and understood in Britain and Europe on all matters affecting the film and television industry.

PEN

152–156 Kentish Town Road, London NW1 9QB
☎020 7267 9444   Fax 020 7267 9304
Email enquiries@englishpen.org
Website www.pen.englishorg
Executive Director *Susanna Nicklin*
Membership cheque/standing order: £45/£40 (London/Overseas); £40/£35 (Country)

English PEN is part of International PEN, a worldwide association of writers and other literary professionals which promotes literature, fights for freedom of expression and speaks out for writers who are imprisoned or harassed for having criticised their governments, or for publishing other unpopular views.

FOUNDED in London in 1921, International PEN now consists of over 130 centres in almost 100 countries. PEN originally stood for poets, essayists and novelists, but membership is now open to all literary professionals. It is also possible to become a 'Friend of English PEN'. A programme of talks and discussions, and other activities such as social gatherings, is supplemented by mailings, website and annual congress at one of the centre countries.

Performing Right Society

29–33 Berners Street, London W1T 3AB
☎020 7580 5544   Fax 020 7306 4455
Email info@prs.co.uk
Website www.prs.co.uk

Collects and distributes royalties arising from the performance and broadcast of copyright music on behalf of its composer, lyricist and music publisher members and members of affiliated societies worldwide.

Periodical Publishers Association (PPA)

Queens House, 28 Kingsway, London WC2B 6JR
☎020 7404 4166   Fax 020 7404 4167
Email info1@ppa.co.uk
Website www.ppa.co.uk

FOUNDED 1913 to promote and protect the interests of magazine publishers in the UK.

The Personal Managers' Association Ltd

1 Summer Road, East Molesey, Surrey KT8 9LX
☎020 8398 9796   Fax 020 8398 9796
Email info@thepma.com
Co-chairs *Marc Berlin, Tim Corrie, Nicholas Young*
Secretary *Angela Adler*
Subscription £250 p.a.

An association of artists' and dramatists' agents (membership not open to individuals). Monthly meetings for exchange of information and discussion. Maintains a code of conduct and acts as a lobby when necessary. Applicants screened. A high proportion of play agents are members of the PMA.

The Picture Research Association

Head Office: 2 Culver Drive, Oxted, Surrey RH8 9HP
☎01883 730123 Fax 01883 730144
Email pra@lippmann.co.uk
Website www.picture-research.org.uk

Chair *Charlotte Lippmann*
Subscription Members: £45 (Introductory); £55 (Full); £50 (Associate).
   Magazine only: £25

FOUNDED 1977 as the Society of Picture Researchers & Editors. The Picture Research Association is a professional body for picture researchers, managers, picture editors and all those involved in the research, management and supply of visual material to all forms of the media. The Association's main aims are to promote the interests and specific skills of its members internationally; to promote and maintain professional standards; to bring together those involved in the research and publication of visual material; to provide a forum for the exchange of information and to provide guidance to its members. Free advisory service for members, regular meetings, quarterly magazine, monthly newsletter and Freelance Register.

Player–Playwrights

9 Hillfield Park, London N10 3QT
☎020 8883 0371
Email P-P@dial.pipex.com

President *Olwen Wymark*
Contact *Peter Thompson* (at the address above)
Subscription £10 (Joining fee); £6 p.a. thereafter, plus £1.50 per attendance

FOUNDED 1948. A society giving opportunity for writers new to stage, radio and television, as well as others finding difficulty in achieving results, to work with writers established in those media. At weekly meetings (7.45 pm–10.00 pm, Mondays, upstairs at the Horse and Groom, 128 Great Portland Street, London W1), members' scripts are read or performed by actor members and afterwards assessed and dissected in general discussion. Newcomers and new acting members are always welcome.

PLS
See **Publishers Licensing Society Ltd**

PMA
See **The Personal Managers' Association Ltd**

Poetry Book Society
See **Organisations of Interest to Poets**

Poetry Ireland
See **Organisations of Interest to Poets**

The Poetry Society
See **Organisations of Interest to Poets**

Press Complaints Commission

1 Salisbury Square, London EC4Y 8JB
☎020 7353 1248 Fax 020 7353 8355
Email pcc@pcc.org.uk
Website www.pcc.org.uk

Director *Guy Black*
Information Officer *Tonia Milton*

FOUNDED in 1991 to deal with complaints from members of the public about the editorial content of newspapers and magazines. Administers the editors' Code of Practice covering such areas as accuracy, privacy, harrassment and intrusion into grief. Publications available: *Code of Practice*, *How to Complain*, and *Annual Review*.

Private Libraries Association

55 Hamilton Park West, London N5 1AE
☎020 7503 9827 Fax 020 7503 9826
Email Frank@plantage.demon.co.uk

Honorary Secretary *James Brown*
Membership £25 p.a.

FOUNDED 1956. An international society of book collectors. The Association's objectives are to promote and encourage the awareness of the benefits of book ownership, and the study of books, their production and ownership; to publish works concerned with this, particularly those which are not commercially profitable, to hold meetings at which papers on cognate subjects can be read and discussed. Lectures and exhibitions are open to non-members.

Producers Alliance for Cinema and Television
See **PACT**

The Publishers Association

29B Montague Street, London WC1B 5BH
☎020 7691 9191 Fax 020 7691 9199
Email mail@publishers.org.uk
Website www.publishers.org.uk

Chief Executive *Ronnie Williams, OBE*

The national UK trade association for books, learned journals, and electronic publications, with around 200 member companies in the industry. Very much a trade body representing the industry to Government and the European Commission, and providing services to publishers. Publishes the *Directory of Publishing* in association with **Continuum**. Also home of the Educational Publishers Council (school books), PA's International Division (BDCI), the Council of Academic and Professional Publishers, and the Electronic Publishers' Forum.

Publishers' Association of South Africa

PO Box 22640, Fish Hoek 7974, South Africa
☎00 27 21 7827677 Fax 00 27 21 7827679
Email pasa@publishsa.co.za
Website www.publishsa.co.za

FOUNDED in 1992 to represent publishing in South Africa, a small but key industry sector. With a membership of approximately 120 companies, the Association includes commercial organisations, university presses, one-person privately-owned publishers as well as importers and distributors.

Publishers Licensing Society Ltd

37–41 Gower Street, London WC1E 6HH
☎020 7299 7730 Fax 020 7299 7780
Email pls@pls.org.uk
Website www.pls.org.uk

Chief Executive *Jens Bammel*
Manager *Caroline Elmslie*

FOUNDED in 1981, the PLS obtains mandates from publishers which grant PLS the authority to license photocopying of pages from published works. Some licences for digitisation of printed works are available. PLS aims to maximise revenue from licences for mandating publishers and to expand the range and repertoire of mandated publishers available to licence holders. It supports the **Copyright Licensing Agency (CLA)** in its efforts to increase the number of legitimate users through the issuing of licences and vigorously pursues any infringements of copyright works belonging to rights' holders.

Publishers Publicity Circle

65 Airedale Avenue, London W4 2NN
☎020 8994 1881
Email ppc-@lineone.net
Website www.publisherspublicitycircle.co.uk

Contact *Heather White*

Enables book publicists from both publishing houses and freelance PR agencies to meet and share information regularly. Meetings, held monthly in central London, provide a forum for press journalists, television and radio researchers and producers to meet publicists collectively. A directory of the PPC membership is published each year and distributed to over 2500 media contacts.

Romance Writers of America

3707 FM 1960 W, Suite 555, Houston, TX 77068, USA
☎001 281 440 6885 Fax 001 281 440 7510
Email info@rwanational.org
Website www.rwanational.org

Communications Assistant *Nicole Kennedy*
Subscriptions $75 p.a. plus $25 joining fee

FOUNDED 1980. RWA, a non-profit association with more than 8400 members worldwide, provides a service to authors at all stages of their careers as well as to the romance publishing industry and its readers. Anyone pursuing a career in romantic fiction may join RWA. Holds an annual conference, and provides contests for both published and unpublished writers through the RITA Awards and Golden Hearts Awards.

The Romantic Novelists' Association

Highcroft, Church Place, Rodborough, Stroud, Gloucestershire GL5 3NF
Email ffordes@aol.com
Website www.rna-uk.org

Contact *Katie Fforde*
Subscription Full & Associate: £28 p.a.;
   £33 (Overseas, non-EU); New
   Writers: £78; £83 (Overseas, non-EU)

Membership is open to published writers of romantic fiction (modern or historical), or those who have had one or more full-length serials published. Associate membership is open to publishers, editors, literary agents, booksellers, librarians and others having a close connection with novel writing and publishing. Membership in the New Writers' Scheme is available to writers who have not yet had a full-length novel published. New Writers must submit a manuscript each year. The mss receive a report from experienced published members and the reading fee is included in the subscription of £78. Meetings are held in London and the regions with guest speakers. The *RNA News* is published quarterly and issued free to members. The Association makes two annual awards: The Major Award for the **Parker Romantic Novel of the Year,** and The New Writers Award for the best published novel by a new writer and the category Romance of the Year.

Royal Festival Hall Literature & Talks

See entry under **Festivals**

Royal Society of Literature

Somerset House, Strand, London WC2R 1LA
☎020 7845 4676 Fax 020 7845 4679
Email info@rslit.org
Website www.rslit.org

Chairman *Ronald Harwood*
Subscription £30 p.a.

FOUNDED 1820. Membership by application to the Secretary. Fellowships are conferred by the Society on the proposal of two Fellows. Membership benefits include lectures, discussion meetings, poetry readings and two annual joint meetings with the Royal Society. Lecturers have included John Carey, Michael Holroyd, P.D. James, Jan Morris and Philip Pullman. Presents the **W.H. Heinemann Award**, the **Winifred Holtby Prize** and the **V.S. Pritchett Memorial Prize**.

Royal Television Society

Holborn Hall, 100 Gray's Inn Road, London WC1X 8AL
☎020 7430 1000 Fax 020 7430 0924
Email info@rts.org.uk
Website www.rts.org.uk

Subscription £70 p.a.

FOUNDED 1927. Covers all disciplines involved in the television industry. Provides a forum for debate and conferences on technical, social and cultural aspects of the medium. Presents various awards including journalism, programmes, technology, design and commercials. *Publishes Television Magazine* nine times a year for members and subscribers.

Science Fiction Foundation

Membership Secretary: D28, Department of Arts and Media, Buckinghamshire Chilterns University College, High Wycombe, Buckinghamshire HP11 2JZ
Email ambutler@enterprise.net
Website www.sf-foundation.org
Membership Secretary *Andrew M. Butler*

The SFF is an international academic body for the furtherance of science fiction studies. *Publishes* a thrice-yearly magazine, *Foundation* (see entry under **Magazines**), which features academic articles and reviews of new fiction. It also has a reference library (see entry under

Library Services), housed at Liverpool University.

Scottish Book Trust

Sandeman House, 55 High Street, Edinburgh EH1 1SR
☎0131 229 3663 Fax 0131 228 4293
Email info@scottishbooktrust.com
Website www.scottishbooktrust.com

Contact *Lindsey Fraser*

FOUNDED 1956. Scottish Book Trust exists to serve readers and writers in Scotland. 'We work to ensure that everyone has access to good books and to related resources and opportunities. We do this by operating the Writers in Scotland Scheme which funds over 1400 vists a year by Scottish writers to a variety of institutions and groups; by supporting Scottish writing through a programme of professional training opportunities for writers; by publishing a wide variety of resources and leaflets to support readership; by promoting initiatives such as National Poetry Day and World Book Day; through our Book Information Service providing free advice and support to readers and writers and the general public.'

Scottish Daily Newspaper Society

48 Palmerston Place, Edinburgh EH12 5DE
☎0131 220 4353 Fax 0131 220 4344
Email info@sdns.org.uk

Director *Mr J.B. Raeburn*

FOUNDED 1915. Trade association representing publishers of Scottish daily and Sunday newspapers.

Scottish Library Association

See **CILIP in Scotland**

Scottish Newspaper Publishers Association

48 Palmerston Place, Edinburgh EH12 5DE
☎0131 220 4353 Fax 0131 220 4344
Email info@snpa.org.uk
Website www.snpa.org.uk

Director *Mr J.B. Raeburn*

The representative body for the publishers of paid-for weekly and associated free newspapers in Scotland. Represents the interests of the industry to Government, public and other bodies and provides a range of services including marketing of *The Scottish Weekly Press*, industrial relations, and education and training. It is an active supporter of the Press Complaints Commission.

Scottish Print Employers Federation

48 Palmerston Place, Edinburgh EH12 5DE
☎0131 220 4353 Fax 0131 220 4344
Email info@spef.org.uk
Website www.spef.org.uk
Director *Mr J.B. Raeburn*

FOUNDED 1910. Employers' organisation and trade association for the Scottish printing industry. Represents the interests of the industry to Government, public and other bodies and provides a range of services including industrial relations, education, training and commercial activities. Negotiates a national wages and conditions agreement with the Graphical, Paper and Media Union. The Federation is a member of Intergraf, the international confederation for employers' associations in the printing industry. In this capacity its views are channelled on the increasing number of matters affecting print businesses emanating from the European Union.

Scottish Publishers Association

Scottish Book Centre, 137 Dundee Street, Edinburgh EH11 1BG
☎0131 228 6866 Fax 0131 228 3220
Email carol.lothian@scottishbooks.org
Website www.scottishbooks.org
Director *Lorraine Fannin*
Member Services Manager *Liz Small*
Financial and Office Administrator
    Carol Lothian
Project Administrator *Caroline Taylor*

The Association represents over 80 Scottish publishers, from multinationals to small presses, in a number of capacities, but primarily in the cooperative promotion and marketing of their books. The SPA also acts as an information and advice centre for both the trade and general public. *Publishes* membership lists and the annual Directory of Publishing in Scotland. Represents members at international book fairs; runs an extensive training programme in publishing skills; carries out market research; and encourages export initiatives.

Scottish Screen

2nd Floor, 249 West George Street, Glasgow G2 4QE
☎0141 302 1700 Fax 0141 302 1778
Email info@scottishscreen.com
Website www.scottishscreen.com
Infomation Manager *Isabella Edgar*

FOUNDED 1997. Scottish Screen develops, encourages and promotes every aspect of film, television and new media in Scotland through script and company development, short film production, distribution of national lottery film production finance, training, education, exhibition funding, film commission locations support and the Scottish Screen Archive.

Scottish Young Playwrights

Scottish Youth Theatre, 3rd Floor, Forsyth House, 111 Union Street, Glasgow G1 3TA
☎0141 221 5127 Fax 0141 221 9123
Email info@scottishyouththeatre.org.
Website www.scottishyouththeatre.org
Artistic Director *Mary McCluskey*

Scottish Youth Theatre is involved in and operates various projects supporting young writers in Scotland. Further details from the address above.

Society for Children's Book Writers & Illustrators

Flat 3, 124 Norwood Road, London SE24 9AY
Email scbwi_bi@hotmail.com
Website www.wordpool.co.uk/scbwi
British Isles Regional Advisor *Natascha Biebow*

FOUNDED in 1968 by a group of Los Angeles-based writers, the SCBWI is the only international professional organisation for the exchange of information between writers, illustrators, editors, publishers, agents and others involved with literature for young people. With a membership of 18,000 worldwide, it holds three annual international conferences plus a number of regional events, *publishes* a bi-monthly newsletter and awards grants for works in progress. The British Isles region meets quarterly for speaker events and holds an Illustrator's Day in the spring and a Writer's Day in the autumn. It facilitates critique groups and *publishes* a quarterly regional newsletter. For membership enquiries, contact the address above.

Society for Editors and Proofreaders (SfEP)

1 Riverbank House, 1 Putney Bridge Approach, London SW6 3JD
☎020 7736 3278 Fax 020 7736 3318
Email administration@sfep.org.uk
Website www.sfep.org.uk
Chair *Naomi Laredo*
Vice-chair *Christina Thomas*
Secretary *Katie Lewis*

Subscription £65 p.a. (Individuals) plus £25 joining fee; Corporate membership available

FOUNDED 1988 in response to the growing number of freelance editors and their increasing importance to the publishing industry. Aims to promote high editorial standards by disseminating information through advice and training, and to achieve recognition of the professional status of its members. The Society also supports moves towards recognised standards of training and accreditation for editors and proofreaders. It launched its own Accreditation in Proofreading test in 2002.

Society for Technical Communications (STC)

901 N. Stuart Street, Suite 904, Arlington, Virginia 22203–1822 USA
☎001 703 522 4114 Fax 001 703 522 2075
Email stc@stc.org *and*
(UK Chapter) stc_uk_chapter@yahoo.co.uk
Website www.stc.org *and*
www.stc-europe.org/uk

UK Chapter Contact *Liz Hale* (07970 649579)
Subscription US$158 p.a. (Individual)

Dedicated to advancing the arts and sciences of technical communication, the STC has 25,000 members world-wide, including technical writers, editors, graphic designers, videographers, multimedia artists, Web and intranet page information designers, translators and others whose work involves making technical information available to those who need it. *Publishes* a quarterly scholarly journal, *Technical Communications* and the magazine, *Intercom*, ten times a year (both available to members only). The UK Chapter, which has about 140 members, hosts meetings and seminars, runs an annual technical publications competition, and publishes its own newsletter six times a year.

The Society of Authors

84 Drayton Gardens, London SW10 9SB
☎020 7373 6642 Fax 020 7373 5768
Email info@societyofauthors.org
Website www.societyofauthors.org

General Secretary *Mark Le Fanu*
Subscription £80/75 p.a.

FOUNDED 1884. The Society of Authors is an independent trade union with some 7000 members. It advises on negotiations with publishers, broadcasting organisations, theatre managers and film companies and any queries or concerns members may have about the business aspects of

their writing; assists with complaints and takes action for breach of contract, copyright infringement, etc. Together with the **Writers' Guild**, the Society has played a major role in advancing the Minimum Terms Agreement for authors. Among the Society's publications are *The Author* (a quarterly journal) and the *Quick Guides* series to various aspects of writing (all free of charge to members). Other services include vetting of contracts, emergency funds for writers, and various special discounts. There are groups within the Society for scriptwriters, children's writers and illustrators, educational writers, academic writers, medical writers and translators. Authors under 35 or over 65, not earning a significant income from their writing, may apply for lower subscription rates. Contact the Society for a free booklet and a copy of *The Author*.

The Society of Authors in Scotland

8 Briar Road, Kirkintilloch, Glasgow G66 3SA
☎0141 776 4280 Fax 0141 776 4280
Email brian@bdosborne.fsnet.co.uk
Website www.writersorg.co.uk

Secretary *Brian D. Osborne*

The Scottish branch of the **Society of Authors**, which organises business meetings, social and bookshop events throughout Scotland.

Society of Civil and Public Service Writers

17 The Green, Corby Glen, Grantham, Lincolnshire NG33 4NP
Email joan@hykin.fsnet.co.uk
Website www.scpsw.co.uk

Membership Secretary *Mrs Joan Lewis*
Subscription £15 p.a.

FOUNDED 1935. Welcomes serving and retired members of the Civil Service, armed forces, Post Office, BT, nursing profession and other public servants who are aspiring or published writers. Offers competitions for short story, article and poetry; postal folios for short story and article; AGM, occasional meetings and luncheon held in London; quarterly magazine, *Civil Service Author*, to which members may submit material; Poetry Workshop (extra £3) offers annual weekend outside London, anthology, newsletter, postal folio, competitions. S.a.e. to Secretary for details.

Society of Editors

University Centre, Granta Place, Mill Lane, Cambridge CB2 1RU
☎01223 304080 Fax 01223 304090

Email info@societyofeditors.org
Website www.societyofeditors.org
Executive Director Bob Satchwell

Formed by a merger of the Association of British Editors and the Guild of Editors, the Society of Editors has nearly 500 members in national, regional and local newspapers, magazines, broadcasting, new media, journalism education and media law. Campaigns for media freedom and self-regulation. For further information contact Bob Satchwell at the address above.

Society of Indexers
John Street, Sheffield, South Yorkshire S2 4SU
☎0114 292 2350   Fax 0114 292 2351
Email admin@indexers.org.uk
Website www.indexers.org.uk
Secretary Ann Kingdom
Administrator Wendy Burrow
Subscription £60 p.a.; Institutions: from £120

FOUNDED 1957. *Publishes The Indexer* (biannual, April and October) and a quarterly newsletter. Issues an annual list of members and *Indexers Available (IA)*, which lists members and their subject expertise. In addition, the Society runs an open-learning course entitled *Training in Indexing* and recommends rates of pay (currently £15–20 per hour).

Society of Picture Researchers & Editors
See **The Picture Research Association**

Society of Women Writers & Journalists
Calvers Farm, Thelverton, Diss, Norfolk IP21 4NG
☎01379 740550   Fax 01379 741716
Email zoe@zoeking.com
Honorary Secretary Zoe King
Subscription £35 (Town); £30 (Country); £25 (Overseas). £15 Joining fee

FOUNDED 1894. The first of its kind to be run as an association of women engaged in journalism. Aims to encourage literary achievement, uphold professional standards, and establish social contacts with other writers. Lectures given at monthly lunchtime meetings. Offers advice to members and has regular seminars, etc. *Publishes* a society journal, *The Woman Writer*.

Society of Young Publishers
c/o The Bookseller, Endeavour House, 189 Shaftesbury Avenue, London WC2H 8JT
Email info@thesyp.org.uk
Website www.thesyp.org.uk
Subscription £25 p.a.; £15 (Student/Unwaged); £30 (Associate)

Provides facilities whereby members can increase their knowledge and widen their experience of all aspects of publishing, and holds regular social events. Open to those in related occupations, with associate membership available for over-35s. *Publishes* a monthly newsletter called *Inprint* and holds meetings on the last Wednesday of each month featuring trade professionals. Please enclose an s.a.e. when writing to the Society.

The South and Mid-Wales Association of Writers (SAMWAW)
c/o I.M.C. Consulting Group, Denham House, Lambourne Crescent, Cardiff CF14 5ZW
☎029 2076 1170   Fax 029 2076 1304
Email info@imcconsultinggroup.co.uk
Subscription £10 (Single); £15 (Joint)

FOUNDED 1971 to foster the art and craft of writing in all its forms. Provides a common meeting ground for writers, critics, editors, adjudicators from all over the UK and abroad. Organises residential weekend conferences and day seminars throughout the year. Holds competitions, two for members only and two which are open to the public, in addition to **The Mathew Prichard Award for Short Story Writing** (see entry under **Prizes**).

Spoken Word Publishing Association (SWPA)
c/o Macmillan Audio, 20 New Wharf Road, London N1 9RR
☎020 7014 6041   Fax 020 7014 6141
Email z.howes@macmillan.co.uk
Website www.swpa.co.uk
Chairman Ali Muirden
Secretary Zoe Howes

FOUNDED 1994. SWPA is the UK trade association for the spoken word industry with membership open to all involved in the publishing of spoken word audio. *Publishes SWPA Resources Directory* available from the address above.

Sports Writers' Association of Great Britain
c/o Sport England External Affairs, 16 Upper Woburn Place, London WC1H 0QP
☎020 7273 1789   Fax 020 7383 0273

Subscription £23.50 p.a. incl. VAT (London); £11.75 (Regional)

FOUNDED 1948 to promote and maintain a high professional standard among journalists who specialise in sport in all its branches and to serve members' interests. *Publishes* a quarterly bulletin for members and promotes jointly with Sport England the annual British Sports Personalities of the Year Awards, the British Sports Journalism Awards and the Sports Photographer of the Year award.

SWPA
See **Spoken Word Publishing Association**

Theatre Writers' Union
See **The Writers' Guild of Great Britain**

The Translators Association
84 Drayton Gardens, London SW10 9SB
☎020 7373 6642 Fax 020 7373 5768
Email info@societyofauthors.org
Website www.societyofauthors.org/translators
Secretary *Dorothy Sym*

FOUNDED 1958 as a subsidiary group within the **Society of Authors** to deal exclusively with the special problems of literary translators into the English language. Benefits to members include free legal and general advice and assistance on all business matters relating to translators' work, including the vetting of contracts and advice on rates of remuneration. Membership is normally confined to translators who have had their work published in volume or serial form or produced in this country for stage, television or radio. The Association administers several prizes for translators of published work (see **Prizes**) and maintains a database to enable members' details to be supplied to publishers who are seeking a translator for a particular work.

Voice of the Listener and Viewer (VLV)
101 Kings Drive, Gravesend, Kent DA12 5BQ
☎01474 352835 Fax 01474 351112
Email vlv@btinternet.com

VLV represents the citizen and consumer interest in broadcasting. It is an independent, non-profit-making society working to ensure independence, quality and diversity in broadcasting. VLV is the only consumer body speaking for listeners and viewers on the full range of broadcasting issues. VLV is funded by its members and is free from sectarian, commercial and political affiliations. Holds public lectures, seminars and conferences, and has frequent contact with MPs, civil servants, the BBC and independent broadcasters, regulators, academics and other consumer groups. Produces a quarterly news bulletin and regular briefings on broadcasting issues. Holds its own archive and those of the former Broadcasting Research Unit (1980–90) and BACTV (British Action for Children's Television). Maintains a panel of speakers, the VLV Forum for Children's Broadcasting, and the VLV Forum for Educational Broadcasting, and acts as secretariat for the European Alliance of Listeners' and Viewers' Associations (EURALVA). VLV has responded to all major public enquiries on broadcasting since 1984 and to all consultation documents issued by the ITC and Radio Authority since 1990. The VLV does not handle complaints.

W.A.T.C.H.
See **Writers, Artists and their Copyright Holders**

Welsh Academy
See **Academi**

Welsh Books Council (Cyngor Llyfrau Cymru)
Castell Brychan, Aberystwyth, Ceredigion SY23 2JB
☎01970 624151 Fax 01970 625385
Email castellbrychan@cllc.org.uk
Website www.cllc.org.uk *and*
   www.gwales.com
Director *Gwerfyl Pierce Jones*
Head of Editorial Department *Dewi Morris Jones*

FOUNDED 1961 to stimulate interest in Welsh literature and to support publishing in Wales. The Council distributes publishing grants and promotes and fosters all aspects of both Welsh and Welsh-interest book production. Its Editorial, Design, Marketing and Children's Books departments and wholesale distribution centre offer central services to publishers in Wales. Writers in Welsh and English are welcome to approach the Editorial Department for advice on how to get their manuscripts published.

Welsh National Literature Promotion Agency
See **Academi**

West Country Writers' Association
High Wotton, Wotton Lane, Lympstone, Exmouth, Devon EX8 5AY
☎01395 222749

Email judy@josser.freeserve.co.uk
Website www.westcountrywriters.co.uk
President *Christopher Fry*
Honorary Secretary *Judy Joss*
FOUNDED 1951 in the interest of published authors with an interest in the West Country. Meets to discuss news and views and to listen to talks. Conference and newsletters.

Women in Publishing
Email info@wipub.org.uk
Contact *Information Officer* (at e-mail address above)

Aims to promote the status of women working in publishing and related trades by helping them to develop their careers. Through WiP there are opportunities for members to learn more about their area of work, share information and expertise, give and receive support and partake in a practical forum for the exchange of information about different industry sectors. Monthly meetings provide a forum for discussion on various topics of interest within the industry while other meetings are oriented towards giving careers advice and networking. Meetings are held on the second Wednesday of each month. See website for further information. *Publishes* monthly newsletter, *WiPlash* and *Women in Publishing Directory*.

Women Writers Network (WWN)
23 Prospect Road, London NW2 2JU
☎020 7794 5861
Membership Secretary *Cathy Smith*
Subscription £40 p.a. (Full); £30 p.a. (Overseas); £25 p.a. ('Newsletter only' UK membership)

FOUNDED 1985. Provides a forum for the exchange of information, support, career and networking opportunities for working women writers. Meetings, seminars, excursions, newsletter and directory. Full membership includes free admission to monthly meetings, a directory of members and a monthly newsletter. Details from the Membership Secretary at the address above.

Writernet
Cabin V, Clarendon Buildings, 25 Horsell Road, Highbury, London N5 1XL
☎020 7609 7474 Fax 020 7609 7557
Email writernet@btinternet.com
Website www.writernet.org.uk
Executive Director *Jonathan Meth*
Subscription (information on rates available by post or on website)

Writernet (formerly the New Playwrights Trust) is the national research and development organisation for writing for all forms of live and recorded performance. *Publishes* a range of information pertinent to writers on all aspects of development and production in the form of pamphlets, and a six-weekly journal which also includes articles and interviews on aesthetic and practical issues. Writernet also runs a script-reading service and a link service between writers and producers, organises seminars and conducts research projects. The latter includes research into the use of bilingual techniques in playwriting (*Two Tongues*), documentation of training programmes for writers (*Going Black Under the Skin*) and an investigation of the relationship between live art and writing (*Writing Live*).

The Writers' Guild of Great Britain
15 Britannia Street, London WC1X 9JN
☎020 7833 0777 Fax 020 7833 4777
Email admin@writersguild.org.uk
Website www.writersguild.org.uk
General Secretary *Bernie Corbett*
Assistant General Secretaries *Anne Hogben, Christine Paris*
Annual subscription 1% of that part of the author's income earned in the areas in which the Guild operates, with a basic subscription of £125 and a maximum of £1250

FOUNDED 1959. The Writers' Guild is the writers' trade union, affiliated to the TUC. It represents writers in film, radio, television, theatre and publishing. The Guild has negotiated agreements on which writers' contracts are based with the BBC, Independent Television companies, and **PACT** (the Producers' Alliance for Cinema and Television). Those agreements are regularly renegotiated, both in terms of finance and conditions. In 1997, the Guild membership joined with that of the Theatre Writers' Union to create a new, more powerful union.

In 1979, together with the Theatre Writers' Union, the Guild negotiated the first ever industrial agreement for theatre writers, the TNC Agreement, which covers the **Royal National Theatre**, the **Royal Shakespeare Company**, and the **Royal Court**. Further agreements have been negotiated with the Theatrical Management Association which covers regional theatre and the **Independent Theatre Council**, the organisation which covers small theatres and the Fringe.

The Guild initiated a campaign over ten years ago which achieved the first ever publishing agreement for writers with the publisher W.H. Allen. Jointly with the **Society of Authors**, that campaign has continued and most years see new agreements with more publishers. Perhaps the most important breakthrough came with **Penguin** on 20 July 1990. The Guild now also has agreements covering **HarperCollins**, **Random House Group**, **Transworld** and others.

The Guild regularly provides individual help and advice to members on contracts, conditions of work, and matters which affect a member's life as a professional writer. Members are given the opportunity of meeting at craft meetings, which are held on a regular basis throughout the year. Writers can apply for Full Membership if they have one piece of written work for which payment has been received under a contract with terms not less than those negotiated by the Guild. Writers who do not qualify for Full Membership can apply for Candidate Membership. This is open to all those who wish to be involved in writing but have not yet had work published. The subscription fee for this is £55.

Writers, Artists and their Copyright Holders (W.A.T.C.H.)
The Library, The University of Reading, PO Box 223, Whiteknights, Reading, Berkshire RG6 6AE
☎0118 931 8783 Fax 0118 931 6636
Website www.watch-file.com

Contact *Dr David Sutton*
FOUNDED 1994. Provides an online database of information about the copyright holders of literary authors and artists. The database is available free of charge on the Internet and the Web. W.A.T.C.H. is the successor project to the Location Register of English Literary Manuscripts and Letters, and continues to deal with location register enquiries.

Yachting Journalists' Association
Booker's Yard, The Street, Walberton, Arundel, West Sussex BN18 0BF
☎01243 555561 Fax 01243 555562
Email ppl@mistral.co.uk
Honorary Secretary *Barry Pickthall*
Subscription £40 p.a.

To further the interest of yachting, sail and power, and to provide support and assistance to journalists in the field; current membership is just over 260 with 31 from overseas. A handbook, listing details of members and subscribing PR organisations, press facility recommendations, forthcoming events and other useful information, is published annually at a cost to non-members and non-advertisers of £10. Information for inclusion should be submitted by the end of August. The YJA organises the Yachtsman of the Year and Young Sailor of the Year Awards, presented annually at the beginning of January.

Yr Academi Gymreig
See **Academi**

What is Mine is Yours – at a Price

Kate Pool, Deputy General Secretary of the Society of Authors, gives an update on the law of copyright

Copyright is the legal right of authors, dramatists, artists and composers to prevent others from exploiting their work without their permission. All original material qualifies for protection, regardless of its artistic merit, immediately it is recorded in writing or in another form. There are no formalities in any country which is a member of the Berne Copyright Union – which now includes virtually all the principal countries of the world. Contrary to some popular misunderstandings, and while it may sometimes be harder to police infringements, copyright applies as much to work appearing on the internet as it does to work appearing anywhere else.

Generally, the owner of the copyright in a work is the author who created it. The main exceptions are when you produce work in the course of your employment, in which case your employer will own the copyright; or when you assign your copyright to someone else. A translator owns copyright in the translation, in addition to any copyright which exists in the original work. Likewise, a screenwriter owns copyright in a screenplay, in addition to any copyright in the work from which the script was adapted.

Length of copyright

Throughout the European Economic Area, and also the USA, copyright lasts until seventy years from the end of the year of the author's death. In most other countries of the world (including Canada and Australia) copyright lasts until fifty years from the end of the year of the author's death. However, there are many exceptions to this general rule. In particular:

Literary, dramatic and musical works *unpublished* during the author's lifetime (including letters and private papers)
If the author died before 1 August 1989, copyright lasts for fifty years from the end of the year of first posthumous publication or until 31 December 2039, whichever is the sooner. If the length of the author's life plus seventy years is longer than that period, then the life plus seventy rule will prevail, but not otherwise. Where the author died after 1 August 1989, the copyright period is seventy years from death, and artistic works, whenever the artist died and whether published or not, are protected for life plus seventy, with the exception of old photographs, portraits and engravings.

The works of non-European authors
These are protected in Europe only for as long as they are protected in their country of origin.

The copyright status of old works in the USA
This is a complex affair. The Society of Authors' *Quick Guide to Copyright and Moral Rights* has a section covering American copyright law as it relates to British authors.

The works of European authors who died between 1 January 1925 and 31 December 1944 which went out of copyright fifty years after their death
On 1 January 1996 these works went back into copyright for what remains of 70 years from the author's death. The new period of protection is known as 'revived copyright'. You may use revived copyright material without permission from the rights holder but you have to give notice of your intentions and may have to pay a reasonable royalty.

The typographical arrangement of a published work is owned by the publisher
This means the work cannot, for example, be photocopied without the publisher's consent. The protection lasts for twenty-five years from the end of the year in which the first edition of the work appeared.

There is no copyright in ideas or information. In general, anyone may use published ideas and facts provided they do not copy the precise wording in which they are expressed. But be careful. It is an infringement of copyright to rely on someone else's 'skill and labour' in creating a work. The second writer is expected to check all facts at their original source.

Protecting your material when submitting it to publishers

Copyright is yours, and applies as soon as something is recorded. When sending out a typescript, you should include a copyright line: © [your name] 2004 (although copyright is not forfeited if you forget to do so). Always send your proposal to a specific person by name (not just the Commissioning Editor), with a covering letter making clear that all rights in the work are yours, you are showing it to them in confidence, and you would be pleased to discuss terms if they are interested in publishing it. Always send a copy, not the original.

You can establish proof of the date your work was created by putting a copy in a sealed, dated envelope, and depositing it with a bank or a solicitor – or even by posting it to yourself and storing it in a safe place.

Submitting an article to a journal
Find out what terms the journal will want before, not after, committing yourself. Ideally you should be granting 'first serial rights' only – which means the

publisher has the right to be the first to publish the article (in paper and electronic form), but having done so, all further rights belong to you. Be aware that many journals seek a wider grant of rights. Indeed, academic and learned journals frequently seek an outright assignment of copyright from their contributors (something that the writers' unions deplore).

A book publishing contract
You should be keeping your copyright and giving the publisher the 'exclusive licence' to publish the work.

Assigning copyright
If you do have to assign copyright, make sure that there is a termination clause under which you can get your rights back if things go wrong, if, for example, you are not paid. Also make sure that no major changes will be made to the text without your agreement; that you will be credited as the author and your moral right of paternity is asserted (see moral rights below); and that if the work is exploited in some further way, you will be paid for and credited on the adaptation. It should also be clear that the assignment is not valid until you have received full payment of any monies due to you.

Small complete items like short stories, poems and illustrations
In most cases it will be appropriate to grant only a non-exclusive licence to reproduce the material in a particular anthology or journal, leaving you free to use the work elsewhere.

Moral rights

The main moral rights conferred by the Copyright, Designs and Patents Act 1988 are the right of paternity (the right of an author to be identified whenever a work is published, performed or broadcast: in other words, book writers, scriptwriters, illustrators and translators must be properly credited); and the right of integrity (the right of an author to object to 'derogatory' treatment of a work). Treatment is 'derogatory' if it amounts to 'distortion or mutilation . . . or is otherwise prejudicial to the honour or reputation of the author . . . '

While the right of integrity is automatic, the right of paternity must be 'asserted' in writing. The easiest way is to include a suitable clause in your publishing contract – the assertion should also appear in the book, generally under the copyright line.

The rights of paternity and integrity do not apply to work published in a newspaper, magazine or similar periodical. Nor do the rights benefit authors contributing to an encyclopaedia, dictionary, yearbook or similar collective work of reference.

When do you need permission to make use of someone else's copyright work?

The simple answer is 'on most occasions', but there are exceptions worth noting.

First, there are special provisions covering educational use – the Society of Authors can give further information on this.

Second, if the quotation has been published previously and can be regarded as 'fair dealing . . . for purposes of criticism or review', whether of the work quoted or of another work, you need not ask permission, but must ensure that either in the text itself or in an acknowledgements page you give the title and author of the work quoted. It is not possible to give specific guidance on what constitutes 'fair dealing'; it is a matter of impression and common sense according to the circumstances. However, it may be relevant to take into account:

- the length and importance of the quotation
- the amount quoted in relation to your commentary
- the extent to which your work competes with or rivals the work quoted
- the extent to which works quoted are saving you work

Some years ago the Society of Authors and the Publishers' Association stated that they would usually regard as 'fair dealing' the use of a single extract of up to 400 words or a series of extracts (of which none exceeds 300 words) to a total of 800 words from a prose work, or of extracts to a total of forty lines from a poem, provided that this did not exceed a quarter of the poem. The words must be quoted in the context of 'criticism or review'. While this statement does not have the force of law, it has carried weight with a judge experienced in copyright in a leading infringement case. It does not mean, however, that a quotation 'for purposes of criticism or review' in excess of these limits cannot rank as 'fair dealing' in some circumstances.

For quotations other than those in the above categories you should ask permission to use any 'substantial' extract from a copyright work. The difficulty, once again, is that the meaning of 'substantial' is not defined, but is a matter of fact and degree. A short extract may be a vital part of a work. It has often been said that the test is much more about the quality than the quantity of what has been used. A few sentences taken from a long novel or biography are unlikely to a 'substantial part' of the original work, but a few lines of poetry may be. The only safe course, if in doubt, is to ask permission.

Permission should be obtained for the use of any quotation of copyright material, however short, to be included in an anthology. And if you want to quote from song lyrics that are in copyright, be aware that permission fees can be much higher than those charged by book publishers.

When reproducing extracts from letters or private papers, remember that they may still be in copyright long after the author's death. The letter itself belongs to the recipient, but the copyright in it belongs to the writer of the letter and, after death, to the writer's estate.

Who grants permission?

With published material, it is best to write first to the publishers of the original edition of the book. Address your letter to the Permissions Department. It is very much in your interest to clear permissions as early as possible. If the publisher cannot help, or if the work is unpublished, the *Society of Authors' Quick Guide to Permissions* (also on its website at www.societyofauthors.org) gives suggestions as to how to track down rights-holders.

What will the fee be?

When assessing fees, copyright owners should bear in mind that they may well on occasion be on the other side of the fence and wish to quote from other authors' works.

The lower figures in the scales given below may be considered as recommended 'basic minimum fees', with the top figures representing the suggested rates appropriate to major works. Factors such as the importance of the author quoted, the proportion of the original work that the user intends to quote, its value to the author or publisher requesting permission and the expected size of the print run will most likely be taken into consideration and may affect the fee.

Rates given are for world rights; where more limited rights are required it is usual for fees to be adjusted proportionately. The rate for UK and Commonwealth, or the USA alone, for example, is usually 50 per cent of the world rate, and for a single major country, 25 per cent of the world rate. The Society of Authors can advise on appropriate rates for other territories.

These fees will generally cover just one edition. An additional fee may be required if material is used in a reset or offset edition or in a new format or new binding, for example a paperback edition, and will certainly be required if the publisher of an anthology sub-licenses publication rights to another publisher.

Prose: £120 to £146 per 1,000 words Where an extract is complete in itself (a chapter or a short story) an additional fee is sometimes charged at half the rate applicable for 1,000 words. It is usual to halve the fees for quotations to be used in critical or scholarly works with low print runs.

Poetry: £90 to £120 for the first ten lines, £2.10 to £2.30 per line for the next twenty lines and £1.30 to £1.50 per line thereafter The rate per line/poem may be reduced by a third if the poem appears in a literary or scholarly journal, or an anthology which contains more than forty poems in copyright, or in a book with a print run of less than 1,500 copies. For subsequent editions or for separate publication elsewhere, for example in the USA, Australasia, Europe, Canada, it is accepted practice to charge further, but reduced fees, of not less than half the original fee when new poets are involved. Established poets may well command full fees.

Further information on copyright

The *Quick Guide to Permissions*, *Quick Guide to Copyright and Moral Right* and the *Quick Guide to Copyright in Artistic Works, including Photographs* are available from the

Society of Authors, 84 Drayton Gardens, London SW10 9SB, ☎020 7373 6642, email info@societyof authors.org (free to members, £2 post free in the UK to non-members).

For details about copyright in the USA refer to the Library of Congress Copyright Office at www.loc.gov/copyright or call the Public Information Office on 001 202 707 3000.

Some useful websites when tracing rights holders:
Authors' Licensing and Collecting Society: www.alcs.co.uk
Association of Authors' Agents: www.agentsassoc.co.uk
British Library http://blpc.bl.uk
Location Register of Literary Mss: http://tyler.hrc.utexas.edu
National Library of Scotland: www.nls.uk
US Library of Congress Copyright Office: www.loc.gov/copyright
WATCH (Writers Artists and Their Copyright Holders): www.watch-file.com

Literary Societies

The Adrian Bell Society

3 The Maltings, Church Close, Coltishall,
Norfolk NR12 7DZ
☎01603 737168
Secretary *Moya Leighton*
Subscription £5 p.a.

FOUNDED 1995, the Society aims to promote the
study and enjoyment of the writing of Adrian
Bell (1901–80); to publish journals twice a year
and hold meetings to help members obtain
copies of out of print titles; to assemble a collection of photocopies of his 1500 *Countryman's
Notebooks* that appeared in the *Eastern Daily Press*
and to index them; to commemorate his career
as *The Times* first crossword compiler; to share
knowledge of the places and factual background
mentioned in his books. The society has 250
members worldwide who keep in touch through
the journal *A Centenary Countryman's Notebook*,
published 2001 (£7.00 + p&p).

Margery Allingham Society

2B Higham Green, Winchelsea, East Sussex
TN36 4HB
☎01797 222363 Fax 01797 222363
Website www.geocities.com/
  margeryallingham
Contact *Mrs Pamela Bruxner*
Subscription £14 p.a.

FOUNDED 1988 to promote interest in and study
of the works of Margery Allingham. The Society
publishes two issues of the newsletter, *The Bottle
Street Gazette*, per year. Contributions welcome.
Two social events a year. Open membership.

Jane Austen Society

22 Belmont Grove, Bedhampton, Havant,
Hampshire PO9 3PU
☎023 9247 5855
Email rosemary@sndc.demon.co.uk
Website www.sndc.demon.co.uk/jas.htm
Membership Secretary *Mrs Rosemary Culley*
Subscription UK: £7.50 (Student); £15
  (Annual); £20 (Joint); £45 (Corporate);
  £250 (Life); Overseas: £18 (Annual by
  credit card or UK banker's order only);
  £50 (Corporate); Overseas Membership
  £50/£75 (for 3 years); £300/450 (Life)

FOUNDED 1940 to promote interest in and

enjoyment of Jane Austen's novels and letters.
The society has branches in Bath and Bristol,
Midlands, London, Oxford, Kent and
Hampshire. There are independent Societies in
North America and Australia.

The Barbara Pym Society

St Hilda's College, Oxford OX4 1DU
☎01865 276867 Fax 01865 276820
Email eileen.roberts@st-hidsas.oxford.ac.uk
Website www.pym.org
Chairman *Kate Charles*
Subscription £15 p.a. (Individual);
  £20 p.a. (Household); £8 p.a. (Concession)

Aims to promote interest in and scholarly
research into the works of Barbara Pym; to
bring together like-minded people to enjoy the
exploration of all aspects of her novels and to
continue to encourage publishers to keep her
novels in print. Annual weekend conference at
St. Hilda's College in September, focusing on a
theme or a particular novel. Annual North
American Conference at Harvard University.
Annual one-day spring meeting in London,
with speaker. *Publishes* a newsletter, *Green
Leaves*, biannually. In addition to reports on
conferences and society activities, the newsletter includes scholarly papers and various
unpublished items from the Pym archives at
the Bodleian Library (i.e. short stories).

The Baskerville Hounds

6 Bramham Moor, Hill Head, Fareham,
Hampshire PO14 3RU
☎01329 667325
Chairman *Philip Weller*
Subscription £6 p.a.

FOUNDED 1989. An international Sherlock
Holmes society specialising solely in studies of
The Hound of the Baskervilles and its Dartmoor
associations. *Publishes* an annual journal and
specialist monographs. It also organises many
social functions, usually on Dartmoor. Open
membership.

The BB Society

8 Park Road, Solihull, West Midlands B91 3SU
☎01564 741847
Email bryan@barbryn.co.uk

Chairman *Bill Humphreys*
Secretary *Bryan Holden* (at address above)
Subscription £10 (Individual); £17.50
(Family); £50 (Corporate); £5 (Student);
£12.50 (Overseas)

FOUNDED in 2000 to bring together devotees
of the writer/illustrator BB (Denys Watkins-
Pitchford). BB's oeuvre included books on
wildfowling, angling, children's fantasy and the
countryside. The Society holds two meetings a
year and publishes newsletters and an annual
journal, *Sky Gypsy*.

The Beckford Society

15 Healey Street, London NW1 8SR
☎020 7267 7750 Fax 01985 213239
Email Sidney.Blackmore@btinternet.com

Secretary *Sidney Blackmore*
Subscription £10 (min.) p.a.

FOUNDED 1995 to promote an interest in the life
and works of William Beckford (1760–1844)
and his circle. Encourages Beckford studies and
scholarship through exhibitions, lectures and
publications, including an annual journal, *The
Beckford Journal*, and occasional newsletters.

Thomas Lovell Beddoes Society

11 Laund Nook, Belper, Derbyshire
DE56 1GY
☎01773 828066 Fax 01773 828066
Email john@beddoes.demon.co.uk
Website www.nortexinfo.net/McDaniel/
tlb.htm

Chairman *John Lovell Beddoes*
Secretary *Christine Hunkinson*

Formed to research the life, times and work of
poet Thomas Lovell Beddoes (1803–1849),
encourage relevant publications, further the
reading and appreciation of his works by a
wider public and liaise with other groups and
organisations. *Publishes* an annual newsletter.

Arnold Bennett Society

106 Scotia Road, Burslem, Stoke on Trent
ST6 4ET
☎01782 816311
Website www.arnoldbennett.co.uk

Secretary *Mrs Jean Potter*
Subscription £7 (Single); £9 (Family) plus
£2 for membership outside the EEC

Aims to promote interest in the life and works
of 'Five Towns' author Arnold Bennett and
other North Staffordshire writers. Annual dinner. Regular functions in and around Burslem

plus annual seminar in London. Three newsletters a year. Open membership.

E.F. Benson Society

The Old Coach House, High Street, Rye,
East Sussex TN31 7JF
☎01797 223114
Website www.efbensonsociety.org

Secretary *Allan Downend*
Subscription £7.50 (UK/Europe);
£12.50 (Overseas)

FOUNDED 1985 to promote the life and work of
E.F. Benson and the Benson family. Organises
social and literary events, exhibitions, talks and
Benson interest walks in Rye. *Publishes* a quarterly newsletter and annual journal, *The Dodo*,
postcards and reprints of E.F. Benson articles and
short stories in a series called 'Bensoniana' plus
other books of Benson interest. Holds an archive
which includes the Seckersen Collection (tran-
scriptions of the Benson collection at the
Bodleian Library in Oxford).

E.F. Benson/The Tilling Society

5 Friars Bank, Guestling, Hastings, East Sussex
TN35 4EJ Fax 01424 813237
Website www.tilling.org.uk/society

Contact *Cynthia Reavell*
Subscription Full starting membership
(members receive all back newsletters) £34
(UK); £38 (Overseas); or annual membership
(members receive only current year's
newsletters) £8 (UK); £10 (Overseas)

FOUNDED 1982 for the exchange of news, information and speculation about E.F. Benson, his
works and, in particular, his *Mapp & Lucia* novels. Readings, talks and journal–length biannual
newsletter. Annual get–together in Rye/
'Tilling'. Acts as a clearing house for every sort of
news and activity concerning E.F. Benson.

The Betjeman Society

7 Copthorn Close, Maidenhead, Berks
SL6 3PN
☎01628 823704

Honorary Secretary *Andrew Curtis*
Subscription £10 (Individual);
£12 (Family); £3 (Student); £3 additional
for Overseas members

Aims to promote the study and appreciation of
the work and life of Sir John Betjeman. Annual
programme includes poetry readings, lectures,
discussions, visits to places associated with
Betjeman, and various social events. Meetings
are held in London and other centres. Regular
newsletter and annual journal, *The Betjemanian*.

The Bewick Society

c/o The Hancock Museum, Newcastle upon
Tyne NE2 4PT
☎01207 562196
Email juneholmes@lineone.net
Membership Secretary *June Holmes*
Subscription £7 p.a. (Individual);
£10 (Family)

FOUNDED 1988 to promote an interest in the life
and work of Thomas Bewick, wood-engraver
and naturalist (1753–1828). Organises related
events and meetings, and is associated with the
Bewick birthplace museum at Cherryburn,
Northumberland.

Birmingham Central Literary Association

23 Arden Grove, Ladywood, Birmingham
B16 8HG
☎0121 454 9352
Email bakerbrum@aol.com
Contact *The Secretary*

Holds fortnightly meetings in central
Birmingham to discuss the lives and work of
authors and poets. Holds an annual dinner to
celebrate Shakespeare's birthday.

The George Borrow Society

60 Upper Marsh Road, Warminster, Wiltshire
BA12 9PN
Email borrow@mskillman.freeserve.co.uk
Website www.clough5.fsnet.co.uk/gb.html
Chairman/Bulletin Editor *Dr Ann M.
Ridler*
Membership Secretary *Michael Skillman*
Honorary Treasurer *David Pattinson*

Bulletin Editor: St Mary's Cottage, 61 Thame
Road, Warborough, Wallingford, Oxford
OX10 7EA
☎01865 858379 Fax 01865 858575
Subscription £12.50 p.a.

FOUNDED 1991 to promote knowledge of the
life and works of George Borrow (1803–81),
traveller, linguist and writer. The Society holds
biennial conferences (with published proceedings) and informal intermediate gatherings, all at
places associated with Borrow. *Publishes* the
George Borrow Bulletin twice yearly, containing
scholarly articles, reviews of publications relating
to Borrow, reports of past events and news of
forthcoming events. Member of the **Alliance of
Literary Societies** and corporate associate
member of the Centre of East Anglian Studies
(CEAS) at the University of East Anglia,
Norwich (Borrow's home city for many years).

Elinor Brent-Dyer

See **Friends of the Chalet School** and **The
New Chalet Club**

British Fantasy Society

201 Reddish Road, South Reddish,
Stockport, Cheshire SK5 7HR
☎0161 476 5368 (after 6pm)
Email faliol@yahoo.com
Website www.britishfantasysociety.org.uk
President *Ramsey Campbell*
Chairman *Gary Couzens*
Secretary *Robert Parkinson*
Subscription from £25 p.a. (apply to
Secretary.)

FOUNDED 1971 for devotees of fantasy, horror
and related fields in literature, art and the cinema. *Publishes* a regular newsletter with information and reviews of new books and films,
plus related fiction and non-fiction magazines.
Annual conference at which the **British
Fantasy Awards** are presented. These awards
are voted on by the membership and are not an
open competition.

The Brontë Society

Brontë Parsonage Museum, Haworth,
Keighley, West Yorkshire BD22 8DR
☎01535 642323 Fax 01535 647131
Email bronte@bronte.org.uk
Website www.bronte.org.uk
Contact *Membership Secretary*
Subscription £18.50 p.a. (UK/Europe);
£10.50 (Student); £5 (Junior to age 14);
£27.50 (Overseas); Joint subscriptions
available

FOUNDED 1893. Aims and activities include the
preservation of manuscripts and other objects
related to or connected with the Brontë family,
and the maintenance and development of the
museum and library at Haworth. The society
holds regular meetings, lectures and exhibitions; and *publishes* information relating to the
family and a biannual *Gazette*. Freelance contributions for either publication should be sent
to the Publications Secretary at the address
above. Members can receive the journal, *Brontë
Studies*, at a reduced subscription of £12 p.a.

The Rupert Brooke Society

The Orchard, 45/47 Mill Way, Grantchester,
Cambridge CB3 9ND
☎01223 845788 Fax 01223 842331
Email rbs@callan.co.uk
Website www.rupert-brooke-society.com
Contact *Robin Callan*

Subscription £7.50 (UK); £10.50 (Overseas)

FOUNDED in 1999 to foster an interest in the work of Rupert Brooke, help preserve places associated with him and to increase the knowledge and appreciation of the village of Grantchester. Members receive a newsletter with information about events, new books and activities.

The Browning Society
163 Wembley Hill Road, Wembley Park, Middlesex HA9 8EL
☎020 8904 8401
Honorary Secretary *Ralph Ensz*
Subscription £15 p.a.

FOUNDED 1969 to promote an interest in the lives and poetry of Robert and Elizabeth Barrett Browning. Meetings are arranged in the London area, one of which occurs in December at Westminster Abbey to commemorate Robert Browning's death.

The John Buchan Society
Greenmantle, Main Street, Kings Newton, Melbourne, Derbyshire DE73 1BX
☎01332 865315
Email kah@greenmantle63.freeserve.co.uk
Secretary *Kenneth Hillier*
Subscription £12 (Full/Overseas);
£5 (Associate); £6 (Junior);
£20 (Corporate); £120 (Life)

To perpetuate the memory of John Buchan and to promote a wider understanding of his life and works. Holds regular meetings and social gatherings, *publishes* a journal, and liaises with the John Buchan Centre at Broughton in the Scottish borders.

The Robert Burns World Federation Ltd
Dean Castle Country Park Dower House, Kilmarnock, Strathclyde KA3 1XB
☎01563 572469 Fax 01563 572469
Email robertburnsfederation@kilmarnock26.freeserve.co.uk
Chief Executive *Shirley Bell*
Subscription £20 p.a.(Individual);
£25 (Family); £40 (Club subscription)

FOUNDED 1885 to encourage interest in the life and work of Robert Burns and keep alive the old Scottish Tongue. The Society's interests go beyond Burns himself in its commitment to the development of Scottish literature, music and arts in general. *Publishes* the quarterly *Burns Chronicle/Burnsian.*

The Byron Society
Byron House, 6 Gertrude Street, London SW10 0JN
☎020 7352 5112
Honorary Director, Byron Society *Mrs Elma Dangerfield CBE*
Subscription £20 p.a.

FOUNDED 1876; revived in 1971. Aims to promote knowledge and discussion of Lord Byron's life and works, and those of his contemporaries, through lectures, readings, concerts, performances and international conferences. *Publishes* annually in April *The Byron Journal*, a scholarly journal – £5.50 plus £2 postage.

Randolph Caldecott Society
Clatterwick House, Little Leigh, Northwich, Cheshire CW8 4RJ
☎01606 891303 (day)/781731 (evening)
Honorary Secretary *Kenneth N. Oultram*
Subscription £8–£12 p.a.

FOUNDED 1983 to promote the life and work of artist/book illustrator Randolph Caldecott. Meetings held in the spring and autumn in Caldecott's birthplace, Chester. Guest speakers, outings, newsletter, exchanges with the society's American counterpart. (Caldecott died and was buried in St Augustine, Florida.) A medal in his memory is awarded annually in the US for children's book illustration.

The Carlyle Society, Edinburgh
Dept of English Literature, The University of Edinburgh, David Hume Tower, George Square, Edinburgh EH8 9JX
Fax 0131 650 6898
Email ian.campbell@ed.ac.uk
President *Ian Campbell*
Subscription £2 p.a.; £10 (Life); $20 (US)

FOUNDED 1929 to examine the lives of Thomas Carlyle and his wife Jane, their writings, contemporaries, and influences. Meetings are held about six times a year and occasional papers are published annually. Enquiries should be addressed to the President of the Society at the address above.

Lewis Carroll Society
69 Cromwell Road, Hertford, Hertfordshire SG13 7DP
☎01992 584530
Email alanwhite@tesco.net
Website aznet.co.uk/lcs
Secretary *Alan White*
Subscription Individual: £13 (UK);
£15 (Europe); £17 (Outside Europe);

£10 (Retired rate); £2 (Additional family members); Institutions: £26 (UK); £28 (Europe); £30 (Outside Europe)

FOUNDED 1969 to bring together people with an interest in Charles Dodgson and promote research into his life and works. *Publishes* bi-annual journal *The Carrollian*, featuring scholarly articles and reviews; a newsletter (*Bandersnatch*) which reports on Carrollian events and the Society's activities; and *The Lewis Carroll Review*, a book-reviewing journal. Regular meetings held in London with lectures, talks, outings, etc.

Lewis Carroll Society (Daresbury)

Clatterwick House, Little Leigh, Northwich, Cheshire CW8 4RJ
☎01606 891303 (day)/781731 (evening)
Honorary Secretary *Kenneth N. Oultram*
Subscription £5 p.a.

FOUNDED 1970. To promote the life and work of Charles Dodgson, author of the world-famous *Alice's Adventures*. Holds meetings in the spring and autumn in Carroll's birthplace, Daresbury, Cheshire. Guest speakers and theatre visits. Appoints annually a 10-year-old 'Alice' who is available for public invitations.

The New Chalet Club

94 Bangor Street, Y Felinheli, Gwynedd LL56 4PJ
Website www.newchaletclub.co.uk
Membership Secretary *Sera Roberts*
Subscription £6 p.a. (UK under 18); £10 (UK Adults & Europe); £12 (RoW)

FOUNDED 1995 for all those with an interest in the books of Elinor Brent-Dyer. *Publishes* a quarterly journal and occasional supplements, including *The A-Z of Chalet Characters*, and regularly holds local and national meetings.

Friends of the Chalet School

4 Rock Terrace, Coleford, Bath, Somerset BA3 5NF
☎01373 812705
Email focs@rockterrace.demon.co.uk
Website www.rockterrace.demon.co.uk/ FOCS
Contacts *Ann Mackie-Hunter, Clarissa Cridland*
Subscription £7.50 p.a.; £6 (Under-18); Outside UK: details on application

FOUNDED 1989 to promote the works of Elinor Brent-Dyer. The society has members worldwide; *publishes* four magazines a year and runs a lending library.

The Chesterton Society UK

11 Lawrence Leys, Bloxham, Near Banbury, Oxfordshire OX15 4NU
☎01295 720869/07747 786428 (mobile)
Honorary Secretary *Robert Hughes, KHS*
Subscription £12.50 p.a.

FOUNDED 1964 to promote the ideas and writings of G.K. Chesterton.

The Children's Books History Society

25 Field Way, Hoddesdon, Hertfordshire EN11 0QN
☎01992 464885   Fax 01992 464885
Email cbhs@abcgarrett.demon.co.uk
Membership Secretary *Mrs Pat Garrett*
Subscription £10 p.a. (UK/Europe); write for Overseas subscription details

ESTABLISHED 1969. Aims to promote an appreciation of children's books and to study their history, bibliography and literary content. The Society holds approximately six meetings per year in London and a summer meeting to a collection, or to a location with a children's book connection. Three substantial newsletters issued annually, with an occasional paper. Review copies should be sent to Newsletter co-editor Mrs Pat Garrett (address above). The Society constitutes the British branch of the Friends of the Osborne and Lillian H. Smith Collections in Toronto, Canada, and also liaises with **CILIP** (formerly The Library Association). In 1990, the Society established its biennial Harvey Darton Award for a book, published in English, which extends our knowledge of some aspect of British children's literature of the past. 2002 winner: Nigel Tattersfield *John Bewick, engraver on wood*.

The John Clare Society

9 The Chase, Ely, Cambs CB6 3DR
☎01353 668438 Website vzone.virgin.net/ linda.curry/jclaresociety.htm *or* human.ntu.ac.uk/clare/clare.html
Honorary Secretary *Miss Sue Holgate*
Subscription £10 (Individual); £13 (Joint); £8 (Fully Retired); £10 (Joint Retired); £13 (Group); £15 (Library); £5 (Student, Full-time); £15 sterling draft/$30 €25 (eurocheque) (Overseas)

FOUNDED 1981 to promote a wider appreciation of the life and works of the poet John Clare (1793–1864). Organises an annual festival in Helpston in July; arranges exhibitions, poetry readings and conferences; and *publishes* an annual society journal and quarterly newsletter.

William Cobbett Society
10 Grenehurst Way, Petersfield, Hampshire
GU31 4AZ
☎01730 262060
Chairman *Molly Townsend*
Subscription £8 p.a.

Also: Boynell House, Outlands Lane,
Curdridge, Southampton SO30 2HR
☎01489 782453

Contact *David Chun*

FOUNDED in 1976 to bring together those with
an interest in the life and works of William
Cobbett (1763–1835) and to extend the interest
to a wider public. Society activities include an
annual Memorial Lecture; publication of an
annual journal (*Cobbett's New Register*) containing
articles on various aspects of his life and times; an
annual expedition retracing routes taken by
Cobbett on his Rural Rides in the 1820s; visits
to his birthplace and his tomb in Farnham,
Surrey. In association with the Society, the
Museum of Farnham holds bound volumes of
Cobbett's *Political Register*, a large collection of
Cobbett's works, books about Cobbett, and has
various Cobbett artefacts on display.

The Friends of Coleridge
87 Richmond Road, Montpelier, Bristol
BS6 5EP
☎0117 942 6366
Email gcddavidson@compuserve.com
Website www.friendsofcoleridge.com

Membership Secretary *Shirley Watters*
(11 Castle Street, Nether Stowey, Somerset
TA5 1LN)

Editor (Coleridge Bulletin) *Graham
Davidson*
Subscription £10 (UK); £15 or
£20 (Overseas)

FOUNDED in 1987 to advance knowledge about
the life, work and times of Samuel Taylor
Coleridge and his circle, and to support his
Nether Stowey Cottage, with the National
Trust, as a centre of Coleridge interest. Holds
literary evenings, study weekends and a biennial
international academic conference. Publishes *The
Coleridge Bulletin* biannually. Short articles on
Coleridge-related topics may be sent to the edi-
tor at the (Bristol) address above.

Wilkie Collins Society
4 Ernest Gardens, London W4 3QU
Email paul@wilkiecollins.org
Website www.wilkiecollins.org
Chairman *Andrew Gasson*

Membership Secretary *Paul Lewis* (at
address above)
Subscription £10 (UK/Europe); £18 (RoW
– remittance must be made in UK sterling)

FOUNDED 1980 to provide information on and
promote interest in the life and works of Wilkie
Collins, one of the first English novelists to deal
with the detection of crime. *The Woman in White*
appeared in 1860 and *The Moonstone* in 1868.
Publishes newsletters, reprints of Collins' work
and an annual academic journal.

The Arthur Conan Doyle Society
PO Box 1360, Ashcroft, British Columbia,
Canada V0K 1A0
☎001 250 453 2045 Fax 001 250 453 2075
Email ashtree@ash-tree.bc.ca
Website www.ash-tree.bc.ca/acdsocy.html

Joint Organisers *Christopher Roden, Barbara
Roden*

FOUNDED 1989 to promote the study and discussion of the life and works of Sir Arthur
Conan Doyle. Occasional meetings, functions
and visits. *Publishes* a biannual journal together
with reprints of Conan Doyle's writings.

Joseph Conrad Society (UK)
c/o P.O.S.K., 238–246 King Street,
Hammersmith, London W6 0RF
Fax 020 8240 4365
Email AllanSimmons@compuserve.com
Website www.bathspa.ac.uk/conrad/

Secretary *Hugh Epstein*
Treasurer/Editor (The Conradian) *Allan
Simmons*
Subscription £15 p.a. (Individual);
£20 p.a. (Institutions)

FOUNDED in 1973 to promote the study of the
works and life of Joseph Conrad (1857–1924).
A scholarly society, supported by the Polish
Library at the Polish Cultural Association
where a substantial library of Conrad texts and
criticism is held in the Study Centre. *Publishes* a
journal of Conrad studies – *The Conradian* –
biannually and holds an annual International
Conference in the first week of July. Awards an
essay prize and travel and study grants to scholars on application.

The David Jones Society
48 Sylvan Way, Sketty, Swansea, West
Glamorgan SA2 9JB
☎01792 206144 Fax 01792 205305
Email anne.price-owen@sihe.ac.uk
Website www.sihe/ac/uk/davidjones

Contact *Anne Price-Owen*

Subscription £18 (Individual);
£30 (Corporate)

FOUNDED 1996, the Society aims to promote and encourage knowledge of the painter-poet David Jones. The Society hosts annual scholarly meetings. The annual subscription includes a copy of the *David Jones Journal*. Unsolicited material relating to David Jones, art, literarure or any of his philosophies may be sent for consideration for publication in the journal.

The Rhys Davies Trust
10 Heol Don, Whitchurch, Cardiff
CF14 2AU
☎029 2062 3359 Fax 029 2052 9202

Contact *Professor Meic Stephens*

FOUNDED 1990 to perpetuate the literary reputation of the Welsh prose writer, Rhys Davies (1901–78), and to foster Welsh writing in English. Organises competitions in association with other bodies such as the **Welsh Academy**, puts up plaques on buildings associated with Welsh writers, offers grant-aid for book production, etc.

Warwick Deeping Appreciation Society
23 Merton Road, Enfield, Middlesex
EN2 0LS
☎020 8367 0263
Email geoffrey@gillam.fsworld.co.uk

Secretary *Geoffrey Gillam*
Subscription £3.50 p.a.

Open to all with an interest in the life and work of Warwick Deeping who produced 70 novels and many short stories. A quarterly newsletter includes reviews of his books and results of research into his life.

The Walter de la Mare Society
Flat 15, Trinity Court, Vicarage Road, Twickenham, Middlesex TW2 5TY
Website www.bluetree.co.uk/wdlmsociety

Honorary President *John Bayley, CBE*
Honorary Secretary & Treasurer *Julie de la Mare*
Subscription £15 p.a.

FOUNDED in 1997 to honour the memory of Walter de la Mare; to promote the study and deepen the appreciation of his works; to widen the readership of his works; to facilitate research by making available the widest range of contacts and information about de la Mare; and to encourage and facilitate new Walter de la Mare publications. Produces a regular newsletter and organises events. Membership information from the address above.

The Dickens Fellowship
48 Doughty Street, London WC1N 2LX
☎020 7405 2127 Fax 020 7831 5175
Email arwilliams33@compuserve.com
Website www.dickens.fellowship.btinternet.co.uk

Joint Honorary General Secretaries
Mrs Thelma Grove, Dr Tony Williams
Subscription £5 (First year); £8.50 (Renewal)

FOUNDED 1902. The Society's particular aims and objectives are: to bring together lovers of Charles Dickens; to spread the message of Dickens, his love of humanity ('the keynote of all his work'); to remedy social injustice for the poor and oppressed; to assist in the preservation of material and buildings associated with Dickens. Annual conference. *Publishes* journal called *The Dickensian* (available at special rate to members) and organises a full programme of lectures, discussions, visits and conducted walks throughout the year. Branches worldwide.

Early English Text Society
Christ Church, Oxford OX1 1DP
Fax 01865 286581
Website www.oets.org.uk

Executive Secretary *R.F.S. Hamer*
  (at address above)
Editorial Secretary *Dr H.L. Spencer*
  (at Exeter College, Oxford OX1 3DP)
Membership Secretary *Mrs J.M. Watkinson*
  (at 12 North End, Durham DH1 4NJ)
Subscription £15 p.a. (UK); $30 (US);
  $35 (Canada)

FOUNDED 1864. Concerned with the publication of early English texts. Members receive annual publications (one or two a year) or may select titles from the backlist in lieu.

The George Eliot Fellowship
71 Stepping Stones Road, Coventry, Warwickshire CV5 8JT
☎024 7659 2231

Contact *Mrs Kathleen Adams*
Subscription £10 p.a.; £100 (Life);
  Concessions for pensioners

FOUNDED 1930. Exists to honour George Eliot and promote interest in her life and works. Readings, memorial lecture, birthday luncheon and functions. Issues a quarterly newsletter and an annual journal. Awards an annual prize for a George Eliot essay.

The John Meade Falkner Society
Greenmantle, Main Street, Kings Newton,
Melbourne, Derbyshire DE73 1BX
☎01332 865315
Email kah@greenmantle63.freeserve.co.uk
Secretary *Kenneth Hillier*
Subscription £5

FOUNDED in 1999 to promote the appreciation
and study of John Meade Falkner's life, times
and works. Produces three newsletters a year
and an annual journal.

Folly (Fans of Light Literature for the Young)
21 Warwick Road, Pokesdown,
Bournemouth, Dorset BH7 6JW
☎01202 432562 Fax 01202 460059
Email folly@sims.abel.co.uk

Contact *Mrs Sue Sims*
Subscription £9 p.a. (UK); £11 (Europe);
£14 (Worldwide)

FOUNDED 1990 to promote interest in a wide
variety of children's authors – with a bias towards
writers of girls' books and school stories. *Publishes*
three magazines a year.

The Ford Madox Ford Society
c/o Dr Sara Haslam, Dept of Literature, The
Open University, Milton Keynes MK7 6AA
☎01908 652472 Fax 01908 653750
Email s.haslan@open.ac.uk
Website www.rialto.com/
fordmadoxford_society

Chairman *Professor Max Saunders*
Treasurer *Dr Sara Haslam*
Subscription £12 or £6 conc.

FOUNDED 1996 to promote the works of Ford
Madox Ford and to increase knowledge of his
writing and impact on writing in the 20th century. Meets for academic conferences and more
popular events annually. Distributes *International
Ford Madox Ford Studies* free to members.
Welcomes all with an interest in Ford and his
works. Has members in the UK, USA, Italy,
France and Germany and holds events in as many
different places as possible.

C.S. Forester Society
11 Park Town, Oxford OX2 6SN
☎01865 512111 Fax 01865 515292
Email csforester@hotmail.com
Website www.csforester.com

Contact *Colin Blogg*
Subscription £10 or $15 p.a.

FOUNDED in 1999 to provide an informal forum
to promote knowledge and enjoyment of the
works and life of C.S. Forester; to write a definitive bibliography and, ultimately, a biography.
Publishes a newsletter 3–4 times a year containing
contributions from members and holds meetings
for film shows, readings and lectures.

The Franco–Midland Hardware Company
6 Bramham Moor, Hill Head, Fareham,
Hampshire PO14 3RU
☎01329 667325
Email franco.midland@btinternet.com
Website www.btinternet.com/~sherlock.fmhc

Chairman *Philip Weller*
Subscription £12 p.a. (UK); £13 (Europe);
£15 (RoW)

FOUNDED 1989. 'The world's leading Sherlock
Holmes correspondence study group and the
most active Holmesian society in Britain.'
Publishes annual journal, a biannual news magazine and an individual case study as a subscription
package. Also publishes at least two specialist
monographs a year. It provides certificated self-
study courses and organises monthly functions at
Holmes-associated locations. Open membership.

The Friends of Shandy Hall (The Laurence Sterne Trust)
Shandy Hall, Coxwold, York YO61 4AD
☎01347 868465 Fax 01347 868465
Website www.shandy-hall.org.uk

Honorary Secretary *Mrs J. Monkman*
Subscription £7 (Annual); £70 (Life)

Promotes interest in the works of Laurence
Sterne and aims to preserve the house in which
they were created (open to the public). *Publishes*
annual journal, *The Shandean*. An Annual
Memorial Lecture is delivered at Shandy Hall
each summer.

The Friends of the Dymock Poets
19 The Southend, Ledbury, Herefordshire
HR8 2EY
☎01531 684796
Email cateluck@btopenworld.com
Website www.dymockpoets.co.uk

Chairman *Roy Palmer*
Hon. Secretary *Catharine Luck*
Membership Secretary *Jeff Cooper*
Subscription £7 (Individuals); £12 (Couples);
£3 (Students); £12 (Societies/Families)

FOUNDED 1993. Established to foster an interest
in the work of the Dymock Poets – Edward
Thomas, Robert Frost, Wilfred Gibson,

Rupert Brooke, John Drinkwater, Lascelles Abercrombie; help preserve places and things associated with them; keep members informed of literary and other matters relating to the poets; increase knowledge and appreciation of the landscape between May Hill (Gloucestershire) and the Malvern Hills. Members are offered lectures, poetry readings, social meetings, a newsletter and annual journal, guided walks in the countryside aroung Dymock; links with other literary societies; and annual event to commemorate the first meeting between Edward Thomas and Robert Frost on 6 October 1913.

The Gaskell Society

Far Yew Tree House, Over Tabley,
Knutsford, Cheshire WA16 0HN
☎01565 634668
Email JoanLeach@aol.com
Website gaskellsociety.users.btopenworld.com
and lang.nagoya-u.ac.jp/~matsuoka/
    EG–Society.html
Honorary Secretary *Joan Leach*
Subscription £12 p.a.; £16 (Corporate &
    Overseas)
FOUNDED 1985 to promote and encourage the study and appreciation of the life and works of Elizabeth Cleghorn Gaskell. Meetings held in Knutsford, Manchester, Bath and London; residential study weekends and visits; annual journal and biannual newsletter. On alternate years holds either a residential weekend conference or overseas visit.

The Ghost Story Society

PO Box 1360, Ashcroft, British Columbia,
Canada V0K 1A0
☎001 250 453 2045 Fax 001 250 453 2075
Email ashtree@ash–tree.bc.ca
Website www.ash-tree.bc.ca/GSShtml
Joint Organisers *Barbara Roden, Christopher Roden*
Subscription UK: £20 (Airmail); $29 (US$);
    $36 (Canadian$)
FOUNDED 1988. Devoted mainly to supernatural fiction in the literary tradition of M.R. James, Walter de la Mare, Algernon Blackwood, E.F. Benson, A.N.L. Munby, R.H. Malden, etc. *Publishes* a thrice-yearly journal, *All Hallows*, which includes new fiction in the genre and non-fiction of relevance to the genre.

Graham Greene Birthplace Trust

Rhenigidale, Ivy House Lane, Berkhamsted,
Hertfordshire HP4 2PP
☎01442 865158
Email secretary@grahamgreenebt.org
Website www.grahamgreenebt.org
Secretary *Ken Sherwood*
Subscription £7.50 (UK, £18 for 3 years);
    £10 (Europe, £25); £14 (RoW, £37)
FOUNDED on 2 October 1997, the 93rd anniversary of Graham Greene's birth, to promote the appreciation and study of his works. *Publishes* a quarterly newsletter, occasional papers, videos and compact discs. Organises the annual four-day Graham Greene Festival during the weekend nearest to the writer's birthday (2nd October) and administrates the Graham Greene Memorial Awards.

Rider Haggard Society

27 Deneholm, Whitley Bay, Tyne & Wear
NE25 9AU
☎0191 252 4516 Fax 0191 252 4516
Email RB27Allen@aol.com
Website www.riderhaggardsociety.org.uk
Contact *Roger Allen*
Subscription £9 p.a. (UK); £10 (Overseas)
FOUNDED 1985 to promote appreciation of the life and works of Sir Henry Rider Haggard, English novelist, 1856–1925. News/books exchange and meetings every 18 months.

James Hanley Network

Old School House, George Green Road,
George Green, Wexham, Buckinghamshire
SL3 6BJ
☎01753 578632
Email gostick@london.com
Website www.jameshanley.mcmail.com/
    index.htm
Network Coordinator *Chris Gostick*
An informal international association FOUNDED in 1997 for all those interested in exploring and publicising the works and contribution to literature of the novelist and dramatist James Hanley (1901–1985). *Publishes* an annual newsletter. Occasional conferences are planned for the future. All enquiries welcome.

The Thomas Hardy Society

PO Box 1438, Dorchester, Dorset DT1 1YH
☎01305 251501 Fax 01305 251501
Email info@hardysociety.org
Website www.hardysociety.org
Honorary Secretary *Mrs Helen Gibson*
Subscription £18 (Individual);
    £25 (Corporate); £22.50 (Individual
    Overseas); £30 (Corporate Overseas)
FOUNDED 1967 to promote the reading and

study of the works and life of Thomas Hardy. Thrice-yearly journal, events and a biennial conference. An international organisation.

The Henty Society

Hayfield, Bourne Fields, Twyford, Winchester
SO21 1NY
☎01962 713164

Honorary Secretary *Bruce Lees*
Subscription £13 p.a. (UK); £16 (Overseas)

FOUNDED 1977 to study the life and work of George Alfred Henty, and to publish research, bibliographical data and lesser-known works, namely short stories. Organises conferences and social gatherings in the UK and North America, and *publishes* bulletins to members. Published in 1996: *G.A. Henty (1832–1902) a Bibliographical Study* by Peter Newbolt.

James Hilton Society

49 Beckingthorpe Drive, Bottesford,
Nottingham NG13 0DN
Website www.jameshiltonsociety.co.uk

Honorary Secretary *J.R. Hammond*
Subscription £10 (UK/EU); £7 Concessions

FOUNDED 2000 to promote interest in the life and work of novelist and scriptwriter James Hilton (1900–1954). *Publishes The James Hilton Newsletter* (quarterly) and organises meetings and conferences.

Sherlock Holmes Society (Northern Musgraves)

Hallas Lodge, Greenside Lane, Cullingworth,
Bradford, West Yorkshire BD13 5AP
☎01535 273468
Email hallaslodge@btinternet.com

Contacts *John Hall, Anne Jordan*
Subscription £17 p.a. (UK)

FOUNDED 1987 to promote enjoyment and study of Sir Arthur Conan Doyle's Sherlock Holmes through publications and meetings. One of the largest Sherlock Holmes societies in Great Britain. Honorary members include Bert Coules, Richard Lancelyn Green, Edward Hardwicke, Clive Merrison and Douglas Wilmer. Past honorary members: Dame Jean Conan Doyle, Peter Cushing, Jeremy Brett and Michael Williams. Open membership. Lectures, presentations and consultation on matters relating to Holmes and Conan Doyle available.

Sherlock Holmes

See **The Franco–Midland Hardware Company**

Hopkins Society

41 North Drive, Rhyl, Denbighshire
LL18 4SW
☎01745 354151
Email carolinemay@hopkinsoc.freeserve.co.uk
Website www.hopkinsoc.freeserve.co.uk

Contact *Imelda Jones*
Subscription £7 p.a. (UK); £10 (Overseas)

FOUNDED 1990 to celebrate the life and work of Gerard Manley Hopkins; to inform members of any publications, courses or events about the poet. Holds an annual lecture on Hopkins in the spring; produces two newsletters a year; sponsors and organises educational projects based on Hopkins' life and works.

Housman Society

80 New Road, Bromsgrove, Worcestershire
B60 2LA
☎01527 874136
Email info@housman–society.co.uk
Website www.housman–society.co.uk

Contact *Jim Page*
Subscription £10 (UK); £12.50 (Overseas)

FOUNDED 1973 to promote knowledge and appreciation of the lives and work of A.E. Housman and other members of his family, and to promote the cause of literature and poetry. Sponsors a lecture at the **Hay Festival** each year under the title of 'The Name and Nature of Poetry'. *Publishes* an annual journal and biannual newsletter.

The Ivor Gurney Society

4 Myton Road, London SE21 8EB
☎0208 761 3180
Email william.marshall@kcl.ac.uk
Website www.ivor.gurney.net

Subscription £12.50 (Individual);
£10 (Retired); £15 (Joint);
£12.50 (Joint retired); £5 (Student);
£12.50 (Group/ Library); £5 (Overseas – sterling equivalent)

To promote interest in Ivor Gurney and his context and to make his music and poetry available to a wider audience by way of performances, readings, conferences, recordings and publications. To enhance and promote informed scholarship on all aspects of his life and work through the publication of a regular newsletter and an annual journal, available to society members. To maintain and expand the Gurney archive at Gloucester Central Library.

W.W. Jacobs Appreciation Society
3 Roman Road, Southwick, West Sussex
BN42 4TP
☎01273 871017   Fax 01273 871017
Contact *A.R. James*

FOUNDED 1988 to encourage and promote the enjoyment of the works of W.W. Jacobs, and stimulate research into his life and works. No subscription charge. Material available for purchase includes *W.W. Jacobs*, a biography published in 1999, price £12, post paid, and *WWJ Book Hunter's Field Guide*, a narrative bibliography published in 2001, price £6, post paid.

Richard Jefferies Society
Eidsvoll, Bedwells Heath, Boars Hill, Oxford
OX1 5JE
☎01865 735678
Website www.bath.ac.uk/~lissmc/rjeffs.htm
Honorary Secretary *Lady Phyllis Treitel*
Membership Secretary *Mrs Margaret Evans*
Subscription £7 p.a. (Individual); £8 (Joint);
   Life membership for those over 50

FOUNDED 1950 to promote understanding of the work of Richard Jefferies, nature/country writer, novelist and mystic (1848–87). Produces newsletters, reports and an annual journal; organises talks, discussions and readings. Library and archives. Assists in maintaining the museum in Jefferies' birthplace at Coate near Swindon. Membership applications should be sent to *Margaret Evans*, 23 Hardwell Close, Grove, Nr Wantage, Oxon OX12 0BN.

Jerome K. Jerome Society
c/o Fraser Wood, Mayo and Pinson,
15/16 Lichfield Street, Walsall, West Midlands
WS1 1TS
☎01922 629000   Fax 01922 721065
Email tonygray@jkj.demon.co.uk
Website www.jeromekjerome.com
Honorary Secretary *Tony Gray*
Subscription £7 p.a. (Ordinary);
   £25 (Corporate); £2.50 (Under 21/
   Over 65)

FOUNDED 1984 to stimulate interest in Jerome K. Jerome's life and works (1859–1927). One of the Society's principal activities is the support of a small museum in the author's birthplace, Walsall. Meetings, lectures, events and a twice-yearly newsletter, *Idle Thoughts*. Annual dinner in Walsall near Jerome's birth date (2nd May).

The Captain W.E. Johns Appreciation Society
Nottingham meeting: Wendover, Windy Harbour Lane, Bromley Cross, Bolton, Lancashire BL7 9AP
☎01204 306051
Email Biggles.uk@LineOne.net
Website website.lineone.net/~biggles.uk
Contacts *Mrs A. Thompson* (Nottingham),
   Joy Tilley (Hertford, ☎01785 240299)
Hertford meeting: 8 Holmes Close,
   Castlefields, Stafford ST16 1AR

Society for the appreciation of W.E. Johns, creator of Biggles. Meets twice a year in Nottingham and Hertford. See contacts above.

Johnson Society
Johnson Birthplace Museum, Breadmarket Street, Lichfield, Staffordshire WS13 6LG
☎01543 264972
Website www.lichfieldrambler.co.uk
Hon. General Secretary *Mrs Norma Hooper*
Subscription £7.50 p.a.; £10 (Joint)

FOUNDED 1910 to encourage the study of the life, works and times of Samuel Johnson (1709–1784) and his contemporaries. The Society is committed to the preservation of the Johnson Birthplace Museum and Johnson memorials.

Johnson Society of London
255 Baring Road, Grove Park, London
SE12 0BQ
☎020 8851 0173
Email JSL@nbbl.demon.co.uk
Website www.nbbl.demon.co.uk/index.html
President *Mary, Viscountess Eccles, PhD, DLitt*
Honorary Secretary *Mrs Z.E. O'Donnell*
Subscription £12.50 p.a.; £15 (Joint)

FOUNDED 1928 to promote the knowledge and appreciation of Dr Samuel Johnson and his works. *Publishes* an annual journal, *New Rambler* and occasional newsletter. Regular meetings from October to April in the meeting room of Wesley's Chapel, City Road, London on the second Saturday of each month, and a commemoration ceremony around the anniversary of Johnson's death (December) held in Westminster Abbey.

The Just William Society
Easter Badbea, Dundonnell, Wester Ross
IV23 2QX
Secretary/Treasurer *Paula Cross*
Subscription £7 p.a. (UK); £10 (Overseas);
   £5 (Juvenile/Student); £15 (Family)

FOUNDED 1994 to further knowledge of Richmal Crompton's *William* and *Jimmy* books. An annual 'William' meeting is held in April. The Honorary President of the Society is Richmal Crompton's niece, Richmal Ashbee.

The Keats–Shelley Memorial Association (Inc)
(Registered office): 1 Satchwell Walk, Royal Priors, Leamington Spa, Warwickshire CV32 4QE
☎01926 427400 Fax 01926 335133
Contact *Honorary Secretary*
Subscription £10 p.a.

FOUNDED 1903 to promote appreciation of the works of Keats and Shelley, and their circle. One of the Society's main tasks is the preservation of 26 Piazza di Spagna in Rome as a memorial to the British Romantic poets in Italy, particularly Keats and Shelley. *Publishes* an annual review of Romantic Studies called the *Keats-Shelley Review*, arranges events and lectures for Friends and promotes bursaries and competitive writing on Romantic Studies (see **Keats–Shelley Prize** under **Prizes**). The *Review* is edited by *Angus Graham-Campbell*, c/o Eton College, Windsor, Berkshire SL4 6EA.

The Kenny/Naughton Society
Aghamore, Ballyhaunis, Co Mayo, Republic of Ireland
Email paulwdrogers@hotmail.com
Website www.aghamorgegaa.com/society/knsociety.htm
Chairman *Paul W.D. Rogers*
Patron *Mrs Erna Naughton*

FOUNDED in 1993 to commemorate two writers who had links with Aghamore: P.D. Kenny (1862–1944), who wrote under the pseudonym 'Pat' and Bill Naughton (1910–1992), best known as the author of *Alfie*. Holds an annual school over the October bank holiday weekend which includes lectures, drama, debate and competition (the **Bill Naughton Short Story Competition** – see entry under **Prizes**).

Kent & Sussex Poetry Society
39 Rockington Way, Crowborough, East Sussex TN6 2NJ
☎01892 662781
Email joyce345@yahoo.co.uk
Publicity Secretary *John Arnold*
Subscription £10 p.a. (Full); £6 (Concessionary – country members

living farther afield, senior citizens, under-16s, unemployed)

FOUNDED 1946 to promote the enjoyment of poetry. Monthly meetings are held in Tunbridge Wells, including readings by major poets, a monthly workshop and an annual writing retreat week. *Publishes* an annual folio of members' work based on Members' Competition, adjudicated and commented upon by a major poet. Runs an annual Open Poetry Competition (see entry under **Prizes**) and Saturday workshops twice a year with leading poets.

The Kilvert Society
The Old Forge, Kinnersley, Hereford HR3 6QB
☎01544 327426
Secretary *Mr M. Sharp*
Subscription £6 p.a.; £9 (2 persons at same address)

FOUNDED 1948 to foster an interest in the Diary, the diarist and the countryside he loved. *Publishes* three journals each year; during the summer holds three weekends of walks, commemoration services and talks.

The Kipling Society
6 Clifton Road, London W9 1SS
☎020 7286 0194 Fax 020 7286 0194
Email jane@keskar.fsworld.co.uk
Website www.kipling.org.uk
Honorary Secretary *Jane Keskar*
Subscription £20 p.a.

FOUNDED 1927. The Society's main activities are: maintaining a specialised library in London; answering enquiries from the public (schools, publishers, writers and the media); arranging a regular programme of lectures, especially in London and in Sussex, and an annual luncheon with guest speaker; maintaining a small museum and reference at The Grange, in Rottingdean near Brighton; issuing a quarterly journal. (For the Kipling mailbox discussion list, e-mail to: Rudyard-Kipling@jiscmail.ac.uk) This is a literary society for all who enjoy the prose and verse of Rudyard Kipling (1865–1936) and are interested in his life and times. Please contact the Secretary by letter, telephone, fax or e-mail for further information.

The Kitley Trust
Woodstock, Litton Dale, Litton, Derbyshire SK17 8QL
☎01298 871564
Email stottie2@waitrose.com

Contact *Rosie Ford*

FOUNDED 1990 by a teacher in Sheffield to promote the art of creative writing, in memory of her mother, Jessie Kitley. Activities include: biannual poetry competitions; a 'Get Poetry' day (distribution of children's poems in shopping malls); annual sponsorship of a writer for a school; campaigns; organising conferences for writers and teachers of writing. Funds are provided by donations and profits (if any) from competitions.

Charles Lamb Society
BM Elia, London WC1N 3XX

Subscription £12 p.a. (Single); £18 (Joint & Corporate); US$28 (Overseas Personal); US$42 (Overseas Corporate)

FOUNDED 1935 to promote the study of the life, works and times of English essayist Charles Lamb (1775–1834). Holds regular bi-monthly meetings and lectures in London and organises society events over the summer. Annual luncheon in February. *Publishes* a quarterly bulletin, *The Charles Lamb Bulletin*. Contributions of Elian interest are welcomed by the editor *Rick Tomlinson* at 669 South Monroe Street, Decatur, Illinois 62522–3225, USA (Email romanticism @ameritech.net). Membership applications should be sent to the box number address above. The Society's library is housed in the **Guildhall Library**, Aldermanbury, London EC2P 2EJ. Requests to consult printed sources must be made 48 hours in advance by letter to the Principal Reference Librarian, in person at the Printed Books Enquiry Desk or by telephone (020 7332 1868/1870). Member of the **Alliance of Literary Societies**. Registered Charity No: 803222.

Lancashire Authors' Association
Heatherslade, 5 Quakerfields, Westhoughton, Bolton, Lancashire BL5 2BJ
☎01942 791390
Email eholt@cwctv.net

General Secretary *Eric Holt*
Subscription £10 p.a.; £12 (Joint); £1 (Junior)

FOUNDED 1909 for writers and lovers of Lancashire literature and history. Aims to foster and stimulate interest in Lancashire history and literature as well as in the preservation of the Lancashire dialect. Meets three times a year on Saturday at various locations. *Publishes* a quarterly journal called *The Record*, which is issued free to members, and holds eight annual competitions (open to members only) for both verse and prose. Comprehensive library with access for research to members.

The Landor Society of Warwick
11 Watersfield Gardens, Sydenham, Leamington Spa, Warwickshire CV31 1NT
☎01926 337874
Email portlandbooks@quicknetuk.com
Honorary Secretary *Mrs Jean Field*
Subscription £5 p.a.

FOUNDED 2000 to promote interest in the life and works of the Warwick-born writer Walter Savage Landor (1775–1864). Holds a Landor Birthday Dinner on 30th January each year, and reading and discussion meetings most months. *Publishes* newsletter twice a year.

The Philip Larkin Society
c/o Department of Humanities, The University of Hull, Hull HU6 7RX
☎01482 465640 Fax 01482 465303
Email j.a.osborne@hull.ac.uk
Website www.philiplarkin.com

Contact *Dr John Osborne*
Subscription £18 (Full rate); £12 (Unwaged/ Senior Citizen); £8 (Student)

FOUNDED in 1995 to promote awareness of the life and work of Philip Larkin (1922–1985) and his literary contemporaries; to bring together all those who admire Larkin's work as a poet, writer and librarian; to bring about publications on all things Larkinesque. Organises a programme of events ranging from lectures to rambles exploring the countryside of Larkin's schooldays and *publishes* a biannual newsletter, *About Larkin*.

The D.H. Lawrence Society
24 Briarwood Avenue, Nottingham NG3 6JQ
☎0115 950 3008

Secretary *Ron Faulks*
Subscription £14; £12 (Concession); £16 (European); £19 (RoW)

FOUNDED 1974 to increase knowledge and the appreciation of the life and works of D.H. Lawrence. Monthly meetings, addressed by guest speakers, are held in the library at Eastwood (birthplace of DHL). Organises visits to places of interest in the surrounding countryside, supports the activities of the D.H. Lawrence Centre at Nottingham University, and has close links with DHL Societies worldwide. *Publishes* two newsletters and one journal each year, free to members.

The T.E. Lawrence Society
PO Box 728, Oxford OX2 6YP
Website www.telsociety.org
Contact *Gigi Horsfield*
Subscription £18 (UK); £23 (Overseas)
FOUNDED 1985 as a non-profit making, educational, registered charity to advance awareness of the life and work of Thomas Edward Lawrence and to promote research into his life and work. *Publishes* four newsletters and two journals per year. A biennial symposium is held, usually in Oxford, to bring members together to share both academic and social interests. The Society encourages the formation of regional groups of which, currently, there are seven: three in England (Northwest, London, Dorset), one in Europe (Netherlands), two in the USA (Eastern and Western States) and one in Japan.

The Leamington Literary Society
52 Newbold Terrace East, Leamington Spa,
Warwickshire CV32 4EZ
☎01926 425733
Honorary Secretary *Mrs Margaret Watkins*
Subscription £10 p.a.
FOUNDED 1912 to promote the study and appreciation of literature and the arts. Holds regular meetings every second Tuesday of the month (except August) at the Royal Pump Rooms, Leamington Spa. The Society has published various books of local interest.

Lewes Monday Literary Club
c/o 12 Little East Street, Lewes, East Sussex
BN7 2NU
☎01273 472658
Email derekmason@onetel.net.uk
Contact *Mrs Christine Mason*
Subscription £15 p.a.; £5 (Guest, per meeting)
FOUNDED in 1948 for the promotion and enjoyment of literature. Seven meetings are held during the winter on the last Monday of each month (from October to April) at the White Hart Hotel in Lewes. The Club attracts speakers of the highest quality and a balance between all forms of literature is aimed for. Guests are welcome to attend meetings.

The George MacDonald Society
The Library, Kings College, Strand, London
WC2R 2LS
☎01342 823859
Email macdonaldsociety@britishlibrary.net
Website www.gmsociety.org.uk *linked with* www.george-macdonald.com
Contact *John Docherty*
Subscription £10 p.a. (Individual);
£13 (Joint); £7 (Unwaged); £11 (Overseas)
FOUNDED 1981 to increase awareness of 'the uniqueness and importance of MacDonald's writings'. Notable among Victorian writers for his radical mixture of genres: MacDonald's fantasy works influenced H.G. Wells, C.S. Lewis and J.R.R. Tolkien, and his 'realistic' novels offered a fascinating glimpse into Victorian Scottish life. The Society organises conferences and workshops in Britain and abroad, often in association with other societies with related interests. *Publishes* an annual journal, *North Wind*, with contributions from most of the leading MacDonald scholars worldwide and a newsletter, *Orts*, three times a year.

The Friends of Arthur Machen
78 Greenwich South Street, Greenwich,
London SE10 8UN
☎020 8691 7836
Email jrc@amaranus.ndo.co.uk
Website www.machensoc.demon.co.uk/
welcome.htm
Contact *Jeremy Cantwell*
Subscription £15 p.a. (UK); £18 (US)
FOUNDED 1998. (Formerly the Arthur Machen Society.) Promotes a wider readership of Arthur Machen and a greater understanding of his life and work. Members receive hardback journals (*Faunus*) and newsletters (*Machenalia*). 'While stocks last', new members also receive *Precious Balms* and a new biography of Machen.

The Marlowe Society
9 Middlefield Gardens, Hurst Green Road,
Halesowen, West Midlands B62 9QH
☎1021 421 1482 Fax 1021 421 1482
Email marsoct@ntlworld.com
Website www.marlowe-society.org
Membership Secretary *Frieda Barker*
Treasurer *Bruce Young*
Subscription £12 p.a. (Individual);
£7 p.a. (Pensioners/Student/Unwaged);
£15 p.a. (Overseas); £200 (Group);
£100 (Individual Life Membership)
FOUNDED 1955. Holds meetings, lectures and discussions, stimulates research into Marlowe's life and works, encourages production of his plays and *publishes* a biannual newsletter. At a ceremony on 11th July 2002 the Society cele-

brated their success in establishing a memorial to the playwright and poet in Poets' Corner in Westminster Abbey.

The John Masefield Society
The Frith, Ledbury, Herefordshire HR8 1LW
☎01531 631647 Fax 01531 631647
Email petercarter@btinternet.com
Website www.my.genie.co.uk/masefield
Chairman *Peter Carter*
Subscription £5 p.a. (Individual);
  £8 (Family, Institutions, Libraries);
  £10 (Overseas); £2.50 (Junior, Student)
FOUNDED in 1992 to stimulate the appreciation of and interest in the life and works of John Masefield (Poet Laureate 1930–1967). The Society is based in Ledbury, the Herefordshire market town of his birth and holds various public events in addition to publishing a journal and occasional papers.

William Morris Society
Kelmscott House, 26 Upper Mall,
Hammersmith, London W6 9TA
☎020 8741 3735 Fax 020 8748 5207
Email william.morris@care4free.net
Website www.morrissociety.org
Contact *Helen Elletson*
Subscription £15 p.a.
FOUNDED 1955 to promote interest in the life, work and ideas of William Morris (1834–1896), English poet and craftsman.

The Neil Munro Society
8 Briar Road, Kirkintilloch, Glasgow G66 3SA
☎0141 776 4280
Email brian@bdosborne.fsnet.co.uk
Website www.neilmunro.co.uk
Secretary *Brian D. Osborne*
Subscription £10 (Annual); £11 (Family);
  £5 (Unwaged); £15 (Institutional)
FOUNDED in 1996 to encourage interest in the works of Neil Munro (1863–1930), the Scottish novelist, short story writer, poet and journalist. An annual programme of meetings is held in Glasgow and Munro's home-town of Inveraray. *Publishes ParaGraphs*, a twice-yearly magazine, sponsors reprints of Munro's work and is developing a Munro archive.

Bill Naughton
See **The Kenny/Naughton Society**

Violet Needham Society
c/o 19 Ashburnham Place, London
SE10 8TZ

☎020 8692 4562
Honorary Secretary *R.H.A. Cheffins*
Subscription £7.50 p.a. (UK & Europe);
  £11 (RoW)
FOUNDED 1985 to celebrate the work of children's author Violet Needham and stimulate critical awareness of her work. *Publishes* thrice-yearly *Souvenir*, the Society journal with an accompanying newsletter; organises meetings and excursions to places associated with the author and her books. The journal includes articles about other children's writers of the 1940s and '50s and on ruritanian fiction. Contributions welcome.

The Edith Nesbit Society
21 Churchfields, West Malling, Kent
ME19 6RJ
Website www.imagix.dial.pipex.com
Chairman *Margaret McCarthy*
Subscription £6 p.a.; £8 (Joint); £75 (Life)
FOUNDED in 1996 to celebrate the life and work of Edith Nesbit (1858–1924), best known as the author of *The Railway Children*. The Society's activities include a regular newsletter, booklets, talks and visits to relevant places.

The Wilfred Owen Association
192 York Road, Shrewsbury, Shropshire
SY1 3QH
☎01743 460089
Website www.1914-19.co.uk/owen
Chairman *Michael Grayer*
Subscription Adults £6 (£10 Overseas);
  £4 (Senior Citizens/Students/Unemployed);
  £15 (UK Groups/Institutions); £25
  (Overseas Groups/Institutions)
FOUNDED 1989 to commemorate the life and works of Wilfred Owen by promoting readings, visits, talks and performances relating to Owen and his work. The Association offers practical support for students of literature and future poets through links with education, support for literary foundations and information on historical and literary background material. Membership is international with 700 members. *Publishes* a regular newsletter and annual Journal. Speakers are available.

The Elsie Jeanette Oxenham Appreciation Society
32 Tadfield Road, Romsey, Hampshire
SO51 5AJ
☎01794 517149 Fax 01794 517149
Email abbey@bufobooks.demon.co.uk

Website www.bufobooks.demon.co.uk/abbeylnk.htm

Contact *Ms Ruth Allen* (Membership Secretary/Treasurer)

Subscription £7.50 p.a.; enquire for Overseas rates

FOUNDED 1989 to promote the works of Elsie J. Oxenham. Publishes a newsletter for members, *The Abbey Chronicle*, three times a year – editor: *Fiona Dyer* (fionadyer@btopenworld.com). 500+ members.

Thomas Paine Society

43 Eugene Gardens, Nottingham NG2 3LF
☎0115 986 0010

President *The Rt. Hon. Michael Foot*
Honorary Secretary *R.W. Morrell, MBE* (at address above)
Treasurer *Stuart Wright*
Subscription (Minimum) £15 p.a. (UK); $35 (Overseas); £5 (Unwaged/Pensioners/Students)

FOUNDED 1963 to promote the life and work of Thomas Paine, and continues to expound his ideals. Meetings, newsletters, lectures and research assistance. Membership badge. The Society has members worldwide and keeps in touch with American and French Thomas Paine associations. *Publishes* magazine, *The Journal of Radical History*, twice yearly (Editor: *R.W. Morrell*) and a newsletter. Holds occasional exhibitions and lectures, including the biannual Thomas Paine Memorial Lecture and the annual Eric Paine Memorial Lecture.

The John Polidori Literary Society

PO Box 6078, Nottingham NG16 4HX
Founder & President *Franklin Bishop*
Subscription on application

FOUNDED 1990 to promote and encourage appreciation of the life and works of John William Polidori MD (1795–1821) – novelist, poet, tragedian, philosopher, diarist, essayist, reviewer, traveller and one of the youngest students to obtain a medical degree (at the age of 19). He was one-time intimate of the leading figures in the Romantic movement and travelling companion and private physician to Lord Byron. He was a pivotal figure in the infamous Villa Diodati ghost story sessions in which he assisted Mary Shelley in the creation of her *Frankenstein* tale. Polidori introduced into literature the enduring icon of the vampire portrayed as an aristocratic, handsome seducer with his seminal

work *The Vampyre – A Tale*, published in 1819. Polidori was honoured in 1998 by the erection of a City of Westminster Plaque at his birthplace – 38 Great Pulteney Street, Westminster, London – officially unveiled by the Italian ambassador. The Society issues unique publications of the rare works of Polidori. International membership in Italy, USA, Canada and Spain.

The Beatrix Potter Society

9 Broadfields, Harpenden, Hertfordshire AL5 2HJ
☎01582 769755 Fax 01582 769755
Email beatrixpottersociety@tiscali.co.uk
Website www.beatrixpottersociety.org.uk
Subscription UK: £15 p.a. (Individual); £20 (Institution); Overseas: £20 (Individual); £25 (Institution)

FOUNDED 1980 to promote the study and appreciation of the life and works of Beatrix Potter (1866–1943). Potter was not only the author of *The Tale of Peter Rabbit* and other classics of children's literature; she was also a landscape and natural history artist, diarist, farmer and conservationist, and was responsible for the preservation of large areas of the Lake District through her gifts to the National Trust. The Society upholds and protects the integrity of the inimitable and unique work of Potter, her aims and bequests; holds regular talks and meetings in London with visits to places connected with Beatrix Potter. International Study Conferences are held in the UK and the USA. The Society has an active publishing programme.

The Anthony Powell Society

76 Ennismore Avenue, Greenford, Middlesex UB6 0JW
☎020 8864 4095 Fax 020 8864 6109
Email secretary@anthonypowell.org.uk
Website www.anthonypowell.org.uk
Patron *John M. A. Powell*
President *Hugh Massingberd*
Honorary Secretary *Dr Keith C. Marshall*
Subscription £20 p.a. (Individual); £30 (Joint/Gold); £12 (Students); £100 (Organisation)

FOUNDED in June 2000 by a group of scholars and enthusiasts following Powell's death earlier that year at the age of 94. The Society's first project was the First Biennial Anthony Powell Conference, held at Eton College (Powell's old school); the second conference was in April 2003 at Balliol College, Oxford (Powell's *alma mater*). Also organises events for members, ranging from 'pub meets' to talks and visits to places of Powell interest. *Publishes* a quarterly newsletter. The Society is a member of the **Alliance of Literary Societies**.

The Powys Society

82 Linden Road, Gloucester GL1 5HD
☎01452 304539
Email pjf@retepssof.freeserve.co.uk
Website www.powys-society.org
Honorary Secretary *Peter J. Foss*
Subscription £13.50 (UK); £16 (Overseas); £6 (Students)

The Society (with a membership of 350) aims to promote public education and recognition of the writings, thought and contribution to the arts of the Powys family; particularly of John Cowper, Theodore and Llewelyn, but also of the other members of the family and their close associates. The Society holds two major collections of Powys published works, letters, manuscripts and memorabilia. *Publishes* the *Powys Society Newsletter* in April, June and November and *The Powys Journal* in August. Organises an annual conference as well as lectures and meetings in Powys places.

The J.B. Priestley Society

Eldwick Crag Farm, High Eldwick, Bingley, West Yorkshire BD16 3BB
☎01274 563078
Email reavill@globalnet.co.uk
Website www.jbpriestley-society.com
President *Roy Hattersley*
Chairman *The Revd. John Waddington-Feather*
Honorary Secretary *R.E.Y. Slater*
Membership Secretary *Tony Reavill*
Subscription £10 (Individual); £5 (Concession); £15 (Group/Family)

FOUNDED 1997 to widen the knowledge and understanding of Priestley's works; promote the study of his life and his social, cultural and political influences; provide members of the Society with lectures, seminars, films, journals and stimulate education projects; promote public performances of his works and the distribution of material associated with him. For further information, contact the Membership Secretary at the address above.

The Queen's English Society

Membership Secretary: Fernwood, Nightingales, West Chiltington, Pulborough, West Sussex RH20 2QT
☎01798 813001

Website www.queens-english-society.com
Hon. Membership Secretary *David Ellis*
Subscription £10 p.a. (Ordinary); £12 (Family/Corporate); £100 (Life member); reduced rates available for students and long-term unemployed

FOUNDED in 1972 to promote and uphold the use of good English and to encourage the enjoyment of the language. Holds regular meetings to which speakers are invited, an annual luncheon and *publishes* a quarterly journal, *Quest*, for which original articles are welcome.

The Arthur Ransome Society Ltd

Abbot Hall Art Gallery & Museum, Kendal, Cumbria LA6 5AL
☎01539 722464 Fax 01539 722494
Email tarsinfo@arthur-ransome.org
Website www.arthur-ransome.org/ar
Trustee Chairman *Robin Anderson*
Company Secretary *Bill Janes*
Subscription UK: £5 (Junior); £10 (Student); £15 (Adult); £20 (Family); £40 (Corporate); Overseas: £5 (Junior); £10 (Student); £20 (Adult); £25 (Family) Payable in local currency in US, Canada, Australia, Japan and New Zealand

FOUNDED in 1990 to celebrate the life and to promote the works and ideas of Arthur Ransome, author of *Swallows and Amazons* titles for children, biographer of Oscar Wilde, works on the Russian Revolution and extensive articles on fishing. TARS seeks to encourage children and adults to engage in adventurous pursuits, to educate the public about Ransome and his works, and to sponsor research into his literary works and life.

The Followers of Rupert

31 Whiteley, Windsor, Berkshire SL4 5PJ
☎01753 865562
Email followersofrupert@hotmail.com
Website www.rupertbear.info
Membership Secretary *Mrs Shirley Reeves*
Subscription UK: £15; £17 (Joint); Europe, airmail: £18 (Individual); £20 (Joint); RoW, airmail: £20 (Individual); £22 (Joint)

FOUNDED in 1983. The Society caters for the growing interest in the Rupert Bear stories, past, present and future. *Publishes* the *Nutwood Newsletter* quarterly which gives up-to-date news of Rupert and information on Society activities. A national get-together of members – the Followers Annual – is held during the autumn.

The Ruskin Society

49 Hallam Street, London W1W 6JP
☎020 7580 1894

Honorary Secretary *Dr Cynthia. J. Gamble*
Honorary Treasurer *The Hon. Mrs Catherine Edwards*
Subscription £10 p.a. (payable on January 1st)

FOUNDED in 1997 to encourage a wider understanding of John Ruskin and his contemporaries. Organises lectures and events which seek not only to explain to the public at large the nature of Ruskin's theories but also to place these in a modern context.

The Ruskin Society of London

351 Woodstock Road, Oxford OX2 7NX
☎01865 310987/515962 Fax 01865 240448

Honorary Secretary *Miss O.E. Forbes-Madden*
Subscription £10 p.a.

FOUNDED 1986 to promote interest in John Ruskin (1819–1900) and his contemporaries. All aspects of Ruskinia are introduced. Functions are held in London. *Publishes* the annual *Ruskin Gazette*, a journal concerned with Ruskin's influence. Affiliated to other literary societies.

The Malcolm Saville Society

78a Windmill Road, Mortimer, Berkshire RG7 3RL
Email mystery@witchend.com
Website www.witchend.com

Membership Secretary *Richard Griffiths*
Subscription £7.50 p.a. (UK); £12 (Overseas)

FOUNDED in 1994 to remember and promote interest in the work of the popular children's author. Regular social activities, booksearch, library, contact directory and three magazines per year.

The Dorothy L. Sayers Society

Rose Cottage, Malthouse Lane,
Hurstpierpoint, West Sussex BN6 9JY
☎01273 833444 Fax 01273 835988
Website www.sayers.org.uk

Contact *Christopher Dean*
Subscription £14 p.a. (UK);
£16.50 (Europe); $28 (US)

FOUNDED 1976 to promote the study of the life, works and thoughts of Dorothy Sayers; to encourage the performance of her plays and publication of her books and books about her; to preserve original material and provide assistance to researchers. Acts as a forum and information centre, providing material for study purposes which would otherwise be unavailable. Annual seminars and other meetings. Co-founder of the Dorothy L. Sayers Centre in Witham. *Publishes* bi-monthly bulletin, annual proceedings and other papers.

The Bernard Shaw Information & Research Service

27 Cavendish Avenue, South Ruislip
HA4 6QJ
Email diane@georgebernardshaw.com
Website www.georgebernardshaw.com

President *Diane S. Uttley*

ESTABLISHED in 1997 by writer and Shaw specialist Diane S. Uttley who was custodian of and lived in the writer's home, Shaw's Corner, from 1989 to 1997. The service is used by enthusiasts and academics; literary, theatrical and biographical.

The Shaw Society

51 Farmfield Road, Downham, Bromley,
Kent BR1 4NF
☎020 8697 3619 Fax 020 8697 3619
Email anthnyellis@aol.com

Honorary Secretary *Ms Barbara Smoker*
Subscription £15 p.a. (Individual);
£22 (Joint)

FOUNDED 1941 to promote interest in the life and works of G. Bernard Shaw. Meetings are held on the last Friday of every month (except July, August and December) at Conway Hall, Red Lion Square, London WC1 (6.30 pm for 7.00 pm) at which speakers are invited to talk on some aspect of Shaw's life or works. Monthly playreadings are held on the first Friday of each month (except August). A 'Birthday Tribute' is held at Shaw's Corner, Ayot St Lawrence in Hertfordshire, on the weekend nearest to Shaw's birthday (26th July). *Publishes* a quarterly newsletter and a magazine, *The Shavian*, which appears approximately every nine months. (No payment for contributors.)

The Robert Southey Society

1 Lewis Terrace, Abergarwed, Neath
SA11 4DL
☎01639 711480

Contact *Robert King*
Subscription £10 p.a.

FOUNDED 1990 to promote the work of Robert Southey. *Publishes* an annual newsletter and arranges talks on his life and work. Open membership.

The Laurence Sterne Trust
See **The Friends of Shandy Hall**

Robert Louis Stevenson Club
37 Lauder Road, Edinburgh EH9 1UE
☎0131 667 6256 Fax 0131 662 0353
Email MBeanConferences@aol.com
Contact *Margaret Bean, MA*
Subscription £15 p.a. (Individual); £20 p.a.
  (Overseas); £100 (Ten-year); £180 (Life)
FOUNDED in 1920 to foster interest in Robert
Louis Stevenson's life and works. The Club
organises an annual lunch and other events.
Publishes RLS Club News twice a year.

The Bram Stoker Society
Regent House, Trinity College, Dublin 2,
Republic of Ireland
Fax 00 353 1 671 9003 (attn: David Lass)
Email dlass@tcd.ie
Website www.benecke.com/stoker
Honorary Secretary *David Lass*
Honorary Treasurer *Dr Albert Power*
  (43 Castle Court, Killiney Hill Road,
  Killiney, Co. Dublin, Republic of Ireland)
Subscription £10 p.a. (UK); €10 (Europe);
  $20 (US/RoW)
FOUNDED 1980. Aims to promote the study and
appreciation of Bram Stoker's works, including
his place in the Gothic horror tradition, and his
influence on later writers in the areas of cinema,
music and theatre. *Publishes* an occasional
newsletter, an annual journal of scholarly articles
and organises a regular programme of activities
with its affiliated body, The Bram Stoker Club of
Trinity College Dublin. These include screenings, annual memorial lectures and the annual
summer school held in July. Subscription payments by cheque or postal order (made out to
The Bram Stoker Society) should be sent to the
Hon. Treasurer at his address above.

The R.S. Surtees Society
Manor Farm House, Nunney, Near Frome,
Somerset BA11 4NJ
☎01373 836937 Fax 01373 836574
Email www.r.s.surteessociety.org
Website www.clique.co.uk/r.s.surteessociety
Contact *Orders and Membership Secretary*
Subscription £10
FOUNDED 1979 to republish the works of R.S.
Surtees and others.

The Tennyson Society
Central Library, Free School Lane, Lincoln
LN2 1EZ
☎01522 552862 Fax 01522 552858
Email kathleenjefferson@lincolnshire.gov.uk
Honorary Secretary *Miss K. Jefferson*
Subscription £8 p.a. (Individual);
  £10 (Family); £15 (Corporate); £125 (Life)
FOUNDED 1960. An international society with
membership worldwide. Exists to promote the
study and understanding of the life and work of
Alfred, Lord Tennyson. The Society is concerned with the work of the Tennyson Research
Centre, 'probably the most significant collection
of mss, family papers and books in the world'.
Publishes annually the *Tennyson Research Bulletin*,
which contains articles and critical reviews; and
organises lectures, visits and seminars. Annual
memorial service at Somersby in Lincolnshire.

The Angela Thirkell Society
54 Belmont Park, London SE13 5BN
☎020 8244 9339
Email penny.aldred@tesco.net
Website www.sndc.demon.co.uk/als.htm *and*
www.angelathirkell.org (N. American branch)
Honorary Secretary *Mrs. P. Aldred*
Subscription £7 p.a.
FOUNDED in 1980 to honour the memory of
Angela Thirkell as a writer and to make her
works available to new generations. *Publishes* an
annual journal, holds an AGM in early October
and a spring meeting which usually takes the
form of a visit to a location associated with
Thirkell. Has a flourishing North American
branch which has frequent contact with the UK
parent society.

The Dylan Thomas Society of Great Britain
5 Church Park, Mumbles, Swansea SA3 4DE
☎01792 520080
Contact *Mrs Eryl Jenkins*
Subscription £5 (Individual); £8 (2 adults
  from same household)
FOUNDED 1977 to foster an understanding of the
work of Dylan Thomas and to extend members'
awareness of other 20th century writers, especially Welsh writers in English. Meetings take
place monthly, mainly in Swansea.

The Edward Thomas Fellowship
1 Carfax, Undercliff Drive, St Lawrence, Isle
of Wight PO38 1XG
☎01983 853366

Email colin.g.thornton@btopenworld.com
Hon. Secretary *Colin G. Thornton*
Subscription £7 p.a. (Single); £10 p.a. (Joint)

FOUNDED 1980 to perpetuate and promote the memory of Edward Thomas and to encourage an appreciation of his life and work. The Fellowship holds a commemorative birthday walk on the Sunday nearest the poet's birthday, 3rd March; issues newsletters and holds various events.

The Tolkien Society

65 Wentworth Crescent, Ash Vale, Surrey
GU12 5LF Fax 0870 0525569
Email membership@tolkiensociety.org
Website www.tolkiensociety.org

Membership Secretary *Trevor Reynolds*
Subscription £20 p.a. (UK); £22 (Overseas)

An international organisation which aims to encourage and further interest in the life and works of the late Professor J.R.R. Tolkien, CBE, author of *The Hobbit* and *Lord of the Rings*. Current membership stands at 900. *Publishes Mallorn* annually and *Amon Hen* bi-monthly.

The Trollope Society

9A North Street, Clapham, London
SW4 0HN
☎020 7720 6789 Fax 020 7978 1815
Email trollsoc@barset.fsnet.co.uk

Contacts *John Letts, Phyllis Eden*

FOUNDED 1987 to study and promote Anthony Trollope's works. *Publishes* the complete works of Trollope's novels and travel books.

Edgar Wallace Society

84 Ridgefield Road, Oxford OX4 3DA
Website www.edgarwallace.org

Organiser *Miss Penny Wyrd*
Subscription £15 p.a.; £10 (Senior Citizen/Student); Overseas: £20; £15 (Senior Citizen/Student)

FOUNDED in 1969 by Wallace's daughter, Penelope, to bring together all who have an interest in Edgar Wallace. Members receive a brief biography of Edgar by Penelope Wallace, with a list of published book titles. A newsletter, *Crimson Circle*, is published three times a year.

The Walmsley Society

April Cottage, No 1 Brand Road, Hampden Park, Eastbourne, East Sussex BN22 9PX
☎01323 506447
Email walmsley@haughshw.demon.co.uk

Honorary Secretary *Fred Lane*

Subscription £10 p.a.; £12 (Family); £9 (Students/Senior Citizens); £15 (Overseas, £25 for 2 years)

FOUNDED 1985 to promote interest in the writings of Leo Walmsley and to foster an appreciation of the work of his father, the artist Ulric Walmsley. Two annual meetings – one held in Robin Hood's Bay on the East Yorkshire coast, spiritual home of the author Leo Walmsley. *Publishes* a journal twice-yearly and newsletters, and is involved in other publications which benefit the aims of the Society. A biography of Leo Walmsley is now available.

Sylvia Townsend Warner Society

2 Vicarage Lane, Dorchester, Dorset DT1 1LH
☎01305 266028
Email tartarus@pavilion.co.uk
Website www.freepages.pavilion.net/users/tartarus/warner1.htm

Contact *Eileen Johnson*
Subscription £10 p.a.; $20 (Overseas)

FOUNDED in 2000 to promote a wider readership and better understanding of the writings of Sylvia Townsend Warner.

Mary Webb Society

8 The Knowe, Willaston, Neston, Cheshire
CH64 1TA
☎0151 327 5843
Email suehigginbotham@yahoo.co.uk
Website www.marywebb.2ya.com

Secretary *Sue Higginbotham*
Subscription £10 p.a. (Individual); £13 p.a. (Joint/Overseas)

FOUNDED 1972. Attracts members from the UK and overseas who are devotees of the literature of Mary Webb and of the beautiful Shropshire countryside of her novels. *Publishes* biannual journal, organises summer schools in various locations related to the authoress's life and works. Archives; lectures; tours arranged for individuals and groups.

H.G. Wells Society

49 Beckingthorpe Drive, Bottesford, Nottingham NG13 0DN
Website hgwellsusa.50megs.com

Honorary Secretary *J.R. Hammond*
Subscription £16 (UK/EU); £19 (Overseas); £20 (Corporate); £10 (Concessions)

FOUNDED 1960 to promote an interest in and appreciation of the life, work and thought of Herbert George Wells. *Publishes The Wellsian* (annual) and *The H.G. Wells Newsletter* (three issues yearly). Organises meetings and conferences.

The Oscar Wilde Society
100 Peacock Street, Gravesend, Kent
DA12 1EQ
☎01474 535978
Email vanessa@salome.co.uk
Honorary Secretary *Vanessa Harris*

FOUNDED 1990 to promote knowledge, appreciation and study of the life, personality and works of the writer and wit Oscar Wilde. Activities include meetings, lectures, readings and exhibitions, and visits to locations associated with Wilde. Members receive a journal, *The Wildean*, twice-yearly and a newsletter, *Intentions* (six per year).

The Charles Williams Society
35 Broomfield, Stacey Bushes, Milton Keynes, Buckinghamshire MK12 6HA
Email charles_wms_soc@yahoo.co.uk
Website www.geocities.com/charles_wms_soc
Contact *Honorary Secretary*

FOUNDED 1975 to promote interest in, and provide a means for the exchange of views and information on the life and work of Charles Walter Stansby Williams (1886–1945).

The Henry Williamson Society
16 Doran Drive, Redhill, Surrey RH1 6AX
☎01737 763228
Email mm@misterman.freeserve.co.uk
Website www.henrywilliamson.org
Membership Secretary *Mrs Margaret Murphy*
Subscription £12 p.a.; £15 (Family);
£5 (Students)

FOUNDED 1980 to encourage, by all appropriate means, a wider readership and deeper understanding of the literary heritage left by the 20th-century English writer Henry Williamson (1895–1977). *Publishes* annual journal.

The P.G. Wodehouse Society (UK)
16 Herbert Street, Plaistow, London E13 8BE
Website www.eclipse.co.uk/wodehouse
Membership Secretary *Helen Murphy*
Subscription £15 p.a.

Relaunched in May 1997 to advance the genius of P.G. Wodehouse. Publications include the *Wooster Source* quarterly journal and the *By The Way* newsletter. Regular national and international group meetings. Members in most countries throughout the world. Society

patrons include Rt. Hon. Tony Blair MP and Stephen Fry. Wodehouse's grandson, Sir Edward Cazalet, is on the committee.

The Parson Woodforde Society
22 Gaynor Close, Wymondham, Norfolk
NR18 0EA
☎01953 604124
Email mabrayne@supanet.com
Website www.parsonwoodforde.org.uk
Membership Secretary *Mrs Ann Elliott*
Subscription £12.50 (UK); £25 (Overseas)

FOUNDED 1968. Aims to extend and develop knowledge of James Woodforde's life and the society in which he lived and to provide the opportunity for fellow enthusiasts to meet together in places associated with the diarist. *Publishes* a quarterly journal and newsletter. The Society is producing a complete edition of the diary of James Woodforde. To date, twelve volumes of diary material have been published covering the period 1759–1790.

The Virginia Woolf Society of Great Britain
Fairhaven, Charnleys Lane, Banks, Southport
PR9 8HJ
Email snclarke@talk21.com
Website orlando.jp.org/vwsgb/index.html
Contact *Stuart N. Clarke*
Subscription £12 p.a.; £15 (Overseas)

FOUNDED 1998 to promote interest in the life and work of Virginia Woolf, author, essayist and diarist. The Society's activities include trips away, walks, reading groups and talks. *Publishes* a literary journal, *Virginia Woolf Bulletin*, three times a year.

WW2 HMSO PPBKS Society
3 Roman Road, Southwick, West Sussex
BN42 4TP
☎01273 871017   Fax 01273 871017
Contact *A.R. James*

FOUNDED 1994 to encourage collectors and to promote research into HMSO's World War II series of paperbacks. Most of them were written by well-known authors, though in many cases anonymously. No subscription charge. Available for purchase: Collectors' Guide (£5); Bibliography (£3); Handbook, *Informing the People* (£10).

The Yeats Society Sligo
Yeats Memorial Building, Douglas Hyde Bridge, Sligo, Republic of Ireland
☎00 353 71 42693   Fax 00 353 71 42780

Email info@yeats-sligo.com
Website www.yeats-sligo.com
President *Michael Keohane*
Subscription €25 (Single); €38 (Couple);
€127 (Corporate)

FOUNDED in 1958 to promote the heritage of
W.B. Yeats and the Yeats family. Attractions
include continuous updated Yeats exhibitions
for public viewing, annual Yeats International
Summer School in August and Yeats Winter
School in January. The Yeats Summer Festival
is held each August and lectures are held in the
winter and spring, sponsored by the Institute of
Technology, Sligo. *Publishes* a newsletter and
organises year-round events/programmes in
arts, culture, education for writers' groups,
poetry/drama groups, etc.

Yorkshire Dialect Society
51 Stepney Avenue, Scarborough, North
Yorkshire YO12 5BW
Secretary *Michael Park*
Subscription £10 p.a.

FOUNDED 1897 to promote interest in and preserve a record of the Yorkshire dialect.
Publishes dialect verse and prose writing. Two
journals to members annually. Details of publications are available from YDS, Rosebank
Cottage, Main Street, Great Heck, West
Yorkshire DN14 0BQ.

Francis Brett Young Society
92 Gower Road, Halesowen, West Midlands
B62 9BT
☎0121 422 8969
Website www.fbysociety.co.uk
Honorary Secretary *Mrs Jean Hadley*
Subscription £7 p.a. (Individuals); £10
(Couples sharing a journal); £5 (Students);
£7 (Organisations/Overseas); £70 (Life);
£100 (Joint, Life)

FOUNDED 1979. Aims to provide a forum for
those interested in the life and works of English
novelist Francis Brett Young and to collate
research on him. Promotes lectures, exhibitions
and readings; *publishes* a regular newsletter.

Arts Councils and Regional Offices

The Arts Council England
14 Great Peter Street, London SW1P 3NQ
☎020 7333 0100 (Textphone: 020 7973 6564) Fax 020 7973 6590
Email enquiries@artscouncil.org.uk
Website www.artscouncil.org.uk
Chairman *Gerry Robinson*
Chief Executive *Peter Hewitt*
Director of Literature *Gary Mckeone*

Arts Council England is the national development agency for the arts in England, distributing public money from government and the National Lottery to artists and arts organisations. Arts Council England works independently and at arm's length from government. Information about Arts Council England funding is available on the website, by e-mail or by contacting the enquiry line on 020 7973 6517.

Arts Council England has 9 regional offices:

Arts Council England, East
Eden House, 48–49 Bateman Street, Cambridge CB2 1LR
☎ 01223 454400 Fax 0870 242 1271
Textphone 01223 306893

Arts Council England, East Midlands
St Nicholas Court, 25–27 Castle Gate, Nottingham NG1 7AR
☎0115 989 7520 Fax 0115 950 2467

Arts Council England, London
2 Pear Tree Court, London EC1R 0DS
☎020 7608 6100 Fax 020 7608 4100
Textphone 020 7608 4101
Head of Literature *Nick McDowell*

Arts Council England, North East
Central Square, Forth Street, Newcastle upon Tyne NE1 3PJ
☎0191 255 8500 Fax 0191 230 1020
Textphone 0191 255 8500

Arts Council England, North West
Manchester House, 22 Bridge Street, Manchester M3 3AB
☎0161 834 6644 Fax 0161 834 6969
Textphone 0161 834 9131

Also at: Graphic House, 107 Duke Street Liverpool L1 4JR
☎0151 709 0671 Fax 0151 708 9034
Director of Visual Arts and Literature
Howard Rifkin

Arts Council England, South East
SovereignHouse, Church Street, Brighton BN1 1RA
☎01273 763000 Fax 0870 242 1257
Textphone: 01273 710659
Director of Visual Arts and Literature
Michael Craven

Arts Council England, South West
Bradninch Place, Gandy Street, Exeter EX4 3LS
☎01392 218188 Fax 01392 229229
Textphone 01392 433503

Arts Council England, West Midlands
82 Granville Street, Birmingham B1 2LH
☎0121 631 3121 Fax 0121 643 7239
Textphone 0121 643 2815
Literature Officer *Adrian Johnson*

Arts Council England, Yorkshire
21 Bond Street, Dewsbury, West Yorkshire WF13 1AX
☎01924 455555 Fax 01924 466522
Textphone 01924 438585
Director of Visual Arts and Literature
Adrian Friedli

The Irish Arts Council/ An Chomhairle Ealaíon
70 Merrion Square, Dublin 2
☎00 353 1 6180200 Fax 00 353 1 6761302
Email info@artscouncil.ie
Website www.artscouncil.ie
Literature Officer *to be appointed*

The Irish Arts Council has programmes under six headings to assist in the area of literature and book promotion: a) Writers; b) Literary Organisations; c) Publishers; d) Literary Magazines; e) Participation Programmes; f) Literary Events and Festivals. It also awards a number of annual bursaries (see **Arts Council Literature Bursaries, Ireland** under **Bursaries, Fellowships and Grants**).

The Arts Council
of Northern Ireland
MacNeice House, 77 Malone Road, Belfast
BT9 6AQ
☎028 9038 5200 Fax 028 9066 1715
Website www.artscouncil-ni.org
Literature and Language Arts Officer
Robbie Meredith

Funds book production by established publishers, programmes of readings, literary festivals, writers-in-residence schemes and literary magazines and periodicals. Occasional schools programmes and anthologies of children's writing are produced. Annual awards and bursaries for writers are available. Holds information also on various groups associated with local arts, workshops and courses.

Scottish Arts Council
12 Manor Place, Edinburgh EH3 7DD
☎0131 226 6051 Fax 0131 225 9833
Email administrator@scottisharts.org.uk
Website www.sac.org.uk
Chairman *James Boyle*
Acting Director *Graham Berry*
Literature Director *Jenny Brown*
Literature Officers *Gavin Wallace,*
Jenny Attala
Literature Secretary *Catherine Allan*

Principal channel for government funding of the arts in Scotland. The Scottish Arts Council (SAC) is funded by the Scottish Executive. It aims to develop and improve the knowledge, understanding and practice of the arts, and to increase their accessibility throughout Scotland. It offers around 1300 grants a year to artists and arts organisations concerned with the visual arts, crafts, dance and mime, drama, literature, music, festivals and traditional, ethnic and community arts. It is also a distributor of National Lottery funds to the arts in Scotland. SAC's support for Scottish-based writers with a track record of publication includes bursaries, writing and translation fellowships and book awards (see entries under **Bursaries, Fellowships and Grants** and **Prizes**). Information offered includes lists of literary awards, literary magazines, agents and publishers.

The Arts Council of Wales
Museum Place, Cardiff CF10 3NX
☎029 2037 6500 Fax 029 2022 1447
Website www.artswales.org.uk/language
Senior Officer: Drama *Sandra Wynne*

On 14 April 2003 the responsibility for funding literary magazines and book production transferred to the **Welsh Books Council**. Services for individual writers including bursaries, mentoring, the critical writers service and writers in residency/writers on tour are provided by the **Welsh Academy, Hay-on-Wye Literature Festival** and **Tŷ Newydd Writers' Centre** at Cricieth. The Council aims to develop theatrical experience among Wales-based writers through a variety of schemes – in particular, by funding writers on year-long attachments.

Writers' Courses, Circles and Workshops

Writer's Courses

UK – ENGLAND

Berkshire

University of Reading
The School of Continuing Education, London Road, Reading, Berkshire RG1 5AQ
☎0118 931 8347
Email Cont-Ed@reading.ac.uk
Website www.reading.ac.uk/ContEd

An expanding programme of creative writing courses, including *Life into Fiction*; *Poetry Workshop*; *Writing Fiction*; and *Scriptwriting*. There is also a public lecture by a writer and a reading by students of their work, and various Saturday workshops. Tutors include novelist Leslie Wilson and poets Jane Draycott, Susan Utting and Paul Bavister. Fees vary depending on the length of course. Concessions available.

Buckinghamshire

Missenden Abbey Adult Learning
Chilterns Consortium, The Misbourne Centre, Great Missenden, HP16 0BN
☎01494 862904 Fax 01494 890087
Email adultlearningchil@bucksee.gov.uk
Website www.aredu.org.uk/missendenabbey

Residential and non-residential weekend workshops and summer school. Programmes have included *Writing Stories for Children*; *Short Story Writing*; *Poetry Workshop*; *Writing for TV and Film*; *Writing Comedy for Television*.

National Film & Television School
Beaconsfield Studios, Station Road, Beaconsfield, Buckinghamshire HP9 1LG
☎01494 731425 Fax 01494 674042
Email admin@nftsfilm-tv.ac.uk
Website www.nftsfilm-tv.ac.uk *and*
www.nftsscreenwriting.org

Two-year programme covering all aspects of screenwriting from the development of ideas through to final production. Studying alongside other filmmaking students allows writers to have their work tested in workshops and productions. The emphasis on practical exploration and filmmaking and degree of contact with industry personnel through seminars and pitching sessions makes the course unique among screenwriting programmes. Year One deals with the basic principles of storytelling, the craft of screenwriting for film and television and the collaborative nature of production, while in Year Two students attend classes part-time while developing a portfolio of screenplays and writing the dissertation. A five-week course – Feature Development – and a one-week course on the First Draft Feature Script are also offered at intervals during the year – details from the school's website.

Cambridgeshire

National Extension College
Michael Young Centre, Purbeck Road, Cambridge CB2 2HN
☎01223 400200 Fax 01223 400399
Email info@nec.ac.uk
Website www.nec.ac.uk

Runs a number of home-study courses on writing. Courses include: *Essential Editing*; *Creative Writing*; *Copywriting*; *Essential Design*. Contact the NEC for copy of the *Guide to Courses* which includes details of fees.

University of Cambridge Institute of Continuing Education
Madingley Hall, Madingley, Cambridge CB3 8AQ
☎01954 280399 Fax 01954 280200
Website www.cont-ed.cam.ac.uk

A wide range of weekend, five-day and week long creative writing courses for adults is offered by the University at the Institute of Continuing Education's residential headquarters at Madingley Hall. Evening courses are also available in Cambridgeshire and surrounding areas. Access the website or phone for details.

Cheshire

Burton Manor
Burton Village, Neston, Cheshire CH64 5SJ
☎0151 336 5172 Fax 0151 336 6586

Email enquiry@burtonmanor.com
Website www.burtonmanor.org

Wide variety of short courses, residential and non-residential on writing and literature, including *Writing About Travel; Unleash Your Writing Power*. Full details in brochure.

The College of Technical Authorship – Distance Learning Course

The College of Technical Authorship, PO Box 7, Cheadle, Cheshire SK8 3BY
☎0161 437 4235 Fax 0161 437 4235
Email crossley@coltecha.u-net.com
Website www.coltecha.com

Contact *John Crossley*

Distance learning courses for City & Guilds Tech 5360, Part 1, Technical Communication Techniques, and Part 2, Technical Authorship. Individual tuition by letter or e-mail. A member of the British Association for Open Learning.

Cornwall

Falmouth College of Arts

Woodlane, Falmouth, Cornwall TR11 4RH
☎01326 211077
Website www.falmouth.ac.uk *and* (magazine) www.bloc-online.com

Contact *Admissions Secretary*

Postgraduate professional writing programme. An intensive vocational writing programme developing skills in fiction, magazine journalism/features, screenwriting. Students work on an extended writing project and form links with other PgDips such as broadcast TV and radio. The course website won a Guardian Media Award in 1999.

The Indian King Arts Centre

Fore Street, Camelford, Cornwall PL32 9PG
☎01840 212111
Email info@indianking.co.uk
Website www.indianking.co.uk

Director *Helen Jagger Wood*

Founded in 1994 to offer the opportunity for exploring and developing creative writing skills with the support of published writers. Residential writing courses start with the annual Poetry Festival, held on the last weekend before Easter, and continue into the autumn. Offers courses with visiting writers in poetry, short and long fiction and drama. The Centre offers writing classes, readings and book launches throughout the year as well as having a poetry library.

Cumbria

Higham Hall College

Bassenthwaite Lake, Cockermouth, CA13 9SH
☎01768 776276 Fax 01768 776013
Email admin@highamhall.com
Website www.highamhall.com

Winter and summer residential courses. Brochure available.

Derbyshire

Real Writers

PO Box 170, Chesterfield, Derbyshire S40 1FE
☎01246 238492 Fax 01246 238492
Email info@real-writers.com
Website www.real-writers.com

Correspondence service with personal tuition from working writers. Also runs an annual short story competition. Send s.a.e. for details.

Swanwick – The Writers' Summer School

The Hayes Conference Centre, Swanwick
Email jean.sutton@lineone.net

Secretary *Jean Sutton*

A six-day Summer School of informal talks, discussion groups, panels and competitions. All levels welcome. Held mid-August from Saturday to Friday morning. Cost (2003) £250 all inclusive. S.a.e. to the secretary at 10 Stag Road, Lake Sandown, Isle of Wight PO36 8PE (01983 406759).

University of Derby

Student Information Centre, Kedleston Road, Derby DE22 1GB
☎01332 622236 Fax 01332 622754
Email J.Bains@derby.ac.uk (for prospectuses only)
Website www.derby.ac.uk

Contact *Graham Parker*

With upwards of 300 students, *Creative Writing* runs 21 modules as part of the undergraduate degree programme including *Poetry; Playwriting; The Short Story; Journalism; Writing for Children*. The courses are all led by practising writers.

Devon

Arvon Foundation (Devon)
See entry under Greater London

Dartington College of Arts
Totnes, Devon TQ9 6EJ
☎01803 862224 Fax 01803 861666
Email registry@dartington.ac.uk
Website www.dartington.ac.uk

BA(Hons) course in *Performance Writing*: exploratory approach to writing as it relates to performance. The course is part of a performance arts programme which encourages interdisciplinary work with arts management, music, theatre and visual performance. Also covered are digital media and emerging art forms. Contact Subject Director, Performance Writing: *Rick Allsopp*.

Exeter Phoenix
Bradninch Place, Gandy Street, Exeter, Devon EX4 3LS
☎01392 667080 Fax 01392 667599
Website www.exeterphoenix.org.uk

Regular literature events, focusing on readings by living poets and other writers, often linked to wider performance programmes including the annual tEXt festival in May. Tutors in a wide range of writing skills run classes and workshops, listed in the brochure of Phoenix activities.

Fire in the Head Creative Writing Programme
PO Box 17, Yelverton, Devon PL20 9YF
☎01822 841081
Email roselleangwin@internet-today.co.uk
Website www.fire-in-the-head.co.uk
Contact *Roselle Angwin*

Imaginative and comprehensive year-round writing programme in poetry, fiction (short and novel-writing), reflective writing and creative development. Roselle Angwin, director and tutor, is a poet and author whose courses have been featured in *The Guardian* and *The Sunday Times*. Also available is an editorial consultancy.

University of Exeter
Exeter, Devon EX4 4QW
☎01392 264580 Fax 01392 264594
Email drama@ex.ac.uk
Website www.ex.ac.uk/drama

Contact *The Secretary* (Drama Department, Thornlea, New North Road, Exeter EX4 4LA)

BA(Hons) in Drama with a third-year option in *Playwriting*. MA in *Theatre Practice* with playwriting pathway. MPhil and PhD in *Performance Practice* (including *Playwriting*).

Dorset

Bournemouth University
Bournemouth Media School, Poole House, Talbot Campus, Fern Barrow, Poole, BH12 5BB
☎01202 595553 Fax 01202 595530
Contact *Katrina King, Programme Administrator*

Three-year, full-time BA(Hons) course in *Scriptwriting for Film and Television*.

Essex

National Council for the Training of Journalists
Latton Bush Centre, Southern Way, Harlow, Essex CM18 7BL
☎01279 430009 Fax 01279 438008
Email info@nctj.com
Website www.nctj.com

For details of journalism courses, both full-time and via distance learning, please send a large s.a.e. or visit the website.

Writing Life
PO Box 4065, Braintree, Essex CM7 9RJ
☎01376 343759
Email writing@talk21.com
Website www.creativewritinglife.co.uk
Contact *Mrs Bernie Ross*

Home study course. Postal and e-mail tuition in *Creative Writing*, from anywhere in the world. Fiction speciality: one-off critiques and on-going mentoring.

Gloucestershire

Chrysalis – The Poet In You with Jay Ramsay, BA Hons (Oxon), PGDip
5 Oxford Terrace, Uplands, Stroud, Gloucestershire GL5 1TW
☎01453 759436/020 7794 8880
Email ramsay@chrysalis37.fsnet.co.uk

Offers postal courses, workshops (including 'The Sacred Space of the Word'), one-to-one editing sessions with the option of accredited individual therapy. The Chrysalis course itself consists of Part 1, 'for those who feel drawn to reading more poetry as well as wanting to start to write their own', and Part 2, 'a more in-depth course designed for those who are already writing and who want to go more deeply into its process and technique'. Editing and information about publication also provided. More information from the address above.

Wye Valley Arts Centre

The Coach House, Mork, St Briavel's, Lydney, Gloucestershire GL15 6QH
☎01594 530214/01291 689463
Fax 01594 530321
Email wyeart@cwcom.net
Website www.wyeart.cwc.net

Residential courses (Monday to Friday) – held at The Coach House near Tintern Abbey – include *Creative Writing* and *Fiction Workshop*. 'All styles and abilities. Companions and other guests not taking the courses are welcome.'

Hampshire

Annual Writers' Conference Winchester

'Chinook', Southdown Road, Winchester, Hampshire SO21 2BY
☎01962 712307
Email WriterConf@aol.com
Website www.gmp.co.uk/writers/conference *and* www.awc-workshops.ndo.co.uk
Conference Director *Barbara Large*

26–28 June 2004. This Festival of Writing, now in its 23rd year, attracts international authors, playwrights, poets, agents and editors who give workshops, mini courses, editor appointments, lectures and seminars to help writers harness their creativity and develop their writing, editing and marketing skills. Fifteen writing competitions are attached to the conference. All first-place winners are published in *The Best of* series annually. The Bookfair offers delegates a wide choice of exhibits including Internet author services, publishers, booksellers, printers and trade associations. See also **Pitstop Refuelling Writers' Weekend Workshops**.

Annual Writers' Weekend Conference

F * F Productions, Carlton House, Binstead Road, Ryde, Isle of Wight PO33 3RD

☎01983 612272 Fax 01983 612272
Email felicityfair@clara.co.uk
Website www.writeplot.co.uk
Contact *Felicity Fair Thompson*

Highbury College, Portsmouth

Dovercourt Road, Cosham, Portsmouth, Hampshire PO6 2SA
☎023 9238 3131 Fax 023 9237 8382
Website www.highbury.ac.uk
Contact *Secretary* (☎023 9231 3287)

The 20-week fast-track courses include: *Pre-entry Magazine Journalism*, *Pre-entry Newspaper Journalism* and a Postgraduate Diploma in *Broadcasting Journalism* run under the auspices of the Periodicals Training Council, the National Council for Training of Journalists and the Broadcast Journalism Training Council respectively.

King Alfred's College

Winchester, Hampshire SO22 4NR
☎01962 841515 Fax 01962 842280
Website www.kingalfreds.ac.uk

Three-year degree course in *Drama, Theatre and Television Studies*, including *Writing for Devised Community Theatre* and *Writing for Television Documentary*. Contact the Admissions Office (☎01962 827262).

MA course in *Theatre for Development* – one year, full-time course with major project overseas or in the UK. MA course in *Writing for Children* available on either a one- or two-year basis. Enquiries: Admissions Officer (☎01962 827235).

University of Southampton New College

The Avenue, Southampton SO17 1BG
☎023 8059 7261 Fax 023 8059 7271
Email vah@soton.ac.uk

Creative writing courses and writers' workshops. Courses are held in local/regional centres.

Hertfordshire

Liberato Breakaway Writing Courses

9 Bishop's Avenue, Bishop's Stortford, Hertfordshire CM23 3EJ
☎01279 833690
Email Liberato@tesco.net
Website www.liberato.co.uk

Contact *Maureen Blundell*

Offers day, weekend and week-long courses to beginner fiction writers from March–November. Day and week courses on poetry and fiction in the Gibberd Garden, Old Henlow, Essex in association with Barbara Wood-Kaczmar and an Arts in Essex grant. Adults and children welcome. Weekend courses on all aspects of fiction writing held at Polstead in Suffolk or Hertford. Five-day fiction and poetry course at Leiston, Suffolk in September. Also offers postal manuscript critiques on all fiction/autobiography.

West Herts College

Creative Industries, Hempstead Road, Watford, Hertfordshire WD17 3EZ
☎01923 812654
Email gaym@westherts.ac.uk
Contact *Admissions*

The college offers a postgraduate diploma in *Publishing*.

Kent

North West Kent College

Oakfield Lane, Dartford, Kent DA1 2JT
☎01322 629436 Fax 01322 629468
Website www.nwkent.ac.uk
Contact *Neil Nixon, Head of Media School*

Two-year, full-time course that explores writing from a number of angles, teaching essential skills, market and academic aspects of the subject. Successful students progress to work or the University of Greenwich, the latter option allowing them to gain a BA(Hons) in Human-ities from a further year of study. Staff include scriptwriters, novelists and a book publisher. Students compile a portfolio in the final year.

University of Kent at Canterbury

Unit for Regional Learning, Keynes College, Canterbury, Kent CT2 7NP
☎01227 827973 Fax 01227 458745
Email part-time@ukc.ac.uk
Website www.ukc.ac.uk/url

Certificate courses in *Practical Writing* and *Imaginative Writing*. Also combined studies – *English and Creative Writing*.

Lancashire

Alston Hall College

Alston Lane, Longridge, Preston, PR3 3BP
☎01772 784661 Fax 01772 785835
Email alston.hall@ed.lancscc.gov.uk
Website www.alstonhall.u-net.com

Holds regular day and residential Creative Writing workshops. Full colour brochure available.

Edge Hill College of Higher Education

St Helen's Road, Ormskirk, L39 4QP
☎01695 575171
Email shepparr@edgehill.ac.uk

Contact *Dr R. Sheppard*

Offers a two-year, part-time MA in *Writing Studies*. Combines advanced-level writers' workshops with closely related courses in the poetics of writing and contemporary writing in English. There is also provision for MPhil and PhD-level research in writing and poetics. Undergraduate creative writing modules in poetry and fiction are available.

Lancaster University

Department of Creative Writing, Lonsdale College, Bailrigg, Lancaster LA1 4YN
☎01524 594169 Fax 01524 843934
Email l.kellett@lancaster.ac.uk

Contact *Lyn Kellett*

Offers practical graduate and undergraduate courses in writing fiction, poetry and scripts. All based on group workshops – students' work-in-progress is circulated and discussed. Distance learning MA now available. Graduates include Andrew Miller, Justin Hill, Alison MacLeod.

Leicestershire

Leicester Adult Education College, Writing School

2 Wellington Street, Leicester LE1 6HL
☎0116 233 4343 Fax 0116 233 4344
Email um1@leicester-adult-ed.ac.uk
Website www.leicester-adult-ed.ac.uk

Contact *Valerie Moore*

Offers a wide range of part time creative writing and journalism courses throughout the year. The programme offers a mix of critical workshops, one-day courses and short craft modules. Supports writers through to publication and has strong links with local media.

Greater London

Arvon Foundation

National Administration: 2nd Floor, 42A Buckingham Palace Road, London SW1W 0RE
☎020 7931 7611 Fax 020 7963 0961
Website www.arvonfoundation.org
Joint Presidents *Terry Hands and Sir Robin Chichester-Clark*

Devon: Totleigh Barton, Sheepwash, Beaworthy, Devon EX21 5NS
☎01409 231338   Fax 01409 231144
Email t-barton@arvonfoundation.org

Yorkshire: Lumb Bank, Heptonstall, Hebden Bridge, West Yorkshire HX7 6DF
☎01422 843714 Fax 01422 843714
Email l-bank@arvonfoundation.org

Invernesshire: Moniack Mhor, Teavarran, Kiltarlity, Beauly, Invernesshire IV4 7HT
☎01463 741675
Email m-mhor@arvonfoundation.org

Shropshire: The Hurst, Clunton, Craven Arms, Shropshire SY7 0JA
☎01588 640658 Fax 01588 640509
Email hurst@arvonfoundation.org

Chairman *Prue Skene, CBE*
National Director *Helen Chaloner*

Founded 1968. Offers people of any age (over 16) and any background the opportunity to live and work with professional writers. Four-and-a-half-day residential courses are held throughout the year at Arvon's four centres, covering poetry, fiction, drama, writing for children, songwriting and the performing arts. Bursaries towards course fees are available for those on low incomes. Runs a biennial poetry competition (see entry under **Prizes**).

Blaze the Trail

2nd Floor, 241 High Street, London E17 7BH
☎020 8520 4569 Fax 020 8520 2358
Email training@coralmedia.co.uk
Website www.blaze-the-trail.com
Contact *Course Administrator*

Offers vocational training including *Script Development*; *Production Management and Research 4 Media* for all levels. Writers, readers, script editors, researchers and production managers acquire broadcast training in television and film screenwriting and production. Works with broadcasters such as the BBC and Channel Four. Coupled with support from Skillset, the company is continually evolving with the film and television industry. *Blaze the Trail* helps develop tailor-made courses for corporate clients. Please call Course Administrator or see our website for full details.

The Central School of Speech and Drama

Embassy Theatre, Eton Avenue, London NW3 3HY
☎020 7722 8183 Fax 020 7722 4132
Email n.wood@cssd.ac.uk
Contact *Nick Wood, Writing and Dramaturgy Tutor*

MA in *Advanced Theatre Practice*. One-year, full-time course aimed at providing a grounding in principal areas of professional theatre practice – *Writing, Dramaturgy, Directing, Performance, Puppetry* and *Design*, with an emphasis on collaboration between the various strands. Prospectus available. Nick Wood is also editor of the Dramaturgy Forum website www.dramforum.net.

The City Literary Institute

Humanities Dept, Stukeley Street, London WC2B 5LJ
☎020 7430 0542 Fax 020 7405 3347
Email humanities@citylit.ac.uk

The Writing School offers a wide range of courses from *Ways Into Creative Writing* and *Writing for Children* to *Playwriting* and *Writing Short Stories*. Various lengths of course available. The Department offers information and advice during term time.

City University

Department of Continuing Education, Northampton Square, London EC1V 0HB
☎020 7040 5060
Email conted@city.ac.uk
Website www.city.ac.uk/conted/cfa.htm

Courses for Adults evening programme includes the three term *Certificate in Novel Writing*; *Novel Writing and Longer Works*; *Towards Publication*; *Writing Crime Fiction*; *Writing for Children*; and *Writing Television Drama*.

The Complete Creative Writing Course at the Groucho Club

☎020 7249 3711 Fax 020 7683 8141
Email maggie.h@blueyonder.co.uk

Website www.creative-writing.pwp.
blueyonder.co.uk

Contact *Maggie Hamand*

Courses of ten two-hour sessions held at the Groucho Club in London's Soho, starting in January, April and September, Monday or Saturday afternoons, 2.30 pm – 4.30 pm. Beginners and advanced courses offered. Courses include stimulating exercises, discussions and weekly homework. The tutors are novelists Maggie Hamand and Henrietta Seredy. £195 for whole course.

The Drill Hall

16 Chenies Street, London WC1E 7EX
☎020 7307 5061 Fax 020 7307 5062
Email admin@drillhall.co.uk

Holds a number of writing classes and workshops. Regular tutors include Carol Burns and Peter Carty.

London College of Printing

Elephant & Castle, London SE1 6SB
☎020 7514 6562
Website www.lcptraining.co.uk

Intensive courses in journalism. Short courses run by DALI (Developments at the London Institute) at the above address include: *News Writing*; *Feature Writing*; *Sub-editing*; *Interviewing Techniques*. Also offers five-day specialist journalism courses in newswriting, subediting, print journalism, radio journalism and online journalism plus a three-week course in broadcast TV journalism. In addition, Effective Copywriting, Effective Writing Techniques for Public Relations and Handling the Media Successfully. For individuals and companies 'tailor-made training' services can be provided. Prospectus and information leaflets available; telephone 020 7514 6770 or access the website to book.

London School of Journalism

22 Upbrook Mews, London W2 3HG
☎020 7706 3790 Fax 020 7706 3780
Email info@lsjournalism.com
Website www.home-study.com

Contact *Student Administration Office*

Distance learning courses with an individual and personal approach. Options include: Short Story Writing; *Writing for Children*; *Freelance Journalism*; *Media Law*; *Cartooning*; *Thriller Writing*. Fees vary but range from £295 for *Enjoying English Literature* to £395 for

Journalism and Newswriting. NUJ-recognised Postgraduate Diploma Courses, taught in London (three month full-time, six month part-time, nine month evening classes).

Middlesex University

School of Humanities, White Hart Lane, London N17 8HR
☎020 8411 5000 Fax 020 8411 6652
Email tmadmissions@mdx.ac.uk
Website www.mdx.ac.uk

The UK's longest established writing degree offers a Single or Joint Honours programme in *Creative and Media Writing* (full- or part-time). This modular programme gives an opportunity to explore journalism, poetry, prose fiction and dramatic writing for a wide range of genres and audiences. Option for work experience in media and publishing. Contact Admissions or *Maggie Butt*, Programme Leader. (E-mail m.butt@mdx.ac.uk)

MA in *Writing* (full-time, part-time; day and evening classes) includes writing workshops; critical seminars on the short story and novel; lectures and workshops from established writers; introduction to agents and publishers. Options in Poetry and Scriptwriting are awaiting validation. Contact *Sue Gee*. Tel 020 8411 5941. (E-mail s.gee@mdx.ac.uk)

PMA Training

The PMA Centre for Media Excellence, 10 Cynthia Street, London N1 9JF
☎020 7278 0606
Email training@pma-group.com
Website www.pma-group.com

One-/two-/three-day editorial, PR, design and publishing courses held in central London. High-powered, intensive courses run by Fleet Street journalists and magazine editors. Courses include: *News-Writing*; *Feature Writing*; *Investigative Reporting*. Fees range from £170 to £750 plus VAT. Special rates for freelancers.

Soho Theatre Company

See entry under **Theatre Producers**

University of Surrey Roehampton

School of Arts, Roehampton Lane, London SW15 5PU
☎020 8392 3230 Fax 020 8392 3289
Website www.roehampton.ac.uk

Three-year BA(Hons) programmes in *Drama and Theatre Studies* and *Film and Television Studies* include courses on writing for stage and screen.

University of Westminster

School of Communication and Creative
Industries, Harrow Campus, Watford Road,
Harrow, Middlesex HA1 3TP
☎020 7911 5903 Fax 020 7911 5955
Email harrow-admissions@wmin.ac.uk
Website www.wmin.ac.uk

Courses include part-time MAs available in
Journalism Studies; *Film and Television Studies*.

Greater Manchester

Manchester Metropolitan University – The Writing School

Department of English, Geoffrey Manton
Building, Rosamond Street West, off Oxford
Road, Manchester M15 6LL
☎0161 247 1732/1 Fax 0161 247 6345
Email m.schmidt@mmu.ac.uk
Course Convenor *Michael Schmidt*

Closely associated with **Carcanet Press Ltd**
and *PN Review*, The Writing School offers
four 'routes' for students to follow: *Poetry,
The Novel, Life Writing* and *Writing for
Children*. Regular readings, lectures, workshops and masterclasses by industry representatives. Tutors include Simon Armitage,
Carol Ann Duffy, Sophie Hannah and Jeffrey
Wainwright.

Password Training Ltd

23 New Mount Street, Manchester M4 4DE
☎0161 953 4071 Fax 0161 953 4001

Password Training provides training for pub-
lishers, writers' groups and individual writers in
Internet publishing, planning, production,
design, marketing, costing and distribution.
Clients have included The Arts Council,
Regional Arts Boards and the Yorkshire Art
Circus.

University of Manchester

Department of English & American Studies,
Arts Building, Oxford Road, Manchester M13
9PL
☎0161 275 3144 Fax 0161 275 3256
Email englishpg@man.ac.uk
Website www.art.man.ac.uk/english/
   pgdegree/ma.htm#novel
Course Director *Suzannah Dunn*

Offers a one-year MA in *Novel Writing*.

University of Salford

Postgraduate Admissions, Dept. of Arts, Media
& Social Sciences, Adelphi Building, Peru
Street, Salford, Greater Manchester M3 6EQ
☎0161 295 6027
Email r.humphrey@salford.ac.uk
Website www.smmp.salford.ac.uk

MA in *Television and Radio Scriptwriting*. Two-
year, part-time course taught by professional
writers and producers. Also offers masterclasses
with leading figures in industry.

The Writers Bureau

Sevendale House, 7 Dale Street, Manchester
M1 1JB
☎0161 228 2362 Fax 0161 236 9440
Email studentservices@writersbureau.com
Website www.writersbureau.com

Comprehensive home-study writing course
with personal tuition service from professional
writers. Fiction, non-fiction, articles, short stories, novels, TV, radio and drama all covered in
detail. Trial period, guarantee and no time limits. ODLQC accredited. Quote Ref. EH04.
Free enquiry line: 0800 856 2008

The Writers Bureau College of Journalism

Address etc. as The Writers Bureau above

Home-study course covering all aspects of
journalism. Real-life assignments assessed by
qualified tutors with the emphasis on getting
into print. Comprises 28 modules and three
handbooks with special introductory offers.
Ref: EHJ04. Free enquiry line: 0800 298 7008.

The Writers College

Address etc. as The Writers Bureau above

The Art of Writing Poetry course from The
Writers Bureau's sister college. A home-study
course with a more 'recreational' emphasis.
The 60,000-word course has 17 modules and
lets you complete six written assignments for
tutorial evaluation. Fees: £99. Quote Ref.
EHP04. Free enquiry line: 0800 856 2008.

The Writer's Muse

5 Churchdale Road, Higher Blackley,
Manchester M9 8NE
☎0161 720 9307
Secretary *Wendy Adeforoye*

Offers courses designed to meet aspiring writers' individual needs. Twelve assignments
marked by qualified teachers/freelance writers

(no poetry). £60 p.a. Certificate of participation. Also offers evaluation service £50 per manuscript. Send A4 s.a.e. for full details.

Merseyside

University of Liverpool

Centre for Continuing Education, 19 Abercromby Square, Liverpool L69 7ZG
☎0151 794 6900/6952 (24 hours)
Fax 0151 794 2544
Website www.liv.ac.uk/conted
Head of Creative Arts *Keith Birch*

Courses include: *Introduction to Creative Writing*; *The Short Story and the Novel*; *Introduction to Writing Poetry*; *Introduction to Scripting for Radio and Television*; *Science Fiction and Fantasy*; *Songwriting*; *Theatre Playwrights Workshop*. Most courses are run in the evening over 10 or 20 weeks but there are some linked Saturday and weekday courses on offer. Students have the option of accreditation towards a university award in Creative Writing. Some of the above courses are also part of the university's part-time Flexible Degree pathway (Comb. Hons., Arts). No pre-entry qualifications required. Fees vary with concessions for the unwaged and those in receipt of benefit.

Northamptonshire

Knuston Hall Residential College for Adult Education

Irchester, Wellingborough, NN29 7EU
☎01933 312104
Email enquiries@knustonhall.org.uk
Website www.knustonhall.org.uk

Writing courses being held in 2003 include: *Reminiscence Writing*; *Writing Poems and Stories*.

Norfolk

University of East Anglia

School of English & American Studies, Norwich, Norfolk NR4 7TJ
☎01603 593262 Fax 01603 593799
Email pheas@uea.ac.uk
Website www.uea.ac.uk/eas
Contact *Kerry Duinford, Postgraduate Admissions*

UEA has a history of concern with contemporary literary culture. Among its MA programmes is one in *Creative Writing*, Stream 1: Prose Fiction; Stream 2: Poetry; Stream 3: Scriptwriting.

Nottinghamshire

The Nottingham Trent University

Humanities Faculty Office (Post Graduate Studies), Clifton Lane, Nottingham NG11 8NS
☎0115 848 6677 Fax 0115 848 6632
Email hum.postgrad@ntu.ac.uk
Website www.human.ntu.ac.uk/writing

MA in *Writing*. Hands-on and workshop-based, the course concentrates primarily on the practice and production of writing. A choice of options from *Fiction*, *Poetry*, *Creative Non-Fiction*, *New Media Writing*, *Children's Writing* and *Scriptwriting*. Assignments and a dissertation, but no formal exams. Staff are all established writers. Also a full programme of visiting speakers. Study either full-time (three evenings per week) or part-time (two evenings per week over two years). Write for further details.

Oxfordshire

University of Oxford Department for Continuing Education

Rewley House, 1 Wellington Square, Oxford OX1 2JA
☎01865 280356 Fax 01865 270309
Website www.conted.ox.ac.uk

Creative writing schools are held during the autumn, spring and summer terms. Courses for 2003/4 are: *Writing Short Stories*, *Writing a Novel*, *The Art of Memory*. Each course is a series of three-day schools with student numbers limited to 20. Early booking is advised. A two year part-time Diploma in Creative Writing is also offered, beginning in October each year.

Shropshire

Arvon Foundation (Shropshire)

See entry under Greater London

Somerset

Ammerdown Centre

The Ammerdown Conference and Retreat Centre, Radstock, Bath BA3 5SW
☎01761 433709 Fax 01761 433094
Email centre@ammerdown.org
Website www.ammerdown.org

Courses held in 2003 included a weekend on *Creative Writing* and a five-day creative writing course. Residential facilities. Brochure available or full details on our website.

Bath Spa University College
Newton Park, Bath BA2 9BN
☎01225 875875 Fax 01225 875444
Email enquiries@bathspa.ac.uk
Website www.bathspa.ac.uk
Admissions Officer *Clare Brandram Jones*

Postgraduate Diploma/MA in *Creative Writing*. A course for creative writers wanting to develop their work taught by published writers. In recent years, several students from this course have received contracts from publishers for novels, awards for poetry and short stories and have had work produced on BBC Radio.

Dillington House
Ilminster, Somerset TA19 9DT
☎01460 52427/Minicom: 01460 258640
Fax 01460 52433
Email dillington@somerset.gov.uk
Website www.dillington.co.uk
Contact *Christine Jacobs*

Offers a range of day schools, residential weekends and a summer school in a variety of writing subjects and literary appreciation. Courses in 2003/4 include *Write On!* (creative writing); *Writing From Experience*; *Writing the Commercial Short Story*; *Creating Fiction Week-end*; *Travel Writing Weekend*. Full details of programme available in free brochure and on the website.

Institute of Copywriting
Honeycombe House, Bagley, Wedmore, Somerset BS28 4TD
☎01934 713563 Fax 01934 713492
Email copy@inst.org
Website www.institute.org/copy

Comprehensive copywriting home-study course including advice on becoming a self-employed copywriter. Each student has a personal tutor who is an experienced copywriter and who provides detailed feedback on the student's assignments.

University of Bristol
Department of English, 3/5 Woodland Road, Bristol BS8 1TB
☎0117 954 6969 Fax 0117 928 8860
Email rowena.fowler@bris.ac.uk
Website www.bris.ac.uk/Depts/English/ce_creat.html

A variety of courses open to the general public including *Women and Writing*, for women who write or would like to begin to write (poetry, fiction, non-fiction, journals). Also offers a *Diploma in Creative Writing*. Detailed brochure available.

Staffordshire
Keele University
The Centre for Continuing and Professional Education, Keele University, (Freepost ST1666), Newcastle under Lyme, Staffordshire ST5 5BG
☎01782 583436

Evening and weekend courses on literature and creative writing. The 2003/4 programme includes courses on novel writing, writing for magazines, writers workshops and poetry writing.

Surrey
Guildford Institute
Guildford Institute of the University of Surrey, Ward Street, Guildford, Surrey GU1 4LH
☎01483 562142 Fax 01483 451034
Email gi-reception@surrey.ac.uk
Website www.surrey.ac.uk/education

Several of the **University of Surrey's** *Creative Writing* courses take place at the Guildford Institute. The courses carry credits at Higher Education Level 1 (first-year undergraduate level). For details contact the Institute (details above), or *Dr Christopher Joyce*, Subject Leader for Creative Writing and Literature, at the University (01483 683122 – c.joyce@surrey.ac.uk).

Royal Holloway
University of London, Department of Drama and Theatre, Egham Hill, Egham, Surrey TW20 0EX
☎01784 443922 Fax 01784 431018
Email drama@rhul.ac.uk
Contacts *Dan Rebellato, David Wiles*

Three-year BA course in *Theatre Studies* with a playwriting option in the second or third year. MA *Theatre (Playwriting)*, a one- or two-year (full- or part-time) postgraduate degree. A new three-year BA course in *Drama and Creative Writing* is expected to be available from September 2004, as is a new three-year BA course in *English and Creative Writing*.

University of Surrey
Adult and Continuing Education, University of Surrey, Guildford, Surrey GU2 7XH
☎01483 683151 Fax 01483 686191
Email ace@surrey.ac.uk
Website www.surrey.ac.uk

The Open Studies programme includes several *Creative Writing* courses. For autumn 2003 these will be held at the **Guildford Institute**, Caterham and Reigate. The courses carry credits and can build to a university award. For details, contact Beryl Northam, Courses Secretary or *Dr Christopher Joyce*, Subject Leader in Creative Writing.

Sussex

The Earnley Concourse

Earnley, Chichester, West Sussex PO20 7JL
☎01243 670392   Fax 01243 670832
Email info@earnley.co.uk
Website www.earnley.co.uk

Offers a range of residential and non-residential courses throughout the year. Previous programme has included *Writing for Publication; You Can Sell What You Write*. Brochure available.

University College Chichester

Bishop Otter Campus, College Lane,
Chichester, West Sussex PO19 4PE
☎01243 816000   Fax 01243 816080
Email s.norgate@ucc.ac.uk

Contact *Stephanie Norgate*, Route Leader, MA in Creative Writing (01243 816296)

Postgraduate Certificate/Diploma/MA in *Creative Writing*, both full- and part-time.

University of Sussex

Centre for Continuing Education, Education Development Building, Falmer, Brighton, East Sussex BN1 9RG
☎01273 678537   Fax 01273 678848
Email y.d.barnes@sussex.ac.uk
Website www.sussex.ac.uk

Contact (for all courses) *Yvonne Barnes*

Postgraduate Diploma in *Dramatic Writing*: the student is treated as a commissioned writer working in theatre, TV, radio or film with professional directors and actors. Includes workshops, masterclasses and a residential weekend. Sixteen-months, part-time. Proposed expansion to two-year M.A. from 2003. Convenor: *Richard Crane*. Certificate in *Creative Writing*: short fiction, novel and poetry for imaginative writers. Two-year, part-time. Convenors: *Richard Crane, Mark Slater*.

Tyne & Wear

University of Newcastle upon Tyne

Centre for Lifelong Learning, Joseph Cowen House, Newcastle upon Tyne NE1 7RU
☎0191 222 5680   Fax 0191 222 7090
Website www.cll.ncl.ac.uk

Courses held have included: *Creative Writing: Fictionalising the Family* and *Writing From the Inside Out*, a workshop for women. Contact the Secretary, Adult Education Programme.

West Midlands

National Academy of Writing

Calthorpe House, 30 Hagley Road,
Edgbaston, Birmingham B16 8QY
Email info@writingacademy.org
Website www.writingacademy.org

The National Academy of Writing is a new teaching institution designed to nurture and promote writing talent for the creative industries: publishing, journalism, theatre, film, radio and television. Summer 2003 courses were in prose narrative, adaptation and advanced screenwriting. Admission is based on a demonstrable talent, and the student's commitment to a writing career is axiomatic. Tuition is augmented by regular public events and masterclasses given by our patrons. The 'Adventures in the Writing Trade' series introduces top writers to young audiences and new writers and encourages them to consider a writing career. The Academy also develops interactive schools events with high-profile writers. Access the website for full details of future courses.

University of Birmingham

School of Education, Selly Oak, Birmingham B29 6LL
☎00121 414 3413 Fax 0121 414 8067
Email S.G.Roseten@bham.ac.uk

Certificate of Higher Education in *Creative Writing* – two years, part-time in Birmingham and Worcester. Classes in theory and practice of writing in a wide range of literary genres. Course brochures are available from the above address. Progression routes to Diploma and Degree. Students who can demonstrate qualifications / writing skills equivalent to Certificate Level may apply to join the Diploma of Creative Writing. Additional courses at the Selly Oak Campus and in Worcestershire.

The University also offers an Mphil in *Playwriting Studies*. Contact *April Di Angelis*,

Course Director at the Department of Drama and Theatre Arts (☎0121 414 5790).

University of Warwick

Open Studies, Continuing Education Department, Coventry, CV4 7AL
☎024 7652 8286
Email k.rainsley@warwick.ac.uk or l.downs@warwick.ac.uk

Creative writing courses held at the university or in regional centres include: *Starting to Write*; *Prose and Poetry Writing*; *Screenwriting for Beginners*. A one-year certificate in *Creative Writing* is available.

Wiltshire

Marlborough College Summer School

Marlborough, Wiltshire SN8 1PA
☎01672 892388/9 Fax 01672 892476
Email admin@mcsummerschool.org.uk
Website www.mcsummerschool.org.uk

Summer School with literature and creative writing included in its programme. Caters for residential and day students. Brochure available giving full details and prices.

Urchfont Manor College

Urchfont, Devizes, Wiltshire SN10 4RG
☎01380 840495 Fax 01380 840005

Short courses – days, residential weeks and weekends offered in a varied programme which includes literature and creative writing. 'Beautiful location; historic environment; delicious home cooking'. Send for a brochure.

Yorkshire

Hull College

Queen's Gardens, Hull, East Yorkshire HU1 3DG
☎01482 329943 Fax 598733219079
Email jbillaney@hull-college.ac.uk
Contact *Daphne Glazer*

Offers part-time day/evening writing courses in *Novel Writing* and *Short Story Writing*, at Hull College, Park Street Centre. Courses begin each academic term. Writers are encouraged to contribute stories for a collection.

Leeds Metropolitan University

H505, City Site, Calverley Street, Leeds, West Yorkshire LS1 3HE
☎0113 283 2600 ext 3330
Email r.hibbert@lmu.ac.uk
Website www.lmu.ac.uk
Administrator *Richard Hibbert*

Offers a Postgraduate Certificate / Diploma / MA in *Screenwriting (Fiction)*.

Open College of the Arts

Unit 1B, Redbrook Business Park, Wilthorpe Road, Barnsley, South Yorkshire S75 1JN
☎01226 730495 Fax 01226 730838
Email open.arts@ukonline.co.uk
Website www.oca-uk.com

The OCA correspondence course, *Starting to Write*, offers help and stimulus from experienced writers/tutors. Emphasis is on personal development rather than commercial genre. Also offers specialist poetry, fiction and autobiographical writing courses. Accredited by the University of Glamorgan. Prospectus and Guide to Courses available on request.

Sheffield Hallam University

School of Cultural Studies, Sheffield Hallam University, Collegiate Crescent, Sheffield S10 2BP
☎0114 225 2607 Fax 0114 225 2603
Email cspgenquiry@shu.ac.uk
Website www.shu.ac.uk/schools/cs/english/english.htm

Offers MA in *Creative Writing* (one-year, full-time; also part-time).

University of Hull

Scarborough Campus, Filey Road, Scarborough, North Yorkshire YO11 3AZ
☎01723 362392 Fax 01723 370815
Website www.hull.ac.uk
Director of Studies *David Hughes*

BA Single Honours in Theatre Studies. Works closely with the Stephen Joseph Theatre and its artistic director Alan Ayckbourn. The theatre sustains a policy for staging new writers. (See entry under **Theatre Producers**.) The campus hosts the annual National Student Drama Festival which includes the International Student Playscript Competition (details from The National Information Centre for Student Drama; E-mail nsdf@hull.ac.uk).

University of Leeds

Springfield Mount, Leeds, LS2 9JT
Email r.k.o'rourke@leeds.ac.uk

Contact *Rebecca O'Rourke*

Also at: Adult Education Centre, 37 Harrow
Road, Middlesborough, Cleveland, TS5 5NT
☎01642 814987

Creative writing courses held throughout
Cleveland, North and West Yorkshire in the
autumn, spring and summer terms. These are
held weekly and as non-residential summer
schools. Courses carrying undergraduate credit
are part-time and are in a range of subjects, at
all levels. Also offered are post-graduate professional development courses for writers.

University of Leeds, Bretton Hall Campus

School of Performance and Cultural
Industries, Bretton Hall Campus, West
Bretton, Wakefield, West Yorkshire WF4
4LG
☎0113 343 9070 or 0113 343 9022
Email rbwatson@leeds.ac.uk

Contact *Rob Watson* or *Secretary Linda Smith*
at pculs@leeds.ac.uk

Offers one-year full-time/two-year part-time
MA course in *Creative Writing* designed for
competent though not necessarily published
writers. Also offers a three-year *Creative Writing*
BA (details from *Simon Ross* s.j.ross@leeds.
ac.uk).

University of Sheffield

Institute for Lifelong Learning, 196–198 West
Street, Sheffield S1 4ET
☎0114 222 7000 Fax 0114 222 7001
Website www.shef.ac.uk/till

Certificate in *Creative Writing* (Degree Level 1)
and a wide range of courses, from foundation
level to specialist writing areas, open to all.
Courses in poetry, prose, journalism,
scriptwriting, comedy, travel writing, writing
using ICT/Web, writing for children.
Brochures and information available from the
address above.

Yorkshire Art Circus

School Lane, Glasshoughton, Castleford
WF10 4QH
☎01977 550401
Email admin@artcircus.org.uk
Website www.artcircus.org.uk

Course Administrator *Lorna Hey*

Offers an annual programme of courses in creative writing, poetry, self-publishing and book
production. Mostly daytime courses. Course
brochures available.

IRELAND

Dingle Writing Courses Ltd

Ballyneanig, Ballyferriter, Tralee, Co. Kerry,
Republic of Ireland
☎00 353 66 9154990 Fax 00 353 66 9154992
Email info@dinglewriting.com
Website www.dinglewriting.com

Directors *Abigail Joffe, Nicholas McLachlan*

A summer and autumn programme of weekend and residential courses for beginners and
experienced writers alike. Tutored by professional writers the courses include poetry, fiction, starting to write and writing for theatre as
well as special themed courses.

Past tutors have included Michael Donaghy,
Paul Durcan, Anne Enright and Jennifer
Johnston. Also organises tailor-made courses
for schools, writers' groups or students on a
Creative Writing programme. **Course Director**
Camilla Dinkel.

Queen's University of Belfast

Institute of Lifelong Learning, Belfast BT7
1NN
☎028 9027 3323 Fax 028 9023 6909
Email ill@qub.ac.uk
Website www.qub.ac.uk/ill

Courses have included *Creative Writing*; *Writing
for Profit and Pleasure*; *Scriptwriting* and *Creative
Writing for Beginners*.

University of Dublin (Trinity College)

Graduate Studies Office, Arts Building,
Trinity College, Dublin 2, Republic of Ireland
☎00 353 1 608 1166 Fax 00 353 1 671 2821
Email gradinfo@tcd.ie
Website www.tcd.ie/owc

Contact *Admissions*

Offers an MPhil *Creative Writing* course. A
one-year, full-time course intended for students who are seriously committed to writing,
or prospective authors.

University of Ulster

Conference & Professional Development
Unit, Room 17C21, University of Ulster,
Belfast BT37 0QB
☎028 9036 5131 Fax 028 9036 6060

Creative writing courses/workshops, usually held in the autumn and spring terms. Concessions available.

SCOTLAND

Arvon Foundation (Invernesshire)
See entry under Greater London

Edinburgh University
Office of Lifelong Learning, 11 Buccleuch Place, Edinburgh EH8 9LW
☎0131 650 4400 Fax 0131 667 6097
Email cce@ed.ac.uk
Website www.cce.ed.ac.uk or www.lifelong.ed.ac.uk

Several writing-orientated courses and summer schools. Course brochure available.

University of Dundee
Continuing Education, Nethergate, Dundee DD1 4HN
☎01382 344128/344809 Fax 01382 221057
Email l.fulton@dundee.ac.uk
Website www.dundee.ac.uk/education

Various creative writing courses held at the University and elsewhere in Dundee, Perthshire and Angus. Detailed course brochure available.

University of Glasgow
Department of Adult and Continuing Education, St Andrews Building, 11 Eldon Street, Glasgow G3 6NH
☎0141 330 4394/1829 (Enquiries/Brochure)
Fax 0141 330 1821
Email enquiry@ace.gla.ac.uk
Website www.gla.ac.uk/Acad/AdultEd

Runs writers' workshops and courses at all levels; all friendly and informal. Tutors are all experienced published writers.

University of St Andrews
School of English, The University, St Andrews, Fife KY16 9AL
☎01334 462666 Fax 01334 462655
Email english@st-andrews.ac.uk
Website www.st-andrews.ac.uk

Offers postgraduate study in *Creative Writing*. Candidates choose two topics from: *Fiction: The Novel*; *Craft and Technique in Poetry* and all take the *Short Story* module. Students submit a dissertation of original writing – prose fiction of 15,000 words or a collection of around 30

short poems. Taught by John Burnside, Kathleen Jamie, A. L. Kennedy and Don Paterson.

7:84 Summer School
See **7:84 Theatre Company Scotland** under **Theatre Producers**

WALES

Tŷ Newydd Writers' Centre
Llanystumdwy, Cricieth, Gwynedd LL52 0LW
☎01766 522811 Fax 01766 523095
Email tynewydd@dial.pipex.com

Residential writers' centre set up by the Taliesin Trust with the support of the **Arts Council of Wales** to encourage and promote writing in both English and Welsh. Weeklong courses with two tutors and a maximum of 16 participants. A wide range of courses for all levels. Early booking essential. Fee: £350 (single)/£335 (shared) inclusive. People on low incomes may be eligible for a grant or bursary. Course leaflet available. (See also **Organisations of Interest to Poets**.)

University of Glamorgan
Treforest, Pontypridd CF37 1DL
☎01443 483598
Website www.glam.ac.uk

Director, The National Centre for Writing *Professor Tony Curtis, FRSL*

MPhil in *Writing* – a two-year part-time Masters degree for writers of fiction and poets. Established 1993. Contact: *Professor Tony Curtis* at the School of Humanities and Social Sciences.
    MA in *Scriptwriting (Theatre, TV or Radio)* – a two-year part-time Masters degree for scriptwriters. Contact: *Dr Richard J. Hand*.
    Also, BA *Creative and Professional Writing* – a three-year course for undergraduates. Contact: *Dr Matthew Francis*.

University of Wales, Aberystwyth
Department of English, Hugh Owen Building, Aberystwyth, Ceredigion SY23 3DY
☎01970 622534 Fax 01970 622530
Website www.aber.ac.uk/~engwww/

BA *English and Creative Writing*, a three-year course taught in part by practising writers, including poet Tiffany Atkinson. Also offers an MA in *Writing* with modules in narratology and poetry, writing and publication

University of Wales, Bangor
Department of English, College Road, Bangor
LL57 2DG
☎01248 382102   Fax 01248 382102
Email els029@bangor.ac.uk
Website www.bangor.ac.uk/ccpa

PhD *Creative and Critical Writing*; *MA Creative Studies* (Creative Writing); *BA English Literature with Creative Writing*; *BA English Language with Creative Writing*; *BA French with Creative Writing*; *BA German with Creative Writing* and new *BA Creative Studies* (pending). Also MA *Creative Studies (Film Practice)*; MA *Creative Studies (Drama Practice)*; MA *Creative Studies (Media Practice)*. The Centre for the Creative and Performing Arts launched the UK national database on creative writing education in universities and colleges and is the location of the research programme, Creative Writing in Universities.

Writers' Holiday at Caerlon
School Bungalow, Church Road,
Pontnewydd, Cwmbran NP44 1AT
☎01633 489438

Email writersholiday@lineone.net
Website www.writersholiday.net
Contact *Anne Hobbs*

Annual six-day conference for writers of all standards held in the summer at the University of Wales' Caerlon Campus. Courses, lectures, concert and excursion all included in the fee. Full board accommodation. Courses have included *Writing Poetry*, *Writing Romantic Fiction* and *Writing for the Radio*.

EUROPE – FRANCE

Creative in Calvados
1 Ormelie Terrace, Joppa, Edinburgh EH15 2EX
☎0131 669 4025
Email steveharvey@creativeincalvados.co.uk
Website www.creativeincalvados.co.uk
Contact *Steve Harvey*

Residential writing courses and retreats, readers' breaks and creative workshops based in an old watermill and outbuildings in a forest valley in Normandy. Friendly and informal courses are tutored by well-known writers. Group numbers are limited to seven per course. Evening meals at excellent local restaurants.

Circles and Workshops

Directory of Writers' Circles
39 Lincoln Way, Harlington, LU5 6NG
☎01525 873197
Email diana@writers-circles.com
Website www.writers-circles.com

Directory of writers' circles in the UK and Republic of Ireland. Contact the editor, *Diana Hayden*, for details.

Writers' Circles Handbook
Oldacre, Horderns Park Road, Chapel-en-le-Frith, High Peak SK23 9SY
☎01298 812305
Website www.btinternet.com/~oldacre

New handbook with a comprehensive list of all known UK circles and groups. Free updates available after initial purchase (£5, post free). Contact *Jill Dick* for further details.

Carmarthen Writers' Circle
Lower Carfab, Tavernspite, Whitland,
Pembrokeshire SA34 0NP
☎01994 240441

Contact *Jenny White*

Founded 1989, the circle meets monthly. All levels and genres welcome.

Chiltern Writers' Group
151 Chartridge Lane, Chesham,
Buckinghamshire HP5 2SE
☎01494 772308
Email chilwriters@netscape.net

Website http://chilternwriters.netfirms.com

Guest speakers and workshops. Monthly meetings, a newsletter and competitions. Annual subscription: £15; concessions: £10. Non-members meeting: £3.

Concordant Poets Folios
17 Stone Close, Braintree, Essex CM7 1LJ
☎01376 342095
Email whogg@onetel.net.uk

An independent postal workshop for poets. Send s.a.e. for details.

The Cotswold Writers' Circle
Bliss's Cottage, Lower Chedworth,
Cheltenham, Gloucestershire GL54 4AN
☎01285 72668
Email elaine@pandelunt.co.uk
Patron *Elizabeth Webster*
Membership *Secretary Elaine Lunt*
Competition Secretary *Mrs Anne Brookes*

Meets Tuesdays in Cirencester. Workshops
with well-known authors and competitions.

Cumbrian Literary Group
'Calgarth', The Brow, Flimby, Maryport,
Cumbria CA15 8TD
☎01900 813444
Acting President *Glyn Matthews*
Secretary *Joyce E. Fisher*

Founded in 1946. Monthly meetings, guest
speakers and competitions. £8 p.a.

'Sean Dorman' Manuscript Society
Cherry Trees, Crosemere Road, Cockshutt,
Ellesmere, Shropshire SY12 0JP
☎01939 270293
Director *Mary Driver*

Founded 1957. Supports aspiring UK writers.
Offers constructive criticism. Send s.a.e for
details. Subscription: £6.50 p.a.

East Anglian Writers
52 Riverside Road, Norwich, NR1 1SR
☎01603 629088 Fax 01603 629088
Email Anthony.Vivis@tesco.net
Contact *Anthony Vivis* (Chair)

A group of local professional writers affiliated
to the **Society of Authors**. Informal pub
meetings and occasional speakers.

Eastbourne's Anderida Writers
20 Vian Avenue, Eastbourne, BN23 6EY
☎01323 737677
Secretary *Stella Freshney*

Creative workshops for Sussex authors. Talks
and competitions. Annual anthology of members' work. Subscription: £15 p.a.

Equinoxe Screenwriting Workshops
Association Equinoxe, 4 Square du Roule
75008, Paris, France
☎00 331 53 53 44 88 Fax: 00 331 53 53 44 89
Email: equinoxe@wanadoo.fr

Contact *Claire Dubert*

Founded 1993, with Jeanne Moreau as chair,
to promote screenwriting, to link European
and American film production and to support
young writers. Open to selected professional
screenwriters with fluent English or French.
To date, Equinoxe has helped 181 authors.

Euroscript
Suffolk House, 1008 Whitfield Place, London
W1P 5SF
☎020 7387 5880 Fax 020 77387 5880
Email euroscript@netmatters.co.uk

Website www.euroscript.co.uk

Offers creative and editorial input to professional writers and producers. Residential script
workshops, script reports, two film story competitions per year.

Gay Authors Workshop
BM Box 5700, London C1N 3XX
☎020 8520 5223
Contact *Kathryn Byrd*

Established 1978. Regular meetings and a
newsletter. GAW gave rise to **Paradise Press**.

Historical Novel Folio
17 Purbeck Heights, Mount Road, Parkstone,
Poole, Dorset BH14 0QP
☎01202 741897
Contact *Doris Myall-Harris*

A postal workshop dealing with any pre-World
War II period. Send s.a.e. for details.

Kops and Ryan Advanced Playwriting Workshops
41B Canfield Gardens, London NW6 3JL
☎020 7624 2940/7263 8740
Tutors *Bernard Kops, Tom Ryan*

Three ten-week terms per year from
September. Small group writing and improvi-
sation workshops. Instruction in film technique
and private tutorials. Call for details.

London Writers' Circle
27 Braycourt Avenue, Walton-on-Thames,
Surrey KT12 2AZ
☎01932 702874
Email wendy@stickler.org.uk
Contact *Wendy Hughes*

Founded 1924. Encourages writers of all grades
in poetry, short story and feature writing.
Monthly meetings, social events and quarterly

magazine. Subscription: £20 (London); £10 (UK); £6 (Overseas).

North West Playwrights (NWP)

18 St Margaret's Chambers, 5 Newton Street, Manchester M1 1HL
☎0161 237 1978 Fax 0161 237 1978
Email newplaysnw@hotmail.com
Website www.newplaysnw.com

Founded 1982. Offers script-reading and classes, disburses grants and publishes *The Lowdown* newsletter. Regional writers only.

Pier Playwrights

PO Box 141, Brighton, East Sussex BN2 1LZ
☎01273 625132
Email: admin@pierplaywrights.co.uk
Website www.pierplaywrights.co.uk

Contact *Chris Taylor*

Run by playwrights for local playwrights. Workshops by visiting professionals and monthly newsletter; Subscription: £15 (Individual); £5 (Unwaged); £30 (Company).

Pitstop Refuelling Writers' Weekend Workshops

'Chinook', Southdown Road, Winchester, Hampshire SO21 2BY
☎01962 712307
Email WriterCon@aol.com
Website www.gmp.co.uk/writers/conference and www.awc-workshops.ndo.co.uk

Director Barbara Large, MBE, FRSA

Small-group writing workshops under professional guidance. 2004 dates are 19-21 March and 22–24 October.

Screenwriters' Workshop

Suffolk House, 1-8 Whitfield Place, London W1T 5JU
☎020 7387 5511
Email screenoffice@tiscali.co.uk
Website www.lsw.org.uk

Established 1983, this educational charity helps writers into the film and TV industries. Membership: £40 p.a. Runs *Feedback* – a script-reading service – contact *R. Wheeler* (e-mail ritaw@tiscali.co.uk).

Scribo

1/31 Hamilton Road, Bournemouth, BH1 4EQ
☎01202 302533

Contact *K. & P. Silvester*

Scribo is a postal workshop for novelists. No annual subscription. Send s.a.e for details.

Short Story Writers' Folio/ Children's Novel Writers' Folio

5 Park Road, Brading, Sandown, PO36 0HU
☎01983 407697
Email dawn.wortley-nott@lineone.net

Contact *Mrs Dawn Wortley-Nott*

Constructive criticism via postal workshops. Send an s.a.e. for further details.

Society of Sussex Authors

Bookends, Lewes Road, Horsted Keynes, Haywards Heath, West Sussex RH17 7DP
☎01825 790755 Fax 01825 790755
Email michael@bookends.claranet.com

Contact *Michael Legat*

Founded 1968. Six meetings per annum in Lewes and social events. Sussex-based published writers only. Subscription: £10 p.a.

South Manchester Writers' Workshop

c/o Didsbury Methodist Church Hall, Sandhurst Road, Didsbury, Manchester M20
☎0161 431 4717
Email philip.caveney@ntlworld.com
Website
    www.manchesterwriters.freeserve.co.uk

Contact *Philip Caveney*

Weekly meetings open to all. Phone or see the website for more details.

Southwest Scriptwriters

☎0117 909 5522
Website www.southwest-scriptwriters.co.uk

Secretary *John Colborn*

Founded 1994 to offer support to regional writers for all media. The group meets at the Theatre Royal, Bristol. Annual subscription: £5.

Speakeasy – Milton Keynes Writers' Group

46 Wealdstone Place, Springfield, Milton Keynes MK6 3JG
☎01908 663 860
Email speakeasy@writerbrock.co.uk
Website www.mkweb.co.uk

Contact *Martin Brocklebank*

Monthly meetings, competitions, readings and performances by local writers and guest speakers. Send s.a.e. for details.

Spread the Word
Unit 8, Eurolink Business Centre, 49 Effra Road, London SW2 1BZ
☎020 7207 2025   Fax 020 7738 4123
Email info@spreadtheword.org.uk
Website www.spreadtheword.org.uk
Development Officer *Emma Hewett*

Supports new writing and live literature in London. Live events, creative writing workshops, talks and one-to-one surgeries.

Sussex Playwrights' Club
2 Brunswick Mews, Hove, BN3 1HD
☎01273 730106
Website www.newventure.org.uk
Secretary *Dennis Evans*

Founded 1935. Monthly readings of members' work by experienced actors. Membership open to all. Meetings held at New Venture Theatre, Brighton. Annual subscription: £7; Guests: £1.

Tally Ho! Writers' Group
124 Fiern Park, London, N12 9PN
Contact *Rosalyn Rappaport* (020 8446 3690)
   or *John Burns* (at the address above)
Open to new and established authors. Meets Tuesdays at the Tally Ho! pub, Finchley.

Ver Poets
Haycroft, 61-63 Chiswell Green Lane, St Albans, Hertfordshire AL2 3AL
☎01727 867005
Email may.badman@virgin.net
Chairman *Ray Badman*
Editor/Organiser *May Badman*

Founded 1966. Postal and local members. Meets in St Albans, publishes members' work and organises competitions. Membership: £12.50 p.a.; £15 or US$30 (Overseas).

Verulam Writers' Circle
46 Gadebridge Lane, Hemel Hempstead, HP1 3HF
☎01442 217741
Email ncook@kodak.com
Website www.judasweb.co.uk/
   verulamwriters

Contact *Nick Cook*

Founded 1956. Offers constructive criticism, talks and workshops. Fortnightly meeting.

Walton Wordsmiths
27 Braycourt Avenue, Walton-on-Thames, Surrey KT12 2AZ
☎01932 702874
Email words@stickler.org.uk
Contact *Wendy Hughes*

Founded in 1999 by Wendy Hughes. Supports writers of all levels and capabilities.

Workers' Educational Association
National Office: Temple House, 17 Victoria Park Square, London E2 9PB
☎020 8983 1515 Fax 020 8983 4840
Email national@wea.org.uk
Website www.wea.org.uk

Founded in 1903 as a voluntary body running courses and workshops. Courses are open to all. Contact the Disctrict Secretary at your district WEA office for courses in your region.

Cheshire, Merseyside & West Lancashire: 7/8 Bluecoat Chambers, School Lane, Liverpool L1 3BX (☎0151 709 8023)

Eastern: Botolph House, 17 Botolph Lane, Cambridge CB2 3RE (☎01223 350978)

East Midlands: 39 Mapperley Road, Mapperley Park, Nottingham NG3 5AQ (☎ 0115 962 8400)

London: 4 Luke Street, London EC2A 4XW (☎020 7613 7550)

Northern: 51 Grainger Street, Newcastle upon Tyne NE1 5JE (☎0191 232 3957)

North Western: 4th Floor, Crawford House, University Precinct Centre, Oxford Road, Manchester M13 9GH (☎0161 277 5400)

South Eastern: 57 Riverside 2, Sir Thomas Longley Road, Rochester, Kent ME2 4DP (☎01634 730101)

South Western: Sandon Court, The Millfields, 1 Craigie Drive, Plymouth, Devon PL1 3JB (☎01752 664989)

Thames & Solent: 6 Brewer Street, Oxford OX1 1QN (☎01865 246270)

Western: 7 York Court, Wilder Street, Bristol, BS2 8QG (☎0117 916 6500)

West Mercia: 78-80 Sherlock Street, Birmingham b5 6LT (☎0121 666 6101)

Yorkshire North: 6 Woodhouse Square, Leeds, W. Yorkshire LS3 1AD (☎0113 245 3304)

Yorkshire South: Chantry Buildings, 6–20 Corporation Street, Rotherham S60 1NG (☎01709 837001)

Scottish Association: Riddle's Court, 322 Lawnmarket, Edinburgh EH1 2PG (☎0131 226 3456)

Writers in Oxford

18 Paradise Square, Oxford OX1 1TW
☎01865 208930
Email rob@satin.co.uk

Membership Secretary *Rob Walters*
Chairman *Janie Hampton*

Founded 1992. Open to published writers. Literary seminars and social functions. Publishes *The Oxford Writer* newsletter. Subscription £20 p.a.

The Writers' Workshop

Cowfields Farm, Rotherfield Greys, Henley-on-Thames, Oxfordshire RG9 4PX
☎01491 628819 Fax 01491 628581

Runs regular daytime creative writing sessions with guest speakers. All levels welcome.

Yorkshire Playwrights

3 Trinity Road, Scarborough, YO11 2TD
☎01723 367449 Fax: 01723 367449
Email ScarTam@aol.com
Website www.yorkshireplaywrights.com

Administrator *Ian Watson*

A group of professional playwrights founded 1989. Open to Yorkshire-based Writers' Guild or Society of Authors members. Contact the Administrator for an information sheet.

The Words Complained Of …

David Hooper gives advice on how to avoid an expensive court appearance

The main area of risk in libel is in non-fiction. The best working test is whether the tendency of the words used is to diminish the reputation of the claimant. If you were in the claimant's position, could you validly object to what was written about you? It is sensible to ask yourself who might complain about what you have written and how you would respond to that complaint bearing in mind that the burden of proving by legally admissible evidence will be upon you. There is unfortunately no substitute for careful research and checking. Some errors pass into mythology. A British police officer called Morton collected damages on no less than three occasions from W.H. Allen, Secker & Warburg and Weidenfeld & Nicolson for the repetition of the canard that he was responsible for the shooting in cold blood of Abram Stern, head of the Stern gang in Palestine. The Court of Appeal has recently rejected attempts to use the freedom of expression principles under the European Convention of Human Rights Article 10, to reduce the strict application of the repetition rule in libel. If you repeat someone else's libel you are liable to have to prove that it is true even if you believed your source of information was reliable.

The issue is what readers would reasonably conclude that the words meant. The fact that the author did not intend to libel the claimant is not a defence. The reader is in any event unlikely to know what the author's intention was and would form his own view on the interpretation of the words on the page. The fact that a libel was the result of an honest mistake rather than deliberate would be relevant to the amount of damages awarded. Unhappily experience shows that libel is, particularly in the area of publishing, usually the product of mistake rather than the product of a failed exposé. Publishers are in any event increasingly reluctant to run the risk of publishing investigative books. Cases involving the exposure of the wrongdoing of footballers, policemen or doctors normally involve newspapers or television companies. Writers need therefore to check the accuracy of what they write. They do well, for example, not to confuse the Chancellor of Glasgow University, Sir Alec Cairncross with his brother, a suspected member of the Cambridge spy ring. Nor is it wise to suggest that a Nigerian-born singer had said that 'it was time to support apartheid' when in reality she had said nothing more sinister than 'it was time to support a party'.

The writer should focus on all people who might bring a claim. Often controversial books successfully avoid an action from the principal target only to invite a claim from some minor character over a relatively trivial indiscretion. Claims can come from unlikely sources. The *Sunday Telegraph* can scarcely have expected to be sued by the son of Qaddafi but when he turned up at court he obtained an apology although no damages. Recently a Russian businessman, Grigori Loutchansky, successfully sued *The Times* over a report linking him with money laundering. The paper may have felt such a claim was unlikely as Loutchansky was banned from this country because his presence was deemed undesirable by the Home Secretary and he had served a lengthy prison sentence for dishonesty in the USSR.

The Loutchansky case was a salutary reminder of the severity of English libel law. Although it is the case that the limitation period for bringing libel actions is one year, the courts upheld – which is bad news for writers of books – what is known as the single publication rule, namely that each book sale or downloading from the Internet is a fresh act of publication with its own one-year limitation period. Journalists whose material might be published electronically in an archive or otherwise accessible on a website should take care to ensure that if there is a valid libel complaint steps are taken to stop any further publication of the material electronically. Otherwise they may face another claim. Unfortunately, the libel laws in this country have attracted a number of libel tourists wishing to impress on the world their spotless reputation. Writers should bear in mind that the libel laws in the United States are unfavourable to plaintiffs with the result that people like Dr Armand Hammer sued the English edition of a hostile biography in this country but decided not to bring a claim in the USA.

If a claim for libel is notified, advice should be sought from a specialist lawyer, preferably one recommended by the publisher. An outraged response can raise the level of damages. If a claim is made, immediate consideration must be given as to whether any amendment or footnote is required in respect of any electronic version of the article which can be accessed by third parties. Section 2 of the Defamation Act 1996 has significantly amended the defence of offer of amends which enables a swift and less expensive resolution of a claim where a mistake has been made. It involves an admission of liability and, if the parties cannot agree, an assessment of damages by the judge but it can stop the greed of the claimant in its tracks. Writers need to discover whether they are covered by the publisher's insurance and, if so, what excess attaches to any claim. If the writer believes that the claim may be covered by insurance, he or she must ensure that the insurers are promptly notified and that any letter of complaint is forwarded to them and that no admission of liability is made without the authority of the insurers. Increasingly, libel insurance only cuts in after the claim has cost five figures – scant consolation for the author who is likely to have warranted in the publishing contract that the book is free from libel. Very often publishers will not enforce that indemnity in the absence of serious blameworthy conduct on the part of the writer but again that is little consolation, as publishers will not commit themselves in advance to their probable reaction to a libel claim. It is important therefore to consider whether the book should be read for libel and, if so, whether it is necessary to have it all read or simply parts of it.

Many publishing contracts are silent on the question of who pays for the libel reading. Writers who try to modify the standard form indemnity given to publishers normally face a thankless task, but it is worth considering whether there is scope for agreeing that the writer's liability should be modified in respect of potential defamations of which the publisher is aware where the writer has complied with all the requirements of the lawyer reading the book for libel. Practical steps which can be taken include considering whether a particular passage should be sent to the person written about. If it can be shown that the person consented to what was written, that is a defence to a claim for libel. The problem, however, is that normally such persons will not give consent.

Libel actions cannot be brought on behalf of those who are dead. The death of a plaintiff in the course of a libel action, as happened with Robert Maxwell's claim against Faber, brings the claim to an immediate halt, but each side is left bearing their own legal costs. Writers are sometimes well advised to consult a helpful volume called *Who Was Who*.

Another defence is justification, which involves the author proving that what was written was true. If what was written was fair comment on a matter of public interest based on facts which were substantially true the writer will have a defence. By virtue of the Human Rights Act 1998 the English courts will increasingly take note of the decisions made under Article 10 of the European Convention of Human Rights which upholds the freedom of speech and which has a greater tendency to rule that criticisms made of a claimant were matters of comment rather than allegations of fact which have to be justified. If a court is told that the disputed passage in a libel claim will be defended, the court will not grant an interim injunction pending trial. The downside is that if the defence fails the damages are likely to be that much greater. Consideration often has to be given to whether it would be appropriate and less expensive to deal with the claim at an early stage, possibly by altering the disputed passage if that can still be done or by revising it in a later edition.

One of the most promising developments has been the expansion of the defence of qualified privilege by the libel action brought by the former Irish Prime Minister Albert Reynolds against the *Sunday Times*. If the writer can prove that on a matter of public interest there was a duty to inform the public who had a corresponding interest in receiving that information, there will be a defence which does not require proving that the particular allegation was true. The Court will, however, look very carefully at the research carried out, the language used and the attempt to put both sides of the matter.

Qualified privilege was the issue in the Loutchansky case, where the newspaper argued that it required the protection of qualified privilege to write about the alleged activities of Loutchansky which were by their nature very difficult to prove. The judge concluded, however, that the paper had made insufficient attempts to contact Loutchansky and should not have published until it had done so. The most helpful development for writers is the recognition by the courts of the importance of freedom of speech. The press has to discharge vital functions as a bloodhound as well as a watchdog and any lingering doubts should be resolved in favour of publication. The courts have recognized that freedom of speech is essential to informed political debate and that restrictions imposed upon that freedom must be proportionate and no more than is necessary to promote the legitimate object of the restriction. The courts also recognize that news is a perishable commodity and that the decision to publish must be assessed in the light of the facts then known.

To date, however, despite all the ringing endorsements of the freedom of the press, the courts have often been unwilling to uphold defences of qualified privilege. Too often they have found that there was some step which ought to have been taken before going into print. Journalists with publication deadlines may have a better prospect of establishing qualified privilege than authors who may be expected to undertake more research to get to the truth of the matter. The existence of the defence and the unpredictability of the view the judge may take of the research carried out are likely to deter many claimants, particularly those in public life. The Court of Appeal has recently held that a balanced account of the allegations, which it termed neutral reportage, made by a Saudi dissident was protected by qualified privilege. However, this defence is more likely to be applicable to the reporting of political matters. Previously, a writer repeating the allegations was likely to have had to prove that they were true. If there is not the pressure of a newspaper deadline the courts are going to expect an even higher standard of research and balance on the part of an author.

Writers of fiction face fewer libel problems. However, their use of auto-biographical material can lead to some of their characters being identifiable. The inadvertent use of the name of a real peer has led to a novel being pulped. Directories should, where possible, be consulted to ensure there are no similarly named people in a comparable occupation. Care should be taken to see on whom characters are based and whether any of the surrounding events actually happened. Often there is much to be said for a carefully worded disclaimer of reference to living individuals. Compton Mackenzie used to pick names from old telephone directories. Unfortunately, even when this expedient was used by the novelist Paul Watkins in his book *Stand Up Before Your God*, a randomly chosen name of a villainous character was by ill-fortune the name of one of his contemporaries at Eton College. Damages had to be paid as checks in the school directories could have avoided this error. Choosing the names of friends or acquaintances and involving them in defamatory escapades may be very difficult to defend and could result in the payment of damages and costs.

Writers of fiction will benefit from the defence of accidental defamation under Section 2 of the Defamation Act which will limit damages and costs by making a suitable offer of amends but, even so, failure to make these checks can be expensive. Derek Jameson's experiences of accidentally changing the name of a sergeant who had been convicted of treason to spare that man's family's feelings to a randomly chosen name which turned out to be that of a journalist showed that the road to libel can be paved with good intentions.

The growth of faction and the introduction of living people into works of fiction do increase the risk of libel claims by blurring the distinction between fact and imagination. A roman-à-clef can present significant libel problems and it was perhaps not surprising that a publisher could not be found for a novel featuring unattractive characteristics of a person described as the wife of a Labour prime minister who as 'a young chap with a phoney smile' was felt not to be sufficiently unrecognizable.

Changes introduced by the Defamation Act 1996 and procedural changes regarding the conduct of libel actions to make them less tortuous and expensive and to require each side to disclose the strengths and weaknesses of their cases at an earlier stage certainly are an improvement. Libel nevertheless remains a very costly pitfall even if the damages awarded are much reduced. Damages are now capped but are slowly moving upwards for the most serious libels. In the last year two nursery workers accused of child abuse were awarded £200,000 each and a company that was falsely linked to al-Qaeda was reputed to have recovered £500,000 from the BBC, although part of those damages may have related to loss of business contracts. On top of that there are the legal costs. Most cases settle for a fraction of that. There are fast-track procedures where libel damages will be capped at £10,000. This is little consolation to writers, as these changes together with the willingness of lawyers to bring libel claims on a conditional fee basis – that is to say the lawyer does not get paid unless he wins the case, but he can recover from the defendant a success fee on top of his not inconsiderable normal legal fees – serve only to encourage the bringing of smaller, but nevertheless expensive, claims. Things are improving but at present the only certainty about libel is its expense.

Article 8 of the European Convention of Human Rights protects the right to respect for private and family life. To date, claims have related either to intrusive tabloid exposés or to celebrities exploiting publicity rights, such as Michael Douglas in his spat with *Hello!* magazine who published unauthorized paparazzi photographs. That case was really about the right to control publicity and to prevent unauthorized breach of confidence in such circumstances where the parties from their commercial dealings were aware of the confidentiality that attached to the private, albeit much hyped, wedding party. The court felt that there was no public interest in such intrusive behaviour on the part of *Hello!* magazine and the Douglases were entitled to damages for distress and with *OK!* magazine for any reduced syndication revenues. The court did not uphold a general right of privacy and to that extent there has been some back-peddling by the courts, which had looked as if they were going to establish a general right of privacy. If there is a remedy it is likely to be under the law of confidence and much will depend on the facts in each case. Where a person has a reasonable expectation of privacy, intrusion into that privacy will need to be justified and the threshold may be that much lower for public figures. The unauthorized use of photographs is more likely to be restrained than the written word. At present the law of privacy and of confidence is likely to present problems, if at all, only for the tabloids and for those who seek to interfere with the legitimate commercial exploitation of what would otherwise be considered private matters. It is a developing area of law but at present it need not cause concern to serious writers. The approach of the court seems to have been that just as the court would have protected a written account by the Douglases of their wedding so they should be able to control the commercial exploitation of the events.

Naomi Campbell recovered £3,500 in respect of photographs of her leaving a drugs rehabilitation clinic and Amanda Holden and her husband received £40,000 from the *Daily Star*, which had published intrusive pictures of them on holiday and Sara Cox, the disc jockey, recovered £50,000 from invasive pictures of her in a jacuzzi while on honeymoon. Although the Court of Appeal has restricted the scope of privacy claims in the case brought by the footballer Gary Flitcroft, claims based in privacy or breach-of-confidence claims can be brought where the writer knew or ought to have known that the other person could reasonably expect his privacy to be protected. Certain kinds of information about a person, for example relating to health, private relationships or finances, might well be viewed by the court as private, as could certain kinds of activity which a reasonable person applying contemporary standards of morals and behaviour would understand to be meant to be unobserved. A useful practical test of what is private is whether the disclosure of that information or conduct would be highly offensive to a reasonable person of ordinary sensibilities. Writers who are publishing details of people's private lives or their personal finances need to be able to justify the publication of such material and they may need to limit the amount of detail they do in fact publish.

David Hooper is media partner of Reynolds Porter Chamberlain and author of Reputations under Fire, *published by Little Brown (2001).*

Miscellany

Arjay Research
20 Rookery View, Little Thurrock, Grays,
Essex RM17 6AS
☎01375 372199 Fax 01375 372199
Email RogWJ@aol.com
Website www.copy-editing.net

Contact *Roger W. Jordan*

All aspects of international merchant shipping
and naval research undertaken by former shipping archivist and editor. Extensive maritime
library and comprehensive databases on *inter
alia* ships wrecked/lost and passenger and cruise
ships. Terms by arrangement.

Authors' Research Services
32 Oak Village, London NW5 4QN
☎020 7284 4316 Fax 020 7284 4316
Email rmwindserv@aol.com

Contact *Richard Wright*

Research and document supply service, particularly to authors, academics and others without
easy access to London libraries and sources of
information. Also indexing of books and journals. Rates negotiable.

Combrógos
10 Heol Don, Whitchurch, Cardiff
CF14 2AU
☎029 2062 3359 Fax 029 2052 9202
Email meic@heoldon.fsnet.co.uk

Contact *Professor Meic Stephens*

FOUNDED 1990. Arts and media research, editorial services, specialising in books about
Wales or by Welsh authors. 'Encyclopaedic
knowledge of Welsh history, language, literature and culture.'

Jacqueline Edwards
104 Earlsdon Avenue South, Coventry,
Warwickshire CV5 6DQ

Contact *Jacqueline Edwards, MA, LLB(Hons)*

Historical research – family, local and 19th and
20th century legal history. Covers Warwickshire, Gloucestershire, Wiltshire, Worcestershire, Cambridgeshire and the Public Record
Office, Kew, London.

Facts&nfo Research Service for Writers
12 Kenbury Street, London SE5 9BS
☎020 7326 4215/07966 386304 (mobile)
Fax 020 7326 4215
Email factsinfo@beeb.net

Contact *Thecla Schreuders*

Facts&nfo specialises in global research for fiction and non-fiction writers. Offers biographical
and character research; social backgrounds and
domestic life; popular culture; medical, scientific
and technical research; and history, from classical
Greece to the late 20th century. Also archive
and journal searches, art and film references; and
source experts of all kinds. Over 12 years' experience in research for factual television.

Impressions of Monmouth
Hadnock Road, Monmouth NP25 3NQ
☎01600 772600 Fax 01600 712896
Email books@impressionsmon.demon.co.uk

Contact *David James*

Advice and technical assistance for those wishing to self-publish with full design, printing
and binding services. Yearbooks, commemorative books, personal, family, local histories, etc.
Print runs as low as 25 copies. Fixed prices

International Booksearch Service
8 Old James Street, London SE15 3TS
☎020 7639 8900
Email scfordham@talk21.com
Website www.scfordham.com

Contact *S.C. Fordham*

FOUNDED 1992. International book search service for out-of-print books. A free service with
no obligation to buy the book when found.
Experienced in finding books for authors,
researchers, TV and film companies, newspapers, magazines, etc.

Caroline Landeau
8 Elystan Place, London SW3 3LF
☎07050 600420 Fax 07050 605641
Email winmacweb@hotmail.com

Contact *Caroline Landeau*

Experienced research and production – films,

multimedia, books, magazines, exhibitions, animation, general interest, art, music, crime, travel, food, film, theatre.

Murder Files

Dommett Hill Farm, Hare Lane, Buckland St. Mary, Chard, Somerset TA20 3JS
☎01460 234065
Email enquiry@murderfiles.com
Website www.murderfiles.com

Contact *Paul Williams*

FOUNDED 1994. Crime writer and researcher specialising in GB murders. Holds information on thousands of well-known and less well-known murders dating from 1400 to the present day. Copies of press cuttings available from 1920 onwards. Details of executions, particularly at the Tyburn and Newgate. Information on British hangmen. CD-Rom *The Ultimate Price – The Unlawful Killing of British Police Officers*, Part 1 (1700–1899) & Part 2 (1900–2000), available £15 each or £26 for both including p&p. Specialist in British police murders since 1700. Service available to general enquirers, writers, researchers, TV, radio, video, etc.

Ormrod Research Services

Weeping Birch, Burwash, East Sussex TN19 7HG
☎01435 882541
Email richardormrod@aol.com

Contact *Richard Ormrod*

ESTABLISHED 1982. Comprehensive research service: literary, historical, academic, biographical, commercial. Verbal quotations available. Also editing, indexing, ghost-writing and critical reading.

Patent Research

Dachsteinstr. 12a, D–81825 Munich, Germany
☎00 49 89 430 7833

Contact *Gerhard Everwyn*

All world, historical patents for researchers, authors, archives, museums and publishers. Rates on application.

Teral Research Services

45 Forest View Road, Moordown, Bournemouth, Dorset BH9 3BH
☎01202 516834 Fax 01202 516834
Email terry@judgetread/fsnet.co.uk

Contact *Terry C. Treadwell*

All aspects of research undertaken but specialises in all military, aviation, naval and defence subjects, both past and present. Extensive book and photographic library, including a leading collection of World War One aviation photographs. Terms by arrangement.

The United Kingdom Copyright Bureau

110 Trafalgar Road, Portslade, East Sussex BN41 1GS
☎01273 277333 Fax 01273 705451
Email info@copyrightbureau.co.uk
Website www.copyrightbureau.co.uk

Contact *Ralph de Straet von Kollman, Petra Ginman*

The UKCB provides a secure copyright service at reasonable cost, enabling multiple copyrights to be registered nominally when required. Prices are advertised on the website including the UKCB's solicitors, etc. Copyrights preferred on floppy disk or CD-Rom; mss are not accepted due to storage space.

Melanie Wilson

72 High Street, Syston LE7 1GQ
☎0116 260 4442 Fax 0116 260 1396
Email MelanieWilson@dragonflight.co.uk

Contact *Melanie Wilson*

Comprehensive research service for books, magazines, newspapers, documentaries, films, radio, education, TV drama. Includes free worldwide booksearch service and groundwork for factual basis for all media presentations, particularly in historical research, costume and textiles, crafts, food and cooking, weapons and uniforms, traditional storytelling, past technology, living history displays and exhibitions.

Press Cuttings Agencies

Durrants

Discovery House, 28—42 Banner Street,
London EC1Y 8QE
☎020 7674 0200 Fax 020 7674 0222
Email contact@durrants.co.uk
Website www.durrants.co.uk

Wide coverage of all print media sectors plus
Internet, newswire and broadcast monitoring;
foreign press in association with agencies
abroad. High speed, early morning press cuttings from the national press e-mailed to your
desktop. Overnight delivery via courier to
most areas or first-class mail. Well presented,
laser printed, A4 cuttings. Rates on application.

International Press–Cutting Bureau

224–236 Walworth Road, London SE17 1JE
☎020 7708 2113 Fax 020 7701 4489
Email ipcb2000@aol.com

Contact *Robert Podro*

Covers national, provincial, trade, technical
and magazine press. Cuttings are normally sent
twice weekly by first-class post . Our basic
charges are £60 per month + 60p per cutting.

Romeike Media Intelligence

Hale House, 290–296 Green Lanes, London
N13 5TP
☎0800 289543 Fax 020 8882 6716
Email info@romeike.com

Website www.romeike.com

Contact *Alistair Hails*

Monitors national and international dailies and
Sundays, provincial papers, consumer magazines, trade and technical journals, teletext
services as well as national radio and TV networks. Back research, advertising checking and
Internet monitoring, plus analysis and editorial
summary service available.

We Find It (Press Clippings)

40 Galwally Avenue, Belfast BT8 7AJ
☎028 9064 6008 Fax 028 9064 6008

Contact *Avril Forsythe*

Specialises in Northern Ireland press and magazines, both national and provincial. Rates on
application.

Xtreme Information

89½ Worship Street, London EC2A 2BF
☎020 7377 1742 Fax 020 7377 6103
Email info@news.xtremeinformation.com
Website www.news.xtremeinformation.com

National and European press monitoring
agency. Cuttings from national and all major
European press available seven days a week,
with early morning delivery. Also monitoring
of internet and newswire channels. Delivery
available online; account management available
24 hours a day.

Bursaries, Fellowships and Grants

Arts Council Literature Bursaries, Ireland

An Chomhairle Ealaíon (The Irish Arts Council), 70 Merrion Square, Dublin 2, Republic of Ireland
☎00 353 1 6180200 Fax 00 353 1 6761302
Email info@artscouncil.ie
Website www.artscouncil.ie

Contact *Literature Officer*

Bursaries in literature awarded to creative writers of fiction, poetry and drama in Irish and English to enable development or completion of, specific projects. A limited number of bursaries may also be given to non-fiction projects of a contemporary nature. Open to Irish citizens or residents only.
Awards up to €12,000.

The Authors' Contingency Fund

The Society of Authors, 84 Drayton Gardens, London SW10 9SB
☎020 7373 6642 Fax 020 7373 5768
Email info@societyofauthors.org
Website www.societyofauthors.org

This fund makes modest grants to published authors who find themselves in sudden financial difficulties. Contact the **Society of Authors** for an information sheet and application form.

The Authors' Foundation

The Society of Authors, 84 Drayton Gardens, London SW10 9SB
☎020 7373 6642 Fax 020 7373 5768
Email info@societyofauthors.org
Website www.societyofauthors.org

Grants to writers whose publisher's advance is insufficient to cover the costs of research involved. Application by letter to The Authors' Foundation giving details, in confidence, of the advance and royalties, together with the reasons for needing additional funding. Grants are sometimes given even if there is no commitment by a publisher, so long as the applicant has had a book published and the new work will almost certainly be published. About £80,000 is distributed each year. Contact the **Society of Authors** for full entry details. Final entry dates: 30 April and 31 October.

The K. Blundell Trust

The Society of Authors, 84 Drayton Gardens, London SW10 9SB
☎020 7373 6642 Fax 020 7373 5768
Email info@societyofauthors.org
Website www.societyofauthors.org

Grants to writers whose publisher's advance is insufficient to cover the costs of research. Author must be under 40, has to submit a copy of his/her previous book and the work must 'contribute to the greater understanding of existing social and economic organisation'. Application by letter. Contact the **Society of Authors** for full entry details. Final entry dates: 30 April and 31 October.

Alfred Bradley Bursary Award

c/o BBC Radio Drama, Room 2129, New Broadcasting House, Oxford Road, Manchester M60 1SJ
☎0161 244 4255 Fax 0161 244 4248

Contact *Coordinator*

ESTABLISHED 1992. Biennial award in commemoration of the life and work of the distinguished radio producer Alfred Bradley. Aims to encourage and develop new radio writing talent in the BBC North region. There is a change of focus for each award, e.g. previous years have targeted comedy drama, verse drama, etc. Entrants must live in the North region. The award is given to help writers to pursue a career in writing for radio. The next award will be launched in spring 2004, with a deadline for scripts in autumn 2004. Previous winners: Lee Hall, Mandy Precious, Peter Straughan, Pam Leeson.
Award Up to £6000 over two years and a BBC Radio Drama commission, the opportunity to develop further ideas with Radio Drama.

British Academy Small Personal Research Grants

10 Carlton House Terrace, London SW1Y 5AH
☎020 7969 5200 Fax 020 7969 5300
Website www.britac.ac.uk

Contact *Assistant Secretary, Research Grants*

Quarterly award to further original academic research at postdoctoral level in the humanities and social sciences. Entrants must no longer be registered for postgraduate study and must be resident in the UK. Final entry dates: end of September, November, February and April.

Award £5000 (maximum).

Lar Cassidy Award

An Chomhairle Ealaíon (The Irish Arts Council), 70 Merrion Square, Dublin 2, Republic of Ireland

☎00 353 1 6180200   Fax 00 353 1 6761302
Email info@artscouncil.ie
Website www.artscouncil.ie

The award commemorates the life and work of the late Lar Cassidy, pioneering arts administrator and former Arts Council Literature and Community Arts Officer. The aim of the award in 2004 is to support an individual writer working on a new or experimental fiction project. (In alternate years, the award will be offered to an arts practitioner working in the field of combined arts.) Information sheet/application form available.

Award €15,000.

Cholmondeley Awards

The Society of Authors, 84 Drayton Gardens, London SW10 9SB

☎020 7373 6642   Fax 020 7373 5768
Email info@societyofauthors.org
Website www.societyofauthors.org

FOUNDED 1965 by the late Dowager Marchioness of Cholmondeley. Annual honorary awards to recognise the achievement and distinction of individual poets. 2002 winners: Moniza Alvi, David Constantine, Liz Lochhead, Brian Patten.

Award £8000 (total).

Tony Doyle New Writers' Bursary

BBC Northern Ireland Drama, Broadcasting House, Ormeau Avenue, Belfast BT2 8HQ

☎02890 338497   Fax 02890 338408
Email tvdrama.ni@bbc.co.uk
Website www.bbc.co.uk/ni/drama

Contacts *Diedre Cartmill, Stephen Wright*

The aim of the bursary is to encourage Irish writers to write for television – the medium in which Tony Doyle had his greatest successes. Its aim is to encourage writing for television, to inform writers of the opportunities that television affords and to nurture long-term creative links between all broadcasters and writers in Ireland. Writers must have an Irish background. The writer must not have had a drama in English previously produced for television. Final entry date is usally 31 January each year

(opens in October). Previous winners: Bill Murphy (2001), Brian Dungan (2002). The winner receives a cash prize of £2000. The finalists are invited to a residential seminar to introduce them to the world of television drama through a series of intensive sessions with the BBC Drama Development Team and experienced practitioners. Two typed copies should be submitted. Only one entry accepted per person. Enties must be in English. Contact the department and ask for criteria as these may change annually.

The Economist/ Richard Casement Internship

The Economist, 25 St James's Street, London SW1A 1HG

☎020 7830 7000
Website www.economist.com

Contact *Science Editor (re. Casement Internship)*

For an aspiring journalist under 25 to spend three months in the summer writing for *The Economist* about science and technology. Applicants should write a letter of introduction along with an article of approximately 600 words suitable for inclusion in the Science and Technology Section. Competition details normally announced in the magazine late January or early February and 4–5 weeks allowed for application.

European Jewish Publication Society

PO Box 19948, London N3 3ZJ

☎020 8346 1668   Fax 020 8346 1776
Email cs@ejps.org.uk
Website www.ejps.org.uk

Contact *Dr Colin Shindler*

ESTABLISHED in 1995 to help fund the publication of books of European Jewish interest which would otherwise remain unpublished. Helps with the marketing, distribution and promotion of such books. Publishers who may be interested in publishing works of Jewish interest should approach the Society with a proposal and manuscript in the first instance. Books which have been supported include: *The Vanished Shtetl* Stanislav Brunstein; *Tidings from Zion* Jennifer Glynn; *Botchki* David Zagier; *Just One More Dance* Ernest Levy, *Cherrie in the Icebox* Shelley Weiner, *Contemporary Hebrew Short Stories* ed. Marian Baraitser, Haya Hoffman. Also supports the publication of poetry, and translations from and into other European languages.

Grant £3000 (maximum).

Fulbright Awards

The Fulbright Commission, Fulbright House,
62 Doughty Street, London WC1N 2JZ
☎020 7404 6880 Fax 020 7404 6834
Website www.fulbright.co.uk

Contact *British Programme Manager*

The Fulbright Commission has a number of scholarships given at postgraduate level and above, open to any field (science and the arts) of study/research to be undertaken in the USA. Length of award is typically an academic year. Application deadline for postgraduate awards is usually late October/early November of preceding year of study; and mid-March/early April for distinguished scholar awards. Further details and application forms are available on the Commission's website. Alternatively, send A4 envelope with sufficient postage for 100g with a covering letter explaining which level of award is of interest.

Fulton Fellowship

David Fulton (Publishers) Ltd, The Chiswick Centre, 414 Chiswick High Road, London W4 5TF
☎020 8996 3610 Fax 020 8996 3622
Email orders@fultonpublishers.co.uk
Website www.fultonpublishers.co.uk

Chairman and Publisher *David Fulton*
Publishing Director *Christopher Glennie*

The Fulton Fellowship in Special Education was ESTABLISHED in 1995 and is administered by the Centre for Special Education, University College, Worcester. The Fellowship, worth £2000, has been extended to offer schools as well as individual teachers the chance to share work their staff have done or are doing collaboratively through written publication to a wider audience. 2000 Fellow: Mordaunt School, Southampton.

Tony Godwin Memorial Trust

c/o 38 Lyttelton Court, Lyttelton Road, London N2 0EB
☎020 8209 1613
Email info@tgmt.org.uk
Website www.tgmt.org.uk

Chairman *Iain Brown*

Biennial award established to commemorate the life of Tony Godwin, a prominent publisher in the 1960s/70s. Open to all young people (under 35 years old) who are UK nationals and working, or intending to work, in publishing. The award provides the recipient with the means to spend at least one month as the guest of an American publishing house in order to learn about international publishing. The recipient is expected to submit a report upon return to the UK. Next award: 2004; final entry date: 31 December 2003. Previous winners: George Lucas (Hodder), Clive Priddle (Fourth Estate), Richard Scrivener (Penguin), Lisa Shakespeare (Weidenfeld & Nicolson), Fiona Stewart (HarperCollins).
Award Bursary of approx. US$5000.

Eric Gregory Trust Fund

The Society of Authors, 84 Drayton Gardens, London SW10 9SB
☎020 7373 6642 Fax 020 7373 5768
Email info@societyofauthors.org
Website www.societyofauthors.org

Annual awards of varying amounts are made for the encouragement of poets under the age of 30 on the basis of a submitted collection. Open only to British-born subjects resident in the UK. Final entry date: 31 October. Contact the **Society of Authors** for full entry details. 2002 winners: Caroline Bird, Christopher James, Jacob Polley, Luke Heeley, Judith Cal, David Briggs, Eleanor Rees, Kathryn Simmonds.
Award £24,000 (total).

The Guardian Research Fellowship

Nuffield College, Oxford OX1 1NF
☎01865 288540 Fax 01865 278676

Contact *The Academic Administrator*

One-year fellowship endowed by the Scott Trust, owner of *The Guardian*, to give someone working in the media the chance to put their experience into a new perspective, publish the outcome and give a *Guardian* lecture. Applications welcomed from journalists and management members, in newspapers, periodicals or broadcasting. Research or study proposals should be directly related to experience of working in the media. Accommodation and meals in college will be provided and a stipend. Advertised biennially in November.

Hawthornden Castle Fellowship

Hawthornden Castle, The International Retreat for Writers, Lasswade, Midlothian EH18 1EG
☎0131 440 2180 Fax 0131 440 1989

Contact *The Administrator*

ESTABLISHED 1982 to provide a peaceful setting where published writers can work without disturbance. The Retreat houses five writers at a time, who are known as Hawthornden Fellows. Writers from any part of the world may apply for the fellowships. No monetary assistance is given, nor any contribution to travelling expenses, but once arrived at Hawthornden, the writer is the guest of the Retreat. Applications on forms provided must be made by the end of September for the following calendar year. Previous winners include: Les Murray, Alasdair Gray, Helen Vendler, Olive Senior, Hilary Spurling.

Francis Head Bequest
The Society of Authors, 84 Drayton Gardens, London SW10 9SB
☎020 7373 6642 Fax 020 7373 5768
Email info@societyofauthors.org
Website www.societyofauthors.org
Provides grants to published British authors over the age of 35 who need financial help during a period of illness, disablement or temporary financial crisis. Contact the **Society of Authors** for an information sheet and application form.

Ralph Lewis Award
University of Sussex Library, Brighton, East Sussex BN1 9QL
☎01273 678158 Fax 01273 678441
Email p.a.ringshaw@sussex.ac.uk
ESTABLISHED 1985. Occasional award set up by Ralph Lewis, a Brighton author and art collector who left money to fund awards for promising manuscripts which would not otherwise be published. The award is given in the form of a grant to a UK-based publisher in respect of an agreed three-year programme of publication of literary works by new authors or by established authors using new styles or forms. No direct applications from writers. Previous winners: **Peterloo Poets**; **Serpent's Tail**; **Stride Publications**.

Macaulay Fellowship
An Chomhairle Ealaíon (The Irish Arts Council), 70 Merrion Square, Dublin 2, Republic of Ireland
☎00 353 1 6180200 Fax 00 353 1 6761302
Email info@artscouncil.ie
Website www.artscouncil.ie
Contact *Literature Officer*
To further the liberal education of a young creative artist. Candidates for this triennial award must be under 30 on 30 June, or 35 in exceptional circumstances, and must be Irish citizens or residents. The Fellowship is offered on rotation between Music, Visual Arts and Literature (Visual Arts in 2003).
Award €5000.

The John Masefield Memorial Trust
The Society of Authors, 84 Drayton Gardens, London SW10 9SB
☎020 7373 6642 Fax 020 7373 5768
Email info@societyofauthors.org
Website www.societyofauthors.org
This trust makes occasional grants to professional poets (or their immediate dependants) who are faced with sudden financial problems. Contact the **Society of Authors** for an information sheet and application form.

Somerset Maugham Trust Fund
The Society of Authors, 84 Drayton Gardens, London SW10 9SB
☎020 7373 6642 Fax 020 7373 5768
Email info@societyofauthors.org
Website www.societyofauthors.org
Annual awards designed to encourage writers under the age of 35 to travel. Given on the basis of a published work of fiction, non-fiction or poetry. Open only to British-born subjects resident in the UK. Final entry date: 20 December. 2002 winners: Charlotte Hobson *Black Earth City*; Marcel Theroux *The Paperchase*.
Awards £12,000 (total).

The Airey Neave Trust
PO Box 36800, 40 Bernard Street, London WC1N 1WJ
☎020 7833 4440
Email hanthoc@aol.com
Contact *Hannah Scott*
INITIATED 1989. Annual research fellowships for up to three years – towards a book or paper – for serious research connected with national and international law, and human freedom. Preferably attached to a particular university in Britain.

Newspaper Press Fund
Dickens House, 35 Wathen Road, Dorking, Surrey RH4 1JY
☎01306 887511 Fax 01306 888212
Email enquiries@pressfund.org.uk
Director/Secretary *David Ilott*
Aims to relieve distress among journalists and their dependants. Continuous and/or occasional financial grants; also retirement homes for eligible beneficiaries. Further information and subscription details available from the Secretary.

North East Literary Fellowship

Arts Council England, North East, Central Square, Forth Street, Newcastle upon Tyne NE1 3PJ
☎0191 255 8500 Fax 0191 230 1020

Contact *Literature Officer*

A competitive fellowship in association with the Universities of Durham and Newcastle upon Tyne. Contact Arts Council England, North East, for details.

Northern Rock Foundation Writer's Award

New Writing North, 7–8 Trinity Chare, Quayside, Newcastle upon Tyne NE1 3DF
☎0191 232 9991 Fax 0191 230 1883
Email mail@newwritingnorth.com
Website www.newwritingnorth.com

Contact *Silvana Michelini*

Annual award ESTABLISHED in 2002 with the aim of liberating established writers who live in the region from work other than writing. Applicants must have at least two books published by a recognised publisher and *must* live in Northumberland, Tyne and Wear, County Durham or Teesside. Closing date November. The first winner of the award in 2002 was poet, Anne Stevenson.

Award £60,000 (£20,000 a year for three years).

Northern Writers' Awards

See **New Writing North** under **Professional Associations and Societies**

PAWS (Public Awareness of Science) Drama Script Fund

The PAWS Office, OMNI Communications, Chancel House, Neasden Lane, London NW10 2TU
☎020 8214 1543 Fax 020 8214 1544
Email pawsomni@globalnet.co.uk

Contacts *Barrie Whatley, Andrew Millington*

ESTABLISHED 1994. Annual award aimed at encouraging television scriptwriters to include science and engineering scenarios in their work. Grants (currently £2000) are given to selected writers to develop their script ideas into full treatments; prizes are awarded for the best of these treatments. The PAWS Fund holds meetings enabling writers to meet scientists and engineers and also offers a contacts service to put writers in 'one-to-one' contact with specialists who can help them develop their ideas. See also the **EuroPAWS Midas Prize** under **Prizes**.

Pearson Playwrights' Scheme

80 Strand, London WC2R 0RL
Website www.pearson.com

Administrator *Jack Andrews, MBE*

Awards four bursaries to playwrights annually, each worth £5000. Applicants must be sponsored by a theatre which then submits the play for consideration by a panel. Each award allows the playwright a twelve-month attachment. Applications invited via theatres in October each year. For up-to-date information, contact *Jack Andrews* (Tel 020 8943 8176).

Charles Pick Fellowship

School of English and American Studies, University of East Anglia, Norwich, Norfolk NR4 7TJ
☎01603 492810 Fax 01603 507728
Email v.striker@uea.ac.uk
Website www.uea.ac.uk/eas/Fellowships/
   fellowschol.html

Contact *Val Striker*

An annual award, FOUNDED in 2001 by the Charles Pick Consultancy in memory of the publisher and literary agent who died in 2000, to support a new unpublished writer of fictional or non-fictional prose. Award of the fellowship, which is residential from August to January, is judged on the quality of writing and reference from a literary agent, editor or accredited creative writing teacher. Previous winner: Tom Frick. Deadline for applications: 31 January each year.

Award £10,000 plus free campus accommodation.

Peggy Ramsay Foundation

Hanover House, 14 Hanover Square, London W1S 1HP
☎020 7667 5000 Fax 020 7667 5100
Email laurence.harbottle@harbottle.com
Website www.peggyramsayfoundation.org

Contact *G. Laurence Harbottle*

FOUNDED 1992 in accordance with the will of the late Peggy Ramsay, the well-known agent. Grants are made to writers for the stage who have some experience and who need time and resources to make writing possible. Grants are also made for writing projects by organisations connected with the theatre. The Foundation does not support production costs or any project that does not have a direct benefit to play-writing. Writers must have some record of successful writing for the stage.

Grants total £150,000 to £200,000 per year.

The Royal Literary Fund
3 Johnson's Court, off Fleet Street, London EC4A 3EA
☎020 7353 7150 Fax 020 7353 1350
Email egunnrl@globalnet.co.uk
Website www.rlf.org.uk

Secretary *Eileen Gunn*

Grants and pensions are awarded to published authors of several works in financial need, or to their dependants. Examples of author's works are needed for assessment by Committee. Contact Secretary for further details and application form.

Scottish Arts Council
Book Awards
Scottish Arts Council, 12 Manor Place, Edinburgh EH3 7DD
☎0131 226 6051 Fax 0131 225 9833
Email gavin.wallace@scottisharts.org.uk
Website www.sac.org.uk

Contact *Gavin Wallace, Literature Officer*

A minimum of three awards is made annually in the spring. Preference is given to literary fiction but literary non-fiction is also considered. Authors should be Scottish or resident in Scotland, but books of Scottish interest by other authors are eligible for consideration. Applications from publishers only.

Scottish Arts Council
Creative Scotland Awards
Scottish Arts Council, 12 Manor Place, Edinburgh EH3 7DD
☎0131 226 6051/ Help Desk: 0845 603 6000
Fax 0131 225 9833
Email helpdesk@scottisharts.org.uk
Website www.sac.org.uk

The details of this scheme are currently under review but substantial awards or commissions will be available to established artists based in Scotland working in any medium, including writing.

Scottish Arts Council
New Writers' Bursaries
Scottish Arts Council, 12 Manor Place, Edinburgh EH3 7DD
☎0131 226 6051 Fax 0131 225 9833

Email gavin.wallace@scottisharts.org.uk
Website www.sac.org.uk

Contact *Gavin Wallace, Head of Literature*

Ten bursaries of £2000 awarded annually to enable previously unpublished writers of literary work more time to devote to their writing. Applicants should be based in Scotland.

Scottish Arts Council
Writers' and Playwrights' Bursaries
Scottish Arts Council, 12 Manor Place, Edinburgh EH3 7DD
☎0131 226 6051 Fax 0131 225 9833
Email gavin.wallace@scottisharts.org.uk
Website www.sac.org.uk

Contact *Gavin Wallace, Head of Literature*

Bursaries to enable published writers of literary work and recognised playwrights to devote more time to their writing. Around 20 bursaries of up to £15,000 awarded annually; deadline for applications in June and December. Application open to writers based in Scotland.

Laurence Stern Fellowship
Department of Journalism, City University, Northampton Square, London EC1V 0HB
☎020 7040 8224 Fax 020 7040 8594
Email B.Jones@city.ac.uk
Website www.city.ac.uk/journalism

Contact *Bob Jones*

FOUNDED 1980. Awarded to a young journalist experienced enough to work on national stories. It gives them the chance to work on the national desk of the *Washington Post*. Benjamin Bradlee, the *Post*'s Vice-President-at-Large, selects from a shortlist drawn up in March/April. 2003 winner: Tania Branigan of *The Guardian*. Full details available on the website.

Tom-Gallon Trust
The Society of Authors, 84 Drayton Gardens, London SW10 9SB
☎020 7373 6642 Fax 020 7373 5768
Email info@societyofauthors.org
Website www.societyofauthors.org

A biennial award made on the basis of a submitted story to fiction writers of limited means who have had at least one short story accepted for publication. Contact the **Society of Authors** for an entry form. Final entry date 20 September 2004.

Award £1000.

The Betty Trask Awards
The Society of Authors, 84 Drayton Gardens,
London SW10 9SB
☎020 7373 6642 Fax 020 7373 5768
Email info@societyofauthors.org
Website www.societyofauthors.org

These annual awards are for authors who are
under 35 and Commonwealth citizens, awarded
on the strength of a first novel (published or
unpublished) of a traditional or romantic nature.
The awards must be used for a period or periods
of foreign travel. Final entry date: 31 January.
Contact the **Society of Authors** for an entry
form. 2002 winners: Hari Kuazru *The
Impressionist*; Rachel Seiffert *The Dark Room*;
Shamin Sarif *The World Unseen*; Helen Cross *My
Summer of Love*; Chloe Hooper *A Child's Book of
True Crime*; Susanna Jones *The Earthquake Bird*;
Gwendoline Riley *Cold Water*.

Award £25,000 (total).

The Travelling Scholarships
The Society of Authors, 84 Drayton Gardens,
London SW10 9SB
☎020 7373 6642 Fax 020 7373 5768
Email info@societyofauthors.org
Website www.societyofauthors.org

Annual honorary grants to established British
writers. 2002 winners: Frank Kuppner, David
Park, George Szirtes.

Award £6000 (total).

UEA Writing Fellowship
School of English and American Studies,
University of East Anglia, University Plain,
Norwich, Norfolk NR4 7TJ
☎01603 592734 Fax 01603 593522
Website www.uea.ac.uk/eas/Fellowships/
fellowschol.html

Director of Personnel & Registry Services
J.R.L. Beck

ESTABLISHED 1971. Awarded to a writer of established reputation in prose fiction and poetry for a
period of six months, January to end June. The
duties of the Fellowship are discussed at an interview. It is assumed that one activity will be the
pursuit of the Fellow's own writing. In addition
the Fellow will be expected to (a) offer an undergraduate creative writing workshop in the
School of English and American Studies during
the Spring semester; (b) make contact with
groups around the county in association with
East England Arts. Office space and some limited
secretarial assistance will be provided, and some
additional funds will be available to help the
Fellow with the activities described above.
Applications for the fellowship should be lodged
with the Director of Personnel & Registry
Services in the autumn; candidates should submit
two examples of recent work. Previous winner:
Jill Dawson.

Award £7500, plus free flat on campus.

David T.K. Wong Fellowship
School of English and American Studies,
University of East Anglia, University Plain,
Norwich, Norfolk NR4 7TJ
☎01603 592810 Fax 01603 507728
Email v.striker@uea.ac.uk
Website www.uea.ac.uk/eas/Fellowships/
fellowschol.html

Contact *Val Striker*

FOUNDED 1998. An annual endowment to
enable a writer of promise to spend a year at
the University writing a work of fiction on
some aspect of life in the Far East. Judged on
the basis of submitted written work, the award
is open to all nationalities. Final entry date:
31 October. 2003 winner: Wendy Law-Yone.

Award £25,000.

Prizes

J.R. Ackerley Prize

English Centre of International PEN, 152–156 Kentish Town Road, London NW1 9QB
☎020 7267 9444 Fax 020 7267 9304
Email enquiries@englishpen.org
Website www.englishpen.org

Commemorating the novelist/autobiographer J.R. Ackerley, this prize is awarded for a literary autobiography, written in English and published in the year preceding the award. Entry restricted to nominations from the Ackerley Trustees only ('please do not submit books'). Previous winner: Michael Foss *Out of India: A Raj Childhood*.
  Prize £1000, plus silver pen.

Acorn–Rukeyser Chapbook Contest

Website www.meklerdeahl.com

This contest has been suspended and will not run in 2003 and 2004, but may resume in 2005. All past contests will be judged and the contest books will be published. Poets who have entered these contests may consult the website where results will be posted as they become available.

Aldeburgh Poetry Festival Prize

Reading Room Yard, The Street, Brockdish, Diss, Norfolk IP21 4JZ
☎01379 668345 Fax 01379 668844

Contact *Naomi Jaffa*

ESTABLISHED 1989 by the Aldeburgh Poetry Trust. Sponsored by the Aldeburgh Bookshop for the best first collection published in Britain or the Republic of Ireland in the preceding twelve months. Open to any first collection of poetry of at least 40 pages. Final entry date: 1 October. Previous winners include: Donald Atkinson, Susan Wicks, Gwyneth Lewis, Glyn Wright, Robin Robertson, Tamar Yoseloff, Colette Bryce, Henry Shukman.
  Prize £500, plus an invitation to read at the following year's festival.

Alexander Prize

Royal Historical Society, University College London, Gower Street, London WC1E 6BT
☎020 7387 7532 Fax 020 7387 7532

Email rhsinfo@sas.ac.uk
Contact *Executive Secretary*

Awarded for a historical essay of not more than 8000 words. Competitors may choose their own subject for the essay. Closing date: 1 November.
  Prize £250 or a silver medal.

ALPSP Awards/ALPSP/ Charlesworth Awards

ALPSP, South House, The Street, Clapham, Worthing, West Sussex BN13 3UU
☎01903 871686 Fax 01903 871457
Email sec-gen@alpsp.org
Website www.alpsp.org

Contact *Sally Morris*

Presented in recognition of significant achievement in the field of learned and professional publishing by the **Association of Learned and Professional Society Publishers** and the Charlesworth Group. The awards were originally for excellence in design and typography in journals but since 2001 they also recognise innovation, contribution to not-for-profit publishing, library-publisher relations and service to ALPSP. The awards are international and open to publishers, organisations and individuals. Details available on the Association's website.

An Duais don bh Filíocht i nGaeilge

An Chomhairle Ealaíon (The Irish Arts Council), 70 Merrion Square, Dublin 2, Republic of Ireland
☎00 353 1 6180200 Fax 00 353 1 6761302
Email info@artscouncil.ie
Website www.artscouncil.ie

Contact *Literature Officer*

Triennial award for the best book of Irish poetry. Works must have been published in the Irish language in the preceding three years. Next award in 2004.
  Prize €4000.

Hans Christian Andersen Awards

IBBY, Nonnenweg 12, Postfach, CH-4003 Basel, Switzerland
☎00 41 61 272 2917 Fax 00 41 61 272 2757

Email ibby@eye.ch
Website www.ibby.org

Executive Director *Leena Maissen*

The highest international prizes for children's literature: The Hans Christian Andersen Award for Writing ESTABLISHED 1956; The Hans Christian Andersen Award for Illustration ESTABLISHED 1966. Candidates are nominated by National Sections of IBBY (The International Board on Books for Young People). Biennial prizes are awarded, in even-numbered years, to an author and an illustrator whose body of work has made a lasting contribution to children's literature. 2002 winners: Award for Writing: Aidan Chambers (UK); Award for Illustration: Quentin Blake (UK).

Award Gold medals.

Angus Book Award

Angus Council Cultural Services, County Buildings, Forfar DD8 3WF
☎01307 461460 Fax 01307 462590
Email cultural.services@angus.gov.uk

Contact *Moyra Hood, Educational Resources Librarian*

ESTABLISHED 1995. Designed to try to help teenagers develop an interest in and enthusiasm for reading. Eligible books are read and voted on by third-year schoolchildren in all eight Angus secondary schools. 2002 winner: Bali Rai *Un(arranged) Marriage*.

Prize £250 cheque, plus trophy in the form of a replica Pictish stone.

Annual Theatre Book Prize

See **The Society for Theatre Research Annual Theatre Book Prize**

Artists' Choice Award for Art Instruction Book of the Year

PO Box 3, Huntingdon, Cambridgeshire PE28 0QX
☎01832 710201 Fax 01832 710488
Email award@acaward.com
Website www.acaward.com

Contact *Henry Malt*

ESTABLISHED 1995. Established by Artists' Choice Book Club to recognise the quality of books published in this specialised field. Books must have an element of art instruction and be first published in the UK. 2002 winner: *The Complete Drawing Course* by John Raynes, published by Collins & Brown.

Prize A cheque is presented to the author and a trophy to the publisher.

Arts Council Children's Award

Arts Council England, 14 Great Peter Street, London SW1P 3NQ
☎020 7333 0100
Website www.artscouncil.org.uk

Contact *Theatre Writing Section*

An annual award for playwrights who write for children. The plays, which must have been produced professionally between 1 July 2003 and 30 June 2004, should be suitable for children up to the age of 12 and be at least 45 minutes long. The playwright must be resident in UK. Closing date for entries: 2 July 2004. Contact the Theatre Writing Section for details and application form.

Award £6000.

Arvon Foundation International Poetry Competition

2nd Floor, 42a Buckingham Palace Road, London SW1W 0RE
☎020 7931 7611 Fax 020 7963 0961
Email london@arvonfoundation.org
Website www.arvonfoundation.org

Contact *National Administration*

ESTABLISHED 1980. Biennial competition (next in the spring of 2004) for poems written in English and not previously broadcast or published. There are no restrictions on the number of lines, themes, age of entrants or nationality. No limit to the number of entries. Entry fee: £5 per poem. Previous winners: Paul Farley *Laws of Gravity*; Don Paterson *A Private Bottling*.

Prize (1st) £5000 and £5000 worth of other prizes sponsored by Duncan Lawrie Limited.

Authors' Club First Novel Award

Authors' Club, 40 Dover Street, London W1S 4NP
☎020 7499 8581 Fax 020 7409 0913

Contact *Mrs Ann de La Grange*

ESTABLISHED 1954. This award is made for the most promising work published in Britain by a British author, and is presented at a dinner held at the Authors' Club in April. Entries for the award are accepted from publishers by the end of November of the year in question and must be full-length – short stories are not eligible. 2002 winner: Carl Tighe *Burning Worm*.

Award £1000 (sponsored by the Marsh Christian Trust).

Aventis Prizes for Science Books

Copus, c/o The Royal Society, 6–9 Carlton House Terrace, London SW1Y 5AG
☎020 7451 2579 Fax 020 7451 2693

Email booksprize@copus.org
Website www.aventissciencebookprizes.com

Contact *Natasha Martineau*

Annual prizes ESTABLISHED in 1988 to celebrate the best in popular science writing. Awarded to books that make science more accessible to readers of all ages and backgrounds. Organised by Copus (The Science Communication Partnership) and sponsored by Aventis Pharma Ltd. All entries must be written in English and their first publication in the UK must have been between 1 January and 31 December; submission by publishers only. Educational textbooks published for professional or specialist audiences are not eligible. 2002 winners: Stephen Hawking *The Universe in a Nutshell* (General Prize); Richard Walker *The DK Guide to the Human Body* (Junior Prize).

Prizes (total) £30,000: £10,000 to each winner (junior and overall); £1000 to each of the other five shortlisted authors in each prize.

The BA/Nielson BookData Author of the Year Award

Booksellers Association Ltd, 272 Vauxhall Bridge Road, London SW1V 1BA
☎020 7802 0801 Fax 020 7802 0803
Email denise.bayat@booksellers.org.uk
Website www.booksellers.org.uk

Contact *Denise Bayat*

Founded as part of the BA Annual Conference to involve authors more closely in the event. Authors must be British or Irish. Not an award open to entry but voted on by the BA's membership. 2002 winner: Philip Pullman.

Award £1000, plus trophy.

BAAL Book Prize

BAAL Publications Secretary, School of Education, University of Leeds, Leeds LS2 9JT
☎0113 233 4569
Email a.g.white@education.leeds.ac.uk
Website www.baal.org.uk

Contact *Gooditu White*

Annual award made by the British Association for Applied Linguistics to an outstanding book in the field of applied linguistics. Final entry at the end of Oct/Nov. Nominations from publishers only. Previous winners: Joshua A. Fishman *Reversing Language Shift*; Deborah Cameron *Verbal Hygiene*; Marco Jacquemet *Credibility in Court*; Ana Celia Zentella *Growing Up Bilingual*; Daniel Nettle and Suzanne Romaine *Vanishing Voices: the extinction of the world's languages*; M. Gorlach *A Dictionary of European Anglicisms*.

Barclays Bank Prize

See **Lakeland Book of the Year Awards**

Verity Bargate Award

The Soho Theatre Company, 21 Dean Street, London W1D 3NE
☎020 7287 5060 Fax 020 7287 5061
Email writers@sohotheatre.com
Website www.sohotheatre.com

Contact *Jo Ingham, Literary Officer*

The award was set up to commemorate the late Verity Bargate, co-founder and director of the **Soho Theatre Company**. This national award is presented biennially for a new and unperformed play (next in 2004). To go on the mailing list, please e-mail or send s.a.e. to *Jo Ingham*. Previous winners include: Shan Khan, Fraser Grace, Lyndon Morgans, Adrian Pagan, Diane Samuels, Judy Upton and Toby Whithouse.

The Herb Barrett Award

Website www.meklerdeahl.com

This contest has been suspended and will not run in 2003 and 2004, but may resume in 2005. All past contests will be judged and the contest books will be published. Poets who have entered these contests may consult the website where results will be posted as they become available.

BBC Wildlife Magazine Awards for Nature Writing

PO Box 229, Bristol BS99 7JN
☎0117 973 8402 Fax 0117 946 7075
Email nina.epton@bbc.co.uk

Contact *Nina Epton*

Annual competition for professional and amateur writers. Entries (no longer than 800 words) should be based on personal observations of, or thoughts about, nature – general or specific. The entry form appears in the magazine; closing date varies. Contact the magazine for entry information.

Prizes Winner: cash prize, plus publication in the magazine; runners-up: cash prizes, plus publication; two young writers' awards.

BBC Wildlife Magazine Poet of the Year Awards

PO Box 229, Bristol BS99 7JN
☎0117 973 8402 Fax 0117 946 7075
Email nina.epton@bbc.co.uk

Contact *Nina Epton*

Annual award for a poem, the subject of which must be the natural world and/or our relationship with it. Entrants may submit one poem only of no more than 50 lines with the entry form which appears in the magazine. Closing date for entries varies from year to year. Contact the magazine for entry information.

Prizes Poet of the Year: £500, publication in the magazine, plus reading of the poem on Radio 4's *Poetry Please*; runners-up: cash prizes, plus publication in the magazine; four young poets awards.

BBC Wildlife Magazine Travel Writing Award
PO Box 229, Bristol BS99 7JN
☎0117 973 8402 Fax 0117 946 7075
Email nina.epton@bbc.co.uk

Contact *Nina Epton*

Awarded to a travel essay that is a true account involving an intimate encounter with wildlife, either local or exotic. The essay should convey a strong impression of the environment and incorporate the idea of travel and discovery. Maximum 800 words. Contact the magaine for entry information.

Prize Publication in the magazine, plus 'holiday of a lifetime'.

The BBCFour Samuel Johnson Prize for Non-fiction
The Booksellers Association, Minster House, 272 Vauxhall Bridge Road, London SW1V 1BA
☎020 7802 0802 Fax 020 7802 0803
Email sharon.down@booksellers.org.uk

Contact *Sharon Down*

ESTABLISHED 1998. Annual prize sponsored by BBCFour. Eligible categories include the arts, autobiography, biography, business, commerce, current affairs, history, natural history, popular science, religion, sport and travel. Entries submitted by publishers only. 2003 winner: Tom Binyon *Pushkin*.

Prize £30,000; £1000 to each shortlisted author.

Bedford Open Poetry Competition
PO Box 6079, Leighton Buzzard, Bedfordshire LU7 2NB
Email stewartga@waitrose.com

Contact *Gavin Stewart*

Annual award, FOUNDED 1997. Open to anyone of 16 years of age and over, competitors may submit an unlimited number of poems for a fee of £3 per poem. Entry information leaflet

available. The aim of the competition is to find good poems for publication in *The Interpreter's House* magazine. Previous winners: Julian Van Hauson and Mary Michaels.

Prizes £300 (1st); £100 (Runners-up); £50 (Bedfordshire Prize).

David Berry Prize
Royal Historical Society, University College London, Gower Street, London WC1E 6BT
☎020 7387 7532 Fax 020 7387 7532
Email rhs.info@sas.ac.uk

Contact *Executive Secretary*

Annual award for an essay of not more than 10,000 words on Scottish history. Closing date: 31 October

Prize £250,

Besterman/McColvin Medal
See **CILIP: The Chartered Institute of Library and Information Professionals Besterman/McColvin Medal**

The Biographers' Club Prize
17 Sutherland Street, London SW1V 4JU
☎020 7828 1274 Fax 020 7828 7608
Email lownie@globalnet.co.uk
Website www.booktrust.org.uk

Contact *Andrew Lownie*

ESTABLISHED 1999 by literary agent, biographer and founder of the Biographers' Club, Andrew Lownie, to finance and encourage first-time writers researching a biography. Sponsored by the *Daily Mail*. Open to previously un-commissioned writers producing a proposal of 15–20 pages, broken down by chapter with a note of author's credentials, the market for the book, sources used and competing/comparable books. 2002 winner: Anna Swan.

Prize £1000.

Birdwatch Bird Book of the Year
c/o Birdwatch Magazine, 3D/F Leroy House, 436 Essex Road, Islington, London N1 3QP
☎020 7704 9495

Contact *Dominic Mitchell*

ESTABLISHED in 1992 to acknowledge excellence in ornithological publishing – an increasingly large market with a high turnover. Annual award. Entries, from publishers, must offer an original and comprehensive treatment of their particular ornithological subject matter and must have a broad appeal to British-based readers. 2002 winner: *A Corporate Guide to Antarctic Wildlife* Hadoram Shirihai.

Biscuit Poetry and Fiction Prizes
Biscuit Publishing, PO Box 123, Washington, Newcastle upon Tyne NE37 2YW
☎0191 431 1263 Fax 0191 431 1263
Email biscuitpub@yahoo.co.uk
Website www.biscuitpublishing.com
Contacts *Brian Lister, Jacqui Lister*
FOUNDED 2000. Annual award that aims to support new writers of short fiction and poetry. The 'Top Twenty' winners from each category are published in an anthology. In addition, the winning poet and fiction author will each have separate publications. Closing date: 31 May. Previous winners: Ruth Henderson *The Art of Living*; Chris Preddle *Bonobos*; Veronica Lloyd *Adrift, from Belize to Havana*; Bob Beagrie *Huginn and Muninn*.
Prizes Publication and advance royalties.

Bisto/Book of the Year Award
See **Children's Books Ireland** under **Professional Associations**

James Tait Black Memorial Prizes
University of Edinburgh, David Hume Tower, George Square, Edinburgh EH8 9JX
☎0131 650 3619 Fax 0131 650 6898
Website www.ed.ac.uk/englit/jtbinf.htm
Contact *Department of English Literature*
ESTABLISHED 1918 in memory of a partner of the publishing firm of **A.&C. Black Ltd**. Two prizes, one for biography and one for fiction. Closing date for submissions: 30 September. Each prize is awarded for a book published or co-published in Britain in the previous 12 months. 2002 winners: Sid Smith *Something Like a House* (fiction); Robert Skidelsky *John Maynard Keynes: Fighting for Britain 1939–1947* (biography).
Prizes £3000 each.

Boardman Tasker Award
Pound House, Llangennith, Swansea, West Glamorgan SA3 1JQ
☎01792 386215 Fax 01792 386215
Email margaretbody@lineone.net
Website www.boardmantasker.com
Contact *Maggie Body, Honorary Secretary*
ESTABLISHED 1983, this award is given for a work of fiction, non-fiction or poetry, whose central theme is concerned with the mountain environment and which can be said to have made an outstanding contribution to mountain literature. Authors of any nationality are eligible, but the book must have been pub-lished or distributed in the UK for the first time between 1 November 2002 and 31 October 2003. Entries from publishers only. 2002 winner: Robert Roper *Fatal Mountaineer*.
Prize £2000 (at Trustees' discretion).

Bollinger Everyman Wodehouse Prize
Everyman Publishers, Gloucester Mansions, 140A Shaftesbury Avenue, London WC2H 8HD
☎020 7539 7608 Fax 020 7379 4060
Email dcampbell@everyman.uk.com
Website www.everyman.uk.com
Contact *Becke Parker*
ESTABLISHED in 2000 by David Campbell, publisher of Everyman's Library, Bollinger and the Hay Festival to celebrate comic writing in memory of P.G. Wodehouse. Books are nominated by readers of the *Sunday Times* and visitors to www.bol.com. Previous winner: Jonathan Coe *The Rotters' Club*.

The Booker Prize for Fiction
See **The Man Booker Prize for Fiction**

Border Television Prize
See **Lakeland Book of the Year Awards**

Harry Bowling Prize
c/o MBA Literary Agents, 62 Grafton Way, London W1T 5DW
☎020 7387 2076 Fax 020 7387 2042
Email ldana@mbalit.co.uk
Contact *Danah Arnott*
ESTABLISHED 2000 in honour of Harry Bowling, 'the king of Cockney sagas' (*d.* 1999). Biennial award, sponsored by **Headline Book Publishing**, to encourage writers of adult fiction set in London. Open to anyone who has not previously been published. Final entry date: 31 March. Entry fee charged; forms from MBA Literary Agents (enclose s.a.e.). 2002 winners: Catherine Woodman *Waking Up*; Mark Latteharry *The Symian Curve*.
Prizes Winner £1000; five runners-up £1000 each.

The BP Natural World Book Prize
See **The Natural World Book Prize**

The Branford Boase Award
9 Bolderwood Close, Bishopstoke, Eastleigh SO50 8TG
☎02380 600439
Email anne@marleyhcl.freeserve.co.uk

Website www.henriettabranford.co.uk
Acting Administrator *Anne Marley*

ESTABLISHED in 2000 in memory of children's novelist, Henrietta Branford and editor and publisher, Wendy Boase. To be awarded annually to encourage and celebrate the most promising novel by a new writer of children's books, while at the same time highlighting the importance of the editor in nurturing new talent. 2003 winners: Kevin Brooks *Martyn Pig* (book); Barry Cunningham (editor) *The Chicken House* (The Branford Boase Award).
Award £1000.

The Bridport Prize

Bridport Arts Centre, South Street, Bridport, Dorset DT6 3NR
☎01308 459444 Fax 01308 459166
Email info@bridport-arts.com
Website www.bridportprize.org.uk
Contact *Frances Everitt, Administrator*

Annual competition for poetry and short story writing. Unpublished work only, written in English. Winning stories are read by a literary agent, the winning poems are put forward to *Poetry Review* and the **Forward Prize**, and an anthology of winning entries is published. Final entry date: 30 June. Send s.a.e. for entry forms.
Prizes £3000, £1000 & £500 in each category, plus 10 supplementary prizes of £50 each.

Katharine Briggs Folklore Award

The Folklore Society, c/o The Warburg Institute, Woburn Square, London WC1H 0AB
☎020 7862 8564/8562
Email folklore-society@talk21.com
Website www.folklore-society.com
Contact *The Convenor*

ESTABLISHED 1982. An annual award in November for the book, published in Britain and Ireland between 1 June in the previous calendar year and 30 May, which has made the most distinguished non-fiction contribution to folklore studies. Intended to encourage serious research in the field which Katharine Briggs did so much to establish. The term folklore studies is interpreted broadly to include all aspects of traditional and popular culture, narrative, belief, custom and folk arts.
Prize £50, plus engraved goblet.

The British Academy Book Prize

10 Carlton House Terrace, London SW1Y 5AH
☎020 7969 5263 Fax 020 7969 5415
Email jbreckon@britac.ac.uk
Contact *Dr Jonathan Breckon*

Annual award FOUNDED in 2001 to celebrate outstanding scholarly books in the humanities and social sciences that are accessible to the general reader. Nominations from publishers only; final entry date: 20 February. 2002 winner: Stanley Cohen *States of Denial: Knowing about Atrocities and Suffering.*

British Book Awards

Publishing News, 39 Store Street, London WC1E 7DB
☎020 7692 2900 Fax 020 7419 2111
Email mailbox@publishingnews.co.uk
Website www.britishbookawards.com

ESTABLISHED 1988. Viewed by the book trade as the one to win, 'The Nibbies' are presented annually in February. The awards are made in various categories. Each winner receives the prestigious Nibbie and the awards are presented to those who have made the most impact in the book trade during the previous year. 2003 winners included: Michael Moore, the late Roy Jenkins, Allison Pearson, Jacqueline Wilson, Michael Palin, the publishers Canongate, and a lifetime achievement award for Alan Bennett. For further information contact: Merric Davidson, 12 Priors Heath, Goudhurst, Cranbrook, Kent TN17 2RE (☎/Fax 01580 212041; e-mail nibbies@mdla.co.uk).

British Czech & Slovak Association

The BCSA Prize Administrator, 24 Ferndale, Tunbridge Wells, Kent TN2 3NS
☎01892 543206
Email prize@bcsa.co.uk
Website www.bcsa.co.uk
Contact *Prize Administrator*

The British Czech & Slovak Association offers an annual prize for the best piece of original writing, in English, on the links between Britain and the Czech and Slovak Republics, or describing society in transition in those republics since the Velvet Revolution in 1989. Entries can be fiction or factual, should not have been previously published, and should be up to 2000 words in length. Submissions are invited from individuals of any age, nationality or educational background; closing date is 30 June. Details for 2004 should be checked with the Prize Administrator.
The 2002 winning entry was *The Most Splendid City – George Eliot in Prague* by Susan Reynolds of Oxford.
Prize £300, presented at the BCSA's annual dinner in London. The winning entry is published in the *British Czech & Slovak Review.*

British Fantasy Awards

201 Reddish Road, South Reddish,
Stockport, Cheshire SK5 7HR
☎0161 476 5368 (after 6.00 pm)
Email faliol@yahoo.com
Website www.britishfantasysociety.org.uk

Secretary *Robert Parkinson*

Awarded by the **British Fantasy Society** by members at its annual conference for Best Novel and Best Short Story categories, among others. Not an open competition. Previous winners include: Ramsey Campbell, Dan Simmons, Michael Marshall Smith, Thomas Ligotti.

British Press Awards

Press Gazette, Quantum House, 19 Scarbrook Road, Croydon, Surrey CR9 1LX
☎020 8565 4539 Fax 020 8565 4395
Email foyhe@quantumbusinessmedia.com
Website www.britishpressawards.com

'The Oscars of British journalism.' Open to all British morning and Sunday newspapers sold nationally and news agencies. March event. Run by *Press Gazette*.

British Science Fiction Association Award

8 Century House, Armoury Road, London SE8 4LH
☎020 8469 3354
Email awards@amaranth.aviators.net
Website www.bsfa.co.uk

Award Administrator *Tanya Brown*

ESTABLISHED 1966. Categories for novel, short story, artwork and non-fiction. The awards are announced and presented at the British Annual SF Convention every Easter. 2002 winners: Christopher Priest *The Separation*; Neil Gaiman *Coraline*; David Langford *Maps: the Uncollected John Sladek*.

British Sports Journalism Awards

See **Sports Writers' Association of Great Britain** under **Professional Associations**

The Caine Prize for African Writing

2 Drayson Mews, London W8 4LY
☎020 7376 0440 Fax 020 7938 3728
Email caineprize@jftaylor.com
Website www.caineprize.com

Administrator *Nick Elam*
Secretary *Jan Hart*

Annual award FOUNDED in 1999 in memory of Sir Michael Caine, former chairman of Booker plc, to recognise worth of African writing in English. Awarded for a short story by an African writer, published in English anywhere in the world. 'An African writer' is someone who was born in Africa, or who is a national of an African country, or whose parents are African, and whose work has reflected African sensibilities. Final entry date: 31 January; submissions by publishers only. 2002 winner: Binyavanga Wainaina *Discovering Home*.

    Prize $15,000.

The Calouste Gulbenkian Prize
See **The Translators Association Awards**

James Cameron Award

City University, Department of Journalism, Northampton Square, London EC1V 0HB
☎020 7477 8221 Fax 020 7477 8594

Contact *The Administrator*

Annual award for journalism to a reporter of any nationality, working for the British media, whose work is judged to have contributed most during the year to the continuance of the Cameron tradition. Administered by the City University Department of Journalism. 2002 winner: Chris McGreal, *The Guardian*.

Canadian Poetry Association Annual Poetry Contest

Box 22571, St George Postal Outlet, 264 Bloor Street West, Toronto, Ontario M5S 1V8, Canada
Website www.mirror.org/cpa

Annual contest open to members and non-members of the CPA worldwide. Submission fee: $5 per poem. See the website for entry details. All winning poems are published on the CPA website.

    Six cash *Prizes* and publication in *Poetmata*.

Canadian Poetry Association Shaunt Basmajian Award

Box 22571, St George Postal Outlet, 264 Bloor Street West, Toronto, Ontario M5S 1V8 Canada
Website www.mirror.org/cpa

Annual poetry contest open to members and non-members of the CPA worldwide. Entry fee: C$15; cheque or money order payable to the Canadian Poetry Association. Submit a manuscript of poems up to 24 pages in length, published or unpublished, and in any style or tradition. See the website for full details. The author of the winning manuscript receives 50 copies of the resulting chapbook as well as C$100 cash.

Cardiff International Poetry Competition

PO Box 438, Cardiff CF10 5YA
☎029 2047 2266 Fax 029 2049 2930
Email post@academi.org
Website www.academi.org

Contact *Peter Finch*

ESTABLISHED 1986. An annual competition for unpublished poems in English of up to 50 lines. Closing date in January.

Prize £5000 (total).

Carey Award

Society of Indexers, Blades Enterprise Centre, John Street, Sheffield, South Yorkshire S2 4SU
☎0114 292 2350 Fax 0114 292 2351
Email admin@indexers.org.uk
Website www.indexers.org.uk

Secretary *Ann Kingdom*

A private award made by the Society to a member who has given outstanding services to indexing. The recipient is selected by Council with no recommendations considered from elsewhere.

Carnegie Medal

See **CILIP: The Chartered Institute of Library and Information Professionals Carnegie Medal**

Sid Chaplin Short Story Competition

Shildon Town Council, Civic Centre Square, Shildon, Co Durham DL4 1AH
☎01388 772563 Fax 01388 775227

Contact *Mrs J.M. Stafford*

ESTABLISHED 1986. Annual themed short story competition (2002 subject was "Life'). Maximum 3000 words; £2 entrance fee (juniors free). All stories must be unpublished and not broadcast and/or performed. Application forms available from September 2003.

Prizes £300 (1st); £150 (2nd); £75 (3rd); £50 (Junior).

Children's Book Circle Eleanor Farjeon Award

See **Eleanor Farjeon Award**

The Children's Laureate

c/o Fraser Ross Associates, 6 Wellington Place, Edinburgh EH6 7EQ
☎0131 553 2759
Email lindsey.fraser@tiscali.org.uk
Website www.childrenslaureate.org

Administrator *Fraser Ross Associates*

ESTABLISHED 1998. The Laureate is awarded biennially to an eminent British writer or illustrator of children's books both in celebration of a lifetime's achievement and to highlight the role of children's book creators in inspiring, informing and entertaining young readers. 2003 winner: Michael Morpurgo.

Award Medal and £10,000.

CILIP: The Chartered Institute of Library and Information Professionals Besterman/McColvin Medal

7 Ridgmount Street, London WC1E 7AE
☎020 7255 0650 Fax 020 7255 0501
Website www.cilip.org.uk/awards

Part of the CILIP/Nielsen BookData Reference Awards. Annual award for an outstanding reference work first published in the UK during the preceding year. Consists of two categories: printed and electronic. Works eligible for consideration include: encyclopedias, general and special dictionaries; annuals, yearbooks and directories; handbooks and compendia of data; atlases. Nominations are invited from members of **CILIP**, publishers and others. 2002 winner (printed): *20th Century Ceramic Designers in Britain* by Andrew Casey; 2002 winner (electronic): *The Visual Culture of Wales: Imaging the Nation* by Peter Lord.

Award Medal and cash prize for each category.

CILIP: The Chartered Institute of Library and Information Professionals Carnegie Medal

7 Ridgmount Street, London WC1E 7AE
☎020 7255 0650 Fax 020 7255 0501
Website www.ckg.org.uk

ESTABLISHED 1936. Presented for an outstanding book for children written in English and first published in the UK during the preceding year. Fiction, non-fiction and poetry are all eligible. Previous winner: *20th Century Ceramic Designers in Britain* by Andrew Casey; 2002 winner: Terry Pratchett *Amazing Maurice and his Educated Rodents.*

Award Medal.

CILIP: The Chartered Institute of Library and Information Professionals Kate Greenaway Medal

7 Ridgmount Street, London WC1E 7AE
☎020 7255 0650 Fax 020 7255 0501

Website www.ckg.org.uk

ESTABLISHED 1955. Presented annually for the most distinguished work in the illustration of children's books first published in the UK during the preceding year. 2002 winner: *Pirate Diary* by Chris Riddell.

Award Medal. The Colin Mears Award (£5000 cash) is given annually to the winner of the Kate Greenaway Medal.

CILIP: The Chartered Institute of Library and Information Professionals Walford Award

7 Ridgmount Street, London WC1E 7AE
☎020 7255 0650 Fax 020 7255 0501
Website www.cilip.org.uk/awards

Part of the CILIP/Nielsen BookData Reference Awards. Awarded to an individual who has made a sustained and continual contribution to British bibliography over a period of years. The nominee need not be resident in the UK. The award is named after Dr A.J. Walford, a bibliograper of international repute. Previous winners include: Prof. J.D. Pearson, Prof. R.C. Alston and Prof. John McIlwaine. 2002 winner: Robin Alston.

Award Cash prize and certificate.

CILIP: The Chartered Institute of Library and Information Professionals Wheatley Medal

7 Ridgmount Street, London WC1E 7AE
☎020 7255 0650 Fax 020 7255 0501
Website www.cilip.org.uk/awards

Part of the CILIP/NielsenBookData Awards. ESTABLISHED 1962. Annual award for an outstanding index first published in the UK during the preceding three years. Whole work must have originated in the UK and recommendations for the award are invited from members of **CILIP**, the **Society of Indexers**, publishers and others. Previous winners include: Paul Nash *The World of Environment 1972–1992*; Richard Raper *The Works of Charles Darwin*; David Crystal and Hilary Crystal *Words on Words*. 2002 winner: *Encyclopedia Britannica 2002*. Revision edited by Dale H. Holberg; published by Encyclopedia Britannica Inc.; indexer: Dale H. Holberg.

Award Medal and cash prize.

Arthur C. Clarke Award for Science Fiction

60 Bournemouth Road, Folkestone, Kent CT19 5AZ
☎01303 252939
Email arthurcclarkeaward@yahoo.com

Website www.clarkeaward.com

Administrator *Paul Kincaid*

ESTABLISHED 1986. The Arthur C. Clarke Award is given annually to the best science fiction novel with first UK publication in the previous calendar year. Both hardcover and paperback books qualify. Made possible by a generous donation from Arthur C. Clarke, this award is selected by a rotating panel of judges nominated by the **British Science Fiction Association**, the **Science Fiction Foundation** and the Science Museum. 2002 winner: Gwyneth Jones *Bold as Love*.

Award £2002 (award increases by £1 per year), plus trophy.

The Commonwealth Writers Prize

Booktrust, Book House, 45 East Hill, London SW18 2QZ
☎020 8516 2972 Fax 020 8516 2978
Email tarryn@booktrust.org.uk
Website www.booktrust.org.uk *or*
   www.commonwealthwriters.com

Contact *Tarryn McKay*

ESTABLISHED 1987. An annual award to reward and encourage the upsurge of new Commonwealth fiction. Any work of prose or fiction is eligible, i.e. a novel or collection of short stories. No drama or poetry. The work must be first written in English by a citizen of the Commonwealth and be first published in the year before its entry for the prize. Entries must be submitted by the publisher to the region of the writer's Commonwealth citizenship. The four regions are: Africa, Eurasia, S.E. Asia and South Pacific, Caribbean and Canada. 2003 winners: Best Book Award – Austin Clarke *The Polished Hoe*; Best First Book Award – Sarah Hull *Haweswater*.

Prizes £10,000 for Best Book; £3000 for Best First Book; 8 prizes of £1000 for each best and first best book in four regions.

The Thomas Cook Travel Book Award

Thomas Cook Publishing, PO Box 227, Peterborough PE3 8XX
☎01733 402009 Fax 01733 416688

ESTABLISHED in 1980 by The Thomas Cook Group. Annual award given to the author of the book, published (in the English language) in the previous year, which most inspires the reader to want to travel. Submissions by publishers only. 2002 winner: Ma Jian *Red Dust*.

Award £10,000.

The Duff Cooper Prize
54 St Maur Road, London SW6 4DP
☎020 7736 3729 Fax 020 7731 7638

Contact *Artemis Cooper*

An annual award for a literary work of biography, history, politics or poetry, published by a recognised publisher (member of the **Publishers Association**) during the previous 12 months. The book must be submitted by the publisher, not the author. Financed by the interest from a trust fund commemorating Duff Cooper, first Viscount Norwich (1890–1954). 2002 winner: Jane Ridley *The Architect and his Wife: a Life of Edwin Lutyens*.
  Prize £3000.

Rose Mary Crawshay Prize
The British Academy, 10 Carlton House Terrace, London SW1Y 5AH
☎020 7969 5200 Fax 020 7969 5300
Website www.britac.ac.uk

Contact *British Academy Secretary*

ESTABLISHED 1888 by Rose Mary Crawshay, this prize is given for a historical or critical work by a woman of any nationality on English literature, with particular preference for a work on Keats, Byron or Shelley. The work must have been published in the preceding three years.
  Prizes Normally two of approximately £500 each.

Crime Writers' Association (Cartier Diamond Dagger)
PO Box 273, Boreham Wood, Hertfordshire WD6 2XA
Email secretary@thecwa.co.uk
Website www.thecwa.co.uk

Contact *The Secretary*

ESTABLISHED 1986. An annual award for a lifetime's outstanding contribution to the genre. 2003 winner: Robert Barnard.

Crime Writers' Association (The CWA Ellis Peters Historical Dagger)
PO Box 273, Boreham Wood, Hertfordshire WD6 2XA
Email secretary@thecwa.co.uk
Website www.thecwa.co.uk

Contact *The Secretary*

ESTABLISHED 1999. Annual award for the best historical crime novel. Nominations from publishers only. 2002 winner: Sarah Waters *Fingersmith*.
  Award Dagger, plus cheque.

Crime Writers' Association (The Ian Fleming Steel Dagger)
PO Box 273, Boreham Wood, Hertfordshire WD6 2XA
Email secretary@thecwa.co.uk
Website www.thecwa.co.uk

Contact *The Secretary*

FOUNDED 2002. Annual award for the best thriller, adventure or spy novel. Sponsored by Ian Fleming (Glidrose) Publications Ltd to celebrate the best of contemporary thriller writing. 2002 winner: John Creed *The Sirius Crossing*.
  Award Dagger, plus cheque.

Crime Writers' Association (The Macallan Gold Dagger for Non-Fiction)
PO Box 273, Boreham Wood, Hertfordshire WD6 2XA
Email secretary@thecwa.co.uk
Website www.thecwa.co.uk

Contact *The Secretary*

Annual award for the best non-fiction crime book published during the year. Nominations from publishers only. 2002 winner: Lillian Pizzichini *Dead Men's Wages*.
  Award Dagger, plus cheque (sum varies).

Crime Writers' Association (The Macallan Gold and Silver Daggers for Fiction)
PO Box 273, Boreham Wood, Hertfordshire WD6 2XA
Email secretary@thecwa.co.uk
Website www.thecwa.co.uk

Contact *The Secretary*

Two annual awards for the best crime fiction published during the year. Nominations for Gold Dagger from publishers only. 2002 winners: José Carlos Somoza *The Athenian Murders* (Gold); James Crumley *The Final Count* (Silver).
  Award Dagger, plus cheque (sum varies).

Crime Writers' Association (The Macallan Short Story Dagger)
PO Box 273, Boreham Wood, Hertfordshire WD6 2XA
Email secretary@thecwa.co.uk
Website www.thecwa.co.uk

Contact *The Secretary*

ESTABLISHED 1993. An award for a published crime story. Publishers should submit three copies of the story by 30 September. 2002 winner: Stella Duffy *Martha Grace*.

Prize Dagger, plus cheque.

Crime Writers' Association (The Creasey Dagger for Best First Crime Novel)
PO Box 273, Boreham Wood, Hertfordshire WD6 2XA
Email secretary@thecwa.co.uk
Website www.thecwa.co.uk

Contact *The Secretary*

ESTABLISHED 1973 following the death of crime writer John Creasey, founder of the **Crime Writers' Association**. This award, sponsored by Chivers Press, is given annually for the best crime novel by an author who has not previously published a full-length work of fiction. Nominations from publishers only. 2002 winner: Louise Welsh *The Cutting Room*.

Award Dagger, plus cheque.

Crime Writers' Association (The Dagger in the Library)
PO Box 273, Boreham Wood, Hertfordshire WD6 2XA
Email secretary@thecwa.co.uk

Contact *The Secretary*

REINSTATED 2002. Annual award (sponsored by Random House) to the author whose work has given most pleasure to readers. Nominated and judged by librarians. 2002 winner: Peter Robinson.

Award Dagger, plus cheque.

Crime Writers' Association (The Debut Dagger)
New Writing Competition, P.O. Box 63, Wakefield WF2 0YW
Email debut.dagger@thecwa.co.uk
Website www.thecwa.co.uk

Contact *The Secretary*

Annual competition (sponsored by Orion) for unpublished writers to submit the first 3000 words and 500 word outline of crime novel (entry fee and form required). For full details see website or send s.a.e. to the address above. 2002 winner: Ilona Van Mil *Sugarmilk Falls*.

Award Dagger, plus cheque.

David Cohen British Literature Prize
Arts Council of England, 14 Great Peter Street, London SW1P 3NQ
☎020 7333 0100 Fax 020 7973 6520
Website www.artscouncil.org.uk
Literature Director *Gary McKeone*
Literature Assistant *Pippa Shoubridge*

ESTABLISHED 1993 by the Arts Council and awarded biennially, the British Literature Prize is one of the most distinguished literary prizes in Britain. It recognises English language writers who are British citizens, encompassing dramatists as well as novelists, poets and essayists. The prize is for a lifetime's achievement and is donated by the David Cohen Family Charitable Trust. Set up in 1980 by David Cohen, GP and son of a property developer, the Trust has helped composers, choreographers, dancers, poets, playwrights and actors. The Council is providing a further £10,000 to enable the winner to commission new work, with the dual aim of encouraging young writers and readers. Previous winners: William Trevor, Dame Muriel Spark, Harold Pinter, V.S. Naipaul, Doris Lessing. The 2003 prize was shared between novelist Beryl Bainbridge and poet Thom Gunn.

Award £30,000, plus £10,000 towards new work.

Hunter Davies Prize
See **Lakeland Book of the Year Awards**

Isaac & Tamara Deutscher Memorial Prize
SML, University of Southampton, Highfield, Southampton, Hampshire SO17 1BJ
Email ed2@soton.ac.uk

Contact *Dr Elizabeth Dore*

An annual award in recognition of, and as an encouragement to, outstanding research in or about the Marxist tradition. Made to the author of a published book. Final entry date: 1 May.

Award £250.

George Devine Award
17A South Villas, London NW1 9BS
☎020 7267 9793 (evenings only)

Contact *Christine Smith*

Annual award for a promising new playwright writing for the stage in memory of George Devine, artistic director of the **Royal Court Theatre**, who died in 1965. The play, which can be of any length, does not need to have been produced. Send two copies of the script, plus outline of work, to Christine Smith. Send s.a.e. for the script to be returned if required. Closing date: March. Information leaflet available from January on receipt of s.a.e.

Prize £10,000.

Denis Devlin
Memorial Award for Poetry
An Chomhairle Ealaíon (The Irish Arts
Council), 70 Merrion Square, Dublin 2,
Republic of Ireland
☎00 353 1 6180200 Fax 00 353 1 6761302
Email info@artscouncil.ie
Website www.artscouncil.ie

Contact *Literature Officer*

Triennial award for the best book of poetry in
English by an Irish poet, published in the pre-
ceding three years. Next award 2004.
Award €2500.

Dingle Prize
British Society for the History of Science,
31 High Street, Stanford in the Vale,
Farringdon, Oxfordshire SN7 8LH
☎01367 718963 Fax 01367 718963
Email bshs@hidex.demon.co.uk
Website www.bshs.org.uk

Biennial award made by the BSHS to the best
book in the history of science (broadly con-
strued) which is accessible to a wide audience
of non-specialists. Next award: 2005. Previous
winners: Deborah Cadbury *The Dinosaur
Hunters*; Steven Shapin *The Scientific Revolution*.
Prize £300.

Drama Association of Wales
Playwriting Competition
The Old Library, Singleton Road, Splott,
Cardiff CF24 2ET
☎029 2045 2200 Fax 029 2045 2277
Email aled.daw@virgin.net

Contact *Teresa Hennessy*

Annual competition held to promote the writing of one-act plays in English and Welsh of
between 20 and 50 minutes' playing time. The
competition format is reviewed annually, looking at different themes, genres and markets.
Application forms from the address above.

The Dryden Competition
(British Comparative Literature Association/
British Centre for Literary Translation)
School of Language, Linguistics and
Translation Studies, University of East Anglia,
Norwich, Norfolk NR4 7TJ
Fax 01603 250599
Email transcomp@uea.ac.uk
Website www.bcla.org

Competition Organiser *Dr Jean Boase-Beier*

ESTABLISHED 1983. Annual competition open

to unpublished literary translations from all languages. Maximum submission: 25 pages.
Prizes £350 (1st); £200 (2nd); £100 (3rd);
plus publication for all winning entries in the
Association's annual journal. Other entries may
receive commendations.

The Dundee Book Prize
City of Discovery Campaign Press Office,
Prospect III Business Centre, Gemini
Crescent, Dundee Technology Park, Dundee
DD2 1SW
☎01382 562883 Fax 01382 562882
Email anne.rendall@beattie-dundee.co.uk
Website www.dundeecity.gov.uk

Contact *Anne Rendall*

LAUNCHED in 1998, this is a biennial award. The
first prize winner was Andrea Murray Scott for
Tumulus. Second prize winner was Claire-Marie
Watson for *The Cirewife*. Entry qualifications are
detailed in the entry form. Final entry date
March 2004.
Prize £6000 plus publication of novel.

S.T. Dupont Golden PEN Award
for Lifetime Distinguished Service
to Literature
English Centre of International PEN, 152–156
Kentish Town Road, London NW1 9QB
☎020 7267 9444 Fax 020 7267 9304
Email enquiries@englishpen.org
Website www.englishpen.org

Awarded to a senior writer, with a distinguished body of work over many years, who
has made a significant and constructive impact
on fellow writers, the reading public and the
literary world. Nominations by members of
English PEN only. Previous winners include
V.S. Pritchett, Iris Murdoch and Francis King.
2002 award winner: Doris Lessing.
Prize £500 and a golden pen awarded by
S.T. Dupont.

The Encore Award
The Society of Authors, 84 Drayton Gardens,
London SW10 9SB
☎020 7373 6642 Fax 020 7373 5768
Email info@societyofauthors.org
Website www.societyofauthors.org

ESTABLISHED 1990. Awarded for the best sec-
ond published novel or novels of the year.
Final entry date: 30 November. Details from
the **Society of Authors**. 2002 winner: Ali
Smith *Hotel World*.
Prize £10,000.

Envoi Poetry Competition

Envoi, 44 Rudyard Road, Biddulph Moor,
Stoke on Trent, Staffordshire ST8 7JN
☎01782 517892

Contact *Roger Elkin*

Run by *Envoi* poetry magazine. Competitions
are featured regularly, with prizes of £300, plus
three annual subscriptions to *Envoi*. Winning
poems along with full adjudication report are
published. Send s.a.e. to Competition Secretary,
17 Millcroft, Bishops Stortford, Hertfordshire
CM23 2BP.

EuroPAWS (European Public Awareness of Science) Midas Prize

The EuroPAWS Office, OMNI
Communications, Chancel House, Neasden
Lane, London NW10 2TU
☎020 8214 1543   Fax 020 8214 1544
Email pawsomni@globalnet.co.uk

Contacts *Barrie Whatley, Andrew Millington*

ESTABLISHED 1998. Annual prize awarded to
the writer and producer of the best television
drama, first transmitted in the year up to the
end of October, that bears in a significant way
on science or engineering. The drama may be a
single play or an episode of a series, serial or
soap. It need not necessarily be centred on a
science or engineering theme, although clearly
it can be. The context and quality of the drama
and the audience size all weigh alongside the
science in making the Award. To enter a programme or suggest that a programme should be
entered, contact the EuroPAWS office above.
Prize £5000.

Euroscript Film Story Competitions

See **Euroscript** under **Writers' Courses, Circles and Workshops**

Geoffrey Faber Memorial Prize

Faber & Faber Ltd, 3 Queen Square, London
WC1N 3AU
☎020 7465 0045   Fax 020 7465 0034

ESTABLISHED 1963 as a memorial to the
founder and first chairman of **Faber & Faber**,
this prize is awarded in alternate years for the
volume of verse and the volume of prose fiction published in the UK in the preceding two
years, which is judged to be of greatest literary
merit. Authors must be under 40 at the time of
publication and citizens of the UK,
Commonwealth, Republic of Ireland or South

Africa. 2002 winner: Greta Stoddart *At Home
in the Dark.*
Prize £1000.

Eleanor Farjeon Award

Children's Book Circle, c/o David Higham
Associates, 5–8 Lower John St, Golden
Square, London W1F 9HA
☎020 7437 7888   Fax 020 7437 1072

This award, named in memory of the much-
loved children's writer, is for distinguished services to children's books either in this country or
overseas, and may be given to a librarian,
teacher, publisher, bookseller, author, artist,
reviewer, television producer, etc. Nominations
from members of the **Children's Book Circle**.
Sponsored by **Scholastic**. 2002 winner: Philip
Pullman.
Award £750.

The Fish Short Story Prize

Fish Publishing, Durrus, Bantry, Co. Cork,
Republic of Ireland
☎00 353 27 61246
Email info@fishpublishing.com
Website www.fishpublishing.com

Contact *Clem Cairns*

FOUNDED 1994. Annual international award
which aims to discover, encourage and publish
exciting new literary talent. The best 15–20
stories are published in an anthology. Previously
unpublished stories up to 5000 words are eli-
gible. Entry fee: £11 (€14) for first, £8 (€10) for
subsequent entries; concession rate: £8 (€10).
Closing date: 30 November. 2003 winner
Andrew Lloyd Jones *Feathers and Cigarettes.*
Previous winners: Gina Oschner *From the Bering
Strait*; Kathy Hughes *Five O'Clock Shadow*;
Maureen O'Neill *Asylum 1928*; Catherine
Dowd *Franklin's Grace.*
First Prize: £1000/€1500; Second Prize: one-
week residence at Anam Cara Writers' and
Artists' Retreat in West Cork.

Sir Banister Fletcher Award

Authors' Club, 40 Dover Street, London
W1S 4NP
☎020 7499 8581   Fax 020 7409 0913

Contact *Mrs Ann de La Grange*

This award was created by Sir Bannister
Fletcher, President of the **Authors' Club** for
many years, and is presented annually. The prize
alternates between books on architecture and
the fine arts. In 2002 the prize was awarded for
the best book on the fine arts published during
the previous two years. Submissions to Mrs Ann

de La Grange at the Authors' Club. Previous winners: Jean Clair *Balthus*; David Alan Brown *Leonardo da Vinci*; Richard Weston *Alvar Aalto*; Dr Megan Aldrich *Gothic Revival*; Professor Thomas Markus *Building and Power*; John Onians *Bearers of Meaning: Classical Orders in Antiquity*; Sir Michael Levey *Gianbattista Tiepolo: his life and art;* John Allan *Berthold Lubetkin – Architecture and The Tradition of Progress*.

The John Florio Prize
See **The Translators Association Awards**

The Forward Prizes for Poetry
Colman Getty PR, Middlesex House, 34–42 Cleveland Street, London W1T 4JE
☎020 7631 2666   Fax 020 7631 2699
Email sophie@colmangettypr.co.uk
Contact *Sophie Rochester*
ESTABLISHED 1992. Three awards: the Forward Prize for Best Collection, the Waterstone's Prize for Best First Collection and the Tolman Cunard Prize for Best Single Poem which is not already part of an anthology or collection. All entries must be published in the UK or Eire and submitted by poetry publishers (collections) or newspaper and magazine editors (single poems). Individual entries of poets' own work are not accepted. 2002 winners: Peter Porter (best collection), Tom French (best first collection), Medbh McGuckian (best single poem).
  Prizes £10,000 for best collection; £5000 for best first collection; £1000 for best single poem.

The Frogmore Poetry Prize
42 Morehall Avenue, Folkestone, Kent CT19 4EF
Website www.frogmorepress.co.uk
Contact *Jeremy Page*
ESTABLISHED 1987. Awarded annually and sponsored by the Frogmore Foundation. The winning poem, runners-up and short-listed entries are all published in the magazine. Previous winners: David Satherley, Caroline Price, Bill Headdon, John Latham, Diane Brown, Tobias Hill, Mario Petrucci, Gina Wilson, Ross Cogan, Joan Benner, Ann Alexander, Gerald Watts.
  Prize The winner receives 200 guineas and a life subscription to the biannual literary magazine, *The Frogmore Papers*.

R.H. Gapper Book Prize
Society for French Studies, Taylor Institution, St Giles, Oxford OX1 3NA
Email french.studies@taylib.ox/ac.uk

Website www.sfs.ac.uk
Contact *The Editor*
ESTABLISHED in 2000 to promote excellence in scholarship in French Studies. Awarded for critical and scholarly distinction and likely impact on wider critical debate. The winner is chosen from all books received for review by *French Studies* quarterly journal in the previous calendar year. The author must be based in an institution of higher education in the UK or Ireland. 2002 winner: Stephen Bann *Parallel Lives: Printmakers, Painters and Photographers in 19th Century France.*
  Prize £2000, presented at the Society for French Studies annual conference.

Martha Gellhorn Trust Prize
Rutherfords, Herbert Road, Salcombe, Devon TQ8 8HN
Annual prize for journalism in honour of one of the twentieth century's greatest reporters. Open for journalism published in English, giving 'the view from the ground – a human story that penetrates the established version of events and illuminates an urgent issue buried by prevailing fashions of what makes news'. The subject matter can involve the UK or abroad. Six copies of each entry should be sent to the above address by 7 March. 2002 winner: Geoffrey Lean.
  Prize £5000.

The Gladstone History Book Prize
Royal Historical Society, University College London, Gower Street, London WC1E 6BT
☎020 7387 7532   Fax 020 7387 7532
Contact *Executive Secretary*
ESTABLISHED 1998. Annual award for the best new work on any historical subject which is not primarily related to British history, published in the UK in the preceding calendar year. The book must be the author's first (solely written) history book and be an original and scholarly work of historical research. Closing date: 31 December. 2002 joint winners: David M. Hopkin *Soldiers and Peasants in French Popular Culture 1766–1870*; Gary Rowlands *The Dynastic State and the Army under Louis XIV: Royal Service and Private Interest 1661–1701.*
  Prize £1000.

Glenfiddich Food & Drink Awards
1 Bedford Avenue, London WC1B 3AU
☎020 7255 1100   Fax 020 7255 5454
Known as the 'Cooker Bookers' or the 'Oscars'

of the gastronomic world, the awards aim to recognise excellence in writing, publishing and broadcasting on the subjects of food and drink. There are 12 category winners from work published or broadcast in the UK and the Republic of Ireland. 2003 winners: Food Book: *Thai Food* David Thompson; Drink Book: *Africa Uncorked* John and Erica Platter; Food Writer: Chandos Elletson for work in *Restaurant Magazine*; Magazine Cookery Writer: Brian Glover for work in *Homes & Gardens*; Newspaper Cookery Writer: Mark Hix for work in *The Independent Magazine*; Restaurant Critic: Tracey MacLeod for work in *The Independent Magazine*; Drink Writer: Andrew Jefford for work in *Harpers* and *Decanter*; Wine Writer: Andrew Jefford for work in *Decanter* and *Waitrose Food Illustrated*; Regional Writer (joint winners): Sue Lawrence for work in *Scotland on Sunday*; Paddy Shennan and Mike Chapple for the *Liverpool Echo Pub Guide*; Bar Writer: Richard Erlich for work in *The Independent on Sunday Review*; Radio Programme: *Food Poverty*, The Food Programme, BBC Radio 4, presented by Sheila Dillon; Television Programme: *Jamie's Kitchen*, Channel 4, featuring Jamie Oliver; Photography: Georgia Glynn Smith for work in *Sainsburys Magazine* and *Living* etc.; Multimedia: www.bbc.co.uk/food, edited by Sue Todd, BBC; GQ/Glenfiddich Food & Drink Personality of the Year: Jamie Oliver; Independent Spirit Award: James Pavitt, co-ordinator of the National Association of Farmers' Markets.

Award Overall winner (chosen from the category winners) £3000, plus the Glenfiddich Trophy (which is held for one year); category winners £1000 each, plus a case of Glenfiddich Single Malt Scotch Whisky.

Golden Kite Award
See **Society for Children's Book Writers & Illustrators** under **Professional Associations**

The Phillip Good Memorial Prize
QWF Magazine, PO Box 1768, Rugby CV21 4ZA
Email jo.good@ntlworld.com
Website www.qwfmagazine.co.uk

Contact *Competition Secretary*

ESTABLISHED in 1997, the competition is run by *QWF Magazine* . The prize commemorates the memory of Phillip Good (late husband of *QWF* editor, Jo Good) and is for short stories of less than 5000 words in any style or genre (except children's). Open entry. Entrants may request in-depth critique of their stories for an extra fee. For entry forms send s.a.e. to the address above. Closing date: 21 August.

Prizes (total) at least £525, plus free subscription to *QWF Magazine*; also book prizes and publication for winning authors.

Edgar Graham Book Prize
c/o Development Studies, School of Oriental and African Studies, Thornhaugh Street, Russell Square, London WC1H 0XG
☎020 7898 4485 Fax 020 7898 4519

Contact *Professor Henry Bernstein*

ESTABLISHED 1984. Biennial award in memory of Edgar Graham. Aims to encourage research work in Third World agricultural and industrial development. At the time of going to press the award was under review.

Kate Greenaway Medal
See **CILIP: The Chartered Institute of Library and Information Professionals Kate Greenaway Medal**

The Griffin Poetry Prize
6610 Edwards Boulevard, Mississauga, Ontario, Canada L5T 2V6
☎001 905 565 5993 Fax 001 905 564 3645
Email info@griffinpoetryprize.com
Website www.griffinpoetryprize.com

Contact *Ruth Smith, Manager*

Annual award ESTABLISHED in 2000 by Toronto-based entrepreneur, Scott Griffin, for books of poetry written in or translated into English. Trustees include Margaret Atwood and Michael Ondaatje. Submissions from publishers only.

Prizes A total of C$80,000, divided into two categories: International and Canadian.

The Guardian Children's Fiction Award
The Guardian, 119 Farringdon Road, London EC1R 3ER
☎020 7239 9694 Fax 020 7713 4366

Children's Book Editor *Julia Eccleshare*

ESTABLISHED 1967. Annual award for an outstanding work of fiction for children aged seven and over by a British or Commonwealth author, first published in the UK in the preceding year, excluding picture books. Final entry date: 1 June. No application form necessary. 2002 winner: Sonya Hartnett *Thursday's Child*.

Award £1500.

The Guardian First Book Award

The Guardian, 119 Farringdon Road, London EC1R 3ER
☎020 7239 9694 Fax 020 7713 4366

Contact *Literary Editor*

ESTABLISHED 1999. Annual award for first time authors published in English in the UK. All genres of writing eligible, apart from academic, guidebooks, children's, educational, manuals, reprints and TV, radio and film tie-ins. 2002 winner: Jonathan Safran Foer *Everything Is Illuminated*.

Award £10,000, plus *Guardian/Observer* advertising package.

Guild of Food Writers Awards

48 Crabtree Lane, London SW6 6LW
☎020 7610 1180 Fax 020 7610 0299
Email awards@gfw.co.uk
Website www.gfw.co.uk

Contact *Christina Thomas*

ESTABLISHED 1985. Annual awards in recognition of outstanding achievement in all areas in which food writers work and have influence. Entry is not restricted to members of the Guild. Entry form available from the address above. 2002 winners: Derek Cooper Award: *Local Food Programme Toolkit* various authors; Michael Smith Award: Colin Spencer *British Food: An Extraordinary Thousand Years of History*; Jeremy Round Award for Best First Book of the Year: Clarissa Hyman *Cucina Siciliana*; Food Journalist of the Year: Kevin Gould for work in *Waitrose Food Illustrated*; Cookery Journalist of the Year: Annie Bell for work in *Country Living*; Food Book of the Year: David Thompson *Thai Food*; Cookery Book of the Year: Monisha Bharadwaj *Stylish Indian in Minutes*.

Gwobr Llyfr y Flwyddyn

See **Arts Council of Wales Book of the Year Awards**

James W. Hackett Award

See **The British Haiku Society** under **Organisations of Interest to Poets**

Hastings National Poetry Competition

See **Hastings International Poetry Festival** under **Festivals**

W.H. Heinemann Award

Royal Society of Literature, Somerset House, Strand, London WC2R 1LA
☎020 7845 4676 Fax 020 7845 4679
Email info@rslit.org
Website www.rslit.org

ESTABLISHED 1945. This prize is most often awarded to works of non-fiction: biography, history, poetry, criticism, through novels, if of sufficient distinction, will not be overlooked. Books must be written in the English language and have been published in the previous year; translations are not eligible for consideration nor are single poems, nor collections of pieces by more than one author, nor may individuals put forward their own work. Publishers must contact the Secretary for details of how to submit works. Final entry date: 15 December. Up to three awards may be given. Previous winner: Miranda Carter *Anthony Blunt – His Lives*.

Prize £5000.

Hellenic Foundation Prize

See **The Translators Association Awards**

Felicia Hemans Prize for Lyrical Poetry

University of Liverpool, PO Box 147, Liverpool, Merseyside L69 3BX
☎0151 794 2458 Fax 0151 794 2454
Email wilderc@liv.ac.uk

Contact *The Registrar*

ESTABLISHED 1899. Annual award for published or unpublished verse. Open to past or present members and students of the University of Liverpool. One poem per entrant only. Closing date 1 May.

Prize £30.

The Hessell-Tiltman Prize for History

English Centre of International PEN, 152–156 Kentish Town Road, London NW1 9QB
☎020 7267 9444 Fax 020 7267 9304
Email enquiries@englishpen.org
Website www.englishpen.org

FOUNDED 2002. Awarded for a history book, written in English (including translations) and aimed at a wide audience. Submissions by publishers only. Previous winner: Margaret MacMillan *Peacemakers*.

Prize £3000 and Silver Dupont pen.

Heywood Hill Literary Prize

10 Curzon Street, London W1J 5HH
☎020 7629 0647

Contact *John Saumarez Smith*

ESTABLISHED 1995 by the Duke of Devonshire to reward a lifetime's contribution to the enjoyment of books. Three judges chosen annually. No applications are necessary for this award. 2002 winner: Michael Frayn.

Prize £15,000.

Hidden Brook Press International Poetry Anthology Contests

412–701 King Street West, Toronto, Ontario, Canada M5V 2W7

☎001 416 504 3966 Fax 001 801 751 1837

Email writers@hiddenbrookpress.com

Website www.HiddenBrookPress.com

International poetry competitions: No Love Lost Poetry Anthology Contest; The Open Window Poetry Anthology Contest and Seeds International Poetry Chapbook Anthology Contest. Electronic and hard copy submissions are required. Closing dates and full entry details can be found on the website. Ten cash prizes, up to 12 Honourable Mentions and up to 300 runners up published in perfect bound colour-cover book.

William Hill
Sports Book of the Year

Greenside House, Station Road, Wood Green, London N22 7TP

☎020 8918 3731 Fax 020 8918 3728

Email pressoffice@williamhill.co.uk

Contact *Graham Sharpe*

ESTABLISHED 1989. Annual award introduced by Graham Sharpe of bookmakers William Hill. Sponsored by William Hill and thus dubbed the 'Bookie' prize, it is the first, and only, Sports Book of the Year award. Final entry date: September. 2002 winner: Donald McRae *In Black and White*.

Prize (reviewed annually) £15,000 package including £12,000 cash, hand-bound copy, £1000 free bet. Runners-up prizes.

Calvin & Rose G. Hoffman Prize

King's School, Canterbury, Kent CT1 2ES

☎01227 595501

Contact *The Headmaster*

Annual award for distinguished publication on Christopher Marlowe, established by the late Calvin Hoffman, author of *The Man Who was Shakespeare* (1955) as a memorial to himself and his wife. For unpublished works of at least 5000 words written in English for their scholarly contribution to the study of Christopher Marlowe and his relationship to William Shakespeare. Final entry date: 1 September. 2002 joint winners: Lukas Erne and Dr Peter Roberts.

Winifred Holtby Prize

Royal Society of Literature, Somerset House, Strand, London WC2R 1LA

☎020 7845 4676 Fax 020 7845 4679

Email info@rslit.org

Website www.rslit.org

ESTABLISHED 1966 by Vera Brittain who gave a sum of money to the RSL to provide an annual prize in honour of Winifred Holtby who died at the age of 37. Administered by the **Royal Society of Literature**. The prize is for the best regional novel of the year written in the English language. The writer must be of British or Irish nationality, or a citizen of the Commonwealth. Translations, unless made by the author himself of his own work, are not eligible for consideration. If in any year it is considered that no regional novel is of sufficient merit the prize money may be awarded to an author, qualified as aforesaid, of a literary work of non-fiction or poetry, concerning a regional subject. Publishers are invited to submit works published during the current year and must contact the Secretary for details. Final entry date: 15 December. Previous winners: Donna Morrissey *Kit's Law*; Eden Robinson *Traplines*; Andrew O'Hagan *Our Fathers*.

Prize £1000.

How do I love thee? Magazine Love Poetry Competition

Poetry Life Publishing, 1 Blue Ball Corner, Water Lane, Winchester, Hampshire SO23 0ER

Contact *Adrian Bishop*

Open competition for original love poems which have not been published in a book. Maximum length of 80 lines. Entry fee of £3 per poem. Send s.a.e. for details.

Prizes £500 (1st); £100 (2nd); £50 each (3rd & 4th).

L. Ron Hubbard's
Writers of the Future Contest

PO Box 218, East Grinstead, West Sussex RH19 4GH

Contest Administrator *Andrea Grant-Webb*

ESTABLISHED 1984 by L. Ron Hubbard to encourage new and amateur writers of science fiction, fantasy and horror. Quarterly awards with an annual grand prize. Entrants must submit a short story of up to 10,000 words, or a novelette less than 17,000 words, which must not have been published previously. The contest is open only to those who have not been published professionally. Previous winners: Roge Gregory, Malcolm Twigg, Tom Brennan, Alan Smale, Janet Barron. Send s.a.e. for entry form.

Prizes £640 (1st), £480 (2nd) and £320 (3rd) each quarter; Annual Grand Prize: £2500. All winners are awarded a trip to the annual L. Ron Hubbard Achievement Awards which include a series of professional writers' workshops, and are published in the *L. Ron Hubbard Presents Writers of the Future* anthology.

The Richard Imison Memorial Award

The Society of Authors, 84 Drayton Gardens, London SW10 9SB
☎020 7373 6642 Fax 020 7373 5768
Email info@societyofauthors.org
Website www.societyofauthors.org
Contact *The Secretary, The Broadcasting Committee*

Annual award established 'to perpetuate the memory of Richard Imison, to acknowledge the encouragement he gave to writers working in the medium of radio, and in memory of the support and friendship he invariably offered writers in general, and radio writers in particular'. Administered by the **Society of Authors** and generally sponsored by the **Peggy Ramsay Foundation**, the purpose is 'to encourage new talent and high standards in writing for radio by selecting the radio drama by a writer new to radio which, in the opinion of the judges, is the best of those submitted.' An adaptation for radio of a piece originally written for the stage, television or film is not eligible. Any radio drama first transmitted in the UK between 1 January and 31 December by a writer or writers new to radio, is eligible, provided the work is an original piece for radio and it is the first dramatic work by the writer(s) that has been broadcast. Submission may be made by any party to the production in the form of two copies of an audio cassette (not-returnable) accompanied by a nomination form. 2003 winners: Nell Lyshon and Steven McAanena *Milk* and Celia Bryce *The Skate Grinder*.

Prize £1500.

The Independent Foreign Fiction Prize

c/o Literature Department, Arts Council of England, 14 Great Peter Street, London SW1P 3NQ
☎020 7973 6442 Fax 020 7973 6590

Awarded for translated fiction by living authors first published in Britain in the year preceding the award. 2002 winner: *Austerlitz* by W.G. Sebald; translated by Anthea Bell.

Prize £10,000 shared equally between author and translator.

Individual Screenwriter Awards

SGRÎN – Media Agency for Wales, The Bank, 10 Mount Stuart Square, Cardiff CF10 5EE
☎029 2033 3300 Fax 029 2033 3320
Email anneli.jones@acw-ccc.org.uk
Contact *Anneli Jones*

FOUNDED 2001. A pilot scheme, offering funding towards the development of a feature-length screenplay. Open to any individual, excluding those in full-time education. Entry requirements: completion of application form and submission of 12-page treatment and c.v.

Prizes Individual awards of up to £5000.

The International IMPAC Dublin Literary Award

Dublin City Public Libraries, Library & Archive Administration, 138–144 Pearse Street, Dublin 2, Republic of Ireland
☎00 353 1 674 4802 Fax 00 353 1 674 4879
Email dubaward@iol.ie
Website www.impacdublinaward.ie

ESTABLISHED 1995. Sponsored by Dublin City Council and a US-based productivity improvement firm, IMPAC, this prize is awarded for a work of fiction written and published in the English language or written in a language other than English and published in English translation. Initial nominations are made by municipal public libraries in major and capital cities worldwide, each library putting forward up to three books to the international panel of judges in Dublin. 2002 winner: Michel Houllebecq *Atomised*; 2003 winner: Orhan Impac *My Name is Red*.

Prize €100,000 (if the winning book is in English translation, the prize is shared €75,000 to the author and €25,000 to the translator).

International Reading Association Literacy Award

International Reading Association, 800 Barksdale Road, PO Box 8139, Newark, Delaware 19714-8139, USA
☎001 302 731 1600 Fax 001 302 731 1057
Executive Director *Alan E. Farstrup*

The International Reading Association is a non-profit education organisation devoted to improving reading instruction and promoting literacy worldwide. In addition to the US $15,000 award presented each year on International Literacy Day (September 8), the organisation gives more than 25 awards in recognition of achievement in reading research, writing for children, media coverage of literacy and literacy instruction.

International Student Playscript Competition
See **University of Hull** under **Writers' Courses, Circles and Workshops**

Irish Times International Fiction Prize
The Irish Times Ltd, 10–16 D'Olier Street, Dublin 2, Republic of Ireland
☎00 353 1 679 2022 Fax 00 353 1 670 9383

Biennial prize awarded for any work of fiction (novel, novella or collection of short stories) in the English language. Books are nominated by literary editors and critics, and are then called in from publishers. Next award to be announced in autumn 2003. Previous winner: Michael Ondaatje *Anil's Ghost*.

Irish Times **Irish Literature Prizes**
The Irish Times Ltd, 10–16 D'Olier Street, Dublin 2, Republic of Ireland
☎00 353 1 679 2022 Fax 00 353 1 670 9383

Administrator, Book Prizes *Gerard Cavanagh*

ESTABLISHED 1989. Biennial prizes awarded in four different categories: fiction (a novel, novella or collection of short stories), non-fiction prose (history, biography, autobiography, criticism, politics, sociological interest, travel, current affairs and belles-lettres), poetry (collection or a long poem or a sequence of poems, or a revised/updated edition of a previously published selection/collection) and for a work in the Irish language (fiction, poetry or non-fiction). The author must have been born in Ireland or be an Irish citizen, but may live in any part of the world. Books are nominated by literary editors and critics, and are then called in from publishers. Next awards to be announced in autumn 2003. Previous winners: William Trevor *The Hill Bachelors* (fiction); Angela Bourke *The Burning of Bridget Cleary* (non-fiction); Michael Longley *The Weather in Japan*; Cathal O'Searcaigh *Ag Tnúth Leis an tSolas* (Irish language).

JazzClaw **Alternative Poetry Competition**
Searle Publishing, 36 Wolfe Road, Norwich, Norfolk NR1 4HT
Email jazzclaw@lycos.co.uk
Website www.searlepublishing.co.uk

Ten finalists are selected by a team of JazzClaw published poets. Entry fee: £2 per poem or £10 for unlimited entries. Cheques must be made out to 'Searle Publishing'. Closing date 30 August 2004. Information leaflet available.
Prizes 1st £100, plus publication; 2nd £30); 3rd £10.

Jewish Quarterly **Literary Prizes**
PO Box 35042, London NW1 7XH
☎020 7284 1117 Fax 020 7284 1117

Contact *Gerald Don*

Formerly the H.H. Wingate Prize. Annual awards (one for fiction and one for non-fiction) for works which best stimulate an interest in and awareness of themes of Jewish interest. Books must have been published in the UK in the year of the award and be written in English by an author resident in Britain, the Commonwealth, Israel, Republic of Ireland or South Africa. 2002 winners: W.G. Sebald *Austerlitz* (fiction); Oliver Sacks *Uncle Tungsten* (non-fiction). Zadie Smith won the *Jewish Quarterly* Wingate Prize 2003 for fiction for her novel *The Autograph Man*. Sebastian Haffner won the non-fiction prize for his posthumously published work *Defying Hitler*.
Prizes £4000 each

Mary Vaughan Jones Award
Cyngor Llyfrau Cymru (Welsh Books Council), Castell Brychan, Aberystwyth, Dyfed SY23 2JB
☎01970 624151 Fax 01970 625385
Email castellbrychan@cllc.org.uk
Website www.wbc.org.uk

Contact *The Administrator*

Triennial award for distinguished services in the field of children's literature in Wales over a considerable period of time. 2000 winner: J. Selwyn Lloyd.
Award Silver trophy.

Keats–Shelley Prize
Keats–Shelley Memorial Association, 117 Cheyne Walk, London SW10 0ES
☎020 7352 2180 Fax 020 7352 6705
Website www.demon.co.uk.heritage/
   Keats.House.Rome

Contact *Harriet Cullen*

ESTABLISHED 1998. Annual award to promote the study and appreciation of Keats and Shelley, especially in the universities, and of creative writing inspired by the younger Romantic poets. Two categories: essay and poem; open to all ages and nationalities. Previous winners: Rukmini Maria Callimachi, James Burton, Cate Parish,

Joe Francis, Antony Nichols, Helena Nelson, Robert Saxton, Toby Venables, Jane Draycott, Ciaran Berry, Katherine Halsey, Sarah Wootton.

Prize £3000 distributed between the winners of the two categories.

The Keeley-Sherrard Translation Award

Poetry Greece, Mitropolitou Athanasiou 10, 3rd Parados, Triklino, Corfu 49100, Greece
☎00 30 661 047990 Fax 00 30 661 047990
Email wendyholborow@hotmail.com
Website users.otenet.gr/~wendyhol/
    poetry_greece/

Contact *Wendy Holborow*

Annual award in memory of the late Philip Sherrard who worked closely with Edmund Keeley translating many Greek poets into English. The award is for Greek poetry translated into English. Potential translators should contact Poetry Greece for further information.

The Petra Kenney Poetry Competition

PO Box 32, Filey, Yorkshire YO14 9YG
Email morgan@petrapoetrycompetition.co.uk
Website www.petrapoetrycompetition.co.uk

Contact *Secretary*

ESTABLISHED 1995. Annual poetry award. Original, unpublished poems up to 80 lines on any theme. Closing date: 1 December. Entry fee: £3 per poem. Send s.a.e. for rules and entry form. Recent winner have included Stephen Heighton, Barry Dempster, John Tatum, Mary Coe, Gary Hyland, Sue Macleod.

Prizes £1000 (1st); £500 (2nd); £250 (3rd) and three highly commended prizes of £125 each; plus publication in *Writers' Forum* and inscribed Royal Brierley Crystal Vase to each winner.

Kent & Sussex Poetry Society Open Competition

13 Ruscombe Close, Southborough, Tunbridge Wells, Kent TN4 0SG
☎01892 543862

Chairman *Clive R. Eastwood*

Annual competition. Entry fee: £3 per poem, maximum 40 lines.

Prizes £1000 (total).

Kent Short Story Competition

4 Shipwrights Lee, Island Wall, Whitstable, Kent CT5 1EW
☎01227 762504

Contact *Competition Organiser 'Connections'*

Competition for a short story of up to 2500 words. Send s.a.e. for entry form and full details.

Kiriyama Pacific Rim Book Prize

Kiriyama Institute, 650 Delancy St, Suite 101, San Francisco, CA 94107
☎00 1 415 777 1428 Fax 00 1 415 777 1646
Email admin@kiriyamaprize.org
Website www.kiriyamaprize.org

Contact *Jeannine Cuevas, Manager*

FOUNDED 1996 with the aim of promoting books that contribute to greater understanding and cooperation among the peoples and nations of the Pacific Rim and South Asia, this annual award takes its name from the Reverend Seiyu Kiriyama. Entry details may be obtained from the above address or from the website. 2002 winners: Fiction – Rohinton Mistry *Family Matters*; Non-Fiction – Pascal Khoo Thwe *The Land of Green Ghosts: A Burmese Odyssey*.

Prizes $30,000 divided between fiction and non-fiction winners.

Kraszna-Krausz Book Awards

122 Fawnbrake Avenue, London SE24 0BZ
☎020 7738 6701 Fax 020 7738 6701
Email awards@k-k.org.uk
Website www.k-k.org.uk

Administrator *Andrea Livingstone*

ESTABLISHED 1985. Annual award to encourage and recognise oustanding achievements in the publishing and writing of books on the art, practice, history and technology of photography and the moving image (film, television, video and related screen media). Books in any language, published worldwide, are eligible. Entries must be submitted by publishers only. Prizes for books on still photography alternate annually with those for books on the moving image (2003: moving image). 2002 winners: Larry Schaaf *The Photographic Art of William Henry Fox Talbot*; Peter Hamilton and Roger Hargreaves *The Beautiful and the Damned*.

Prizes £5000 in each of the main categories; £1000 special commendations.

Lakeland Book of the Year Awards

Cumbria Tourist Board, Ashleigh, Holly Road, Windermere, Cumbria LA23 2AQ
☎01539 444444 Fax 01539 444041
Email mail@cumbria-tourist-board.co.uk
Website www.golakes.co.uk

Contact *Annette Vidler*

Six annual awards set up by Cumbrian author

Hunter Davies and the Cumbria Tourist Board. The **Hunter Davies Prize** was established in 1984 and is awarded for the book which best helps visitors or residents enjoy a greater love or understanding of any aspect of life in Cumbria and the Lake District. The **Barclays Bank Prize**, established in 1993, is for the best researched book on any aspect of Cumbrian life, its people or culture. The **Border Television Prize**, also established in 1993, is for the book which best illustrates the beauty and character of Cumbria. A further two prizes were established in 1999: the **Ron Sands Prize**, for the best book on a cultural theme; and the **Titus Wilson and Son Prize**, for the best book on people. The **Bill Rollinson Award** was given in 2001 for the best book on the Cumbrian landscape and tradition. Final entry date mid-March. Past winners have included: John and Eilean Malden; David A. Cross; Helen Caldwell, John Caldwell, Jennifer Forsyth and Beryl Offley; John Batchelor; David W.V. Weston.
Prize £100 and certificate.

Lancashire County Library Children's Book of the Year Award
Lancashire County Library Headquarters, County Hall, PO Box 61, Preston, Lancashire PR1 8RJ
☎01772 264040 Fax 01772 264043
Email jean.wolstenholme@lcl.lancscc.gov.uk
Manager, Young People's Service *Jean Wolstenholme*
ESTABLISHED 1986. Annual award, presented in June for a work of original fiction suitable for 12–14-year-olds. The winner is chosen by 13–14-year-old secondary school pupils in Lancashire. Books must have been published between 1 September and 31 August in the previous year of the award and authors must be UK residents. Final entry date: 1 September each year. 2003 winner: Julie Bertagna *Exodus*.
Prize £500, plus engraved glass decanter.

Lannan Literary Award
Lannan Foundation, 313 Read Street, Santa Fe, New Mexico 87501, USA
☎001 505 986 8160
Website www.lannan.org
ESTABLISHED 1989. Annual awards given to writers of exceptional poetry, fiction and non-fiction who have made a significant contribution to English-language literature, as well as emerging writers of distinctive literary merit who have demonstrated potential for outstanding future

work. On occasion, the Foundation recognises a writer for lifetime achievement. Candidates for the awards are recommended to the Foundation by a network of writers, literary scholars, publishers and editors. Applications for the awards are not accepted.

Legend Writing Award
Hastings Writers' Group, 39 Emmanuel Road, Hastings, East Sussex TN34 3LB
Website www.hwg.supanet.com
Contact *Legend Coordinator*
ESTABLISHED 2001. Annual award to encourage new fiction writers resident in the UK. Entries (2000 words maximum) may be either short stories or openings of novels. Closing date: 31 August. Entry fee: £4.50. Rules/entry form (essential) can be obtained from website or by sending s.a.e. to the above address. The competition is organised by Hastings Writers' Group and prize-winning entries are selected by its patron, author David Gemmell.
Prizes £500 (1st); £250 (2nd); £100 (3rd); plus three runners-up prizes of £50.

The Library Association Awards
See **CILIP: The Chartered Institute of Library and Information Professionals** individual awards

Lichfield Prize
Lichfield Garrick, Castle Duke, Lichfield WS13 6HR
☎01543 308225
Email lichfield-prize@lichfielddc./gov.uk
Contact *Maria Whatton*
FOUNDED 1989. An entry must be a novel and an original work of fiction. No entered manuscript should have been previously published. The judges are looking for a quality manuscript with wide audience appeal and commercial sales potential. Short-listed authors will be invited to the Lichfield Prize presentation during the Lichfield Festival in July 2004.
Prize £5000.

Literary Review Grand Poetry Competition
See *Literary Review* under **Magazines**

The London Writers Competition
Room 224a, The Town Hall, Wandsworth High Street, London SW18 2PU
☎020 8871 8711 Fax 020 8871 7630
Email arts@wandsworth.gov.uk
Website www.wandsworth.gov.uk

Contact *Wandsworth Arts Office*

Arranged by Wandsworth Borough Council in association with Waterstone's. An annual competition, open to all writers of 16 or over who live, work or study in the Greater London area. Work must not have been published previously. There are four sections: poetry, short story, play and fiction for children.

Prizes £1000 for each section, with a first prize of £600. Poetry and story winners are published and the winning play is showcased in a London venue.

Elizabeth Longford Prize

The Society of Authors, 85 Drayton Gardens, London SW10 9SB
☎020 7373 6642 Fax 020 7373 5768
Email info@societyofauthors.org
Website www.societyofauthors.org

Historical biography prize established in memory of Elizabeth Longford. Submissions are not accepted. Inaugural winner: David Gilmour *The Long Recessional*.

Prize £3000

Longman-*History Today* Book of the Year Award

c/o History Today, 20 Old Compton Street, London W1D 4TW
☎020 7534 8000

Contacts *Peter Furtado, Marion Soldan*

ESTABLISHED 1993. Annual award set up as joint initiative between the magazine *History Today* and the publisher Longman (**Pearson Education**) to mark the past links between the two organisations, to encourage new writers, and to promote a wider public understanding of, and enthusiasm for, the study and publication of history. Submissions are made by publishers only. 2003 joint winners: Margo Todd *The Culture of Protestantism in Early Modern Scotland* and Elizabeth A. Fenn *Pox Americana: The Great Smallpox Epidemic of 1775–82*.

Prize £1000 (see *History Today* from July 2003).

Sir William Lyons Award

The Guild of Motoring Writers, 30 The Cravens, Smallfield, Surrey RH6 9QS
☎01342 843294 Fax 01342 844093
Email sharon@scott-fairweather.freeserve.co.uk

Contact *Sharon Scott-Fairweather*

An annual competitive award to encourage young people in automotive journalism and to foster interests in motoring and the motor industry. Entrance by two essays and interview with Awards Committee. Applicants must be British, aged 17–23 and resident in UK. Final entry date: 31 August. Presentation date in December.

Award £1000 plus trophy.

The Macallan/*Scotland on Sunday* Short Story Competition

Scotland on Sunday, 108 Holyrood Road, Edinburgh EH8 8AS
☎0131 620 8620 Fax 0131 523 0330

Contact *Competition Administrator*

ESTABLISHED 1990. Annual competition to recognise the best in new Scottish writing. Stories are accepted from those who were born or are living in Scotland, or from Scots living abroad. Up to three stories per applicant permitted. Maximum 3000 words per story. Final entry date: end of August. Previous winners: David Strachan, Alan Spence, Ali Smith, Chris Dolan, Michel Faber, Anne Donovan.

Prizes £6000 (1st); £2000 (2nd); four runners-up receive £500 each. Winning story is published in *Scotland on Sunday*.

McColvin Medal

See **CILIP: The Chartered Institute of Library and Information Professionals Besterman/McColvin Medal**

W.J.M. Mackenzie Book Prize

Political Studies Association, Department of Politics, University of Newcastle, Newcastle upon Tyne NE1 7RU
☎0191 222 8021 Fax 0191 222 3499
Email psa@ncl.ac.uk
Website www.psa.ac.uk

PSA Executive Director *Jack Arthurs*

ESTABLISHED 1987. Annual award to best work of political science published in the UK during the previous year. Submissions from publishers only. Final entry date: 31 October. Prizes are judged in the year following publication and awarded the year after that. The 2001 winner was David McKay for *Designing Europe: Comparative Lessons from the Federal Experience*.

McKitterick Prize

Society of Authors, 84 Drayton Gardens, London SW10 9SB
☎020 7373 6642 Fax 020 7373 5768
Email info@societyofauthors.org
Website www.societyofauthors.org

Contact *Awards Secretary*

Annual award for a full-length novel in the English language, first published in the UK or unpublished. Open to writers over 40 who have not had any novel published other than the one submitted (excluding works for children). Closing date: 20 December. 2002 winner: Manil Suri *The Death of Vishnu*.

Prize £4000.

Enid McLeod Prize
Franco-British Society, Room 623, Linen Hall, 162–168 Regent Street, London W1R 5TB
☎020 7734 0815 Fax 020 7734 0815
Executive Secretary *Kate Brayn*

ESTABLISHED 1982. Annual award to the author of the work of literature published in the UK which, in the opinion of the judges, has contributed most to Franco-British understanding. Any full-length work written in English by a citizen of the UK, Commonwealth, Republic of Ireland, Pakistan, Bangladesh and South Africa. No English translation of a book written originally in any other language will be considered. Nominations from publishers for books published between 1 January and 31 December of the year of the prize. 2001 winner: Antonia Fraser *Marie Antoinette*.

Prize Cheque.

Macmillan Prize for a Children's Picture Book Illustration
Macmillan Children's Books, 20 New Wharf Road, London N1 9RR
☎020 7014 6124 Fax 020 7014 6142
Website www.panmacmillan.com
Contact *Marketing Dept., Macmillan Children's Books*

Set up in order to stimulate new work from young illustrators in art schools, and to help them start their professional lives. Fiction or non-fiction. **Macmillan** have the option to publish any of the prize winners.

Prizes £1000 (1st); £500 (2nd); £250 (3rd).

Macmillan Silver PEN Award
The English Centre of International PEN, 152–156 Kentish Town Road, London NW1 9QB
☎020 7267 9444 Fax 020 7267 9304
Email enquiries@englishpen.org
Website www.englishpen.org

Sponsored by **Macmillan Publishers**. An annual award for a volume of short stories written in English by a British author and published in the UK in the year preceding the prize. Nominations by the PEN Executive Committee only. Please do not submit books. 2002 winner: Bill Broady *In This Block There Lives a Slag*.

Prize £500, plus silver pen.

The Mail on Sunday Novel Competition
Postal box address changes each year (see below)

Annual award ESTABLISHED 1983. Judges look for a story/character that springs to life in the 'tantalising opening 50–150 words of a novel'. Details of the competition, including the postal box address, are published in *The Mail on Sunday* in July/August. 2002 winner: Christine Morrey.

Awards (1st) £400 book tokens and a writing course at the **Arvon Foundation**; (2nd) £300 tokens; (3rd) £200 tokens; three further prizes of £150 tokens each.

The Mail on Sunday/ John Llewellyn Rhys Prize
Booktrust, Book House, 45 East Hill, London SW18 2QZ
☎020 8516 2972 Fax 020 8516 2978
Email tarryn@booktrust.org.uk
Website www.booktrust.org.uk
Contact *Tarryn McKay*

ESTABLISHED 1942. An annual young writer's award for a memorable work of any kind. Entrants must be under the age of 35 at the time of publication; books must have been published in the UK in the year of the award. The author must be a citizen of the UK or the Commonwealth, writing in English. 2002 winner: Susanna Jones *The Earthquake Bird*.

Prize £5000 (1st); £500 for shortlisted entries.

The Man Booker Prize for Fiction
Colman Getty PR, Middlesex House, 34–42 Cleveland Street, London W1T 4JE
☎020 7631 2666 Fax 0207631 2699
Email pr@colmangettypr.co.uk
Website www.colmangettypr.co.uk
Contact *Cathryn Summerhayes (Submissions)*

The Booker Prize for Fiction was originally set up by Booker plc in 1968 to reward merit, raise the stature of the author in the eyes of the public and encourage an interest in contemporary fiction. In April 2002 it was announced that the Man Group had been chosen by the

Booker Prize Foundation as the new sponsor of the Booker Prize. The sponsorship is due to run for five years during which time the prize will be known as the Man Booker Prize for Fiction. United Kingdom publishers may enter up to two full-length novels, with scheduled publication dates between 1 October 2002 and 30 September 2003. In addition, any title by an author who has previously won the Booker or Man Booker Prize and any title by an author who has been shortlisted in the last ten years may be submitted. The 2002 winner was *The Life of Pi* by Yann Martel.

Prize The winner receives £50,000. The six shortlisted authors each receive £2500.

Marsh Award for Children's Literature in Translation

National Centre for Research in Children's Literature, University of Surrey Roehampton, Digby Stuart College, Roehampton Lane, London SW15 5PH
☎020 8392 3008   Fax 020 8392 3819
Email g.lathey@roehampton.ac.uk
Contact *Dr Gillian Lathey*

ESTABLISHED 1995 and sponsored by the Marsh Christian Trust, the award aims to encourage translation of foreign children's books into English. It is a biennial award (next award: 2005), open to British translators of books for 4–16-year-olds, published in the UK by a British publisher. Any category will be considered with the exception of encyclopedias and reference books. No electronic books. 2003 winner: Anthea Bell for her translation of *Where Were You Robert?* by Hans Magnus Enzenberger.
Prize £750.

Marsh Biography Award

The English-Speaking Union, Dartmouth House, 37 Charles Street, London W1J 5ED
☎020 7529 1565   Fax 020 7495 6108
Email tim_rolph@esu.org
Website www.esu.org
Contact *Ann Ferrier-Ilic*

A biennial award for the most significant biography published over a two-year period by a British publisher. Next award October 2003. 2001 winner: Anthony Sampson *Mandela: The Authorised Biography*. Previous winners: Richard Holmes *Coleridge: Darker Reflections*; Jim Ring *Erskine Childers*; Selina Hastings *Evelyn Waugh*; Patrick Marnham *The Man Who Wasn't Maigret*.
Award A year's membership of the ESU and £4000, plus a silver trophy presented at a dinner.

Colin Mears Award

See **CILIP: The Chartered Institute of Library and Information Professionals Kate Greenaway Medal**

Medical Book Awards

The Society of Authors, 84 Drayton Gardens, London SW10 9SB
☎020 7373 6642   Fax 020 7373 5768
Email info@society of authors.org
Website www.societyofauthors.org
Contact *Secretary, Medical Writers Group*

Annual awards sponsored by the Royal Society of Medicine. Nine categories for medical texts published in the twelve months preceding the deadline. Contact the **Society of Authors** for entry details. Closing date: 30 April.
Prizes £6500 (total).

The Mercedes–Benz Award for the Montagu of Beaulieu Trophy

Guild of Motoring Writers, 30 The Cravens, Smallfield, Surrey RH6 9QS
☎01342 843294   Fax 01342 844093
Email sharon@scott-fairweather.freeserve.co.uk
Contact *Sharon Scott-Fairweather*

First presented by Lord Montagu on the occasion of the opening of the National Motor Museum at Beaulieu in 1972. Awarded annually to a member of the **Guild of Motoring Writers** who, in the opinion of the nominated jury, has made the greatest contribution to recording in the English language the history of motoring or motor cycling in a published book or article, film, television or radio script, or research manuscript available to the public. Cash prize sponsored by Mercedes–Benz UK.
Prize £1000, plus trophy.

Mere Literary Festival Open Competition

'Lawrences', Old Hollow, Mere, Wiltshire BA12 6EG
☎01747 860475
Contact *Mrs Adrienne Howell (Events Organiser)*

Annual open competition which alternates between short stories and poetry. Winners are announced at the Mere Literary Festival during the second week of October. In 2004 the prize is for a short story; closing date for entries in July. For further details, including entry fees and form, apply with s.a.e. from 1 March
Cash prizes.

Meyer-Whitworth Award

Arts Council England, 14 Great Peter Street, London SW1P 3NQ
☎020 7333 01001
Website www.artscouncil.org.uk

Contact *Theatre Writing Section*

This annual award is intended to help further the careers of UK playwrights who are not yet established, and to draw contemporary theatre writers to the public's attention. Nominations are from professional theatre companies. Plays must have been written in the English language and produced professionally in the UK in the 12 months between 1 August 2003 and 31 July 2004. Candidates will have had no more than two of their plays professionally produced. No writer who has won the award previously may reapply and no play that has been submitted previously for the award is eligible. For further details and application form contact Theatre Writing Section.
Award £8000.

MIND Book of the Year

Granta House, 15–19 Broadway, London E15 4BQ
☎020 8519 2122 Fax 020 8522 1725
Email publications@mind.org.uk
Website www.mind.org.uk

ESTABLISHED 1981. Annual award, in memory of Sir Allen Lane, for the author of a book published in the current year (fiction or non-fiction), which furthers public understanding of mental health problems. 2002 winner: Andrew Solomon *The Noonday Demon*.

The Mitchell Prize for Art History/ The Eric Mitchell Prize

c/o The Burlington Magazine, 14–16 Duke's Road, London WC1H 9SZ
☎020 7388 8157 Fax 020 7388 1230

Executive Director *Caroline Elam*

ESTABLISHED 1977 by art collector, philanthropist and businessman, Jan Mitchell, to draw attention to exceptional achievements in the history of art. Consists of two prizes: The Mitchell Prize, given for an outstanding and original contribution to the study and understanding of visual arts, and The Eric Mitchell Prize, given for the outstanding exhibition catalogue of the year. The prizes are awarded to authors of books in English that have been published in the previous 12 months. Books are submitted by publishers before the end of February. Previous winners: The Mitchell Prize: *Nicolas Poussin* Elizabeth Cropper and Charles Dempsey; The Eric Mitchell Prize: *The Triumph of Vulcan* Suzanne Brown Butters.
Prizes $10,000 each.

Scott Moncrieff Prize

See **The Translators Association Awards**

The Oscar Moore Screenwriting Prize

The Oscar Moore Foundation, c/o Screen International, 33–39 Bowling Green Lane, London EC1R 0DA
☎020 7505 8080 Fax 020 7505 8087
Email annmarie.oconnor@media.emap.com
Website www.screendaily.com

Coordinator *Annemarie O'Connor*

ESTABLISHED 1997. Annual prize in honour of Oscar Moore, former *Guardian* columnist and editor-in-chief of *Screen International*, who died in 1996. The genre for the competition changes each year (drama for 2003, thriller for 2004), as does the closing date. Contact the Foundation to obtain an entry form. 2002 winners: Jason and Brendan Butler *Ton of Money*.
Award £10,000 cash, plus week-long script development course courtesy of Arista, and performance of the winning script by the Script Factory.

Shiva Naipaul Memorial Prize

The Spectator, 56 Doughty Street, London WC1N 2LL
☎020 7405 1706 Fax 020 7242 0603
Email emma@spectator.co.uk

Contact *Emma Bagnall*

ESTABLISHED 1985. Annual prize given to an English language writer of any nationality under the age of 35 for an essay of not more than 4000 words describing a culture alien to the writer. Final entry date is 30 April.
Prize £3000.

NASEN Special Educational Needs Book Awards

NASEN House, 4–5 Amber Busisness Village, Amber Close, Amington, Tamworth B77 4RP
☎01827 311 500 Fax 01827 313 005
Email welcome@nasen.org.uk
Website www.nasen.org.uk

Organised by the National Association for Special Education Needs (NASEN) and the Times Educational Supplement (TES). Three awards: *The Children's Book Award*, for the book that most successfully provides a positive image of children with special educational needs; *The Academic Book Award* celebrates the work of authors and editors who have made an outstanding contribution to the theory and practice of special education; The *Books for Teaching and Learning Award* is presented for curriculum materials for pupils or teachers in early years, primary or secondary phases.

Eligibility: Books must have been published in the UK within the year preceding the award (Academic).

Prize £500 each category.

National Poetry Anthology

United Press, Admail 3735, London EC1B 1JB
☎0870 240 6190 Fax 0870 240 6191

Contact *Peter Quinn, Publishing Director*

Free-to-enter annual poetry competition. Entrants may submit three poems (of 160 words and 20 lines maximum each) by annual closing date of 30 June. Organisers select around 200 regional winners which are published in the annual book, the *National Poetry Anthology*. The 200 winners all receive a free copy of the book and vote for one overall champion. This person receives the prize when the book is published in the spring.

Prize £1000 plus trophy to keep in perpetuity.

National Poetry Competition

The Poetry Society, 22 Betterton Street, London WC2H 9BX
☎020 7420 9880 Fax 020 7240 4818
Email info@poetrysociety.org.uk
Website www.poetrysociety.org.uk

Contact *Competition Organiser (WH)*

One of Britain's major open poetry competitions. Closing date: 31 October. Poems on any theme, up to 40 lines. For rules and entry form send s.a.e. to the competition organiser at the address above or enter the competition via the website.

Prizes £5000 (1st); £1000 (2nd); £500 (3rd); plus 10 commendations of £50.

The Natural World Book Prize (formerly The BP Natural World Book Prize)

Booktrust, Book House, 45 East Hill, London SW18 2QZ
☎020 8516 2972 Fax 020 8516 2978
Email tarryn@booktrust.org.uk
Website www.booktrust.org.uk

Contact *Tarryn McKay*

ESTABLISHED in 1996 as an amalgamation of the Natural World Book Prize (the magazine of the Wildlife Trusts) and the BP Conservation Book Prize. Award for a book which most imaginatively promotes the conservation of the natural environment and all its animals and plants. Entries from UK publishers only. 2002 winner: Edward O. Wilson *The Future of Life*.

Prizes £5000; a runner-up prize may be awarded at the judge's discretion.

Bill Naughton Short Story Competition

Box No. 2004, Aghamore, Ballyhaunis, Co. Mayo, Republic of Ireland
Website www.aghamoregaa.com/society/knschool.htm

Organised by the **Kenny/Naughton Society** (see entry under **Literary Societies**). Stories may be on any topic and no more than 2500 words in length. All work must be unpublished; typed scripts only with no name or address appearing on the work. Entry fee: £4 of €5 per story; three stories may be submitted for the price of two. Closing date: 1 September each year. No entry form required.

Prizes £150 (€200) (1st); £100 (€130) (2nd); £50 (€65) (3rd). Best stories published in a collection entitled *Splinters*.

Nestlé Smarties Book Prize

Booktrust, Book House, 45 East Hill, London SW18 2QZ
☎020 8516 2972 Fax 020 8516 2978
Email tarryn@booktrust.org.uk
Website www.booktrusted.com

Contact *Tarryn McKay*

ESTABLISHED 1985 to encourage high standards and stimulate interest in books for children, this prize is given for a children's book (fiction or poetry), written in English by a citizen of the UK or an author resident in the UK, and published in the UK in the year ending 31 October. There are three age-group categories: 5 and under, 6–8 and 9–11. Uniquely, the shortlist for each age category is judged by classes of schoolchildren, who enter a competition to win a chance to be Young Judges. 50 classes from each age category judge the books, deciding who gets Gold, Silver and Bronze. The class projects entered for the judging process are then judged to see which classes will come to London for the prize presentation. 2002 Gold Award winners: Lucy Cousins *Jazzy in the Jungle* (5 and under); Lauren Child *That Pesky Rat* (6–8); Philip Reeve *Mortal*

Engines (9–11); Lauren Child *That Pesky Rat* (Kids' Club Network Special Award).

Prizes in each category: £2500 (gold); £1000 (silver); £500 (bronze).

The New Writer
Prose & Poetry Prizes

The New Writer, PO Box 60, Cranbrook, Kent TN17 2ZR
☎01580 212626 Fax 01580 212041
Email admin@thenewwriter.com
Website www.thenewwriter.com

Contact *Merric Davidson*

ESTABLISHED 1997. Annual award founded by *The New Writer* poetry editor and poet, Abi Hughes-Edwards. Open to all poets writing in the English language for an original, previously unpublished poem or collection of six to ten poems. Also open to writers of short stories and novellas/serials, features, articles, essays and interviews. Final entry date: 30 November. Previous winners: Mark Granier, Ros Barber, Celia de Fréine, John Hilton.

Prizes (total) £2000, plus publication in collection.

Newham Lesbian & Gay
Writing Out Award

Email info@writingout.com
Website www.writingout.com

FOUNDED 2000. Annual international competition for plays on lesbian, gay, bisexual and transgender themes. Welcome previously unperformed plays and screenplays of any length. Final entry date: December 2003. (At the time of going to press the 2003 competition was not confirmed; check website in October for details.) Previous winner: Troy Fairclough *You Don't Kiss.*

Prizes £1500 (1st) plus showcase at London theatre; two runner-up prizes of £500 each.

'The Nibbies'
See **British Book Awards**

No Love Lost
Poetry Anthology Contest
See **Hidden Brook Press International Poetry Anthology Contest**

Nobel Prize

The Nobel Foundation, PO Box 5232, 102 45 Stockholm, Sweden
☎00 46 8 663 0920 Fax 00 46 8 660 3847
Website www.nobel.se

Contact *Information Section*

Awarded yearly for outstanding achievement in physics, chemistry, physiology or medicine, literature and peace. FOUNDED by Alfred Nobel, a chemist who proved his creative ability by inventing dynamite. In general, individuals cannot nominate someone for a Nobel Prize. The rules vary from prize to prize but the following are eligible to do so for Literature: members of the Swedish Academy and of other academies, institutions and societies similar to it in constitution and purpose; professors of literature and of linguistics at universities or colleges; Nobel Laureates in Literature; presidents of authors' organisations which are representative of the literary production in their respective countries. British winners of the literature prize, first granted in 1901, include Rudyard Kipling, John Galsworthy and Winston Churchill. Recent winners: Nadine Gordimer (South Africa); Derek Walcott (St Lucia); Toni Morrison (USA); Kenzaburo Oe (Japan); Seamus Heaney (Ireland); Wislawa Szymborska (Poland); Dario Fo (Italy); José Saramago (Portugal); Günter Grass (Germany); Gao Xingjian (France); V.S. Naipaul (Great Britain). Nobel Laureate in Literature 2002: Imre Kertész (Hungary).

The Noma Award for
Publishing Africa

PO Box 128, Witney, Oxfordshire OX8 5XU
☎01993 775235 Fax 01993 709265
Email maryljay@aol.com
Website www.nomaaward.org

Contact *Mary Jay, Secretary to the Managing Committee*

ESTABLISHED 1979. Annual award, founded by the late Shoichi Noma, President of Kodansha Ltd, Tokyo. The award is for an outstanding book, published in Africa by an African writer, in three categories: scholarly and academic; literature and creative writing; children's books. Entries, by publishers only, by 31 March for a title published in the previous year. Maximum number of three entries. Previous winners: Kitia Touré *Destins Parallèles*; A. Adu Boahen *Mfantsipim and the Making of Ghana: A Centenary History 1876–1976*; Peter Adwok Nyaba *The Politics of Liberation in South Sudan; An Insider's View*; Djibril Samb *L'intérpretation des rêves dans la région Sénégambienne. Suivi de la clef des songes de la Sénégambie, de l'Egypte pharaonique et de la tradition islamique*; Kimari Njogu and Rocha Chimerah *Ufundishaji wa Fasihi. Nadharia na Mbinu*; Abosede Emanuel *Odun Ifa/Ifa Festival.*

Prize US$10,000 and presentation plaque.

C.B. Oldman Prize
Aberdeen University Library, Queen Mother Library, Meston Walk, Aberdeen AB24 3UE
☎01224 272590 Fax 01224 487048
Email r.turbet@abdn.ac.uk

Contact *Richard Turbet*

ESTABLISHED 1989 by the International Association of Music Libraries, UK & Ireland Branch. Annual award for best book of music bibliography, librarianship or reference published the year before last (i.e. books published in 2002 considered for the 2003 prize). Previous winners: Michael Talbot, Donald Clarke, John Parkinson, John Wagstaff, Stanley Sadie, William Waterhouse, Richard Turbet, John Gillaspie, David Fallows, Arthur Searle, Graham Johnson.
Prize £150.

Open Window Poetry Anthology Contest
See **Hidden Brook Press International Poetry Anthology Contests**

Orange Prize for Fiction
Booktrust, 45 East Hill, London SW18 2QZ
☎020 8516 2972 Fax 020 8516 2978
Email tarryn@booktrust.org.uk
Website www.orangeprize.com

Contact *Tarryn McKay*

ESTABLISHED 1996. Annual award founded by a group of senior women in publishing to 'create the opportunity for more women to be rewarded for their work and to be better known by the reading public'. Awarded for a full-length novel written in English by a woman of any nationality, and published in the UK between 1 April and 31 March of the following year. 2003 winner: Valerie Martin *Property*.
Prize £30,000 and a work of art (a limited edition bronze figurine known as 'The Bessie' in acknowledgement of anonymous prize endowment).

The Orwell Prize
Simage Communications Ltd, Fulton House, Fulton Road, Wembley Park, Middlesex HA9 0TF
☎020 8584 0444 Fax 020 8584 0443
Email orwell@simage-comms.co.uk
Website www.simage-comms.co.uk

Contact *Sue Dowsett*

Jointly ESTABLISHED in 1993 by the George Orwell Memorial Fund and the *Political Quarterly* to encourage and reward writing in the spirit of Orwell's 'What I have most wanted to do ... is to make political writing into an art'. Two categories: book or pamphlet; newspaper and/or articles, features, columns, or sustained reportage on a theme. Submissions by editors, publishers or authors. 2002 winner: Francis Wheen *Hoo-Haas and Passing Frenzies: Collected Journalism 1991–2001.*
Prizes £1000 for each category.

Outposts Poetry Competition
Outposts, 22 Whitewell Road, Frome, Somerset BA11 4EL
☎01373 466653

Contact *Roland John*

Annual competition for an unpublished poem of not more than 60 lines run by **Hippopotamus Press**.
Prizes £500 (1st), £200 (2nd), £100 (3rd).

The Wilfred Owen Award for Poetry
192 York Road, Shrewsbury, Shropshire SY1 3QH
☎01743 460089
Website www.1914-18.co.uk/owen

Contact *Michael Grayer*

ESTABLISHED in 1988 by the **Wilfred Owen Association**. Given to a poet whose poetry reflects the spirit of Owen's work in its thinking, expression and inspiration. Applications are not sought; the decision is made by the Association's committee. Previous winner: Seamus Heaney.
Award A silver and gunmetal work of art, suitably decorated and engraved.

OWG Awards for Excellence
Outdoor Writers' Guild, PO Box 520, Bamber Bridge, Preston, Lancashire PR5 8LF
☎01772 696732 Fax 01772 696732

Contact *Terry Marsh*

ESTABLISHED 1980. Annual awards by the **Outdoor Writers' Guild** to raise the standard of outdoor writing, journalism and broadcasting. Winning categories include guidebook, outdoor book, feature (one-off), feature (regular), photography. Open to OWG members only. Final entry date: May.

The Oxford Weidenfeld Translation Prize
St Anne's College, Oxford OX2 6HS
☎01865 274820 Fax 01865 274899
Email patrick.mcguinness@st-annes.ox.ac.uk

Contact *The Fellows' Secretary*

ESTABLISHED in 1996 by publisher Lord Weidenfeld to encourage good translation into English. Annual award to the translator(s) of a work of fiction, poetry or drama written in any living European language. Translations must have been published in the previous year. Submissions from publishers only. For further information, contact Dr Patrick McGuiness at the address above. 2002 winners: Patrick Thursfield and Katalin Bánffy-Jelen for their translation of *They Were Divided* by Miklós Bánffy.

Prize £1000.

Catherine Pakenham Award

The Sunday Telegraph, 1 Canada Square, Canary Wharf, London E14 5DT
☎020 7538 6257 Fax 020 7513 2512
Email charlotte.ibarra@telegraph.co.uk

Contact *Emma Gilbert-Harris*

ESTABLISHED in 1970, the award is designed to ecourage women journalists as they embark on their careers. Open to women aged 18–25 who have published work, however small. Prizes were presented by Joanna Trollope at a reception in London in the summer of 2003.

Award £1000 and a writing commission with one of the Telegraph publications; three runner-up prizes of £200 each.

The Parker Romantic Novel of the Year

57 Coniger Road, London SW6 3TB
☎020 7736 4968

Award Organiser *Mary de Laszio*

ESTABLISHED 1960. Formerly known as the Romantic Novelists' Association Major Award. Sponsorship for the 2003 award is by Parker Pen. Annual award for the best romantic novel of the year, open to non-members as well as members of the **Romantic Novelists' Association**. Novels must be published in the UK between specified dates. Authors must be based in the UK unless members of the RNA. 2002 winner: Philippa Gregory *The Other Boleyn Girl*. Send s.a.e. to the Organiser for entry form.

Award £10,000.

PEN Awards

See **J.R. Ackerley Prize**; **Golden PEN Award for Lifetime Distinguished Services to Literature**; **The Hessell-Tiltman Prize for History**; **Macmillan Silver PEN Award**

Peterloo Poets Open Poetry Competition

The Old Chapel, Sand Lane, Calstock, Cornwall PL18 9QX
☎01822 833473
Email poets@peterloo.fsnet.co.uk
Website www.peterloopoets.co.uk

Contact *Harry Chambers*

ESTABLISHED 1986. Annual competition for unpublished English language poems of not more than 40 lines. Final entry date: 1 March. Send s.a.e. for rules and entry form. Previous winners: John Watts, Jem Poster, David Craig, Rodney Pybus, Debjani Chatterjee, Donald Atkinson, Romesh Gunesekera, Anna Crowe, Carol Ann Duffy, Mimi Khalvati, John Lyons, M.R. Peacocke, Alison Pryde, Carol Shergold, Maureen Wilkinson, Chris Woods.

Prizes £2000 (1st); £1000 (2nd); £500 (3rd); £100 (4th); plus 10 prizes of £50; 15–19 age group: 5 prizes of £100.

Poetry Business Competition

The Studio, Byram Arcade, Westgate, Huddersfield, West Yorkshire HD1 1ND
☎01484 434840 Fax 01484 426566
Email edit@poetrybusiness.co.uk
Website www.poetrybusiness.co.uk

Contact *The Competition Administrator*

ESTABLISHED 1986. Annual award which aims to discover and publish new writers. Entrants should submit a manuscript of poems. Winners will have their work published by the **Poetry Business** under the Smith/Doorstop imprint. Final entry date: end of October. Contact for conditions of entry. Previous winners include: Pauline Stainer, Michael Laskey, Minmi Khalvati, David Morley, Julia Casterton, Liz Cashdan, Moniza Alvi, Selima Hill.

Prizes Publication of full collection; runners-up have pamphlets; 20 complimentary copies. Also cash prize (£1000) to be shared equally between all winners.

Poetry Life Poetry Competition

1 Blue Ball Corner, Water Lane, Winchester, Hampshire SO23 0ER
Email adrian.abishop@virgin.net
Website freespace.virgin.net/poetry.life/

Contact *Adrian Bishop*

ESTABLISHED 1993. Open competition for original poems in any style which have not been published in a book. Maximum length of 80 lines. Entry fee of £4 per poem. Send s.a.e. for details.

Prizes £3000 (1st); £500 (2nd); £250 (3rd)

plus 20 Special Commendations winning £25 book token.

The Poetry Society's National Poetry Competition
See **National Poetry Competition**

Peter Pook Humorous Novel Competition
See **Emissary Publishing** under **UK Publishers**

The Portico Prize
The Portico Library, 57 Mosley Street, Manchester M2 3HY
☎0161 236 6785 Fax 0161 236 6803
Email librarian@theportico.org.uk
Website www.theportico.org.uk
Contact *Miss Emma Marigliano*
ESTABLISHED 1985. Administered by the Portico Library in Manchester. Biennial award for a work of fiction or non-fiction published between the two closing dates. Set wholly or mainly in the North-West of England, including Cumbria and the High Peak District of Derbyshire. Next award: June 2004. Previous winners include: Anthony Burgess *Any Old Iron*; John Stalker *Stalker*; Jenny Uglow *Elizabeth Gaskell: A Habit of Stories*.
Prize £3000.

The Dennis Potter Screenwriting Award
BBC Broadcasting House, Whiteladies Road, Bristol BS8 2LR
☎0117 974 7586
Editor *Jeremy Howe*
Annual award ESTABLISHED in 1995 in memory of the late television playwright to 'nurture and encourage the work of new writers of talent and personal vision'. Submissions should be made through a BBC TV drama producer or an independent production company (no start date confirmed; contact the editor for further information).

The Premio Valle Inclán
See **The Translators Association Awards**

The Mathew Prichard Award for Short Story Writing
Competition Secretary, 2 Rhododendron Close, The Greenways, Cyn Coed, Cardiff CF23 7HS
Website www.samwaw.org.uk

Competition Organiser *Philip Beynon*
Competition Secretary *Marjorie Williams*
ESTABLISHED 1996 to provide sponsorship and promote Wales and its writers. Entry fee: £5; NB scripts are not returned. Competition open to all writers in English; the final entry date is 28 February each year. Entry forms and information from website.
Prizes A total of £2000.

V.S. Pritchett Memorial Prize
Royal Society of Literature, Somerset House, Strand, London WC2R 1LA
☎020 7845 4676 Fax 020 7845 4679
Email info@rslit.org
Website www.rslit.org
ESTABLISHED 1999. Awarded for a previously unpublished short story of between 2000 and 5000 words. For entry forms, please contact the Secretary.

Pulitzer Prizes
The Pulitzer Prize Board, 709 Journalism, Columbia University, New York, NY 10027, USA
☎001 212 854 3841/2 Fax 001 212 854 3342
Email pulitzer@www.pulitzer.org
Website www.pulitzer.org
Awards for journalism in US newspapers, and for published literature, drama and music by American nationals. Deadlines: 1 February (journalism); 1 March (music); 1 March (drama); 1 July for books published between 1 Jan–30 June, and 1 Nov for books published between 1 July–31 Dec (literature). Previous winners include: Michael Chabon *The Amazing Adventures of Kavalier & Clay*; Joseph J. Ellis *Founding Brothers: The Revolutionary Generation*; David Levering Lewis *W.E.B. Du Bois: The Fight for Equality and the American Century, 1919–1963*; Stephen Dunn *Different Hours*; Herbert P. Bix *Hirohito and the Making of Modern Japan*. 2003 winners include: Jeffrey Eugenides *Middlesex* (fiction); Paul Muldoon *Moy, Sand and Gravel* (poetry).

The Red House Children's Book Award
The Federation of Children's Book Groups, The Old Malt House, Aldbourne, Wiltshire SN8 2DW
☎01672 540629 Fax 01672 541280
Email marianneadey@aol.com
Coordinator *Marianne Adey*
ESTABLISHED 1980. Awarded annually for best

book of fiction suitable for children. Unique in that it is judged by the children themselves. 2003 winner: Anthony Horowitz *Skeleton Key*.

Award Portfolio of letters, drawings and comments from the children who took part in the judging. Silver bowls and trophy.

Trevor Reese Memorial Prize

Institute of Commonwealth Studies, University of London, 28 Russell Square, London WC1B 5DS
☎020 7862 8844 Fax 020 7862 8820

Contact *Events & Publicity Officer*

ESTABLISHED 1979 with the proceeds of contributions to a memorial fund to Dr Trevor Reese, Reader in Commonwealth Studies at the Institute and a distinguished scholar of imperial history (d.1976). Biennial award (next award 2004) for a scholarly work, usually by a single author, in the field of Imperial and Commonwealth History published in the preceding two academic years. All correspondence relating to the prize should be marked 'Trevor Reese Memorial Prize'.
Prize £1000.

Regional Press Awards

Press Gazette, Quantum House, 19 Scarbrook Road, Croydon, Surrey CR9 1LX
☎020 8565 4359 Fax 020 8565 4462
Email foyh@quantumbusinessmedia.com

Comprehensive range of journalist and newspaper awards for the regional press. Five newspapers of the year, by circulation and frequency, and a full list of journalism categories. Open to all regional journalists, whether freelance or staff. July event. Run by the *Press Gazette*.

Renault UK Journalist of the Year Award

Guild of Motoring Writers, 30 The Cravens, Smallfield, Surrey RH6 9QS
☎01342 843294 Fax 01342 844093
Email sharon@scott-fairweather.freeserve.co.uk

Contact *Sharon Scott-Fairweather*

Originally the Pierre Dreyfus Award and ESTABLISHED 1977. Awarded annually by Renault UK Ltd in honour of Pierre Dreyfus, president director general of Renault 1955–75, to the member of the **Guild of Motoring Writers** who is judged to have made the most outstanding journalistic effort during the year.
Prize (1st) £1500, plus trophy.

John Llewellyn Rhys Prize

See **The Mail on Sunday/John Llewellyn Rhys Prize**

Bill Rollinson Award

See **Lakeland Book of the Year Awards**

Romantic Novelists' Association Major Award

See **The Parker Romantic Novel of the Year**

Rooney Prize for Irish Literature

Rooney Prize, Strathin, Templecarrig, Delgany, Co. Wicklow, Republic of Ireland
☎00 353 1 287 4769/287 4376
Fax 00 353 1 287 2595
Email rooneyprize@ireland.com

Contacts *Jim Sherwin, Thelma Cloake*

ESTABLISHED 1976. Annual award to encourage young Irish writing to develop and continue. Authors must be Irish, under 40 and published. A non-competitive award with no application procedure.
Prize €8000.

Royal Economic Society Prize

c/o University of York, York YO10 5DD
☎01904 433575 Fax 01904 433575

Contact *Professor Mike Wickens*

Annual award for the best article published in *The Economic Journal*. Open to members of the Royal Economic Society only. Previous winners: Professors Kip Viscusi, Mark Armstrong, Jim Heckman, Jeffrey Smith, Richard Dickens and Casey Mulligan.
Prize £3000.

Royal Society of Literature Awards

See **Winifred Holtby Memorial Prize** and **W.H. Heinemann Prize**

Runciman Award

The Anglo-Hellenic League, c/o The Hellenic Centre, 16–18 Paddington Street, London W1U 5AS
☎020 7486 9410 Fax 020 7486 4254

Contact *The Administrator*

ESTABLISHED 1985. Annual award, sponsored by the National Bank of Greece. Founded by the Anglo-Hellenic League to promote Anglo-Greek understanding and friendship, for a work wholly or mainly about some aspect of Greece or the Hellenic scene, which has been published in its first English edition in the UK during the previous year and listed in Whitaker's Books in Print. Named after the late Sir Steven Runciman, former chairman of the Anglo-Hellenic League. The Award may be given for a work of fiction, poetry, drama or non-fiction; concerned academically or non-academically with the history of any period; biography or autobiography, travel and topography; the arts, architecture, archaeology and the environment; the social and political sciences and current affairs; a guide book or a translation from the Greek of any period. Final entry date in February; award presented in May/June. 2002 winner: James Whitley *The Archaeology of Ancient Greece*.

Award £5000.

Sagittarius Prize

Society of Authors, 84 Drayton Gardens, London SW10 9SB
☎020 7373 6642 Fax 020 7373 5768
Email info@societyofauthors.org
Website www.societyofauthors.org

ESTABLISHED 1990. For first published novel by an author over the age of 60. Final entry date: 20 December. Full details available from the **Society of Authors**. 2002 winner: Svi Jagendorf *Wolfy and the Strudelbakers*.

Prize £2000.

Sainsbury's Baby Book Award

Booktrust, Book House, 45 East Hill, London SW18 2QZ
☎020 8516 2972 Fax 020 8516 2978
Email tarryn@booktrust.org.uk
Website www.booktrust.org.uk

Contact *Tarryn McKay*

ESTABLISHED 1999. Annual award, set up by **Booktrust** with sponsorship from Sainsbury's, for the best book for a baby under one year old, published in the UK. 2002 winner: Annie Kubler *Head, Shoulders, Knees and Toes*.

Prize £2000 and trophy to the winner; certificate and trophy to the winning publisher.

The David St John Thomas Charitable Trust Competitions and Awards

PO Box 6055, Nairn IV12 4YB
☎01667 453351

Competition & Awards Manager *Lorna Edwardson*

A large programme of writing competitions and awards including annual ghost story and love story competitions (each 1600–1800 words with £1000 first prize), and open poetry competition (poems up to 32 lines, total prize money £1000). Publication of winning entries is guaranteed, usually in *Writers' News/Writing Magazine* and/or annual anthology. The awards are led by the annual Self-Publishing Award, ESTABLISHED in 1993, which is open to anyone who has self-published a book during the preceding calendar year. There are four categories each with a £250 prize; the overall winner is declared self-publisher of the year with a total award of £1000. For full details, send large s.a.e. to the address above.

The Saltire Literary Awards

Saltire Society, 9 Fountain Close, 22 High Street, Edinburgh EH1 1TF
☎0131 556 1836 Fax 0131 557 1675
Email saltire@saltiresociety.org.uk
Website www.saltiresociety.org.uk

Administrator *Kathleen Munro*

ESTABLISHED 1982. Annual awards, one for Book of the Year, the other for Best First Book by an author publishing for the first time. Open to any author of Scottish descent or living in Scotland, or to anyone who has written a book which deals with either the work and life of a Scot or with a Scottish problem, event or situation. Nominations are invited from editors of leading newspapers, magazines and periodicals. Previous winners: Saltire Scottish Book of the Year: Janice Galloway *Clara*; The Post Office/Saltire Best First Book: Liam McIlvanney *Burns the Radical*. Saltire Society History Book of the year: Dr Roland Tanner *The Late Medieval Scottish Parliament: Politics and the Three Estates, 1424–1488*.

Prizes £5000 (Scottish Book); £1500 (First Book).

Sandburg-Livesay Anthology Contest

Mekler & Deahl, Publishers, 237 Prospect Street South, Hamilton, Ontario, Canada L8M 2Z6
☎001 905 312 1779 Fax 001 905 312 8285
Email james@meklerdeahl.com
Website www.meklerdeahl.com

This contest has been suspended and will not run in 2003 and 2004, but may resume in 2005. All past contests will be judged and the contest books will be published. Poets who have entered these contests may consult the website where results will be posted as they become available.

Ron Sands Prize
See **Lakeland Book of the Year Awards**

The Biennial Sasakawa Prize
British Haiku Society, Lenacre Ford,
Woolhope, Hereford HR1 4RF
☎01432 860328
Email davidawalker@btinternet.com
Website www.britishhaikusociety.org

Contact *David Walker*

ESTABLISHED 1999. Biennial prize (next in
2003) for original contributions in the field of
haikai (haiku and related genres). Open to
entrants domiciled in either the UK or Japan.
Closing date: 31 December 2003. Entry details
available from the British Haiku Society at the
address above or on the website.

Prize £2500, partly in the form of a return
air ticket to Japan (or to the UK for a Japanese
winner).

Schlegel–Tieck Prize
See **The Translators Association Awards**

Science Writer Awards
The Daily Telegraphy, 1 Canada Square,
Canary Wharf, London E14 5DT
☎020 7538 6257   Fax 020 7704 5315
Email enquiries@science-writer.co.uk
Website www.science-writer.co.uk

Contact *Emma Gilbert-Harris*

ESTABLISHED 1987, this award is designed to
bridge the gap between science and writing,
challenging the writer to come up with a piece
of no more than 700 words that is friendly,
informative and, above all, understandable.
Sponsosred by BASF, the award is open to two
age groups: 16–19 and 20–28.

Award Winners and runners-up receive cash
prizes and have the opportunity to have their
pieces published on the science pages of *The
Daily Telegraph*. The winner in each category also
gets an all expenses paid trip to the USA for the
meeting of the American Association for the
Advancement of Science and an invitation to
meet Britain's most distinguished scientists at the
British Association's Festival of Science. There is
also a prize for schools and new to this year a
prize for teachers (for further details see the website). Visit the website, telephone the hotline
number or e-mail for further information.

Scottish Arts Council Book Awards
Scottish Arts Council, 12 Manor Place,
Edinburgh EH3 7DD
☎0131 226 6051   Fax 0131 225 9833
Email gavin.wallace@scottisharts.org.uk
Website www.scottisharts.org.uk

Head of Literature *Gavin Wallace*

Awards are made annually and are given in
recognition of high standards in fiction, poetry,
non-fiction and literary non-fiction. Authors
should be Scottish or resident in Scotland, but
books of Scottish interest by other authors are
eligible for consideration. Applications are
made by publishers only, and the closing date is
31 January for books published in the previous
calendar year.

Awards Three shortlisted adult and three
shortlisted children's writers each receive an
award of £2000. The Scottish Arts Council
Book of the Year Award is worth a total of
£10,000 and the Children's Book of the Year
Award is a total of £5000.

Scottish Book of the Year
See **The Saltire Literary Awards**

Scottish Historical Book of the Year
The Saltire Society, 9 Fountain Close,
22 High Street, Edinburgh EH1 1TF
☎0131 556 1836   Fax 0131 557 1675
Email saltire@saltiresociety.org.uk
Website www.saltiresociety.org.uk

Administrator *Kathleen Munro*

ESTABLISHED 1965. Annual award in memory of
the late Dr Agnes Mure Mackenzie for a published work of distinguished Scottish historical
research of scholarly importance (including intellectual history and the history of science).
Editions of texts are not eligible. Nominations
are invited and should be sent to the Administrator. Previous winner: Marcus Merriman *The
Rough Wooings: Mary Queen of Scots 1542–1551*.

Prize Bound and inscribed copy of the winning publication.

SEEDS International Poetry Chapbook Anthology Contest
See **Hidden Brook Press International
Poetry Anthology Contests**

SES Book Prizes
University of Sunderland, School of Education
& Lifelong Learning, Gray Road, Hammerton
Hall, Sunderland SR2 8JB
☎0191 515 2364   Fax 0191 515 2629
Email gill.crozier@sunderland.ac.uk

Contact *Professor Gill Crozier*

Annual awards given by the Society for Educational Studies for the best books on education published during the preceding year. Nomination by members of the Society for Educational Studies and publishers or by individual authors based in the UK.

Prizes £1000, £800 and £400.

Bernard Shaw Translation Prize
See **The Translators Association Awards**

André Simon Memorial Fund Book Awards
5 Sion Hill Place, Bath BA1 5SJ
☎01225 336305 Fax 01225 421862
Email tessa@tantraweb.co.uk

Contact *Tessa Hayward*

ESTABLISHED 1978. Awards given annually for the best book on drink, best on food and special commendation in either. Previous winners: Stephen Skelton *The Wines of Britain and Ireland*; Hugh Fearnley-Whittingstall *River Cottage Cookbook*; Bennet Alan Weinberg and Bonnie K. Bealer *The World of Caffeine* (special commendation); Tom Jaine (special award).

Awards £2000 (best books); £1000 (special commendation); £200 to shortlisted books.

WHSmith's Thumping Good Read Award
WHSmith PLC, Greenbridge Road, Swindon, Wiltshire SN3 3LD
☎01793 616161 Fax 01793 562590

Contact *Award Administrator*

ESTABLISHED 1992 to promote writers of popular fiction. Books must have been published in the twelve months preceding the award. Submissions, made by publishers, are judged by a panel of customers to be the most un-put-down-able from a shortlist of ten. 2002 winner: Mo Hayder *The Treatment*.

Award £5000.

WHSmith 'People' Choice' Awards
WHSmith PLC, Nations House, 103 Wigmore Street, London W1U 1WH
☎020 7514 9623 Fax 020 7514 9635
Email elizabeth.walker@group-whsmith.co.uk
Website www.whsmith.co.uk/bookawards2003

Contact *Elizabeth Walker, Awards Manager*

The only UK book awards where the winners are voted for entirely by the public, celebrating good books from all genres of literature. 'With over 120,000 votes cast in the first two years of the awards, we can lay claim to be the "people's choice" for the book industry in this country.'

There are nine award categories in total. Eight are voted for by the public: Autobiography/Biography; Travel Writing; Business; General Knowledge; Fiction; New Talent; Home & Leisure and Children's. The ninth category, The Literary Award, is not put out to public vote but decided by a panel led by the Professor of English Literature at Merton College, Oxford, and Chief Book Reviewer for the *Sunday Times*, John Carey. Recent winners have included Nick Hornby, Nigella Lawson, Pamela Stephenson, Ian McEwan and Eoin Colfer.

Prizes Each winning author receives £5000.

The Society for Theatre Research Annual Theatre Book Prize
c/o The Theatre Museum, 1e Tavistock Street, London WC2E 7PR
Email e.cottis@btinternet.com
Website www.str.org.uk

ESTABLISHED 1997. Annual award for books, in English, of original research into any aspect of the history and technique of the British Theatre. Not restricted to authors of British nationality nor books solely from British publishers. Books must be first published in English (no translations) during the calendar year. Play texts and those treating drama as literature are not eligible. Publishers submit books directly to the independent judges and should contact the Book Prize Administrator for further details.

Award £400.

Sony Radio Academy Awards
Alan Zafer & Associates, 47–48 Chagford Street, London NW1 6EB
☎020 7723 0106 Fax 020 7724 6163
Email secretariat@radioawards.org
Website www.radioawards.org

Contact *The Secretariat*

ESTABLISHED 1982 in association with the **Society of Authors** and Sony UK. Presented in association with the Radio Academy. Annual awards to recognise excellence in radio broadcasting. Entries must have been broadcast in the UK between 1 January and 31 December in the year preceding the award. The categories for the awards are reviewed each year.

Southport Writers' Circle Poetry Competition
32 Dover Road, Southport, Merseyside PR8 4TB
Contact *Mrs Hilary Tinsley*

For previously unpublished work. Entry fee: £2 per poem. Any subject, any form; maximum 40 lines. Closing date: end April. Poems must be entered anonymously, accompanied by a sealed envelope marked with the title of poem, containing s.a.e. Entries must be typed on A4 paper and be accompanied by the appropriate fee payable to Southport Writers' Circle. No application form is required. Envelopes should be marked 'Poetry Competition'. Postal enquiries only. No calls.

Prizes £250 (1st); £50 (2nd); £25 (3rd); additional £25 Humour Prize.

The Spoken Word Awards

The Spoken Word Publishing Association, Macmillan Audio Books, 20 New Wharf Road, London N1 9RR
☎020 7014 6041
Email z.howes@macmillan.co.uk

Contact *Zoe Howes*

Hosted by the **Spoken Word Publishing Association**, the Awards are for excellence in the spoken word industry and recognise the valuable work of all those involved with the production of audio books. There are 22 categories of award, consisting of 14 Consumer Awards (including Drama, Biography, Poetry, Children's and Comedy), four Trade Awards (including Best Retailer and Best Media Coverage) and four Performance Awards (Male and Female Performer of the Year, Publisher of the Year and Spoken Word Audio of the Year).

Prizes Glass trophy for the 'Gold' awards; certificates for Silver and Bronze.

Bram Stoker Awards for Superior Achievement

Horror Writers Association, PO Box 50577, Palo Alto, CA 94303, USA
☎001 650 322 4610
Email hwa@horror.org
Website www.horror.org

Contact *Nancy Etchemendy*

FOUNDED 1988 and named in honour of Bram Stoker, author of *Dracula*. Presented annually by the **Horror Writers Association** (HWA) for works of horror first published in the English language. Works are eligible during their first year of publication. HWA members recommend works for consideration in twelve categories: novel, first novel, short fiction, long fiction, fiction collection, anthology, non-fiction, illustrated narrative, screenplay, work for young readers, poetry and other media. In addition, Lifetime Achievement Stokers are occasionally presented to individuals whose entire body of work has substantially influenced horror.

Strokestown International Poetry Prize

Strokestown Poetry Festival, Strokestown, Co. Roscommon, Republic of Ireland
☎00 353 78 33759
Email twiggezvous@eircom.net
Website www.strokestownpoetryprize.com

Contacts *M. Harpur, Pat Compton*

Annual poetry festival and competition now in its fifth year. Established to reward excellence in poetry. Festival takes place the first weekend in May. Readings and competitions over three days. A centrepiece of the festival is the Strokestown International Poetry prize. Closing date mid February. Entry fee €4 (£3 or $5).

Prizes €4000 (£2500); runners-up prizes of €2000 (2nd) and €1000 (3rd) with €450 reading fee for seven other shortlisted poets. Also prizes totalling €2400 for winning poems in the Irish language. There is also €1000 for a political satire in verse.

Sunday Times Award for Small Publishers

Independent Publishers Guild, PO Box 93, Royston, Hertfordshire SG8 5GH
Fax 01763 246293
Email sheila@ipg.uk.com

Contact *Sheila Bounford*

ESTABLISHED 1988, the first winner was **Fourth Estate**. Open to any publisher producing between five and forty titles a year, which must primarily be original titles, not reprints. Annual turnover must not exceed £1.5 million p.a. Entrants are invited to submit their catalogues for the last twelve months, together with two representative titles. 2002 winner: **Arcadia Books**. Previous winners include: **Hambledon and London**; **Carcanet Press**; **Profile Books**; **Nick Hern Books**; **Tarquin Publications**; Ellipsis; **Bradt Publications**.

Sunday Times Writer of the Year Award

The Sunday Times, 1 Pennington Street, London E1 9XW
☎020 7782 5770 Fax 020 7782 5798
Website www.societyofauthors.org

ESTABLISHED 1987. Annual award to fiction and non-fiction writers. The panel consists of *Sunday Times* journalists and critics. Previous winners: Anthony Burgess, Seamus Heaney, Stephen Hawking, Ruth Rendell, Muriel Spark, William Trevor, Martin Amis, Margaret

Atwood, Ted Hughes, Harold Pinter, Tom Wolfe, Robert Hughes. No applications; prize at the discretion of the Literary Editor.

Sunday Times Young Writer of the Year Award
The Society of Authors, 84 Drayton Gardens, London SW10 9SB
☎020 7373 6642 Fax 020 7373 5768
Email info@societyofauthors.org
Contact *Awards Secretary*

ESTABLISHED 1991. Annual award given on the strength of the promise shown by a full-length published work of fiction, non-fiction, poetry or drama. Entrants must be British citizens, resident in Britain and under the age of 35. The panel consists of *Sunday Times* journalists and critics. Closing date: 20 December. The work must be by one author, in the English language, and published in Britain. Applications by publishers via the **Society of Authors**.

Reginald Taylor and Lord Fletcher Essay Prize
Journal of the British Archaeological Association, Institute of Archaelogy, 36 Beaumont Street, Oxford OX1 2PG
Contact *Dr Martin Henig*

A biennial prize, in memory of the late E. Reginald Taylor and of Lord Fletcher, for the best unpublished essay, not exceeding 7500 words, on a subject of archaeological, art history or antiquarian interest within the period from the Roman era to AD 1830. The essay should show *original* research on its chosen subject, and the author will be invited to read the essay before the Association. The essay may be published in the Journal of the Association if approved by the Editorial Committee. Closing date for entries is 1 June 2004. All enquiries by post please. No phone calls. Send s.a.e. for details.
Prize £300 and a medal.

The Tir Na N-Og Award
Cyngor Llyfrau Cymru (Welsh Books Council), Castell Brychan, Aberystwyth, Dyfed SY23 2JB
☎01970 624151 Fax 01970 625385
Email castellbrychan@cllc.org.uk
Website www.wbc.org.uk

An annual award given to the best original book published for children in the year prior to the announcement. There are three categories: Best Welsh Fiction; Best Welsh Non-fiction; Best English Book with an authentic Welsh background.
Awards £1000 (each category).

TLS/Blackwells Poetry Competition
Times Literary Supplement, Admiral House, 66–68 East Smithfield, London E1W 1BX
☎020 7782 3000
Website www.the-tls.co.uk
Contact *Mick Imlah (Poetry Editor, TLS)*

ESTABLISHED 1997. Annual open competition. Final entry date in July. Previous winner: Jane Griffiths.
Prizes £2000; three runners-up £500 each.

Tolman Cunard Prize
See **The Forward Prizes for Poetry**

Marten Toonder Award
An Chomhairle Ealaíon (The Irish Arts Council), 70 Merrion Square, Dublin 2, Republic of Ireland
☎00 353 1 6180200 Fax 00 353 1 6761302
Email info@artscouncil.ie
Website www.artscouncil.ie
Contact *Music Officer*

The award, made possible by Dutch artist Marten Toonder, honours established artists in music, literature and the visual arts. In 2002 the award was made for visual art; in 2003 for music with literature being the subject in 2004. Applicants should enclose a detailed c.v. as well as an excerpt or copy of their work. The standard application form for individuals should be used and is available on request.
Award €10,000.

The Translators Association Awards
The Translators Association, 84 Drayton Gardens, London SW10 9SB
☎020 7373 6642 Fax 020 7373 5768
Email info@societyofauthors.org
Website www.societyofauthors.org
Contact *Awards Secretary*

Various awards for published translations into English from Dutch and Flemish (The Vondel Translation Prize), French (Scott Moncrieff Prize), German (Schlegel-Tieck Prize), Greek (Hellenic Foundation Prize), Italian (The John Florio Prize), Portuguese (The Calouste Gulbenkian Prize), Spanish (The Premio Valle Inclán), Swedish (Bernard Shaw Translation

Prize) and Japanese (Sasakawa Prize). Contact the **Translators Association** for full details.

The Betty Trask Awards

See entry under **Bursaries, Fellowships and Grants**

The Trewithen Poetry Prize

Chy-an-Dour, Trewithen Moor, Stithians, Truro, Cornwall TR3 7DU
Website www.trewithenpoetry.co.uk

Contact *Competition Secretary*

ESTABLISHED 1995 in order to promote poetry with a rural theme. The competition supports one environmental and one animal welfare charity. Now a biennial competition, next one in 2004. Entry forms available from the address above (enclose s.a.e.) or can be downloaded from the website. Closing date: 31 October. Entry fee of £3.50 for first poem, £2.50 for subsequent poems. Previous winners include: Elizabeth Rapp, David Smart, Ann Drysdale, Roger Elkin, Lesley Quayle.
Prizes (total) £800.

The Trollope Society Short Story Prize

9A North Street, London SW4 0HN
☎020 7720 6789 Fax 020 7978 1815
Email pamela@tvdox.com
Website www.trollopestoryprize.org

Contacts *Pamela Neville-Sington, John Williams*

ESTABLISHED in 2001 to encourage interest in Trollope's novels among young people with the emphasis on reading – and writing – for fun. The competition, which is held annually, focuses on a different Trollope book each year; visit the website for details. Open to pre-university students of all countries. Final entry date: 15 January. The winning story will be published in the Society's quarterly journal, *Trollopiana*.
Prize £1000.

UNESCO Prize for Children's and Young People's Literature in the Service of Tolerance

Division of Arts and Cultural Enterprise, UNESCO, 1 rue Miollis, 75732–Paris, Cedex 15 France
☎00 33 1 45 68 43 40
Fax 00 33 1 45 68 55 95
Email m.bulos@unesco.org
Website www.unesco.org/culture/
   toleranceliterature

Contact *Ms Maha Bulos*

The UNESCO Prize is awarded every two years in recognition of works for the young that 'best embody the concepts and ideals of tolerance and peace, and promote mutual understanding based on respect for other people and cultures'. The works may be novels, collections of short stories or illustrated picture books, and fall within two categories: for children up to the age of 12 and for young people aged 13 to 18. Submissions by publishers only. The International Jury will select the 2005 winners in December 2003.
Prizes US$8000 in each category.

Sir Peter Ustinov Television Scriptwriting Award

The International TV Academy Foundation, 142 West 57th Street, New York City, NY 10019, USA
☎00 1 212 489 6969
Fax 00 1 212 489 6557
Email ludovic@iemmys.tv
Website www.iemmys.tv

Contact *Ludovic Attal*

ESTABLISHED 1998. The International TV Academy, recognised worldwide since 1969 for its celebration of world-class international programming through its International Emmy Awards, will also recognise excellence in the writing of television programmes for a family audience. Sir Peter Ustinov, the quintessential writer, director and performer, has graciously given his name to the International TV Academy Foundation's Television Scriptwriting Award. This annual competition is designed to motivate novice writers worldwide. The scriptwriter cannot be a United States citizen nor resident and must be below 30 years of age. Final date for entry 1 September. Previous winners: 2000: Sylke Rene Meyer (Germany); 2001 Colm Mahon (Ireland); 2002 Howard Hund (UK).
Prize The award winner will receive US$5000 and the opportunity to work with an established writer as mentor.

The V.B. Poetry Prize

20 Clifton House, Club Row, London E2 7HB
Email LOOKLEARN@aol.com
Website www.looklearn.com

Contact *Nicholas Morgan*

Annual open competition for original single unpublished poem, any style, maximum length 40 lines. Entry fee: £3 for first two poems, £1.50 for each additional poem. Closing date:

30 June. Send s.a.e. for full details and entry form.

Prizes £400 (1st), £150 (2nd), £50 (3rd). Winning poems will be published on the Look and Learn Productions' website.

Ver Poets Open Competition

Haycroft, 61–63 Chiswell Green Lane, St Albans, Hertfordshire AL2 3AL
☎01727 867005

Contact *May Badman*

Various competitions are organised by **Ver Poets**, the main one being the annual Open for unpublished poems of no more than 30 lines written in English. Entry fee: £3 per poem. Entries must be made under a pseudonym, with name and address on form or separate sheet. Two copies of poems typed on A4 white paper. *Vision On*, the anthology of winning and selected poems, and the adjudicators' report are normally available from mid-June. Final entry date: 30 April. Back numbers of the anthology are available for £3, post-free; one copy each free to those included.

Prizes £500 (1st); £300 (2nd); two runner-up prizes of £100.

Vogue Talent Contest

Vogue, Vogue House, Hanover Square, London W1S 1JU
☎020 7152 3003 Fax 020 7408 0559

Contact *Frances Bentley*

ESTABLISHED 1951. Annual award for young writers and journalists (under 25 on 1 January in the year of the contest). Final entry date is in April. Entrants must write three pieces of journalism on given subjects.

Prizes £1000, plus a month's paid work experience with *Vogue*; £500 (2nd).

The Vondel Translation Prize

See **The Translators Association Awards**

Wadsworth Prize for Business History

Business Archives Council, c/o Ms Fiona Maccoll, Records Manager, Rio Tinto plc, 6 St James Square, London SW1Y4LD
☎020 7753 2123 Fax 020 7753 2211

Contact *Mrs Lenore Symons*

ESTABLISHED 1978. Annual award for the best book published on British business history. 2003 winner: Margaret Ackrill and Leslie Hannah *Barclays – The Business of Banking 1690–1990*.

Prize £500.

Arts Council of Wales Book of the Year Awards

Arts Council of Wales, Museum Place, Cardiff CF10 3NX
☎029 2037 6500 Fax 029 2022 1447
Email info@artswales.org.uk

Annual non-competitive prizes awarded for works of exceptional literary merit written by Welsh authors (by birth or residence), published in Welsh or English during the previous calendar year. There is one major prize in English, the Book of the Year Award, and one major prize in Welsh, Gwobr Llyfr y Flwyddyn. From April 2003 the Welsh Academy will be managing the Book of the Year.

Prizes £3000 (each); £1000 to each of four runners-up.

Walford Award

See **CILIP: The Chartered Institute of Library and Information Professionals Walford Award**

Waterstone's Prize

See **The Forward Prizes for Poetry**

The David Watt Prize

Rio Tinto plc, 6 St James's Square, London SW1Y 4LD
☎020 7753 2316 Fax 020 7930 3249
Email davidwattprize@riotinto.com

Contact *The Administrator*

INITIATED in 1987 to commemorate the life and work of David Watt. Annual award, open to writers currently engaged in writing for English language newspapers and journals, on international and national affairs. The winners are judged as having made 'outstanding contributions towards the greater understanding of national, international or global issues'. Entries must have been published during the year preceding the award. Final entry date 31 March. The 2002 winner was Philip Stephens for *Vulnerability of a Superpower*.

Prize £7500.

The Harri Webb Prize

10 Heol Don, Whitchurch, Cardiff CF14 2AU
☎029 2062 3359 Fax 029 2052 9202
Email meic@heoldon.fsnet.co.uk

Contact *Professor Meic Stephens*

ESTABLISHED 1995. Annual award to commemorate the Welsh poet, Harri Webb (1920–94), for a single poem in any of the categories in which he wrote: ballad, satire, song, polemic or a first collection of poems. The poems are chosen by three adjudicators; no submissions. Previous winner: Grahame Davies.

Prizes £100/£200.

Westminster Medal for Military Literature

Royal United Services Institute, Whitehall, London SW1A 2ET

☎020 7930 5854 Fax 020 7321 0943
Email sam@rusi.org
Website www.rusi.org

Contact *Sam Leathers*

ESTABLISHED 1997 this annual award is sponsored by the Duke of Westminster and its aim is to mark a notable and original contribution to the study of international or national security. Work must be in English and must have been published in the preceding or next six months of the closing date for entries. Previous winners: 2000: Colonel Michael Hickey; 2001: Norman Friedman; 2002: Sir Percy Cradock.

Prize Silver medal, £1000. Winning author is invited to give lecture at RUSI and collect medal from the Duke of Westminster.

Wheatley Medal

See **CILIP: The Chartered Institute of Library and Information Professionals Wheatley Medal**

Whitbread Book Awards

The Booksellers Association, Minster House, 272 Vauxhall Bridge Road, London SW1V 1BA

☎020 7802 0802 Fax 020 7802 0803
Email nicola.tarling@booksellers.co.uk
Website www.whitbread-bookawards.co.uk

Contact *Nicola Tarling*

ESTABLISHED 1971. The awards celebrate and promote the best contemporary British writing. They are judged in two stages and offer a total of £50,000 prize money. The awards are open to novel, first novel, biography, poetry and children's book, each judged by a panel of three judges, with two young judges joining the panel for the Whitbread Children's Book Award. The winner of each award receives £5000. The Whitbread Book of the Year (£25,000) is chosen from the category winners. Writers must have lived in Britain and Ireland for three or more years. Submissions received from publishers only. Closing date: early July. Sponsored by

Whitbread PLC. 2002 winners: Hilary Mckay *Saffy's Angel* (children's); Michael Frayn *Spies* (novel); Norman Lebrecht *The Song of Names* (first novel); Claire Tomalin *Samuel Pepys: The Unequalled Self* (biography and overall winner); Paul Farley *The Ice Age* (poetry).

Whitfield Prize

Royal Historical Society, University College London, Gower Street, London WC1E 6BT

☎020 7387 7532 Fax 020 7387 7532
Email rhs.info@sas.ac.uk

Contact *Executive Secretary*

ESTABLISHED 1977. An annual award for the best new work within a field of British history, published in the UK in the preceding calendar year. The book must be the author's first (solely written) history book and be an original and scholarly work of historical research. Final entry date: 31 December. Previous winners: John Goodall *God's House at Ewelme: Life, Devotion and Architecture in a Fifteenth-Century Almshouse*; Frank Salmon *Building on Ruins: The Rediscovery of Rome and English Architecture*.

Prize £1000.

John Whiting Award

Arts Council of England, 14 Great Peter Street, London SW1P 3NQ

☎020 7333 0100
Email jemima.lee@artscouncil.org.uk
Website www.artscouncil.org.uk

Contact *Theatre Writing Section*

FOUNDED 1965. Annual award to commemorate the life and work of the playwright John Whiting (*The Devils, A Penny for a Song*). Any writer who has received during 2003 and 2004: (a) an award through the **Arts Council's Theatre Writing Schemes**; (b) a commission from a theatre company in receipt of an annual or revenue subsidy from either the Arts Council or a Regional Arts Board; or (c) a première production by a theatre company in receipt of annual subsidy is eligible to apply. The play must have been written during 2003 and/or 2004. Awarded to the writer whose play most nearly satisfies the following criteria: a play in which the writing is of special quality; a play of relevance and importance to contemporary life; a play of potential value to the British theatre. No writer who has won the award previously may reapply and no play that has been submitted for the award previously is eligible. Contact the theatre writing section for full details and application form.

Prize £6000.

Alfred and Mary Wilkins Memorial Poetry Competition and Lecture

Birmingham & Midland Institute, 9 Margaret Street, Birmingham B3 3BS
☎0121 236 3591 Fax 0121 212 4577
Administrator *Mr P.A. Fisher*

Alternating competition and lecture. The next competition, to be held in 2004, is for an unpublished poem, not exceeding 40 lines, written in English by an author not over the age of 15. The poem should not have been entered for any other poetry competition. Details from the address above.

Prizes (total) £1000.

Titus Wilson and Son Prize

See **Lakeland Book of the Year Awards**

H.H. Wingate Prize

See **Jewish Quarterly Literary Prizes**

Wolf Web

PO Box 136, Norwich, Norfolk NR3 3NJ
☎01603 440940 Fax 01603 440940
Email poems@sayanawolf.org
Website www.sayanawolf.org
Contact *Tricia Frances*

Sayana Wolf Trust publishes *Wolf Web* twice a year and runs one poetry competiton annually. Closing date: 12 December. Unpublished poems only on the theme of 'wolf'. All profits go to the work of The Sayana Wolf Trust which funds personal development, educational and community projects for British and North American children and adults. For more details, write to the address above (no replies without s.a.e.).

Prizes One-year's membership to Wolf Web and publication in *Wolf Web*.

Wolfson History Prizes

Wolfson Foundation, 8 Queen Anne Street, London W1G 9LD
☎020 7323 5730 Fax 020 7323 3241
Contact *Executive Secretary*

The Wolfson History Prize, ESTABLISHED in 1972, is awarded annually to promote and encourage standards of excellence in the writing of history for the general reading public. 2003 winners: *Marianne in Chains: In Search of the German Occupation 1940–1945* Robert Gildea (*Prize* £15,000); *White Mughals: Seduction and Betrayal in 18th-Century India* William Dalrymple *Prize* £10,000).

The David T.K. Wong Short Story Prize

International PEN, 9/10 Charterhouse Buildings, Goswell Road, London EC1M 7AT
☎020 7253 4308 Fax 020 7253 5711
Email intpen@dircon.co.uk
Website www.internatpen.org
Contact *Gilly Vincent*

ESTABLISHED 2000. An international, biannual prize to promote literary excellence in the form of the short story written in English. Unpublished stories (6000 words maximum) are welcome from writers worldwide, as long as their entries are submitted via their local PEN Centre and incorporate one or more of International PEN's ideals as set out in its Charter. Writers in those few countries without a PEN Centre can be directed to the nearest appropriate centre by International PEN. See website for full prize details and PEN Centres. 2001 winner: Rachel Seiffert *The Crossing*.

Prize £7500 (1st).

World Wide Writers Award

PO Box 3229, Bournemouth, Dorset BH1 1ZS
☎01202 589828 Fax 01202 587758
Email writintl@globalnet.co.uk
Website www.worldwidewriters.com
Contacts *John Jenkins, Mary Hogarth*

ESTABLISHED 1997. Quarterly and annual competitions for original, unpublished short stories of between 2500 and 5000 words. Entries are published in *World Wide Writers* magazine. Entry fee: £10 (£6 for subscribers to *World Wide Writers*). Entry fee includes back issue of the magazine. Closing dates: end of January, March, June and September. Previous winners: Sally Zigmond, Shirley Nunes, Judi Moore, Gerald Phillipson, Brian Dixon, L. Morgana Braveraven.

Annual *prize* £3000 and medal. *Writers' Forum* Short Story Competition: £150 to £250 with an annual trophy and a cheque for £1000 for the best story of the year.

The Writers Bureau Poetry and Short Story Competition

The Writers Bureau, Sevendale House, 7 Dale Street, Manchester M1 1JB
☎0161 228 2362 Fax 0161 228 3533
Email studentservices@writersbureau.com
Website www.writersbureau.com
Competition Secretary *Angela Cox*

ESTABLISHED 1994. Annual award. Poems should be no longer than 40 lines and short stories no more than 2000 words. £5 entry fee. Closing date: 31 July 2004.

Prizes in each category: £1000 (1st); £400 (2nd); £200 (3rd); £100 (4th); £50 x 6.

Yorkshire Post
Book of the Year Award
The Rectory, Ripley, Near Harrogate, North Yorkshire HG3 3AY

☎01423 772217   Fax 01423 772217

Contact *Margaret Brown*

An annual award for the book (either fiction or non-fiction) which, in the opinion of the judges, is the best work published in the preceding year. Closing date: 31 December. Previous winner: Steven Pinker *The Blank State – the Modern Denial of Human Nature.*

Prize £1200.

The Cost of Borrowing

Where we are with Public Lending Right

We all make mistakes. A year ago *The Writer's Handbook* confidently predicted that Public Lending Right (PLR), the fund that compensates authors for loans of their books from public libraries, had had its day. There was not enough money in the kitty to sustain the enterprise, we argued, and no chance that Chancellor Brown would favour an increased handout to a profession not noted for exercising political muscle. But this was to underestimate the grit of the Society of Authors, that noble institution that has been leading a campaign to re-establish PLR on a sound financial footing. Furious lobbying secured a leap in funding from £5.2 million to £7 million with more to come. The figure goes up to £7.38 million for 2004/5 with at least proportionate increases expected thereafter. This follows a Department of Culture review that gives full backing to PLR and its administration which is judged, quite properly, to be a notable exercise in cost-effective bureaucracy.

How far individual writers will notice any difference depends, of course, on the popularity of their titles. As always, the calculation is based on a sample of thirty library authorities across the UK while the rate for the loan is worked out by dividing the amount in the PLR pot by the total number of loans. For this last year the rate was 4.21 pence, up from the previous year's rate of 2.67 pence. Just over 19,000 authors get their just reward, though for the great majority, nearly 13,000, this is under £100. For the explanation, look no further than library statistics. While more books are being published and more authors registering for PLR, fewer readers are using the libraries or maybe using them less frequently. Total UK loans are down from 430 million in 2001 to 406 million last year. And the trend shows no sign of reversing. This suggests that PLR is in need of an update to bring it into line with contemporary reading habits. As a start the maximum payout, £5,000–£6,000, which goes to the rich list of top writers could be reduced, say, to £1,000 allowing for an extra million or so to be shared between authors who have to scramble for a living. Then again PLR, as presently constituted, continues for the life of the author plus seventy years, bringing joy to the heirs of such as Agatha Christie and Catherine Cookson. Would it not be fairer to restrict the time frame to ten years?

While the argument over the future of PLR hots up, there is encouraging news for authors from the Authors' Licensing & Collecting Society (ALCS) which distributes fees to writers whose work has been copied, broadcast or recorded. A long drawn-out fight with the universities over the page rate for copying has ended with an agreed blanket fee of £4 per student per year for a fixed period of five years to allow for the copying of up to five per cent of any work. Authors of academic books, not to mention poets, playwrights and novelists are now getting a welcome addition to income. This year ALCS has achieved its biggest distribution figure ever with £5.3 million split between 25,000 authors, 20 per cent up on last year. And this is where the future lies. Copying and, longer term, online transmission will take over from the traditional library loan system as the meaty bone of contention between authors and readers.

PLR application forms and details can be obtained from the Registrar of Public Lending Right at Richard House, Sorbonne Close, Stockton-on-Tees TS17 6DA. ☎*01642 604699; fax 01642 615641; email authorservices@plr.uk.com website: www.plr.uk.com*

The PLR Office has recently published its own report on the operation of PLR with practical information about the past, present and future. Copies are available free of charge from the PLR Office at the above address; or email jim.parker@plr.uk.com

The Authors' Licensing & Collecting Society Ltd (ALCS) is at Marlborough Court, 14–18 Holborn, London EC1N 2LE. ☎*020 7395 0600; fax 020 7395 0660; email alcs@alcs.co.uk; website www.alcs.co.uk*

Library Services

Aberdeen Central Library

Rosemount Viaduct, Aberdeen AB25 1GW
☎01224 652500 Fax 01224 641985
Email centlib@arts-rec.aberdeen.net.uk

Open 9.00 am to 7.00 pm Monday to
Thursday; 9.00 am to 5.00 pm Friday
(Reference & Local Studies: 9.00 am to
8.00 pm); 9.00 am to 5.00 pm Saturday.
Branch library opening times vary

Open access
General reference and loans. Books, pamphlets, periodicals and newspapers; videos, CDs; arts equipment lending service; Internet and Learning Centre for public access; photographs of the Aberdeen area; census records, maps; online database, patents and standards. The library offers special services to housebound readers. Non-resident administrative fee.

Armitt Library

Ambleside, Cumbria LA22 9BL
☎015394 31212 Fax 015394 31313
Website www.armitt.com

Open 10.00 am to 12.30 pm and 1.30 pm to
4.00 pm Monday to Friday

Free access (To view original material please give prior notice)
A small but unique reference library of rare books, manuscripts, pictures, antiquarian prints and museum items, mainly about the Lake District. It includes early guidebooks and topographical works, books and papers relating to Ruskin, H. Martineau, Charlotte Mason and others; fine art including work by W. Green, J.B. Pyne, John Harden, K. Schwitters, and Victorian photographs by Herbert Bell; also a major collection of Beatrix Potter's scientific watercolour drawings and microscope studies. Museum and Exhibition open seven days per week from 10.00 am to 5.00 pm. Entry charge.

The Athenaeum, Liverpool

Church Alley, Liverpool L1 3DD
☎0151 709 7770 Fax 0151 709 0418
Email library@athena.force9.net
Website www.athena.force9.co.uk

Open 9.00 am to 4.00 pm Monday to Friday

Access To club members; researchers by application only

General collection, with books dating from the 15th century, now concentrated mainly on local history with a long run of Liverpool directories and guides. *Special collections* Liverpool playbills; William Roscoe; Blanco White; Robert Gladstone; 18th-century plays; 19th-century economic pamphlets; the Norris books; Bibles; Yorkshire and other genealogy. Some original drawings, portraits, topographical material and local maps.

Bank of England Information Centre

Threadneedle Street, London EC2R 8AH
☎020 7601 4715 Fax 020 7601 4356
Email informationcentre@bankofengland.co.uk
Website www.bankofengland.co.uk

Open 9.30 am to 5.30 pm Monday to Friday

Access For research workers by prior arrangement only, when material is not readily available elsewhere
50,000 volumes of books and periodicals. 2000 periodicals taken. UK and overseas coverage of banking, finance and economics. *Special collections* Central bank reports; UK 17th–19th-century economic tracts; Government reports in the field of banking.

Barbican Library

Barbican Centre, London EC2Y 8DS
☎020 7638 0569 Fax 020 7638 2249
Email barbicanlib@corpoflondon.gov.uk
Website www.cityoflondon.gov.uk/libraries

Open 9.30 am to 5.30 pm Monday,
Wednesday, Thursday, Friday; 9.30 am to
7.30 pm Tuesday; 9.30 am to 12.30 pm
Saturday

Open access
Situated on Level 2 of the Barbican Centre, this is the Corporation of London's largest lending library. Study facilities are available plus free Internet access. In addition to a large general lending department, the library seeks to reflect the Centre's emphasis on the arts and includes strong collections (including DVDs, videos and CD-ROMs), on painting, sculpture, theatre, cinema and ballet, as well as a large music library with books, scores and CDs (sound recording

loans available at a small charge). Also houses the City's main children's library and has special collections on finance, natural resources, conservation, socialism and the history of London. Service available for housebound readers. A literature events programme is organised by the Library which supplements and provides cross-arts planning opportunities with the Barbican Centre artistic programme. Reading groups meet in the library on the first Tuesday and Thursday of every month.

Barnsley Public Library
Central Library, Shambles Street, Barnsley, South Yorkshire S70 2JF
☎01226 773930 Fax 01226 773955
Email barnsleylibraryenquiries@barnsley.gov.uk
Website www.barnsley.gov.uk/service/libraries/index.asp

Open Lending & Reference: 9.30 am to 7.00 pm Monday and Wednesday; 9.30 am to 5.30 pm Tuesday and Friday; 9.30 am to 4.00 pm Saturday. Please telephone to check hours of other departments.

Open access
General library, lending and reference. Archive collection of family history and local firms; local studies: coal mining, local authors, Yorkshire and Barnsley; large junior library. (Specialist departments are closed on certain weekday evenings and Saturday afternoons.)

BBC Written Archives Centre
Peppard Road, Caversham Park, Reading, Berkshire RG4 8TZ
☎0118 948 6281 Fax 0118 946 1145
Email wac.enquiries@bbc.co.uk
Website www.bbc.co.uk/thenandnow
Contact *Jacqueline Kavanagh*
Open 9.30 am to 5.30 pm Monday to Friday
Access For reference, by appointment only on Wednesday to Friday.
Holds the written records of the BBC, including internal papers from 1922 to 1979 and published material to date. 20th century biography, social history, popular culture and broadcasting. Charges for certain services.

Bedford Central Library
Harpur Street, Bedford MK40 1PG
☎01234 350931/270102 (Reference Library)
Fax 01234 342163
Website www.bedfordshire.gov.uk

Open 9.30 am to 7.00 pm Monday and Wednesday; 9.30 am to 5.30 pm Tuesday, Thursday, Friday; 9.30 am to 5.00 pm Saturday
Open access
Lending library with a wide range of stock, including books, music (CDs and cassettes), audio books and videos; reference and information library, children's library, local history library and Internet facilities.

Belfast Public Libraries: Central Library
Royal Avenue, Belfast BT1 1EA
☎028 9050 9150 Fax 028 9033 2819
Email info.belb@ni-libraries.net
Website www.belb.org.uk

Open 9.00 am to 9.00 pm Monday and Thursday; 9.00 am to 5.30 pm Tuesday, Wednesday, Friday; 9.00 am to 1.00 pm Saturday
Open access To lending libraries; reference libraries by application only
Over two million volumes for lending and reference. *Special collections* United Nations depository; complete British Patent Collection; Northern Ireland Newspaper Library; British and Irish government publications. The Central Library provides the following Reference Departments: General Reference; Belfast, Ulster and Irish Studies; Music. A Learning Gateway includes public Internet facilities and a Learndirect Centre. The Lending Library is one of over 20 branches along with a range of outreach services to hospitals, care homes and housebound readers.

BFI National Library
21 Stephen Street, London W1T 1LN
☎020 7255 1444 Fax 020 7436 2338
Email library@bfi.org.uk
Website www.bfi.org.uk

Open 10.30 am to 5.30 pm Monday and Friday; 10.30 am to 8.00 pm Tuesday and Thursday; 1.00 pm to 8.00 pm Wednesday; Telephone Enquiry Service operates from 10.00 am to 5.00 pm
Access For reference only; annual, 5-day and limited day membership available
The world's largest collection of information on film and television including periodicals, cuttings, scripts, related documentation, personal papers. Main library catalogue available via website.

Birmingham and Midland Institute

9 Margaret Street, Birmingham B3 3BS
☎0121 236 3591 Fax 0121 212 4577
Website www.bmi.org.uk

Administrator & General Secretary *Philip Fisher*

Access Members only
ESTABLISHED 1854. Later merged with the Birmingham Library which was founded in 1779. Specialises in the humanities, with approximately 100,000 volumes in stock. Founder member of the **Association of Independent Libraries**. Meeting-place of many affiliated societies devoted to poetry and literature.

Birmingham Library Services

Central Library, Chamberlain Square, Birmingham B3 3HQ
☎0121 303 4511
Email central.library@birmingham.gov.uk
Website www.birmingham.gov.uk/libraries

Open 9.00 am to 8.00 pm Monday to Friday; 9.00 am to 5.00 pm Saturday

Over a million volumes. *Research collections* include the Shakespeare Library; War Poetry Collection; Parker Collection of Children's Books and Games; Johnson Collection; Milton Collection; Cervantes Collections; Early and Fine Printing Collection (including the William Ridler Collection of Fine Printing); Joseph Priestley Collection; Loudon Collection; Railway Collection; Wingate Bett Transport Ticket Collection; Labour, Trade Union and Co-operative Collections. Photographic archives: Sir John Benjamin Stone; Francis Bedford; Francis Frith; Warwickshire Photographic Survey; Boulton and Watt Archive. Also, Charles Parker Archive; Birmingham Repertory Theatre Archive and Sir Barry Jackson Library; Local Studies (Birmingham); Patents Collection; Song Sheets Collection; Oberammergau Festival Collection.

Bournemouth Library

22 The Triangle, Bournemouth, Dorset BH2 5RQ
☎01202 454848 Fax 01202 454840

Open 10.00 am to 7.00 pm Monday; 9.30 am to 7.00 pm Tuesday, Thursday, Friday; 9.30 am to 5.00 pm Wednesday; 9.00 am to 1.00 pm Saturday

Open access
Main library for Bournemouth with lending, reference and music departments, plus the Heritage Zone – local and family history.

Bradford Central Library

Princes Way, Bradford, West Yorkshire BD1 1NN
☎01274 753600 Fax 01274 395108
Email public.libraries@bradford.gov.uk

Open 9.00 am to 7.30 pm Monday to Friday; 9.00 am to 5.00 pm Saturday

Open access
Wide range of books and media loan services. Comprehensive reference and information services, including major local history collections and specialised business information service. Bradford Libraries run *Reader2Reader*, a groundbreaking, reader-centred literature development project (www.Reader2Reader.com)

Brighton Central Library

Vantage Point, New England Street, Brighton, East Sussex BN1 2GW
☎01273 290800 Fax 01273 296951

Local Studies Library: Church Street, Brighton BN1 2UE

Open 10.00 am to 7.00 pm Monday to Friday (closed Wednesday); 10.00 am to 4.00 pm Saturday

Access Limited stock on open access; material for reference use and lending
FOUNDED 1869, the library has a large stock covering most subjects. Specialisations include art and antiques, history of Brighton and Sussex, family history, local illustrations, TSO, business and large bequests of antiquarian books and ecclesiastical history.

Bristol Central Library

College Green, Bristol BS1 5TL
☎0117 903 7200 Fax 0117 922 1081
Website www.bristol-city.gov.uk *or* www.digitalbristol.org

Open 9.30 am to 7.30 pm Monday, Tuesday and Thursday; 9.30 am to 5.00 pm Wednesday, Friday and Saturday; 1.00 pm to 4.00 pm Sunday

Open access
Lending, reference, art, music, business and local studies are particularly strong. Facilities available: PCs (large screen with Jaws and Zoomtext), Internet, printing; videophone on site.

British Architectural Library

Royal Institute of British Architects, 66 Portland Place, London W1B 1AD
☎020 7580 5533 Fax 020 7631 1802
Email info@inst.riba.org

Website www.architecture.com

Members' Information Line: 020 7307 3600 (membership number required);

Public Information Line (50p per min.): 0906 302 0400

Open 10.00 pm to 8.00 pm Tuesday; 10.00 am to 5.00 pm Wednesday to Friday; 10.00 am to 1.30 pm Saturday; Closed Sunday, Monday and any Saturday preceding a Bank Holiday; full details on the website

Access Free to RIBA members; non-members must buy a day ticket (£10/£6 concessions, but on Tuesdays between 5.00 pm–8.00 pm and Saturdays £6/£3); subscriber membership available (write for details); loans available to RIBA and library members only

Collection of books, drawings, manuscripts, photographs and periodicals. All aspects of architecture, current and historical. Material both technical and aesthetic, covering related fields including: interior design, landscape architecture, topography, the construction industry and applied arts. Brochure available; queries by telephone, letter, e-mail or in person. Charge for research (min. charge £30).

The British Library

Admission to St Pancras Reading Rooms

The British Library does not provide access to all those who request admission to use its research facilities but operates an admissions policy which grants access to those who need to use the collection because they cannot find the material they require in other libraries.

Admission is by interview and applicants are required to demonstrate that they need access to the reading rooms because: (a) material they need to consult is not available elsewhere; (b) their work or studies require the facilities of a large research library; (c) they need access to the Library's public records.

For further information, contact the Reader Admissions Office, The British Library, 96 Euston Road, London NW1 2DB E-mail reader-admissions@bl.uk ☎020 7412 7677 Fax 020 7412 7794

British Library Business Information Service (BIS)

96 Euston Road, London NW1 2DB
Email business-information@bl.uk
Website www.bl.uk/bis

Free enquiry service ☎020 7412 7977
Fax 020 7412 7453
Free enquiry service: ☎020 7412 7977
Fax 020 7412 945

Priced enquiry service: ☎020 7412 7457
Fax 020 7412 7453

Open 10.00 am to 8.00 pm Monday; 9.30 am to 8.00 pm Tuesday to Thursday; 9.30 am to 5.00 pm Friday and Saturday; closed for public holidays

Access Pass required for access

BIS holds the most comprehensive collection of business information literature in the UK. This includes market research reports and journals, directories, company annual reports, trade and business journals, house journals, trade literature and CD-ROM services.

British Library Early Printed Collections/Rare Book and Music Reading Room

96 Euston Road, London NW1 2DB
☎020 7412 7676 Fax 020 7412 7577
Email rare-books@bl.uk
Website www.bl.uk

General enquiries about reader services and advance reservations: ☎020 7412 7676 Fax 020 7412 7609 Email reader-services@bl.uk

Open 10.00 am to 8.00 pm Monday; 9.30 am to 8.00 pm Tuesday to Thursday; 9.30 am to 5.00 pm Friday and Saturday; closed for public holidays

Access By British Library reader's pass

Early Printed Collections, which is an integral part of British Library Scholarship and Collections, selects, acquires, researches and provides access to material printed in the British Isles to 1914 and in Western European languages before 1851. The collections are available in the Rare Books and Music Reading Room at St Pancras which also functions as the focus for the British Library's extensive collection of humanities microforms.

Further information about Early Printed Collections can be found at the British Library website.

British Library Humanities Reading Room

96 Euston Road, London NW1 2DB
☎020 7412 7676 Fax 020 7412 7609
Email reader-services-enquiries@bl.uk
Website www.bl.uk/resources/humanities

Open 10.00 am to 8.00 pm Monday; 9.30 am to 8.00 pm Tuesday, Wednesday, Thursday; 9.30 am to 5.00 pm Friday and Saturday; closed for public holidays

Access By British Library reader's pass

This reading room is the focus for the

Library's modern collections service in the humanities. It is on two levels, Humanities 1 and Humanities 2 and provides access to the Library's comprehensive collections of books and periodicals in all subjects in the humanities and social sciences and in all languages apart from Oriental. These collections are not available for browsing at the shelf. Material is held in closed access storage and needs to be identified and ordered from store using an online catalogue. A selective open access collection on most humanities subjects can be found in Humanities 1 whilst in Humanities 2 there are open access reference works relating to periodicals and theses, to recorded sound and to librarianship and information science.

To access British Library catalogues, go to the website.

British Library Manuscript Collections
96 Euston Road, London NW1 2DB
☎020 7412 7513 Fax 020 7412 7745
Email mss@bl.uk
Website www.bl.uk

Open 10.00 am to 5.00 pm Monday; 9.30 am to 5.00 pm Tuesday to Saturday; closed for public holidays

Access Reading facilities only, by British Library reader's pass; a written letter of recommendation and advance notice is required for certain categories of material

Two useful publications, *Index of Manuscripts in the British Library*, Cambridge 1984–6, 10 vols, and *The British Library: Guide to the Catalogues and Indexes of the Department of Manuscripts* by M.A.E. Nickson, help to guide the researcher through this vast collection of manuscripts dating from Ancient Greece to the present day. Approximately 300,000 mss, charters, papyri and seals are housed here.

For information on British Library collections and services and to access British Library catalogues, including the Manuscripts online catalogue, visit the website.

British Library Map Collections
96 Euston Road, London NW1 2DB
☎020 7412 7702 Fax 020 7412 7780
Email maps@bl.uk
Website www.bl.uk/collections/maps

Open 10.00 am to 5.00 pm Monday; 9.30 am to 5.00 pm Tuesday to Saturday; closed for public holidays

Access By British Library reader's pass
A collection of about 4.5million maps, charts and globes, manuscript, printed and, increasingly, digital, with particular reference to the history of British cartography. Maps for all parts of the world in a wide range of scales, formats and dates, including the most comprehensive collection of Ordnance Survey maps and plans. *Special collections* King George III Topographical Collection and Maritime Collection, the Crace Collection of maps and plans of London and the cartographic archive of the Ministry of Defence (i.e. GSGS).

For information on British Library collections and services, visit the website.

To access main British Library catalogues, go to the website at blpc.bl.uk (NB Map Library catalogue on CD-ROM; not yet available online.)

British Library Music Collections
96 Euston Road, London NW1 2DB
☎020 7412 7772 Fax 020 7412 7751
Email music-collections@bl.uk
Website www.bl.uk

Open 10.00 am to 8.00 pm Monday; 9.30 am to 8.00 pm Tuesday to Thursday; 9.30 am to 5.00 pm Friday and Saturday; closed for public holidays

Access By British Library reader's pass
Special collections The Royal Music Library (containing almost all Handel's surviving autograph scores), The Zweig Collection of Music & Literary Mss, The Royal Philharmonic Society Archive and the Paul Hirsch Music Library. Also a large collection (about one and a quarter million items) of printed music (UK via legal deposit) and about 100,000 items of manuscript music, both British and foreign.

The British Library website contains details of collections and services, and provides access to the catalogues.

British Library National Sound Archive
96 Euston Road, London NW1 2DB
☎020 7412 7440 Fax 020 7412 7441
Email nsa@bl.uk
Website www.bl.uk/nsa
Online catalogue cadenza.bl.uk

Open 10.00 am to 8.00 pm Monday; 9.30 am to 8.00 pm Tuesday to Thursday; 9.30 am to 5.00 pm Friday and Saturday; closed for public holidays

Listening service (by appointment)

Northern Listening Service:
British Library Document Supply Centre,

Boston Spa, West Yorkshire: 9.15 am to 4.30 pm Monday to Friday

Open access

An archive of over 1,000,000 discs and more than 200,000 hours of tape recordings, including all types of music, oral history, drama, literature, poetry, wildlife, selected BBC broadcasts and BBC Sound Archive material. Produces a twice-yearly newsletter, *Playback*.

For information on British Library National Sound Archive collections and services, visit the website.

British Library Newspaper Library

Colindale Avenue, London NW9 5HE
☎020 7412 7353 Fax 020 7412 7379
Email newspaper@bl.uk
Website www.bl.uk/collections/
newspapers.html

Open 10.00 am to 4.45 pm Monday to Saturday (last newspaper issue 4.15 pm); closed for public holidays

Access By British Library reader's pass or Newspaper Library pass (available from and valid only for Colindale)

Major collections of English provincial, Scottish, Welsh, Irish, Commonwealth and selected overseas foreign newspapers from *c*.1700 are housed here. Some earlier holdings are also available. London newspapers from 1801 and many weekly and fortnightly periodicals are also in stock. (London newspapers pre-dating 1801 are housed at the new library building in St Pancras – 96 Euston Road, NW1 2DB – though many are available at Colindale Avenue on microfilm.) Readers are advised to check availability of material in advance.

For information on British Library Newspaper Library collections and services, visit the website.

British Library Oriental and India Office Collections

96 Euston Road, London NW1 2DB
☎020 7412 7873 Fax 020 7412 7641
Email oioc-enquiries@bl.uk
Website www.bl.uk

Open 10.00 am to 5.00 pm Monday; 9.30 am to 5.00 pm Tuesday to Saturday; closed for public holidays

Access By British Library reader's pass (identification required)

A comprehensive collection of printed volumes and manuscripts in the languages of North Africa, the Near and Middle East and all of Asia, plus records of the East India Company

and British government in India until 1947. Also prints, drawings and paintings by British artists of India.

For information on British Library collections and services, visit the website.

To access British Library catalogues, go to the website at blpc.bl.uk

British Library Science, Technology and Innovation Information Services

96 Euston Road, London NW1 2DB
☎020 7412 7288/7494 (General Enquiries)
Fax 020 7412 7495
Email scitech@bl.uk
Website www.bl.uk

British/EPO patent enquiries:
☎020 7412 7919

Business enquiries: ☎020 7412 7454/7977
(Business quick enquiry line available 9.00 am to 5.00 pm Monday to Friday)

Open 10.00 am to 8.00 pm Monday; 9.30 am to 8.00 pm Tuesday to Thursday; 9.30 am to 5.00 pm Friday and Saturday; closed for public holidays

Engineering, business information on companies, markets and products, physical science and technologies. British, European and Patent Co-operation Treaty patents and trade marks.

For information on British Library collections and services, visit the website.

To access British Library catalogues go to the website at blpc.bl.uk

British Library Social Policy Information Service

96 Euston Road, London NW1 2DB
☎020 7412 7536 Fax 020 7412 7761
Website www.bl.uk/services/stb/spis.html

Open 10.00 am to 8.00 pm Monday; 9.30 am to 8.00 pm Tuesday to Thursday; 9.30 am to 5.00 pm Friday and Saturday; closed for public holidays

Access By British Library reader's pass

Provides an information service on social policy, public administration, and current and international affairs, and access to current and historical official publications from all countries and intergovernmental bodies, including House of Commons sessional papers, UK legislation, UK electoral registers, up-to-date reference books on official publications and on the social sciences, a major collection of statistics and a browsing collection of recent social science books and periodicals. Also offers a priced research service providing literature surveys, current awareness and topic briefings for clients on demand.

To access British Library catalogues, go to the website at blpc.bl.uk

British Psychological Society Library

c/o Psychology Library, University of London Library, Senate House, Malet Street, London WC1E 7HU
☎020 7862 8451/8461 Fax 020 7862 8480
Email enquiries@ull.ac.uk
Website www.ull.ac.uk

Open Term-time: 9.00 am to 9.00 pm Monday to Thursday; 9.00 am to 6.30 pm Friday; 9.30 am to 5.30 pm Saturday (Holidays: 9.00 am to 6.00 pm Monday to Friday; 9.30 am to 5.30 pm Saturday)

Access Members only; Non-members £7 day ticket

Reference library, containing the British Psychological Society collection of periodicals – over 140 current titles housed alongside the University of London's collection of books and journals. Largely for academic research. General queries referred to **Swiss Cottage Library** in London which has a good psychology collection.

Bromley Central Library

London Borough of Bromley – Leisure & Community Services, High Street, Bromley, Kent BR1 1EX
☎020 8460 9955 Fax 020 8313 9975
Email reference.library@bromley.gov.uk
Website www.bromley.gov.uk

Open 9.30 am to 6.00 pm Monday, Wednesday, Friday; 9.30 am to 8.00 pm Tuesday and Thursday; 9.30 am to 5.00 pm Saturday

Open access

A large selection of fiction and non-fiction books for loan, both adult and children's. Also DVDs, videos, CDs, cassettes, language courses, open learning packs, CD-ROM and Playstation games for hire. Other facilities include a business information service (e-mail bis@bromley.gov. uk), CD-ROM, computer hire, Internet, local studies library, 'Upfront' teenage section, large reference library with photocopying, fax, microfiche and film facilities, 'Signpost' – online community information. *Specialist collections* include: H.G. Wells, Walter de la Mare, Crystal Palace, The Harlow Bequest, and the history and geography of Asia, America, Australasia and the Polar regions.

Bromley House Library

Angel Row, Nottingham NG1 6HL
☎0115 947 3134

Librarian *Julia Wilson*

Open 9.30 am to 5.00 pm Monday to Friday; also first Saturday of each month from 10.00 am to 12.30 pm

Access For members only
FOUNDED 1816 as the Nottingham Subscription Library. Collection of 30,000 books including local history, topography, biography, travel and fiction.

CAA Library and Information Centre

Aviation House, Gatwick Airport, West Sussex RH6 0YR
☎01293 573725 Fax 01293 573181
Website www.caa.co.uk

Open 9.30 am to 4.30 pm Monday to Friday; 10.00 am to 4.30 pm first Wednesday of the month

Open access

Books, periodicals and reports on air transport, air traffic control, electronics, radar and computing.

Cambridge Central Library (Reference Library & Information Service)

7 Lion Yard, Cambridge CB2 3QD
☎01223 712000 Fax 01223 712036
Email cambridge.central.library@ cambridgeshire.gov.uk
Website www.cambridgeshire.gov.uk/library

Open 9.00 am to 7.00 pm Monday to Friday; 9.00 am to 5.30 pm Saturday

Open access

Large stock of books, periodicals, newspapers, maps, plus comprehensive collection of directories and annuals covering UK, Europe and the world. Microfilm and fiche reading and printing services. Online access to news and business databases. News databases on CD-ROM; Internet access. Monochrome and colour photocopiers.

Camomile Street Library

12–20 Camomile Street, London EC3A 7EX
☎020 7247 8895

Open 9.30 am to 5.30 pm Monday to Friday

Open access

Corporation of London lending library.

Wide range of fiction and non-fiction books and language courses on cassette, foreign fiction, paperbacks, maps and guides for travel at home and abroad, children's books, a selection of large print, and collections of DVDs, videos and music CDs. Free Internet access.

Cardiff Central Library
Frederick Street, St David's Link, Cardiff CF10 2DU
☎029 2038 2116 Fax 029 2087 1599
Email robboddy@hotmail.com
Website www.libraries.cardiff.gov.uk

Open 9.00 am to 6.00 pm Monday, Tuesday, Wednesday, Friday; 9.00 am to 7.00 pm Thursday; 9.00 am to 5.30 pm Saturday

General lending library with the following departments: leisure, music, children's, local studies, information, science and humanities.

Carmarthen Public Library
St Peter's Street, Carmarthen SA31 1LN
☎01267 224830 Fax 01267 221839
Email dpthomas@carmarthenshire.gov.uk

Open 9.30 am to 7.00 pm Monday, Tuesday, Wednesday, Friday; 9.30 am to 5.00 pm Thursday and Saturday

Open access
Comprehensive range of fiction, non-fiction, children's books and reference works in English and in Welsh. Large local history library. Free Internet access and CD-ROM facilities. Large Print books, books on tape, CDs, CD-ROMs, cassettes and videos available for loan.

Catholic Central Library
Lancing Street, London NW1 1ND
☎020 7383 4333 Fax 020 7388 6675
Email librarian@catholic-library.org.uk
Website www.catholic-library.org.uk

Open 10.30 am to 5.00 pm Monday, Tuesday, Thursday, Friday; 10.30 am to 7.00 pm Wednesday

Open access For reference (non-members must sign in; loans restricted to members)
Contains books, many not readily available elsewhere, on theology, religions worldwide, scripture and the history of churches of all denominations.

The Centre for the Study of Cartoons and Caricature
See entry under **Picture Libraries**

City Business Library
1 Brewers' Hall Garden, London EC2V 5BX
☎020 7332 1812 Fax 020 7332 1847
Email cbl@corpoflondon.gov.uk
Website www.cityoflondon.gov.uk/libraries
Open 9.30 am to 5.00 pm Monday to Friday

Open access
Local authority public reference library run by the Corporation of London. Books, pamphlets, periodicals and newspapers of current business interest, mostly financial. Aims to satisfy the day-to-day information needs of the City's business community, and in so doing has become one of the leading public resource centres in Britain in its field. Strong collection of directories for both the UK and overseas, plus companies information, market research sources, management, law, banking, insurance, statistics and investment. Public internet access. No academic journals or textbooks.

Commonwealth Secretariat Library
Marlborough House, Pall Mall, London SW1Y 5HX
☎020 7747 6164 Fax 020 7747 6168
Email library@commonwealth.int
Website www.thecommonwealth.org
Librarian *David Blake*
Open 9.15 am to 5.00 pm Monday to Friday

Access For reference only, by appointment
Extensive reference source concerned with economy, development, trade, production and industry of Commonwealth countries; also human resources including women, youth, health, management and education. Includes the archives of the Secretariat.

Corporation of London Libraries
See **Barbican Library; Camomile Street Library; City Business Library; Guildhall Library**

Coventry Central Library
Smithford Way, Coventry, Warwickshire CV1 1FY
☎024 7683 2314/2395 (Minicom)
Fax 024 7683 2440
Email central.library@coventry.gov.co.uk
Website www.coventry.gov.uk/accent.htm

Open 9.00 am to 8.00 pm Monday to Friday; 9.00 am to 4.30 pm Saturday; 12.00 am to 4.00 pm Sunday.

Open access
Located in the middle of the city's main shopping centre. Approximately 120,000 items

(books, cassettes, CDs and DVDs) for loan; plus reference collection of business information and local history. *Special collections* Cycling and motor industries; George Eliot; Angela Brazil; Tom Mann Collection (trade union and labour studies); local newspapers on microfilm from 1740 onwards. Over 300 periodicals taken. 'Peoplelink' community information database available.

Department for Environment, Food and Rural Affairs

Nobel House, 17 Smith Square, London SW1P 3JR
☎020 7238 3000 Fax 020 7238 6591

DEFRA Helpline 08459 335577 (local call rate) – general contact point which can provide information on the work of DEFRA, either directly or by referring callers to appropriate contacts. Available 9.00 am to 5.00 pm Monday to Friday (excluding Bank Holidays)

Open 9.30 am to 5.00 pm Monday to Friday

Access For reference (but at least 24 hours notice must be given for intended visits)
  Large stock of volumes on temperate agriculture.

Derby Central Library

Wardwick, Derby DE1 1HS
☎01332 255398 Fax 01332 369570
Website www.derby.gov.uk/libraries

Open 9.30 am to 7.00 pm Monday, Tuesday, Thursday, Friday; 9.30 am to 1.00 pm Wednesday and Saturday

LOCAL STUDIES LIBRARY
25B Irongate, Derby DE1 3GL
☎01332 255393 Fax 01332 255381

Open 9.30 am to 7.00 pm Monday and Tuesday; 9.30 am to 5.00 pm Wednesday, Thursday, Friday; 9.30 am to 1.00 pm Saturday

Open access
  General library for lending, information and Children's Services. The Central Library also houses specialist private libraries: Derbyshire Archaeological Society; Derby Philatelic Society. The Local Studies Library houses the largest multimedia collection of resources in existence relating to Derby and Derbyshire. The collection includes mss deeds, family papers, business records including the Derby Canal Company, Derby Board of Guardians and the Derby China Factory. Both libraries offer Internet access for a small charge.

Devon & Exeter Institution Library

7 Cathedral Close, Exeter, Devon EX1 1EZ
☎01392 251017
Email M.Midgley@exeter.ac.uk
Website www.devonandexeterinstitution.org.uk

Open 9.00 am to 5.00 pm Monday to Friday

Access Members only (Temporary membership available)
  FOUNDED 1813. Under the administration of Exeter University Library. Contains over 36,000 volumes, including long runs of 19th-century journals, theology, history, topography, early science, biography and literature. Large and growing collection of books, journals, newspapers, prints and maps relating to the South West.

Doncaster Libraries and Information Services

Central Library, Waterdale, Doncaster, South Yorkshire DN1 3JE
☎01302 734305 Fax 01302 369749
Email Reference.Library@doncaster.gov.uk

Open 9.30 am to 6.00 pm Monday; 9.00 am to 6.00 pm Tuesday to Friday; 9.00 am to 4.00 pm Saturday

Open access
  Books, cassettes, CDs, videos, picture loans. Reading aids unit for people with visual handicap; activities for children during school holidays, including visits by authors, etc. Occasional funding available to support literature activities. Also reference library.

Dorchester Library (part of Dorset County Library)

Colliton Park, Dorchester, Dorset DT1 1XJ
☎01305 224440 (lending)/224448 (reference)
Fax 01305 266120
Email Dorchesterreflibrary@dorset-cc.gov.uk

Open 10.00 am to 7.00 pm Monday; 9.30 am to 7.00 pm Tuesday, Wednesday, Friday; 9.30 am to 5.00 pm Thursday; 9.00 am to 4.00 pm Saturday

Open access
  General lending and reference library, including Local Studies Collection, special collections on Thomas Hardy, the Powys Family and William Barnes. Periodicals, children's library, CD-ROMs, free Internet access. Video lending service.

Dundee Central Library

The Wellgate, Dundee DD1 1DB
☎01382 434318 Fax 01382 434642

Email central.library@dundeecity.gov.uk
Website www.dundeecity.gov.uk

Open Lending & Local Studies Departments: 9.30 am to 6.00 pm Monday, Tuesday, Friday; 10.00 am to 6.00 pm Wednesday; 9.30 am to 8.00 pm Thursday; 9.30 am to 5.00 pm Saturday. General Reference Department: 9.30 am to 9.00 pm Monday, Tuesday, Thursday, Friday; 10.00 am to 9.00 pm Wednesday; 9.30 am to 5.00 pm Saturday.

Access Reference services available to all; lending services to those who live, work, study or were educated within Dundee City

Adult lending, reference and children's services. Art, music, audio, video and DVD lending services. Internet access. Schools service (Agency). Housebound and mobile services. *Special collections*: The Wighton Collection of National Music; The Wilson Photographic Collection; The Lamb Collection.

Durning-Lawrence Library
See **University of London Library**

English Nature
Northminster House, Peterborough, Cambridgeshire PE1 1UA
☎01733 455000 Fax 01733 568834
Email enquiries@english-nature.org.uk
Website www.english-nature.org.uk

Open 8.30 am to 5.00 pm Monday to Thursday; 8.30 am to 4.30 pm Friday

Access To *bona fide* students only. Telephone library for appointment on 01733 455094

Information on nature conservation, nature reserves, SSSIs, planning, legislation, etc. English Nature is the government-funded body whose purpose is to promote the conservation of England's wildlife and natural features.

Equal Opportunities Commission
Arndale House, Arndale Centre, Manchester M4 3EQ
☎0845 601 5901 Fax 0161 838 8303
Email info@eoc.org.uk
Website www.eoc.org.uk

The EOC is open to the public via the Helpline (0845 601 5901) 9am–5pm Mondays to Fridays. The Customer Contact Point is available to deal with/pass on calls or mail publications.

Essex County Council Libraries
County Library Headquarters, Goldlay Gardens, Chelmsford, Essex CM2 0EW
☎01245 284981 Fax 01245 492780

Email essexlib@essexcc.gov.uk
Website www.essexcc.gov.uk

Essex County Council Libraries has 74 static libraries throughout Essex as well as 13 mobile libraries and three special-needs mobiles. Services to the public include books, newspapers, periodicals, CDs, cassettes, videos, pictures, CD-ROMs and Internet access as well as postal cassettes for the blind and subtitled videos. Specialist subjects and collections are listed below at the relevant library.

Chelmsford Library
PO Box 882, Market Road, Chelmsford, Essex CM1 1LH
☎01245 492758 Fax 01245 492536

Open 9.00 am to 7.00 pm Monday, Tuesday, Thursday, Friday; 10.00 am to 7.00 pm Wednesday; 9.00 am to 5.00 pm Saturday; 1.00 pm to 4.00 pm Sunday

Science and technology, business information and social sciences.

Colchester Library Trinity Square, Colchester, Essex CO1 1JB T
☎01206 245900 Fax 01206 245901

Open 9.00 am to 7.30 pm Monday, Tuesday, Friday; 10.00 am to 7.30 pm Wednesday; 9.00 am to 5.00 pm Thursday and Saturday; 1.00 pm to 4.00 pm Sunday

Local studies, music scores and education. Harsnett collection (early theological works 16th/17th-century); Castle collection (18th-century subscription library); Cunnington collection; Margaret Lazell collection; Taylor collection.

Harlow Library
The High, Harlow, Essex CM20 1HA
☎ 01279 413772 Fax 01279 424612

Open 9.00 am to 7.00 pm Monday, Tuesday, Thursday, Friday; 10.00 am to 7.00 pm Wednesday; 9.00 am to 5.00 pm Saturday; 1.00 pm to 4.00 pm Sunday

Fiction, language and literature. Sir John Newson Memorial collection; Maurice Hughes Memorial collection.

Loughton Library
Traps Hill, Loughton, Essex IG10 1HD
☎020 8502 0181 Fax 020 8508 5041

Open 9.30 am to 7.00 pm Monday and Friday; 10.00 am to 7.00 pm Tuesday and Wednesday; 9.30 am to 1.30 pm Thursday; 9.00 am to 5.00 pm Saturday; 11.00 am to 5.00 pm Sunday

National Jazz Foundation Archive.

Saffron Walden Library
2 King Street, Saffron Walden, Essex CB10 1ES
☎01799 523178 Fax 01799 513642

Open 9.00 am to 7.00 pm Monday, Tuesday,
Thursday, Friday; 9.00 am to 5.00 pm
Saturday; 1.00 pm to 4.00 pm Sunday
(closed Wednesday)

Victorian studies collection.

Witham Library
18 Newland Street, Witham, Essex CM8 2AQ
☎01376 519625 Fax 01376 501913

Open 9.00 am to 7.00 pm Monday, Tuesday,
Thursday, Friday; 9.00 am to 5.00 pm
Saturday (closed Wednesday); 1.00 pm to
4.00 pm Sunday

Drama. Dorothy L. Sayers and Maskell collections.

The Fawcett Library
See **The Women's Library**

Foreign and Commonwealth Office Library
King Charles Street, London SW1A 2AH
☎020 7008 3925 Fax 020 7008 3270
Website www.fco.gov.uk

Access By appointment only
An extensive stock of books, pamphlets and
other reference material on all aspects of historical, socio-economic and political subjects relating to countries covered by the Foreign and
Commonwealth Office. Particularly strong on
colonial history, early works on travel, and photograph collections, mainly of Commonwealth
countries and former colonies, c. 1850s–1960s.

Forestry Commission Library
Forest Research Station, Alice Holt Lodge,
Wrecclesham, Farnham, Surrey GU10 4LH
☎01420 22255 Fax 01420 23653
Email library@forestry.gsi.gov.uk
Website www.forestry.gov.uk/forest_research

Open 9.00 am to 5.00 pm Monday to
Thursday; 9.00 am to 4.30 pm Friday

Access By appointment for personal visits
Approximately 20,000 books on forestry and
arboriculture, plus 500 current journals. CD-ROMS include TREECD (1939 onwards).
Offers a Research Advisory Service for advice
and enquiries on forestry (☎01402 23000)
with a charge for consultations and diagnosis of
tree problems exceeding ten minutes.

French Institute Library
Institut français, 17 Queensberry Place,
London SW7 2DT
☎020 7073 1350 Fax 020 7073 1363
Email library@ambafrance.org.uk
Website www.institut.ambafrance.org.uk

Open 12 noon to 7.00 pm Tuesday to Friday;
12 noon to 6.00 pm Saturday; Children's
Library: 12 noon to 6.00 pm Tuesday to
Saturday

Open access For reference and consultation
(loans restricted to members)
A collection of over 55,000 volumes mainly
centred on French cultural interests with special
emphasis on language, literature and history.
Books in French and English. Collection of
videos, periodicals, CDs (French music), CD-ROMs; special collections: 'France Libre',
microfilms and CD-ROMs of *Le Monde*
(1944–2002). Denis Saurat MSS, recordings of
lectures, press–cuttings on French current affairs.
Inter-library loans; quick information service;
Internet access to members. Group visits on
request. Children's library (8,000 documents).

John Frost Newspapers
22b Rosemary Avenue, Enfield, Middlesex
EN2 0SS
☎020 8366 1392/0946 Fax 020 8366 1379
Email andrew@johnfrostnewspapers.com
Website www.johnfrostnewspapers.co.uk

Contacts *Andrew Frost, John Frost*
A collection of 80,000 original newspapers (1630
to the present day) and 200,000 press cuttings
available, on loan, for research and rostrum/stills
work (TV documentaries, book and magazine
publishers and audiovisual presentations).
Historic events, politics, sports, royalty, crime,
wars, personalities, etc., plus many in-depth files.

Gloucestershire County Council Library and Information Services
Quayside House, Shire Hall, Gloucester
GL1 2HY
☎01452 425020 Fax 01452 425042
Email gclams@gloscc.gov.uk
Website www.gloscc.gov.uk

Head of Library Services and Information
David Paynter

Open access
The service includes 39 local libraries and six
mobile libraries. The website (GlosNet)
includes library opening hours, mobile library
route schedules; the library catalogue; and a
book renewal/reservations facility.

Goethe-Institut Library

50 Princes Gate, Exhibition Road, London SW7 2PH

☎020 7596 4040 Fax 020 7594 0230

Email Library@London.goethe.org

Website www.goethe.de/london

Librarian *Gerlinde Buck*

Open 12.00 am to 8.00 pm Monday to Thursday; 11.00 am to 5.00 pm Saturday

Library specialising in German literature and books/audiovisual material on German culture and history: 25,000 books (4800 of them in English), 140 periodicals, 14 newspapers, 2800 audiovisual media (including 1000 videos), selected press clippings on German affairs from the German and UK press, information service, photocopier, video facility. Also German language teaching material for teachers and students of German.

Goldsmiths' Library

See **University of London Library**

Greater London Record Office

See **London Metropolitan Archives**

Guildford Institute of the University of Surrey Library

Ward Street, Guildford, Surrey GU1 4LH

☎01483 562142

Email c.miles@surrey.ac.uk

Librarian *Clare Miles*

Open 10.00 am to 3.00 pm Tuesday to Friday

Open access To members only but open to enquirers for research purposes

FOUNDED 1834. Some 12,000 volumes of which 7500 were printed before the First World War. The remaining stock consists of recently published works of fiction and non-fiction. Newspapers and periodicals also available. *Special collections* include an almost complete run of the *Illustrated London News* from 1843–1906, a collection of Victorian and early 20th century scrapbooks, and about 400 photos and other pictures relating to the Institute's history and the town of Guildford. Publishes Library newsletter twice-yearly.

Guildhall Library

Aldermanbury, London EC2P 2EJ

☎See below Fax 020 7600 3384

Website www.cityoflondon.gov.uk

Access For reference (but much of the material is kept in storage areas and is supplied to readers on request; proof of identity is required for consultation of certain categories of stock)

Part of the Corporation of London libraries. Seeks to provide a basic general reference service but its major strength, acknowledged worldwide, is in its historical collections. The library is divided into three sections, each with its own catalogues and enquiry desks. These are: Printed Books; Manuscripts; the Print & Maps Room.

PRINTED BOOKS

☎020 7332 1868/1870

Open 9.30 am to 5 pm Monday to Saturday; NB closes on Saturdays preceding Bank Holidays; check for details

Strong on all aspects of London history, with wide holdings of English history, topography and genealogy, including local directories, poll books and parish register transcripts. Also good collections of English statutes, law reports, parliamentary debates and journals, and House of Commons papers. Home of several important collections deposited by London institutions: the Marine collection of the Corporation of Lloyd's, the Stock Exchange's historical files of reports and prospectuses, the Clockmakers' Company library and museum, the Gardeners' Company, Fletchers' Company, the Institute of Masters of Wine, International Wine and Food Society and Gresham College.

MANUSCRIPTS

☎020 7332 1862/3

Email manuscripts.guildhall@corpoflondon.gov.uk

Website ihr.sas.ac.uk/gh/

Open 9.30 am to 4.45 pm Monday to Saturday (no requests for records after 4.30 pm; no manuscripts can be produced between 12 noon and 2 pm on Saturdays); NB closes Saturdays preceding Bank Holidays; check for details

The official repository for historical records relating to the City of London (except those of the Corporation of London itself, which are housed at the Corporation Records Office). Records date from the 11th century to the present day. They include archives of most of the City's parishes, wards and livery companies, and of many individuals, families, estates, schools, societies and other institutions, notably the Diocese of London and St Paul's Cathedral, as well as the largest collection of business archives in any public repository in the UK. Although mainly of City interest, holdings include material for the London area as a whole and beyond.

PRINT & MAPS ROOM
☎020 7332 1839
Email print&maps@corpoflondon.gov.uk
Website http://collage-cityoflondon.gov.uk

Open 9.30 am to 5.00 pm Monday to Friday

An unrivalled collection of prints and drawings relating to London and the adjacent counties. The emphasis is on topography, but there are strong collections of portraits and satirical prints. The map collection includes maps of the capital from the mid-16th century to the present day and various classes of Ordnance Survey maps. Other material includes photographs, theatre bills and programmes, trade cards, book plates and playing cards as well as a sizeable collection of Old Master prints. Over 30,000 items have been digitally imaged on Collage, including topographical prints, some maps, a small number of photographs and all the Guildhall Art Gallery collection.

Free, *limited* enquiry service available. Also a fee-based service for in-depth research: ☎020 7332 1854 Fax 020 7600 3384 E-mail search. guildhall@corpoflondon.gov.uk Website www. cityoflondon.gov.uk/search_guildhall

Guille–Alles Library

Market Street, St Peter Port, Guernsey, Channel Islands GY1 1HB
☎01481 720392 Fax 01481 712425
Email ga@library.gg
Website www.library.gg

Open 9.00 am to 5.00 pm Monday, Thursday, Friday, Saturday; 10.00 am to 5.00 pm Tuesday; 9.00 am to 8.00 pm Wednesday

Open access For residents; payment of returnable deposit by visitors. Music CD collection: £10 for two-year subscription

Lending, reference and information services. Public Internet service.

Herefordshire Libraries and Information Service

Shirehall, Hereford HR1 2HY
☎01432 359830 Fax 01432 260744
Website www.libraries.herefordshire.gov.uk

Open Opening hours vary in the libraries across the county

Access Information and reference services open to anyone; loans to members only (membership criteria: resident, being educated, working, or an elector in the county or neighbouring authorities; temporary membership to visitors. Proof of identity and address required)

Information service, reference and lending libraries. Non-fiction and fiction for all age groups, including normal and large print, spoken word cassettes, sound recordings (CD and cassette), videos, maps, local history, CD-ROMs for reference at Hereford and Leominster Libraries. Internet access at all libraries. *Special collections* Cidermaking; Beekeeping; Alfred Watkins; John Masefield; Pilley.

University of Hertfordshire Library

College Lane, Hatfield, Hertfordshire AL10 9AB
☎01707 284678 Fax 01707 284666
Website www.herts.ac.uk/lis

Open See website for term-time and vacation opening hours

Access For reference use of printed collections. Appropriate ID required for Visitor's pass.

For further information please refer to our website.

Highgate Literary and Scientific Institution Library

11 South Grove, London N6 6BS
☎020 8340 3343 Fax 020 8340 5632
Email admin@hlsi.net

Open 10.00 am to 5.00 pm Tuesday to Friday; 10.00 am to 4.00 pm Saturday (closed Sunday and Monday)

Annual membership £50 (individual); £80 (household)

25,000 volumes of general fiction and non-fiction, with a children's section and extensive local archives. *Special collections* on local history, London, and local poets Samuel Taylor Coleridge and John Betjeman.

Highland Libraries, The Highland Council, Education, Culture and Sport Service

Library Support Unit, 31a Harbour Road, Inverness IV1 1UA
☎01463 235713 Fax 01463 236986
Email libraries@highland.gov.uk
Website www.highland.gov.uk

Open Library opening hours vary to suit local needs. Contact administration and support services for details (8.00 am to 6.00 pm Monday to Friday)

Open access

Comprehensive range of lending and reference stock: books, pamphlets, periodicals, newspapers, compact discs, audio and video cassettes, maps, census records, genealogical records, photographs, educational materials, etc. Highland Libraries provides the public library service throughout the Highlands with a network of 43 static and 12 mobile libraries.

Holborn Library
32–38 Theobalds Road, London
WC1X 8PA
☎020 7974 6345/6

Open 10.00 am to 7.00 pm Monday and Thursday; 10.00 am to 6.00 pm Tuesday and Friday; 10.00 am to 5.00 pm Saturday (closed all day Wednesday)

Open access
London Borough of Camden public library. Includes a law collection and the London Borough of Camden Local Studies and Archive Centre.

Sherlock Holmes Collection (Westminster)
Marylebone Library, Marylebone Road, London NW1 5PS
☎020 7641 1206 Fax 020 7641 1019
Email ccooke@westminster.gov.uk
Website www.westminster.gov.uk/libraries/special/sherlock.cfm

Open 9.30 am to 8.00 pm Monday, Tuesday, Thursday, Friday; 10.00 am to 8.00 pm Wednesday; Closed Saturday and Sunday (unless by prior arrangement)

Access By appointment only
Located in Westminster's Marylebone Library. An extensive collection of material from all over the world, covering Sherlock Holmes and Sir Arthur Conan Doyle. Books, pamphlets, journals, newspaper cuttings and photos, much of which is otherwise unavailable in this country. Some background material.

Imperial College Central Library
See **Science Museum Library**

Imperial War Museum
Department of Printed Books, Lambeth Road, London SE1 6HZ
☎020 7416 5342 Fax 020 7416 5246
Email books@iwm.org.uk
Website www.iwm.org.uk

Open 10.00 am to 5.00 pm Monday to Saturday (restricted service Saturday; closed on Bank Holiday Saturdays and two weeks during the year for annual stock check)

Access For reference (but at least 24 hours' notice must be given for intended visits)
A large collection of material on British and Commonwealth 20th-century life with detailed coverage of the two world wars and other conflicts. Books, pamphlets and periodicals, including many produced for short periods in unlikely wartime settings; also maps, biographies and privately printed memoirs, and foreign language material. Additional research material available in the following departments: Art, Documents, Exhibits and Firearms, Film, Sound Records, Photographs. Active publishing programme based on reprints of rare books held in library. Catalogue available.

Instituto Cervantes
102 Eaton Square, London SW1W 9AN
☎020 7201 0757 Fax 020 7235 0329
Email biblon@cervantes.es
Website www.cervantes.es

Open 12 noon to 6.30 pm Monday to Thursday; 9.30 am to 1.30 pm Saturday (closed Friday)

Open access For reference and lending
Spanish literature, history, art, philosophy. The library houses a collection of books, periodicals, videos, slides, tapes, CDs, cassettes, films and CD-ROMs specialising entirely in Spain and Latin America.

Italian Institute Library
39 Belgrave Square, London SW1X 8NX
☎020 7396 4425 Fax 020 7235 4618
Website www.italcultur.org.uk

Open 10.00 am to 1.00 pm and 2.00 pm to 5.00 pm Monday to Friday

Open access For reference
A collection of over 21,000 volumes relating to all aspects of Italian culture. Texts are mostly in Italian, with some in English.

Jersey Library
Halkett Place, St Helier, Jersey JE2 4WH
☎01534 759991 (lending)/759992 (reference)
Fax 01534 769444
Email library@jsylib.gov.je
Website www.jsylib.gov.je

Open 9.30 am to 5.30 pm Monday, Wednesday, Thursday, Friday; 9.30 am to 7.30 pm Tuesday; 9.30 am to 4.00 pm Saturday

Open access
Books, periodicals, newspapers, CDs, cassettes, CD-ROMs, videos, microfilm, spe-

cialised local studies collection, public Internet access. Branch Library at Les Quennevais School, St Brelade. Mobile library and homes services. Open Learning Centre.

Kent County Central Library
Kent County Council Arts & Libraries, Springfield, Maidstone, Kent ME14 2LH
☎01622 696511 Fax 01622 696494
Website www.kent.gov.uk/edl/artslib
Open 9.30 am to 5.30 pm Monday, Wednesday, Friday; 9.30 am to 6.00 pm Tuesday; 9.30 am to 7.00 pm Thursday; 10.00 am to 5.00 pm Saturday

Open access
50,000 volumes available on the floor of the library plus 250,000 volumes of non-fiction, mostly academic, available on request to staff. English literature, poetry, classical literature, drama (including play sets), music (including music sets). Strong, too, in sociology, art history, business information and government publications. Loans to all who live or work in Kent; those who do not may consult stock for reference or arrange loans via their own local library service.

Leeds Central Library
Calverley Street, Leeds, West Yorkshire LS1 3AB
☎0113 247 8911 Fax 0113 247 8426
Website www.leeds.gov.uk/libraries
Open 9.00 am to 8.00 pm Monday, Tuesday, Wednesday; 9.30 am to 5.30 pm Thursday; 9.00 pm to 5.00 pm Saturday; 12.00 am to 4.00 pm Saturday

Open access to lending libraries; reference material on request
   Lending Library covering all subjects. Telephone number as above.
   Music Library contains scores, books, video and audio. ☎0113 247 8273
   Business & Research Library Company information, market research, statistics, directories, journals and computer-based information. Extensive files of newspapers and periodicals plus all government publications since 1960. *Special collections* include military history, Judaic, early gardening books and mountaineering.☎0113 247 8426/8282 Email information.for.business @leeds.gov.uk *and* research.and.studies@leeds.gov.uk
   Art Library Major collection of material on fine and applied arts. ☎0113 247 8247
   Local Studies Library Extensive collection

on Leeds and Yorkshire, including maps, books, pamphlets, local newspapers, illustrations and playbills. Census returns for the whole of Yorkshire also available. International Genealogical Index and parish registers. Free public Internet access. ☎0113 247 8290 Email local.studies@leeds.gov.uk

Leeds City Libraries has an extensive network of 65 branch and mobile libraries.

Leeds Library
18 Commercial Street, Leeds, West Yorkshire LS1 6AL
☎0113 245 3071 Fax 0113 243 8218
Open 9.00 am to 5.00 pm Monday to Friday

Access To members; research use upon application to the librarian
   FOUNDED 1768. Contains over 125,000 books and periodicals from the 15th century to the present day. *Special collections* Reformation pamphlets, Civil War tracts, Victorian and Edwardian children's books and fiction, European language material, spiritualism and psychical research, plus local material.

Lincoln Central Library
Free School Lane, Lincoln LN2 1EZ
☎01522 510800 Fax 01522 535882
Email lincoln.library@lincolnshire.gov.uk
Website www.lincolnshire.info
Open 9.30 am to 7.00 pm Monday to Friday; 9.30 am to 4.00 pm Saturday

Open access to the library; appointment required for the Tennyson Research Centre
   Lending and reference library. Special collections include Lincolnshire local history (printed and published material, photographs, maps, directories and census data) and the Tennyson Research Centre (contact *Susan Gates*).

Linen Hall Library
17 Donegall Square North, Belfast BT1 5GB
☎028 9032 1707 Fax 028 9043 8586
Email info@linenhall.com
Website www.linenhall.com
Librarian *John Gray*
Open 9.30 am to 5.30 pm Monday to Friday; 9.30 am to 4.00 pm Saturday

Open access For reference (loans restricted to members)
   FOUNDED 1788.Contains about 200,000 books. Major Irish and local studies collections, including the Northern Ireland Political Collection relating to the current troubles (c. 250,000 items).

Literary & Philosophical Society of Newcastle upon Tyne

23 Westgate Road, Newcastle upon Tyne
NE1 1SE
☎0191 232 0192 Fax 0191 261 4494
Email library@litandphil.org.uk
Website www.litandphil.org.uk

Librarian *Kay Easson*

Open 9.30 am to 7.00 pm Monday,
Wednesday, Thursday, Friday; 9.30 am to 8.00
pm Tuesday; 9.30 am to 1.00 pm Saturday

Access Members; research facilities for *bona fide* scholars on application to the Librarian
200-year-old library of 140,000 volumes, periodicals (including 130 current titles), classical music on vinyl recordings and CD, plus a collection of scores. A programme of lectures and recitals provided. Recent publications include: *The Reverend William Turner: Dissent and Reform in Georgian Newcastle upon Tyne* Stephen Harbottle; *History of the Literary and Philosophical Society of Newcastle upon Tyne, Vol. 2 (1896–1989)* Charles Parish; *Bicentenary Lectures 1993* ed. John Philipson.

Liverpool City Libraries

William Brown Street, Liverpool L3 8EW
☎0151 233 5829 Fax 0151 233 5886
Email refbt.central.library@liverpool.gov.uk
Website www.liverpool.gov.uk

Open 9.00 am to 8.00 pm Monday to
Thursday; 9.00 am to 7.00 pm Friday; 9.00
am to 5.00 pm Saturday; 12 noon to 4.00
pm Sunday

Open access

Humanities Reference Library A total stock in excess of 120,000 volumes and 24,000 maps, plus book plates, prints and autographed letters. *Special collections* Walter Crane and Edward Lear illustrations, Kelmscott Press, Audubon.

Business and Technology Reference Library Extensive stock dealing with all aspects of science, commerce and technology, including British and European standards and patents and trade directories.

Audio Visual Library Extensive stock relating to all aspects of music. Includes 128,000 volumes and music scores, over 3000 CDs, 2000 videos and 600 DVDs.

Record Office and Local History Department Material relating to Liverpool, Merseyside, Lancashire and Cheshire, together with archive material mainly on Liverpool. Proof of name and address required to obtain reader's ticket.

University of London Library

Senate House, Malet Street, London
WC1E 7HU
☎020 7862 8461/62 (Information Centre)
Fax 020 7862 8480
Email enquiries@ull.ac.uk (Information Centre)
Website www.ull.ac.uk

Membership Desk: ☎020 7862 8439/40
Email userservices@ull.ac.uk

Open Term-time: 9.00 am to 9.00 pm
Monday to Thursday; 9.00 am to 6.30 pm
Friday; 9.30 am to 5.30 pm Saturday.
Vacation: 9.00 am to 6.00 pm Monday to
Friday; 9.30 am to 5.30 pm Saturday. The
Library is closed on Sundays and at certain
periods during Bank Holidays

The University of London Library is a major academic research library predominantly based across the Humanities and Social Sciences. Housed within its 16 floors in Senate House are some two million titles including 5500 current periodicals and a wide range of electronic resources. It contains a number of outstanding research collections which, as well as supporting the scholarly activities of the University, attract researchers from throughout the United Kingdom and internationally. These include: English (e.g. the Durning-Lawrence Library and Sterling Collection of first editions); Economic and Social History (the Goldsmiths' Library, containing 70,000 items ranging from 15th to early 19th century); Modern Languages (primarily Romance and Germanic); Palaeography (acclaimed as being the best open access collection in its field in Europe); History (complementary to the Institute of Historical Research); Music; Philosophy (acts as the Library of the Royal Institute of Philosophy); Psychology (includes the BPS library); Major area studies collections (Latin-American – including Caribbean; United States and Commonwealth Studies, British Government Publications and maps). The Library has a wide range of Special Collections holdings. Check the website for full details of collections and current access arrangements.

The London Institute – London College of Printing: Library and Learning Resources

Elephant and Castle, London SE1 6SB
☎020 7514 6527 (Elephant)/6882 (Back Hill)
Fax 020 7514 6597
Website www.linst.ac.uk/library

Access By arrangement

Library and Learning Resources provides books, periodicals, slides, CD-ROMs, videos and computer software on all aspects of the art of the book, printing, management, film/photography, graphic arts, plus retailing. *Special collections* history and development of published and unpublished scripts and the art of the western book.

The London Library

14 St James's Square, London SW1Y 4LG
☎020 7930 7705   Fax 020 7766 4766
Email membership@londonlibrary.co.uk
Website www.londonlibrary.co.uk

Librarian *Miss Inez Lynn*

Open 9.30 am to 5.30 pm Monday, Friday, Saturday; 9.30 am to 7.30 pm Tuesday, Wednesday, Thursday

Access For members only (£170 p.a., 2003)

With over a million books and 8400 members, The London Library 'is the most distinguished private library in the world; probably the largest, certainly the best loved'. Founded in 1841, it is a registered charity and wholly independent of public funding. Its permanent collection embraces most European languages as well as English. Its subject range is predominantly within the humanities, with emphasis on literature, history, fine and applied art, architecture, bibliography, philosophy, religion, and topography and travel. Some 6000–7000 titles are added yearly. Most of the stock is on open shelves to which members have free access. Members may take out up to 10 volumes; 15 if they live more than 20 miles from the Library. The comfortable Reading Room has an annexe for users of personal computers. There are photocopiers, CD-ROM workstations, free access to the Internet, and the Library also offers a postal loans service.

Prospective members are required to submit a refereed application form in advance of admission, but there is at present no waiting list for membership. The London Library Trust may make grants to those who are unable to afford the full annual fee; details on application.

London Metropolitan Archives

40 Northampton Road, London EC1R 0HB
☎020 7332 3820   Fax 020 7833 9136
Email ask.lma@corpoflondon.gov.uk
Website www.cityoflondon.gov.uk
Minicom 020 7278 8703

Open 9.30 am to 4.45 pm Monday, Wednesday, Friday; 9.30 pm to 7.30 pm Tuesday and Thursday; call the Archives for details of Saturday opening hours

Access For reference only

Formerly, the Greater London Record Office Library. Covers all aspects of the life and development of London, specialising in the history and organisation of local government in general, and London in particular. Books on London history and topography, covering many subjects. Also London directories dating back to 1677, plus other source material including Acts of Parliament, Hansard reports, statistical returns, atlases, yearbooks and periodicals.

Lord Louis Library

Orchard Street, Newport, Isle of Wight PO30 1LL
☎01983 527655/823800 (Reference Library)
Fax 01983 825972
Email reflib@llouis.demon.co.uk

Open 9.00 am to 5.30 pm Monday to Wednesday and Friday; 9.00 am to 8.00 pm Thursday; 9.00 am to 5.00 pm Saturday; 10.00 am to 4.00 pm Sunday

Open access

General adult and junior fiction and non-fiction collections; local history collection and periodicals. Also the county's main reference library.

Manchester Central Library

St Peters Square, Manchester M2 5PD
☎0161 234 1900   Fax 0161 234 1963
Email mclib@libraries.manchester.gov.uk
Website www.manchester.gov.uk/libraries

Open 10.00 am to 8.00 pm Monday to Thursday; 10.00 am to 5.00 pm Friday and Saturday; Commercial and European Units: 10.00 am to 6.00 pm Monday to Thursday; 10.00 am to 5.00 pm Friday and Saturday

Open access

One of the country's leading reference libraries with extensive collections covering all subjects. Departments include: Commercial, European, Technical, Social Sciences, Arts, Music, Local Studies, Chinese, General Readers, Language & Literature. Large lending stock and VIP (visually impaired) service available.

Marylebone Library (Westminster)

See **Sherlock Holmes Collection**

The Mitchell Library

North Street, Glasgow G3 7DN
☎0141 287 2999   Fax 0141 287 2915
Website www.glasgowlibraries.org

Open 9.00 am to 8.00 pm Monday to Thursday; 9.00 am to 5.00 pm Friday and Saturday

Open access
One of Europe's largest public reference libraries with stock of over 1,200,000 volumes. It subscribes to 48 newspapers and more than 2000 periodicals. There are collections in microform, records, tapes and videos, as well as CD-ROMs, electronic databases, illustrations, photographs, postcards, etc.

The library contains a number of special collections, e.g. the Robert Burns Collection (5000 vols), the Scottish Poetry Collection (12,000 items) and the Scottish Drama Collection (1650 items).

Morrab Library
Morrab House, Morrab Gardens, Penzance, Cornwall TR18 4DA
☎01736 364474

Librarian *Annabelle Read*
Open 10.00 am to 4.00 pm Tuesday to Friday; 10.00 am to 1.00 pm Saturday

Access Non-members may use the library for a small daily fee, but may not borrow books

Formerly known as the Penzance Library. An independent subscription lending library of over 40,000 volumes covering virtually all subjects except modern science and technology, with large collections on history, literature and religion. There is a comprehensive Cornish collection of books, newspapers and manuscripts including the Borlase letters; a West Cornwall photographic archive; many runs of 18th- and 19th-century periodicals; a collection of over 2000 books published before 1800.

The National Archives
Kew, Richmond, Surrey TW9 4DU
☎020 8876 3444
Fax 020 8878 8905
Email enquiry@pro.gov.uk
Website www.pro.gov.uk
The Family Record Centre, 1 Myddleton Street, London EC1R 1UW

Open 9.00 am to 5.00 pm Monday, Wednesday, Friday; 10.00 am to 7.00 pm Tuesday; 9.00 am to 7.00 pm Thursday; 9.30 am to 5.00 pm Saturday

Access for reference, by reader's ticket, available free of charge on production of proof of identity (UK citizens: banker's card or driving licence; non-UK: passport or national identity card. Telephone for further information)

Over 168 kilometres of shelving house the national repository of records of central government in the UK and law courts of England and Wales, which extend in time from the 11th–20th century. Medieval records and the records of the State Paper Office from the early 16th–late 18th century, plus the records of the Privy Council Office and the Lord Chamberlain's and Lord Steward's departments. Modern government department records, together with those of the Copyright Office dating mostly from the late 18th century. Under the Public Records Act, records are normally only open to inspection when they are 30 years old.

National Library of Scotland
George IV Bridge, Edinburgh EH1 1EW
☎0131 226 4531 Fax 0131 622 4803
Email enquiries@nls.uk
Website www.nls.uk

Open Main Reading Room: 9.30 am to 8.30 pm Monday, Tuesday, Thursday, Friday; 10.00 am to 8.30 pm Wednesday; 9.30 am to 1.00 pm Saturday. Map Library: 9.30 am to 5.00 pm Monday, Tuesday, Thursday, Friday; 10.00 am to 5.00 pm Wednesday; 9.30 am to 1.00 pm Saturday.

Access To all reading rooms, for research not easily done elsewhere, by reader's ticket

Collection of over seven million volumes. The library receives all British and Irish publications. Large stock of newspapers and periodicals. Many special collections, including early Scottish books, theology, polar studies, baking, phrenology and liturgies. Also large collections of maps, music and manuscripts including personal archives of notable Scottish persons.

National Library of Wales
Aberystwyth, Ceredigion SY23 3BU
☎01970 632800 Fax 01970 615709
Website www.llgc.org.uk

Open 9.30 am to 6.00 pm Monday to Friday; 9.30 am to 5.00 pm Saturday (closed Bank Holidays and first week of October)

Access To reading rooms by reader's ticket, available on application. Open acess to regular exhibition programme and to permanent exhibition 'The Treasures of the Nation'

Collection of over four million books and including large collections of periodicals, maps, manuscripts and audiovisual material. Particular emphasis on humanities in printed foreign material, and on Wales and other Celtic areas in all collections.

National Meteorological Library and Archive

London Road, Bracknell, Berkshire RG12 2SZ
☎01344 854841 Fax 01344 854840
Email metlib@metoffice.com
Website www.metoffice.com

Open Library & Archive: 8.30 am to 4.30 pm Monday to Friday; Archive closed between 1.00 pm and 2.00 pm

Access By Visitor's Pass available from the reception desk; advance notice of a planned visit is appreciated

The major repository of most of the important literature on the subjects of meteorology, climatology and related sciences from the 16th century to the present day. The Library houses a collection of books, journals, articles and scientific papers, plus published climatological data from many parts of the world. The Technical Archive (The Scott Building, Sterling Centre, Eastern Road, Bracknell, Berks RG12 2PW, ☎01344 855960; Fax 01344 855961) holds the document collection of meteorological data and charts from England, Wales and British overseas bases, including ships' weather logs. Records from Scotland are stored in Edinburgh and those from Northern Ireland in Belfast.

The Natural History Museum Library

Cromwell Road, London SW7 5BD
☎020 7942 5460 Fax 020 7942 5559
Email library@nhm.ac.uk
Website www.nhm.ac.uk/library/index.html

Open 10.00 am to 4.30 pm Monday to Friday

Access To *bona fide* researchers, by reader's ticket on presentation of identification (telephone first to make an appointment)

The library is in five sections: general; botany; zoology; entomology; earth sciences. The sub-department of ornithology is housed at the Zoological Museum, Akeman Street, Tring, Herts HP23 6AP (☎01442 834181). Resources available include books, journals, maps, manuscripts, drawings and photographs covering all aspects of natural history, including palaeontology and mineralogy, from the 14th century to the present day. Also archives and historical collection on the museum itself.

Newcastle upon Tyne City Library

Princess Square, Newcastle upon Tyne
NE99 1DX
☎0191 277 4100 Fax 0191 277 4168
Email city.information@newcastle.gov.uk *or*

city.reference.library@newcastle.gov.uk *or*
information@newcastle.gov.uk

Open 9.30 am to 8.00 pm Monday and Thursday; 9.30 am to 5.00 pm Tuesday, Wednesday, Friday; 9.00 am to 5.00 pm Saturday

Open access

Extensive local studies collection, including newspapers, illustrations and genealogy. Also business, science, humanities and arts.

Nielsen BookData Ltd

Globe House, 1 Chertsey Road,
Twickenham, Middlesex TW1 1LR
☎020 8843 8620 Fax 020 8843 8744
Email sales@bookdata.co.uk
Website www.bookdata.co.uk *and*
  www.ehaus.co.uk

Contact *Sales Department*

The leading supplier of high-quality, content-rich book information and other published media to the book industry. Nielsen BookData takes information from publishers and creates a unique title record which includes bibliographic details, text summaries, tables of contents, extensive subject-related information, market-rights details, jacket images and reviews. This bibliographic information is then available through a variety of services worldwide. Data can be supplied as a direct feed, as a range of CD-ROMs, DVDs or online: BookFind-Online, Whitaker-Web, LibWeb, PubWeb and print versions. The company also offers routing services through TeleOrdering and EDI services through *first* Edition. e-haus creates websites for the industry and can provide a complete service – for web design, hosting and maintenance.

Norfolk Library & Information Service

Norfolk and Norwich Millennium Library,
The Forum, Millennium Plain, Norwich,
Norfolk NR2 1AW
Website www.norfolk.gov.uk/council/
  departments/lis/libhome.htm

Open Lending Library, Reference and Information Service and Norfolk Studies: 9.00 am to 8.00 pm Monday to Friday; 9.00 am to 5.00 pm Saturday. EXPRESS: 9.00 am to 10.30 pm Monday to Friday; 9.00 am to 8.30 pm Saturday; 10.30 am to 4.30 pm Sunday.

Open access

Reference lending library (stock merged together) with wide range, including books, recorded music, music scores, plays and videos. Houses the 2nd Air Division Memorial Library and has a strong Norfolk Heritage Library. Extensive range of reference stock including business information. Online database and CD-ROM services. Public fax and colour photocopying, free access to the Internet. EXPRESS (fiction, sound & vision library within a library) – selection of popular fiction, videos, CDs and DVDs available, with extended opening hours.

Northamptonshire Libraries & Information Service

Library HQ, PO Box 216, John Dryden House, 8–10 The Lakes, Northampton
NN4 7DD
☎01604 237959 Fax 01604 237937
Email nrowland@northamptonshire.gov.uk

Since 1991, the Libraries and Information Service has offered its 'Words Work' diary of literature events. The programme now attracts exciting literary names as well as new and locally-based writers. There are three diaries each year for an adult audience. Poets have an opportunity to read at a variety of venues. Literature workshops, activities and other events are supported. Regular book displays and dedicated notice boards in libraries support the programme across the county.

Northumberland Central Library

The Willows, Morpeth, Northumberland
NE61 1TA
☎01670 534518/534514 Fax 01670 534513
Email referencelibrary@northumberland.gov.uk
Website www.northumberland.gov.uk

Open 10.00 am to 8.00 pm Monday,
Tuesday, Wednesday, Friday; 9.30 am to
12.30 pm Saturday (closed Thursday)

Open access
Books, periodicals, newspapers, story cassettes, DVDs, CDs, videos, Free Internet access, word processing facilities, prints, microforms, vocal scores, playsets, community resource equipment. *Special collections* **Northern Poetry Library**: 15,000 volumes of modern poetry (see entry under **Organisations of Interest to Poets**); Cinema: comprehensive collection of about 5000 volumes covering all aspects of the cinema; Family History.

Nottingham Central Library

Angel Row, Nottingham NG1 6HP
☎0115 915 2828 Fax 0115 915 2850
Email arts.library@nottinghamcity.gov.co.uk
Website www.nottinghamcity.gov.uk

Open 9.30 am to 7.00 pm Monday to Friday;
9.00 am to 1.00 pm Saturday

Open access
General public lending library: business information, online information, the arts, local studies, religion, community languages, literature. Videos, periodicals, spoken word, recorded music, CD-ROM service – textual information on CD-ROM on public access machines. People's Network Internet, providing free public access. *Special collection* on D.H. Lawrence. Extensive back-up reserve stocks. Drama and music sets for loan to groups. Art gallery – contemporary exhibitions; coffee shop.

Nottingham Subscription Library Ltd

See **Bromley House Library**

Office for National Statistics, National Statistics Information and Library Service

1 Drummond Gate, London SW1V 2QQ
☎0845 601 3034/Minicom: 01633 812399
Fax 01633 652747
Email info@statistics.gov.uk
Website www.statistics.gov.uk

Open 9.00 am to 5.00 pm; no appointment
required

Also: National Statistics Information and Library Service, Government Buildings, Cardiff Road, Newport NP9 1XG

Open as above
Wide range of government statistical publications and access to government Internet-based data. Census statistical data from 1801; population and health data from 1837; government social survey reports from 1941; recent international statistical data (UN, Eurostat, etc.); monograph and periodical collections of statistical methodology. The library in south Wales holds a wide range of government economic and statistical publications.

Orkney Library

Laing Street, Kirkwall, Orkney KW15 1NW
☎01856 873166 Fax 01856 875260
Email orkney.library@orkney.gov.uk
Website www.orkneylibrary.org.uk

Open 9.00 am to 7.00 pm Monday,
Wednesday, Thursday; 9.00 am to 5.00 pm
Tuesday, Friday, Saturday. Archives: 9.00
am to 1.00 pm and 2.00 pm to 4.45 pm
Tuesday to Friday

Open access
Local studies collection. Archive includes sound and photographic departments.

Oxford Central Library

Westgate, Oxford OX1 1DJ
☎01865 815549 Fax 01865 721694
Email centlib.occdla@dial.pipex.com
Website www.oxfordshire.gov.uk
Open Call 01865 815509 for details

General lending and reference library including the Centre for Oxfordshire Studies. Also periodicals, audio visual materials, music library, children's library and Business Information Point.

PA News Centre

Central Park, New Lane, Leeds, West Yorkshire LS11 5DZ
☎0870 830 6824 Fax 0870 830 6801
Email palibrary@pa.press.net
Website www.pa.press.net
Open 8.00 am to 8.00 pm Monday to Friday;
    10.00 am to 6.00 pm Saturday and Sunday

Open access
    PA News, the 24-hour national news and information group, offers public access to its press cuttings archive. Covering a wide range of subjects, the library includes over 14 million cuttings dating back to 1928. Personal callers welcome or research undertaken by in-house staff.

Penzance Library

See **Morrab Library**

City of Plymouth Library and Information Services

Central Library, Drake Circus, Plymouth, Devon PL4 8AL
Website www.plymouthlibraries.info *or*
www.plymouth.gov.uk/star/library.htm
Open access
CENTRAL LIBRARY LENDING DEPARTMENTS:
Lending ☎01752 305912
Children's Department ☎01752 305916
Email childrens.library@plymouth.gov.uk
Music & Drama Department ☎01752 305914 Email music@plymouth.gov.uk
Open 9.30 am to 7.00 pm Monday and Friday; 9.30 am to 5.30 pm Tuesday, Wednesday, Thursday; 9.30 am to 4.00 pm Saturday

The Lending departments offer books on all subjects; language courses on cassette and foreign language books; the Holcenberg Jewish Collection; books on music and musicians, drama and theatre; music parts and sets of music parts; play sets; DVDs, videos; song index; cassettes and CDs; public Internet access.

CENTRAL LIBRARY REFERENCE DEPARTMENTS:
Reference ☎01752 305907/8
Email ref@plymouth.gov.uk
Business Information ☎01752 305906
Email keyinfo@plymouth.gov.uk
Local Studies & Naval History Department
☎01752 305909
Email localstudies@plymouth.gov.uk
Open 9.00 am to 7.00 pm Monday to Friday;
    9.00 am to 4.00 pm Saturday

The Reference departments include an extensive collection of Ordnance Survey maps and town guides; community and census information; marketing and statistical information; Patents; books on every aspect of Plymouth; naval history; Mormon Index on microfilm; Baring Gould manuscript of 'Folk Songs of the West'; public Internet access.

Plymouth Proprietary Library

Alton Terrace, 111 North Hill, Plymouth, Devon PL4 8JY
☎01752 660515
Librarian *John R. Smith*
Open Monday to Saturday from 9.30 am
    (closing time varies)
Access To members; visitors by appointment only
    FOUNDED 1810. The library contains approximately 17,000 volumes of mainly 20th-century work. Member of the **Association of Independent Libraries**.

The Poetry Library

See entry under **Organisations of Interest to Poets**

Polish Library

238–246 King Street, London W6 0RF
☎020 8741 0474 Fax 020 8741 7724
Email bibliotekapolska@posklibrary.fsnet.co.uk
Librarian *Mrs Jadwiga Szmidt*
Open 10.00 am to 8.00 pm Monday and Wednesday; 10.00 am to 5.00 pm Friday; 10.00 am to 1.00 pm Saturday (library closed Tuesday and Thursday)
Access For reference to all interested in Polish affairs; limited loans to members and *bona fide* scholars only through inter-library loans
    Books, pamphlets, periodicals, maps, music, photographs on all aspects of Polish history and culture. *Special collections* Emigré publications; Joseph Conrad and related works; Polish underground publications; bookplates.

Poole Central Library

Dolphin Centre, Poole, Dorset BH15 1QE
☎01202 262424 Fax 01202 262442
Email poolelibrary@poole.gov.uk

Open 8.00 am to 7.00 pm Monday; 8.30 am
to 6.30 pm Tuesday, Wednesday, Thursday;
8.00 am to 7.00 pm Friday; 9.00 am to 5.00
pm Saturday

Open access
General lending and reference library,
including Healthpoint health information centre, business information, children's library,
periodicals and newspapers, cafe, IT suite and
meeting room.

Press Association Library
See **PA News Centre**

Public Record Office
See **The National Archives**

Reading Central Library

Abbey Square, Reading, Berkshire RG1 3BQ
☎0118 901 5955 Fax 0118 901 5954
Email info@readinglibraries.org.uk
Website www.readinglibraries.org.uk

Open 9.30 am to 5.30 pm Monday and
Friday; 9.30 am to 7.00 pm Tuesday and
Thursday; 9.30 am to 5.00 pm Wednesday
and Saturday

Open access
Ground Floor: Fiction, popular non-fiction,
audio-visual material, children's library; First
Floor: Non-fiction, newspapers; business section; Second Floor: Non-fiction, art, music,
literature, meeting room for hire; Third floor:
Non-fiction, world history, national history,
local history, family history. Magazines and
periodicals and Internet access on all floors.

Religious Society of Friends Library

Friends House, 173 Euston Road, London
NW1 2BJ
☎020 7663 1135 Fax 020 7663 1001
Email library@quaker.org.uk
Website www.quaker.org.uk

Access arrangements 1.00 pm to 5.00 pm
Monday, Tuesday, Thursday, Friday; 10.00
am to 5.00 pm Wednesday

Open access A letter of introduction from a
college/employer/publisher/Friends meeting
is required for researchers who are not members of the Society

Quaker history, thought and activities from
the 17th century onwards. Supporting collections on peace, anti-slavery and other subjects
in which Quakers have maintained long-standing interest. Also archives and manuscripts
relating to the Society of Friends.

Richmond Central Reference Library

Old Town Hall, Whittaker Avenue,
Richmond, Surrey TW9 1TP
☎020 8940 5529 Fax 020 8940 6899
Email reference.services@richmond.gov.uk
Website www.richmond.gov.uk

Open 10.00 am to 6.00 pm Monday,
Thursday, Friday (Tuesday until 1.00 pm;
Wednesday until 8.00 pm and Saturday
until 5.00 pm)

Open access
General reference library serving the needs
of local residents and organisations. Internet
access and online databases for public use.

Royal Geographical Society Library (with the Institute of British Geographers)

1 Kensington Gore, London SW7 2AR
☎020 7591 3040 Fax 020 7591 3001
Website www.rgs.org

The Library and Map Room are closed for major
refurbishment until Spring 2004. The Archives
remain open to Fellows and non-Fellows by
appointment only on Mondays and Tuesdays.
All enquiries should be made in writing to the
Archives Assistant (archives@rgs.org). For information on the Picture Library see entry under
Picture Libraries.

Royal Institute of Philosophy
See **University of London Library**

Royal Society Library

6–9 Carlton House Terrace, London
SW1Y 5AG
☎020 7451 2606 Fax 020 7930 2170
Email library@royalsoc.ac.uk
Website www.royalsoc.ac.uk

Open 10.00 am to 5.00 pm Monday to Friday

Access Open to all researchers with an interest
in the history of science, the Fellowship of the
Royal Society and science policy. Researchers
are advised to contact the Library in advance of
their first visit.

History of science, scientists' biographies,
science policy reports, and publications of

international scientific unions and national academies from all over the world.

RSA (Royal Society for the Encouragement of Arts, Manufactures & Commerce)
8 John Adam Street, London WC2N 6EZ
☎020 7930 5115 Fax 020 7839 5805
Website www.theRSA.org

Open Library: 8.30 am to 8.00 pm every weekday. Archive material by appointment

Access to Fellows of RSA; by application and appointment to non-Fellows (Contact Librarian, ☎020 7451 6874 or e-mail library@rsa.org.uk)
Archives of the Society since 1754. A collection of approximately 10,000 volumes; international exhibition material.

Royal Society of Medicine Library
1 Wimpole Street, London W1G 0AE
☎020 7290 2940 Fax 020 7290 2939
Email library@rsm.ac.uk
Website www.rsm.ac.uk

Director of Information Services *Ian Snowley*
Head of Customer Services *Sheron Burton*

Open 9.00 am to 8.30 pm Monday to Friday; 10.00 am to 5.00 pm Saturday

Access For reference only, on introduction by Fellow of the Society or temporary membership is available to non-members; £12 per day; £35 per week; £90 per month. Identification required.
Books, periodicals, databases on postgraduate biomedical information. Extensive historical collection dating from the fifteenth century and medical portrait collection.

Eric Frank Russel Archive
See **Science Fiction Foundation Research Library**

St Bride Printing Library
Bride Lane, London EC4Y 8EE
☎020 7353 4660 Fax 020 7583 7073
Email stbride@corpoflondon.gov.uk
Website www.stbride.org

Open 9.30 am to 5.30 pm Monday to Friday

Open access
Corporation of London public reference library. Appointments advisable for consultation of special collections. Every aspect of printing and related matters: publishing and bookselling, newspapers and magazines, graphic design, calligraphy and type, papermaking and bookbinding. One of the world's largest specialist collections in its field, with over 50,000 volumes, over 3000 periodicals (200 current titles), and extensive collection of drawings, manuscripts, prospectuses, patents and materials for printing and typefounding. Noted for its comprehensive holdings of historical and early technical literature.

Science Fiction Foundation Research Library
Liverpool University Library, PO Box 123, Liverpool L69 3DA
☎0151 794 3142 Fax 0151 794 2681
Email asawyer@liverpool.ac.uk
Website www.liv.ac.uk/~asawyer/ sffchome.html

Contact *Andy Sawyer*

Access For research, by appointment only (telephone first)
This is the largest collection outside the US of science fiction and related material – including autobiographies and critical works. *Special collection* Runs of 'pulp' magazines dating back to the 1920s. Foreign-language material (including a large Russian collection), and the papers of the Flat Earth Society. The collection also features a growing range of archive and manuscript material, including the Eric Frank Russell archive. The University of Liverpool also holds the Olaf Stapledon and John Wyndham archives.

Science Museum Library
Imperial College Road, London SW7 5NH
☎020 7942 4242 Fax 020 7942 4243
Email smlinfo@nmsi.ac.uk
Website www.nmsi.ac.uk/library

Open 9.30 am to 9.00 pm Monday to Friday (closes 5.30 pm outside academic terms); 9.30 am to 5.30 pm Saturday

Open access Reference only; no loans
National reference library for the history and public understanding of science and technology, with a large collection of source material. Operates jointly with Imperial College Central Library.

Scottish Poetry Library
See entry under **Organisations of Interest to Poets**

2nd Air Division Memorial Library
See **Norfolk Library & Information Service**

Sheffield Libraries, Archives and Information

Central Library, Surrey Street, Sheffield
S1 1XZ
☎0114 273 4712 Fax 0114 273 5009

Central Lending Library
☎0114 273 4727 (enquiries)/4729 (book renewals)

Open 10.00 am to 8.00 pm Monday; 9.30 am to 5.30 pm Tuesday, Thursday and Friday; 9.30 am to 8.00 pm Wednesday; 9.30 am to 5.30 pm Saturday

Books, talking books, large print, language courses, European fiction, books in cultural languages, play sets. Writers' Resource Centre, Wednesday evenings, 5.00 pm to 7.00 pm. Proof of signature and a separate proof of address required to join.

Sheffield Archives
52 Shoreham Street, Sheffield S1 4SP
☎0114 203 9395 Fax 0114 203 9398
Email sheffield.archives@dial.pipex.com

Open 10.00 am to 5.30 pm Monday; 9.30 am to 5.30 pm Tuesday to Thursday; 9.30 am to 1.00 pm and 2.00 pm to 5.00 pm Saturday (documents should be ordered by 5.00 pm Thursday for Saturday); closed Friday

Access By reader's pass
Holds documents relating to Sheffield and South Yorkshire, dating from the 12th century to the present day, including records of the City Council, churches, businesses, landed estates, families and individuals, institutions and societies.

Arts and Social Sciences and Sports Reference Service
☎0114 273 4747/8
Email sportslibrary@dial.pipex.com

Open 10.00 am to 8.00 pm Monday; 9.30 am to 5.30 pm Tuesday, Thursday and Friday; 9.30 am to 8.00 pm Wednesday; 9.30 am to 5.30 pm Saturday

Access For reference only
A comprehensive collection of books, periodicals and newspapers covering all aspects of arts (excluding music) and social sciences.

Music and Video Service
☎0114 273 4733

Open as for Arts and Social Sciences above

Access For reference and lending
An extensive range of books, CDs, cassettes, scores, etc. related to music. Also a video cassette and DVD loan service.

Local Studies Service
☎0114 273 4753

Open as for Arts & Social Sciences above (except Wednesday 9.30 am to 5.30 pm)

Access For reference
Extensive material covering all aspects of Sheffield and its population, including maps, photos and videos.

Business, Science and Technology Reference Services
☎0114 273 4736/7 or 273 4742

Open as for Arts & Social Sciences above

Access For reference only
Extensive coverage of science and technology as well as commerce and commercial law. British patents and British and European standards with emphasis on metals. Hosts the World Metal Index. The business section holds a large stock of business and trade directories, plus overseas telephone directories and reference works with business emphasis.

Sheffield Information Service
☎0114 273 4761/4712 Fax 0114 275 7111
Email nd54@dial.pipex.com
Website dis.shef.ac.uk/help_yourself

Open 10.00 am to 5.30 pm Monday; 9.30 am to 5.30 pm Tuesday, Wednesday, Thursday and Friday; 9.30 am to 5.30 pm Saturday

Full local information service covering all aspects of the Sheffield community and a generalist advice service on a sessional basis.

Children's and Young People's Library Service
☎0114 273 4734

Open 10.30 am to 5.00 pm Monday and Friday; 1.00 pm to 5.00 pm Tuesday, Wednesday and Thursday; 9.30 am to 4.30 pm Saturday

Books, spoken word sets, videos; under-five play area; teenage reference section; readings and promotions; storytime sessions.

Shetland Library

Lower Hillhead, Lerwick, Shetland
ZE1 0EL
☎01595 693868 Fax 01595 694430
Email info@shetland-library.gov.uk
Website www.shetland-library.gov.uk

Open 10.00 am to 7.00 pm Monday, Wednesday, Thursday; 10.00 am to 5.00 pm Tuesday, Friday, Saturday
General lending and reference library; exten-

sive local interest collection including complete set of *The Shetland Times, The Shetland News* and other local newspapers on microfilm and many old and rare books; audio collection including talking books/newspapers. Junior room for children. Disabled access and Housebound Readers Service (delivery to reader's home). Mobile library services to rural areas. Open Learning Service. Same day photocopying service. Publishing programme of books in dialect, history, literature. Learning centre providing access to learning opportunities including Internet.

Shoe Lane Library

Hill House, Little New Street, London EC4A 3JR
☎020 7583 7178   Fax 020 7353 0884
Email shoelane@corpoflondon.gov.uk
Website www.corpoflondon.gov.uk

Open 9.00 am to 5.30 pm Monday, Wednesday, Thursday, Friday; 9.00 am to 6.30 pm Tuesday

Open access
Corporation of London general lending library, with a comprehensive stock of 50,000 volumes, most of which are on display.

Shrewsbury Library and Reference & Information Service

Castlegates, Shrewsbury, Shropshire SY1 2AS
☎01743 255300   Fax 01743 255309
Email shrewsbury.library@shropshire-cc.gov.uk
Website www.shropshire-cc.gov.uk/library.nsf

Open 9.30am–5.00pm Monday, Wednesday & Friday; 9.30am–7.00pm Tuesday & Thursday; 9.30am–7.00pm Thursday; 9.30am–4.00pm Saturday

Open access
The largest public library in Shropshire. Books, cassettes, CDs, talking books, DVDs, videos, language courses. Open Learning and study centre with three public use computers for word processing, CD-ROMs and Internet access. Music, literature and art book collection for lending and reference. The West Midlands Literary Heritage Collection is housed at Shrewsbury Library.

Spanish Institute Library
See **Instituto Cervantes**

Sterling Collection
See **University of London Library**

Suffolk County Council Libraries & Heritage

St Andrew House, County Hall, St Helens Street, Ipswich, Suffolk IP4 1LJ
☎01473 584564   Fax 01473 584549
Email infocentre.ipswich@libher.suffolkcc.gov.uk
Website www.suffolkcc.gov.uk/libraries

Open Details on application to St Andrew House above. Major libraries open six days a week

Access A single user registration card gives access to the lending service of 42 libraries across the county

Full range of lending and reference services. Free public access to the Internet and multimedia CD-ROMs in all libraries. Catalogue with self-service facilities for registered borrowers available on the website. *Special collections* include Suffolk Archives and Local History Collection; Benjamin Britten Collection; Edward Fitzgerald Collection; Seckford Collection and Racing Collection (Newmarket). The Suffolk Infolink service gives details of local groups and societies and is available in libraries throughout the county and on the website.

Sunderland City Library and Arts Centre

28–30 Fawcett Street, Sunderland, Tyne & Wear SR1 1RE
☎0191 514 1235   Fax 0191 514 8444
Email enquiry.desk@edcom.sunderland.gov.uk
Website www.sunderland.gov/libraries

Open 9.30 am to 7.30 pm Monday and Wednesday; 9.30 am to 5.00 pm Tuesday, Thursday, Friday; 9.30 am to 4.00 pm Saturday

The city's main library for lending and reference services. Local studies and children's sections, plus Sound and Vision department (CDs, cassettes, videos, CD-ROMs, talking books). The City of Sunderland also maintains community libraries of varying size, offering a range of services, plus mobile libraries. Free Internet access is available in all libraries across the city. A Books on Wheels service is available to housebound readers; the Schools Library Service serves teachers and schools. Two writers' groups meet at the City Library and Arts Centre: Janus Writers, every Wednesday, 1.30 pm to 3.30 pm. Tuesday Writers, every Tuesday, 7.30 pm to 9.30 pm.

LIBRARY SERVICES   679

Swansea Central Reference Library

Alexandra Road, Swansea SA1 5DX
☎01792 516753/516757 Fax 01792 615759
Email central.library@swansea.gov.uk
Website www.swansea.gov.uk/culture/
  libraries/libraryIntro.htm

Open 9.00 am to 7.00 pm Monday, Tuesday,
  Wednesday, Friday; 9.00 am to 5.00 pm
  Thursday and Saturday. The library has a
  lending service but hours tend to be shorter
  – check in advance (☎01792 516750/1)

Access For reference only (Local Studies
closed access: items must be requested on forms
provided)
  General reference material; also British standards, statutes, company information, maps,
European Community information. Local
studies: comprehensive collections on Wales;
Swansea & Gower; Dylan Thomas. Local
maps, periodicals, illustrations, local newspapers from 1804. B&w and colour photocopying facilities, access to the Internet and micro-
film/microfiche copying facility.

Swiss Cottage Central Library

88 Avenue Road, London NW3 3HA
☎020 7974 6522 Fax 020 7974 6522

Open 10.00 am to 7.00 pm Monday and
  Thursday; 10.00 am to 6.00 pm Tuesday,
  Wednesday, Friday; 10.00 am to 5.00 pm
  Saturday

Open access
  Over 300,000 volumes in the lending and reference libraries. Home of the London Borough
of Camden's Information and Reference
Services.

Theatre Museum Library & Archive

1e Tavistock Street, London WC2E 7PR
☎020 7943 4727 Fax 020 7943 4777
Website theatremuseum.org

Open 10.30 am to 4.30 pm Wednesday to
  Friday

Access By appointment only
  The Theatre Museum was founded as a separate department of the Victoria & Albert
Museum in 1974 and moved to its own building
in Covent Garden in 1987. The museum (open
Tuesday to Sunday 10.00 am to 6.00 pm) houses
permanent displays, temporary exhibitions, a studio theatre, and organises a programme of special
events, performances, lectures, guided visits and

workshops. The library houses the UK's largest
performing arts research collections, including
books, photographs, designs, engravings, programmes, press cuttings, etc. All the performing
arts are covered but strengths are in the areas of
theatre, dance, musical theatre and stage design.
A large store in West London houses the
Museum's special collections of archives. A separate reading room there provides access to them.

Thurrock Council Leisure, Libraries & Cultural Services Department

Grays Library, Orsett Road, Grays, Essex
RM17 5DX
☎01375 383611 Fax 01375 370806
Email grays.library@thurrock.gov.uk

Virtual Enquiry Desk:
  acairns@thurrock.gov.uk
Open 9.00 am to 7.00 pm Monday, Tuesday,
  Thursday; 9.00 am to 5.00 pm Wednesday,
  Friday, Saturday; branch library opening
  times vary

Open access
  General library lending and reference through
ten libraries and a mobile library. Services
include books, magazines, newspapers, audio-
cassettes, CDs, videos and language courses.
Large collection of Thurrock materials. Internet
and word processing.

Truro Library

Union Place, Pydar Street, Truro, Cornwall
TR1 1EP
☎01872 279205 (lending)/272702 (reference)
Email truro.library@cornwall.gov.uk
Website www.cornwall.gov.uk/library

Open 9.00 am to 6.00 pm Monday to Friday;
  9.00 am to 4.00 pm Saturday
  Books, cassettes, CDs, videos and DVDs for
loan through branch or mobile networks.
Study centre and IT suite. Reference collection. *Special collections* on local studies.

United Nations Depository
See **Belfast Public Libraries**

United Nations Information Centre

Millbank Tower (21st Floor), 21–24 Millbank,
London SW1P 4QH
☎020 7630 1981 Fax 020 7976 6478
Email info@uniclondon.org
Website www.unitednations.org.uk

Open Library: 9.00 am to 1.00 pm and 2.00 pm to 5.00 pm Monday to Thursday

Access By appointment only

A full stock of official publications and documentation from the United Nations.

Western Isles Libraries
Public Library, 19 Cromwell Street, Stornoway, Isle of Lewis HS1 2DA
☎01851 708631 Fax 01851 708676

Open 10.00 am to 5.00 pm Monday to Wednesdayday; 10.00 am to 6.00 pm Thursday and Friday; 10.00 am to 5.00 pm Saturday

Open access

General public library stock, plus local history and Gaelic collections including maps, videos, printed music, cassettes and CDs; census records and Council minutes; music collection (CDs and cassettes). Branch libraries on the isles of Barra, Benbecula, Harris and Lewis.

City of Westminster
Archives Centre
10 St Ann's Street, London SW1P 2DE
☎020 7641 5180/Minicom: 020 7641 4879
Fax 020 7641 5179
Email archives@westminster.gov.uk
Website www.westminster.gov.uk

Open 9.30 am to 5.00 pm Monday, Friday, Saturday; 9.30 am to 7.00 pm Tuesday, Wednesday, Thursday

Access For reference

Comprehensive coverage of the history of Westminster and selective coverage of general London history. 22,000 books, together with a large stock of maps, prints, photographs, local newspapers, theatre programmes and archives.

Westminster Music Library
Victoria Library, 160 Buckingham Palace Road, London SW1W 9UD
☎020 7641 4292 Fax 020 7641 4281
Email westmuslib@dial.pipex.com
Website www.westminster.gov.uk/libraries/special/music

Open 11.00 am to 7.00 pm Monday to Friday; 10 am to 5.00 pm Saturday

Open access

Located at Victoria Library, this is the largest public music library in the South of England, with extensive coverage of all aspects of music, including books, periodicals and printed scores. No recorded material, notated only. Lending library includes a small collection of CDs and videos.

Westminster Reference Library
35 St Martin's Street, London WC2H 7HP
☎020 7641 4636 Fax 020 7641 4606
Email referencelibraryws2@westminster.gov.uk
Website www.westminster.gov.uk/libraries/libraries/westref

General Reference & Performing Arts
☎020 7641 4636

Art & Design
☎020 7641 4638

Business and Official Publications
☎020 7641 4634

Open 10.00 am to 8.00 pm Monday to Friday; 10.00 am to 5.00 pm Saturday

Access For reference only

A general reference library with emphasis on the following: Art & Design – fine and decorative arts, architecture, graphics and design; Performing Arts – theatre, cinema, radio, television and dance; Official Publications – major collection of HMSO publications from 1947, plus parliamentary papers dating back to 1906; Business – UK directories, trade directories, company and market data; Official EU Depository Library – carries official EU material; Periodicals – long files of many titles. One working day's notice is required for some government documents, some monographs and most older periodicals.

Blanco White Collection
See **Athenaeum, Liverpool**

The Wiener Library
4 Devonshire Street, London W1W 5BH
☎020 7636 7247 Fax 020 7436 6428
Email info@wienerlibrary.co.uk
Website wienerlibrary.co.uk

Director *Ben Barkow*
Education and Outreach Coordinator *Katherin Klinger*

Open 10.00 am to 5.30 pm Monday to Friday

Access By letter of introduction (readers needing to use the Library for any length of time should become members)

Private library – one of the leading research centres on European history since the First World War, with special reference to the era of totalitarianism and to Jewish affairs. Founded by Dr Alfred Wiener in Amsterdam in 1933, it holds material that is not available elsewhere.

Books, periodicals, press archives, documents, pamphlets, leaflets and brochures. Much of the material can be consulted on microfilm.

Vaughan Williams Memorial Library

English Folk Dance and Song Society, Cecil Sharp House, 2 Regent's Park Road, London NW1 7AY
☎020 7485 2206 ext. 18/19
Fax 020 7284 0523
Email library@efdss.org
Website www.efdss.org

Contact *Elinor Pearson*

Open 9.30 am to 5.30 pm Tuesday to Friday; 10.00 am to 4.00 pm 1st & 3rd Saturday (sometimes closed between 1.00 pm and 2.00 pm)

Access For reference to the general public, on payment of a daily fee; members may borrow books and use the library free of charge

A multimedia collection: books, periodicals, manuscripts, tapes, records, CDs, films, videos. Mostly British traditional culture and how this has developed around the world. Some foreign language material, and some books in English about foreign cultures. Also, the history of the English Folk Dance and Song Society.

Dr Williams's Library

14 Gordon Square, London WC1H 0AR
☎020 7387 3727
Email enquiries@dwlib.co.uk

Open 10.00 am to 5.00 pm Monday, Wednesday, Friday; 10.00 am to 6.30 pm Tuesday and Thursday

Open access to reading room (loans restricted to subscribers). Visitors required to supply identification

Annual subscription £10; ministers of religion and certain students £5

Primarily a library of theology, religion and ecclesiastical history. Also philosophy, history (English and Byzantine). Particularly important for the study of English Nonconformity. Trustees of Dr William's Library manage the Congregational Library on behalf of the Memorial Hall Trustees.

Wolverhampton Central Library

Snow Hill, Wolverhampton WV1 3AX
☎01902 552025 (lending)/552026 (reference)
Fax 01902 552024
Email wolverhampton.libraries@dial.pipex.com

Website www.wolverhampton.gov.uk

Open 9.00 am to 7.00 pm Monday to Thursday; 9.00 am to 5.00 pm Friday and Saturday

Archives & Local Studies Collection
42–50 Snow Hill, Wolverhampton WV2 4AB
☎01902 552480

Open 10.00 am to 5.00 pm Monday, Tuesday, Friday, 1st and 3rd Saturday of each month; 10.00 am to 7.00 pm Wednesday; closed Thursday

General lending and reference libraries, plus children's library and audiovisual library holding cassettes, CDs, videos and music scores. Internet access.

The Women's Library

London Metropolitan University, Old Castle Street, London E1 7NT
☎020 7320 2222 Fax 020 7320 2333
Email moreinfo@thewomenslibrary.ac.uk
Website www.thewomenslibrary.ac.uk

Open Reading Room: 9.30 am to 5.00 pm Tuesday to Friday (8.00 pm Thursday); 10.00 am to 4.00 pm Saturday

Open access. Exhibition: 9.30 am to 5.30 pm Monday to Friday (8.00 pm Thursday); 10.00 am to 4.00 pm Saturday. Director: *Antonia Byatt*

The Women's Library, national research library for women's history, is the UK's oldest and most comprehensive research library on all aspects of women in society, with both historical and contemporary coverage. The Library includes materials on feminism, work, education, health, the family, law, arts, sciences, technology, language, sexuality, fashion and the home. The main emphasis is on Britain but many other countries are represented, especially the Commonwealth and the developing countries. Established in 1926 as the library of the London Society of Women's Service (formerly Suffrage), a non-militant organisation led by Millicent Fawcett. In 1953 the Society was renamed after her and the library became the Fawcett Library.

Collections include: women's suffrage, work, education, women and the church, the law, sport, art, music, abortion, prostitution. Mostly British materials but some American, Commonwealth and European works. Books, journals, pamphlets, archives, photographs, posters, postcards, audiovisual materials, artefacts, scrapbooks, albums and press cuttings dating mainly from the 19th century although some materials date from the 17th century.

The Library's new building, which opened in February 2002, includes a reading room, exhibition space, café, education areas and a conference room, and is the cultural and research centre for anyone interested in women's lives and achievements.

Worcestershire Libraries and Information Service

Cultural Services, Worcestershire County Council, County Hall, Spetchley Road, Worcester WR5 2NP
☎01905 766231 Fax 01905 766244
Website www.worcestershire.gov.uk/libraries

Open Opening hours vary in the 22 libraries, the History Centre and mobile libraries covering the county; all full-time libraries open at least one evening a week until 7.00 pm or 8.00 pm, and on Saturday until 1 pm; 8 largest libraries open until 4.00 pm on Saturday; part-time libraries vary

Access Information and reference services open to anyone; loans to members only (membership criteria: resident, being educated, working, or an elector in the county or neighbouring authorities; temporary membership to visitors. Proof of identity and address required. No charge for membership or for borrowing books.)

Information service, and reference and lending libraries. Non-fiction and fiction for all age groups, including normal and large print, spoken word cassettes, sound recordings (CD, cassette), videos, maps, local history, CD-ROMs for reference at main libraries, free public Internet access in all libraries. Joint Libraries Service/County Record Office History Centre with resources for local and family history. *Special collections* Carpets and Textiles; Needles & Needlemaking; Stuart Period; A.E. Housman.

John Wyndham Archive
See **Science Fiction Foundation Research Library**

York Central Library
Museum Street, York YO1 7DS
☎01904 655631 Fax 01904 611025
Email reference.library@york.gov.uk

Lending Library
Open 9.30 am to 8.00 pm Monday, Tuesday, Friday; 9.30 am to 5.30 pm Wednesday and Thursday; 9.30 am to 4.00 pm Saturday

General lending library including videos, CDs, music cassettes, audio books, children's story-tapes language courses and printed music. Photocopying and fax facilities.

Reference Library
Open 9.00 am to 8.00 pm Monday, Tuesday, Wednesday, Friday; 9.00 am to 5.30 pm Thursday; 9.00 am to 4.00 pm Saturday

General reference library; organisations database; local studies library for York and surrounding area; business information service; microfilm/fiche readers for national and local newspapers; census returns and family history resource; general reference collection. Maintains strong links with other local history resource centres, namely the Borthwick Institute, York City Archive and York Minster Library. CD-ROM and Internet facilities. Room 18: IT resource centre available to the public. In addition, 14 branch libraries and one mobile, serving the City of York Council area.

York City Archive
See **York Central Library**

York Minster Archive
See **York Central Library**

Young Booktrust Children's Reference Library
Book House, 45 East Hill, London SW18 2QZ
☎020 8516 2985 Fax 020 8516 2978
Email ed@booktrust.org.uk

Website www.booktrust.org.uk *and* www.booktrusted.com

Contact *Mr E. Zaghini*
Open 9.00 am to 5.00 pm Monday to Friday (by appointment only)

Access For reference only
A comprehensive collection of children's literature, related books and periodicals. Aims to hold most of all children's titles published within the last two years. An information service covers all aspects of children's literature, including profiles of authors and illustrators. Reading room facilities.

Zoological Society Library
Regent's Park, London NW1 4RY
☎020 7449 6293 Fax 020 7586 5743
Email library@zsl.org
Website www.zsl.org

Open 9.30 am to 5.30 pm Monday to Friday

Access To members and staff; non-members by application and on payment of fee

160,000 volumes on zoology including 5000 journals (1300 current) and a wide range of books on animals and particular habitats. Slide collection available and many historic zoological prints.

Picture Libraries

A–Z Botanical Collection Ltd
192 Goswell Road, London EC1V 7DT
☎020 7253 0991 Fax 020 7253 0992
Email sales@azbotanical.com
Website www.azbotanical.com

Contact *Anna Gibson*

300,000 transparencies, specialising in plants and related subjects.

Acme
See **Popperfoto**

Action Plus
54–58 Tanner Street, London SE1 3PH
☎020 7403 1558 Fax 020 7403 1526
Email info@actionplus.co.uk
Website www.actionplus.co.uk

FOUNDED 1986. Specialist sports and action library with a vast comprehensive collection of small-format colour and b&w images covering all aspects of over 130 professional and amateur sports from around the world. As well as personalities, events, venues, etc, also covers themes such as success, celebration, dejection, teamwork, effort and exhaustion. 35mm colour stock and online digital archive.

Lesley & Roy Adkins
Picture Library
Ten Acre Wood, Whitestone, Exeter, Devon EX4 2HW
☎01392 811357 Fax 01392 811435
Email mail@adkinsarchaeology.com
Website www.adkinsarchaeology.com

Colour coverage of archaeology, antiquity, heritage and related subjects in the UK, Europe, Egypt and Turkey. Subjects include towns, villages, housing, landscape and countryside, churches, temples, castles, monasteries, art and architecture, gravestones and tombs, inscriptions and antiquarian views. No service charge if pictures are used.

The Advertising Archive Limited
45 Lyndale Avenue, London NW2 2QB
☎020 7435 6540 Fax 020 7794 6584
Email suzanne@advertisingarchives.co.uk
Website www.advertisingarchives.co.uk

Contacts *Suzanne Viner, Larry Viner*

With over one million images, the largest collection of British and American press ads, TV commercial stills and magazine cover illustrations in Europe. Material spans the period from 1850 to the present day. Expert in-house research; rapid service, competitive rates. On-line database and digital delivery available. Visitors by appointment.

AKG images Ltd, The Arts and History Picture Library
5 Melbray Mews, 158 Hurlingham Road, London SW6 3NS
☎020 7610 6103 Fax 020 7610 6125
Email enquiries@akg-images.co.uk
Website www.akg-images.co.uk

Contact *Julia Engelhardt*

Collection of 250,000 images with direct access to ten million (100,000 available via ISDN as high resolution scans) kept in the Berlin AKG Library. *Specialises* in art, archaeology, history, topography, music, personalities and film.

Bryan & Cherry Alexander Photography
Higher Cottage, Manston, Sturminster Newton, Dorset DT10 1EZ
☎01258 473006 Fax 01258 473333
Email alexander@arcticphoto.co.uk
Website www.arcticphoto.co.uk

Contact *Cherry Alexander*

Arctic and Antarctic specialists; indigenous peoples, wildlife and science in polar regions; Norway, Iceland, Siberia and Alaska.

Alpine Garden Society
AGS Centre, Avon Bank, Pershore, Worcester WR10 3JP
☎01386 554790 Fax 01386 554801
Email ags@alpinegardensociety.org
Website www.alpinegardensociety.org

Contact *Peter Sheasby*

Over 17,000 colour transparencies (35mm) covering plants in the wild from many parts of the world; particularly strong in plants from mountain and sub-alpine regions, and from Mediterranean climates – South Africa, Australia, California and the Mediterranean. Extensive coverage of show alpines in pots and in gardens and of European orchids. Full slide list available.

Alvey & Towers
Enterprise House, Ashby Road, Coalville, Leicestershire LE67 3LA
☎01530 450011 Fax 01530 450011
Email alveytower@aol.com
Website www.alveyandtowers.com
Contact *Emma Rowen*

Houses one of the country's most comprehensive collections of transport images depicting not only actual transport systems but their surrounding industries as well. Also specialist modern railway image collection.

Andalucia Slide Library
Apto 499, Estepona, Malaga 29 680, Spain
☎00 34 952 793647 Fax 00 34 952 880138
Email info@andaluciaslidelibrary.com
Website www.andaluciaslidelibrary.com
Library Manager *Michelle Chaplow*

Specialist library covering all aspects of Spain and Spanish life and culture. Cities, white villages, landscapes, festivals, art, gastronomy, leisure, tourism. Also images of Portugal, Madiera and Malta. Commissions undertaken.

Andes Press Agency
26 Padbury Court, London E2 7EH
☎020 7613 5417 Fax 020 7739 3159
Email apa@andespressagency.com
Website www.andespressagency.com
Contacts *Val Baker, Carlos Reyes*

80,000 colour transparencies and 300,000 b&w, specialising in social documentary, world religions, Latin America and Britain.

Heather Angel/Natural Visions
Highways, 6 Vicarage Hill, Farnham, Surrey GU9 8HJ
☎01252 716700 Fax 01252 727464
Email hangel@naturalvisions.co.uk
Website www.naturalvisions.co.uk
Contact *Valerie West*

Constantly expanding worldwide natural history, wildlife and landscapes: polar regions, tropical rainforest flora and fauna, all species of plants and animals in natural habitats from Africa, Asia (notably China and Malaysia), Australasia, South America and USA, urban wildlife, pollution, biodiversity, global warming. Also worldwide gardens and cultivated flowers. Transparencies only loaned to publishers after contract exchanged with author.

Ansel Adams
See **Corbis Images**

Aquarius Library
PO Box 5, Hastings, East Sussex TN34 1HR
☎01424 721196 Fax 01424 717704
Email aquarius.lib@clara.net
Website www.aquariuscollection.com
Contact *David Corkill*

Over one million images specialising in cinema past and present, television, pop music, ballet, opera, theatre, etc. The library includes various American showbiz collections. Film stills date back to the beginning of the century. Interested in film stills, the older the better.

Architectural Association Photo Library
36 Bedford Square, London WC1B 3ES
☎020 7887 4066 Fax 020 7414 0782
Email valerie@aaschool.ac.uk
Website www.aaschool.ac.uk
Contacts *Valerie Bennett, Sarah Franklin, Wayne Henderson*

100,000 35mm transparencies on architecture, historical and contemporary. Archive or large-format b&w negatives from the 1920s and 1930s.

ArenaPAL
Lambert House, 55 Southwark Street, London SE1 1RU
☎020 7403 8542 Fax 020 7403 8561
Email enquiries@arenapal.com
Website www.arenapal.com

'All the entertainment pictures you'll ever need'. Continually updated specialist performing arts image collection covering classical music, opera, theatre, musicals, film, pop, rock, jazz, instruments, festivals, venues, circus, ballet and contemporary dance, props and personalities. Over two million images from late 19th century onwards. Please phone, fax or e-mail to make a selection.

Art Directors & Trip Photo Library
57 Burdon Lane, Cheam, Surrey SM2 7BY
☎020 8642 3593 Fax 020 8395 7230
Email images@artdirectors.co.uk
Website www.artdirectors.co.uk
Contacts *Helene Rogers, Bob Turner*

Extensive coverage, with over 750,000 images, of all countries, lifestyles, peoples, etc. with detailed coverage of all religions. Backgrounds a speciality. Catalogues available free to professionals.

Aspect Picture Library Ltd
40 Rostrevor Road, London SW6 5AD
☎020 7736 1998/7731 7362
Fax 020 7731 7362
Email Aspect.Ldn@btinternet.com
Website www.aspect-picture-library.co.uk

Colour and b&w worldwide coverage of countries, events, industry and travel, with large files on art, namely paintings, space, China and the Middle East.

Atlantic Syndication
See **Solo Syndication Ltd**

Australia Pictures
28 Sheen Common Drive, Richmond TW10 5BN
☎020 7602 1989 Fax 020 7602 1989
Contact *John Miles*

Collection of 4000 transparencies covering all aspects of Australia: Aboriginal people, paintings, Ayers Rock, Kakadu, Tasmania, underwater, reefs, Arnhem Land, Sydney. Also Africa, Middle East and Asia.

Aviation Images – Mark Wagner
42B Queens Road, London SW19 8LR
☎020 8944 5225 Fax 020 8944 5335
Email mark.wagner@aviation-images.com
Website www.aviation-images.com
Contacts *Mark Wagner, Mark Steele*

500,000+ aviation images, civil and military, technical and generic. Mark Wagner is the photographer for *Flight International* magazine. Member of **BAPLA** and RAeS.

Aviation Photographs International
15 Downs View Road, Swindon, Wiltshire SN3 1NS
☎01793 497179 Fax 01793 434030

The 250,000 photographs comprise a comprehensive coverage of army, naval and airforce hardware ranging from early pistols to the latest ships. Extensive coverage of military and civil aviation includes modern together with many air-to-air views of vintage/warbird types. Collections available on disk. Commissions undertaken for additional photography and research. CD-ROM available of part of the library collection.

Aviation Picture Library
116 The Avenue, St Stephens, West Ealing, London W13 8JX
☎020 8566 7712 (Mobile: 07860 670073)
Fax 020 8566 7714
Email avpix@aol.com
Contact *Austin John Brown*

Specialists in the aviation field but also a general library which includes travel, architecture, transport, landscapes and skyscapes. *Special collections* Aircraft and all aspects of the aviation industry, including the archival collection of John Stroud; aerial obliques of Europe, USA, Caribbean and West Africa; architectural and town planning. Photographers for *Flyer* magazine in the UK. Commissions undertaken on the ground and in the air.

Axel Poignant Archive
115 Bedford Court Mansions, Bedford Avenue, London WC1B 3AG
☎020 7636 2555 Fax 020 7636 2555
Email Rpoignant@aol.com
Contact *Roslyn Poignant*

Anthropological and ethnographic subjects, especially Australia and the South Pacific. Also Scandinavia (early history and mythology), Sicily and England.

Barnaby's Picture Library
See **Mary Evans Picture Library**

Barnardos Photographic and Film Archive
Tanners Lane, Barkingside, Ilford, Essex IG6 1QG
☎020 8550 8822 Fax 020 8550 0429
Email marissa.dowling@barnardos.org.uk
Website www.barnardos.org.uk
Contact *Stephen Povers*

Specialises in social history (1874 to present day), child care, education, emigration/migration, war years. Half a million prints, slides, negatives, mainly b&w, colour since late 1940s/early '50s. Archive of 200 films dating back to 1905. Visitors by appointment Mon–Fri, 9.30 am to 4.30 pm.

Colin Baxter Photography Limited
Woodlands Industrial Estate, Grantown-on-Spey PH26 3NA
☎01479 873999 Fax 01479 873888
Email sales@colinbaxter.co.uk
Website www.colinbaxter.co.uk
Contacts *Colin B. Kirkwood* (Marketing), *Mike Rensner* (Editorial)

Over 50,000 images specialising in Scotland. Also the Lake District, Yorkshire, France, Iceland and a special collection on Charles Rennie Mackintosh's work. *Publishes* guidebooks plus books, calendars, postcards and greetings cards on landscape, cityscape and natural history containing images which are primarily, but not exclusively, Colin Baxter's. Also publishers of the *Worldlife Library* of natural history books.

BBC Natural History Unit Picture Library
See **Nature Picture Library**

The Photographic Library Beamish, The North of England Open Air Museum
The North of England Open Air Museum, Beamish, County Durham DH9 0RG
☎0191 370 4000 Fax 0191 370 4001
Email museum@beamish.org.uk
Website www.beamish.org.uk
Keeper of Resource Collections *Jim Lawson*
Comprehensive collection; images relate to the North East of England and cover agricultural, industrial, topography, advertising and shop scenes, people at work and play. Also on laser disk for rapid searching. Visitors by appointment weekdays.

Francis Bedford
See **Birmingham Library Services** under **Library Services**

Ivan J. Belcher Colour Picture Library
57 Gibson Close, Abingdon, Oxfordshire OX14 1XS
☎01235 521524 Fax 01235 521524
Extensive colour picture library specialising in top-quality medium-format transparencies depicting the British scene. Particular emphasis on tourist, holiday and heritage locations, including famous cities, towns, picturesque harbours, rivers, canals, castles, cottages, rural scenes and traditions photographed throughout the seasons. Mainly of recent origin and constantly updated.

Andrew Besley PhotoLibrary
'Trenerth Barton', Fraddam, Near Hayle, Cornwall TR27 5EP
☎01736 850086 Fax 01736 850086
Email bes.pix@btinternet.com
Website www.andrewbesley-photolibrary.co.uk
Contact *Andrew Besley*

Specialist library of 20,000 images of West Country faces, places and moods.

Bettmann Archive
See **Corbis Images**

BFI Stills, Posters and Designs
British Film Institute, 21 Stephen Street, London W1T 1LN
☎020 7957 4797 Fax 020 7323 9260
Email stills.films@bfi.org.uk
Website ww.bfi.org.uk/collections/stills/index.html
A unique collection of photographs from cinema and TV containing over seven million stills and transparencies from over 80,000 titles. Capturing on and off screen moments, the material features not only portraits of the world's most famous stars – and those behind the camera who made them famous – but shots of studios, cinemas and special events. The collection provides a comprehensive visual history of film and TV from their inception to the present day. Also holds original posters, set and costume designs. Research requests can be made by e-mail, telephone, fax or letter. Visits by appointment only (Tuesday to Thursday, 11 am to 4 pm).

Blackwoods Picture Library
See **Geoslides Photography**

Anthony Blake Photo Library
20 Blades Court, Deodar Road, Putney, London SW15 2NU
☎020 8877 1123 Fax 020 8877 9787
Email info@abpl.co.uk
Website ww.abpl.co.uk
'Europe's premier source' of food and wine-related images. From the farm and vineyard to the plate and the bottle. Cooking and kitchens, top chefs and restaurants, country trades and markets, worldwide travel with an extensive Italian section. Many recipes available to accompany transparencies. Free brochure available.

Peter Boardman Collection
See **Chris Bonington Picture Library**

Boats & Boating Features (Keith Pritchard)
9 High Street, Southwell, Portland, Dorset DT5 2EH
☎01305 861006 Fax 0870 132 4192
Email boats@btinternet.com
Website www.boats.btinternet.co.uk
Contact *Keith Pritchard*

Marine lifestyle, maritime heritage and inland waterways – worldwide. Search, license, download.

Chris Bonington Picture Library

Badger Hill, Nether Row, Hesket Newmarket, Wigton, Cumbria CA7 8LA
☎016974 78286 Fax 016974 78238
Email frances@bonington.com
Website www.bonington.com

Contact *Frances Daltrey*

Based on the personal collection of climber and author Chris Bonington and his extensive travels and mountaineering achievements; also work by Doug Scott and other climbers, including the Peter Boardman and Joe Tasker Collections. Full coverage of the world's mountains, from British hills to Everest, depicting expedition planning and management stages, the approach march showing inhabitants of the area, flora and fauna, local architecture and climbing action shots on some of the world's highest mountains.

Boulton and Watt Archive

See **Birmingham Library Services** under **Library Services**

The Bridgeman Art Library

17–19 Garway Road, London W2 4PH
☎020 7727 4065 Fax 020 7792 8509
Email london@bridgeman.co.uk
Website www.bridgeman.co.uk

Head of Picture Research *Jenny Page*

Fine art photo archive acting as an agent to more than 1000 museums, galleries and picture owners around the world. Large-format colour transparencies of private collections, artists, paintings, sculptures, prints, manuscripts, antiquities and the decorative arts. The Library is currently expanding at the rate of 500 new images each week and has offices in Paris and New York. Collections represented by the library include the British Library, the National Galleries of Scotland, the National Library of Australia, and the National Gallery of South Africa. Fully searchable catalogue online.

British Library Picture Library and Images Online/Reproductions

British Library, 96 Euston Road, London NW1 2DB
Images Online: ☎020 7412 7614
Fax 020 7412 7771 Email imagesonline@bl.uk
Website www.bl.uk/imagesonline
Reproductions: ☎020 7412 7613
Fax 020 7412 7596 Email reproductions@bl.uk

Website www.bl.uk/reproductions

The Picture Library holds a growing number of images from the British Library's collections of manuscripts, books, maps, music and philately. Transparencies or prints are available for hire and printouts are supplied free for selection purposes.

The fully searchable website, Images Online, includes images scanned from the library's existing transparencies. High-resolution images are available on CD-ROM; smaller JPEGs can be purchased online and downloaded instantly.

Reproductions offers high quality paper copying, microfilming, photographic and digital services to customers who require copies from the following collection areas: Maps, Music, Printed Books, Manuscripts and the Oriental and India Office Collections. There are two levels of copying service: standard 25 working days, and express 10 working days. For commercial reproduction please use the contact details.

Brooklands Museum Picture Library

Brooklands Museum, Brooklands Road, Weybridge, Surrey KT13 0QN
☎01932 857381 Fax 01932 855465
Email info@brooklandsmuseum.com
Website www.brooklandsmuseum.com

Contacts *John Pulford* (Curator of Collections), *Julian Temple* (Curator of Aviation)

About 40,000 b&w and colour prints and slides. Subjects include: Brooklands Motor Racing 1907–1939; British aviation and aerospace 1908–present day – particularly BAC, Hawker, Sopwith and Vickers aircraft built at Brooklands.

Hamish Brown MBE, D.Litt, FRSGS Scottish Photographic

26 Kirkcaldy Road, Burntisland, Fife KY3 9HQ
☎01592 873546

Contact *Hamish Brown*

Coverage of most topics and areas of Scotland (sites, historic, buildings, landscape, mountains), also travel and mountains abroad, Ireland and Morocco. Commissions undertaken.

Capital Pictures

49–51 Central Street, London EC1V 8AB
☎020 7253 1122 Fax 020 7253 1414
Email sales@capitalpictures.com
Website www.capitalpictures.com

Contact *Phil Loftus*

500,000 images. *Specialises* in photographs of

famous people from the worlds of show-business, rock and pop, television, politics, royalty and film stills.

The Centre for the Study of Cartoons and Caricature

The Templeman Library, University of Kent at Canterbury, Canterbury, Kent CT2 7NU
☎01227 823127 Fax 01227 823127
Email N.P.Hiley@ukc.ac.uk *or* J.M.Newton@ukc.ac.uk
Website library.ukc.ac.uk/cartoons/

Contacts *Dr Nicholas Hiley, Jane Newton*

A national research archive of over 85,000 twentieth century cartoons and caricatures, supported by a library of books, papers, journals, catalogues and assorted ephemera. A computer database of 90,000 cartoons provides quick and easy catalogued access. A source for exhibitions and displays as well as a picture library service. *Specialises* in historical, political and social cartoons from British newspapers.

Cephas Picture Library

Hurst House, 157 Walton Road, East Molesey, Surrey KT8 0DX
☎020 8979 8647 Fax 020 8224 8095
Email pictures@cephas.co.uk
Website www.cephas.com

The wine industry and vineyards of the world is the subject on which Cephas has made its reputation. 100,000 images, mainly original 6×7″ make this the most comprehensive and up-to-date archive in Britain. Almost all wine-producing countries and all aspects of the industry are covered in depth. Spirits, beer and cider also included. A major food and drink collection now also exists, through preparation and cooking, to eating and drinking.

Giles Chapman Library

2 Peacock Yard, Iliffe Street, London SE17 3LH
☎020 7708 5818 Fax 020 7701 8672
Email chapman.media@virgin.net

Contact *Giles Chapman*

Around 125,000 colour and b&w images of cars and motoring, from 1945 to the present day. No research fees.

Christel Clear Marine Photography

5 Providence Place, Stoke Damerel, Plymouth PL1 5QS
☎01752 297598 Fax 07931 157717
Email julianne@cristelclear.co.uk
Website www.cristelclear.co.uk

Contact *Julie-Anne Putt*

Over 70,000 images on 35mm and 645 transparencies: yachting and boating from Grand Prix sailing to small dinghies, cruising locations and harbours. Recent additions include angling, fly fishing and travel. Visitors by appointment.

Christian Aid Photo Section

PO Box 100, London SE1 7RT
☎020 7523 2235 Fax 020 7620 0719

Contacts *J. Cabon, B. Nicholson*

Pictures, mainly from Africa, Asia, Latin America, relating to small-scale, community-based programmes. Mostly development themes: agriculture, health, education, urban and rural life.

Christie's Images Ltd

1 Langley Lane, London SW8 1TJ
☎020 7582 1282 Fax 020 7582 5632
Email imageslondon@christies.com
Website www.christiesimages.com

Contact *Emma Strouts*

The UK's largest fine art photo library. 150,000 images of fine and decorative art. An extensive list of subjects is covered through paintings, drawings and prints of all periods as well as silver, ceramics, jewellery, sculpture, textiles and many other decorative and collectable items. Staff will search files and database to locate specific requests or supply a selection for consideration. Visits by appointment. Search fee.

Chrysalis Images

64 Brewery Road, London N7 9NT
☎020 7697 3000 Fax 020 7697 3001
Email Tforshaw@chrysalisbooks.co.uk

Contact *Terry Forshaw*

One million photographs and illustrations, colour and b&w, on military, history, transport, cookery, crafts, natural history, space and travel.

The Cinema Museum

The Master's House, Old Lambeth Workhouse, off Renfrew Road, London SE11 4TH
☎020 7840 2200 Fax 020 7840 2299
Email martin@cinemamuseum.org.uk

Colour and b&w coverage (including stills) of the motion picture industry throughout its history, including the Ronald Grant Archive. Smaller collections on theatre, variety, television and popular music.

John Cleare/Mountain Camera

Hill Cottage, Fonthill Gifford, Salisbury, Wiltshire SP3 6QW
☎01747 820320 Fax 01747 820320

Email cleare@btinternet.com
Website www.mountaincamera.com

Colour and b&w coverage of mountains and wild places, climbing, ski-touring, trekking, expeditions, wilderness travel, landscapes, people and geographical features from all continents. *Specialises* in the Himalaya, Andes, Antarctic, Alps and the British countryside, and a range of topics from reindeer in Lapland to camels in Australia, from whitewater rafting in Utah to ski-mountaineering in China. Commissions and consultancy work undertaken. Researchers welcome by appointment. Member of **BAPLA** and the **OWG**.

Michael Cole Camerawork
The Coach House, 27 The Avenue,
Beckenham, Kent BR3 2DP
☎020 8658 6120   Fax 020 8658 6120
Email mikecole@dircon.co.uk
Contacts *Michael Cole, Derrick Bentley*

Probably the largest and most comprehensive collection of tennis pictures in the world. Over 50 years' coverage of the Wimbledon Championships. M.C.C. incorporates the tennis archives of Le Roye Productions, established in 1945.

Collections
13 Woodberry Crescent, London N10 1PJ
☎020 8883 0083   Fax 020 8883 9215
Email collections@btinternet.com
Website www.collectionspicturelibrary.com
Contact *Brian Shuel*

Extensive coverage of the British and Ireland from the Shetlands to the Channel Islands, and Connemara to East Anglia, including people, traditional customs, workers, religions and pastimes, as well as places both well known and obscure, and an extensive collection of 'things'. Includes the landscapes of Fay Godwin. Visitors are welcome but please make an appointment.

Concannon Golf History Library
See **Phil Sheldon Golf Picture Library**

Corbis Images
111 Salusbury Road, London NW6 6RG
☎020 7644 7644 (0800 731 9995 Toll Free)
Fax 020 7644 7645
Email info@uk.corbis.com
Website www.corbis.com
Contact *Anna Calvert*

A unique and comprehensive resource containing more than 65 million images, with over 2.1

million of them available online. The images come from professional photographers, museums, cultural institutions and public and private collections worldwide, including images from the Bettmann Archive, Ansel Adams, Lynn Goldsmith, the Turnley Collection and Hulton Deutsch. Subjects include history, travel, celebrities, events, science, world art and cultures. Free catalogues are available or register for a free password to search, save and order online.

Sylvia Cordaiy Photo Library
45 Rotherstone, Devizes, Wiltshire SN10 2DD
☎01380 728327   Fax 01380 728328
Email stock@sylvia-cordaiy.com
Website www.sylvia-cordaiy.com

Over 160 countries on file from the obscure to main stock images – Africa, North, Central and South America, Asia, Atlantic, Indian and Pacific Ocean islands, Australasia, Europe, polar regions. Covers travel, architecture, ancient civilisations, people worldwide, environment, wildlife, natural history, Antarctica, domestic pets, livestock, marine biology, veterinary treatment, equestrian, ornithology, flowers. UK files cover cities, towns villages, coastal and rural scenes, London collection. Transport, railways, shipping and aircraft (military and civilian). Aerial photography. Backgrounds and abstracts. Also the Paul Kaye B/W archive.

Country Collections
Unit 9, Ditton Priors Trading Estate,
Bridgnorth, Shropshire WV16 6SS
☎01746 712533   Fax 01746 861330
Contact *Robert Foster*

Small select collection of colour transparencies specialising in sundials, Celtic culture, villages, churches and ancient monuments. Assignments undertaken.

Country Images Picture Library
27 Camwood, Bamber Bridge, Preston,
Lancashire PR5 8LA
☎01772 321243   Fax 0870 137 8888
Email mail@countryimages.uk.net
Website www.countryimages.uk.net
Contact *Terry Marsh*

35mm and medium format colour coverage of landscapes and countryside features generally throughout the UK (Cumbria, North Yorkshire, Lancashire, southern Scotland, Isle of Skye, Scottish islands, Wales, Cornwall), France (French Alps, French Pyrenees, Provence) and Australia. Commissions undertaken.

Country Life Picture Library

King's Reach Tower, Stamford Street,
London SE1 9LS
☎020 7261 6337 Fax 020 7261 6216
Email camilla_costello@ipcmedia.com
Website www.clpicturelibrary.co.uk

Contact *Camilla Costello*

Over 150,000 b&w negatives dating back to
1897, and 80,000 colour transparencies. Country
houses, stately homes, churches and town houses
in Britain and abroad, interiors of architectural
interest (ceilings, fireplaces, furniture, paintings,
sculpture), and exteriors showing many land-
scaped gardens, sporting and social events, crafts,
people and animals. Visitors by appointment.
Open Tuesday to Friday.

Philip Craven
Worldwide Photo-Library

Surrey Studios, 21 Nork Way, Nork,
Banstead, Surrey SM7 1PB
☎0870 220 2121
Website www.philipcraven.com

Contact *Philip Craven*

Extensive coverage of British scenes, cities,
villages, English countryside, gardens, historic
buildings and wildlife. Worldwide travel and
wildlife subjects on medium- and large-format
transparencies.

CTC Picture Library

CTC Ltd, Longfield, Midhurst Road,
Fernhurst, Haslemere, Surrey GU27 3HA
☎01428 661441 Fax 01428 641071
Email mail@crightonthomascreative.com
Website www.crightonthomascreative.com

Contact *Vic Thomas*

One of the biggest specialist libraries in the UK
with 250,000 slides covering world and UK
agriculture, horticulture, and environmental
subjects. Also a small section on travel.

Cumbria Picture Library

See **Eric Whitehead Photography**

Sue Cunningham Photographic

56 Chatham Road, Kingston upon Thames,
Surrey KT1 3AA
☎020 8541 3024 Fax 020 8541 5388
Email pictures@scphotographic.com
Website www.scphotographic.com

Extensive coverage of many geographical areas:
South America (especially Brazil), Eastern
Europe from the Baltic to the Balkans, various

African countries, Western Europe including the
UK. Colour and b&w. Member of **BAPLA**.

Dalton–Watson Collection

See **The Ludvigsen Library Limited**

James Davis Travel Photography

65 Brighton Road, Shoreham, West Sussex
BN43 6RE
☎01273 452252 Fax 01273 440116
Email library@eyeubiquitous.com
Website www.eyeubiquitous.com

Travel collection: people, places, emotive scenes
and tourism. Constantly updated by James Davis
and a team of photographers, both at home and
abroad. Same-day service available.

The Defence Picture Library

8 Creykes Court, Craigie Drive, The
Millfields, Plymouth, Devon PL1 3JB
☎01752 401800/01752 312061
Fax 01752 402800
Email picdesk@defencepictures.com
Website www.defencepictures.com

Contacts *David Reynolds, Jessica Kelly, James
Rowlands, Andrew Chittock*

Leading source of military photography covering
all areas of the UK Armed Forces, supported by a
research agency of facts and figures. More than
500,000 images with a significant number on
CD-ROM. Campaigns in Aden, the Falklands,
Ulster, the Gulf and Kosovo. Specialist collections include the Chinese Armed Forces, US
Special Forces, as well as military units of Italy,
Spain and France. Visitors welcome by appointment.

Douglas Dickins Photo Library

2 Wessex Gardens, Golders Green, London
NW11 9RT
☎020 8455 6221

Sole Proprietor *Douglas Dickins, FRPS*

Worldwide colour and b&w coverage, specialising in Asia, particularly India, Indonesia and
Japan. *In Grandpa's Footsteps,* highly illustrated
book of world travel published by Book Guild
in 2000.

CM Dixon

The Orchard, Marley Lane, Kingston,
Canterbury, Kent CT4 6JH
☎01227 830075 Fax 01227 831135

Colour coverage of ancient civilisations,
archaeology and art, ethnology, mythology,
world religion, museum objects, geography,
geology, meteorology, landscapes, people and

places from many countries including most of Europe, former USSR, Ethiopia, Iceland, Jordan, Morocco, Sri Lanka, Tunisia, Turkey, Egypt, Uzbekistan.

Dominic Photography
4B Moore Park Road, London SW6 2JT
☎020 7381 0007 Fax 020 7381 0008

Contacts *Zoë Dominic, Catherine Ashmore*

Colour and b&w coverage of the entertainment world from 1957 onwards: dance, opera, theatre, ballet, musicals and personalities.

E&E Picture Library – Ecclesiastical and Eccentricities
Beggars Roost, Woolpack Hill, Brabourne Lees, Ashford, Kent TN25 6RR
☎01303 812608 Fax 01303 812608
Email isobel@picture-library.freeserve.co.uk
Website www.picture-library.freeserve.co.uk

Contact *Isobel Sinden*

Specialises in world religions, buildings, artifacts, clothes, festivals, clergy, arts, culture, history, pilgrimages, ancient stones, Bible lands, death and burial worldwide, ancient to modern. Curiosities such as follies, mazes, towers, pyramids. Also wind and water.

Patrick Eagar Photography
1 Queensberry Place, Richmond, Surrey TW9 1NW
☎020 8940 9269 Fax 020 8332 1229
Email patrick@patrickeagar.com
Website www.patrickeagar.com

The cricket library consists of Patrick Eagar's work over the last 30 years with coverage of over 250 Test matches worldwide, unique coverage of all seven World Cups, countless one-day internationals and player action portraits of over 2000 cricketers. The wine library consists of vineyards, grapes and festivals from Argentina to New Zealand. France and Australia are specialist areas. Photographs can be supplied by ISDN, on CD, prints and transparencies.

Ecoscene
The Oasts, Passfield, Liphook, Hampshire GU30 7RX
☎01428 751056 Fax 01428 751057
Email sally@ecoscene.com
Website www.ecoscene.com

Contact *Sally Morgan*

Expanding colour library of over 80,000 transparencies specialising in all aspects of the environment: pollution, conservation, recycling, restoration, wildlife (especially underwater), habitats, education, landscapes, industry and agriculture. All parts of the globe are covered with specialist collections covering Antarctica, Australia, North America. Sally Morgan, who runs the library, is a professional ecologist and expert source of information on all environmental topics. Photographic and writing commissions undertaken. Images delivered by post, on CD-ROM and by e-mail.

Edifice
14 Doughty Street, London WC1N 2PL
☎020 7242 0740 Fax 020 7267 3632
Email info@edificephoto.com
Website www.edificephoto.com

Contacts *Philippa Lewis, Gillian Darley*

Colour coverage of architecture, buildings of all possible descriptions, gardens, urban and rural landscape. *Specialises* in details of ornament, period style and material. British Isles, USA, Africa, Europe and Japan all covered. Detailed list available; visits by appointment. Website is searchable on line.

Education Photos
April Cottage, Warners Lane, Albury Heath, Guildford, Surrey GU5 9DE
☎01483 203846 Fax 01483 203846
Email johnwalmsley@educationphotos.co.uk
Website www.educationphotos.co.uk

Formerly the John Walmsley Photo Library. Specialist library of learning/training/working subjects. Comprehensive coverage of learning environments such as playgroups, schools, colleges and universities. Images reflect a multi-racial Britain. Commissions undertaken. Subject list and CD available on request.

English Heritage Photo Library
23 Savile Row, London W1S 2ET
☎020 7973 3338/9 Fax 020 7973 3027
Email celia.sterne@english-heritage.org.uk
Website www.english-heritage.org.uk

Contact *Celia Sterne*

Images of English castles, abbeys, houses, gardens, Roman remains, ancient monuments, battlefields, industrial and post-war buildings, interiors, paintings, artifacts, architectural details, conservation, archaeology, scenic views, landscapes.

Mary Evans Picture Library
59 Tranquil Vale, Blackheath, London SE3 0BS
☎020 8318 0034 Fax 020 8852 7211
Email lib@mepl.co.uk

Website www.mepl.co.uk

Collection of historical illustrations documenting social, political, cultural, technical, geographical and biographical themes from ancient times to the recent past (up to mid-20th century). Photographs, prints and ephemera backed by large book and magazine collection. Many special collections including Sigmund Freud, the **Women's Library** (women's rights), the paranormal, the Meledin Collection (20th-century Russian history) and individual photographers such as Roger Mayne and Grace Robertson. Recently acquired the Weimar Archive and Barnaby's Picture Library. Brochure sent on request. Compilers of the *Picture Researcher's Handbook* by Pira International.

Exile Images

1 Mill Row, West Hill Road, Brighton BN1 3SU
☎01273 208741 Fax 01273 382782
Email pics@exileimages.co.uk
Website www.exileimages.co.uk
Contact *Howard Davies*

Over 15,000 b&w and colour 35mm slides of refugees, asylum seekers, conflict, Third World development and daily life, UK protests, travel. CD-ROM available via the website to picture editors and researchers. Search and download high resolution pictures online.

Express Newspapers Syndication

Ludgate House, 245 Blackfriars Road, London SE1 9UX
☎020 7922 7884 Fax 020 7922 7871
Email syndication@express.co.uk
Manager *Adam Williams*

Two million images updated daily, with strong collections on personalities, royalty, showbiz, sport, fashion, nostalgia and events. Also includes the *OK! Magazine* collection. Electronic transmission available. Daily news and feature service.

Eye Ubiquitous

65 Brighton Road, Shoreham, East Sussex BN43 6RE
☎01273 440113 Fax 01273 440116
Email library@eyeubiquitous.com
Website www.eyeubiquitous.com
Contact *Stephen Rafferty*

General stock specialising in social documentary worldwide, including the work of Tim Page, and now incorporating the **James Davis Travel** library (see entry).

EyeWire

See **Getty Images**

Famous Pictures & Features Agency

13 Harwood Road, London SW6 4QP
☎020 7731 9333 Fax 020 7731 9330
Email info@famous.uk.com
Website www.famous.uk.com

Pictures and features agency with a growing library of interviews and colour transparencies dating back to 1985. Portrait, party and concert shots of rock and pop stars plus international entertainers, film and TV celebrities. The library is supplied by a team of photographers and journalists from the UK and around the world, keeping it up-to-date on a daily basis. 'We are always looking out for new writers who specialise in celebrity material.'

ffotograff

10 Kyveilog Street, Pontcanna, Cardiff CF11 9JA
☎029 2023 6879
Email ffotograff@easynet.co.uk
Website www.ffotograff.com
Contact *Patricia Aithie*

Library and agency specialising in travel, exploration, the arts, architecture, traditional culture, archaeology and landscape. Based in Wales but specialising in the Middle and Far East; Africa, Central and South America; Yemen and Wales are strong aspects of the library. Churches and cathedrals of Britain and Crusader castles.

Financial Times Pictures

One Southwark Bridge, London SE1 9HL
☎020 7873 3671 Fax 020 7873 4606
Email richard.pigden@ft.com

Photographs from around the world ranging from personalities in business, politics and the arts, people at work and other human interests and activities. 'FT Graphics are outstanding in their ability to make complex issues comprehensible.' Delivery via ISDN or e-mail.

Fine Art Photographic Library Ltd

2A Milner Street, London SW3 2PU
☎020 7589 3127 Fax 020 7584 1944
Email info@fineartphotolibrary.com
Website www.fineartphotolibrary.com
Contact *Linda Hammerbeck*

Over 30,000 large-format transparencies, with a specialist collection of 19th and 20th century paintings. CD-ROM available.

Firepix International
68 Arkles Lane, Anfield, Liverpool,
Merseyside L4 2SP
☎0151 260 0111/0777 5930419 (mobile)
Fax 0151 260 0111
Email info@firepix.com
Website www.firepix.com
Contact *Tony Myers*

The UK's only fire photo library. 23,000
images of fire-related subjects, firefighters, fire
equipment manufacturers. Website contains 15
categories from industrial fire, domestic, digital
images and abstract flame. Member of
BAPLA.

Fogden Wildlife Photographs
16 Locheport, North Uist, Western Isles
HS6 5EU
☎01876 580245 Fax 01876 580777
Email susan.fogden@virgin.net
Website www.fogdenphotos.com
Contact *Susan Fogden*

Natural history collection, with special reference to rain forests and deserts. Emphasis on
quality rather than quantity; growing collection of around 15,000 images.

Food Features
Farnham Forge, 5 Upper Church Lane,
Farnham, Surrey GU9 7PW
☎01252 735240 Fax 01252 735242
Email frontdesk@foodpix.co.uk
Website www.foodpix.co.uk
Contacts *Steve Moss, Alex Barker*

Specialised high-quality food and drink photography, features and tested recipes. Clients'
specific requirements can be incorporated into
regular shooting schedules.

FoodPix
See **Getty Images**

Christine Foord
Colour Picture Library
155B City Way, Rochester, Kent ME1 2BE
☎01634 847348 Fax 01634 847348

Specialist library with over 1000 species of
British and European wild flowers, plus garden
flowers, trees, indoor plants, pests and diseases,
mosses, lichen, cacti and the majority of larger
British insects.

Forest Life Picture Library
231 Corstorphine Road, Edinburgh EH12 7AT
☎0131 314 6411 Fax 0131 314 6285

Email neill.campbell@forestry.gsi/gov.uk
Website www.forestry.gov.uk/pictures
Contacts *Douglas Green, Neill Campbell*

The official image bank of the Forestry Commission, the library provides a single source for
all aspects of forest and woodland management.
The comprehensive subject list includes tree
species, scenic landscapes, employment, wildlife,
flora and fauna, conservation, sport and leisure.

Werner Forman Archive Ltd
36 Camden Square, London NW1 9XA
☎020 7267 1034 Fax 020 7267 6026
Email wfa@btinternet.com
Website www.werner-forman-archive.com

Colour and b&w coverage of ancient civilisations, oriental and primitive societies around
the world. A number of rare collections.
Searchable website.

Formula One Pictures
2013 Pomaz, Buzavirag U.6., Hungary
☎00 36 26 322 826
(Mobile +44 7905 819 555)
Email jt@f1pictures.com
Website www.f1pictures.com
Contacts *John Townsend, Erika Townsend*

500,000 35mm colour slides, b&w and colour
negatives of all aspects of Formula One grand
prix racing including driver profiles and portraits.

Robert Forsythe Picture Library
16 Lime Grove, Prudhoe, Northumberland
NE42 6PR
☎01661 834511 Fax 01661 834511
Email robert@forsythe.demon.co.uk
Website www.forsythe.demon.co.uk
Contacts *Robert Forsythe, Fiona Forsythe*

25,000 transparencies of industrial and transport
heritage; plus a unique collection of 70,000 items
of related publicity ephemera from 1945. Image
finding service available. Robert Forsythe is a
transport/industrial heritage historian and consultant. Nationwide coverage, particularly strong
on Northern Britain. A bibliography of published material is available.

Fortean Picture Library
Henblas, Mwrog Street, Ruthin LL15 1LG
☎01824 707278 Fax 01824 705324
Email janet.bord@forteanpix.demon.co.uk
Website www.forteanpix.demon.co.uk
Contact *Janet Bord*

30,000 colour and 45,000 b&w images: mysteries and strange phenomena worldwide, including

ghosts, UFOs, witchcraft and monsters; also antiquities, folklore and mythology. Subject list available.

The Fotomas Index
12 Pickhurst Rise, West Wickham, Kent BR4 0AL
☎020 8776 2772 Fax 020 8776 2236/2772
Contact *John Freeman*

General historical collection, mostly pre-1900. Subjects include London, topography, art, satirical, social and political history. Large portrait section.

The Francis Frith Collection
Frith's Barn, Teffont, Salisbury, Wiltshire SP3 5QP
☎01722 716376 Fax 01722 716881
Email john_buck@francisfrith.co.uk
Website www.francisfrith.co.uk
Contact *John Buck*

Publishers of *Frith's Photographic Memories* series of illustrated local books, all featuring nostalgic photographs from the archive, founded by Frith in 1860. The archive now contains over 360,000 images of 7000 British towns.

John Frost Newspapers
See entry under **Library Services**

Andrew N. Gagg's Photo Flora
Town House Two, Fordbank Court, Henwick Road, Worcester WR2 5PF
☎01905 748515
Email a.n.gagg@ntlworld.com
Website homepage.ntlworld.com/a.n.gagg/
    photo/photoflora.html

Specialist in British and European wild plants, flowers, ferns, grasses, trees, shrubs, etc. with colour coverage of most British and many European species (rare and common) and habitats; also travel in India, Sri Lanka, Nepal, Egypt, China, Mexico, Thailand, Tibet, Vietnam and Cambodia.

Galaxy Picture Library
34 Fennels Way, Flackwell Heath, High Wycombe, Bucks HP10 9BY
☎01628 521338 Fax 01628 520132
Email robin@galaxypix.com
Website www.galaxypix.com
Contact *Robin Scagell*

Specialises in astronomy, space, telescopes, observatories, the sky, clouds and sunsets. Composites

of foregrounds, stars, moon and planets prepared to commission. Editorial service available.

Garden and Wildlife Matters Photo Library
'Marlham', Henley's Down, Battle, East Sussex TN33 9BN
☎01424 830566 Fax 01424 830224
Email gardens@gmpix.com
Website www.gardenmatters.uk.com *and*
    www.gmpix.com
Contact *Dr John Feltwell*

Collection of 110,000 6×4″ and 35mm images. General gardening techniques and design; cottage gardens and USA designer gardens. 9000 species of garden plants and over 1000 species of trees. Flowers, wild and house plants, trees and crops. Environmental, ecological and conservation pictures, including sea, air, noise and freshwater pollution, SE Asian and Central and South American rainforests; Eastern Europe, Mediterranean. Recycling, agriculture, forestry, horticulture and oblique aerial habitat shots from Europe and USA. 24/7 service. Digital images supplied worldwide by ISDN.

Garden Picture Library
Unit 12, Ransome's Dock, 35 Parkgate Road, London SW11 4NP
☎020 7228 4332 (ISDN available on request)
Fax 020 7924 3267
Email info@gardenpicture.com
Website www.gardenpicture.com
Picture Research Manager *Lorraine Shill*

'Our inspirational images of gardens, plants and gardening lifestyle offer plenty of scope for writers looking for original ideas to write about.' The collection covers all garden related subjects; everything from plant portraits to floral graphics and garden design details to whole landscapes. Bringing together the work of over 150 professional photographers from across the gardening globe our Picture Editors select the very best images from each individual portfolio, creating an outstanding range of images by photographic style as well as subject for all possible media requirements. We hold approximately 400,000 fully captioned images of which around 15,000 are available digitally. In-house picture research can be undertaken on request or searches can be made online via keyword or subject category to create lightboxes which can be emailed or downloaded. Visitors to the library are welcome by appointment and copies of promotional literature are available on request.

Ed Geldard Photo Collection
9 Sunderland Bridge Village, Durham
DH6 5HB
☎0191 378 2592

Contact *Ed Geldard*

Approximately 20,000 colour transparencies
and b&w negs, all by Ed Geldard, specialising
in mountain landscapes: particularly the mountain regions of the Lake District; and the
Yorkshire limestone areas, from valley to sum-
mit. Commissions undertaken. Books published: *Wainwright's Tour of the Lake District*;
Wainwright in the Limestone Dales; *The Lake
District*.

Genesis Space Photo Library
Greenbanks, Robins Hill, Raleigh, Bideford,
Devon EX39 3PA
☎01237 471960 Fax 01237 472060
Email tim@spaceport.co.uk
Website www.spaceport.co.uk

Contact *Tim Furniss*

Contemporary and historical colour and b&w
spaceflight collection including rockets, space-
craft, spacemen, Earth, moon and planets.
Catalogue of 775 images on website.

Geo Aerial Photography
4 Christian Fields, London SW16 3JZ
☎020 8764 6292/0115 981 9418
Fax 020 8764 6292/0115 981 9418
Email geo.aerial@geo-group.co.uk
Website www.geo-group.co.uk

Contact *Kelly White*

Established 1990 and now a growing collection
of aerial oblique photographs from the UK,
Scandinavia, Asia and Africa – landscapes,
buildings, industrial sites, etc. Commissions
undertaken.

GeoScience Features
6 Orchard Drive, Wye, Kent TN25 5AU
☎01233 812707 Fax 01233 812707
Email gsf@geoscience.demon.co.uk
Website www.geoscience.demon.co.uk

Fully computerised and comprehensive library
containing the world's principal source of vol-
canic phenomena. Extensive collections, providing scientific detail with technical quality, of
rocks, minerals, fossils, microsections of botanical and animal tissues, animals, biology, birds,
botany, chemistry, earth science, ecology,
environment, geology, geography, habitats,
landscapes, macro/microbiology, peoples, sky,

weather, wildlife and zoology. Over 300,000
original colour transparencies in medium- and
35mm-format. Subject lists and CD-ROM
catalogue available on application. Incorporates
the RIDA photolibrary.

Geoslides Photography
4 Christian Fields, London SW16 3JZ
☎020 8764 6292/0115 981 9418
Fax 020 8764 6292/0115 981 9418
Email geoslides@geo-group.co.uk
Website www.geo-group.co.uk

Contact *John Douglas*

Established in 1968. Landscape and human
interest subjects from the Arctic, Antarctica,
Scandinavia, UK, Africa (south of Sahara),
Middle East, Asia (south and southeast); also
Australia, via Blackwoods Picture Library. Also
specialist collections of images from British
India (the Raj) and Boer War.

Getty Images
101 Bayham Street, London NW1 0AG
☎020 7544 2987 Fax 020 7544 3373
Email john.hagelin@gettyimages.com
Website www.gettyimages.com

Contact *Sales Dept.*

Hosts a variety of collections including The
Image Bank, EyeWire, FoodPix, Hulton
Archive, Illustration Works and Tony Stone
Images. With over 15 million images, Getty
Images is the largest picture resource in Europe
with coverage from ancient history through
the early years of photography up to the present day. As well as many old newspaper
archives, the extensive contemporary collections cover lifestyles, travel, science, business.

Getty Images News & Sport
116 Bayham Street, London NW1 0AG
☎0800 376 7981 Fax 020 7428 6175
Email europeannewsandsport@gettyimages.com
Website www.gettyimages.com

Getty Images News & Sport provides up-to-
the-minute imagery of the latest news, sport
and entertainment events as they unfold
around the world. 'Award winning photography distinguishes our imagery as we deliver
unique shots of moments that count in digital
format in real time. To receive a customised
experience on our site tailored to your exact
photography needs and publication style you
will need to register. Only then can you download high-resolution images and gain access to
the features on our site.'

Lynn Goldsmith
See **Corbis Images**

Martin and Dorothy Grace
40 Clipstone Avenue, Mapperley, Nottingham
NG3 5JZ
☎0115 920 8248   Fax 0115 962 6802
Email graces@lineone.net

Colour coverage of Britain's natural history,
specialising in trees, shrubs and wild flowers.
Also ferns, birds and butterflies, habitats, landscapes, ecology.

Ronald Grant Archive
See **The Cinema Museum**

Sally and Richard Greenhill
357 Liverpool Road, London N1 1NL
☎020 7607 8549   Fax 020 7607 7151
Email sr.greenhill@virgin.net
Website www.srgreenhill.co.uk

Photo Librarian *Denise Lalonde*

Social documentary photography in colour and
b&w of working lives: pregnancy and birth,
child development, education, work, old people,
medical, urban. Also Modern China, 1971 to the
present; most London statues. Some material
from Borneo, USA, India, Israel, Philippines and
Sri Lanka.

V.K. Guy Ltd
Silver Birches, Troutbeck, Windermere,
Cumbria LA23 1PN
☎015394 33519   Fax 015394 32971
Email vic@vk.guy.co.uk
Website www.vk.guy.co.uk

Contacts *Vic Guy, Pauline Guy, Mike Guy,
Paul Guy, Nicola Guy*

British landscapes and architectural heritage.
20,000 5x4" transparencies, suitable for tourism
brochures, calendars, etc. Colour catalogue
available.

Angela Hampton
'Family Life Picture Library'
Holly Tree House, The Street, Walberton,
Arundel, West Sussex BN18 0PH
☎01243 555952   Fax 01243 555952

Contact *Angela Hampton*

Over 50,000 transparencies on all aspects of
contemporary lifestyle, including pregnancy,
childbirth, babies, children, parenting, behaviour, education, medical, holidays, pets, family
life, relationships, teenagers, women and men's
health, over-50s and retirement. Also domestic

and farm animal life. Environmental and travel
pictures in 35mm. Commissions undertaken.
Offers fully illustrated text packages on most
subjects and welcomes ideas for collaboration
from writers with proven, successful background.

Tom Hanley
41 Harefield, Esher, Surrey KT10 9TG
☎020 8972 9165   Fax 020 8972 9164
Email Tomhanley31@hotmail.com

Colour and b&w coverage of London, England,
Europe, Canada, India, the Philippines, Brazil,
China, Japan, Korea, Taiwan, the Seychelles,
Cayman Islands, USA. Also pop artists of the
'60s, First World War trenches, removal of
London Bridge to America, and much more.
Current preoccupation with Greece, Turkey,
Spain and Egypt, ancient and modern.

Robert Harding Picture Library
58–59 Great Marlborough Street, London
W1F 7JY
☎020 7478 4000   Fax 020 7631 1070
Email info@robertharding.com
Website www.robertharding.com

A leading source of stock photography with
over two million colour images covering a wide
range of subjects – worldwide travel and culture,
geography and landscapes, people and lifestyle,
architecture, business and industry, medicine,
sports, food and drink. Rights protected and
royalty-free images. Can supply images as transparencies, on CD or ISDN. Visitors welcome;
telephone or visit the website.

Dennis Hardley Photography,
Scottish Photo Library
Rosslynn, Benderloch, Oban, Argyll PA37 1ST
☎01631 720434   Fax 01631 720434
Email dennis.hardley@btinternet.com *and*
info@scotphoto.com
Website www.scotphoto.com

Contacts *Dennis Hardley, Tony Hardley*

ESTABLISHED 1974. About 30,000 images
(6×7, 6×9 format colour transparencies) of
Scotland: castles, historic, scenic landscapes,
islands, transport, etc. Also English views –
Liverpool, Chester, Bath, Weston Super Mare,
Sussex, Somerset and Cambridge.

Jim Henderson
Photographer & Publisher
Crooktree, Kincardine O'Neil, Aboyne,
Aberdeenshire AB34 4JD
☎01339 882149   Fax 01339 882149

Email JHende7868@aol.com
Website www.jimhendersonphotography.com
Contact *Jim Henderson, AMPA, ARPS*

Scenic and general activity coverage of the north east Scotland/Grampian region and Highlands for tourist, holiday and activity illustration. Specialist collection of over 150 Aurora Borealis displays from 1989–2003 in Grampian and co-author of *The Aurora* (pub. 1997). Large collection of recent images of Egypt: Cairo through to Abu-Simbel. Commissions undertaken.

Heritage and Natural History Photographic Library

37 Plainwood Close, Summersdale, Chichester, West Sussex PO195YB
☎01243 533822 Fax 01243 533822
Contact *Dr John B. Free*

Specialises in insects (particularly bees and bee-keeping), tropical and temperate agriculture and crops, archaeology and history worldwide.

John Heseltine Archive

Mill Studio, Frogmarsh Mill, South Woodchester, Gloucestershire GL5 5ET
☎01453 873792 Fax 01453 873793
Email john@heseltine.co.uk
Website www.heseltine.co.uk
Contact *John Heseltine*

Over 200,000 colour transparencies and digital files of landscapes, architecture, food and travel with particular emphasis on Italy and the UK.

Christopher Hill Photographic Library

17 Clarence Street, Belfast BT2 8DY
☎028 9024 5038 Fax 028 9023 1942
Email ChrisHillPhotographic@btclick.com
Website www.scenicireland.com
Contact *Christopher Hill*

A comprehensive collection of landscapes of Northern Ireland, from Belfast to the Giant's Causeway, updated daily. Images of farming, food and industry. 'We will endeavour to supply images overnight.'

Hobbs Golf Collection

5 Winston Way, New Ridley, Stocksfield, Northumberland NE43 7RF
☎01661 842933 Fax 01661 842933
Email hobbs.golf@btinternet.com
Website www.hobbsgolfcollection.com

Contact *Michael Hobbs*

Specialist golf collection: players, courses, art, memorabilia and historical topics (1300–present). 40,000+ images – mainly 35mm colour transparencies and b&w prints. Commissions undertaken. Author of 30 golf books.

David Hoffman Photo Library

c/o BAPLA, 18 Vine Hill, London EC1R 5DZ
☎020 8981 5041 Fax 020 8980 2041
Email info@hoffmanphotos.com
Website www.hoffmanphotos.com
Contact *David Hoffman*

Commissioned photography and stock library with a strong emphasis on social issues built up from 35mm journalistic and documentary work dating from the late 1970s. Files on drugs and drug use, policing, disorder, riots, youth, protest, homelessness, housing, environmental demonstrations and events, waste disposal, alternative energy, industry and pollution. Wide range of images especially from UK and Europe but also USA, Canada, Venezuela, Mexico and Thailand. General files on topical issues and current affairs plus specialist files from leisure cycling to local authority services. Some photographs available for online delivery from www.alamy.com

Holt Studios International Ltd

The Courtyard, 24 High Street, Hungerford, Berkshire RG17 0NF
☎01488 683523 Fax 01488 683511
Email library@holt-studios.co.uk
Website www.holt-studios.co.uk
Director *Nigel Cattlin*

Specialist photo library covering world agriculture, horticulture, gardens and gardening from pictorial and technical aspects. Worldwide assignments undertaken.

Houghton's Horses/ Kit Houghton Photography

Radlet Cottage, Spaxton, Bridgwater, Somerset TA5 1DE
☎01278 671362 Fax 01278 671739
Email kit@enterprise.net
Website www.houghtonshorses.com
Contacts *Kit Houghton, Debbie Cook*

Specialist equestrian library of over 300,000 transparencies on all aspects of the horse world, with images ranging from the romantic to the practical, step-by-step instructional and competition pictures in all equestrian disciplines worldwide. Online picture delivery with ISDN facility.

Houses and Interiors

192 Goswell Road, London EC1V 7DT
☎020 7253 0991 Fax 020 7253 0992
Email anna@botanical.com
Website www.idspicturedesk.com
  (access by registration)

Manager *Anna Gibson*

Stylish house interiors and exteriors, home dossiers, renovations, architectural details, interior design, gardens, houseplants and cookery. Also step-by-step photographic sequences of DIY subjects and gardening techniques. Large format and 35mm. Member of **BAPLA**.

Chris Howes/
Wild Places Photography

51 Timbers Square, Cardiff CF24 3SH
☎029 2048 6557 Fax 029 2048 6557
Email photos@wildplaces.co.uk

Contacts *Chris Howes, Judith Calford*

Expanding collection of over 50,000 colour transparencies and b&w prints covering travel, topography and natural history worldwide, plus action sports such as climbing. *Specialist areas* include caves, caving and mines (with historical coverage using engravings and early photographs), wildlife, landscapes and the environment, including pollution and conservation. Europe (including Britain), USA, Africa and Australia are all well represented within the collection. Commissions undertaken.

Hulton Archive

See **Getty Images**

Hulton Deutsch

See **Corbis Images**

Huntley Film Archive

191 Wardour Street, London W1F 82E
☎020 7287 8000 Fax 020 7287 8001
Email films@huntleyarchives.com
Website www.huntleyarchives.com

Contact *Amanda Huntley*

Originally a private collection, the library is now a comprehensive archive of rare and vintage documentary film dating from 1895. 30,000–35,000 films on all subjects of a documentary nature, plus 50,000 feature film stills. Hollywood and the British film studios plus a television archive of rare stills and films. Online catalogue available.

Jacqui Hurst

66 Richford Street, Hammersmith, London W6 7HP
☎020 8743 2315/07970 781336 (mobile)
Fax 020 8743 2315
Email jacquih@dircon.co.uk

Contact *Jacqui Hurst*

A specialist library of traditional and contemporary applied arts, regional food producers and markets. The photos form illustrated essays of how something is made and finish with a still life of the completed object. The collection is always being extended and a list is available on request. Commissions undertaken.

Hutchison Picture Library

118B Holland Park Avenue, London W11 4UA
☎020 7229 2743 Fax 020 7792 0259
Email library@hutchisonpic.demon.co.uk
Website www.hutchisonpictures.co.uk

Worldwide contemporary images from the straight-forward to the esoteric and quirky. With over half a million documentary colour photographs on file and more than 200 photographers continually adding new work, this is an ever-growing resource covering people, places, customs and faiths, agriculture, industry and transport. *Special collections* include the environment and climate, family life (including pregnancy and birth), ethnic minorities worldwide (including Disappearing World archive), conventional and alternative medicine, and music around the world. Search service available.

Illustrated London News
Picture Library

20 Upper Ground, London SE1 9PF
☎020 7805 5585 Fax 020 7805 5905
Email iln.pictures@ilng.co.uk
Website www.ilng.co.uk

Engravings, photographs and illustrations from 1842 to the present day, taken from magazines published by Illustrated Newspapers: *Illustrated London News*; *Graphic*; *Sphere*; *Tatler*; *Sketch*; *Illustrated Sporting and Dramatic News*; *Illustrated War News 1914–18*; *Bystander*; *Britannia & Eve*. Social history, London, Industrial Revolution, wars, travel. CD-ROM available. Visitors by appointment.

Illustration Works

See **Getty Images**

The Image Bank

See **Getty Images**

Images of Africa Photobank

11 The Windings, Lichfield, Staffordshire
WS13 7EX
☎01543 262898 Fax 01543 417154
Email info@imagesofafrica.co.uk
Website www.imagesofafrica.co.uk

Contact *Jacquie Shipton*
Owner *David Keith Jones, FRPS*

Over 135,000 images covering Botswana, Chad, Egypt, Ethiopia, Kenya, Lesotho, Madagascar, Malawi, Morocco, Namibia, Rwanda, South Africa, Swaziland, Tanzania, Uganda, Zaire, Zambia, Zanzibar and Zimbabwe. 'Probably the best collection of photographs of Kenya in Europe.' A wide range of topics are covered. Strong on African wildlife with over 80 species of mammals including many sequences showing action and behaviour. Popular animals like lions and elephants are covered in encyclopædic detail. More than 100 species of birds and many reptiles are included. Other strengths include National Parks and reserves, natural beauty, tourism facilities, traditional and modern people. Most work is by David Keith Jones, FRPS; several other photographers are represented. An attractive colour brochure is available. The Library offers next day delivery by post or same day by e-mail when requested.

ImageState Europe

Ramillies House, 1–2 Ramillies Street, London W1F 7LN
☎020 7734 7344 Fax 020 7287 3933
Email sales@imagestate.co.uk
Website www.imagestate.co.uk

Markets royalty free and rights protected images, footage, music and sound effects. Image and footage subjects include people and lifestyles, business and industry, sport, travel, nature and animals and more. Visit the website for details.

Imperial War Museum Photograph Archive

All Saints Annexe, Austral Street, London SE1 4SL
☎020 7416 5333 Fax 020 7416 5355
Email photos@iwm.org.uk
Website www.iwm.org.uk

A national archive of over six million photographs illustrating all aspects of 20th century conflict. Emphasis on the two world wars but includes material from other conflicts involving Britain and the Commonwealth. Majority of material is b&w, although holdings of colour material increases with more recent conflicts. Visitors welcome by appointment, Monday to Friday, 10.00 am. to 5.00 pm.

Infoterra

Arthur Street, Barwell, Leicestershire LE9 8GZ
☎01455 849214 Fax 01455 841785
Email davidread@infoterra-global.com
Website www.infoterra-global.com

Contact *David Read*

Leading supplier of earth observation data, including satellite imagery, aerial photography and airborne remote sensing.

International Photobank

Loscombe Barn Farmhouse, West Knighton, Dorchester, Dorset DT2 8LS
☎01305 854145 Fax 01305 853065
Email peter@internationalphotobank.co.uk
Website www.internationalphotobank.co.uk

Over 385,000 transparencies, mostly medium-format. Colour coverage of travel subjects: places, people, folklore, events. Assignments undertaken for guide books and brochure photography. ISDN digital service available for newspapers, magazines and other users.

Robbie Jack Photography

45 Church Road, Hanwell, London W7 3BD
☎020 8567 9616 Fax 020 8567 9616
Email robbie@robbiejack.com
Website www.robbiejack.com

Contact *Robbie Jack*

Built up over the last 20 years, the library contains over 300,000 colour transparencies of the performing arts – theatre, dance, opera and music. Includes West End shows, the RSC and Royal National Theatre productions, English National Opera and Royal Opera. The dance section contains images of the Royal Ballet, English National Ballet, the Rambert Dance Company, plus many foreign companies. Also holds the largest selection of colour material from the Edinburgh International Festival. Researchers are welcome to visit by appointment. From 2001 we began offering our colour transparencies as digital images which are being added to on a daily basis.

Trevor Jones Thoroughbred Photography

The Hornbeams, 2 The Street, Worlington, Suffolk IP28 8RU
☎01638 713944 Fax 01638 713945
Email trevorjones@thoroughbredphoto.com
Website www.thoroughbredphoto.com

Contacts *Trevor Jones, Gill Jones, Laura Green*

Extensive library of high-quality colour transparencies depicting all aspects of thoroughbred horse racing dating from 1987. Major group races, English classics, studs, stallions, mares and foals, early morning scenes, personalities, jockeys, trainers and prominent owners. Also international work: USA Breeders Cup, Arc de Triomphe, French Classics, Irish Derby, Dubai racing scene, Japan Cup and Hokkaido stud farms; and more unusual scenes such as racing on the sands at low tide, Ireland, and on the frozen lake at St Moritz. Visitors by appointment.

Katz Pictures/FSP
109 Clifton Street, London EC2A 4LD
☎020 7749 6000 Fax 020 7749 6001
Email katzpictures@katzpictures.com
Website www.katzpictures.com
Contact *Sarah Bennett*

Contains an extensive collection of colour and b&w material covering a multitude of subjects from around the world – business, environment, industry, travel, lifestyles, politics plus celebrity portraits from the entertainment world. Also Hollywood portraits and film stills dating back to the twenties.

David King Collection
90 St Pauls Road, London N1 2QP
☎020 7226 0149 Fax 020 7354 8264
Email davidkingcollection@btopenworld.com
Contact *David King*

250,000 b&w original and copy photographs and colour transparencies of historical and present-day images. Russian history and the Soviet Union from 1900 to the fall of Khrushchev; the lives of Lenin, Trotsky and Stalin; the Tzars, Russo-Japanese War, 1917 Revolution, World War I, Red Army, the Great Purges, Great Patriotic War, etc. Special collections on China, Eastern Europe, the Weimar Republic, John Heartfield, American labour struggles, Spanish Civil War. Open to qualified researchers by appointment, Monday to Friday, 10.00 am to 6.00 pm. Staff will undertake research; negotiable fee for long projects. David King's latest photographic book, *The Commissar Vanishes*, documents the falsification of photographs and art in Stalin's Russia.

The Kobal Collection
2 The Quadrant, 135 Salusbury Road,
London NW6 6RJ
☎020 7624 3300 Fax 020 7624 3311
Email info@picture-desk.com

Website www.picture-desk.com

Colour and b&w coverage of Hollywood films: portraits, stills, publicity shots, posters, ephemera. Visitors by appointment.

Kos Picture Source Ltd
7 Spice Court, Ivory Square, Plantation Wharf, London SW11 3UE
☎020 7801 0044 Fax 020 7801 0055
Email images@kospictures.com
Website www.kospictures.com

Specialists in water-related images including international yacht racing and cruising, classic boats and superyachts, and extensive range of watersports. Also worldwide travel including seascapes, beach scenes, underwater photography and the weather.

Ed Lacey Collection
See **Phil Sheldon Golf Picture Library**

Frank Lane Picture Agency Ltd
Pages Green House, Wetheringsett,
Stowmarket, Suffolk IP14 5QA
☎01728 860789 Fax 01728 860222
Email pictures@flpa-images.co.uk
Website www.flpa-images.co.uk

Colour and b&w coverage of natural history, environment, pets and weather. Represents Sunset from France, Foto Natura from Holland, Minden Pictures from the US and works closely with Eric and David Hosking, plus 270 freelance photographers.

Last Resort Picture Library
Manvers Studios, 12 Ollerton Road, Tuxford,
Newark, Nottinghamshire NG22 0LF
☎01777 870166 Fax 01777 871739
Email LRPL@dmimaging.co.uk
Website www.dmimaging.co.uk
Contact *Jo Makin*

Subject areas include agriculture, architecture, computing, education, food, industry, landscape, people at work, skiing, trees, flowers. Images cover a wide variety of topics rather than specialising, ranging from the everyday to the obscure. Bespoke service available through our linked photographic studio. Contact us for details

LAT Photographic
Somerset House, Somerset Road, Teddington TW11 8RU
☎020 8251 3000 Fax 020 8251 3001
Email lat.photo@haynet.com
Website www.latphoto.co.uk

Motor sport collection of over nine million images dating from 1895 to the present day.

André Laubier Picture Library

4 St James Park, Bath BA1 2SS
☎01225 420688 Fax 01225 420688

An extensive library of photographs from 1935 to the present day in 35mm and medium-format. Main subjects are: archaeology and architecture, art and artists (wood carving, sculptures, contemporary glass), botany, historical buildings, sites and events, landscapes, nature, leisure sports, events, experimental artwork and photography, people and travel. Substantial stock of many other subjects including: birds, buildings and cities, folklore, food and drink, gardens, transport. Special collection: Images d'Europe (Austria, Britain, France, Greece, S.W. Ireland, Italy, Spain, Turkey, Egypt – from Cairo to Abu Simbel, Norway and former Yugoslavia). Africa and Kenyan safari. Private collection: World War II to D-Day. List available on request. Correspondence welcome in English, French or German.

Lebrecht Music Collection

58b Carlton Hill, London NW8 0ES
☎020 7625 5341/7372 8233
Fax 020 7625 5341
Email pictures@lebrecht.co.uk
Website www.lebrecht.co.uk

Contact *Elbie Lebrecht*

50,000 prints and transparencies covering music, from antiquity to 21st century minimalists. Instruments, opera singers, concert halls and opera houses, composers and musicians jazz and rock plus historical and social context images. High resolution imagery download from website.

The Erich Lessing Archive of Fine Art & Culture

c/o ak-images London Ltd, The Arts and History Picture Library, 5 Melbray Mews, 158 Hurlingham Road, London SW6 3NS
☎020 7610 6103 Fax 020 7610 6125
Email enquiries@akg-images.co.uk
Website www.akg-images.co.uk

Archive of large-format transparencies depicting the contents of many of the world's finest art galleries as well as ancient archaeological and biblical sites. High resolution scans available via ISDN. Mac and PC-compatible CD-ROMs. Represented by **AKG Images Ltd**.

Life File Ltd

26 Ambleside Drive, Oxford OX3 0AQ
Fax 020 8672 8879
Contact *Simon Taylor*

300,000 images of people and places, lifestyles, industry, environmental issues, natural history and customs, from Afghanistan to Zimbabwe. Stocks most of the major tourist destinations throughout the world, including the UK.

Lindley Library, Royal Horticultural Society

80 Vincent Square, London SW1P 2PE
☎020 7821 3053 Fax 020 7821 3051

Contact *Picture Librarian*

20,000 original drawings and approx. 8000 books with hand-coloured plates of botanical illustrations. Appointment is absolutely essential; all photography is done by own photographer.

Link Picture Library

33 Greyhound Road, London W6 8NH
☎020 7381 2261/2433 Fax 020 7385 6244
Email lib@linkpicturelibrary.com
Website www.linkpicturelibrary.com

Contact *Orde Eliason*

100,000 images of South Africa, India, China, Vietnam and Israel. A more general collection of colour transparencies from 100 countries worldwide. Link Picture Library has an international network and can source material not in its file from Japan, Scandinavia, India and South Africa. Original photographic commissions undertaken.

London Aerial Photo Library

PO Box 25, Ashwellthorpe, Norwich, Norfolk NR16 1HL
☎01508 488320 Fax 01508 488282
Email aerialphotos@btinternet.com
Website www.londonaerial.co.uk

Contact *Sandy Stockwell*

100,000 colour negatives of aerial photographs covering most of Britain, with particular emphasis on London and surrounding counties. No search fee. E-mailed library prints are supplied free of charge to enquirers. Welcomes enquiries in respect of either general subjects or specific sites and buildings.

The London Film Archive

78 Mildmay Park, Islington, London N1 4PR
☎020 7923 4074 Fax 020 7241 4929
Email info@londonfilmarchive.org
Website www.londonfilmarchive.org

Contact *Robert Dewar*

Archive which concentrates on all aspects of commercial, political and social life in the City and suburbs of London. The collection is primarily a film collection but also has stills, glass plate negatives, posters, advertising and documents of London interest.

London Metropolitan Archives

40 Northampton Road, London
EC1R 0HB
☎020 7332 3820 Fax 020 7833 9136
Email ask.lma@corpoflondon.gov.uk
Website www.cityoflondon.gov.uk

Contact *The Senior Librarian*

London Metropolitan Archives (LMA) is the largest local authority record office in the United Kingdom. 'There are 32 miles of archives in our strongrooms – an enormous amount of information about the capital and its people. We hold records of London government, hospitals, charities, businesses and parish churches. We have books, documents, photographs, maps and drawings. Nearly 900 years of London history can be brought to life at LMA.' There is also a 100,000 volume reference library specialising in London history. See entry under **Library Services**.

London's Transport Museum Photographic Library

39 Wellington Street, London WC2E 7BB
☎020 7379 6344 Fax 020 7565 7252
Website www.ltmuseum.co.uk

Contacts *Hugh Robertson, Simon Murphy*

Around 100,000 b&w images from the 1860s and 20,000 colour images from c.1975. *Specialist collections* Poster archive, Underground construction, corporate design and architecture, street scenes, London Transport during the war. Collection available for viewing by appointment on Monday and Tuesday. No loans system but prints and transparences can be purchased. Digital images available on CD-ROM.

Lonely Planet Images

See **Lonely Planet Publications** under **UK Publishers**

Ludvigsen Library Limited

Scoles Gate, Hawkendon, Bury St Edmunds, Suffolk IP29 4AU
☎01284 789246 Fax 01284 789246
Email library@ludvigsen.com *or*
  karlcars@btinternet.com

Website www.ludvigsen.com

Contact *Karl Ludvigsen*

Extensive information research facilities for writers and publishers. Approximately 400,000 images (both b&w and many colour transparencies) of automobiles and motorsport, from 1890s through 1980s. Glass plate negatives from the early 1900s; Formula One, Le Mans, motor car shows, vintage, antique and classic cars from all countries. Includes the Dalton–Watson Collection and the work of noted photographers such as John Dugdale, Edward Eves, Peter Keen, Max le Grand, Karl Ludvigsen, Rodolfo Mailander, Ove Nielsen, Stanley Rosenthall and others.

MacQuitty International Photographic Collection

7 Elm Lodge, River Gardens, Stevenage Road, London SW6 6NZ
☎020 7385 5606 Fax 020 7385 5606
Email miranda.macquitty@btinternet.com

Contact *Dr Miranda MacQuitty*

Colour and b&w collection on aspects of life in over 70 countries: dancing, music, religion, death, archaeology, buildings, transport, food, drink, nature. Visitors by appointment.

Magnum Photos Ltd

Moreland Buildings, 2nd Floor, 5 Old Street, London EC1V 9HL
☎020 7490 1771 Fax 020 7608 0020
Email magnum@magnumphotos.co.uk
Website www.magnumphotos.com

Head of Library *Hamish Crooks*

FOUNDED 1947 by Cartier Bresson, George Rodger, Robert Capa and David 'Chim' Seymour. Represents over 50 of the world's leading photo-journalists. Coverage of all major world events from the Spanish Civil War to present day. Also a large collection of personalities.

The Raymond Mander & Joe Mitchenson Theatre Collection

Jerwood Library of the Performing Arts, Trinity College of Music, King Charles Court, Old Royal Naval College, London SE10 9JF
☎020 8305 4426 Fax 020 8305 3993
Email rmangan@tcm.ac.uk
Website www.mander-and-mitchenson.co.uk

Contact *Richard Mangan*

Enormous collection covering all aspects of the theatre: plays, actors, dramatists, music hall, theatres, singers, composers, etc. Visitors welcome by appointment.

S&O Mathews Photography
Solent Cottage, High Street, Yarmouth, Isle of Wight PO41 0PN
☎01983 761983 Fax 01983 761982
Email oliver@mathews-photography.com
Website www.mathews-photography.com
Library of colour transparencies of gardens, plants and landscapes.

Institution of Mechanical Engineers
1 Birdcage Walk, London SW1H 9JJ
☎020 7973 1265 Fax 020 7222 8762
Email k_moore@imeche.org.uk
Website www.imeche.org.uk
Senior Librarian & Archivist *Keith Moore*
Historical and contemporary images on mechanical engineering. Open 9.15 am to 5.30 pm, Mon. to Fri. Telephone for appointment.

Meledin Collection
See **Mary Evans Picture Library**

The MerseySlides Collection
c/o Tropix Photo Library, 156 Meols Parade, Meols, Wirral CH47 6AN
☎0151 632 1698 Fax 0151 632 1698
Email tropixphoto@talk21.com
Website www.tropix.co.uk
Contact *Veronica Birley*
The MerseySlides Collection comes from **Tropix Photo Library** and contains powerful images of Liverpool, Merseyside, Wirral, Cheshire and much of North West England. Also North Wales, Scotland, other parts of England, Ireland and some Europe. Assignment and studio photography are regularly undertaken for a wide range of clients, both commercial and editorial. Photography is available in all formats including digital and panoramic.

Lee Miller Archives
Farley Farm House, Chiddingly, Near Lewes, East Sussex BN8 6HW
☎01825 872691 Fax 01825 872733
Email archives@leemiller.co.uk
Website www.leemiller.co.uk
The work of Lee Miller (1907–77). As a photo-journalist she covered the war in Europe from early in 1944 to VE Day with further reporting from the Balkans. Collection includes photographic portraits of prominent Surrealist artists: Ernst, Eluard, Miró, Picasso, Penrose, Carrington, Tanning, and others. Surrealist and contemporary art, poets and writers, fashion, the Middle East, Egypt, the Balkans in the 1930s, London during the Blitz, war in Europe and the liberation of Dachau and Buchenwald.

Mirrorpix
22nd Floor, 1 Canada Square, Canary Wharf, London E14 5AP
☎020 7293 3700 Fax 020 7293 2712
Email desk@mirrorpix.com
Website www.mirrorpix.com
General Manager *John Churchill*
'For the past 100 years the skilled photographers of the *Daily Mirror* and her sister titles have documented both the light and dark sides of British life, in startling detail. The stories of the people, places, events and movements that have shaped modern Britain can be found within this impressive and comprehensive catalogue. The full range of British life is expressed in perhaps the most significant photographic archive ever assembled within the UK.'

Monitor Picture Library
The Forge, Roydon, Harlow, Essex CM19 5HH
☎01279 792700 Fax 01279 792600
Email info@monitorpicturelibrary.com
Website www.monitorpicturelibrary.com
Colour and b&w coverage of leading international personalities. Politics, entertainment, royals, judicial, commerce, religion, trade unions, well-known buildings. Also an archive library dating back to 1840, and a specialist file on Lotus cars. Syndication to international, national and local media.

Moroccan Scapes
Seend Park, Seend, Wiltshire SN12 6NZ
☎01380 828533 Fax 01380 828630
Email chris@morocco-travel.com
Website www.realmorocco.com
Contact *Chris Lawrence*
Specialist collection of Moroccan material: scenery, towns, people, markets and places, plus the Atlas Mountains. Over 18,000 images.

Motoring Picture Library
National Motor Museum, Beaulieu, Hampshire SO42 7ZN
☎01590 614656 Fax 01590 612655
Email motoring.pictures@beaulieu.co.uk
Website www.alamay.com/mpl *and*
   www.heritage-images.com
Contact *Jonathan Day*
Three-quarters of a million b&w images, plus

90,000 colour transparencies covering all forms of motoring history from the 1880s to the present day. Commissions undertaken. Own studio.

Mountain Camera
See **John Cleare**

Moving Image Communications
61 Great Titchfield Street, London W1W 7PP
☎020 7580 3300 Fax 020 7580 2242
Email mail@milibrary.com
Website www.milibrary.com

Contact *Nathalie Banaigs*

Over 11,350 hours of quality archive and contemporary footage, including: Channel X Communications; TVAM Archive 1983–92; Leo & Mandy Dickinson Action & Adventure Sports Archive; The Lonely Planet (TV travel series); Shark Bay Films (tropical and sub-aqua); British Tourist Authority – BTA (1930 to present day); TIDA Public Information Films (BTA's predecessor); Buff Films (aviation archive/NATO planes and ships); Drummer Films (travel classics, 1950–70); Universal Newsreels (1950s-60s); The Freud Archive (1930–39); Natural World; Stockshots (time-lapse, cityscapes, land and seascapes, chroma-key); Space Exploration (NASA); Wild Islands; Flying Pictures; National Trust.

Museum of Antiquities Picture Library
University and Society of Antiquaries of Newcastle upon Tyne, Newcastle upon Tyne NE1 7RU
☎0191 222 7846 Fax 0191 222 8561
Email m.o.antiquities@ncl.ac.uk
Website www.ncl.ac.uk/antiquities

Contact *Lindsay Allason-Jones*

25,000 images, mostly b&w, of special collections including: Hadrian's Wall Archive (b&ws taken over the last 100 years); Gertrude Bell Archive (during her travels in the Near East, 1900–26); and aerial photographs of archaeological sites in the North of England. Visitors welcome by appointment.

Museum of London Picture Library
150 London Wall, London EC2Y 5HN
☎020 7814 5604 Fax 020 7600 1058
Email picturelib@museumoflondon.org.uk

The Museum of London Picture Library tells the story of London from its earliest settlers to the present day. Suffragettes: photographs and

memorabilia; Museum Objects: gallery and reserve collections – Prehistoric, Roman, Saxon, Medieval, Tudor, Stuart, Georgian, Victorian, London Now; Photographs: social history of the capital – working life, East End, inter-war years, the Blitz, post-war; Prints and Caricatures: political and social satire, architecture; Paintings: dating from the 17th century, portraits, landscapes, cityscapes.

National Galleries of Scotland Picture Library
The Dean Gallery, Belford Road, Edinburgh EH4 3DS
☎0131 624 6258/6260 Fax 0131 623 7135
Email picture.library@nationalgalleries.org

Contact *Deborah Hunter*

Over 80,000 b&w and several thousand images in colour of works of art from the Renaissance to present day. Specialist subjects cover fine art (painting, sculpture, drawing), portraits, Scottish, historical, still life, photography and landscape. Colour leaflet, scale of charges and application forms available on request.

National Maritime Museum Picture Library
Greenwich, London SE10 9NF
☎020 8312 6631/6704 Fax 020 8312 6533
Email picturelibrary@nmm.ac.uk
Website www.nmm.ac.uk

Contacts *David Taylor, Lucy Waitt*

Over three million maritime-related images and artefacts, including oil paintings from the 16th century to present day, prints and drawings, historic photographs, plans of ships built in the UK since the beginning of the 18th century, models, rare maps and charts, instruments, etc. Over 50,000 items within the collection are now photographed and with the Historic Photographs Collection form the basis of the picture library's stock.

National Meteorological Library and Archive
See entry under **Library Services**

National Monuments Record
National Monuments Record Centre, Kemble Drive, Swindon, Wiltshire SN2 2GZ
☎01793 414600 Fax 01793 414606
Email nmrinfo@english-heritage.org.uk
Website www.english-heritage.org.uk

The National Monuments Record is the first

stop for photographs and information on England's heritage. Over 10 million photographs, documents and drawings are held. English architecture from the first days of photography to the present, air photographs covering every inch of England from the first days of flying to the present, and archaeological sites. The record is the public archive of English Heritage. The London office specialises in the architecture of the capital city – for more information e-mail (nmrlondon@english-heritage. org.uk) or phone 020 7208 8200.

National Portrait Gallery Picture Library

St Martin's Place, London WC2H 0HE
☎020 7312 2474/5/6 Fax 020 7312 2464
Email picturelibrary@npg.org.uk
Website www.npg.org.uk

Contact *Tom Morgan*

Access to portraits of famous British men and women dating from the middle ages to the present. Images can be searched, viewed and ordered on the website.

National Railway Museum Picture Library

Leeman Road, York YO26 4XJ
☎01904 621261 Fax 01904 611112
Email nrm@nmsi.ac.uk
Website www.nrm.org.uk

1.5 million images, mainly b&w, covering every aspect of railways from 1850s to the present day. Visitors by appointment.

The National Trust Photo Library

36 Queen Anne's Gate, London SW1H 9AS
☎020 7447 6788/9 Fax 020 7447 6767
Email photolibrary@ntrust.org.uk
Website www.nationaltrust.org.uk/
 photolibrary

Contact *Chris Lacey*

Collection of mixed-format transparencies covering landscape and coastline throughout England, Wales and Northern Ireland; also architecture, interiors, gardens, paintings and conservation, plus a new collection of wildlife photographs. Award-winning brochure available on request. Profits from the picture library are reinvested in continuing the work of the Trust.

Natural History Museum Picture Library

Cromwell Road, London SW7 5BD
☎020 7942 5401/5324 Fax 020 7942 5443

Email nhmpl@nhm.ac.uk
Website www.nhm.ac.uk/piclib

Contacts *Hillary Smith, Dawn Hathaway*

Pictures from the Museum's collections, including dinosaurs, man's evolution, extinct species and fossil remains. Also pictures of gems, minerals, birds and animals, plants and insect specimens, plus historical artworks depicting the natural world.

Natural History Photographic Agency

See **NHPA**

Natural Science Photos

33 Woodland Drive, Watford, Hertfordshire WD17 3BY
☎01923 245265 Fax 01923 246067

Colour coverage of natural history subjects worldwide. The work of some 150 photographers, it includes angling, animals, birds, reptiles, amphibia, fish, insects and other invertebrates, habitats, plants, fungi, geography, weather, scenics, horticulture, agriculture, farm animals and registered dog breeds. Researched by experienced scientists, Peter and Sondra Ward. Visits by appointment. Commissions undertaken.

Nature Photographers Ltd

West Wit, New Road, Little London, Tadley, Hampshire RG26 5EU
☎01256 850661 Fax 01256 851157
Email info@naturephotographersco.uk
Website www.naturephotographers.co.uk

Contact *Dr Paul Sterry*

Over 150,000 images on worldwide natural history and environmental subjects. The library is run by a trained biologist and experienced author on his subject.

Nature Picture Library

BBC Broadcasting House, Whiteladies Road, Bristol BS8 2LR
☎0117 974 6720 Fax 0117 923 8166
Email info@naturepl.com
Website www.naturepl.com

Contact *Helen Gilks*

A collection of 120,000 transparencies of wildlife from around the world, especially animal portraits and behaviour. Other subjects covered include plants, landscapes, environmental issues and photos relating to the making of the BBC natural history films. Thousands of images can be viewed online and downloaded for reproduction.

Peter Newark's Picture Library
3 Barton Buildings, Queen Square, Bath
BA1 2JR
☎01225 334213 Fax 01225 480554

Over one million images covering world history from ancient times to the present day. Includes an extensive military collection of photographs, paintings and illustrations. Also a special collection on American history covering Colonial times, exploration, social, political and the Wild West and Native-Americans in particular. Subject list available. Telephone, fax or write for further information.

NHPA (Natural History Photographic Agency)
Little Tye, 57 High Street, Ardingly,
West Sussex RH17 6TB
☎01444 892514 Fax 01444 892168
Email nhpa@nhpa.co.uk
Website www.nhpa.co.uk

Library Manager *Tim Harris*

Extensive coverage on all aspects of natural history – animals, plants, landscapes, environmental issues, gardens and pets. Over 150 photographers worldwide provide a steady input of high-quality images. Specialist files include the unique high-speed photography of Stephen Dalton, extensive coverage of African and American wildlife, also rainforests, marine life and the polar regions. UK agents for the ANT collection of Australasian material. Loans are generally made direct to publishers; individual writers must request material via their publisher. See our website to view over 10,000 pictures.

Odhams Periodicals Library
See **Popperfoto**

Offshoot
See **Skishoot**

Only Horses Picture Agency
27 Greenway Gardens, Greenford, Middlesex
UB6 9TU
☎020 8578 9047 Fax 020 8575 7244
Email onlyhorsespics@aol.com
Website www.onlyhorsespictures.com

Colour and b&w coverage of all aspects of the horse. Foaling, retirement, racing, show jumping, eventing, veterinary, polo, breeds, personalities.

Oxford Picture Library
15 Curtis Yard, North Hinksey Lane, Oxford
OX2 0LX
☎01865 723404 Fax 01865 725294
Email opl@cap-ox.com
Website www.cap-ox.co.uk

Contacts *Chris Andrews, Annabel Webb*

Specialist collection on Oxford: the city, university and colleges, events, people, spires and shires. Also, the Cotswolds, architecture and landscape from Stratford-upon-Avon to Bath; the Thames and Chilterns, including Henley on Thames and Windsor; Channel Islands, especially Guernsey and Sark. Aerial views of all areas specified above. General collection includes wildlife, trees, plants, clouds, sun, sky, water and teddy bears. Commissions undertaken.

Oxford Scientific Films Photo Library
Lower Road, Long Hanborough, Oxfordshire
OX29 8LL
☎01993 881881 Fax 01993 882808
Email photo.library@osf.uk.com
Website www.osf.uk.com

Head of Film & Photo Library *Suzanne Aitzetmuller*
Account Managers *Arnaud Letresor, Rebecca Warren, Ruth Blair*

Collection of 350,000 colour transparencies and digital files of wildlife and natural science images supplied by over 300 photographers worldwide, covering all aspects of wildlife plus landscapes, weather, seasons, plants, environment, anthropology, habitats, industry, space, creative textures and backgrounds, and geology. Macro and micro photography. UK agents for Animals Animals, USA, Okapia, Germany and Dinodia, India. Research by experienced researchers for specialist and creative briefs. Visits welcome, by appointment.

PA Photos
PA News Centre, 292 Vauxhall Bridge Road,
London SW1V 1AE
☎020 7963 7990 Fax 020 7963 7066
Email paphotos@pa.press.net
Website www.paphotos.com

PA Photos is the photographic agency of the Press Association, the national news agency of the UK and Ireland. Therefore it is the comprehensive resource for news, entertainment, celebrity and sport images from the UK and across the globe. Photographs date from 1890 to the present day.

Hugh Palmer

21 Walton House, Oxford OX1 2JG
Email hugh@hughpalmer.com
Website www.hughpalmer.com

Extensive collection of landscapes, rural life and architecture from Britain and Europe, as featured in *The Most Beautiful Villages* series of books published by Thames & Hudson.

Panos Pictures

Studio 3b, 38 Southwark Street, London
SE1 1UN
☎020 7234 0010 Fax 020 7357 0094
Email pics@panos.co.uk
Website www.panos.co.uk

Documentary colour and b&w library specialising in Third World and Eastern Europe, with emphasis on environment and development issues. Leaflet available. Fifty per cent of all profits from this library go to the Panos Institute to further its work in international sustainable development.

Charles Parker Archive

See **Birmingham Library Services** under **Library Services**

Ann & Bury Peerless
Picture Library

St David's, 22 King's Avenue, Minnis Bay, Birchington-on-Sea, Kent CT7 9QL
☎01843 841428 Fax 01843 848321
Website www.peerlessimages.com

Contacts *Ann or Bury Peerless*

Specialist collection on world religions: Hinduism, Buddhism, Confucianism, Taoism, Jainism, Christianity, Islam, Sikhism, Zoroastrianism (Parsees of India). Geographical areas covered: India, Afghanistan (Bamiyan Valley of the Buddhas), Pakistan, Bangladesh, Sri Lanka, Cambodia (Angkor), Java (Borobudur), Bali, Thailand, Russia, Republic of China, Spain, Poland, Uzbekistan (Samarkand and Bukhara), Vietnam. Basis of collection (35mm colour transparencies), historical, cultural, extensive coverage of art (sculpture and miniature paintings), architecture including Pharaonic Egypt.

Photo Resources

The Orchard, Marley Lane, Kingston, Canterbury, Kent CT4 6JH
☎01227 830075 Fax 01227 831135

Colour and b&w coverage of archaeology, art, ancient art, ethnology, mythology, world religion, museum objects.

Photofusion

17A Electric Lane, London SW9 8LA
☎020 7733 3500 Fax 020 7738 5509
Email library@photofusion.org
Website www.photofusion.org

Contact *Liz Somerville*

Colour and b&w coverage of contemporary social and environmental UK issues including babies and children, disability, education, the elderly, environment, family, health, housing, homelessness, people and work. Brochure available.

The Photolibrary Wales

2 Bro-nant, Church Road, Pentyrch, Cardiff
CF15 9QG
☎029 2089 0311 Fax 029 2089 2650
Email info@photolibrarywales.com
Website www.photolibrarywales.com

Contacts *Steve Benbow, Kate Benbow*

Over 60,000 colour transparences covering all areas and subjects of Wales. Represents the work of 140 photographers, living and working in Wales.

Photos Horticultural

PO Box 105, Ipswich, Suffolk IP1 4PR
☎01473 257329 Fax 01473 233974
Email library@photos.keme.co.uk
Website www.photos-horticultural.co.uk

Wide coverage of gardens and all aspects of gardening from library established in 1968. Illustrated features to order. Commissions undertaken. 'Extensive travelling ensures the best material from around the world is on file.'

PictureBank Photo Library Ltd

Parman House, 30–36 Fife Road, Kingston upon Thames, Surrey KT1 1SY
☎020 8547 2344 Fax 020 8974 5652
Email info@picturebank.co.uk
Website www.picturebank.co.uk

Over 400,000 colour transparencies covering people (girls, couples, families, children), travel and scenic (UK and world), moods (sunsets, seascapes, deserts, etc.), industry and technology, environments and general. Commissions undertaken. Visitors welcome. Member of **BAPLA**. New material on medium/large format welcome.

Pictures Colour Library

10 James Whatman Court, Turkey Mill, Ashford Road, Maidstone, Kent ME14 5SS
☎01622 609809 Fax 01622 609806

Email Researcher@PicturesColourLibrary.co.uk
Website www.picturescolourlibrary.co.uk

Travel and travel-related images depicting lifestyles and cultures, people and places, attitudes and environments from around the world, including a comprehensive section on Great Britain.

H.G. Ponting
See **Popperfoto**

Popperfoto.com
The Old Mill, Overstone Farm, Overstone, Northampton NN6 0AB
☎01604 670670 Fax 01604 670635
Email enquiries@popperfoto.com
Website www.popperfoto.com

Home to over 14 million images, covering 150 years of photographic history. Renowned for its archival material, a world-famous sports library and stock photography. Popperfoto's credit line includes Reuters, Bob Thomas Sports Photography, UPI, Acme, INP, Planet, Paul Popper, Exclusive News Agency, Victory Archive, Odhams Periodicals Library, Illustrated, Harris Picture Agency, and H.G. Ponting which holds the Scott 1910–1912 Antarctic expedition. Colour from 1940, b&w from 1870 to the present. Major subjects covered worldwide include events, personalities, wars, royalty, sport, politics, transport, crime, history and social conditions. Material available on the same day to clients throughout the world. Mac-desk available. Researchers welcome by appointment. Free catalogue available.

PPL (Photo Agency) Ltd
Bookers Yard, The Street, Walberton, Arundel, West Sussex BN18 0PF
☎01243 555561 Fax 01243 555562
Email ppl@mistral.co.uk
Website www.pplmedia.com
Contacts *Barry Pickthall, Jo Bennett*

Two million pictures covering watersports, business and commerce, travel and tourism and a fast growing archive on Sussex and the home counties. Pictures available in high resolution directly from website.

Premaphotos Wildlife
Amberstone, 1 Kirland Road, Bodmin, Cornwall PL30 5JQ
☎01208 78258 Fax 01208 72302
Email authors@premaphotos.co.uk
Website www.premaphotos.co.uk

Contact *Jean Preston-Mafham, Library Manager*

Natural history worldwide. Subjects include flowering and non-flowering plants, fungi, slime moulds, fruits and seeds, galls, leaf mines, seashore life, mammals, birds, reptiles, amphibians, insects, spiders, habitats, scenery and cultivated cacti. Commissions undertaken. Visitors welcome. 'Make sure your name is on our mailing list to receive regular, colourful mailers.'

Professional Sport UK Ltd
18–19 Shaftesbury Quay, Hertford, Hertfordshire SG14 1SF
☎01992 505000 Fax 01992 505020
Email pictures@prosport.co.uk
Website www.professionalsport.com

Photographic coverage of tennis, soccer, athletics, golf, cricket, rugby, winter sports and many minor sports. Major international events including the Olympic Games, World Cup soccer and all Grand Slam tennis events. Also news and feature material supplied worldwide. Online photo archive; photo transmission services available for editorial and advertising.

Public Record Office Image Library
Ruskin Avenue, Kew, Richmond, Surrey TW9 4DU
☎020 8392 5225 Fax 020 8392 5266
Email image-library@pro.gov.uk
Contacts *Paul Johnson, Hugh Alexander*

British and colonial history from the Domesday Book to the 1960s, shown in photography, maps, illuminations, posters, advertisements, textiles and original manuscripts. Approximately 30,000 5x4″ and 35mm colour transparencies and b&w negatives. Open: 9.00 am to 5.00 pm, Monday to Friday.

Punch Cartoon Library
87–135 Brompton Road, London SW1X 7XL
☎020 7225 6710/6793 Fax 020 7225 6712
Email punch.library@harrods.com
Website www.punch.co.uk
Owner *Liberty Publishing*

Gives access to the 500,000 cartoons published in *Punch* magazine between 1841–1992. The library has a 500+ subject listing and can search on any topic. Social history, politics, fashion, fads, famous people and more by the world's most famous cartoonists, including Tenniel, du Maurier, Pont, Fougasse, E.H. Shepard and Emmett.

PWA International Ltd

City Gate House, 399–425 Eastern Avenue,
Gants Hill, Ilford, Essex IG2 6LR
☎020 8518 2057 Fax 020 8518 2241
Email pwaint@dircon.co.uk

Contact *Terry Allen*

Leading comprehensive library of story illustrations comprising work by some of the UK's best-known illustrators, including book covers and magazines. Also over half a million images of beauty, cookery and craft.

Railfotos

Millbrook House Ltd., Unit 1, Oldbury
Business Centre, Pound Road, Oldbury, West
Midlands B68 8NA
☎0121 544 2970
Fax 0121 253 6836 (quote Millbrook House)

One of the largest specialist libraries dealing with railway subjects worldwide. Colour and b&w dating from the turn of the century to present day. Up-to-date material on UK, South America and Far East. Visitors by appointment.

Redferns Music Picture Library

7 Bramley Road, London W10 6SZ
☎020 7792 9914 Fax 020 7792 0921
Email info@redferns.com
Website www.musicpictures.com

Music picture library covering every aspect of 18th century classical music to present day pop. Over 18,000 artists on file plus other subjects including musical instruments, recording studios, crowd scenes, festivals, etc. Brochure available.

Retna Pictures Ltd

West Complex, Pinewood Studios, Pinewood
Road, Iver Heath, Buckinghamshire SL0 0NH
☎01753 785450 Fax 01753 785 451
Email ukinfo@retna.com
Website www.retna.com

ESTABLISHED 1978, Retna Pictures Ltd is a leading picture agency with two libraries: celebrity and lifestyle. The former specialises in images of international and national celebrities, early and contemporary music, films and personalities. The lifestyle library specialises in people, family life, work, leisure and food. Both libraries are constantly receiving new material from established and up and coming photographers.

Rex Features Ltd

18 Vine Hill, London EC1R 5DZ
☎020 7278 7294 Fax 020 7696 0974
Email library@rexfeatures.com
Website www.rexfeatures.com

Contact *Glen Marks, Library Sales Manager*

Extensive picture library established in the 1950s. Daily coverage of news, politics, personalities, show business, glamour, humour, art, medicine, science, landscapes, royalty, etc.

Royal Air Force Museum

Grahame Park Way, Hendon, London
NW9 5LL
☎020 8205 2266 Fax 020 8200 1751
Email photographic@rafmuseum.com

Contact *Christine Gregory*

About a quarter of a million images, mostly b&w, with around 1500 colour in all formats, on the history of aviation. Particularly strong on the activities of the Royal Air Force from the 1870s to 1970s. Researchers are requested to enquire in writing only.

The Royal Collection, Photographic Services

Windsor Castle, Windsor, Berks SL4 1NJ
☎01753 868286 Fax 01753 620046
Email photoservices@royalcollection.org.uk

Contact *Shruti Patel*

Photographic material of items in the Royal Collection, particularly oil paintings, drawings and watercolours, works of art, and interiors and exteriors of royal residences. 35,000 colour transparencies, plus 25,000 b&w negatives.

Royal Geographical Society Picture Library

1 Kensington Gore, London SW7 2AR
☎020 7591 3060 Fax 020 7591 3061
Email pictures@rgs.org
Website www.rgs.org/picturelibrary

Contact *Joanna Wright*

A strong source of geographical and historical images, both archival and modern, showing the world through the eyes of photographers and explorers dating from the 1830s to the present day. The RGS Contempory Collection provides up-to-date transparencies from around the world, highlighting aspects of cultural activity, environmental phenomena, anthropology, architectural design, travel, mountaineering and exploration. Offers a professional and comprehensive service for both commercial and academic use.

RSPB Images

PO Box 7515, Billericay, Essex CM11 1WR
☎01268 71171 Fax 01268 710353
Email rspb@thatsgood.biz

Website www.rspb-images.com
Contact *Wendy Hollis*

Colour and b&w images of birds, butterflies, moths, mammals, reptiles and their habitats. Also colour images of all RSPB reserves. Growing selection of various habitats. Over 52,000 slides available digitally or in any desired format.

RSPCA Photolibrary

RSPCA Trading Limited, Wilberforce Way, Southwater, Horsham, West Sussex RH13 9RS
☎0870 754 0150 Fax 0870 753 0048
Email pictures@rspcaphotolibrary.com
Website www.rspcaphotolibrary.com

Photolibrary Manager *Andrew Forsyth*

Over 70,000 colour transparencies and over 5000 b&w/colour prints. A comprehensive collection of natural history images whose subjects include mammals, birds, domestic and farm animals, amphibians, insects and the environment, as well as a unique photographic record of the RSPCA's work. Also includes the Wild Images collections. Catalogue available. No search fees.

Russia and and Eastern Images

'Sonning', Cheapside Lane, Denham, Uxbridge, Middlesex UB9 5AE
☎01895 833508 Fax 01895 831957
Email easteuropix@btinternet.com
Website www.easteuropix.com

Architecture, cities, landscapes, people and travel images of Russia and the former Soviet Union. Considerable background knowledge available and Russian language spoken.

Peter Sanders Photography

24 Meades Lane, Chesham, Buckinghamshire HP5 1ND
☎01494 773674/771372 Fax 01494 773674
Email photos@petersanders.com
Website www.petersanders.com

Contacts *Peter Sanders, Hafsa Garwatuk*

Specialises in the world of Islam in all its aspects from culture, arts, industry, lifestyles, celebrations, etc. Areas included are north, east and west Africa, the Middle East (including Saudi Arabia), China, Asia, Europe and USA. A continually expanding library.

Science & Society Picture Library

Science Museum, Exhibition Road, London SW7 2DD
☎020 7942 4400 Fax 020 7942 4401

Email piclib@nmsi.ac.uk
Website www.nmsi.ac.uk/piclib/

Contact *Angela Murphy*

25,000 reference prints and 100,000 colour transparencies, incorporating many from collections at the Science Museum, the National Railway Museum and the National Museum of Photography, Film & Television. Collections illustrate the history of science, industry, technology, medicine, transport and the media. Plus three archives documenting British society in the twentieth century.

Science Photo Library

327–329 Harrow Road, London W9 3RB
☎020 7432 1100 Fax 020 7286 8668
Email info@sciencephoto.com
Website www.sciencephoto.com

Subjects covered include the human body, health and medicine, research, genetics, technology and industry, space exploration and astronomy, earth science, satellite imagery, environment, nature and wildlife and the history of science. The whole collection, more than 100,000 images, is available online.

Seaco Picture Library

Sea Containers House, 20 Upper Ground, London SE1 9PF
☎020 7805 5831 Fax 020 7805 5807
Email seaco.pictures@seacontainers.com

Contact *Maureen Elliott*

Approx. 250,000 images of containerisation, shipping, fast ferries, manufacturing, fruit farming, ports, hotels and leisure.

Mick Sharp Photography

Eithinog, Waun, Penisarwaun, Caernarfon, Gwynedd LL55 3PW
☎01286 872425 Fax 01286 872425
Email mick.jean@virgin.net

Contacts *Mick Sharp, Jean Williamson*

Colour transparencies (6×4.5cm and 35mm) and black & white prints (5×4" and 6×4.5cm negatives) of subjects connected with archaeology, ancient monuments, buildings, churches, countryside, environment, history, landscape, past cultures and topography from Britain and abroad. Photographs by Mick Sharp and Jean Williamson, plus access to other specialist collections on related subjects. Commissions undertaken.

Phil Sheldon Golf Picture Library

40 Manor Road, Barnet, Hertfordshire
EN5 2JQ
☎020 8440 1986 Fax 020 8440 9348
Email gill@philsheldongolfopics.co.uk *or*
  phil@philsheldongolfpics.co.uk

An expanding collection of over 500,000 quality images of the 'world of golf'. In-depth worldwide tournament coverage including every Major championship and Ryder Cup since 1976. Instruction, portraits, trophies and over 400 golf courses from around the world. Also the Dale Concannon collection covering the period 1870 to 1940, the classic 1960s collection by photographer Sidney Harris and the Ed Lacey Collection.

Skishoot–Offshoot

Hall Place, Upper Woodcott, Whitchurch,
Hampshire RG28 7PY
☎01635 255527 Fax 01635 255528
Email skishootsnow@aol.com
Website www.skishoot.co.uk
Contacts *Kate Parker, Jo Crossley*

Skishoot ski and snowboarding picture library has 400,000 images. Offshoot travel library specialises in France.

The Skyscan Photolibrary

Oak House, Toddington, Cheltenham,
Gloucestershire GL54 5BY
☎01242 621357 Fax 01242 621343
Email info@skyscan.co.uk
Website www.skyscan.co.uk

As well as the Skyscan Photolibrary collection of unique balloon's-eye views of Britain, the library now includes the work of photographers from across the aviation spectrum; air to ground, aviation, aerial sports – 'in fact, anything aerial!' Links have been built with photographers across the world; photographs can be handled on an agency basis and held in house, or as a brokerage where the collection stays with the photographer; terms 50/50 for both. Commissioned photography arranged. Enquiries welcome.

SMG Newspapers Ltd

200 Renfield Street, Glasgow G2 3PR
☎0141 302 7364 Fax 0141 302 7383
Email piclib@smg.plc.uk

Over six million images: b&w and colour photographs from *c.*1900 from the *Herald* (Glasgow) and *Evening Times*. Current affairs, Scotland, Glasgow, Clydeside shipbuilding and engineering, personalities, World Wars I and II, sport.

Snookerimages (Eric Whitehead Photography)

Postal Buildings, Ash Street, Bowness-on-Windermere, Cumbria LA23 3EB
☎015394 48894 Fax 015394 48294
Email eric@snookerimages.co.uk
Website www.snookerimages.co.uk

Over 20,000 images of snooker from 1982 to the present day. The agency covers local news events, PR and commercial material.

SOA Photo Library

Lovells Farm, Dark Lane, Stoke St Gregory,
Taunton, Somerset TA3 6EU
☎0870 333 6062 Fax 0870 333 6082
Email info@soaphotoagency.com
Website www.soaphotoagency.com
Contact *Sabine Oppenlander*

85,000 colour slides, 15,000 b&w photos covering *Stern* productions, sports, travel and geographic, advertising, social subjects. Representatives of Voller Ernst, Interfoto, Picture Press, Look and many freelance photographers. Free catalogues available.

Solo Syndication Ltd (trading as Atlantic Syndication)

17–18 Haywards Place, Clerkenwell, London
EC1R 0EQ
☎020 7566 0360 Fax 020 7566 0388
Syndication Director *Trevor York*
Sales *Danny Howell, Nick York*
Online transmissions *Geoff Malyon*
  (☎020 7566 0370)

Three million images from the archives of the *Daily Mail, Mail on Sunday, Evening Standard* and *Evening News*. Hard prints or Mac-to-Mac delivery. 24-hour service.

Sotheby's Picture Library

34-35 New Bond Street, London W1A 2AA
☎020 7293 5383 Fax 020 7293 5062
Email piclib.london@sothebys.com
Contact *Joanna Ling*

The library consists of over 200,000 selected transparencies of pictures sold at Sotheby's. Images from the 15th to the 20th century. Oils, drawings, watercolours, prints and decorative items. 'Happy to do searches or, alternatively, visitors are welcome by appointment.'

South American Pictures

48 Station Road, Woodbridge, Suffolk
IP12 4AT
☎01394 383963/380423 Fax 01394 380176

Email morrison@southamericanpictures.com
Website www.southamericanpictures.com *and
specialist site:* www.nonesuchinfo.info

Contact *Marion Morrison*

Colour and b&w images of South/Central America, Cuba, Mexico, New Mexico (USA), Dominican Republic and Haiti, including archaeology and the Amazon. There is an archival section, with pictures and documents from most countries. Now with 40 contributing photographers.

The Special Photographers Library

236 Westbourne Park Road, London
W11 1EL
☎020 7221 3489 Fax 020 7792 9112
Email info@specialphotographers.com
Website www.specialphotographers.com

Contacts *Chris Kewbank*

Represents over 100 contemporary fine art photographers who are unusual in style, technique or subject matter. The content could be anything!

The Still Moving Picture Co.

157 Broughton Road, Edinburgh EH7 4JJ
☎0131 557 9697 Fax 0131 557 9699
Email info@stillmovingpictures.com
Website www.stillmovingpictures.com

Contact *John Hutchinson*

Over 150,000 colour images of Scotland and sport. Scottish agents for **Allsport (UK) Ltd**. (Fully digitised service via www.stilldigital.co.uk)

Still Pictures' Whole Earth Photolibrary

199 Shooters Hill Road, Blackheath, London
SE3 8UL
☎020 8858 8307 Fax 020 8858 2049
Email info@stillpictures.com
Website www.stillpictures.com

Contacts *Kate Watson, Mark Edwards*

FOUNDED 1970, the library is a leading source of pictures illustrating the human impact on the environment, Third World development issues, industrial ecology, nature and wildlife, endangered species and habitats. 400,000 colour medium-format transparencies, 100,000 b&w prints. Over 400 leading photographers from around the world supply the library with stock pictures. Write, phone or fax for Still Pictures' Environment and Third World catalogue and Still Pictures' Nature and Wildlife catalogue.

Stockfile

5 High Street, Sunningdale, Berkshire
SL5 0LX
☎01344 872249 Fax 01344 872263
Email info@stockfile.co.uk
Website www.stockfile.co.uk

Contacts *Jill Behr, Steven Behr*

Specialist cycling collection with emphasis on mountain biking. Expanding adventure sports section covering snow, land, air and water activities.

Stockscotland Photo Library

Croft Roy, Crammond Brae, Tain, Ross-shire
IV19 1JG
☎01862 892298 Fax 01862 892298
Email info@stockscotland.com
Website www.stockscotland.com

Contact *Hugh Webster*

150,000 colour transparencies of Scotland. Not just a travel library; images cover industry, agriculture, fisheries and many other subjects. Submissions from photographers welcome. Commissions undertaken. Call for CD catalogue.

Sir John Benjamin Stone

See **Birmingham Library Services** under **Library Services**

Tony Stone Images

See **Getty Images**

Jessica Strang Photo Library

504 Brody House, Strype Street, Spitalfields,
London E1 7LQ
☎020 7247 8982 Fax 020 7247 8982
Email Jessica.Strang@virgin.net

Contact *Jessica Strang*

Approximately 60,000 transparencies covering architecture, interiors (contemporary), gardens, 'obsessive and not just small but tiny, or from almost no space at all', men, women, couples and animals in architecture, and vanishing London details. Recycled ideas for the home.

Joe Tasker Collection

See **Chris Bonington Picture Library**

Tate Enterprises Picture Library

20 John Islip Street, London SW1P 4LL
☎020 7887 8867 Fax 020 7887 8805
Email picture.library@tate.org.uk
Website www.tate.org.uk

Contact *Chris Webster*

Approximately 8000 images of British art from the 16th century; international 20th century painting and sculpture. Artists include William Blake, William Hogarth, J.M.W. Turner, Dante Gabriel Rossetti, Barbara Hepworth, Henry Moore, Stanley Spencer, Pablo Picasso, Mark Rothko, Salvador Dali, Lucien Freud and David Hockney. Colour transparencies of more than half the works in the main collection are available for hire. For a fee, new photography is available depending on the location and condition of the art work. B&w prints of nearly all the works in the collection can be purchased. Colour slides and prints can be made on request providing a colour transparency exists. Picture researchers must make an appointment to visit the library. All applications must be made by e-mail, fax or letter.

Bob Thomas Sports Photography
See **Popperfoto**

Rick Tomlinson
Marine Photo Library
18 Hamble Yacht Services, Port Hamble, Hamble, Southampton, Hampshire SO31 4NN
☎023 8045 8450 Fax 023 8045 8350
Email ricktom@compuserve.com
Website www.rick-tomlinson.com

Contacts *Rick Tomlinson*

ESTABLISHED 1985. *Specialises* in marine subjects. 100,000 35mm transparencies of yachting, racing, cruising, Whitbread Round the World Race, Volvo Ocean Race, Americas Cup, Tall Ships, RNLI Lifeboats, Antarctica, wildlife and locations.

Topham Picturepoint
PO Box 33, Edenbridge, Kent TN8 5PB
☎01732 863939 Fax 01732 860215
Email admin@topfoto.co.uk
Website www.topfoto.co.uk

Contact *Alan Smith*

Eight million contemporary and historical images, ideal for advertisers, publishers and the travel trade. Delivery online.

B.M. Totterdell Photography
Constable Cottage, Burlings Lane, Knockholt, Kent TN14 7PE
☎01959 532001 Fax 01959 532001
Email btrial@btinternet.com

Contact *Barbara Totterdell*

Specialist volleyball library covering all aspects of the sport.

Tessa Traeger Library
7 Rossetti Studios, 72 Flood Street, London SW3 5TF
☎020 7352 3641 Fax 020 7352 4846
Food, gardens, travel and artists.

Travel Ink Photo & Feature Library
The Old Coach House, 14 High Street, Goring on Thames, Nr Reading, Berkshire RG8 9AR
☎01491 873011 Fax 01491 875558
Email info@travel-ink.co.uk
Website www.travel-ink.co.uk

Contact *Felicity Bazell*

Around 100,000 colour images covering about 130 countries (including the UK). Close links with other specialist libraries mean most topics can be accessed. Subjects include travel, tourism, lifestyles, business, industry, transport, children, religion, history, activities. Specialist collections on Hong Kong (including construction of the Tsing Ma bridge), Greece, North Wales, Germany, the Cotswolds, France and many others.

Peter Trenchard's Image Store Ltd
The Studio, West Hill, St Helier, Jersey, Channel Islands JE2 3HB
☎01534 769933 Fax 01534 789191
Email peter-trenchard@supnet.com
Website www.peter-trenchard.com

Contact *Peter Trenchard, FBIPP, AMPA, PPA*

Slide library of the Channel Islands – mainly tourist and financial-related. Commissions undertaken.

Tropix Photo Library
156 Meols Parade, Meols, Wirral CH47 6AN
☎0151 632 1698 Fax 0151 632 1698
Email tropixphoto@talk21.com
Website www.tropix.co.uk

Contact *Veronica Birley*

Specialises in images of developing nations: travel and editorial pictures emphasising the attractive and progressive, not just the problems. Evocative photos concerning the economies, environment, culture and society of 100+ countries across Africa, Central and South America, Caribbean, Eastern Europe, Middle East, Indian sub-continent, South East Asia, CIS and Far East; also Antarctica. Also incorporating **MerseySlides Collection** (see entry). Assignment photography available worldwide. All photos supplied with detailed captions. Rapid response with one-hour digital delivery available. Established 22 years. **BAPLA** member.

True North Picture Source

26 New Road, Hebden Bridge, West Yorkshire HX7 8EF
☎01422 845532
Email john@trunorth.demon.co.uk

Contact *John Morrison*

30,000 transparencies on 35mm and 6×4.5cm format on the life and landscape of the north of England, photographed by John Morrison.

Turnley Collection
See **Corbis Images**

Ulster Museum Picture Library

Botanic Gardens, Belfast BT9 5AB
☎028 9038 3000 ext 3113 Fax 028 9038 3103
Email patricia.mclean.um@nics.gov.uk
Website www.ulstermuseum.org.uk

Contact *Mrs Pat McLean*

Specialist subjects: art – fine and decorative, late 17th–20th century, particularly Irish art, archaeology, ethnography, treasures from the Armada shipwrecks, geology, botany, zoology, local history and industrial archaeology. Commissions welcome for objects not already photographed.

Universal Pictorial
Press & Agency Ltd

29–31 Saffron Hill, London EC1N 8SW
☎020 7421 6000 Fax 020 7421 6006
Email peter.dare@photoshot.com
Website www.uppa.co.uk

News Editor *Peter Dare*

Photo archive dates back to 1944 and contains approximately four million pictures. Colour and b&w coverage of news, royalty, politics, sport, arts, and many other subjects. Commissions undertaken for press and public relations. Fully interactive digital photo archive in addition to bulletin board accessible via ISDN or modem. Full digital scanning, retouching and transmission facilities.

UPI
See **Popperfoto**

V&A Images

Victoria and Albert Museum, Cromwell Road, South Kensington, London SW7 2RL
☎020 7942 2483/6/9 Fax 020 7942 2482
Email vanda.images@vam.ac.uk
Website www.vandaimages.com

A vast collection of photographs from the world's largest museum of decorative and applied arts, reflecting culture and life style spanning over 1000 years of history to the present time. Digital delivery of large format transparencies of contemporary and historical textiles, costumes and fashions, ceramics, furniture, metalwork, glass, sculpture, toys, and games, design and photographs from around the world. Their unique photographs include 1960s fashion by John French, Harry Hammond's behind the scenes pop idols, Houston Rogers theatrical world of the 1930s to 1970s, images of royalty by Lafayette, Cecil Beaton, and the 19th century pioneer photographers. Images from the inexhaustible shelves of the National Art Library and Library of Art & Design, and from the Theatre Museum and Museum of Childhood are readily available.

Valley Green

Barn Ley, Valley Lane, Buxhall, Stowmarket, Suffolk IP14 3EB
☎01449 736090 Fax 01449 736090
Email pics@valleygreen.co.uk

Contacts *Joseph Barrere, Colette Barrere*

'Profusion of perennials – all correctly labelled.' Over 10,000 hardy plant transparencies in stock, plus watercolours and line drawings available. Commissions undertaken as well as creative copywriting.

Victory Archive
See **Popperfoto**

Vin Mag Archives Ltd

84–90 Digby Road, London E9 6HX
☎020 8533 7588 Fax 020 8533 7283
Email piclib@vinmag.com
Website www.vinmagarchive.com

Formerly the Vintage Magazine Company. A large collection of movie stills and posters, photographs, illustrations and advertisements covering music, glamour, social history, theatre posters, ephemera, postcards.

John Walmsley Photo Library
See **Education Photos**

Christopher Ware Pictures

65 Trinity Street, Barry, Glamorgan CF62 7EX
☎01446 732816/07802 865999 (mobile)
Email crware@ntlworld.com

Contact *Christopher Ware*

Large collection of images (b&w and colour) of S.E. Wales, including Barry docks and the Steam

Graveyard, railways, Vale of Glamorgan land-scapes, civil and military aircraft over the last 40 years. Images available on CD-ROM or via e-mail. Digital post-production. Commissions. Other photographers' work not accepted. Also broadcast camera operation.

Warwickshire Photographic Survey
See **Birmingham Library Services** under **Library Services**

Waterways Photo Library
39 Manor Court Road, Hanwell, London W7 3EJ
☎020 8840 1659 Fax 020 8567 0605
Email watphot39@aol.com

Contact *Derek Pratt*

A specialist photo library on all aspects of Britain's inland waterways. Top-quality 35mm and medium-format colour transparencies, plus a large collection of b&w. Rivers and canals, bridges, locks, aqueducts, tunnels and waterside buildings. Town and countryside scenes, canal art, waterway holidays, boating, fishing, wind-mills, watermills, watersports and wildlife.

Philip Way Photography
2 Green Moor Link, Winchmore Hill, London N21 2ND
☎020 8360 3034

Contact *Philip Way*

Over 10,000 images of St Paul's Cathedral – historical exteriors, interiors and events (1686–2002).

Weimar Archive
See **Mary Evans Picture Library**

The Wellcome Trust Medical Photographic Library
210 Euston Road, London NW1 2BE
☎020 7611 8348 Fax 020 7611 8577
Email photolib@wellcome.ac.uk
Website http://medphoto.wellcome.ac.uk

Contacts *Michele Minto*

Approximately 180,000 images on the history of medicine and human culture worldwide, including modern clinical medicine, health-care, family life and biomedica.

Eric Whitehead Photography
Postal Buildings, Ash Street, Bowness-on-Windermere, Cumbria LA23 3EB
☎015394 48894 Fax 015394 48284
Email info@ewphotography.com

Website www.ewphotography.com
Incorporates the Cumbria Picture Library. The agency covers local news events, PR and com-mercial material, also leading library of snooker images (see **Snookerimages**).

Wild Images
See **RSPCA Photolibrary**

Wilderness Photographic Library
Mill Barn, Broad Raine, Sedbergh, Cumbria LA10 5ED
☎015396 20196 Fax 015396 21293
Email wildernessphoto@btinternet.com

Contact *John Noble*

Striking colour images from around the world, from polar wastes to the Himalayas and Amazon jungle. Subjects: mountains, Arctic, deserts, ice-bergs, wildlife, rainforests, glaciers, geysers, exploration, caves, rivers, eco-tourism, people and cultures, canyons, seascapes, marine life, weather, volcanoes, mountaineering, skiing, geology, conservation, adventure sports, national parks.

David Williams Picture Library
50 Burlington Avenue, Glasgow G12 0LH
☎0141 339 7823 Fax 0141 337 3031

Specialises in travel photography with wide coverage of Scotland, Iceland and Spain. Many other European countries also included plus smaller collections of Western USA and Canada. The main subjects in each country are: cities, towns, villages, 'tourist haunts', buildings of architectural or historical interest, landscapes and natural features. The Scotland and Iceland collections include many pictures depicting physical geography and geology. Photographic commissions and illustrated travel articles undertaken. Catalogue available.

The Neil Williams Classical Collection
22 Avon, Hockley, Tamworth, Staffordshire B77 5QA
☎01827 286086 Fax 01827 286086
Email neil@classicalcollection.co.uk

Contact *Neil Williams, PGCertMus, BA(Hons), DipMus.*

Archive specialising in classical music ephemera, particularly portraits of composers, musicians, conductors and opera singers com-prising of old and sometimes very rare pho-tographs, postcards, antique prints, cigarette cards, stamps, First Day Covers, concert programmes, Victorian newspapers, etc. Also modern photos of composer references such as museums, statues, busts, paintings, monuments, memorials and graves. Other subjects covered include ballet, musical instruments, concert halls, opera houses, 'music in art', manuscripts, opera scenes, music-caricatures, bands, orchestras and other music groups. Also writer of concert programme notes and CD inserts for classical music, as well as being a commissionable composer.

Vaughan Williams Memorial Library

English Folk Dance and Song Society, Cecil Sharp House, 2 Regent's Park Road, London NW1 7AY
☎020 7485 2206 ext. 18/19
Fax 020 7284 0523
Email library@efdss.org
Website www.efdss.org

Mainly b&w coverage of traditional/folk music, dance and customs worldwide, focusing on Britain and other English-speaking nations. Photographs date from the late 19th century to the 1990s.

The Wilson Photographic Collection

See **Dundee Central Library** under **Library Services**

Windrush Photos, Wildlife and Countryside Picture Agency

99 Noah's Ark, Kemsing, Sevenoaks, Kent TN15 6PD
☎01732 763486 Fax 01732 763285
Email dt@windrushphotos.demon.co.uk
Website www.windrushphotos.com
Contact *David Tipling*

Specialists in birds (worldwide) and British wildlife. Photographic and features commissions are regularly undertaken for publications in the UK and overseas. The agency acts as ornithological consultants for all aspects of the media. **BAPLA** member.

Woodfall Wild Images

17 Bull Lane, Denbigh, Denbighshire LL16 3SN
☎01745 815903 Fax 01745 814581
Email wwimages@btinternet.com
Website www.woodfall.com
Contacts *David Woodfall, Donna Westwood*

A comprehensive and specialist collection of

wildlife, landscape and environmental photographs from both the UK and the rest of the world. Award winning photography by the world's more imaginative photographers. All formats, 35mm to panoramic. 'Personal and friendly service.' Subjects include: birds, animals, insects and marine life, trees and forests, wildflowers and meadows, wetlands, heathlands, moorlands and Downs, the coast, rivers, waterfalls, lakes and canals. Environmental issues such as pollution, conservation and habitat destruction, the weather and climate, landscapes and scenics.

World Pictures

25 Gosfield Street, London W1W 6HP
☎020 7437 2121/7436 0440
Fax 020 7439 1307
Email worldpictures@btinternet.com
Website www.worldpictures.co.uk
Contacts *David Brenes, Carlo Irek*

600,000 colour transparencies of travel and emotive material.

WWF UK Photolibrary

Panda House, Weyside Park, Catteshall Lane, Godalming, Surrey GU7 1XR
☎01483 412336 Fax 01483 861360
Email psunters@wwf.org.uk
Contact *Paul Sunters*

Specialist library covering natural history, endangered species, conservation, environment, forests, habitats, habitat destruction, and pollution in the UK and abroad. 25,000 colour slides (35mm).

Yemen Pictures

28 Sheen Common Drive, Richmond TW10 5BN
☎020 7602 1989 Fax 020 7602 1989

Large collection (4000 transparencies) covering all aspects of Yemen – culture, people, architecture, dance, qat, music. Also Africa, Australia, Middle East, and Asia.

York Archaeological Trust Picture Library

Cromwell House, 13 Ogleforth, York YO1 7FG
☎01904 663000 Fax 01904 663024
Email enquiries@yorkarchaeology.co.uk
Website www.yorkarchaeology.co.uk

Specialist library of rediscovered artifacts, historic buildings and excavations, presented by the creators of the highly acclaimed Jorvik

Viking Centre. The main emphasis is on the Roman, Anglo–Saxon and Viking periods.

The John Robert Young Collection
61 De Montfort Road, Lewes, East Sussex BN7 1SS
☎01273 475216 Fax 01273 475216
Email johnrobert@pxvobiscum.fsnet.co.uk

Website http://johnrobertyoung.members.beeb.net

Contact *Jennifer Barrett*

50,000 transparencies and monochrome prints on religion, travel and military subjects. Major portfolios: religious communities; the French Foreign Legion; the Spanish Legion; the Royal Marines; the People's Liberation Army (China).

Settling Accounts

*Ian Spring takes an expert look at the latest Budget
and explains how writers can be tax wise*

'No man in the country is under the smallest obligation, moral or other, to
arrange his affairs as to enable the Inland Revenue to put the largest possible shovel in his stores.

The Inland Revenue is not slow, and quite rightly, to take every advantage which is open to it ... for the purpose of depleting the taxpayer's
pockets. And the taxpayer is, in like manner, entitled to be astute to prevent as far as he honestly can the depletion of his means by the Inland
Revenue.'

Lord Clyde, *Ayrshire Pullman v Inland Revenue Commissioners, 1929*

Income Tax

What is a professional writer for tax purposes?

Writers are professionals while they are writing regularly with the intention of
making a profit; or while they are gathering material, researching or otherwise
preparing a publication.

A professional freelance writer is taxed under Case II of Schedule D of the
Income and Corporation Taxes Act 1988. The taxable income is the amount
receivable, either directly or by an agent, on his behalf, less expenses wholly and
exclusively laid out for the purpose of the profession. If expenses exceed
income, the loss can either be set against other income of the same or preceding
years or carried forward and set against future income from writing. If tax has
been paid on that other income, a repayment can be obtained, or the sum can be
offset against other tax liabilities. Special loss relief can apply in the opening
years of the profession. Losses made in the first four years can be set against
income of up to three earlier years.

Where a writer receives very occasional payments for isolated articles, it may
not be possible to establish that these are profits arising from carrying on a continuing profession. In such circumstances these 'isolated transactions' may be
assessed under Case VI of Schedule D of the Income and Corporation Taxes Act
1988. Again, expenses may be deducted in arriving at the taxable income but, if
expenses exceed income, the loss can only be set against the profits from future
isolated transactions, or other income assessable under Case VI.

In the tax year 1996/97 a new tax system came into effect called Self Assessment.
Under Self Assessment the onus is on the individual to declare income and

expenses correctly. Each writer therefore has to decide whether profits arise from a professional or occasional activity. The consequences of getting it wrong can be expensive by way of interest, penalties and surcharges on additional tax subsequently found to be due. If in any doubt the writer should seek professional advice.

Income

A writer's income includes fees, advances, royalties, commissions, sale of copyrights, reimbursed expenses, etc., from any source anywhere in the world whether or not brought to the UK (non UK resident or domiciled writers should seek professional advice).

Agents

It should be borne in mind that the agent stands in the shoes of the principal. It is not always realised that when the agent receives royalties, fees, advances, etc. on behalf of the author those receipts became the property of the author on the date of their receipt by the agent. This applies for Income Tax and Value Added Tax purposes.

Expenses

A writer can normally claim the following expenses:

(a) Secretarial, typing, proofreading, research. Where payment for these is made to the author's wife or husband they should be recorded and entered in the spouse's tax return as earned income which is subject to the usual personal allowances. If payments reach relevant levels, PAYE should be operated.

(b) Telephone, faxes, Internet costs, computer software, postage, stationery, printing, equipment maintenance, insurance, dictation tapes, batteries, any equipment or office requisites used for the profession.

(c) Periodicals, books (including presentation copies and reference books) and other publications necessary for the profession, but amounts received from the sale of books should be deducted.

(d) Hotels, fares, car running expenses (including repairs, petrol, oil, garaging, parking, cleaning, insurance, road fund tax, depreciation), hire of cars or taxis in connection with:

(i) business discussions with agents, publishers, co-authors, collaborators, researchers, illustrators, etc.

(ii) travel at home and abroad to collect background material.

As an alternative to keeping details of full car running costs, a mileage rate can be claimed for business use. This rate depends on the engine size and varies from year to year. This is known as the Fixed Profit Car Scheme and is available to writers whose turnover does not exceed the VAT registration limit, currently £56,000.

(e) Publishing and advertising expenses, including costs of proof corrections, indexing, photographs, etc.

(f) Subscriptions to societies and associations, press cutting agencies, libraries, etc., incurred wholly for the purpose of the profession.

(g) Rent, council tax and water rates, etc., the proportion being determined by the ratio of the number of rooms used exclusively for the profession, to the total number of rooms in the residence. But see note on Capital Gains Tax below.

(h) Lighting, heating and cleaning. A carefully calculated figure of the business use of these costs can be claimed as a proportion of the total.

(i) Agent's commission, accountancy charges and legal charges incurred wholly in the course of the profession including cost of defending libel actions, damages in so far as they are not covered by insurance, and libel insurance premiums. However, where in a libel case damages are awarded to punish the author for having acted maliciously the action becomes quasi-criminal and costs and damages may not be allowed.

(j) TV and video rental (which may be apportioned for private use), and cinema or theatre tickets, if wholly for the purpose of the profession.

(k) Capital allowances for business equipment. These are now divided into three categories:

  (i) Computer equipment including printers, scanners, cabling, etc. For any such equipment purchased subsequent to 1 April 2000 there is a First Year Allowance of 100%. We know that this 100% allowance will remain for purchases at least until 31 March 2004. Prior to that the First Year Allowance was 40% of the cost of the equipment purchased after 1 July 1998 and 50% on equipment purchased after 1 July 1997. For equipment purchased prior to 1 April 2000, after the first year there is an annual Writing Down Allowance of 25% of the reducing balance.

  (ii) On motor cars the allowance is 25% in the first year and 25% of the reducing balance in each successive year limited to £3000 each year.

  (iii) For all other business equipment, e.g. TV, radio, hi-fi sets, tape and video recorders, Dictaphones, office furniture, photographic equipment, etc. there is a First Year Allowance of 40%. After the first year there is an annual Writing Down Allowance of 25% of the reducing balance. The allowances for all the three categories mentioned above will be reduced to exclude personal (non-professional) use where necessary.

(l) Lease rent. The cost of lease rent of equipment is allowable; also on cars, subject to restrictions for private use, and for expensive cars.

(m) Other expenses incurred wholly and exclusively for professional purposes. (Entertaining expenses are not allowable in any circumstances.)

NB It essential to keep detailed records. Diary entries of appointments, notes of fares and receipted bills are much more convincing to the Inland Revenue who are very reluctant to accept estimates.

The Self Assessment regime makes it a legal requirement for proper accounting records to be kept. These records must be sufficient to support the figures declared in the tax return.

In addition to the above, tax relief is available on:

(a) Premiums to pension schemes such as the Society of Authors Retirement Benefits Scheme. Depending on age, up to 40% of net earned income can be paid into a personal pension plan.

(b) Covenants to charities. (Deeds executed prior to 6 April 2000.)

(c) Gift Aid payments to charities. Any amount.

Capital Gains Tax

The exemption from Capital Gains Tax which applies to an individual's main residence does not apply to any part of that residence which is used exclusively for business purposes. The appropriate proportion of any increase in value of the residence, since purchase or 31 March 1982 if later, can be taxed when the residence is sold, subject to adjustment for inflation to March 1998 and subsequent length of ownership, at the individual's highest rate of tax.

Writers who own their houses should bear this in mind before claiming expenses for the use of a room for writing purposes. Arguments in favour of making such claims are that they afford some relief now, while Capital Gains Tax in its present form may not stay for ever. Also, where a new house is bought in place of an old one, the gain made on the sale of the first study may be set off against the cost of the study in the new house, thus postponing the tax payment until the final sale. For this relief to apply, each house must have a study and the author must continue his profession throughout. On death there is an exemption of the total Capital Gains of the estate.

Alternatively, writers can claim that their use is non-exclusive and restrict their claim to the cost of extra lighting, heating and cleaning to avoid any Capital Gains Tax liability.

Can a writer average out his income over a number of years for tax purposes?

The Budget in March 2001 introduced measures which will enable writers to average their profits (made wholly or mainly from creative works) over two or more consecutive years. If the profits of the lower year are less than 70% of the profits of the higher year or the profits of one year (but not both) are nil, the author will be able to claim to have the profits averaged. Where the profits of the lower year are more than 70% but less than 75% of the profits of the higher year a pro-rata adjustment is made to both years to reduce the difference between them.

The first years that can be averaged are 2000/1 and 2001/2.

It is also possible to average out income within the terms of publishers' contracts, but professional advice should be taken before signature. Where a husband and wife collaborate as writers, advice should be taken as to whether a formal partnership agreement should be made or whether the publishing agreement should be in joint names.

Is a lump sum paid for an outright sale of the copyright or is part of the copyright exempt from tax?

No. All the money received from the marketing of literary work, by whatever means, is taxable. Some writers, in spite of clear judicial decisions to the contrary, still seem to think that an outright sale of, for instance, the film rights in a book is not subject to tax. The averaging relief described above should be considered.

Remaindering

To avoid remaindering authors can usually purchase copies of their own books from the publishers. Monies received from sales are subject to income tax but the cost of books sold should be deducted because tax is only payable on the profit made.

Is there any relief where old copyrights are sold?

No. There was relief available until April 2001 but was then withdrawn. The averaging relief described above should be considered.

Are royalties payable on publication of a book abroad subject to both foreign tax as well as UK tax?

Where there is a Double Taxation Agreement between the country concerned and the UK, then on the completion of certain formalities no tax is deductible at source by the foreign payer, but such income is taxable in the UK in the ordinary way. When there is no Double Taxation Agreement, credit will be given against UK tax for overseas tax paid. A complete list of countries with which the UK has conventions for the avoidance of double taxation may be obtained from FICO, Inland Revenue, St John's House, Merton Road, Bootle, Merseyside L69 9BB, or a local tax office.

Residence abroad

Writers residing abroad will, of course, be subject to the tax laws ruling in their country of residence, and as a general rule royalty income paid from the United Kingdom can be exempted from deduction of UK tax at source, providing the author is carrying on his profession abroad. A writer who is intending to go and live abroad should make early application for future royalties to be paid without deduction of tax to FICO, address as above. In certain circumstances writers resident in the Irish Republic are exempt from Irish Income Tax on their authorship earnings.

Are grants or prizes taxable?

The law is uncertain. Some Arts Council grants are now deemed to be taxable, whereas most prizes and awards are not, though it depends on the conditions in each case. When submitting the Self Assessment annual returns, such items should be excluded, but reference made to them in the 'Additional Information' box on the self-employment (or partnership) pages.

What is the item 'Class 4 N.I.C.' which appears on my Self Assessment return?

All taxpayers who are self-employed pay an additional national insurance contribution if their earned income exceeds a figure which varies each year. This contribution is described as Class 4 and is calculated when preparing the return. It is additional to the self-employed Class 2 contribution but confers no additional benefits and is a form of levy. It applies to men aged under 65 and women under 60.

Should an author use a limited company?

Changes in the tax regime has made the incorporation of businesses more and more attractive and there are advantages in so doing for businesses with relatively low levels of profit. However, there are disadvantages in all cases and particular considerations for authors. The advice of an accountant, knowledgeable about the affairs of authors, should be sought if incorporation is contemplated.

Value Added Tax

Value Added Tax (VAT) is a tax currently levied at 17.5% on:

(a) the total value of taxable goods and services supplied to consumers,
(b) the importation of goods into the UK,
(c) certain services or goods from abroad if a taxable person receives them in the UK for the purpose of their business.

Who is taxable?

A writer resident in the UK whose turnover from writing and any other business, craft or art on a self-employed basis is greater than £56,000 annually, before deducting agent's commission, must register with HM Customs & Excise as a taxable person. Turnover includes fees, royalties, advances, commissions, sale of copyright, reimbursed expenses, etc. A business is required to register:

- at the end of any month if the value of taxable supplies in the past twelve months has exceeded the annual threshold; or
- if there are reasonable grounds for believing that the value of taxable supplies in the next twelve months will exceed the annual threshold.

Penalties will be claimed in the case of late registration. In his 2003 Budget, the Chancellor announced a penalty amnesty for people registering late between 10 April 2003 and 30 September 2003. A writer whose turnover is below these limits is exempt from the requirements to register for VAT but may apply for voluntary registration and this will be allowed at the discretion of HM Customs & Excise.

A taxable person collects VAT on outputs (turnover) and deducts VAT paid on inputs (taxable expenses) and where VAT collected exceeds VAT paid, must remit the difference to HM Customs & Excise. In the event that input exceeds output, the difference will be refunded by HM Customs & Excise.

Outputs (Turnover)

A writer's outputs are taxable services supplied to publishers, broadcasting organisations, theatre managements, film companies, educational institutions, etc. A taxable writer must invoice, i.e. collect from, all the persons (either individuals or organisations) in the UK for whom supplies have been made, for fees, royalties or other considerations plus VAT. An unregistered writer cannot and must not invoice for VAT. A taxable writer is not obliged to collect VAT on

Inputs

Taxable at the standard rate if supplier is registered	Taxable at the zero or special rate	Not liable to VAT
Rent of certain commercial premises	Books (zero)	Rent of non-commercial premises
Advertisements in newspapers, magazines, journals and periodicals	Coach, rail and air travel (zero)	Postage
Agent's commission (unless it relates to monies from overseas)	Agent's commission (on monies from overseas)	Services supplied by unregistered persons
Accountant's and solicitor's fees for business matters	Domestic gas and electricity (5%)	Subscriptions to the Society of Authors, PEN, NUJ, etc.
Agency services (typing, copying, etc.)		Insurance
Word processors, typewriters and stationery		
Artists' materials		
Photographic equipment		
Tape recorders and tapes		
Hotel accommodation		*Outside the scope of VAT*
Taxi fares		
Motorcar expenses		PLR (Public Lending Right)
Telephone		Profit shares
Theatres and concerts		Investment income
NB This list is not exhaustive		

royalties or other fees paid by publishers or others overseas. In practice, agents usually collect VAT for the registered author.

Remit to Customs

The taxable writer adds up the VAT which has been paid on taxable inputs, deducts it from the VAT received and remits the balance to Customs. Business with HM Customs is conducted through the local VAT offices of HM Customs which are listed in local telephone directories, except for VAT returns which are sent direct to the Customs & Excise VAT Central Unit, Alexander House, 21 Victoria Avenue, Southend on Sea, Essex SS99 1AA.

Accounting

A taxable writer is obliged to account to HM Customs & Excise at quarterly intervals. Returns must be completed and sent to VAT Central Unit by the dates shown on the return. Penalties can be charged if the returns are late.

It is possible to account for the VAT liability under the Cash Accounting Scheme (leaflet 731), whereby the author accounts for the output tax when the invoice is paid or royalties, etc., are received. The same applies to the input tax, but as most purchases are probably on a 'cash basis', this will not make a considerable difference to the author's input tax. This scheme is only applicable to those with a taxable turnover of less than £600,000 and, therefore, is available to the majority of authors. The advantage of this scheme is that the author does not have to account for VAT before receiving payments, thereby relieving the author of a cash flow problem.

It is also possible to pay VAT by nine estimated direct debits, with a final balance at the end of the year (see leaflet 732). This annual accounting method also means that only one VAT return is submitted.

Flat Rate Scheme

Small businesses can elect to pay VAT under a flat rate scheme (FRS). This is open to businesses with business income up to £150,000 a year. Under the normal VAT accounting rules, each item of turnover and every claimed expense must be recorded and supported by evidence, e.g. invoices, receipts, etc. Under the FRS, detailed records of sales and purchases do not have to be kept. A record of gross income (including zero rated and exempt income) is maintained and a flat rate percentage is applied to the total. This percentage is then paid over to HM Customs. The percentage varies from one profession or business to another but for authors is 11%. The aim of the scheme is to reduce the amount of time and money spent in complying with VAT regulations and this is to be welcomed. However, there are disadvantages:

- The detailed records of income and expenses are still going to be required for taxation purposes.
- Invoices on sales are issued in the normal way.

- The percentage is applied to all business income. So 11% VAT will effectively be paid on income from abroad, zero rated under the normal basis, and PLR, otherwise exempt.

For many authors, normal VAT accounting has imposed a good, timely discipline for dealing with accounting and taxation matters.

Registration

A writer will be given a VAT registration number which must be quoted on all VAT correspondence. It is the responsibility of those registered to inform those to whom they make supplies of their registration number. The taxable turnover limit which determines whether a person who is registered for VAT may apply for cancellation of registration is £54,000.

Voluntary registration

A writer whose turnover is below the limits may apply to register. If the writer is paying a relatively large amount of VAT on taxable inputs – agent's commission, accountant's fees, equipment, materials, or agency services, etc. – it may make a significant improvement in the net income to be able to offset the VAT on these inputs. A writer who pays relatively little VAT may find it easier, and no more expensive, to remain unregistered.

Fees and royalties

A taxable writer must notify those to whom he makes supplies of the VAT Registration Number at the first opportunity. One method of accounting for and paying VAT on fees and royalties is the use of multiple stationery for 'self-billing', one copy of the royalty statement being used by the author as the VAT invoice. A second method is for the recipient of taxable outputs to pay fees, including authors' royalties, without VAT. The taxable writer then renders a tax invoice for the VAT element and a second payment, of the VAT element, will be made. This scheme is cumbersome but will involve only taxable authors. Fees and royalties from abroad will count as payments of the exported services and will accordingly be zero-rated.

Agents and accountants

A writer is responsible to HM Customs for making VAT returns and payments. Neither an agent nor an accountant nor a solicitor can remove the responsibility, although they can be helpful in preparing and keeping VAT returns and accounts. Their professional fees or commission will, except in rare cases where the adviser or agent is himself unregistered, be taxable at the standard rate and will represent some of a writer's taxable inputs.

Income Tax – Schedule D

An unregistered writer can claim some of the VAT paid on taxable inputs as a business expense allowable against income tax. However, certain taxable inputs fall into categories which cannot be claimed under the income tax regulations. A taxable writer, who has already claimed VAT on inputs, cannot charge it as a business expense for the purposes of income tax.

Certain services from abroad

A taxable author who resides in the United Kingdom and who receives certain services from abroad must account for VAT on those services at the appropriate tax rate on the sum paid for them. Examples of the type of services concerned include: services of lawyers, accountants, consultants, provision of information and copyright permissions.

Inheritance Tax

Inheritance Tax was introduced in 1984 to replace Capital Transfer Tax, which had in turn replaced Estate Duty, the first of the death taxes of recent times. Paradoxically, Inheritance Tax has reintroduced a number of principles present under the old Estate Duty.

The general principle now is that all assets owned at death are chargeable to tax (currently 40%) except the first £255,000 of the estate and any assets passed to a surviving spouse or a charity. Gifts made more than seven years before death are exempt, but those made within this period may be taxed on a sliding scale. No tax is payable at the time of making the gift.

In addition, each individual may currently make gifts of up to £3000 in any year and these will be considered to be exempt. A further exemption covers any number of annual gifts not exceeding £250 to any one person.

If the £3000 is not fully utilised in one year, any unused balance can be carried forward to the following year (but no later). Gifts out of income, which do not reduce one's living standards, are also exempt if they are part of normal expenditure.

At death all assets are valued; they will include any property, investments, life policies, furniture and personal possessions, bank balances and, in the case of authors, the value of copyrights. All, with the sole exception of copyrights, are capable (as assets) of accurate valuation and, if necessary, can be turned into cash. The valuation of copyright is, of course, complicated and frequently gives rise to difficulty. Except where they are bequeathed to the owner's husband or wife, very real problems can be left behind by the author.

Experience has shown that a figure based on two to three years' past royalties may be proposed by the Inland Revenue in their valuation of copyright. However, this may not be reasonable and may require negotiation. If a book is running out of print or if, as in the case of educational books, it may need revision at the next reprint, these factors must be taken into account. In many cases the fact that the author is no longer alive and able to make personal appearances, or provide publicity, or write further works, will result in lower or slower sales. Obviously, this is an area in which help can be given by the publishers, and in particular one needs to know what their future intentions are, what stocks of the books remain, and what likelihood there will be of reprinting.

There is a further relief available to authors who have established that they have been carrying on a business, normally assessable under Case II of Schedule D, for at least two years prior to death. It has been possible to establish that copyrights are treated as business property and in these circumstances, Inheritance Tax 'business property relief' is available. This relief at present is 100% so that the tax saving can be quite substantial. The Inland Revenue may wish to be assured that the business is continuing and consideration should therefore be given to the appointment, in the author's will, of a literary executor who should be a qualified business person or, in certain circumstances, the formation of partnership between the author and spouse, or other relative, to ensure that it is established the business is continuing after the author's death.

If the author has sufficient income, consideration should be given to building up a fund to cover future Inheritance Tax liabilities. One of a number of ways would be to take out a whole life assurance policy which is assigned to the children, or other beneficiaries, the premiums on which are within the annual exemption of £3000. The capital sum payable on the death of the assured is exempt from inheritance tax.

Anyone wondering how best to order his affairs for tax purposes should consult an accountant with specialised knowledge in this field. Experience shows that a good accountant is well worth his fee which, incidentally, so far as it relates to professional matters, is an allowable expense.

The information contained in this section has been prepared by Ian Spring of Moore Stephens, Chartered Accountants, who will be pleased to answer questions on tax problems. Please write to Ian Spring, c/o The Writer's Handbook, 34 Ufton Road, London N1 5BX.

Company Index

Subject Index

Kansas, University Press of, 468
Kent State University Press, 469
Louisiana State University Press, 470
Mississippi, University Press of, 471
Nevada Press, University of, 472
Oklahoma Press, University of, 473
Virginia Press, University of, 480
Washington State University Press, 480

Value Added Tax, 724–728

Vanity Publishing, 109–111

Vegetarian: Agents (UK)
Martinez Literary Agency, 234

Vegetarian: Magazines
Vegan, The, 341

Veterinary: Agents (UK)
Martinez Literary Agency, 234

Veterinary: Picture Libraries
Cordaiy (Sylvia) Photo Library, 690
Only Horses Picture Agency, 707

Veterinary: Publishers (Commonwealth)
Affiliated East West Press Pvt Ltd, 512
Harcourt Australia Pty Ltd, 508

Veterinary: Publishers (UK)
Blackwell Publishing, 13
Manson Publishing Ltd, 59

Veterinary: Publishers (US)
Iowa State University Press, 468

Video: Agents (UK)
International Scripts, 230
Levy (Barbara) Literary Agency, 232
Sharland Organisation Ltd, The, 239

Video: Film, TV & Video Producers
Greenwich Village Productions, 386
Monty Funk Productions Ltd, 391
Taylor Made Broadcasts Ltd, 400

Video: Magazines
Camcorder User, 279
Empire, 292
Screen International, 331
Sight & Sound, 333

Video: Packagers (UK)
Direct Image Publishing, 210

Video: Prizes
Kraszna-Krausz Book Awards, 630

Video: Professional Associations
British Film Institute, 523
IVCA, 532

Video: Publishers (Commonwealth)
Currency Press Pty Ltd, 508
McGraw-Hill, 509

Video: Publishers (European)
Bulzoni Editore SRL (Le Edizioni Universitarie d'Italia), 449
Cappelli (Nuova Casa Editrice Licinio) GEM srl, 449
Gremese (Ernesto) Editore SRL, 449
Heyne (Wilhelm) Verlag, 447
Propylän Verlag, Zweigniederlassung Berlin der Ullstein Buchverlage GmbH, 448

Video: Publishers (UK)
Artech House, 8
Fitzgerald Publishing, 37
Guild of Master Craftsman Publications Ltd, 43
Halsgrove, 44
Omnibus Press, 67
Phaidon Press Limited, 71
Reardon Publishing, 77

Video: Publishers (US)
Houghton Mifflin Co., 467
Random House, Inc., 475
Reader's Digest Association Inc, 475
Tyndale House Publishers, Inc., 479
Zondervan Publishing House, 481

Video: Writer's Courses, Circles & Workshops
Screenwriters' Workshop, 592

Virtual Reality: Agents (UK)
Curtis Brown Group Ltd, 223
Sharland Organisation Ltd, The, 239

Volcanoes: Agents (UK)
Curtis Brown Group Ltd, 223

Volcanoes: Picture Libraries
GeoScience Features, 696
Wilderness Photographic Library, 716

Voluntary Sector: Publishers (UK)
NCVO Publications, 63

Wales/Welsh Interest: Agents (UK)
Curtis Brown Group Ltd, 223
International Scripts, 230

Wales/Welsh Interest: Arts Councils & Regional Arts Boards
Arts Council of Wales, The, 575

Wales/Welsh Interest: Audio Books
Spokenbooks Audio, 117

Wales/Welsh Interest: Electronic Publishers
Deunant Books, 196

Wales/Welsh Interest: Film, TV & Video Producers
Teliesyn, 400

Wales/Welsh Interest: Libraries
Carmarthen Public Library, 661
National Library of Wales, 671
Swansea Central Reference Library, 678

Wales/Welsh Interest: Literary Societies
Davies (Rhys) Trust, The, 558
Thomas (Dylan) Society of Great Britain, The, 570

Wales/Welsh Interest: Magazines
New Welsh Review, 318

Wales/Welsh Interest: Miscellany
Combrógos, 601

Wales/Welsh Interest: Picture Libraries
Country Matters Picture Library, 690
ffotograff, 693
MerseySlides Collection, The, 704
National Trust Photo Library, The, 706
Photolibrary Wales, The, 708
Travel Ink Photo & Feature Library, 714
Ware (Christopher) Pictures, 715

Wales/Welsh Interest: Poetry Magazines
Barddas, 157
New Welsh Review, 162
Planet, 164
Poetry Wales, 165
Red Poets' Society, 167
Skald, 168

Wales/Welsh Interest: Poetry Presses
Parthian Books, 152

Wales/Welsh Interest: Prizes
Drama Association of Wales Playwriting Competition, 622
Jones (Mary Vaughan) Award, 629
Prichard (Mathew) Award for Short Story Writing, The, 640
Tir Na N-Og Award, The, 646
Wales (Arts Council of) Book of the Year Awards, 648
Webb (Harri) Prize, The, 649